NEW!

for *Psychology*

Engaging Every Student.   Supporting Every Instructor.   Setting the New Standard for Teaching and Learning.

Achieve for *Psychology* sets a whole new standard for integrating **assessments**, **activities**, and **analytics** into your teaching. It brings together all of the features that instructors and students loved about our previous platform, LaunchPad — interactive e-book, LearningCurve adaptive quizzing and other assessments, interactive learning activities, extensive instructor resources — in a powerful new platform that offers:

- A cleaner, more intuitive, mobile-friendly interface.
- Powerful analytics.
- Self-regulated learning and goal-setting surveys.
- A fully integrated iClicker classroom response system, with questions available for each chapter or the option to integrate your own.
- A **NEW Video Collection for *Psychology*!**

Our resources were **co-designed with instructors and students**, on a foundation of *years* of **learning research**, and rigorous testing over multiple semesters. The result is superior content, organization, and functionality. Achieve's pre-built assignments engage students both *inside* and *outside of class*. And Achieve is effective for students of *all levels* of motivation and preparedness, whether they are high achievers or need extra support.

Macmillan Learning offers **deep platform integration** of Achieve with all LMS providers, including Blackboard, Brightspace, Canvas, and Moodle. With integration, students can access course content and their grades through one sign-in. And you can pair Achieve with course tools from your LMS, such as discussion boards and chat and Gradebook functionality. LMS integration is also available with Inclusive Access. For more information, visit www.macmillanlearning.com/college/ca/solutions/LMS-Integration or talk to your local sales representative.

Achieve was built with **accessibility** in mind. Macmillan Learning strives to create products that are usable by all learners and meet universally applied accessibility standards. In addition to addressing product compatibility with assistive technologies such as screen reader software, alternative keyboard devices, and voice recognition products, we are working to ensure that the content and platforms we provide are fully accessible. For more information visit www.macmillanlearning.com/college/ca/our-story/accessibility

Mobile: Based on user data, we know that lots of students use parts of Achieve on a mobile device. As such, activities such as e-book readings, videos, and LearningCurve adaptive quizzes are easily used across devices with different screen sizes.

Achieve for *Psychology*:   Assessments

LearningCurve Adaptive Quizzing

Based on extensive learning and memory research proven effective for hundreds of thousands of students, LearningCurve focuses on the core concepts in every chapter, providing individualized question sets and feedback for correct and incorrect responses. The system adapts to each student's level of understanding, with follow-up quizzes targeting areas where the student needs improvement. Each question is tied to a learning objective and linked to the appropriate section of the e-book to encourage students to discover the right answer for themselves. LearningCurve has consistently been rated the #1 resource by instructors and students alike.

- LearningCurve's game-like quizzing promotes retrieval practice through its unique delivery of questions and its point system.

- Students with a firm grasp on the material get plenty of practice but proceed through the activity relatively quickly.

- Unprepared students are given more questions, therefore requiring that they do what they should be doing anyway if they're unprepared—practice some more.

- Instructors can monitor results for each student and the class as a whole, to identify areas that may need more coverage in lectures and assignments.

E-Book

Macmillan Learning's e-book is an interactive version of the textbook that offers highlighting, bookmarking, and note-taking. Built-in, low-stakes self-assessments allow students to test their level of understanding along the way, and learn even more in the process thanks to the *testing effect*. Students can download the e-book to read offline, or to have it read aloud to them. Achieve allows instructors to assign chapter sections as homework.

Test Bank

Test banks for Macmillan Learning's psychology textbooks offer thousands of questions, all meticulously reviewed. Instructors can assign out-of-the-box exams or create their own by:

- Choosing from thousands of questions in our database.
- Filtering questions by type, topic, difficulty, and Bloom's level.
- Customizing multiple-choice questions.
- Integrating their own questions into the exam.

Exam/Quiz results report to a Gradebook that lets instructors monitor student progress individually and classwide.

Practice Quizzes

Practice Quizzes mirror the experience of a quiz or test, with questions that are similar but distinct from those in the test bank. Instructors can use the quizzes as is or create their own, selecting questions by question type, topic, difficulty, and Bloom's level.

Achieve for *Psychology*: Activities

Achieve is designed to support and encourage active learning by connecting familiar activities and practice out of class with some of the most effective and approachable in-class activities, curated from a variety of active learning sources.

© 2016 MACMILLAN

New! Video Collection for *Psychology*

This collection offers classic as well as current, in-demand clips from high-quality sources, with original content to support *Psychology*, Canadian Sixth Edition.

Accompanying assessment makes these videos assignable, with results reporting to the Achieve Gradebook. Our faculty and student consultants were instrumental in helping us create this diverse and engaging set of clips. All videos are closed-captioned and found only in Achieve.

Immersive Learning Activities

Focusing on student engagement, these immersive learning activities invite students to apply what they are learning to their own lives, or to play the role of researcher — exploring experimental methods, analyzing data, and developing scientific literacy and critical thinking skills.

The Visualizing Data features have been updated in Achieve. These activities invite students to engage with the material by answering questions the way psychologists do — namely, by looking at data. Each activity presents an interactive graph that displays real data from a published study, followed by questions that allow students to test their understanding of the study, as well as test their ability to reason about the data.

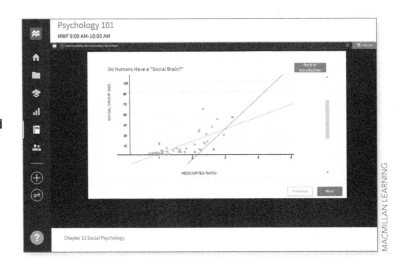

MACMILLAN LEARNING

Concept Practice Tutorials

Achieve includes dozens of these dynamic, interactive mini-tutorials that teach and reinforce the course's foundational ideas. Each of these brief activities (only 5 minutes to complete) addresses one or two key concepts, in a consistent format—review, practice, quiz, and conclusion.

Instructor Activity Guides

Instructor Activity Guides provide instructors with a structured plan for using Achieve's active learning opportunities in both face-to-face and remote learning courses. Each guide offers step-by-step instructions—from pre-class reflection to in-class engagement to post-class follow-up. The guides include suggestions for discussion questions, group work, presentations, and simulations, with estimated class time, implementation effort, and Bloom's taxonomy level for each activity.

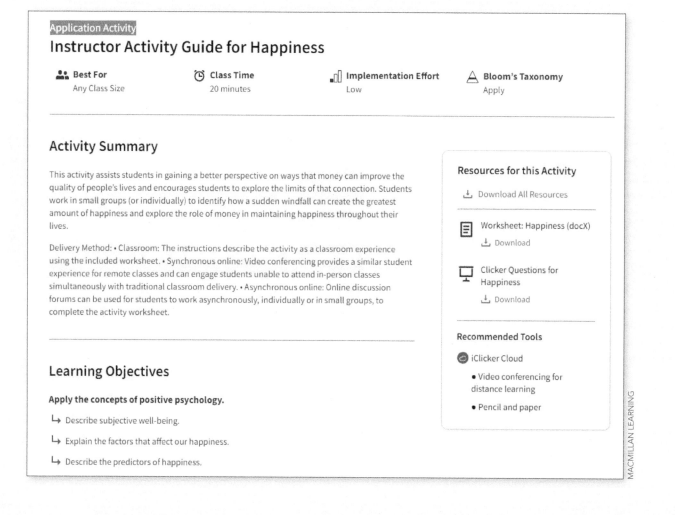

iClicker Classroom Response System

Achieve seamlessly integrates iClicker, Macmillan Learning's highly acclaimed classroom response system. iClicker can help make any classroom — in-person or virtual — more lively, engaging, and productive:

- iClicker's attendance feature helps you make sure students are actually attending in-person classes.
- Instructors can choose from flexible polling and quizzing options to engage students, check their understanding, and get their feedback in real time.
- iClicker allows students to participate using laptops, mobile devices, or in-class remotes.
- iClicker easily integrates with instructors' existing slides and polling questions — there is no need to re-enter them.
- Instructors can take advantage of the questions in our In-Class Activity Guides, and our book-specific questions within Achieve to improve the opportunities for all students to be active in class.

MACMILLAN LEARNING

Achieve for *Psychology*:   Analytics

Learning Objectives, Reports, and Insights

Content in Achieve is tagged to specific Learning Objectives, aligning the coursework with the textbook and with the APA Learning Goals and Outcomes. Reporting within Achieve helps students see how they are performing against objectives, and it helps instructors determine if any student, group of students, or the class as a whole needs extra help in specific areas. This enables more efficient and effective instructor interventions.

Achieve provides reports on student activities, assignments, and assessments at the course level, unit level, subunit level, and individual student level, so instructors can identify trouble spots and adjust their efforts accordingly. Within Reports, the Insights section offers snapshots with high-level data on student performance and behaviour, to answer such questions as:

- What are the top Learning Objectives to review in this unit?
- What are the top assignments to review?
- What's the range of performance on a particular assignment?
- How many students aren't logging in?

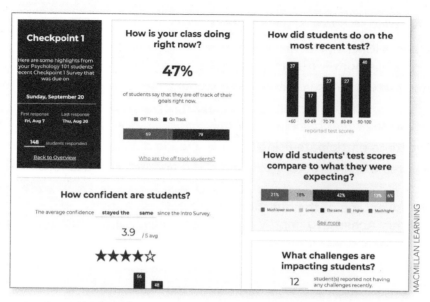

Achieve's **Innovation Lab** offers surveys that help students self-direct and develop confidence in their own learning:

- The **Introductory survey** asks students to consider their goals for the class and how they plan to manage their time and learning strategies.
- **Checkpoint surveys** ask students to reflect on what's been working and where they need to make changes.
- **Each completed survey generates a report** that reveals how each student is doing, beyond the course grade.

These tools help instructors engage their students in a discussion on soft skills, such as metacognition, effective learning and time management strategies, and other non-cognitive skills that impact student success.

Additional Instructor Resources in Achieve: All Within One Place

Image Slides and Tables

Presentation slides feature chapter photos, illustrations, and tables and can be used as is or customized to fit an instructor's needs. Alt text for images is available upon request via WebAccessibility@Macmillan.com.

Instructor's Resource Manuals

Downloadable PDF manuals include a range of resources, such as chapter outlines or summaries, teaching tips, discussion starters, sample syllabi, assignment suggestions, and classroom activities.

Lecture Slides

Accessible, downloadable presentation slides provide support for key concepts and themes from the text and can be used as is or customized to fit an instructor's needs.

Customer Support

Our Achieve Client Success Team—dedicated platform experts—provides collaboration, software expertise, and consulting to tailor each course to fit your instructional goals and student needs. Start with a demo at a time that works for you to learn more about how to set up your customized course. Talk to your sales representative or visit www.macmillanlearning.com/college/ca/contact-us/training-and-demos for more information.

Pricing and bundling options are available at the Macmillan student store: store.macmillanlearning.com/ca

PSYCHOLOGY

PSYCHOLOGY

CANADIAN SIXTH EDITION

Daniel L. Schacter

Harvard University

Daniel T. Gilbert

Harvard University

Matthew K. Nock

Harvard University

Ingrid S. Johnsrude

The University of Western Ontario

worth publishers

Macmillan Learning

New York

Executive Vice President, General Manager: Charles Linsmeier
Vice President, Social Sciences and High School: Shani Fisher
Senior Executive Program Manager: Carolyn Merrill
Development Editor: Marita Bley
Editorial Assistant: Emily Kelly
Executive Marketing Manager: Katherine Nurre
Marketing Assistant: Claudia Cruz
Director of Media Editorial and Assessment: Noel Hohnstine
Lead Media Project Manager: Joseph Tomasso
Senior Director, Content Management Enhancement: Tracey Kuehn
Senior Managing Editor: Lisa Kinne
Senior Content Project Manager: Vivien Weiss
Senior Project Manager: Arindam Bose, Lumina Datamatics, Inc.
Senior Workflow Project Supervisor: Paul Rohloff
Director of Design, Content Management: Diana Blume
Senior Design Services Manager: Natasha Wolfe
Interior Designer: Jerilyn DiCarlo
Senior Cover Design Manager: John Callahan
Executive Permissions Editor: Robin Fadool
Art Manager: Matthew McAdams
Illustrations: Lumina Datamatics, Inc.
Composition: Lumina Datamatics, Inc.
Printing and Binding: Lakeside Book Company

Library of Congress Control Number: 2022945787

Student Edition:
ISBN-13: 978-1-319-34053-7
ISBN-10: 1-319-34053-9

Loose-leaf:
ISBN-13: 978-1-319-46977-1
ISBN-10: 1-319-46977-9

Printed in the United States of America.

1   2   3   4   5   6   28   27   26   25   24   23

Worth Publishers
120 Broadway
New York, NY 10271
www.macmillanlearning.com

Dedication

We dedicate this sixth edition to Daniel Wegner—*collaborator, colleague, and dear friend. His name has left our cover, but his brilliant ideas and beautiful words remain in our pages. And in our hearts.*

ABOUT THE AUTHORS

COURTESY OF DANIEL SCHACTER

Daniel Schacter is William R. Kenan Jr. Professor of Psychology at Harvard University. Dan received his BA degree from the University of North Carolina at Chapel Hill. He subsequently developed a keen interest in amnesic disorders associated with various kinds of brain damage. He continued his research and education at the University of Toronto, where he received his PhD in 1981. He taught on the faculty at Toronto for the next 6 years before joining the psychology department at the University of Arizona in 1987. In 1991, he joined the faculty at Harvard University. His research explores the relationship between conscious and unconscious forms of memory, the nature of distortions and errors in remembering, and the ways in which we use memory to imagine future events. Many of his studies are summarized in his 1996 book, *Searching for Memory: The Brain, the Mind, and the Past,* and his 2001 book, *The Seven Sins of Memory: How the Mind Forgets and Remembers,* both winners of the American Psychological Association's William James Book Award. He has also received awards for his teaching and research, including the Harvard-Radcliffe Phi Beta Kappa Teaching Prize, the Distinguished Scientific Contributions Award from the American Psychological Association, and the William James Fellow Award from the Association for Psychological Science for "a lifetime of significant intellectual contributions to the basic science of psychology." In 2013, he was elected to the National Academy of Sciences.

JOANNE GILBERT

Daniel Gilbert is the Edgar Pierce Professor of Psychology at Harvard University. Dan received his BA from the University of Colorado at Denver in 1981 and his PhD from Princeton University in 1985. He taught at the University of Texas at Austin, and in 1996 joined the faculty of Harvard University. He has received the Distinguished Scientific Award for an Early Career Contribution to Psychology from the American Psychological Association; the Diener Award for "outstanding contributions to social psychology" from the Foundation for Personality and Social Psychology; the Campbell Award for "distinguished scholarly achievement and sustained excellence in research in social psychology" from the Society for Personality and Social Psychology; and the William James Fellow Award for "a lifetime of significant intellectual contributions to the basic science of psychology" from the Association for Psychological Science. He teaches introductory psychology and has won teaching awards that include the Phi Beta Kappa Teaching Prize and the Harvard College Professorship. His research focuses on how and how well people think about their emotional reactions to future events. He is the author of the best seller *Stumbling on Happiness,* which won the Royal Society's General Prize for best popular science book of the year, and the cowriter and host of the award-winning PBS television series *This Emotional Life.*

NICOLAS GUEVARA

Matthew Nock is the Edgar Pierce Professor of Psychology at Harvard University. Matt received his BA from Boston University in 1995 and his PhD from Yale University in 2003. He completed his clinical internship at Bellevue Hospital and the New York University Child Study Center, and then joined the faculty of Harvard University in 2003. While an undergraduate, he became interested in understanding why people do things to intentionally harm themselves, and he has been conducting research to answer that question ever since. His research is multidisciplinary and uses a wide range of methodological approaches (e.g., epidemiologic surveys, laboratory-based experiments, and clinic-based studies) to understand how these behaviours develop, how to predict them, and how to prevent their occurrence. He has received many teaching awards at Harvard, as well as four Early Career awards recognizing his research. In 2011, he was named a MacArthur Fellow.

FRANK NEUFELD

Ingrid Johnsrude is Western Research Chair in Cognitive Neuroscience at The University of Western Ontario. Ingrid received her BSc from Queen's University in 1989 and her PhD in clinical psychology from McGill University in 1997, supervised by pioneering neuropsychologist Brenda Milner. After 7 years in the UK, first as a postdoctoral fellow at University College London and then as a research scientist at Cambridge University, she returned to her alma mater, Queen's, where she held a Canada Research Chair and taught Introductory Psychology. She moved to the University of Western Ontario in 2014. Individuals in her group study how people manage to understand speech when there is background noise, such as in a bar or restaurant, or at a party. She has received multiple teaching awards and early career awards for her research, and is a Fellow of the Canadian Academy of Health Sciences. Her many years of experience across the broad discipline of psychology—in animal behaviour, neuropsychology, clinical psychology, cognitive science, cognitive neuroscience, and research methods—as well as her experience teaching Introductory Psychology, make her well equipped to serve as Canadian author for this textbook.

BRIEF CONTENTS

CONTENTS

A NOTE TO STUDENTS

Dear Student,

The world is full of mysteries—from stars to fossils, from quarks to cells. But for us, the greatest mystery has always been other people, and that's what drew each of us into our first psychology course in university. What we remember about those courses is that we were blown away by the ideas we encountered and by the lectures we heard, but what we don't remember are the textbooks. That's probably because they were little more than jargon-filled encyclopedias of names and dates that we eagerly sold to some other unsuspecting sucker the moment we finished our final exams.

After we became psychology professors, we started to wonder why textbooks had to be like that. We decided they didn't, so in 2008 we wrote the first edition of *Psychology*—the textbook that we wished we'd been given when we were students. The reaction to it was nothing short of astounding. We'd never written a textbook before, so we had no idea what to expect, but never in our wildest dreams did we imagine that we would end up winning *the Pulitzer Prize*!

Which was good, because we didn't. But what actually happened was even better. Okay, just as good. Okay, almost as good. Anyway, what happened is that we started getting e-mails from students all over the place who told us (with seeming surprise) that they actually *liked* reading our textbook. They liked the content, of course, because psychology is inherently fascinating, but they liked other things too. They liked the fact that our textbook didn't *sound* like a textbook and wasn't written in the stodgy dad-voice of that guy who seems to be the narrator in every high school biology film ever made ("Behold the side-stripped jackal, nature's furry little scavenger"). Rather, it was written in *our* voices—the same voices we use when we talk to our students, friends, families, and pets (which is why Chapter 12 was originally titled "Stop Chewing My Shoes and Get Off the Couch"). Students also liked the fact that we told the *story* of psychology—that we integrated topics rather than just listing them, that we illustrated ideas rather than just describing them, and that we made fun of ourselves and anyone else who didn't run away fast enough. That kind of feedback is what's kept us going for six editions.

Of course, a textbook has to do more than just tell an interesting and entertaining story. It also has to *help you learn*. That's why in addition to all the stuff that novels, cookbooks, and owner's manuals have—words and sentences, graphs and diagrams—textbooks also have features that are meant to help you understand and remember the material you're reading. Designing these features requires a keen understanding of how human beings learn, and, as luck would have it, that's one of the subjects on which psychologists happen to be expert. The features in our textbook all make use of basic principles of psychology. To introduce you to those features, we'll start by giving you six tips for reading our textbook, and then, after you've read those tips, we'll explain how our textbook's features will help you implement them.

Six Tips for Reading This Textbook

Reading just happens. You look at a printed page and your eyes instantly start to glide across it, turning black squiggles into words and sentences without any help from you. Unlike reading, understanding and remembering don't just happen, which is why you can read a sentence, look up, and ten seconds later have no freaking idea what you just read. (If that's happening now, please start this section over.) Research shows that the best way to turn *reading* into *understanding and remembering* is to not just let reading happen but, rather, to take an active role in reading. Here are five ways to do that.

- **Rehearse.** No, we don't mean dress up and recite Shakespeare. In psychology, rehearsal simply means repeating information to yourself, and if you do it right, it turns out to be a remarkably useful way to memorize facts. For example, suppose you wanted to remember the name of the person who built the first psychology laboratory (which you may want to do when you read Chapter 1). First you might say something like "Wilhelm Wundt built the first psychology laboratory" a few times to yourself, wait a few seconds, then say it a few times again, wait even longer, then say it again, then . . . well, you get the idea. By increasing the interval between rehearsals you will be making it a little bit harder to remember the fact each time—kind of like doing bench presses and adding increasing amounts of weight with each set of repetitions—and research shows that this is an effective way to commit information to memory.

- **Interpret.** Rehearsal is good for memorizing facts, but if you want to learn psychology, you're going to need to understand *ideas*. Research shows that one of the best ways to understand and remember ideas is to stop reading for a moment and *interpret* them—that is, to think about what they mean and how they relate to you. For example, suppose you wanted to learn the basic ideas behind behaviourism (which you will definitely want to do when you read Chapter 7). You will be tempted to read what we've written about behaviourism and move on, but you'd be better off pausing and asking yourself a question such as "How would a behaviourist explain my choice of degree program?" To answer this question, you will not only need to recall what you read about behaviourism, but you will also need to relate it to other things that you already know (e.g., that you struggled to decide whether you should major in psychology or in something your parents incorrectly told you was more important). It turns out that it is much easier to remember new information when you relate it to something with which you are already familiar.

- **Organize.** If someone asked you to memorize the words "Greet, Ask, Beg, Sign, Fold, Insert, Lick," in that order, you might find it difficult—unless you noticed that these are the steps involved in composing a letter that asks for money and then mailing it to your parents. Organizing information in a meaningful way is one of the best methods for learning and remembering it, which is why after reading each chapter, you should try telling yourself its story. This doesn't just mean rehearsing the facts or interpreting the various ideas, but rather, it means linking them together and asking how one leads to the other.

- **Test.** You may be tempted to use a yellow highlighter as you read, and then to study by re-reading the material you highlighted. This is a mistake (especially if you have an electronic copy of the textbook) because as you re-read the highlighted material it will start to seem more and more familiar to you, and you will mistakenly assume that because the material is familiar, you know it pretty well. But the fact is that you only "know it" when you're reading it! A much better way to learn is to *test yourself* on the material while you are *not* looking at the textbook. Better yet, study with someone else and test each other.

- **Space.** *When* should you do all this stuff? The wrong answer is "The night before the exam." Research shows that you are much more likely to remember what you learn if you read a bit of the textbook every day and do these exercises while you're reading. Cramming the night before an exam is not only a painful experience (as you might have guessed from the word *cramming*), it is also one of the very worst things you can do if you want to learn, remember what you've learned, and do well on an exam. Reading the textbook the night before is only slightly better than not reading it at all.

- **Sleep.** You already know that it's a good idea to get plenty of sleep the night before an exam. But as you will discover in Chapter 6, it is equally important to get plenty of sleep on the days that you do the study exercises we've just described. When you sleep, your brain rehearses information you encountered during the day, sifting through it, finding patterns in it, and storing it efficiently. Letting your brain "sleep on it" is nearly as important as letting your brain read it in the first place.

Features That Help You Implement These Tips

So yes, those are six excellent pieces of advice. But how in the world are you supposed to remember them—or remember to use them? Don't worry. We've got your back. Our textbook contains a variety of features that we specifically designed to help you implement these and other research-based learning strategies. In fact, we even wrote one really boring chapter just to help you sleep! (Kidding.)

For example, you'll notice that every chapter is divided into a few major sections, and at the beginning of each major section are a set of **Learning Outcomes** that allow you to "be on the lookout" for key concepts as you are reading. This will help you organize the material in your mind—kind of like how knowing beforehand that Romeo and Juliet are star-crossed lovers can help you make sense of the play when you are watching it. Just as the Learning Outcomes tell you what to look for before you read, the **Chapter Review** (which you'll find at the end of each chapter) can help you decide whether you actually found it. By briefly summarizing the major points in each section, it can help you determine whether your reading has produced the level of understanding you desire—and that your instructor will require! If not, then you can go back and re-read the section until you are all learned out.

We've also built features to help you interpret the material you're reading. For instance, at the end of each chapter, you will find a series of **Changing Minds** scenarios that describe everyday situations in which misconceptions about human behaviour arise, and that then ask you to use the chapter's material to correct them. The **Visualizing Data Activities** that are available in Macmillan's Learning online platform **Achieve** invite you to engage with the material by answering questions the way psychologists do—namely, by looking at data! Each activity presents an interactive graph that displays real data from a published study, followed by questions that allow you to test your understanding of the study as well as your ability to reason about the data. The **LearningCurve** adaptive quizzing system will also allow you to test yourself—and it will design quizzes just for you.

A Box of Words

You may have noticed that when people tell stories ("When I was in Rome this summer, I saw the Trevi Fountain, the Sistine Chapel, and the Colosseum"), they occasionally pause to tell you some related thing that they found especially interesting ("Did you know that in the 16th century, the Pope tried to turn the Colosseum into a wool factory?"). Then when they're done, they pick up their story again. Well, every chapter in our textbook also tells a story, and once in a while we pause that story to tell you some related thing that we found especially interesting—not about Italian wool factories, but about psychology. The way you'll know we're pausing is that you will bump into a big box full of words. These boxes come in four flavours, and we've given each a name.

- One box is called **A World of Difference.** People differ in countless ways—by culture, gender, race, religion, age, wealth, sexual orientation, and a whole host of other differences. These sources of diversity influence just about everything people think, feel, and do, so in every chapter we pause our story to highlight one or more of them.

- A second box is called **Other Voices.** Long before psychologists appeared on earth, poets, pundits, playwrights, and philosophers were having insights into human nature. So we decided to invite some of them to share their insights with you. In every chapter, you will find a short essay by someone who writes beautifully, has something to say, and most importantly, isn't us.

- A third box is called **The Real World**. From rats in mazes to humans in brain scanners, a textbook can sometimes seem like a report from places that aren't much like the place you live. That's why in every chapter we have included a box that shows how the material you are reading can be applied to the stuff of everyday life—from dating to studying to going on a job interview.

- Finally, in every chapter you will bump into a box called **Hot Science.** When we wrote the previous edition of this textbook 3 years ago, QAnon was an illegal Scrabble word and a coronavirus was something you might get from a Mexican beer. Which is to say, the world changes fast. That's why in every chapter, we take a moment to share with you a new scientific finding that has changed the way we think—and that might change the way you think as well.

Those are the features and those are the boxes and that's probably enough for one note. We could drone on because, after all, we *are* professors, but we trust you get the point: We love the science of psychology and we've written a book that we hope makes you fall in love with it as well. Happy reading!

A NOTE TO INSTRUCTORS

Dear Instructor,

Why do we do this to ourselves? You've spent days and days browsing textbooks when you could have been baking cookies, reading poetry, or binge-watching *The Walking Dead*. We've spent years and years reading papers, writing chapters, and finding photographs when we could have been listening to music, visiting museums, or binge-watching *The Walking Dead*. Why have we all chosen to get lost in Textbookland when there are so many zombies to stream?

For the love of science. You and we may be different ages, genders, races, and religions; we may come from different places or speak different first languages; but much greater than our differences is our common bond, and that is our shared and unshakeable belief that science provides the best tools for understanding the mysteries of human behaviour. Somewhere along the way, we all stumbled on a field called psychology and got stuck there because we fell in love with a simple idea, which is that the methods scientists use to figure out what causes cancer or to understand how butterflies migrate can also be used to answer age-old questions about the hearts and minds of our kind. Honestly, anyone who stumbles on that idea and isn't excited by it just has to be a zombie.

Is our textbook right for you? We don't know. But we do know that when you choose a textbook you are entrusting part of your students' education to someone else, and that trust needs to be earned. We've tried to do that by writing a textbook that has a single overarching goal: To make your students fall in love with this amazing young science for just the reasons that you did and we did. Whatever they do with that passion—become psychologists, or just become better parents, smarter consumers, and more informed citizens—our job is to ignite it by spreading the good news about our science. That's what we try to do on every one of the pages that follow, and you will decide if we've succeeded.

Okay, give us a minute to dry our eyes. There, that's better. Now let's get into some of the nutsy-boltsy stuff you'll want to know about our textbook, and about our sixth edition in particular.

Building on What Works

The words *new* and *improved* sell a lot of mobile phones and coffee makers, and they probably sell a lot of textbooks too. But we won't use them. After all, this is the sixth edition of our textbook, and if everything in it were new and improved, then everything in the previous editions would have to be obsolete or in desperate need of repair. That's simply not the case. We've spent more than 15 years crafting this textbook, and we've learned a lot in the process—not just from writing and re-writing it, but also from the many instructors and students across the country who have taken the time to tell us what they liked, what they didn't like, and how we could turn the latter into the former.

We've listened, and the reason our sixth edition is the best one ever is that rather than *changing* everything just so we could point to three new bells and a shiny whistle, we put most of our energies into *perfecting* the things that were already working well. Instructors told us that our pedagogical tools were strong, so we sharpened them rather than replacing them. They told us that our coverage was right on target, so we steadied our aim rather than aiming elsewhere. And they told us that their students enjoyed our casual and sometimes irreverent narrative voice, so we updated our jokes rather than admitting to ourselves that they were just really, really bad. If the sixth edition looks familiar to you, that's because with each edition we've learned to make more babies and less bathwater.

With that said, the sixth edition is by no means the fifth with a new cover. In every chapter you will find several dozen updates to the basic science we cover, as well as a variety of changes that are meant to reflect our rapidly changing times, like the effects of the COVID-19 pandemic. Before the book even got started we inserted a new section called "Words Matter" that not only explains our use of words denoting sex, gender, and race, but also encourages students to think about how they use these words in their everyday lives. Here are some of the highlights of what's new in each chapter.

About the Sixth Canadian Edition

Writing a Canadian edition of an American psychology textbook is not simply a matter of putting a lot of extra *u*'s in words like *color* and *behavior*. Although the principles of psychology are universal, behaviour depends on demographics, history, geography, and culture. The United States may be culturally familiar to Canadians, but Canadian students deserve a book that reflects their own experience. Cultural references need to be relatable, and information about incidence and prevalence should be appropriate for the society in which our students live. Canada is a multicultural and outward-looking place, and a Canadian book should reflect that also. Finally, Canadian scientists have made foundational discoveries in psychology, and these should be highlighted so they can inspire the Canadian scientists of tomorrow who are reading this book.

This new edition retains the highly engaging examples and international perspective of the fifth Canadian edition while incorporating the new research and features of the American sixth edition. Wherever possible, U.S. statistics have been replaced with ones from Statistics Canada, and Canadian or international examples or topics have been substituted for those that had a specifically American focus and context.

In the Canadian edition, we have aimed to maintain the benefits of the parent text and its narrative while appealing to Canadian students. Psychology is an international endeavour, and research foundational to the field has been conducted in many countries outside the United States. Consequently, we did not "Canadianize" the textbook as much as make it less America-centric. To highlight the international dimension, we have indicated the nationality of non-American scientists responsible for particularly important discoveries. When these happened in Canada, we have also indicated the university. We have also tried to highlight the remarkable scientific discoveries made by pioneering Canadian scientists such as Albert Bandura, Alain Dagher, Donald Hebb, Ronald Melzack, Brenda Milner, Wilder Penfield, Gordon Pennycook, Hans Selye, Shepard Siegel, and others.

We have also tried to reflect the diversity of the people who live across this large country. We have worked to recognize and reflect the experience of the Indigenous peoples who are the traditional stewards of the land we call Canada.

To illustrate how we have incorporated Canadian, and Indigenous, perspectives, we highlight some of the specific information included in each chapter:

Chapter 1 Psychology: Evolution of a Science

- The book begins by noting the year 1860, and a reference to both the Cariboo Gold Rush and the death of an important Indigenous chief are used as temporal place markers.
- An emphasis on William James as the founder of psychology has been altered to take a more international view.
- Instead of a Harvard-specific history of cognitive psychology, we now discuss Tolman and his demonstration of cognitive maps.
- Besides the American Psychological Association, we include descriptions of Canadian psychological organizations, such as the Canadian Psychological Association; the Canadian Society for Brain, Behaviour and Cognitive Science; and the Canadian Association of Neuroscience. We also indicate career paths for psychologists in Canada.

Chapter 2 Methods in Psychology

- We use examples in our explanations that appeal beyond the United States.
- We present the ethical guidelines that all Canadian psychologists are to follow, whether in conducting research or dealing with clients using the wording of the TriCouncil TCPS 2, the Canadian Psychological Association Code of Ethics, and the Canadian Council on Animal Care.

Chapter 3 Neuroscience and Behaviour

- We start with a story about Steve Montador, a professional hockey player, to illustrate the issue of sports-related head trauma and chronic traumatic encephalopathy.
- We put the issue of opioid dependence and addiction in a Canadian context with new statistics.
- We mention new research about the importance of the cerebellum to cognition, mentioning Canadian researcher Jorn Diedrichsen.
- We highlight the contributions of Montreal neurosurgeon Wilder Penfield in mapping the somatosensory and motor cortex.
- We have replaced U.S. statistics on the prevalence of Alzheimer's dementia with Canadian information.
- We highlight McGill researcher Michael Meaney's work demonstrating that maternal caretaking behaviour has a profound influence on the stress response in offspring.

Chapter 4 Sensation and Perception

- The foundational work of Western researcher Mel Goodale related to perception and action and the complementary specializations of the dorsal and ventral pathways is highlighted.

Chapter 5 Consciousness

- We have added a section on disorders of consciousness (i.e., coma, vegetative state, minimally conscious state, and locked-in syndrome).

- We present the story of French journalist Jean-Dominique Bauby, who wrote *The Diving Bell and the Butterfly,* a memoir about being completely paralyzed after suffering a massive stroke, by blinking his left eyelid.

- The temperance movement is discussed in a Canadian, not American, context.

- The Real World feature "Anyone for Tennis?" presents the story of Scott Routley, who was diagnosed as being in a persistent vegetative state after a car accident. Adrian Owen (The University of Western Ontario) and his team used fMRI technology to show that Scott was conscious, but was locked in by his injury.

- We've rewritten the Hot Science piece "Why Is There an Opioid Epidemic and What Can We Do About It?" to explain the harm done by poor-quality published studies in the 1980s and 1990s, and we've set the epidemic in a Canadian context.

- We describe the harm-reduction evidence for the Canadian government's policy decision to legalize marijuana.

- We have replaced American statistics on drug and alcohol use and abuse with Canadian data.

- We include a new Other Voices piece on how Canadian legalization of pot might benefit research.

Chapter 6 Memory

- We cover the foundational research on the levels-of-processing account (Fergus Craik and Endel Tulving, University of Toronto), which has been so influential in our understanding of how humans encode information.

- We discuss Brenda Milner's discovery, through her early work with Henry Molaison (H.M.), of the role of the hippocampus in long-term memory.

- We highlight Hebb's idea, crystallized as "cells that fire together wire together," that is the neural basis of long-term memory.

- We highlight the discovery of priming by British scientists Elizabeth Warrington and Larry Weiskrantz.

- In the section Memory Failures: The Seven Sins of Memory, we present memory transience through the example of Wilder Penfield's erroneous conclusions about memory being a complete and permanent record of all experience, based on anecdotal observations made while electrically stimulating the brains of his patients. This serves to illustrate to students that our understanding of how the brain works changes over time, based on evidence.

- We have replaced very specifically American examples throughout the chapter with scenarios that Canadian students can relate to more easily.

Chapter 7 Learning

- The Real World: Understanding Drug Overdoses presents some of McMaster University researcher Shepard Siegel's work on classical conditioning and how it can be used to explain how drug overdoses occur in people who are experienced with abusing drugs.

- We have included the discovery of brain stimulation reward in rats by McGill University researchers Peter Milner and James Olds: the first demonstration of brain "pleasure centres."
- We have included Albert Bandura and Paul Gribble's work on observational learning.
- We discuss observational learning as a mechanism for the perpetuation of intergenerational trauma amongst Indigenous peoples.
- The new Other Voices: The Dangers of Learning Loss from Canadian researchers Wendy Cukier, Kelly Gallagher-Mackay, and Karen Mundy makes the point that Canada needs to invest in tutoring to make up for pandemic-related learning loss.

Chapter 8 Emotion and Motivation

- We use a Canadian geographic example to introduce multidimensional scaling.
- Specifically American examples have been replaced with ones that Canadian students can relate to more easily.
- The Hot Science box highlights a study of eating behaviour conducted at the Montreal Neurological Institute by Alain Dagher and his team.
- We've replaced the Other Voices piece, on American political outrage on social media, with a piece from the *New York Times* by Frans de Waal, on emotions in dogs.
- We've replaced the text in the World of Difference to reflect a more global perspective, making the same point about communication.
- We highlight Kang Lee's studies of lying in very young children.
- Statistics about anorexia and obesity are anchored in a Canadian context.
- We discuss sexuality using Canadian statistics and studies.

Chapter 9 Language and Thought

- We highlight the remarkable finding made by McGill researchers Laura Petitto and Paula Marentette (1991) that deaf babies "babble" with their hands.
- We highlight the finding by McGill researcher Denise Klein that a child's first language leaves lasting traces in the brain, even when they are adopted out of their first culture and so never speak it again.
- The discussion on bilingualism is placed in a global context—we make the point that speaking more than one language is the rule, not the exception, globally.
- We emphasize that the discussion of bilingualism in the book is based on Canadian science.
- We have replaced the Other Voices piece on fighting misinformation in social media with one by Gordon Pennycook from the University of Regina.

Chapter 10 Intelligence

- A new The Real World piece features a UK study that demonstrates the surprising plasticity of the brain in adolescence when it comes to cognitive ability.

- We've removed specifically American examples and statistics, and replaced these with Canadian ones.
- Other Voices: Not by Intelligence Alone features Barry Schwartz, on what attributes, besides intelligence, are required for a happy, productive, and successful life.

Chapter 11 Development

- We present Canadian statistics on prenatal factors and health care.
- A new Other Voices piece by Cindy Blackstock, executive director of the First Nations Child and Family Caring Society of Canada, explores how social welfare policies in Canada damage the development of Indigenous youth, contributing to intergenerational trauma in this group.
- We highlight the work of University of Toronto/McGill University researcher Tomas Paus on brain development.
- We present Canadian statistics on substance use and texting while driving among Canadian adolescents.
- We present Canadian statistics on gender identity.
- We have replaced information on American attitudes towards homosexuality with information about attitudes around the world, and with Canadian statistics.
- We highlight that Canada was the first country to legalize same-sex marriage.
- We highlight the work of Queen's University psychologist Meredith Chivers on the effects of sexual orientation on arousal.
- We discuss the term *two spirit* — which is used by some Indigenous people to describe their sexual, gender, and/or spiritual identity — in the Real World piece on gender and sexual orientation, "Coming to Terms with Ourselves."
- We use Canadian statistics and information in the discussion about sexual activity in adolescence.
- The exclusive emphasis on marriage in the section on adult committed relationships has been altered to be more inclusive, since many couples (particularly in Quebec) in long-term committed relationships do not get married.
- We rely on Canadian sources for statistics on happiness and information about factors influencing happiness.

Chapter 12 Personality

- Specifically American examples have been replaced with scenarios that Canadian students can relate to more easily.
- We have changed the example of implicit egoism to an amusing anecdote about Henry Head and Lord Walter Russell Brain, two British neurologists who were editors of the journal *Brain*.

Chapter 13 Social Psychology

- Specifically American information has been replaced with its Canadian equivalent, and specifically American examples throughout have been replaced with examples that Canadian students can relate to.

- American violent crime statistics have been replaced with Canadian ones.
- Figure 13.5 on altruism in American states was replaced with a figure showing organ donation rates by province.
- A new Other Voices piece on the use of solitary confinement in Canadian prisons features Canadian criminologists Anthony Doob and Jane Sprott.
- We highlight the Vancouver Capilano Bridge experiment in which University of British Columbia researchers Donald Dutton and Arthur Aron demonstrated that physiological arousal accompanying fear can be mistaken for attraction.
- The section on love and marriage has been revised to discuss long-term committed relationships generally, not just marriages.
- Canadian statistics for committed long-term relationships and breakups have replaced American marriage and divorce statistics.
- The section on stereotyping and unconscious bias is set in a Canadian context—for instance, Figure 13.10 has been replaced with Canadian data. Twitter sensation Gurdeep Pandhar of the Yukon is used as an example of stereotype violation.
- The discussion of implicit bias has been widened beyond a consideration of Black and white Americans, and put into a Canadian context with Canadian statistics.
- We discuss how implicit bias in Canada has created systemic barriers for Indigenous people and include a specific example on how legislation has resulted in structural inequalities that make health care less accessible and of poorer quality for Indigenous people.

Chapter 14 Stress and Health

- Specifically American information has been replaced with its Canadian equivalent, and specifically American examples throughout have been replaced with examples that Canadian students can relate to.
- In the text as well as in the World of Difference piece "Can Discrimination Cause Stress and Illness?" we present evidence indicating how racism and discrimination against the Black, Indigenous, and other people of colour (BIPOC) population in Canada leads to increased stress and poorer health.
- We highlight the work of University of Montreal researcher Hans Selye in developing the general adaptation syndrome.
- We include Canadian statistics on religious beliefs, lifestyle factors in health and wellness, and the health of immigrant and Indigenous groups in Canada.

Chapter 15 Psychological Disorders

- Specifically American information has been replaced with its Canadian equivalent, and specifically American examples throughout have been replaced with examples that Canadian students can relate to more easily.
- We include incidence and prevalence statistics for psychological disorders in Canada instead of the United States throughout.
- We include a discussion of posttraumatic stress disorder (PTSD) in Canadian veterans of the war in Afghanistan.
- We use the war in Ukraine as an example to highlight recent research on the link between moral injury and PTSD.

- We discuss the large demographic and geographic differences in suicide rates across the country.
- We include a new paragraph that provides evidence for elevated rates of suicide among Indigenous groups and discusses contributing factors.

Chapter 16 Treatment of Psychological Disorders

- Specifically American information has been replaced with its Canadian equivalent, and specifically American examples throughout have been replaced with examples that Canadian students can relate to.
- We provide evidence of the cost of mental disorders to the Canadian economy.
- We provide statistics for provision, access, and use of mental health services by different demographic groups in Canada.
- A new Other Voices piece by Kevin Berube explores the intergenerational trauma amongst Indigenous residential school survivors and their descendants.
- The explanation for why people fail to seek treatment is presented in a Canadian context, since health service provision differs widely between Canada and the United States.
- The training and practice of psychotherapy differs substantially between Canada and the United States, so the Real World box on types of psychotherapists provides Canadian information about how practitioners are trained, the regulatory frameworks, and what types of therapy orientations are popular.
- Similarly, Figure 16.1, on approaches to psychotherapy in the 21st century, provides information about the popularity of different theoretical orientations in Canada, and approaches that are popular in Canada but not mentioned in the American edition (e.g., family systems therapy) are described briefly in the text.
- We discuss the CPA guidelines, together with the APA guidelines, for the use of empirically supported treatments, as well as the Canadian Code of Ethics for treating vulnerable individuals with mental disorders.

You Do the Teaching—We'll Do the Rest

Our primary job as textbook authors is to give your students a solid overview of the vast literature in psychological science so that you can spend your class time focusing on the things you really want to tell them, or ask them, or do with them, rather than trying to cover all that territory yourself. Maybe that's all you wanted from us, in which case . . . um, thanks for stopping in!

But if you think textbook authors can do more than that for you, well then, we happen to agree. That's why we (and *we* of course means "a team of dedicated people at Macmillan Learning whose hard work we will now take credit for") have developed a variety of resources to make your job easier and your teaching more effective. Here are just a few of them:

- One of the many features of **Achieve** that we personally like best is the **LearningCurve** adaptive quizzing system. This system measures a student's performance and then chooses quiz questions based on how well they are doing, which means that every student in your class can take a quiz that has been custom-designed for them. What's more, LearningCurve gives students instant feedback about their performance, while providing you with a report on the progress of individual students and on your class as a whole. You really have to see how beautiful the platform is and how easily it works.

- Students hate taking exams. What they don't realize is that we hate making them even more. That's why our book comes with a **Test Bank** (overseen by Dominique Hubbard of Northern Virginia Community College-Alexandria) that includes more than 250 multiple-choice, true/false, and essay questions for every chapter. You may have designed your class around the APA's outcomes for introductory psychology students, and, if so, you'll be happy to know that we link the test bank questions to these outcomes, making it easy for you to see which goals are being achieved.

- Can we help you make some **lecture slides**? We hope so, because our book comes with a fully updated set. Can we suggest some **lecture topics and class activities**? We hope so, because our book also comes with a download-able **Instructor's Resource Manual** (created by Julie Lazzara of Paradise Valley Community College), which contains plenty of them. Can we get you a cup of coffee? Just checking to see if you were still with us.

- Is there a doctor in the house? Some of your students may be preparing to take the **MCAT,** and if so, we've got them covered. We prepared a special resource that connects the contents of our textbook to the specific topics that are covered on the MCAT exam. Furthermore, our test bank includes a special set of questions for each chapter that test quantitative reasoning ability in the style of the MCAT.

These are just a few of the resources that help make our textbook more than the sum of its chapters. You can find more details online at macmillanlearning.com.

ACKNOWLEDGEMENTS

Despite what you might guess by looking at our photographs, we all found partners who were willing to marry us after some special pleading. We are grateful to Susan McGlynn, Marilynn Oliphant, and Keesha Nock, who never complained about those long nights and weekends when we were writing this textbook rather than hanging out with them. We assume they missed us and we are smart enough not to ask.

Although ours are the only names on the cover, writing a textbook is a team sport, and we've been fortunate to have a terrific group of professionals in our dugout. They have helped us on this edition and past editions more than we can say, and more than they probably realize:

Suman Ali
Oakton Community College

Ersin Asliturk
Douglas College

Joan T. Bihun
University of Colorado, Denver

Scott David Eaton
Mohawk Valley Community College

Gisel Flores-Montoya
Carleton College

Johnathan D. Forbey
Ball State University

Sherona Garrett-Ruffin
Bowling Green State University-Main Campus

Alicia M. Grande
Western Carolina University

Stephanie Griffiths
Okanagan College

Ryan Hjelle
University of Minnesota-Duluth

Paul Johnson
Oakton Community College

George Martinez
Somerset Community College

Liza Meredith
University of Minnesota-Twin Cities

Ryan Messatzzia
Wor Wic Community College

Peter Mezo
University of Toledo

Kristen Mudge
Jackson Community College

Erin M. Myers
Western Carolina University

Neelam Rattan
California State University San Jose

Jolina H. Ruckert
Lewis & Clark College

Albert K. Toh
University of Arkansas at Pine Bluff

Adriana Uruena-Agnes
University of South Florida–Tampa

Frank Wagenblast
Middlesex County College

Benjamin White
Blinn College–Bryan Campus

Past Editions
Rebecca Addington
University of Wisconsin–Madison

Christine Bartholomew
Kent State University

Dave Baskind
Delta College

Elizabeth A. Becker
St. Joseph's University

Dawn Brinkley
University of Texas–Dallas

Jennifer L. Butler
Case Western Reserve University

Marci Campbell
Salt Lake Community College

Diana L. Ciesko
Valencia College

Emily Cohen-Shikora
Washington University–St. Louis

Rebecca DesRoches
Regis College

Chris De La Ronde
Austin Community College

Michael Disch
St. Edwards University

Kimberly Duff
Cerritos College

April K. Dye
Carson-Newman University

John E. Edlund
Rochester Institute of Technology

Kim Ernst
Loyola University New Orleans

Lauren Ethridge
University of Oklahoma

Celeste Favela
El Paso Community College

Mark Ferguson
University of Wisconsin–Stevens Point

Sara Finley
Pacific Lutheran University

Jocelyn R. Folk
Kent State University

Jim Fryer
SUNY Pottsdam

Sophie A. George
Dixie State University

Afshin Gharib
Dominican University of California

Jerry Green
Tarrant County College

Maria E. Guarneri-White
Pacific Lutheran University

Jane S. Halonen
University of West Florida

Edward Hansen
Florida State University

Shani N. Harris
Spelman College

Erin Henshaw
Denison University

L. E. Holliman
*Georgia State University at Perimeter–
Clarkston Campus*

Keith Holyoak
*University of California–
Los Angeles*

George-Harold Jennings
Drew University

Janna Kline
Rutgers University

Michael M. Knepp
University of Mount Union

Karen Kwan
Salt Lake Community College

Christopher B. Mayhorn
North Carolina State University

Michael Jason McCoy
Cape Fear Community College

Wendy Mendes
*University of California San
Francisco*

Dennis K. Miller
University of Missouri–Columbia

Rikki L. A. Miller
University of Southern Maine

Khu Nguyen
Washington University in St. Louis

Bradley M. Okdie
*Ohio State University–
Newark*

Caroline Olko
Nassau Community College

Natasha Otto
Morgan State University

Doug A. Peterson
University of South Dakota

Jessica Petok
St. Olaf College

Catherine Phillips
Northwest Vista College

Gary Popoli
Stevenson University

Mixalis Poulakis
University of Indianapolis

G. A. Radvansky
University of Notre Dame

Marjorie Rhodes
New York University

Kiefer Rich
San Diego City College

Blake Riek
Calvin College

Gwendolyn Scott-Jones
Delaware State University

Keith M. Shafritz
Hofstra University

Shubam Sharma
University of Florida

Michelle Shiota
Arizona State University

Hiroko Sotozaki
Western Illinois University

Jonathan N. Sparks
Vance-Granville Community College

Peter Sparks
Oregon State University–Cascades

Helen T. Sullivan
Rider University

Donald Tellinghuisen
Calvin College

David G. Thomas
Oklahoma State University

Travis Tubré
University of Wisconsin–River Falls

Lora Vasiliauskas
Virginia Western Community College

Constance Walsh
Fullerton College

Megan Kozak Williams
Linfield College

James Thomas Wright
Forsyth Technical Community College

Dasa Zeithamova
University of Oregon

As always, we are deeply grateful to our good friends at Macmillan Learning, with whom we have happily worked for so many years. They include:

- Executive Vice President and General Manager Chuck Linsmeier, who has been providing guidance, encouragement, and alcohol since the first day of the first edition.

- Our executive program manager, Carolyn Merrill, who has managed our project (and us) with wisdom and good humor while keeping all the trains, planes, automobiles, submarines, and pachyderms running on time.

- Our development editor, Marita Bley, whose clear vision and deft touch kept us from making a variety of mistakes, from the conceptual to the rhetorical to the typlographlical. Oh damn.

- Our senior content project manager Vivien Weiss, Lumina project manager Arindam Bose, senior workflow project supervisor Paul Rohloff, and editorial assistant Emily Kelly, all of whom seem to know some magic spell that turns a bunch of disorganized text files into a set of beautiful pages.

- Our senior design services manager Natasha Wolfe, our cover design manager John Callahan, our art manager Matt McAdams, our photo manager Robin Fadool, and our photo researcher Donna Ranieri, who worked together to make our textbook as delightful to look at as it is to read.

- Our media project manager Joseph Tomasso, who expertly guided the development and creation of our superb supplements package.

- Our executive marketing manager Kate Nurre and marketing assistant Claudia Cruz, who have always been and continue to be tireless public advocates for our vision.

What would we have done without all of you? Gracias, arigato, danke, merci, xie xie, and a way big thanks!

Daniel L. Schacter
Cambridge, 2022

Daniel T. Gilbert
Cambridge, 2022

Matthew K. Nock
Cambridge, 2022

Ingrid S. Johnsrude
London, Ontario, 2022

DS MATTER WO
VORDS MATTER
WO
TER

Every human group has a name. Usually more than one. Some of these names acknowledge and honour the group, some misrepresent and demean it. In this book, we talk about many kinds of human groups—groups based on sex and gender, on race and ethnicity, on religion and political affiliation and mental health—and we follow a simple rule: Call people what they want to be called and what they call themselves. In our view, people are the first, best, and final arbiters of their own names.

In most cases, this is an easy rule to follow—or at least not to break. For example, most style manuals now allow authors to use the word *they* as a singular pronoun, so rather than describing a hypothetical person as *he* (which is what most authors did until the late 20th century and which leaves out half the human race) or as *he/she* (which is not just ugly, but which also leaves out all the humans who don't identify with one of these labels), we describe them as . . . well, *them*. Similarly, we generally avoid nouns that seem to define people by their conditions. People with depression generally prefer to be called people with depression rather than depressives, and the same goes for people with schizophrenia, autism, phobia, and just about every other condition you can think of.

Those are the easy cases. In other cases, it is hard for authors to know what to do. For example, as you'll learn in the Development chapter, *sex* refers to the bodies we are born with, and *gender* refers to our identities—how we see ourselves and how we want others to see us. The terms *male* and *female* describe most people's sex, and the terms *man* and *woman* describe most people's gender. Not all, but most. Using these terms properly is easy when we are talking about people we know, but it gets complicated when we are talking about participants in studies that were published some time ago because, until very recently, most researchers reported the number of "male and female participants" in their studies without specifying whether they were reporting sex or gender. So how should we describe those participants now? We suspect that in most cases, researchers were reporting gender and not sex, because in most cases, researchers were reporting what their participants had *told* them—and most people tell researchers their genders, even when researchers ask, "What is your sex?" That's our best guess anyway, and therefore, as a rule, we refer to the participants in studies as men and women unless we have good reason to do otherwise. Of course, this isn't entirely right either because there are more than two genders. But once again, it is only recently that psychologists have begun providing their participants with more than two response options, which means that we simply can't know the nonbinary identities of past participants. So for now, at least, the words *men* and *women* seem like the best compromise between truth and ignorance.

This doesn't mean that we'll never use the terms *male* and *female*. For example, you will learn that females reach puberty earlier than males do, that males have more testosterone than females do and that this makes them more prone to violence, and so on. The words *male* and *female* are appropriate in these instances because we are talking about groups defined by their shared biology, and not by their shared identity.

Finding the best words for racial and ethnic groups can also be tricky when the people being described were participants in studies published long ago. In those cases, we've also had to make our best guesses based on what we know. So you'll notice that we generally refer to "Black participants" rather than "African American participants," and that's because we typically don't know whether all the Black participants in a particular study were Americans—and if they were, whether they were Americans with ancestral roots in the Caribbean who might not identify as African American. So as a rule, we refer to Black participants as Black participants, unless we happen to know that they identify themselves otherwise. But this rule quickly breaks down when describing other groups. For example, the word *Asian* is typically used to describe people who live in Asia, whereas *Asian American* is typically used to describe U.S. citizens with Asian heritage—people who would probably object to being called *Asian* because that word seems to deny their American citizenship and identity. Alas, there is no word for "participants with Asian roots who took part in a study conducted in the United States but whose place of birth and residence is unknown to textbook authors." In cases like this one, we use the term that we *think* the person being described would use to describe themselves.

One more thing: You may notice that throughout this book we capitalize the word *Black*, but not the word *white*. Why? Because the word *Black* refers to a human group with a shared history, culture, and identity and the word *white* does not. The white people in Sweden and the white people in Argentina have virtually nothing in common except for their hatred of Brazil's soccer team. Style manuals disagree about whether the word *white* should or should not also be capitalized, but the big-*B*-small-*w* rule was recently adopted by the Associated Press, the *Wall Street Journal*, and the *New York Times*, and who are we to argue with a bunch of smart people who type for a living?

Words matter, and now you know how and why we use them the way we do in the pages that follow. Will we sometimes get it wrong? Undoubtedly. There is a word for the group that makes mistakes despite having good intentions, and that word is *human*. We've been members of that group for our entire lives.

The Evolution of Psychological Science

IN 1860, the Cariboo gold rush was about to begin in British Columbia, one of the principal chiefs of the Blackfoot tribe in Canada, A'kow-muk-ai ("Old Swan") died, and the cornerstone of a new Parliament was laid in Ottawa, the capital of the British colony of Canada. In the United States, Abraham Lincoln became president, and a woman named Anne Kellogg had just given birth to a child who would grow up to invent the cornflake. On the U.S. East Coast, an 18-year-old named William James (1842–1910) started worrying about what to do with the rest of his life. He loved to paint and draw, but realized that he wasn't talented enough to become a serious artist. At his father's urging, he decided to go to school to study chemistry, but he soon found that chemistry didn't interest him. So he switched to physiology and then to medicine, only to find that those subjects didn't interest him either. Finding so little of interest in school, William took a leave of absence and joined a scientific expedition to the Amazon, hoping to discover his true passion. But all he discovered was that he passionately hated leeches. So William returned to school and quickly became so depressed that he was required to take another leave of absence.

This time, however, instead of heading south, he headed east—to what is now Germany, which at that time was a leading centre for scientific enquiry, especially in the field of physiology. As he talked and listened, he learned about a new science called psychology (from a combination of the Greek *psyche* [soul] and *logos* [to study]). He saw that this developing field was taking a modern, scientific approach to age-old questions about human nature—questions that had become painfully familiar to him during his personal search for meaning but to which only poets and philosophers had ever before offered answers. Excited about the new discipline, James returned to America and quickly finished his medical degree. But he never practiced medicine and never intended to. Rather, he became a professor at Harvard University and devoted the rest of his life to philosophy and psychology. His landmark book *The Principles of Psychology* is still widely read and remains one of the most influential books ever written on the subject (James, 1890).

- **Psychology's Philosophical Roots**
- **The Late 1800s: Towards a Science of the Mind**
- **The Early 1900s: Psychoanalysis and Behaviourism**
- **The Early 1900s: Resistance to Behaviourism**
- **The Late 1900s: The Cognitive Revolution**
- **The Early 2000s: New Frontiers**
- **Becoming a Psychologist**

HISTORY AND ART COLLECTION/ALAMY STOCK PHOTO

"Six Blackfeet Chiefs," painted by Irish-Canadian painter Paul Kane in 1859. Kane travelled and recorded for three years among the wilderness and Indigenous peoples of what is now western Canada. This painting was based on a sketch made along the North Saskatchewan River.

"This is no science," James said of psychology in 1892, "it is only the hope of a science."[1] And at that time, he was right. But now, more than a century later, that hope has been realized and the book you hold in your hand is the evidence. How did it happen? How did we get here from there? How did the psychology taught in William James's classroom become the psychology taught in yours? This chapter tells that story. We'll start by examining psychology's intellectual roots in philosophy, and then we'll explore the early attempts to develop a science of psychology by some of the people whom William James met when he travelled to Germany. Next, we'll see how in the 1900s, two utterly incompatible approaches to psychology arose—one in Europe that viewed the mind as an infinitely complex mystery, and one in America that viewed the mind as an irrelevant fiction. We'll see how the latter approach came to dominate experimental psychology in the 20th century, and how it was ultimately ended by the invention of a machine. Finally, we'll examine the profession of modern psychology and see who the people who call themselves psychologists really are.

THOSE PEOPLE, BY THE WAY, ARE REMARKABLY DIVERSE: Women currently outnumber men in Canadian psychology graduate programs. But it wasn't always so. One of the things you will notice in this chapter is that the *history* of psychology is mainly the story of White men. That's because until the last half of the 20th century arrived, everyone else's opportunities to contribute to psychology's development were severely limited by gender norms, social conventions, sexism, and racism. History is the story of the past, and the past can't be changed; but as you'll see at the end of this chapter, things have changed dramatically in the last few decades—and decidedly for the better.

Psychology's Philosophical Roots

Learning Outcomes

WHAT YOU NEED TO KNOW

- Explain the distinction between dualism and materialism.
- Explain the distinction between realism and idealism.
- Explain the distinction between empiricism and nativism.

Psychology is *the scientific study of mind and behaviour.* The word *mind* refers to a set of private events that happen inside a person—the thoughts and feelings that we experience at every moment but that no one else can see—and the word *behaviour* refers to a set of public events—the things we say and do that can potentially be observed by others. Both human minds and human behaviours have been around for quite a while, and psychologists were not the first to try to make sense of them. That distinction belongs to philosophers, who have been thinking deeply about these topics for several thousand years. Although their ideas could fill several volumes (and if you study philosophy, you'll find that they do), three of these ideas are especially important to understanding modern psychology.

Dualism and Materialism

Our bodies are physical objects that can be seen, smelled, and touched. Our minds are not. The word *mind* refers to a set of subjective events—perceptions and memories, thoughts and feelings—that have no actual physical presence. You can't hear an

---

psychology The scientific study of mind and behaviour.

[1]From *The Letters of William James*, edited by his nephew Henry James, first published by *Atlantic Monthly Press*, Boston, 1920, and now found in a variety of formats and editions.

emotion or taste a belief. The philosopher René Descartes (1596–1650) thought the "mind-stuff in here" and the "stuff-stuff out there" were so different that they must be made of different substances. The body, he argued, is made of a material substance, the mind is made of an immaterial substance, and every person is therefore a material container of an immaterial thing—or what the philosopher Gilbert Ryle (1949) later called the "ghost in the machine." Like most philosophers of his time, Descartes embraced **philosophical dualism,** which is *the view that mind and body are fundamentally different things.*

But if the mind and the body are fundamentally different things, then how do they interact? How does the immaterial mind tell the material body to put its best foot forward? And when the material body steps on a rusty nail, why does the immaterial mind feel pain? Descartes came up with some answers to these questions that satisfied no one, including himself, but they especially dissatisfied philosophers like Thomas Hobbes (1588–1679), who argued that the mind and body aren't fundamentally different things at all. Rather, the mind *is* what the brain *does.* From Hobbes's perspective, looking for a place in the brain where the mind meets the body is like looking for the place on your phone where the picture meets the screen. The picture *is* what the screen *does,* and they don't "meet" in some third place. The brain is a physical object whose activity is known as "the mind," and therefore all mental phenomena—every thought and feeling, every sight and sound—is the result of some physical activity in the physical brain. **Philosophical materialism** is *the view that all mental phenomena are reducible to physical phenomena.*

So which philosopher was right? The debate between dualism and materialism is not readily settled by facts. Many people believe that the body is a material container of an immaterial spirit, and science can provide no objective evidence that requires them to abandon that belief. The truth is that this is just one of those debates in which people choose their own sides, and most of the world's religions—from Christianity and Judaism to Hinduism and Islam—have chosen to side with the dualists and embrace the notion of a nonphysical soul. Most psychologists have gone the other way and have embraced materialism (Ecklund et al., 2007). As you will see throughout this book, psychologists typically believe that all mental phenomena—from attention and memory to belief and emotion—are ultimately explainable in terms of the physical processes that produce them. The mind is what the brain does—nothing less and certainly nothing more. We are remarkably complex machines whose operations somehow give rise to consciousness, and one of psychology's jobs is to figure out what that "somehow" is.

René Descartes was a dualist who believed that the mind was a nonphysical entity—a "substance incorporeal"—that met the physical body in a structure called the pineal gland (shown in the diagram above from his 1662 book *Treatise of Man*). But Thomas Hobbes was a materialist who thought that "substance incorporeal" was an oxymoron. "Substance and body signify the same thing," he wrote, "and therefore substance incorporeal are words which, when they are joined together, destroy one another."

Realism and Idealism

You probably have the sense that "you" are somewhere inside your skull—not inside your foot or your knee—and that right now you are "looking out" through your eye sockets and reading the words on this page. It *feels* as though our eye is some sort of camera, and that "you" are "in here" seeing pictures of the things "out there." The philosopher John Locke (1632–1704) referred to this idea as **philosophical realism,** which is the

philosophical dualism The view that mind and body are fundamentally different things.

philosophical materialism The view that all mental phenomena are reducible to physical phenomena.

philosophical realism The view that our perceptions of the physical world are a faithful copy of information from the world that enters our brains through our sensory apparatus.

John Locke was a British philosopher and physician who championed philosophical realism. Locke was also a political theorist whose writings about the separation of church and state, religious freedom, and liberty strongly influenced liberal democratic systems, like Canada's. Locke's phrase "the pursuit of happiness" is also the name of a Canadian power pop group from the late 1980s to early 1990s.

PAUL NATKIN/ARCHIVE PHOTOS/GETTY IMAGES

view that *our perceptions of the physical world are a faithful copy of information from the world that enters our brains through our sensory apparatus.* According to this account, light is right now bouncing off the text in front of you and hitting your eye, and that light contains all the information necessary to produce your perception of the text you are seeing. In essence, your eye is a camera that sends a picture of the world to your brain. What could be simpler?

The philosopher Immanuel Kant (1724–1804) agreed that this theory was simple, but he also believed it was simply wrong. Kant suggested that our perceptions of the world are less like photographs that provide an image of the world, and more like paintings that provide an *interpretation* of the world. **Philosophical idealism** is the view that *our perceptions of the physical world are our brain's best interpretation of the information that enters through our sensory apparatus.* According to the idealist account, light is bouncing off the text and is hitting your eye, and your brain is using that information—plus all the other information it has about the world—to produce your perception of the text. It is not just *reflecting* the information that entered your eye, but *interpreting* it, and although your perception of the object feels like a perfect copy of the object itself, it is actually a painting of what your brain *believes* the object looks like.

philosophical idealism The view that our perceptions of the physical world are our brain's best interpretation of the information that enters through our sensory apparatus.

It is said that Immanuel Kant (1724–1804) never ventured more than a few miles from his home in Konigsberg, Prussia (shown here) where, in 1781, he wrote his masterpiece, *The Critique of Pure Reason.* In this book, Kant argued that the mind comes hard-wired with certain kinds of knowledge (which he called conceptions) and that it uses this knowledge to create people's perceptions of the world. "Perceptions without conceptions are blind," Kant wrote, meaning that without prior knowledge of the world, people would be unable to perceive it.

La Maison de Kant, à Kœnigsberg. — Dessin de Freeman 1724—1804

So which philosopher was right? Modern psychology has come down strongly on the side of idealism. As you will see in many of the upcoming chapters, your perception of the world is an *inference*—your brain's best guess about what's probably out there. Because your brain is such a good guesser and such a fast guesser, you typically don't realize it is guessing at all. You feel like your eye is a camera that shoots super-high-definition video, but that's only because the artist between our ears can paint so realistically and at lightning speed. Psychologists have devised all sorts of clever ways to catch the artist in the act, and in subsequent chapters you will learn about many of them.

Empiricism and Nativism

Here are some things you know about coffee mugs: You know that four coffee mugs are more than two, that a coffee mug can't pass through a solid brick wall, that if you push a coffee mug off a table it will fall down rather than up. How do you know all this stuff? **Philosophical empiricism** is *the view that all knowledge is acquired through experience*. Philosophers such as Locke believed that a newborn baby is a *tabula rasa,* or "blank slate" upon which experience writes its story. As Locke wrote in his 1690 *Essay on Human Understanding*:

> If we will attentively consider newborn children, we shall have little reason to think that they bring many ideas into the world with them. . . . One may perceive how, by degrees, afterwards, ideas come into their minds; and that they get no more, nor other, than what experience, and the observation of things that come in their way, furnish them with; which might be enough to satisfy us that they are not original characters stamped on the mind.

In other words, you know about coffee mugs—and about coffee pots and coffee tables and coffee ice cream and a huge number of other objects that don't involve coffee—because you've seen them, or interacted with them, or seen someone else interact with them.

Kant thought Locke was wrong about this, too. **Philosophical nativism** is *the view that some knowledge is innate rather than acquired*. Kant argued that human beings must be born with some basic knowledge of the world that allows them to acquire additional knowledge of the world. After all, how could you learn that pushing a coffee mug off a table *causes* it to fall if you didn't already know what causation was? The fact that you can acquire knowledge about what coffee mugs do when pushed suggests that your mind came with at least a few bits of knowledge already programmed into it. For Kant, those few preprogrammed bits of knowledge were not about specific objects such as coffee mugs, ducks, or doorbells, but about basic concepts such as space, time, causality, and number. You can't learn these concepts, Kant argued, and yet you have to have them in order to learn anything else, which means that they must come factory installed.

Which philosopher was right? Most modern psychologists embrace some version of nativism. It is obvious that much of what we know—for example, that coffee mugs are smaller than coffee makers—is acquired through experience, and no psychologist thinks otherwise. But research suggests that at least *some* of what we know is indeed hard-wired into our brains, just as Kant suspected. As you'll see in the Development chapter, even newborn infants seem to have some basic knowledge of the laws of physics and mathematics. The tabula is not rasa and the slate is not blank, which leads to some interesting questions, such as *What exactly is written on the slate at birth? How and when in our evolutionary history did it get there? Can experience erase the slate as well as write on it?* Psychologists refer to these types of questions as "nature-versus-nurture" questions, and as you will see in some of the upcoming chapters, they have a host of techniques for answering them.

philosophical empiricism The view that all knowledge is acquired through experience.

philosophical nativism The view that some knowledge is innate rather than acquired.

Other Voices | **How Should We Judge Historical Figures?**

This chapter celebrates the ideas of several historical figures who were inarguably brilliant, but who held some opinions that today most of us find abhorrent. Immanuel Kant's development of idealism was a stroke of genius, but that same genius argued that women were incapable of reasoning from moral principles and then went on to discuss at some length which Africans made the best slaves. How should we think about people like Kant, whose intellectual contributions are as undeniable as his sexist and racist views?

Writer and director Paul Ratner believes this question has no easy answer, and he grapples with it by considering the controversy over the removal of statues of people who supported the institution of slavery in the American (confederate) South from public places. Ratner's views are also relevant to discussions in Canada around removing monuments to the first prime minister, Sir John A. MacDonald, and Ontario educator Egerton Ryerson, who were both supporters of residential schools for Indigenous children.

> How much are current American citizens responsible for the sins of their ancestors? Which men (and yes, mostly these are men) are allowed to stay up as bronze reminders of some heroic past, and which ones need to finally go to the far reaches of our collective unconscious? Do Confederate monuments and statues deserve to stay as part of the legacy of the South, or does it make any sense that a period of history that lasted about 5 years and produced attitudes that were actually defeated in a bloody Civil War is allowed to percolate in the minds of the population?
>
> There is a big danger, on the other hand, that as the conversation turns to exorcising ghosts of currently unpopular attitudes, we are doing it through the lens of "presentism." It's a bias of judging the behaviour of historical people through the standards of today. Oxford helpfully defines it as "uncritical adherence to present-day attitudes, especially the tendency to interpret past events in terms of modern values and concepts." We tend to view our present time as the best, most advanced socially and intellectually. And as such judge all others as inferior. While that may be true (certainly debatable), it's unfair to view how people reacted to situations around them within the constraints and prejudices of the society of their day. It's

probably how people of a couple of hundred years from now will judge us, who still eat meat, as some kind of utter barbarians, a lesser human.

> Our present knowledge comes at the heels of wisdom gathered by generations before us. It is accumulated over time and by that standard should be richer, informed by greater experience and examination. Yet, is it fair to say that a person living 150 years ago should not have had the attitude shared by most people of their time, who only knew what they could know by that point in history? The intelligence of societies grows not only intellectually, reshaping their governments, but emotionally. It has taken the world a while to grow in that regard, to become mature in empathy and it's obviously nowhere near where it should be in such evolution.

Paul Ratner is a writer, educator, and filmmaker whose award-winning films include *Moses on the Mesa* and *The Caveman of Atomic City.*

> As it is biased to judge a person from a different era for not having the moral foresight to stand up to their peers and end the tyranny of injustice, that is also no excuse to celebrate attitudes and statements that go squarely against what we believe in now. [. . .] Respecting and learning from historical figures is extremely useful and necessary, but putting anyone up on a pedestal is generally a losing proposition. Eastern Europe saw a whole century of statues being torn down every few years in the 1900s—from monarchic rulers to Communist heroes who would fall in and out of favor, then a whole period of pulling down Lenin and Stalin figures in the 90's. Western Europe had its own idol carousel. Many other countries across the world, who've had tumultuous histories and had to undergo historical reckonings did the same. It's a process that happens in societies that experience change.
>
> Of course, the big question is—how far should this go?

Reproduced with permission of Big Think.

The Late 1800s: Towards a Science of the Mind

Learning Outcomes

WHAT YOU NEED TO KNOW

- Define introspection and explain how it was used in structuralism.
- Define natural selection and explain how it influenced functionalism.

The psychologist Hermann Ebbinghaus (1908) once remarked that "psychology has a long past but a short history." Indeed, psychology's philosophical roots go back thousands of years, but its history as an independent science began a mere 150 or so years ago, when a few German scientists began to wonder whether the methods of the physical and natural sciences might be used to study the human mind.

Structuralism: What Is the Mind Like?

During his visit to Berlin in 1867, William James sent a letter to a friend:

> It seems to me that perhaps the time has come for psychology to begin to be a science. . . . I am going on to study what is already known and perhaps may be able to do some work at it. Helmholtz and a man called Wundt at Heidelberg are working at it, and I hope I live through this winter to go to them in the summer.

Who were the people James was talking about? Hermann von Helmholtz (1821–1894) was a physician and physicist who mainly studied the mathematics of vision and hearing, but who had taken to asking people to close their eyes and respond as quickly as possible when he touched different parts of their legs. That's not as creepy as it sounds. Helmholtz recorded each person's **reaction time,** or *the amount of time between the onset of a stimulus and a person's response to that stimulus,* and discovered that people generally took longer to respond when he touched their toes than when he touched their thighs. Why? When something touches your body, your nerves transmit a signal from the point of contact to your brain, and when that signal arrives at your brain, you "feel" the touch. Because your thighs are closer to your brain than your toes are, the signal from your thigh has a shorter distance to travel. By carefully measuring how long it took people to feel a thigh touch and a toe touch and then comparing the two measurements, Helmholtz was able to do something remarkable: He calculated the speed at which nerves transmit information!

But if Helmholtz's experiments set the stage for the birth of psychology, it was his research assistant, Wilhelm Wundt (1832–1920), who wrote the play. Wundt (pronounced "Voont") taught the world's first course in scientific or "experimental" psychology at the University of Heidelberg in Germany in 1867, published the world's first psychology textbook in 1874, and opened the world's first psychology laboratory at the University of Leipzig in 1879. Wundt believed that the primary goal of psychology should be to understand "the facts of consciousness, its combinations and relations, so that it may ultimately discover the laws which govern these relations and combinations" (Wundt, 1912/1973, p. 1). Natural scientists had had great success in understanding the physical world by breaking it down into its basic elements, such as cells and molecules and atoms, and Wundt decided to take the same approach to understanding the mind. His approach later came to be known as **structuralism,** which was *an approach to psychology that attempted to isolate and analyze the mind's basic elements.*

How could these elements be discovered? Wundt's student Edward Titchener (1867–1927) pioneered a technique he called "systematic self-observation" but that everyone since has called **introspection,** which is *the analysis of subjective experience by trained observers.* Titchener trained his research assistants to report on the contents of their moment-to-moment experience, teaching them to report their "raw experience" rather than their interpretation of it. He presented his trained observers with a wide variety of stimuli, from patches of colour to musical tones, and then asked them to describe what was happening in their minds. The observer might describe the hue and luminance of the colour, the feelings they had when they heard the tone, and so on. Titchener believed that by carefully analyzing the reports from many trained observers who had been exposed to many stimuli, he would eventually discover the basic building blocks of subjective experience. This method led to some successes. For example, Wundt himself used it to identify three basic dimensions of sensation—pleasure/pain, strain/relaxation, and excitation/quiescence—and these three dimensions have, in fact, been shown to underlie the words people use to describe subjective experiences in many languages (Osgood et al., 1967).

But structuralism didn't last long as the only way to explore psychology, and you can probably guess why. Natural scientists had indeed been (and continue to be) successful in understanding the natural world by breaking it into small

Wilhelm Wundt (1832–1920) taught the world's first psychology course and published the world's first psychology textbook. He also opened the world's first psychology laboratory at the University of Leipzig (where you can still visit his laboratory and sit at his famous desk, shown above). Wundt was the advisor to a remarkable 184 PhD students, many of whom went on to become well-known psychologists, which is why a large percentage of modern psychologists can trace their intellectual lineage back to him. It is fair to say that modern psychology just *Wundt* be the same without him. (Sorry.)

reaction time The amount of time between the onset of a stimulus and a person's response to that stimulus.

structuralism An approach to psychology that attempted to isolate and analyze the mind's basic elements.

introspection The analysis of subjective experience by trained observers.

functionalism An approach to psychology that emphasized the adaptive significance of mental processes.

natural selection The process by which the specific attributes that promote an organism's survival and reproduction become more prevalent in the population over time.

parts, but that approach is successful only when we know what those parts are. When two biologists looked at blood under a microscope, they saw the same blood cells. This wasn't true of everyone who looked at the colour green or heard C# played on a piano. The problem with Titchener's introspection was that each person's inner experience was an inherently private event—a 3-D movie with an audience of one. As such, there was simply no way to tell if a person's description of their experience was accurate, and no way to tell if their experience was the same as or different from someone else's. So one of structuralism's problems was the method that some of its influential followers, such as Titchener, used. But an even bigger problem was its competition, because while the structuralists were busy introspecting, a young upstart was taking a very different approach to the study of the mind.

Charles Darwin (1809–1882) and Alfred Russel Wallace (1823–1913) independently developed the theory of evolution and then announced it in a joint publication of the Linnean Society in 1858. As the text from that publication (shown above) states, "These gentlemen having, independently and unknown to one another, conceived the same very ingenious theory to account for the appearance and perpetuation of varieties and of specific forms on our planet, may both fairly claim the merit of being original thinkers in this important line of inquiry." But the next year, Darwin published the theory in a book called *On the Origin of Species* and became one of the most famous scientists of all time, while the world pretty much forgot about good old Wallace.

Functionalism: What Is the Mind For?

During William James's time in Heidelberg, Wundt sold him on psychology, but not on structuralism. James felt that subjective experience was less like a molecule made of atoms and more like a river—a "stream of consciousness" as he called it—and that trying to isolate its basic elements was a losing proposition. James thought psychologists should worry less about what mental life was *like,* and more about what it was *for.* Together with psychologists such as John Dewey (1859–1952) and James Angell (1869–1949), James developed a new approach to psychology called **functionalism,** which was *an approach to psychology that emphasized the adaptive significance of mental processes.* What does "adaptive significance" mean?

As one historian wrote, functionalism "inherited its physical body from German experimentalism, but it got its mind from Darwin" (Boring, 1929). Charles Darwin (1809–1882) was a naturalist who had recently published a book entitled *On the Origin of Species by Means of Natural Selection* (1859). In it, Darwin had proposed the principle of **natural selection,** which refers to *the process by which the specific attributes that promote an organism's survival and reproduction become more prevalent in the population over time.* How does natural selection work? Animals pass their physical attributes to their offspring, and those attributes that are most "adaptive"—that is, those that promote the offspring's survival and reproduction—are more likely to be passed along from one generation to the next. Over time, these adaptive attributes become increasingly prevalent in the population simply because "the population" refers to those animals that have managed to survive and reproduce.

Darwin's reasoning was brilliantly circular. Humans have fingers instead of flippers because at some point in the distant past, those of our ancestors who developed fingers were better able to survive and reproduce than those who did not, and they passed their flipperless fingeredness on to us. That's the principle of natural selection at work, shaping the human body. James reasoned that if our physical characteristics had evolved because they were adaptive, then the same should be true of our psychological characteristics. In other words, natural selection should also have shaped the mind. "Consciousness," James wrote in 1892, "has in all probability been evolved, like all other functions, for a use." The mind serves a function and according to James, the task for psychologists was to figure out what that function was.

The Early 1900s: Psychoanalysis and Behaviourism

Structuralism and functionalism were important ideas—to the hundred or so people who knew anything about them. While 19th-century academics debated the best way to study the mind, the rest of the world paid approximately no attention. But all that would change in the next century, when a restless neurologist from Vienna and a failed writer from Pennsylvania would pull psychology in opposite directions and, in the process, take their places on the public stage and eventually become two of the most influential thinkers of all time.

Psychoanalysis: The Mind Does Not Know Itself

While experimental psychologists were trying to understand the mind, physicians were trying to heal it. The French physicians Jean-Martin Charcot (1825–1893) and Pierre Janet (1859–1947) became interested in patients who had an odd collection of symptoms—some were blind, some were paralyzed, and some were unable to remember their identities—but who had no obvious physical illness or injury. They found that when these patients were hypnotized, their symptoms disappeared, and when the patients emerged from their hypnotic trances, their symptoms returned. Charcot and Janet referred to their patients' condition as **hysteria,** which is *a loss of function that has no obvious physical origin.* What could possibly explain it?

　　Enter Sigmund Freud (1856–1939), a young Viennese physician in his late 20s who began his career studying the effects of cocaine and the sexual anatomy of eels (though not at the same time). In 1885, Freud went to Paris on a fellowship to study with Charcot, and when he returned to Vienna he began treating patients who suffered from hysteria and other "nervous disorders." Freud suspected that many of these patients had had a childhood experience so painful that they couldn't allow themselves to remember it. These memories, he reasoned, had been hidden from consciousness and relegated to a place Freud called the **unconscious,** which is *the part of the mind that contains information of which people are not aware.* Freud felt confident that these exiled or "repressed" memories were the source of his patients' hysterical symptoms, and he spent the next several years developing an elaborate theory of the mind known as **psychoanalytic theory,** which is *a general theory that emphasizes the influence of the unconscious on feelings, thoughts, and behaviours.*

　　Freud's theory was complex, and you'll learn more about it in the Consciousness, Personality, Disorders, and Treatment chapters. But in brief, Freud saw the mind as a set of processes that were largely hidden from our view, and he regarded the conscious thoughts and feelings that the structuralists had worked so hard to identify as little more than flotsam and jetsam, bobbing on the surface of a vast and mysterious ocean. To understand the ocean, Freud suggested, you can't just skim the surface. You have to dive—and when you do, you should expect to encounter some frightening things. For Freud, those frightening things were the person's anxieties and impulses—the fear of death, the desire to kill, forbidden sexual urges, and so on—all of which were lurking beneath the waves.

　　Freud believed that the only way to confront these denizens of the deep was through **psychoanalysis,** which is *a therapy that aims to give people insight into the contents of their unconscious minds.* A therapeutic session with Sigmund Freud began with the patient lying on a couch and Freud sitting just behind them (probably smoking a cigar). He might ask the patient to describe their dreams or to "free associate"

Learning Outcomes

WHAT YOU NEED TO KNOW

- Outline the basic ideas behind Freud's psychoanalytic theory.
- Define the basic idea behind behaviourism.
- Explain the principle of reinforcement.

hysteria A loss of function that has no obvious physical origin.

unconscious The part of the mind that contains information of which people are not aware.

psychoanalytic theory A general theory that emphasizes the influence of the unconscious on feelings, thoughts, and behaviours.

psychoanalysis A therapy that aims to give people insight into the contents of their unconscious minds.

Sigmund Freud's first major book, *The Interpretation of Dreams*, sold only 600 copies in the first 8 years. In a despairing letter to a friend, Freud wrote, "Do you suppose that someday a marble tablet will be placed on the house, inscribed with these words: 'In this house on July 24, 1895, the secret of dreams was revealed to Dr. Sigm. Freud'?" Today the site of that house bears a memorial plaque with precisely that inscription.

John B. Watson (1878–1958) was the founder of behaviourism, which revolutionized American psychology in the early 20th century. Watson was married, and his academic career was cut short when a scandalous love affair led Johns Hopkins University to dismiss him in 1920. He took a job in advertising, where he spent the remainder of his life working on campaigns for products such as Maxwell House coffee, Johnson & Johnson baby powder, and Pebeco toothpaste.

behaviourism An approach to psychology that restricts scientific inquiry to observable behaviour.

by talking about anything they wanted or by responding quickly to a word ("What pops into your head when I say 'mother?'"). Freud believed that his patients' dreams and free associations offered a glimpse into the contents of their unconscious minds, and that if he could see what was there, he could heal them.

Freud's theories had little impact on some people and an astonishing impact on others. The people on whom they had little impact were the experimental psychologists. William James, for instance, admired some of Freud's insights but thought most of his theorizing was nonsense. "I strongly suspect Freud, with his dream theory, of being a regular hallucine," he wrote in a letter to a friend in 1909. *Hallucine* is an old-fashioned word for "lunatic," so this was not meant as a compliment. Most experimental psychologists shared James's assessment and paid scant attention to Freud's ideas. On the other hand, clinicians paid a lot of attention, and within a decade, Freud's psychoanalytic movement had attracted a virtual army of disciples, including people like Carl Jung (1875–1961) and Alfred Adler (1870–1937). Indeed, Freud's thinking may not have influenced experimental psychology, but it influenced just about everything else in the 20th century—from history and philosophy to literature, art, and popular culture.

Behaviourism: The Mind Does Not Matter

James had a somewhat dim view of Freud, but as the 20th century got rolling, another, much younger psychologist took an even dimmer view of Freud—and of James, Wundt, Titchner, and everyone else who had ever talked about the "science of the mind." That young psychologist had been born in the tiny town of Traveler's Rest, South Carolina, and went on to the University of Chicago to study the behaviour of rats. When his interest changed to the behaviour of people, his changing interest changed the world.

Pavlov and Watson

His name was John Broadus Watson (1878–1958). Watson thought that everything worth knowing about a rat—how it feeds and mates, how it builds its nest and rears its young—could be known just by watching it, and he wondered why human beings couldn't be known the same way. Why should the study of human behaviour require a bunch of idle speculation about the human mind? Mental life was idiosyncratic, undefinable, and unmeasurable, and Watson felt that if psychology wanted to become a real science, it should limit itself to studying the things people *do* rather than the things they claim to think and feel. Watson called this idea **behaviourism,** which is *an approach to psychology that restricts scientific inquiry to observable behaviour.*

What might a purely "behaviourist" psychology look like? Watson was impressed by the work of the Russian physiologist Ivan Pavlov (1849–1936), about whom you will hear more in the Learning chapter. Pavlov studied digestion in dogs, and he knew that dogs naturally start salivating when they are presented with food. But one day Pavlov noticed something curious: The dogs in his laboratory had started salivating *before* their food arrived—in fact, they seemed to start salivating when they heard the footsteps of the research assistant who was coming down the hall to feed them! Pavlov suspected that his dogs had come to associate the feeder's footsteps with the arrival of food and that the dogs were responding to the footsteps as though they were the food itself. He devised an experiment to test this hypothesis. First, he sounded a tone every time he fed his dogs. Then, after a few days, he sounded the tone without feeding the dogs. What happened? The dogs salivated when they heard the tone. Pavlov called the tone a *stimulus* and the salivation a *response.*

When Watson read about this research, he quickly realized that these two concepts—stimulus and response—could be the building blocks of a new behaviourist approach. Psychology, Watson argued, should be the scientific study of the relationship between stimuli and responses—nothing less, and certainly nothing more. In his 1919 book, *Psychology from the Standpoint of a Behaviourist*, he wrote: "The goal of psychological study is the ascertaining of such data and laws that, given the stimulus, psychology can predict what the response will be; or, on the other hand, given the response, it can specify the nature of the effective stimulus." He proudly noted that in *his* book "the reader will find no discussion of consciousness and no reference to such terms as sensation, perception, attention, will, image and the like" because "I frankly do not know what they mean, nor do I believe that anyone else can use them consistently."

Watson's arguments were not just persuasive—they were *wildly* persuasive. As one historian wrote, "Some conservatives were Wundtians (structuralists), some radicals were functionalists, more psychologists were agnostics. Then Watson touched a match to the mass, there was an explosion, and only behaviourism was left" (Boring, 1929). By the 1930s, experimental psychology *was* behaviourism. But if Watson had convinced psychologists that behaviourism was the one and only proper way to study human behaviour, it would take a skinny kid from Pennsylvania to convince the rest of the world of the same thing.

This photo shows Baika, one of Ivan Pavlov's famous dogs. Pavlov won the Nobel Prize in 1904 for his research on digestion, and Baika was immortalized in a 1971 song by the Rolling Stones ("Yeah when you call my name, I salivate like a Pavlov dog"). There is some debate about which of them earned the greater honour.

Skinner

That kid was named Burrhus Frederick Skinner (1904–1990). He grew up in Pennsylvania and graduated from Hamilton College in 1926 with the intention of becoming a writer, and like many young people with that particular aspiration, he took a job at a bookstore in New York City. One day while browsing the shelves he came across some books by Pavlov and by Watson. He was captivated. He abandoned his nascent writing career and, in 1928, enrolled as a graduate student in the psychology department at Harvard University—the same department from which William James had retired 20 years earlier.

Skinner greatly admired the work of Pavlov and Watson, but as he studied them, he started to suspect that their simple stimulus–response psychology was missing something important. Pavlov's dogs lived in a laboratory where they sat around and waited to be fed, but in the real world, animals had to *act* on their environments to find food. How did they learn to do that? Skinner sought to answer this question by building two devices. The first was a cage for laboratory animals that the world would soon come to call a "Skinner Box." The cage had a lever that, when pressed by a hungry rat, delivered food through a tube. The second device was a "cumulative recorder," which recorded the frequency of the rat's lever-presses in real time. These inventions don't sound like much today, but in 1930 they were serious technology. Moreover, they allowed Skinner to discover something remarkable.

Skinner observed that when he put a rat in one of his special cages, it would typically wander around for a while, sniffing and exploring, until it accidentally bumped the lever, causing a food pellet to appear as if by magic. After this happy accident had happened a few times, the rat would suddenly start *pressing* the lever—tentatively at first, then more quickly and more often, until it basically looked like the conga player in a hot Latin jazz band. Unlike Pavlov's dogs, which had learned to monitor their environments and anticipate food, Skinner's rats had learned to *operate* on their environments to *produce* food. When the rat's behaviour produced food (which Skinner called a "reinforcement"), the rat would repeat the behaviour; and when it didn't, the rat wouldn't. Animals do what they are rewarded for doing, Skinner concluded, and he called this the **principle of reinforcement,** which states that *any behaviour that is rewarded will be repeated and any behaviour that isn't rewarded won't be repeated.*

Skinner argued that this simple principle could explain how rats learn to find food, but that it could also explain the most complex human behaviours, and he made it the

principle of reinforcement A principle stating that any behaviour that is rewarded will be repeated and any behaviour that isn't rewarded won't be repeated.

Among B. F. Skinner's (1904–1990) many inventions was the Skinner Box, shown here. He died in 1990 at the age of 86, and though psychology had long since renounced its allegiance to behaviourism, he remained a staunch defender: "The appeal to cognitive states and processes is a diversion which could well be responsible for much of our failure to solve our problems. We need to change our behaviour and we can do so only by changing our physical and social environments. We choose the wrong path at the very start when we suppose that our goal is to change the 'minds and hearts of men and women' rather than the world in which they live" (Skinner, 1977).

centrepiece of his theorizing. In a relatively short time, Skinner's theories about the effects of reward came to dominate psychology. Indeed, by the 1940s, the majority of experimental psychologists had been converted to Skinner's "radical behaviourism" and were busy studying how an animal's behaviour was shaped by the consequences it produced. Structuralism, functionalism, and every other -ism that mentioned the human mind had quietly disappeared, and "behaviourism was viewed as the one right way to do psychological science" (Baars, 1986, p. 32).

Like Freud, Skinner's influence went far beyond the academy. His theories spread across the globe and became the foundation of classroom education, government programs, psychological therapies, and even child-rearing practices. He extended his influence by writing two controversial best-sellers — *Walden II* (1948) and *Beyond Freedom and Dignity* (1971) — in which he laid out his vision for a utopian society in which all human behaviour was controlled by the judicious application of the principle of reinforcement. In these books, Skinner claimed that free will was an illusion, and that the world could solve its most pressing social problems by acknowledging that behaviour is nothing more than the sum of its consequences, that people do what they are rewarded for doing, and that their sense of "choosing" and "deciding" is a dangerous fiction. "In the behaviouristic view," wrote Skinner (1974), "man can now control his destiny because he knows what must be done and how to do it."

As you might expect, Skinner's critics were many and fierce. *Time* magazine featured him on its cover beneath the words "B. F. Skinner Says: We Can't Afford Freedom." One reviewer called his 1971 book "fascism without tears," and another called it "a corpse patched with nuts, bolts and screws from the junkyard of philosophy." Even the normally nonpartisan *TV Guide* got into the act, warning that Skinner was advocating "the taming of mankind through a system of dog obedience schools for all." These attacks were predictable but mistaken. Skinner did not want to turn classrooms into obedience schools or strip citizens of their civil rights. Rather, he simply believed that a scientific understanding of the principles that govern behaviour could be used to improve social welfare and that behaviourists knew what those principles were.

The Early 1900s: Resistance to Behaviourism

For the first few decades of the 20th century, behaviourism was king; but not all the subjects were loyal. In fact, several pockets of resistance could be found throughout the kingdom—groups of psychologists who refused to swear allegiance to the crown and whose work would soon foment a counterrevolution. Who were these dissidents?

Gestalt Psychology and Developmental Psychology

Many of them were in Europe. The German psychologist Max Wertheimer (1880–1943) was interested in how people perceive motion, and in one of his experiments, participants were shown two lights that flashed quickly on a screen, one after the other. When the time between the flashes was relatively long, the participant would correctly report that the two lights were flashing in sequence; but when the time between flashes was reduced to about 1/5th of a second, participants reported that a single light was moving back and forth (Fancher, 1979; Sarris, 1989). Wertheimer argued that this "illusory motion" occurs because the mind has theories about how the world works (e.g., "when an object is in one location and then instantly appears in a contiguous location, it probably moved") and it uses these theories to make sense of incoming sensory data. (You've already encountered this idea under the name "philosophical idealism.") In both conditions of Wertheimer's experiment, participants had been shown exactly the same physical stimuli, but they had *seen* different things. Physical stimuli, Wertheimer concluded, are part of the perceptual experience, but the whole is more than the sum of its parts. The German word for "whole" is *gestalt,* and Wertheimer and his colleagues called their approach **Gestalt psychology,** which is *an approach to psychology that emphasized the way in which the mind creates perceptual experience.*

While German psychologists were studying why people sometimes see things as they aren't, the British psychologist Sir Frederic Bartlett (1886–1969) was studying why people sometimes remember things as they weren't. Bartlett asked participants to read stories and then try to remember what they had read after varying amounts of time had passed—from 15 minutes to several years. When Bartlett analyzed their errors, he found that participants

If you look up at a "news ticker," the words in the headlines seem to be scrolling by, moving from right to left. But they aren't really moving. Rather, contiguous lights are going on and off in rapid succession. This is the phenomenon that the Gestalt psychologist Max Wertheimer (1880–1943) was studying in Germany in 1912.

Learning Outcomes

WHAT YOU NEED TO KNOW

- Explain why several European psychologists resisted behaviourism.

- Explain why American social psychologists resisted behaviourism.

Gestalt psychology An approach to psychology that emphasized the way in which the mind creates perceptual experience.

developmental psychology The study of the ways in which psychological phenomena change over the life span.

social psychology The study of the causes and consequences of sociality.

Jean Piaget (1896–1980) studied the mistakes children make in thinking about objects in the world. In one of his studies, he showed that young children mistakenly believe that when an object changes shape, it also changes mass—that a ball of clay becomes "more clay" when it is flattened into a log.

often remembered what they had *expected* to read rather than what they had actually read, and that this tendency became more pronounced with the passage of time. For example, some of his participants read a story called "War of the Ghosts," which described a group of Native American men hunting seals—an exotic activity that was unfamiliar to most of Bartlett's British participants in 1932. When asked to recount the story later, many of these participants mistakenly said that the men had been fishing—an activity that most of these participants would have *expected* men to do. Bartlett argued that memory is not a simple recording device, but rather, that our minds use their theories of how the world usually works ("Most men fish") to construct our memories of past experience (see The Real World: Beneath the Ocean of Memory).

While German and British psychologists were trying to understand the minds of adults, Swiss psychologist Jean Piaget (1896–1980) was trying to understand the minds of children, which he often did by examining the mistakes they made. For example, in one study, Piaget showed 3-year-olds two equally large mounds of clay and then broke one mound into little pieces. When the children were asked which mound now had "more clay," they typically said that the unbroken one did. By the age of 6 or 7, children no longer made this mistake. Piaget concluded that the mind has theories about how the world works ("Breaking a material object into pieces doesn't change the amount of material in it") and that because small children have not yet learned these theories, they see the world in a fundamentally different way than adults do. Along with psychologists such as Lev Vygotsky (1896–1934), Piaget helped create an area of experimental psychology called **developmental psychology,** which is *the study of the ways in which psychological phenomena change over the life span.*

In short, while many early 20th-century psychologists, particularly those in the United States, were flying the behaviourist flag, a small number of European psychologists were quietly doing the very thing that behaviourism forbade: studying people's perceptions, memories, and judgements in order to understand the nature of an unobservable entity called the mind.

Social Psychology

Not all the dissidents were in Europe; some had already come to America. Like many Jews, Kurt Lewin (1890–1947) had fled Europe in the early 1930s when Hitler came to power. He had studied with the Gestalt psychologists and had inherited their interest in mental phenomena, but he was less interested in how people treated moving lights and more interested in how they treated each other. So after taking a job as a professor at the Massachusetts Institute of Technology in the United States, Lewin started the Institute for Group Dynamics and began studying topics such as leadership, communication, attitude change, and racial prejudice. At the heart of his many different research projects was a single, simple idea: Behaviour is not a function of the environment, but of the person's *subjective construal* of the environment. Responses do not depend on stimuli, as the behaviourists claimed; rather, they depend on how people *think* about those stimuli.

After fleeing Germany, Kurt Lewin (1890–1947) became interested in the psychological differences between autocracy (in which one person has power over all others) and democracy (in which all people share power). In a series of studies, he assigned 10-year-old boys to work together in autocratic groups on some days and in democratic groups on other days. He observed that "the change from autocracy to democracy seemed to take somewhat more time than from democracy to autocracy" and concluded that this was because "Autocracy is imposed upon the individual. Democracy he has to learn" (Lewin, 1948).

Lewin's research and theorizing gave birth to a new area of experimental psychology called **social psychology,** which is *the study of the causes and consequences of sociality.* Although behaviourism was ascendant, Lewin and the other social psychologists pretty much ignored it as they sought to understand how people see the social world. For example, Solomon Asch (1907–1996) told a group of participants about a man who was envious, stubborn, critical, impulsive, industrious, and intelligent—a string of adjectives that went from bad to good. He told another group about a man who was intelligent, industrious, impulsive, critical, stubborn, and envious—exactly the same list of adjectives but in the opposite order. Asch discovered that the participants who heard the man's good traits first liked him more. Asch argued that this "primacy effect" occurred because the early words in each list created a theory ("*Intelligent* and *industrious*—wow, this is a really great guy") that the mind then used to interpret the later words in that list ("*Stubborn* probably means that he sticks to his principles"). Asch's studies led to an avalanche of research on how people draw inferences about others.

Other social psychologists studied similarly "mentalistic" phenomena. Carl Hovland (1912–1961) and Irving Janis (1918–1990) studied how people persuade each other to change their beliefs; Gordon Allport (1897–1967) studied how people form stereotypes and prejudices; Muzafer Sherif (1906–1988) studied how people create identities based on their social groups; Fritz Heider (1896–1988) studied how people infer each other's intentions; and the list goes on. Beliefs, stereotypes, prejudices, identities, intentions—concepts like these had been banished from behaviourism but were the heart and soul of social psychology. Understanding the richness and complexity of social life in terms of lever-pressing never struck most social psychologists as a realistic possibility, so they banded together, created their own scientific journals and academic societies, and went their separate way. "The power, the honours, the authority, the textbooks, the money, everything in psychology was owned by the behaviouristic school," psychologist George Miller later remembered (Baars, 1986, p. 203). "Those who didn't give a damn, in clinical or social psychology, went off and did their own thing." What the social psychologists didn't know at the time was that their thing would soon be everybody's thing because the behaviourist kingdom was about to be attacked, invaded, and conquered.

Solomon Asch (1907–1996) was one of many social psychologists who were influenced by Gestalt psychology and who resisted the edicts of behaviourism by studying how people think about each other. His early studies of the "primacy effect" showed that early information about a person changes the interpretation of later information. If you saw the photo on the left before the photo on the right, you'd form one impression of the man ("He's a fairly straight-ahead guy who likes to party on weekends"); but if you saw the photos in the opposite order, you'd probably form a very different impression ("He's a hipster who covers his ink for his day job").

The Real World ⦙ Beneath the Ocean of Memory

Sir Frederic Bartlett was interested in how memory worked in "the real world," and despite the ascendance of behaviourism, he spent his life studying it. During World War II, he established the Applied Psychology Unit in Cambridge, England, to help the British military in their efforts to defeat Hitler. So it was more than fitting that nearly a half century after his death, Bartlett's pioneering studies of human memory helped solve a naval mystery.

During World War II, the Australian warship *Sydney* (shown in the photo) battled the German warship *Kormoran*, and both ships sank in the Indian Ocean. There were just a few survivors, and when they were interrogated months later, each had a different memory of the precise spot where the two ships went down. Despite numerous attempts to locate the ships, the wreckage remained lost at the bottom of the sea.

Then, in 1998, psychologists John Dunn and Kim Kirsner decided to see if they could use Bartlett's research to estimate how the survivors' memories might

have become distorted over time (Dunn & Kirsner, 2011). "What we found was that there was a correspondence—that our data looked like the kind of data that Bartlett had generated in his study," said Dunn (Spiegel, 2011). By combining the survivors' testimony with Bartlett's ideas about memory distortion, the psychologists were able to make a prediction about where the ships might actually be.

"I never really thought that I would ever find out whether it would be right or wrong," said Dunn. But he did find out, because in 2008, a team of shipwreck-hunters found the ships on the ocean floor—just about where the two psychologists had predicted they would be. Despite what his behaviourist colleagues had claimed, Sir Frederic Bartlett's mentalistic research was "real science" after all.

The Late 1900s: The Cognitive Revolution

Learning Outcomes

WHAT YOU NEED TO KNOW

- Summarize Chomsky's critique of Skinner.
- Explain what cognitive psychology is and how it emerged.
- Explain what evolutionary psychology is and why it emerged.

As the 20th century moved from its first to second half, Skinner (1957) published a book called *Verbal Behaviour,* in which he offered a behaviourist account of how children learn language. The linguist Noam Chomsky decided that there had been enough passive resistance to behaviourism over the last 40 years and that it was time to mount a full-scale attack. In 1959, he published a devastating 33-page critique of Skinner's book, arguing that behaviourist principles could *never* explain some of the most obvious features of language-learning.

For example, children create novel sentences that they have never heard before. How do they produce them? The obvious answer is that they use grammar—a complex set of rules that tells them which of an infinitely large number of possible sentences are permissible ("The girl ran after the ball") and which are not ("The girl after the ball ran"). So how do they learn these rules? Using formal mathematical logic, Chomsky showed that a purely behaviourist account of learning could never explain how children learn grammar. It wasn't just that the behaviourist account *didn't* work; Chomsky showed that it *couldn't* work—not today, not tomorrow, not ever. Chomsky (1959) suggested that it was time to toss behaviourism into the dustbin of history: "If the study of language is limited in these ways," he wrote, "it seems inevitable that major aspects of verbal behaviour will remain a mystery."

The world was listening. But "Out with the old!" is a successful rallying cry only when followed by "In with the new!" and there was indeed something new happening in the 1960s that would spark a flame and push behaviourism to psychology's back burner. It wasn't a new philosophy, scientific discovery, or social movement. It was a mindless, soulless machine.

Cognitive Psychology

ENIAC (pronounced "ee-knee-ack"), the first general-purpose electronic digital computer, was built in 1945. It weighed 30 tons, was the size of a small house, cost the equivalent of $7,000,000, and didn't do anything that a regular human could possibly care about, which meant that it was of interest mainly to a handful of engineers, the U.S. Army, and a few random nerds. But by the 1960s, computers were becoming smaller and more widely available, and a small group of scientists and mathematicians were starting to wonder whether computers could ever be made to think. Norbert Wiener (1894–1964) was busy inventing cybernetics, Marvin Minsky (1927–2016) and John McCarthy (1927–2011) were busy inventing artificial intelligence, and Allen Newell (1927–1992) and Herb Simon (1916–2001) were busy teaching computers to play chess. Those early computers performed remarkable calculations at lightning speed, but for psychologists, they did something much more important: They gave them permission once again to talk about the mind. How did they do that?

A computer's observable behaviour is as simple as a rat's. Present the computer with a stimulus ("2 + 2 = ?") and it will produce a response ("4"). But unlike a rat, the *way* the computer produces its response is neither hidden nor mysterious. It produces its response by processing information—that is, by encoded information, storing it in memory, retrieving it on demand, and combining it in lawful ways. Computers contain circuits, not ghosts, and those circuits allow computers to do things that from the outside look a whole lot like *learning, reasoning, remembering*—and maybe even *thinking.* If those words could legitimately be used to describe the physical information-processing operations that happen inside a machine, why couldn't they also be used

In this 1946 photo, Marlyn Wescoff (*left*) and Ruth Lichterman (*right*) are programming ENIAC, the world's first digital computer. This revolutionary device did many things, but one of the most important is that it gave psychologists a scientifically respectable way to talk about mental processes.

to describe the physical information-processing operations that happen inside a brain? If the brain is hardware, then the mind is software — and there is nothing spooky or unmeasurable about the way a software program works.

With the digital computer as their liberator, existence proof, and guiding metaphor, psychologists of the 1950s and 1960s suddenly felt emboldened to study topics that everyone but the dissidents had ignored for decades. Donald Broadbent (1926–1993) and Anne Triesman (1935–2018) began studying how people allocate their attention; George Miller (1920–2012) began studying how people expand their capacity to process information by combining it into chunks; Jerome Bruner (1915–2016) began studying how a person's desires can shape their perceptions of physical objects; George Sperling (b. 1934) began studying the nature of brief visual memory; and the list went on. This dramatic shift in psychology's orientation came to be known — for better or for worse — as "the cognitive revolution." In 1967, Ulric Neisser (1928–2012) summarized this new way of thinking in a book titled *Cognitive Psychology,* and in so doing, christened a new field. **Cognitive psychology** is *the study of human information-processing,* and for more than 50 years it has been producing deep insights into the nature of the human mind — many of which you will learn about in the chapters to come.

Evolutionary Psychology

Behaviourism set the mind aside and cognitive psychology brought it back. But behaviourism also set something else aside: the past. Behaviourists viewed individuals as blank slates who came into the world with nothing but a readiness to be shaped by their environments. As John Watson (1930, p. 89) wrote:

> Give me a dozen healthy infants, well-formed, and my own specified world to bring them up in and I'll guarantee to take any one at random and train him to become any type of specialist I might select — doctor, lawyer, artist, merchant-chief and, yes, even beggar-man and thief, regardless of his talents, penchants, tendencies, abilities, vocations, and race of his ancestors.

Watson's view was egalitarian, optimistic, and wrong. In the 1960s, the psychologist John Garcia (1917–2012) was studying how rats react to radiation sickness. He noticed that his rats instantly learned to associate their nausea with the taste of the food they ate just before getting sick, and they instantly developed an aversion to that food. On the other hand, no matter how much training they received, his rats could not learn to associate their nausea with a flashing light or the sound of a buzzer. That just didn't make sense. Pavlov had shown that when two stimuli are paired (e.g., a researcher's footsteps and the appearance of food), animals will learn to associate one with the other — and it wasn't supposed to matter whether those stimuli were foods, footsteps, lights, or buzzers. It wasn't *supposed* to matter, but it *did*. What could that mean?

Garcia thought it meant that every organism is evolved to respond to particular stimuli in particular ways — that animals come into the world "biologically prepared" to learn some associations more easily than others. In the real world of forests and sewers, a rat's nausea is *usually* caused by eating spoiled food, and although Garcia's rats had been born in a laboratory and had never eaten spoiled food, their ancestors had. Millions of years of evolution had designed the rat brain so that it would quickly learn to associate an episode of nausea with the taste of food, and that's why rats learned *this* association so much more quickly and easily than they learned others. Rats, it turned out, were not blank slates — so why should psychologists think of people that way?

The biologist E. O. Wilson (1929–2021) was an admirer of Garcia's experiments, and in 1975 he published a book entitled *Sociobiology: The New Synthesis* in which he brought together research from many areas of science to support

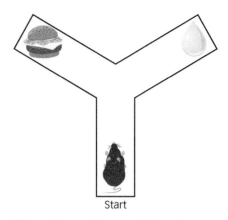

Start

Although cognitive psychology is concerned with human information processing, it doesn't pertain only to humans. Edward C. Tolman (1886–1959) was working with animals at the same time as Skinner and other behaviourists, but he thought behaviourism wasn't sufficient — psychology needed cognition, too. He conducted many experiments to demonstrate that rats have knowledge that cannot be described in behaviourist terms. One of the simplest demonstrations used a simple Y-maze, shown here. Opposite to the starting arm are two goal arms — water was placed in the right and food in the left. Rats first explored the maze neither hungry nor thirsty, several times a day for several days. Then, on test day, rats were deprived of food or water for a time before being placed in the maze — now completely empty. Hungry animals went at once to the left, where the food had been, more frequently than to the right; and the thirsty group went to the right, where the water had been, more frequently than to the left. The animals knew where the food and water were typically located, even though they had not shown this knowledge earlier through any overt behaviour (Tolman, 1948).

cognitive psychology The study of human information-processing.

John Garcia's (1917–2012) experiments showed that the ease with which associations are learned can be influenced by an organism's evolutionary history. Because nausea and vomiting are usually caused by the ingestion of food, nature has programmed mammals to instantly develop an aversion to any food they happened to eat just before getting sick to their stomachs.

his claim that social behaviour had been shaped by natural selection. Although the book primarily discussed the social behaviour of rats, birds, and ants (Wilson's specialty), its brief, final chapter speculated about the evolutionary origins of human behaviour, and that speculation had two consequences. First, it led to a groundswell of protest and criticism by those who felt that Wilson was offering a "biological justification" for sexism and racism. Second, it led to a wave of interest from psychologists, who argued that the best way to understand the mind was to understand the specific problems it had been "designed" by evolution to solve. Why did people save their children even when it cost them their own lives? Why were people all over the world afraid of snakes and spiders, even if they'd never seen one? Questions like these seemed difficult to answer unless one considered how the hunter-gatherers from whom modern humans descended had coped with the challenges of survival and reproduction.

And so psychologists created a new area of experimental psychology called **evolutionary psychology,** which is *the study of the ways in which the human mind has been shaped by natural selection.* Donald Symons (b. 1942) began studying gender differences in sexual promiscuity; Leda Cosmides (b. 1957) and John Tooby (b. 1952) began studying how people detect cheaters in a social exchange; David Buss (b. 1953) began to study how people select their ideal mate; and the list went on. Evolutionary psychology "is not a specific subfield of psychology, such as the study of vision, reasoning, or social behaviour. It is a way of thinking about psychology that can be applied to any topic within it" (Cosmides & Tooby, 2000, p. 115), and, as you will see in the upcoming chapters, modern psychologists now apply evolutionary thinking to a wide array of topics.

After the Revolution

Behaviourism was a valuable approach that led to many important discoveries about human behaviour, but it ignored the mind and it ignored the past—both of which are just too important to stay ignored for long. Although many modern psychologists still study how rats learn and how reinforcement shapes behaviour, few are behaviourists who regard humans as blank slates or who believe that mental processes are unmeasurable fictions. In the aftermath of the cognitive revolution, most modern psychologists are concerned with some aspect of mental life, and most agree that mental life is influenced by its evolutionary origins. Ironically, the emergence of cognitive and evolutionary psychology has in some ways brought psychology full circle. Like the structuralists, cognitive psychologists now ask what the mind is like; and like the functionalists, evolutionary psychologists now ask what the mind is for. Apparently, some questions are just too interesting to go gentle into that good night.

The Early 2000s: New Frontiers

Learning Outcomes

WHAT YOU NEED TO KNOW

- Define neuroscience and explain how modern psychologists study the brain.
- Define cultural psychology and explain why it matters.

The cognitive revolution fundamentally changed psychology at the close of the 20th century. But science doesn't stand still. In the 20 or so years since the present century began, psychology has continued to evolve, and several new and exciting areas have emerged. We'll discuss two of them — one that has psychologists looking "down a level" to biology as they search for the neural substrates of mental life, and another that has psychologists looking "up a level" to sociology and anthropology as they seek to understand its cultural origins.

Neuroscience

The mind is what the brain does. But until recently, knowledge of the brain was based primarily on studies of brains that had been damaged. For instance, in 1861, the French physician Paul Broca (1824–1880) performed an autopsy on a man who had been able to understand words but not produce them; he found damage in a small region on the left side of that man's brain. Broca concluded that the ability to speak somehow depended on this particular region — and the fact that this region is today called Broca's area tells you that he was right. Psychologists learned from brains that were damaged by nature, but they also learned from brains that they damaged themselves. In the 1930s, for instance, the psychologist Karl Lashley (1890–1958) taught rats to run a maze and then surgically damaged different parts of the rats' cerebral cortices and measured changes in their performance. To his surprise, he found that while brain damage impaired performance, it didn't really matter *where* on the cortex the damage was inflicted, which led Lashley to conclude that learning is *not* "localized" or tied to a specific brain area in the same way that language seemed to be.

Of course, damaged brains can only teach us so much. Imagine how hard it would be to figure out how an engine works if all you could do was examine wrecks, or hit it in different places with a hammer and then see how well it drove. Fortunately, the last few decades have seen the invention of new technologies that allow psychologists to observe the undamaged brain in action. For example, functional magnetic resonance imaging (fMRI) is a technology that produces the "brain scans" you often read about in the news. Despite their name, these scans are not photos of the brain; they are maps showing the amount of blood that was flowing in different parts of a person's brain at a particular moment in time. Because neural activity requires oxygen, and because blood supplies it, these scans can tell us which areas of a brain were processing the most information at any particular time, and this has taught us things we could never have learned by merely examining damaged brains.

For instance, Broca would not have been surprised to learn that people using their hands to speak American Sign Language (ASL) show increased neural activity in the same region of the left hemisphere that he identified in 1861. But he might have been surprised by research that has used fMRI to show that this left-hemisphere activity occurs only in the brains of speakers who became deaf in adulthood. Speakers who were *born* deaf show increased neural activity in both the left and right hemispheres, suggesting that they are speaking ASL in a very different way (Newman et al., 2002). The advent of fMRI and other technologies that you'll learn about in the Neuroscience and Behaviour chapter has given birth to two new areas of psychology: **cognitive neuroscience,** which is *the study of the relationship between the brain and the mind (especially in humans),* and **behavioural neuroscience,** which is *the study of the relationship between the brain and behaviour (especially in nonhuman animals).*

evolutionary psychology The study of the ways in which the human mind has been shaped by natural selection.

cognitive neuroscience The study of the relationship between the brain and the mind (especially in humans).

behavioural neuroscience The study of the relationship between the brain and behaviour (especially in nonhuman animals).

Technologies such as fMRI allow cognitive neuroscientists to determine which areas of the brain are most and least active when people perform various mental tasks, such as reading, writing, thinking, or remembering. The machine (*left*) produces what are commonly called "brain scans" (*right*).

Donald Olding Hebb (1904–1985) was a Canadian psychologist whose work has had a profound impact on cognitive neuroscience. He studied how brain cells (neurons) contribute to psychological processes. Hebb suggested, in a nutshell, that "neurons that fire together, wire together." This famous rule is now widely considered to describe one of the most important cellular mechanisms of learning and memory. Although Hebb made the suggestion in 1949, the biological techniques required to observe it were not available until the late 1960s.

Montreal: A Birthplace of Cognitive Neuroscience

The 1940s and 1950s were great decades for the Montreal Canadiens hockey team. Maurice "Rocket" Richard joined the team in 1942, and played with the Canadiens for 18 seasons—the Canadiens made it to the Stanley Cup Finals 12 times in those years and won the Cup 8 times. Roch Carrier's iconic story "The Hockey Sweater" pivots on the legend of the Rocket and vividly describes the passion that Canadians, especially kids, felt for the game.

Just a few kilometers from the Montreal Forum where the Rocket and the Canadiens were making hockey history, a trio of scientists were working together to take the first steps in a new field of inquiry that would come to be known as cognitive neuroscience. They were Donald Hebb, Wilder Penfield, and Brenda Milner.

One of the first graduate students in the Department of Psychology (founded in 1922) at McGill University was Donald Olding Hebb (1904–1985) from Nova Scotia. Hebb was working as a school principal in a troubled Montreal suburb and pursued a Master's thesis at McGill part time. He fell in love with physiological psychology (as cognitive neuroscience was then called) and applied to pursue a PhD in the United States with Karl Lashley, whom you met earlier in this chapter. After obtaining his PhD (he studied the effects on the development of vision in rats that were being reared in darkness), he applied to work in Montreal with Wilder Penfield, one of the most famous neurosurgeons in the world. Hebb wanted to study the effects on psychological processes of the very specific brain removals that Penfield was producing in neurological patients. He moved back to Montreal in 1937.

Wilder Penfield (1891–1976) founded the Montreal Neurological Institute in the 1920s and pioneered the surgical removal of brain tissue to relieve seizure disorders—his approach became known as "the Montreal procedure." By stimulating the brain of awake patients during surgery, Penfield discovered how different parts of the brain support different mental functions and behaviours. You'll learn more about Penfield's work in the Neuroscience and Behaviour chapter.

By 1948, Hebb was Chair of the Department of Psychology at McGill, and in 1949 he published his landmark book *The Organization of Behaviour*, in which he lays out his theory of the neural basis of learning. As you will learn in the Memory chapter, this theory was extraordinarily prescient, and Hebb's ideas are now the basis of our understanding of how the physical structure of the brain changes with experience.

Brenda Milner (1918–), a Cambridge-trained psychologist, came to Canada as a bride in 1944. Her husband was an engineer who had been invited to help develop Canada's first nuclear reactors. Milner enrolled as a PhD student with Hebb and worked with Penfield's patients, studying how the removal of specific parts of the brain affected perception and memory. Over her long career, she has made several fundamental contributions to our understanding of how human thinking and behaviour depend on different parts of the brain. She is probably best known for the discovery of the brain basis of long-term memory   a topic that you will learn more about in the Memory chapter.

Brenda Milner (1918–) is a Canadian psychologist, best known for her discovery of the critical importance of a specific part of the brain, the hippocampus, to memory. She studied patients who had undergone removal of different parts of the brain (usually to relieve seizure disorders), in order to understand how the different regions contribute to human cognition and behaviour.

Cultural Psychology

Although we're all more alike than we are different, human beings vary dramatically in social practices, customs, and ways of living. *Culture* refers to the values, traditions, and beliefs that are shared by a particular group of people, and although we usually think of culture in terms of nationality and ethnicity, it can also be defined by age (e.g., youth culture), sexual orientation (e.g., gay culture), religion (e.g., Jewish culture), occupation (e.g., academic culture), and many of the other dimensions on which people differ (see A World of Difference: To Have or Have Not).

A World of Difference • To Have or Have Not

When we think about "other cultures," most of us imagine faraway lands filled with people eating exotic foods, wearing unfamiliar clothes, and speaking languages we can't understand. But you don't have to board an airplane to visit a culture different from your own, because in just about every place on earth, there are two distinctly different cultures living side by side: those who have more — more money, more education, more prestige — and those who have less (Kraus et al., 2011). In even the most egalitarian societies, people can be divided into higher and lower social classes, and as it turns out, social class is a powerful determinant of human behaviour.

Consider an example. Because upper-class people have ample material resources, they don't need to depend much on others. When problems arise, upper-class people rely on their bank accounts, whereas lower-class people rely on family, friends, and neighbours with whom they must maintain good relationships. In a way, one of the luxuries that upper-class people enjoy is the luxury of not worrying too much about what others feel or think. Does having that luxury influence their behaviour?

Indeed it does. In laboratory studies, upper-class people often prove to be less generous, less charitable, less trusting, and less helpful towards others (Piff et al., 2010), as well as more likely to lie and cheat for personal gain (Gino & Pierce, 2009; Piff et al., 2012). This "me first" orientation is easy to see outside of the laboratory, too. For example, in one study, researchers stood near the intersection

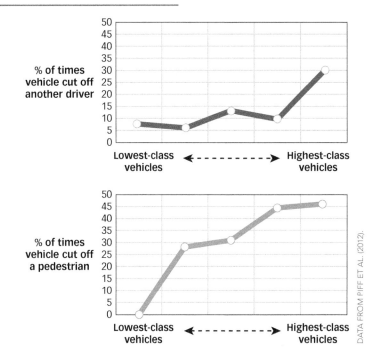

DATA FROM PIFF ET AL. (2012).

of two busy streets and recorded the make, model, and year of the cars that approached. They then watched to see whether the drivers cut off other cars and pedestrians in the intersection. As the two graphs show, the drivers of new, expensive cars were considerably more likely to zip through intersections without regard for others. Is this because being upper-class makes people selfish? Or is it because being selfish makes people upper-class? Some studies suggest that the first explanation is the right one. For instance, when participants in experiments are randomly assigned to *think* of themselves as upper-class — for instance,

when they are asked to compare their incomes to those who have less — they also behave more selfishly (Piff et al., 2012).

Social class matters. So do gender, race, religion, age, and most of the other dimensions on which human beings differ. Psychological science often produces conclusions about "people on average," but it is important to keep in mind that while averages are useful for understanding and predicting behaviour, people actually come in nearly infinite varieties, and the things that distinguish them are often as interesting as the things they have in common.

Scholars have been interested in cultural differences since at least the days of the ancient Greeks, but modern *anthropology* (the study of human societies and cultures) really got its start in the 19th century, when scholars such as Franz Boaz (1858–1942) and James Frazer (1854–1941) began to develop detailed theories to explain the psychological differences they observed among the people of different nations. Some early psychologists such as Wundt recognized the importance of these anthropological insights for psychology, but most 19th-century psychologists were content to ignore them and to assume that what they were studying was universal, or that exceptions to the rule didn't really matter. With

FROM CULTURE AND POINT OF VIEW, RICHARD E. NISBETT, TAKAHIKO MASUDA. PROCEEDINGS OF THE NATIONAL ACADEMY OF SCIENCES SEP 2003, 100 (19), 11163–11170. © 2003 NATIONAL ACADEMY OF SCIENCES, USA.

Culture can influence how and what we see. Participants in a study were shown this scene and then another version of this scene in which something was changed. American participants were more likely to spot changes to the red car, but Japanese participants were more likely to spot changes to the buildings.

the rise of behaviourism in the 20th century, culture became a topic of great interest to the social psychologists (e.g., the *Handbook of Social Psychology* has contained chapters on culture since 1935), but the rest of psychology ignored it. After all, how important could culture be if rats didn't have any?

All of that has now changed. **Cultural psychology** is *the study of how culture influences mental life,* and in the last few decades, research has shown that those influences can be quite profound. For example, in one study, American and Japanese participants were shown two drawings that differed in a few small details and were then asked to spot the differences. The Americans detected more differences in the foreground objects, whereas the Japanese detected more differences in the background objects (Masuda & Nisbett, 2001). Why? Because while Americans live in an independent and individualistic society, the Japanese live in an interdependent society with many role prescriptions that require them to attend to relationships and context, and this cultural difference appears to influence the kinds of visual information to which they naturally attend. Whereas Westerners tend to process visual information "analytically" by attending to objects in the foreground, Easterners tend to process visual information "holistically" by attending to the background. Because culture can influence just about everything psychologists study, you'll learn about work in cultural psychology in every one of the upcoming chapters.

Becoming a Psychologist

Learning Outcomes

WHAT YOU NEED TO KNOW

- Describe the diversity of psychology.
- Outline the different kinds of training psychologists may receive.
- Identify the careers available to psychologists.

If you tell someone you're a psychologist, they typically (a) run away or (b) ask if you are analyzing them. And then run away. Although most ordinary people don't know exactly what psychology is, they have a sneaking suspicion that psychologists can look directly into their minds and read their thoughts, especially the sexual ones. In fact, psychologists can't do this, but they can do other things that are much more useful, such as helping people, doing research, and making lists with three examples. Now that you know where psychology came from, and how it went from there to here, we'll close this chapter by looking at modern psychology as a profession.

Who Becomes a Psychologist?

In July of 1892, William James and six other American psychologists decided to form an organization that represented psychology as a profession, and so the American Psychological Association (APA) was born. James and his buddies would not have guessed that today their little club would boast more than 75,000 members—or that in 1988, a second professional organization would form, and that this Association for Psychological Science (APS) would soon expand to 30,000 members. James and his friends would never have guessed how massive their profession would soon become, or that by 2017, about 70% of the people receiving PhDs in psychology would be women (National Science Foundation, 2018).

You probably noticed that a chapter like this one, on the history of psychology, doesn't feature many women, and that's because for most of its existence, the profession was largely closed to them. But history chapters will start to look different in the coming years, because today there are plenty of women in psychology and they are most definitely making history.

Although many Canadian psychologists belong to the APA and/or the APS, Canada also has the Canadian Psychological Association (CPA; like the APA) and

cultural psychology The study of how culture influences mental life.

the Canadian Society for Brain, Behaviour and Cognitive Science (CSBBCS) for psychologists oriented towards scientific research. Finally, the Canadian Association for Neuroscience — association canadienne de neuroscience (CAN-ACN) — is a rapidly growing society of neuroscientists, including many psychologists. Today, about half of all APA and CPA members are women, and the percentage of non-White members continues to grow. Clearly, North American psychology is increasingly reflecting the diversity of society.

How Do People Become Psychologists?

University students who major in psychology usually come away with a bachelor's degree. They can call themselves educated, they can call themselves graduated, and if they really want to, they can call themselves bachelors. But they can't call themselves psychologists. To be called a psychologist requires earning an additional advanced degree. Two of the most common of these are the master's degree and the PhD in psychology. This abbreviation stands for "doctor of philosophy" (which actually has nothing to do with philosophy and a lot to do with the history of 19th-century German universities — don't ask).

To earn a master's or a PhD, students must attend graduate school, where they take classes and learn to do original research by collaborating with professors. Although William James was able to master the entire field of psychology in just a few years because the body of knowledge was so small, graduate students today typically concentrate their training in a specific area of psychology (e.g., social, cognitive, developmental, or clinical). Graduate (master's and PhD) students in the United States and Canada spend an average of 6 years in graduate school before attaining their degrees (National Science Foundation, 2018), and afterwards many go on for even more training in a laboratory or a hospital.

All that training is nice, but at some point, parents, spouses, and accountants will usually suggest that the graduate student get a job. For some of those who attain an advanced degree in psychology, that job is a professorship at a university, where they usually do some combination of teaching and scientific research. You are probably taking a class from one of those people right now, and may we take just a moment to say that they have excellent taste in textbooks? But many people who receive an advanced degree in psychology do not become professors, and instead work primarily as clinical psychologists, assessing or treating people with cognitive or psychological problems. They work in hospitals, schools, clinics, correctional facilities, employee assistance programs, and private offices. Some clinical psychologists have academic positions in universities and are active in both research and clinical practice.

Clinical psychologists often work in partnership with other mental health professionals, such as psychiatrists (who have earned an MD or a medical doctor degree) and counselors (who have usually earned a master's degree or a PhD). There are many other advanced degrees that allow people to call themselves psychologists and provide therapy, such as the PsyD (doctor of psychology) and the MEd (master of education). Why does a practice need so many different kinds of people? First, different degrees come with different privileges: People with an MD can prescribe medications, but people with a master's degree or a PhD cannot. Second, most clinical psychologists specialize in treating specific problems such as depression, anxiety, eating disorders, and so on, and they may even specialize in treating specific populations, such as children, older adults, or particular ethnic groups (see **FIGURE 1.1**). It takes a village to look after people's mental health.

So some psychologists become professors, and others become clinical psychologists. Does that account for all of them? Not by a long shot. Psychologists are

Figure 1.1

The Subfields of Psychology
Percentage of PhDs awarded by American universities in various subfields of psychology in 2019. Statistics are not available for Canadian universities, but are probably similar.

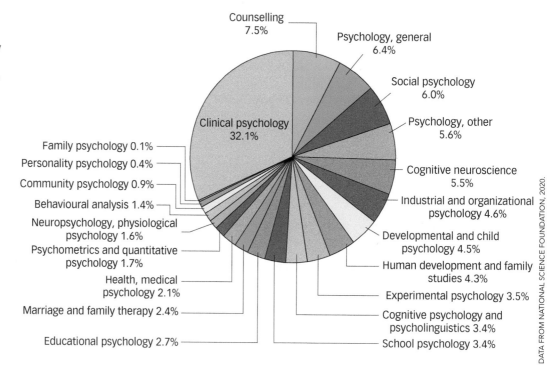

Counselling 7.5%

Psychology, general 6.4%

Social psychology 6.0%

Psychology, other 5.6%

Cognitive neuroscience 5.5%

Industrial and organizational psychology 4.6%

Developmental and child psychology 4.5%

Human development and family studies 4.3%

Experimental psychology 3.5%

Cognitive psychology and psycholinguistics 3.4%

School psychology 3.4%

Clinical psychology 32.1%

Family psychology 0.1%
Personality psychology 0.4%
Community psychology 0.9%
Behavioural analysis 1.4%
Neuropsychology, physiological psychology 1.6%
Psychometrics and quantitative psychology 1.7%
Health, medical psychology 2.1%
Marriage and family therapy 2.4%
Educational psychology 2.7%

DATA FROM NATIONAL SCIENCE FOUNDATION, 2020.

employed in a wide variety of other settings. For example, *school psychologists* offer guidance to students, parents, and teachers; *industrial/organizational psychologists* help businesses and organizations hire employees and maximize the employees' performances; *sports psychologists* help athletes train and compete; *forensic psychologists* assist attorneys and courts in dealing with crime; *consumer psychologists* help companies develop and market new products; and the list goes on. Indeed, it is difficult to think of any major institution or enterprise that *doesn't* employ psychologists in some capacity—and that includes Canada Post and the NHL. The fact is that modern psychologists are a diverse set of people who teach, do research, help those in distress, and aid the missions of public and private institutions. If you like what you learn in the upcoming chapters, you might even to decide to become one of them.

A person earning an advanced degree in psychology can go on to a wide range of fields, such as these three individuals did (from left to right): Lynne Madden is a clinical psychologist who works with both individuals and groups. Gloria Balague applies her training as a clinical psychologist to her work with athletes. Lynne Owens Mock directs a community mental health centre.

Chapter Review

Psychology's Philosophical Roots

- Psychology is the scientific study of mind and behaviour, and it has deep philosophical roots.

- Some philosophers have embraced philosophical dualism, which is the view that mind and body are fundamentally different things, whereas others have embraced philosophical materialism, which is the view that all mental phenomena are reducible to physical phenomena. Most modern psychologists are philosophical materialists.

- Some philosophers have embraced philosophical realism, which is the view that perceptions of the physical world are produced entirely by information from the sensory organs, whereas others have embraced philosophical idealism, which is the view that perceptions of the physical world are the brain's interpretation of information from the sensory organs. Most modern psychologists are philosophical idealists.

- Some philosophers have embraced philosophical empiricism, which is the view that all knowledge is acquired through experience, whereas others have embraced philosophical nativism, which is the view that some knowledge is innate rather than acquired. Most modern psychologists are philosophical nativists.

The Late 1800s: Towards a Science of the Mind

- In the late 19th century, many European psychologists embraced structuralism, which was an approach to psychology that attempted to isolate and analyze the mind's basic elements.

- Structuralism soon gave way to functionalism, which was an approach to psychology that was influenced by Darwin's theory of natural selection, emphasizing the adaptive significance of mental processes.

The Early 1900s: Psychoanalysis and Behaviourism

- In the early 20th century, Sigmund Freud developed psychoanalytic theory, which emphasized the influence of the unconscious on feelings, thoughts, and behaviours. He devised a therapy called psychoanalysis that he believed could help people gain insight into the contents of their unconscious minds.

- Freud had little impact on experimental psychology, but a tremendous impact on the treatment of psychological disorders and on the intellectual climate of the Western world.

- John Watson admired Ivan Pavlov's research on dogs, and he developed behaviourism, which was an approach to psychology that restricted scientific inquiry to observable behaviour. Behaviourism soon came to dominate experimental psychology in America.

- B. F. Skinner took a behaviourist approach to understanding how organisms learn to operate on their environments, and he developed the principle of reinforcement. He believed this principle could explain complex human behaviour, including how people learn language.

The Early 1900s: Resistance to Behaviourism

- In the first half of the 20th century, behaviourism reigned in America, but some European psychologists resisted it and continued to do research on "mentalistic" phenomena such as perception, memory, and judgement.

- At the same time, social psychologists also resisted behaviourism and continued to do research on mentalistic phenomena such as beliefs, attitudes, stereotypes, identity, and intention.

The Late 1900s: The Cognitive Revolution

- In the 1950s and 1960s, Noam Chomsky's critique of Skinner's theory of language, as well as the advent of the digital computer, helped spark the "cognitive revolution." The emergence of cognitive psychology allowed psychologists to use the language of information processing to study mentalistic phenomena.

- In the 1970s and 1980s, psychologists began to incorporate theories from evolutionary biology into their work, which led to the emergence of evolutionary psychology.

The Early 2000s: New Frontiers

- In the 21st century, several new areas of psychology have emerged. Cognitive neuroscientists study the relationship between psychological processes and neural activity, behavioural neuroscientists study the relationship between behaviour and neural activity, and cultural psychologists study the ways in which culture influences mental life.

Becoming a Psychologist

- Psychology is a diverse science. In North America, women earn more than half of all PhDs in psychology.

- To become a psychologist, one must attain an advanced degree. Many psychologists become therapists or clinicians, but some become professors; and many are employed in government, industry, and a variety of other enterprises and institutions.

Changing Minds

1. While scrolling through your newsfeed, you come across a story describing some research that shows that when people feel love, particular regions of their brains "light up." You scroll down and see that someone has commented: "This is crazy. Love is more than brain chemistry. It's about the heart!" Given what you know about materialism, dualism, and fMRI, how would you respond?

2. Sigmund Freud is often described in the media as "the father of modern psychology." How accurate is that title? Who else might deserve it more?

3. One of your friends is a chemistry major. They see your psychology textbook on your desk and starts flipping through it. "Psychology is just so stupid," your friend says. "I mean, how can it claim to be a science when it studies things no one can see, like thoughts and memories and emotions? Why don't they just stick to studying what they can actually measure?" Given what you know about the history of psychology, what would you tell your friend?

4. High school students are touring your campus today—and you get to meet them. Yippie! One of them tells you they are considering a major in psychology. "I figure I can get my degree in four years and then start doing therapy." Given what you've learned about careers in psychology, what should you tell them?

5. **Visualizing Data** Another student touring the campus says, "I'd like to study psychology, but I understand it is a field in decline." Use the DATA to convince the student that they are wrong.

Key Terms

psychology (p. 2)

philosophical dualism (p. 3)

philosophical materialism (p. 3)

philosophical realism (p. 3)

philosophical idealism (p. 4)

philosophical empiricism (p. 5)

philosophical nativism (p. 5)

reaction time (p. 7)

structuralism (p. 7)

introspection (p. 7)

functionalism (p. 8)

natural selection (p. 8)

hysteria (p. 9)

unconscious (p. 9)

psychoanalytic theory (p. 9)

psychoanalysis (p. 9)

behaviourism (p. 10)

principle of reinforcement (p. 11)

Gestalt psychology (p. 13)

developmental psychology (p. 14)

social psychology (p. 14)

cognitive psychology (p. 17)

evolutionary psychology (p. 18)

cognitive neuroscience (p. 19)

behavioural neuroscience (p. 19)

cultural psychology (p. 22)

Methods in Psychology

WHEN LOUISE HAY DIED IN 2017, her net worth was estimated at around $50 million. Her most popular book, *You Can Heal Your Life*, had sold over 35 million copies. In it, she explained that everything that happens to people—including diseases, accidents, and other misfortunes—is a result of the thoughts they choose to think. She claimed that she had been diagnosed with incurable cancer, but that she had cured herself nonetheless by changing the way she thought, and she amassed a fortune by promising people that they could learn to do the same thing if only they attended one of her seminars or bought a few of her videos or books. In a 2010 television interview with one of the authors of this textbook, Hay was asked why she believed her techniques were effective.

> **Gilbert:** How do you know what you're saying is right?
> **Hay:** Oh, my inner ding.
> **Gilbert:** Ding?
> **Hay:** My inner ding. It speaks to me. It feels right or it doesn't feel right. Happiness is choosing thoughts that make you feel good. It's really very simple.
> **Gilbert:** But I hear you saying that even if there were no proof for what you believed, or even if there were scientific evidence against it, it wouldn't change?
> **Hay:** Well, I don't believe in scientific evidence, I really don't. Science is fairly new. It hasn't been around that long. We think it's such a big deal, but it's, you know, it's just a way of looking at life.

Louise Hay didn't believe in scientific evidence—but what could that possibly mean? After all, if her techniques really did cure cancer, then people with cancer who practice her techniques should on average live longer than those who don't. That isn't "a way of looking at life." It's just plain old common sense—exactly the kind of common sense that lies at the heart of science. Science tells us that there is one and only one way to know for sure whether claims like Louise Hay's are true, and that's to gather evidence. Inner dings don't count. If we want to know what's true about the world, then we actually have to go there and take a look around.

But what exactly should we be looking for? Should we ask people who attended one of Hay's seminars whether they think they've been healed by her techniques? Should we examine the medical records of people who have and haven't bought one of her books? Should we invite people to sign up for a class that teaches her techniques and then wait to see how many of them get cancer over the next few years? All of these may strike you as decent ways to test Louise Hay's claim, but in fact, not one of them is. There are a few good ways to test claims

- **Empiricism: How to Know Stuff**
- **Methods of Observation: Discovering What People Do**
- **Methods of Explanation: Discovering Why People Do What They Do**
- **Thinking Critically About Evidence**
- **The Ethics of Science: Doing What's Right**

Louise Hay claimed that people can cure cancer with their minds. How can we tell whether her claim is right or wrong?

MICHELE ASSELIN/CONTOUR BY GETTY IMAGES

like these and a whole lot more bad ways, and the main point of this chapter is to teach you the difference between them. Scientists have developed powerful tools for determining when a claim is right and when it is wrong, and these tools are what make science different from every other way of knowing. As the British philosopher Bertrand Russell (1945, p. 527) wrote, "It is not what the man of science believes that distinguishes him, but how and why he believes it." That goes for all the scientists who aren't men as well.

WE'LL START BY EXAMINING THE GENERAL PRINCIPLES THAT GUIDE scientific research and distinguish it from other human enterprises. Next, we'll see how the methods of psychology allow us to answer two basic questions: What do people do, and why do they do it? Psychologists answer the first question by measuring things, and they answer the second question by looking for relationships between the things they measure. We'll see that scientific evidence allows us to draw certain kinds of conclusions but not others, and that thinking critically about scientific evidence doesn't come naturally to most people. Finally, we'll consider some of the unique ethical questions that confront scientists who study human beings and other animals.

Empiricism: How to Know Stuff

Learning Outcomes

WHAT YOU NEED TO KNOW

- Explain why direct observation is essential to an accurate understanding of nature.
- Outline the process of the scientific method.
- Identify the challenges to studying human behaviour.

empiricism The conviction that accurate knowledge of the world can be acquired by observing it.

scientific method A procedure for using empirical evidence to establish facts.

theory An explanation of a natural phenomenon.

When ancient Greeks sprained their ankles, caught the flu, or accidentally set their hair on fire, they had to choose between two kinds of doctors. The dogmatists (from *dogmatikos,* meaning "belief") thought the best way to understand illness was to develop theories of the body's functions, and the empiricists (from *empeirikos,* meaning "experience") thought the best way was to examine sick people. The rivalry between these two schools of medicine didn't last long because the people who went to see dogmatists tended to die a lot, which was bad for business. That's why today we use the word *dogmatism* to describe the tendency to cling to one's beliefs and we use the word **empiricism** to describe *the conviction that accurate knowledge of the world can be acquired by observing it.* The fact that we can answer questions about the natural world by observing it probably seems obvious to you, but this obvious fact has only recently gained wide acceptance. For most of human history, people trusted authority to provide answers to questions such as "How did we get here?" and "What are we made of?" and "Why do some of us ask more questions than others?" It is only in the last millennium (and especially in the past three centuries) that people have begun to trust their eyes and their ears more than their elders.

The Scientific Method

Empiricism is the backbone of the **scientific method,** which is *a procedure for using empirical evidence to establish facts.* Essentially, the scientific method suggests that when we have an idea about how something in the world works—about how bats navigate, or where the moon came from, or why people can't forget traumatic events—we must go out into the world, make observations, and then use those observations to determine whether our idea is true. Scientists generally refer to these "ideas about how something works" as **theories,** which are *explanations of natural phenomena.* So, for instance, we might theorize that bats navigate by making sounds and then listening for the echo, or that the moon was formed when a small planet collided with the earth, or that the brain responds to traumatic events by producing chemicals that facilitate memory. Each of these theories is an explanation of how something in the natural world works and why it works that way.

How do we decide if a theory is right? A good theory makes specific predictions about what we should observe in the world if the theory is true. For example, if bats really do navigate by making sounds and then listening for echoes, then deaf bats should not be able to navigate very well. That "should" statement is technically known as a **hypothesis,** which is *a falsifiable prediction made by a theory.* The word *falsifiable* is a critical part of that definition. Some theories, such as "Things happen the way they do because that's how God wants it," do not tell us what we should observe if the theory is true; therefore, no amount of observation can ever falsify them. That doesn't mean the theory is wrong. It just means that we can't use the scientific method to evaluate its veracity.

So good theories give rise to hypotheses that can be falsified, and when that happens, the theory is proved wrong. But how can it be proved *right*? Alas, a theory can *never* be proved right, and here's why. Imagine that you decided to test the theory that bats navigate by using sound. The theory gives rise to a falsifiable hypothesis: Deaf bats should navigate poorly. Now, if you observed a deaf bat navigating perfectly well, that observation would be *inconsistent* with your hypothesis, and so your theory must be wrong. On the other hand, if you observed deaf bats navigating poorly, your observation would be *consistent* with your hypothesis, but it would not prove that your theory was right. Why? Because even if you didn't see a deaf bat navigating perfectly well today, it is always possible that you will see one tomorrow—or the day after that, or maybe 30 years from now. You observed one bat, but you didn't observe every bat that has ever been and will ever be, so even if today's observation didn't prove your theory wrong, there is always a chance that some future observation will. The point is that observations that are consistent with a theory can increase our confidence that the theory is right, but they can never make us 100% confident that it is right. So the next time you see a headline that says "Scientists prove theory X," you are hereby authorized to roll your eyes.

The scientific method tells us that the only way to learn the truth about the world is to (1) develop a theory, (2) derive a falsifiable hypothesis from it, and (3) test that hypothesis by observing the world—or, in fancier language, by gathering empirical evidence. You now know about parts one and two—the theories and hypotheses parts—so let's now see what this third "evidence gathering" part is all about.

The Art of Looking

Looking isn't as easy as it looks. For example, people argued for centuries about whether all four feet of a galloping horse leave the ground at the same time. They would all go out and watch the same horse run, and then some would swear that all four feet left the ground at the same time, some would swear that they didn't, and some would just swear. Then, in 1877, a man named Eadweard Muybridge invented a technique for taking photographs in rapid succession. His photos showed that when horses gallop, they really do become airborne for a split second. And that was that. Never again did a group of people engage in a flying-horse debate because Muybridge's pictures had settled the matter forever.

But why did it take so long? Human beings had been watching horses gallop for centuries, so why were some of them sure that horses left the ground while others were equally sure they didn't? Because as wonderful as human eyes may be, there are many things they see inaccurately and many other things they don't

The astronomer Galileo Galilei (1564–1642) was excommunicated and sentenced to prison for sticking to his empirical observations of the solar system rather than accepting the teachings of the Catholic Church. In 1597, he wrote to his friend and fellow astronomer Johannes Kepler (1571–1630), "What would you say of the learned here, who, replete with the pertinacity of the asp, have steadfastly refused to cast a glance through the telescope? What shall we make of this? Shall we laugh, or shall we cry?" As he later learned, the answer was cry.

Classical thinkers such as Euclid and Ptolemy believed that our eyes work by emitting rays that go out and "touch" the objects we see. But the Persian genius Ibn al-Haytham (965–1039) argued that if this theory was right, then when we open our eyes it should take longer to see something far away than something nearby. And guess what? It doesn't. The classical theory of vision gave rise to a hypothesis, that hypothesis was disconfirmed by observation, and an ancient theory vanished in the blink of an eye.

hypothesis A falsifiable prediction made by a theory.

LIBRARY OF CONGRESS PRINTS AND PHOTOGRAPHS DIVISION, REPRODUCTION NUMBER LC-USZ62-52703 (B&W FILM COPY NEG.)

If anyone ever tells you that horses keep one foot on the ground at all times, just say nay, and then trot out Frames 2 and 3 of this historic series of photos by Eadweard Muybridge (1830–1904).

PRAHL/TURGEON SPLASHNEWS/NEWSCOM

People are highly reactive—that is, they behave differently when they know they are being observed. For example, if actor Chris Hemsworth had realized that a photographer was lurking nearby, he might have found a more discreet way to deal with his itchy nose.

empirical method A set of rules and techniques for observation.

see at all. From where you are sitting right now, the earth looks perfectly flat when it is in fact imperfectly round. From where you are sitting right now, you can't see a microbe, or ultraviolet light, or the 14 moons of Neptune, but all of them are real and all of them are there. As Muybridge knew, empiricism is the right approach to testing hypotheses, but to do it properly requires more than a set of eyes. It requires an **empirical method,** which is *a set of rules and techniques for observation.*

In many sciences, the word *method* refers to technologies that enhance the powers of the senses. Biologists use microscopes and astronomers use telescopes because the things they want to observe are invisible to the naked eye. Human behaviour, on the other hand, is easy to see, so you might expect psychology's methods to be relatively simple. But they aren't, and that's because human beings have three qualities that make them more difficult to study than either cells or stars. First, people are extremely *complex*. Scientists can describe the birth of a star or the death of a cell in exquisite detail, but they can barely begin to say how the 100 billion interconnected neurons that constitute the human brain give rise to the thoughts, feelings, and actions that are psychology's core concerns. Second, people are extremely *variable*. One ribosome may be a lot like another, but no two people ever do, say, think, or feel exactly the same thing under exactly the same circumstances. Third, people are extremely *reactive*. A cesium atom oscillates at the same rate regardless of who might be watching, but people tend to think, feel, and act differently when they think they are being observed and when they think they are not.

The fact that human beings are extremely complex, variable, and reactive presents a challenge to the scientific study of their behaviour. Psychologists have met this challenge by developing two kinds of methods: *methods of observation,* which allow them to discover what people do, and *methods of explanation,* which allow them to discover why people do it. We'll examine each of these methods in the sections that follow.

A World of Difference | Are Heroes and Sheroes Divided by Zeroes?

Galileo, Newton, Mendel, Darwin, Faraday, Einstein, Turing, Tesla, Skinner—what do all these people have in common? First, they were all brilliant scientists. And second, they were all men. The history of science is pretty much the history of smart men having big ideas and making big discoveries. So where are all the women? There are two answers to this question. The first is that, until quite recently, educational and employment opportunities for women were limited. For most of history, women were either subtly discouraged or actively prohibited from studying science—and you really can't win the Nobel Prize in Physics if they won't let you take algebra. As the sociologist Leta Hollingworth cheekily noted in 1914, "Women bear and rear the children, and this has had as an inevitable sequel the occupation of housekeeping, a field where eminence is not possible."

The second answer is that men and women may have different interests and talents, and the interests and talents that men have may be the ones people need to become great scientists. That sounds like a troubling suggestion. Is there any truth to it? A few years ago, a group of scientists (whose leader was a woman) got together, surveyed all the scientific evidence on this topic, and drew a striking conclusion: Yes, they concluded, the evidence does show that men and women differ with regard to certain interests and talents (Halpern et al., 2007). First, men are often more interested in the topics that scientists study. Second, men and women differ in scientifically relevant abilities: Specifically, men are more *variable* than women on most measures of quantitative ability (the ability to use numbers) and visuo-spatial ability (the ability to use images), both of which are important to success in many sciences.

Being more variable doesn't mean being better, however. It means that although men and women have the same average amount of talent on these dimensions, there are more men at both the very lowest and very highest ends of the spectrum. If great scientists tend to come from the highest end of the spectrum, then men will naturally be overrepresented among great scientists. In support of this conclusion, recent data show that while men are overrepresented in scientific fields that are "math intensive"—such as geoscience, engineering, economics, mathematics, computer science, and the physical sciences—they are not overrepresented in scientific fields that place less emphasis on math, such as biology, psychology, and sociology (Ceci et al., 2014). Indeed, while women earn fewer than 20% of the degrees in computer science and engineering, they earn the *majority* of degrees in the life and social sciences. With regard to having different interests, it is worth noting that the largest gender gaps in the "hard sciences" emerge in the nations with the *highest* gender equality, suggesting that when women have a choice, they tend not to choose those fields (Stoet & Geary, 2018).

So yes, men do seem to be more interested in certain topics and more variable on certain dimensions. The question is: Why? Is it because there is some innate difference in the structure or function of male and female brains, or is it simply because men are encouraged to develop their interests and hone their quantitative skills by parents who buy them video games instead of dolls, and by teachers who encourage them to join the math team rather than the debate team? Once again, a group of experts reviewed the evidence and concluded that "sex differences in spatial and mathematical reasoning need not stem from biological bases, that the gap between average

female and male math ability is narrowing (suggesting strong environmental influences), and that sex differences in math ability at the right tail [which is the 'high' end of the ability spectrum] show variation over time and across nationalities, ethnicities, and other factors, indicating that the ratio of males to females at the right tail can and does change" (Ceci et al., 2014, p. 75). In other words, men may be more interested in certain scientific topics and may be more likely to be unusually talented (or untalented!) when it comes to math, but there is *no compelling evidence to suggest that these sex differences are innate*. We agree with the experts who concluded that "there are no single or simple answers to the complex questions about sex differences in science and mathematics" (Halpern et al., 2007, p. 75).

In 1834, William Whewell coined the word *scientist* to describe a remarkable astronomer, physicist, and chemist named Mary Somerville. Few people remember that the world's first scientist was a woman.

Methods of Observation: Discovering What People Do

Learning Outcomes

WHAT YOU NEED TO KNOW

- Name the properties of a good operational definition.

- Identify some of the methods psychologists use to avoid demand characteristics and observer bias.

- Explain what a frequency distribution is, and describe the two main types of descriptive statistics.

Define the Property

Generate an operational definition that has construct validity

Detect the Property

Design an instrument that has reliability and power

Figure 2.1
Measurement There are two steps in the measurement of a property.

operational definition A description of a property in measurable terms.

construct validity A feature of operational definitions whose specified operations are generally considered good indicators of the specified properties.

power A detector's ability to detect the presence of differences or changes in the magnitude of a property.

reliability A detector's ability to detect the absence of differences or changes in the magnitude of a property.

When you look at an apple, your brain uses the pattern of light that enters your eyes to make inferences about the apple's colour, shape, and size. That kind of everyday observation is good enough for buying fruit, but not for doing science. Why? First, everyday observations are often *inconsistent:* The same apple can appear red in the daylight and crimson at night, or spherical from one angle and elliptical from another. Second, everyday observations are often *incomplete,* which is to say that they can't provide all the information we want. No matter how long and hard you stare at an apple, you will never be able to determine its melting point or pectin content. Luckily, scientists have devised techniques that allow them to overcome these two limitations. In the sections that follow, we'll first see how psychologists measure the things that everyday observation misses (Measurement), and then we'll see what psychologists do with their measurements once they've made them (Description).

Measurement

We live in a world of clocks and calendars, scales and yardsticks, odometers and thermometers. Measurement is not just a part of modern science, it is a part of modern life. But regardless of what we want to measure—the intensity of an earthquake, the size of an elephant, or the happiness of a citizen—we must always do the same two things. First, we must *define* the property we want to measure, and second, we must find a way to *detect* it (**FIGURE 2.1**). For example, to measure a person's level of happiness, we would start by generating an **operational definition,** which is *a description of a property in measurable terms.* So, for example, we might operationally define happiness as "the amount of dopamine in a person's brain" or "the number of times a person smiles in an hour" or just "how happy a person says they are." Once we have this definition in hand, we need to find a detector—that is, some sort of instrument or device that can detect the property as we just defined it—such as a carbon electrode (to detect dopamine in the brain) or an electromyograph (to detect a smile) or a simple rating scale (to detect how happy a person says they are). What makes a good operational definition, and what makes a good detector?

- One of the key features of a good operational definition is **construct validity,** which is *a feature of operational definitions whose specified operations are generally considered good indicators of the specified properties.* For example, most of us would consider the frequency with which a person smiles to be an appropriate way to operationally define the property called "happiness" because we all know from our own experience that happy people tend to smile more than unhappy people do. But do they also eat more or talk more or spend more money? Well, maybe—or maybe not. And that's why most psychologists would consider "smiles per hour" to be an appropriate way to operationally define happiness, but would not feel similarly about "number of chocolates eaten" or "number of words spoken" or "number of dollars spent." To a large extent, construct validity is in the eye of the beholder, and an operational definition is said to have construct validity when most beholders agree that it is an indicator of the property.

- The two key features of a good detector are **power,** which refers to *a detector's ability to detect the presence of differences or changes in the magnitude of a property,* and **reliability,** which refers to *a detector's ability to detect the absence of differences or changes in the magnitude of a property.* If a person smiles a

KYODO NEWS/GETTY IMAGES

DAVID J. PHILLIP/AP PHOTO

Power and Reliability at the Olympics Usain Bolt ran the 100 metre race in 9.58 seconds, and Yohan Blake ran it in 9.75 seconds. If judges did not have *powerful* speed-detectors, they might have mistakenly concluded that the two men were tied. Judges in the sport of ice dancing rate qualities of performance related to athleticism and artistry, and they are consistent (reliable) in their ratings: Tessa Virtue and Scott Moir, champion ice dancers, clearly measure up.

bit more often on Tuesday than on Wednesday, a powerful smile-detector will detect different amounts of smiling on those two days. If a person smiles exactly as much on Wednesday as they did on Tuesday, then a reliable smile-detector will detect identical amounts of smiling on those two days. A good detector detects differences or changes in the magnitude of a property whenever they exist (power), but it does not detect differences or changes when they don't exist (reliability).

Demand Characteristics: Doing What Is Expected

Once we have an operational definition that has construct validity, and a detector that is both powerful and reliable, are we *finally* ready to measure some behaviour? Yes — as long as we want to measure the behaviour of a worm, a thunderstorm, a stock market, or anything else that doesn't care about being observed. If we want to measure the behaviour of a human being, then we still have some work to do because when human beings know they are being observed, they will often try to behave as they think the observer wants or expects them to behave. **Demand characteristics** are *those aspects of an observational setting that cause people to behave as they think someone else wants or expects.* If a friend asked, "Do you think I'm smart?" you would probably say yes whether you meant it or not. You know what your friend is hoping to hear and so you dutifully supply it. Similarly, if a researcher asked, "Do you think it is wrong to cheat on exams?" then you would probably say yes as well, if only because you know that's the response the researcher expects of you. A study that asked participants such questions would be said to have demand characteristics because the questions "demand" that participants give a response that may or may not reflect their true feelings. How can we avoid demand characteristics? Here are three techniques:

- **Naturalistic Observation** One way that psychologists avoid demand characteristics is by using **naturalistic observation,** which is *a technique for gathering information by unobtrusively observing people in their natural environments.* Naturalistic observation has shown that the biggest groups leave the smallest tips in restaurants (Freeman et al., 1975), that golfers are most likely to cheat when they play several opponents at once (Erffmeyer, 1984), that men usually don't approach the most beautiful woman at a club (Glenwick et al., 1978), and that Olympic athletes smile more when they win the bronze medal than the silver medal (Medvec et al., 1995). Each of these conclusions is the result of measurements made by psychologists who observed people who didn't know they were being observed by psychologists, and it seems unlikely that the diners, golfers, clubbers, and athletes would have behaved the same way if they'd known a psychologist was watching. Of course, naturalistic observation isn't always practical. First, some events just don't occur naturally (e.g., if we wanted to know whether people who have undergone sensory deprivation perform poorly on fine-motor tasks, we would have to stand on the street corner for a very long time before we just so happened to spot a bunch of blindfolded people with earplugs trying to text with one hand); and second, some

demand characteristics Those aspects of an observational setting that cause people to behave as they think someone else wants or expects.

naturalistic observation A technique for gathering information by unobtrusively observing people in their natural environments.

Countries that have a faster pace of life tend to have higher rates of heart disease. How do researchers measure the "pace of life"? They make naturalistic observations—in this case, by measuring the average walking speed of pedestrians in different cities. By the way, the fastest pedestrians are the Irish (*left*) and the slowest are the Romanians (*right*) (Levine & Norenzayan, 1999).

One way to avoid demand characteristics is to measure behaviours that people are unable or unlikely to control. For example, our pupils contract when we are bored (top photo) and dilate when we are interested (bottom photo), which makes pupillary dilation a useful measure of a person's level of engagement in a task.

things can only be observed through direct interaction with people (e.g., if we wanted to know how accurately people can remember their high school graduations, just watching them with binoculars won't do). What can we do when naturalistic observation isn't possible?

- **Privacy and Control** People are less likely to be influenced by demand characteristics when they can't be identified as the authors of their actions, and psychologists often take advantage of this fact by allowing participants in their studies to respond privately (e.g., by having them complete questionnaires when they are alone) and/or anonymously (e.g., by not collecting personal information, such as people's names or addresses). In addition, psychologists may avoid demand characteristics by measuring behaviours that are not under a person's voluntary control. If a psychologist asked whether you were interested in stupid celebrity gossip, you might lie and say no. But if the psychologist instead gauged your interest in stupid celebrity gossip by measuring the dilation of your pupils as you paged through the latest issue of *People* magazine, there would be no way for you to hide the fact that you are shipping Zendaya and Tom Holland. C'mon. You know you are.

- **Unawareness** One of the best ways to avoid demand characteristics is to make sure that the people who are being observed are unaware of the true purpose of the observation. People can't try to behave how they should behave if they don't *know* how they should behave. For example, if you didn't know that a psychologist was studying the effects of classical music on mood, you wouldn't feel obligated to smile when Bach's *Concerto #1 in F Major* started playing in the background. That's why psychologists typically don't reveal the true purpose of an observation to the people being observed until the study is over. And it's also why psychologists sometimes mislead people by telling them that they are studying one thing when they are really studying another, or by giving people pointless tasks or asking pointless questions simply so that people can't easily guess the study's true purpose. (We will discuss the ethical implications of misleading a study's participants later in this chapter.)

Observer Bias: Seeing What Is Expected

More than half a century ago, students in a psychology class were asked to measure the speed with which a rat learned to navigate a maze (Rosenthal & Fode, 1963). Some students were told that their rat had been specially bred to be a slow learner while others were told that their rat had been specially bred to be a fast learner. The truth was that the rats were all exactly the same breed. Nonetheless, students who *thought* they were measuring the speed of a slow learner reported that their rats took

3.47 minutes to navigate the maze, whereas students who *thought* they were measuring the speed of a fast learner reported that their rats took 2.35 minutes to navigate the maze. In other words, the measurements revealed precisely what the students had expected them to reveal, even though those expectations had no basis in reality. This happened for two reasons.

- First, *expectations can influence observations.* Just think about all the decisions the students had to make when they were measuring the speed of their rat. If a rat puts one leg over the finish line, does that count as finishing, or does it have to have all four legs over the line? If a rat stops to urinate, should the stopwatch keep running or should it be stopped until the rat finishes its business? If a rat runs the maze in 18.5 seconds, should that number be rounded up to 19 or down to 18 before it is recorded? How students made these decisions depended on whether they thought their rats were fast or slow learners. "Micky is a fast learner, so let's just call it 18" or "Topo sure is a slow learner. When will he ever drag his last leg over the finish line?"

- Second, *expectations can influence reality.* Students who expected their rats to be fast learners unwittingly did things that might have helped that learning along. For instance, students handled their rats more often and more gently when they thought they were fast learners, and the rats may well have responded to this superior treatment by turning in a superior performance.

Robert Parker is one of the world's foremost wine critics. His ratings indicate how good a wine tastes—but can they also *influence* how good a wine tastes? Researchers gave participants a glass of wine and told some of them that Parker had awarded that wine 92 out of 100 points; others were told that he had awarded it only 72 points (Siegrist & Cousin, 2009). Sure enough, participants who thought the wine was highly rated thought the wine tasted much better and were willing to pay about 50% more for a bottle.

The students probably tried their best to be fair and objective, but their expectations nonetheless seem to have influenced both their rat's behaviour and their observations of it. Psychologists call this **observer bias,** which is *the tendency for observers' expectations to influence both what they believe they observed and what they actually observed.* To avoid observer bias, psychologists use a number of techniques, the most common of which is called the **double-blind study,** which is *a study in which neither the researcher nor the participant knows how the participants are expected to behave.* For example, if we wanted to know whether people smile more when listening to classical music than to hip-hop, we might give participants a task to do while one of these two kinds of music played in the background, and have a research assistant watch them and record how often they smiled. We would take steps to ensure that our participants did not know what we were studying so that they would not feel obligated to behave as we expected them to, and we would also take steps to ensure that the research assistants did not know how the participants were expected to behave, perhaps by having the research assistants wear noise-cancelling headphones so that they wouldn't know which kind of music was playing as they recorded the participants' rate of smiling. If research assistants don't *have* expectations, then their expectations cannot influence either their observations or their participants' behaviour. That's why psychologists typically make sure that the people who are making the observations in a study are as "blind" to the hypothesis as are the people who are being observed.

Description

You now know how to measure—that is, you know how to generate an operational definition of a property that has construct validity, you know how to find a reliable and powerful detector of that property, and you know how to use that detector while avoiding demand characteristics and observer bias. So who are you going to measure? Psychologists rarely measure the properties of an entire **population,** which is *a complete collection of people*—such as the population of human beings

observer bias The tendency for observers' expectations to influence both what they believe they observed and what they actually observed.

double-blind study A study in which neither the researcher nor the participant knows how the participants are expected to behave.

population A complete collection of people.

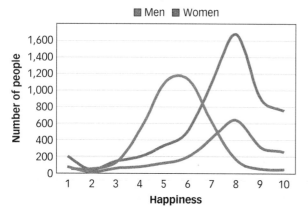

Figure 2.2

Frequency Distributions The graph in the top panel uses bars to show the number of male residents (shown in green) and female residents (shown in brown) in a suburb of Boston, United States, who rated their happiness at each value on a 10-point scale. The graph in the middle panel shows the same data using smoothed lines. The graph in the bottom panel shows how these real data compare to a hypothetical normal distribution (shown in purple).

sample A partial collection of people drawn from a population.

frequency distribution A graphic representation showing the number of times that the measurement of a property takes on each of its possible values.

(about 7 billion), the population of Canadians (about 38 million), or the population of Nova Scotians (about 1 million). Rather, they tend to measure the properties of a **sample,** which is *a partial collection of people drawn from a population.* We'll talk later about how psychologists typically get their samples, but for now, just imagine you have taken a sample and measured its properties.

Congratulations! You are now the proud owner of some *data.* Your data probably take the form of a big spreadsheet filled with numbers that represent things like the frequency with which 211 people smiled in an hour, or the amount of time it took 37 rats to run a maze. And if you are like most researchers, you will look at your data and feel precisely as ignorant as you were before you started because, for most researchers, a big spreadsheet full of numbers just isn't very informative. But that's okay, because psychologists have two techniques for making sense out of big spreadsheets full of numbers: graphic representations and descriptive statistics. Let's have a look at each of these.

Graphic Representations: Picturing the Data

Ever wonder why a map is so much better than a list of step-by-step directions? Vision is our most sophisticated sense, so most people find it easier to understand facts when those facts are represented visually rather than by numbers or words. That's why scientists typically make sense of their data by creating pictures or *graphic representations.* The most common kind of graphic representation is called a **frequency distribution,** which is *a graphic representation showing the number of times that the measurement of a property takes on each of its possible values.*

The frequency distribution in the top panel of **FIGURE 2.2** shows the results of a city-wide census in which residents of Somerville, Massachusetts (a suburb of Boston), were asked to report their current level of happiness by using a rating scale that ranged from 1 (very unhappy) to 10 (very happy). The property being measured was happiness, the operational definition of happiness was a scale rating, and all the possible values of that rating (1 through 10) are shown on the horizontal axis. The vertical axis shows the number of men and women who responded to the census and used each of these values to rate their happiness. (The data from the small number of people who did not identify as men or women are not shown in this graph.) So, for example, the graph shows that 1,677 women and 646 men rated their happiness as 8 on a 10-point scale. The middle panel shows exactly the same data, but it uses smooth lines rather than bars, which is an equally common way to display a frequency distribution.

In a single glance, these graphs reveal things about the sample that a page full of numbers does not. For instance, when you look at the shape of the distributions, you instantly know that the people in this sample tend to be fairly happy. Your eyes also tell you that far fewer men than women responded to the census, but that the general shapes of the two distributions are roughly the same, which suggests that the men in this sample are generally about as happy as the women on average. You can see other things too—for instance, that 8 is the most popular rating for both men and women, and that both genders are about 3 times as likely to rate their happiness as 10 than to rate it as 1. All that information from a simple drawing!

The distributions in the middle panel are *negatively skewed* (which means that they lean to the right) rather than *positively skewed* (which means that they lean to the left) because very few people use numbers that are below the midpoint of the scale to rate their happiness. Although a frequency distribution can have just about any shape, a special shape is shown in purple in the bottom panel of Figure 2.2. As you can see, this distribution has a peak exactly in the middle and then trails off in the same way at both ends. This distribution is unskewed or *symmetrical,* which is to say that the left half is a mirror image of the right half. Although frequency distributions showing data from the real world are rarely as symmetrical as the purple one is, they are often fairly close, especially when the amount of data used to construct them is quite large. That's why the distribution shown in purple is called the **normal distribution,** which is *a mathematically defined distribution in which the frequency of measurements is highest in the middle and decreases symmetrically in both directions.* The normal distribution is often called a *bell curve,* but if you'd like to be single for the rest of your life you can tell everyone you know that it is also called a *Gaussian distribution.*

Descriptive Statistics: Summarizing the Data

A frequency distribution depicts every measurement in a sample and thus provides a full and complete picture of that sample. But sometimes a full and complete picture is more than we want to know. When we ask a friend how they've been doing lately, we don't really want them to show us a frequency distribution of their happiness ratings on each day of the previous 6 months. Rather, we want them to provide a brief summary statement that captures the essential information from that graph—for example, "I've been doing pretty well," or maybe "I've been having a few ups and downs." In psychology, brief summary statements that capture the essential information from a frequency distribution are called *descriptive statistics.*

The two most common kinds of descriptive statistics are those that describe the *central tendency* of a frequency distribution, and those that describe the *variability* in a frequency distribution. What do these terms mean? Descriptions of central tendency are statements about the value of the measurements that *tend* to lie near the *centre* or midpoint of the frequency distribution. When a friend says that they've been "doing pretty well," they are describing the central tendency (or approximate location of the midpoint) of the frequency distribution of their happiness ratings over time (see **FIGURE 2.3**). Descriptions of variability, on the other hand, are statements about the extent to which the measurements in a frequency distribution differ from each other. When your friend says that they have been "having some ups and downs," they are describing the variability among their happiness ratings. Let's dig a little deeper into each of these concepts.

Central Tendency: Where Is the Middle of the Distribution? The three most common descriptions of central tendency are: the **mode** (*the value of the most frequently observed measurement*); the **mean** (*the average value of all the measurements*); and the **median** (*the value that is in the middle, i.e., greater than or equal to half the measurements and less than or equal to half the measurements*). **FIGURE 2.4** shows how each of these descriptive statistics is calculated.

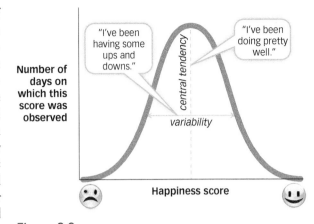

Figure 2.3
Two Kinds of Descriptive Statistics The most common descriptive statistics describe a frequency distribution's central tendency (where do most of the measurements lie?) and variability (how much do the measurements differ from one another?).

normal distribution A mathematically defined distribution in which the frequency of measurements is highest in the middle and decreases symmetrically in both directions.

mode The value of the most frequently observed measurement.

mean The average value of all the measurements.

median The value that is in the middle (i.e., greater than or equal to half the measurements and less than or equal to half the measurements).

- Mode = 5 because there are four 5's, and fewer of every other value.
- Mean = 5.95 because (1+2+3+4+4+5+5+5+5+6+6+7+7+7+8+8+8+9+9+10) / 20 = 5.95
- Median = 6 because 11 of the values are ≥ 6 and 11 of the values are ≤ 6.

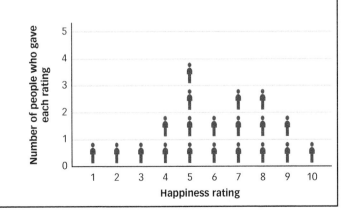

Figure 2.4
Calculating Descriptive Statistics This frequency distribution shows the data from 20 individuals who rated their happiness on a 10-point scale. Descriptive statistics include measures of central tendency (such as the mean, median, and mode) and measures of variability (such as the range and the standard deviation).

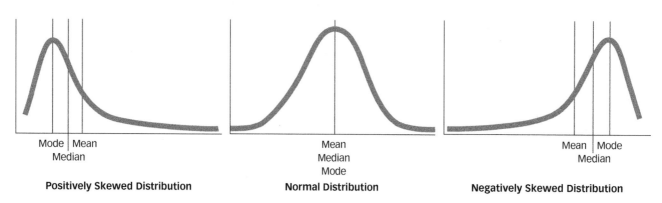

Mode	Mean		Mean		Mean	Mode
Median			Median			Median
			Mode			
Positively Skewed Distribution			**Normal Distribution**		**Negatively Skewed Distribution**	

Figure 2.5
Differently Shaped Distributions
When a frequency distribution is normal, the mean, median, and mode all have the same value, but when it is positively or negatively skewed, these three measures of central tendency have quite different values.

Why do we need three different measures of central tendency? When a distribution is normal, we don't, because these three measures all have exactly the same value. But when a distribution is skewed, the mean gets dragged towards the end of the long tail, the median follows it but doesn't get as far, and the mode stays put at the hump (see **FIGURE 2.5**). When these three measures have different values, calculating just one of them can provide a misleading picture of the data. For instance, if you measured the annual income of the roughly 961,000 households in Vancouver, British Columbia, you'd find that the mean is about just under $100,000. But that sample includes many households with unusually high, and unusually low, income. In 2015, 8 out of every 100 households (8%) earned more than $200,000 (StatsCan, 2016 Census), while 12 out of every 100 households (12%) earned less than $20,000 a year.

Vancouver is home to a few thousand rich people, including several of Canada's billionaires, so considering the mean alone might lead you to overestimate the affluence of the typical Vancouverite. But if, in addition to the mean, you also calculated the median, you'd find it has the considerably lower value of $73,000. Each measure can potentially be misleading in isolation, but when considered together, they paint a much more accurate picture of Vancouver as a middle-class city with some wealthy residents. You should be very suspicious whenever you hear some new fact about the "average person" but don't hear anything about the median, the mode, or the shape of the frequency distribution.

Variability: How Wide Is the Distribution? Descriptions of central tendency are statements about where the measurements in a frequency distribution tend to lie relative to the values on the vertical axis. Descriptions of variability, on the other hand, are statements about where the measurements in a frequency distribution tend to lie relative to each other. Descriptions of variability tell us how much the measurements differ from each other, or roughly how *wide* the distribution is. Variability is important: knowing that the mean temperature in Winnipeg is 2.6°C and that the median temperature is 4.4°C tells you nothing about how hot it gets in the summer or how cold in the winter. To know about that is to know about the variability in temperature.

The simplest measure of variability is the **range,** which is *the value of the largest measurement in a frequency distribution minus the value of the smallest measurement.* When the range is small, the distribution has less variability than when the range is large. The range is easy to compute, but like the mean it can be dramatically influenced by a few extreme measurements. If someone told you that the temperature in San Diego, California, ranged from −4 to +44°C, you might get the mistaken impression that San Diego has a remarkably varied climate when, in fact, it has a remarkably stable climate, rarely getting warmer than 25°C or colder than 10°C. The temperature in San Diego has hit −4°C and +44°C, but just once in the last 100 years.

Other measures of variability aren't as easily distorted by extreme values, but they are a little trickier to compute. One such measure is the **standard deviation,** which is a statistic that describes *how each of the measurements in a frequency distribution*

range The value of the largest measurement in a frequency distribution minus the value of the smallest measurement.

standard deviation A statistic that describes how each of the measurements in a frequency distribution differs from the mean.

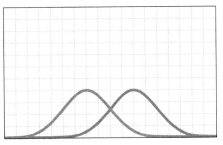

Figure 2.6
Distributions Can Differ in Variability or Central Tendency The panel on the left shows two distributions with the same central tendency but different amounts of variability. The panel on the right shows two distributions with the same amount of variability but different central tendencies.

differs from the mean. (Technically, it is the square root of the averaged squared difference between each measurement and the mean, and if you say that three times backwards you will enter a hypnotic trance that requires medical attention.) In other words, the standard deviation is an estimate of how far, on average, the various measurements are from the centre of the distribution. The standard deviation of average monthly temperatures over the year in Winnipeg is about 13°C, while in San Diego it is much lower, at about 3°C. It is worth noting that variability and central tendency are independent features of a frequency distribution. As **FIGURE 2.6** shows, two frequency distributions can have the same central tendencies but different amounts of variability, just as they can have the same amounts of variability but different central tendencies.

Methods of Explanation: Discovering Why People Do What They Do

In 1639, a pastor named John Clarke suggested that "Early to bed and early to rise, makes a man healthy, wealthy, and wise." People have been repeating this little rhyme ever since, but is there any truth to it? The methods you've learned about so far would allow you to measure the health, wealth, and wisdom of a sample of people. They would also allow you to draw some pictures of those measurements and make some summary statements about them. What they will *not* allow you to do is answer the central question: Does getting in and out of bed early *cause* people to be healthier, wealthier, and wiser? Is there any way to use your shiny new measurement skills to answer this question and others like it?

Indeed there is, and that's what this part of the chapter is all about. In the first section (Correlation), we'll examine a technique that can tell us whether two properties — such as wisdom and bedtime — are in fact related. In the second section (Causation), we'll examine a technique that can tell us whether one of these properties (e.g., bedtime) actually *causes* the other (e.g., wisdom). And in the third and final section (Drawing Conclusions) we'll examine the kinds of conclusions these two techniques do and do not allow us to draw.

Correlation

Speaking of early to bed and early to rise, how much sleep did you get last night? Okay, now, how many of the world's countries can you name in one minute (without asking Alexa or Siri)? If you were to ask a dozen university students those two questions, you'd probably find that the students who got a solid 8 hours the night before could recall more country names, on average, than students who had pulled an all-nighter. In fact, if you kept careful track of their responses (which means writing them down), you would have a series of measurements that would probably look a lot like the ones you can see in **TABLE 2.1**. And from those measurements, you would likely conclude that sleep deprivation causes poor memory.

Learning Outcomes

WHAT YOU NEED TO KNOW

- Explain what you can and cannot conclude from correlational research.
- Outline the essential ingredients of an experiment and explain how experiments solve the third-variable problem.
- Distinguish the kinds of conclusions that can and cannot be drawn from experimental evidence.
- Define both Type I and Type II errors in the context of psychological research.
- Explain why psychologists should worry if the replication rate is too low or too high.

TABLE 2.1

HYPOTHETICAL DATA SHOWING THE RELATIONSHIP BETWEEN SLEEP AND MEMORY

Participant	Hours of Sleep	No. of Countries Named in One Minute
A	0	11
B	0	17
C	2.7	16
D	3.1	21
E	4.4	17
F	5.5	16
G	7.6	31
H	7.9	41
I	8	40
J	8.1	35
K	8.6	38
L	9	43

Whoa! Not so fast. The measurements you took told you only *how much* sleeping and remembering the people in your sample did—so what in the world led you to conclude that there was a *causal relationship* between sleeping and remembering? The answer is that when you looked at your measurements, you instantly noticed a "synchronized pattern of variation." How did you notice that if you don't even know what it is? Read on.

Synchronized Patterns of Variation

When you asked a dozen university students how much they slept the night before and then asked them to name as many countries as possible, you may not have realized that you were doing three important things:

- First, you were measuring a pair of **variables,** which are *properties that can have more than one value.* A variable is basically anything that can . . . well, vary, such as the number of days in a month (which varies from 28 to 31) or the number of legs on an insect (which varies from 0 to 750), but not the number of days in a week (which is always 7) or the number of syllables in a haiku (which is always 17). When you asked students about sleep, you were measuring a variable whose value could vary from 0 to 24, and when you asked them about countries, you were measuring a second variable whose value could vary from 0 to 195.[1]

- Second, you did this again. And then again. And then again. That is, you made a *series* of measurements rather than just one.

- Third and last, you looked at the measurements you made and saw a pattern. If you look at the second column of Table 2.1, you will see that as you move your eyes from top to bottom, the numbers vary from small to large. We could say that this column of numbers has a particular *pattern of variation.* Now, if you compare the third column with the second, you will notice the numbers there have a similar (though not identical) pattern of variation. With just a few exceptions, they also tend to vary from small to large as you move your eyes from top to bottom. The patterns of variation in these two columns are somewhat synchronized—that is, the two columns vary together—and this synchrony is known as a **correlation,** which is *a relationship between variables in which variations in the value of one variable are synchronized with variations in the value of the other.* When patterns of variation are synchronized, two variables are said to be "co-related" or correlated.

Now here's why this is so cool: When two variables are correlated, you can use your knowledge of the value of one variable to predict the value of the other variable *without actually having to measure it!* For example, imagine that after you collected your sleep and memory data, you ran into a friend who lamented that they'd only gotten 2 hours of sleep the previous night. Without even asking them to name countries, you would have a fairly good idea of how many they could name in one minute—somewhere in the 15 to 25 range, right? And if you ran into another friend, asked them to name countries for one minute, and found that they named 42, you wouldn't have to ask them how many hours they'd slept the night before, because you could be pretty sure the answer was somewhere in the 7 to 9 range, right?

Correlations are the ultimate time savers because they allow us to make educated guesses about measurements without having to do the hard work of going out and measuring things. If you know that a man is 201 centimeters (6′7″) tall, you can predict that he probably weighs more than 90 kilograms because height and weight are highly correlated. If you know that a woman earns $1 million per year, you can guess that she probably went to university because income and education are highly correlated. Correlations are knowledge, and knowledge is power, and power is obviously pretty great or else why would so many villains in the Marvel Cinematic Universe want it?

variable A property that can have more than one value.

correlation A relationship between variables in which variations in the value of one variable are synchronized with variations in the value of the other.

[1]Reciting all 195 of them in one minute would require some very fast talking, and relatively few people know them all, so the practical upper bound is probably more like 60.

So correlations are power—but how much power? If you predict that a rich woman went to university, that a tall man is heavy, or that a sleep-deprived person won't be able to name many countries in one minute, you will be right far more often than you'll be wrong. But you won't be right every time. Oprah Winfrey didn't finish university and she is worth $4 billion; Terrance Ferguson played in the NBA and is 6′ 7″, but he weighs just 184 pounds; and even a sleepy Antonio Guterres, secretary general of the United Nations, can probably name way more countries than your average fully rested university student. The point is that correlations do allow us to make predictions, but those predictions are not always perfectly accurate.

r = 1
Perfect Positive Correlation

Measuring the Direction and Strength of a Correlation

Okay then, how accurate are those predictions? Statisticians have developed a way to estimate how accurate predictions based on correlations are likely to be by measuring the *direction* and *strength* of the correlation. Direction is easy to measure because the direction of a correlation is either positive or negative. A positive correlation exists when two variables have a "more-is-more" relationship. So, for example, people who have more education also tend to have more income, which means that education and income are positively correlated. Conversely, a negative correlation exists when two variables have a "more-is-less" relationship. People who have more education have fewer health problems, which means that education and health problems are negatively correlated.

r = −1
Perfect Negative Correlation

The direction of a correlation is easy to measure, but the strength is a little more complicated. The **correlation coefficient** is *a mathematical measure of both the direction and strength of a correlation,* and it is symbolized by the letter *r.* The first thing to know about it is that like most measures, *r* has a *limited range.* If you measure the number of hours of sunshine you experience tomorrow, the value of your measurement will absolutely, certainly, definitely, and for sure be somewhere in the range of 0 to 24. It cannot possibly be −7 or 329—values outside the range of 0 to 24 are impossible. Similarly, the value of *r* can range from −1 to 1, and values outside that range are impossible.

So what do the numbers *inside* that range mean? Let's start by saying what the two most extreme numbers (1 and −1) and the middle number (0) mean.

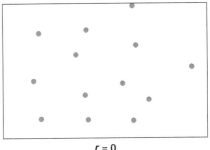

r = 0
No Correlation

Figure 2.7
Graphing Correlations This is what three different kinds of correlations look like when graphed.

- If every time the value of a variable increases by a certain amount, the value of a second variable also increases by a certain amount, then the variables have a *perfect positive correlation* and *r* = 1 (see the top graph in **FIGURE 2.7**). For example, if every *x*-unit increase in education was associated with a *y*-unit increase in income, then the correlation between these two variables would be perfectly positive. In this case, if you knew exactly how educated a person was, you could predict down to the penny how much money they earn.

- If every time the value of a variable increases by a certain amount, the value of a second variable decreases by a certain amount, then the variables have a *perfect negative correlation* and *r* = −1 (see the middle graph in Figure 2.7). For example, if every *x*-unit increase in education were associated with a *y*-unit decrease in health problems, then the correlation between these two variables would be perfectly negative. In this case, too, if you knew exactly how educated a person was, you could predict precisely how many health problems they had.

- If every time the value of a variable increases by a certain amount, the value of a second variable neither increases nor decreases systematically, then the variables have *no correlation* and *r* = 0 (see the bottom graph in Figure 2.7). For example, if an *x*-unit increase in education was sometimes associated with an increase in income, sometimes associated with a decrease in income, and sometimes associated with no change in income at all, then there would be no correlation between the two variables. In this case, knowing how educated a person was would not allow you to predict anything about their income.

correlation coefficient (r) A mathematical measure of both the direction and strength of a correlation, which is symbolized by the letter *r.*

$r = .5$

$r = .3$

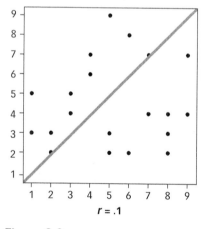

$r = .1$

Figure 2.8
Positive Correlations of Different Strengths The diagonal lines on each of these three graphs shows "the rule." When the exceptions to the rule are few and small, then the positive correlation is strong, and *r* moves towards 1. But when the exceptions are many and large, the positive correlation is weak, and *r* moves towards 0.

natural correlation A correlation that is observed in the natural world.

Correlations of 1 and −1 are extremely common—in textbooks. But they are almost unheard of in the real world. Yes, in the real world, education and income *are* positively correlated—that is, people who have more of one tend to have more of the other—but they have an *imperfect* positive correlation. A person with an extra unit of education probably also has some extra units of income, but that extra unit of education doesn't tell us *exactly* how much extra income that person has. Statements like "Increases in education are associated with increases in income" do not mean that when the education of a group of people increases by 1 unit, every single individual in that group also experiences a 1-unit increase in income. Rather, we mean that for *most* of the people in the group, when education increases by 1 unit then income increases too—sometimes by a little and sometimes by a lot.

You can think of "A 1-unit increase in education is always associated with a 1-unit increase in income" as a rule to which, in the real world, there are exceptions, and the number and size of these exceptions determines where in that range of 0 to 1 the value of *r* will actually lie. If there are just a few exceptions to the rule, then *r* will be closer to 1 than to 0, and predictions about someone's income based solely on knowledge of their education will be fairly accurate. But as the number of exceptions increases, then the value of *r* will begin to move towards 0 and such predictions will become less and less accurate. When *r* finally hits 0, your predictions will become no better than random guesses.

FIGURE 2.8 illustrates three cases in which two variables are positively correlated but have different numbers of exceptions. In each graph, the diagonal line shows the data you would expect to see if the two variables were perfectly positively correlated. The diagonal line represents the rule that "A 1-unit increase in one variable is always associated with a 1-unit increase in the other variable," and therefore every dot that is not on the diagonal line is an exception to the rule. The farther a dot is from the line, the greater that exception is. As you can see, the size and number of the exceptions change the value of *r* quite dramatically. The two variables shown in the graph at the top of Figure 2.8 have a strong correlation of $r = .5$, the two variables shown in the graph in the middle have a moderate correlation of $r = .3$, and the two variables shown in the graph at the bottom have a weak correlation of $r = .1$. The only difference between the graphs of the strong and weak correlations is that the latter has more exceptions—that is, more data points that are farther from the line.

We've come a long way. A few pages ago, you thought *r* was just another Sesame Street letter of the day. Now you know that *r* is a measure of both the *direction* and *strength* of the relationship between two variables. The sign of *r* (plus or minus) tells you the direction of the relationship (positive or negative), and the absolute value of *r* (between 0 and 1) tells you about the number and size of the exceptions to the rule—hence, about how accurate you are likely to be when using knowledge of one variable to make predictions about the other. Big Bird would be so proud.

Causation

The mathematics of correlation may have been new to you, but the concept surely was not. You've been noticing correlations all your life—between height and weight, between sleep and memory, between age and musical preference, and so on. A **natural correlation** is *a correlation that is observed in the natural world*, and although a natural correlation can tell us whether two variables have a relationship, it cannot tell us whether they have a *causal* relationship. For example, many studies (Anderson & Bushman, 2002; C. A. Anderson et al., 2003, 2017; Huesmann et al., 2003) have observed a positive correlation between the aggressiveness of a child's behaviour and the amount of violence to which that child is exposed through media such as television, movies, and video games. The more violence children see, the more aggressively they tend to behave. These two variables clearly have a relationship, but *why* are they correlated?

The Third-Variable Problem: Correlation Is Not Causation

One reason these two variables may be correlated is that exposure to media violence (let's call it variable X) may cause aggressiveness (let's call it variable Y). For instance, media violence may teach children that aggression is an acceptable way to vent anger or solve problems. We'll denote this possible relationship as $X \rightarrow Y$, which simply means X *causes* Y. A second possibility is that $Y \rightarrow X$, which is to say that aggressiveness may cause exposure to media violence. For example, children who are naturally aggressive may be especially inclined to play violent video games and watch violent movies. When you first heard that exposure to media violence and aggressiveness were positively correlated, you probably thought of these two possibilities yourself.

But there is an additional possibility you might not have considered. It is possible that another variable—a heretofore unnamed "third variable" that we will call variable Z—causes children to behave aggressively *and also* causes children to be exposed to media violence (see **FIGURE 2.9**). For instance, a lack of adult supervision (Z) may allow children to get away with playing violent video games that adults would normally prohibit ($Z \rightarrow X$), and may also allow children to get away with bullying others simply because no adult is around to stop them ($Z \rightarrow Y$). If so, then X and Y may be correlated only because $Z \rightarrow X$ & Y, which is to say that being exposed to media violence and behaving aggressively may be two independent effects of the lack of adult supervision and may not be causally related to each other at all.

How can we tell if the natural correlation between X and Y exists because both X and Y are caused by this third variable Z (or perhaps by some other third variable)? We can't. The **third-variable problem** refers to the fact that *the natural correlation between two variables cannot be taken as evidence of a causal relationship between them because a third variable might be causing them both*. What this means is that if we want to know about the causal relationship between two variables, then observing a natural correlation between them can never tell us what we want to know. Luckily, another technique can.

Experimentation: Establishing Causation

That technique is called **experimentation,** which is *a technique for establishing the causal relationship between variables.* The logic underlying experimentation is simple: There are three possible causes of any natural correlation ($X \rightarrow Y$, $Y \rightarrow X$, or $Z \rightarrow X$ & Y), so if we can eliminate two of them, then the one that remains must be the real one. If we know that X did not cause Y, and if we know that Z did not cause X and Y, then we know for sure that Y must have caused X. The logic is simple, but exactly *how* do experiments eliminate two of the three possible causes? They do this by using a pair of techniques called *manipulation* and *random assignment*. Let's explore each of them in turn.

Manipulation: Making Different Conditions

Imagine that one evening you are working on your laptop when you notice that your Internet connection has suddenly slowed to a crawl. Your roommate is upstairs playing with their new Xbox, which you suspect could be sucking up bandwidth, which is making your browser run slow. How would you test your suspicion? You now know that simply observing a natural correlation won't be of much help because even if your browser ran slow every time your roommate used their Xbox and ran fast every time they didn't, the third-variable problem would prevent you from concluding that the Xbox was *causing* the slowdown. For instance, maybe your roommate only uses their Xbox in the evenings, which happens to be the time when a whole lot of other people in your neighbourhood are home watching Netflix, playing video games, downloading music, and otherwise sucking up bandwidth. "Evening" may be a third variable that causes your roommate to fire up the Xbox and that also causes your browser to slow down.

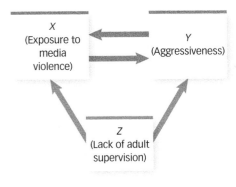

Figure 2.9
Causes of Correlation Three possible reasons X and Y are correlated: $X \rightarrow Y$, $Y \rightarrow X$, or $Z \rightarrow X$ & Y.

In 1949, American physician Dr. Benjamin Sandler noticed a correlation between the incidence of polio and the consumption of ice cream. He concluded that sugar made children susceptible to the disease. Public health officials were so convinced by his findings that they issued public warnings. But as it turned out, the correlation was caused by a third variable: Warm weather had caused an increase in the incidence of polio (because viruses become more active in the summer) and an increase in the consumption of ice cream (because children become more active in the summer).

third-variable problem The fact that the natural correlation between two variables cannot be taken as evidence of a causal relationship between them because a third variable might be causing them both.

experimentation A technique for establishing the causal relationship between variables.

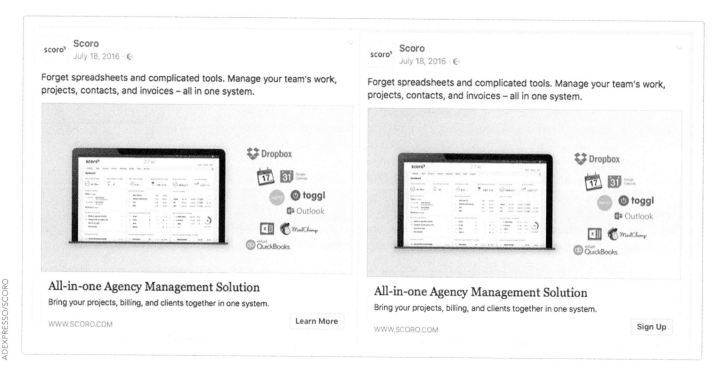

Can you see the difference between these two ads? Don't worry. It's subtle. The one and only difference is that the ad on the left has a "Learn More" button and the ad on the right has a "Sign Up" button. By manipulating the label on the button, the advertiser was able to determine whether a label can cause people to click. And it can! The "Learn More" label led 15% more Facebook users to click (Karlson, 2016).

So how can you tell whether your slowdown is actually being caused by the Xbox? Rather than observing the natural correlation between your roommate's Xbox usage and your browser's speed, you could go upstairs when your roommate isn't home and turn their Xbox on and off while observing the speed of your browser. If your browser slowed down every time you turned the Xbox on and then sped up again every time you turned the Xbox off, you would know that the Xbox was in fact the cause of the slowdown. When you turned the Xbox on and off you performed a **manipulation,** which is *a technique for determining the causal power of a variable by actively changing its value.* Rather than measuring two variables, as we do when we observe natural correlations, experiments require that we *manipulate* one variable—that is, actively change its value—and then measure the other. Changing the value of the Xbox from on to off is an example of manipulation.

We could use this same technique to determine whether exposure to media violence causes aggressiveness. For instance, we could invite some children to our laboratory and give them one of two experiences: Half could be given a violent video game to play, and the other half could be given a nonviolent video game to play. These two experiences are called the *conditions* of our experiment, and we could refer to them as "the violent exposure condition" and "the nonviolent exposure condition." At the end of an hour of game playing, we could then measure the children's aggressiveness, perhaps by observing whether they push to get to the front of a line or by asking whether they think it's okay for someone to kick a growling dog. Then we could compare the measurements of aggressiveness in one condition with the measurements of aggressiveness in the other condition.

When we compare these measurements across conditions, we are essentially asking whether the value of aggressiveness went from low to high when exposure to media violence went from low to high. Essentially, we are computing the correlation between the variable we manipulated (exposure) and the variable we measured (aggressiveness). Now here is the cool part: Because we *manipulated* exposure rather than just *measuring* it as we do when we observe a natural correlation, we have eliminated two of the possible causes of the correlation we observed. Specifically, we know for sure that aggressiveness did not cause exposure to media violence, and we know for sure that lack of adult supervision did not cause exposure to media violence—and

manipulation A technique for determining the causal power of a variable by actively changing its value.

we know these two things because we know what *did* cause exposure to media violence: We did! And that leaves just one possibility: Exposure to media violence *must* have caused aggressiveness—which is the thing we wanted to know! Can we just take a moment to congratulate ourselves?

Experimentation is an invaluable technique that allows us to establish the causal relationship between variables by doing three things:

1. *Manipulate*: The first step in an experiment is to manipulate a variable. *The variable that is manipulated in an experiment* is called the **independent variable** because its value is determined entirely by the experimenter and therefore does not depend on—or is "independent of"—everything else. The value of the independent variable does not depend on the time, or the weather, or anything else except what the experimenter does. A manipulation always creates at least two conditions. In our example, the independent variable was exposure to media violence and the manipulation created a violent exposure condition and a nonviolent exposure condition.

2. *Measure*: The second step in an experiment is to measure a variable. *The variable that is measured in an experiment* is called the **dependent variable** because its value "depends on" the value of the independent variable. In our example, the dependent variable was aggressiveness.

3. *Compare*: The third step in an experiment is to compare the value of the dependent variable in one condition with the value of the dependent variable in the other. If the values differ on average, then we know that changes to the value of the independent variable *caused* changes to the value of the dependent variable. **FIGURE 2.10** shows exactly how manipulation works (and the Hot Science box shows how nature occasionally does experiments by manipulating independent variables of its own).

Violent exposure condition		
	Exposed to media violence?	Aggression
	Yes	High
	Yes	High
	Yes	High
	Yes	High

Nonviolent exposure condition		
	Exposed to media violence?	Aggression
	No	Low
	No	Low
	No	Low
	No	Low

Figure 2.10
The Three Steps of Experimentation Manipulate the independent variable, measure the dependent variable, then compare the values across conditions.

Random Assignment: Making Sure Conditions Differ in Just One Way

Manipulation is an essential ingredient in experimentation. But what kind of recipe has just one ingredient? In fact, experimentation has a second and equally important ingredient, and to understand what it is and what it does, let's return to the hypothetical study we just designed in which children were given violent or nonviolent video games to play and then their aggressiveness was measured an hour later. When the children show up at our laboratory to participate in our study, how should we decide which child will play which game?

One possibility is that we could be polite and ask each child which kind of game they would prefer to play. Imagine we did that, and that half the children chose to play a violent game and the other half chose to play a nonviolent game. Imagine that we then let them play their preferred game for an hour and then measured their aggressiveness, and we discovered that the children who played the violent game were in fact more aggressive than those who played the nonviolent game. Could we now conclude that playing violent video games caused aggressiveness? No! But why not? After all, we manipulated exposure to media violence, switching it on and off as though it were an Xbox, and then we measured aggressiveness and found that it went on and off too. We manipulated, we measured, and we compared—we did all three of the three steps. So where did we go wrong?

We went wrong by letting the children *select* which video game to play. Our independent variable was not truly independent because it depended on the children's choices—and children who *select* violent video games probably differ in many ways from children who don't. They may be older or meaner. They may be younger or sweeter. They may have different brain chemistry, different home environments, different genes, different talents, different numbers of siblings, or different levels

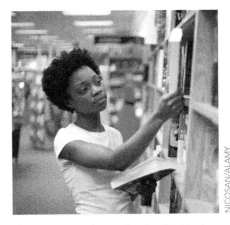

There is no evidence that Louise Hay's techniques can cure cancer. But even if people with cancer who bought her books did show a higher rate of remission than those who didn't, there would still be no evidence because buyers are self-selected and thus may differ from nonbuyers in countless ways.

independent variable The variable that is manipulated in an experiment.

dependent variable The variable that is measured in an experiment.

Hot Science • Hate Posts and Hate Crimes: Not Just a Correlation

In 2004, a university student named Mark Zuckerberg built a Web site called "The Facebook" so that he and his fellow students could learn about each other online. He had no idea that only a decade or so later his company would be one of the most powerful and profitable in human history, and that he would be one of the richest people on earth. Facebook has been very good for its inventor, but has it been very good for the rest of us? It lets us post videos of our pets, share stories of our vacations, and find out what people we barely know had for lunch—and who could possibly argue with the goodness of that? But has it also become a platform in which people's worst impulses are brought together, amplified, and then unleashed upon the world? Do Facebook posts lead people to do terrible things in the real world, such as commit arson, or assault, or even murder?

Karsten Müller and Carlo Schwarz (2018) worried that the answer might be yes. So they conducted a study in Germany, where a right-wing anti-immigrant party (the Alternative für Deutschland, or AfD) had recently developed a significant presence on Facebook. The study involved nothing more than measuring the correlation between two variables: the number of anti-refugee Facebook posts that appeared on the AfD Web site each week and the number of violent crimes against refugees that occurred each week. The accompanying figure shows what they found. As you can see, the two variables were indeed positively correlated: The more "hate posts" that appeared on AfD's Facebook page at any moment in time, the more "hate crimes" happened on German streets.

But wait a minute. What about the third-variable problem? Hate posts and

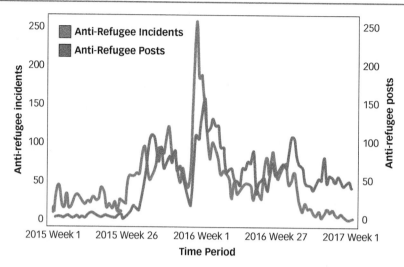

The number of hate crimes and hate posts in Germany from 2015 to 2017.

hate crimes may well be correlated, but that doesn't mean the former *caused* the latter. Maybe the hate crimes caused the hate posts, or maybe some third variable—such as a change in the weather or the parliament or the stock market—caused them both. Drawing conclusions about the causal relationship between two variables requires that one of those variables be *manipulated*, right?

Yes, it does, but luckily for the researchers, nature did just that. Internet service in Germany is sometimes unreliable, and German Facebook users experience frequent interruptions that can knock everyone offline for hours or even days at a time. So what happens when Internet access is randomly turned on and off and then on again? When the researchers analyzed the historical data on service interruptions, they discovered that when Facebook went down, hate crimes went down too; and when Facebook came back up again, so did hate crimes. Because service

interruptions are basically random events, they serve as a manipulation of one variable (the number of hate posts) whose impact on the other variable (the number of hate crimes) can then be measured. When the researchers did that, the impact was clear. As the researchers themselves concluded, "Social media has not only become a fertile soil for the spread of hateful ideas but also motivates real-life action" (Müller & Schwarz, 2018, p. 40).

Psychologists are often faced with a tough choice: They can either (a) observe a correlation in the real world but be unsure about causation, or (b) firmly establish causation in the laboratory but be unsure about whether it generalizes to the real world. But every once in a while, nature resolves this dilemma by randomly manipulating a variable in the real world. When that happens, clever researchers may take advantage of the situation and use it to answer pressing social questions—and to produce some very hot science.

of adult supervision. The list of possible differences is endless. The whole point of doing the experiment was to create two conditions whose participants differed from each other in *one and only one way*, namely, in terms of how much media violence they were exposed to in our laboratory. By letting the children decide for themselves which condition of the experiment they would experience, we ended up with two conditions whose participants may have differed in many ways—and every one of those differences is a third variable that could potentially have caused the differences in aggressiveness that we observed when comparing across conditions. Apparently, it just doesn't pay to be polite. **Self-selection** is *a problem that occurs when anything about a participant determines the value of the independent variable to which the participant was exposed,* and as you can see, it is a problem that leaves us with the same unanswered question that led us to do an experiment in the first place.

So how should we determine which video game each child will play? We should flip a coin. **Random assignment** is *a procedure that assigns participants to conditions by chance.* Just think about what would happen if we used a coin flip to randomly assign each child to play either a violent or nonviolent video game. As **FIGURE 2.11** shows, the first thing that would happen is that roughly half the children would be assigned to play violent video games and roughly half would be assigned to play nonviolent video games. Coins land heads up about as often as they land tails up, so if we use a coin to randomly assign children to one of two conditions, then the two conditions should have roughly equal numbers of children.

Second — and *much* more important — we could expect the two conditions to have roughly equal numbers of mean children and sweet children, of older children and younger children, of children who have a lot of adult supervision at home and children who have little, and so on. In other words, we could expect the two conditions to have roughly equal numbers of children who are anything-you-can-ever-name-and-everything-you-can't! Because the children in the two conditions will be the same *on average* in terms of meanness, age, adult supervision, and every other variable in the known universe *except the independent variable we manipulated,* we could be sure that the independent variable was the cause of the differences in the dependent variable. Because exposure to media violence would be the *only* difference between the two conditions when we started the experiment, it *must* be the cause of any differences in aggressiveness we observed at the end of the experiment.

Statistical Testing: Making Sure Conditions Don't Differ by Chance

Random assignment is a powerful tool. Unfortunately, like a lot of tools, it doesn't work every time you use it. If we randomly assigned children to two conditions, we could expect the two conditions to have roughly equal numbers of mean children, young children, supervised children, and so on. But the key word in that sentence is *roughly.* When you flip a coin 100 times, you expect it to come up heads *roughly* 50 of those times. But every once in a very, very long while, it will come up heads 60 times, or 70 times, or even 100 times, by sheer chance alone (see The Real World: The Surprisingly High Likelihood of Unlikely Coincidences). This will not happen often, of course, but if you execute 100 coin flips enough times, it will eventually happen.[2]

Because random assignment is achieved by using a randomizing device such as a coin, every once in a long while the coin will assign more unsupervised kids to play violent video games and more supervised kids to play nonviolent video games by sheer chance alone. When this happens, scientists say that "random assignment has failed" (though they should actually say that the coin has randomly produced a highly unlikely assignment). When random assignment fails, we are right back where we started when we politely allowed the children to self-select their conditions, and as you will recall, that is not a very good place to be right back to.

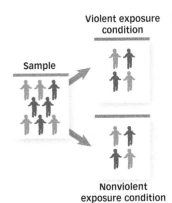

Violent exposure condition	Exposed to media violence?	Adult supervision?	Aggression
	Yes	Yes	High
	Yes	No	High
	Yes	Yes	High
	Yes	No	High

Nonviolent exposure condition	Exposed to media violence?	Adult supervision?	Aggression
	No	Yes	Low
	No	No	Low
	No	Yes	Low
	No	No	Low

Figure 2.11
Random Assignment Random assignment ensures that participants in the two conditions are, on average, equal in terms of all possible third variables.

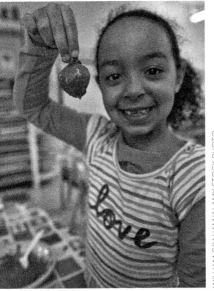

WILLIAM GRAHAM/ALAMY STOCK PHOTO

Do strawberries taste better when dipped in chocolate? If you dip the big juicy ones and don't dip the small dry ones, then you won't know if the chocolate is what made the difference. But if you randomly assign some to be dipped and others not to be dipped, and if the dipped ones taste better on average, then you will have demonstrated scientifically what every 7-year-old already knows.

self-selection A problem that occurs when anything about a participant determines the value of the independent variable to which the participant was exposed.

random assignment A procedure that assigns participants to conditions by chance.

---

[2]How long is "eventually"? Odds are that you would have to execute the 100 coin flips 12,680,000,000,000,000,000, 000,000,000,000 times in order for the coin to come up heads every time by chance alone. Assuming you could flip one coin per second, this would take you about 4^{25} years, which is considerably longer than the universe has existed. In other words, don't try this at home.

The Real World • The Surprisingly High Likelihood of Unlikely Coincidences

Roughly half of all Canadians believe in extrasensory perception, or ESP, and it is easy to understand why (Angus Reid Institute, 2016). Just consider the case of the Truly Amazing Coincidence. One night you dream that a panda is piloting an airplane over the Indian Ocean, and the next day you tell a friend, who says, "Wow, I had exactly the same dream!" One morning you wake up humming an old Taylor Swift tune (probably "Love Story"), and an hour later you hear it playing in the mall. You and your roommate are sitting around watching Netflix when suddenly you turn to each other and say in perfect unison, "Wanna pizza?" Coincidences like these might make anyone believe in strange and spooky supernatural weirdness.

Well, not anyone. While the Nobel laureate Luis Alvarez was reading the newspaper one day, a particular story got him thinking about an old university friend whom he hadn't seen in years. A few minutes later, he turned the page and was shocked to see the very same friend's obituary. But before concluding that he had suddenly developed an acute case of ESP, Alvarez decided to use probability theory to determine just how amazing this coincidence really was. He estimated the number of friends an average person has, estimated how often an average person thinks about each of those friends, did a few simple calculations, and determined the probability that someone would think about a friend

5 minutes before learning about that friend's death. The odds were astonishing. In a country the size of the United States, Alvarez calculated that this coincidence should happen to 10 people every day (Alvarez, 1965). A fellow Nobel laureate put the number closer to 80 people a day (Charpak & Broch, 2004)!

"In ten years, there are five million minutes," says the statistics professor Irving Jack. "That means each person has plenty of opportunity to have some remarkable coincidences in his life" (Neimark, 2004). If 38 million Canadians dream for about 2 hours every night, that's 76 million hours of dreaming, so it isn't really surprising that two people might have the same dream, or that someone would dream about something that actually happened the next day. As the mathematics professor John Paulos noted, "In reality, the most astonishingly incredible coincidence imaginable would be the complete absence of all coincidence" (Neimark, 2004).

If all of this seems surprising to you, then you are not alone. Research shows that people routinely underestimate the likelihood of coincidences (Diaconis & Mosteller, 1989; Falk & McGregor, 1983;

"Idaho! What a coincidence—I'm from Idaho."

Hintzman et al., 1978). If you want to profit from this fact, just assemble a group of 24 or more people and offer to bet anyone $1 that at least two of the people in the group share a birthday. The odds are in your favour, and the bigger the group, the better those odds are. In fact, in a group of 35 people, the odds are a remarkable 85%. When everyone starts handing you their loonies and asking how in the world you knew that two of the people in your group shared a birthday, you can honestly tell them it was ESP—also known as Especially Sneaky Psychology.

How can we know whether random assignment has failed—that is, whether the differences we observed between the conditions in our experiment were actually due to our manipulation of the independent variable rather than dumb luck? Unfortunately, we can never know for sure. But what we *can* do is calculate the *odds* that these differences are due to dumb luck. It's not important for you now to know how to do this calculation (be grateful for that), but it is important for you to understand how psychologists interpret its results. Psychologists perform this calculation every time they do an experiment, and they generally do not accept the results of their experiments unless the calculation suggests that there is less than a 5% chance that those results were due to dumb luck. Such results are said to be *statistically significant,* and psychologists typically indicate this by writing "$p < .05$." (p stands for the *probability* that the differences were due to dumb luck.)

Psychologists have several other ways to figure out whether differences between conditions were due to dumb luck, but this calculation is the most common.[3]

Drawing Conclusions

If we applied all the techniques discussed so far, we could design an experiment that had a very good chance of establishing the causal relationship between two variables. That experiment would be said to have **internal validity,** which is *an attribute of an experiment that allows it to establish causal relationships.* When we say that an experiment is high in internal validity, we mean that everything *inside* the experiment is working exactly as it should in order for us to use its results to draw conclusions about the causal relationship between the independent and dependent variables. But exactly *what* conclusions are we entitled to draw? If our imaginary experiment revealed a difference between the aggressiveness of children who were exposed to high or low levels of media violence and *p* was less than .05, could we conclude that differences in exposure to media violence cause differences in aggressiveness?

Actually, no. The conclusion we'd be entitled to draw would have to be a bit more restricted than that. What we *could* conclude is this: "It is likely that media violence as we defined that variable caused aggressiveness as we defined that variable in the people we studied." That sentence is obnoxiously long and sounds a little too much like a legal disclaimer because it contains these phrases: *as we defined that variable, and in the people we studied, and it is likely that.* But each phrase describes an important restriction on the conclusions we can draw from this or any other experimental result. Let's consider them in turn, as well as the kinds of restrictions they place on our conclusions.

The Representativeness Restriction: "As We Defined That Variable . . ."

The results of an experiment naturally depend on how the independent and dependent variables are operationally defined. For instance, we are more likely to find that exposure to media violence causes aggressiveness if we operationally define exposure as "watching 2 hours of gory axe murders" rather than "watching 10 minutes of football," or if we define aggressiveness as "interrupting another person who is talking" rather than "beating someone with a tire iron." The way we operationally define variables can have a profound influence on what we find, so which of these ways of operationally defining them is the *right* way?

A natural answer is that we should operationally define variables in an experiment as they are defined in the real world. **External validity** is *an attribute of an experiment in which variables have been operationally defined in a representative way.* It seems pretty clear that the kind of aggressive behaviour that concerns teachers and parents lies somewhere between an interruption and an assault, and that the kind of media violence to which children are typically exposed lies somewhere between sports and torture. If the goal of an experiment is to determine whether the kinds of media violence to which children are typically exposed causes the kinds of aggressiveness with which societies are typically concerned, then external validity is important. When variables are defined in an experiment as they typically are in the real world, we say that the variables are *representative* of the real world.

Does piercing make a person more or less attractive? The answer, of course, depends entirely on your operational definition of piercing.

internal validity An attribute of an experiment that allows it to establish causal relationships.

external validity An attribute of an experiment in which variables have been operationally defined in a representative way.

---

[3]Here is a more technical explanation of *p* < .05. If the manipulation of the value of an independent variable causes changes in the value of the dependent variable, then the values of the dependent variable in the two conditions should not look like they were randomly drawn from the same distribution of numbers. Technically, *p* < .05 means that there is less than a 5% chance that the measurements in the two conditions were randomly drawn from the same distribution of numbers, which means there is a 95% or greater chance that they weren't—which means that there was a 95% or greater chance that the differences between conditions were caused by the manipulation of the independent variable and a 5% or less chance that they were caused by dumb luck. Aren't you glad you read footnotes?

External validity sounds like such a good idea that you may be surprised to learn that most psychology experiments are externally *invalid*—and that most psychologists don't consider this a problem (Mook, 1983). To understand why, consider a simple example from physics. Physicists have a theory: *Heat is the result of the rapid motion of molecules.* This theory gives rise to a falsifiable hypothesis: *When the molecules that constitute an object are slowed, the object should become cooler.* Imagine that a physicist tested this hypothesis by performing a laboratory experiment in which they used a laser to slow the motion of the molecules in a steel ball, measured the temperature of the ball before and after, and found that the temperature of the ball decreased by a large amount when its molecules were slowed. Are you worried about external invalidity? Are you thinking, "How can this experiment teach us anything about the real world when in the real world no one uses lasers to slow the movement of the molecules in steel balls?"

Probably not, and that's because you intuitively understand that the physicist's theory led to a clear hypothesis about *what would happen in the laboratory,* and that the events the physicist manipulated and measured in the laboratory therefore tested the hypothesis quite nicely. Similarly, a well-thought-out theory about the causal relationship between exposure to media violence and aggressiveness should lead to hypotheses about how children *in a laboratory* will behave after playing a violent video game, and thus their behaviour tests that hypothesis quite nicely. If children who play *Left 4 Dead* in a laboratory are more likely to shove each other than are children who play *Minecraft* in creative mode, then any theory claiming that media violence cannot influence aggressiveness has just been proved wrong.

In short, theories allow us to generate hypotheses about what can, must, or will happen under particular circumstances; and experiments are usually meant to create some of those circumstances, test the hypotheses, and thereby provide evidence for or against the theories that generated them (see also Hot Science: Hate Posts and Hate Crimes: Not Just a Correlation). Experiments are not usually meant to be miniature versions of everyday life, and as such, their lack of external validity is not necessarily a problem.

The Generalizability Restriction: "In the People We Studied . . ."

You already know that psychologists rarely measure an entire population, but instead measure a sample from that population. How big should that sample be? The size of a population is signified by the uppercase letter N, the size of a sample is signified by the lowercase letter n, and therefore $0 < n < N$. However, in most studies, n is a whole lot closer to 0 than it is to N, and indeed, in some cases $n = 1$.

For example, some individuals are so remarkable that they deserve close study, and the psychologists who study them are using the **case method,** which is *a procedure for gathering scientific information by studying a single individual.* We can learn a lot about, say, memory by studying someone such as Akira Haraguchi, who memorized the first 100,000 digits of pi; about consciousness by studying someone such as Henry Molaison, whose ability to look backward and forward in time was impaired by brain surgery; about creativity by studying someone such as Alma Deutscher, who wrote her first piano sonata at the age of 6; a violin concerto at 9; and her first full length opera, *Cinderella,* when she was 10. Such people are not only interesting in their own right, but their remarkable abilities can also provide important insights into how the rest of us work.

With that said, the vast majority of studies you will read about in this textbook use samples of 10; 100; 1,000; or even many thousands of people. Psychologists typically use the largest samples they can get because the larger the sample, the more confidence they can have in their findings. Why? Well, if a coin came up

RICK FINDLER—PA IMAGES/GETTY IMAGES

Alma Deutscher wrote the opera *Cinderella* for an ensemble of 20 musicians when she was 10. It premiered at the State Opera in Vienna when Alma was 11, and was recorded for commercial release by Sony Classical the next year. She is currently 16 years old, and plays violin and piano in addition to composing.

case method A procedure for gathering scientific information by studying a single individual.

heads 7 out of 10 times, you might *suspect* it was an unfair coin—that is, that the coin was slightly heavier on the tail than the head. But you would not be highly confident in that conclusion because it was based on a small sample of coin flips. If the same coin came up heads 700 out of 1,000 times, however, you would be extremely confident that it was an unfair coin. Because large samples allow us to be more confident in our results, in an ideal world, *n* would be very close to *N* itself. Alas, psychologists in the real world have limited time, limited research funds, and limited access to participants, so they have to settle for the largest *n* that circumstances allow.

So how do psychologists determine which people they will include in their sample and which people they won't? One method is by **random sampling,** which is *a technique for selecting participants that ensures that every member of a population has an equal chance of being included in the sample.* (Note to self: Do not confuse random sampling with random assignment. The only thing they have in common is the word *random.*) When we randomly sample participants from a population, the sample is said to be *representative* of the population. This allows us to *generalize* from the sample to the population—that is, to conclude that what we observed in our sample would also have been observed if we had measured the entire population.

You probably already have solid intuitions about the value of random sampling. For example, if you stopped at a roadside farm stand to buy a bag of cherries and the farmer offered to let you taste a few that they had carefully selected from the bag, you'd be reluctant to generalize from that sample to the population of cherries in the bag because you'd know that the cherries you were offered had been . . . well, cherry-picked. But on the other hand, if the farmer invited you to close your eyes and pull a few cherries from the bag at random, you'd probably consider those cherries to be a representative sample and you'd naturally generalize from that sample ("The cherries I tasted were quite sweet") to the population ("I bet most of the cherries in the bag are sweet too").

Like external validity, random sampling sounds like an obviously good idea, so you may be surprised (once again) to find that most psychological studies involve *non*random samples. Indeed, virtually every participant in every psychology experiment you will ever read about was a volunteer, and a large share were university students who were significantly younger, smarter, healthier, and wealthier than the average Earthling. About 96% of the people psychologists study come from countries that have just 12% of the world's population, and 70% come from the United States alone (Henrich et al., 2010). Why do psychologists sample people nonrandomly?

Because they have to. Even if there were a list of all the world's human inhabitants from which we could randomly sample our research participants (and there isn't), how would we locate the 5-year-old Bedouin girl whose family roams the desert so that we could measure the electrical activity in her brain while she watched cartoons? How would we convince an illiterate farmer in South Sudan to complete a lengthy questionnaire about his political beliefs? How could we sample the Ayoreo-Totobiegosode tribe of Paraguay, which has never had any contact with the outside world? Most psychology experiments are conducted by professors and graduate students at universities in the Western Hemisphere, and as much as they might *like* to randomly sample the population of our planet, the fact is that they are pretty much stuck studying the local folks who volunteer for their studies.

Is this a fatal flaw in psychological science? No, and there are two reasons why. First, *sometimes the representativeness of a sample doesn't matter.* If one pig flew over the Calgary Saddledome just one time, it would instantly disprove the Standard

random sampling A technique for selecting participants that ensures that every member of a population has an equal chance of being included in the sample.

It is often a mistake to generalize from a nonrandom sample. In the American presidential election of 1948, pollsters mistakenly predicted that the Republican Party candidate, Thomas Dewey, would beat Democratic Party candidate Harry Truman (shown here holding a newspaper that prematurely printed the mispredicted the result). Why? Because polling was done by telephone, and Dewey Republicans were more likely to have telephones than were Truman Democrats.

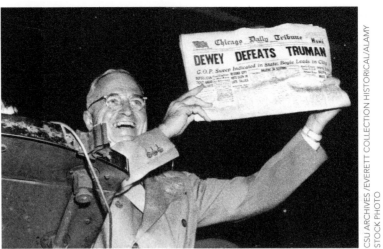

CSU ARCHIVES /EVERETT COLLECTION HISTORICAL/ALAMY STOCK PHOTO

Theory of Porcine Locomotion, and it really wouldn't matter if other pigs could do the same trick. Similarly, if playing *Left 4 Dead* for an hour caused a group of 5th graders from a public school in St. John's to start shoving other kids in the laboratory, then even if the game did not have a similar effect on 9th graders from a private school in Saskatoon, we would still know that media violence *can* influence aggressiveness—which means that any theory that says it can't is just plain wrong. Sometimes psychologists aren't concerned with whether *everyone* does something; they just want to know if *anyone* does it.

The second reason why nonrandom sampling is not a fatal flaw is that *sometimes the representativeness of the sample is a reasonable starting assumption.* Instead of asking, "Do I have a compelling reason to believe that the way the people in my sample behaved is *the same* as everyone else would?" we could just as well ask, "Do I have a compelling reason to believe that the people in my sample behave *differently* than everyone else would?" For example, few of us would be willing to take a new medicine if a nonrandom sample of participants took it and died. Indeed, we would probably refuse to take the medicine even if those participants were mice! Although these nonrandomly sampled participants would be different from us in many ways (e.g., tails and whiskers), most of us would assume that anything that kills them has some reasonable chance of killing us. Similarly, if a psychology experiment demonstrated that a sample of American children behaved aggressively after playing violent video games, we might ask whether there is a compelling reason to suspect that Ecuadorian university students or middle-aged Australians would respond any differently? If the answer is yes, then we can conduct new experiments to test that possibility.

The bottom line is that learning about *some people* does not necessarily tell us about *all people,* but it can still tell us a lot—and it certainly tells us more than learning about *no people* at all, which is often our only other choice.

The Reliability Restriction: "It Is Likely That . . ."

A **replication** is *an experiment that uses the same procedures as a previous experiment but with a new sample from the same population.* In the last few years, many major media outlets have reported that when psychologists replicate the experiments of other psychologists, they *usually* fail to replicate their results, which suggests that the initial result was some sort of fluke. Could that be right? Are the headlines true?

replication An experiment that uses the same procedures as a previous experiment but with a new sample from the same population.

Estimating Psychology's Replication Rate If a researcher finds that children who were randomly assigned to play violent video games are more aggressive than those who were randomly assigned to play nonviolent video games, we would expect that other researchers who use the same video games and the same measures of aggressiveness under the same conditions should get the same result. We might not expect this to happen every single time, but we would expect it to happen most of the time—and if it happened a whole lot less than most of the time, we would have good reason to suspect that the original finding was due to dumb luck—in other words, a fluke. You already know that psychologists publish their results only when the odds that their findings are due to dumb luck are less than 5%, but that means that 5% of the time, the original result was indeed due to dumb luck and therefore we would not expect it to be replicated. We can live with that. But what if these flukes happen way more than 5% of the time? What if they happen the *majority* of the time, just as the headlines suggest?

In the last few years, teams of psychologists have tried to estimate the proportion of flukes in the scientific literature by selecting a sample of published studies and then attempting to replicate them. Some teams have found the replication rate in their samples to be frighteningly low (Open Science Collaboration et al., 2015) while others have found it to be reasonably high (Klein et al., 2014). But do any of these findings tell us the actual replication rate of studies in psychology? Probably not (Gilbert et al., 2016). First, the teams who did these replications did not randomly sample the population of published studies in psychology. Rather, they chose studies of particular kinds (e.g., those that are easy for anyone to do rather than those that require a lot of time, money, or expertise) from particular areas of psychology (e.g., almost always from social, and almost never from neuroscience, developmental, or clinical). Because the studies they chose are not representative of psychology as a whole, their results may tell us something about the replicability of the specific studies in the samples, but they are unlikely to tell us much about the replication rate of the entire discipline.

Second, the teams did not always use the same methods that were used in the original studies—sometimes because details of the original methods were not known, and sometimes because the teams made mistakes. This means that some of their studies were not really replications at all; and yet, the results of these "bad replications" are typically included when journalists report that there is a "replication crisis" in psychology. Journalists may be fooled, but careful scientists are not. The National Academies of Sciences, Engineering, and Medicine is the United States' single most prestigious body of scientists, and when they recently considered all the evidence about replicability in psychology, they concluded that contrary to what you read in the news, "It is not helpful, or justified, to refer to psychology as in a state of 'crisis' " (National Academies of Sciences, Engineering, and Medicine, 2019, p. 124). The bottom line is that no one knows the actual replication rate of experiments in psychology—or any other science for that matter.

Type I and Type II Errors If we can't answer the question about the real replication rate, then maybe we can answer an easier one: What is the *ideal* replication rate? What percentage of the results published in scientific journals do we *wish* would replicate perfectly? You are probably tempted to say 100%, but that answer is wrong. To understand why that answer is wrong requires understanding the two errors researchers can make when they draw conclusions from evidence.

A **Type I error** occurs *when researchers conclude that there is a causal relationship between two variables when in fact there is not.* If a psychologist concluded that playing violent video games increased aggressiveness in children when in fact it hadn't, that conclusion would be a Type I error, also known as a *false positive*.

Headlines suggest that the results of most psychology studies can't be replicated. Should you believe them?

PHOTO RESEARCHERS/SCIENCE SOURCE

Type I error An error that occurs when researchers conclude that there is a causal relationship between two variables when in fact there is not.

A **Type II error** occurs *when researchers conclude that there is not a causal relationship between two variables when in fact there is.* If a psychologist concluded that playing violent video games did not increase aggressiveness in children when in fact it had, that conclusion would be a Type II error, also known as a *false negative.* You can think of these mistaken conclusions as *flukes* and *flunks:* A fluke happens when we detect a causal relationship between variables when there really isn't one, and a flunk happens when we fail to detect a causal relationship between variables when there really is one.

Now, the annoying thing about flukes and flunks is that anything you do to reduce the likelihood of one will increase the likelihood of the other. Why? Well, just consider a home security system that sounds an alarm whenever the motion detector is triggered. If you set the sensitivity of the motion detector to *high,* the alarm will always ring when a burglar opens a window (no flunks), but sometimes it will ring when a houseplant drops a leaf (lots of flukes). You will always detect a burglar when they are really there, but sometimes you'll also detect them when they're not. On the other hand, if you set the detector's sensitivity to *low,* the alarm will never mistakenly ring for a houseplant (no flukes), but sometimes it will fail to ring when a burglar opens a window (lots of flunks). You will never detect a burglar when they aren't really there, but sometimes you'll fail to detect them when they are. See the problem? If you want to catch every single burglar, then you'll just have to put up with a few false alarms (flukes), and if you want to eliminate every single false alarm then you'll just have to put up with a few uncaught burglars (flunks). Flukes are known as Type I errors, and flunks are known as Type II errors. When setting the sensitivity of your motion detector, you just have to decide which of these errors worries you the most.

Psychologists worry too—not about burglars and houseplants, but about flukes and flunks in their experiments. They don't want to draw false conclusions from their experiments, but they also don't want to miss the chance to draw true ones. If psychologists designed their experiments to avoid all Type II errors, they would rarely miss discovering a real and important fact about human behaviour, but a sizeable chunk of those "facts" would turn out to be flukes and the replication rate would be very low. On the other hand, if psychologists designed their experiments to avoid all Type I errors, they would never be fooled by flukes and the replication rate would be very high, but a lot of their studies would be flunks that failed to discover real and important facts about human behaviour.

Neither of these are happy outcomes, so psychologists do exactly what you would do if you were setting up a home security system: They try to strike a balance between the two mistakes they are in danger of making by minimizing the risk of whichever mistake seems worse in a particular situation and accepting an elevated risk of its opposite (Finkel et al., 2017). The U.S. National Academies of Sciences, Engineering, and Medicine noted that "even if there were a definitive estimate of replicability in psychology, no one knows the expected level of non-replicability in a healthy science" (2019, p. 124). In other words, we do not know what the replication rate should be, but we do know that if it were 100%, psychologists would be flunking—that is, failing to make some of the most important discoveries.

Replication serves an important function in psychology, as it does in every science. And it reminds us that even the best experimental evidence does not allow us to conclude that two variables *are* causally related; rather, it allows us to conclude that two variables *are likely to be* causally related. The more easily and more often that evidence is reproduced, the more confident we can be in the causal relationship between the variables. We can never be completely confident in any result, of course, but replications can move us ever closer to certainty (see Other Voices: Psychology Is Not in Crisis).

Type II error An error that occurs when researchers conclude that there is not a causal relationship between two variables when in fact there is.

Other Voices ⦁ **Psychology Is Not in Crisis**

Is psychology in the midst of a research crisis?

An initiative called the Reproducibility Project at the Center for Open Science in Charlottesville, Virginia, USA, reran 100 psychology experiments and found that over 60% of them failed to replicate—that is, their findings did not hold up the second time around. The results, published in August 2015 in *Science*, have generated alarm (and in some cases, confirmed suspicions) that the field of psychology is in poor shape.

But the failure to replicate is not a cause for alarm; in fact, it is a normal part of how science works.

Suppose you have two well-designed, carefully run studies, A and B, that investigate the same phenomenon. They perform what appear to be identical experiments, and yet they reach opposite conclusions. Study A produces the predicted phenomenon, whereas Study B does not. We have a failure to replicate.

Does this mean that the phenomenon in question is necessarily illusory? Absolutely not. If the studies were well designed and executed, it is more likely that the phenomenon from Study A is true *only under certain conditions*. The scientist's job now is to figure out what those conditions are, in order to form new and better hypotheses to test.

A number of years ago, for example, scientists conducted an experiment on fruit flies that appeared to identify the gene responsible for curly wings. The results looked solid in the tidy confines of the lab, but out in the messy reality of nature, where temperatures and humidity varied widely, the gene turned out not to reliably have this effect. In a simplistic sense, the experiment "failed to replicate." But in a grander sense, as the evolutionary biologist Richard Lewontin has noted, "failures" like this helped teach biologists that a single gene produces different characteristics and behaviours, depending on the context.

Similarly, when physicists discovered that subatomic particles didn't obey Newton's laws of motion, they didn't cry out that Newton's laws had "failed to replicate." Instead, they realized that Newton's laws were valid only in certain contexts, rather than being universal, and thus the science of quantum mechanics was born.

In psychology, we find many phenomena that fail to replicate if we change the context. One of the most famous is called "fear learning," which has been used to explain anxiety disorders like posttraumatic stress. Scientists place a rat into a small box with an electrical grid on the floor. They play a loud tone and then, a moment later, give the rat an electrical shock. The shock causes the rat to freeze and its heart rate and blood pressure to rise. The scientists repeat this process many times, pairing the tone and the shock, with the same results. Eventually, they play the tone without the shock, and the rat responds in the same way, as if expecting the shock.

Originally this "fear learning" was assumed to be a universal law, but then other scientists slightly varied the context and the rats stopped freezing. For example, if you restrain the rat during the tone (which shouldn't matter if the rat is going to freeze anyway), its heart rate goes down instead of up. And if the cage design permits, the rat will run away rather than freeze.

These failures to replicate did not mean that the original experiments were worthless. Indeed, they led scientists to the crucial understanding that a freezing rat was actually responding to the uncertainty of threat, which happened to be engendered by particular combinations of tone, cage, and shock.

Much of science still assumes that phenomena can be explained with universal laws and therefore context should not matter. But this is not how the world works. Even a simple statement like "the sky is blue" is true only at particular times of day, depending on the mix of molecules in the air as they reflect and scatter light, and on the viewer's experience of colour.

Psychologists are usually well attuned to the importance of context. In our experiments, we take great pains to avoid any irregularities or distractions that might affect the results. But when it comes to replication, psychologists and their critics often seem to forget the powerful and subtle effects of context. They ask simply, "Did the experiment work or not?" rather than considering a failure to replicate as a valuable scientific clue.

As with any scientific field, psychology has some published studies that were conducted sloppily, and a few bad eggs who have falsified their data. But contrary to the implication of the Reproducibility Project, there is no replication crisis in psychology. The "crisis" may simply be the result of a misunderstanding of what science is.

Science is not a body of facts that emerge, like an orderly string of light bulbs, to illuminate a linear path to universal truth. Rather, science (to paraphrase Henry Gee, an editor at *Nature*) is a method to quantify doubt about a hypothesis, and to find the contexts in which a phenomenon is likely. Failure to replicate is not a bug; it is a feature. It is what leads us along the path—the wonderfully twisty path—of scientific discovery.

MARK KARLSBERG OF STUDIO ELEVEN/LISA FELDMAN BARRETT

Lisa Feldman Barrett is the University Distinguished Professor of Psychology and Director of the Interdisciplinary Affective Science Laboratory at Northeastern University in Boston, Massachusetts, United States. Her newest book is called *7½ Lessons About the Brain.*

Thinking Critically About Evidence

Learning Outcomes

WHAT YOU NEED TO KNOW

- Identify the psychological tendencies that make critical thinking so difficult.
- Describe the two steps people can take to help them think critically.

Sir Francis Bacon (1561–1626) devised the scientific method, but underestimated its occupational hazards. While conducting experiments to determine the effect of low temperatures on the preservation of meat, he caught pneumonia and died.

In 1620, Sir Francis Bacon published a book called *Novum Organum,* in which he described a new method for discovering facts about the natural world. What was once called the "Baconian method" is now widely known as the *scientific method,* and that method has allowed human beings to learn more about themselves and the world in the last four centuries than in all the previous centuries combined.

As you've seen in this chapter, the scientific method produces empirical evidence. But empirical evidence is useful only if we know how to think about it—and the fact is that most of us don't. Using evidence requires *critical thinking,* which involves asking ourselves tough questions about whether we have interpreted the evidence in an unbiased way, and about whether the evidence tells not just the truth, but the *whole* truth. Research suggests that most of us have trouble doing these two things and that educational programs designed to teach or improve our critical thinking skills are not particularly effective (Willingham, 2007). Why do we have so much trouble thinking critically?

Consider the armadillo. Some animals freeze when threatened; others duck, run, or growl. Armadillos jump. This natural tendency served armadillos quite well for millennia because for millennia the most common threat to an armadillo's well-being was a rattlesnake. Alas, this natural tendency serves armadillos rather poorly today, because when they wander onto a Texas highway and are threatened by a speeding car, they jump up and hit the bumper. No armadillo makes this mistake twice. Human beings also have natural tendencies that once served them well but no longer do. Our natural and intuitive ways of thinking about evidence, for example, worked just fine when we were hunter-gatherers living in small groups on the African savannah. But today, most of us live in large, complex societies, and our natural ways of thinking about the world don't always serve us well. Sir Francis Bacon understood this. In the very same book in which he developed the scientific method, he argued that two natural human tendencies—the tendency to see what we expect or want to see, and the tendency to ignore what we can't see—are the main enemies of critical thinking. Let's examine each of these tendencies and see how they thwart us.

We See What We Expect and Want to See

When two people are presented with the same evidence, they often draw different conclusions, and Sir Francis Bacon knew why: "The human understanding, once it has adopted opinions . . . draws everything else to support and agree with them . . . [and therefore our] first conclusion colours and brings into conformity with itself all that come after." In other words, our beliefs colour our view of new evidence, causing us to see what we expect to see. As such, evidence often seems to confirm what we believed all along.

This tendency has been documented thousands of times in psychological science. For instance, participants in one study (Darley & Gross, 1983) learned about a little girl named Hannah. One group of participants was told that Hannah came from an affluent family, while the other group was told that Hannah came from a poor family. All participants were then shown some evidence about Hannah's academic abilities (specifically, they watched a video of Hannah taking a reading test) and were then asked to rate Hannah. Although the video was exactly the same for all participants, those who believed that Hannah's family was affluent rated her performance more positively than did those who believed that her family was poor. What's more, both groups of participants defended their conclusions by citing evidence from the video! Experiments like this one suggest that when we consider evidence, what we see often depends on what we *expected* to see.

Our beliefs aren't the only things that colour our views of evidence. They are also coloured by our preferences and prejudices, our ambitions and aversions, our hopes and needs and wants and dreams (Hornsey, 2020). As Bacon noted, "The human understanding is not a dry light, but is infused by desire and emotion which give rise to wishful science. For man prefers to believe what he wants to be true." Research suggests that Bacon was right about this, too. For example, participants in one study (Lord et al., 1979) were shown some scientific evidence about the effectiveness of the death penalty in deterring crime. Some of the evidence suggested that the death penalty deterred crime, some suggested it did not. What did participants make of this mixed bag of evidence? Participants who originally supported the death penalty became even *more* supportive, and participants who originally opposed the death penalty became even *more* opposed. In other words, when presented with exactly the same evidence, participants saw what they *wanted* to see and ended up feeling even more sure about their initial views. Subsequent research has shown that the same pattern emerges when professional scientists are asked to rate the quality of scientific studies that either confirm or disconfirm what they want to believe (Koehler, 1993).

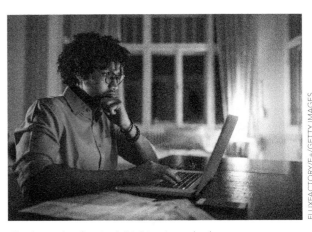

The first rule of critical thinking is to doubt your own conclusions—but that's hard to do when everyone tells you you're right! Recent research shows that Facebook users create "echo chambers" by sharing stories and links mainly with friends who already share their points of view (Del Vicario et al., 2016).

Exactly how do beliefs and desires shape our view of the evidence? One way is that we tend to hold different kinds of evidence to different standards (McPhetres & Zuckerman, 2017). When evidence confirms what we believe or want to believe, we ask ourselves, "*Can* I believe this evidence?" But when evidence disconfirms what we believe or want to believe, we ask ourselves, "*Must* I believe this evidence?" (Gilovich, 1991). The problem is that *can* is a low standard and *must* is a high one: You *can* believe almost anything, but you *must* believe almost nothing. For instance, *can* you believe that people with university degrees are happier than people without them? Of course. Plenty of surveys show that just such a relationship exists, and a reasonable person who studied the evidence could easily defend this conclusion. Now, *must* you believe it? Well, no. After all, those surveys didn't measure every single person on earth, did they? And if the survey questions had been asked differently, they might well have produced different answers, right? A reasonable person who studied the evidence could easily conclude that the relationship between education and happiness is not yet clear enough to compel a strong conclusion.

A second way in which our beliefs and desires shape our view of the evidence is by influencing *which* evidence we consider in the first place. Most people surround themselves with others who believe the same things they believe and want the same things they want, which means that our friends and families are much more likely to validate our beliefs and desires than to challenge them. Studies also show that when given the opportunity to search for evidence, people preferentially search for evidence that confirms their beliefs and fulfills their desires (Hart et al., 2009). What's more, when people find evidence that confirms their beliefs and fulfills their desires, they tend to stop looking, but when they find evidence that does the opposite, they keep searching for more evidence (Gesiarz et al., 2019; Kunda, 1990).

These and other studies suggest that most evidence leaves room for interpretation, and that's the room in which our beliefs and desires just love to hang out. Because it is so easy to see what we expect to see, or to see what we want to see, the first rule of critical thinking is this: *Doubt your own conclusions.* One of the best ways to find the truth about the world is to seek out people who don't see the world your way and then listen carefully to what they have to say. Most of us find this painful, but the outcome is often worth the pain. Scientists go out of their way to expose themselves to criticism by sharing their results with colleagues who are likely to disagree with them, and they do this largely so that they can achieve a more balanced view of their own conclusions (as well as their self-worth). If you want to be happy, take a friend to lunch; but if you want to be right, take an enemy.

We Don't Consider What We Don't See

In another part of his remarkable book, Francis Bacon recounted an old story about a man who visited a Roman temple. The priest showed the man a portrait of several sailors who had taken religious vows and then miraculously survived a shipwreck, and suggested that this was clear evidence of the power of the gods. The visitor paused a moment and then asked precisely the right question: "But where are the pictures of those who perished after taking their vows?" According to Bacon, most of us never ask this kind of question. We consider the evidence we can see and forget about the evidence we can't. Bacon claimed that "little or no attention is paid to things invisible" and argued that this natural tendency was "the greatest impediment and aberration of the human understanding."

Bacon was right when he claimed that people rarely pay attention to what is missing (Kardes & Sanbonmatsu, 2003). For example, participants in one study (Newman et al., 1980) played a game in which they were shown a set of trigrams, which are three-letter combinations such as *SXY, GTR, BCG,* and *EVX.* On each trial, the experimenter pointed to one of the trigrams in the set and told the participants that *this* trigram was the special one. The participants' job was to figure out what made the special trigram so special. How many trials did it take before participants figured it out? It depended on the trigram's special feature. For half the participants, the special trigram was always the one that contained the letter *T,* and participants in this condition needed to see about 34 sets of trigrams before they figured out that the presence of *T* was what made the trigram special. But for the other half of the participants, the special trigram was always the one that *lacked* the letter *T.* How many trials did it take before participants figured it out? They *never* figured it out. That's right. Never. And that's because it is much easier to think about what *is* there than about what *isn't.*

The tendency to ignore missing evidence can lead us to draw erroneous conclusions (Wainer & Zwerling, 2006). For instance, some universities in Canada have reputations as party schools. The bar graph in **FIGURE 2.12**, shows the number of hours per week that students at different Canadian universities said they spend partying. You might look at this graph and think "Wow, Queen's

The second rule of critical thinking is to consider what you don't see. Businesses often provide testimonials from satisfied customers—but where are all the dissatisfied customers, and what might they have to say?

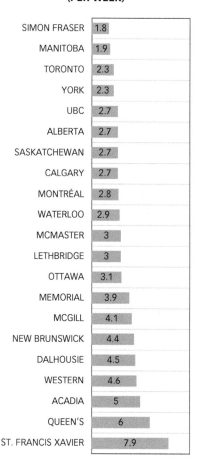

HOURS SPENT PARTYING (PER WEEK)

University	Hours
SIMON FRASER	1.8
MANITOBA	1.9
TORONTO	2.3
YORK	2.3
UBC	2.7
ALBERTA	2.7
SASKATCHEWAN	2.7
CALGARY	2.7
MONTRÉAL	2.8
WATERLOO	2.9
MCMASTER	3
LETHBRIDGE	3
OTTAWA	3.1
MEMORIAL	3.9
MCGILL	4.1
NEW BRUNSWICK	4.4
DALHOUSIE	4.5
WESTERN	4.6
ACADIA	5
QUEEN'S	6
ST. FRANCIS XAVIER	7.9

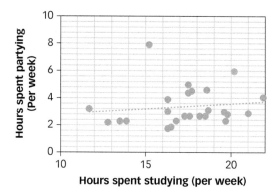

Figure 2.12

Hours Spent Partying or Studying at Some Canadian Universities. The bar graph at left shows the hours per week that students at various Canadian universities reported they spend partying. Queen's, with the second-most hours, must be full of slackers, right? Wrong. The scatterplot above compares hours spent partying and studying at Canadian universities—and there is no relationship between the two variables. Queen's is shown in orange. Ignoring the missing data (about study habits) would lead to the wrong conclusion about the academic rigour of one of Canada's oldest universities. Data from Brown (2017).

University must be a pretty slack school — students there spend a lot of time having fun."

That's a reasonable hypothesis based on the evidence, but it's not quite correct, because of evidence *not* shown in Figure 2.12. How many hours per week do students spend hitting the books? You might have assumed that the more time students spend partying, the less time they spend studying (in other words, that these two variables are negatively correlated), but that is not true. The scatterplot in Figure 2.12 shows the relationship between hours spent partying and hours spent studying at different schools. There is no correlation between these two variables. Queen's students do spend a lot of time partying, but they are also near the top in terms of reported hours spent studying per week. These students play hard — and work harder!

Someone who is shown the evidence in the bar graph in Figure 2.12 and who forgets to ask about the missing evidence in the scatterplot would draw the wrong conclusion about the relationship between partying and dedication to academic pursuits. And yet, forgetting to ask for missing evidence is something that happens all the time. Much of World War II was fought in the air, and the question of how best to armour planes to protect them from enemy fire was something that people worried about. Too much armour, and the plane is too heavy to fly well. Too little armour — and bye, bye airplane. The Allied military collected data on airplanes that returned from engagements. There were regularly more bullet holes in the fuselage than in the engines. Officers reasoned that it would be most efficient to concentrate armour where the need was greatest: clearly the fuselage, right? The officers consulted Alexander Wald, a refugee mathematician from eastern Europe. He did not agree. Dr. Wald instead wondered about the *missing* holes — the ones that should have been in the engines but weren't. He guessed pretty quickly where those holes were — on the engines of the planes that did *not* return. These planes probably crashed because of the damage. After he explained his reasoning, the armour went on the engines, not the fuselage. If the first rule of critical thinking is to doubt what you *do* see, then the second rule is to consider what you *don't* see.

The Skeptical Stance

Science is a human enterprise and humans make mistakes: They see what they expect to see, they see what they want to see, and they often fail to consider what they can't see at all. What makes science different from most other human enterprises is that scientists actively seek to discover and remedy their mistakes. Scientists are constantly striving to make their observations more accurate and their reasoning more rigorous, and they invite anyone and everyone to examine their evidence and challenge their conclusions. As a result, science is the ultimate democracy in which the lowliest nobody can triumph over the most celebrated somebody. When an unknown Swiss patent clerk with a vivid imagination challenged the greatest physicists of his day, he didn't have a famous father, a fancy degree, powerful friends, or a fat wallet. Albert Einstein won the scientific debate for one reason and one reason alone: He was right.

So think of the remaining chapters in this textbook as a report from the field — a description of the work that psychological scientists have done so far as they stumble towards knowledge. These chapters tell the story of Francis Bacon's intellectual progeny — the people who have put their faith in the scientific method and used it to pry loose pieces of the truth about who we are, how we think, feel, and behave, and what we are all doing together here on the third rock from the sun. Some of their reports will turn out to be flukes, others will turn out to be flunks, but every one of them is our current best guess about the way people work. Read these reports with interest but think critically about their claims — and for that matter, about everything else.

The Ethics of Science: Doing What's Right

Learning Outcomes

WHAT YOU NEED TO KNOW

- Identify the three basic principles that ethical research must follow.

- Summarize the ways in which psychologists ensure that their research respects people.

- Explain the ways in which psychologists ensure that their research respects truth.

Why is the man at this bar so upset? He just saw another man slip a drug into a woman's drink and he is alerting the bartender. What he doesn't know is that all the people at the bar are actors and that he is being filmed for the television show *What Would You Do?* The man behaved ethically, but what about the producers of the show? Was it ethical for them to put the man in such a stressful situation without his consent?

informed consent A verbal agreement to participate in a study made by an adult who has been informed of all the risks that participation may entail.

Somewhere along the way, someone probably told you that it isn't nice to treat people like objects. And yet, psychologists may appear to be doing just that when they create experimental situations that cause people to feel fearful or sad, to do things that are embarrassing or immoral, or to learn things about themselves and others that they might not really want to know. Don't be fooled by appearances. The fact is that psychologists go to great lengths to protect the well-being of their research participants, and they are bound by a code of ethics that is as detailed and demanding as the professional codes that bind physicians, lawyers, and accountants. That code requires psychologists to show respect for people, for animals, and for the truth. Let's examine each of these obligations in turn.

Respecting People

During World War II, Nazi doctors performed barbaric experiments on human subjects, such as removing organs without anesthesia or submerging people in ice water to see how long it would take them to die. The international community was appalled, and after the war ended they developed the Nuremberg Code of 1947 and then the Declaration of Helsinki in 1964, both of which spelled out rules for the ethical treatment of the people who participate in experiments. Unfortunately, not everyone obeyed the rules. For example, from 1932 until 1972, the U.S. Public Health Service conducted the infamous Tuskegee experiment, in which 399 Black men with syphilis were denied treatment so that researchers could observe the progression of the disease. As one journalist noted, the government "used human beings as laboratory animals in a long and inefficient study of how long it takes syphilis to kill someone" (Jones, 1993, p. 10).

Over time, the basic tenets of the Declaration of Helsinki have become increasingly enshrined in national legislation and regulations. In Canada, all research involving human persons or tissue is covered by the Tri-Council Policy Statement (TCPS): Ethical Conduct for Research Involving Humans. "Tri-Council" refers to the three federal research funding agencies: CIHR (Canadian Institutes of Health Research), NSERC (Natural Sciences and Engineering Research Council), and SSHRC (Social Sciences and Humanities Research Council), which cover health-related, basic science, and social science–related research, respectively. (See Other Voices: Can We Afford Science? for more on the federal funding of psychological science.) The TCPS describes the core principles, based on respect for human dignity, that all research involving human participants must follow. First, research should show *respect for persons* and their right to make decisions for and about themselves without undue influence or coercion. Second, research should *show concern for welfare* which means that it should attempt to maximize benefits and reduce risks to the participant. Third, research should be *just,* which means that it should distribute benefits and risks equally to participants without prejudice towards particular individuals or groups.

The specific ethical code that psychologists follow incorporates these basic principles and expands them. (You can find the American Psychological Association's *Ethical Principles of Psychologists and Code of Conduct* [2017] at https://www.apa.org /ethics/code; the Canadian Psychological Association's *Canadian Code of Ethics for Psychologists* is very similar and can be accessed at https://cpa.ca/docs/File/Ethics /CPA_Code_2017_4thEd.pdf.) Here are a few of the most important rules that govern the conduct of psychological research:

- *Informed consent:* Participants may not take part in a psychological study unless they have given **informed consent,** which is *a verbal agreement to participate in a study made by an adult who has been informed of all the risks* *that participation may entail.* This doesn't mean that the person must know everything about the study (e.g., the hypothesis), but it does mean that the person must know about anything that might potentially be harmful or painful. If people cannot give informed consent (e.g., because they are minors or are mentally incapable), then informed consent must be obtained from their legal guardians. And even after people give informed consent, they always have the right to withdraw from the study at any time without penalty.

- *Freedom from coercion:* Psychologists may not coerce participation. Coercion not only means physical and psychological coercion but monetary coercion as well. It is unethical to offer people large amounts of money to do something that they might otherwise decline to do. University students may be invited to participate in studies as part of their training in psychology, but they are ordinarily offered the option of learning the same things by other means.

- *Protection from harm:* Psychologists must take every possible precaution to protect their research participants from physical or psychological harm. If there are two equally effective ways to study something, the psychologist must use the safer method. If no safe method is available, the psychologist may not perform the study.

- *Risk–benefit analysis:* Although participants may be asked to accept small risks, such as a minor shock or a small embarrassment, they may not even be *asked* to accept large risks, such as severe pain, psychological trauma, or any risk that is greater than the risks they would ordinarily take in their everyday lives. Furthermore, even when participants are asked to take small risks, the psychologist must first show that these risks are outweighed by the social benefits of the new knowledge that might be gained from the study.

- *Deception:* Psychologists may use deception only when it is justified by the study's scientific, educational, or applied value and when alternative procedures are not feasible. They may never deceive participants about any aspect of a study that could cause them physical or psychological harm or pain.

- *Debriefing:* If a participant is deceived in any way before or during a study, the psychologist must afterwards provide them with a **debriefing,** which is *a verbal description of the true nature and purpose of a study.* If the participant was changed in any way (e.g., made to feel sad), the psychologist must attempt to undo that change (e.g., ask the person to do a task that will make them happy) and restore the participant to the state they were in before the study.

- *Confidentiality:* Psychologists are obligated to keep private and personal information obtained during a study confidential.

These are just some of the rules that psychologists must follow. But how are those rules enforced? Almost all psychology studies are performed by psychologists who work at universities. These institutions have research ethics boards (REBs) that are composed of researchers, university staff, and laypeople from the community (e.g., business leaders or members of the clergy). If the research is federally funded, the law requires that the REB include at least one nonscientist and one person who is not affiliated with the institution. A psychologist may conduct a study only after the REB has reviewed and approved it.

As you can imagine, the code of ethics and the procedure for approval are so strict that many studies simply cannot be performed anywhere, by anyone, at any time. For example, psychologists would love to know how growing up without exposure to language affects a person's subsequent ability to speak and think, but they cannot ethically manipulate that variable in an experiment. They can only study the natural correlations between language exposure and speaking ability, and so may never be able to firmly establish the causal relationships between these variables. Indeed, there are many questions that psychologists will never be able to answer definitively because doing so would require unethical experiments that violate basic human rights. But treating people ethically is more important than gaining scientific knowledge, so this is a limit on research that psychologists gladly accept.

debriefing A verbal description of the true nature and purpose of a study.

Respecting Animals

Not all research participants have human rights because not all research participants are humans. Some are macaque monkeys, rats, pigeons, or other nonhuman animals. The Canadian Council on Animal Care (CCAC) is the national organization responsible for establishing standards for the ethical use and care of animals in research. It describes the special rights of these nonhuman participants, and provides guidelines that all research must follow. The Three Rs tenet (Replacement, Reduction, and Refinement) guides the ethical use of animals in science, ensuring appropriate consideration of the animals' comfort, health, and humane treatment.

Replacement means that researchers have to prove there is no alternative to using animals in research and that the use of animals is justified by the scientific or clinical value of the study. *Reduction* means that researchers must use the smallest number of animals possible to achieve the research. *Refinement* means that procedures must be modified to minimize discomfort, infection, illness, and pain of animals. This requires that animals be treated humanely, with comfortable housing and the ability to satisfy their basic instincts (e.g., mice have to make nests, and primates require perching or elevated areas in their enclosures), and appropriate administration of painkillers.

That's good—but is it good enough? Some people don't think so. For example, philosopher Peter Singer (1975) has argued that all creatures capable of feeling pain have the same fundamental rights, and that treating nonhumans differently from humans is a form of "species-ism" that is every bit as abhorrent as racism or sexism. Singer's philosophy has inspired groups such as People for the Ethical Treatment of Animals to call for an end to all research involving nonhuman animals. Unfortunately, it has also inspired some groups to attack psychologists who conduct such research, legally and ethically. As two of these researchers (Ringach & Jentsch, 2009, p. 11417) reported:

> We have seen our cars and homes firebombed or flooded, and we have received letters packed with poisoned razors and death threats via e-mail and voicemail. Our families and neighbours have been terrorized by angry mobs of masked protesters who throw rocks, break windows, and chant that "you should stop or be stopped" and that they "know where you sleep at night." Some of the attacks have been catalogued as attempted murder. Adding insult to injury, misguided animal-rights militants openly incite others to violence on the Internet, brag about the resulting crimes, and go as far as to call plots for our assassination "morally justifiable."

Where do most people stand on this issue? A 2013 Nanos poll conducted on behalf of the CCAC (Canadian Council on Animal Care) revealed that most Canadians (at least 57–64%) support the use of animals in research. Indeed, most Canadians eat meat, wear leather, and support the rights of hunters, which is to say that most Canadians see a sharp distinction between animal and human rights. Science is not in the business of resolving moral controversies, and every individual must draw their own conclusions about this issue. But whatever position you take, it is important to note that only a small percentage of the people who champion animal rights engage in abusive or illegal behaviour. It is also important to note that only a small percentage of psychological studies involve animals, and that only a small percentage of those studies cause animals any pain or harm. Psychologists mainly study people, and when they do study animals, they mainly study their behaviour.

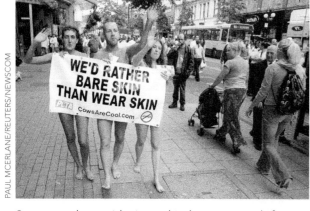

Some people consider it unethical to use animals for clothing or research. Others see an important distinction between these two purposes.

PAUL MCERLANE/REUTERS/NEWSCOM

Respecting Truth

Research ethics boards ensure that data are collected ethically. But once the data are collected, who ensures that they are honestly analyzed and thoroughly reported? No one. Psychology, like all sciences, works on the honour system. No authority is charged with monitoring what psychologists do with the data they've collected, and no authority is charged with checking to see if the claims they make are true. You may find that a bit odd. After all, we don't use the honour system in stores ("Take the microwave home and pay us next time you're in the neighbourhood"), banks ("I don't need to look up your account, just tell me how much money you want to withdraw"), or courtrooms ("If you say you're innocent, well then, that's good enough for me"), so why would we expect it to work in science? Are scientists more honest than everyone else?

Maybe, or maybe not. But it doesn't really matter because the honour system doesn't depend on scientists being more honest than everyone else; it depends on the fact that science is a community enterprise. When scientists claim to have discovered something important, other scientists don't just applaud: They start studying it too. When the physicist Jan Hendrik Schön announced in 2001 that he had produced a molecular-scale transistor, other physicists were deeply impressed—that is, until they tried to replicate his work and discovered that Schön had fabricated his data (Agin, 2007). Schön lost his job and his PhD was revoked, but the important point is that such frauds can't last long because one scientist's conclusion is the next scientist's research question.

This doesn't mean that all frauds are uncovered swiftly, however. The psychologist Diederik Stapel lied, cheated, and made up his data for decades before people became suspicious enough to investigate (Levelt Committee et al., 2012), but that's mainly because the discoveries he claimed to have made were not particularly important to begin with and so few people had attempted to replicate his work. Not all frauds are uncovered, but all of the *important* ones are. The psychologist who fraudulently claims to have shown that chimps are smarter than goldfish may never get caught because no one is likely to follow up on such an obvious finding, but the psychologist who fraudulently claims to have shown the opposite will soon have a lot of explaining to do.

What exactly are psychologists on their honour to do? At least three things. First, when writing reports of their studies and publishing them in scientific journals, psychologists are obligated to report truthfully on what they did and what they found. They can't fabricate results (e.g., by claiming to have performed studies that they never really performed) or fudge results (e.g., by changing records of data that were actually collected), and they can't mislead by omission (e.g., by reporting only the results that confirm their hypothesis and saying nothing about the results that don't). Second, psychologists are obligated to share credit fairly by including as co-authors of their reports the other people who contributed to the work, as well as by mentioning in their reports the other scientists who have done related work. And third, psychologists are obligated to share their data. The American Psychological Association's code of conduct states that ethical psychologists "do not withhold the data on which their conclusions are based from other competent professionals who seek to verify the substantive claims through reanalysis." Most scientific frauds have been uncovered by fellow scientists who became suspicious when they looked closely at the fraudster's data. The fact that anyone can check up on anyone else is one of the reasons the honour system works as well as it does.

Chapter Review

Empiricism: How to Know Stuff

- Empiricism is the belief that the best way to understand the world is to observe it firsthand. It is only in the past few centuries that people have begun to systematically collect and evaluate evidence to test the accuracy of their beliefs about the world.

- Observation doesn't just mean "looking." It requires a method. The scientific method involves (a) developing a theory that gives rise to a falsifiable hypothesis; and then (b) making observations that serve to test that hypothesis. Although these tests may prove that a theory is false, they can never prove that it is true.

- The methods of psychology are special because human beings are more complex, variable, and reactive than almost anything else that scientists study.

Methods of Observation: Discovering What People Do

- Measurement involves (a) defining a property in measurable terms and then (b) using a device that can detect that property. A good definition has construct validity (the concrete condition being measured adequately characterizes the property), and a good detector has both power (it can tell when properties are different) and reliability (it can tell when properties are the same).

- When people know they are being observed, they may behave as they think they should. Demand characteristics are aspects of an observational setting that cause people to behave as they think someone else wants or expects them to. Psychologists try to reduce or eliminate demand characteristics by observing participants in their natural habitats or by hiding their expectations from the participant. Observer bias is the tendency for observers' expectations to influence both what they believe they observed and what actually happened. Psychologists try to avoid observer bias by conducting double-blind studies.

- Psychologists usually measure samples rather than entire populations. They often describe their measurements with a graphic representation called a frequency distribution, which often has a special shape known as the normal distribution. They also describe their measurements with descriptive statistics; the most common are descriptions of central tendency (such as the mean, median, and mode) and descriptions of variability (such as the range and the standard deviation).

Methods of Explanation: Discovering Why People Do What They Do

- To determine whether two variables are causally related, we must first determine whether they are related at all. This can be done by measuring each variable many times and then comparing the patterns of variation within each series of measurements. If the patterns are synchronized, then the variables are correlated. Correlations allow us to predict the value of one variable from knowledge of the value of the other. The direction and strength of a correlation are measured by the correlation coefficient (r).

- Even when we observe a correlation between two variables, we can't conclude that they are causally related because a "third variable" could be causing them both. Experiments solve this third-variable problem by manipulating an independent variable, randomly assigning participants to the conditions that this manipulation creates, and then measuring a dependent variable. These measurements are then compared across conditions. If calculations show that the results would only happen 5% of the time by

dumb luck alone, then the differences in the measurements across conditions are assumed to have been caused by the manipulation.

- An internally valid experiment establishes the likelihood of a causal relationship between variables as they were defined and among the participants who were studied. When an experiment mimics the real world, it is externally valid. But most psychology experiments are not attempts to mimic the real world; rather, they test hypotheses derived from theories.

- Random sampling allows researchers to generalize from their samples to the populations from which the samples were drawn, but most psychology studies cannot use random sampling and therefore there are restrictions on the conclusions that can be drawn from them. One restriction is that we can never be absolutely sure that a result is not a fluke, yet replications do help to increase our confidence.

- Replication is an attempt to reproduce a result by using the same procedures and sampling from the same population as the original study. Although no one knows the real replication rate in psychological science, the fact that researchers must balance the risk of Type I and Type II errors means that we would not expect the rate to be—or want it to be—100%.

Thinking Critically About Evidence

- Thinking critically about evidence is difficult because people have a natural tendency to see what they expect to see, to see what they want to see, and to consider what they see but not what they don't see.

- Critical thinkers consider evidence that disconfirms their own opinions. They also consider the evidence that is absent, not just the evidence that is present.

- One thing that makes science different from most other human enterprises is that science actively seeks to discover and remedy its own biases and errors.

The Ethics of Science: Doing What's Right

- Research ethics boards (REBs) ensure that the rights of human beings who participate in scientific research are based on the principles of respect for persons, concern for welfare, and justice.

- Psychologists are obligated to uphold these principles by getting informed consent from participants, not coercing their participation, protecting participants from harm, weighing benefits against risks, avoiding deception, and keeping information confidential.

- Psychologists are obligated to respect the rights of animals and to treat them humanely. Most people are in favour of using animals in scientific research.

- Psychologists are obligated to tell the truth about their studies, to share credit appropriately, and to grant others access to their data.

Changing Minds

1. A research study shows that getting a good night's sleep increases people's performance on almost any kind of task. You tell a classmate about this study and they shrug. "Who didn't already know that? If you ask me, psychology is just common sense. Why conduct experiments to show what everyone already knows?" How would you explain the value of studying something that seems like common sense?

2. Your friend texts you a link to a study showing that Europeans who work longer hours are less happy than those who work shorter hours, but that in the United States and Canada it's the other way around. The text reads "Cool experiment!" so you reply "Study—not experiment," either because you are very wise or because you don't know much about friendship. Why aren't all research studies experiments? What can't you learn from this study that you *could* learn from an experiment?

3. After the first exam, your professor says they've noticed a positive correlation between the location of students' seats and their exam scores: "The closer students sit to the front of the room, the higher their scores on the exam," your professor announces. After class, your friend suggests that the two of you should sit up front for the rest of the semester to improve your grades. Having read about correlation and causation, should you be skeptical? What are some possible reasons for the correlation between seating position and good grades? Could you design an experiment to test whether sitting up front actually causes good grades?

4. A classmate in your criminal justice course suggests that mental illness is a major cause of violent crimes in Canada. As evidence, they mention a highly publicized murder trial in which the convicted defendant was diagnosed with schizophrenia. What scientific evidence would your classmate need to support this claim?

5. You ask your friend if they want to go to the gym with you. "No," they say, "I never exercise." You tell your friend that regular exercise has all kinds of health benefits, including greatly reducing the risk of heart disease. "I don't believe that," they reply. "I had an uncle who got up at 6 a.m. every day of his life to go jogging, and he still died of a heart attack at age 53." What would you tell your friend? Does their uncle's case prove that exercise really doesn't protect against heart disease after all?

6.
Visualizing Data
A first-year psychology student says: "Once a correlation between two variables is established, conclusions can be drawn only on a general level, not an individual level." Use the DATA to support or dispute this statement.

Key Terms

empiricism (p. 28)

scientific method (p. 28)

theories (p. 28)

hypothesis (p. 29)

empirical method (p. 30)

operational definition (p. 32)

construct validity (p. 32)

power (p. 32)

reliability (p. 32)

demand characteristics (p. 33)

naturalistic observation (p. 33)

observer bias (p. 35)

double-blind study (p. 35)

population (p. 35)

sample (p. 36)

frequency distribution (p. 36)

normal distribution (p. 37)

mode (p. 37)

mean (p. 37)

median (p. 37)

range (p. 38)

standard deviation (p. 38)

variable (p. 40)

correlation (p. 40)

correlation coefficient (r) (p. 41)

natural correlation (p. 42)

third-variable problem (p. 43)

experimentation (p. 43)

manipulation (p. 44)

independent variable (p. 45)

dependent variable (p. 45)

self-selection (p. 47)

random assignment (p. 47)

internal validity (p. 49)

external validity (p. 49)

case method (p. 50)

random sampling (p. 51)

replication (p. 52)

Type I error (p. 53)

Type II error (p. 54)

informed consent (p. 60)

debriefing (p. 61)

Neuroscience and Behaviour

Steve "The Matador" Montador played for teams in the National Hockey League for 10 years. He died 3 years after retirement, and postmortem analysis revealed widespread chronic traumatic encephalopathy in his brain, due to repeated blows to the head.

MIKE BLAKE/REUTERS/ALAMY STOCK PHOTO

S TEVE MONTADOR GREW UP IN MISSISSAUGA PLAYING HOCKEY. He was a talented player: By the age of 16, he was playing Junior Hockey in Ontario, then turned professional, joining the Calgary Flames of the National Hockey League, when he was 22. He played in the NHL for 13 years and was known for his willingness to fight. During his NHL career, he sustained at least 15 documented concussions, including four in early 2012, and probably experienced thousands more minor brain traumas that were not documented. After the fourth concussion in February 2012, he was unable to play for over a year, and became depressed. He died suddenly at his home in Mississauga in February 2015, 4 days before the birth of his only child. He was 35. An autopsy at the Krembil Brain Institute in Toronto revealed the widespread presence of a condition now known as chronic traumatic encephalopathy (CTE), a form of progressive brain damage that has been linked to repeated concussions (Montenigro et al., 2015). According to his family, Montador had struggled with memory loss, sleep changes, and other mood changes, as well as depression, in the years before his death. These are all established symptoms of CTE. First called "punch drunk syndrome" after being observed in former boxers nearly 100 years ago (Martland, 1928), CTE has also been observed after repeated head injuries in wrestling, football, and rugby (Costanza et al., 2011; Daneshvar et al., 2011; Lakhan & Kirchgessner, 2012; McKee et al., 2009).

In December 2015, attention to CTE was heightened further by the release of the movie *Concussion,* which focuses on the story of Bennet Omalu (played by Will Smith), the pathologist who first uncovered evidence for CTE in the brain of an NFL (National Football League) player. Although statements by the Omalu character in the movie imply that CTE has caused the decline and death of former NFL players, others have claimed that the science linking CTE and bad outcomes after football is inconclusive and even flawed (Barr & Karantzoulis, 2019; Hoge, 2018). In fact, we don't know whether playing football or hockey causes CTE, or whether CTE causes such extreme outcomes as suicide. Indeed, former NFL players are at lower risk for suicide than men in the general population (Iverson, 2015), and scientists are actively debating the nature and consequences of CTE (Castellani et al., 2015; LoBue et al., 2020;

McKee, 2020). However, we do know that CTE is associated with an array of cognitive and emotional deficits in afflicted individuals, including inability to concentrate, memory loss, irritability, and depression, usually beginning within a decade after repeated concussions and worsening with time (McKee et al., 2009; Montenigro et al., 2015). Fortunately, growing awareness of CTE and its associated symptoms is leading professional sports organizations, as well as universities, schools, and others involved in youth sports, to take steps to address the problem.

The symptoms of CTE are reminders that our psychological, emotional, and social well-being depend critically on the health and integrity of the brain. They also highlight that understanding neuroscience isn't just an academic exercise confined to scientific laboratories: The more we know about the brain, and the more people who know it, the better our chances of finding solutions to problems such as CTE.

IN THIS CHAPTER, WE'LL CONSIDER HOW THE BRAIN WORKS, what happens when it doesn't, and how both states of affairs determine behaviour. First, we'll introduce the basic unit of information processing in the brain, the neuron. The electrical and chemical activities of neurons are the starting point of all behaviour, thought, and emotion. Next, we'll consider the anatomy of the central nervous system, focusing especially on the brain, including its overall organization, and the key structures that perform its different functions. We'll then examine the interplay between genetics and the environment, and the role they play in directing behaviour. Finally, we'll discuss methods that allow us to study both damaged and healthy brains.

Neurons: The Origin of Behaviour

An estimated 1 billion people watch the final game of World Cup soccer every 4 years. That's a whole lot of people, but to put it in perspective, it's only a little over 14% of the estimated 7 billion people currently living on earth. But a really, really big number is inside your skull right now, helping you make sense of these big numbers you're reading about. Scientists estimate that there are as many as *86 billion* nerve cells (von Bartheld et al., 2016) in your brain. All of your thoughts, feelings, and behaviours spring from cells in the brain that take in information and produce some kind of output trillions of times a day. These cells are **neurons,** *cells in the nervous system that communicate with each other to perform information-processing tasks.*

Learning Outcomes

WHAT YOU NEED TO KNOW

- Explain the function of neurons.
- Outline the components of the neuron.
- Differentiate the three major types of neurons by their function.

Components of the Neuron

During the 1800s, philosophers wrote poetically about an "enchanted loom" that mysteriously wove a tapestry of behaviour, and many scientists confirmed that metaphor (Corsi, 1991). To those scientists, the brain looked as though it were composed of a continuously connected lattice of fine threads, leading them to conclude that it was one big woven web of material. However, in the late 1880s, the

neurons Cells in the nervous system that communicate with each other to perform information-processing tasks.

OXFORD SCIENTIFIC/GETTY IMAGES

Figure 3.1

Golgi-Stained Neurons Santiago Ramón y Cajal used a Golgi stain (like the one shown here) to highlight the appearance of neurons. He was the first to see that each neuron is composed of a body with many threads extending outward towards other neurons. In a surprising finding, he also saw that the threads of each neuron do not actually touch other neurons.

cell body (soma) Component of the neuron that coordinates information-processing tasks and keeps the cell alive.

dendrite Receives information from other neurons and relays it to the cell body.

axon Carries information to other neurons, muscles, or glands.

myelin sheath An insulating layer of fatty material.

glial cells Support cells found in the nervous system.

synapse The junction or region between the axon of one neuron and the dendrites or cell body of another.

sensory neurons Receive information from the external world and convey this information to the brain via the spinal cord.

motor neurons Carry signals from the spinal cord to the muscles to produce movement.

Spanish physician Santiago Ramón y Cajal (1852–1934) learned about a new technique for staining neurons in the brain (DeFelipe & Jones, 1988). The stain highlighted the appearance of entire cells, revealing that they came in different shapes and sizes (see **FIGURE 3.1**).

Ramón y Cajal discovered that neurons are complex structures composed of three basic parts: the cell body, the dendrites, and the axon (see **FIGURE 3.2**). Like cells in all organs of the body, neurons have a **cell body** (also called the *soma*), the largest *component of the neuron that coordinates the information-processing tasks and keeps the cell alive*. Functions such as protein synthesis, energy production, and metabolism take place here. The cell body contains a *nucleus,* which houses chromosomes that contain your DNA, the genetic blueprint of who you are. The cell body is enclosed by a porous cell membrane that allows some molecules to flow into and out of the cell.

Unlike other cells in the body, neurons have two types of specialized extensions of the cell membrane that allow them to communicate: dendrites and axons. **Dendrites** *receive information from other neurons and relay it to the cell body*. The term *dendrite* comes from the Greek word for "tree"; indeed, most neurons have many dendrites that look like tree branches. The **axon** *carries information to other neurons, muscles, or glands*. Axons can be very long, even stretching up to a meter from the base of the spinal cord down to the big toe.

In many neurons, the axon is covered by a **myelin sheath,** *an insulating layer of fatty material*. The myelin sheath is composed of **glial cells** (named for the Greek word for "glue"), which are *support cells found in the nervous system*. Glial cells serve a variety of roles critical to the function of the nervous system (von Bartheld et al., 2016). Some glial cells digest parts of dead neurons, while others provide physical and nutritional support for neurons, and still others form the myelin that insulates the axons of nearby neurons and allows those neurons to carry information more efficiently. In fact, *demyelinating diseases,* such as multiple sclerosis, cause the myelin sheath to deteriorate, slowing communication from one neuron to another (Schwartz & Westbrook, 2000). This slowdown leads to a variety of problems, including loss of feeling in the limbs, partial blindness, and difficulties in coordinated movement and cognition (Butler et al., 2009).

Ramón y Cajal also observed that the dendrites and axons of neurons do not actually touch each other. There's a small gap between the axon of one neuron and the dendrites or cell body of another. This gap is part of the **synapse,** *the junction or region between the axon of one neuron and the dendrites or cell body of another* (see Figure 3.2). Many of the billions of neurons in your brain have a few thousand synaptic junctions, so it should come as no shock that adults have trillions of synapses. As you'll read shortly, the transmission of information across the synapse is fundamental to communication between neurons, a process that allows us to think, feel, and behave.

Neurons Specialized by Function

There are three major types of neurons, each performing a distinct function: sensory neurons, motor neurons, and interneurons.

- **Sensory neurons** *receive information from the external world and convey this information to the brain via the spinal cord*. They have specialized endings on their dendrites that receive signals for light, sound, touch, taste, and smell. For example, the endings of sensory neurons in our eyes are sensitive to light.

- **Motor neurons** *carry signals from the spinal cord to the muscles to produce movement*. These neurons often have long axons that reach to muscles at our extremities.

Neural impulse

Dendrites
Dendrites receive information from other neurons and relay it to the cell body.

Cell Body
The **cell body** coordinates the information-processing tasks and keeps the cell alive.

Terminal branches of the axon

Lying within the cell body, the *nucleus* houses chromosomes that contain DNA.

Axon
The **axon** carries information to other neurons, muscles, or glands.

Sending neuron

Receiving neuron

Vesicles

The *synapse* is the small gap between the axon of one neuron and the dendrites or cell body of another across which information is transmitted.

Receptor

Neurotransmitter

The *myelin sheath* is an insulating layer of fatty material composed of *glial cells.*

Figure 3.2
Components of a Neuron A neuron is made up of three parts: a cell body, dendrites, and an axon. Notice that neurons do not actually touch one another: There is a small synaptic space between them across which information is transmitted.

- **Interneurons** *connect sensory neurons, motor neurons, or other interneurons.* Most of the nervous system is composed of the interneurons. Some carry information from sensory neurons into the nervous system, while others carry information from the nervous system to motor neurons, and still others perform a variety of information-processing functions within the nervous system. Interneurons work together in small circuits to perform simple tasks, such as identifying the location of a sensory signal, and much more complicated ones, such as recognizing a familiar face.

interneurons Connect sensory neurons, motor neurons, or other interneurons.

Other Voices | **Neuromyths**

You've no doubt heard the phrase "We only use 10% of our brains," and perhaps you've wondered whether there is anything to it. Chabris and Simons (2012) discussed this and other statements about the brain that they believe to be merely myths, based in part on a contemporaneous study by Dekker et al. (2012).

Pop quiz: Which of these statements is false?

1. We use only 10% of our brain.
2. Environments rich in stimuli improve the brains of preschool children.
3. Individuals learn better when they receive information in their preferred learning style, whether auditory, visual, or kinesthetic.

If you picked the first one, congratulations. The idea that we use only 10% of our brain is patently false. Yet it so permeates popular culture that, among psychologists and neuroscientists, it is known as the "10% myth." Contrary to popular belief, the entire brain is put to use—unused neurons die and unused circuits atrophy. Reports of neuroimaging research might perpetuate the myth by showing only a small number of areas "lighting up" in a brain scan, but those are just areas that have more than a baseline level of activity; the dark regions aren't dormant or unused.

Did you agree with the other two statements? If so, you fell into our trap. All three statements are false—or at least not substantiated by scientific evidence. Unfortunately, if you got any of them wrong, you're hardly alone.

These "neuromyths," along with others, were presented to 242 primary and secondary school teachers in the Netherlands and the United Kingdom as part of a study by Sanne Dekker and colleagues at VU University Amsterdam and Bristol University. They found that 47% of the teachers believed the 10% myth. Even more, 76%, believed that enriching children's environments will strengthen their brains.

This belief might have emerged from evidence that rats raised in cages with amenities like exercise wheels, tunnels, and other rats showed better cognitive abilities and improvements in brain structure compared with rats that grew up isolated in bare cages. But such experiments show only that a truly impoverished and unnatural environment leads to poorer developmental outcomes than a more natural environment with opportunities to play and interact. It follows that growing up locked in a closet or otherwise cut off from human contact will impair a child's brain development. It does not follow that "enriching" a child's environment beyond what is already typical (e.g., by constant exposure to "Baby Einstein"–type videos) will boost cognitive development.

The myth about learning styles was the most popular: 94% of the teachers believed that students perform better when lessons are delivered in their preferred learning style. Indeed, students do have preferences about how they learn; the problem is that these preferences have little to do with how effectively they learn . . .

Our own surveys of the U.S. population have found even more widespread belief in myths about the brain. About two-thirds of the public agreed with the 10% myth. Many also believed that memory works like a video recording or that they can tell when someone is staring at the back of their head.

Christopher Chabris (*left*) is a professor and co-director at the Behavioural and Decision Sciences Program, Geisinger Health System. Daniel Simons (*right*) is a professor of psychology at the University of Illinois. Chabris and Simons coauthored *The Invisible Gorilla: And Other Ways Our Intuitions Deceive Us* (2010).

Ironically, in the Dekker group's study, the teachers who knew the most about neuroscience also believed in the most myths. Apparently, teachers who are (admirably) enthusiastic about expanding their knowledge of the mind and brain have trouble separating fact from fiction as they learn. Neuromyths have so much intuitive appeal, and they spread so rapidly in fields like business and self-help, that eradicating them from popular consciousness might be a Sisyphean task. But reducing their influence in the classroom would be a good start.

If for some perverse reason you wanted to annoy the instructor of your psychology course, you probably could do no better than to claim that "we use only 10% of our brains." Even though, as pointed out by Chabris and Simons (2012), a surprisingly high proportion of elementary and secondary schoolteachers in the Netherlands and the United Kingdom subscribe to this myth, we don't know any psychologists teaching courses like the one you are taking who would endorse it, and we hope that there aren't any. How did the myth get started? Nobody really knows. Some think it may have arisen from a quotation by the great psychologist William James ("We are making use of only a small part of our possible mental and physical resources") or that it possibly arises from Albert Einstein's attempt to make sense of his own massive intellect (Boyd, 2008).

The key point for our purposes is that when you hear such bold claims from, say, a friend who heard it from somebody else, it's time for you to put into action the kinds of critical thinking skills that we focus on in this text and start asking questions: What's the evidence for the claim? Is there a specific study or studies that your friend can name to provide evidence in support of the claim? Are any such studies published in peer-reviewed scientific journals? What kind of sample was used in the study? Is the sample large enough to support a clear conclusion? Has the finding been replicated? Tall tales such as the 10% myth don't stand much chance of surviving for long if claims for their existence are met head on with critical thinking.

Christopher Chabris and Daniel Simons, "Using Just 10% of Your Brain? Think Again" *Wall Street Journal*, November 16, 2012. Reprinted by permission of the authors.

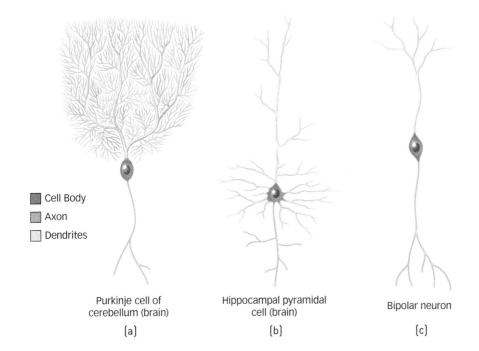

■ Cell Body
■ Axon
□ Dendrites

Purkinje cell of
cerebellum (brain)

(a)

Hippocampal pyramidal
cell (brain)

(b)

Bipolar neuron

(c)

Figure 3.3
Neurons Specialized by Location
Neurons have a cell body, an axon, and at least one dendrite. The size and shape of neurons vary considerably, however. The Purkinje cell has an elaborate treelike assemblage of dendrites (*a*). Pyramidal cells have a triangular cell body and a single, long dendrite with many smaller dendrites (*b*). Bipolar cells have only one dendrite and a single axon (*c*).

Neurons Specialized by Location

Besides specialization for sensory, motor, or connective functions, neurons are also somewhat specialized depending on their location (see **FIGURE 3.3**). For example, *Purkinje cells* are a type of interneuron that carries information from the cerebellum to the rest of the brain and the spinal cord. These neurons have dense, elaborate dendrites that resemble bushes. *Pyramidal cells,* found in the cerebral cortex, have a triangular cell body and a single, long dendrite among many smaller dendrites. *Bipolar cells,* a type of sensory neuron found in the retinas of the eye, have a single axon and a single dendrite. The brain processes different types of information, so a substantial amount of specialization at the cellular level has evolved to handle these tasks.

The Electrochemical Actions of Neurons: Information Processing

Our thoughts, feelings, and actions depend on neural communication. Neurons use both electrical and chemical signals to communicate. First, an electric signal is *conducted* inside the neuron, from the dendrites to the cell body, and then down the axon. Second, a chemical signal is *transmitted* from one neuron to another, across the synapse. Together, these stages are what scientists generally refer to as the *electrochemical action* of neurons. Let's look at each stage in more detail.

Electric Signaling: Conducting Information Inside a Neuron

The neuron's cell membrane has small pores that act as channels to allow *ions* to flow into and out of the cell. Ions are atoms or molecules that carry a small positive (+) or negative (−) electric charge. The flow of ions across the neuron's cell membrane creates the conduction of electric current within the neuron. How does it happen?

Learning Outcomes

WHAT YOU NEED TO KNOW

- Describe how an electric signal moves down an axon.

- Outline the steps in synaptic transmission.

- Explain how drugs are able to mimic neurotransmitters.

resting potential The difference in electric charge between the inside and outside of a neuron's cell membrane.

action potential An electric signal that is conducted along the length of a neuron's axon to a synapse.

The Resting Potential: The Origin of the Neuron's Electrical Properties

Normally (when a neuron is "at rest"), some ions, such as positively charged potassium ions (K^+) and negatively charged protein ions (A^-), are more abundant *inside* the neuron than outside in the fluid-filled space between neurons (see **FIGURE 3.4a**). Other ions, such as positively charged sodium ions (Na^+), are more abundant *outside* the neuron. The net result is that the inside of the neuron has a slight negative electric charge, relative to the outside. This small imbalance is known as the **resting potential,** *the difference in electric charge between the inside and outside of a neuron's cell membrane.* The resting potential, discovered by biologists working with the squid giant axon in the 1930s, is usually about −70 millivolts. By comparison, a typical AA battery has about 1.5 volts (1,500 millivolts).

One reason for the difference in concentrations of ions inside and outside the neuron's cell membrane is that special channels in the cell membrane restrict the movement of the ions in and out of the cell. But, like the floodgates of a dam, which hold back a river until they are released, these channels in the cell membrane can be opened, allowing ions to rush across the membrane in a fraction of a second.

The Action Potential: Sending Signals Across the Neuron

The biologists working with the squid giant axon noticed something strange. When they stimulated the axon with an electric shock, it set off a much larger electrical impulse, a spike in voltage that travelled down the axon in a wave without losing any intensity along the way (Häusser, 2000; Hodgkin & Huxley, 1939). This electric impulse is called an **action potential,** *an electric signal that is conducted along the length of a neuron's axon to a synapse.* The action potential isn't just some curious

Figure 3.4
The Resting and Action Potentials Neurons have a natural electric charge called a resting potential. Electric stimulation causes an action potential.

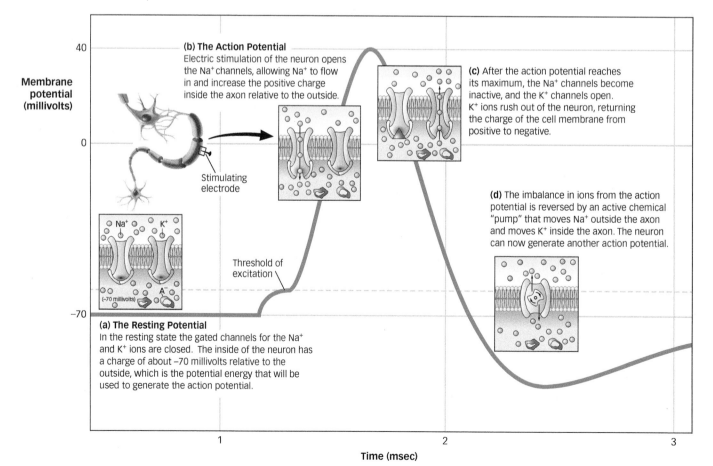

feature of the squid giant axon — it is a fundamental basis for just about everything that we think, feel, or do, and so it is important to understand how it works.

The action potential occurred only when the electric shock reached a certain level, or *threshold*. Above that threshold, increases in the electric shock did *not* increase the strength of the action potential. The action potential is *all or none*: Electric stimulation below the threshold fails to produce an action potential, whereas electric stimulation at or above the threshold always produces the action potential and always at the same strength. Because of the rapid, all-or-nothing nature of an action potential, scientists sometimes say that a neuron "fires" when it produces an action potential. (By way of analogy, a revolver ejects one bullet at a constant velocity whenever the trigger is pulled with sufficient force. Pulling on the trigger with sufficient force causes the revolver to fire — but, beyond that point, extra force on the trigger will not cause the bullet to be ejected more forcefully or at greater speed; the firing event is all-or-nothing.)

The Action Potential Moves Across the Neuron in a Domino Effect The action potential occurs due to changes in the axon's membrane channels. During the resting potential, the membrane channels for sodium ions are closed. However, when the electrical charge across the cell membrane reaches the threshold, sodium channels in that area of the cell membrane open up like the floodgate of a dam, and Na^+ ions rush in almost instantaneously (see Figure 3.4b). This inrush of positively charged ions causes the local electric charge to surge from −70 millivolts to +40 millivolts in less than one millisecond.

And this starts a domino effect. As the first Na^+ ions rush in, they spread inside the cell, increasing the electric charge in neighbouring areas too. When the electric charge in those areas reaches the threshold, channels in the adjacent cell membrane open and let in more Na^+ ions, spreading the charge even farther. Just as one domino knocks over another, the influx of Na^+ ions triggers nearby channels to open, and the process repeats down the entire axon.

In many neurons, the conduction of the action potential is greatly increased by the presence of a myelin sheath around the axon. The myelin sheath prevents electric current from leaking out of the axon, in much the same way as insulation covers the wires on a power cord to keep the electric current from leaking out. But unlike the insulation on a power cord, myelin doesn't cover the entire axon; rather, it clumps around the axon with little break points between clumps, looking kind of like sausage links. These breakpoints are called the *nodes of Ranvier*, after the French pathologist Louis-Antoine Ranvier, who discovered them (see **FIGURE 3.5**). The current seems to "jump" quickly from node to node (Poliak & Peles, 2003). This process is called *saltatory conduction* (*saltare* is Latin for "hop" or "leap"), and it helps speed the flow of information down the axon.

The action potential always spreads onward, never backward, because the Na^+ channels in each region of the axon are temporarily inactivated after the action potential passes over them, just as a domino that has already been knocked over cannot be knocked over twice. This brief period of inactivation is called a **refractory period,** *the time following an action potential during which a new action potential cannot be*

AGE FOTOSTOCK/GETTY IMAGES

The British biologists Alan Hodgkin and Andrew Huxley discovered the resting potential in the summer of 1939 while studying marine invertebrates — sea creatures that lack a spine, such as clams, squid, and lobsters (Stevens, 1971). Hodgkin and Huxley worked with the squid giant axon because it is 100 times larger than the biggest axon in humans. They inserted a thin wire into the squid axon so that it touched the jellylike fluid inside. Then they placed another wire just outside the axon in the watery fluid that surrounds it. They found a substantial difference between the electric charges inside and outside the axon, which they called the resting potential.

refractory period The time following an action potential during which a new action potential cannot be initiated.

Axon

Nodes of Ranvier

Myelin

Figure 3.5
Myelin and Nodes of Ranvier Myelin is formed by a type of glial cell. It wraps around a neuron's axon to speed the movement of the action potential along the length of the axon. Breaks in the myelin sheath are called the nodes of Ranvier. The electric impulse jumps from node to node, thereby speeding the conduction of information down the axon.

terminal buttons Knoblike structures that branch out from an axon.

neurotransmitters Chemicals that transmit information across the synapse to a receiving neuron's dendrites.

receptors Parts of the cell membrane that receive the neurotransmitter and either initiate or prevent a new electric signal.

initiated. During the refractory period, the electrical and chemical balance of the neuron is restored. To restore the electrical balance, Na^+ channels inactivate themselves for several milliseconds, stopping the inrush of Na^+ ions, and K^+ channels open, allowing excess K^+ ions in the cell to escape (see Figure 3.4c). The rapid exit of positively charged K^+ ions returns the electrical charge of the membrane to a negative state. Then, to restore the chemical balance, a series of special channels, called ion pumps, work to redistribute the ions (e.g., pushing all that excess Na^+ back out of the cell and pulling some K^+ back in), until the concentrations are rebalanced and the resting potential is restored (see Figure 3.4d). At this point, the dominoes are set back up—and ready to be knocked over again if triggered. The entire process is so fast that some neurons fire more than 100 times in a single second.

Chemical Signaling: Transmission Between Neurons

When the action potential reaches the end of an axon, you might think that it stops there. After all, the synaptic space between neurons means that the axon of one neuron and the neighbouring neuron's dendrites do not actually touch one another. However, the electric action potential takes a form that crosses the synaptic gap by relying on a bit of chemistry.

Although a neuron has only one axon, the axon may have hundreds or even thousands of branches that reach out to other neurons and organs. Axons usually end in **terminal buttons,** *knoblike structures that branch out from an axon.* Each terminal button is filled with tiny *vesicles* or bags that contain **neurotransmitters,** *chemicals that transmit information across the synapse to a receiving neuron's dendrites.* The dendrites of the receiving neuron contain **receptors,** *parts of the cell membrane that receive the neurotransmitter and either initiate or prevent a new electric signal.*

The action potential in the sending neuron, or *presynaptic neuron,* travels down the length of the axon to the terminal buttons, where it stimulates the release of neurotransmitters from vesicles into the synapses. The neurotransmitters quickly float across the synapse and bind to receptor sites on the nearby dendrite of the receiving neuron, or *postsynaptic neuron.* The sending and receiving of chemical neurotransmitters is called *synaptic transmission* (see **FIGURE 3.6**), and it ultimately underlies your thoughts, emotions, and behaviour. When the postsynaptic neuron receives a neurotransmitter, it may activate nearby ion channels, which can either raise or lower the voltage across the membrane. Depending on the combination and timing of the neurotransmitters acting on the neuron, the voltage inside the cell body membrane may reach the threshold and trigger a new action potential. In this way, the neurotransmitters' chemical messages create an electrical signal, and the electrochemical process of neuronal communication continues.

Now that you understand the basic process of how information moves from one neuron to another, let's refine things a bit. If a given neuron makes a few thousand synaptic connections with other neurons, what tells the dendrites which of the neurotransmitters flooding into the synapse they should receive? First, neurons tend to form pathways in the brain that are characterized by specific types of neurotransmitters;

Figure 3.6
Synaptic Transmission (1) The action potential travels down the axon and (2) stimulates the release of neurotransmitters from vesicles. (3) The neurotransmitters are released into the synapse, where they float to bind with receptor sites on a dendrite of a postsynaptic neuron, initiating a new action potential. The neurotransmitters are cleared out of the synapse by (4) reuptake into the sending neuron, (5) being broken down by enzymes in the synapse, or (6) diffusion away from the synapse. (7) Neurotransmitters bind to autoreceptors on the sending neuron, stopping the release of more neurotransmitters.

one neurotransmitter might be prevalent in one part of the brain, whereas a different neurotransmitter might be prevalent in a different part of the brain.

Second, neurotransmitters and receptor sites act like a lock-and-key system. Just as a particular key will fit only in a particular lock, so too will only some neurotransmitters bind to specific receptor sites on a dendrite. The molecular structure of the neurotransmitter must fit the molecular structure of the receptor site.

Another question is: What happens to the neurotransmitters left in the synapse after the chemical message is relayed to the postsynaptic neuron? Something must make neurotransmitters stop acting on neurons; otherwise, there would be no end to the signals that they send. Neurotransmitters leave the synapse through three processes (see Figure 3.6). First, *reuptake* occurs when neurotransmitters are absorbed by the terminal buttons of the presynaptic neuron's axon or by neighbouring glial cells. Second, neurotransmitters can be destroyed by enzymes in the synapse in a process called *enzyme deactivation,* in which specific enzymes break down specific neurotransmitters. Third, *diffusion* occurs when neurotransmitters drift out of the synapse and can no longer reach receptors.

Neurotransmitters can also bind to receptor sites on the presynaptic neuron called *autoreceptors.* Autoreceptors detect how much of a neurotransmitter has been released into a synapse and may stop the release of more.

Types and Functions of Neurotransmitters

Given the important role of neurotransmitters, you might wonder how many types of neurotransmitters are floating across synapses in your brain right now. Today, we know that more than 100 chemicals play a role in transmitting information throughout the brain and body and affect thought, feeling, and behaviour in different ways. Simple actions such as waving hello, enjoying a bite of ice cream, or falling asleep involve the combined action of many different types of neurotransmitters flowing across synapses in different parts of the nervous system. Researchers have identified a few major classes of neurotransmitters that are most common in the nervous system and play key roles in certain fundamental behaviours. We'll summarize those here, and you'll encounter some of these neurotransmitters again in later chapters.

- **Acetylcholine (ACh)** is *a neurotransmitter involved in a number of functions, including voluntary motor control.* Acetylcholine is found in neurons of the brain and in the synapses where axons connect to muscles and body organs, such as the heart. Acetylcholine activates muscle movements, and it also contributes to the regulation of attention, learning, sleeping, dreaming, and memory (Gais & Born, 2004; Hasselmo, 2006; Wrenn et al., 2006). Alzheimer's disease, a medical condition involving severe memory impairments (Salmon & Bondi, 2009), is associated with the deterioration of ACh-producing neurons.

- **Dopamine** is *a neurotransmitter that regulates motor behaviour, motivation, pleasure, and emotional arousal.* Because of its role in basic motivated behaviours, such as seeking pleasure or associating actions with rewards, dopamine plays a role in drug addiction (Baler & Volkow, 2006). High levels of dopamine in some brain pathways are linked to schizophrenia (Winterer & Weinberger, 2004), whereas low levels in other areas are linked to Parkinson's disease.

- **Glutamate** is the *major excitatory neurotransmitter in the brain,* meaning that it enhances the transmission of information between neurons. **GABA (gamma-aminobutyric acid),** in contrast, is *the primary inhibitory neurotransmitter in the brain,* meaning that it tends to prevent the firing of neurons. Too much glutamate, or too little GABA, can cause neurons to become overactive, causing seizures.

- Two related neurotransmitters influence mood and arousal: norepinephrine and serotonin. **Norepinephrine** is *involved in states of vigilance, or*

acetylcholine (ACh) A neurotransmitter involved in a number of functions, including voluntary motor control.

dopamine A neurotransmitter that regulates motor behaviour, motivation, pleasure, and emotional arousal.

glutamate The major excitatory neurotransmitter in the brain.

GABA (gamma-aminobutyric acid) The primary inhibitory neurotransmitter in the brain.

norepinephrine Involved in states of vigilance or heightened awareness of dangers in the environment.

SAM BARNES/GETTY IMAGES

When long-distance runners complete a marathon, they may experience the subjective highs that result from the release of endorphins—chemical messengers acting in emotion and pain centres that elevate mood and dull the experience of pain.

heightened awareness of dangers in the environment (Ressler & Nemeroff, 1999). **Serotonin** is *involved in the regulation of sleep and wakefulness, eating, and aggressive behaviour* (Dayan & Huys, 2009; Kroeze & Roth, 1998). Because both neurotransmitters affect mood and arousal, low levels of each have been implicated in mood disorders such as depression (Tamminga et al., 2002).

- **Endorphins** *are chemicals that act within the pain pathways and emotion centres of the brain* (Keefe et al., 2001). The term *endorphin* is a contraction of *endogenous morphine,* which is a pretty apt description. Morphine is a drug that has an intensely pleasurable and pain-relieving effect; an endorphin is an internally produced substance that has similar but less intense properties, such as dulling the experience of pain and elevating moods. The "runner's high" experienced by many athletes as they push their bodies to painful limits of endurance can be explained by the release of endorphins in the brain (Boecker et al., 2008).

Each of these neurotransmitters affects thought, feeling, and behaviour in different ways, so typical functioning involves a delicate balance of each. Even a slight imbalance—too much of one neurotransmitter or not enough of another—can dramatically affect behaviour. These imbalances can occur naturally: Sometimes the brain doesn't produce enough serotonin, for example, which contributes to depressed or anxious moods. Other times a person may actively seek to cause imbalances. People who smoke, drink alcohol, or take drugs (legal or not) are altering the balance of neurotransmitters in their brains. The drug LSD, for example, is structurally similar to serotonin, so it binds easily with serotonin receptors in the brain, producing similar effects. In the next section, we'll look at how some drugs are able to "trick" receptor sites in just this way.

How Drugs Mimic Neurotransmitters

Many drugs that affect the nervous system operate by increasing, interfering with, or mimicking the manufacture or function of neurotransmitters (Cooper et al., 2003; Sarter, 2006). **Agonists** are *drugs that increase the action of a neurotransmitter.* **Antagonists** are *drugs that diminish the function of a neurotransmitter.* If, by binding to a receptor, a drug activates the neurotransmitter, it is an agonist; if it prevents the neurotransmitter from acting or lessens its effect, it is an antagonist (see **FIGURE 3.7**).

Some drugs alter a step in the production or release of the neurotransmitter, whereas others have a chemical structure so similar to a neurotransmitter that the drug is able to bind to that neuron's receptor. For example, the drug L-dopa, which is made from dopamine, is used to treat Parkinson's disease, a movement disorder characterized by tremors and difficulty initiating movement. Public awareness of Parkinson's disease and L-dopa increased during the 1980s and 1990s when celebrities such as the late American boxer Muhammad Ali and the Canadian actor Michael J. Fox were diagnosed with the condition. Fox, who takes L-dopa, described in his memoir the simple act of trying to brush his teeth:

Grasping the toothpaste is nothing compared to the effort it takes to coordinate the two-handed task of wrangling the toothbrush and strangling out a line of paste onto the bristles. By now, my right hand has started up again, rotating at the wrist in a circular motion, perfect for what I'm about to do. My left hand guides my right hand up to my mouth, and once the back of the Oral-B touches the inside of my upper lip, I let go. It's like releasing the tension on a slingshot and compares favorably to the most powerful state-of-the-art electric toothbrush on the market. With no off switch, stopping means seizing my right wrist with my left hand, forcing it down to the sink basin, and shaking the brush loose as though disarming a knife-wielding attacker. (Fox, 2009, pp. 2–3)

Parkinson's disease is caused by the loss of neurons that make the neurotransmitter dopamine by modifying L-dopa produced naturally in the body. Ingesting L-dopa as

serotonin Involved in the regulation of sleep and wakefulness, eating, and aggressive behaviour.

endorphins Chemicals that act within the pain pathways and emotion centres of the brain.

agonists Drugs that increase the action of a neurotransmitter.

antagonists Drugs that diminish the function of a neurotransmitter.

Agonists increase the action of a neurotransmitter.

Drugs such as clonidine bind to autoreceptors and block their inhibitory effect

Autoreceptor

Neurotransmitters

Drugs such as L-dopa increase production of neurotransmitters

Vesicle

Drug molecule

Action potential

Receptor sites

Drugs such as amphetamines increase release of neurotransmitters

Drugs such as Prozac block the reuptake of neurotransmitters

Drugs such as nicotine bind to postsynaptic receptor sites and activate them or increase the neurotransmitter effect

Antagonists block the function of a neurotransmitter.

Drugs such as caffeine activate autoreceptors so they inhibit release of neurotransmitters

Autoreceptor

Neurotransmitters

Vesicle

Drug molecule

Action potential

Receptor sites

Drugs such as botulinum toxin block release of neurotransmitters

Drugs such as AMPT block production of neurotransmitters

Drugs such as naloxone bind to receptor sites and block neurotransmitters

a drug elevates its concentration in the brain and spurs the surviving neurons to produce more dopamine. In other words, L-dopa acts as an agonist for dopamine by increasing its production. The use of L-dopa has been reasonably successful in the alleviation of Parkinson's disease symptoms (Muenter & Tyce, 1971; Schapira et al., 2009). However, its effectiveness typically decreases when used over a long period of time, so many longtime users experience some symptoms of the disease. However, new treatments for the disease are becoming available.

Many other drugs, including drugs sold illegally on the street, alter the actions of neurotransmitters. *Amphetamine* is a popular drug that stimulates the release of norepinephrine and dopamine and also blocks their reuptake. This combination creates an excess of neurotransmitters that flood the synapse, activating their receptors over and over. *Cocaine* is another drug that acts by preventing the reuptake of neurotransmitters. Both of these drugs therefore are agonists, although their psychological effects differ because of where and how each acts on the brain. Norepinephrine and dopamine play a critical role in mood control, such that an increase in either neurotransmitter results in euphoria, wakefulness, and a burst of energy. However, norepinephrine also increases heart rate. An overdose of amphetamine or cocaine can cause the heart to contract so rapidly that heartbeats do not last long enough to pump blood effectively, leading to fainting and sometimes death.

Opioids are a class of chemically similar drugs either derived naturally from the opium poppy (such as morphine and heroin) or made synthetically (such as oxycodone, hydrocodone, and fentanyl). Most opioids work in part by acting as agonists for endorphins, which creates powerful feelings of calm and euphoria. Opioids have been widely prescribed for pain relief because they are also highly effective antagonists that decrease the release of neurotransmitters involved in the perception of pain. At the same time, opioids also diminish the brainstem's sensitivity to rising

Figure 3.7

The Actions of Agonist and Antagonist Drugs Agonist and antagonist drugs can enhance or interfere with synaptic transmission at every point in the process: in the production of neurotransmitters, in the release of neurotransmitters, at the autoreceptors, in reuptake, in the postsynaptic receptors, and in the synapse itself.

Muhammad Ali and Michael J. Fox have increased public awareness of Parkinson's disease and spurred greater efforts towards finding a cure.

levels of carbon dioxide in the blood, which depresses breathing. In the case of an overdose, this can lead to asphyxiation and death.

These properties, as well as the availability of opioids both as pharmaceuticals and street drugs, have raised opioid addiction to the level of a public health crisis in many parts of Canada. According to the Public Health Agency of Canada, opioid overdose claimed the lives of 19 Canadians a day in the first six months of 2021, and more than 25,000 Canadians have died from overdosing since 2016 (PHAC, 2021). One widespread response is to equip first responders with the drug naloxone, the active ingredient in the nasal spray Narcan. Technically, naloxone is also an opioid but one that acts as an antagonist: It binds with opioid receptors, blocking agonists like heroin and preventing their effects on neurons.

Prozac, a drug commonly used to treat depression, is another example of a neurotransmitter agonist. Prozac blocks the reuptake of the neurotransmitter *serotonin*, making it part of a category of drugs called *selective serotonin reuptake inhibitors,* or *SSRIs* (Wong et al., 1995). People suffering from clinical depression typically have reduced levels of serotonin in their brains. By blocking reuptake, more of the neurotransmitter remains in the synapse longer and produces greater activation of serotonin receptors. Serotonin elevates mood, which can help relieve depression (Mann, 2005).

An antagonist with important medical implications is a drug called *propanolol,* one of a class of drugs called *beta blockers*. These drugs obstruct receptor sites in the heart for norepinephrine, a neurotransmitter that increases one's heartbeat. Because norepinephrine cannot bind to these receptors, the heart rate slows down, which is helpful for disorders in which the heart beats too fast or irregularly. Beta blockers are also prescribed to reduce the agitation, racing heart, and nervousness associated with stage fright (Mills & Dimsdale, 1991). (For additional discussion of antianxiety and antidepression drug treatments, see the Treatment of Psychological Disorders chapter.)

The Organization of the Nervous System

Learning Outcomes

WHAT YOU NEED TO KNOW

- Differentiate the functions of the central and peripheral nervous systems.

- Understand the nature of the reflex arc.

- Demonstrate the hierarchical structure of the central nervous system.

nervous system An interacting network of neurons that conveys electrochemical information throughout the body.

central nervous system (CNS) Composed of the brain and spinal cord.

We've seen how individual neurons communicate with each other. What's the bigger picture? Neurons work by forming circuits and pathways in the brain, which in turn influence circuits and pathways in other areas of the body. Without this kind of organization and delegation, neurons would be churning away with little purpose. The **nervous system** is *an interacting network of neurons that conveys electrochemical information throughout the body*. In this section, we'll look at the major divisions and components of the nervous system.

Divisions of the Nervous System

There are two major divisions of the nervous system: the central nervous system and the peripheral nervous system (see **FIGURE 3.8**). The **central nervous system (CNS)** is *composed of the brain and spinal cord*. It receives sensory information from the external world, processes and coordinates this information, and sends commands to the skeletal and muscular systems for action. At the top of the CNS rests the brain, which contains structures that support the most complex perceptual, motor, emotional, and cognitive functions of the nervous system. The spinal cord branches down from the brain; nerves that process sensory information and relay commands to the body connect to the spinal cord.

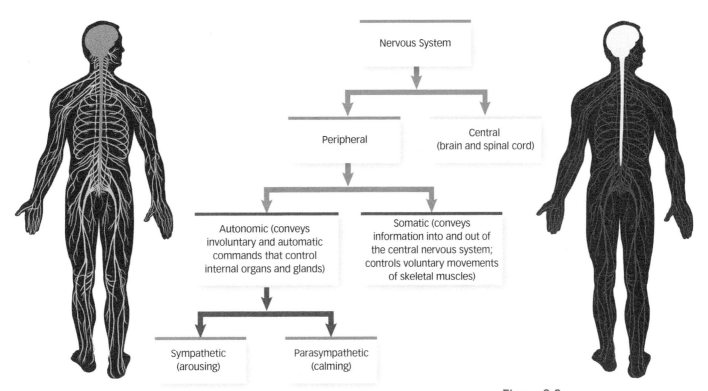

Figure 3.8
The Human Nervous System The nervous system is organized into the peripheral and central nervous systems. The peripheral nervous system is further divided into the autonomic and somatic nervous systems.

The **peripheral nervous system (PNS)** *connects the central nervous system to the body's organs and muscles.* The peripheral nervous system is itself composed of two major subdivisions, the somatic nervous system and the autonomic nervous system. The **somatic nervous system** is *a set of nerves that conveys information between skeletal muscles and the central nervous system.* Humans have conscious control over this system and use it to perceive, think, and coordinate their behaviours. For example, reaching for your morning cup of coffee involves the elegantly orchestrated activities of the somatic nervous system: Information from the receptors in your eyes travels to your brain, registering that a cup is on the table; signals from your brain travel to the muscles in your arm and hand; feedback from those muscles tells your brain that the cup has been grasped, and so on.

In contrast, the **autonomic nervous system (ANS)** is *a set of nerves that carries involuntary and automatic commands that control blood vessels, body organs, and glands.* As suggested by its name, this system works on its own to regulate bodily systems, largely outside of conscious control. The ANS has two major subdivisions, the sympathetic nervous system and the parasympathetic nervous system. Each exerts a different type of control on the body. The **sympathetic nervous system** is *a set of nerves that prepares the body for action in challenging or threatening situations* (see **FIGURE 3.9**). For example, imagine that you are walking alone late at night and are frightened by footsteps behind you in a dark alley. Your sympathetic nervous system kicks into action at this point: It dilates your pupils to let in more light, increases your heart rate and respiration to pump more oxygen to your muscles, diverts blood flow to your brain and muscles, and activates sweat glands to cool your body. To conserve energy, the sympathetic nervous system inhibits salivation and bowel movements, suppresses the body's immune responses, and suppresses responses to pain and injury. The sum total of these fast, automatic responses is that they increase the likelihood that you can escape.

The **parasympathetic nervous system** *helps the body return to a normal resting state.* When you're far away from your would-be attacker, your body doesn't need to remain on red alert. Now the parasympathetic nervous system kicks in to reverse the effects of the sympathetic nervous system and return your body to its normal state.

peripheral nervous system (PNS) Connects the central nervous system to the body's organs and muscles.

somatic nervous system A set of nerves that conveys information between skeletal muscles and the central nervous system.

autonomic nervous system (ANS) A set of nerves that carries involuntary and automatic commands that control blood vessels, body organs, and glands.

sympathetic nervous system A set of nerves that prepares the body for action in challenging or threatening situations.

parasympathetic nervous system Helps the body return to a normal resting state.

Figure 3.9
Sympathetic and Parasympathetic Systems The autonomic nervous system is composed of two subsystems that complement each other. Activation of the sympathetic system serves several aspects of arousal, whereas the parasympathetic nervous system returns the body to its normal resting state.

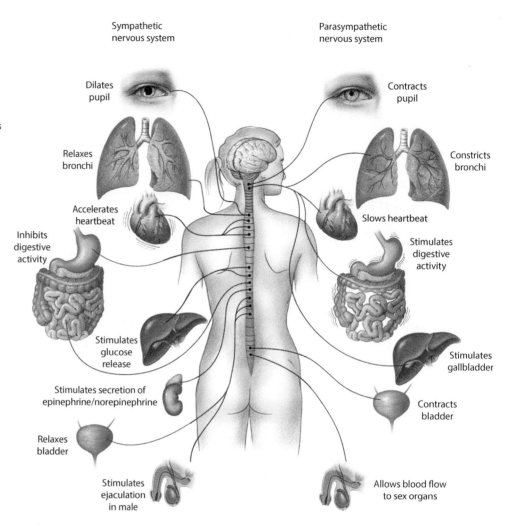

The parasympathetic nervous system generally mirrors the connections of the sympathetic nervous system. For instance, the parasympathetic nervous system constricts your pupils, slows your heart rate and respiration, diverts blood flow to your digestive system, and decreases activity in your sweat glands.

As you might imagine, the sympathetic and parasympathetic nervous systems coordinate to control many bodily functions. One example is sexual behaviour. In men, the parasympathetic nervous system engorges the blood vessels of the penis to produce an erection, but the sympathetic nervous system is responsible for ejaculation. In women, the parasympathetic nervous system produces vaginal lubrication, but the sympathetic nervous system underlies orgasm. In both men and women, a successful sexual experience depends on a delicate balance of these two systems; in fact, anxiety about sexual performance can disrupt this balance. For instance, sympathetic nervous system activation caused by anxiety can lead to premature ejaculation in males and lack of lubrication in females.

Components of the Central Nervous System

Compared with the many divisions of the peripheral nervous system, the central nervous system may seem simple. After all, it has only two elements: the brain and the spinal cord. But those two elements are ultimately responsible for most of what we do as humans.

The spinal cord often seems like the brain's poor relation: The brain gets all the glory, and the spinal cord just hangs around, doing relatively simple tasks. Those tasks, however, are pretty important: They keep you breathing, respond to pain, and

spinal reflexes Simple pathways in the nervous system that rapidly generate muscle contractions.

reflex arc A neural pathway that controls reflex actions.

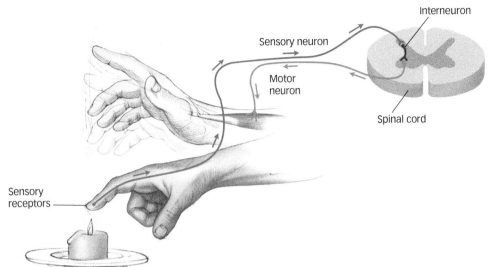

Figure 3.10

The Pain Withdrawal Reflex Many actions of the central nervous system don't require the brain's input. For example, withdrawing from pain is a reflexive activity controlled by the spinal cord. Painful sensations (such as the heat of fire) travel directly to the spinal cord via sensory neurons, which then issue an immediate command to motor neurons to retract the hand.

move your muscles, allowing you to walk. What's more, without the spinal cord, the brain would not be able to put any of its higher processing into action.

Do you need your brain to tell you to pull your hand away from a hot stove? For some very basic behaviours such as this, the spinal cord doesn't need input from the brain at all. Connections between the sensory inputs and motor neurons in the spinal cord mediate **spinal reflexes,** *simple pathways in the nervous system that rapidly generate muscle contractions*. If you touch a hot stove, the sensory neurons that register pain send inputs directly into the spinal cord (see **FIGURE 3.10**). Through just a few synaptic connections within the spinal cord, interneurons relay these sensory inputs to motor neurons that connect to your arm muscles and direct you to quickly retract your hand. These spinal reflexes illustrate the operation of a **reflex arc,** *a neural pathway that controls reflex actions*. Reflex arcs can include sensory neurons, interneurons, and motor neurons, but some simple reflex arcs are comprised of only sensory and motor neurons.

Beyond reflexes, more elaborate tasks require the collaboration of the spinal cord and the brain. The peripheral nervous system sends messages from sensory neurons through the spinal cord into the brain. The brain sends commands for voluntary movement through the spinal cord to motor neurons, whose axons project out to skeletal muscles. Damage to the spinal cord severs the connection from the brain to the sensory and motor neurons that are essential to sensory perception and movement. The location of the spinal injury often determines the extent of the abilities that are lost. As you can see in **FIGURE 3.11**, different regions of the spinal cord control different systems of the body. Individuals with damage at a particular level of the spinal cord lose sensations of touch and pain in body parts below the level of the injury, as well as a loss of motor control of the muscles in the same areas. A spinal injury higher up the cord usually predicts a much poorer prognosis, such as quadriplegia (loss of sensation and motor control over all limbs), breathing through a respirator, and lifelong immobility.

The late actor Christopher Reeve, who starred as Superman in four *Superman* movies, damaged his spinal cord in a horseback riding accident in 1995, resulting in loss of sensation and motor control in all of his body parts below the neck. Despite great efforts over several years, Reeve made only modest gains in his motor control and sensation, highlighting the extent to which we depend on communication from the brain through the spinal cord to the body, and showing how difficult it is to compensate for the loss of these connections (Edgerton et al., 2004). Unfortunately, Christopher Reeve died at age 52 in 2004 from complications due to his paralysis. On a brighter note, researchers are making progress in understanding the nature of spinal cord injuries and how to treat them by focusing on how the brain changes in response to injury (Blesch & Tuszynski, 2009; Dunlop, 2008), a process that is

Figure 3.11

Regions of the Spinal Cord The spinal cord is divided into four main sections; each controls different parts of the body. Damage higher on the spinal cord usually means greater impairment.

closely related to the concept of brain plasticity that we will examine later in this chapter. Progress in constructing brain–machine interfaces could also improve the lives of people who have suffered paralysis from spinal cord injuries (see The Real World: The Power of Thought: Brain–Computer Interfaces).

The Real World | The Power of Thought: Brain–Computer Interfaces

In the wildly popular James Cameron movie *Avatar*, the paraplegic marine Jake Sully's brain is able to control, via computer, the actions of an avatar body. Though this scenario is seemingly far-fetched, scientists recently have been taking steps to bring this type of science-fiction fantasy closer to reality.

Experiments with monkeys provided initial evidence that the brain can control mechanical devices through thoughts alone (Carmena et al., 2003). The researchers implanted multiple wires into the monkeys' motor cortices and trained them to obtain a juice reward by moving a joystick that controlled a cursor on a computer screen. Using the activity patterns of many neurons, they created a computer model of the neural activity that corresponded to different directions of joystick movements. Then they disconnected the joystick from the computer and instead connected directly to the computer the signals that their model extracted from the monkey's motor cortex activity. With just a few days of practice, the monkeys learned to adjust their motor cortex activity patterns to hit the targets successfully. In effect, the monkeys were controlling the cursor with their thoughts.

These findings raised the possibility that cortical recordings and state-of-the-art computer programs could be developed into a kind of neuroprosthesis to help people with brain or spinal injuries that have left them paralyzed. Mounting evidence from studies using brain–computer interfaces (BCIs) supports this idea. For example, Hochberg et al. (2012) studied a 58-year-old woman and a 66-year-old man who had suffered strokes to the brainstem that produced quadriplegia: paralysis resulting in the loss of use of all limbs. They examined whether the patients could use a BCI to control a robotic arm for performing reaching and grasping movements. In order to guide movement, the researchers sent the robotic arm signals

that were decoded by a computer program from a small population of neurons in each individual's motor cortex. The participants' task was to reach for and grasp purple spheres that were elevated above a table. Both participants were able to perform the task with relatively high levels of accuracy and speed, though they were not as accurate or as fast as able-bodied participants. Using signals decoded from her motor cortex, the female patient was even able to use the robotic arm to drink her coffee! Researchers have continued to develop new ways to improve the accuracy with which BCIs can guide a robotic arm (Iturrate et al., 2015).

More recently, Willett et al. (2021) asked whether the same type of approach could work for handwriting, which involves a much more rapid sequence of movements than in previous BCI studies. The researchers tested a 65-year-old tetraplegic man, referred to as T5, who had two BCI chips, each containing about 100 electrodes, surgically implanted in his left motor cortex. To train the BCI, Willett and colleagues had T5 "write" letters on a computer screen by imagining writing them with a pen on imaginary paper while they recorded neural signals in T5's left motor cortex. This training enabled the BCI to learn which neural signals were associated with which letters. After training, T5 mentally copied new sentences to which the BCI had not been exposed previously. Impressively, T5 was able to type quite rapidly — about 90 characters per minute, not far off from the typical physical typing speed of 115 characters/minute achieved by non-paralyzed individuals of T5's age. He achieved an accuracy rate of 94% online, which improved to 99% offline when using an autocorrect feature similar to that on many smartphones. T5 was also able to mentally type answers to open-ended questions, albeit at a somewhat slower rate, reflecting time needed to compose his responses.

Although these studies do not quite take us all the way to the world envisioned in *Avatar*, they provide clear evidence that what we once thought of as pure science fiction is well on its way to becoming science fact.

To assess the neural representation of attempted handwriting, participant T5 attempted to handwrite each character one at a time, following the instructions given on a computer screen. (Bottom panels depict what is shown on the screen, following the timeline.) Decoded pen trajectories are shown for all 31 tested characters. Orange circles denote the start of the trajectory.
REPRINTED BY PERMISSION FROM SPRINGER NATURE: NATURE 593, 249–254. HIGH-PERFORMANCE BRAIN-TO-TEXT COMMUNICATION VIA HANDWRITING, WILLETT, F.R., AVANSINO, D.T., HOCHBERG, L.R. ET AL., 2021.

Structure of the Brain

The human brain, weighing in at about 1,300–1,400 grams, is really not much to look at. You already know that its neurons and glial cells are busy humming away, giving you potentially brilliant ideas, consciousness, and feelings. But which neurons in which parts of the brain control which functions?

To answer that question, neuroscientists had to find a way of describing the brain that allows researchers to communicate with one another. It can be helpful to talk about areas of the brain from "bottom to top," noting how the different regions are specialized for different kinds of tasks. In general, simpler functions are performed at the "lower" levels of the brain, whereas more complex functions are performed at successively "higher" levels (see **FIGURE 3.12a**). Or, as you'll see shortly, the brain can also be approached in a "side-by-side" fashion: Although the two sides of the brain are roughly mirror-symmetric, one half of the brain specializes in some tasks that the other half doesn't. Although these divisions make it easier to understand areas of the brain and their functions, keep in mind that none of these structures or areas in the brain can act alone. Individual regions within the brain are organized into larger scale *networks*, which consist of interacting and interdependent regions that work together to support complex psychological functions (Avena-Koenigsberger et al., 2018; Sporns & Betzel, 2016). Individual regions make specific contributions to these networks that reflect their specialized nature, but they operate as part of an interdependent unit.

Let's look first at the divisions of the brain, and the responsibilities of each part, moving from the bottom to the top. Using this view, we can divide the brain into three parts: the hindbrain, the midbrain, and the forebrain (see Figure 3.12a).

The Hindbrain

If you follow the spinal cord from your tailbone to where it enters your skull, you'll find it difficult to determine where your spinal cord ends and your brain begins. That's because the spinal cord is continuous with the **hindbrain,** *an area of the brain that coordinates information coming into and out of the spinal cord.* The hindbrain looks like a stalk on which the rest of the brain sits, and it controls the most basic functions of life: respiration, alertness, and motor skills. The structures that make up the hindbrain include the medulla, the reticular formation, the cerebellum, and the pons (see Figure 3.12b).

The **medulla** is *an extension of the spinal cord into the skull that coordinates heart rate, circulation, and respiration.* Beginning inside the medulla and extending upward is a small cluster of neurons called the **reticular formation,** which *regulates sleep, wakefulness, and levels of arousal.* In one early experiment, researchers stimulated the reticular formation of a sleeping cat. This caused the animal to awaken almost instantaneously and remain alert. Conversely, severing the connections between the reticular formation and the rest of the brain caused the animal to lapse into an irreversible coma (Moruzzi & Magoun, 1949). The reticular formation maintains the same delicate balance between alertness and unconsciousness in humans. In fact, many general anesthetics work by reducing activity in the reticular formation, rendering the patient unconscious.

Behind the medulla is the **cerebellum,** *a large structure of the hindbrain that controls fine motor skills.* (*Cerebellum* is Latin for "little brain," and this structure does look like a small replica of the brain.) The cerebellum orchestrates the proper sequence of movements when we ride a bike, play the piano, or maintain balance while walking and running. It contributes to the fine-tuning of behaviour: smoothing our actions to allow their graceful execution rather than initiating the actions (Smetacek, 2002). The initiation of behaviour involves other areas of the brain; as you'll recall, different brain systems interact with and are independent of each other.

Learning Outcomes

WHAT YOU NEED TO KNOW

- Differentiate the functions of the major divisions of the brain.
- Explain the functions of the cerebral cortex according to organization across hemispheres, within hemispheres, and within specific lobes.
- Identify the causes and consequences of brain plasticity.

ARNO BALZARINI/KEYSTONE/AP IMAGES

The high-wire artist Freddy Nock relied on his cerebellum to coordinate the movements necessary to walk on the rope of the Corvatsch cable car from more than 10,000 feet over sea level down to the base station in Silvaplana, Switzerland.

hindbrain The area of the brain that coordinates information coming into and out of the spinal cord.

medulla An extension of the spinal cord into the skull that coordinates heart rate, circulation, and respiration.

reticular formation Regulates sleep, wakefulness, and levels of arousal.

cerebellum A large structure of the hindbrain that controls fine motor skills.

Forebrain

Midbrain

Hindbrain

(a)
The Major Divisions of the Brain
The brain can be organized into three parts, moving from the
bottom to the top, from simpler functions to the more complex:
the hindbrain, the midbrain, and the forebrain.

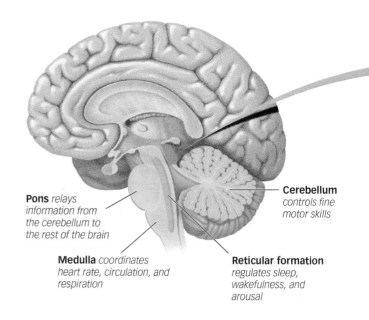

Pons *relays
information from
the cerebellum to
the rest of the brain*

Cerebellum
*controls fine
motor skills*

Medulla *coordinates
heart rate, circulation, and
respiration*

Reticular formation
*regulates sleep,
wakefulness, and
arousal*

(b)
The Hindbrain
The hindbrain coordinates information coming into and out of
the spinal cord and controls the basic functions of life.

**Figure 3.12
Structure of the Brain**

SCIENCE SOURCE

The human brain weighs only 1,300–1,400
grams and isn't much to look at, but its
accomplishments are staggering.

pons A brain structure that relays
information from the cerebellum to the
rest of the brain.

tectum Orients an organism in the
environment.

tegmentum Involved in movement
and arousal.

Recent research, capitalizing on advances in brain imaging, reveals that the cerebellum is involved in a much broader range of cognitive, social, and emotional functions beyond motor control (e.g., see Diedrichsen, King, Hernandez-Castillo, Sereno, & Ivry, 2019). Perhaps the cerebellum is a timing device that serves to coordinate the brain processes required for any complex cognition or behaviour (Bareš et al., 2019; Braitenberg, 1961). Cerebellum function is an area of active investigation.

The last major area of the hindbrain is the **pons,** *a structure that relays information from the cerebellum to the rest of the brain.* (*Pons* means "bridge" in Latin.) Although the detailed functions of the pons remain poorly understood, it essentially acts as a relay station or bridge between the cerebellum and other structures in the brain.

The Midbrain

Sitting on top of the hindbrain is the *midbrain,* which is relatively small in humans. As you can see in Figure 3.12c, the midbrain contains two main structures: the tectum and the tegmentum. The **tectum** *orients an organism in the environment.* The tectum receives stimulus input from the eyes, ears, and skin and moves the organism in a coordinated way towards the stimulus. For example, when you're studying in a quiet room and you hear a *click* behind and to the right of you, your body will swivel and orient to the direction of the sound; this is your tectum in action. The **tegmentum** is *involved in movement and arousal*; it also helps to orient an organism towards sensory stimuli.

The midbrain may be relatively small, but it is a central location of neurotransmitters involved in arousal, mood, and motivation and the brain structures that rely on them (White, 1996). You could survive if you had only a hindbrain and a midbrain. The structures in the hindbrain would take care of all the bodily functions necessary to sustain life, and the structures in the midbrain would orient you towards or away from pleasurable or threatening stimuli in the environment. But this wouldn't be much of a life. To understand where the abilities that make us fully human come from, we need to consider the last division of the brain: the forebrain.

Cerebral cortex

Subcortical structures:

Basal ganglia *a set of subcortical structures that directs intentional movements*

Thalamus *receives and transmits information from the senses to the cerebral cortex*

Hippocampus *critical for creating and integrating new memories*

Amygdala *plays a role in emotional processes*

Hypothalamus *regulates body temperature, hunger, thirst, and sexual behaviour*

Pituitary gland *releases hormones that direct many other glands*

Tegmentum *involved in movement and arousal*

Tectum *orients into the environment*

Corpus callosum

(c)
The Midbrain
The midbrain is important for orientation and movement.

(d)
The Forebrain
The forebrain is the highest level of the brain and is critical for complex cognitive, emotional, sensory, and motor functions. The forebrain is divided into two parts: the cerebral cortex and the underlying subcortical structures. The cerebral cortex, the outermost layer of the brain, is divided into two hemispheres, connected by the corpus callosum (see Figure 3.15).

The Forebrain

When you appreciate the beauty of a poem, detect the sarcasm in a friend's remark, plan to go skiing next winter, or notice the faint glimmer of sadness on a loved one's face, you are enlisting the forebrain. The *forebrain* is the highest level of the brain—literally and figuratively—and controls complex cognitive, emotional, sensory, and motor functions. The forebrain itself is divided into two main sections: the cerebral cortex and the subcortical structures.

The **cerebral cortex** is *the outermost layer of the brain, visible to the naked eye, and divided into two hemispheres*. The **subcortical structures** are *areas of the forebrain housed under the cerebral cortex near the centre of the brain* (see Figure 3.12d). We'll have much more to say about the two hemispheres of the cerebral cortex and the functions they serve in the next section, with the highest level of the brain fittingly saved for last. First, we'll examine the subcortical structures.

Subcortical Structures

The subcortical (meaning "beneath the cortex") structures are nestled deep inside the brain, where they are quite protected. If you imagine sticking an index finger in each of your ears and pushing inward until they touch, that's about where you'd find the *thalamus,* three components of the limbic system (the *hypothalamus,* the *hippocampus,* and the *amygdala*), the basal ganglia, and the pituitary gland, which is part of the endocrine system (see Figure 3.12d). Each of these subcortical structures plays an important role in relaying information throughout the brain, as well as in performing specific tasks that allow us to think, feel, and behave as humans. Here we'll give you a brief introduction to each, and you'll read more about many of these structures in later chapters.

Thalamus and Hypothalamus The thalamus and hypothalamus, located in the centre of the brain, interact closely with several other brain structures. They relay signals to and from these structures and also help to regulate them.

cerebral cortex The outermost layer of the brain, visible to the naked eye and divided into two hemispheres.

subcortical structures Areas of the forebrain housed under the cerebral cortex near the centre of the brain.

The thalamus receives inputs from all the major senses except smell. You can thank your thalamus when you see the red apple, feel its smoothness in your hand, hear the crunch as you bite into it, and taste its sweetness.

The **thalamus** *relays and filters information from the senses and transmits the information to the cerebral cortex.* The thalamus receives inputs from all the major senses except smell, which has direct connections to the cerebral cortex. The thalamus acts as a kind of computer server in a networked system, taking in multiple inputs and relaying them to a variety of locations (Guillery & Sherman, 2002). However, unlike the mechanical operations of a computer ("send input A to location B"), the thalamus actively filters sensory information, giving more weight to some inputs and less weight to others. The thalamus also closes the pathways of incoming sensations during sleep, providing a valuable function in *not* allowing information to pass to the rest of the brain.

The **hypothalamus,** located below the thalamus (*hypo-* is Greek for "under"), *regulates body temperature, hunger, thirst, and sexual behaviour.* Although the hypothalamus is a tiny area of the brain, clusters of neurons in the hypothalamus oversee a wide range of basic behaviours, keeping body temperature, blood sugar levels, and metabolism within an optimal range for typical human functioning. Lesions to some areas of the hypothalamus result in overeating, whereas lesions to other areas leave an animal with no desire for food at all, highlighting that the hypothalamus plays a key role in regulating food intake (Berthoud & Morrison, 2008). Also, when you think about sex, messages from your cerebral cortex are sent to the hypothalamus to trigger the release of hormones. Finally, electric stimulation of some areas of the hypothalamus in cats can produce hissing and biting, whereas stimulation of other areas in the hypothalamus can produce what appears to be intense pleasure for an animal (Siegel et al., 1999).

The researchers James Olds and Peter Milner, working at McGill University, found that a small electric current delivered to a certain region of a rat's hypothalamus was extremely rewarding for the animal (Olds & Milner, 1954). In fact, when allowed to press a bar attached to the electrode to initiate their own stimulation, rats would do so several thousand times an hour, often to the point of exhaustion!

The Limbic System The hypothalamus is also part of the limbic system, a group of forebrain structures that includes the hypothalamus, the hippocampus, and the amygdala, which are involved in motivation, emotion, learning, and memory (Maclean, 1970; Papez, 1937). The limbic system is where the subcortical structures meet the cerebral cortex.

The **hippocampus** (from Latin for "sea horse," due to its shape) is *critical for creating new memories and integrating them into a network of knowledge so that they can be stored indefinitely in other parts of the cerebral cortex.* Individuals with damage to the hippocampus can acquire new information and keep it in awareness for a few seconds, but as soon as they are distracted, they forget the information and the experience that produced it (Scoville & Milner, 1957; Squire, 2009). This kind of disruption is limited to everyday memory for facts and events that we can bring to consciousness; memory of learned habitual routines or emotional reactions remains intact (Squire et al., 1993). For example, people with damage to the hippocampus can remember how to drive and talk, but they cannot recall where they have recently driven or a conversation they have just had (see A World of Difference regarding implications for Alzheimer's disease, p. 95). You will read more about the hippocampus and its role in creating, storing, and combining memories in the Memory chapter.

The **amygdala** (from Latin for "almond," also due to its shape), *located at the tip of each horn of the hippocampus, plays a central role in many emotional processes, particularly the formation of emotional memories* (Aggleton, 1992). The amygdala attaches significance to previously neutral events that are associated with fear, punishment, or reward (LeDoux, 1992). For example, think of the last time something scary or unpleasant happened to you: A car came barrelling towards you as you started walking into an intersection, or a ferocious dog leaped out of an alley as you passed by. Those stimuli—a car or a dog—are fairly neutral; you don't have a panic attack every time you walk by a used car lot. The emotional significance attached

thalamus Relays and filters information from the senses and transmits the information to the cerebral cortex.

hypothalamus Regulates body temperature, hunger, thirst, and sexual behaviour.

hippocampus Critical for creating new memories and integrating them into a network of knowledge so that they can be stored indefinitely in other parts of the cerebral cortex.

amygdala Located at the tip of each horn of the hippocampus, plays a central role in many emotional processes, particularly the formation of emotional memories.

to events involving those stimuli is the work of the amygdala (McGaugh, 2006, 2015). When we are in emotionally arousing situations, the amygdala stimulates the hippocampus to remember many details surrounding the situation (Kensinger & Schacter, 2005).

For instance, people who are old enough to remember the terrorist attacks on New York City and Washington, D.C., of September 11, 2001, remember vivid details about where they were, what they were doing, and how they felt when they heard the news, even years later (Hirst et al., 2009, 2015). In particular, the amygdala seems to be especially involved in encoding events as *fearful* (Adolphs et al., 1995; Sigurdsson et al., 2007). We'll have more to say about the amygdala in the Emotion and Motivation chapter. For now, keep in mind that a group of neurons the size of a lima bean buried deep in your brain help you to laugh, weep, or shriek in fright when the circumstances call for it.

A scary movie is designed to stimulate your amygdala, but only a little.

The Basal Ganglia There are several other structures in the subcortical area, but we'll consider just one more. The **basal ganglia** is not one structure but *a set of subcortical structures that directs intentional movements and plays a role in reward processing.* Located near the thalamus and hypothalamus, the basal ganglia receive input from the cerebral cortex and send outputs to the motor centres in the brainstem (Nelson & Kreitzer, 2015). One part of the basal ganglia, the *striatum,* has an important role in the control of posture and movement. As we saw in the excerpt from Michael J. Fox's book, people who suffer from Parkinson's disease typically show symptoms of uncontrollable shaking and sudden jerks of the limbs and are unable to initiate a sequence of movements to achieve a specific goal. This happens because Parkinson's disease damages parts of the midbrain that normally supply the striatum with dopamine (Dauer & Przedborski, 2003). The undersupply of dopamine impairs the function of the striatum, which in turn leads to the visible tremors of Parkinson's.

So what's the problem in Parkinson's: the jerky movements, the ineffectiveness of the striatum in directing behaviour, or the underproduction of dopamine at the neuronal level? The answer is all of these (Weiner et al., 2013). This disease clearly illustrates two themes of the brain and behaviour. First, actions at the microscopic level of neurons in the brain can produce substantial effects at the level of observable behaviour. Second, the structures in the hindbrain, midbrain, and forebrain don't function in isolation; they are interdependent, and damage in one area affects other areas in turn.

In addition to its role in movement, the striatum also plays a role in reward processing (Schultz, 2016). As just noted, the midbrain supplies the striatum with dopamine, which we saw earlier plays a role in pleasure and motivation as well as in movements. A part of the striatum known as the *nucleus accumbens* has been linked to various kinds of rewards, including social rewards such as approval from others (Kohls et al., 2013; Williams et al., 2020; see The Real World: What the Brain Likes: The Instagram Effect).

The Endocrine System

The **endocrine system** is *a network of glands that produce and secrete into the bloodstream chemical messages known as hormones, which influence a wide variety of basic functions, including metabolism, growth, and sexual development.* The endocrine system is distinct from the nervous system but works closely with it, especially the limbic system, to regulate thoughts, emotions, and behaviours. Some of the main glands in the endocrine system include the thyroid, which regulates bodily functions such as body temperature and heart rate; the adrenals, which regulate stress responses; the pancreas, which controls digestion; and the pineal, which secretes melatonin, influencing the sleep-wake cycle. The overall functioning of the endocrine system is orchestrated by the **pituitary gland,** *the*

basal ganglia A set of subcortical structures that directs intentional movements and plays a role in reward processing.

endocrine system A network of glands that produce and secrete into the bloodstream chemical messages known as hormones, which influence a wide variety of basic functions, including metabolism, growth, and sexual development.

pituitary gland The "master gland" of the body's hormone-producing system, which releases hormones that direct the functions of many other glands in the body.

The Real World | What the Brain Likes: The Instagram Effect

On May 26, 2021, Instagram announced that everyone on Instagram and Facebook would have the option to hide their like counts, a feature that they had been testing since 2019 on Instagram (https://about.fb.com/news/2021/05/giving-people-more-control/). This move reflects the potentially harmful power of like counts on these platforms, which can create intense social pressure and possibly mental health problems for users, as highlighted in the title of a 2019 article: "An Instagram With No 'Likes' Could Have A Big Impact On Mental Health" (Wong, 2019). This negative effect is powerful in adolescents. In one recent study (Lee et al., 2020), ninth-grade students interacted for 3 minutes with an electronic partner (who, unknown to the students, was a member of the research team) during an experimentally devised social media task. Students who were randomly assigned to a condition in which they received few likes in response to their posts from the partners reported more negative feelings and thoughts about themselves, and even greater depressive symptoms, than students who were randomly assigned to a condition that yielded many likes. This effect was particularly strong among adolescents who had experienced peer victimization at school.

Research using fMRI (see the section Investigating the Brain in this chapter) to examine activity in the adolescent brain during social media interactions has provided an initial glimpse into the possible basis of the potent effects wielded by the varying numbers of likes during social media interactions. Sherman et al. (2016) scanned adolescent participants while they performed a social media task designed to simulate Instagram. Participants submitted photos from their own Instagram accounts, and were told that their photos would be combined with photos from other participants to form a social network. The participants viewed some of their own photos, along with a standardized set of publicly available photos selected by the researchers. They were further informed that they would see how often each photo had been liked by previous participants, though in reality the number of likes was assigned and manipulated by the researchers. Participants were able to add their own likes to any of the photos as they wished.

Participants more frequently liked photos that were shown as having received more versus fewer likes by others, highlighting the social influence on adolescents' "like" responses. Analysis of fMRI data revealed that photos with more likes elicited greater activity in a variety of brain regions than photos with fewer likes, including the hippocampus and parts of the frontal lobe involved in attention and social processing. The researchers were particularly interested in responses in the nucleus accumbens, a part of the striatum in the basal ganglia that is a critical component of the brain's reward circuitry. This region showed increased activity for photos that received many likes versus few likes, and showed an especially strong response when participants viewed photos of their own that received many likes. In a subsequent study, Sherman et al. (2018) found that providing likes to others' photos was also associated with increased activity in reward processing regions, notably once again in the striatum.

Another way of phrasing these results is that reward processing regions showed *less* activity for photos that received (or were given) fewer likes versus many likes. That finding is of interest in relation to a result from the aforementioned study of Lee et al. (2020). They reported that feelings of rejection among adolescents were linked to insufficient positive feedback, as opposed to explicitly negative feedback, during their experimental social media interaction. Lee et al.'s finding suggests that the reward associated with receiving likes on Instagram or Facebook, linked to the engagement of underlying reward processing regions, is something that adolescents crave and that is missed acutely when it is not delivered. We don't yet know whether the new Instagram policies allowing users to hide like counts will alleviate the distress associated with receiving few likes in adolescents (or anyone else), but the new policy corresponds well with the recent findings from studies of the adolescent brain and mind (Crone & Kronjin, 2018).

DZMITRY KLIAPITSKI/ALAMY STOCK PHOTO

861 likes

"master gland" of the body's hormone-producing system, which releases hormones that direct the functions of many other glands in the body (see **FIGURE 3.13**).

The hypothalamus sends hormonal signals to the pituitary gland, which in turn sends hormonal signals to other glands to control stress, digestive activities, and reproductive processes. For example, when we sense a threat, sensory neurons send

Figure 3.13
Major Glands of the Endocrine System The endocrine system is a network of glands that works with the nervous system and impacts many basic functions by releasing hormones into the bloodstream.

signals to the hypothalamus, which stimulates the release of adrenocorticotropic hormone (ACTH) from the pituitary gland. ACTH, in turn, stimulates the adrenal glands to release hormones that activate the sympathetic nervous system (Selye & Fortier, 1950). As you read earlier in this chapter, the sympathetic nervous system prepares the body either to meet the threat head on or to flee from the situation.

The endocrine system also plays a key role in sexual behaviour and reproduction. The sexual reproductive glands are the ovaries in females, which make the hormone *estrogen*, and the testes in males, which make the hormone *testosterone* (see Figure 3.13). However, testosterone is not exclusive to males, and estrogen is not exclusive to females: The ovaries generate small amounts of testosterone, and the testes generate small amounts of estrogen (Davis & Wahlin-Jacobsen, 2015; Wibowo & Wassersug, 2014). Although it is widely believed that fluctuations in sexual desire are closely linked to fluctuations in sex hormones, recent research has failed to reveal a strong link between testosterone levels and sexual desire in men or women (Roney & Simmons, 2013; van Anders, 2012), whereas there is evidence for a link between estrogen levels and sexual desire in women (Gangestad & Haselton, 2015; Roney & Simmons, 2013).

The Cerebral Cortex

Our tour of the brain has taken us from the very small (neurons) to the somewhat bigger (major divisions of the brain) to the very large: the cerebral cortex. The cortex is the highest level of the brain, and it is responsible for the most complex aspects of perception, emotion, movement, and thought (Fuster, 2003). It sits over the rest

DONNA RANIERI

Crumpling a newspaper allows the same amount of surface area to fit into a much smaller space, just as the wrinkles and folds in the cortex allow a great deal of brain power to fit inside the human skull.

Figure 3.14
Cerebral Cortex and Lobes The four major lobes of the cerebral cortex are the occipital lobe, the parietal lobe, the temporal lobe, and the frontal lobe. The smooth surfaces of the cortex are called gyri, and the indentations are called sulci.

Figure 3.15
Cerebral Hemispheres The corpus callosum connects the two hemispheres of the brain and supports communication between them.

corpus callosum Connects large areas of the cerebral cortex on each side of the brain and supports communication of information across the hemispheres.

occipital lobe Processes visual information.

parietal lobe Processes information about touch.

of the brain, like a mushroom cap shielding the underside and stem, and it is the wrinkled surface you see when looking at the brain with the naked eye.

The smooth surfaces of the cortex—the raised part—are called *gyri* (*gyrus* if you're talking about just one), and the indentations or fissures are called *sulci* (*sulcus* when singular). The sulci and gyri are a triumph of evolution. The cerebral cortex occupies roughly the area of a newspaper page, so fitting that much cortex into a human skull is a tough task. But if you crumple a sheet of newspaper, you'll see that the same surface area now fits compactly into a much smaller space. The cortex, with its wrinkles (sulci) and folds (gyri), holds a lot of brainpower in a relatively small package that fits comfortably inside the human skull (see **FIGURE 3.14**). The functions of the cerebral cortex can be understood at three levels: the separation of the cortex into two hemispheres, the functions of each hemisphere, and the role of specific cortical areas.

Organization Across Hemispheres The first level of organization divides the cortex into the left and right hemispheres. The two hemispheres are more or less symmetrical in their appearance and, to some extent, in their functions. However, each hemisphere controls the functions of the opposite side of the body. This is called *contralateral control,* meaning that your right cerebral hemisphere perceives stimuli from and controls movements on the left side of your body, whereas your left cerebral hemisphere perceives stimuli from and controls movement on the right side of your body.

The cerebral hemispheres are connected to each other by *commissures,* bundles of axons that make possible communication between parallel areas of the cortex in each half. The largest of these commissures is the **corpus callosum,** which *connects large areas of the cerebral cortex on each side of the brain and supports communication of information across the hemispheres* (see **FIGURE 3.15**). This means that information received in the right hemisphere, for example, can pass across the corpus callosum and be registered, virtually instantaneously, in the left hemisphere.

Organization Within Hemispheres The second level of organization in the cerebral cortex distinguishes the functions of the different regions within each hemisphere of the brain. Each hemisphere of the cerebral cortex is divided into four areas, or *lobes:* From back to front, these are the occipital lobe, the parietal lobe, the temporal lobe, and the frontal lobe, as shown in Figure 3.14. We'll examine the functions of these lobes in more detail in later chapters, noting how scientists have used a variety of techniques to understand the operations of the brain. For now, here's a brief overview of the main functions of each lobe.

The **occipital lobe,** located at the back of the cerebral cortex, *processes visual information.* Sensory receptors in the eyes send information to the thalamus, which in turn sends information to the primary areas of the occipital lobe, where simple features of the stimulus are extracted, such as the location and orientation of an object's edges (see the Sensation and Perception chapter for more details). These features are then processed into a more complex "map" of the stimulus onto the occipital cortex, leading to comprehension of what's being seen. As you might imagine, damage to the primary visual areas of the occipital lobe can leave a person with partial or complete blindness. Information still enters the eyes, which work just fine. But without the ability to process and make sense of the information at the level of the cerebral cortex, the information is as good as lost (Zeki, 2001).

Whereas the occipital lobe processes visual information, the other three main lobes process information from multiple modalities. The **parietal lobe,** located in front of the occipital lobe, carries out several functions that include *processing information about touch.* The parietal lobe contains the *somatosensory cortex,* a strip of brain tissue running from the top of the brain down to the sides (see **FIGURE 3.16**). Within each

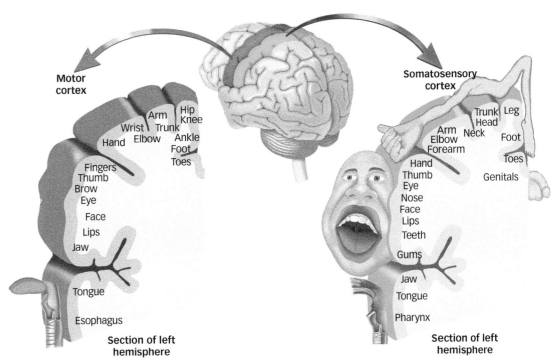

Figure 3.16
Somatosensory and Motor Cortices The motor cortex, a strip of brain tissue in the frontal lobe, represents and controls different skin and body areas on the contralateral side of the body. Directly behind the motor cortex, in the parietal lobe, lies the somatosensory cortex. Like the motor cortex, the somatosensory cortex represents skin areas of particular parts on the contralateral side of the body.

hemisphere, the somatosensory cortex represents the skin areas on the contralateral surface of the body. Each part of the somatosensory cortex maps onto a particular part of the body. If a body area is more sensitive, a larger part of the somatosensory cortex is devoted to it. For example, the part of the somatosensory cortex that corresponds to the lips and tongue is larger than the area corresponding to the feet. The somatosensory cortex can be illustrated as a distorted figure, called a *homunculus* ("little man"), in which the body parts are rendered according to how much of the somatosensory cortex is devoted to them (Penfield & Rasmussen, 1950). This map of the body in the brain was developed by Montreal neurosurgeon Wilder Penfield, by stimulating the brains of his awake patients during surgery and recording where the patient reported feeling a sensation. Directly in front of the somatosensory cortex, in the frontal lobe, is a parallel strip of brain tissue called the *motor cortex.*

As in the somatosensory cortex, different parts of the motor cortex correspond to different body parts. The motor cortex initiates voluntary movements and sends messages to the basal ganglia, cerebellum, and spinal cord. The motor and somatosensory cortices, then, are akin to sending and receiving areas of the cerebral cortex, taking in information and sending out commands, as the case might be.

The **temporal lobe,** located on the lower side of each hemisphere, is *responsible for hearing and language.* The *primary auditory cortex* in the temporal lobe is analogous to the somatosensory cortex in the parietal lobe and the primary visual areas of the occipital lobe: It receives sensory information from the ears based on the frequencies of sounds. Secondary areas of the temporal lobe then process the information into meaningful units, such as speech and words. The temporal lobe also houses areas that interpret the meaning of visual stimuli and help us recognize common objects in the environment (Martin, 2007).

The **frontal lobe,** which sits behind the forehead, has *specialized areas for movement, abstract thinking, planning, memory, and judgement.* As you just read, it contains the motor cortex, which coordinates movements of muscle groups throughout the body. Other areas in the frontal lobe coordinate thought processes that help us manipulate information and retrieve memories, which we can use to plan our behaviours and interact socially with others. In short, the frontal cortex functions as a kind of executive that allows us to do the kind of thinking, imagining, planning, and

temporal lobe Responsible for hearing and language.

frontal lobe Specialized areas for movement, abstract thinking, planning, memory, and judgement.

anticipating that sets humans apart from most other species (Schoenemann et al., 2005; Stuss & Benson, 1986; Suddendorf & Corballis, 2007).

Organization Within Specific Lobes The third level of organization in the cerebral cortex involves the representation of information within specific lobes in the cortex. A hierarchy of processing stages from primary areas handles fine details of information all the way up to **association areas,** which are *composed of neurons that help provide sense and meaning to information registered in the cortex.* For example, neurons in the primary visual cortex are highly specialized: Some detect features of the environment that are in a horizontal orientation, others detect movement, and still others process information about human versus nonhuman forms. Association areas interpret the information extracted by these primary areas (shape, motion, etc.) to make sense of what's being perceived—in this case, perhaps a large cat leaping towards your face (Martin, 2007). Similarly, neurons in the primary auditory cortex register sound frequencies, but it's the association areas of the temporal lobe that allow you to turn those noises into the meaning of your friend screaming, "Look out for the cat!" Association areas, then, help stitch together the threads of information in the various parts of the cortex to produce a meaningful understanding of what's being registered in the brain.

A striking example of this property of association areas comes from the discovery of the mirror-neuron system. **Mirror neurons** are *active when an animal performs a behaviour, such as reaching for or manipulating an object, and are also activated when another animal observes that animal performing the same behaviour.* Mirror neurons are found in the frontal lobe (near the motor cortex) and in the parietal lobe (Rizzolatti & Craighero, 2004; Rizzolatti & Sinigaglia, 2010). They have been identified in birds, monkeys, and humans, and their name reflects the function they serve. Neuroimaging studies with humans have shown that mirror neurons are active when people watch someone perform a behaviour, such as grasping in midair. But they are more highly activated when that behaviour has some purpose or context, such as grasping a cup to take a drink (Iacoboni et al., 2005), and they seem to be related to recognizing the goal someone has in carrying out an action and the outcome of the action, rather than to the particular movements a person makes while performing that action (Hamilton & Grafton, 2006, 2008; Iacoboni, 2009; Rizzolatti & Sinigaglia, 2010).

There is controversy about how to interpret the activity of mirror neurons, particularly in humans (Hickok, 2009, 2014), and about whether, as claimed by some researchers, impairments to the mirror neuron system contribute to difficulties with understanding the minds of other people, as occurs in autism spectrum disorder (Hamilton, 2013; see the chapter on Psychological Disorders). Nonetheless, the existence of mirror neurons is supported by experimental evidence (Rizzolatti & Rozzi, 2018). In the Learning chapter we'll find out more about the role of mirror neurons in learning.

Finally, neurons in the association areas are usually less specialized and more flexible than neurons in the primary areas. Thus, they can be shaped by learning and experience to do their job more effectively. This kind of shaping of neurons by environmental forces allows the brain flexibility, or plasticity, our next topic.

Brain Plasticity

The cerebral cortex may seem to be a fixed structure, one big sheet of neurons designed to help us make sense of our external world. Remarkably, however, sensory cortices are not fixed. They can adapt to changes in sensory inputs, a quality that researchers call *plasticity* (i.e., the ability to be molded). As an example, if you lose your middle finger in an accident, the part of the somatosensory area that represents that finger is initially unresponsive (Kaas, 1991). After all, there's no longer any sensory input going from that location to that part of the brain. You might expect the left middle-finger neurons of the somatosensory cortex to wither away. However, over time, that area in the

When one animal observes another engaging in a particular behaviour, some of the same neurons become active in the observer's brain as in the brain of the animal exhibiting the behaviour. These mirror neurons seem to play an important role in social behaviour.

association areas Composed of neurons that help provide sense and meaning to information registered in the cortex.

mirror neurons Neurons that are active when an animal performs a behaviour, such as reaching for or manipulating an object, and are also activated when another animal observes that animal performing the same behaviour.

somatosensory cortex becomes responsive to stimulation of the fingers *adjacent* to the missing finger. The brain is plastic: Functions that were assigned to certain areas of the brain may be capable of being reassigned to other areas of the brain to accommodate changing input from the environment (Feldman, 2009). This suggests that sensory inputs "compete" for representation in each cortical area.

New Mapping

A striking example comes from amputees who continue to experience sensations where the missing limb would be, a phenomenon called *phantom limb syndrome.* Patients can feel their missing limbs moving, even in coordinated gestures such as shaking hands. Some even report feeling pain in their phantom limbs (Kuffler, 2018; Ramachandran & Brang, 2015). Why does this happen?

To find out, researchers stimulated the skin surface in various regions around the face, torso, and arms while monitoring brain activity in amputees and nonamputee volunteers (Ramachandran & Blakeslee, 1998; Ramachandran et al., 2010; Ramachandran et al., 1992). Brain-imaging techniques displayed the somatosensory cortical areas that were activated when the skin was stimulated, enabling the researchers to map how touch is represented in the somatosensory cortex for different areas of the body. For instance, when the face was touched, the researchers could determine which areas in the somatosensory cortex were most active; when the torso was stimulated, they could see which areas responded, and so on.

Brain scans of the amputees revealed that stimulating areas of the face and upper arm activated an area in the somatosensory cortex that previously would have been activated by a now-missing hand (**FIGURE 3.17**). The face and arm were represented in the somatosensory cortex in an area adjacent to where the person's hand—now amputated—would have been represented. Stimulating the face or arm produced phantom limb sensations in the amputees; they reported "feeling" a sensation in their missing limbs.

Brain plasticity can explain these results (Pascual-Leone et al., 2005). The cortical representations for the face and the upper arm normally lie on either side of the representation for the hand (Figure 3.16). The somatosensory areas for the face and upper arm were larger in amputees and had taken over the part of the cortex normally representing the hand. Indeed, the new face and arm representations were now contiguous with each other, filling in the space occupied by the hand representation. Some of these new mappings were quite concise. For example, in some amputees, when specific areas of the facial skin were activated, the patient reported sensations in just one finger of the phantom hand (Figure 3.17)!

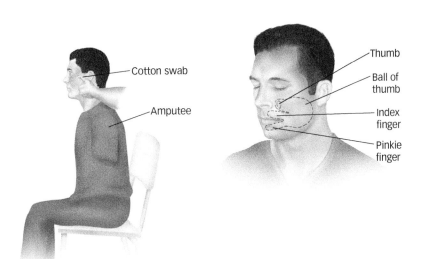

Figure 3.17
Mapping Sensations in Phantom Limbs Researchers lightly touch an amputee's face with a cotton swab, eliciting sensations in the missing hand. Touching different parts of the cheek can even result in sensations in particular fingers or the thumb of the missing hand.

Herbie Hancock is a virtuoso who has been playing piano for more than 70 years. Compared with those of a novice, the brain regions that control his fingers are relatively less active when he plays.

The Influence of Practice

Plasticity doesn't occur only to compensate for missing digits or limbs, however. An extraordinary amount of stimulation of one finger can result in that finger's "taking over" the representation of the part of the cortex that usually represents other, adjacent fingers (Merzenich et al., 1990). Based on this work, it is likely that concert pianists have highly developed cortical areas for finger control: The continued input from the fingers commands a larger area of representation in the somatosensory cortices in the brain. Consistent with this idea, recent research indicates greater plasticity within the motor cortex of professional musicians compared with nonmusicians, perhaps reflecting an increase in the number of motor synapses as a result of extended practice (Rosenkranz et al., 2007). Similar findings have been obtained with quilters (who have highly developed areas for the thumb and forefinger, which are critical to their profession) and taxi drivers (who have overdeveloped brain areas in the hippocampus that are used during spatial navigation) (Maguire et al., 2000).

The Influence of Exercise

Plasticity is also related to a question you might not expect to find in a psychology textbook: How much have you been exercising lately? Although we expect that you are spending countless happy hours reading this textbook, we also hope that you've been finding enough time for physical exercise. A large number of studies in rats and other nonhuman animals indicate that physical exercise can increase the number of synapses and even promote the development of new neurons in the hippocampus (Hillman et al., 2008; van Praag, 2009). Recent studies with people have begun to document beneficial effects of cardiovascular exercise on aspects of brain function and cognitive performance (Colcombe et al., 2004, 2006; Prakash et al., 2015).

Although these effects tend to be seen most clearly in older adults (okay, so it's time for your textbook authors to get on a treadmill), benefits have also been documented throughout the life span (Hertig & Nagel, 2012; Hillman et al., 2008). Some evidence indicates that even a single session of moderate-to-intensive exercise can boost aspects of memory and motor skills (Roig et al., 2012; Statton et al., 2015). In fact, some researchers believe that this kind of activity-dependent brain plasticity is relevant to treating spinal cord injuries (which, as we have seen, have a devastating impact on people's lives) because understanding how to maximize plasticity through exercise and training may help to guide rehabilitation efforts (Dunlop, 2008). It should be clear by now that the plasticity of the brain is not just an interesting theoretical idea; it has potentially important applications to everyday life (Bryck & Fisher, 2012).

The Influence of Culture

Another example of brain plasticity comes from examining the impact of culture on psychological and neural processes. As you learned in The Evolution of Psychological Science chapter, *culture* refers to the values, traditions, and beliefs that are shared by a particular people, and *cultural psychology* is the study of how culture influences mental life. **Cultural neuroscience** is *the study of how culture and neurobiological processes influence one another* (Chiao & Ambady, 2007; Kim & Sasaki, 2014).

Findings from cultural psychology and neuroscience studies have provided growing evidence that culture does indeed exert a notable impact on neurobiological processes (Park & Huang, 2010). For example, studies of visual perception that have compared the responses of people from Western cultures (e.g., North Americans) and Eastern cultures (i.e., China, Japan, and Korea) have consistently revealed differences in how they process visual information (Gutchess & Sekuler, 2019). When presented with visual displays comprised of an object and a background context, such as a fish swimming underwater, Westerners tended to focus more on the focal

cultural neuroscience The study of how culture and neurobiological processes influence one another.

A World of Difference • Alzheimer's Disease and the Hippocampus: Sex Differences

Alzheimer's disease (AD) is a devastating progressive brain disorder that gradually impairs and ultimately wipes out memory and other cognitive functions. Among older adults in Canada and other countries, it is a leading cause of death. In 2017 alone, over 6,675 deaths in Canada were attributed to it (Statistics Canada, www.statcan.ca, Table 13-10-0394-01) on people and societies across the globe, with 90 million cases expected worldwide by 2050 (Prince et al., 2015).

But AD does not affect men and women equally. A report by a large group of leading experts concluded that AD is more prevalent among women than men in many regions of the world (Mazure & Swendsen, 2016; Winblad et al., 2016). Although scientists are just beginning to unravel the reasons why this is so, some evidence indicates that the hippocampus, a brain region critical for learning and memory, shows potentially important sex differences.

Using measurements from a technique called magnetic resonance imaging (MRI), which you will learn more about later in this chapter, one study analyzed the volume of the hippocampus in 43 patients who had been diagnosed with probable AD and in 23 cognitively intact older adults (Ardekani et al., 2016). Importantly, hippocampal volume was measured several times in each individual during the course of a year, allowing

researchers to assess possible changes that occurred during this time. Overall, hippocampal volume was reduced in the AD group compared to the controls, and the measurements also showed a larger volume decline over the year in the AD patients. However, the magnitude of the volume decline among the AD patients was significantly larger in women: Hippocampal atrophy progressed about 1.5 times faster in women than in men during the year. A more recent study found that changes in hippocampal volume over time in individuals who were cognitively intact when assessed initially are more predictive of an eventual diagnosis of probable AD in women than in men (Burke et al., 2019).

These findings are potentially important clinically because they suggest that measurements of hippocampal volume might be a particularly reliable early indication of the onset of AD in women. Some earlier evidence consistent with this idea comes from an analysis of hippocampal volume in an intriguing project known as "the Nun study" (Snowdon, 2003). The Nun study is a large scale, ongoing longitudinal study of members of the School Sisters of Notre Dame living in various parts of the United States. It is important because researchers obtained a broad range of cognitive and neural measures from a large group of women with relatively similar lifestyles and environments, and they have shown that signs of

AD could be detected in writing samples of sisters decades before they were diagnosed with AD (Snowden et al., 1996). For example, sisters whose writing samples when they were young were grammatically simple and contained few ideas were more likely to later develop AD than those whose writing samples when young were grammatically complex and contained lots of ideas. Goshe and colleagues (2002) obtained postmortem MRI scans of 56 participants in the Nun study, and they found that reduced hippocampal volume was a strong indicator of the presence of AD pathology even in the brains of sisters who were not demented while alive, providing further evidence that hippocampal volume is a sensitive indicator of AD in women.

Changes in hippocampal volume are not the only sex difference related to AD. Compared with men, women exhibit greater rates of brain atrophy in several other regions (Hua et al., 2010) and faster cognitive decline (Ferretti et al., 2018). Researchers and clinicians are increasingly coming to realize that these sex differences likely have important implications for diagnosis and treatment, which should ultimately help scientists craft sex-specific approaches to both diagnosis and treatment of AD (Ferretti et al., 2018; Fisher et al., 2018). Given the worldwide impact of AD, it is difficult to imagine a more important arena for the investigation of sex differences.

object (the fish) and Easterners tended to focus more on the background information (qualities of the water; Masuda & Nisbet, 2001). Such cognitive differences are accompanied by differing neural responses in visual cortex to objects and backgrounds by Westerners and Easterners (Gutchess et al., 2006; Ksander et al., 2018). These cognitive and neural differences are thought to reflect the greater emphasis in Western cultures on analytic processing (i.e., focusing on a primary object independent of its context) and a greater emphasis in Eastern cultures on holistic processing (i.e., focusing on the relationship between an object and its context; Nisbett & Miyamoto, 2005). More generally, evidence for cultural differences in cognitive and neural responses highlights again that the brain is plastic and that culture plays a key role in its wiring (Park & Huang, 2010).

Genes, Epigenetics, and the Environment

Learning Outcomes

WHAT YOU NEED TO KNOW

- Outline the structure of a gene.
- Differentiate between monozygotic and dizygotic twins.
- Explain how epigenetic influences work.
- Give examples of the influence of genetics and the environment to human behaviour.

gene The major unit of hereditary transmission.

chromosomes Strands of DNA wound around each other in a double-helix configuration.

Is it genetics (nature) or the environment (nurture) that reigns supreme in directing a person's behaviour? The emerging picture from current research is that both nature *and* nurture play a role in directing behaviour, and the focus has shifted to examining the interaction of the two rather than the absolute contributions of either alone (Gottesman & Hanson, 2005; Rutter & Silberg, 2002; Zhang & Meaney, 2010).

What Are Genes?

A **gene** is *the major unit of hereditary transmission.* Over time, the term *gene* has been used to refer to two distinct but related concepts. The initial, relatively abstract concept of a gene referred to units of inheritance that specify traits such as eye colour. More recently, genes have been defined as sections on a strand of DNA (deoxyribonucleic acid) that code for the protein molecules that affect traits. Genes are organized into large threads called **chromosomes,** *strands of DNA wound around each other in a double-helix configuration* (see **FIGURE 3.18a**). The DNA in our chromosomes produces protein molecules through the action of a molecule known as messenger RNA (ribonucleic acid; mRNA), which communicates a copy of the DNA code to cells that produce proteins. Chromosomes come in pairs, and humans have 23 pairs each. These pairs of chromosomes are similar but not identical: You inherit one of each pair from your father and one from your mother. There's a twist, however: The selection of *which* of each pair is given to you is random.

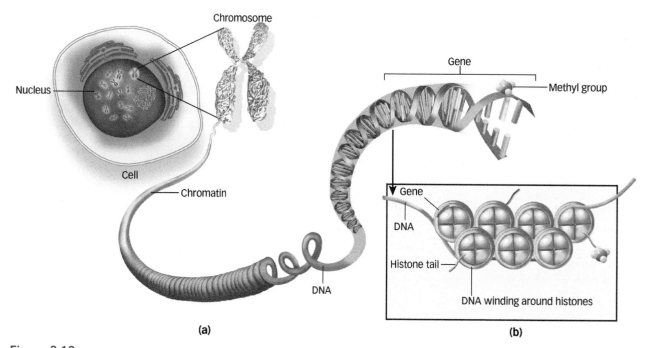

(a) (b)

Figure 3.18

Genes and Epigenetics *(a)* **Genes and Chromosomes.** The cell nucleus houses chromosomes, which are made up of double-helix strands of DNA. Every cell in our bodies has 23 pairs of chromosomes. Genes are segments on the strand of DNA. *(b)* **Epigenetics.** Studies suggest that DNA methylation and histone modification play a key role in the long-lasting effects of early life experiences for both rodents and humans.

Perhaps the most striking example of this random distribution is the determination of sex. In mammals, the chromosomes that determine sex are the X and Y chromosomes; females have two X chromosomes, whereas males have one X and one Y chromosome. You inherited an X chromosome from your mother because she has only X chromosomes to give. Your biological sex, therefore, was determined by whether you received an additional X chromosome or a Y chromosome from your father.

As a species, we share about 99% of the same DNA (and almost as much with other apes), but a portion of DNA varies across individuals. Children share more of this variable portion of DNA with their parents than with more distant relatives or with nonrelatives: They share half their genes with each parent, a quarter of their genes with their grandparents, an eighth of their genes with cousins, and so on. The probability of sharing genes is called *degree of relatedness*. The most genetically related people are *monozygotic twins* (also called *identical twins*), who develop from the splitting of a single fertilized egg and therefore share 100% of their genes. *Dizygotic twins* (*fraternal twins*) develop from two separate fertilized eggs and share 50% of their genes, the same as any two siblings born separately.

Many researchers have tried to determine the relative influence of genetics on behaviour. One way to do this is to compare a trait shown by monozygotic twins with that same trait among dizygotic twins. This type of research usually enlists twins who were raised in the same household, so that the impact of their environment (their socioeconomic status, access to education, parental child-rearing practices, environmental stressors) remains relatively constant. Finding that monozygotic twins have a higher presence of a specific trait suggests a genetic influence (Boomsma et al., 2002).

For example, the likelihood that the dizygotic twin of a person who has schizophrenia (a mental disorder we'll discuss in greater detail in the Psychological Disorders chapter) will *also* develop schizophrenia is 27%. However, this statistic rises to 50% for monozygotic twins. This observation suggests a substantial genetic influence on the likelihood of developing schizophrenia. Monozygotic twins share 100% of their genes, and if one assumes environmental influences are relatively consistent for both members of the twin pair, the 50% likelihood can be traced to genetic factors. That sounds scarily high—until you realize that the remaining 50% probability must be due to environmental influences. In short, genetics can contribute to the development, likelihood, or onset of a variety of traits. But a more complete picture of genetic influences on behaviour must always take the environmental context into consideration. Genes express themselves within an environment, not in isolation.

"The title of my science project is 'My Little Brother: Nature or Nurture.'"

MICHAEL SHAW/CARTOON STOCK

Monozygotic twins (*left*) share 100% of their genes in common, whereas dizygotic twins (*right*) share 50% of their genes, the same as other siblings. Studies of monozygotic and dizygotic twins help researchers estimate the relative contributions of genes and environmental influences on behaviour.

PAUL AVIS/STOCKBYTE/GETTY IMAGES

JBPHOTO1/ALAMY

A Role for Epigenetics

The idea that genes are expressed within an environment is central to an important and rapidly growing area of research known as **epigenetics**: *the study of environmental influences that determine whether or not genes are expressed, or the degree to which they are expressed, without altering the basic DNA sequences that constitute the genes themselves.* To understand how epigenetic influences work, it is useful to think about DNA as analogous to a script for a play or a movie. The biologist Nessa Carey (2012) offers the example of Shakespeare's *Romeo and Juliet*, which was made into a movie back in 1936 starring the classic actors Leslie Howard and Norma Shearer, and in 1996 starring Leonardo DiCaprio and Claire Danes. Shakespeare's tragedy formed the basis of both screenplays, but the directors of the two films used Shakespeare's material in different ways, and the actors in the two films gave different performances. Thus, the final products departed from Shakespeare's play and were different from one another, even though Shakespeare's original play still exists. Something similar happens with epigenetics: Depending on the environment, a gene can be expressed or not expressed without altering the underlying DNA code.

The environment can influence gene expression through **epigenetic marks,** *chemical modifications to DNA that can turn genes on or off.* You can think of epigenetic marks as analogous to notes that the movie directors made on Shakespeare's play that determined how the play was used in a particular film. There are two widely studied epigenetic marks:

- **DNA methylation** involves *adding a methyl group to DNA.* There are special enzymes, referred to as *epigenetic writers,* whose role is to add methyl groups to DNA. Although adding a methyl group doesn't alter the basic DNA sequence, it switches off the methylated gene (see Figure 3.18b). This process is roughly analogous to Claire Danes's director making notes that instruct her to ignore a certain portion of the Shakespeare play. That portion of the play—like the switched-off gene—is still there, but its contents are not expressed.

- **Histone modification** involves *adding chemical modifications to proteins called histones that are involved in packaging DNA.* We tend to visualize DNA as the free-floating double helix shown in Figure 3.18a, but DNA is actually tightly wrapped around groups of histone proteins, as shown in Figure 3.18b. However, whereas DNA methylation switches genes off, histone modification can either switch genes off or turn them on. But just like DNA methylation, histone modifications influence gene expression without altering the underlying DNA sequence (Carey, 2012).

One interesting implication of these processes is that experience can create epigenetic differences between monozygotic twins; although they are epigenetically indistinguishable early in life, as they accumulate experience, they are no longer truly identical (Fraga et al., 2005).

The Relevance of Epigenetics to the Brain, Psychology, and Everyday Life

So far, you have learned a lot of strange new terms and may have wondered which Timothée Chalamet movie to watch next. But we now know that epigenetics is highly relevant to the brain, psychology, and everyday life. Experiments with rats and mice have shown that epigenetic marks left by DNA methylation and histone modification play a role in learning and memory (Bredy et al., 2007; Day & Sweatt, 2011; Levenson & Sweatt, 2005). Several studies have linked epigenetic changes with responses to stress (Zhang & Meaney, 2010), including recent research with humans. For example, studies of nurses working in high-stress versus low-stress environments found differences between the two groups in DNA methylation (Alasaari et al., 2012). Subjective levels of stress in a sample of 92 Canadian adults, as well as physiological signs of stress, were correlated with levels

epigenetics The study of environmental influences that determine whether or not genes are expressed, or the degree to which they are expressed, without altering the basic DNA sequences that constitute the genes themselves.

epigenetic marks Chemical modifications to DNA that can turn genes on or off.

DNA methylation Adding a methyl group to DNA.

histone modification Adding chemical modifications to proteins called histones that are involved in packaging DNA.

of DNA methylation (Lam et al., 2012). Other studies have suggested that epigenetics might even play a role in transmitting the consequences of trauma across generations: Research with Holocaust survivors has revealed reduced DNA methylation of a particular gene, known as FKBP5, in survivors' offspring compared with a control group (Bierer et al., 2020; Yehuda et al., 2016). The psychological significance of this finding remains to be determined, but FKBP5 has been associated with regulation of stress responses (Zannas et al., 2016).

Epigenetics and Early Life Experiences

DNA methylation and histone modifications also play a key role in the long-lasting effects of early experiences for both rats and humans. Key early work from the laboratory of McGill researcher Michael Meaney and his colleagues (Francis et al., 1999; Liu et al., 1997) built on the finding that there are notable differences in the mothering styles of rats: Some mothers spend a lot of time licking and grooming their young pups (high LG mothers), which rat pups greatly enjoy, whereas others spend little time doing so (low LG mothers). The researchers found that pups of high LG mothers are much less fearful as adults when placed in stressful situations than are the adult pups of low LG mothers. Perhaps this simply reflects the effects of a genetic profile shared by the mother and her pups? Not so: The same effects were obtained when the offspring of high LG mothers are raised by low LG mothers, and vice versa.

These effects were accompanied by physiological changes. When placed in fear-inducing situations, adult rats raised by the high LG mothers showed lower levels of several stress-related hormones than did adult rats that had been raised by low LG mothers. There was also increased evidence of hippocampal serotonin in the adult pups of high LG mothers; as you learned earlier in this chapter, increased levels of serotonin are associated with elevated mood. In other words, the high LG pups grow up to become "chilled out" adults. But exactly how did these effects persist from infancy to adulthood? This is where epigenetics comes in. The increased serotonin response produced by high LG mothers triggers a decrease in DNA methylation of the glucocorticoid receptor gene (see the Stress and Health chapter for a discussion of glucocorticoids and stress), which leads to greater expression of the gene and a corresponding ability to respond more calmly to stress (Weaver et al., 2004).

Rodent pups raised by mothers who spend a lot of time licking and grooming them are less fearful as adults in stressful situations.

The rats raised by low LG mothers showed relatively increased DNA methylation of the glucocorticoid receptor gene, which leads to reduced expression of the gene and a corresponding inability to respond calmly to stress. Because DNA methylation can be very stable over time, these studies with rats provided the foundation for more recent studies with humans. The human equivalent of high LG is probably loving and attentive parenting, and the equivalent of low LG is probably childhood neglect and abuse. Indeed, studies show a role for epigenetics in the persisting effects of childhood abuse in adult men (McGowan et al., 2009). Related studies suggest that the effects of early experience are not restricted to a single gene, but occur more broadly (McGowan et al., 2011; Suderman et al., 2012). And a recent large-scale study of over 1,600 children in Great Britain has provided evidence that children raised in economically disadvantaged neighbourhoods showed greater DNA methylation in genes linked to inflammation and smoking than children raised in more economically advantaged neighbourhoods, leading the authors to suggest that epigenetic changes may constitute a "biological pathway through which neighbourhood disadvantage gets under the skin to engender long-term health disparities" (Reuben et al., 2020).

These kinds of results have led both clinicians and researchers to increasingly recognize the importance of epigenetics for various psychological disorders in which early life stress is a risk factor, including depression, schizophrenia, and posttraumatic stress disorder (Kundakovic et al., 2015; Provencal & Binder, 2015; Schiele et al., 2020). Although we are far from fully understanding the complex relationship between epigenetic changes and psychological phenomena, scientists are increasingly recognizing the relevance of epigenetics for psychology (Jones et al., 2018; Sweatt, 2019; Zhang & Meaney, 2010).

The Role of Environmental Factors

Genes set the range of possibilities that can be observed in a population, but the characteristics of any individual within that range are determined by environmental factors and experience. The genetic capabilities that another species might enjoy, such as being able to breathe underwater, are outside the range of *your* possibilities, no matter how much you might desire them.

With these parameters in mind, behavioural geneticists use calculations based on relatedness to compute the heritability of behaviours (Plomin et al., 2001). **Heritability** is *a measure of the variability of behavioural traits among individuals that can be accounted for by genetic factors*. Heritability is calculated as a proportion, and its numerical value (index) ranges from 0 to 1.00. A heritability of 0 means that genes do not contribute to individual differences in the behavioural trait; a heritability of 1.00 means that genes are the *only* reason for the individual differences. As you might guess, scores of 0 or 1.00 occur so infrequently that they are theoretical limits rather than realistic values; almost nothing in human behaviour is completely due to the environment or owed *completely* to genetic inheritance. Scores between 0 and 1.00, then, indicate that individual differences are caused by varying *degrees* of genetic and environmental contributions — a little stronger influence of genetics here, a little stronger influence of the environment there — but each always within the context of the other (Moffitt, 2005; Zhang & Meaney, 2010).

For human behaviour, almost all estimates of heritability are in the moderate range, between .30 and .60. For example, a heritability index of .50 for intelligence indicates that half of the variability in intelligence test scores is attributable to genetic influences and the remaining half is due to environmental influences. Smart parents often (but not always) produce smart children; genetics certainly plays a role. But smart and not-so-smart children attend good or not-so-good schools, practice their piano lessons with more or less regularity, study or don't study as hard as they might, have good and not-so-good teachers and role models, and so on. Genetics is only half the story in intelligence. Environmental influences also play a significant role in predicting the basis of intelligence (see the Intelligence chapter).

Heritability has proven to be a theoretically useful and statistically sound concept in helping scientists understand the relative genetic and environmental influences on behaviour. However, there are four important points about heritability to bear in mind.

- *Heritability is an abstract concept*: It tells us nothing about the *specific* genes that contribute to a trait.
- *Heritability is a population concept*: It tells us nothing about an individual. Heritability provides guidance for understanding differences across individuals in a population rather than abilities within an individual.
- *Heritability is dependent on the environment*: Just as behaviour occurs within certain contexts, so do genetic influences. For example, intelligence isn't an unchanging quality. People are intelligent within a particular learning context, a social setting, a family environment, a socioeconomic class, and so on. Heritability, therefore, is meaningful only for the environmental conditions in which it was computed, and heritability estimates may change dramatically under other environmental conditions.
- *Heritability is not fate*: It tells us nothing about the degree to which interventions can change a behavioural trait. Heritability is useful for identifying behavioural traits that are influenced by genes, but it is not useful for determining how individuals will respond to particular environmental conditions or treatments.

heritability A measure of the variability of behavioural traits among individuals that can be accounted for by genetic factors.

Investigating the Brain

So far, you've read a great deal about the nervous system: how it's organized, how it works, what its components are, and what those components do. But one question remains largely unanswered: *How* do we know all of this? Anatomists can dissect a human brain and identify its structures, but they cannot determine which structures play a role in producing which behaviours by dissecting a nonliving brain.

Scientists use a variety of methods to understand how the brain affects behaviour. Let's consider three of the main ones: studying people with brain damage; studying the brain's electrical activity; and using brain imaging to study brain structure and watch the brain in action. Let's examine each of these ways of investigating the brain.

Studying the Damaged Brain

To better understand the successful operation of a process, it is instructive to identify what happens when that process fails. Much research in neuroscience seeks to link the loss of specific perceptual, motor, emotional, or cognitive functions with specific areas of brain damage (Andrewes, 2001; Kolb & Whishaw, 2015). By studying these instances, neuroscientists can theorize about the functions those brain areas normally perform. Note that the concept of a *damaged* brain is different from that of an *atypical* brain. Scientists are increasingly embracing the concept of *neurodiversity*, that is, the idea that there are natural variations in the structure and function of the brain that produce variations across individuals in cognitive, social, and emotional functions that should be distinguished from a disorder or from a damaged brain (Baron-Cohen, 2017). From this perspective, rather than referring to a "normal" brain, it is more appropriate to refer to a neurotypical brain (Armstrong, 2015). While keeping these important ideas in mind, let's look at how studies of the damaged brain have provided key insights into the neurotypical brain.

The modern history of neuroscience can be dated to the work of Paul Broca (1824–1880) (see The Evolution of Psychological Science chapter). In 1861, Broca described a patient who had lost the capacity to produce spoken language (but not the ability to understand language) due to damage in a small area in the left frontal lobe. In 1874, Carl Wernicke (1848–1905) described a patient with an impairment in language comprehension (but not the ability to produce speech) associated with damage to an area in the upper-left temporal lobe. These areas were named, respectively, *Broca's area* and *Wernicke's area* (see Figure 9.3 in the Language and Thought chapter), and they provided the earliest evidence that the brain locations for speech production and speech comprehension are separate and that for most people, the left hemisphere is critical to producing and understanding language (Young, 1990).

The Emotional Functions of the Frontal Lobes

As you've already seen, the human frontal lobes are a remarkable evolutionary achievement. However, psychology's first glimpse at some functions of the frontal lobes came from a rather unremarkable fellow. He was so unremarkable, in fact, that a single event in his life defined his place in the annals of psychology's history (Macmillan, 2000). Phineas Gage was a muscular 25-year-old railroad worker. On September 13, 1848, in Cavendish, Vermont, he was packing an explosive charge into a crevice in a rock when the powder exploded, driving a 3-foot, 13-pound iron rod through his head at high speed (Harlow, 1868). As **FIGURE 3.19** shows, the rod entered through his lower left jaw and exited through the middle top of his head. Incredibly, Gage lived to tell the tale. But his personality underwent a significant change.

Learning Outcomes

WHAT YOU NEED TO KNOW

- Identify the three main ways that researchers study the human brain.

- Compare and contrast advantages and disadvantages of techniques used to study the brain in action.

(a)

(b)

WARREN ANATOMICAL MUSEUM IN THE FRANCIS A. COUNTWAY LIBRARY OF MEDICINE. GIFT OF JACK AND BEVERLY WILGUS

Figure 3.19

Phineas Gage (*a*) Phineas Gage's traumatic accident allowed researchers to investigate the functions of the frontal lobe and its connections with emotion centres in the subcortical structures. (*b*) The likely path of the metal rod through Gage's skull is reconstructed here.

Before the accident, Gage had been mild-mannered, quiet, conscientious, and a hard worker. After the accident, however, Harlow (1868) reported that he became irritable, irresponsible, indecisive, and given to profanity. The sad change in Gage's personality and emotional life nonetheless provided an unexpected benefit to psychology. His case study was the first to allow researchers to investigate the hypothesis that the frontal lobe is involved in emotion regulation, planning, and decision making. Furthermore, because the connections between the frontal lobe and the subcortical structures of the limbic system were affected, scientists were able to better understand how the amygdala, hippocampus, and related brain structures interacted with the cerebral cortex (Damasio, 2005).

The Distinct Roles of the Left and Right Hemispheres

You'll recall that the cerebral cortex is divided into two hemispheres, although typically the two hemispheres act as one integrated unit. Sometimes, however, disorders can threaten the ability of the brain to function, and the only way to stop them is with radical methods. This is sometimes the case for people who suffer from severe, intractable epilepsy. Seizures that begin in one hemisphere cross the corpus callosum (the thick band of nerve fibers that allows the two hemispheres to communicate) to the opposite hemisphere and start a feedback loop that results in a kind of firestorm in the brain. To alleviate the severity of the seizures, surgeons can sever the corpus callosum in an operation called a *split-brain procedure*. The result is that a seizure that starts in one hemisphere is isolated in that hemisphere because there is no longer a connection to the other side. This procedure helps people with epilepsy but also produces some unusual, if not unpredictable, behaviour.

Normally, any information that initially enters the left hemisphere is also registered in the right hemisphere and vice versa: The information comes in and travels across the corpus callosum, and both hemispheres understand what's going on (see **FIGURE 3.20**). But in a person with a split brain, information entering one hemisphere stays there. Without an intact corpus callosum, there's no way for that information to reach the other hemisphere. The Nobel Laureate Roger Sperry (1913–1994) and his colleagues used this understanding in a series of experiments (Sperry, 1964). For example, they asked a person with a split brain to look at a spot in the centre of a screen and then projected a stimulus either on the left side of the screen (the left visual field) or the right side of the screen (the right visual field), isolating the stimulus to the opposite hemisphere. (See Figure 4.10 in the Sensation and Perception chapter for more details about how information from one visual field enters the opposite hemisphere.)

The hemispheres themselves are specialized for different kinds of tasks. You've just learned about Broca's and Wernicke's areas, which revealed that language processing is largely a left-hemisphere activity. So, imagine that some information came into the left hemisphere of a person with a split brain, and they were asked to describe verbally what it was. No problem: The left hemisphere has the information, it's the "speaking" hemisphere, and so they should have no difficulty verbally describing what they saw. But suppose they were asked to reach behind the screen with their left hand and pick up the object they just saw. Remember that the hemispheres exert contralateral control over the body, meaning that the left hand is controlled by the right hemisphere. Yet this person's right hemisphere has no clue what the object was because that information was received in the left hemisphere and was unable to travel to the right hemisphere! So even though they saw the object and could verbally describe it, they would be unable to use the right hemisphere to perform other tasks regarding that object, such as correctly selecting it from a group with their left hand (see Figure 3.20).

Figure 3.20

Split-Brain Experiment When a person with a split brain is presented with the picture of a ring on the right and a picture of a key on the left side of a screen, they can verbalize "ring" but not "key" because the left hemisphere "sees" the ring and language is usually located in the left hemisphere. They would be able to choose a key with their left hand from a set of objects behind a screen. They would not, however, be able to pick out a ring with their left hand because what the left hemisphere "sees" is not communicated to the left side of their body.

Of course, information presented to the right hemisphere would produce complementary deficits. In this case, they might be presented with a familiar object in their left hand (e.g., a key), be able to demonstrate that they knew what it was (by twisting and turning the key in midair), yet be unable to verbally describe what they were holding. In this case, the information in the right hemisphere is unable to travel to the left hemisphere, which controls the production of speech.

Furthermore, suppose a person with a split brain was briefly flashed the unusual face in **FIGURE 3.21** while they were staring straight ahead. This is called a *chimeric face,* assembled from half-face components of the full faces also shown in the figure. When asked to indicate which face was presented, their answer would depend on how they were asked to respond (Levy et al., 1972). If they were asked to name who they saw, the response would depend on the left, language-dominant, hemisphere; they would report that they saw whoever's half-face had been presented on the right (Leonardo DiCaprio in Figure 3.21). In contrast, if they were asked to point with their left hand (controlled by the right hemisphere), they would indicate the picture of Brad Pitt, because Brad's half-face had been flashed to only the right hemisphere.

These split-brain studies reveal that the two hemispheres perform different functions and can work together seamlessly as long as the corpus callosum is intact. Without a way to transmit information from one hemisphere to the other,

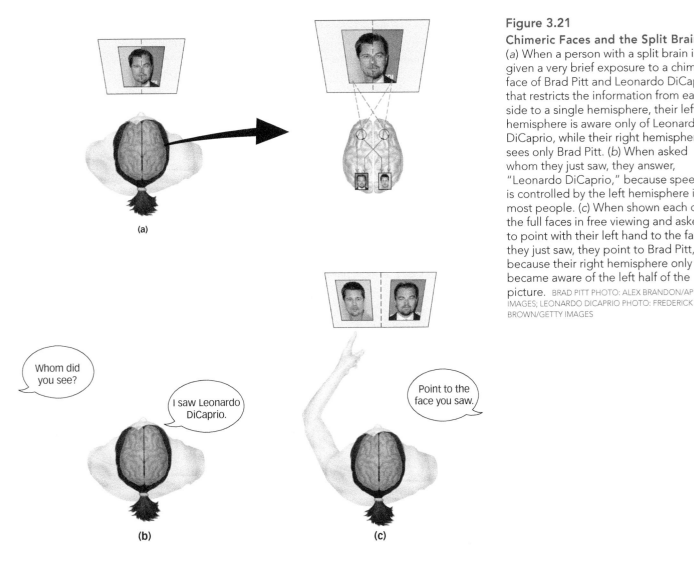

Figure 3.21
Chimeric Faces and the Split Brain
(*a*) When a person with a split brain is given a very brief exposure to a chimeric face of Brad Pitt and Leonardo DiCaprio that restricts the information from each side to a single hemisphere, their left hemisphere is aware only of Leonardo DiCaprio, while their right hemisphere sees only Brad Pitt. (*b*) When asked whom they just saw, they answer, "Leonardo DiCaprio," because speech is controlled by the left hemisphere in most people. (*c*) When shown each of the full faces in free viewing and asked to point with their left hand to the face they just saw, they point to Brad Pitt, because their right hemisphere only became aware of the left half of the picture. BRAD PITT PHOTO: ALEX BRANDON/AP IMAGES; LEONARDO DICAPRIO PHOTO: FREDERICK M. BROWN/GETTY IMAGES

Figure 3.22

Does the EEG Read Minds? The electroencephalograph (EEG) records electrical activity in the brain but cannot discern the content of your thoughts. Many states of consciousness, such as wakefulness and stages of sleep, are characterized by particular types of brain waves. This allows researchers to measure variables like a person's level of attention over time. Medically, the EEG can reveal abnormal patterns of activity associated with brain injuries and disorders.

David Hubel (*left*, b. 1926) and Torsten Wiesel (*right*, b. 1924) received the Nobel Prize in physiology in 1981 for their work on mapping the visual cortex.

electroencephalograph (EEG) A device used to record electrical activity in the brain.

information remains in the hemisphere it initially entered, and we become acutely aware of the different functions of each hemisphere. Of course, a person with a split brain can adapt to this by simply moving their eyes a little so that the same information independently enters both hemispheres. Split-brain studies have continued over the past few decades and continue to play an important role in shaping our understanding of how the brain works (Gazzaniga, 2006).

Studying the Brain's Electrical Activity

A second approach to studying the link between brain structures and behaviour involves recording the pattern of electrical activity of neurons. An **electroencephalograph (EEG)** is *a device used to record electrical activity in the brain*. Typically, electrodes are placed on the outside of the head, and even though the source of electrical activity in synapses and action potentials is far removed from these wires, the EEG can amplify the electric signals several thousand times. This provides a visual record of the underlying electrical activity, as shown in **FIGURE 3.22**.

Using this technique, researchers can determine the amount of brain activity during different experiences and states of consciousness. For example, as you'll read in the Consciousness chapter, the brain shows distinctive patterns of electrical activity when awake versus asleep; in fact, different brain-wave patterns are even associated with different stages of sleep. EEG recordings allow researchers to make these fundamental discoveries about the nature of sleep and wakefulness (Dement, 1978). The EEG can also be used to examine the brain's electrical activity when individuals who are awake engage in a variety of psychological functions, such as perceiving, learning, and remembering. Because the EEG is noninvasive and relatively inexpensive, it is also widely used in research, medicine, and industry to understand brain processes involved in social interactions, sleep problems, and other everyday activities.

A different approach to recording electrical activity resulted in a more refined understanding of the brain's division of responsibilities, even at a cellular level. The Nobel laureates David Hubel and Torsten Wiesel used a technique in which they inserted electrodes into the occipital lobes of anesthetized cats and observed the patterns of action potentials of individual neurons (Hubel, 1988). Hubel and Wiesel amplified the action potential signals through a loudspeaker so that they could hear the signals as clicks, as well as see them on an oscilloscope. While flashing lights in front of the animal's eye, Hubel and Wiesel recorded the resulting activity of neurons in the occipital cortex. They discovered that neurons in the primary visual cortex are activated whenever a contrast between light and dark occurs in part of the visual field, seen particularly well when the visual stimulus was a thick line of light against a dark background. They then found that each neuron responded vigorously only when presented with a contrasting edge at a particular orientation. Since then, many studies have shown that neurons in the primary visual cortex respond to particular features of visual stimuli, such as contrast, shape, and colour (Zeki, 1993).

These neurons in the visual cortex are known as *feature detectors* because they selectively respond to certain aspects of a visual image. For example, some neurons fire only when detecting a vertical line in the middle of the visual field, other neurons fire when a line at a 45° angle is perceived, and still others in response to wider lines, horizontal lines, lines in the periphery of the visual field, and so on (Livingstone & Hubel, 1988). The discovery of this specialized function for neurons was a huge leap forward in our understanding of how the visual cortex works. Feature detectors identify basic dimensions of a stimulus ("slanted line . . . other slanted line . . . horizontal line"); those dimensions are then combined during a later stage of visual processing to allow recognition and perception of a stimulus ("Oh, it's a letter *A*").

Other studies have identified a variety of features that are detected by sensory neurons. For instance, some visual processing neurons in the temporal lobe are activated only when detecting faces (Kanwisher, 2000; Perrett et al., 1982). Neurons in this area are specialized for processing faces; damage to this area results in an inability to perceive faces. These complementary observations (showing that the type of function that is lost or altered when a brain area is damaged corresponds to the kind of information processed by neurons in that cortical area) provide the most compelling evidence linking the brain to behaviour.

Using Brain Imaging to Study Structure and to Watch the Brain in Action

The third major way that neuroscientists can peer into the workings of the human brain involves *neuroimaging techniques* that use advanced technology to create images of the living, healthy brain (Posner & Raichle, 1994; Raichle & Mintun, 2006). *Structural brain imaging* provides information about the basic structure of the brain and allows clinicians or researchers to see changes or abnormalities in brain structure. *Functional brain imaging,* in contrast, provides information about the activity of the brain while people perform various kinds of cognitive or motor tasks.

Structural Brain Imaging

One of the first neuroimaging techniques developed was the *computerized axial tomography (CT) scan,* in which a scanner rotates a device around a person's head and takes a series of X-ray photographs from different angles. Computer programs then combine these images to provide views from any angle. CT scans show different densities of tissue in the brain. For example, the higher-density skull looks white on a CT scan, the cortex shows up as gray, and the least-dense fissures and ventricles in the brain look dark (see **FIGURE 3.23**). CT scans are used to locate lesions or tumours, which typically appear darker because they are less dense than the cortex.

Magnetic resonance imaging (MRI) uses a strong magnetic field to line up the nuclei of specific molecules in the brain tissue. Brief but powerful pulses of radio waves cause the nuclei to rotate out of alignment. When a pulse ends, the nuclei snap back in line with the magnetic field and give off a small amount of energy in the process. Different molecules have unique energy signatures when they snap back in line with the magnetic field, so these signatures can be used to reveal brain structures with different molecular compositions. MRI produces pictures of soft tissue at a better resolution than a CT scan, as you can see in Figure 3.23. These techniques give psychologists a clearer picture of the structure and volume of the brain (see Hot Science: Big Brain, Smart Brain?) and can help localize brain damage (as when someone suffers a stroke), but they reveal nothing about the functions of the brain.

Diffusion tensor imaging (DTI) is a type of MRI, developed relatively recently, that is used to visualize white matter pathways, which are fiber bundles that connect both nearby and distant brain regions to each other. DTI measures the rate and direction of diffusion or movement of water molecules, which reveal where a white matter pathway goes. DTI is a critical tool in mapping the connectivity of the human brain and it plays a central role in an ambitious undertaking known as the Human Connectome Project. This is an international (largely British and American) collaborative effort that began in 2009 and aims to provide a complete map of the connectivity of neural pathways in the brain: the human connectome (Toga et al., 2012).

Figure 3.23
Structural Imaging Techniques (CT and MRI) CT (*left*) and MRI (*right*) scans are used to provide information about the structure of the brain and can help to spot tumours and other kinds of damage. Each scan shown here provides a snapshot of a single slice in a healthy brain. Note that the MRI scan provides a clearer, higher-resolution image than the CT scan. (See the text for further discussion of how these images are constructed and what they depict.)

Hot Science | Big Brain, Smart Brain?

Is a bigger brain a smarter brain? This seemingly straightforward question has fascinated psychologists, neuroscientists, and philosophers for centuries. For example, the British psychologist Sir Francis Galton noted that measurements of head volume in University of Cambridge undergraduates who obtained high honours revealed that these students "had considerably larger brains than others at the age of nineteen" (Galton, 1869, p. 156). Does that mean you should grab a tape measure to try to predict how you and your friends will do on an upcoming exam? Not so fast. A century later, a literature review uncovered deficiencies in previous studies that had claimed to find a positive correlation between brain volume and intelligence; the review also highlighted more recent evidence that failed to establish any such relationship (Stott, 1983).

These discrepancies are perhaps not surprising, because early studies used indirect and inadequate methods, such as attempting to estimate brain volume by measuring head circumference. However, the advent of modern brain-imaging techniques such as MRI has made it possible to obtain direct and precise measurements of brain volume. Indeed, studies using MRI have typically reported a positive correlation between overall brain volume and various measures of intelligence (Gignac & Bates, 2017; Pietschnig et al., 2015). But there is still debate about the strength of that correlation. As you learned in the Methods in Psychology chapter, a positive correlation can fall anywhere from very weak (near 0) to very strong (near +1.00); we would think differently about the relation between brain volume and intelligence depending on whether the actual correlation between them is +.05, +.25, or +.75. Also, some or all of the correlation between brain volume and intelligence could be due to third variables such as age, socioeconomic status, height, or sex. As you also learned in the Methods chapter, interpreting correlations can be difficult because of the third-variable problem—that is, a relationship between two variables may be caused by an unmeasured third variable.

Recent large-scale studies have taken a large step forward in attempting to resolve these issues. The researchers used a valuable new resource known as the UK Biobank (UKB), a massive database of health-related information from volunteer participants being built in the United Kingdom (Miller et al., 2016). UKB has already acquired genetic data from approximately 500,000 adults and, as of early 2020, had acquired structural MRI scans from about 45,000 adults (Littlejohns et al., 2020). Nave et al. (2019) analyzed MRI-measured brain volume in 13,608 UKB participants and related it to several cognitive measures that were obtained from those same participants. This sample dwarfs all other previous studies on this topic: In fact, it is 70% larger than the sample size from all previous studies combined! This is important, because with such a large sample, the data obtained are likely to be very stable, and if there is a correlation between brain volume and cognitive measures, the researchers should be able to detect it. A large sample size also helps the researchers to control statistically for the possible influence of variables such as age, socioeconomic status, height, and sex.

The most important of the cognitive measures analyzed by Nave et al. (2019) focused on the ability to solve novel problems that demand logic and reasoning ability, which is known as *fluid intelligence* (discussed in more detail in the Intelligence chapter). After controlling for other variables, Nave et al. (2019) found a significant correlation of +.19 between brain volume and fluid intelligence. In a related study using a slightly different sample from the UKB and a different approach to estimating intelligence, Cox et al. (2019) reported a significant and slightly larger correlation of +.27. These findings are important because they clearly establish a relationship between brain volume and intelligence that cannot be explained by age, socioeconomic status, height, or sex. However, the correlations are not large, and suggest that brain volume accounts for only a small portion of the variation in intelligence across the samples investigated. Moreover, because the data are correlational, we still don't know whether larger overall brain volume causes increases in intelligence or vice versa—it is conceivable that people with higher levels of intelligence use their brain in a way that produces increased volume. Although these results provide a solid basis for evaluating the extent to which a bigger brain is a smarter brain, you should still leave your tape measure in the drawer next time you try to predict your academic success or anyone else's.

Measuring your head circumference won't tell you much about your cognitive abilities.

A unique and exciting feature of the Human Connectome Project is that the researchers have made available some of the results at their Web site (www.humanconnectomeproject.org), which includes fascinating colourful images of some of the connection pathways they have discovered.

Functional Brain Imaging

Functional brain-imaging techniques show researchers much more than just the structure of the brain—they allow us to watch the brain in action. These techniques rely on the fact that activated brain areas demand more energy, which is supplied by increased blood flow; and functional-imaging techniques can detect such changes in blood flow. For instance, in *positron emission tomography* (*PET*), a harmless radioactive substance is injected into a person's bloodstream. The brain is then scanned by radiation detectors as the person performs perceptual or cognitive tasks, such as reading or speaking. Areas of the brain that are activated during these tasks demand more energy and greater blood flow, resulting in a higher amount of radioactivity in that region. The radiation detectors record the level of radioactivity in each region, producing a computerized image of the activated areas (see **FIGURE 3.24**).

For psychologists today, the most widely used functional brain-imaging technique is *functional magnetic resonance imaging* (*fMRI*), which detects the difference between oxygenated hemoglobin and deoxygenated hemoglobin when exposed to magnetic pulses. Hemoglobin is the molecule in the blood that carries oxygen to our tissues, including the brain. When active neurons demand more energy and blood flow, oxygenated hemoglobin concentrates in the active areas; fMRI detects the oxygenated hemoglobin and provides a picture of the level of activation in each brain area (see Figure 3.24).

Both fMRI and PET enable researchers to localize changes in the brain very accurately, but fMRI has a couple of advantages over PET. First, fMRI does not require any exposure to a radioactive substance. Second, fMRI can localize changes in brain activity across briefer periods than PET, which makes it more useful for analyzing psychological processes that occur extremely quickly, such as reading a word or recognizing a face. With fMRI, researchers can design experiments that more closely resemble the ones they carry out in the psychology laboratory.

Functional MRI can also be used to explore the relationship of brain regions with each other, using a recently developed technique referred to as *resting state functional connectivity*. As implied by the name, this technique does not require participants to perform a task; they simply rest quietly while fMRI measurements are made. Functional connectivity measures the extent to which spontaneous activity in different brain regions is correlated over time; brain regions whose activity is highly correlated are thought to be functionally connected with each other (Biswal et al., 1995; Lee et al., 2013).

Functional connectivity measures have been used extensively in recent years to identify brain *networks*, which, as you learned earlier in the chapter, are sets of brain

DTI allows researchers to visualize white matter pathways in the brain, the fiber bundles that play an important role by connecting brain regions to one another.

Figure 3.24
Functional Imaging Techniques (PET and fMRI) PET and fMRI scans provide information about the function of the brain by revealing which brain areas become more or less active in different conditions. The PET scan (directly below) shows areas in the left hemisphere (Broca's area, left; lower parietal—upper temporal area, right) that become active when people hold in mind a string of letters for a few seconds. The red areas in the fMRI scans (all views to the left) indicate activity in the auditory cortex of a person listening to music.

PET scan

Bharat Biswal pioneered the method of resting state functional connectivity, which has been an indispensable tool in allowing neuroscientists to map brain networks.

regions that are closely connected to each other (Yeo et al., 2011). For example, functional connectivity helped to identify the *default network* (Gusnard & Raichle, 2001; Raichle, 2015), a group of interconnected regions in the frontal, temporal, and parietal lobes that is involved in internally focused cognitive activities, such as remembering past events, imagining future events, daydreaming, and mind wandering (Buckner et al., 2008; Buckner & DiNicola, 2019) (see the chapters on Memory and Consciousness).

Functional connectivity, along with DTI (which measures structural connectivity), is used in studies conducted by the Human Connectome Project and will contribute important information to the map of the human connectome. It also has potentially important applications because researchers believe that advances in understanding brain connectivity can enhance our ability to predict and characterize the clinical course of brain disorders, such as Alzheimer's disease (Fornito et al., 2015).

Caution Is Needed Before Jumping to Conclusions Although the insights being obtained from fMRI are exciting, it is important that we don't get too carried away with them, as sometimes happens in media depictions of fMRI results (Marcus, 2012; Poldrack, 2018). FMRI (and PET) images typically result from a comparison between an experimental task and a control task, so when we see increased activation in a particular brain region, this does *not* mean that we are only using that small part of our brain to perform the experimental task. Consider also as an example the topic of memory accuracy and distortion. Using experimental paradigms that you'll learn about in the chapter on Memory, fMRI studies have shown that activity in some parts of the brain is greater during the retrieval of accurate rather than inaccurate memories (Schacter & Loftus, 2013). Does that mean we are ready to use fMRI in the courtroom to determine whether a witness is recounting an accurate memory or an inaccurate memory?

Schacter and Loftus argued that the answer to this question is an emphatic no. For instance, we don't yet know whether the results of laboratory fMRI studies of memory, which typically use simple materials like words or pictures, generalize to the kinds of complex everyday events that are relevant in the courtroom. Furthermore, evidence that fMRI can distinguish accurate from inaccurate memories comes from studies in which brain activity is averaged across a *group* of participants. But in the courtroom, we need to determine whether an *individual* is remembering accurately or not, and there is little evidence yet that fMRI can do so. More generally, it is important to think carefully about how fMRI evidence is obtained before we leap to conclusions about how that evidence can be used in everyday life (Poldrack, 2018).

Transcranial Magnetic Stimulation

We noted earlier that researchers have learned a lot about the brain by studying the behaviour of people with brain injuries. Scientists have discovered a way to mimic brain damage with a benign technique called *transcranial magnetic stimulation (TMS)* (Barker et al., 1985; Hallett, 2000). TMS delivers a magnetic pulse that passes through the skull and deactivates neurons in the cerebral cortex for a short period. Researchers can direct TMS pulses to particular brain regions (essentially turning them off) and then measure temporary changes in the way a person moves, sees, thinks, remembers, speaks, or feels. By manipulating the state of the brain, scientists can perform experiments that establish causal relationships.

For example, as mentioned earlier, fMRI studies have linked the default network with remembering past experiences and imagining future experiences. But these observations don't tell us whether particular regions in the default network play a *causal* role in remembering or imagining. In recent studies, researchers used TMS to interfere with

Transcranial magnetic stimulation (TMS) activates and deactivates regions of the brain with a magnetic pulse, temporarily mimicking brain damage.

the operation of a particular region in the default network, the angular gyrus in the parietal lobe, just before people performed memory and imagination tasks (Bonnici et al., 2018; Thakral et al., 2017). TMS reduced the number of details that people remembered from past experiences and imagined in future experiences, thereby providing evidence that this part of the default network may play a causal role in remembering and imagining.

Scientists have also begun to combine TMS with fMRI, allowing them to localize precisely where in the brain TMS is having its effect (Parkin et al., 2015). Studies suggest that TMS has no harmful side effects (Anand & Hotson, 2002; Pascual-Leone et al., 1993), and this tool has changed the study of how our brains create our thoughts, feelings, and actions. The picture of human brain activity that emerges from these methods should help to dispel common myths about the brain that remain popular even today (see Other Voices: Neuromyths).

Perhaps the most important takeaway from our review of methods for studying the brain is that each method provides psychologists with a specific type of tool for exploring how various aspects of brain structure or function are related to psychological constructs. Each method has strengths and weaknesses, so an important task for researchers is to decide which of the available tools is the most appropriate for their particular scientific question. Making that decision requires both an understanding of the possibilities and limitations of each tool, as well as framing a scientific question clearly enough to make an informed choice among the available tools.

Chapter Review

Neurons: The Origin of Behaviour

- Neurons are the building blocks of the nervous system: They process information received from the outside world, communicate with each other, and send messages to the body's muscles and organs.

- Neurons are composed of three major parts: the cell body, dendrites, and the axon. The cell body contains the nucleus, which houses the organism's genetic material. Dendrites receive sensory signals from other neurons and transmit this information to the cell body. Each axon carries signals from the cell body to other neurons or to muscles and organs in the body.

- Neurons don't actually touch. They are separated by a small gap, which is part of the synapse across which signals are transmitted from one neuron to another.

- Glial cells provide support for neurons, usually in the form of the myelin sheath, which coats the axon to facilitate the transmission of information. In demyelinating diseases, the myelin sheath deteriorates.

- Neurons are differentiated according to the functions they perform. The three major types of neurons include sensory neurons (e.g., bipolar neurons), motor neurons, and interneurons (e.g., Purkinje cells).

The Electrochemical Actions of Neurons: Information Processing

- The neuron's resting potential is due to differences in the potassium (K^+) concentrations inside and outside the cell membrane, resulting from open channels that allow K^+ to flow outside the membrane while closed channels prevent sodium ions (Na^+) and other ions from flowing into the neuron. The conduction of an electric signal within a neuron happens when the resting potential is reversed by an electric impulse called an action potential.

- If electric signals reach a threshold, this initiates an action potential, an all-or-none signal that moves down the entire length of the axon. The action potential occurs when K^+ channels in the axon membrane close and Na^+ channels open, allowing the Na^+ ions to flow inside the axon.

- After the action potential has reached its maximum, a chemical pump reverses the imbalance in ions, returning the neuron to its resting potential. For a brief refractory period, the action potential cannot be reinitiated. Once it is initiated, the action potential spreads down the axon, jumping across the nodes of Ranvier to the synapse.

- Communication between neurons takes place through synaptic transmission, where an action potential triggers release of neurotransmitters from the terminal buttons of the sending neuron's axon, which travel across the synapse to bind with receptors in the receiving neuron's dendrite. Neurotransmitters bind to dendrites on specific receptor sites; they leave the synapse through reuptake, through enzyme deactivation, and by binding to autoreceptors.

- Some of the major neurotransmitters are acetylcholine (ACh), dopamine, glutamate, GABA, norepinephrine, serotonin, and endorphins.

- Drugs can affect behaviour by acting as agonists—that is, by facilitating or increasing the actions of neurotransmitters—or as antagonists, by blocking the action of neurotransmitters. Recreational drug use can have an effect on brain function.

The Organization of the Nervous System

- Neurons make up nerves, which in turn form the human nervous system.

- The nervous system is divided into the peripheral and the central nervous systems. The central nervous system is composed of the spinal cord and the brain.

- The peripheral nervous system connects the central nervous system with the rest of the body and is itself divided into the somatic nervous system and the autonomic nervous system. The somatic nervous system, which conveys information into and out of the central nervous system, controls voluntary muscles, whereas the autonomic nervous system automatically controls the body's organs.

- The autonomic nervous system is further divided into the sympathetic and parasympathetic nervous systems, which complement each other in their effects on the body. The sympathetic nervous system prepares the body for action in threatening situations, and the parasympathetic nervous system returns the body to its normal state.

- The spinal cord can control some basic behaviours such as spinal reflexes without input from the brain.

Structure of the Brain

- The brain can be divided into the hindbrain, midbrain, and forebrain.

- The hindbrain generally coordinates information coming into and out of the spinal cord with structures such as the medulla, the reticular formation, the cerebellum, and the pons. These structures, respectively, coordinate breathing and heart rate, regulate sleep and arousal levels, coordinate fine motor skills, and communicate this information to the cortex.

- The structures of the midbrain, the tectum and tegmentum, generally coordinate functions such as orientation to the environment and movement and arousal towards sensory stimuli.

- The forebrain generally coordinates higher-level functions, such as perceiving, feeling, and thinking. The forebrain houses subcortical structures, such as the thalamus, hypothalamus, limbic system (including the hippocampus and amygdala), and basal ganglia; all these structures perform a variety of functions related to motivation and emotion.

- The endocrine system works closely with the nervous system to regulate thoughts, emotions, and behaviours through the release of hormones. The pituitary gland orchestrates the functioning of the endocrine system by releasing hormones that direct the functions of other glands.

- Also in the forebrain, the cerebral cortex, composed of two hemispheres with four lobes each (occipital, parietal, temporal, and frontal), performs tasks that help make us fully human: thinking, planning, judging, perceiving, and behaving purposefully and voluntarily.

- Neurons in the brain can be shaped by experience and by the environment, making the human brain amazingly plastic.

Genes, Epigenetics, and the Environment

- The gene, or the unit of hereditary transmission, is built from strands of DNA in a double-helix formation that is organized into chromosomes. Humans have 23 pairs of chromosomes, half of which come from each parent. A child shares 50% of their genes with each parent.

- Monozygotic twins share 100% of their genes, whereas dizygotic twins share 50%, the same as any other siblings. Because of their genetic relatedness, twins are often participants in genetic research.

- Epigenetics refers to the study of environmental influences that determine whether or not genes are expressed, without altering the basic DNA sequences that constitute the genes themselves. Epigenetic marks such as DNA methylation and histone modification influence whether specific genes are switched on or off. Epigenetic influences have been shown to play a critical role in the persisting effects of early experiences in rats and humans.

- The study of genetics indicates that both genes and the environment work together to influence behaviour. Genes set the range of variation in populations within a given environment, but they do not predict individual characteristics; experience and other environmental factors play a crucial role as well.

Investigating the Brain

- There are three major approaches to studying the link between the brain and behaviour, outlined as follows.

- One approach is to observe how perceptual, motor, intellectual, and emotional capacities are affected after brain damage. By carefully relating specific psychological and behavioural disruptions to damage in particular areas of the brain, researchers can better understand how the brain area normally plays a role in producing those behaviours.

- A second approach is to examine global electrical activity in the brain and the activity patterns of single neurons. The patterns of electrical activity in large brain areas can be examined from outside the skull using the electroencephalograph (EEG). Single-cell recordings taken from specific neurons can be linked to specific perceptual or behavioural events, suggesting that those neurons represent particular kinds of stimuli or control particular aspects of behaviour.

- The third approach is to use brain imaging to scan the brain as people perform different perceptual or intellectual tasks. Correlating energy consumption in particular brain areas with specific cognitive and behavioural events suggests that those brain areas are involved in specific types of perceptual, motor, cognitive, or emotional processing.

Changing Minds

1. While watching late-night TV, you come across an infomercial for all-natural BrainGro. "It's a well-known fact that most people use only 10% of their brain," the spokesman promises, "but with BrainGro you can increase that number from 10% to 99%!" Why should you be skeptical of the claim that we use only 10% of our brains? What would happen if a drug actually increased neuronal activity tenfold?

2. Your friend has been feeling depressed and has gone to a psychiatrist for help. "He prescribed a medication that's supposed to increase serotonin in my brain. But my feelings depend on me, not on a bunch of chemicals in my head," she said. What examples could you give your friend to convince her that hormones and neurotransmitters really do influence our cognition, mood, and behaviour?

3. A classmate has read the section in this chapter about the evolution of the central nervous system. "Evolution is just a theory," they say. "Not everyone believes in it. And even if it's true that we're all descended from monkeys, that doesn't have anything to do with the psychology of humans alive today." What is your friend misunderstanding about evolution? How would you better explain to your friend the relevance of evolution to modern psychology?

4. A news program reports on a study (Hölzel et al., 2011) in which people who practiced meditation for about 30 minutes a day for 8 weeks showed changes in their brains, including increases in the size of the hippocampus and the amygdala. You tell a friend about the study, who's skeptical. "The brain doesn't change like that. Basically, the brain you're born with is the brain you're stuck with for the rest of your life," your friend says. Why is their statement wrong? What are several specific ways in which the brain does change over time?

5. A friend of yours announces that he's figured out why he's bad at math. "I read it in a book," he says. "Left-brained people are analytical and logical, but right-brained people are creative and artistic. I'm an art major, so I must be right-brained, and that's why I'm not good at math." Why is your friend's view too simplistic?

6. **Visualizing Data** A friend says, "I'll play any other sport than football. I don't want to risk a concussion!" Using the DATA, respond to your friend.

Key Terms

neurons (p. 67)
cell body (soma) (p. 68)
dendrite (p. 68)
axon (p. 68)
myelin sheath (p. 68)
glial cells (p. 68)
synapse (p. 68)
sensory neurons (p. 68)
motor neurons (p. 68)
interneurons (p. 69)
resting potential (p. 72)
action potential (p. 72)
refractory period (p. 73)
terminal buttons (p. 74)
neurotransmitters (p. 74)
receptors (p. 74)
acetylcholine (ACh) (p. 75)
dopamine (p. 75)

glutamate (p. 75)
GABA (gamma-aminobutyric acid) (p. 75)
norepinephrine (p. 75)
serotonin (p. 76)
endorphins (p. 76)
agonists (p. 76)
antagonists (p. 76)
nervous system (p. 78)
central nervous system (CNS) (p. 78)
peripheral nervous system (PNS) (p. 79)
somatic nervous system (p. 79)
autonomic nervous system (ANS) (p. 79)
sympathetic nervous system (p. 79)
parasympathetic nervous system (p. 79)

spinal reflexes (p. 81)
reflex arc (p. 81)
hindbrain (p. 83)
medulla (p. 83)
reticular formation (p. 83)
cerebellum (p. 83)
pons (p. 84)
tectum (p. 84)
tegmentum (p. 84)
cerebral cortex (p. 85)
subcortical structures (p. 85)
thalamus (p. 86)
hypothalamus (p. 86)
hippocampus (p. 86)
amygdala (p. 86)
basal ganglia (p. 87)
endocrine system (p. 87)
pituitary gland (p. 87)

corpus callosum (p. 90)
occipital lobe (p. 90)
parietal lobe (p. 90)
temporal lobe (p. 91)
frontal lobe (p. 91)
association areas (p. 92)
mirror neurons (p. 92)
cultural neuroscience (p. 94)
gene (p. 96)
chromosomes (p. 96)
epigenetics (p. 98)
epigenetic marks (p. 98)
DNA methylation (p. 98)
histone modification (p. 98)
heritability (p. 100)
electroencephalograph (EEG) (p. 104)

Sensation and Perception

DANIEL KISH IS A MIDDLE-AGED CALIFORNIAN with master's degrees in psychology and education. Growing up, he wanted to be either a pilot or Batman. He enjoys making music, solo hiking, and mountain biking. He founded and now leads a nonprofit organization and spends much of his time working with and teaching children. Daniel is also totally blind.

When Daniel was a year old, he had to have both eyes removed because of cancer. He "sees" using a form of echolocation, or sonar, rather like that used by bats and dolphins. He clicks his tongue quietly against the roof of his mouth (once every few seconds) as he moves around the world. The clicks are reflected off physical surfaces—trees, walls, fences, lampposts—and Daniel uses the echoes of these clicks to create a mental image of his environment. The echoes inform Daniel about the location of objects, their size and shape, and even what they are made of. The images that are created using this "flash sonar" technique are not as precise as vision would be, but they are informative about the space around him. Daniel says, "You do get a continuous sort of vision, the way you might if you used flashes to light up a darkened scene. It comes into clarity and focus with every flash, a kind of three-dimensional fuzzy geometry. . . . You have a depth of structure, and you have position and dimension. You also have a pretty strong sense of density and texture that are sort of like the color, if you will, of flash sonar" (Hurst, 2017). The visual analogies are apt: Recent brain-imaging studies demonstrate that blind users of flash sonar, including Daniel, activate the "visual" parts of their brain, in the occipital lobe, when they are actively echolocating (Norman & Thaler, 2019; Thaler et al., 2011).

Daniel taught himself flash sonar as a child so that he could be active and independent. He now teaches blind people of all ages to use echolocation through his nonprofit World Access for the Blind. Daniel, and other blind people who use echolocation, teach us all that, with enough practice, we can all change our brains to do amazing things, even "see" like bats, though we can't all be Batman.

WORLD ACCESS FOR THE BLIND

Daniel Kish, who has been totally blind since birth, enjoys solo trips in the mountains of his native California.

IN THIS CHAPTER, WE'LL EXPLORE THE NATURE of sensation and perception. These experiences are basic to survival and reproduction; we wouldn't last long without the ability to accurately make sense of the world around us. Indeed, research on sensation and perception is the basis for much of psychology, a pathway towards understanding more complex cognition and behaviour such as memory, emotion, motivation, and decision making.

We'll look at how physical energy in the world around us is encoded by our senses and converted into electrical activity that is sent to the brain; it then enters our conscious awareness.

We'll devote a fair amount of space to understanding how the visual system works. Then we'll discuss how we perceive sounds such as words and music and noise, followed by the body senses, emphasizing touch, pain, and balance. We'll end with the chemical senses of smell and taste, which together allow you to savour the foods you eat. But before doing any of that, we will first distinguish between sensation and perception, to illustrate how perception depends on knowledge and experience as well as on sensory information.

Sensation and Perception Are Distinct Activities

Imagine the taste of chocolate. Imagine the feeling of stroking a purring kitten. Imagine your favorite song. In all cases, you are remembering *perceptions* that originated, in part, as sensory information (*sensations*) in your mouth, on your skin, and in your ears. Sensation and perception may appear to us to be one seamless event, but sensation precedes, and is transformed by, perception.

- **Sensation** is *simple stimulation of a sense organ*. It is the basic registration of light, sound, pressure, odour, or taste as parts of your body interact with the physical world.
- **Perception** occurs in your brain as sensation is registered there. It is *the organization, identification, and interpretation of a sensation in order to form a mental representation*.

For example, your eyes are coursing across these sentences right now. The sensory receptors in your eyeballs are registering different patterns of light reflecting off the page. Your brain, however, is integrating and processing that light information into the meaningful perception of words, such as *meaningful, perception,* and *words*. Your eyes — the sensory organs — aren't really seeing words; they're simply encoding different lines and curves on a page. Your brain — the perceptual organ — is transforming those lines and curves into a coherent mental representation of words and concepts.

Consciously, it may *seem* as if you're reading words directly, but reading is a learned skill. You may remember how slow and confusing reading was when you first started. After years of practice, it now may feel automatic. But without that learning, the sensory information — the lines and curves on the page — would be meaningless. Particular kinds of damage to the visual processing centres in the brain can interfere with reading and with the interpretation of information coming from the eyes: In this case, the senses are intact, but perceptual ability is compromised.

Sensory Energy and Transduction

How do sensory receptors communicate with the brain? It all depends on the process of **transduction,** which occurs *when sense receptors convert physical signals from the environment into neural signals that are sent to the central nervous system.* In vision, light reflected from surfaces provides the eyes with information about the shape, colour, and position of objects. In hearing, vibrations (e.g., from vocal cords or a guitar string) cause changes in air pressure that propagate through space to a listener's ears. In touch, the pressure of a surface against the skin signals its shape, texture, and temperature. In taste and smell, molecules dispersed in the air or dissolved in saliva reveal the identity of substances that we may or may not want to eat.

Learning Outcomes

WHAT YOU NEED TO KNOW

- Distinguish between sensation and perception.
- Explain what transduction is.
- Give examples of how sensation and perception are measured.

sensation Simple stimulation of a sense organ.

perception The organization, identification, and interpretation of a sensation in order to form a mental representation.

transduction The process whereby sense receptors convert physical signals from the environment into neural signals that are sent to the central nervous system.

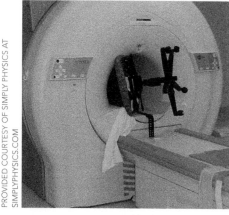

When someone accidentally rolled an office chair into a room containing an MRI system, it flew across the room to the magnet and got stuck as soon as it entered the strong field of the magnet. People can't sense this strong magnetic field, which is why accidents like this happen. Why do you think that we've evolved in such a way that we are not able to detect all the information there is "out there"? Surely, more information would be better than less and would confer a survival advantage, don't you think?

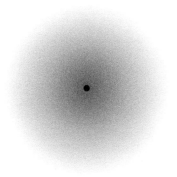

Stare at the central black dot in the image above. After several seconds, the grey cloud around the dot will disappear. This phenomenon, called Troxler fading (see Simons et al., 2006), is another example of adaptation.

sensory adaptation The process whereby sensitivity to prolonged stimulation tends to decline over time as an organism adapts to current (unchanging) conditions.

In each case, physical energy from the world is converted to electrical signals, which are interpreted by your brain to construct what you perceive as the world "out there."

Each type of sensory receptor is uniquely sensitive to a particular type of energy. The eye is sensitive to light (but not to sound); the skin to mechanical pressure (but not to visible light). The eye is sensitive to mechanical pressure, too, but only a little bit. If you close your eye and push on your eyelid with your finger, you might see sparkly dots. This mechanical pressure is registered by the receptors in your eye as light, not touch. Think about what that means: You *perceived* light when sensory receptors in the eye were stimulated, even though the stimulus *was not light*. The physical energy of your finger was transduced into electrical signals that were carried along axons, crossed synapses, and were interpreted by your brain as light. Although perception "feels" direct and immediate, it is not. We'll discuss in more detail how transduction works in different sensory domains including vision, hearing, touch, taste, and smell in separate sections later in this chapter.

The Illusion of Perception

Bats, rats, and mice communicate with each other using high sound frequencies that humans cannot hear; bees and butterflies find food by seeing "colours" we cannot see. In fact, as you'll learn later in this chapter we can see only a very small portion of electromagnetic frequencies—those that generate visible light. But there's nothing about these specific frequencies that makes them inherently visible; we can see them because those are the frequencies for which we have visual receptors. Some animals navigate by sensing the earth's magnetic field. We cannot sense even strong magnetic fields, like those in magnetic resonance imaging (MRI) systems, although they can be very dangerous.

Your mother is probably grateful that your head wasn't any bigger when you were born. Humans have evolved so that, at birth, all bits of them can fit through a woman's pelvis. That limits maximum head size, which in turn limits the number of neurons your brain can have and, therefore, its capacity for processing sensory information. The senses act like gates. They allow a limited amount of information in and do not admit other information. The illusion of perception is that we perceive a rich, detailed, and complete world around us, despite the sensory signals that we detect being a small subset of what is "out there."

Sensory Adaptation

When you walk into a bakery, the aroma of freshly baked bread overwhelms you, but after a few minutes the smell fades. If you dive into cold water, the temperature is shocking at first, but after a few minutes you get used to it. When you wake up in the middle of the night for a drink of water, the bathroom light blinds you, but after a few minutes you no longer squint. These are all examples of **sensory adaptation,** whereby *sensitivity to prolonged stimulation tends to decline over time as an organism adapts to current (unchanging) conditions.*

Sensory adaptation is a useful process. Imagine what your sensory and perceptual world would be like without it. When you put on your jeans in the morning, the feeling of rough cloth against your bare skin would be as noticeable hours later as it was in the first few minutes. If you had to be constantly aware of how your tongue feels while it is resting in your mouth, you'd be driven to distraction.

Our sensory systems respond more strongly to changes in stimulation than to constant stimulation. A change in stimulation often signals a need for action—that is, if you are walking across a street and suddenly hear squealing brakes, you move! A sensory signal that doesn't change usually doesn't require any action, and your body discards such signals. This is another way that our bodies only perceive a subset of what is "out there."

Psychophysics

When shopping around for a new computer, you consider different models in terms of their performance: What is the resolution of the screen? What is the processing speed? How much data can it store? How long does its battery last? These characteristics can be measured. Similarly, even though you already own a human body, you might be interested in the performance of your sensory systems. How sensitive are they? How fast can information be registered? How quickly does adaptation happen? These are all questions that can be answered using **psychophysics,** *methods that systematically relate the physical characteristics of a stimulus to an observer's perception.* In a simple psychophysics experiment, researchers might ask people to decide whether or not they see a faint spot of light, for example. The intensity of the light is changed systematically, and the responses of the observer (yes or no) are recorded as a function of intensity.

Measuring Thresholds

The simplest quantitative measurement in psychophysics is the **absolute threshold,** *the minimal intensity needed to just barely detect a stimulus in 50% of the trials.* A *threshold* is a boundary. Just as the doorway that separates the inside from the outside of a house is a threshold, so is the boundary between two psychological states (awareness and unawareness, or perceiving and not perceiving, in this case). **TABLE 4.1** lists the approximate absolute thresholds for the five senses.

To measure the absolute threshold for detecting a sound, for example, an observer wears headphones linked to a computer. The experimenter repeatedly presents a tone at different intensities and records how often the observer reports hearing the tone at each intensity level. The outcome of such an experiment is graphed in **FIGURE 4.1**. Notice from the shape of the curve that the transition from *not hearing* to *hearing* is gradual rather than abrupt. We define the sound intensity at which the observer is correct (i.e., says the tone is present) half the time as the absolute threshold.

If we repeat this experiment for many different tones, we can observe and record the absolute thresholds for tones ranging from very low to very high pitch. It turns out that people tend to be most sensitive (have the lowest thresholds) to the range of tones corresponding to the human voice. Our thresholds are higher for tones that are lower or higher in pitch than voices. We need more sound energy to hear these sounds. In fact, if the tone is low enough, such as the lowest note on a pipe organ, most humans cannot hear it at all; we can only feel it. If the tone is high enough, we also cannot hear it, but dogs and many other animals can.

psychophysics Methods that systematically relate the physical characteristics of a stimulus to an observer's perception.

absolute threshold The minimal intensity needed to just barely detect a stimulus in 50% of trials.

TABLE 4.1	
APPROXIMATE SENSORY THRESHOLDS	
Sense	**Absolute Threshold**
Vision	A candle flame 48 kilometres away on a clear, dark night
Hearing	A clock's tick 6.1 metres away when all is quiet
Touch	A fly's wing falling on the cheek from 1 centimetre away
Smell	A single drop of perfume diffused through an area equivalent to the volume of six rooms
Taste	A teaspoon of sugar dissolved in 7.6 litres of water

Research from Galanter (1962).

Physical intensity of stimulus tone

Figure 4.1
Absolute Threshold Absolute threshold is graphed here as the point at which the increasing intensity of the stimulus enables an observer to detect it on 50% of the trials. As its intensity gradually increases, we detect the stimulus more frequently.

The absolute threshold is useful for assessing **sensitivity,** *how responsive we are to faint stimuli;* but sometimes we also want to know about **acuity,** *how well we can distinguish two very similar stimuli,* such as two tones that differ slightly in loudness or two lights that differ slightly in brightness. The **just noticeable difference (JND)** is *the minimal change in a stimulus (e.g., its loudness or brightness) that can just barely be detected.*

The JND is not a fixed quantity; it depends on the particular sense being measured, as well as on the intensity of the original stimulus. Consider measuring the JND for the brightness of a light. An observer in a dark room is shown a light of fixed intensity, called the *standard* (S), next to a comparison light that is slightly brighter or dimmer than the standard. When S is very dim, observers can perceive even a very small difference in brightness between the two lights: The JND is small. But if S is bright, a much larger increment is needed to detect the difference: The JND is larger.

It turns out that for any sensory domain, the ratio between the JND and the standard stimulus is a constant value—except when the standard takes extreme values—e.g., is hard to perceive, or is overwhelming. This relationship was first noticed in 1834 by the German physiologist Ernst Weber (Watson, 1978). Gustav Fechner, who developed the field of psychophysics and the methods we still use today, applied Weber's insight directly to psychophysics (Fechner, 1860/1966). He described a formal relationship called **Weber's law,** which states that *for every sense domain, the change in a stimulus that is just noticeable is a constant proportion despite variation in intensities.* As an example, if you picked up a 25-gram envelope, then a 50-gram envelope, you'd probably notice the difference between them. But if you picked up a 10-kilogram package, then a package 25 grams heavier, you'd probably detect no difference at all between them.

Signal Detection

Measuring absolute and difference thresholds requires a critical assumption: that a threshold exists! But humans don't suddenly and rapidly switch between perceiving and not perceiving; in fact, the very same physical stimulus, such as a dim light or a quiet tone, presented on several different occasions, may be perceived by the same person on some occasions but not on others. Remember, an absolute threshold is operationalized as perceiving the stimulus 50% of the time, which means that the other 50% of the time it might go undetected (Figure 4.1).

Our accurate perception of a sensory stimulus, then, can be somewhat haphazard. Whether in the psychophysics lab or out in the world, sensory signals face a lot of competition, or *noise,* which refers to all the other stimuli coming from the internal and external environments. Memories, moods, and motives intertwine with what you are seeing, hearing, and smelling at any given time. This internal "noise" competes with your ability to detect a stimulus with perfect, focused attention. Other sights, sounds, and smells in the world at large also compete for attention. As a consequence of noise, you may not perceive everything that you sense, and you may even perceive things that you haven't sensed.

An approach to psychophysics called **signal detection theory** holds that *the response to a stimulus depends both on a person's sensitivity to the stimulus in the presence of noise and on a person's decision criterion.* That is, observers consider the sensory evidence evoked by the stimulus and compare it with an internal decision criterion (Green & Swets, 1966; Macmillan & Creelman, 2005). If the sensory evidence exceeds the criterion, the observer responds by saying, "Yes, I detected the stimulus," and if it falls short of the criterion, the observer responds by saying, "No, I did not detect the stimulus."

Signal detection theory has practical applications at home, school, and work, and even while driving. For example, a radiologist may have to decide whether a mammogram shows that a patient has breast cancer. The radiologist knows that certain features, such as a mass of a particular size and shape, are associated with the presence of cancer. But noncancerous features can have a very similar

sensitivity How responsive we are to faint stimuli.

acuity How well we can distinguish two very similar stimuli.

just noticeable difference (JND) The minimal change in a stimulus (e.g., its loudness or brightness) that can just barely be detected.

Weber's law For every sense domain, the change in a stimulus that is just noticeable is a constant proportion despite variation in intensities.

signal detection theory An approach that holds that the response to a stimulus depends both on a person's sensitivity to the stimulus in the presence of noise and on a person's decision criterion.

appearance to cancerous ones. The radiologist may decide on a strictly liberal criterion and check every possible case of cancer with a biopsy. This decision strategy minimizes the possibility of missing a true cancer but leads to many unnecessary biopsies. A strictly conservative criterion will cut down on unnecessary biopsies but will miss some treatable cancers. These different types of errors have to be weighed against each other in setting the decision criterion.

For an example of a common everyday task that can interfere with signal detection, see The Real World: Multitasking.

The Real World | **Multitasking**

By one estimate, using a cell phone while driving makes having an accident four times more likely (McEvoy et al., 2005). In response to highway safety experts' concerns, and statistics such as this, provincial and territorial legislative assemblies have passed laws that restrict, and sometimes ban, using mobile phones while driving. You might think that's a fine idea . . . for everyone else on the road. But surely you can manage to punch in a number on a phone, carry on a conversation, or maybe even text-message while simultaneously driving in a safe and courteous manner. Right? In a word, wrong.

The issue here is *selective attention*, or perceiving only what's currently relevant to you. Perception is an active, moment-to-moment exploration for relevant or interesting information, not a passive receptacle for whatever happens to come along. Talking on a cell phone while driving demands that you juggle two independent sources of sensory input — vision and hearing — at the same time. This is problematic, because research has found that when attention is directed to hearing, activity in visual areas decreases (Shomstein & Yantis, 2004).

This kind of *multitasking* creates problems when you need to react suddenly, as you often do while driving. Researchers have tested experienced drivers in a highly realistic driving simulator, measuring their response times to brake lights and stop signs while they listened to the radio or carried on phone conversations about a political issue, among other tasks (Strayer et al., 2003). These experienced drivers reacted significantly more slowly during phone conversations than during the other tasks. This is because a phone conversation requires memory retrieval, deliberation, and planning what to say and often

carries an emotional stake in the conversation topic. Tasks such as listening to the radio require far less attention.

The tested drivers became so engaged in their conversations that their minds no longer seemed to be in the car. Their slower braking response translated into an increased stopping distance that, depending on the driver's speed, would have resulted in a rear-end collision. Whether the phone was handheld or hands free made little difference, and similar results have been obtained in field studies of actual driving (Horrey & Wickens, 2006). A more recent meta-analysis of 93 studies with over 4,300 participants confirms these findings (Caird et al., 2018). This suggests that laws requiring drivers to use hands-free phones may have little effect on reducing accidents. Even after drivers had extensive practice at driving while using a hands-free cell phone in a simulator, the disruptive effects of cell phone use were still observed (Cooper & Strayer, 2008).

The situation is even worse when text messaging is involved: Compared with a no-texting control condition, when either sending or receiving a text message in the simulator, drivers spent dramatically less time looking at the road, had a much harder time staying in their lane, missed numerous lane changes, and had greater difficulty maintaining an appropriate distance behind the car ahead of them (Hosking et al., 2009). Another review concluded that the impairing effect of texting while driving is comparable with that of alcohol consumption and greater than that of smoking marijuana (Pascual-Ferra et al., 2012). Browsing a Facebook page while driving is, not surprisingly, also detrimental to driving performance,

Superior temporal lobe   Fusiform gyrus

(a)   (b)

SHOMSTEIN AND YANTIS, 2004, CONTROL OF ATTENTION SHIFTS BETWEEN VISION AND AUDITION IN HUMAN CORTEX, THE JOURNAL OF NEUROSCIENCE, 24 NOVEMBER 2004, 24(47): 10702-10706; DOI: 10.1523/JNEUROSCI.2939-04.2004.

Shifting attention participants received fMRI scans as they performed tasks that required them to shift their attention between visual and auditory information. (a) When participants focused on auditory information, a region in the superior (upper) temporal lobe involved in auditory processing showed increased activity (yellow/orange). (b) In striking contrast, a visual region, the fusiform gyrus, showed decreased activity when participants focused on auditory information (blue).

but still not quite as harmful as texting (Hashash et al., 2019).

Impairments from multitasking are not restricted to driving. People who report that they multitask frequently in everyday life have difficulty in laboratory tasks that require focusing attention in the face of distractions, compared with individuals who do not multitask much in daily life (Ophir et al., 2009), and these lapses of attention in habitual multitaskers often result in memory failures (Madore et al., 2020). Frequent multitasking in academic settings (via texting or Facebook use) can have a negative impact on learning (Chen & Yan, 2015; Judd, 2014; Wammes et al., 2019). So how well do we multitask in several thousand pounds of metal hurtling down the highway? Unless you have two heads with one brain each — one to talk and one to concentrate on driving — you would do well to keep your eyes on the road and not on the phone.

Visual Pathways: Connections Between the Eye and the Brain

Learning Outcomes

WHAT YOU NEED TO KNOW

- Discuss how the physical properties of light relate to the psychological dimensions of brightness, colour, and saturation.

- Describe how the eye converts light waves into neural impulses.

- Discuss how we perceive colour.

- Describe what happens once the neural impulses reach the brain.

- Describe the functions of the dorsal and ventral visual streams.

Your sophisticated visual system has evolved to transduce visual energy in the world into neural signals in the brain. Humans have sensory receptors in their eyes that respond to wavelengths of light energy. When we look at people, places, and things, patterns of light and colour give us information about where one surface stops and another begins. The array of light reflected from those surfaces preserves their shapes and enables us to form a mental representation of a scene (Rodieck, 1998; Snowdon et al., 2012). Understanding vision, then, starts with understanding light.

Sensing Light

Visible light is simply that portion of the electromagnetic spectrum that we can see, and as noted earlier, it is an extremely small slice (see **FIGURE 4.2**). You can think of light as waves of energy. Like ocean waves, light waves vary in height and in the distance between their peaks, or *wavelengths*. Light waves vary on three physical dimensions. Changes in these physical dimensions produce systematic changes in perception (psychological dimensions) (see **TABLE 4.2**). Length and amplitude are properties of the light waves themselves. The *length* of a light wave determines its hue, or what humans perceive as colour. The intensity, or *amplitude*, of a light wave—how high the peaks are—determines what we perceive as the brightness of light.

Purity is a third dimension that refers to the degree to which a light source is emitting just one wavelength, or a mixture of wavelengths. It also influences how colour is perceived. Some synthetic light sources (such as lasers) produce light that is *pure*, consisting of just one wavelength. These lights have high *saturation*, meaning that they are perceived by humans as having very rich colours. Most light sources (such as the sun, fire, luminescent algae, incandescent light bulbs) are composed of many different wavelengths of light at the same time: The colour that is perceived depends on the relative amounts of different wavelengths in the (impure) mixture.

Figure 4.2

Electromagnetic Spectrum The sliver of light waves visible to humans as a rainbow of colours from violet-blue to red is bounded on the short end by ultraviolet rays, which honeybees can see, and on the long end by infrared waves, on which night-vision equipment operates. Someone wearing night-vision goggles, for example, can detect another person's body heat in complete darkness. Light waves are tiny, but the scale along the bottom of this chart offers a glimpse of their varying lengths, measured in nanometres (nm)—1 nm = 1 billionth of a metre.

TABLE 4.2

PROPERTIES OF LIGHT WAVES

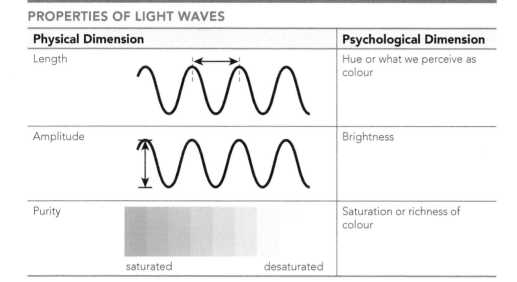

Physical Dimension	Psychological Dimension
Length	Hue or what we perceive as colour
Amplitude	Brightness
Purity (saturated — desaturated)	Saturation or richness of colour

The Eye Detects and Focuses Light

Eyes have evolved as specialized organs to detect light. **FIGURE 4.3a** shows the human eye in cross-section. Light that reaches the eyes passes first through a clear, smooth outer tissue called the *cornea,* which bends the light wave and sends it through the *pupil,* a hole in the coloured part of the eye. This coloured part is the *iris,* which is a translucent, doughnut-shaped muscle that controls the size of the pupil and hence the amount of light that can enter the eye.

Immediately behind the iris, muscles inside the eye control the shape of the *lens* to bend the light again and focus it onto the **retina,** *a layer of light-sensitive tissue lining the back of the eyeball.* The muscles change the shape of the lens to focus objects at different distances, making the lens flatter for objects that are far away or rounder for nearby objects. This change is called **accommodation,** *the process whereby the eye maintains a clear image on the retina.* Figure 4.3b shows how accommodation works.

If your eyeballs are a little too long or a little too short, the lens will not focus images properly on the retina. If the eyeball is too long, images are focused in front of the retina, leading to nearsightedness (*myopia*). If the eyeball is too short, images are focused behind the retina, and the result is farsightedness (*hyperopia*). Eyeglasses, contact lenses, and surgical procedures can correct either condition. Eyeglasses and contact lenses both provide an additional lens to help focus light more appropriately, and procedures such as LASIK physically reshape the eye's existing lens.

Light Is Converted into Neural Impulses in the Retina

How does light become a meaningful image? The retina is the interface between the world of light outside the body and the world of vision inside the central nervous system. Two types of *photoreceptor cells* in the retina contain light-sensitive proteins that absorb light and transduce it into electrical signals. **Cones** *detect colour, operate under normal daylight conditions, and allow us to focus on fine detail.* **Rods** *become active only under low-light conditions, for night vision* (see Figure 4.3c).

Rods are much more sensitive photoreceptors than cones, but they provide no information about colour and sense only shades of grey. Think about this the next time you wake up in the middle of the night and make your way to the bathroom for a drink of water. Using only the moonlight from the window to light your way, do you see the room in colour or in shades of grey? Rods and cones differ in several

HURONPHOTO/GETTY IMAGES

HURONPHOTO/GETTY IMAGES

The full-colour image on the top is what you'd see if your rods and cones are fully at work. The greyscale image on the bottom is what you'd see if only your rods are functioning.

retina A layer of light-sensitive tissue lining the back of the eyeball.

accommodation The process whereby the eye maintains a clear image on the retina.

cones Photoreceptors that detect colour, operate under normal daylight conditions, and allow us to focus on fine detail.

rods Photoreceptors that become active under low-light conditions for night vision.

a. The Eye Captures Light Waves Reflected From an Object's Surface

Light reflected from an object's surface enters the eyes via the transparent **cornea**, bending to pass through the **pupil** at the centre of the coloured **iris**.

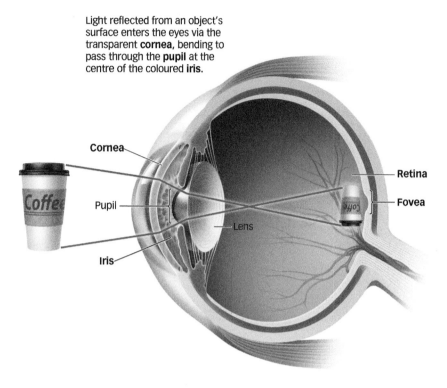

Behind the iris, the thickness and shape of the **lens** adjust to focus light on the **retina**, where the image appears upside down and backwards. Vision is clearest at the **fovea**.

Figure 4.3
The Eye Transduces Light Waves into Neural Activity

b. Muscles Change the Shape of the Lens to Focus Objects at Different Distances, a Process Called Accommodation

People with **normal vision** focus the image on the retina at the back of the eye, both for near and far objects.

Nearsighted people see clearly what's nearby, but distant objects are blurry because light from them is focused in front of the retina.

For **farsighted** people, distant objects are clear, but those nearby are blurry because their point of focus falls beyond the surface of the retina.

---

other ways as well, most notably in their numbers. About 120 million rods are distributed more or less evenly around each retina except at the very centre, known as the **fovea,** *an area of the retina where vision is clearest and there are no rods at all.* The absence of rods in the fovea decreases the sharpness of vision in reduced light, but the benefit is enhanced sensitivity to faint light in the rest of the retina outside the fovea (the *periphery*). For example, when amateur astronomers view dim stars through their telescopes at night, they know to look a little off to the side of the target so that the image will fall not on the rod-free fovea but on some other part of the retina that contains many highly sensitive rods.

Cones are far less numerous than rods. Each retina contains only about 6 million cones, which are densely packed in the fovea and much more sparsely distributed over the rest of the retina, as you can see in Figure 4.3c. Light reflected off of objects that you look at directly falls on your fovea. The high density of cones in the fovea means that these objects are seen in great detail, rather like images produced by a state-of-the-art smartphone camera. Objects outside of your direct focus—in other words, objects in your *peripheral vision*—aren't so clear. The light reflecting from those peripheral objects falls outside the fovea where the cell density is lower, resulting in a fuzzier, grainier image, more like a low-end smartphone camera.

fovea An area of the retina where vision is clearest and there are no rods at all.

c. The Retina Is the Interface Between the Eye and the Brain

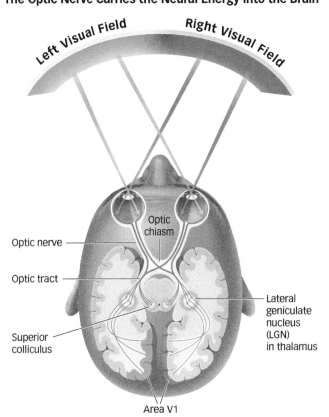

RGC axon | Retinal ganglion cell | Bipolar cell | Cone | Rod

Retina

Cones | Rods

OMIKRON/SCIENCE SOURCE

The surface of the retina is composed of photoreceptor cells, the rods and cones, beneath a layer of transparent neurons, the bipolar and retinal ganglion cells (RGCs), connected in sequence. The axon of a retinal ganglion cell joins with all other RGC axons to form the **optic nerve**. The optic nerve creates the blind spot on the retina.

The **fovea**, the area of greatest visual acuity, is where most colour-sensitive cones are concentrated, allowing us to see fine detail as well as colour. Rods, the predominant photoreceptors activated in low-light conditions, are distributed everywhere else on the retina.

d. The Optic Nerve Carries the Neural Energy into the Brain

Left Visual Field | Right Visual Field

Optic chiasm

Optic nerve

Optic tract

Superior colliculus

Lateral geniculate nucleus (LGN) in thalamus

Area V1

Objects in the right visual field stimulate the left half of each retina, and objects in the left visual field stimulate the right half of each retina. Just before the optic nerves enter the brain about half the nerve fibers from each eye cross. The left half of each optic nerve (representing the right visual field) runs through the brain's left hemisphere via the thalamus, and the right half of each optic nerve (representing the left visual field) travels this route through the right hemisphere. So, information from the right visual field ends up in the left hemisphere and information from the left visual field ends up in the right hemisphere.

The retina consists of several layers of cells. As seen in Figure 4.3c, the photoreceptor cells (rods and cones) form the innermost layer, beneath a layer of transparent neurons called the bipolar and retinal ganglion cells. The *bipolar cells* collect electrical signals from the rods and cones and transmit them to the outermost layer of the retina, where neurons called *retinal ganglion cells (RGCs)* organize the signals and send them to the brain.

BACKYARDPRODUCTION/THINKSTOCK/ISTOCK/GETTY IMAGES

The image on the left was taken at a higher resolution than the image on the right. The difference in quality is analogous to light falling on the fovea, rather than on the periphery of the retina.

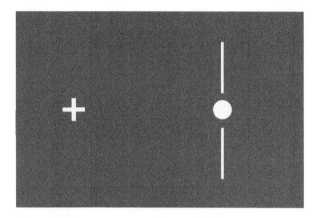

Figure 4.4

Blind Spot Demonstration To find the blind spot in your right eye, close your left eye and stare at the cross with your right eye. Hold this book 6 to 12 inches (15 to 30 centimetres) away from your eyes and move it slowly towards and away from you until the dot disappears. When that happens, the dot is in your blind spot and so is not visible. At this point the vertical lines may appear as one continuous line, because your visual perceptual system fills in the area occupied by the missing dot! To test your left eye's blind spot, turn the book upside down and repeat the experiment with your right eye closed.

blind spot A location in the visual field that produces no sensation on the retina.

area V1 The part of the occipital lobe that contains the primary visual cortex.

The bundled RGC axons—about 1.5 million per eye—form the *optic nerve,* which leaves the eye through a hole in the retina. Because it contains neither rods nor cones and therefore has no mechanism for sensing light, this hole in the retina creates a **blind spot,** *a location in the visual field that produces no sensation on the retina.* The area of the blind spot makes quite a big hole in the visual field. Imagine looking at a full moon high in the night sky. Now imagine another 11 moons lined up right beside it; if all 12 moons fell on your blind spot, you would not see them (Anstis, 2010). Why don't we notice these big holes in the world we see? Our perceptual system automatically "fills in," using knowledge of the colour or texture around the blind spot, rather like the "paint bucket" in a graphics program might do. Try the demonstration in **FIGURE 4.4** to find the blind spot in your own eyes.

The Optic Nerve Carries Neural Impulses to the Brain

Streams of action potentials (neural impulses) containing information encoded by the retina travel to the brain along the optic nerve. Half of the axons in the optic nerve that leave each eye come from retinal ganglion cells (RGCs) that code information in the right visual field, whereas the other half code information in the left visual field. The right visual field information is relayed to the left hemisphere of the brain, while the left visual field information is relayed to the right hemisphere (see Figure 4.3d). Information first goes to the *lateral geniculate nucleus (LGN),* located in the thalamus of each hemisphere. As you will recall from the Neuroscience and Behaviour chapter, the thalamus receives inputs from all of the senses except smell. From the LGN, the visual signals travel to the back of the brain, to a location called **area V1** (pronounced "vee-one"), the *part of the occipital lobe that contains the primary visual cortex.*

Perceiving Colour

Around 1670, Sir Isaac Newton pointed out that colour is not something "in" light waves. In fact, the perception of colour is created by our brain (see Figure 4.2). If we see pure light (i.e., only one wavelength at a time), we perceive the shortest visible ones as deep purple. As wavelengths become longer, the colours we perceive change gradually and continuously to blue, then green, yellow, orange, and, with the longest visible wavelengths, red. This rainbow of hues and accompanying wavelengths is called the *visible spectrum,* illustrated in Figure 4.2 and **FIGURE 4.5**. The perception of colour from mixtures of wavelengths (as emitted by most light sources) depends on the relative amounts of different wavelengths in the mixture. For example, light

Figure 4.5

Seeing in Colour We perceive a spectrum of colour because objects selectively absorb some wavelengths of light and reflect others. Colour perception corresponds to the relative activity of the three types of cones. The sensitivity of the three types of cones is shown by the three coloured lines. Each type is most sensitive to a range of wavelengths in the visible spectrum—short (bluish light), medium (greenish light), or long (reddish light). (Data from Stockman & Sharpe, 2000.)

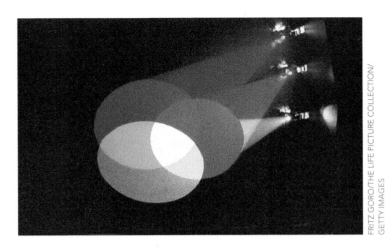

Figure 4.6
Colour Mixing The millions of shades of colour that humans can perceive are products of the mixture of wavelengths that sources emit or that objects reflect. Coloured spotlights work by causing the surface to reflect light of a particular wavelength, which stimulates the red, blue, or green photopigments in the cones. When all visible wavelengths are present, we see white.

is seen as white in colour if it contains about the same amounts of many different wavelengths across the visible spectrum, as shown in **FIGURE 4.6**. Notice that in the centre of the figure, where the red, green, and blue lights overlap, the surface looks white. This is because the surface is reflecting a broad range of visible wavelengths of light, from long (red) through medium (green) to short (blue).

You'll recall that all rods are ideal for low-light vision but cannot distinguish colours. Why? Think of a garden water tap, and compare it to the mixer tap you might have in a kitchen or bathroom (Snowdon et al., 2012). The garden tap only moves one way—that is, it allows you to control the flow of water, but you cannot control the temperature. With a mixer tap, you can go up and down, and side to side; you can control both flow and temperature. With only one type of photopigment, the rod receptor is like the garden tap. Rods can signal only the brightness, not the colour, of the dim light to which they are sensitive. Cones, by contrast, come in three types; one type is especially sensitive to long wavelengths (L-cones), one to medium wavelengths (M-cones), and one to short wavelengths (S-cones). When light (direct from a source, or reflected off an object) hits a region of the retina, the L-, M-, and S-cones in that region are each excited to the degree that the light contains the wavelengths to which they are sensitive, as shown in Figure 4.5. Just as a mixer tap with two channels (up–down, and left–right) allows control of both flow and temperature, three cone types allow the brain to interpret brightness, signaled by the total amount of activity across all three cone types, and colour, signaled by the relative levels of activity between pairs of cone types.

You can think of the three types of cones in the retina (L-, M-, and S-cones) as three channels of information. The relative amount of activity in each channel provides a unique code for each colour you see. Genetic disorders in which one of the cone types is missing—and, in some very rare cases, two or all three cone types are missing—cause a *colour vision deficiency*. Such disorders are sex linked, affecting men much more often than women.

Colour vision deficiency is often referred to as *colour blindness,* but in fact, people who lack only one type of cone can still distinguish many colours, just not as many as someone who has the full complement of three cone types. You can create a kind of temporary colour deficiency by exploiting the idea of sensory adaptation. Just like the rest of your body, cones need an occasional break, too. Staring too long at one colour fatigues the cones that respond to that colour, producing a form of sensory adaptation that results in a *colour afterimage.* To demonstrate this effect for yourself, follow these instructions for **FIGURE 4.7**:

- Stare at the small cross between the two colour patches for about 1 minute. Try to keep your eyes as still as possible.
- After a minute, look at the lower cross. You should see a vivid colour aftereffect that lasts for a few seconds. Pay particular attention to the colour in the afterimage.

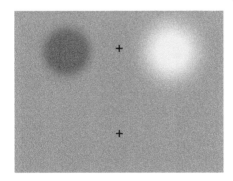

Figure 4.7
Colour Afterimage Demonstration Follow the accompanying instructions in the text, and sensory adaptation will do the rest. When the afterimage fades, you can get back to reading the chapter.

Were you puzzled that the pink-red patch produces a greenish afterimage and the yellow patch produces a blue afterimage? This result reveals something important about colour perception. The explanation stems from the **colour-opponent system,** in which *pairs of cone types (channels) work in opposition:* the L-cone channel against the M-cone channel (as in Figure 4.7) and the S-cone channel against the M-cone channel (Hurvich & Jameson, 1957). The colour-opponent system explains colour aftereffects. For example, you see "green" when your M-cones are more active than your L-cones, and "red" when your L-cones are more active than your M-cones. If you stare at a red patch, the cones that are firing most strongly (the L-cones) become fatigued over time (recall sensory adaptation). Now, when you stare at a white or grey patch, which reflects all the wavelengths equally and should make L-, M-, and S-cones equally active, the fatigued L-cones respond relatively weakly compared to the M-cones. Since the M-cones are more active than the L-cones, you perceive the patch as tinted green.

The Visual Brain

We have seen that a great deal of processing takes place within the retina itself, including spots of light and colour. More complex aspects of vision, however, require more powerful processing, and that enlists the brain.

Neural Systems for Perceiving Shape

One of the most important functions of vision involves perceiving the shapes of objects; our day-to-day lives would be a mess if we couldn't distinguish individual shapes. Imagine not being able to differentiate reliably between a warm glazed doughnut and a straight stalk of celery and you'll get the idea. Perceiving shape depends on the location and orientation of an object's edges. It is not surprising, then, that area V1 (see Figure 4.3d) is sensitive to edge orientation. As you also read in the Neuroscience and Behaviour chapter, neurons in the primary visual cortex (V1) selectively respond to bars and edges in specific orientations in space (Hubel & Wiesel, 1962, 1998). The **visual receptive field,** meaning *the region of the visual field to which each neuron responds,* is also very small for neurons in V1. In effect, area V1 contains populations of neurons, each "tuned" to respond to edges oriented a particular way, in a particular location in space. This means that some neurons fire when we perceive a vertical edge (like the side of a door or window) in a particular location in space; other neurons fire when we perceive a horizontal edge (like the top of a door or window) in that location; still other neurons fire when we perceive edges at a diagonal orientation of 45°; and so on (see **FIGURE 4.8**). Those orientations at other locations in space activate

colour-opponent system Theory stating that pairs of cone types (channels) work in opposition.

visual receptive field The region of the visual field to which each neuron responds.

Figure 4.8

Single-Neuron Feature Detectors
Area V1 contains neurons that respond to specific orientations of edges. Here, a single neuron's responses (action potentials shown as pink lines) are recorded (*left*) as a monkey views bars at different orientations (*right*). This neuron fires action potentials at a high rate when the bar is pointing to the right at 45°, less often when it is vertical, and hardly at all when it is pointing to the left at 45°.

FRITZ GORO/THE LIFE PICTURE COLLECTION/GETTY IMAGES

other neurons. All of these edge detectors in V1 work together to allow you to distinguish between a doughnut and a celery stalk.

Pathways for What, Where, and How

From area V1, visual information spreads out and is processed through 32 or more (!) distinct brain areas (Felleman & van Essen, 1991). Neurons in V1 and its neighbouring brain regions respond to only a small region of the visual field (i.e., they have small *receptive fields*) and are tuned to relatively simple features, like edges. As signals are processed and transformed in progressively later areas farther away from V1, receptive fields become larger, and the features to which neurons respond become more complex. The many visual processing areas can be simplified into two functionally distinct pathways, or *visual streams* (see **FIGURE 4.9**):

Figure 4.9
Visual Streams One pathway courses from the occipital visual regions into the lower temporal lobe. This ventral pathway enables us to identify what we see. Another pathway travels from the occipital lobe through the upper regions of the temporal lobe into the parietal regions. This dorsal pathway allows us to locate objects, to track their movements, and to act on them.

- The *ventral* (lower) *stream* travels across the occipital lobe into the lower levels of the temporal lobes and includes brain areas that represent an object's shape and identity. Because this stream represents *what* an object is, it is often called the "what" pathway (Kravitz et al., 2013; Ungerleider & Mishkin, 1982).

- The *dorsal* (upper) *stream* travels up from the occipital lobe to the parietal lobes (including some of the middle and upper levels of the temporal lobes) and includes brain areas that identify where an object is and how it is moving (Kravitz et al., 2011). Because the dorsal stream allows us to perceive spatial relations, researchers originally dubbed it the "where" pathway (Ungerleider & Mishkin, 1982). Neuroscientists later argued that because the dorsal stream is crucial for guiding actions, such as aiming, reaching, or tracking with the eyes, the "where" pathway is more appropriately called a "perception for action" pathway (Milner & Goodale, 1995).

How do we know there are two pathways? The most dramatic evidence comes from studying people with brain injuries within either of the two pathways.

For example, a woman known as DF suffered permanent damage to a large region of the lateral occipital cortex, an area in the ventral stream (Goodale et al., 1991). Her ability to identify objects by sight was greatly impaired, although her ability to identify them by touch was normal. This suggests that her *visual representation* of objects, but not her *memory* for objects, was damaged. DF represents a striking example of **visual form agnosia,** *the inability to recognize objects by sight* (Goodale & Milner, 1992; Whitewell et al., 2014). DF could still accurately *guide* her actions by sight to an object, even though she could not say what the object was, as demonstrated in **FIGURE 4.10**. When DF's brain was scanned using fMRI, researchers found that regions within the dorsal stream exhibited normal activity during guided movement (James et al., 2003).

visual form agnosia The inability to recognize objects by sight.

Figure 4.10
Testing Visual Form Agnosia (*left*) When researchers asked DF to look at the slot in the testing apparatus at various angles, and then turn a handheld card until its orientation matched, she was unable to comply. (*right*) However, when asked to actually insert the card into the slot at various angles, DF accomplished the task almost perfectly.

Other people with brain damage to the parietal lobe, a section of the dorsal stream, have difficulty using vision to guide reaching and grasping (Perenin & Vighetto, 1988). However, they can still identify objects they see because their ventral streams are intact. We can conclude from these two patterns of impairment that the ventral and dorsal visual streams are functionally distinct. One stream may be damaged, whereas the other remains intact, but the two streams must still work together during visual perception in order to integrate perception for identification (ventral) and perception for action (dorsal).

When perceiving an object—say, a coffee cup—we are simultaneously aware of what it is, where it is located, and how to reach for it to pick it up. These are not features that are separated in our conscious awareness, despite being represented by different parts of the brain. This is an instance of what researchers call the **binding problem,** which is *how the brain links features together so that we see unified objects in our visual world rather than free-floating or miscombined features* (Treisman, 1998, 2006). How do we perceive the world as an integrated, seamless whole, when different features are processed and represented in different, specialized, parts of the brain? This binding problem pertains to all sensory domains, but it has been studied most in the context of the visual system.

A concept of "binding neurons" in the visual system has been proposed, which may provide a solution to the problem (Eguchi et al., 2018). These are neurons in the ventral visual stream that receive coincident (simultaneous) input from other neurons involved in representing different features of an object. They participate in a larger array of neurons that signal a whole object by engaging in an intricate and repeatable dance of action potentials. Solving the binding problem is essential to understanding how our brains make sense of complex visual scenes, and this is an area of active research.

Visual Perception: Recognizing What We See

Learning Outcomes

WHAT YOU NEED TO KNOW

- List the factors that allow us to recognize objects by sight.
- Describe the visual cues essential for depth perception.
- Discuss how we perceive motion and change.

binding problem How the brain links features together so that we see unified objects in our visual world rather than free-floating or miscombined features.

parallel processing The brain's capacity to perform multiple activities at the same time.

Our journey into the visual system has already revealed how it accomplishes some pretty astonishing feats. But the system needs to do much more in order for us to be able to interact effectively with our visual world. Let's now consider in more detail how the system links together individual visual features into whole objects, allows us to recognize what those objects are, organizes objects into visual scenes, and detects motion and change in those scenes.

Binding Individual Features into a Whole

Specialized feature detectors in different parts of the visual system analyze each of the multiple features of a visible object: orientation, colour, size, shape, and so forth. **Parallel processing** is *the brain's capacity to perform multiple activities at the same time.* Ultimately, though, parallel processing of these different features must somehow be integrated into a single, unified perception of an object (Nassi & Callaway, 2009). We have already discussed how different features of one object might be bound together in perception. But usually we see multiple objects at the same time—what allows us to perceive so easily and correctly that a young man is wearing a grey shirt and a young woman is wearing a red shirt? Why don't we see free-floating patches of grey and red, or even incorrect combinations, such as the young man wearing a red shirt and the young woman wearing a grey shirt? This is another aspect of the binding problem.

Illusory Conjunctions: Perceptual Mistakes

In everyday life, we correctly combine features into unified objects so automatically and effortlessly that it may be difficult to appreciate that binding is ever a problem at all. However, researchers have discovered errors in binding that reveal important clues about how the process works. One such error is known as an **illusory conjunction,** *a perceptual mistake whereby the brain incorrectly combines features from multiple objects.* In a pioneering study of illusory conjunctions, Anne Treisman and Hilary Schmidt (1982) briefly showed study participants visual displays in which black digits flanked coloured letters, then instructed them first to report the black digits and second to describe the coloured letters. Participants frequently reported illusory conjunctions, claiming to have seen, for example, a blue *A* or a red *X* instead of the red *A* and the blue *X* that had actually been shown (see **FIGURE 4.11a, b**).

These illusory conjunctions were not just the result of guessing; they occurred more frequently than other kinds of errors, such as reporting a letter or colour that was not present in the display (see Figure 4.11c). The illusory conjunctions looked real to the participants, who were just as confident about seeing them as they were about the actual coloured letters they perceived correctly. (See A World of Difference: The Experience of Synesthesia for an example of subjectively compelling perceptions that occur in a small percentage of people, including some well-known musical and literary figures.)

Why do illusory conjunctions occur? Treisman and her colleagues have tried to explain them by proposing a **feature-integration theory** (Treisman, 1998, 2006; Treisman & Gelade, 1980; Treisman & Schmidt, 1982), which holds that *focused attention is not required to detect the individual features that make up a stimulus (e.g., the colour, shape, size, and location of letters), but it is required to bind those individual features together.* From this perspective, **attention,** which is *the active and conscious processing of particular information,* provides the "glue" necessary to bind features together. Illusory conjunctions occur when it is difficult for participants to pay full attention to the features that need to be glued together. For example, in the experiments we just considered, participants were required to process the digits that flanked the coloured letters, thereby reducing attention to the letters and allowing illusory conjunctions to occur. When experimental conditions are changed so that participants can pay full attention to the coloured letters, and they are able to correctly bind those features together, illusory conjunctions disappear (Treisman, 1998; Treisman & Schmidt, 1982).

Illusory conjunctions are important for feature integration theory, but may also have broader implications for everyday life. Consider a study in which experimenters used the basic illusory conjunction experimental paradigm, but instead of showing participants letters flanked by numbers, they briefly flashed faces of Black and white males that had either a neutral or angry expression, flanked by numbers (Becker et al., 2010). On each trial, one of the two faces had a neutral expression, and one had an angry expression. Participants first reported the sum of the flanking numbers. On some trials, participants also judged the expression of one of the faces (the target) while ignoring the expression of the other face (the distractor). When judging the expression of a neutral target face, participants showed evidence of an illusory conjunction: Sometimes they reported that the neutral face had an angry expression, although the angry expression was only on the distractor face. Critically, anger from a distractor face was more likely to move to a Black target face than to a white target face. In other words, the illusory conjunction of a face and expression was affected by the kind of racial stereotype that you will learn more about later in this textbook (see the Social Psychology chapter). You can imagine how such an illusory conjunction might occur in everyday life; for example, in a bustling crowd in which a fight breaks out, an angry expression on a white face is seen as originating from a Black face.

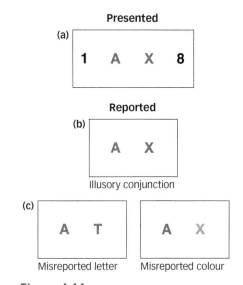

Figure 4.11

Illusory Conjunctions Illusory conjunctions occur when features such as colour and shape are combined incorrectly. For example, when participants are shown a red A and a blue X, they sometimes report seeing a blue A and a red X. Other kinds of errors, such as a misreported letter (e.g., reporting T when no T was presented) or misreported colour (reporting green when no green was presented) occur rarely, indicating that illusory conjunctions are not the result of guessing (based on Robertson, 2003).

illusory conjunction A perceptual mistake whereby the brain incorrectly combines features from multiple objects.

feature-integration theory The idea that focused attention is not required to detect the individual features that make up a stimulus (e.g., the colour, shape, size, and location of letters), but it is required to bind those individual features together.

attention The active and conscious processing of particular information.

With only a quick glance, you recognize all these letters as G, but their varying sizes, shapes, angles, and orientations ought to make this recognition task difficult. What is it about the process of object recognition that allows us to perform this task effortlessly?

Recognizing Objects by Sight

Take a quick look at the letters "G" in the accompanying illustration. Even though they're quite different from each other, you probably effortlessly recognized all of them as examples of the letter *G.* Now consider the same kind of demonstration but using your best friend's face. Suppose one day your friend gets a dramatic new haircut—or adds glasses, hair dye, or a nose ring. Even though your friend now looks strikingly different, you still recognize that person with ease. Just like the variability in *G*s, you somehow are able to extract the underlying features of the face that allow you to accurately identify your friend.

This thought exercise may seem trivial, but it's no small perceptual feat. Machines still have difficulty recognizing objects from different points of view, or recognizing different instances of a thing (like your friend with different haircuts) as the thing itself. The field of *machine learning,* which involves computers learning from very large data sets (e.g., many different instances of your friend's face) to identify patterns (what makes your friend unique, despite variations in dress, hair, and accessories), is developing rapidly, but such systems still fail in unexpected ways (Goodfellow et al., 2016). How do we humans recognize patterns, extracting the essential information that makes a *G* a *G* so accurately and effortlessly? Researchers have been addressing the issue from different but complementary perspectives.

Some researchers argue for a modular view, in which specialized brain areas, or modules, detect and represent faces or houses, body parts, and even other objects (Kanwisher, 2010). For example, a classic study using fMRI to examine visual processing in healthy young adults identified a subregion in the temporal lobe that responds more strongly to faces than to just about any other object category, whereas a nearby area responds most strongly to buildings and landscapes (Kanwisher et al., 1997). Much research since is compatible with the idea that different regions of the ventral stream respond preferentially to different kinds of objects, such as faces, bodies, scenes, and tools (Kanwisher, 2010; Hutchison et al., 2014). Other researchers argue for a more *distributed representation* of object categories. In this view, it is the pattern of activity across multiple brain regions that identifies any viewed object, including faces (Haxby et al., 2001). Each of these views explains some data better than the other one, and both may ultimately be necessary to explain object recognition (Duchaine & Yovel, 2015).

Another perspective on this issue is provided by studies that examine how single neurons in the human brain respond to objects and faces (Quiroga, 2016; Suthana & Fried, 2012). For example, in a study by Quiroga et al. (2005), electrodes were placed in the temporal lobes of people suffering from epilepsy to help identify the source of their seizures and so improve treatment. While the electrodes were in place, patients were also shown photographs of faces and objects as the researchers recorded their neural responses. The researchers found that neurons in the temporal lobe respond to specific objects viewed from multiple angles, as well as to people wearing different clothing and facial expressions, and photographed from various angles. In some cases, the neurons also responded to the words for these same objects. For example, a neuron that responded to photographs of the Sydney Opera House also responded when the words *Sydney Opera* were displayed, but not when the words *Eiffel Tower* were displayed.

These studies also provide examples of the principle of **perceptual constancy,** the idea that *even as aspects of sensory signals change, perception remains constant.* Sometimes we may recognize our friend (constancy) and still notice changes in hair colour or style, or the addition of facial jewelry, but often constancy acts such that we don't even notice that the object has changed. When you pick up a coffee cup, then put it down with the handle pointing in a slightly different direction, and later go to pick it up again, you probably don't notice that it looks slightly different than it did the last time you reached for it. Similarly, if you see a friend outside in bright

perceptual constancy A perceptual principle stating that even as aspects of sensory signals change, perception remains consistent.

perceptual organization The process of grouping and segregating features to create whole objects organized in meaningful ways.

sunlight, and then illuminated under blacklight in a dark club, she looks pretty much the same despite the light reflecting off your friend's face (and thus the signals from your retinas to your brain) being very different in the two situations. Perceptual constancy is the result of your perceptual system organizing the sensory information into meaningful objects, then supplementing that with information about novel features or stripping away potentially distracting, unnecessary, sensory data entirely.

Recently, researchers have been exploring the importance of *conceptual knowledge* in recognizing objects — the rich store of facts and other meaningful knowledge we have about a familiar object (Clarke & Tyler, 2015; Schwartz & Yovel, 2016). According to this view, when we perceive an object, we don't merely recognize what it looks like, but we understand what it *is* — its characteristics and significance to our behaviour. There wouldn't be much use in recognizing that the thing approaching you as you cross the street is a car, not a canary, if you don't also know that cars are made of unyielding metal, travel fast, and probably cause some damage if they hit you. An object's visual properties are analyzed in the ventral visual stream, which leads to activation of conceptual knowledge at higher levels of the ventral stream, closer to the front of the brain.

Principles of Perceptual Organization

Researchers in the Gestalt psychology movement, whom you read about in The Evolution of Psychological Science chapter, were the first to recognize that we tend to perceive not just collections of separate features but whole objects, organized in meaningful ways. We perceptually *group* features that belong together into one object, while we *segregate* features that belong to different objects. The *process of grouping and segregating features to create whole objects organized in meaningful ways* is called **perceptual organization.** There are usually multiple ways of perceptually organizing a complex scene, but our perceptual system automatically delivers to us the interpretation that is the simplest and most meaningful, consistent with our experience and expectations.

The Gestalt *perceptual grouping rules* govern how humans are likely to perceptually organize things, even though the information could, in theory, be organized in some other way (Koffka, 1935). Here's a sampling (see **FIGURE 4.12**):

- *Simplicity*: When confronted with two or more possible interpretations of an object's shape, the visual system tends to select the simplest or most likely interpretation. In Figure 4.12a, we perceive the complex shape as an arrow.

Our visual systems allow us to identify people as the same individuals even when they change such features as hairstyle and skin colour. Despite the extreme changes in these two photos, you can probably tell that they both portray Emma Stone.

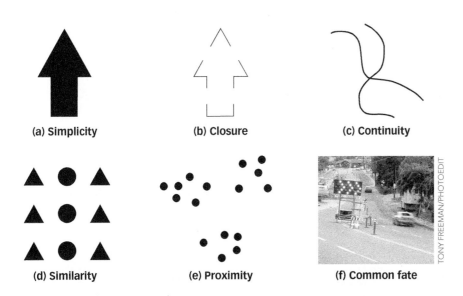

(a) Simplicity   (b) Closure   (c) Continuity

(d) Similarity   (e) Proximity   (f) Common fate

Figure 4.12

Perceptual Grouping Rules Principles first identified by Gestalt psychologists and now supported by a wealth of experimental evidence demonstrate that the brain is predisposed to impose order on incoming sensations in particular ways. This is probably largely due to experience gathered while moving around and interacting with the world, although some principles may be hard-wired from birth.

Figure 4.13

Gestalt Principles at Work! Above, you may see a meaningless collection of grey and white shapes. The same shapes below (but where the white has been turned to black) give a very different impression. You probably perceptually organize them as an outline of an airplane, superimposed on a bunch of Bs. You have a lot of experience with Bs, and with the shapes of aircraft, and with what things look like when other things are in front of them. Your perceptual system uses the sensory information in this image, and your knowledge, to organize it (probably effortlessly and automatically) into this novel scene.

- *Closure:* We tend to fill in missing elements of a visual scene, allowing us to perceive edges that are separated by an interruption (e.g., a gap) as belonging to complete objects. In Figure 4.12b, we see an arrow despite the gaps.
- *Continuity:* Edges or contours that have the same orientation have what the Gestalt psychologists called *good continuation,* and we tend to group them together perceptually. In Figure 4.12c, we perceive two crossing lines instead of two V shapes.
- *Similarity:* Regions that are similar in colour, lightness, shape, or texture are perceived as belonging to the same object. In Figure 4.12d, we perceive three columns—a column of circles flanked by two columns of triangles.
- *Proximity:* Objects that are close together tend to be grouped together. In Figure 4.12e, we perceive three groups or "clumps" of 5 or 6 dots each, not just 16 dots.
- *Common fate:* Elements of a visual image that move together are perceived as parts of a single moving object. In Figure 4.12f, the series of flashing lights in the road sign are perceived as a moving arrowhead.

As an example, in **FIGURE 4.13**, we may see a mess of meaningless shapes above, but below, the principle of simplicity means we see two kinds of shapes (airplane and the letter *B*) instead. The principle of closure is at work when we see the *B*s as whole, behind the airplane. That we see the contour of the whole airplane, instead of just a bunch of black lines, reflects the principles of continuity and similarity. Finally, the principle of proximity enables us to group the right features of each *B* together—we aren't tempted to "see" a *B* except where the component bits are close together.

Separating Figure from Ground

Perceptual organization is a powerful aid to our ability to recognize objects by sight. Grouping and segregation involve visually separating an object from its surroundings. In Gestalt terms, this means identifying a *figure* apart from the (back)*ground* in which it resides. For instance, you perceive the words on this page as figural: They stand out from the ground of the sheet of paper on which they're printed. You certainly can perceptually organize these elements differently, of course: The words *and* the paper together are all part of an object you perceive as *a page.* Typically, our perceptual systems focus attention on some objects, while disregarding others as background.

Size provides one clue to what's figure and what's ground: Smaller regions are likely to be figures, such as tiny letters on a big sheet of paper. Movement also helps: Your instructor is (we hope) a dynamic lecturer, moving around in a static environment, so you perceive your instructor as figure against the background of the classroom.

Figure and ground can also swap roles. Edgar Rubin (1886–1951), a Danish psychologist, developed a famous illusion called the *Rubin vase* or, more generally, a *reversible figure–ground relationship.* You can view this "face–vase" illusion in **FIGURE 4.14** in two ways: either as a vase on a black background or as a pair of silhouettes facing each other. Your visual system settles on one or the other interpretation and fluctuates between them every few seconds. This happens because the edge that separates figure and ground equally defines the contours of the vase and the contours of the faces. Evidence from fMRI brain imaging studies shows, quite nicely, that when people are seeing the Rubin image as faces, there is greater activity in the face-selective region of the temporal lobe discussed earlier than when they are seeing it as a vase (Hasson et al., 2001).

Figure 4.14

Ambiguous Edges Here's how Rubin's classic reversible figure–ground illusion works: Fix your eyes on the centre of the image. Your perception will alternate between a vase and facing silhouettes, even as the sensory stimulation remains constant.

Perceiving Depth and Size

Objects in the world (e.g., tables) generally have three dimensions—length, width, and depth—but the retinal image contains only two dimensions, length and width. How does the brain process a flat, 2-D retinal image so that we perceive the depth of an object and how far away it is? How can we tell whether something is a large object far away, or a small object that is much closer? The answer is that we have to make an educated guess. It is a guess because we have no way to sense visual depth (or real image size) directly; educated because we've all been alive for many years, moving around in a 3-D world, which has taught us that various visual cues indicate depth and distance. Some of these can be picked up with just one eye (monocular cues) and some rely on a comparison of the images in the two eyes (binocular cues).

Monocular Depth Cues

Monocular depth cues are *aspects of a scene that yield information about depth when viewed with only one eye.* There are many different cues that work this way, and they have been exploited by visual artists for centuries. For instance, even when you have one eye closed, the retinal image of an object you've focused on grows smaller as that object moves farther away and larger as it moves closer. Our brains routinely use these differences in retinal image size, or *relative size,* to perceive distance; this really only works if the typical size of an object is familiar, so this cue is also called "familiar size." Most adults, for example, fall within a narrow range of heights (perhaps 5–6 feet tall), so retinal image size alone is usually a reliable cue to how far away they are. Our perceptual system automatically corrects for size differences and attributes them to differences in distance. **FIGURE 4.15** demonstrates the strength of this perceptual correction for familiar size.

In addition to familiar size, there are several more monocular depth cues (see **FIGURE 4.16**), such as:

- *Linear perspective,* which describes the phenomenon that parallel lines seem to converge as they recede into the distance (see Figure 4.16a).

- *Texture gradient,* which describes how textures such as parched ground look more detailed close up but more uniform and smooth when farther away (see Figure 4.16b).

- *Interposition,* which occurs when one object partly blocks another (see Figure 4.16c). You can infer that the blocking object (bowl of cherries) is closer than the blocked object (basket of apples). However, interposition by itself cannot provide information about how far apart the two objects are.

- *Relative height in the image* depends on your field of vision (see Figure 4.16d). Objects that are closer to you tend to be lower in a visual scene (or in your visual field of view), whereas faraway objects are higher up in your field of view.

monocular depth cues Aspects of a scene that yield information about depth when viewed with only one eye.

THE PHOTO WORKS

THE PHOTO WORKS

Figure 4.15
Familiar Size When you view images of things that have a familiar size, such as the people in the left-hand photo, your perceptual system automatically interprets the smaller object as the same size as the nearer one, but farther away. With a little image manipulation, you can see in the right-hand photo that the relative size difference projected on your retinas is far greater than you perceive. The image of the person in the black vest is exactly the same size in both photos. This is an example of perceptual constancy—we perceive all people to be about the same size, even though the size on the retina is very different.

Figure 4.16
Pictorial Depth Cues Visual artists rely on a variety of monocular cues to make their work come to life. You can rely on cues in an image such as linear perspective (a), texture gradient (b), interposition (c), and relative height (d) to infer distance, depth, and position, even with only one eye.

(a)

(b)

(c)

(d)

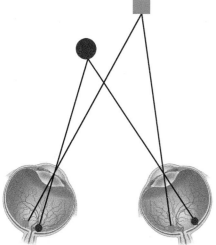

Figure 4.17
Binocular Disparity We see the world in three dimensions because our eyes are a distance apart, so the image of an object falls on a slightly different place on the retina of each eye. In this two-object scene, the images of the square and the circle fall on different points of the retina in each eye. The disparity in the positions of the circle's retinal images provides a compelling cue to depth.

binocular disparity The difference in the retinal images of the two eyes that provides information about depth.

Binocular Depth Cues

We can also use **binocular disparity,** *the difference in the retinal images of the two eyes that provides information about depth.* Because our eyes are slightly separated, each registers a slightly different view of the world. Your brain computes the difference (disparity) between the two retinal images and uses this to perceive how far away objects are, as shown in **FIGURE 4.17**. If the images fall in very similar places on the two retinas, demonstrating little disparity, the object is perceived as farther away; if the images are more disparate in their retinal location, the object is perceived as closer.

Binocular disparity as a cue to depth perception was first discussed by Sir Charles Wheatstone in 1838. Wheatstone went on to invent the stereoscope, essentially a holder for a pair of photographs or drawings taken from two horizontally displaced locations. (Wheatstone did not lack for original ideas; he also invented the accordion and an early telegraph, and coined the term *microphone.*) When viewed, one by each eye, the pairs of images evoked a vivid sense of depth; 3-D movies are based on this same idea.

Illusions of Depth and Size

The ambiguous relation between size and distance has been used to create elaborate illusions that depend on fooling the visual system about how far away objects are. All these illusions depend on the same principle: When you view two objects that project the same retinal image size, the object you perceive as farther away will be perceived as larger. Such illusions are typically constructed to be viewed from just one vantage point—for this reason, they are called *forced perspective illusions.* A famous example is the Ames room, a room that is trapezoidal in shape rather than square: Only two sides are parallel (see **FIGURE 4.18a**). A person standing in one corner of an Ames room is physically twice as far away from the viewer as a person standing in the other corner. But when viewed with one eye through the small peephole placed in one wall, the Ames room looks square because the shapes of the windows and the flooring tiles are carefully crafted to *look* square from the viewing port (Ittelson, 1952).

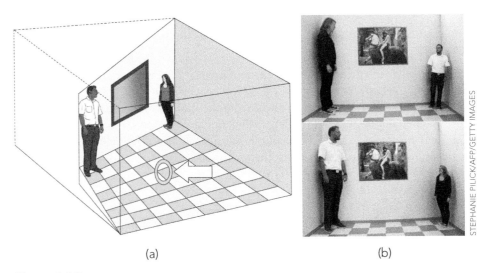

(a)   (b)

Figure 4.18
The Amazing Ames Room (a) A diagram showing the actual proportions of the Ames room reveals its secrets. The sides of the room form a trapezoid with parallel sides but a back wall that's way off square. The uneven floor makes the room's height shorter in the far back corner than in the nearer corner. Add misleading cues such as specially designed windows and flooring and position the room's occupants in each corner, and you're ready to lure an unsuspecting observer. (b) Looking into the Ames room through the viewing port (see yellow arrow in part a) with only one eye, the observer infers a normal size–distance relationship—that both people are the same distance away. And so the image sizes they project on the retina lead the viewer to conclude that one person is very small and the other is very large.

The perceptual system interprets the far wall as perpendicular to the line of sight, such that people standing at different positions along that wall appear to be at the same distance. The viewer interprets the retinal image size so that the person standing in the right corner appears to be much larger than the person standing in the left corner (see Figure 4.18b). Forced perspective is also commonly used in filmmaking, to make objects or people in the same frame appear to be of different sizes. For example, the actors in the *Lord of the Rings* movies are not very different in size in real life, but you perceive the hobbits as much smaller than the humans, wizards, and elves.

Can you see that, by constructing the wagon as a trapezoid similar to an Ames room, Frodo the hobbit (*left*) appears to be much smaller than Gandalf the wizard (*right*) in this scene from *The Fellowship of the Ring* (Warner Brothers)?

Perceiving Motion and Change

You should now have a good sense of how we see what and where objects are, a process made substantially easier when the objects stay in one place. But real life, of course, is full of moving targets. Objects change position over time: Birds fly, horses gallop; rain and snow fall; trees bend in the wind. Understanding how we perceive motion and why we sometimes fail to perceive change can bring us closer to appreciating how visual perception works in everyday life.

Motion Perception

To sense motion, the visual system must encode information about both space and time. The simplest case to consider is an observer who is not moving, looking at an object that is.

As an object moves across a stationary observer's visual field, it first stimulates one location on the retina, then soon after stimulates another location on the retina. Neural circuits in the brain can detect this change in position over time and respond to specific speeds and directions of motion (Emerson et al., 1992). A region near the back of the temporal lobe, referred to as *MT* (part of the dorsal stream we discussed earlier), is specialized for the perception of visual motion (Born & Bradley, 2005; Newsome & Paré, 1988), and brain damage in this area causes a deficit in normal motion perception (Zihl et al., 1983).

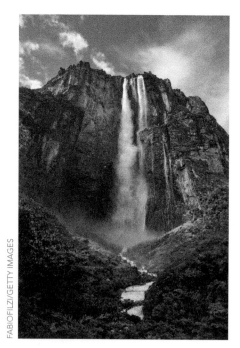

Colour perception and motion perception both rely on opponent processing, which is why we fall prey to colour aftereffects and to the waterfall illusion, which also depends on neural adaptation.

Of course, in the real world, rarely are you a stationary observer: As you move around, your head and eyes move all the time. The motion-perception system must take into account the position and movement of your eyes, and ultimately of your head and body, in order to perceive the motions of objects correctly and allow you to approach or avoid them. The brain accomplishes this by monitoring your eye and head movements and "subtracting" them from the motion in the retinal image.

Motion perception, like colour perception, operates in part through opponent processes and is subject to sensory adaptation. A motion aftereffect called the *waterfall illusion* is analogous to colour aftereffects. If you stare at the downward rush of a waterfall for several seconds, you'll experience an upward motion aftereffect when you then look at stationary objects near the waterfall, such as trees or rocks. What's going on here?

This process is similar to seeing green after staring at a patch of red. Just like your perception of colour depends on the relative activity in opposing sets of cones, perception of motion depends on relative activity in opposing sets of motion detector cells. If there is no motion, activity in the two sets of cells is equal. If one set of motion detector cells is fatigued through adaptation to motion in one direction, then, when motion ceases, there is relatively greater firing in the opposing, less fatigued, set of cells, which is interpreted by your perceptual system as motion in the opposite direction. Evidence from studies using fMRI to study brain activity indicates that when people experience the waterfall illusion while viewing a stationary stimulus, there is increased activity in region MT, which plays a key role in motion perception (Tootell et al., 1995).

The movement of objects in the world is not the only event that can evoke the perception of motion. The successively flashing lights of a Las Vegas casino sign can evoke a strong sense of motion because people perceive a series of flashing lights as a whole moving object (see Figure 4.12f). This *perception of movement as a result of alternating signals appearing in rapid succession in different locations* is called **apparent motion.**

Of course, we don't only perceive the motion of objects in the world—we also perceive the motions of other people. Classic studies have shown that adults, children, and even young infants are capable of detecting human motion from minimal cues such as a set of dots moving in a typically human pattern (Johannsen, 1973). **Biological motion perception** refers to *our ability to perceive biological motion critical for identifying individuals and various socially relevant features, such as their emotional state, personality characteristics, whether they are vulnerable to attack, or are engaging in deceptive actions* (Blake & Shiffrar, 2007; Gunns et al., 2002; Heberlein et al., 2004). FMRI studies have revealed that a region in the back of the temporal lobe, the posterior superior temporal sulcus, is strongly linked to biological motion perception (Bellot et al., 2021; Pelphrey et al., 2005). This region is anatomically adjacent to, and functionally connected with, the temporo-parietal junction, a region that plays a key role in social processing (Meyer, 2019; Van Overwalle, 2009). In fact, interactions between these regions are thought to play a key role in a variety of social abilities (Patel et al., 2019), which makes them a likely brain substrate for the social functions of biological motion perception (see **FIGURE 4.19**).

Figure 4.19

Areas of the Brain That Play a Role in Perceiving the Motion of Objects Area MT plays a key role in perceiving the motion of objects, whereas STS is important for biological motion perception and is closely connected to the TPJ, which is important for social cognition.

Sensory Superpowers

Filmmaking and animation depend on apparent motion. Motion pictures flash 24 still frames per second (fps). A slower rate would produce a much choppier sense of motion; a faster rate would be a waste of resources because we would not perceive the motion as any smoother than it appears at 24 fps. As you will learn in the next section, our auditory system is much more sensitive to rapid changes than our visual system. Although we cannot see the difference between 24 and 50 frames in a second, we can very easily hear the difference between 24 and 50 clicks in a second. Every sensory domain has its superpower. Your visual system has amazing **spatial acuity,** or *ability to distinguish two stimuli that are very close together in space,* while your auditory system rocks at **temporal acuity,** the *ability to distinguish two stimuli that are very close together in time.*

In our everyday life, we capitalize on these strengths. Many events in the world are **multisensory,** *stimulating multiple senses at the same time.* We take sensory information into account according to how good it is. For example, when you watch a movie with surround sound, you attribute voices to characters on the screen: You hear them coming from what you can see, even though you know they are coming from speakers elsewhere. This is called the **ventriloquist illusion.** You depend on your visual system for reliable information about spatial location; when you see a moving mouth, simultaneously with hearing speech, you perceive the speech as coming from that mouth. We "believe" our visual system over our auditory system when it comes to determining the spatial location of an event.

Change Blindness and Inattentional Blindness

The visual world is very rich—so rich, in fact, that our perceptual system cannot take it all in, although intuitively we may feel that at any moment we have full awareness of what is around us. However, our comfortable intuitions have been challenged by experimental demonstrations of **change blindness,** which occurs *when people fail to detect changes to the visual details of a scene* (Rensink, 2002; Simons & Rensink, 2005). Change blindness occurs even when major details of a scene are changed—changes that we incorrectly believe we couldn't possibly miss (Beek et al., 2007).

In a study that dramatically illustrates this idea, an experimenter asked a person on a university campus for directions (Simons & Levin, 1998). While they were talking, two men walked between them, carrying a door that hid a second experimenter (see **FIGURE 4.20**). Behind the door, the two experimenters traded places, so that when the men carrying the door moved on, a different person was asking for directions than the one who had been there just a second or two earlier. Remarkably, only 7 of 15 participants noticed this change.

Although it is surprising that people can be blind to such dramatic changes, these findings once again illustrate the illusion of perception; we think we are aware of much more of what is "out in the world" than we really are. They also illustrate the

apparent motion The perception of movement as a result of alternating signals appearing in rapid succession in different locations.

biological motion perception The ability to perceive biological motion critical for identifying individuals and various socially relevant features.

spatial acuity The ability to distinguish two features that are very close together in space.

temporal acuity The ability to distinguish two features that are very close together in time.

multisensory Events that stimulate multiple senses at the same time.

ventriloquist illusion The fact that you depend on your visual system for reliable information about spatial location.

change blindness Failure to detect changes to the visual details of a scene.

(a)   (b)   (c)

Figure 4.20

Change Blindness The white-haired man was giving directions to one experimenter (a), who disappeared behind the moving door (b), only to be replaced by another experimenter (c). Like many other people, the man failed to detect a seemingly obvious change.

A World of Difference • The Experience of Synesthesia

Lorde and Billie Eilish are two of the biggest musical superstars to emerge during the past decade. In addition to their phenomenal success, the two have something else in common that makes their perceptual worlds quite different from most of ours. Lorde doesn't just hear her songs, she sees them. "From the moment I start something, I can see the finished song," Lorde reflected in an interview with the *New York Times*, adding that for her, composing a song is "about getting the actual thing to sound like what I've been seeing" (Weiner, 2017). Billie Eilish describes something similar, commenting that she sees her songs in particular colours, for example, she sees the song "Bury a Friend" in dark colours: grey, black, or brown (Nattress, 2019). This kind of experience is known as **synesthesia**, *when one attribute of a stimulus, such as its sound or shape, leads to the conscious experience of an additional attribute, often in a different sensory modality than the initiating stimulus* (Ward, 2013).

Some people with synesthesia, like Lorde and Eilish, experience visual sensations in response to sounds. They are not alone among musicians: Tori Amos, Mary J. Blige, Billy Joel, and Kanye West are just a few other well-known musicians who report synesthetic experiences. Similarly, the great Russian novelist Vladimir Nabokov described a coloured alphabet in which he associated the sound of each letter to a specific colour (Hupé, 2020). Other people with synesthesia experience specific tastes or smells in response to sounds or sights. Still others see printed letters or numbers in specific colours, such as always seeing the letter *A* as red and *C* as green (see figure). Once dismissed as a rare curiosity, research indicates that synesthesia is more common than previously believed and that certain kinds of synesthesia occur more frequently than others. For example, synesthesia in which people see specific letters in specific colours occurs in about 1 in 100 people (Carmichael et al., 2015; Watson et al., 2017), and is more common than, say, a smell evoked by seeing or touching a particular shape. There is also some evidence that synesthetes — especially those who link sound and colour — are more likely than non-synesthetes to pursue artistic activities (Lunke & Meier, 2019).

The differing subjective experiences of synesthetes and non-synesthetes can produce striking differences in how they perform basic perceptual tasks. An early study showed that synesthetes who see the digits 2 and 4 as pink and 3 as green find it easier to pick out a 2 among a bunch of 3s than among a bunch of 4s, whereas nonsynesthetes perform these two tasks equally well (Palmieri et al., 2002). Synesthetes who experience subjective colour in response to letters or numbers show an enhanced ability to discriminate objective colours compared with non-synesthetes (Banissy et al., 2009), and this enhanced perceptual ability plays a role in synesthetes' enhanced memories for colours (Lunke & Meier, 2020; Ovalle-Fresa et al., 2021). When asked to assess the brightness of printed letters, letter-colour synesthetes judged those letters that they typically saw with bright synesthetic colours to be brighter than those letters that they typically saw with dark synesthetic colours, but no such effects on brightness perception occurred in non-synesthetes who assessed the brightness of the same letters (Uno & Yokosawa, 2020).

Scientists are attempting to understand how brain activity may differ in synesthetes

(a) Usual appearance

(b) Appearance to a person with synesthesia

Most of us see letters printed in black as they appear in (a). Some people with synesthesia link their perceptions of letters with certain colours and perceive letters as printed in different colours, as shown in (b). In synesthesia, brain regions for different sensory modalities cross-activate one another.

and non-synesthetes, but results to date are conflicting. For example, some fMRI studies suggest that synesthetes who experience colours in response to letters show increased activity in parts of the visual cortex that are responsible for processing colours, but not all studies show this effect (Hupé & Dojat, 2015; Ruiz et al., 2020). Although we don't yet have a full understanding of why only some people experience synesthesia, there is evidence for a genetic contribution: In three families characterized by sound–colour synesthesia, researchers identified a shared set of rare alterations in genes that influence the development of neural connections in the brain (Tilot et al., 2018).

Synesthesia in its various forms highlights that basic properties of perceptual experience can differ substantially across individuals. And in gifted performers such as Lorde and Billie Eilish, the ability to see sounds is far more than a perceptual anomaly — it's an integral part of their creative process.

---

synesthesia When one attribute of a stimulus, such as its sound or shape, leads to the conscious experience of an additional attribute, often in a different sensory modality than the initiating stimulus.

importance of focused attention for visual perception. (See the earlier discussion of feature-integration theory.) Just as focused attention is critical for binding together the features of objects, it is also necessary for detecting changes to objects and scenes (Rensink, 2002; Simons & Rensink, 2005). Change blindness is most likely to occur when people fail to focus attention on the object that undergoes a change (Rensink et al., 1997).

The role of focused attention in conscious visual experience is also dramatically illustrated by the closely related phenomenon of **inattentional blindness,** *a failure to perceive objects that are not the focus of attention* (Simons & Chabris, 1999). We've already seen that the use of cell phones is a bad idea when driving (see The Real World: Multitasking). Ira Hyman and colleagues (2010) asked whether cell phone use results in inattentional blindness in other situations. They recruited a clown to ride a unicycle in the middle of a large courtyard on the Western Washington University campus. On a pleasant afternoon, the researchers asked 151 students who had just walked through the square whether they saw the clown. Seventy-five percent of the students who were using cell phones failed to notice the clown, compared with less than 50% who were not using cell phones.

In a follow-up study, walkers using cell phones were less aware than others of obstacles in their path and even failed to notice a tree with money hanging from it (Hyman et al., 2014)! Using cell phones draws on focused attention, resulting in inattentional blindness and emphasizing again that our conscious experience of our visual environment is restricted to those features or objects selected by focused attention.

University students who were using their cell phones while walking through campus failed to notice the unicycling clown more frequently than did students who were not using their cell phones.

Hearing: More Than Meets the Ear

Ray Charles (1930–2004) was a pioneering American soul-music singer and songwriter who went blind at the age of 6. He said, "I look at blindness like an inconvenience. I can do 98 percent of everything I want to do in my life . . .[but] it would be a real [expletive deleted] if I ever lost my hearing" (Sager, 2007). It is understandable that a musician would feel this way, but you don't have to be a blind musician to appreciate what hearing adds to your life. Just close your eyes for a few minutes and notice what sounds you hear. Unlike vision, hearing works in the dark, through walls, and around corners. We are social animals, who typically rely on sound as our primary means of communicating with each other.

The sense of hearing depends on **sound waves,** *changes in air pressure unfolding over time.* Plenty of things produce sound waves: the impact of two hands clapping, the vibration of vocal cords during a stirring speech, the resonance of a bass guitar string during a thrash metal concert. Just as vision is about the perception of meaningful visual objects, hearing involves transforming changes in air pressure into meaningful sound objects (or sources).

Sensing Sound

Striking a tuning fork produces a *pure tone,* a simple sound wave that consists of regularly alternating regions of higher and lower air pressure, radiating outward in all directions from the source. If your ear is in the path of this spreading sound, the alternating pressure wave causes your eardrum to vibrate in time with the wave, hundreds or even thousands of times per second. Just as there are three physical dimensions of light waves that influence visual perception, so, too, are there three physical dimensions of a sound wave that correspond to dimensions of auditory perception: frequency, amplitude, and complexity (see **TABLE 4.3**).

- The *frequency* (or *repetition rate*) of the sound wave depends on how often the peak in air pressure passes the ear or a microphone, measured in cycles per second, or hertz (Hz). The repetition rate of a sound wave is perceived as the **pitch,** *how high or low a sound is.*

Learning Outcomes

WHAT YOU NEED TO KNOW

- Describe the physical properties of sound waves.

- Describe how the ear converts sound waves into neural impulses.

- Explain how pitch, timbre, and loudness of a sound relate to its physical properties.

- Compare the main causes of hearing loss.

inattentional blindness A failure to perceive objects that are not the focus of attention.

sound waves Changes in air pressure unfolding over time.

pitch How high or low a sound is.

TABLE 4.3

PROPERTIES OF SOUND WAVES

Frequency (repetition rate) Corresponds to our perception of pitch	Low frequency (low-pitched sound)	High frequency (high-pitched sound)
Amplitude Corresponds to our perception of loudness	High amplitude (loud sound)	Low amplitude (soft sound)
Complexity Corresponds to our perception of timbre	Simple (pure tone)	Complex (mix of frequencies)

- The *amplitude* of a sound wave refers to its intensity, relative to the threshold for human hearing (which is set at zero decibels, or dB). **Loudness** is *the perception of a sound's intensity.* To give you an idea of the relation between the physical property of intensity (measured in dB) and your subjective impression of loudness, the rustling of leaves in a soft breeze is about 20 dB, normal conversation is about 60 dB, a busy restaurant is about 85 dB, and a Slayer concert is about 130 dB. That's loud enough to cause permanent damage to the auditory system and is well above the pain threshold; in fact, sounds above 85 dB can cause hearing damage, depending on the length of exposure.

- The *complexity* of sound waves, or the mixture of frequencies, influences perception of **timbre,** *the quality of sound that allows you to distinguish two sources with the same pitch and loudness.* Timbre (pronounced "TAM-ber") allows you to tell the difference between a piano and a guitar both playing the same melody in the same key, at the same loudness. Very few sources (other than tuning forks and artificial tone generators) emit pure tones, consisting of just one frequency. Nearly all everyday sounds consist of a broad range of frequencies present at the same time. Timbre (whether it's a piano, guitar, or human voice) is determined, in part, by the relative amounts of the different frequencies in the sound mixture, rather like how colour depends on the relative amounts of different wavelengths in an impure light.

The auditory world is a busy place. Imagine being in a coffee shop, conversing with a friend. In addition to your friend's voice and your own, you hear music in the background; the voices and laughter of strangers conversing at adjacent tables; as well as the clatter of dishes, the hiss of the espresso machine, and the rumble of traffic outside. The different sounds combine in the air to create very complex sound waves in your two ears.

Most sound sources that you encounter in real life are a mixture of many different frequencies, and different sources may have frequencies in common. These mix together into a complex wave that produces an intricate pattern of vibration in the eardrum. Somehow, we perceive auditory scenes not as incoherent jumbles, but as discrete, recognizable sound sources—such as voices, espresso machines, and traffic—in different auditory locations. How does your brain reconstruct the original

GETTY IMAGES

The process of auditory perception is very different from visual perception. This is not surprising: Light is a form of electromagnetic radiation, whereas sound is a physical change in air pressure over time. Different forms of energy require different processes of transduction.

loudness Perception of a sound's intensity.

timbre The quality of sound that allows you to distinguish two sources with the same pitch and loudness.

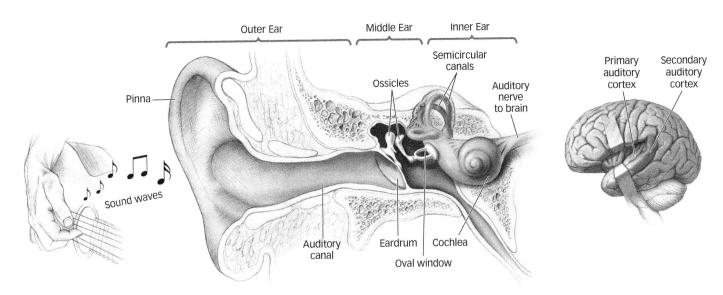

Figure 4.21

Anatomy of the Human Ear The pinna funnels sound waves into the auditory canal, causing the eardrum to vibrate in time with the sound wave. In the middle ear, the ossicles pick up the eardrum vibrations, amplify them, and pass them along, causing vibration of the oval window, and therefore of the fluid-filled cochlea in the inner ear. Here, fluid carries the wave energy to the auditory receptors (inner hair cells) that transduce it into electrical activity, exciting the neurons that form the auditory nerve, leading to the brain.

sounds such that you can hear and understand your friend over all the other sounds? This is the central problem of auditory perception; to answer it, we need to understand how the auditory system converts sound waves into neural signals.

The Outer Ear Funnels Sound Waves to the Middle Ear

The human ear is divided into three distinct parts, as shown in **FIGURE 4.21**. The *outer ear* collects sound waves and funnels them towards the *middle ear*, which transmits the vibrations to the *inner ear,* embedded in the skull, where they are transduced into neural impulses.

The outer ear consists of the visible part on the outside of the head (called the *pinna*); the auditory canal; and the eardrum, an airtight flap of skin that vibrates in response to sound waves gathered by the pinna and channelled into the canal. The middle ear, a tiny, air-filled chamber behind the eardrum, contains the three smallest bones in the body, called *ossicles*. Named for their appearance as hammer, anvil, and stirrup, the ossicles fit together into a lever that mechanically transmits and amplifies vibrations from the eardrum to the inner ear. Amplification is required because the ossicles push against the oval window, which is a membrane that separates the middle ear from the cochlea of the inner ear. The ossicles take the airborne pressure wave at the eardrum and transfer it into a pressure wave in fluid. Fluid requires more energy to vibrate; if you've ever been poolside, trying to talk to someone who is underwater, you know you have to really shout in order for the pressure wave of your voice to carry under the water.

Sound Is Converted into Neural Impulses in the Inner Ear

The inner ear contains the spiral-shaped **cochlea** (Latin for "snail"), *a fluid-filled tube that contains cells that transduce sound vibrations into neural impulses.* The cochlea is divided along its length by the **basilar membrane,** *a structure in the inner ear that moves up and down in time with vibrations relayed from the ossicles, transmitted through the oval window* (see **FIGURE 4.22**). Sound causes the basilar membrane to move up and down in a **travelling wave** (see Figure 4.22) (Békésy, 1960). The frequency of the stimulating sound determines where on the basilar membrane the up-and-down motion is highest. When the frequency is low, the wide, floppy tip (*apex*) of the basilar membrane moves the most; when the frequency is high, the narrow, stiff end closest to the oval window (*base*) moves the most.

When the basilar membrane moves up and down, the cochlear fluid moves back and forth. This stimulates thousands of **inner hair cells,** which are *specialized auditory receptor neurons embedded in the basilar membrane.* The hair cells have long

cochlea A fluid-filled tube that contains cells that transduce sound vibrations into neural impulses.

basilar membrane A structure in the inner ear that moves up and down in time with vibrations relayed from the ossicles, transmitted through the oval window.

travelling wave The up-and-down movement that sound causes in the basilar membrane.

inner hair cells Specialized auditory receptor neurons embedded in the basilar membrane.

Figure 4.22

Auditory Transduction Inside the cochlea (shown here as though the coiled part was uncoiled—note that this never actually happens!), the basilar membrane undulates in response to wave energy in the cochlear fluid. Different locations along the membrane are sensitive to different frequency components, from low frequencies at the apex of the cochlea to high frequencies at the base, and the movement of the basilar membrane causes the hairs of the hair cells at those locations to bend. This bending generates action potentials in the attached auditory nerve axons, which together form the auditory nerve that emerges from the cochlea.

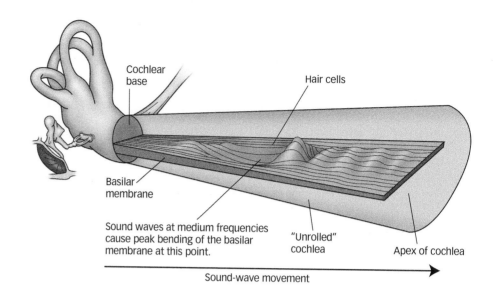

hairs sticking out their tops that bend back and forth in the cochlear fluid, like seaweed in a current. This back-and-forth bending generates rhythmic action potentials in the auditory nerve axons that travel to the brain, and these action potentials are precisely timed with the pressure peaks of the original sound wave. The auditory nerve axons that fire the most are those connected to hair cells in the area of the basilar membrane that moves the most.

The Auditory Nerve Carries the Neural Impulses to the Brain

From the inner ear, action potentials in the auditory nerve travel to several regions of the brainstem in turn, and then to the thalamus and ultimately to an area of the cerebral cortex called **area A1,** *the primary auditory cortex in the temporal lobe* (see **FIGURE 4.23**). There is some evidence that the auditory cortex is composed of two distinct streams, roughly analogous to the dorsal and ventral streams of the visual system. Spatial ("where") auditory features, which allow you to locate the source of a sound in space, are handled by areas towards the back of the temporal lobe and

area A1 The primary auditory cortex in the temporal lobe.

Figure 4.23

Primary Auditory Cortex Area A1, also known as the primary auditory cortex, is folded into the temporal lobe beneath the lateral fissure in each hemisphere. The area A1 cortex has a topographic organization (inset), with lower frequencies mapping towards the front of the brain and higher frequencies towards the back, mirroring the organization of the basilar membrane along the cochlea (see Figure 4.22).

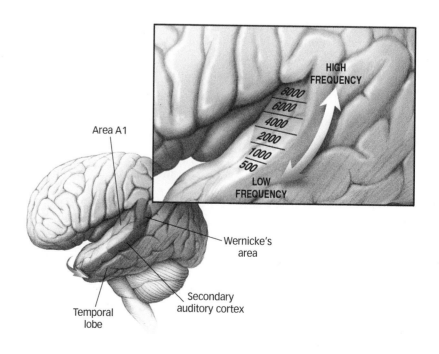

in regions that may overlap with the visual dorsal stream. Features that allow you to identify the sound (what it is) are handled by areas in the lower (ventral) part of the temporal lobe, and this pathway may overlap with the ventral visual pathway.

Perceiving Sound Sources

Just as visual objects can be identified based on their shape and size and their colour and location, sound sources—like voices, or clapping hands, or a guitar—have particular perceptual attributes that allow you to identify them. These include loudness, pitch, timbre, and location.

Perceiving Pitch, Loudness, Timbre, and Location

Your brain uses patterns of action potentials in the auditory nerve to perceive sounds in terms of their loudness, pitch, timbre, and location. How does it accomplish this?

- The perceptual attribute of loudness is signaled by the total amount of activity in hair cells, rather like how brightness of light is signaled by the total amount of activity in photoreceptors.

- How we perceive pitch (e.g., of musical notes or voices) has been studied extensively, and it seems to depend on two aspects of auditory nerve activity (Plack, 2018a). First, different frequencies stimulate neural signals at specific places along the basilar membrane. This provides a **place code,** whereby *the brain uses information about the relative activity of hair cells (e.g., which ones are more active and which are less active) across the whole basilar membrane to help determine the pitch you hear.* Second, the hair cell hairs move in time with the incoming sound wave, so auditory nerve axons fire synchronously with the sound-wave peaks, which happen regularly at the sound's repetition rate. This provides a **temporal code,** whereby *the brain uses the timing of the action potentials in the auditory nerve to help determine the pitch you hear.*

- Timbre depends, in part, on the relative amounts of different frequency components in a sound and thus, like pitch, depends on the relative activity of hair cells across the whole basilar membrane.

- How we determine the location of a sound has also been studied extensively (Plack, 2018b). As in vision, there are monaural (one ear) and binaural (two ear) cues to location. First, your pinnas aren't simply handy places to hook your sunglasses. Their intricate folds alter sound, emphasizing some frequency components over others, depending on where the sound is coming from. You have learned to interpret these changes as indicating a sound's location. Second, the speed of sound is much slower than the speed of light. Sounds arrive a little sooner at the ear nearer to the source than at the far ear. This time difference is effective for indicating the location of lower-frequency components of a sound, even when it is only a little off to one side. Third, the higher-frequency components of a sound are more intense in the ear closer to the sound than in the ear farther away, because the listener's head blocks higher frequencies. The farther a sound is off to the side, the greater the between-ear difference in the level of these high-frequency components.

Sometimes you may find yourself turning your head from side to side to localize a sound. By doing this, you are changing the relative intensity and timing of sound waves arriving in your ears and collecting better information about the likely source of the sound. Turning your head also allows you to use your eyes to locate the source of the sound—and, as you learned earlier in this chapter, your visual system is much better at pinpointing the location of things than your auditory system is.

place code The process by which the brain uses information about the relative activity of hair cells (e.g., which ones are more active and which are less active) across the whole basilar membrane to help determine the pitch you hear.

temporal code The process whereby the brain uses the timing of the action potentials in the auditory nerve to help determine the pitch you hear.

Organizing Sound Features into Sources

In hearing, your auditory system first analyzes a complex sound wave (like that resulting from the mixture of different coffee shop sounds) into its component frequencies, which activate different regions of the basilar membrane and auditory nerve. Then the brain has to figure out which frequency components belong together in a single source (perceptual grouping) and which frequency components belong to different sources (perceptual segregation). Just as in vision, our perceptual system organizes and automatically delivers to us the interpretation that is the simplest and most meaningful, consistent with expectations based on experience.

The Gestalt rules you learned about earlier in this chapter also apply to sound. For example, sounds that are *similar* in the physical properties of frequency or intensity, or that are similar in the perceptual attributes of loudness, pitch, timbre, or location, are grouped together into one source, as are sounds that occur close together in time (proximity). Furthermore, sounds that start together and stop together (like the different frequencies emitted simultaneously by a musical instrument, or a voice) are perceived as coming from the same source.

Hearing Loss

Hearing loss has two main causes. *Conductive hearing loss* arises because the eardrum or ossicles are damaged to the point that they cannot conduct sound waves effectively to the cochlea. The cochlea itself, however, is normal, making this a kind of "mechanical problem" with the moving parts of the ear: the hammer, anvil, stirrup, or eardrum. In many cases, medication or surgery can correct the problem. Sound amplification from a hearing aid also can improve hearing through conduction via the bones around the ear directly to the cochlea.

Sensorineural hearing loss is caused by damage to the cochlea, the hair cells, or the auditory nerve, and it happens to almost all of us as we age. It has two main effects: Sensitivity decreases so sounds have to be more intense to be heard, and acuity decreases so sounds smear together on the basilar membrane, making voices harder to understand, especially if other sounds are present. Sensorineural hearing loss has many causes, including genetic disorders, premature birth, infections, medications, accumulated damage from sound exposure (particularly intense sounds), and aging (these last two causes are hard to tease apart since older people have been exposed to sound for longer). Hearing aids amplify sounds, helping with decreased sensitivity, but, unlike glasses, which can fix blurry vision, hearing aids cannot fix the acuity problem.

When hearing loss is severe, a *cochlear implant* may restore some hearing. A cochlear implant is an electronic device that replaces the function of the hair cells (Waltzman, 2006). The external parts of the device include a microphone and a processor and transmitter (a little bigger than a two-dollar coin), worn on the scalp near the ear. The implanted parts include a receiver just inside the skull and a thin wire containing electrodes inserted into the cochlea to stimulate the auditory nerve. Sound picked up by the microphone is transformed into electric signals by the processor, which is essentially a small computer. The signal is transmitted to the implanted receiver, which activates the electrodes in the cochlea. Cochlear implants are now in routine use and can improve hearing to the point that the wearer can understand speech, although background sound still poses a real challenge. (See Hot Science: Big Technology in Little Ears for how cochlear implants are allowing babies to learn the language of their parents and caregivers.)

Hot Science · Big Technology in Little Ears

More than 90% of infants who are born deaf are born to hearing parents, who communicate using spoken language, which their babies can't hear. Such children are vulnerable to language disorders because communication with parents and other caregivers in the first few years is crucial if language is to develop normally, as you'll learn in the Development chapter. Some of these parents compensate by learning a signed language, such as American Sign Language, so they can teach it to, and use it with, their baby. Recent evidence indicates that when deaf children of hearing parents are exposed to American Sign Language by 6 months of age, they later show age-appropriate growth of vocabulary (Caselli et al., 2021). But if you have ever attempted to learn a second language, you know how difficult it can be. Now imagine trying to learn a second language while also caring for a new baby! This requires an extraordinary commitment of time and resources that is sometimes not practical or even possible. Furthermore, even if parents and child successfully learn to use a sign language together, what about that child's relationships with grandparents, family friends, and others in the hearing community?

Giving a baby cochlear implants allows parents and others to interact with the child using their native spoken language, enabling language development. Hearing screening programs for newborns now mean that deafness can be identified at birth, and babies are routinely implanted around their first birthday, and sometimes even earlier. This is a serious decision for parents to make; although it enables hearing, cochlear implantation does have risks, such as a higher chance of the child contracting a serious infection like meningitis. So, it might make sense to wait as long as

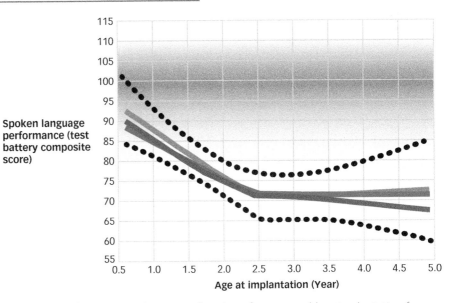

Language performance is shown as a function of age at cochlear implantation for children who received follow-up testing at three different times after implantation: 4 years (blue), 5 years (maroon), or 6 years (orange).

possible, perhaps until the child is 4 or 5 or even older, before giving the child an implant.

Are there any disadvantages to language development, if a family waits to have their child implanted? Researchers tested 160 children implanted between the ages of 6 months and 5 years of age to examine the link between spoken language ability, assessed using a battery of tests, and the age at which the implant was received (Tobey et al., 2013). The results are shown in the figure. The performance of normally hearing children, adjusted for age, is given by the grey-shaded rectangle (average of 100, with two-thirds of children falling between scores of 85 and 115). Whether the kids were tested at 4, 5, or 6 years after implantation didn't really affect the data: The blue (4 years), maroon (5 years), and orange (6 years) lines, showing average

performance at these test time points, are all pretty similar to each other. What mattered was age at implantation. The dotted lines are the upper and lower bounds of performance for 95% of the kids implanted at each age. The children implanted at the youngest ages (starting from the left side of figure) show average performance in the normal range (grey, shaded rectangle), whereas those implanted at older ages, over 1½ years or so, do not. Consistent with these findings on spoken language ability, more recent studies have shown that early cochlear implantation in deaf children is also associated with enhanced auditory comprehension (Mitchell et al., 2020) and reading comprehension (Guerzoni et al., 2020). Taken together, these studies highlight that there are disadvantages to waiting to have a child implanted at an older age.

The Body Senses: More Than Skin Deep

Learning Outcomes

WHAT YOU NEED TO KNOW

- Describe how touch receptors transmit messages to the brain.

- Discuss why pain is a psychological perception.

- Explain how we use various senses to keep our balance.

Vision and hearing provide information about the world at a distance. By responding to light and sound energy in the environment, these "distance" senses allow us to identify and locate the objects and people around us. In comparison, the body senses, also called *somatosenses* (*soma* from the Greek for "body"), are up close and personal. **Haptic perception** is the *active exploration of the environment by touching and grasping objects with our hands*. We use sensory receptors in our muscles, tendons, and joints as well as a variety of receptors in our skin to get a feel for the world around us (see **FIGURE 4.24**).

Sensing Touch

Touch begins with the transduction of skin sensations into neural signals. Receptors located under the skin's surface enable us to sense pain, pressure, texture, pattern, or vibration against the skin (see Figure 4.24). Each receptor has a **tactile receptive field,** *a small patch of skin that relates information about pain, pressure, texture, pattern, or vibration to a receptor.* These specialized cells work together to provide a rich tactile (from Latin, "to touch") experience when you explore an object by feeling it or attempting to grasp it. In addition, *thermoreceptors,* nerve fibres that sense cold and warmth, respond when your skin temperature changes. All these sensations blend seamlessly together in perception, of course, but detailed physiological studies have successfully isolated the parts of the touch system (Hollins, 2010; Johnson, 2002).

There are three important principles regarding the neural representation of the body's surface. First, the left half of the body is represented in the right half of the brain and vice versa. Second, refer back to Figure 3.16 in the Neuroscience and Behaviour chapter; you'll recall that different locations on the body send sensory signals to different locations in the somatosensory cortex in the parietal lobe. Just as more of the visual brain is devoted to foveal vision, where acuity is greatest, more of

haptic perception The active exploration of the environment by touching and grasping objects with our hands.

tactile receptive field A small patch of skin that relates information about pain, pressure, texture, pattern, or vibration to a receptor.

Figure 4.24

Touch Receptors Specialized sensory neurons form distinct groups of haptic receptors that detect pressure, temperature, and vibrations against the skin. Each touch receptor responds to stimulation within its receptive field, and the long axons enter the brain via the spinal or cranial nerves. Pain receptors populate all body tissues that feel pain; they are distributed around bones and within muscles and internal organs, as well as under the skin surface. Sensory signals on the body travel to the somatosensory cortex.

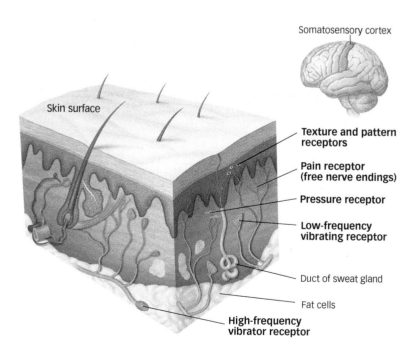

Somatosensory cortex

Skin surface

Texture and pattern receptors

Pain receptor (free nerve endings)

Pressure receptor

Low-frequency vibrating receptor

Duct of sweat gland

Fat cells

High-frequency vibrator receptor

the tactile brain is devoted to parts of the skin surface where sensitivity to fine spatial detail (acuity) is greatest. Regions such as the fingertips and lips have high acuity, whereas acuity is lower in areas such as the calf. You can test this yourself: If you put two chopsticks together so that their tips are about a centimetre apart, and gently press them into the skin of your fingertip, you should be able to tell that there are two tips, not one. If you do the same on your calf, how far apart do the tips have to be before you can tell them apart? Third, there is mounting evidence for a distinction between "what" and "where" pathways in touch, analogous to similar distinctions we've already considered for vision and hearing. The "what" system for touch provides information about the properties of surfaces and objects; the "where" system provides information about the location in external space that is being touched or a location on the body that is being stimulated (Lederman & Klatzky, 2009).

Sensing Pain

Does the possibility of a life free from pain seem appealing? Although pain is arguably the least pleasant of sensations, this aspect of touch is among the most important for survival: Pain indicates damage or potential damage to the body. Without the ability to feel pain, we might ignore infections, broken bones, or serious burns. Congenital insensitivity to pain, a rare inherited disorder that specifically impairs pain perception, is more of a curse than a blessing: Children who experience this disorder often accidentally mutilate themselves (e.g., biting into their tongues or gouging their skin while scratching) and are at increased risk of dying in childhood (Nagasako et al., 2003).

Tissue damage is transduced by the free nerve endings shown in Figure 4.24 that sense painful stimuli. In addition, researchers have distinguished between fast-acting *A-delta fibres*, which are axons that transmit initial sharp pain, and slower *C fibres*, which are axons that transmit the longer-lasting, duller persistent pain. If you were running barefoot outside and stubbed your toe against a rock, you would first feel a sudden stinging pain transmitted by A-delta fibres that would die down quickly, only to be replaced by the throbbing but longer-lasting pain carried by C fibres.

Perceiving Pain

As you'll remember from the chapter on Neuroscience and Behaviour, the pain-withdrawal reflex is coordinated by the spinal cord. No brainpower is required when you touch a hot stove; you retract your hand almost instantaneously. But neural signals for pain—such as wrenching your elbow as you brace yourself to keep from falling—travel to two distinct areas in the brain and evoke two distinct psychological experiences (see **FIGURE 4.25**) (Treede et al., 1999). One pain pathway sends signals to the somatosensory cortex, identifying where the pain is occurring and what sort of pain it is (sharp, burning, or dull). The second pain pathway sends signals to the motivational and emotional centres of the brain, such as the hypothalamus and amygdala, as well as to the frontal lobe. This is the aspect of pain that is unpleasant and motivates us to escape from, or relieve, the pain.

Interestingly, fMRI has demonstrated that some of the brain areas that respond to our own physical pain, particularly in the frontal lobe, also respond when we witness others experiencing pain and feel concern for them (Lamm et al., 2011). Precisely what common features of experiencing pain and witnessing pain result in this overlap (Zaki et al., 2016), and whether or not the overlap extends to perceiving the *social pain* (such as embarrassment or social exclusion) of others, are areas of active research (Bruneau et al., 2015).

Pain typically feels as though it comes from the site of the tissue damage that caused it. If you burn your finger, you will perceive the pain as originating there. But

A rather unimposing geodesic dome sits on the floor of the Exploratorium, a world-renowned science museum in San Francisco. Called the Tactile Dome, it was created in 1971 by August Coppola (brother of the director Francis Ford Coppola and father of the actor Nicolas Cage) and Carl Day, who wanted to create an environment in which only haptic perception could be used. The inside of the dome is pitch black; visitors must crawl, wiggle, slide, and otherwise navigate the unfamiliar terrain using only their sense of touch. How would you feel being in that environment for an hour or so?

Figure 4.25
Pain Travels Along Two Pathways
Neural signals for pain travel along two pathways: one to the somatosensory cortex, where the location and type of pain are determined; the other to the motivational and emotional centres of the brain.

referred pain Feeling of pain on the surface of the body, but due to internal damage; occurs because sensory information from internal and external areas converges on the same nerve cells in the spinal cord.

gate-control theory A theory of pain perception based on the idea that signals arriving from pain receptors in the body can be stopped, or *gated*, by interneurons in the spinal cord via feedback from the skin or from the brain.

we have pain receptors in many areas besides the skin, such as around bones and within muscles and internal organs as well. When pain originates internally, in a body organ, for instance, we can feel it on the surface of the body. This kind of **referred pain** occurs when *sensory information from internal and external areas converges on the same nerve cells in the spinal cord.* One common example is a heart attack: Victims often feel pain radiating from the left arm rather than from inside the chest.

Pain intensity cannot always be predicted solely from the extent of the injury that causes the pain (Keefe et al., 2005). For instance, *turf toe* sounds like the mildest of ailments; it is pain at the base of the big toe as a result of bending or pushing off repeatedly, as a runner or football player might do during a sporting event. This small-sounding injury in a small area of the body can nonetheless sideline an athlete for a month with considerable pain. On the other hand, you've probably heard a story or two about someone treading bone-chilling water for hours on end, or dragging their shattered legs a mile down a country road to seek help after a tractor accident, or performing some other incredible feat despite searing pain and extensive tissue damage. Pain type and pain intensity show a less-than-perfect correlation, a fact that intrigues researchers.

One influential account of pain perception is known as the **gate-control theory,** which holds that *signals arriving from pain receptors in the body can be stopped, or gated, by interneurons in the spinal cord via feedback from the skin or from the brain* (Melzack & Wall, 1965). Pain can be gated by the skin receptors, for example, by rubbing the affected area. Rubbing your stubbed toe activates neurons that "close the gate" to stop pain signals from travelling to the brain. Pain can also be gated from the brain, which can modulate the activity of pain-transmission neurons.

The brain's feedback to the spinal cord comes from a region in the midbrain called the *periaqueductal grey* (PAG). Under extreme conditions, such as high stress, naturally occurring endorphins can activate the PAG to send inhibitory signals to neurons in the spinal cord that then suppress pain signals to the brain, thereby modulating the experience of pain. The PAG also responds to the action of opiate drugs, such as morphine.

A different kind of feedback signal from the brain can *increase* the sensation of pain. This system is activated by events such as infection and learned danger signals. When we are quite ill, what we otherwise might experience as mild discomfort can feel quite painful. This pain facilitation signal presumably evolved to motivate people who are ill to rest and avoid strenuous activity, allowing their energy to be devoted to healing.

Although some details of the gate-control theory of pain have been challenged, a key concept underlying the theory—that perception is a two-way street—has broad implications. The senses feed information such as pain sensations to the brain, which processes these sensory data into perceptions, as you have learned in this chapter.* But, as you have also learned, perceptions are not just shaped by sense data—they are affected by your knowledge, by your expectations, and by other factors such as your mood and motivational state. Visual illusions and the Gestalt principles of closure (filling in what isn't really there) provide some examples. This kind of *top-down control* also explains how the brain influences the experience of touch and pain (Kucyi & Davis, 2015; Wager & Atlas, 2013).

Body Position, Movement, and Balance

Shut your eyes and notice the position of your legs and feet, and arms and hands. Can you feel where they are in space? This is a sense that isn't often talked about—**proprioception** is *your sense of bodily position*. After all, you need some way to sense your position in physical space other than moving your eyes constantly to see the location of your limbs. Your perception of the position (and movement) of your torso, limbs, hands, and feet in space depends on stimulation of receptors in the muscles, tendons, and joints of your body, whereas information about which way is up and about head movement (to serve your balance) originates in the inner ear.

Sensory receptors provide the information we need to perceive the position and movement of our limbs, head, and body. These receptors also provide feedback about whether we are performing a desired movement correctly and how resistance from held objects may be influencing the movement. For example, when you swing a baseball bat, the weight of the bat affects how your muscles move your arm, as well as the sensation when the bat hits the ball. You can use muscle, joint, and tendon feedback about how your arms actually moved to improve performance through learning.

Maintaining balance depends primarily on the **vestibular system,** *the three fluid-filled semicircular canals and adjacent organs located next to the cochlea in each inner ear* (see Figure 4.21). The semicircular canals are arranged in three perpendicular orientations and studded with hair cells that detect movement of the fluid when the head moves or accelerates. The bending of the hairs of these cells generates activity in the vestibular nerve that is then conveyed to the brain. This detected motion enables us to maintain our balance (Lackner & DiZio, 2005).

Vision also helps us keep our balance. If you see that you are swaying relative to a vertical orientation, such as the walls of a room, you adjust your posture to keep from falling over. Psychologists have experimented with this visual aspect of balance by placing people in rooms where the floor is stationary but the walls

*Perceptual psychologists call control of perception by senses bottom-up control.

RICK RYCROFT/AP IMAGES

Hitting a ball with a bat or racquet provides feedback about where your arms and body are in space, as well as how the resistance of these objects affects your movement and balance. Successful athletes, such as Serena Williams, have particularly well-developed body senses.

proprioception Your sense of bodily position.

vestibular system The three fluid-filled semicircular canals and adjacent organs located next to the cochlea in each inner ear.

sway forwards and backwards (Bertenthal et al., 1977). If the room sways enough, people—particularly small children—will topple over as they try to compensate for what their visual system is telling them. When a mismatch between the information provided by visual cues and vestibular feedback occurs, motion sickness can result. Remember this the next time you try reading in the back seat of a moving car!

The Chemical Senses: Adding Flavour

Learning Outcomes

WHAT YOU NEED TO KNOW

- Describe how odourant molecules are converted into neural impulses.
- Explain the importance of smell in personal and social experiences.
- Describe how taste sensations are converted into neural impulses by the tongue.
- Explain what senses contribute to the perception of flavour.

Vision and hearing begin with physical energy in the world—light and sound waves—and touch is activated by physical energy in or on the body surface. The last set of senses we'll consider rely on chemicals that enter our mouths (the sense of taste, or gustation) or float into our noses (the sense of smell, or olfaction). Some have called smell "taste at a distance," and taste and smell have a common, ancient evolutionary basis that allowed our distant ancestors, the earliest cells, to sense beneficial and dangerous chemicals in the seawater around them. Smell and taste combine to produce the perceptual experience we call *flavour*.

Sense of Smell

Olfaction is the least understood sense, and one of the most fascinating. Recall from the Neuroscience and Behaviour chapter that whereas the other senses connect first to the thalamus, olfactory information enters the frontal lobe, amygdala, hippocampus, and other forebrain structures almost directly. This anatomy indicates that smell has a close relationship with areas involved in emotional and social behaviour, as well as memory. Smell can signal whether a creature is unfriendly or friendly (or is a potential mate); it can tell us whether a substance is probably delicious or is more likely to be toxic and dangerous; and it has an uncanny ability to remind us of long-ago places and people. Helen Keller (1880–1968), a blind and deaf writer, said: "Smell is a potent wizard that transports you across thousands of miles and all the years you have lived. The odors of fruits waft me to my southern home, to my childhood frolics in the peach orchard. Other odors, instantaneous and fleeting, cause my heart to dilate joyously or contract with remembered grief" (Keller, 1908, p. 75).

Countless substances release odours into the air. Just as natural lights and sounds are mixtures of wavelengths and frequencies, most natural odours (such as baking bread, coffee, and farts) are actually mixtures of different *odourant molecules*. Odourants are chemicals such as hydrogen sulfide (which on its own smells like rotten eggs), benzaldehyde (which smells like almonds), and vanillin (which gives vanilla its distinctive smell). Odourant molecules make their way into our noses, drifting in on the air we breathe. Situated along the top of the nasal cavity, shown in **FIGURE 4.26**, is a mucous membrane called the *olfactory epithelium*, which contains about 10 million **olfactory receptor neurons (ORNs),** *receptor cells that transduce odourant molecules into neural impulses* (Dalton, 2003). Each ORN has receptors that bind to some odourants but not to others, as if the receptor is a lock and the odourant is the key (see Figure 4.26). Groups of ORNs sensitive to the same odourant send their axons from the olfactory epithelium into the **olfactory bulb,** *a brain structure located above the nasal cavity beneath the frontal lobes.* Humans possess about 350 different ORN types that permit us to discriminate up to one trillion (!) odours through the unique patterns of neural activity each odour evokes (Bushdid et al., 2014). This setup is similar to our ability to see a vast range of colours through only a small number of retinal receptor cell types or to feel a range of skin sensations through only a handful of touch-receptor cell types.

olfactory receptor neurons (ORNs) Receptor cells that transduce odourant molecules into neural impulses.

olfactory bulb A brain structure located above the nasal cavity beneath the frontal lobes.

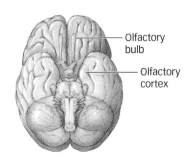

Figure 4.26

Anatomy of Smell Along the roof of the nasal cavity, odourant molecules dissolve in the mucous membrane that forms the olfactory epithelium. Odourants may then bind to olfactory receptor neurons (ORNs) embedded in the epithelium. Different ORNs have receptors for different odourant molecules. Once activated, ORNs relay action potentials to the olfactory bulb, located just beneath the frontal lobes. The output from the olfactory bulb is to axons that form the olfactory nerve, which projects directly into the brain.

Dogs and mice have up to 900 different ORN types, and up to 100 times as many ORNs; they have a correspondingly sharpened *olfactory sensitivity* (ability to detect odours) and *olfactory acuity* (ability to discriminate among odours). Nevertheless, humans are sensitive to the smells of some substances in extremely small concentrations. For example, we can sense mercaptan, a chemical compound that is added to natural gas to help detect gas leaks, at a concentration of just 0.0003 part per million. By contrast, acetone (nail polish remover), something most people regard as pungent, can be detected only if its concentration is 15 parts per million or greater.

Perceiving Smell

Just as the output of the final stage of retinal processing is retinal ganglion cell axons that form the optic nerve, the output of the final stage of olfactory bulb processing is in the axons that form the olfactory nerve. The olfactory bulb sends outputs to various centres in the brain, including the parts that are responsible for controlling basic drives, emotions, and memories. The relationship between smell and emotion explains why smells can have immediate, strongly positive or negative effects on us. Fortunately, sensory adaptation is at work when it comes to smell, just as it is with the other senses. Whether the associations are good or bad, after just a few minutes the smell fades. Smell adaptation makes sense: It allows us to detect new odours that may require us to act, but after that initial evaluation has occurred, it may be best to reduce our sensitivity to allow us to detect other smells.

Our experience of smell is determined not only by bottom-up influences, such as odourant molecules binding to sites on ORNs, but also by top-down influences, such as our previous experiences with an odour (Gottfried, 2008; Rolls, 2015). Consistent with this idea, people rate the identical odour as more pleasant when it is paired with an appealing verbal label such as *cheddar cheese* rather than an unappealing one such as *body odour* (de Araujo et al., 2005; Herz & von Clef, 2001).

Smell may also play a role in social behaviour. Other animals can detect odours from **pheromones,** *biochemical odourants emitted by other members of an animal's species that can affect its behaviour or physiology.* Pheromones play an important role in reproductive and social behaviour in insects and in several mammalian species, including mice, dogs, and primates (Brennan & Zufall, 2006). What about humans?

Since humans are mammals, it is possible—perhaps even probable—that we, like other mammals, both secrete and sense pheromones. However, evidence for human pheromones from well-conducted and replicable experiments is scant (Wyatt, 2015). Studies have tended to use small sample sizes (which raises the risk of a result that isn't true) and they have not been successfully replicated. In order to prove the existence of human pheromones, we would first want to observe a behavioural or physiological response that could be attributed to an airborne chemical, then identify and synthesize the active molecule, and ultimately confirm that humans have a specialized cell receptor and transduction mechanism for that chemical (Wyatt, 2015). Tristan Wyatt, a zoologist at Oxford points out, "We become smellier in puberty, apart from other changes in sexual development (the growth of more visible secondary sexual characteristics such as hair in our armpits and groins, for example). The changes in the smells we give off before and after puberty might give us clues as to what molecules might be signals" (Wyatt, 2015).

Some evidence for a human pheromone comes from breastfeeding mothers and babies. Nursing in mammals is known to depend on smell (Schaal & Al Aïn, 2014). Human mothers produce a substance from the glands around their nipples. If this secretion, taken from a lactating mother, is put under the nose of a 3-day-old newborn (not their own child), the baby responds with head and mouth movements consistent with nursing behaviour (Doucet et al., 2009). This suggests that one of the compounds in the secreted substance might be a pheromone that encourages nursing behaviour in babies; indeed, the degree to which first-time mothers secrete this substance seems to correlate with the rate of weight gain in the babies in the first days after birth (Doucet et al., 2012).

Sense of Taste

The sense of taste evolved from the sense of smell. Whereas smell analyzes the chemical composition of things outside the body, taste does the same for things taken into the body. One of the primary responsibilities of the chemical sense of taste is identifying things that are bad for you—as in poisonous and lethal. Some aspects of taste perception are genetic, such as an aversion to extreme bitterness (which may indicate poison), and some are learned, such as an aversion to a particular food that once caused nausea. In either case, the direct contact between the tongue and possible foods allows us to anticipate whether something will be harmful or nutritious.

The taste system contains just five main types of taste receptors, corresponding to five primary taste sensations: salt, sour, bitter, sweet, and *umami* (savoury). The first four are probably familiar to you, but *umami* may not be. The umami receptor was discovered by Japanese scientists who attributed its stimulation to the rich savoury tastes evoked by foods containing a high concentration of protein, such as miso, meats, and cheeses like blue cheese or old cheddar (Yamaguchi, 1998).

The tongue is covered with thousands of small bumps, called *papillae,* which are easily visible to the naked eye. Within most of the papilla are hundreds of **taste buds,** *the organs of taste transduction* (see **FIGURE 4.27**). The mouth contains 5,000 to 10,000 taste buds fairly evenly distributed over the tongue, the roof of the mouth, and the upper throat (Bartoshuk & Beauchamp, 1994; Halpern, 2002). Each taste bud contains 50 to 100 taste receptor cells, and receptors for the different tastes are also pretty evenly distributed—any taste can be detected by any part of the tongue. Taste perception

pheromones Biochemical odourants emitted by other members of an animal's species that can affect its behaviour or physiology.

taste buds The organs of taste transduction.

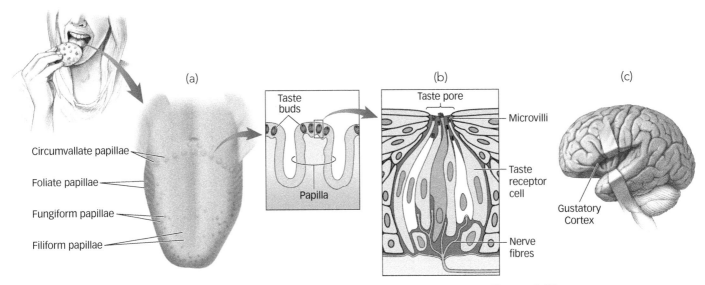

(a)

Circumvallate papillae

Foliate papillae

Fungiform papillae

Filiform papillae

(b)

Taste buds

Taste pore

Papilla

Microvilli

Taste receptor cell

Nerve fibres

(c)

Gustatory Cortex

Figure 4.27

A Taste Bud (a) Taste buds stud the bumps (papillae) on the tongue, shown here, as well as the back, sides, and roof of the mouth. (b) Each taste bud contains a range of receptor cells that respond to varying chemical components of foods called tastants. (c) Tastant molecules dissolve in saliva and stimulate the microvilli that form the tips of the taste receptor cells. Each taste bud connects to a cranial nerve that carries taste information to the brainstem, then to the thalamus, and then to the primary gustatory cortex in the brain's frontal lobe.

fades with age (Methven et al., 2012; Barragán et al., 2018). This may help explain why young children seem to be "fussy eaters," since they may have greater sensitivity to taste sensations.

Each taste bud contains several types of taste receptor cells whose tips, called *microvilli,* react with *tastant molecules* in food. Just as odours are typically composed of a mixture of odourants, foods usually contain a mixture of tastants. Salt receptors are most strongly activated by sodium chloride (table salt). Sour receptors respond to acids, such as vinegar or lime juice. Bitter, sweet, and umami receptors also respond to tastants that give rise to these tastes in food.

Research suggests that there may be a sixth basic taste, fat, that is elicited by fatty acids and is distinct from the five primary taste sensations (Running et al., 2015). The researchers noted that the sensation people experience in response to fatty acids is not necessarily consistent with expectations of "fattiness," so they proposed a new word for this taste sensation, *oleogustus.* (*Oleosus* is Latin for "fatty" or "oily," and *gustus* signifies "taste.")

Taste experiences vary widely across individuals. About 50% of people report a mildly bitter taste in caffeine, saccharine, certain green vegetables, and other substances, whereas roughly 25% report no bitter taste. Members of the first group are called *tasters;* members of the second group are called *nontasters.* The remaining 25% of people are *supertasters,* who report that such substances, especially dark green vegetables, are extremely bitter, to the point of being inedible (Bartoshuk, 2000). Because supertasters tend to avoid fruits and vegetables that contain tastes they experience as extremely bitter, they may be at increased health risk for diseases such as colon cancer. On the other hand, because they also tend to avoid fatty, creamy foods, they tend to be thinner and may have decreased risk of cardiovascular disease (Bartoshuk, 2000). There is evidence that genetic factors contribute to individual differences in taste perception (Kim et al., 2003), but much remains to be learned about the specific genes that are involved (Hayes et al., 2008; Reed, 2008).

People also vary dramatically in their tolerance of food textures and spicy food. Some people hate the texture of eggplant ("slimy!") or of bubble tea ("frogspawn!). Some people really love hot spicy food; others do not. In addition to the five (or six) tastes to which receptors in the mouth are sensitive, information about the temperature, spiciness, and texture (mouthfeel) of food is transduced and relayed from the mouth via touch receptors and thermoreceptors such as those discussed earlier.

Fussy eater? Or just too sensitive? Our taste perception declines with age. That can make childhood a time of either savoury delight or sensory overload of taste.

LESLIE BANKS/ISTOCKPHOTO

"We would like to be genetically modified to taste like Brussels sprouts."

Perceiving Flavour

Of course, the variety of taste experiences greatly exceeds the five basic taste receptors discussed here. Any food molecules dissolved in saliva evoke specific, combined patterns of activity in the five taste receptor types. Furthermore, taste isn't quite the same thing as flavour. Taste is the contribution made by receptors in your mouth alone. Taste and smell collaborate to produce the complex perception of flavour. Have you ever eaten a meal while suffering through a severe head cold that blocks your sense of smell? In that case, food tastes bland, right? The loss of smell and taste is a jarring and upsetting experience, as many people have learned for themselves during the COVID-19 pandemic (see Other Voices: A World without Smell and Taste).

Food perception is multisensory, involving taste, smell, and texture. Do these different sensory channels combine in one area of the brain to produce the perception of flavour? Or are they each processed separately, such that perception of flavour depends on binding information across systems, rather like visual perception depends on binding information from dorsal and ventral streams? Neuroimaging, particularly fMRI, has been very helpful in letting us get "inside the heads" (literally!) of people while they're eating, to begin to answer this question. This work indicates that areas sensitive to odours from food include not only primary olfactory cortex (near the amygdala) but also primary gustatory (taste) cortex (in the frontal lobe) and the mouth region of primary somatosensory cortex (in the parietal lobe) (Cerf-Ducastel & Murphy, 2001; Small et al., 2005). Indeed, primary olfactory and gustatory cortex are interconnected, and gustatory cortex passes "taste" information directly to olfactory cortex.

Multisensory effects on the perception of flavour also include visual and auditory influences. Many studies have shown that the colour of food and drinks can alter ratings of how they taste (Spence, 2015), and similar effects have been observed even for packaging and labels (Spence, 2018). For example, in a study on beer tasting Barnett and Spence (2016) reported that participants gave higher ratings of citrus and fruity tastes to a beer that was poured from a bottle with a yellow-green label designed to highlight the citrus notes in the beer, versus the same beer poured from a bottle with a brown label or no label. You've probably eaten many times in loud environments, such as noisy restaurants or an airline cabin at 30,000 feet. In a study that was designed to simulate the kind of loud background noise that you typically experience in an airplane cabin, Yan and Dando (2015) found that participants who rated a variety of taste solutions gave lower sweet intensity ratings and higher umami taste intensity ratings in the noisy condition as compared to a control condition. More recent research using similar levels of loud noise has shown that it affects how people experience drinking a cup of coffee: Participants reported that coffee tasted less bitter and had less aroma in noisy than in quiet conditions (Bravo-Mancayo et al., 2020).

One last point about flavour: It is a very easy thing to learn about! In the Learning chapter, we discuss how a strong, lifelong aversion to a food (e.g., hummus) can develop after only one nasty experience with a tainted bowl of it. This makes sense — if something is bad for you once, it probably will be again, and you learn quickly to stay well away. Learned preferences in food are also important in determining flavour, and they depend dramatically on culture and experience. "It's an acquired taste" is something you may have heard about a food you find disgusting: Acquired tastes include toasted grasshoppers in Mexico (chapulines); fermented fish in Scandinavia (lutefisk, hakarl, surströmming); fetal ducks still in the shell in Vietnam and Philippines (balut) — even cheese in many parts of the world. One person's "yecch!" is another person's "yummy!"

The full experience of a wine's flavour cannot be appreciated without a finely trained sense of smell. When you raise a glass to your mouth, odourants from the wine enter the nasal cavity via the nostrils, as well as through the back of the throat. Wine aficionados are taught to pull air in over wine held in the mouth; it allows the wine's odourant molecules to enter the nasal cavity through this "back door." The same happens with other foods.

Other Voices | **A World without Smell and Taste**

It's difficult to imagine what our lives would be like without the ability to smell or taste. Unfortunately, beginning with the onset of the COVID-19 pandemic in early 2020, many infected people reported a highly disturbing loss of these abilities (Marshall, 2021). In September 2020, the writer Krista Diamond vividly described her own struggle with losing smell and especially taste as a result of COVID-19, as well as some of the experiences of people in a Facebook group she joined comprised of more than 5,000 individuals who were going through something similar.

After I tested positive for COVID-19, I ordered panang curry. When the food arrived, I lifted the plastic lid, expecting the scent of makrut lime, lemongrass and ginger. But there was nothing. I plucked a forkful of tofu from the sauce. It was flavorless.

My abilities to smell and taste had suddenly evaporated. And in the month since I've been sick, they have yet to return.

Earlier in the pandemic, my husband and I developed a ritual of ordering comfort food every Friday. We live in Las Vegas — a city that has been hit hard by the virus — and found meals from beloved local restaurants to be small but crucial gifts in a glittering landscape that was losing its luster. In March, my husband was laid off from a casino, and I lost a majority of my clients as a freelance writer. In June, the Strip reopened to unmasked tourists drunk on margaritas and the falsehood of a world without disease. By August, we were sick.

Unable to get out of bed days later, I sent out a tweet bemoaning COVID-19. Someone replied, "Whatever you do, don't Google 'When will I get my smell and taste back.'" I did exactly that and was met with article after article about anosmia — smell blindness — many of which suggested its impact could be long-term.

My existing symptoms worsened while new ones appeared: body aches, paralyzing nausea, 12-hour headaches, difficulty breathing and exhaustion that lingered like a hangover. But despite the physical pain of the illness, losing my ability to taste hurt the most. For months before I got the virus, I was locked inside my house. I saw friends and family through my computer screen. I watched the lights of downtown Las Vegas flicker off from my bedroom window. I felt the heartbeat of my career flatline.

Throughout this sea change, my only sense of joy was the taste of food. The red velvet cake I ate on my birthday in lieu of a canceled California vacation. The balsamic roasted brussels sprouts I cooked after I lost another client. The spicy bourbon fried chicken from the sun-drenched cafe where I used to read on leisurely Sundays.

Las Vegas is a city centered around pleasure, and so much of that pleasure is taste — the bright citrus of champagne, the brine of fresh oysters, the impossible luxury of Kobe beef. And what is Las Vegas without pleasure? A desert.

The ability to taste was my connection to life before the coronavirus. And suddenly it was — and still is — gone.

My first week without taste and smell, I searched constantly for flashes of my lost senses. I sniffed candles, opened leftovers in my refrigerator, buried my face in my dog's fur in search of that puppy smell. Even spoonfuls of hot sauce, pinches of salt, amounted to nothing. I worried — if I ate spoiled food, would I know? If there was a gas leak in my house, would it kill me?

Krista Diamond is a freelance writer whose essays, features, and short fiction have been published widely.

In desperation I turned to a Facebook group for people with COVID-19 experiencing smell and taste loss. It had more than 5,000 members.

"Today marks exactly 5 months since losing my taste/smell completely," someone reported.

"There is hope," another said, sharing that she had regained the ability to smell.

Some expressed sadness over seeing friends enjoying meals. Others floated conspiracies — had masks caused this? Many discussed smell training, a method requiring anosmia sufferers to sniff scents like eucalyptus, lemon and rose every day in hopes of turning the memory of them into reality.

Occasionally, someone would celebrate the return of taste and smell only to lose the sensations again or find that they had changed. Suddenly sugar was unbearably sweet, wine intolerably bitter. Phantom scents filled their nostrils — cleaning chemicals, gas.

I read the group's Facebook posts for hours, commiserating with strangers around the world who shared this one strange loss. In a way it felt frivolous. After all, many of us have already recovered and will avoid panicked emergency rooms. We will continue to live our lives — even if they are lives where chocolate tastes like chalk and whiskey tastes like water.

But what is life without taste, without smell? If I never regain these abilities, will the question "What do you want for dinner" mean anything? Will a nice restaurant still have value? How will it feel when someone cooks for me, watches me take the first bite and waits for my reaction? What is the point of perfume, of piney mountain air?

In a way, anosmia is the perfect metaphor for the world during COVID 19: devoid of pleasures we didn't realize we might not always have.

But still I try. I lift my husband's shirt to my nose and breathe in. I cook meals — seared ahi tuna, pasta carbonara, strawberry pastries — and eat them, closing my eyes and trying to remember what they taste like.

Each day I hope for the familiar aromas and flavors to come back. I wait like the rest of us, for the things I love to return.

Scientists are still trying to determine precisely how and why COVID-19 produces the kinds of taste and smell losses described so well by Krista Diamond (Santos et al., 2021). Her loss of taste and smell persisted for a month after she was no longer sick, and a member of the Facebook group she joined had not recovered these abilities after 5 months. By summer 2021, about a year after Krista contracted COVID-19, she had fully recovered her ability to smell (although she occasionally smells odours that aren't actually there, such as stale cigarette smoke) and mostly recovered her sense of taste (Krista Diamond, personal communication, August 3, 2021). Fortunately, research shows that most COVID-19 patients recover taste and smell within a month (Reiter et al., 2020). Nonetheless, as the pandemic dragged on and the dangerous Delta variant spread during summer 2021, concern about possible loss of taste and smell grew: Internet searches for "loss of taste" and "loss of smell" showed a sharp increase during July 2021 (Sherman, 2021). Preliminary reports suggest that loss of taste and smell is quite infrequent after infection by the Delta variant (Bonfiglio, 2021), so hopefully few patients who are infected by Delta will have to experience the disruptive losses of taste and smell that afflicted Krista Diamond and too many other people.

Chapter Review

Sensation and Perception Are Distinct Activities

- Sensation and perception are critical to survival. Sensation is the simple stimulation of a sense organ, whereas perception organizes, identifies, and interprets sensation at the level of the brain.

- All of our senses depend on the process of transduction, which converts physical signals from the environment into neural signals carried by sensory neurons into the central nervous system.

- In the 19th century, researchers developed psychophysics, an approach to studying perception that measures the strength of a stimulus and an observer's sensitivity to that stimulus. Psychophysicists have developed procedures for measuring an observer's absolute threshold, which is the smallest intensity needed to just barely detect a stimulus, as well as the just noticeable difference (JND), which is the smallest change in a stimulus that can just barely be detected.

- Signal detection theory allows researchers to distinguish between an observer's perceptual sensitivity to a stimulus and criteria for making decisions about that stimulus.

- Sensory adaptation occurs when sensitivity to unchanging stimulation declines over time.

Visual Pathways: Connections Between the Eye and the Brain

- Light travels in waves that pass through several layers in the eye to reach the retina. In a process called accommodation, the eye muscles change the shape of the lens to focus objects at different distances on the retina.

- Two types of photoreceptor cells in the retina transduce light into neural impulses: Cones operate under normal daylight conditions and sense colour; rods are active under low-light conditions for night vision. The neural impulses travel along the optic nerve to the brain.

- The retina consists of several layers; the innermost consists of retinal ganglion cells (RGCs) that collect and send signals to the brain. Bundles of RGC axons form the optic nerve.

- Information encoded by the retina travels to the brain along the optic nerve, which connects to the lateral geniculate nucleus in the thalamus and then to the primary visual cortex (area V1) in the occipital lobe.

- Light striking the retina causes a specific pattern of response in each of three cone types that are critical to colour perception: short-wavelength (bluish) light, medium-wavelength (greenish) light, and long-wavelength (reddish) light. The overall pattern of response across the three cone types results in a unique code for each colour.

- The shapes of objects are perceived when different neurons in the visual cortex fire in response to different orientations of the object's edges.

- Two functionally distinct pathways project from the occipital lobe to visual areas in other parts of the brain. The ventral stream travels into the lower levels of the temporal lobes and includes brain areas that represent an object's shape and identity. The dorsal stream goes from the occipital lobes to the parietal lobes, connecting with brain areas that identify the location and motion of an object.

Visual Perception: Recognizing What We See

- Illusory conjunctions occur when features from separate objects are mistakenly combined. According to feature-integration theory, attention provides the glue necessary to bind features together. The parietal lobe is important for attention and contributes to feature binding.

- Some regions in the occipital and temporal lobes respond selectively to specific object categories, supporting the modular view that specialized brain areas detect particular classes of objects, such as faces or houses or body parts.

- The principle of perceptual constancy holds that even as sensory signals change, perception remains consistent.

- Gestalt principles of perceptual grouping, such as simplicity, closure, and continuity, govern how features are perceptually organized into meaningful objects.

- Depth perception depends on monocular cues, such as familiar size and linear perspective; binocular cues, such as retinal disparity; and motion-based cues, which are based on the movement of the head over time.

- We experience a sense of motion through the differences in the strengths of output from neurons sensitive to motion in different directions. These processes can give rise to illusions such as apparent motion.

- Change blindness and inattentional blindness occur when we fail to notice visible and even salient features of our environment, emphasizing that our conscious visual experience depends on focused attention.

Hearing: More Than Meets the Ear

- Perceiving sound depends on three physical dimensions of a sound wave: The frequency of the sound wave determines the pitch; the amplitude determines the loudness; and differences in the complexity, or mix, of frequencies determine the sound quality, or timbre.

- Auditory pitch perception begins in the ear, which consists of an outer ear that funnels sound waves towards the middle ear, which in turn sends the vibrations to the inner ear, which contains the cochlea. Action potentials from the inner ear travel along an auditory pathway through the thalamus to the primary auditory cortex (area A1) in the temporal lobe.

- Auditory perception depends on both a place code and a temporal code. Our ability to localize sound sources depends critically on the placement of our ears on opposite sides of the head.

- Some hearing loss can be overcome with hearing aids that amplify sound. When hair cells are damaged, a cochlear implant is a possible solution.

The Body Senses: More Than Skin Deep

- Sensory receptors on the body send neural signals to locations in the somatosensory cortex, a part of the parietal lobe, which the brain translates as the sensation of touch. Different locations on the body project sensory signals to different locations in the cortex, and some areas are better at discriminating details.

- The experience of pain depends on signals that travel along two distinct pathways. One pathway sends signals to the somatosensory cortex to indicate the location and type of pain, and another sends signals to the emotional centres of the brain that result in unpleasant feelings that we wish to escape. The experience of pain varies across individuals, which is explained by bottom-up and top-down aspects of the gate-control theory of pain.

- Balance and acceleration depend primarily on the vestibular system but are also influenced by vision.

The Chemical Senses: Adding Flavour

- Our experience of smell, or olfaction, is associated with odourant molecules that bind to sites on specialized olfactory receptors, which converge within the olfactory bulb. The olfactory bulb in turn sends signals to parts of the brain that control drives, emotions, and memories, which helps to explain why smells can have immediate and powerful effects on us.

- Smell is also involved in social behaviour, as illustrated by pheromones, which are related to reproductive behaviour and sexual responses in several species.

- Sensations of taste depend on taste buds, which are distributed across the tongue, the roof of the mouth, and the upper throat, as well as on taste receptors which correspond to the five primary taste sensations of salt, sour, bitter, sweet, and umami.

- Taste experiences vary widely across individuals and, like olfactory experiences, depend in part on cognitive influences.

Changing Minds

1. A friend of yours is taking a class in medical ethics. "We discussed a tough case today," your friend says. "It has to do with a patient who's been in a vegetative state for several years, and the family has to decide whether to take him off life support. The doctors say he has no awareness of himself or his environment, and he is never expected to recover. But when light is shone in his eyes, his pupils contract. That shows he can sense light, so he has to have some ability to perceive his surroundings, doesn't he?" Without knowing any of the details of this particular case, how would you explain to your friend that a patient might be able to sense light but not perceive it? What other examples from the chapter could you use to illustrate the difference between sensation and perception?

2. In your philosophy class, the professor discusses the proposition that "perception is reality." From the point of view of philosophy, reality is the state of things as they actually exist, whereas perception is how they appear to the observer. What does psychophysics have to say about this issue? What are three ways in which sensory transduction can alter perception, causing perceptions that may differ from absolute reality?

3. A friend comes across the story of an American soldier, Sergeant Leroy Petry, who received the Medal of Honor for saving the lives of two of his men. The soldiers were in a firefight in Afghanistan when a live grenade landed at their feet; Petry picked up the grenade and tried to toss it away from the others, but it exploded, destroying his right hand. According to the news report, Petry didn't initially feel any pain; instead, he set about applying a tourniquet to his own arm while continuing to shout orders to his men as the firefight continued. "That's amazingly heroic," your friend says, "but that bit about not feeling the pain—that's crazy. He must just be so tough that he kept going despite the pain." What would you tell your friend? How can the perception of pain be altered?

4. **Visualizing Data** You wonder why you like spicy food so much, but your cousin can't tolerate the slightest bit of spice in their food. Review the DATA to try to explain these varied taste perceptions.

Key Terms

sensation (p. 113)

perception (p. 113)

transduction (p. 113)

sensory adaptation (p. 114)

psychophysics (p. 115)

absolute threshold (p. 115)

sensitivity (p. 116)

acuity (p. 116)

just noticeable difference (JND) (p. 116)

Weber's law (p. 116)

signal detection theory (p. 116)

retina (p. 119)

accommodation (p. 119)

cones (p. 119)

rods (p. 119)

fovea (p. 120)

blind spot (p. 122)

area V1 (p. 122)

colour-opponent system (p. 124)

visual receptive field (p. 124)

visual form agnosia (p. 125)

binding problem (p. 126)

parallel processing (p. 126)

illusory conjunction (p. 127)

feature-integration theory (p. 127)

attention (p. 127)

perceptual constancy (p. 128)

perceptual organization (p. 129)

monocular depth cues (p. 131)

binocular disparity (p. 132)

apparent motion (p. 134)

biological motion perception (p. 134)

spatial acuity (p. 135)

temporal acuity (p. 135)

multisensory (p. 135)

ventriloquist illusion (p. 135)

change blindness (p. 135)

synesthesia (p. 136)

inattentional blindness (p. 137)

sound waves (p. 137)

pitch (p. 137)

loudness (p. 138)

timbre (p. 138)

cochlea (p. 139)

basilar membrane (p. 139)

travelling wave (p. 139)

inner hair cells (p. 139)

area A1 (p. 140)

place code (p. 141)

temporal code (p. 141)

haptic perception (p. 144)

tactile receptive field (p. 144)

referred pain (p. 146)

gate-control theory (p. 146)

proprioception (p. 147)

vestibular system (p. 147)

olfactory receptor neurons (ORNs) (p. 148)

olfactory bulb (p. 148)

pheromones (p. 150)

taste buds (p. 150)

Consciousness

UNCONSCIOUSNESS IS SOMETHING YOU DON'T REALLY appreciate until you need it. Belle Riskin needed it one day on an operating table, when she awoke just as doctors were pushing a breathing tube down her throat. She felt she was choking, but she couldn't see, breathe, scream, or move. Unable even to blink an eye, she couldn't signal to the surgeons that she was conscious. "I was terrified. Why is this happening to me? Why can't I feel my arms? I could feel my heart pounding in my head. It was like being buried alive, but with somebody shoving something down your throat," she explained later. "I knew I was conscious, that something was going on during the surgery. I had just enough awareness to know I was being intubated" (Groves, 2004).

How could this happen? Anaesthesia for surgery is supposed to leave the patient unconscious, "feeling no pain," yet in this case—and in about 1 in every 20,000 surgical procedures (Pandit et al., 2014)—the patient regains consciousness at some point and even remembers the experience. Some patients remember pain; others remember the clink of surgical instruments in a pan or the conversations of doctors and nurses. This is not how modern surgery is supposed to go, but the problem arises because muscle-relaxing drugs are used to keep the patient from moving involuntarily and making unhelpful contributions to the operation. Yet when the drugs that are given to induce unconsciousness fail to do their job, the patient with extremely relaxed muscles is unable to show or tell doctors that there is a problem.

Waking up in the middle of surgery sounds pretty rough all by itself, but it can cause additional complications. The conscious patient could become alarmed and emotional during the operation, spiking blood pressure and heart rate to dangerous levels. Awareness also might lead to later emotional problems. Fortunately, there are new methods of monitoring wakefulness by measuring the electrical activity of the brain. One system uses sensors attached to the patient's head and gives readings on a scale from 0 (no electrical activity in the brain) to 100 (fully alert), providing a kind of "consciousness metre."

Anaesthesiologists using this index deliver anaesthetics to keep the patient in the recommended range of 40 to 60 for general anaesthesia during surgery. They have found that this system reduces postsurgical reports of consciousness and memory of the surgical experience (Myles et al., 2004), and

- **The Mysteries of Consciousness**

- **The Nature of Consciousness**

- **The Unconscious Mind**

- **Sleep and Dreaming: Good Night, Mind**

- **Drugs and Consciousness: Artificial Inspiration**

- **Hypnosis: Open to Suggestion**

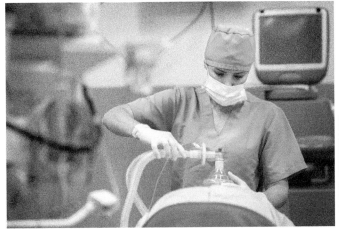

When it's time for surgery, it's great to be unconscious.

ANDRESR/E+/GETTY IMAGES

157

that letting patients fall below 45 on this index for prolonged periods increases the risk of negative postoperative outcomes, including death (Kertai et al., 2010). One of these devices in the operating room might have helped Belle Riskin settle into the unconsciousness she so sorely needed.

MOST OF THE TIME, OF COURSE, CONSCIOUSNESS IS SOMETHING we cherish. How else could we experience a favourite work of art, the familiar lyrics of our favourite song, the taste of chocolate, or the touch of a loved one's hand? **Consciousness** is a *person's subjective experience of the world and the mind.* Although you might think of consciousness as simply "being awake," the defining feature of consciousness is experience, which you have when you're awake or when you're having a vivid dream. Conscious experience is essential to what it means to be human. The anaesthesiologist's dilemma in trying to monitor Belle Riskin's consciousness is a stark reminder, though, that it is impossible for one person to experience another's consciousness.

How can this private world be studied? We'll begin by examining consciousness directly, trying to understand what it is like and how it compares with the mind's *unconscious* processes. Then we'll examine how it departs from normal by exploring altered states: sleep and dreams, intoxication with alcohol and other drugs, hypnosis, and disorders of consciousness resulting from brain damage. Like the traveller who learns the meaning of *home* by roaming far away, we can learn the meaning of *consciousness* by exploring its exotic variations.

The Mysteries of Consciousness

Learning Outcomes

WHAT YOU NEED TO KNOW

- Explain the two dimensions of mind perception.
- Outline the relationship between brain activity, thinking, and acting.

consciousness A person's subjective experience of the world and the mind.

phenomenology The study of how things seem to the conscious person.

What does it feel like to be you right now? It probably feels as though you are somewhere inside your head, looking out at the world through your eyes. You can notice the position of your body in your chair as you read or the sounds in the room when you orient yourself towards them. If you shut your eyes, you may be able to imagine things in your mind, even though all the while thoughts and feelings come and go, passing through your imagination. But where are "you," really? And how is it that this theatre of consciousness gives you a view of some things in your world and your mind but not others? The theatre in your mind doesn't have seating for more than one, making it difficult to share what's on your mental screen.

Other sciences, such as physics, chemistry, and biology, have the great luxury of studying *objects,* things that we all can see. Psychology studies objects, too, looking at people and their brains and behaviours, but it has the unique challenge of also trying to make sense of *subjects.* A physicist is not concerned with what it is like to be a neutron, but psychologists hope to understand what it is like to be a human—that is, they seek to understand the subjective perspectives of the people whom they study.

Psychologists hope to include an understanding of **phenomenology,** *the study of how things seem to the conscious person,* in their understanding of mind and behaviour. After all, consciousness is an extraordinary human property. But including phenomenology in psychology brings up mysteries pondered by great thinkers since the beginning of thinking. Let's look at two of the more vexing mysteries of consciousness: the problem of other minds and the mind–body problem.

The Problem of Other Minds

One great mystery in psychology is called the **problem of other minds,** *the fundamental difficulty we have in perceiving the consciousness of others.* How do you know that anyone else is conscious? They tell you that they are conscious, of course, and are often willing to describe in depth how they feel, how they think, what they are experiencing, and how good or how bad it all is. But perhaps they are just *saying* these things. There is no clear way to distinguish a conscious person from someone who might do and say all the same things as a conscious person but who is *not* conscious. Philosophers have called this hypothetical nonconscious person a *zombie,* in reference to the living-yet-dead creatures of horror films (Chalmers, 1996). A philosopher's zombie could talk about experiences ("The lights are so bright!") and even seem to react to them (wincing and turning away) but might not be having any inner experience at all. No one knows whether there could be such a zombie, but then again, because of the problem of other minds, none of us will ever know for sure that another person is *not* a zombie.

Even the consciousness metre used by anaesthesiologists falls short. It certainly doesn't give the anaesthesiologist any special insight into what it is like to be the patient on the operating table; it only predicts whether patients will *say* they were conscious. We simply lack the ability to directly perceive the consciousness of others. In short, *you* are the only thing in the universe that you will ever truly know what it is like to be.

The problem of other minds also means there is no way you can tell if another person's experience of anything is at all like yours. Although you know what the colour red looks like to you, for instance, you cannot know whether it looks the same to other people. Maybe they're seeing what you see as blue and just calling it red in a consistent way. Of course, most people have come to trust each other in describing their inner lives, reaching the general assumption that other human minds are pretty much like their own. But they don't know this for a fact, and they can't know it firsthand.

How do people perceive other minds? Researchers conducting a large online survey asked people to compare the minds of 13 different targets — such as a baby, chimp, or robot — on 18 different mental capacities, such as feeling pain, pleasure, hunger, and consciousness (see **FIGURE 5.1**) (Gray et al., 2007). Respondents who were judging the mental capacity to feel pain, for example, compared pairs of targets: Is a frog or a dog more able to feel pain? Is a baby

problem of other minds The fundamental difficulty we have in perceiving the consciousness of others.

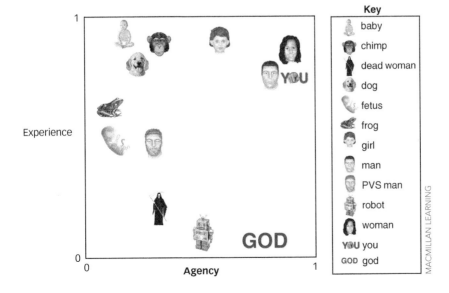

Figure 5.1

Dimensions of Mind Perception When participants judged the mental capacities of 13 targets, two dimensions of mind perception were discovered (Gray et al., 2007). Participants perceived minds as varying in the capacity for experience (such as abilities to feel pain or pleasure) and in the capacity for agency (such as abilities to plan or exert self-control). They perceived normal adult humans (male, female, or "you," the respondent) to have minds on both dimensions, whereas other targets were perceived to have reduced experience or agency. The man in a persistent vegetative state ("PVS man"), for example, was judged to have only some experience and very little agency.

MACMILLAN LEARNING

or a robot more able to feel pain? When the researchers examined all the comparisons on the different mental capacities with the computational technique of factor analysis (see the Intelligence chapter), they found two dimensions of mind perception. People judge minds according to the capacity for *experience* (such as the ability to feel pain, pleasure, hunger, consciousness, anger, or fear) and the capacity for *agency* (such as the ability for self-control, planning, memory, or thought).

As shown in Figure 5.1, respondents rated some targets as having little experience or agency (the dead woman), others as having experiences but little agency (the baby), and yet others as having both experience and agency (adult humans). Still others were perceived to have agency without experiences (the robot, God). The perception of minds, then, involves more than just whether something has a mind. People appreciate that minds both have experiences and lead us to perform actions.

Ultimately, the problem of other minds is a problem for psychological science. As you'll remember from the Methods chapter, the scientific method requires that any observation made by one scientist should, in principle, be available for observation by any other scientist. But if other minds aren't observable, how can consciousness be a topic of scientific study? One radical solution is to eliminate consciousness from psychology entirely and follow the other sciences into total objectivity by renouncing the study of *anything* mental. This was the solution offered by behaviourism, and it turned out to have its own shortcomings, as you saw in The Evolution of Psychological Science chapter. Despite the problem of other minds, modern psychology has embraced the study of consciousness. The astonishing richness of mental life simply cannot be ignored.

Pineal gland

Figure 5.2

Seat of the Soul Descartes imagined that the seat of the soul—and consciousness—might reside in the pineal gland located behind the third ventricle of the brain. This original drawing from Descartes (1662) shows the pineal gland (H) nicely situated for a soul, right in the middle of the brain.

mind–body problem The issue of how the mind is related to the brain and body.

The Mind–Body Problem

Another mystery of consciousness is the **mind–body problem,** *the issue of how the mind is related to the brain and body.* The French philosopher and mathematician René Descartes (1596–1650) is famous for proposing, among other things, that the human body is a machine made of physical matter but that the human mind or soul is a separate entity made of a "thinking substance." He suggested that the mind has its effects on the brain and body through the pineal gland, a small structure located near the centre of the brain (see **FIGURE 5.2**). It turns out that the pineal gland is not even a nerve structure but rather is an endocrine gland, and thus is poorly equipped to serve as a centre of human consciousness. We now know that, far from the tiny connection between mind and brain in the pineal gland that Descartes proposed, the mind and brain are connected everywhere to each other. In other words, "the mind is what the brain does" (Minsky, 1986, p. 287).

But Descartes was right in pointing out the difficulty of reconciling the physical body with the mind. Most psychologists assume that mental events are intimately tied to brain events, such that every thought, perception, or feeling is associated with a particular pattern of activation of neurons in the brain (see the Neuroscience and Behaviour chapter). Thinking about a particular person, for instance, occurs with a unique array of neural connections and activations. If the neurons repeat that pattern, then you must be thinking of the same person; conversely, if you think of the person, the brain activity occurs in that pattern.

One telling set of studies, however, suggests that the brain's activities *precede* the activities of the conscious mind. Researchers measured the electrical activity in the brains of volunteers by placing sensors on their scalps as they repeatedly decided when to move their hand (Libet, 1985). Participants were also asked to indicate exactly when they consciously chose to move by reporting the position of a dot moving rapidly around the face of a clock just at the point of the decision (**FIGURE 5.3a**).

Brain activity begins (EEG)	Conscious wish to act is experienced (clock reading)	Finger movement occurs (EMG)

Time ⟶ −535 msec −204 msec 0

(a) (b)

As a rule, the brain begins to show electrical activity about half a second before a voluntary action (535 milliseconds, to be exact) and about one-third of a second (331 milliseconds) before the person's conscious decision to move (as shown in Figure 5.3b). The feeling that you are consciously willing your actions, it seems, may be a result rather than a cause of your brain activity. Although your personal intuition is that you *think* of an action and *then* do it, these experiments suggest that your brain is getting started before *either* the thinking or the doing, paving the way for both thought and action (Haggard & Tsakiris, 2009; Wegner, 2002).

Consciousness has its mysteries, but psychologists like a challenge. Over the past several decades, psychologists have tried to solve this problem by working with computer scientists and others to attempt to create machines that can mimic human consciousness and intelligence. This work has led to the creation of the field of "artificial intelligence" (AI), which refers to the study and use of machines (including computers) that can independently operate in ways that mimic human intelligence and interactions. AI is used increasingly in our daily lives in ways that attempt to mimic the behaviour of human agents—such as through Apple's "Siri" and Amazon's "Alexa." Siri and Alexa already act more like humans than the zombies mentioned earlier (who mostly just grunt and moan), but are they really displaying human-like intelligence?

Back in 1950, Alan Turing famously proposed that to conclude that a machine can exhibit human-like intelligence, it must be able to act in ways that are indistinguishable from humans. His proposed method of demonstrating this, which has come to be called the "Turing test," is by having a person observe a conversation between a person and a computer, such as by reading out their responses to questions posed in that conversation. The machine/computer is said to have passed the test if the observer is unable to accurately determine which is the machine/computer and which is the human.

Over the past several decades, psychological scientists have continued to work towards the development of increasingly sophisticated AI methods to better understand, and mimic, various aspects of human consciousness, such as the abilities for learning, decision making, attention, memory, and planning for the future (Hassabis et al., 2017). To date, there is agreement that current robots and AI do not yet have human-like consciousness (Hildt, 2019). If and when they do, we will have to address a range of new ethical questions, such as: If a computer has consciousness, is it acceptable for us to shut it off (e.g., is this murder?). Although there is still much progress to be made, since researchers may not yet be able to know exactly how consciousness arises from the brain, this has not prevented them from also collecting people's reports of conscious experiences and learning how these reports reveal the nature of consciousness.

Figure 5.3

The Timing of Conscious Will (a) In Benjamin Libet's experiments, the participant was asked to move fingers at will while watching a dot move around the face of a clock to mark the moment at which the action was consciously willed. Meanwhile, EEG sensors timed the onset of brain activation, and EMG sensors timed the muscle movement. (b) The experiment showed that brain activity (EEG) precedes the willed movement of the finger (EMG) but that the reported time of consciously willing the finger to move follows the brain activity.

Do Alexa or Siri have human consciousness? How could you find out?

FRANK DUENZL/PICTURE-ALLIANCE/DPA/AP IMAGES

The Nature of Consciousness

Learning Outcomes

WHAT YOU NEED TO KNOW

- Describe the four basic properties of consciousness.
- Compare the three levels of consciousness.
- Explain why we can't always control our conscious thoughts.

How would you describe your own consciousness? Researchers examining people's descriptions suggest that consciousness has four basic properties (intentionality, unity, selectivity, and transience); that it occurs on three different levels; and that it includes a range of different contents. Let's examine each of these points in turn.

Four Basic Properties

Researchers have identified four basic properties of consciousness, based on people's reports of conscious experience.

1. Consciousness has *intentionality,* which is the quality of being directed towards an object. Consciousness is always *about* something. Despite all the lush detail you see in your mind's eye, the kaleidoscope of sights and sounds and feelings and thoughts, the object of your consciousness at any one moment is focused on just a small part of all of this. To describe how this works, psychologists refer to three other properties of consciousness: unity, selectivity, and transience.

2. Consciousness has *unity,* which is resistance to division, or the ability to integrate information from all of the body's senses into one coherent whole (see **FIGURE 5.4**). As you read this book, your five senses are taking in a great deal of information. Your eyes are scanning lots of black squiggles on a page (or screen) while also sensing an enormous array of shapes, colours, depths, and textures in your periphery; your hands are gripping a heavy book (or computer); your butt and feet may sense pressure from gravity pulling you against a chair or floor; and you may be listening to music or talking in another room while smelling the odour of freshly made popcorn (or your roommate's dirty laundry). Although your body is constantly sensing an enormous amount of information from the world around you, your brain—amazingly—integrates all of this information into the experience of one unified consciousness (or two, in the case of the split-brain patients described in the Neuroscience and Behaviour chapter).

3. Consciousness has *selectivity,* the capacity to include some objects but not others. You may recall from the Sensation and Perception chapter that while binding the many sensations around you into a coherent whole, your mind must make decisions about which pieces of information to include and

Figure 5.4

Bellotto's *Dresden* and Closeup (*left*) The people on the bridge in the distance look very finely detailed in *View of Dresden with the Frauenkirche* by Bernardo Bellotto (1721–1780). However, when you examine the detail closely (*right*), you discover that the people are made of brushstrokes merely suggesting people—an arm here, a torso there. Consciousness produces a similar impression of "filling in," as it seems to consist of extreme detail even in areas that are peripheral (Dennett, 1991).

which to exclude. This property is shown through studies of **dichotic listening,** *a task in which people wearing headphones hear different messages in each ear.* Research participants were instructed to repeat aloud the words they heard in one ear while a different message was presented to the other ear (Cherry, 1953). As a result of focusing on the words they were supposed to repeat, participants noticed little of the second message, often not even realizing that at some point it changed from English to German! So consciousness *filters out* some information. At the same time, participants did notice when the voice in the unattended ear changed from a man's to a woman's, suggesting that the selectivity of consciousness can also work to *tune in* other information.

How does consciousness decide what to tune in and what to filter out? The conscious system is most inclined to select information of special interest to the listener; for example, in what has come to be known as the **cocktail-party phenomenon,** *a phenomenon in which people tune in one message even while they filter out others nearby.* In the dichotic listening situation, for example, research participants are especially likely to notice if their own name is spoken into the unattended ear (Moray, 1959). Perhaps you, too, have noticed how abruptly your attention is diverted from whatever conversation you are having when someone else within earshot at a party mentions your name. Selectivity is not only a property of waking consciousness: The mind works this way in other states. People are more sensitive to their own name than to others' names, for instance, even during sleep (Oswald et al., 1960). This is why, when you are trying to wake someone, it is best to use the person's name.

4. Consciousness has *transience,* or the tendency to change. Consciousness wiggles and fidgets like a toddler in the seat behind you on an airplane. The mind wanders not just sometimes, but incessantly, from one "right now" to the next "right now" and then on to the next (Wegner, 1997). William James, whom you met way back in The Evolution of Psychological Science chapter, famously described consciousness as a "stream" (James, 1890). Prose written in the "stream of consciousness" style illustrates the whirling, chaotic, and constantly changing flow of consciousness. Perhaps because it resembles our own experience of consciousness, this style is widely used, appearing in classic books such as Virginia Woolf's *Mrs. Dalloway* (1925):

> *Quiet descended on her, calm, content, as her needle, drawing the silk smoothly to its gentle pause, collected the green folds together and attached them, very lightly, to the belt. So on a summer's day waves collect, overbalance, and fall; collect and fall; and the whole world seems to be saying "that is all" more and more ponderously, until even the heart in the body which lies in the sun on the beach says too, that is all. Fear no more, says the heart. Fear no more, says the heart, committing its burden to some sea, which sighs collectively for all sorrows, and renews, begins, collects, lets fall. And the body alone listens to the passing bee; the wave breaking; the dog barking, far away barking and barking. "Heavens, the front-door bell!" exclaimed Clarissa, staying her needle. Roused, she listened.*

Whether or not you have encountered books or stories using stream of consciousness writing, you almost certainly have encountered it in poetry and musical lyrics. For instance, think about the lyrics to your favourite song. Whether you currently are listening to Cardi B, The Weeknd, Ariana Grande, Post Malone, or someone else, chances are you will find a lot of songs using a stream of consciousness style. Our own stream of consciousness may flow in this way partly because of the limited capacity of the conscious mind. We humans can hold only so much information in mind at one time, after all, so when we select more information, some of what is currently there must disappear. As a result, our focus of attention keeps changing.

Participants in a dichotic listening experiment hear different messages played to the right and left ears and may be asked to "shadow" one of the messages by repeating it aloud.

The contents of our conscious thoughts are constantly changing, like water in a stream. This might be why we so enjoy the "stream of consciousness" presentation of words used in most popular songs. The artist Black Thought of the musical group The Roots provided a classic example of such a presentation in a 10-minute freestyle performance so impressive that it was recommended listening by the *New York Times.*

Levels of Consciousness

Consciousness can also be understood as having levels, ranging from minimal consciousness to full consciousness to self-consciousness. These levels of consciousness would probably all register as "conscious" on that wakefulness metre for surgery patients you read about at the beginning of this chapter. The levels of consciousness that psychologists distinguish among involve different qualities of awareness of the world and of the self.

In its minimal form, consciousness is just a connection between the person and the world. When you sense the sun coming in through the window, for example, you might turn towards the light. Such **minimal consciousness** is *a low-level kind of sensory awareness and responsiveness that occurs when the mind inputs sensations and may output behaviour* (Armstrong, 1980). This kind of sensory awareness and responsiveness could even happen when someone pokes you while you're asleep and you turn over. Something seems to register in your mind, at least in the sense that you experience it, but you may not think at all about having had the experience. It could be that animals can have this minimal level of consciousness. But because of the problem of other minds and the notorious reluctance of animals and plants to talk to us, we can't know for sure that they *experience* the things that make them respond. At least in the case of humans, we can safely assume that there is something it "feels like" to be them and that when they're awake, they are at least minimally conscious.

Human consciousness is often more than minimal, of course, but what exactly gets added? Consider the glorious feeling of waking up on a spring morning as rays of sun stream across your pillow. It's not just that you are having this experience: Being fully conscious means that you are also *aware* that you are having this experience. The critical ingredient that accompanies **full consciousness** is that you *know and are able to report your mental state*. That's a subtle distinction: Being fully conscious means that you are aware of having a mental state while you are experiencing the mental state itself. When you have a hurt leg and mindlessly rub it, for instance, your pain may be minimally conscious. After all, you seem to be experiencing pain because you have acted and are indeed rubbing your leg. It is only when you realize that it hurts, though, that you become fully conscious of the pain.

Have you ever been driving a car and suddenly realized that you don't remember the past 15 minutes of driving? Chances are that you were not unconscious, but instead minimally conscious. When you are completely aware and thinking about your driving, you have moved into the realm of full consciousness.

Full consciousness involves a certain consciousness of oneself; the person notices the self in a particular mental state. ("Here I am, reading this sentence.") However, this is not quite the same thing as *self*-consciousness. Sometimes consciousness is entirely flooded with the self. ("Not only am I reading this sentence, but I have a pimple on the end of my nose today that makes me feel like I'm guiding a sleigh.") Self-consciousness focuses on the self to the exclusion of almost everything else. William James (1890) and other theorists have suggested that **self-consciousness** is yet another *distinct level of consciousness in which the person's attention is drawn to the self as an object* (Morin, 2006). Most people report experiencing such self-consciousness when they are embarrassed; when they find themselves the focus of attention in a group; when someone focuses a camera on them; or when they are deeply introspective about their thoughts, feelings, or personal qualities.

Self-consciousness brings with it a tendency to evaluate yourself and notice your shortcomings. Looking in a mirror, for example, is all it takes to make people evaluate themselves — thinking not just about their looks, but also about whether they are good or bad in other ways. People go out of their way to avoid mirrors when they've done something they are ashamed of (Duval & Wicklund, 1972). Mirrors also can prevent people from doing something they are ashamed of in the first place. In a recent study, children had an opportunity to peek at a toy when the adult

PHOTOMONDO/PHOTODISC/
GETTY IMAGES

Full consciousness involves a consciousness of oneself, such as thinking about the act of driving while driving a car. How is this different from self-consciousness?

minimal consciousness A low-level kind of sensory awareness and responsiveness that occurs when the mind inputs sensations and may output behaviour.

full consciousness A level of consciousness in which you know and are able to report your mental state.

self-consciousness A distinct level of consciousness in which the person's attention is drawn to the self as an object.

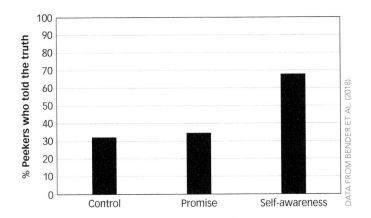

Figure 5.5
Mirrors Increase Honesty Children who peeked at a toy when an adult experimenter was out of the room were much more likely to tell the truth about doing so if they were first asked to look in a mirror to increase their self-awareness than were children who promised to tell the truth or who engaged in a control task.

Self-consciousness is a curse and a blessing. Looking in a mirror can make people evaluate themselves on deeper attributes such as honesty as well as superficial ones such as appearance.

experimenter left the room (Bender et al., 2018). Upon returning to the room, the experimenter either had the child look in a mirror, promise to tell the truth, or participate in a control task. The experimenter then asked the child if they peeked at the toy (which was confirmed via hidden camera). Children who looked in the mirror were significantly more likely to tell the truth than children in the other two conditions (see **FIGURE 5.5**).

Most animals can't follow this path to civilization. The typical dog or cat seems mystified by a mirror, ignoring it or acting as though there is some other critter back there. However, chimpanzees that have spent time with mirrors sometimes behave in ways that suggest they recognize themselves in a mirror. To examine this, researchers painted an odourless red dye over the eyebrow of an anaesthetized chimp and then watched when the awakened chimp was presented with a mirror (Gallup, 1977). If the chimp interpreted the mirror image as a representation of some other chimp with an unusual approach to cosmetics, we would expect it just to look at the mirror or perhaps to reach towards it. But the chimp reached towards its *own eye* as it looked into the mirror — not the mirror image — suggesting that it recognized the image as a reflection of itself.

Versions of this experiment have now been repeated with many different animals, and it turns out that, like humans, animals such as chimpanzees and orangutans (Gallup, 1997), possibly dolphins (Reiss & Marino, 2001), and maybe even elephants (Plotnik et al., 2006) and magpies (Prior et al., 2008) recognize their own mirror images. Dogs, cats, crows, and gorillas have been tested, too, but don't seem to know they are looking at themselves. However, there is current debate about whether the mirror test is an accurate method of inferring self-consciousness as it may be that some animals may lack familiarity with, and ability to use, a mirror to locate any objects. One study showed that after training monkeys in how to use a mirror to locate objects in space, they gained the ability to pass the mirror test (Chang et al., 2017). Psychologists are trying to develop new ways of more accurately measuring self-awareness that can be used across species.

Disorders of Consciousness

So far, we've been talking about normal levels of consciousness during wakefulness, in people with a normal brain. Severe brain damage, caused by illness or accident, can produce a transient or permanent change in the maximum level of consciousness that an individual is capable of. Improvements in medical intensive care over the last few decades means that more patients are surviving severe brain injury but, as a result, experience either a temporary or permanent *disorder of consciousness*, in which the patient is not able to demonstrate either full consciousness or self-consciousness. Doctors distinguish different *disorders of consciousness*, which can either be transient stages on the road to recovery, or more permanent conditions.

1. Patients in a *coma* look a bit like they are deeply asleep. Their eyes are closed, they do not communicate, and they do not respond when someone shouts their name, or pinches their toe (which would generally waken a sleeping person!). They seem to be completely unaware.

2. Patients in a *vegetative state* alternate between eyes-open and eyes-closed states: There are regular periods of time in which they appear to be "awake." Patients may move their limbs and eyes, swallow, smile, cry, grunt, moan, or scream, but — and this is key to the diagnosis — none of these behaviours is *produced reliably in response to external stimulation*. In other words, no evidence exists that patients are aware of themselves or their surroundings, as demonstrated by reliable, purposeful responding to sensory stimulation (such as being touched or hearing their name called).

3. Patients in a *minimally consciousness state* can respond reliably, but somewhat inconsistently, to sensory stimulation.

Locked-in syndrome is a rare condition in which patients have full awareness but cannot demonstrate it, because they cannot move any voluntary muscles. This is not a disorder of consciousness, but it can easily be mistaken for one. The French journalist Jean-Dominique Bauby wrote *The Diving Bell and the Butterfly* after he suffered a massive stroke that left him with locked-in syndrome. The book was written by Bauby blinking his left eyelid, which he did for 4 hours a day over 10 months. Patients with locked-in syndrome can, like Bauby, sometimes move their eyes voluntarily up and down, and can use this movement to communicate. Some locked-in patients do not have even this minimal control of voluntary muscles.

How do doctors determine whether a patient is aware? The problem is even more complex because disorders of consciousness can be transient, as a patient recovers from brain damage, or can be permanent. It can be very difficult to observe when a severely injured patient is recovering awareness. Traditionally, physicians observe a patient's behaviour and judge whether the patient is repeatedly able to respond to commands (like "raise your left arm"), or to the sound of their name being spoken. If the patient has trouble controlling their body, then this test can be misleading. Recently, brain-imaging methods have given researchers and physicians a direct window into brain activity (see The Real World: Anyone for Tennis?). Brain activity is, after all, the wellspring of behaviour — for the left arm to be raised, there first must be a specific pattern of arm-raising activity in the brain. We now know that, out of every 100 people diagnosed as being in a vegetative state using traditional bedside assessment, between 10 and 40 will turn out to be conscious to some degree when assessed using these more sensitive measures (Monti et al., 2010), and about a third of patients diagnosed as minimally conscious may be fully conscious (Cruse et al., 2012).

Conscious Contents

What's on your mind? For that matter, what's on everybody's mind? One way to learn what is on people's minds is to ask them, and much research has called on people simply to *think aloud* while in a psychological laboratory. A more modern approach is the use of *experience-sampling* or *ecological momentary assessment (EMA)* techniques, in which people are asked to report their conscious experiences at particular times. Equipped with survey apps loaded onto their smartphone, for example, participants often are asked to record their current thoughts when prompted (e.g., via a push notification) at random times throughout the day (Stone, 2018).

The Real World • Anyone for Tennis?

In 1999, Scott Routley was seriously injured in a car accident that resulted from him pulling out in front of a Sarnia, Ontario, police cruiser. For 12 years, he was considered by doctors to be in a vegetative state: showing periods of apparent eyes-open wakefulness, but without any signs of awareness of himself or his environment and without any apparent ability to communicate. Definitely not (it was thought) in any state to play tennis. This view of Scott changed dramatically when he underwent a series of fMRI scans at the University of Western Ontario.

For many years, Adrian Owen and his colleagues at the University of Western Ontario, working with researchers in Cambridge, UK, and in Liège, Belgium, have been evaluating whether, and how, fMRI can be used to detect signs of consciousness in brain-damaged patients. Traditional bedside measures of awareness rely on the patient being able to make observable movements, which some patients just cannot do, leading to conscious, aware patients being mistaken for vegetative ones. First, the researchers used fMRI to show that two mental imagery tasks reliably activate very different brain regions in healthy "control" individuals. The control group was asked to imagine moving their arms as though swinging a tennis racquet at a ball, which activated motor areas of the brain. Then, they were asked to imagine wandering from room to room in their house, and visualizing what they might see in each place, which activated visual and motor areas (Owen et al., 2006).

Next, the researchers demonstrated that some patients who had been diagnosed as vegetative were also able to reliably generate these distinct patterns. Out of 54 patients diagnosed as vegetative, 5 were able to reliably generate a tennis-playing pattern of activity when asked to imagine playing tennis, and a spatial-navigation pattern of activity when asked to imagine going from room to room in their house. This is voluntary command following—conceptually equivalent to correctly raising your left or right arm when asked to do so—and is a hallmark of agency, which was identified on page 174 as one of the characteristics of conscious awareness (Monti et al., 2010).

When the researchers used this fMRI method with Scott, he was able to reliably generate the tennis and spatial-navigation patterns of activity on command. This indicated, much to the surprise of his doctors, that Scott was not in a vegetative state after all. The researchers went a step further and used this method to ask Scott simple yes-or-no questions. They did this by instructing Scott to imagine playing tennis if he wished to respond *yes* to a question, and to imagine navigating around his house if he wished to respond *no*. The distinct patterns of brain activity for these two tasks could then be interpreted as meaning *yes* or *no*. The researchers started by asking Scott questions to which they knew the answers, such as whether his father's name was Jim (it was). He correctly answered many such questions, indicating that he was fully conscious. The researchers then did something they had never tried with a patient before: They asked Scott

Thirty-nine-year-old Scott Routley was considered to be in a vegetative state for 12 years following a car crash. However, in an experiment conducted by researchers at the University of Western Ontario using fMRI, he was asked to imagine swinging a tennis racquet at a ball. Brain-imaging results showed that the areas of his brain that were activated during this task were the same as those for the control group. This demonstrated that Scott is aware and can answer questions.

a question that only he could know the answer to, "Are you in pain?" Much to everyone's relief, the answering brain activity indicated *no*.

This image shows the distinct patterns of activity in a healthy control participant and in a brain-damaged patient, resulting from two different mental imagery tasks. The patient, previously diagnosed as being in a vegetative state, was able to follow commands to "imagine playing tennis" or "imagine moving around the rooms of your house," and generated the same patterns as the healthy controls. This ability to reliably engage in purposeful mental activity indicates awareness.

Experience-sampling studies show that consciousness is dominated by the immediate environment—what we see, feel, hear, taste, and smell. What do you experience while actually carrying out the events of your daily life? Researchers who use experience-sampling methods to record the emotions people experience during everyday activities have found interesting results. One study collected data from over 900 working women by asking them to reflect on the events of the past day and record how they felt while engaging in each activity (Kahneman et al., 2004).

Some of the results are as expected. For instance, as shown in **TABLE 5.1**, people score lowest on positive affect when commuting, working, and doing housework. Unfortunately, this is how we spend a large part of our day. The American women in this study reported having the most positive affect while being intimate with another person, although they only did this for 12 minutes of the day. Some less intuitive findings are related to the activities that fell in between the two. In survey studies, parents often report that they are happiest when spending time with their children; but when asked about actual events of the prior day using these daily experience-sampling methods, being with one's children ranked just two ticks above housework and well below other activities such as shopping, watching TV, and making more children.

Experience-sampling is increasingly being used to study what it is like to be human by focusing on a range of different aspects of conscious experiences. For instance, one study used experience-sampling to zoom in on one all too familiar aspect of daily life: boredom (Chin et al., 2017). The authors of this study used experience-sampling to follow 1.1 million people over a 10-day period to better understand, among other things, what situations are most associated with the experience of boredom. As shown in **FIGURE 5.6** and sadly for you, people

TABLE 5.1

HOW WAS YOUR DAY? WOMEN'S RATINGS OF LEVEL OF POSITIVE AFFECT AND AMOUNT OF TIME IN DAILY ACTIVITIES

Activities	Mean Affect Rating	
	Positive Affect	Mean Hours/Day
Intimate relations	5.1	0.2
Socializing	4.6	2.3
Relaxing	4.4	2.2
Pray/worship/meditate	4.4	0.4
Eating	4.3	2.2
Exercising	4.3	0.2
Watching TV	4.2	2.2
Shopping	4.0	0.4
Preparing food	3.9	1.1
On the phone	3.9	2.5
Napping	3.9	0.9
Taking care of my children	3.9	1.1
Computer/e-mail/Internet	3.8	1.9
Housework	3.7	1.1
Working	3.6	6.9
Commuting	3.5	1.6

Data from Kahneman et al. (2004).

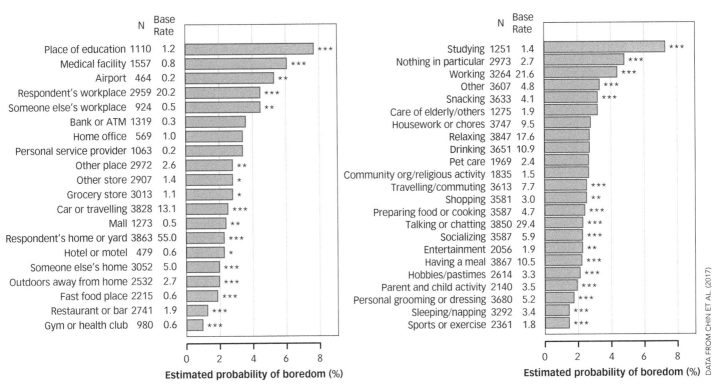

N	Base Rate	Estimated probability of boredom (%)
Place of education 1110	1.2	***
Medical facility 1557	0.8	***
Airport 464	0.2	**
Respondent's workplace 2959	20.2	***
Someone else's workplace 924	0.5	**
Bank or ATM 1319	0.3	
Home office 569	1.0	
Personal service provider 1063	0.2	
Other place 2972	2.6	**
Other store 2907	1.4	*
Grocery store 3013	1.1	*
Car or travelling 3828	13.1	***
Mall 1273	0.5	**
Respondent's home or yard 3863	55.0	***
Hotel or motel 479	0.6	*
Someone else's home 3052	5.0	***
Outdoors away from home 2532	2.7	***
Fast food place 2215	0.6	***
Restaurant or bar 2741	1.9	***
Gym or health club 980	0.6	***

N	Base Rate	Estimated probability of boredom (%)
Studying 1251	1.4	***
Nothing in particular 2973	2.7	***
Working 3264	21.6	***
Other 3607	4.8	***
Snacking 3633	4.1	***
Care of elderly/others 1275	1.9	
Housework or chores 3747	9.5	
Relaxing 3847	17.6	
Drinking 3651	10.9	
Pet care 1969	2.4	
Community org/religious activity 1835	1.5	
Travelling/commuting 3613	7.7	***
Shopping 3581	3.0	**
Preparing food or cooking 3587	4.7	***
Talking or chatting 3850	29.4	***
Socializing 3587	5.9	***
Entertainment 2056	1.9	**
Having a meal 3867	10.5	***
Hobbies/pastimes 2614	3.3	***
Parent and child activity 2140	3.5	***
Personal grooming or dressing 3680	5.2	***
Sleeping/napping 3292	3.4	***
Sports or exercise 2361	1.8	***

DATA FROM CHIN ET AL (2017)

Figure 5.6

Situations and Activities Associated with Boredom An experience-sampling study of more than 1 million people revealed the locations and activities associated with the highest (and lowest) probability of being bored. N is the number of people (out of 3,867) who reported engaging in that activity. Base rate denotes the percent of all reports during which that activity occurred.

reported the highest likelihood of boredom while at their place of education (e.g., school)—even more so than while in an airport or doctor's office. In terms of activities, people reported the highest likelihood of boredom while studying—an activity that was rated as even more boring than doing nothing at all (fortunately, you have this very stimulating book to keep you from getting bored!).

Daydreams: The Brain Is Always Active

One reason that we often avoid boredom when doing nothing is that our mind shifts into a period of *daydreaming,* a state of consciousness in which a seemingly purposeless flow of thoughts comes to mind. When thoughts drift along this way, it may seem as if you are just wasting time. The brain, however, is active even when it has no specific task at hand. The mental work done in daydreaming was examined in an fMRI study of people resting in the scanner (Mason et al., 2007). Usually, people in brain-scanning studies don't have time to daydream much because they are kept busy with mental tasks; scans cost money and researchers want to get as much data as possible for their bucks. But when people are *not* busy, they still show a widespread pattern of activation in many areas of the brain—now known as the *default network* (Gusnard & Raichle, 2001). The study by Mason and colleagues revealed that this network became activated whenever people worked on a mental task that they knew so well that they could daydream while doing it (see **FIGURE 5.7**). The areas of the default network are known to be involved in thinking about social life, about the self, and about the past and future—all the usual haunts of the daydreaming mind (Buckner & DiNicola, 2019).

Efforts to Suppress Current Concerns Can Backfire

The current concerns that populate consciousness can sometimes get the upper hand, transforming daydreams or everyday thoughts into rumination and worry. Thoughts that return again and again, or problem-solving attempts that never seem to succeed, can come to dominate consciousness. When this happens, people

DATA FROM SCIENCE FROM WONDERING MINDS, MASON, ET AL., VOL. 315, JANUARY 19, 2007, PP. 393–305.

Figure 5.7

The Default Network Activated During Daydreaming An fMRI scan shows that many areas, known as the default network, are active when the person is not given a specific mental task to perform during the scan.

may exert **mental control,** *the attempt to change conscious states of mind.* For example, someone troubled by a recurring worry about the future ("What if I can't get a decent job when I graduate?") might choose to try *not* to think about this because it causes too much anxiety and uncertainty. Whenever this thought comes to mind, the person engages in **thought suppression,** the *conscious avoidance of a thought.* This may seem like a perfectly sensible strategy because it eliminates the worry and allows the person to move on to think about something else.

Or does it? The great Russian novelist Fyodor Dostoyevsky (1863/1988, p. 49) remarked on the difficulty of thought suppression: "Try to pose for yourself this task: not to think of a polar bear, and you will see that the cursed thing will come to mind every minute." Inspired by this observation, Daniel Wegner and his colleagues (1987) gave people this exact task in the laboratory. Participants were asked to try not to think about a white bear for 5 minutes while they recorded all their thoughts aloud into a tape recorder. In addition, they were asked to ring a bell if the thought of a white bear came to mind. On average, they mentioned the white bear or rang the bell (indicating the thought) more than once per minute. Thought suppression simply didn't work and instead produced a flurry of returns of the unwanted thought.

What's more, when some research participants later were specifically asked to change tasks and deliberately *think* about a white bear, they became oddly preoccupied with it. A graph of their bell rings in **FIGURE 5.8** shows that for these participants, the white bear came to mind far more often than it did for people who had only been asked to think about the bear from the outset, with no prior suppression. This **rebound effect of thought suppression,** *the tendency of a thought to return to consciousness with greater frequency following suppression,* suggests that attempts at mental control may be difficult indeed. The act of trying to suppress a thought may itself cause that thought to return to consciousness in a robust way.

Go ahead, look away from this book for a minute and try not to think about a white bear.

LARRY WILLIAMS/GETTY IMAGES

mental control The attempt to change conscious states of mind.

thought suppression The conscious avoidance of a thought.

rebound effect of thought suppression The tendency of a thought to return to consciousness with greater frequency following suppression.

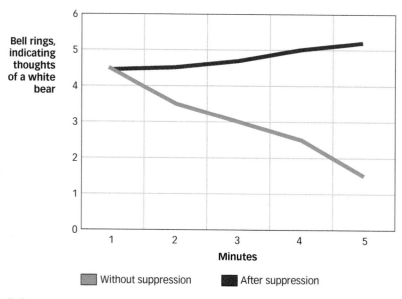

Figure 5.8

Rebound Effect Research participants were asked to try to think about a white bear and to ring a bell whenever it came to mind. Compared to those who were simply asked to think about a bear without prior suppression (bottom line), those people who first suppressed the thought (top line) showed a rebound of increased thinking about the bear (Wegner et al., 1987).

Processes Outside of Consciousness Can Stymie
Attempts at Conscious Control

As with thought suppression, other attempts to steer consciousness in any direction can result in mental states that are precisely the opposite of those desired. How ironic: Trying to consciously achieve one task may produce precisely the opposite outcome! These ironic effects seem most likely to occur when the person is distracted or under stress. People who are distracted while they are trying to get into a good mood, for example, tend to become sad (Wegner et al., 1993), and those who are distracted while trying to relax actually become more anxious than those who are not trying to relax (Wegner et al., 1997). Likewise, an attempt not to overshoot a golf putt, undertaken during distraction, often yields the unwanted overshot (Wegner et al., 1998). The theory of **ironic processes of mental control** proposes that such *ironic errors occur because the mental process that monitors errors can itself produce them* (Wegner, 1994a, 2009). The irony about the attempt not to think of a white bear, for instance, is that a small part of the mind is *searching* for the white bear.

This ironic monitoring process is not present in consciousness. After all, trying *not* to think of something would be useless if monitoring the progress of suppression required keeping that target in consciousness. For example, if trying not to think of a white bear meant that you consciously kept repeating to yourself, "No white bear! No white bear!" then you've failed before you've begun: That thought is present in consciousness even as you strive to eliminate it. Rather, the ironic monitor is a process of the mind that works *outside* of consciousness, making us sensitive to all the things we do not want to think, feel, or do so that we can notice and consciously take steps to regain control if these things come back to mind.

As this unconscious monitoring whirs along in the background, it unfortunately increases the person's sensitivity to the very thought that is unwanted. Ironic processes are mental functions that are needed for effective mental control—they help in the process of banishing a thought from consciousness—but they can sometimes yield the very failure they seem designed to overcome. Ironic effects of mental control arise from processes that work outside of consciousness, so they remind us that much of the mind's machinery may be hidden from our view, lying outside the fringes of our experience.

ironic processes of mental control A mental process that can produce ironic errors because monitoring for errors can itself produce them.

The Unconscious Mind

Many mental processes are unconscious, in the sense that they occur without our experience of them. When we speak, for instance, "We are not really conscious either of the search for words, or of putting the words together into phrases, or of putting the phrases into sentences. . . . The actual process of thinking . . . is not conscious at all . . . only its preparation, its materials, and its end result are consciously perceived" (Jaynes, 1976, p. 41). To put the role of consciousness in perspective, think for a moment about the mental processes involved in simple addition. What happens in consciousness between hearing a problem (what's 4 + 5?) and thinking of the answer (9)? Probably nothing—the answer just appears in the mind. But this is a piece of calculation that must take at least a bit of thinking. After all, at a very young age you may have had to solve such problems by counting on your fingers. Now that you don't have to do that anymore (please tell me you don't have to do that anymore), the answer seems to pop into your head automatically, by virtue of a process that doesn't require

Learning Outcomes

WHAT YOU NEED TO KNOW

- Compare Freud's conception of the unconscious with the modern view.

- Explain the dual process perspective.

There are no conscious steps between hearing an easy problem (what's 4 + 5?) and thinking of the answer—unless you have to count on your fingers.

you to be aware of any underlying steps and, for that matter, doesn't even *allow* you to be aware of the steps. The answer just suddenly appears.

In the early part of the 20th century, when structuralist psychologists such as Edward Tichener believed that introspection was the best method of research (see The Evolution of Psychological Science chapter), research volunteers trained in describing their thoughts tried to discern what happens when a simple problem brings to mind a simple answer (Watt, 1905). They drew the same blank you probably did. Nothing conscious seems to bridge this gap, but the answer comes from somewhere, and this emptiness points to the unconscious mind. To explore these hidden recesses, we can look at the classical theory of the unconscious, introduced by Sigmund Freud, and then at the modern cognitive psychology of unconscious mental processes.

Freudian Unconscious

The true champion of the unconscious mind was Sigmund Freud. As you read in The Evolution of Psychological Science chapter, Freud's psychoanalytic theory viewed conscious thought as the surface of a much deeper mind made up of unconscious processes—but far more than just a collection of hidden processes. Freud described a **dynamic unconscious**—*an active system encompassing a lifetime of hidden memories, the person's deepest instincts and desires, and the person's inner struggle to control these forces.* The dynamic unconscious might contain hidden sexual thoughts about one's parents, for example, or destructive urges aimed at a helpless infant—the kinds of thoughts people keep secret from others and may not even acknowledge to themselves. According to Freud's theory, the unconscious is a force to be held in check by something he called **repression,** *a mental process that removes unacceptable thoughts and memories from consciousness and keeps them in the unconscious.* Freud believed that without repression, a person might think, do, or say every unconscious impulse or animal urge, no matter how selfish or immoral. With repression, these desires are held in the recesses of the dynamic unconscious.

Freud looked for evidence of the unconscious mind in speech errors and lapses of consciousness, or what are commonly called *Freudian slips.* Forgetting the name of someone you dislike, for example, is a slip that seems to have special meaning. Freud believed that errors are not random and instead have some surplus meaning that may appear to have been created by an intelligent unconscious mind, even though the person consciously disavows them. Of course, suggesting that there is special meaning to any one thing a person says, or that there is a pattern to a series of random events is not the same as scientifically predicting and explaining when and why an event should happen. Anyone can offer a reasonable, compelling explanation for an event after it has already happened ("That must have been a Freudian slip!"), but the true work of science is to offer testable hypotheses that can be evaluated based on reliable evidence. Unfortunately, Freud's theories about the unconscious have not been supported by scientific research over the past 100 years.

dynamic unconscious An active system encompassing a lifetime of hidden memories, the person's deepest instincts and desires, and the person's inner struggle to control these forces.

repression A mental process that removes unacceptable thoughts and memories from consciousness and keeps them in the unconscious.

cognitive unconscious All the mental processes that give rise to a person's thoughts, choices, emotions, and behaviour even though they are not experienced by the person.

A Modern View of the Cognitive Unconscious

Modern psychologists share Freud's interest in the impact of unconscious mental processes on consciousness and on behaviour. However, rather than seeing Freud's vision of the unconscious as a teeming menagerie of animal urges and repressed thoughts, the current study of the unconscious mind views it as a rapid, automatic information processor that influences our thoughts, feelings, and behaviours. The **cognitive unconscious** includes *all the mental processes that give rise to a person's thoughts, choices, emotions, and behaviour even though they are not experienced by the person.*

Our Brains Are Wired for Both Fast and Slow Thinking

Modern views of cognition propose that we have two different types of minds wired into our one little brain. **Dual process theories** *suggest that we have two different systems in our brains for processing information: one dedicated to fast, automatic, and unconscious processing; and the other dedicated to slow, effortful, and conscious processing.* The first, which is now commonly referred to as System 1 (Stanovich & West, 2000), is at work when you effortlessly engage in activities such as reading these words; solving problems such as 2 + 2 = ___; and walking down the street avoiding people, cars, and other obstacles. You use the second, System 2, when you rationally and intentionally work to complete a task, such as answering this chapter's quiz questions, solving problems such as 245 × 32 = ___, and placing an order at a restaurant. These systems, and the important roles they play, are outlined in detail in the psychologist and Nobel laureate Daniel Kahneman's book *Thinking Fast and Slow* (Kahneman, 2011).

Kahneman (2011) suggests that Systems 1 and 2 are both continuously active whenever we are awake: System 1 helps you efficiently navigate your daily life, and System 2 becomes engaged when more serious mental effort is involved. For instance, if you are walking around campus from one class to another—a walk that you have taken dozens of times—System 1 will guide you. However, if you happen upon a clown holding a fist full of rubber chickens, System 2 may come online to help you resolve this apparent conflict between what System 1 expected and what it observed. In this way, System 2 uses information and inputs from System 1 to help guide your future behaviour.

This dual process perspective is similar in some ways to Freud's idea of the split between the unconscious and the conscious mind. However, dual process theories do not incorporate all of Freud's beliefs about hidden urges, defense mechanisms, Freudian slips, and the like. Instead, they simply propose that we have these two different ways of processing information that draw on different neural pathways. Dual process theories have been used to understand the workings of different cognitive processes, such as attention, learning, and memory, and they continue to guide thinking and research in many different areas of psychology. (For example, see the discussions of implicit and explicit learning and memory in later chapters on these topics.)

The Unconscious Mind: Smart or Not So Smart?

If System 1 can handle only simple tasks, should we think of it as an unintelligent system? Freud attributed great intelligence to the unconscious, believing that it harbours complex motives and inner conflicts and that it expresses these in an astonishing array of thoughts and emotions, as well as psychological disorders (see the Disorders chapter). Contemporary cognitive psychologists wonder whether the unconscious is so smart after all, pointing out that some unconscious processes even seem downright "dumb" (Loftus & Klinger, 1992). For example, the unconscious processes that underlie the perception of subliminal visual stimuli do not seem able to understand the combined meaning of word pairs, although they can understand single words. To the *conscious* mind, for example, a word pair such as *enemy loses* is somewhat positive—it is good to have your enemy lose. However, subliminal presentations of this word pair make people think of negative things, as though the unconscious mind is simply adding together the unpleasantness of the single words *enemy* and *loses* (Greenwald, 1992). So System 1 appears to be able to help us think fast, but in very simple terms.

dual process theories Theories that suggest that we have two different systems in our brains for processing information: one dedicated to fast, automatic, and unconscious processing, and the other dedicated to slow, effortful, and conscious processing.

Sleep and Dreaming: Good Night, Mind

Learning Outcomes

WHAT YOU NEED TO KNOW

- Describe the stages of sleep.
- Identify the types of sleep disorders.
- Compare the two leading theories of why we dream.

What's it like to be asleep? Sometimes it's like nothing at all. Sleep can produce a state of unconsciousness in which the mind and brain apparently turn off the functions that create experience: The theatre in your mind is closed. But this is an oversimplification because the theatre seems to reopen during the night for special shows of bizarre cult films—in other words, dreams. Dream consciousness involves a transformation of experience that is so radical it is commonly considered an **altered state of consciousness:** *a form of experience that departs significantly from the normal subjective experience of the world and the mind.* Such altered states can be accompanied by changes in thinking, disturbances in the sense of time, feelings of loss of control, changes in emotional expression, alterations in body image and sense of self, perceptual distortions, and changes in meaning or significance (Ludwig, 1966). The world of sleep and dreams, the two topics in this section, provides two unique perspectives on consciousness: a view of the mind without consciousness and a view of consciousness in an altered state.

Sleep

Consider a typical night. As you begin to fall asleep, the busy, task-oriented thoughts of the waking mind are replaced by wandering thoughts and images and odd juxta-positions, some of them almost dreamlike. This pre-sleep consciousness is called the *hypnagogic state.* On some rare nights you might experience a *hypnic jerk,* a sudden quiver or sensation of dropping, as though missing a step on a staircase. No one is quite sure why these happen. Eventually, your presence of mind goes away entirely. Time and experience stop, you are unconscious, and in fact there seems to be no "you" there to have experiences. But then come dreams, whole vistas of a vivid and surrealistic consciousness you just don't get during the day, a set of experiences that occur with the odd prerequisite that there is nothing "out there" that you are actually experiencing. More patches of unconsciousness may occur, with more dreams here and there. And finally, the glimmerings of waking consciousness return again in a foggy and imprecise form as you enter post-sleep consciousness (the *hypnopompic state*) and then awake, often with bad hair.

Sleep Cycle

The sequence of events that occurs during a night of sleep is part of one of the major rhythms of human life, the cycle of sleep and waking. This **circadian rhythm** is *a naturally occurring 24-hour cycle,* from the Latin *circa* ("about") and *dies* ("day"). Even people sequestered in underground buildings without clocks (known as time-free environments), who are allowed to sleep when they want, tend to have a rest–activity cycle of about 25.1 hours (Aschoff, 1965). This slight deviation from 24 hours is not easily explained (Lavie, 2001), but it seems to underlie the tendency many people have to want to stay up a little later each night and wake up a little later each day. We're 25.1-hour people living in a 24-hour world.

Research Reveals Five Stages of Sleep The sleep cycle is far more than a simple on–off routine, however, since many bodily and psychological processes ebb and flow in this rhythm. In 1929, researchers made EEG (electroencephalograph) recordings of the human brain for the first time (Berger, 1929) (see the Neuroscience and Behaviour chapter). Before this, many people had offered descriptions of their night-time experiences, and researchers knew that there were deeper and lighter periods

altered state of consciousness A form of experience that departs significantly from the normal subjective experience of the world and the mind.

circadian rhythm A naturally occurring 24-hour cycle.

of sleep, as well as dream periods. But no one had been able to measure much of anything about sleep without waking up the sleeper and totally disrupting the experience of sleep. The EEG recordings revealed a regular pattern of changes in electrical activity in the brain accompanying the circadian cycle. During waking, these changes involve alternating between high-frequency activity (*beta waves*) during alertness and lower-frequency activity (*alpha waves*) during relaxation.

The largest changes in EEG occur during sleep. These changes show a regular pattern over the course of the night that allowed sleep researchers to identify five sleep stages (see **FIGURE 5.9**). In the first stage of sleep, the EEG moves to frequency patterns even lower than alpha waves (*theta waves*). In the second stage of sleep, these patterns are interrupted by short bursts of activity called *sleep spindles* and *K complexes,* and the sleeper becomes somewhat more difficult to awaken. The deepest stages of sleep are stages 3 and 4, known as slow-wave sleep, in which the EEG patterns show activity called *delta waves.*

The fifth sleep stage is **REM sleep,** which is *a stage of sleep characterized by rapid eye movements and a high level of brain activity,* during which EEG patterns become high-frequency sawtooth waves, similar to beta waves. This suggests that at this time, the mind is as active as it is during waking (see Figure 5.9). Using an **electrooculograph (EOG)** — *an instrument that measures eye movements during sleep* — researchers found that sleepers who were awakened during REM periods reported having dreams much more often than those awakened during non-REM periods (Aserinsky & Kleitman, 1953). During REM sleep, the pulse quickens, blood

REM sleep A stage of sleep characterized by rapid eye movements and a high level of brain activity.

electrooculograph (EOG) An instrument that measures eye movements.

Awake
Beta waves

Drowsy, Relaxed
Alpha waves

Stage 1 Sleep
Theta waves

Theta waves

Stage 2 Sleep
Sleep spindles,
K complexes

Sleep spindle

K complex

Stage 3/Stage 4 Sleep
Delta waves

Delta activity

REM Sleep
Fast, random

Sawtooth waves

50 μv
1 sec.

Figure 5.9
EEG Patterns During the Stages of Sleep The waking brain shows high-frequency beta wave activity, which changes during drowsiness and relaxation to lower-frequency alpha waves. Stage 1 sleep shows lower-frequency theta waves, which are accompanied in stage 2 by irregular patterns called sleep spindles and K complexes. Stages 3 and 4 are marked by the lowest frequencies, delta waves. During REM sleep, EEG patterns return to higher-frequency sawtooth waves that resemble the beta waves of waking.

Psychologists learn about what happens when we sleep by collecting EOG, EEG, and other measurements from research volunteers while they sleep in sleep laboratories such as this one.

pressure rises, and there are telltale signs of sexual arousal. At the same time, measurements of muscle movements indicate that the sleeper is very still, except for a rapid side-to-side movement of the eyes. (Watch someone sleeping and you may be able to see the REMs through their closed eyelids. But be careful doing this with strangers down at the bus station.)

Although many people believe that they don't dream much (if at all), some 80% of people awakened during REM sleep report dreams. If you've ever wondered whether dreams actually take place in an instant or whether they take as long to happen as the events they portray might take, the analysis of REM sleep offers an answer. The sleep researchers William Dement and Nathaniel Kleitman (1957) woke volunteers either 5 minutes or 15 minutes after the onset of REM sleep and asked them to judge, on the basis of the events in the remembered dream, how long they had been dreaming. Sleepers in 92 of 111 cases were correct, suggesting that dreaming occurs in "real time." The discovery of REM sleep has offered many insights into dreaming, but not all dreams occur in REM periods. Some dreams are also reported in other sleep stages, and the dreams that occur at those times are described as less wild than REM dreams and more like normal thinking.

A Typical Night's Sleep Putting EEG and REM data together produces a picture of how a typical night's sleep progresses through cycles of sleep stages (see **FIGURE 5.10**). In the first hour of the night, you fall all the way from waking to the fourth and deepest stage of sleep, the stage marked by delta waves. These slow waves indicate a general synchronization of neural firing, as though the brain is doing one thing at this time rather than many: the neuronal equivalent of "the wave" moving through the crowd at a stadium as lots of individuals move together in synchrony. You then return to lighter sleep stages, eventually reaching REM and dreamland. Note that although REM sleep is lighter than that of lower stages, it is deep enough that you may be difficult to awaken. You then continue to cycle between REM and slow-wave sleep stages every 90 minutes or so throughout the night. Periods of REM last longer as the night goes on, and lighter sleep stages predominate between these periods, with the deeper slow-wave stages 3 and 4 disappearing halfway through the night. Although you're either unconscious or dream-conscious at the time, your brain and mind cycle through a remarkable array of different states each time you have a night's sleep.

Sleep Needs and Deprivation

How much do people sleep? The answer depends on the age of the sleeper (Dement, 1999). Newborns will sleep six to eight times in 24 hours, often totaling more than 16 hours. Their napping cycle gets consolidated into "sleeping through the night,"

Figure 5.10

Stages of Sleep During the Night Over the course of a typical night, sleep cycles into deeper stages early on and then more shallow stages later. REM periods become longer in later cycles, and the deeper slow-wave sleep of stages 3 and 4 disappears halfway through the night.

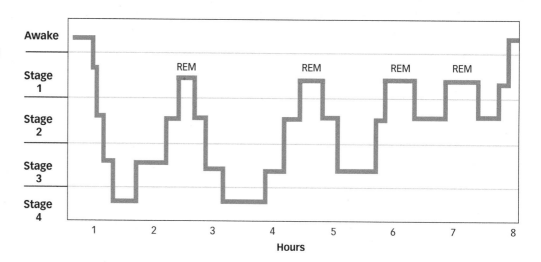

usually sometime between 9 and 18 months, but occasionally even later. The typical 6-year-old child might need 11 or 12 hours of sleep, and the progression to less sleep then continues into adulthood, when the average is about 7 to 7.5 hours per night. With aging, people can get along with even a bit less sleep than that. Over a whole lifetime, we get about 1 hour of sleep for every 2 hours we are awake.

This is a lot of sleeping. Could we tolerate less? Monitored by William Dement, Randy Gardner stayed up for 264 hours and 12 minutes (just over 11 days) in 1965 for a science project. When 17-year-old Randy finally did go to sleep, he slept only 14 hours and 40 minutes and awakened essentially recovered (Dement, 1978).

Feats such as this one suggest that sleep might be expendable. This is the thinking behind the classic all-nighter that you may have tried just before a big exam. But be careful because, as it turns out, this is not the case. Robert Stickgold and his colleagues (2000) found that when people learning a difficult perceptual task are kept up all night after they have finished practicing the task, their learning of the task is wiped out. Even after two nights of catch-up sleep, they show little indication of their initial training on the task. Sleep following learning appears to be essential for memory consolidation (see Hot Science: Can Sleep Enhance Learning? Yes!, in the Memory chapter). It is as though memories normally deteriorate unless sleep occurs to help keep them in place. Studying all night may help you cram for the exam, but it won't make the material stick, which pretty much defeats the whole purpose.

Sleep turns out to be a necessity rather than a luxury in other ways as well. At the extreme, sleep loss can be fatal. When rats are forced to break Randy Gardner's human waking record and stay awake even longer, they have trouble regulating their body temperature and lose weight although they eat much more than normal. Their bodily systems break down and they die, on average, in 21 days (Rechtschaffen et al., 1983). Shakespeare called sleep "nature's soft nurse," and it is clear that even for healthy young humans, a few hours of sleep deprivation each night can have a cumulative detrimental effect: It reduces mental acuity and reaction time, increases irritability and depression, and increases the risk of accidents and injury (Coren, 1997).

Some researchers have deprived people of different sleep stages selectively by waking them whenever certain stages are detected. Studies of REM sleep deprivation indicate that this part of sleep is psychologically important. Memory problems and excessive aggression are observed in both humans and rats after only a few days of being awakened whenever REM activity starts (Ellman et al., 1991). The brain must value something about REM sleep because REM deprivation causes a rebound of more REM sleep the next night (Brunner et al., 1990). Deprivation from slow-wave sleep (in stages 3 and 4), in turn, has more physical effects, with just a few nights of deprivation leaving people feeling tired, fatigued, and hypersensitive to muscle and bone pain (Lentz et al., 1999).

It's clearly dangerous to neglect the need for sleep. But why would we have such a need in the first place? All animals appear to sleep, although the amount of sleep required varies quite a bit (see **FIGURE 5.11**). Giraffes sleep less than 2 hours daily, whereas brown bats snooze for almost 20 hours. These variations in sleep needs, and the very existence of a need, are hard to explain. Is the restoration that happens during the unconsciousness of sleep something that simply can't be achieved during consciousness? Sleep is, after all, potentially costly in the course of evolution. The sleeping animal is easy prey, so the habit of sleep would not seem to have developed so widely across species unless it had significant benefits that made up for this vulnerability. Theories of sleep have not yet determined why the brain and body have evolved to need these recurring episodes of unconsciousness. One possibility is that the brain performs required maintenance while we sleep. Scientists discovered a system in the brain called the "glymphatic system" that eliminates potentially neurotoxic waste products and distributes necessary compounds through the brain such as glucose, lipids, and amino acids (Jessen et al., 2015). The glymphatic system

Sleep following learning is essential for memory consolidation. Sleep during class, on the other hand, not so much.

Figure 5.11

Average Daily Sleep Totals All animals and insects seem to require sleep, although in differing amounts. Next time you oversleep and someone accuses you of "sleeping like a baby," you might tell them instead that you were sleeping like a tiger, or a brown bat.

AVERAGE DAILY SLEEP TOTALS

GIRAFFE — 1.9
ELEPHANT — 3.5
HUMAN — 8.0
CHIMPANZEE — 9.7
BOTTLENOSE DOLPHIN — 10.4
RABBIT — 11.4
GERBIL — 13.1
TIGER — 15.8
BROWN BAT — 19.9

HOURS

LJERKA ILIC/HERMERA/THINKSTOCK

operates mainly during sleep, leading researchers to suggest that the brain may need sleep, and the decreased activity that comes with it, to allow itself the time and resources to perform this daily maintenance.

Sleep Disorders

In answer to the question "Did you sleep well?" the comedian Stephen Wright said, "No, I made a couple of mistakes." Sleeping well is something everyone would love to do, but for many people, sleep disorders are deeply troubling. The most common disorders that plague sleep include insomnia, sleep apnea, and somnambulism.

Insomnia, *difficulty in falling asleep or staying asleep,* is perhaps the most common sleep disorder. Approximately 11% of adults meet diagnostic criteria for insomnia within the past month (Aernout et al., 2021). Unfortunately, insomnia often is a persistent problem; most people with insomnia experience it for at least a year (Morin et al., 2009).

Insomnia has many potential causes. In some instances, it results from lifestyle choices such as working night shifts (self-induced insomnia), whereas in other cases it occurs in response to depression, anxiety, or some other condition (secondary insomnia). In still other cases, there are no obvious causal factors (primary insomnia). Regardless of type, insomnia can be exacerbated by worrying about insomnia (Blake et al., 2018). No doubt you've experienced some nights when sleeping was a high priority, such as before a class presentation or an important interview, and you've found that you were unable to fall asleep. The desire to sleep initiates an ironic process of mental control—a heightened sensitivity to signs of sleeplessness—and this sensitivity interferes with sleep. In fact, participants in an experiment who were instructed to go to sleep quickly became hypersensitive and had more difficulty sleeping than those who were not instructed to hurry (Ansfield et al., 1996). The paradoxical solution for insomnia in some cases, then, may be to give up the pursuit of sleep and instead find something else to do.

Giving up on trying so hard to sleep is probably better than another common remedy—the use of sleeping pills. Although sedatives can be useful for brief sleep problems associated with emotional events, their long-term use is not effective. To begin with, most sleeping pills are addictive. People become dependent on the pills to sleep and may need to increase the dose over time to achieve the same effect.

INSOMNIA JEOPARDY

WAYS IN WHICH PEOPLE HAVE WRONGED ME	STRANGE NOISES	DISEASES I PROBABLY HAVE	MONEY TROUBLES	WHY DID I SAY/DO THAT?	IDEAS FOR A SCREENPLAY
$10	$10	$10	$10	$10	$10
$20	$20	$20	$20	$20	$20
$30	$30	$30	$30	$30	$30
$40	$40	$40	$40	$40	$40
$50	$50	$50	$50	$50	$50

R. Chast

ROZ CHAST/CARTOON STOCK

insomnia Difficulty in falling asleep or staying asleep.

Even in short-term use, sedatives can interfere with the normal sleep cycle. Although they promote sleep, they can reduce the proportion of time spent in REM and slow-wave sleep (Qureshi & Lee-Chiong, 2004), robbing people of dreams and their deepest sleep stages. As a result, the quality of sleep achieved with pills may not be as high as without them, and people may experience side effects such as grogginess and irritability during the day. Finally, stopping the use of sleeping pills suddenly can produce insomnia that is worse than before.

Sleep apnea is *a disorder in which the person stops breathing for brief periods while asleep.* A person with apnea usually snores because apnea involves an involuntary obstruction of the breathing passage. When episodes of apnea occur for over 10 seconds at a time and recur many times during the night, they may cause many awakenings and sleep loss or insomnia. Apnea occurs most often in middle-aged, overweight men (Punjabi, 2008) and may go undiagnosed because it is not easy for the sleeper to notice. Bed partners may be the ones who finally get tired of the snoring and noisy gasping for air when the sleeper's breathing restarts, or the sleeper may eventually seek treatment because of excessive sleepiness during the day. Therapies involving weight loss, drugs, sleep masks that push air into the nasal passage, or surgery may solve the problem.

Somnambulism (or **sleepwalking**) *occurs when a person arises and walks around while asleep.* Sleepwalking is more common in children (5%) than adults (1.5%) (Stallman & Kohler, 2016). Sleepwalking tends to happen early in the night, usually during slow-wave sleep. Sleepwalkers may awaken during their walk or return to bed without waking, in which case they will probably not remember the episode in the morning. The sleepwalker's eyes are usually open in a glassy stare. Walking with hands outstretched is uncommon except in cartoons. Sleepwalking is not usually linked to any additional problems and is problematic only in that sleepwalkers sometimes engage in strange or unwise behaviours such as urinating in places other than the toilet and leaving the house while still sleeping. People who walk while they are sleeping do not tend to be very coordinated and can trip over furniture or fall down stairs. After all, they're sleeping. Contrary to popular belief, it is safe to wake sleepwalkers or lead them back to bed.

Other sleep disorders are less common. **Narcolepsy** is *a disorder in which sudden sleep attacks occur in the middle of waking activities.* Narcolepsy involves the intrusion of sleep (with REM) into wakefulness and is often accompanied by unrelenting excessive sleepiness and uncontrollable sleep attacks lasting from 30 seconds to 30 minutes. This disorder appears to have a genetic basis because it runs in families, and it can be treated effectively with medication. **Sleep paralysis** is *the experience of waking up unable to move* and is sometimes associated with narcolepsy. This eerie experience usually happens as you are awakening from REM sleep but before you have regained motor control. This period typically lasts only a few seconds or minutes and can be accompanied by hypnopompic (when awakening) or hypnagogic (when falling asleep) hallucinations in which dream content may appear to occur in the waking world. A very clever series of studies suggests that sleep paralysis accompanied by hypnopompic hallucinations of figures being in one's bedroom seems to explain many perceived instances of alien abductions and recovered memories of sexual abuse (aided by therapists who used hypnosis to help the sleepers — incorrectly — piece it all together) (McNally & Clancy, 2005).

Sleep terrors (or **night terrors**) are *abrupt awakenings with panic and intense emotional arousal.* These terrors are experienced by up to 6.5% of children, and occur less frequently among adults (Leung et al., 2020). Sleep terrors happen most often in non-REM sleep early in the sleep cycle and do not usually have dream content the sleeper can report.

Sleepwalkers in cartoons have their arms outstretched and eyes closed, but that's just for cartoons. A real-life sleepwalker usually walks normally with eyes open, sometimes with a glassy look.

sleep apnea A disorder in which the person stops breathing for brief periods while asleep.

somnambulism (sleepwalking) Occurs when a person arises and walks around while asleep.

narcolepsy A disorder in which sudden sleep attacks occur in the middle of waking activities.

sleep paralysis The experience of waking up unable to move.

sleep terrors (night terrors) Abrupt awakenings with panic and intense emotional arousal.

To sum up, a lot happens when we close our eyes for the night. Humans follow a pretty regular sleep cycle, going through the five stages of sleep during the night. Disruptions to that cycle, either from sleep deprivation or sleep disorders, can produce consequences for waking consciousness. But something else happens during a night's sleep that affects our consciousness, both while asleep and when we wake up.

Dreams

The pioneering sleep researcher William C. Dement (1959) said, "Dreaming permits each and every one of us to be quietly and safely insane every night of our lives." Indeed, dreams do seem to have a touch of insanity about them. We experience crazy things in dreams, but even more bizarre is the fact that we are the writers, producers, and directors of the crazy things we experience. Just what are these experiences, and how can they be explained?

Dream Consciousness

Dreams depart dramatically from reality. You may dream of being naked in public, of falling from a great height, of your teeth falling out, or of being chased. These things don't happen much in reality unless you're having a terrible, horrible, no good, very bad day. The quality of consciousness in dreaming is also altered significantly from waking consciousness. Five major characteristics of dream consciousness distinguish it from the waking state (Hobson, 1988):

1. We intensely feel *emotion,* whether it is bliss or terror or love or awe.
2. Dream *thought* is illogical: The continuities of time, place, and person don't apply. You may find you are in one place and then another without any travel in between—or people may change identity from one dream scene to the next.
3. *Sensation* is fully formed and meaningful; visual sensation is predominant, and you may also deeply experience sound, touch, and movement (although pain is uncommon).
4. Dreaming occurs with *uncritical acceptance,* as though the images and events are perfectly normal rather than bizarre.
5. We have *difficulty remembering* the dream after it is over. People often remember dreams only if they are awakened during the dream and, even then, may lose recall for the dream within just a few minutes of waking. If your waking memory were this bad, you'd be standing around half-naked in the street much of the time, having forgotten your intended destination, clothes, and lunch money.

Dreams often are quite intense, vivid, and illogical. This can lead to very cool experiences, such as that depicted in this scene from the movie *Inception.*

Not all of our dreams are fantastic and surreal, however. We often dream about mundane topics that reflect prior waking experiences or "day residue." Conscious concerns experienced during the day can continue into our dream (Scarpelli et al., 2021), along with images from the recent past. A dream may even incorporate sensations experienced during sleep, as when sleepers in one study were led to dream of water when drops were sprayed on their faces during REM sleep (Dement & Wolpert, 1958). The day residue does not usually include episodic memories, that is, complete daytime events replayed in the mind. Instead, dreams that reflect the day's experience tend to single out sensory experiences or objects from waking life. Rather than simply being a replay of that event, dreams often consist of "interleaved fragments of experience" from different times and places that our mind weaves together into a single story (Wamsley & Stickgold, 2011). For instance, after a fun day at the beach with your roommates, your dream that night might include cameo appearances by bouncing beach balls or a flock of seagulls. One study had research participants play the computer game Tetris and found that participants often reported dreaming about the Tetris geometrical figures falling down—even though they seldom reported dreams about being in the experiment or playing the game (Stickgold et al., 2001). Even severely amnesic individuals who couldn't recall playing the game at all reported Tetris-like images appearing in their dreams (Stickgold et al., 2000). The content of dreams takes snapshots from the day rather than retelling the stories of what you have done or seen. This means that dreams often come without clear plots or story lines, so they may not make a lot of sense.

Some of the most memorable dreams are nightmares, and these frightening dreams can wake up the dreamer (Levin & Nielsen, 2009). Children have more nightmares than adults, and people who have experienced traumatic events are inclined to have nightmares that relive those events. Following the 1989 earthquake in the San Francisco Bay area of California, for example, university students who had experienced the quake reported more nightmares than those who had not and often reported that the dreams were about the quake (Wood et al., 1992). This effect of trauma may not only produce dreams of the traumatic event: When police officers experience "critical incidents" of conflict and danger, they tend to have more nightmares in general (Neylan et al., 2002).

Dream Theories

Dreams are puzzles that cry out to be solved. How could you not want to make sense out of these experiences? Although dreams may be fantastic and confusing, they are emotionally riveting, filled with vivid images from your own life, and they seem very real. The search for dream meaning goes all the way back to biblical figures, who interpreted dreams and looked for prophecies in them. In the Old Testament, the prophet Daniel (a favourite of three of the authors of this book) curried favour with King Nebuchadnezzar of Babylon by interpreting the king's dreams. The question of what dreams mean has been burning since antiquity, mainly because the meaning of dreams is usually far from obvious.

Freud's View: Dreams Hold Meaning In the first psychological theory of dreams, Freud (1900/1965) proposed that dreams are confusing and obscure because the dynamic unconscious creates them precisely *to be* confusing and obscure. According to Freud, dreams represent wishes, and some of these wishes are so unacceptable, taboo, and anxiety-inducing that the mind can express them only in disguised form. Freud believed that many of the most unacceptable wishes are sexual. For instance, he would interpret a dream of a train going into a tunnel as symbolic of sexual intercourse. According to Freud, the **manifest content** of a dream, or *its apparent topic or superficial meaning,* is a smoke screen for its **latent content,** *a dream's true underlying meaning.* The problem with Freud's approach is that any dream has infinite potential interpretations. Finding the "correct" one is a matter of guesswork—and of convincing the dreamer that one interpretation is superior to the others.

Although dreams may not represent elaborately hidden wishes, there is evidence that they do feature the return of suppressed thoughts. Researchers asked volunteers to think of a personal acquaintance and then to spend 5 minutes before going to bed writing down whatever came to mind (Wegner et al., 2004). Some participants were asked to suppress thoughts of this person as they wrote, others were asked to focus on thoughts of the person, and still others were asked to just write freely about anything. The next morning, participants wrote dream reports. All participants mentioned dreaming more about the person they had named than about other people. But they most often dreamed of the person they named if they were in the group that had been assigned to

***The Nightmare,* by Henry Fuseli (1790)** Fuseli depicts not only a mare in this painting but also an incubus—an imp perched on the dreamer's chest that is traditionally associated with especially horrifying nightmares.

manifest content A dream's apparent topic or superficial meaning.

latent content A dream's true underlying meaning.

suppress thoughts of the person the night before. This finding suggests that dreams may indeed harbour unwanted thoughts. Perhaps this is why travellers often dream of getting lost, students often dream of missing tests, and professors often dream of forgetting their lectures.

The Activation–Synthesis Model: The Brain Imposes Meaning on Random Neural Activity Another key theory of dreaming is the **activation–synthesis model** (Hobson & McCarley, 1977), which is *the theory that dreams are produced when the brain attempts to make sense of random neural activity that occurs during sleep*. During waking consciousness, the mind is devoted to making sense of the wide range of information that arrives through the senses. You figure out that the odd noise you're hearing during class is your cell phone vibrating, for example, or you realize that the strange smell in the hall outside your room must be from burned popcorn. In the dream state, the mind doesn't have access to external sensations, but it keeps on doing what it usually does: interpreting information. Because that information now comes from neural activations that occur in the now-closed system of the brain, without the continuity provided by the perception of reality, the brain's interpretive mechanisms can run free.

This might be why, for example, a person in a dream can sometimes change into someone else. No actual person is being perceived to help the mind keep a stable view. In the mind's effort to perceive and give meaning to brain activation, the person you view in a dream about a grocery store might seem to be a clerk, but then change to be your favourite teacher. The great interest people have in interpreting their dreams the next morning may be an extension of the interpretive activity they've been doing all night.

The Freudian and the activation–synthesis theory differ in the significance they place on the meaning of dreams. In Freud's theory, dreams begin with meaning, whereas in the activation–synthesis theory, dreams begin randomly — but meaning can be added as the mind lends interpretations in the process of dreaming. Several other theoretical models of dreaming also have been proposed. The *neurocognitive theory of dreams* proposes that dreaming is enabled by the default network (described earlier), which supports imagination and daydreaming while awake, and leads to the experience of "embodied simulations" in which a person experiences being in personal and interpersonal scenarios similar to the ones experienced while awake (Domhoff, 2001, 2019). The *threat-simulation theory of dreams* proposes that the purpose of dreams is to simulate threatening situations that a person is likely to experience and to practice escape and avoidance from those situations (Revonsuo, 2000). This could explain why we dream about scary situations — and how to survive them. Dream research has not yet sorted out whether one of these theories, or yet another, might be the best account of the meaning of dreams. Sleep researchers are attempting to do so by studying the dreaming brain and the dreams it creates.

The Dreaming Brain

What happens in the brain when we dream? Numerous studies have involved fMRI scanning of people's brains during sleep, focusing on the areas of the brain that show changes in activation during REM periods. These studies show that the brain changes that occur during REM sleep correspond with certain alterations of consciousness that occur in dreaming. **FIGURE 5.12** shows some of the patterns of activation and deactivation found in the dreaming brain (Nir & Tononi, 2010; Schwartz & Maquet, 2002).

In dreams there are heights to look down from, dangerous people lurking about, the occasional monster, some minor worries, and at least once in a while that major exam you've forgotten about until you walk into class. These themes suggest that the

Freud theorized that dreams represent unacceptable wishes that the mind can only express in disguised form. The activation–synthesis model proposes that dreams are produced when the mind attempts to make sense of random neural activity that occurs during sleep. Suppose you are expecting a visit from an over-bearing relative or acquaintance; the night before that person's arrival, you dream that a bus is driven through the living room window of your house. How might Freud have interpreted such a dream? How might the activation–synthesis model interpret such a dream?

activation–synthesis model The theory that dreams are produced when the brain attempts to make sense of random neural activity that occurs during sleep.

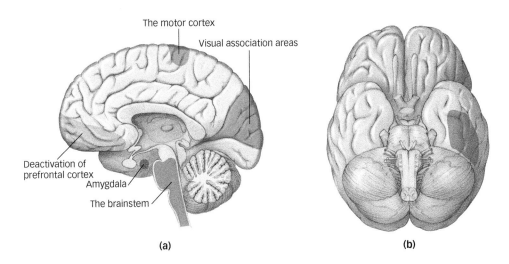

The motor cortex

Visual association areas

Deactivation of prefrontal cortex

Amygdala

The brainstem

(a)   (b)

Figure 5.12

Brain Activation and Deactivation During REM Sleep Brain areas shaded red are activated during REM sleep; those shaded blue are deactivated. (a) The medial view shows activation of the amygdala, the visual association areas, the motor cortex, and the brainstem, and deactivation of the prefrontal cortex. (b) The ventral view shows activation of other visual association areas and deactivation of the prefrontal cortex (Schwartz & Maquet, 2002).

brain areas responsible for fear or emotion somehow work overtime in dreams, and it turns out that this is clearly visible in fMRI scans. The amygdala is involved in responses to threatening or stressful events, and indeed the amygdala is quite active during REM sleep.

The typical dream is also a visual wonderland, with visual events present in almost all dreams. However, there are fewer auditory sensations, even fewer tactile sensations, and almost no smells or tastes. Moreover, people differ dramatically in how much of each sensation they experience in their dreams, as described in A World of Difference: Dreaming Blind. This dream "picture show" doesn't involve actual perception, of course, just the imagination of visual events. It turns out that the areas of the brain responsible for visual perception are *not* activated during dreaming, whereas the visual association areas in the occipital lobe that are responsible for visual imagery *do* show activation (Braun et al., 1998). Your brain is smart enough to realize that it's not really seeing bizarre images but acts instead as though it's imagining bizarre images.

During REM sleep, the prefrontal cortex shows relatively less arousal than it usually does during waking consciousness. What does this mean for the dreamer? As a rule, the prefrontal areas are associated with planning and executing actions, and often dreams seem to be unplanned and rambling. Perhaps this is why dreams often don't have very sensible story lines—they've been scripted by an author whose ability to plan is inactive. One exception to this is seen in the case of *lucid dreaming*, a state in which a person becomes aware that they are dreaming while still in a sleep and dream state. Lucid dreams have been described for decades but are only recently becoming better understood via brain activation studies, which show that people who experience lucid dreams show greater connectivity between the prefrontal cortex and the association areas of the brain that typically are deactivated during sleep (Baird et al., 2018).

Another odd fact of dreaming is that although the eyes are moving rapidly, the body is otherwise very still. During REM sleep, the motor cortex is activated, but spinal neurons running through the brainstem inhibit the expression of this motor activation (Lai & Siegal, 1999). This turns out to be a useful property of brain activation in dreaming; otherwise, you might get up and act out every dream! Individuals suffering from one rare sleep disorder, in fact, lose the normal muscular inhibition accompanying REM sleep and so act out their dreams, thrashing around in bed or stalking around the bedroom (Mahowald & Schenck, 2000). However, most people who are moving during sleep are probably not dreaming. The brain specifically inhibits movement during dreams, perhaps to keep us from hurting ourselves.

A World of Difference | **Dreaming Blind**

What are your dreams like? Are they mostly visual? Do you hear sounds? Do you experience the sense of touch? Taste? Smell? We all differ in our experience of dreaming, just as we do in our waking life. Most people have the ability to experience all of their senses during dreaming. But what about people who lack the ability to experience one of their senses? What is the experience of dreaming like for those who are blind? Researchers have examined this question by asking people who are blind to keep dream journals each day for several weeks, and to compare their reports of their dreams with those of people with sight. For instance, a study by Meaidi and colleagues (2014) revealed that 100% of dreams among sighted people contain visual impressions, compared with only about 75% of dreams among those who had sight and then lost it ("late blind") and 20% of dreams among those who were born blind ("congenitally blind"). It is perhaps not surprising that people who could never see are less likely to "see" during their dreams, but it is interesting

that in 20% of their dreams they can see (although these visual impressions occur only in blind individuals who have at least some amount of light perception).

The lack of visual content in the dreams of people who are blind is made up for by a higher percentage of dreams containing auditory and tactile impressions, as shown in the figure.

Unfortunately, those who are congenitally blind also have a much higher frequency of nightmares, which occur in

nearly 25% of their dreams. These nightmares often have the theme that the blind person is doing something wrong (as a result of their lack of sight), which leads to aggressive responses from others (Maeidi et al., 2014). Virtually all of psychology is focused on understanding the waking mind; however, there appear to be a wide range of important individual differences in the experience of the dreaming mind that are just beginning to be understood.

Drugs and Consciousness: Artificial Inspiration

Learning Outcomes

WHAT YOU NEED TO KNOW

- Explain the dangers of addiction.

- Identify categories of psychoactive drugs and their effects on the body.

psychoactive drugs Chemicals that influence consciousness or behaviour by altering the brain's chemical message system.

The British author of the dystopian novel *Brave New World*, Aldous Huxley (1932), once wrote of his experiences with the drug mescaline. His book *The Doors of Perception* described the intense experience that accompanied Huxley's departure from normal consciousness. He described "a world where everything shone with the Inner Light, and was infinite in its significance. The legs, for example, of a chair—how miraculous their tubularity, how supernatural their polished smoothness! I spent several minutes—or was it several centuries?—not merely gazing at those bamboo legs, but actually *being* them" (Huxley, 1954, p. 22).

Being the legs of a chair? This probably is better than being the seat of a chair, but it still sounds like an odd experience. Nevertheless, many people seek out such experiences, often through the use of drugs. **Psychoactive drugs** are *chemicals that influence consciousness or behaviour by altering the brain's chemical message system.* You read about several such drugs in the Neuroscience and Behaviour chapter when we explored the brain's system of neurotransmitters. And you will read about them in a different light when we turn to their role in the treatment of psychological disorders in the Treatment chapter. Whether these drugs are used for entertainment, for treatment, or for other reasons, they each exert their influence by increasing the activity of a neurotransmitter (the agonists) or decreasing its activity (the antagonists).

Some of the most common neurotransmitters are serotonin, dopamine, gamma-aminobutyric acid (GABA), and acetylcholine. Drugs alter the functioning of neurotransmitters by preventing them from binding to sites on the postsynaptic neuron, by inhibiting their reuptake to the presynaptic neuron, or by enhancing their binding and transmission. Different drugs can intensify or dull transmission patterns, creating changes in brain electrical activities that mimic natural operations of the brain. For example, a drug such as Valium (benzodiazepine) induces sleep but prevents dreaming and so induces a state similar to slow-wave sleep—that is, what the brain naturally develops several times each night. Other drugs prompt patterns of brain activity that do not occur naturally, however, and their influence on consciousness can be dramatic. Like Huxley, who perceived himself becoming the legs of a chair, people using drugs can have experiences unlike any they might find in normal waking consciousness or even in dreams. To understand these altered states, let's explore how people use and abuse drugs, and examine the major categories of psychoactive drugs.

Drug Use and Addiction

Why do children sometimes spin around until they get dizzy and fall down? There is something strangely attractive about states of consciousness that depart from the norm, and people throughout history have sought out these altered states by dancing, fasting, chanting, meditating, and ingesting various chemicals to intoxicate themselves (Crocq, 2007). People pursue altered consciousness even when there are costs, from the nausea that accompanies dizziness to the life-wrecking obsession with a drug that can come with addiction. In this regard, the pursuit of altered consciousness can be a fatal attraction.

Often, drug-induced changes in consciousness begin as pleasant and spark an initial attraction. Researchers have measured the attractiveness of psychoactive drugs by seeing how hard laboratory animals will work to get them. In one study researchers allowed rats to administer cocaine to themselves intravenously by pressing a lever (Bozarth & Wise, 1985). Rats given free access to cocaine increased their use over the course of the 30-day study. They not only continued to self-administer at a high rate but also occasionally binged to the point of giving themselves convulsions. They stopped grooming themselves and eating until they lost on average almost a third of their body weight. About 90% of the rats died by the end of the study.

Rats are not tiny humans, of course, so such research is not a complete basis for understanding human responses to cocaine. But these results do make it clear that cocaine is addictive and that the consequences of such addiction can be dire. Studies of self-administration of drugs in laboratory animals show that animals will work to obtain not only cocaine but also alcohol, amphetamines, barbiturates, caffeine, opiates (such as morphine and heroin), nicotine, phencyclidine (PCP), MDMA (Ecstasy), and THC (tetrahydrocannabinol, the active ingredient in marijuana). There are some psychoactive drugs that animals won't work for (such as mescaline or the antipsychotic drug phenothiazine), suggesting that these drugs have less potential for causing addiction (Bozarth, 1987).

Dangers of Addiction

People usually do not become addicted to a psychoactive drug the first time they use it. They may experiment a few times, then try again, and eventually find that their

Why do kids enjoy spinning around until they get so dizzy that they fall down? Even when we are young, there seems to be something enjoyable about altering states of consciousness.

MATTHEW NOCK

Figure 5.13
Drug Addiction Often Occurs as the Motivation to Use Drugs Shifts from Positive to Negative Reinforcement Research suggests that people often start out using drugs because of the positive experiences they have as a result. But over time, addiction can result if people continue to use drugs to avoid the unpleasant effects of drug withdrawal (George & Koob, 2017).

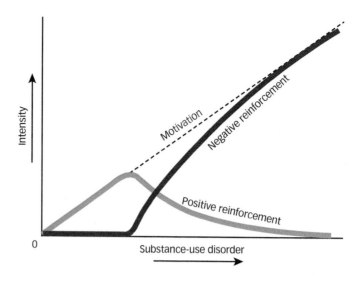

tendency to use the drug increases over time. Research suggests that drug use is initially motivated by *positive reinforcement,* which refers to an increase in the likelihood of a behaviour following the presentation of a reward. In other words, people often try and then repeat the use of psychoactive drugs because those drugs induce a positive psychological state (for reasons described below). Over time, however, some drugs become less rewarding and the motivation to continue to take them is driven by *negative reinforcement,* which refers to an increase in the likelihood of a behaviour following the removal of an aversive state (see **FIGURE 5.13**). That is, people often continue to use psychoactive drugs to reduce or eliminate withdrawal symptoms that arise after the drug leaves their system (George & Koob, 2017). Three primary factors are influential in this process:

1. **Drug tolerance** refers to *the tendency for larger drug doses to be required over time to achieve the same effect.* Physicians who prescribe morphine to control pain in their patients are faced with tolerance problems because steadily greater amounts of the drug may be needed to dampen the same pain. With increased tolerance comes the danger of drug overdose; recreational users find they need to use more and more of a drug to produce the same high. But then, if a new batch of heroin or cocaine is more concentrated than usual, the "normal" amount the user takes to achieve the same high can be fatal.

2. *Physical dependence* refers to the pain, convulsions, hallucinations, or other unpleasant symptoms that accompany withdrawal from drug use. People who suffer from physical dependence may seek to continue drug use to avoid becoming physically ill. A common example is the "caffeine headache" some people complain of when they haven't had their daily jolt of java.

3. *Psychological dependence* refers to a strong desire to return to the drug even when physical withdrawal symptoms are gone. Drugs can create an emotional need over time that continues to prey on the mind, particularly in circumstances that are reminders of the drug. Some ex-smokers report longing wistfully for an after-dinner smoke, for example, even years after they've successfully quit the habit.

There Are Individual Differences in Risk for Addiction

There continues to be a great deal of debate about the extent to which we should think of addiction as a choice (i.e., a person can simply decide to use drugs or not),

drug tolerance The tendency for larger doses of a drug to be required over time to achieve the same effect.

or as a disease over which a person has little or no control. Those who suggest that choice plays a prominent role in addiction note that large-scale studies conducted in the 1980s, 1990s, and 2000s consistently show that approximately 75% of those with substance use disorders overcome their addiction, with the biggest drop in use occurring between ages 20 and 30 (Heyman, 2009).

For instance, one classic study of American soldiers who became addicted to heroin while serving in Vietnam during the Vietnam War (1955–1975) found that, years after their return, only 12% remained addicted (Robins et al., 1980). Resuming the activities, attractions, and obligations of normal life, as well as leaving behind the places and faces associated with their old drug habit, made it possible for returning soldiers to quit successfully—or so the argument goes. More recent, carefully controlled laboratory studies, in which participants are asked to select between a hit of their drug of choice or a small monetary reward (e.g., $5), show that people addicted to drugs such as crack cocaine and methamphetamine very often choose a small monetary reward over taking the drug. Some suggest this means that the decision to use addictive drugs often can be under a person's control (Hart, 2013).

On the other hand, those who argue that addiction is a disease note research over the past several decades suggesting that some people have clear genetic, neurobiological, and social predispositions to have deficits in their ability to resist the urge to engage in drug use, even when doing so has extremely negative consequences such as losing one's home or family (Volkow & Boyle, 2018; Volkow et al., 2016). Not everyone has these predisposing factors; approximately half of all 12th graders report that they have tried at least one illicit drug (Miech et al., 2018), but only a small percentage go on to develop a drug addiction. Like the nature-versus-nurture debate more generally, the reality about drug addiction seems not to be an either-or situation. Rather, it seems that most people do not have a genetic, neurobiological,

Many American soldiers serving in Vietnam became addicted to heroin while there. Robins and colleagues (1980) found that after returning home to the United States, however, the vast majority left their drug habit behind and were no longer addicted.

The temperance movement was an international social and political movement in the 1800s and early 1900s. It was based on the belief that drinking alcohol was responsible for many urban problems, and that banning it was essential to a healthy economy, to a sense of community, and to moral and religious purity. By the 1840s, about 1 person in 10 in Canada was a member of a temperance group. The *Canada Temperance Act* (CTA) of 1878 gave local governments the option to ban the sale of alcohol. Prince Edward Island was the first province to ban alcohol, in 1901, and all of Canada had followed suit by the end of World War I in 1918 (see graph). During prohibition, alcohol could still be obtained for industrial, scientific, mechanical, artistic, and medical uses. Prescription alcohol use "for illness" skyrocketed at this time, and illegal drinking establishments, known as speakeasies, were common. Prohibition was always controversial, and support weakened after the war. By 1925, prohibition laws had been repealed in most provinces. Prohibition happened later in the United States, lasting from 1920 to 1933. Why did prohibition fail, do you think?

or social predisposition to drug addiction; therefore, even if exposed to addictive drugs, they will be able to resist their short- or long-term use. However, some people are more strongly predisposed to have difficulties resisting the urge to use drugs — difficulties that, at the extreme end of the spectrum, can take the form of a disease that appears beyond a person's behavioural control.

What's Considered "Addictive" Can Change

Although "addiction" as a concept is familiar to most of us, there is no standard clinical definition of what an addiction actually is. The concept of addiction has been extended to many human pursuits beyond drugs and alcohol, giving rise to such terms as *sex addict*, *gambling addict*, *workaholic*, and, of course, *chocoholic*. Societies react to mind-altering substances differently at different times. For instance, in the early 17th century, tobacco use was punishable by death in Germany, by castration in Russia, and by decapitation in China (Corti, 1931). Not a good time or place to be a smoker. By contrast, at several points throughout history, marijuana, cocaine, and heroin have all been popular and even recommended as medicines, each without any stigma of addiction attached (Inciardi, 2001).

In Western society today, the use of some drugs is ignored (e.g., caffeine), others regulated (alcohol), others simply taxed (tobacco), and still others subjected to intense prohibition (cocaine, and heroin) (see Hot Science for further discussion of drug use in our society). Rather than viewing *all* drug use as a problem, we need to consider the costs and benefits of such use, as well as establish ways to help people choose behaviours that are informed by this knowledge (Parrott et al., 2005).

Types of Psychoactive Drugs

Approximately 80% of North Americans use caffeine in some form every day, but not all psychoactive drugs are this familiar. To learn how both the well-known and lesser-known drugs influence the mind, let's consider several broad categories of drugs: depressants, stimulants, narcotics, hallucinogens, and marijuana. **TABLE 5.2** summarizes what is known about the potential dangers of these different types of drugs.

Depressants

Depressants are *substances that reduce the activity of the central nervous system.* The most commonly used depressant is alcohol; others include barbiturates, benzodiazepines, and toxic inhalants (such as glue or gasoline). Depressants have a sedative or calming effect, tend to induce sleep in high doses, and can arrest breathing in extremely high doses. Depressants can produce both physical and psychological dependence.

Alcohol Alcohol is king of the depressants, with its worldwide use beginning in prehistory. It is easily available in most cultures, and has widespread acceptance as a socially approved substance. In 2017, approximately 78% of Canadians age 15 and older reported drinking alcohol at least once in the past year, and 21% reported exceeding low-risk drinking guidelines. Those guidelines stipulate no more than 10 drinks a week for women, with no more than 2 drinks a day most days; and 15 drinks a week for men, with no more than 3 drinks a day most days (Canadian Centre on Substance Use and Addiction, 2019).

Alcohol's initial effects, euphoria, and reduced anxiety, feel pretty positive. As alcohol is consumed in greater quantities, however, intoxication results, bringing with it slowed reactions, slurred speech, poor judgement, and other reductions in the effectiveness of thought and action. The exact way in which alcohol influences neural mechanisms is still not understood, but, like other depressants, alcohol

depressants Substances that reduce the activity of the central nervous system.

TABLE 5.2

DANGERS OF DRUGS

Drug	Dangers		
	Overdose (Can taking too much cause death or injury?)	Physical Dependence (Will stopping use make you sick?)	Psychological Dependence (Will you crave it when you stop using it?)
Depressants			
Alcohol	X	X	X
Benzodiazepines/barbiturates	X	X	X
Toxic inhalants	X	X	X
Stimulants			
Amphetamines	X	X	X
MDMA (Ecstasy)	X		?
Nicotine	X	X	X
Cocaine	X	X	X
Narcotics (opium, heroin, morphine, methadone, codeine)	X	X	X
Hallucinogens (LSD, mescaline, psilocybin, PCP, ketamine)	X		?
Marijuana		?	?

increases activity of the neurotransmitter GABA (Koob & Volkow, 2016). As you read in the Neuroscience and Behaviour chapter, GABA normally inhibits the transmission of neural impulses; thus one effect of alcohol is as an inhibitor—a chemical that stops the firing of other neurons. Yet people react very differently to alcohol. Some become loud and aggressive, others become emotional and weepy, others become sullen, and still others turn giddy—and the same person can experience each of these effects in different circumstances. How can one drug do all this? Two theories have been offered to account for these variable effects: *expectancy theory* and *alcohol myopia*.

1. **Expectancy theory** refers to the *idea that alcohol effects can be produced by people's expectations of how alcohol will influence them in particular situations* (Marlatt & Rohsenow, 1980). So, for instance, if you've watched friends or family drink at weddings and notice that this often produces hilarity and gregariousness, you could well experience these effects yourself should you drink alcohol on a similarly festive occasion. Seeing people get drunk and fight in bars, on the other hand, might lead to aggression after drinking. The expectancy theory has been tested in experiments using a **balanced placebo design,** *a study design in which behaviour is observed following the presence or absence of an actual stimulus and also following the presence or absence of a placebo stimulus.* In such a study, participants are given drinks containing alcohol or a substitute nonalcoholic liquid (adjusted for scent and colour); some people in each group are led to believe they drank alcohol while others are led to believe they did not. These experiments often show that the mere *belief* that one has had alcohol can influence behaviour as strongly as the ingestion of alcohol itself (Goldman et al., 1987).

expectancy theory The idea that alcohol effects can be produced by people's expectations of how alcohol will influence them in particular situations.

balanced placebo design A study design in which behaviour is observed following the presence or absence of an actual stimulus and also following the presence or absence of a placebo stimulus.

Which theory, expectancy theory or alcohol myopia, views a person's response to alcohol as being (at least partially) learned, through a process similar to observational learning?

2. The theory of **alcohol myopia** is *a condition that results when alcohol hampers attention, leading people to respond in simple ways to complex situations* (Steele & Josephs, 1990). This theory recognizes that life is filled with complicated pushes and pulls, and our behaviour is often a balancing act. Imagine that you are really attracted to someone who is dating your friend. Do you make your feelings known or focus on your friendship? The myopia theory holds that when you drink alcohol, your judgement is impaired. It becomes hard to appreciate the subtlety of these different options, and the inappropriate response is to veer full tilt one way or the other. In one study on the alcohol myopia theory, men (half of whom were drinking alcohol) watched a video showing an unfriendly woman and then were asked how acceptable it would be for a man to act in a sexually aggressive way towards a woman (Johnson et al., 2000). The unfriendly woman seemed to remind them that sex was out of the question, and, indeed, men who were drinking alcohol and had seen this video were no more likely to think sexual advances were acceptable than were men who were sober. However, when the same question was asked of a group of men who had seen a video of a *friendly* woman, those who were drinking were more inclined to recommend sexual overtures than those who were not, even when these overtures might be unwanted.

Both the expectancy and myopia theories suggest that people using alcohol will often go to extremes (Cooper, 2006). In fact, it seems that drinking is a major contributing factor to social problems that result from extreme behaviour. Driving after drinking alcohol is a major cause of auto accidents. In 2016, nearly 2,000 people in Canada were killed in alcohol-related car crashes (Canadian Council of Motor Transport Administrators, 2016). Alcohol also has been linked to increased aggression towards others in dozens of studies, including increased likelihood of aggression in general, as well as sexual violence and intimate partner violence (Crane et al., 2015).

Barbiturates, Benzodiazepines, and Toxic Inhalants Compared to alcohol, the other depressants are much less popular but are still widely used and abused. Barbiturates such as Seconal or Nembutal are prescribed as sleep aids and as anaesthetics before surgery. Benzodiazepines such as Valium and Xanax are also called minor tranquilizers and are prescribed as antianxiety drugs. These drugs are prescribed by physicians to treat anxiety or sleep problems, but they are dangerous when used in combination with alcohol because they can cause respiratory depression (slowed breathing). Physical dependence is possible because withdrawal from long-term use can produce severe symptoms (including convulsions), and psychological dependence is common as well. Finally, toxic inhalants are perhaps the most alarming substances in this category (Ridenour & Howard, 2012). These drugs are easily accessible, even to children, in the vapors of inexpensive household products such as glue, hair spray, nail polish remover, or gasoline. Sniffing or "huffing" vapors from these products can promote temporary effects that resemble drunkenness, but overdoses can be lethal, and continued use holds the potential for permanent neurological damage (Howard et al., 2011). Perhaps because these products are so easily accessible, inhalant abuse often affects children at younger ages, compared to other forms of substance abuse, and it is especially common in individuals from minority and economically and socially marginalized groups.

Stimulants

Stimulants are *substances that excite the central nervous system, heightening arousal and activity levels.* They include caffeine, amphetamines, nicotine, cocaine,

alcohol myopia A condition that results when alcohol hampers attention, leading people to respond in simple ways to complex situations.

stimulants Substances that excite the central nervous system, heightening arousal and activity levels.

modafinil, and Ecstasy, some of which sometimes have a legitimate pharmaceutical purpose. Amphetamines (also called *speed*), for example, were originally prepared for medicinal uses and as diet drugs; however, amphetamines such as Methedrine and Dexedrine are widely abused, causing insomnia, aggression, and paranoia with long-term use. Stimulants increase the levels of dopamine and norepinephrine in the brain, thereby inducing higher levels of activity in the brain circuits that depend on these neurotransmitters. As a result, they increase alertness and energy in the user, often producing a euphoric sense of confidence and a kind of agitated motivation to get things done. Stimulants produce physical and psychological dependence, and their withdrawal symptoms involve depressive effects such as fatigue and negative emotions.

Cocaine is derived from leaves of the coca plant, which has been cultivated by indigenous peoples of the Andes for millennia and chewed as a medication. And yes, the urban legend is true: Coca-Cola did contain cocaine until 1903 and may still use coca leaves to this day (with cocaine removed) as a flavouring—although the company's not telling. (Pepsi-Cola never contained cocaine and is probably made from something brown.) Sigmund Freud tried cocaine and wrote effusively about it for a while. Cocaine (usually snorted) and crack cocaine (smoked) produce exhilaration and euphoria and are seriously addictive, both for humans and the rats you read about earlier. Withdrawal takes the form of an unpleasant crash; dangerous side effects of cocaine use include psychological problems (e.g., insomnia, depression, aggression, and paranoia) as well as physical problems (e.g., death from a heart attack or hyperthermia) (Marzuk et al., 1998). Although cocaine has been used for many years as a party drug, its extraordinary potential to create dependence and its potentially lethal side effects should be taken very seriously.

Ecstasy (also known as MDMA, "X," or "E"), an amphetamine derivative, is a stimulant, but it has additional effects somewhat like those of hallucinogens. (We'll talk about those shortly.) Ecstasy is particularly known for making users feel empathic and close to those around them. It is often used as a party drug to enhance the group feeling at dance clubs and raves, but it can have unpleasant side effects, such as causing jaw clenching and elevating body temperature. The rave culture popularized pacifiers and juices as remedies for these problems, but users remain highly susceptible to heat stroke and exhaustion. Emergency medical treatment is required for 0.6% of users and approximately once per every 800 pills consumed (van Amsterdam et al., 2020). Ecstasy's potentially toxic effect on serotonin neurons in the human brain is under debate, although mounting evidence from animal and human studies suggests that sustained use is associated with damage to serotonergic neurons and potential associated problems with mood, attention and memory, and impulse control (Kish et al., 2010; Urban et al., 2012).

The popularity of nicotine is something of a puzzle, however. This is a drug with almost nothing to recommend it to the newcomer. It usually involves inhaling smoke that doesn't smell that great, at least at first, and there's not much in the way of a high, either—at best, some dizziness or a queasy feeling. So why do people use it? Tobacco use is motivated far more by the unpleasantness of quitting than by the pleasantness of using. The positive effects people report from smoking—relaxation and improved concentration, for example—come chiefly from relief from withdrawal symptoms (Baker et al., 2004). The best approach to nicotine is to never get started.

Narcotics

Opium, which comes from poppy seeds, and its derivatives heroin, morphine, methadone, and codeine (as well as prescription drugs such as Demerol and Oxycontin)

Because of the known dangers of smoking cigarettes, many are turning to electronic cigarettes (e-cigarettes) under the assumption that they are a safe alternative. However, an investigation of the chemicals contained in flavoured e-cigarettes revealed that 92% of them contain the dangerous chemical diacetyl, which has been linked to severe and irreversible medical problems such as "popcorn lung" (Allen et al., 2016).

People will often endure significant inconveniences to maintain their addictions, which in the case of smoking means puffing smoke to avoid the withdrawal symptoms that come with quitting.

are known as **narcotics** (or **opiates**), *highly addictive drugs derived from opium that relieve pain.* Narcotics induce a feeling of well-being and relaxation that is enjoyable, but they can also induce stupor and lethargy. The addictive properties of narcotics are powerful, and long-term use produces both tolerance and dependence. Because these drugs are often administered with hypodermic syringes, they also introduce the danger of diseases such as hepatitis and HIV when users share syringes. Unfortunately, these drugs are especially alluring because they mimic the brain's own internal relaxation and well-being system.

The brain produces endogenous opioids or endorphins, which are neuropeptides closely related to opiates. As you learned in the Neuroscience and Behaviour chapter, endorphins play a role in how the brain copes internally with pain and stress. These substances reduce the experience of pain naturally. When you exercise for a while and start to feel your muscles burning, for example, you may also find that a time comes when the pain eases—sometimes even *during* exercise. Endorphins are secreted in the pituitary gland and other brain sites as a response to injury or exertion, creating a kind of natural remedy, sometimes referred to as "runner's high," that subsequently reduces pain and increases feelings of well-being. Interesting research suggests that runner's high also seems to be induced in part by activation of the brain's endocannabinoid system—the same one involved in response to smoking marijuana (Fuss et al., 2015).

When people use narcotics, the brain's endorphin receptors are artificially flooded, however, reducing receptor effectiveness and possibly also depressing the production of endorphins. When external administration of narcotics stops, withdrawal symptoms are likely to occur. Withdrawal symptoms can be especially difficult to cope with when using narcotics, which might partially explain the current opioid epidemic sweeping the United States and Canada (see Hot Science: Why Is There an Opioid Epidemic and What Can We Do About It? for more on this important topic).

Hallucinogens

The drugs that produce the most extreme alterations of consciousness are the **hallucinogens,** *drugs that alter sensation and perception and often cause visual and auditory hallucinations.* These include LSD (lysergic acid diethylamide, or acid), mescaline, psilocybin, PCP (phencyclidine), and ketamine (an animal anaesthetic). Some of these drugs are derived from plants (mescaline from peyote cactus, psilocybin or "shrooms" from mushrooms) and have been used by people since ancient times. For example, the ingestion of peyote plays a prominent role in some Native American religious practices. The other hallucinogens are largely synthetic. LSD was first made by the chemist Albert Hofmann in 1938, leading to a rash of experimentation that influenced popular culture in the 1960s. Timothy Leary, at the time a lecturer in the Department of Psychology at Harvard, championed the use of LSD to "turn on, tune in, and drop out"; the Beatles sang of "*Lucy in the Sky with Diamonds*" (denying, of course, that this might be a reference to LSD); and the wave of interest led many people to experiment with hallucinogens.

The experiment was not a great success. These drugs produce profound changes in perception. Sensations may seem unusually intense, stationary objects may seem to move or change, patterns or colours may appear, and these perceptions may be accompanied by exaggerated emotions ranging from blissful transcendence to abject terror. These are the "I've-become-the-legs-of-a-chair!" drugs. But the effects of hallucinogens are dramatic and unpredictable, creating a psychological roller-coaster ride that some people find intriguing and others find deeply disturbing. Hallucinogens are the main class of drugs that animals won't work to self-administer, so it is not surprising that in humans these drugs are unlikely to be addictive. Hallucinogens do not induce significant tolerance or dependence, and overdose deaths are rare.

narcotics (opiates) Highly addictive drugs derived from opium that relieve pain.

hallucinogens Drugs that alter sensation and perception and often cause visual and auditory hallucinations.

Hot Science ╎ Why Is There an Opioid Epidemic and What Can We Do About It?

Opioids have been around in one form or another for thousands of years. For instance, an early medicine called theriac was used for over 1,500 years to treat a range of illnesses, including anxiety and depression. Its more than 100 ingredients often included things like viper's flesh, roses, and carrots, but it turns out there was only one active ingredient: opium. Although opium and its derivatives have been consumed in some fashion for some time, our society has seen an absolutely startling rise in the use of opioids in just the past few years. The rate of opioid overdoses has increased dramatically in the past few years; over 6,300 people in Canada died of opioid overdose in 2020 alone (see map).

Faulty reporting of research in the 1980s and 1990s suggested that the risk of addiction to opioids prescribed for pain relief was low. Pharmaceutical companies pushed this reassuring message about the new opioid drugs they were introducing, and prescribing of opioids for pain increased sharply in the 1990s. Subsequently, the drugs were extensively misused: about 10 to 12% of individuals with prescriptions would become addicted, but the presence of large quantities of these drugs in homes increased access to vulnerable family members, friends, and others. It soon became clear that these drugs could indeed be highly addictive—but by then, addiction and overdose deaths were widespread, and those afflicted had turned to nonprescription forms such as heroin and the powerful synthetic opioid fentanyl.

So, what can be done to turn the tide on this epidemic? Scientists and policy makers are arguing for obvious fixes, such as implementing physician training and policy changes to decrease inappropriately high prescription of these drugs, developing less addictive pain medications, addressing social disparities that can increase risk of drug use and abuse, and initiating public education campaigns that alert communities and individuals to the dangers of potential opioid addiction (Volkow et al., 2021; Volkow, 2021). These strategies may help prevent new addictions. Harm from opioid addiction can be reduced through the introduction of supervised consumption facilities and by making naloxone, a drug that rapidly reverses opioid overdoses, more accessible and easier to use by those without extensive training. What are some other approaches that might be tried?

Psychedelic art and music of the 1960s were inspired by some visual and auditory effects of drugs such as LSD.

Over the past few years, there has been a resurgence of research on hallucinogens, and on the potential therapeutic benefits of these substances. For instance, one recent randomized controlled trial showed that the administration of psilocybin was as effective as a commonly used anti-depressant at decreasing symptoms of depression over a 6-week period (Carhart-Harris et al., 2021). Another recent trial demonstrated the effectiveness of MDMA in the treatment of posttraumatic stress disorder (Mitchell et al., 2021). Although these substances are still illegal to possess and consume, researchers are testing their potential therapeutic value with the hope that they can be packaged and distributed in a way that maximizes the benefits and minimizes the potential harm of their use.

Marijuana

Marijuana (or **cannabis**) is *the leaves and buds of the hemp plant, which contain a psychoactive drug called tetrahydrocannabinol (THC).* When smoked or eaten, either as is or in concentrated form as *hashish,* this drug produces an intoxication that is mildly hallucinogenic. Users describe the experience as euphoric, with heightened senses of sight and sound and the perception of a rush of ideas. Marijuana affects judgement and short-term memory and impairs motor skills and coordination—making driving a car or operating heavy equipment a poor choice during its use. ("Dude, where's my bulldozer?") Researchers have found that receptors in the brain that respond to THC (Stephens, 1999) are normally activated by a neurotransmitter called *anandamide* that is naturally produced in the brain (Wiley, 1999). Anandamide is involved in the regulation of mood, memory, appetite, and pain perception and has been found to temporarily stimulate overeating in laboratory animals, much as marijuana does in humans (Williams & Kirkham, 1999). Some chemicals found in dark chocolate also mimic anandamide, although very weakly, perhaps accounting for the well-being some people claim they enjoy after a "dose" of chocolate.

The addiction potential of marijuana is not strong because tolerance does not seem to develop, and physical withdrawal symptoms are minimal. Psychological dependence is possible, however, and some people do become chronic users. Marijuana use has been widespread throughout the world throughout recorded history, both as a medicine for pain and/or nausea and as a recreational drug, but its use remains controversial. Marijuana abuse and dependence have been linked with increased risk of depression, anxiety, and other forms of psychopathology. Many people also are concerned that marijuana (along with alcohol and tobacco) is a **gateway drug,** *a drug whose use increases the risk of the subsequent use of more harmful drugs.* The gateway theory has gained mixed support, with research studies challenging the notion and suggesting that early-onset drug use in general, regardless of type of drug, increases the risk of later drug and mental-health problems (Degenhardt et al., 2008).

In 2014, Canada's leading hospital for mental illness, the Centre for Addiction and Mental Health (CAMH) in Toronto, published evidence-based recommendations concerning cannabis policy in Canada (Cannabis Policy Framework, 2014). It concluded that a public health approach involving legalization and regulation, such as exists for alcohol and tobacco, would allow for the most control over the risk factors associated with cannabis-related harm. Perhaps this report, as well as the fact that more than 50% of Canadians supported legalization, is why the federal government legalized marijuana in 2018 (see Other Voices: Canada's Grand Cannabis Experiment Has Set Scientists Free).

marijuana (cannabis) The leaves and buds of the hemp plant, which contain a psychoactive drug called tetrahydrocannabinol (THC).

gateway drug A drug whose use increases the risk of the subsequent use of more harmful drugs.

Other Voices | Canada's Grand Cannabis Experiment Has Set Scientists Free

When Canada fully legalized recreational cannabis on Oct. 17, the internet giddily reimagined the CN Tower in Toronto peeking out from a thick haze and swapped the flag's red maple leaf for its jagged-edged green cousin. Outsiders might titter about an entire populace turning into potheads, but legalization means some of the country's brightest can now turn their minds to pot.

As the first G-7 nation to slacken cannabis laws, Canada has bolted to the front lines of the plant's methodical scrutiny and investigation. No longer at risk of censure or lacking access to specimens, researchers can transcend the narrow parameters of scientific study once considered acceptable, namely, clinical research, to explore social, biological, genetic and agricultural questions. From botanists to phytochemists, microbiologists to epidemiologists, scientists of all sorts are free to openly pursue a greater quantity and quality of cannabis science than ever before.

Canada's brand-new legislation, the Cannabis Act, replaces a restrictive system that treated researchers like would-be drug dealers. Scientists intending to cultivate their own plants can now simply apply for a specific class of license rather than toil for an exemption from the retrograde Controlled Drugs and Substances Act, which, among other demands, required criminal record checks.

The Canadian government, once unwilling to touch the stuff, has stepped up to properly examine how cannabis affects the body and brain. It's funding 14 new studies and has set aside millions more for research grants that could ask questions like, Will a pregnant mother using cannabis harm her baby's development? Does smoking affect drivers' reaction time behind the wheel? And at what threshold does teenagers' pot consumption become destructive?

With the legal barriers torn down, a path has been cleared for Canadians to stake a global claim in the emerging field of research. New science projects are taking shape in Europe, Israel and Australia, many the fruit of joint ventures with Canadian companies, others made possible only with imported dried medical marijuana and cannabis oil from Canada. The country has become "the de facto source of research-grade cannabis around the world," contends Philippe Lucas, who is the head of research for the Canadian producer Tilray, which has completed exports to 10 countries.

Canada's grand experiment has already been a catalyst for smarter science in the United States, where its federal prohibition has choked research. Although 33 states have relaxed their marijuana laws, only one facility in Mississippi is federally licensed to supply dried cannabis, and its product is often derided by researchers as lackluster.

Enter Tilray, which, in a rare first this September, was approved by the Drug Enforcement Administration to supply cannabis extract from Canada to a California neurologist who's developing a treatment for tremors in the elderly. (Tilray has also built a greenhouse in a Portugal research park, expanding the science into the European Union.) America's cannabis entrepreneurs, however, aren't so keen on the prospective northern pot pipeline. One multistate medical grower has pleaded with President Trump for domestic regulation in a full-page Wall Street Journal ad, fretting that "America is rapidly losing its competitive advantage to Canada!"

As bidding wars replace the drug war, legalization promises empirical evidence for policymakers caught between popular sensibilities and a paucity of data. Canada's statistical agency and the country's health ministry are already gathering information from a newly visible population of cannabis users. The metrics could enable jurisdictions worldwide to devise policy reforms and public health programs that minimize legalization's potentially negative impacts.

The scholarship on cannabis will finally advance now that a developed, Western society has welcomed back an ancient drug plant, says Jonathan Page, a Vancouver-based plant biologist and a leader of the cannabis genome project. Therapeutic marijuana application dates back thousands of years, according to archaeological and historical records.

"Marijuana's hard-won return to the Canadian mainstream suggests that psychoactive plants matter to modern lives and will continue to shape human culture," he said. "Prohibition was just a blip on the timeline of civilization and a dark age for science."

In an age of global paranoia, Canada's decisive leadership has produced a veritable green-field opportunity. It's incumbent on our scientists to do the plowing.

Amanda Siebert is a Vancouver-based freelance journalist and author of *The Little Book of Cannabis: How Marijuana Can Improve Your Life.*

PHOTO BY JACKIE DIVES, COURTESY AMANDA SIEBERT

Hypnosis: Open to Suggestion

You may have never been hypnotized, but you have probably heard or read about it. People often describe its wonders with an air of amazement; demonstrations of stage hypnosis make it seem very powerful and mysterious. When you think of hypnosis, you may envision people completely under the power of a hypnotist, who is ordering them to dance like a chicken or perhaps "regress" to early childhood and talk in childlike voices. Many common beliefs about hypnosis are incorrect. **Hypnosis** refers to *a social interaction in which one person (the hypnotist) makes suggestions that lead to a change in another person's (the participant's) subjective experience of the world* (Kirsch et al., 2011). The essence of hypnosis is in leading people to expect that certain things will happen to them that are outside their conscious will (Wegner, 2002).

Induction and Susceptibility

To induce hypnosis, a hypnotist may ask the person being hypnotized to sit quietly and focus on some item, such as a spot on the wall (or a swinging pocket watch) and may then make suggestions to the person about what effects hypnosis will have (e.g., "Your eyelids are slowly closing" or "Your arms are getting heavy"). Even without hypnosis, some suggested behaviours might commonly happen just because a person is concentrating on them. Just thinking about their eyelids slowly closing, for instance, may make many people shut their eyes briefly or at least blink. In hypnosis, however, suggestions may be made — and followed by people in a susceptible state of mind — for very unusual behaviour that most people would not normally do, such as flapping their arms and making loud clucking sounds.

Not everyone is equally hypnotizable. Susceptibility varies greatly. Susceptibility is not easily predicted by a person's personality traits. A hypnotist will typically test someone's hypnotic susceptibility with a series of suggestions designed to put a person into a more easily influenced state of mind. One of the best indicators of a person's susceptibility is the person's own judgement. So if you think you might be hypnotizable, you may well be (Hilgard, 1965). People respond most strongly to hypnotic suggestions not only when they are highly susceptible, but also when hypnotic suggestions are made very specifically and in the context of hypnotic induction rituals (Landry et al., 2017).

Hypnotic Effects

From watching stage hypnotism, you might think that the major effect of hypnosis is making people do peculiar things. So what do we actually know to be true about hypnosis? Some impressive demonstrations suggest that real changes occur in those under hypnosis. At the 1849 birthday festivities for Albert, Prince Consort of the British monarch, Queen Victoria, for example, a hypnotized guest was asked to ignore any loud noises and then didn't even flinch when a pistol was fired near his face. These days, hypnotists are discouraged from using firearms during stage shows, but they often have volunteers perform other impressive feats. One common claim for superhuman strength under hypnosis involves asking a hypnotized person to become "stiff as a board" and lie unsupported with shoulders on one chair and feet on another while the hypnotist stands on the hypnotized person's body.

Studies have demonstrated that hypnosis can undermine memory, but with important limitations. People susceptible to hypnosis can be led to experience

hypnosis A social interaction in which one person (the hypnotist) makes suggestions that lead to a change in another person's (the participant's) subjective experience of the world.

posthypnotic amnesia, *the failure to retrieve memories following hypnotic suggestions to forget.* For instance, Ernest Hilgard (1986) taught a hypnotized person the populations of some remote cities and then suggested that the participant forget the study session; after the session, the person was quite surprised at being able to give the census figures correctly. Asked how he knew the answers, the individual decided he might have learned them from a TV program. Such amnesia can then be reversed in subsequent hypnosis.

Some important research has found that only memories that were lost while under hypnosis can be retrieved through hypnosis. The false claim that hypnosis helps people unearth memories they are not able to retrieve in normal consciousness seems to have surfaced because hypnotized people often make up memories to satisfy the hypnotist's suggestions. For example, Paul Ingram, an American sheriff's deputy accused of sexual abuse by his daughters in the 1980s, was asked by interrogators in session after session to relax and imagine having committed the crimes. He emerged from these sessions having confessed to dozens of horrendous acts of "satanic ritual abuse." These confessions were called into question, however, when the independent investigator Richard Ofshe used the same technique to ask Ingram about a crime that Ofshe had simply made up out of thin air, something of which Ingram had never been accused. Ingram produced a three-page handwritten confession, complete with dialogue (Ofshe, 1992). Still, prosecutors in the case accepted Ingram's guilty plea; he was released only in 2003 after a public outcry and years of work on his defense. After a person claims to remember something, even under hypnosis, it is difficult to convince others that the memory was false (Loftus & Ketchum, 1994).

Hypnosis also can lead to measurable physical and behavioural changes in the body. One well-established effect is **hypnotic analgesia,** *the reduction of pain through hypnosis in people who are susceptible to hypnosis.* For example, one classic study (see **FIGURE 5.14**) found that for pain induced in volunteers in the laboratory, hypnosis was more effective than morphine, diazepam (Valium), aspirin, acupuncture, or placebos (Stern et al., 1977). The pain-reducing properties of hypnosis have been demonstrated repeatedly over the years, with recent research from controlled trials suggesting that it can even reduce the experience of pain in brain surgery during which the patient is awake (Frati et al., 2019).

It therefore appears that people under hypnotic suggestion are not merely telling the hypnotist what they want to hear. Rather, they seem to be experiencing what they have been asked to experience.

Hypnotic paralysis and posthypnotic amnesia were both on display, with evil intent, in the hit movie *Get Out*.

posthypnotic amnesia The failure to retrieve memories following hypnotic suggestions to forget.

hypnotic analgesia The reduction of pain through hypnosis in people who are susceptible to hypnosis.

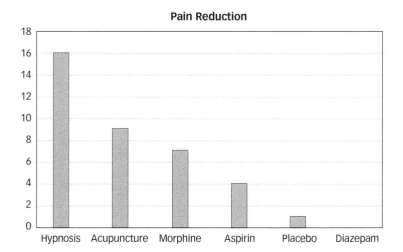

Pain Reduction

[Bar chart showing pain reduction values for different techniques: Hypnosis ≈ 16, Acupuncture ≈ 9, Morphine ≈ 7, Aspirin = 4, Placebo = 1, Diazepam = 0. Y-axis ranges from 0 to 18.]

Figure 5.14

Hypnotic Analgesia The degree of pain reduction (values represent differences between experimental and control conditions on a self-reported pain scale) reported by people using different techniques for the treatment of laboratory-induced pain. Hypnosis wins (Stern et al., 1977).

Chapter Review

The Mysteries of Consciousness

- People judge mind perception according to the capacities for experience and agency.
- Research suggests that mental activity happens first, paving the way for both conscious thought and action.

The Nature of Consciousness

- Consciousness has four basic properties: intentionality, unity, selectivity, and transience. It can also be understood in terms of levels: minimal consciousness, full consciousness, and self-consciousness.
- Disorders of consciousness result from illness or severe brain damage and include coma, vegetative state, and minimally conscious state. In locked-in syndrome, people can have normal conscious awareness but be unable to signal it behaviourally.
- Conscious contents can include current concerns, daydreams, and unwanted thoughts. Efforts to suppress a thought—such as of a white bear—may backfire as the mind searches for thoughts of that white bear to suppress.

The Unconscious Mind

- Unconscious processes are sometimes understood as expressions of the Freudian dynamic unconscious, but they are more commonly viewed as processes of the cognitive unconscious that create our conscious thought and behaviour.
- The cognitive unconscious is at work when subliminal perception and unconscious decision processes influence thought or behaviour without the person's awareness.

Sleep and Dreaming: Good Night, Mind

- Sleeping and dreaming present a view of the mind in an altered state of consciousness. During a night's sleep, the brain passes in and out of five stages of sleep; most dreaming occurs in the REM sleep stage.

- Sleep needs decrease over the life span, but being deprived of sleep and dreams has psychological and physical costs. Sleep can be disrupted through disorders that include insomnia, sleep apnea, somnambulism, narcolepsy, sleep paralysis, and night terrors.
- Dream consciousness differs from the waking state in that we feel emotion intensely, thought is illogical, and sensation is fully formed and meaningful; images and events occur with uncritical acceptance; and dreams are difficult to remember.
- Theories of dreaming include Freud's psychoanalytic theory and the activation–synthesis model. FMRI studies of the brain while dreaming reveal activations associated with visual imagery, increased sensitivity to emotions such as fear, lessened capacities for planning, and the prevention of motor movement.

Drugs and Consciousness: Artificial Inspiration

- Psychoactive drugs influence consciousness by altering the brain's chemical messaging system and intensifying or dulling the effects of neurotransmitters. Drug tolerance can result in overdose, and physical and psychological dependence can lead to addiction.
- Depressants reduce activity of the central nervous system (CNS); stimulants excite the CNS; narcotics relieve pain; hallucinogens alter sensation and perception; and marijuana is mildly hallucinogenic.

Hypnosis: Open to Suggestion

- Hypnosis is an altered state of consciousness characterized by suggestibility.
- Although many claims for hypnosis overstate its effects, hypnosis can create the experience that one's actions are occurring involuntarily and even relieve pain, suggesting that hypnotic experiences are more than imagination.

Changing Minds

1. "I had a really weird dream last night," your friend tells you. "I dreamed that I was trying to fly like a bird but I kept flying into clotheslines. I looked it up online, and dreams where you're struggling to fly mean that there is someone in your life who's standing in your way and preventing you from moving forward. I suppose that has to be my boyfriend, so maybe I'd better break up with him." Applying what you've read in this chapter, what would you tell your friend about the reliability of dream interpretation?

2. During an early-morning class, you notice your friend yawning, and you ask if they slept well the night before. "On weekdays, I'm in class all day, and I work the night shift," your friend says. "So I don't sleep much during the week. But I figure it's okay because I make up for it by sleeping late on Saturday mornings." Is it realistic for your friend to assume that one can balance regular sleep deprivation with rebound sleep on the weekends?

3. You and a friend are watching the 2010 movie *Inception,* starring Leonardo DiCaprio as a corporate spy. DiCaprio's character is hired by a businessman named Saito to plant an idea in the unconscious mind of a competitor while he sleeps. According to the plan, when the competitor awakens, he'll be compelled to act on the idea, to the secret benefit of Saito's company. "It's a cool idea," your friend says, "but it's pure science fiction. There's no such thing as an unconscious mind, and no way that unconscious ideas could influence the way you act when you're conscious." What would you tell your friend? What evidence do we have that the unconscious mind does exist and can influence conscious behaviour?

4. **Visualizing Data** A friend says, "I have so many classes and so much homework to do, I just can't take much time to sleep." Using the DATA, convince your friend whether or not this is a good way to think.

Key Terms

consciousness (p. 158)

phenomenology (p. 158)

problem of other minds (p. 159)

mind–body problem (p. 160)

dichotic listening (p. 163)

cocktail-party phenomenon (p. 163)

minimal consciousness (p. 164)

full consciousness (p. 164)

self-consciousness (p. 164)

mental control (p. 170)

thought suppression (p. 170)

rebound effect of thought suppression (p. 170)

ironic processes of mental control (p. 171)

dynamic unconscious (p. 172)

repression (p. 172)

cognitive unconscious (p. 172)

dual process theories (p. 173)

altered state of consciousness (p. 174)

circadian rhythm (p. 174)

REM sleep (p. 175)

electrooculograph (EOG) (p. 175)

insomnia (p. 178)

sleep apnea (p. 179)

somnambulism (sleepwalking) (p. 179)

narcolepsy (p. 179)

sleep paralysis (p. 179)

sleep terrors (night terrors) (p. 179)

manifest content (p. 181)

latent content (p. 181)

activation–synthesis model (p. 182)

psychoactive drugs (p. 184)

drug tolerance (p. 186)

depressants (p. 188)

expectancy theory (p. 189)

balanced placebo design (p. 189)

alcohol myopia (p. 190)

stimulants (p. 190)

narcotics (opiates) (p. 192)

hallucinogens (p. 192)

marijuana (cannabis) (p. 194)

gateway drug (p. 194)

hypnosis (p. 196)

posthypnotic amnesia (p. 197)

hypnotic analgesia (p. 197)

Memory

Jill Price can accurately remember just about everything that has happened to her during the past 30 years, as confirmed by her diary.

DAN TUFFS/GETTY IMAGES

JILL PRICE WAS 12 YEARS OLD when she began to suspect that she possessed an unusually good memory. While she was studying for a seventh-grade science final on May 30, her mind drifted and she became aware that she could recall vividly everything she had been doing on May 30 of the previous year. Remembering specifics of events that occurred a year ago may not seem so extraordinary—you can probably recall what you did for your last birthday or where you spent last Thanksgiving. But can you recall the details of what you did exactly 1 year ago today? Or what you did a week, a month, 6 months, or 6 years before that day? Probably not, but Jill Price can.

Jill can recall clearly and in great detail what has happened to her *every single day since early 1980* (Price & Davis, 2008). This is not just Jill's subjective impression. Dr. James McGaugh, a well-known memory researcher based at the University of California–Irvine, and his colleagues tested Jill's memory over a period of a few years and came up with some shocking results (E. S. Parker et al., 2006). For example, they asked Jill to recall the dates of each Easter from 1980 to 2003, which is a pretty tough task considering that Easter can fall on any day between March 22 and April 15. Even though she had no idea that she would be asked this question, Jill recalled the correct dates quickly and easily; nobody else the researchers tested came close. The researchers also asked Jill about the details of what she had been doing on various randomly chosen dates, and they checked Jill's recall against her personal diary. Again, Jill answered quickly and accurately: *July 1, 1986?*— "I see it all, that day, that month, that summer. Tuesday. Went with (friend's name) to (restaurant name)." *October 3, 1987?*— "That was a Saturday. Hung out at the apartment all weekend, wearing a sling—hurt my elbow." (E. S. Parker et al., 2006, pp. 39–40).

Researchers still don't understand all the reasons that Jill Price can remember her past so much more fully than the rest of us, but it turns out that Jill is not alone. Jill's extraordinary memory abilities became widely known after a *60 Minutes* story that featured her and Dr. McGaugh. That story elicited a flurry of inquiries to Dr. McGaugh from other people around the world who thought that they, too, possessed the spectacular memory abilities demonstrated by Jill. Although most of them did not, McGaugh and his colleagues

(LePort et al., 2012) identified 11 other individuals with "highly superior autobiographical memory" (HSAM) abilities that resemble those they had seen in Jill Price. The researchers discovered differences in the structure of several brain regions known to be involved in memory in the HSAM group compared with a control group. More recent work using functional MRI has revealed that people with HSAM show increased coupling between memory-related brain regions when they recall past experiences (De Marco et al., 2021; Santangelo et al., 2018). These findings suggest that further study of these unusual individuals might help to unravel the nature of memory more generally.

THE EASE WITH WHICH SOMEONE SUCH AS JILL CAN INSTANTLY REMEMBER HER PAST shouldn't blind us to appreciating how complex that act of remembering really is. Because memory is so remarkably complex, it is also remarkably fragile (Schacter, 1996). We all have had the experience of forgetting something we desperately wanted to remember or of remembering something that never really happened. Why does memory serve us so well in some situations and play such cruel tricks on us in other cases? Is there just one kind of memory, or are there many? These are among the questions that psychologists have asked and answered, and that we'll discuss in this chapter. We'll start by answering the fundamental question: What is memory?

What Is Memory?

Memory is *the ability to store and retrieve information over time.* Even though few of us possess the extraordinary memory abilities of Jill Price and the handful of others with highly superior autobiographical memory, each of us has a unique identity that is intricately tied to the things we have thought, felt, done, and experienced. Memories are the residue of those events, the enduring changes that experience makes in our brains and leaves behind when it passes. If an experience passes without leaving a trace, it might just as well not have happened.

As you've seen in other chapters, the mind's mistakes provide key insights into its fundamental operation, and there is no better illustration of this than in the realm of memory. There are three key functions of memory: **encoding,** *the process of transforming what we perceive, think, or feel into an enduring memory;* **storage,** *the process of maintaining information in memory over time;* and **retrieval,** *the process of bringing to mind information that has been previously encoded and stored.*

memory The ability to store and retrieve information over time.

encoding The process of transforming what we perceive, think, or feel into an enduring memory.

storage The process of maintaining information in memory over time.

retrieval The process of bringing to mind information that has been previously encoded and stored.

Encoding: Transforming Perceptions Into Memories

Learning Outcomes

WHAT YOU NEED TO KNOW

- Explain how memory is a construction and not a recording of new information.
- Describe the three main ways that information is encoded into the brain.
- Give reasons why we remember survival-related information so well.

```
     2 8
    6 9 1
   0 4 7 3
  8 7 4 5 4
 9 0 2 4 8 1
5 7 4 2 2 9 6
 6 4 7 1 9 3 0 4
3 5 6 7 1 8 4 8 5
1 0 2 8 8 3 4 7 2 9
4 7 2 0 8 2 7 4 2 6 4
7 3 1 0 9 3 4 3 5 1 3 8
```

Figure 6.1

Digit Memory Test How many digits can you remember? Start on the first row and cover the rows below it with a piece of paper. Study the numbers in the row for 1 second and then cover that row back up again. After a couple of seconds, try to repeat the numbers. Then uncover the row to see if you were correct. If so, continue down to the next row, using the same instructions, until you can't recall all the numbers in a row. The number of digits in the last row you can remember correctly is your digit span. Bubbles P. could remember 20 random numbers, or about five rows deep. How did you do?

semantic encoding The process of relating new information in a meaningful way to knowledge that is already stored in memory.

Bubbles P., a professional gambler with no formal education who spent most of his time shooting craps at local clubs or playing high-stakes poker, had no difficulty rattling off 20 numbers, in either forward or backward order, after just a single glance (Ceci et al., 1992). Most people can listen to a list of numbers and then repeat them from memory—as long as the list is no more than about seven items long. (Try it for yourself using **FIGURE 6.1**.)

How did Bubbles accomplish his astounding feats of memory? For at least 2,000 years, people have thought of memory as a recording device that makes exact copies of the information that comes in through our senses and then stores those copies for later use. This idea is simple and intuitive. It is also completely incorrect. We make memories by combining information we *already* have in our brains with new information that comes in through our senses. In this way, memory is like cooking; starting from a recipe but improvising along the way, we add old information to new information, mix, shake, and bake, and out pops a memory. Memories are *constructed*, not recorded, and encoding is the process by which we transform what we perceive, think, or feel into an enduring memory. Let's look at three types of encoding processes—semantic encoding, visual imagery encoding, and organizational encoding—and then consider how encoding had possible survival value for our ancestors.

Semantic Encoding

Because memories are a combination of old and new information, the nature of any particular memory depends as much on the old information already in our memories as it does on the new information coming in through our senses. In other words, how we remember something depends on how we think about it at the time. For example, as a professional gambler, Bubbles found numbers unusually meaningful, so when he saw a string of digits, he tended to think about their meanings. However, when Bubbles was tested with materials other than numbers—faces, words, objects, or locations—his memory performance was no better than average. Most of us, unlike Bubbles, can't remember 20 digits, but we can remember 20 experiences (a favourite camping trip, a 16th birthday party, a first day at university, and so on). One reason is that we often think about the meaning behind our experiences, so we semantically encode them without even trying (Craik & Tulving, 1975). **Semantic encoding** is *the process of relating new information in a meaningful way to knowledge that is already stored in memory* (Brown & Craik, 2000).

In a seminal experiment, Toronto researchers Fergus Craik and Endel Tulving presented participants with a series of words and asked them to make one of three types of judgements (Craik & Tulving, 1975):

- *Semantic judgements* required the participants to think about the meaning of the words (Is *hat* a type of clothing?).
- *Rhyme judgements* required the participants to think about the sound of the words (Does *hat* rhyme with *cat*?).
- *Case judgements* required the participants to think about the appearance of the words (Is *HAT* written in uppercase or lowercase?).

The type of judgement task influenced how participants thought about each word—what old information they combined with the new—and had a powerful impact on their memories. Those participants who made semantic judgements (i.e., thought about the meaning of the words) had much better memory for the words than did participants who thought about how the words looked or sounded.

The results of these and many other studies have shown that long-term retention is greatly enhanced by semantic encoding.

So where does this semantic encoding take place? What's going on in the brain when this type of information processing occurs? Studies reveal that semantic encoding is uniquely associated with increased activity in the lower left part of the frontal lobe and the inner part of the left temporal lobe (**FIGURE 6.2a**) (Demb et al., 1995; Kapur et al., 1994; Wagner et al., 1998). In fact, the amount of activity in each of these two regions during encoding is directly related to whether people later remember an item. The more activity there is in these areas, the more likely the person will remember the information.

a. Semantic Judgements

b. Visual Judgements

c. Organizational Judgements

Figure 6.2
Brain Activity During Different Types of Judgements Evidence from fMRI studies reveals that different parts of the brain are active during different types of judgements: (a) During semantic encoding, the lower left frontal lobe is active; (b) during visual imagery encoding, the occipital lobe is active; and (c) during organizational encoding, the upper left frontal lobe is active.

Alex Mullen, world memory champion, can quickly remember the order of a deck of playing cards and much more.

Pen and paper are optional for some servers who have figured out how to use organizational encoding.

visual imagery encoding The process of storing new information by converting it into mental pictures.

organizational encoding The process of categorizing information according to the relationships among a series of items.

Visual Imagery Encoding

In Athens in 477 BCE, the Greek poet Simonides had just left a banquet when the ceiling collapsed and killed all the people inside. Simonides was able to name every one of the dead simply by visualizing each chair around the banquet table and recalling the person who had been sitting there. Simonides wasn't the first—but he was among the most proficient at it—to use **visual imagery encoding,** *the process of storing new information by converting it into mental pictures.*

Numerous experiments have shown that visual imagery encoding can substantially improve memory. In one experiment, participants who studied lists of words by creating visual images of them later recalled twice as many items as participants who just mentally repeated the words (Schnorr & Atkinson, 1969). Contemporary "memory athletes," who compete in increasingly popular memory championships, typically rely on visual imagery encoding to accomplish astounding feats of memorization (Dresler et al., 2017). Alex Mullen, an American medical student, used visual imagery encoding to memorize the order of a deck of playing cards in under 16 seconds! This world record helped Alex to win the World Memory Championship in 2017. Researchers recently tested a smartphone app that provided training in using visual imagery to encode new information for adults ranging in age from 20 to 90 years (Sandberg et al., 2021). They found that the training improved memory performance on a task that required encoding and recalling the order of a sequence of pictures in all but the oldest adults.

Why does visual imagery encoding work so well? First, visual imagery encoding does some of the same things that semantic encoding does: When you create a visual image, you relate incoming information to knowledge already in memory. For example, a visual image of a fireworks finale might help you create a link to your memory of last July 1, or your first trip to Disney World.

Second, when you use visual imagery to encode words and other verbal information, you end up with two different mental *placeholders* for the items—a visual one and a verbal one—which gives you more ways to remember the items than just a verbal placeholder alone (Paivio, 1971, 1986). Visual imagery encoding activates visual processing regions in the occipital lobe (see Figure 6.2b), which suggests that people actually enlist the visual system when forming memories based on mental images (Kosslyn et al., 1993; Pearson & Kosslyn, 2015). Neuroimaging evidence shows that training ordinary people to use visual imagery encoding produces neural changes in visual and memory networks that support enhanced memory performance (Dresler et al., 2017). However, visual imagery encoding requires a great deal of cognitive effort to use successfully, which can limit its practical use for real-world activities such as studying for exams (see the Learning in the Classroom section in the Learning chapter).

Organizational Encoding

Have you ever ordered dinner with a group of friends and watched in amazement as your server took the order without writing anything down and yet brought everyone the food they ordered? To find out how this is done, one researcher wired servers in a restaurant with microphones and asked them to think aloud, that is, to say what they were thinking as they walked around all day doing their jobs (Stevens, 1988). Recordings showed that as soon as the server left a customer's table, they immediately began *grouping* or *categorizing* the orders into hot drinks, cold drinks, hot foods, and cold foods. The servers remembered their orders by relying on **organizational encoding,** *the process of categorizing information according to the relationships among a series of items.*

For example, suppose you had to memorize the words *peach, cow, chair, apple, table, cherry, lion, couch, horse, desk.* The task seems difficult, but if you organize the

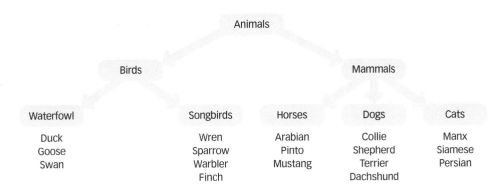

Figure 6.3
Organizing Words Into a
Hierarchy Organizing words into
conceptual groups and relating them
to each other—as in this example
of a hierarchy—makes it easier to
reconstruct the items from memory
later (Bower et al., 1969). Keeping
track of the 17 items in this example
can be facilitated by remembering the
hierarchical groupings they fall under.

items into three categories—fruit (*peach, apple, cherry*), animals (*cow, lion, horse*), and furniture (*chair, table, couch, desk*)—the task becomes much easier. Studies have shown that instructing people to sort items into categories is an effective way to enhance their subsequent recall of those items (Mandler, 1967). Even more complex organizational schemes have been used, such as the hierarchy in **FIGURE 6.3** (Bower et al., 1969). People can improve their recall of individual items by organizing them into multiple-level categories, all the way from a general category such as *animals,* through intermediate categories such as *birds* and *songbirds,* down to specific examples such as *wren* and *sparrow.*

Of course, organizational encoding is not just for word lists. In everyday life, we organize our current experiences by segmenting the ongoing flow of events into meaningful units (Kurby & Zacks, 2008). For example, we might segment a shopping trip into event units such as driving to the mall, walking from the parking lot, returning a gift to H&M, checking out the Apple store, and so forth. A recent study showed that when people view movies composed of everyday activities, segmenting the movie into meaningful event units during encoding enhanced subsequent memory for those events, compared to encoding without event segmentation; the memory benefit was evident at delays ranging from 10 minutes to 1 month (Flores et al., 2017).

Just as semantic and visual imagery encoding activate distinct regions of the brain, so, too, does organizational encoding. As you can see in Figure 6.2c, organizational encoding activates the upper surface of the left frontal lobe (Fletcher et al., 1998; Savage et al., 2001). Different types of encoding strategies appear to rely on the activation of different areas of the brain. However, all three forms of encoding can be used as **mnemonics,** which are *encoding strategies that improve subsequent retrieval.* The semantic encoding strategy used by Bubbles P. to recall numbers, the visual imagery encoding strategy used by Alex Mullen to memorize a deck of cards, and the organizational encoding strategy used by restaurant servers to remember orders are all examples of mnemonics that greatly aid subsequent memory.

Encoding of Survival-Related Information

Encoding new information is critical to many aspects of everyday life: Prospects for attaining your degree would be pretty slim without this ability. According to the evolutionary perspective, which is based on Darwin's principle of natural selection, features of an organism that help it survive and reproduce are more likely than other features to be passed on to subsequent generations (see The Evolution of Psychological Science chapter). Therefore, memory mechanisms that help us survive and reproduce should be preserved by natural selection. Our memory systems should be built in a way that allows us to remember especially well the encoded information that is relevant to our survival, such as sources of food and water and the location of predators.

mnemonics Encoding strategies that improve subsequent retrieval.

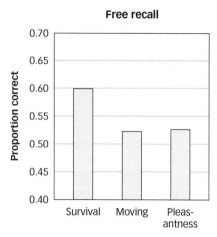

Free recall

Figure 6.4
Encoding of Survival-Related Information Enhances Later Recall
People recall more words after survival-encoding tasks than after moving or pleasantness-encoding tasks (Nairne et al., 2007). Explain this from your understanding of the three main kinds of encoding discussed in this chapter.

To test this idea, researchers gave participants three different encoding tasks (Nairne et al., 2007). In the first task, a survival-encoding condition, participants were asked to imagine they were stranded in the grasslands of a foreign land without any survival materials. They were told that over the next few months, they would need supplies of food and water and also need to protect themselves from predators. The researchers then showed participants randomly chosen words (e.g., *stone, meadow, chair*) and asked them to rate on a 1–5 scale how relevant each item would be to survival in the hypothetical situation. In a second task, a moving-encoding condition, a second group of participants was asked to imagine that they were planning to move to a new home in a foreign land, and to rate on a 1–5 scale how useful each item might be in helping them set up a new home. In the third task, the pleasantness-encoding condition, a third group was shown the same words and asked to rate on a 1–5 scale the pleasantness of each word.

The findings, displayed in **FIGURE 6.4**, show that participants recalled more words after the survival-encoding task than after either the moving or pleasantness tasks. In later studies, the researchers found that survival encoding resulted in higher levels of recall than several other non–survival-encoding tasks (Nairne et al., 2008). Exactly what about survival encoding produces such high levels of memory?

One advantage of encoding survival-related information is that it draws on elements of semantic, visual imagery, and organizational encoding (Burns et al., 2011), which together produce high levels of subsequent memory. Also, survival encoding encourages participants to think in detail about the goals they want to achieve and thus engage in extensive planning, which in turn benefits memory and may account for much of the benefit of survival encoding (Bell et al., 2015). For example, survival scenarios that *do* involve planning produce superior subsequent memory compared with survival scenarios that do *not* involve planning. It is critical that superior recall is also observed for scenarios that *involve planning but not survival,* such as planning a dinner party (Klein et al., 2011). Of course, planning for the future is itself critical for our long-term survival, so these findings are still broadly consistent with the evolutionary perspective that memory is built to enhance our chances of survival (Klein et al., 2011; Schacter, 2012; Suddendorf & Corballis, 2007).

Storage: Maintaining Memories Over Time

Learning Outcomes

WHAT YOU NEED TO KNOW

- Distinguish sensory memory from short-term memory.

- Describe the elements of the model of working memory.

- Explain the interrelationship between memory and the hippocampus.

- Summarize the role of the neural synapse in long-term memory storage.

Encoding is the process of turning perceptions into memories. But one of the hallmarks of a memory is that you can bring it to mind on Tuesday, not bring it to mind on Wednesday, and then bring it to mind again on Thursday. So where are our memories when we aren't using them? Clearly, those memories are stored in some form in your brain. As pointed out earlier, *storage is the process of maintaining information in memory over time.* There are three major kinds of memory storage: sensory, short-term, and long-term. As these names suggest, the three kinds of storage are distinguished primarily by the amount of time over which a memory is retained.

Sensory Storage

Sensory memory is *a type of storage that holds sensory information for a few seconds or less.* In a series of classic experiments, research participants were asked to remember rows of letters (Sperling, 1960). In one version of the procedure, participants viewed three rows of four letters each, as shown in **FIGURE 6.5**. The researcher flashed the letters on a screen for just 1/20th of a second. When asked to remember all 12 of the letters they had just seen, participants recalled fewer than half. There were two possible explanations for this:

- People simply couldn't encode all the letters in such a brief period of time.
- People encoded the letters but forgot them while trying to recall everything they had seen.

To test the two ideas, the researcher relied on a clever trick. Just after the letters disappeared from the screen, a tone sounded that cued the participants to report the letters in a particular row. A *high* tone cued participants to report the contents of the top row, a *medium* tone cued participants to report the contents of the middle row, and a *low* tone cued participants to report the contents of the bottom row. When asked to report only a single row, people recalled almost all of the letters in that row! Because the tone sounded after the letters disappeared from the screen and the participants had no way of knowing which of the three rows would be cued, the researcher inferred that virtually all the letters had been encoded. In fact, if the tone was substantially delayed, participants couldn't perform the task because the information had slipped away from their sensory memories. Like the afterimage of a flashlight, the 12 letters flashed on a screen are visual icons, a lingering trace stored in memory for a very short period.

Because we have more than one sense, we have more than one kind of sensory memory. **Iconic memory** is *a fast-decaying store of visual information.* **Echoic memory** is *a fast-decaying store of auditory information.* When you have difficulty understanding what someone has just said, you probably find yourself replaying the last few words — listening to them echo in your "mind's ear," so to speak. What you are actually doing is accessing information that is being held in your echoic memory store. The hallmark of both the iconic and echoic memory stores is that they hold information for a very short time. Iconic memories usually decay in about 1 second or less, and echoic memories usually decay in about 5 seconds (Darwin et al., 1972).

These two sensory memory stores are a bit like doughnut shops: The products come in, they sit briefly on the shelf, and then they are discarded. If you want one, you have to grab it fast. But how to grab it? If information from sensory memory is quickly lost, how do we recall it at all? The key is attention, which brings us to short-term memory (see **FIGURE 6.6**).

Short-Term Storage and Working Memory

A second kind of memory storage is **short-term memory,** *a type of storage that holds nonsensory information for more than a few seconds but less than a minute.* We need to attend to incoming information for it to enter short-term memory, but as soon as we attend to something else, the information is quickly lost. For example, if someone tells you a telephone number and you pay attention to what they say, you can usually

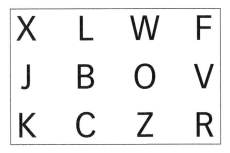

Figure 6.5

Iconic Memory Test When a grid of letters is flashed on screen for only 1/20th of a second, it is difficult to recall individual letters. But if prompted to remember a particular row immediately after the grid is shown, research participants will do so with high accuracy. Sperling used this procedure to demonstrate that although iconic memory stores the whole grid, the information fades away too quickly for a person to recall everything (Sperling, 1960).

sensory memory A type of storage that holds sensory information for a few seconds or less.

iconic memory A fast-decaying store of visual information.

echoic memory A fast-decaying store of auditory information.

short-term memory A type of storage that holds nonsensory information for more than a few seconds but less than a minute.

Figure 6.6

The Flow of Information Through the Memory System Information moves through several stages of memory as it gets encoded, stored, and made available for later retrieval.

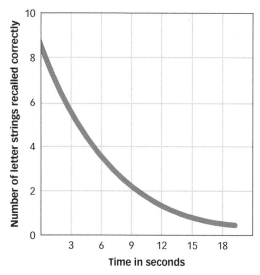

Figure 6.7

The Decline of Short-Term Memory
A 1959 experiment showed how quickly short-term memory fades without rehearsal. On a test for memory of three-letter strings, research participants were highly accurate when tested a few seconds after exposure to each string, but if the test was delayed another 15 seconds, people barely recalled the strings at all (Peterson & Peterson, 1959).

Which of the books in the Harry Potter series are you likely to most easily recall, according to the serial position effect?

rehearsal The process of keeping information in short-term memory by mentally repeating it.

serial position effect The observation that the first few and last few items in a series are more likely to be recalled than the items in the middle.

chunking Combining small pieces of information into larger clusters or chunks that are more easily held in short-term memory.

repeat it back with ease—but you will quickly lose the information as soon as your attention focuses on anything else. In one study, research participants were given consonant strings to remember, such as DBX and HLM. After seeing each string, participants were asked to count backward from 100 by 3 for varying amounts of time and were then asked to recall the consonant strings (Peterson & Peterson, 1959). As shown in **FIGURE 6.7**, memory for the consonant strings declined rapidly, from approximately 80% after a 3-second delay to virtually nothing after a 20-second delay. These results suggest that information can be held in the short-term memory store for about 15 to 20 seconds.

Rehearsal and "Chunking" Strengthen Memory

What if 15 to 20 seconds isn't enough time? What if we need the information for a while longer? We can use a trick that allows us to get around the natural limitations of our short-term memories. **Rehearsal** is *the process of keeping information in short-term memory by mentally repeating it*. If someone gives you a telephone number and you can't immediately enter it into your cell phone or write it down, you say it over and over to yourself until you can. Each time you repeat the number, you are reentering it into short-term memory, giving it another 15 to 20 seconds of shelf life.

Rehearsal can play a role in the **serial position effect,** which refers to *the observation that the first few and last few items in a series are more likely to be recalled than the items in the middle*. Enhanced recall of the first few items in, say, a list of words is called the *primacy effect*. It occurs because these items receive more rehearsals than subsequent items in the middle of the list and thus are more likely to be encoded into long-term storage. Enhanced recall of the last few items is called the *recency effect* and can result from rehearsing items that are still in short-term storage (Atkinson & Shiffrin, 1968). Consistent with this interpretation, classic studies showed that the recency effect—but not the primacy effect—is eliminated when participants count backward by 3s after the final list item is presented, which prevents them from relying on short-term storage to rehearse the last few items (Glanzer & Cunitz, 1966). However, both primacy and recency effects can be observed in situations that involve only long-term storage, such as recalling the order of the seven Harry Potter books (Kelley et al., 2013). When participants who were familiar with the Harry Potter series were asked to recall the order in which the seven books were published, they were quite accurate in recalling that *Harry Potter and the Sorcerer's Stone* and *Harry Potter and the Chamber of Secrets* were the first two books in the series and that *Harry Potter and the Half-Blood Prince* and *Harry Potter and the Deathly Hallows* were the last two, but were less accurate in remembering the order of the middle three books. These kinds of findings indicate that serial position effects occur in everyday life.

Short-term memory is limited in *how long* it can hold information, as well as in *how much* information it can hold. Not only can most people keep approximately seven numbers in short-term memory but also if they put more new numbers in, then old numbers begin to fall out (Miller, 1956). Short-term memory isn't limited to numbers, of course. It can also hold about seven letters or seven words—even though those seven words contain many more than seven letters. In fact, short-term memory can hold about seven *meaningful items* at once (Miller, 1956). Therefore, one way to increase storage is to group several letters into a single meaningful item. **Chunking** involves *combining small pieces of information into larger clusters or chunks that are more easily held in short-term memory*. Servers in restaurants who use organizational encoding to organize customer orders into groups are essentially chunking the information, giving themselves less to remember.

Working Memory Stores and Manipulates Information

Short-term memory was originally conceived as a kind of "place" where information is kept for a limited amount of time. More recently, researchers have developed

Figure 6.8
A Refined Model of Working Memory
The working memory system consists of a central executive that controls the flow of information through the system; a visuo-spatial sketchpad and phonological loop that temporarily hold visual/spatial images and verbal/auditory information, respectively; and an episodic buffer that integrates the various kinds of information that are maintained by the visuo-spatial sketchpad and phonological loop (Baddeley et al., 2011).

and refined a more dynamic model of a limited-capacity memory system, called **working memory,** which refers to *active maintenance of information in short-term storage* (Baddeley & Hitch, 1974). As illustrated in **FIGURE 6.8**, working memory includes two subsystems that store and manipulate information—one for visual images (the *visuo-spatial sketchpad*) and another for verbal information (the *phonological loop*). It also involves an *episodic buffer* that integrates visual and verbal information from the subsystems into a multidimensional code, as well as a *central executive* that coordinates the subsystems and the episodic buffer (Baddeley, 2001; Baddeley et al., 2011).

In practical terms, say you were using Google Maps on your phone to walk to a new destination and wanted to keep the arrangement of locations on the map in mind as you contemplated your next move. You'd be relying on your visuo-spatial sketchpad to hold the visual representation of the locations on the map. You might also enlist the phonological loop to hold onto the upcoming street names and rely on your central executive to control mental manipulation of the directions and awareness of the flow of information into and out of memory, all stored for a limited amount of time. In short, the working memory model acknowledges both the limited nature of this kind of memory storage and the activities that are commonly associated with it.

Research conducted in the context of this model has taught us that working memory plays an important role in many aspects of our cognitive lives (Baddeley, 2012). For example, studies of individuals with neurological damage to the phonological loop subsystem of working memory reveal that not only do those individuals have problems holding on to strings of digits and letters for a few seconds, but they also have difficulty learning novel words. This suggests a link between this part of the working memory system and the ability to learn language (Baddeley & Hitch, 2019; Gathercole, 2008). Recent research has even linked working memory to compliance with social distancing guidelines during the early stages of the COVID-19 pandemic (Xie et al., 2020). In two online studies conducted in March 2020 that included 850 participants, Xie and colleagues found that a measure of working memory capacity predicted individual differences in self-reported compliance with social distancing guidelines, even when accounting for other influences such as education, intelligence, age, and socioeconomic status. Participants with higher working memory capacity were more likely to report having engaged in social distancing practices during the past week, such as avoiding social gatherings and refraining from handshakes, hugs, and kisses when greeting others, than participants with lower working memory capacity. A possible explanation for this relationship is that compliance with social distancing guidelines requires prioritizing the benefits of social distancing over its costs, which likely requires holding, manipulating, and comparing multiple bits of information in working memory (Xie et al., 2020).

Brain-imaging studies indicate that the central executive component of working memory depends on regions within the frontal lobe that are important for controlling and manipulating information on a wide range of cognitive tasks (Baddeley, 2001; D'Esposito & Postle, 2015). Children who score low on working memory tasks have difficulty learning new information and performing well in the classroom (Alloway et al., 2009), which has led researchers to focus increasingly on trying to understand the impact of working memory problems on cognitive development (Alloway, 2018).

In everyday life, we draw on working memory when using our phones to navigate novel environments.

working memory Active maintenance of information in short-term storage.

Researchers only recently have begun to study the episodic buffer. In a typical experiment, people perform tasks in which they need to combine different kinds of information, such as colours, shapes, and sounds, and hold that information over a brief period of time. Evidence from such experiments suggests that the episodic buffer automatically combines separate items into an integrated whole (Baddeley et al., 2011) and is a gateway to long-term memory, which we will discuss at length in the section on explicit memory later in this chapter. The episodic buffer plays a role in learning to recognize words, which requires combining visual and verbal information. Recent studies of grade school children and young adults showed that the ability to link together visual and auditory information and hold it in working memory, a task thought to depend on the episodic buffer, shows marked increases with age and is associated with word recognition skills, even when controlling for the ability to hold the individual items in working memory (Wang & Allen, 2018; Wang et al., 2015). Baddeley and colleagues (2011) have suggested that the episodic buffer also integrates other kinds of sensory information, such as smell and taste (see Figure 6.8), but research is needed to explore this possibility.

Examining the Link Between Working Memory Training and Cognitive Functioning

Can working memory skills be improved through training, and can such training enhance cognitive functioning? This question has become a hot research topic over the past decade (Klingberg, 2010; Pappa et al., 2020; Shipstead et al., 2012; Soveri et al., 2017). In typical studies, participants are first given extensive practice in performing working memory tasks that require the maintenance and manipulation of visual or verbal information. They are then tested on new working memory tasks for which they have not been specifically trained, as well as on other cognitive tasks (reasoning, comprehension, or paying sustained attention). Some encouraging results have been reported. For example, elementary school students who were trained on several working memory tasks (about 35 minutes/day for at least 20 days over a 5- to 7-week period) showed improvement on other working memory tasks when compared with untrained children (Holmes et al., 2009). These gains were evident even when the children were tested 6 months after training. There was also some evidence of improvement on math tasks. However, many working memory training studies are inconclusive as to whether the training in particular is responsible for the effects that are observed (Slagter, 2012).

Furthermore, several studies have found that working memory training improved performance on the working memory task that was "trained" but did not result in improvements on other cognitive tasks (Redick et al., 2013), including other working memory tasks (De Simoni & von Bastian, 2018). More research will be needed to determine whether working memory training produces any general improvements in cognitive performance and, if so, whether the improvements are large enough to affect performance on everyday cognitive tasks (Au et al., 2015; Redick, 2015; Shipstead et al., 2012). However, the current evidence is consistent with the conclusion that in working memory training studies, people learn specific strategies to perform specific tasks, and not much more than that (De Simoni & von Bastian, 2018; Soveri et al., 2017).

Long-Term Storage

In contrast to the time-limited sensory and short-term storage stores, **long-term memory** is *a type of storage that holds information for hours, days, weeks, or years.* In contrast to both sensory and short-term storage, long-term memory has no known capacity limits (see Figure 6.6). For example, most people can recall 10,000 to 15,000 words in their native language; tens of thousands of facts (the capital of France is Paris, and $3 \times 3 = 9$); and an untold number of personal experiences. Just think of all the song lyrics you can recite by heart, and you'll understand that you've got a lot of information tucked away in your long-term memory!

long-term memory A type of storage that holds information for hours, days, weeks, or years.

More amazing, people can recall items from long-term memory even if they haven't thought of those items for years. For instance, researchers have found that even 50 years after graduation, people can accurately recognize about 90% of their high school classmates from yearbook photographs (Bahrick, 2000). Such a feat is more remarkable when you consider that the people in the study probably had not accessed most of this information for years before the experiment.

The Hippocampus as Index: Linking Pieces Into One Memory

Where is long-term memory located in the brain? The clues to answering this question come from individuals who are unable to store long-term memories. In 1953, a 27-year-old man, known then by the initials HM, suffered from intractable epilepsy (Scoville & Milner, 1957). In a desperate attempt to stop the seizures, HM's doctors removed parts of his temporal lobes, including the hippocampus and some surrounding regions (**FIGURE 6.9**). After the operation, HM could converse easily, use and understand language, and perform well on intelligence tests, but he could not remember anything that happened to him after the operation. HM could repeat a telephone number with no difficulty, suggesting that his short-term memory store was just fine (Corkin, 2002, 2013; Hilts, 1995; Squire, 2009). But after information left the short-term store, it was gone forever. For example, he would often forget that he had just eaten a meal or fail to recognize the hospital staff who helped him on a daily basis. Studies of HM and others have shown that the hippocampal region of the brain is critical for putting new information into the long-term store (Clark & Maguire, 2016; Smith et al., 2013). Individuals who have sustained damage to this region suffer from a condition known as **anterograde amnesia,** which is *the inability to transfer new information from the short-term store into the long-term store.* HM's own words best describe what anterograde amnesia must be like: "Right now I'm wondering, have I done or said anything amiss? You see, at this moment everything looks clear to me, but what happened just before? That's what worries me. It's like waking from a dream; I just don't remember" (Milner, 1970).

Some individuals with amnesia also suffer from **retrograde amnesia,** which is *the inability to retrieve information that was acquired before a particular date, usually the date of an injury or surgery.* The fact that HM had much worse anterograde than retrograde amnesia suggests that the hippocampal region is not the site of long-term memory. Indeed, research has shown that different aspects of a single memory — its sights, sounds, smells, emotional content — are stored in different places in the

anterograde amnesia The inability to transfer new information from the short-term store into the long-term store.

retrograde amnesia The inability to retrieve information that was acquired before a particular date, usually the date of an injury or surgery.

Areas removed

Figure 6.9
The Hippocampus Patient HM had his hippocampus and adjacent structures of the medial temporal lobe (indicated by the shaded areas) surgically removed to stop his epileptic seizures (*left*). As a result, he could not remember things that happened after the surgery. Henry Molaison (*right*), better known to the world as patient HM, passed away on December 2, 2008, at the age of 82 at a nursing home near Hartford, Connecticut. Molaison's catastrophic inability to encode new long-term memories was discovered by Montreal psychologist Brenda Milner in 1953, and he participated in countless memory experiments between that time and his death. In so doing, he made fundamental contributions to our understanding of memory and the brain (Corkin, 2013).

cortex (Damasio, 1989; Schacter, 1996; Squire & Kandel, 1999). Some psychologists have argued that the hippocampal region acts as a kind of "index" that links together all these otherwise separate bits and pieces so that we remember them as one memory (Schacter, 1996; Squire, 1992; Teyler & DiScenna, 1986). Neuroscience studies support this "index view." Evidence from fMRI shows that activity in the hippocampus relates to retrieving as a holistic unit the separate elements, such as a person, a location, and an object, which were initially encoded by distinct regions in the cortex (Horner et al., 2015). Evidence from hippocampal cell firing patterns in mice also supports the idea that these cells are involved in memory formation and serve as an index that ties together memory contents stored elsewhere (Tanaka et al., 2018).

Over time, however, the hippocampal index may become less necessary. Returning to our cooking analogy, you can think of the hippocampal region index as a printed recipe. The first time you make a pie, you need the recipe to help you retrieve all the ingredients and then mix them together in the right amounts. As you bake more and more pies, though, you don't need to rely on the printed recipe anymore. Similarly, although the hippocampal region index is critical when a new memory is first formed, it may become less important as the memory ages. Another possibility is that the hippocampal index remains involved over long periods of time with some memories (highly detailed recollections of personal experiences, the kinds of memories that give us the feeling that we are almost reliving a past experience), but it does not stay involved in less detailed, more general memories (Harand et al., 2012; Winocur et al., 2010).

In terms of the cooking analogy again, you might need to rely on a recipe each time you cook a complex meal with many details, but not when you cook a simpler meal with a less detailed recipe. Scientists are still debating the extent to which the hippocampal region helps us remember details of our old memories (Bayley et al., 2005; Gilmore et al., 2021; Kirwan et al., 2008; Moscovitch et al., 2016; Squire & Wixted, 2011; Winocur et al., 2010). However, the notion of the hippocampus as an index explains why people such as HM cannot make new memories and why they can remember many old ones.

Consolidation Stabilizes Memories

The idea that the hippocampus becomes less important over time for maintaining memories is closely related to the concept of **consolidation,** *the process by which memories become stable in the brain* (McGaugh, 2000, 2015). Shortly after encoding, memories exist in a fragile state that can be disrupted easily; once consolidation has occurred, they are more resistant to disruption. One type of consolidation operates over seconds or minutes. For example, when someone experiences a head injury in a car crash and later cannot recall what happened during the few seconds or minutes before the crash—but can recall other events normally—the head injury probably prevented consolidation of short-term memory into long-term memory. Another type of consolidation occurs over much longer periods of time—days, weeks, months, and years—and likely involves transfer of information from the hippocampus to more permanent storage sites in the cortex. The operation of this longer-term consolidation process is why individuals who have retrograde amnesia with hippocampal damage can recall memories from childhood relatively normally but are impaired when recalling experiences that occurred just a few years prior to the time they became amnesic (Kirwan et al., 2008; Squire & Wixted, 2011).

How does a memory become consolidated? The act of recalling a memory, thinking about it, and talking about it with others probably contributes to consolidation (Moscovitch et al., 2006). And though you may not be aware of it, consolidation gets a boost from something that you do effortlessly every night: sleep. As explained in Hot Science: Can Sleep Enhance Learning? Yes!, mounting evidence gathered during the past decade indicates that sleep plays an important role in memory consolidation.

consolidation The process by which memories become stable in the brain.

Recalled Memories May Be Disrupted During Reconsolidation

Many researchers have long believed that a fully consolidated memory becomes a permanent fixture in the brain, more difficult to get rid of than a computer virus. But another line of research that has developed rapidly in recent years suggests that things are not so simple. Experiments have shown that even seemingly consolidated *memories can become vulnerable to disruption when they are recalled, thus requiring them to be consolidated again.* This process is called **reconsolidation** (Dudai, 2012; Nader & Hardt, 2009).

Early evidence for reconsolidation came from experiments with rats showing that when animals are cued to retrieve a new memory that was acquired a day earlier, giving the animal a drug (or an electrical shock) that prevents initial consolidation will cause forgetting (Nader et al., 2000; Sara, 2000). It is critical that if the animal is not actively retrieving the memory, the same drug (or shock) has no effect when given a day after initial encoding. Researchers have produced similar effects using electrical shocks in studies with people (Elsey et al., 2018; Schiller et al., 2010). This finding is surprising because it was once thought that when memories have been consolidated, drugs or shock that can prevent initial consolidation no longer have any impact. On the contrary, it now appears that each time memories are retrieved, they become vulnerable to disruption and must be reconsolidated.

Disrupting Reconsolidation May Reduce Traumatic Memories

Might it be possible one day to eliminate or modify painful memories by disrupting reconsolidation? Recent research from McGill University suggests it could be. When a traumatic event was reactivated in traumatized individuals who had been given a drug to reduce anxiety, there was a subsequent reduction in traumatic symptoms (Brunet et al., 2008, 2018). However, drugs are not necessary to disrupt reconsolidation of painful memories. Consider the traumatic events of April 15, 2013, when two bombs exploded near the finish line of the Boston Marathon, a famous international sporting event, killing three people and injuring over 250 others. Several months later, researchers asked undergraduates at Boston University (located near the site of the bombing) to recall where they were when they learned of the bombing, what they were doing, and how they felt (Kredlow & Otto, 2015). The students' memories were detailed, and they recalled feeling considerable distress at the time. One minute after this memory reactivation, during the reconsolidation phase when memories are vulnerable to disruption, some students read a negative story, others read either a positive or neutral story, and still others (the control group) did nothing.

The Boston Marathon bombings produced detailed and disturbing memories in people at or near the site of the bombings. However, research shows that the amount of detail in those memories can be reduced by interfering with their reconsolidation.

KEN MCGAGH/METROWEST DAILY NEWS/ AP IMAGES

All the students returned a week later and recalled their memories of the bombing again. Compared with the students in the control group, the students who read a negative story shortly after memory reactivation recalled significantly fewer details about the bombing than they had initially, whereas those who read positive or neutral stories showed smaller, nonsignificant reductions in recalled details. Reading the negative story appeared to interfere with reconsolidation of students' negative memories of the bombing. More recent research has revealed that similar approaches aimed at disrupting reconsolidation can reduce the impact of painful memories following a motor vehicle accident (Iyadurai et al., 2018).

Related work using fMRI indicates that disrupting reconsolidation can seemingly eliminate a fear memory in a part of the brain called the *amygdala,* which, as we will learn later in this chapter, plays a key role in emotional memory (Agren et al., 2012). Reconsolidation thus appears to be a key memory process with many important implications.

reconsolidation The process whereby memories can become vulnerable to disruption when they are recalled, thus requiring them to be consolidated again.

By studying the sea slug *Aplysia Californica's* extremely simple nervous system, researchers were able to determine that long-term memory storage depends on the growth of new synaptic connections between neurons.

Nobel Prize–winning neuroscientist Eric Kandel took a risk and studied the tiny sea slug *Aplysia* based in part on a lesson he had learned from his wife regarding their recent marriage, which encouraged him to trust his intuition: "Denise was confident that our marriage would work, so I took a leap of faith and went ahead. I learned from that experience that there are many situations in which one cannot decide on the basis of cold facts alone—because the facts are often insufficient. One ultimately has to trust one's unconscious, one's instincts, one's creative urge. I did this again in choosing *Aplysia*" (Kandel, 2006, p. 149).

long-term potentiation (LTP)
A process whereby repeated communication across the synapse between neurons strengthens the connection, making further communication easier.

Memories, Neurons, and Synapses

We've already discussed parts of the brain that are related to memory storage, but we haven't said much about how or where memories are stored. Research suggests that memory storage depends critically on the *spaces* between neurons. You'll recall from the Neuroscience and Behaviour chapter that a *synapse* is the small space between the axon of one neuron and the dendrite of another and that neurons communicate by sending neurotransmitters across these synapses. As it turns out, sending a neurotransmitter across a synapse isn't like sending a toy boat across a pond, because the act of sending actually *changes* the synapse. Specifically, it strengthens the connection between the two neurons, making it easier for them to transmit to each other the next time. This is why the famous Canadian neuroscientist Donald Hebb said, "Cells that fire together wire together" (Hebb, 1949).

The idea that the connections between neurons are strengthened by their communication, making communication easier the next time, provides the neurological basis for long-term memory—and much of what we know about this comes from the sea slug *Aplysia*. The story of *Aplysia* and memory is closely linked with the work of the neuroscientist Eric Kandel, who won the Nobel Prize in 2000 for his work with the creature. When Kandel first became interested in *Aplysia* back in the late 1950s, only two researchers in the entire world were studying it. But *Aplysia* was attractive to Kandel because it is relatively uncomplicated and has an extremely simple nervous system consisting of only 20,000 neurons (compared with roughly 100 billion in the human brain), so Kandel followed his intuition and studied *Aplysia* (Kandel, 2006).

When an experimenter stimulates *Aplysia's* tail with a mild electric shock, the slug immediately withdraws its gill; if the experimenter does it again a moment later, *Aplysia* withdraws its gill even more quickly. If the experimenter comes back an hour later and shocks *Aplysia*, the withdrawal of the gill happens as slowly as it did the first time, as if *Aplysia* can't "remember" what happened an hour earlier (Abel et al., 1995). But if the experimenter shocks *Aplysia* over and over, it does develop an enduring "memory" that can last for days or even weeks. Research suggests that this long-term storage involves the growth of new synaptic connections between neurons (Abel et al., 1995; Kandel, 2006; Squire & Kandel, 1999). Thus, learning in *Aplysia* is based on changes involving the synapses for both short-term storage (enhanced neurotransmitter release) and long-term storage (growth of new synapses). Any experience that results in memory produces physical changes in the nervous system—even if you are a slug.

If you're something more complex than a slug—say, a chimpanzee or your roommate—a similar process of synaptic strengthening happens in the hippocampus, which we've seen is an area crucial for storing new long-term memories. In the early 1970s, researchers applied a brief electrical stimulus to a neural pathway in a rat's hippocampus (Bliss & Lømo, 1973). They found that the electrical current produced a stronger connection between synapses that lay along the pathway and that the strengthening lasted for hours or even weeks. They called this effect **long-term potentiation** (more commonly known as **LTP**), *a process whereby repeated communication across the synapse between neurons strengthens the connection, making further communication easier.* Long-term potentiation has a number of properties that indicate to researchers the important role it plays in long-term memory storage: It occurs in several pathways within the hippocampus; it can be induced rapidly; and it can last for a long time. In fact, drugs that block LTP can turn rats into rodent versions of patient HM: The animals have great difficulty remembering where they've been recently and become easily lost in a maze (Bliss, 1999; Morris et al., 1986).

Hot Science | Can Sleep Enhance Learning? Yes!

Thinking about pulling an all-nighter before your next big test? Here's a reason to reconsider: Our minds don't simply shut off when we sleep (see the Consciousness chapter). In fact, sleep may be as important to our memories as wakefulness.

Nearly a century ago, Jenkins and Dallenbach (1924) reported that recall of recently learned information is greater immediately after sleeping than after the same amount of time spent awake. But Jenkins and Dallenbach did not think that sleep played an active role in strengthening or consolidating memory. They argued instead that being asleep passively protects us from encountering information that interferes with our ability to remember. As is explained by retroactive interference, that's a valid argument. In recent years, some evidence has accumulated that sleep plays an active role in memory consolidation, doing more than simply protecting us from waking interference (Diekelmann & Born, 2010; Ellenbogen et al., 2006; Vorster & Born, 2015), but other studies have failed to document such effects (Cordi & Rasch, 2021). More research will be needed to determine whether the benefits of sleep on memory reflect its active role in memory consolidation or protection from interference.

However, another more recent and robust line of evidence shows that memory consolidation during sleep can be enhanced by presenting sounds during sleep that reactivate specific memories, a procedure known as *targeted memory reactivation* (TMR) (Cellini & Capuozzo, 2018; Oudiette & Paller, 2013). Before sleep, participants learned to associate an object, such as a kettle, with a particular location on a screen; they saw a picture of the kettle and also heard its characteristic whistling sound. During a subsequent period of sleep, researchers played for participants the sounds of some of the studied objects in an attempt to reactivate their memories of the object–location associations. In a remarkable result, when tested after awakening, participants showed more accurate memory for the location of the objects whose characteristic sounds were presented during sleep than for the locations of objects whose characteristic sounds were not presented—even though participants were not aware that any sounds had been presented while they slept. Such targeted memory reactivation effects are strongest for those associations that are not well learned initially (Creery et al., 2015).

These findings suggest that it may be possible to use TMR during sleep to boost learning. To examine this possibility, researchers tested whether TMR could help people acquire new foreign vocabulary (Schreiner & Rasch, 2015). Participants were young adult native German speakers who did not know any items of Dutch vocabulary. While awake in the late evening, all participants learned a series of Dutch words, each paired with their German translation. Some of the participants then slept for 3 hours; one group received TMR in which some of the previously studied Dutch words were presented auditorily, whereas the other group was not exposed to the studied Dutch words while sleeping. After waking up, all participants were given a vocabulary test for the German translation of the Dutch words. Exposure to the Dutch word during sleep improved learning of the German translation during subsequent waking. In a more recent vocabulary learning study done in a home setting, beneficial effects of TMR were observed (Göldi & Rasch, 2019).

Given these promising results, studies of TMR have rapidly accumulated during the past few years, but do TMR effects hold up across studies? To address this question, researchers pulled together data from 91 separate experiments (Hu et al., 2020). They found that TMR effects are statistically significant across experiments, but only when TMR is administered during stage 2 and slow-wave sleep; the effects are not observed during rapid eye movement sleep (REM; see Consciousness chapter). An important task for future research will be to explain why TMR is effective during non-REM but not during REM sleep.

So when you find yourself nodding off after hours of studying for your exam, the science is on the side of a good night's sleep.

Retrieval: Bringing Memories to Mind

There is something fiendishly frustrating about piggy banks. You can put money in them, you can shake them around to assure yourself that the money is there, but you can't easily get the money out. If memories were like pennies in a piggy bank, stored but inaccessible, what would be the point of saving them in the first place? Retrieval is the process of bringing to mind information that has been previously encoded and stored, and it is perhaps the most important of all memory processes (Roediger & McDermott, 2000; Schacter, 2001a).

Retrieval Cues: Reinstating the Past

One of the best ways to retrieve information from *inside* your head is to encounter information *outside* your head that is somehow connected to it. The information

Learning Outcomes

WHAT YOU NEED TO KNOW

- Explain the encoding specificity principle.

- Explain how memories can be changed by the act of retrieval.

- Describe the difference in brain activity when trying to recall versus successfully recalling information.

Retrieval cues are hints that help bring stored information to mind. How does this explain the fact that most students prefer multiple-choice exams to fill-in-the-blank exams?

outside your head is called a **retrieval cue,** *external information that is associated with stored information and helps bring it to mind.* Retrieval cues can be incredibly effective. How many times have you said something such as, "I *know* who played the white cop who stood in for the black cop to infiltrate the Ku Klux Klan in *BlacKkKlansman,* but I just can't remember his name," only to have a friend give you a hint ("He was in *The Last Jedi*"), which instantly brings the answer to mind ("Adam Driver!")?

In one experiment, undergraduates studied lists of words, such as *table, peach, bed, apple, chair, grape,* and *desk* (Tulving & Pearlstone, 1966). Later, the students were asked to write down all the words from the list that they could remember. When they were absolutely sure that they had emptied their memory stores of every last word, the experimenters again asked the students to remember the words on the list. This time, however, the experimenters provided retrieval cues, such as "furniture" or "fruit." The students who were sure that they had done all the remembering they possibly could were suddenly able to remember more words. These results suggest that information is sometimes *available* in memory even when it is momentarily *inaccessible* and that retrieval cues help us bring inaccessible information to mind.

In this and many other lab experiments, participants use retrieval cues in a deliberate attempt to recall studied information; in everyday life, however, retrieval cues sometimes spontaneously elicit involuntary memories of past experiences (Berntsen, 2010). Encountering a friend may automatically remind you of the movie you recently saw with her, or hearing a song on the radio may remind you of a concert you attended by that band. Involuntary memories occur even more often in everyday life than memories that we voluntarily try to retrieve (Rasmussen & Bernsten, 2011), underscoring the power of retrieval cues to unlock our personal pasts.

External Context Provides Cues

Hints are one kind of retrieval cue, but they are not the only kind. The **encoding specificity principle** states that *a retrieval cue can serve as an effective reminder when it helps re-create the specific way in which information was initially encoded* (Tulving & Thomson, 1973). External contexts often make powerful retrieval cues (Hockley, 2008). For example, in one study divers learned some words on land and some other words underwater; they recalled the words best when they were tested in the same dry or wet environment in which they had initially learned them, because the environment itself was a retrieval cue (Godden & Baddeley, 1975). Recovering alcoholics often experience a renewed urge to drink when visiting places in which they once drank because those places are retrieval cues. There may even be some wisdom to finding a seat in a classroom, sitting in it every day, and then sitting in it again when you take the test. The feel of the chair and the sights you see may help you remember the information you learned while you sat there.

Inner States Also Provide Cues

Retrieval cues need not be external contexts—they can also be inner states. **State-dependent retrieval** is *the process whereby information tends to be better recalled when the person is in the same state during encoding and retrieval.* For example, retrieving information when you are in a sad or happy mood increases the likelihood that you will retrieve sad or happy episodes (Eich, 1995). Why should that be? Because a person's physiological or psychological state at the time of encoding is associated with the information that is encoded. For instance, being in a good mood affects patterns of electrical activity in parts of the brain responsible for semantic processing, suggesting that mood has a direct influence on semantic encoding (Kiefer et al., 2007). If the person's state at the time of retrieval matches the person's state at the time of encoding, the state itself is a retrieval cue. It is a bridge that connects the moment at which we experience something to the moment at which we remember it. Retrieval cues can even be thoughts themselves, as when one thought calls to mind another, related thought (Anderson et al., 1976).

retrieval cue External information that is associated with stored information and helps bring it to mind.

encoding specificity principle The idea that a retrieval cue can be an effective reminder when it helps re-create the specific way in which information was initially encoded.

state-dependent retrieval The process whereby information tends to be better recalled when the person is in the same state during encoding *and* retrieval.

Matching Encoding and Retrieval Contexts Improves Recall

The encoding specificity principle makes some unusual predictions. For example, you learned earlier that making semantic judgements about a word (e.g., what does *brain* mean?) usually produces a more durable memory for the word than does making rhyme judgements (e.g., what rhymes with *brain*?). Suppose you were shown a cue card of the word *brain* and were then asked to think of a word that rhymes, while your friend was shown the same card and asked to think about what *brain* means. The next day, if we simply asked you both, "Hey, what was that word you saw yesterday?" we would expect your friend to remember it better. However, if instead we asked both of you, "What was that word that rhymed with *train*?" the retrieval cue would match your encoding context better than your friend's, and we would expect you to remember it better than your friend did (Fisher & Craik, 1977). This is a fairly astounding finding. The principle of **transfer-appropriate processing** is *the idea that memory is likely to transfer from one situation to another when the encoding and retrieval contexts of the situations match* (Morris et al., 1977; Roediger et al., 1989).

These and other findings concerning the importance of matching encoding and retrieval contexts have been incorporated into a procedure called the Cognitive Interview (CI; Fisher & Geiselman, 1992) that was developed in order to enhance the memory of eyewitnesses for everyday experiences. A key procedure used during the CI is context reinstatement, where people are encouraged to try to reconstruct the physical setting of a particular event and their psychological state during the event. Numerous studies have shown that the CI increases the number of accurate details people remember about an event (Memon et al., 2010), including stressful real-world events (Dodier et al., 2021). Recent work has also shown that during a contact tracing interview, where individuals are questioned about all the people they have come in contact with during a recent time period in order to try to stop the spread of an infectious disease, the CI boosted the number of contacts retrieved (Mosser & Evans, 2019). Contact tracing interviews were important during the early stages of the COVID-19 pandemic, leading researchers to suggest that the CI could be a useful tool to help control the spread of the virus (Mosser & Evans, 2020).

Consequences of Retrieval

Human memory differs substantially from computer memory. Simply retrieving a file from my computer doesn't have any effect on the likelihood that the file will open again in the future. Not so with human memory. Retrieval doesn't merely provide a readout of what is in memory; it also changes the state of the memory system in important ways.

Retrieval Can Improve Subsequent Memory

Psychologists have known for some time that the act of retrieval can strengthen a retrieved memory, making it easier to remember that information at a later time (Bjork, 1975). Does this finding surprise you? Probably not. Does studying information twice have the same benefit as retrieving information twice? This finding probably *will* surprise you. It turns out that retrieving information from memory has different effects from studying it again. This point was made dramatically in an experiment in which participants studied brief stories and then either studied them again or were given a test that required retrieving the stories (Roediger & Karpicke, 2006). Participants were then given a final recall test for the stories either 5 minutes, 2 days, or 1 week later. As shown in **FIGURE 6.10**, at the 5-minute delay, studying the stories twice resulted in slightly higher recall than did studying paired with retrieval (testing). In a critical finding, the opposite occurred at the 2-day and 1-week delays: Retrieval produced much higher levels of recall than did an extra study exposure.

transfer-appropriate processing The idea that memory is likely to transfer from one situation to another when the encoding and retrieval contexts of the situations match.

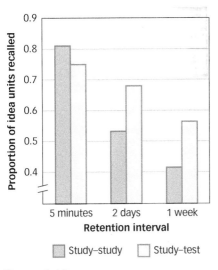

Figure 6.10

Memory Testing Benefits Long-Term Retention With a 5-minute retention interval, the study–study condition results in slightly higher recall. But the results change dramatically with retention intervals of 2 days and 1 week. With these longer delays, the study–test condition yields much higher levels of recall than does the study–study condition (Roediger & Karpicke, 2006).

A subsequent experiment using foreign vocabulary items also revealed that retrieval of the items produced a much bigger benefit on a delayed vocabulary test than did further study (Karpicke & Roediger, 2008). The benefits of retrieval on subsequent retention occur not only in adults but also in grade school children (Jaeger et al., 2015). Although there are specific situations in which testing produces little or no benefit for subsequent retention (Van Gog et al., 2015), the benefits of retrieval have been documented across many different memory tasks and with both simple and complex materials (Karpicke & Aue, 2015). Furthermore, students are able to learn to use this kind of retrieval practice spontaneously and on their own (Ariel & Karpicke, 2018). These findings have potentially important implications for learning in educational contexts (Karpicke, 2012; McDermott, 2021), which we will explore further in the Learning chapter.

Retrieval Can Also Impair Subsequent Memory

As much as retrieval can help memory, that's not always the case. **Retrieval-induced forgetting** is *a process by which retrieving an item from long-term memory impairs subsequent recall of related items* (Anderson, 2003; Anderson et al., 1994; Murayama et al., 2014).

Let's see how a typical experiment on retrieval-induced forgetting works (Anderson et al., 1994). Participants first studied word pairs consisting of a category name and an example of an item from that category (e.g., *fruit–orange, fruit–apple, tree–elm, tree–birch*). Then they practiced recalling some of the items in response to a category cue and the initial letters of the target item. For instance, the fruit category participants would practice recalling *orange* to the cue "fruit or _____," but would not practice recalling *apple*. The general idea was that while they were practicing recall of *orange*, participants suppressed the competitor item *apple*. For other categories (e.g., *trees*), no retrieval practice was given for any of the studied pairs. Later, the participants were given a final test for all the words they initially studied. It was not surprising that on the final test, participants remembered words that they practiced (e.g., *orange*) better than words from categories that they did not practice (e.g., *elm*).

But what happened on the final test to the items such as *apple*, which were not practiced and which participants presumably had to suppress while they practiced recall of related items? Those items were recalled most poorly of all, indicating that retrieving the similar target items (e.g., *orange*) caused subsequent forgetting of the related but suppressed items (e.g., *apple*). In fact, even if you don't successfully retrieve the target item, the act of suppressing the competitors while you attempt to retrieve the target still reduces your ability to retrieve the competitors at a later time (Storm et al., 2006).

Can you think of any examples of how retrieval-induced forgetting could affect memory in everyday life? Here are two. First, retrieval-induced forgetting can occur during conversations: When a speaker selectively talks about some aspects of memories shared with a listener and doesn't mention related information, the listener later has a harder time remembering the omitted events, as does the speaker (Cuc et al., 2007; Hirst & Echterhoff, 2012). This effect occurs even for very important or vivid memories, such as those for major world events (Coman et al., 2009). Second, retrieval-induced forgetting can affect eyewitness memory. When witnesses to a staged crime are questioned about some details of the crime scene, their ability to later recall related details that they were not asked about is impaired, compared with that of witnesses who initially were not questioned at all (MacLeod, 2002; Shaw et al., 1995). These findings suggest that initial interviews with eyewitnesses should be as complete as possible in order to avoid potential retrieval-induced forgetting of significant details that are not probed during an interview (MacLeod & Saunders, 2008).

retrieval-induced forgetting
A process by which retrieving an item from long-term memory impairs subsequent recall of related items.

Retrieval Can Change Subsequent Memory

In addition to improving and impairing subsequent memory, the act of retrieval also can change what we remember from an experience. In one experiment, participants went on a tour of a museum, where they viewed designated exhibits, each of which contained several different stops (St. Jacques & Schacter, 2013). The participants each wore a camera that, every 15 seconds, automatically took pictures of what was in front of them. Two days later, the participants visited the memory laboratory (in a separate building) for a "reactivation session." Memories of some of the stops were reactivated by showing photos and asking the participants to rate how vividly they reexperienced what had happened at each stop. The participants were also shown novel photos of *unvisited* stops within the exhibit and were asked to judge how closely these novel photos were related to the photos of the stops they had actually seen in that exhibit. Two days after the reactivation session, the participants were given a memory test.

Participants sometimes incorrectly remembered that the stop shown in the novel photo had been part of the original tour. Most important, participants who tended to make this mistake also tended to have more vivid recollections during the reactivation session. In other words, retrieving and vividly reexperiencing memories of what participants actually did see at the museum led them to incorporate into their memory information that was *not* part of their original experience. This finding may be related to the phenomenon of reconsolidation that we discussed earlier, where reactivating a memory temporarily makes it vulnerable to disruption and change. At the very least, this finding reinforces the idea that retrieving a memory involves far more than a simple readout of information.

As part of an experiment, participants wore cameras that took pictures every 15 seconds as the participants toured a museum.

Separating the Components of Retrieval

Before leaving the topic of retrieval, let's look at how the process actually works. There is reason to believe that *trying* to recall an incident and *successfully* recalling one are fundamentally different processes that occur in different parts of the brain (Moscovitch, 1994; Schacter, 1996). For example, regions in the left frontal lobe show heightened activity when people *try* to retrieve information that was presented to them earlier (Oztekin et al., 2009; Tulving et al., 1994). This activity may reflect the mental effort of struggling to dredge up the past event (Lepage et al., 2000). However, *successfully* remembering a past experience tends to be accompanied by activity in the hippocampal region (see **FIGURE 6.11**) (Eldridge et al., 2000; Giovanello et al., 2004; Schacter et al., 1996). Furthermore, successful recall also activates parts

High recall minus baseline **Low recall minus baseline**

Hippocampus

Left frontal lobe

(a) (b)

Figure 6.11
PET Scans of Successful and Unsuccessful Recall (a) When people successfully remembered words they had seen earlier in an experiment (achieving high levels of recall on a test), the hippocampus showed increased activity. (b) When people tried but failed to recall words they had seen earlier (achieving low levels of recall on a test), the left frontal lobe showed increased activity.
SCHACTER DL. ALPERT NM, SAVAGE CR. RAUCH SL, ALBERT MS. CONSCIOUS RECOLLECTION AND THE HUMAN HIPPOCAMPAL FORMATION: EVIDENCE FROM POSITRON EMISSION TOMOGRAPHY. PROC NATL ACAD SCI USA 1996; 93: 321–5.

of the brain that play a role in processing the sensory features of an experience. For instance, recall of previously heard sounds is accompanied by activity in the auditory cortex (the upper part of the temporal lobe), whereas recall of previously seen pictures is accompanied by activity in the visual cortex (in the occipital lobe) (Wheeler et al., 2000). Although retrieval may seem like a single process, neuroimaging studies suggest that separately identifiable processes are at work.

This finding sheds some light on the phenomenon we just discussed: retrieval-induced forgetting. Evidence from fMRI studies indicates that during memory retrieval, regions within the frontal lobe that are involved in retrieval effort play a role in suppressing competitors (Benoit & Anderson, 2012; Kuhl et al., 2007; Wimber et al., 2009). Indeed, repeated attempts to retrieve target items result in a suppression of the specific neural patterns that are uniquely associated with competitors (Wimber et al., 2015). So, for example, when hippocampal activity during retrieval practice signals successful recall of an unwanted competitor, frontal lobe mechanisms are recruited that help suppress the competitor. Once the competitor is suppressed, the frontal lobe no longer has to work as hard to control retrieval, ultimately making it easier to recall the target item (Kuhl et al., 2007). In addition, successful suppression of an unwanted memory causes reduced activity in the hippocampus (Anderson et al., 2004; Gagnepain et al., 2017). These findings make sense as we understand the specific roles played by particular brain regions in the retrieval process.

Forms of Long-Term Memory: More Than One Kind

Learning Outcomes

WHAT YOU NEED TO KNOW

- Distinguish between explicit memory and implicit memory.
- Give examples of both semantic memories and episodic memories.
- Describe the pros and cons of collaborative memory.

In 1977, the neurologist Oliver Sacks interviewed a young man named Greg who had a tumour in his brain that wiped out his ability to remember day-to-day events. One thing Greg could remember, however, was his life during the 1960s in New York's Greenwich Village, years before the tumour formed, when Greg's primary occupation seemed to be attending rock concerts by his favourite band, the Grateful Dead. Greg's memories of those Dead concerts stuck with him over the ensuing years, when he was living in a long-term care hospital and was interviewed regularly by Dr. Sacks. In 1991, Dr. Sacks took Greg to a Dead concert at New York's Madison Square Garden, wondering whether such a momentous event might jolt his memory into action. "That was fantastic," Greg told Dr. Sacks as they left the concert. "I will always remember it. I had the time of my life." But when Dr. Sacks saw Greg the next morning and asked him whether he recalled the previous night's Dead concert at the Garden, Greg drew a blank: "No, I've never been to the Garden" (Sacks, 1995, pp. 76–77).

Although Greg was unable to make new memories, some of the new things that happened to him did seem to leave a mark. For example, Greg did not recall learning that his father had died, but he did seem sad and withdrawn for years after hearing the news. Similarly, HM could not make new memories after his surgery, but if he played a game in which he had to track a moving target, his performance gradually improved with each round (Milner, 1962). Greg could not consciously remember hearing about his father's death, and HM could not consciously remember playing the tracking game, but both showed clear signs of having been permanently changed by experiences that they so rapidly forgot. In other words, they *behaved* as though they were remembering things while claiming to remember nothing at all. This suggests that there must be several kinds of memory—some that are accessible to conscious recall and some that we cannot consciously access (Eichenbaum & Cohen, 2001; Schacter & Tulving, 1994; Schacter et al., 2000; Squire & Kandel, 1999).

Memories can be broken down into two types. **Explicit memory** occurs *when people consciously or intentionally retrieve past experiences.* Recalling last summer's vacation, incidents from a novel you just read, or facts you studied for a test all involve explicit memory. Indeed, anytime you start a sentence with "I remember . . . ," you are talking about an explicit memory. **Implicit memory** occurs when *past experiences influence later behaviour and performance, even without an effort to remember them or an awareness of the recollection* (Graf & Schacter, 1985; Schacter, 1987). (See **FIGURE 6.12**.) Let's look next at both of these.

Implicit Memory

Implicit memories are not consciously recalled, but their presence is "implied" by our actions. Greg's persistent sadness after his father's death, even though he had no conscious knowledge of the event, is an example of implicit memory. So is HM's improved performance on a tracking task that he didn't consciously remember having done before.

The ability to ride a bike or tie your shoelaces or play the guitar are other examples of implicit memory. You may know how to do these things, but you probably can't describe *how* to do them. Such knowledge reflects a particular kind of implicit memory called **procedural memory,** which refers to *the gradual acquisition of skills as a result of practice, or "knowing how" to do things.*

One of the hallmarks of procedural memory is that the things you remember are automatically translated into actions. Sometimes you can explain how it is done (put one finger on the third fret of the E string, one finger . . .), and sometimes you can't (get on the bike and . . . well, uh . . . just balance). The fact that people who have amnesia can acquire new procedural memories suggests that the hippocampal structures that are usually damaged in these individuals may be necessary for explicit memory, but they aren't needed for implicit procedural memory. In fact, it appears that brain regions outside the hippocampal area (including areas in the motor cortex) are involved in procedural memory. The Learning chapter discusses this evidence further, and you will also see that procedural memory is crucial for learning various kinds of motor, perceptual, and cognitive skills.

explicit memory The act of consciously or intentionally retrieving past experiences.

implicit memory The influence of past experiences on later behaviour and performance, even without an effort to remember them or an awareness of the recollection.

procedural memory The gradual acquisition of skills as a result of practice, or "knowing how" to do things.

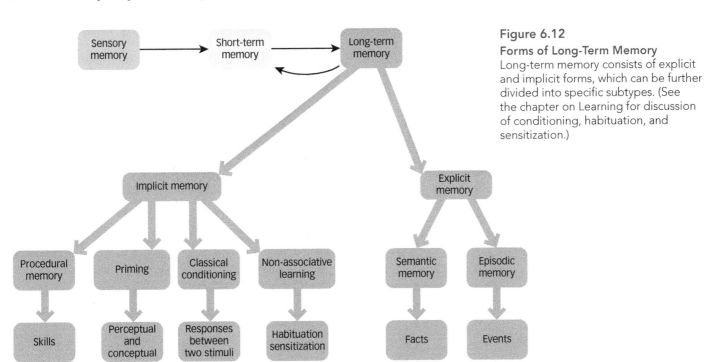

Figure 6.12
Forms of Long-Term Memory
Long-term memory consists of explicit and implicit forms, which can be further divided into specific subtypes. (See the chapter on Learning for discussion of conditioning, habituation, and sensitization.)

Guitarists such as Janelle Monáe rely heavily on procedural memory to acquire and use the skills they need to play their music at a high level.

Priming Makes Some Information More Accessible

Not all implicit memories are procedural or "how to" memories. For example, **priming** refers to *an enhanced ability to think of a stimulus, such as a word or object, as a result of a recent exposure to the stimulus during an earlier study task* (Tulving & Schacter, 1990). In one experiment, university students were asked to study a long list of words, including items such as *avocado, mystery, climate, octopus,* and *assassin* (Tulving et al., 1982). Later, explicit memory was tested by showing participants some of these words along with new ones they hadn't seen and asking them which words were on the list. To test implicit memory, participants received word fragments and were asked to come up with a word that fit the fragment. Try the test yourself:

c h – – – – n k   o – t – p – –   – o g – y – – –   – l – m – t e

You probably had difficulty coming up with the answers for the first and third fragments (*chipmunk, bogeyman*) but had little trouble coming up with answers for the second and fourth (*octopus, climate*). Seeing *octopus* and *climate* on the original list made those words more accessible later, during the fill-in-the-blanks test. Just as priming a pump makes water flow more easily, priming the memory system makes some information more accessible. In the fill-in-the-blanks experiment, people showed priming for studied words even when they failed to remember consciously that they had seen them earlier. This suggests that priming is an example of implicit, not explicit, memory.

A truly stunning example of this point comes from a study by Mitchell (2006) in which participants first studied black-and-white line drawings depicting everyday objects. Later, the participants were shown fragmented versions of the drawings that were difficult to identify; some of them depicted objects that they had studied earlier in the experiment, whereas others depicted new objects that they had not studied. Mitchell found that participants correctly identified more fragmented drawings of studied than new objects, and identified more studied objects than did participants in a control group who had never seen the pictures—a clear demonstration of priming (see **FIGURE 6.13**). This is not so surprising in itself—such priming had been demonstrated by British researchers nearly 40 years earlier (Warrington & Weiskrantz, 1968). Here's the stunning part: The fragmented drawing test was given 17 years after presentation of the study list! By that time, participants had little or no explicit memory of having seen the drawings, and some had no recollection that they had ever participated in the experiment! "I'm sorry—I really don't remember this experiment at all," said one 36-year-old man who showed a strong priming effect. A 36-year-old woman who showed even more priming stated simply, "Don't remember anything about it" (Mitchell, 2006, p. 929). Mitchell and colleagues (2018) replicated these findings in a different sample of participants. These observations confirm that priming is an example of implicit memory, and also that priming can persist over very long periods of time.

Procedural Memory and Priming Do Not Rely on the Hippocampus

Because priming is an example of implicit memory, not explicit memory, you'd expect amnesic individuals such as HM and Greg to show priming. In fact, many experiments have shown that amnesic individuals can show substantial priming effects—often as great as healthy, nonamnesic individuals—even though they have no explicit memory for the items they studied (Warrington & Weiskrantz, 1968). Squire and colleagues (2021) used a picture priming procedure with amnesic patients that is similar to the one employed by Mitchell and colleagues (2006, 2018) in the aforementioned experiments, and found that despite their severe explicit memory impairments, amnesic patients showed normal priming effects, even after a 5-month retention interval. These and other similar results suggest that priming, like procedural memory, does not require the hippocampal structures that are damaged in cases of amnesia (Schacter & Curran, 2000).

If the hippocampal region isn't required for procedural memory and priming, which parts of the brain *are* involved? Experiments have revealed that priming is associated

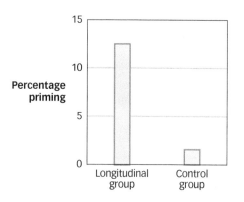

Figure 6.13

Long-Term Priming of Visual Objects Participants who viewed drawings of common objects and were then given a test 17 years later, in which they tried to identify the objects from fragmented drawings (longitudinal group), showed a strong priming effect. In contrast, participants who had not seen the drawings 17 years earlier (control group) showed nonsignificant priming (Mitchell, 2006).

priming An enhanced ability to think of a stimulus, such as a word or object, as a result of a recent exposure to that stimulus during an earlier study task.

with *reduced* activity in various regions of the cortex that are activated when people perform an unprimed task. For instance, when research participants are shown the word stem *mot* _____ or *tab* _____ and are asked to provide the first word that comes to mind, parts of the occipital lobe involved in visual processing and parts of the frontal lobe involved in word retrieval become active. But if people perform the same task after being primed by seeing *motel* and *table,* there's less activity in these same regions (Buckner et al., 1995; Schott et al., 2005). Something similar happens when people see pictures of everyday objects on two different occasions. On the second exposure to a picture, there's less activity in parts of the visual cortex that were activated by seeing the picture initially. Priming seems to make it easier for parts of the cortex that are involved in perceiving a word or object to identify the item after a recent exposure to it (Schacter et al., 2004; Wiggs & Martin, 1998). This suggests that the brain saves a bit of processing time after priming (see **FIGURE 6.14**).

Neuroimaging studies also indicate that different brain systems are involved in two distinct forms of priming: *perceptual priming,* which reflects implicit memory for the sensory features of an item (e.g., the visual characteristics of a word or picture), and *conceptual priming,* which reflects implicit memory for the meaning of a word or how you would use an object. Studies using fMRI indicate that perceptual priming depends primarily on regions towards the back of the brain, such as the visual cortex, whereas conceptual priming depends more on regions towards the front of the brain, such as the frontal lobes (Wig et al., 2009). There is also some evidence that perceptual priming is associated primarily with the right cerebral hemisphere, whereas conceptual priming is associated with the left hemisphere (Schacter et al., 2007).

Explicit Memory: Semantic and Episodic

Consider these two questions: (1) What do we remember at 11 a.m. on November 11 every year? (2) What was the most memorable Remembrance Day activity in which you participated during your elementary school years? Most Canadians know the answer to the first question (we honour those who lost their lives in military service), but we all have our own answers to the second. Both of these are explicit memories, consciously or intentionally retrieved from past experiences. But the first one requires you to dredge up a fact that every Canadian schoolchild knows and that is not part of your personal autobiography, while the second requires you to revisit a particular time and place—or episode—from your personal past. These memories are called *semantic* and *episodic* memories, respectively (Tulving, 1972, 1983, 1998).

- **Semantic memory** is *a network of associated facts and concepts that make up our general knowledge of the world.*

- **Episodic memory** is *the collection of past personal experiences that occurred at a particular time and place.*

semantic memory A network of associated facts and concepts that make up our general knowledge of the world.

episodic memory The collection of past personal experiences that occurred at a particular time and place.

(a)   (b)   (c)   (d)

Left frontal lobe   Occipital/frontal lobe

Figure 6.14
Primed and Unprimed Processing of Stimuli Priming is associated with reduced levels of activation in the cortex on a number of different tasks. In each pair of fMRIs, the images on the upper left (*a, c*) show brain regions in the frontal lobe (*a*) and occipital/temporal lobe (*c*) that are active during an unprimed task (in this case, providing a word response to a visual word cue). The images on the lower right within each pair (*b, d*) show reduced activity in the same regions during the primed version of the same task.
DATA FROM SCHACTER & BUCKNER FROM PRIMING AND THE BRAIN, NEURON 20, 185–195. ELSEVIER FIGURE 1.(1998).

These new Canadians are participating in a citizenship ceremony after passing a citizenship test that would have required them to use their semantic memories.

Episodic memory is special because it is the only form of memory that allows us to engage in mental time travel, projecting ourselves into the past and revisiting events that have happened to us. This ability allows us to connect our pasts and our presents to construct a cohesive story of our lives (see A World of Difference: Do We All Reexperience Our Personal Pasts?). People who have amnesia can usually travel back in time and revisit episodes that occurred before they became amnesic, but they are unable to revisit episodes that happened later. For example, Greg couldn't travel back to any time after 1969, because that's when he stopped being able to create new episodic memories. But can people with amnesia create *new* semantic memories?

British researchers have studied three young adults who suffered damage to the hippocampus during birth as a result of difficult deliveries that interrupted oxygen supply to the brain (Brandt et al., 2009; Vargha-Khadem et al., 1997). Their parents noticed that the children could not recall what happened during a typical day, had to be constantly reminded of appointments, and often became lost and disoriented. In view of their hippocampal damage, you might also expect that they would perform poorly in school and might even be classified as learning disabled. Remarkably, however, all three children learned to read, write, and spell; developed normal vocabularies; and acquired other kinds of semantic knowledge that allowed them to perform well in school. On the basis of this evidence, researchers have concluded that the hippocampus is not necessary for acquiring new *semantic* memories.

Episodic Memory Contributes to Imagination and Creativity

We've already seen that episodic memory allows us to travel backward in time, but it turns out that episodic memory also plays a role in allowing us to travel forward in time. An amnesic man known by the initials KC provided an early clue. KC could not recollect any specific episodes from his past, and when he was asked to imagine a future episode — such as what he might do tomorrow — he reported a complete "blank" (Tulving, 1985). Consistent with this observation, more recent findings from individuals with hippocampal amnesia reveal that many of them have difficulty imagining new experiences, such as sunbathing on a sandy beach (Hassabis et al., 2007), or events that might happen in their everyday lives (Race et al., 2011).

Something similar happens with aging. When asked either to recall episodes that actually occurred in their pasts or to imagine new episodes that might occur in their futures, older adults provided fewer details about what happened, or what might happen, than did university students (Addis et al., 2008; Schacter et al., 2013). Consistent with these findings, neuroimaging studies reveal that a *core network* (Benoit & Schacter, 2015) of brain regions known to be involved in episodic memory — including the hippocampus — shows similarly increased activity when people remember the past and imagine the future (Addis et al., 2007; Okuda et al., 2003; Schacter et al., 2012; Szpunar et al., 2007) (see **FIGURE 6.15**).

Taken together, these observations strongly suggest that we rely heavily on episodic memory to envision our personal futures (Schacter et al., 2008; Szpunar, 2010). Episodic memory is well suited to the task because it is a flexible system that allows us to recombine elements of past experience in new ways, so that we can mentally try out different versions of what might happen (Schacter, 2012; Schacter & Addis, 2007; Suddendorf & Corballis, 2007). For example, when you imagine having a difficult conversation with a friend that will take place in a couple of days, you can draw on past experiences to envision different ways in which the conversation might unfold — and hopefully avoid saying things that, based

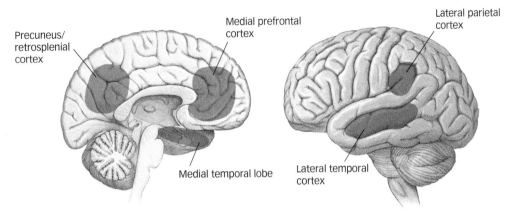

Precuneus/
retrosplenial
cortex

Medial prefrontal
cortex

Lateral parietal
cortex

Medial temporal lobe

Lateral temporal
cortex

Figure 6.15

Remembering the Past and Imagining the Future Depend on a Common Core Network of Brain Regions A common brain network is activated when people remember episodes that actually occurred in their personal pasts and when they imagine episodes that might occur in their personal futures. This network includes the hippocampus, a part of the medial temporal lobe long known to play an important role in episodic memory (Schacter et al., 2007).

on past experience, are likely to make the situation worse. After receiving brief training in recalling details of past experience, a procedure known as an *episodic specificity induction* (Schacter & Madore, 2016), people were subsequently better able to imagine different ways in which they could approach a possible future experience, suggesting that increased episodic memory retrieval was responsible for more flexible future imagining (Jing et al., 2017). As we'll discuss later, however, this flexibility of episodic memory might also be responsible for some kinds of memory errors.

Imagining the future by recombining elements of past experiences sounds a lot like what psychologists refer to as *divergent creative thinking*: generating creative ideas by combining different types of information in new ways (Guilford, 1967). One common test of divergent creative thinking, the Alternate Uses Task (AUT) (Guilford, 1967), requires participants to generate unusual uses of common objects, such as a brick.

When people perform the AUT during an fMRI scan, parts of the core brain network that supports episodic memory and future imagining, including the hippocampus, show increased activity (Beaty et al., 2016, 2018; Benedek et al., 2014), suggesting that episodic memory may contribute to divergent creative thinking. In findings consistent with this idea, amnesic patients with hippocampal damage and episodic memory deficits perform poorly on tests that tap divergent creative thinking (Duff et al., 2013). Moreover, a study of healthy young adults revealed that brief training in retrieving details from episodic memory using the episodic specificity induction discussed in the previous section enhances divergent creative thinking on the AUT (Madore et al., 2015). Training in how to recall episodic details led participants to rely more on their episodic memories during the AUT, helping them recombine information in novel ways and come up with more unusual uses for objects. Evidence from an fMRI study revealed that this episodic induction effect is accompanied by increased activity in the hippocampus, as well as increased coupling between the core brain network that supports episodic processing and an executive network that supports working memory and related control functions (Madore et al., 2019). This finding fits well with other evidence indicating that coupling between core and executive networks is a signature feature of divergent creative thinking (Beaty et al., 2016, 2018). Finally, a recent study that used transcranial magnetic stimulation (TMS; see the section on Transcranial Magnetic Stimulation in the Neuroscience and Behaviour chapter) to inhibit hippocampal activity revealed that TMS impaired performance on both the AUT and also on a task that involved imagining future experiences, further strengthening the link between divergent thinking and imagining the future (Thakral et al., 2020).

How many unusual uses of a brick can you think of? On the AUT, you would receive credit for coming up with such novel uses as a doorstop, a paperweight, or even a weapon.

A World of Difference • Do We All Reexperience Our Personal Pasts?

Think back to your dinner last night. What did you eat and where? What did the dining room look like? Who else was there? You probably didn't have much difficulty answering these questions and reexperiencing at least a few happenings from dinner last night. But some otherwise high-functioning people seem to lack the ability to vividly reexperience past events, even though they know those events happened. Researchers who discovered this condition named it *severely deficient autobiographical memory* (SDAM) (Palombo et al., 2015).

The three SDAM individuals who were studied are each middle-aged adults (one woman, two men) employed at full-time jobs; one has a PhD degree. All three perform normally on a standard battery of cognitive tasks that assess general intellectual abilities, and they even perform well on laboratory tests of verbal memory, showing that they can retain information over time. But they each lack the ability to travel back in time and *reexperience* their personal pasts, a hallmark of episodic memory. When tasked with recalling a particular

autobiographical memory from everyday life, they recall few episodic details about what happened and are particularly unable to retrieve visual details, which for most people is an integral part of successful episodic recollection.

Given the established link between the hippocampus and successful recollection, you might expect hippocampal abnormalities in SDAM individuals — and indeed structural MRI scans showed reduced volume in the right hippocampus of SDAM individuals compared with controls (Palombo et al., 2015). Importantly, a more recent study (Palombo et al., 2018) of 30 healthy young adults showed that individual differences in the ability to recall episodic details on the same autobiographical memory task that had been given to the SDAM group are positively correlated with the volume of a particular subregion within the hippocampus known as DG/CA$_{2/3}$ (dentate gyrus/cornu ammonis regions 2 and 3). Previous neuroimaging research had suggested that the DG/CA$_{2/3}$ subregion may be particularly important for episodic memory, and this new research on

individual differences provides additional support for that hypothesis.

The finding that people with SDAM have a particularly hard time recalling visual details of past experiences suggests that it may be related to another intriguing condition known as *aphantasia*, which involves an inability to generate mental visual images (Keogh & Pearson, 2018; Zeman et al., 2015) and is also characterized by sketchy episodic memories that lack visual detail (Dawes et al., 2020). Nicholas Watkins, a physicist with both SDAM and aphantasia, describes what it is like to try to remember a movie he saw recently: "I have a feeling that I can form and store some sort of unseen quasi-spatial memories. What I don't have is the experience that people describe of feeling that they are back in another time and re-living it" (Watkins, 2019, p. 44). Further research will be needed to assess how often people with SDAM also experience aphantasia (and vice versa), but these findings are important because they highlight that different people may have fundamentally different experiences when reflecting on their personal pasts.

Collaborative Memory: Social Influences on Remembering

So far, we've focused mainly on memory in individuals functioning on their own. But remembering also serves important social functions, which is why we get together with family to talk about old times, or share our memories with friends by posting our vacation photos on Instagram. And we are quick to communicate our memories to others: In a diary study in which university students recorded a memorable event each day for a week, they disclosed 62% of these events to others before the end of the day on which the event occurred (Pasupathi et al., 2009). Sharing memories with others can strengthen them (Hirst & Echterhoff, 2012), but we've already seen that talking about some aspects of a memory, yet omitting other related events, can also produce retrieval-induced *forgetting* (Coman et al., 2009; Cuc et al., 2007). Psychologists have become increasingly interested in how people remember in groups, which is now referred to as *collaborative memory* (Meade et al., 2018; Rajaram, 2011).

Groups Can Recall More Than a Single Individual, but Less Than Multiple Individuals Working on Their Own

In a typical collaborative memory experiment, participants first encode a set of target materials, such as a list of words, on their own (just as in the traditional memory experiments that we've already considered). Things start to get interesting at the time of retrieval, when participants work together in small groups (usually two or three participants) to try to remember the target items. The number of items recalled by this group can then be compared with the number of items recalled by individuals who are trying to recall items on their own, without any help from others. The collaborative group typically recalls more target items than any individual (Hirst & Echterhoff, 2012; Weldon, 2001), suggesting that collaboration benefits memory. That makes a lot of sense and generally fits with our intuitions about what should happen in such a situation (Rajaram, 2011). For example, Tim might recall an item that Emily forgot, and Eric might remember items that neither Tim nor Emily recalled, so the sum total of the group will exceed what any one person can recall.

Remembering as a collaborative group leads to greater recall than any single member of the group would achieve alone, but less than that produced by a nominal group of individuals remembering on their own.

But things get really interesting when we compare the performance of the collaborative group with the performance of what is called a *nominal group*: the combined recall of several individuals recalling target items on their own. Let's consider a nominal group of three compared with a collaborative group of three. In the nominal group, let's assume that after studying a list of eight words, Tim recalls items 1, 2, and 8; Emily recalls items 1, 4, and 7; and Eric recalls items 1, 5, 6, and 8. Functioning on their own, Tim, Emily, and Eric recalled in combination seven of the eight items that were presented. (Nobody recalled item 3.) The surprising finding now reported by many studies is that the collaborative group typically recalls fewer items than the nominal group; that is, when they remember together, Tim, Emily, and Eric will come up with fewer total items than when they remember on their own (Basden et al., 1997; Hirst & Echterhoff, 2012; Rajaram, 2011; Rajaram & Pereira-Pasarin, 2010; Weldon, 2001). This negative effect of group recall on memory is known as *collaborative inhibition*: The same number of individuals working together recall fewer items than they would on their own.

What's going on here? Most people believe, on the basis of intuition, that working together should increase rather than decrease recall (Rajaram, 2011). Why does it turn out otherwise? One possibility is that, in a group, some individuals are prone to "social loafing": They let others do the work and don't pull their own weight. Although social loafing is well known to occur in groups (Karau & Williams, 1993), memory researchers have tested this account of collaborative inhibition and rejected it (Barber et al., 2012).

A more likely explanation is that when recalling items together, the retrieval strategies used by individual members of the group disrupt those used by others (Basden et al., 1997; Hirst & Echterhoff, 2012; Rajaram, 2011). For instance, suppose that Tim goes first and recalls items in the order that they were presented. This retrieval strategy may be disruptive to Emily, who prefers to recall the last item first and then work backward through the list. Research indicates that the negative effects of collaborative inhibition on memory persist even when individual members of a group later try to recall studied items on their own, without the disruption of retrieval strategies by other group members (Barber et al., 2015). These findings suggest that collaborative inhibition produces a lasting reduction in the accessibility of individuals' memories.

Collaborative Recall Has Other Benefits

Despite the effects of collaborative inhibition, when individuals recall information together in a group, they are exposed to items recalled by others that they may not recall themselves. This exposure improves their memory when they are retested at a later time (Blumen & Rajaram, 2008). And when group members discuss what they have recalled, they can help each other to correct and reduce memory errors

(Ross et al., 2008). These observations fit with earlier work showing that couples in close relationships often rely on collaborative remembering (also called *transactive memory*) (Wegner et al., 1991), whereby each member of the couple remembers certain kinds of information that they can share with the other. So the next time you are sharing memories of a past activity with friends, you will be shaping your memories for both better and worse.

The Real World • Is GPS Hurting Our Memories?

Like many of us, the journalist Steven Petrow happily relied on GPS navigation when driving because it allowed him to get to his destination quickly and with little effort. But he began to realize that in doing so he had lost touch with the world around him: "I blindly followed my car's GPS navigator without paying attention to my surroundings. Since I never turned on my brain's own map, I couldn't find my way back to the same location a second time. I'd become like the Steve Carrell character in *The Office*, in which the GPS orders him to drive his car right into a lake" (Petrow, 2018). Sounds far-fetched—until you read that in June 2021, a man in Newton, Massachusetts, actually *did* follow directions from his Waze app onto a golf course at night, where his SUV became stuck on the sixth tee at Brae Burn Country Club (Anderson, 2021)! Because of incidents like this one, Petrow's worry is shared by others, as evidenced by popular press articles with such titles as "Ditch the GPS. It's ruining your brain" (O'Connor, 2019). Are these concerns justified? Let's examine some relevant research.

In the early 2000s, the neuroscientist Eleanor Maguire and her colleagues published famous studies of London taxicab drivers, who rely extensively on their spatial navigation and memory abilities (Maguire et al., 2000; Maguire et al., 2006; see also The Influence of Practice in the Neuroscience and Behaviour chapter). Maguire and associates reported that the volume of the posterior part of the hippocampus, a region linked to both memory and spatial navigation, was larger in the taxi drivers than in control

participants, and that this increased volume was positively correlated with more experience driving taxis. These findings suggested that greater reliance on navigation and memory abilities can yield increased volume in a key brain region that supports those abilities. If that's so, it follows that reliance on GPS could possibly lessen the engagement of the hippocampus, and over time, produce impaired memory abilities.

Relevant data come from another study of spatial memory and navigation in London (Javadi et al., 2017). Participants went on a tour of London's Soho area in order to learn about its spatial layout. The next day, they underwent fMRI scanning while viewing a filmed simulation of Soho. Each participant performed two tasks during scanning. In one task, they relied on their memories of the previous day's tour to plan how they would navigate through Soho; in the other, they simply followed navigation instructions that the experimenters provided, much like relying on GPS. Critically, the hippocampus was strongly activated during the task that required memory-based navigation, but not during the task that used GPS-like instructions. Because the hippocampus plays a critical role in spatial memory, these findings suggest that people who relied on GPS were likely to remember less about their Soho tour than those that did not rely on GPS.

Consistent with this idea, an earlier, purely cognitive study that showed that reliance on GPS produced impaired memory for the route travelled during a virtual navigation task (Gardony et al., 2015). We've probably all had similar experiences, where we follow GPS directions

and realize that we don't recall much of the route we've just navigated, just like the journalist Steven Petrow. That still leaves open the question of whether repeated reliance on GPS over a long period of time has broader negative effects on our memory abilities. Dahmani and Bohbot (2020) addressed this question by asking 50 drivers about their lifetime GPS experience, and examining their performance on two virtual maze tasks that required spatial navigation and memory without relying on GPS. Drivers who reported more lifetime GPS experience performed more poorly on these tasks than did drivers who reported less lifetime GPS experience. Do these findings demonstrate that long-term use of GPS impairs spatial memory? Or could it be that people with poor spatial navigation and memory skills rely more on GPS in the first place? Dahmani and Bohbot (2020) followed up with 13 of the drivers 3 years after the initial testing, and found that drivers who relied more on GPS during that time showed a steeper decline in spatial memory during the follow-up than drivers who relied less on GPS since initial testing. These findings provide suggestive evidence that more reliance on GPS can produce an impairment of spatial memory abilities.

Additional research will be needed to sort out the long-term effects of GPS on navigation and memory abilities. While it's unlikely that many of us will end up in the same dire straits as the Steve Carrell character in *The Office* or the man who crashed his SUV on the golf course, the evidence so far suggests that concerns that GPS could be hurting our memories have some empirical basis.

Memory Failures: The Seven "Sins" of Memory

You probably haven't given much thought to breathing today, and the reason is that from the moment you woke up, you've been doing it effortlessly and well. But the moment breathing fails, you are reminded of just how important it is. Memory is like that. Every time we see, think, notice, imagine, or wonder, we are drawing on our ability to use information stored in our brains, but it isn't until this ability fails that we become acutely aware of just how much we should treasure it. Such memory errors—the seven "sins" of memory—cast similar illumination on how memory normally operates and how often it operates well (Schacter, 1999, 2001b, 2021). We'll discuss each of the seven "sins" in detail below.

1. Transience

Wilder Penfield was a famous Canadian neurosurgeon who founded the Montreal Neurological Institute and developed the effective surgical treatment of epilepsy. Before operating on a patient, he would stimulate regions of their brain with electrical probes. This was done while the patient was awake on the operating table (under local anaesthesia). His intent was to identify the regions of the brain responsible for generating the seizures, but in the process he was able to create detailed maps of the function of the human cortex. Stimulation in one area would cause the left hand to twitch. Stimulation in another area would cause the patient to report a tingling in their right leg.

Many of the experiences reported by patients after stimulation had the character of amazingly detailed, vivid memories. For example, a patient might hear the voice of a cousin in Africa, or see a man and dog walking along a road near their place in the country. During such experiences, the patient was simultaneously aware of being in the operating room. These "memories" (as they seemed to be) were so detailed that, to Penfield, it seemed as though the cortex must contain a permanent record of all past experience (Penfield & Perot, 1963). In fact, only a small minority of his patients reported such experiences, and whether or not they are memories is impossible to know—it now seems very likely that they were not memories at all.

Contrary to what Penfield believed, we now know that memories can and do degrade with time. The culprit here is **transience:** *forgetting what occurs with the passage of time.* Transience occurs during the storage phase of memory, after an experience has been encoded and before it is retrieved. You've already seen the workings of transience—rapid forgetting—in sensory storage and short-term storage. Transience also occurs in long-term storage, as was first illustrated in the late 1870s by Hermann Ebbinghaus, a German philosopher who, after studying lists of nonsense syllables, measured his own memory for those syllables at different delays (Ebbinghaus, 1885/1964). Ebbinghaus charted his recall of the syllables over time, creating the forgetting curve shown in **FIGURE 6.16**. He noted a rapid drop-off in retention during the first few tests, followed by a slower rate of forgetting on later tests—a general pattern confirmed by many subsequent memory researchers (Wixted & Ebbensen, 1991). So, for example, when English-speakers were tested for memory of Spanish vocabulary acquired during high school or university courses taken 1 to 50 years earlier, there was a rapid drop-off in memory during the first 3 years after the students' last class, followed by tiny losses in later years (Bahrick, 1984, 2000). In all these studies, memories didn't fade at a constant rate as time passed; most forgetting happened soon after an event occurred, with increasingly less forgetting as more time passed.

Learning Outcomes

WHAT YOU NEED TO KNOW

- Identify each of the memory "sins."
- Describe possible benefits of each memory "sin."

transience Forgetting what occurs with the passage of time.

Figure 6.16

The Curve of Forgetting
Hermann Ebbinghaus
measured his retention at
various delay intervals after
he studied lists of nonsense
syllables. He measured
retention in percent savings,
that is, the percentage of time
he needed to relearn the list
compared with the time he
needed to learn it initially.

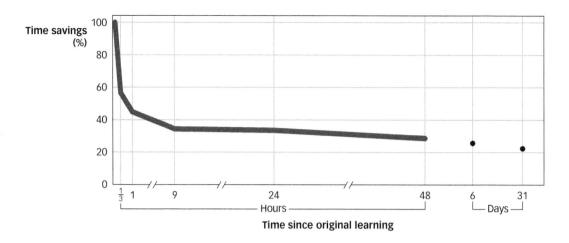

An interesting exception to the general rule that memories fade over time comes from studies of people like Jill Price, the woman described in the chapter opener who showed extraordinary recall of personal experiences. A study of 30 similar individuals with highly superior autobiographical memory revealed that they remembered about as many details of personal events as did people with ordinary memory abilities for events that occurred a day or a week earlier. However, the individuals with highly superior autobiographical memory recalled many more details than did the control participants about personal events that occurred a month, a year, and 10 years earlier (LePort et al., 2016). In other words, they showed much less forgetting over time, perhaps because people with highly superior autobiographical memory spend more time thinking about past personal events than other people do, which shields these experiences from forgetting.

Not only do most of us forget memories with the passage of time, but the quality of our memories also changes. At early time points on the forgetting curve—minutes, hours, and days—memory preserves a relatively detailed record, allowing us to reproduce the past with reasonable if not perfect accuracy. But with the passing of time, we increasingly rely on our general memories for what usually happens and attempt to reconstruct the details by inference and even sheer guesswork. Transience involves a gradual switch from specific to more general memories (Brewer, 1996; Eldridge et al., 1994; Thompson et al., 1996).

Yet another way that memories can be forgotten is by interference from other memories. For example, if you carry out the same activities at work each day, by the time Friday rolls around, it may be difficult to remember what you did on Monday because later activities blend in with earlier ones. This is an example of **retroactive interference,** *situations in which later learning impairs memory for information acquired earlier* (Postman & Underwood, 1973). **Proactive interference,** in contrast, refers to *situations in which earlier learning impairs memory for information acquired later*. For instance, if you use the same parking lot each day at work or at

retroactive interference Situations in which later learning later impairs memory for information acquired earlier.

proactive interference Situations in which earlier learning impairs memory for information acquired later.

First memories are seen later in cultures that place less emphasis on talking about the past.

school, you've probably gone out to find your car and then stood there confused by the memories of having parked it on previous days.

Finally, one of the most common types of forgetting over time is due to *childhood amnesia,* or *infantile amnesia,* the fact that most of us have few or no memories from the first few years of life. On average, an individual's first memory dates to about 3 to 3½ years of age (Dudycha & Dudycha, 1933; Waldfogel, 1948), with women reporting slightly earlier first memories (3.07 years of age) than men (3.4 years) (Howes et al., 1993). These estimates are based on individuals from Western (i.e., North American and European) cultures, which emphasize talking about the past. First memories are seen at even later ages in Asian cultures that place less emphasis on talking about the past, such as Korea and China (MacDonald et al., 2000; Mullen, 1994; Peterson et al., 2009). Culture may thus impact how long our memories last (Wang, 2021).

2. Absentmindedness

The great cellist Yo-Yo Ma put his treasured $2.5 million instrument in the trunk of a taxicab in New York City and then rode to his destination. After a 10-minute trip, he paid the driver and left the cab, forgetting his cello. Minutes later, Mr. Ma realized what he had done and called the police. Fortunately, they tracked down the taxi and recovered the instrument within hours (Finkelstein, 1999). But how had the celebrated cellist forgotten about something so important that had occurred only 10 minutes earlier? Transience is not a likely culprit. As soon as Mr. Ma realized what he'd done with his instrument, he recalled where he had put it. This information had not disappeared from his memory (which is why he was able to tell the police where the cello was). Instead, Yo-Yo Ma was a victim of **absentmindedness,** *a lapse in attention that results in memory failure.*

What makes people absentminded? One common cause is lack of attention. Attention plays a vital role in encoding information into long-term memory. Without proper attention, material is much less likely to be stored properly and recalled later. In studies of divided attention, research participants are given materials to remember, such as a list of words, a story, or a series of pictures. At the same time, they are required to perform an additional task that draws their attention away from the material. For example, participants in one study listened to lists of 15 words for a later memory test (Craik et al., 1996). They were allowed to pay full attention to certain lists, but while hearing other lists, they had to simultaneously view a visual display that contained four boxes; they were told to press different keys to indicate where an asterisk was appearing and disappearing. On a later test, participants recalled far fewer words from the list they had heard while their attention was divided (for research on the effects of attention in the classroom, see the section Testing Aids Attention in the Learning chapter).

There Is Less Activity in the Left Frontal Lobe When Attention Is Divided

What happens in the brain when attention is divided? As we saw earlier, greater activity in the lower left frontal region during encoding is associated with better memory. But participants show less activity in the lower left frontal lobe when their attention is divided (Shallice et al., 1994). Dividing attention, then, prevents the lower left frontal lobe from playing its normal role in semantic encoding, and the result is absentminded forgetting. Divided attention also leads to less hippocampal involvement in encoding (Kensinger et al., 2003; Uncapher & Rugg, 2008). Given the importance of the hippocampus to episodic memory, this finding may help to explain why absentminded forgetting is sometimes so extreme, as when we forget where we put our keys or glasses only moments earlier.

Yo-Yo Ma with his $2.5 million cello. The famous cellist lost the instrument when he absentmindedly forgot that he'd placed it in a taxicab's trunk minutes earlier.

Talking on a cell phone while driving is a common occurrence and an example of divided attention in everyday life; texting is even worse. Texting while driving is illegal because it is dangerous. It entails hefty fines and even license suspension in Canada.

absentmindedness A lapse in attention that results in memory failure.

External memory aids such as Google Calendar can enhance prospective memory in healthy individuals, as well as in patients experiencing memory deficits attributable to traumatic brain injury or Alzheimer's disease.

Most people watching the Macy's Thanksgiving Day Parade will easily recall this character's name, closely associated with a grumpy attitude: The Grinch!

prospective memory Remembering to do things in the future.

blocking A failure to retrieve information that is available in memory even though you are trying to produce it.

We Don't Always Remember to Remember

Another common cause of absentmindedness is forgetting to carry out actions that we plan to do in the future. On any given day, you need to remember the times and places that your classes meet, you need to remember with whom and where you are having lunch, you need to remember which grocery items to pick up for dinner, and you need to remember which page of this book you were on when you fell asleep. In other words, you have to remember to remember, which is called **prospective memory,** *remembering to do things in the future* (Einstein & McDaniel, 1990, 2005).

Failures of prospective memory are a major source of absentmindedness in everyday life (Dismukes, 2012). Avoiding these problems often requires having a cue available at the very moment you need to remember to carry out an action. Because external reminders are so important for enhancing prospective memory, and thereby reducing absentminded memory errors, it is perhaps not surprising in this era of smartphones and Google Calendar that we are increasingly relying on external devices to remind us to carry out future tasks in everyday life, a process referred to as *intention offloading* (Risko & Gilbert, 2016). People are particularly likely to engage in intention offloading when task demands are high and when they lack confidence in their memory abilities, but this self-initiated reliance on external reminders improves prospective memory performance (Gilbert, 2015).

Prospective memory failures are especially common after brain injuries, so it is important to determine whether novel kinds of external reminders, such as Google Calendar, can help brain-injured patients who suffer from high rates of absentminded forgetting. One study of 12 patients who had serious memory impairments as a consequence of various kinds of brain injuries showed that training these patients to use Google Calendar to set reminders improved their prospective memory performance in everyday life more than did training them to use a diary (McDonald et al., 2011). More recent case studies of patients with memory problems resulting from traumatic brain injury (Baldwin & Powell, 2015) and Alzheimer's disease (El Haj et al., 2017) have shown positive effects on everyday prospective memory from training the patients to use Google Calendar synched to their smartphones. These advantages of technology for improving prospective memory failures are balanced by the costs discussed in The Real World: Is GPS Hurting Our Memories?

3. Blocking

Have you ever tried to recall the name of a famous movie actor or a book you've read—and felt that the answer was on the tip of your tongue, rolling around in your head *somewhere* but just out of reach at that moment? This tip-of-the-tongue experience is a classic example of **blocking,** *a failure to retrieve information that is available in memory even though you are trying to produce it.* The sought-after information has been encoded and stored, and a cue is available that would ordinarily trigger recall of it. The information has not faded from memory, and you aren't forgetting to retrieve it. Rather, you are experiencing a full-blown retrieval failure, which makes this memory breakdown especially frustrating. Researchers have described the tip-of-the-tongue state, in particular, as "a mild torment, something like [being] on the brink of a sneeze" (Brown & McNeill, 1966, p. 326).

Blocking occurs especially often for the names of people and places (Cohen, 1990; Semenza, 2009; Valentine et al., 1996). Why? Because their links to related concepts and knowledge are weaker than for common names. That somebody's last name is Baker doesn't tell us much about the person, but saying that he *is* a baker does. To illustrate this point, researchers showed people pictures of cartoon and comic strip characters, some with descriptive names that highlight key features of the character (e.g., Grumpy, Snow White, Scrooge) and others with arbitrary names (e.g., Aladdin, Mary Poppins, Pinocchio) (Brédart & Valentine, 1998). Even though the two types of names were equally familiar to participants in the experiment, they blocked less often on the descriptive names than on the arbitrary names.

Although it's frustrating when it occurs, blocking is a relatively infrequent event for most of us. However, it occurs more often as we grow older, and it is a very common complaint among people in their 60s and 70s (Burke et al., 1991; Schwartz, 2002). Even more striking, some individuals with brain damage live in a nearly perpetual tip-of-the-tongue state (Semenza, 2009). One such individual could recall the names of only 2 of 40 famous people when she saw their photographs, compared with 25 of 40 for healthy volunteers in the control group (Semenza & Zettin, 1989). Yet she could still recall correctly the occupations of 32 of these people—the same number as healthy people could recall. This case and similar ones have given researchers important clues about what parts of the brain are involved in retrieving proper names. Name blocking usually results from damage to parts of the left temporal lobe on the surface of the cortex, most often as a result of a stroke. In fact, studies that show strong activation of regions within the temporal lobe when people recall proper names support this idea (Damasio et al., 1996; Gorno-Tempini et al., 1998).

4. Memory Misattribution

In 1971, musician George Harrison (formerly of The Beatles) had a huge hit worldwide with the song "My Sweet Lord." Because of its similarity to the earlier Chiffons hit "He's So Fine" (written by Ronnie Mack), Harrison was sued. In 1976, the court found that he had "subconsciously" copied the earlier song, but that the lack of awareness was not a mitigating factor—the court recommended that he pay $U.S.1.6 million in damages to the copyright owner of "He's So Fine" (equivalent to about $8.7 million in today's Canadian dollars). Harrison was a victim of **memory misattribution,** *assigning a recollection or an idea to the wrong source* (see **FIGURE 6.17**).

Memory misattribution errors are a primary cause of eyewitness misidentifications. Harrison's case, though dramatic, is not an isolated occurrence: Faulty eyewitness memory was a factor in more than 75% of the first 250 cases in which individuals were shown to be innocent through DNA evidence after being convicted of crimes they did not commit (Garrett, 2011) (see Other Voices: Memories Inside Out).

Correct Memories Can Be Attributed to the Wrong Source

Part of memory is knowing where our memories came from. This is known as **source memory,** *recall of when, where, and how information was acquired* (Johnson et al., 1993; Mitchell & Johnson, 2009; Schacter et al., 1984). People sometimes correctly recall a fact they learned earlier or accurately recognize a person or object they have seen before but misattribute the source of this knowledge—just as happened to George Harrison. Such misattribution could be the cause of déjà vu experiences, when you suddenly feel that you have been in a situation before even though you can't recall any details. A present situation that is similar to a past experience may trigger a general sense of familiarity that is mistakenly attributed to having been in the exact situation previously, which can give rise to the unsettling sensation of déjà vu (Brown, 2004; Cleary & Claxton, 2018; Reed, 1988).

Individuals with damage to the frontal lobes are especially prone to memory misattribution errors (Schacter et al., 1984; Shimamura & Squire, 1987). This is probably because the frontal lobes play a significant role in effortful retrieval

AP PHOTO

Figure 6.17

Memory Misattribution George Harrison made a memory misattribution when he thought that he had composed a melody that was actually created by someone else, and the mistake cost him nearly $9 million. He still found reasons to smile, however.

memory misattribution Assigning a recollection or an idea to the wrong source.

source memory Recall of when, where, and how information was acquired.

Other Voices | Memories Inside Out

There's a good chance that sometime during the summer of 2015 you saw and enjoyed the hit Pixar movie *Inside Out*, which portrays the emotional struggles of the 11-year-old Riley after her family moves to a new home by drawing on psychological research that distinguishes among basic emotions (see the chapter on Emotion and Motivation). The movie also delves into Riley's memories and provides some realistic insights into how memories can be used to regulate emotions. But as Karen Daniel points out in an opinion piece published when the movie opened, the film's depiction of memory ignored some key findings and ideas from psychological research on memory, with potentially serious consequences:

Let me begin by saying that I love, love, love Pixar movies. Like many adults, I began watching them as part of my parental duties. There was a time when I could recite all the dialogue from *Monsters Inc.* and the first two *Toy Story* films.

It was thus with great anticipation that I tuned in to a radio interview of Pete Docter, the director of the latest Pixar release, *Inside Out*. What a fabulous idea: animating the emotions inside the mind of an 11-year-old child named Riley who is undergoing a major life transition. Docter explained that he researched many aspects of psychology to make the film accurate. When it came to human memory, however, Docter departed from science for the sake of the story line.

As shown in a trailer for *Inside Out*, Riley's memories are portrayed as mini-animations safely preserved inside little globes, which can be pulled out and replayed exactly the way they happened. The character Joy explains that certain of these globes contain "core memories" that form the basis of Riley's personality. This representation of memory is essential to the plot but is not true, as Docter candidly admitted.

I couldn't help but cringe. Given the wide appeal of Pixar movies, a new generation may grow up internalizing the profoundly false notion that memory works like a video recording and that perfect memories of events can be recalled at will. In reality, memory is fallible, malleable, and subject to suggestion and distortion. Docter noted that learning this was a revelation to him, even though he chose not to depict memory that way in *Inside Out*.

One may ask, "Who cares? It's just a movie." In the world of criminal justice, it matters a great deal. One of the most critical moments in a criminal trial is when a victim or witness points at the defendant and declares, "I will never forget that face." The witness usually professes complete certainty, and the prosecutor highlights this as proof of the defendant's guilt—even though experts tell us courtroom certainty does not necessarily correlate to accuracy.

In fact, mistaken identification is a leading cause of conviction of the innocent. Myriad factors that are not necessarily obvious to the average person can affect the reliability of an eyewitness identification, such as distractions at the time of the event, lapse of time, post-event discussions with police, and limitations inherent in cross-racial identifications. Expert witnesses can help explain these factors, but most judges exclude expert testimony on the ground [sic] that eyewitness identifications are a matter of "common sense" and expert assistance is not

Karen L. Daniel was a prominent attorney in Chicago and director of Northwestern University Law School's Center on Wrongful Convictions. She died in a car accident in 2019.

necessary. (The Illinois Supreme Court is now reviewing a case that challenges this approach.)

Which brings us back to *Inside Out*. Absent the input of an expert, jurors are left to draw on personal experiences in evaluating testimony. Today's children (and their parents) may become tomorrow's jurors who believe, incorrectly, that memories are stored intact, and that witnesses can simply compare the pictures within their little memory globes to the person sitting at the defendant's table. Docter explained that this comports with most people's sense of how memory works—which is why relying on "common sense" in criminal trials falls short.

We can never entirely eliminate human error from the justice system, but overconfidence in witnesses and misunderstanding by factfinders leads to many wrongful convictions. Let's enjoy Pixar's new film, but when we return from the movie theater, let's ensure that those charged with deciding guilt or innocence in the courtroom are armed with scientific information about eyewitness identifications rather than with the snow globe concept of memory.

SOURCE: Daniel, K. (2015, June 16). Pixar movie teaches future jurors wrong lesson on memory. *Chicago Sun-Times*. Reprinted with permission of the author.

As Daniel and the text point out, faulty eyewitness memories are frequently at work in wrongful convictions. It would be unfortunate if the naive view of memory communicated by *Inside Out* has a lasting influence on any prospective jurors. On a more encouraging note, there are signs that some of the important findings regarding memory's fallibility, such as the seven sins of memory that you learned about in this chapter, are being communicated to participants in the legal system. For example, in 2014 the American National Academy of Sciences published a report written by a distinguished committee composed of experts in both psychology and law titled *Identifying the Culprit: Assessing Eyewitness Identification*, which is intended to convey the findings of psychological research on eyewitness memory to participants in the legal system. Though no doubt many more people saw *Inside Out* than will read this important report, it seems likely that accurate characterizations of memory research such as those contained in the National Academy of Sciences' report will ultimately be more influential in the courtroom than the entertaining though misleading depictions of Riley's memory globes.

processes, which are required to dredge up the correct source of a memory. These individuals sometimes produce bizarre misattributions. In 1991, a British photographer in his mid-40s known as MR was overcome with feelings of familiarity about people he didn't know. He kept asking his wife whether each new passing stranger was "somebody"—a screen actor, television news announcer, or local celebrity. MR's feelings were so intense that he often could not resist approaching strangers and asking whether they were indeed famous celebrities. When given formal tests, MR recognized the faces of actual celebrities as accurately as did healthy volunteers in the control group. But MR also "recognized" more than 75% of unfamiliar faces, whereas healthy volunteers hardly ever did. Neurological exams revealed that MR suffered from multiple sclerosis, which had caused damage to his frontal lobes (Ward et al., 1999). Psychologists call MR's type of memory misattribution **false recognition,** *a feeling of familiarity about something that hasn't been encountered before.*

Memory Misattribution Happens to Us All, but Can Be Influenced by Culture

We are all vulnerable to memory misattribution. Take the following test and there is a good chance that you will experience false recognition for yourself. First, study the two lists of words presented in **TABLE 6.1** by reading each word for about 1 second. When you are done, return to this paragraph for more instructions, but don't look back at the table! Now try to recognize which of the following words appeared in the list you just studied: *taste, bread, needle, king, sweet, thread.* If you think that *taste* and *thread* were on the lists you studied, you're right. And if you think that *bread* and *king* weren't on those lists, you're also right. But if you think that *needle* or *sweet* appeared in the lists, you're dead wrong.

Most people make exactly the same mistake, claiming with confidence that they saw *needle* and *sweet* on the list. This occurs because all the words in the lists are associated with *needle* or *sweet.* Seeing each word in the study list activates related words. Because *needle* and *sweet* are related to all of the associates, they become more activated than other words—so highly activated that only minutes later, people swear that they actually studied the words (Deese, 1959; Gallo, 2006, 2010; Roediger & McDermott, 1995, 2000). This error is extremely powerful: Even people with "highly superior autobiographical memory" (see chapter opening), who have an extraordinary ability to recall everyday experiences accurately, are as susceptible to this type of memory misattribution as the rest of us (Patihis et al., 2013). In fact, neuroimaging studies of this false recognition error show that many of the same brain regions are active during false recognition and true recognition (Cabeza et al., 2001; Schacter et al., 1996; Slotnick & Schacter, 2004).

Recent cross-cultural work using a similar experimental procedure (with associated pictures instead of associated words) has shown that both European and Chinese participants show roughly the same overall level of false recognition (Wang et al., 2021). However, European participants were more likely than Chinese participants to claim that they had a specific, detailed recollection of having seen a nonpresented picture, whereas Chinese participants were more likely than Europeans to claim that they just knew that a nonpresented picture appeared earlier on the study list. Similarly, European participants were more likely than Chinese participants to claim that they had a specific recollection of pictures that actually were presented. These differences in the quality of false (and true) recognition parallel other findings showing that Westerners tend to retrieve more specific details about actual past events than do East Asians (Millar et al., 2013; Wang, 2021), and suggest that culture plays an important role in shaping how people construct memories.

TABLE 6.1

FALSE RECOGNITION

sour	thread
candy	pin
sugar	eye
bitter	sewing
good	sharp
taste	point
tooth	prick
nice	thimble
honey	haystack
soda	pain
chocolate	hurt
heart	injection
cake	syringe
tart	cloth
pie	knitting

false recognition A feeling of familiarity about something that hasn't been encountered before.

In 1992, an El Al cargo plane crashed into an apartment building in a suburb of Amsterdam. When Dutch psychologists asked students if they had seen the television film of the plane crashing, a majority said they had. In fact, no such footage exists (Crombag et al., 1996).

5. Suggestibility

On October 4, 1992, an El Al cargo plane crashed into an apartment building in a southern suburb of Amsterdam, killing 39 residents and all 4 members of the airline crew. The disaster dominated news in the Netherlands for days as people viewed footage of the crash scene and read about the catastrophe. Ten months later, Dutch psychologists asked a simple question of university students: "Did you see the television film of the moment the plane hit the apartment building?" Fifty-five percent answered yes (Crombag et al., 1996). All of this might seem perfectly normal except for one key fact: There was no television film of the moment when the plane actually crashed. The researchers had asked a suggestive question, one that implied that television film of the crash had been shown. Respondents may have viewed television film of the *postcrash* scene, and they may have read, imagined, or talked about what might have happened when the plane hit the building, but they most definitely did not see it. The suggestive question led participants to misattribute information from these or other sources to a film that did not exist. **Suggestibility** is *the tendency to incorporate misleading information from external sources into personal recollections.*

If misleading details can be implanted in people's memories, is it also possible to suggest entire episodes that never occurred? The answer seems to be yes (Loftus, 1993, 2003). In one study, the research participant, a teenager named Chris, was asked by his older brother, Jim, to try to remember the time Chris had been lost in a shopping mall at age 5. He initially recalled nothing, but after several days, Chris produced a detailed recollection of the event. He recalled that he "felt so scared I would never see my family again" and remembered that a kindly old man wearing a flannel shirt found him crying (Loftus, 1993, p. 532). But according to Jim and other family members, Chris was never lost in a shopping mall. Of 24 participants in a larger study on implanted memories, approximately 25% falsely remembered being lost as a child in a shopping mall or in a similar public place (Loftus & Pickrell, 1995).

In response to suggestions, people develop false memories for some of the same reasons memory misattribution occurs. We do not store all the details of our experiences in memory, making us vulnerable to accepting suggestions about what might have happened or should have happened. In addition, visual imagery plays an important role in constructing false memories (Goff & Roediger, 1998). Asking people to imagine an event like spilling punch all over the bride's parents at a wedding increases the likelihood that they will develop a false memory of it (Hyman & Pentland, 1996). Social pressure can also enhance suggestibility, as in cases in which people falsely confess to crimes they did not commit after repeated interrogations by authority figures such as police who are convinced of their guilt and press for a confession (Kassin, 2015). In some instances, these wrongly accused individuals develop false memories of the crime (Kassin, 2007).

All of these factors were operating in a study that provides some of the most dramatic evidence for the misleading effects of suggestion. Consider the following question: Did you ever commit a crime when you were between the ages of 11 and 14 years old? Assuming that you did not, do you think that you could ever be convinced that you did? Shaw and Porter (2015) asked university students about an experience that actually occurred between ages 11 and 14, and also about a crime that they supposedly committed during those years (theft, assault, or assault with a weapon). Although none of the students had actually committed any crimes, during three separate interviews, the experimenters required them repeatedly to imagine that they had. The researchers also applied social pressure techniques, such as telling students

suggestibility The tendency to incorporate misleading information from external sources into personal recollections.

that their parents or caregivers said they had committed the crime and stating that most people can retrieve seemingly lost memories if they try hard enough. By the end of the third interview, 70% of the students came to believe that they had committed the crime, and some of them even developed detailed false memories of having done so (Shaw & Porter, 2015; Wade et al., 2018).

Studies such as these can help us understand the key role that suggestibility played in a controversy that arose during the 1980s and 1990s, concerning the accuracy of childhood memories that people recalled during psychotherapy. One highly publicized example involved a woman named Diana Halbrooks (Schacter, 1996). After a few months in psychotherapy, she began recalling disturbing incidents from her childhood—for example, that her mother had tried to kill her and that her father had abused her sexually. Although her parents denied these events had ever occurred, her therapist encouraged her to believe in the reality of her memories. Eventually, Diana Halbrooks stopped therapy and came to realize that the "memories" she had recovered were inaccurate.

How could this have happened? Victims of sexual abuse and other traumas typically remember these deeply disturbing events (McNally, 2021; Rubin et al., 2016), and it is important for trauma survivors to express their memories in order to help therapy and healing (Hitchcock et al., 2017). However, a number of the techniques used by psychotherapists to try to pull up forgotten childhood memories during the 1980s and 1990s were clearly suggestive (Poole et al., 1995), as was the case for Diana Halbrooks. Importantly, memories that people remember spontaneously on their own are corroborated by other people at about the same rate as the memories of individuals who never forgot their abuse, whereas memories recovered in response to suggestive therapeutic techniques are virtually never corroborated by others (McNally & Geraerts, 2009).

6. Bias

Bias refers to *the distorting influences of present knowledge, beliefs, and feelings on recollection of previous experiences.* Sometimes what people remember from their pasts says less about what actually happened than about what they think, feel, or believe now about themselves or others (Levine et al., 2018). Researchers have also found that our current moods can bias our recall of past experiences (Bower, 1981; Buchanan, 2007; Eich, 1995). So, in addition to helping you recall actual sad memories (as you saw earlier in this chapter), a sad mood can also bias your recollections of experiences that may not have been so sad. *Consistency bias* is the bias to reconstruct the past to fit the present. One researcher asked people in 1973 to rate their attitudes towards a variety of controversial social issues, including legalization of marijuana, women's rights, and aid to equity-deserving groups (Marcus, 1986). They were asked to make the same rating again in 1982 and also to indicate what their attitudes had been in 1973. Researchers found that participants' recollections in 1982 of their 1973 attitudes were more closely related to what they believed in 1982 than to what they had actually said in 1973.

A recent study provides evidence for the operation of consistency bias in how people "remember" fake news. In May 2018, Ireland held a vote that resulted in the repeal of the 8th amendment to the Irish constitution, which was responsible for restrictive abortion laws to protect the rights of unborn children. A week before the vote, researchers administered an online survey to over 3,000 adults that included headlines and accompanying photos of four true and two fake news stories that related either to the "no" campaign, which wanted to preserve the 8th amendment, or to the "yes" campaign, which wanted to repeal it (Murphy et al., 2019). The researchers created two versions of each of the fake news stories; one showed the "no" side in a bad light and one showed the "yes" side in a bad light. Although none of the participants could have actually experienced the events depicted in the

bias The distorting influences of present knowledge, beliefs, and feelings on recollection of previous experiences.

Supporters of the "yes" campaign to repeal Ireland's restrictive abortion laws celebrate the results of the May 2018 vote. Both "yes" and "no" vote supporters developed false memories of fake news stories that showed the other side in a bad light.

fake news stories, Murphy and colleagues found that nearly half claimed to remember at least one of the fake events! Reflecting the operation of consistency bias, a higher percentage of "no" supporters reported a false memory for fake news about the "yes" side, and a higher percentage of "yes" supporters reported a false memory for fake news about the "no" side.

Egocentric bias refers to the tendency to exaggerate the change between present and past in order to make ourselves look good in retrospect. For example, students sometimes remember feeling more anxious before taking an exam than they actually reported at the time (Keuler & Safer, 1998), and blood donors sometimes recall being more nervous about giving blood than they actually were (Breckler, 1994). In both cases, change biases colour memory and make people feel that they behaved more bravely or courageously than they actually did in order to overcome the exaggerated levels of anxiety and nervousness that they remember feeling. Similarly, when university students tried to remember high school grades and their memories were checked against their actual transcripts, they were highly accurate for grades of A (89% correct) and extremely inaccurate for grades of D (29% correct) (Bahrick et al., 1996). The same kind of egocentric bias occurs with memory for university grades: 81% of errors inflated the actual grade, and this bias was evident even when participants were asked about their grades soon after graduation (Bahrick et al., 2008). People were remembering the past as they wanted it to be rather than the way it actually was.

7. Persistence

The artist Melinda Stickney-Gibson awoke in her apartment to the smell of smoke. She jumped out of bed and saw black plumes rising through cracks in the floor. Raging flames had engulfed the entire building, and she had no chance to escape except by jumping from her third-floor window. Shortly after she crashed to the ground, the building exploded into a brilliant fireball. Although she survived the fire and the fall, Melinda became overwhelmed by memories of the fire. When she sat down in front of a blank canvas to start a new painting, her memories of that awful night intruded. Her paintings, which were previously bright, colourful abstractions, became dark meditations that included only black, orange, and ochre—the colours of the fire (Schacter, 1996).

Melinda Stickney-Gibson's experiences illustrate memory's seventh and most deadly sin, **persistence:** *the intrusive recollection of events that we wish we could forget.* Melinda's experience is far from unique; persistence frequently occurs after disturbing or traumatic incidents, such as the fire that destroyed her home. Although being able to recall memories quickly is usually considered a good thing, in the case of persistence, that ability mutates into an unwelcome burden.

Emotional Experiences Are Easiest to Remember

Emotional experiences tend to be better remembered than nonemotional ones. For instance, memory for unpleasant pictures, such as mutilated bodies, or pleasant ones, such as attractive men and women, is more accurate than for emotionally neutral pictures, such as household objects (Ochsner, 2000). Emotional arousal seems to focus our attention on the central features of an event. In one experiment, people who viewed an emotionally arousing sequence of slides involving a bloody car accident remembered more of the central themes and fewer peripheral details than people who viewed a nonemotional sequence (Christianson & Loftus, 1987).

persistence The intrusive recollection of events that we wish we could forget.

flashbulb memories Detailed recollections of when and where we heard about shocking events.

Intrusive memories are undesirable consequences of emotional experiences because emotional experiences generally lead to more vivid and enduring recollections than nonemotional experiences do. One line of evidence comes from the study of **flashbulb memories,** which are *detailed recollections of when and where we heard about shocking events* (Brown & Kulik, 1977). For example, most North Americans born in the early 1990s or earlier can recall exactly where they were and how they heard about the September 11, 2001, terrorist attacks in which four passenger aircraft were hijacked. Two planes were deliberately flown into the World Trade Center in New York City, and two crashed elsewhere in the United States. Memories for that day seem so clear that it is almost as if a mental flashbulb had gone off automatically and recorded the event in long-lasting and vivid detail (Kvavilashvili et al., 2009). Several studies have shown that flashbulb memories are not always entirely accurate, but they are generally better remembered than mundane news events from the same time (Larsen, 1992; Neisser & Harsch, 1992). Enhanced retention of flashbulb memories is partly attributable to the emotional arousal elicited by events such as the 9/11 terrorist attacks, and partly attributable to the fact that we tend to talk and think a lot about these experiences. Recall that semantic encoding enhances memory: When we talk about flashbulb experiences, we elaborate on them and thus further increase the memorability of those aspects of the experience that we discuss (Hirst et al., 2009, 2015).

The Amygdala Plays a Role

Why do our brains succumb to persistence? A key player in the brain's response to emotional events is a small, almond-shaped structure called the *amygdala*, shown in **FIGURE 6.18**. The amygdala influences hormonal systems that kick into high gear when we experience an arousing event; these stress-related hormones, such as adrenaline and cortisol, mobilize the body in the face of threat—and they also enhance memory for the experience. Damage to the amygdala does not result in a general memory deficit. Individuals with amygdala damage, however, do not remember emotional events any better than they remember nonemotional events (Cahill & McGaugh, 1998).

Consider what happened when research participants viewed a series of photographic slides that began with a mother walking her child to school and later included an emotionally arousing event: the child being hit by a car. When tested later, the participants remembered the arousing event better than the mundane ones. But individuals with amygdala damage remembered the mundane and emotionally arousing events equally well (Cahill & McGaugh, 1998). Neuroimaging studies show that when healthy people view a slide sequence that includes an emotionally arousing event, the level of activity in the amygdala at the time they see it is a good predictor of their subsequent memory for the slide. When there is heightened activity in the amygdala as people watch emotional events, there's a better chance that they will recall those events on a later test (Cahill et al., 1996; Kensinger & Schacter, 2005, 2006). And when people are given a drug that interferes with the amygdala-mediated release of stress hormones, their memory for the emotional sections is no better than their memory for the mundane sections (Lonegran et al., 2013). Recall our discussion of reconsolidation earlier in this chapter, where we saw that interfering with reconsolidation can reduce the impact of traumatic memories, which most often give rise to persistence. The same drug that interferes with the release of stress-related hormones is the one used to interfere with reconsolidation of traumatic memories (Brunet al., 2018), suggesting a possible role for reduced amygdala activity in this effect.

In many cases, there are clear benefits to forming strong memories for highly emotional events, particularly those that are life-threatening. In the case of persistence,

Some events are so emotionally charged—such as the terrorist attack on the World Trade Center—that we form unusually detailed memories of when and where we heard about them. These flashbulb memories generally persist much longer than memories for more ordinary events.

Figure 6.18
The Amygdala's Influence on Memory
The amygdala, located next to the hippocampus, responds strongly to emotional events. Individuals with amygdala damage are unable to remember emotional events any better than they can remember nonemotional ones (Cahill & McGaugh, 1998).

though, such memories may be too strong—strong enough to interfere with other aspects of daily life.

Are the Seven "Sins" Vices or Virtues?

You may have concluded that evolution has burdened us with an extremely inefficient memory system so prone to error that it often jeopardizes our well-being. Not so. The seven sins are the price we pay for the many benefits that memory provides, the occasional result of the normally efficient operation of the human memory system (Schacter, 2001b).

Consider transience, for example. Wouldn't it be great to remember all the details of every incident in your life, no matter how much time had passed? Not necessarily: If we didn't gradually forget information over time, our minds would be cluttered with details that we no longer need, such as an old phone number (Bjork, 2011; Bjork & Bjork, 1988; Norby, 2015). Information that we use infrequently is less likely to be needed in the future than is information we use more frequently over the same period (Anderson & Schooler, 1991, 2000). Also, relieving ourselves of outdated information can enhance our ability to make decisions based on memory (Richards & Frankland, 2017). Memory, in essence, makes a bet that when we haven't used information recently, we probably won't need it in the future. We win this bet more often than we lose it, making transience an adaptive property of memory.

Similarly, absentmindedness and blocking can be frustrating, but they are side effects of our memory's usually successful attempt to sort through incoming information, preserving details that are worthy of attention and recall while discarding those that are less worthy.

Memory misattribution and suggestibility both occur because we often fail to recall the details of exactly when and where we saw a face or learned a fact. Our memories carefully record such details only when we think we may need them later, and most of the time we are better off for it. Furthermore, we often use memories to anticipate possible future events. As discussed earlier, memory is flexible, allowing us to recombine elements of past experience in new ways, so that we can mentally try out different versions of what might happen. Researchers have hypothesized that this very flexibility—a strength of memory—may sometimes produce misattribution errors in which elements of past experience are miscombined (Schacter & Addis, 2007; Schacter et al., 2011). Recent studies provide experimental evidence that supports this hypothesis (Carpenter & Schacter, 2017; Dewhurst et al., 2016; see Hot Science: Memory Misattribution: When Accurate Inferences Produce Mistaken Recollections).

Bias skews our memories so that we depict ourselves in an overly favourable light, but it can also produce the benefit of contributing to our overall sense of contentment. Holding positive illusions about ourselves can lead to greater psychological well-being (Taylor, 1989). Although persistence can cause us to be haunted by traumas that we'd be better off forgetting, overall, it is probably adaptive to remember threatening or traumatic events that could pose a threat to survival.

Although each of the seven sins can cause trouble in our lives, each has an adaptive side as well. You can think of the seven sins as costs we pay for benefits that allow memory to work as well as it does most of the time.

Hot Science ⦁ Memory Misattribution: When Accurate Inferences Produce Mistaken Recollections

Examples of people, objects, and settings used in the associative inference experiments.

Imagine that you are enjoying a quiet breakfast at an outdoor café on a summer morning when a man walks by pushing a stroller with a smiling baby girl. A few days later, you return to the café and a woman of about the same age as the man walks by pushing the same stroller with the same baby. You recall the man and baby from a few days ago, and combining that event with the one you just experienced, infer that the man and the woman are probably a couple. Psychologists call this process *associative inference*: the ability to combine information acquired in different episodes to make new connections that we have not experienced directly (Zeithamova et al., 2012). Associative inference is an adaptive process that relies on our ability to use information stored in memory in a flexible way. But, the flexibility of memory can sometimes result in mistaken recollections.

Recent studies conducted in the lab of one of your textbook authors showed that making correct associative inferences can indeed lead to memory misattribution errors (Carpenter & Schacter, 2017), and used fMRI to reveal what is happening in the brain when people make those errors (Carpenter et al., 2021). Let's first consider the experimental paradigm that links associative inference with memory errors. Participants encoded a series of scenes that each contains a person and an object in a particular background setting. For example, as shown in the accompanying photo, in one scene a man holds a yellow construction toy in a living room with a white couch. Each scene is connected to another one in which a different person is paired with the same object — here, a little boy holds the same yellow construction

toy in a different living room with a brown couch. Participants were instructed to try to remember the individual scenes and also to try to associate the individuals who were linked by a common object. On a subsequent memory test for scene details, participants sometimes mixed up elements of related scenes, such as remembering that the man was in a living room with a brown couch. Critically, participants committed more of these misattribution errors when they made *correct* associative inferences about people and objects (e.g., correctly inferred that the man and boy were associated) than when they made *incorrect* inferences. The most likely explanation for these results is that when participants made correct associative inferences, they also mistakenly recombined elements of the two scenes.

To test this idea further, Carpenter and colleagues (2021) conducted an fMRI study in which they first measured patterns of brain activity when participants viewed pictures of scenes without the people and objects in them, such as a living room scene with a brown couch, but no boy and no construction toy. After that, participants encoded scenes with people

and objects, as in the above-described study. The next day, participants were scanned while they performed associative inference and scene memory tests. The key question was: When participants made a misattribution error on the scene memory test — for example, when they mistakenly remembered that the man was in a room with a brown couch — would the fMRI scans reveal evidence of the neural pattern previously elicited by the living room scene that contained a brown couch? And if so, would there be more evidence of this neural pattern after participants made a correct associative inference than after they made an incorrect associative inference? The answer to both questions was "Yes"! These fMRI findings support the idea that successful associative inference led people to confuse elements of the scenes they had studied, resulting in the wrong pattern being reinstated on the scene memory test.

Here we can see that memory misattribution — one of the seven sins of memory — sometimes reflects the operation of an adaptive process, associative inference, that helps us to make sense of our worlds.

Chapter Review

What Is Memory?

- Memory is the ability to store and retrieve information over time.

Encoding: Transforming Perceptions Into Memories

- Encoding is the process of transforming the information received through our senses into a lasting memory.

- A new memory is made and automatically semantically encoded when new information mixes with old information that already has meaning to us.

- Semantic encoding is characterized by relating new information to previous knowledge in a meaningful way.

- Visual imagery encoding also relates new information to previous knowledge, but features both a visual and a verbal placeholder.

- Organizational encoding is a process of finding relationships between items to make them easier to retrieve.

- Encoding information with respect to its survival value is a particularly effective method for increasing subsequent recall, perhaps because our memory systems have evolved in a way that allows us to remember especially well information that is relevant to our survival, and perhaps because survival scenarios used in memory experiments draw on elements of semantic, visual imagery, and organizational encoding, as well as require extensive planning.

Storage: Maintaining Memories Over Time

- Because research participants could recall the same number of letters from any row of the grid, the iconic memory test suggests that sensory memory holds information for a second or two. Rehearsal helps keep memories in short-term storage, and "chunking" combines information into a single, meaningful item.

- Working memory is the active maintenance of information in short-term storage, where information is retained for about 15 to 20 seconds. A model of working memory describes the subsystems that store and manipulate visual and verbal information, the episodic buffer that integrates information, and the central executive that coordinates them.

- The hippocampus functions as an index to put information into long-term memory, but evidence from amnesiacs indicates that it is not the site of long-term memory storage.

- The act of recalling, thinking, and talking about a memory leads to consolidation. Sleep also is an important factor. However, when memories are retrieved, they may also become vulnerable to disruption.

- Memory storage depends on changes in synapses, and long-term potentiation (LTP) increases synaptic connections.

Retrieval: Bringing Memories to Mind

- Whether or not we remember a past experience depends on whether retrieval cues are available to trigger recall. Retrieval cues are effective when they are given in the same context as when we encoded an experience. Moods and inner states can become retrieval cues.

- Retrieving information from memory has consequences for later remembering. Retrieval improves subsequent memory of the retrieved information, as the benefits of testing on later recall show. However, fMRI evidence shows that regions of the frontal lobe involved with retrieving information also play a role in suppressing related information that is not retrieved. This finding underscores the importance of eyewitness interviews being as complete as possible.

- Research shows that retrieving and vividly reexperiencing memories of objects that were seen makes memory vulnerable to disruption, such that unseen objects may be wrongly incorporated into the memory.

- Retrieval can be separated into the effort we make while trying to remember what happened in the past, and the successful recovery of stored information. Neuroimaging studies suggest that trying to remember activates the left frontal lobe, whereas successful recovery of stored information activates the hippocampus and regions in the brain related to the sensory aspects of an experience.

Forms of Long-Term Memory: More Than One Kind

- Long-term memory consists of several different forms.

- Implicit memory refers to the unconscious influence of past experiences on later behaviour and performance, such as procedural memory and priming. Procedural memory involves the acquisition of skills as a result of practice, and priming is a change in the ability to recognize or identify an object or a word as the result of past exposure to it. People who have amnesia are able to retain implicit memory, including procedural memory and priming, but they lack explicit memory.

- Explicit memory is the act of consciously or intentionally retrieving past experiences. Episodic memory is the collection of personal experiences from a particular time and place; it allows us to both recollect the past and imagine the future. Semantic memory is a networked, general, impersonal knowledge of facts, associations, and concepts.

- Collaborative memory refers to remembering in groups. Collaborative remembering can both impair memory (collaborative inhibition) and enhance it by exposing people to new information and helping to correct errors.

Memory Failures: The Seven "Sins" of Memory

- Memory's mistakes can be classified into seven "sins."

- Transience is reflected by a rapid decline in memory, followed by more gradual forgetting. With the passing of time, memory switches from detailed to general. Both decay and interference contribute to transience.

- Absentmindedness results from failures of attention, shallow encoding, and the influence of automatic behaviours; it is often associated with forgetting to do things in the future.

- Blocking occurs when stored information is temporarily inaccessible, as when information is on the "tip of the tongue."

- Memory misattribution happens when we experience a sense of familiarity but don't recall, or mistakenly recall, the specifics of when and where an experience occurred. Misattribution can result in eyewitness misidentification or false recognition. Individuals suffering from frontal lobe damage are especially susceptible to false recognition.

- Suggestibility gives rise to implanted memories of small details or entire episodes. Suggestive techniques such as hypnosis or visualization can promote vivid recall of suggested events, and therapists' use of suggestive techniques may be responsible for some individuals' false memories of childhood traumas. Bias reflects the influence of current knowledge, beliefs, and feelings on memory of past experiences.

- Bias can lead us to make the past consistent with the present, to exaggerate changes between past and present, or to remember the past in a way that makes us look good.

- Persistence reflects the fact that emotional arousal generally leads to enhanced memory, whether we want to remember an experience or not. Persistence is partly attributable to the operation of hormonal systems influenced by the amygdala. Although each of the seven sins can cause trouble in our lives, each has an adaptive side as well.

- You can think of the seven "sins" as costs we pay for benefits that allow memory to work as well as it does most of the time.

Changing Minds

1. A friend of yours lost their father to cancer when they were a very young child. "I really wish I remembered him better," your friend says. "I know all the memories are locked in my head. I'm thinking of trying hypnotism to unlock some of those memories." You explain that we don't, in fact, have stored memories of everything that ever happened to us locked in our heads. What examples could you give of ways in which memories can be lost over time?

2. Your older cousin has a very vivid memory of sitting with his parents in the living room on September 11, 2001, watching live TV as the Twin Towers of the World Trade Center in New York City fell during the terrorist attacks. "I remember my mother was crying," he says, "and that scared me more than the pictures on the TV." Later, he discusses the events of 9/11 with his mother—and is stunned when she assures him that he was actually in school on the morning of the attacks and was only sent home at lunchtime, after the towers had fallen. "I don't understand," he tells you afterwards. "I think she must be confused, because I have a perfect memory of that morning." Assuming your aunt is recalling events correctly, how would you explain to your cousin the ways in which his snapshot memory could be wrong? What memory sin might be at work?

3. You ask one of your psychology classmates if they want to form a study group to prepare for an upcoming exam. "No offense," your friend says, "but I can study the material best by just reading the chapter eight or nine times, and I can do that without a study group." What's wrong with your classmate's study plan? In what ways might the members of a study group help each other learn more effectively?

4. You and a friend go to a party on campus where you meet a lot of new people. After the party, your friend says, "I liked a lot of the people we met, but I'll never remember all their names. Some people just have a good memory, and some don't, and there's nothing I can do about it." What advice could you give your friend to help them remember the names of people they meet at the next party?

5. A friend of yours who is taking a criminal justice class reads about a case in which the conviction of an accused murderer was later overturned on the basis of DNA evidence. "It's a travesty of justice," your friend says. "An eyewitness clearly identified the man by picking him out of a lineup and then identified him again in court during the trial. No results from a chemistry lab should count more than eyewitness testimony." What is your friend failing to appreciate about eyewitness testimony? What sin of memory could lead an eyewitness to honestly believe they are identifying the correct man when they are actually making a false identification?

6. **Visualizing Data** A colleague who is looking for a research project asks about the results of a location information and gender study. Review the data and report the results.

Key Terms

memory (p. 201)

encoding (p. 201)

storage (p. 201)

retrieval (p. 201)

semantic encoding (p. 202)

visual imagery encoding (p. 204)

organizational encoding (p. 204)

mnemonics (p. 205)

sensory memory (p. 206)

iconic memory (p. 207)

echoic memory (p. 207)

short-term memory (p. 207)

rehearsal (p. 208)

serial position effect (p. 208)

chunking (p. 208)

working memory (p. 209)

long-term memory (p. 210)

anterograde amnesia (p. 211)

retrograde amnesia (p. 211)

consolidation (p. 212)

reconsolidation (p. 213)

long-term potentiation (LTP) (p. 214)

retrieval cue (p. 216)

encoding specificity principle (p. 216)

state-dependent retrieval (p. 216)

transfer-appropriate processing (p. 217)

retrieval-induced forgetting (p. 218)

explicit memory (p. 221)

implicit memory (p. 221)

procedural memory (p. 221)

priming (p. 222)

semantic memory (p. 223)

episodic memory (p. 223)

transience (p. 229)

retroactive interference (p. 230)

proactive interference (p. 230)

absentmindedness (p. 231)

prospective memory (p. 232)

blocking (p. 232)

memory misattribution (p. 233)

source memory (p. 233)

false recognition (p. 235)

suggestibility (p. 236)

bias (p. 237)

persistence (p. 238)

flashbulb memories (p. 239)

Learning

CHAPTER

7

JENNIFER, A 45-YEAR-OLD AMERICAN MILITARY NURSE, lived quietly in a rural area of the United States with her spouse of 21 years and their two children before she served 19 months abroad during the Iraq war. In Iraq, she provided care to soldiers from many countries, as well as to Iraqi civilians, prisoners, and militant extremists. Jennifer served 4 months of her assignment in a prison hospital near Baghdad, where she witnessed many horrifying events. The prison was the target of relentless mortar fire, resulting in numerous deaths and serious casualties, including bloody injuries and loss of limbs. Jennifer worked 12- to 14-hour shifts, trying to avoid incoming fire while tending to some of the most gruesomely wounded cases. She frequently encountered the smell of burned flesh and the sight of "young, mangled bodies" as part of her daily duties (Feczer & Bjorklund, 2009, p. 285).

This repetitive trauma took a toll on Jennifer; when she returned home, it became evident that she had not left behind her war experiences. Jennifer thought about them repeatedly, and they profoundly influenced her reactions to many aspects of everyday life. The sight of blood or the smell of cooking meat made her sick to her stomach, to the point that she had to stop eating meat. The previously innocent sound of a helicopter approaching, which in Iraq signaled that new wounded bodies were about to arrive, now created in Jennifer heightened feelings of fear and anxiety. She regularly awoke from nightmares concerning the most troubling aspects of her Iraq experiences, such as tending to soldiers with multiple amputations. In the words of the authors who described her case, Jennifer was "forever changed" by her Iraq experiences (Feczer & Bjorklund, 2009). That is one reason why Jennifer's story is a compelling, though disturbing, introduction to the topic of learning.

Much of what happened to Jennifer after she returned home reflects the operation of a kind of learning based on association. Sights, sounds, and smells in Iraq had become associated with negative emotions in a way that created an enduring bond, such that encountering similar sights, sounds, and smells at home elicited similarly intense negative feelings.

LEARNING IS SHORTHAND FOR A COLLECTION OF DIFFERENT YET RELATED PROCESSES and outcomes that produce changes in an organism's behaviour. Learning psychologists have identified and studied as many as 40 different types of learning. In this chapter, we'll discuss the development and basic psychological principles behind two

- **What Is Learning?**
- **Classical Conditioning: One Thing Leads to Another**
- **Operant Conditioning: Reinforcements from the Environment**
- **Observational Learning: Look at Me**
- **Implicit Learning: Under the Radar**
- **Learning in the Classroom**

During the 4 months that she served at a prison hospital near Baghdad during the Iraq war, Jennifer learned to associate the sound of an arriving helicopter with wounded soldiers. That learned association had a long-lasting influence on her.

245

major approaches to learning: classical conditioning and operant conditioning. We'll then move on to see that some important kinds of learning occur when we simply watch others and that such observational learning plays an important role in the cultural transmission of behaviour. Next, we'll discover that implicit learning can occur entirely outside of awareness. We'll conclude with a discussion of learning in a context that should matter a lot to you: the classroom. We kick off the chapter, however, with some basic insights and definitions.

What Is Learning?

Learning Outcomes

WHAT YOU NEED TO KNOW

- Define learning.
- Demonstrate that even the simplest organisms appear to learn.

Despite the many different kinds of learning that psychologists have discovered, there is a basic principle at the core of all of them. **Learning** involves *the acquisition, from experience, of new knowledge, skills, or responses that results in a relatively permanent change in the state of the learner.* This definition emphasizes these key ideas:

- Learning is based on experience.
- Learning produces changes in the organism.
- These changes are relatively permanent.

Think about Jennifer's time in Iraq and you'll see all of these elements: Experiences that led Jennifer to associate the sound of an approaching helicopter with the arrival of wounded soldiers changed the way she responded to certain situations in a way that lasted for years.

Learning can also occur in much simpler, nonassociative forms. You are probably familiar with the phenomenon of **habituation,** *a general process in which repeated or prolonged exposure to a stimulus results in a gradual reduction in responding.* If you've ever lived under the flight path of your local airport, near railroad tracks, or by a busy highway, you've probably noticed the deafening roar of a Boeing 737 coming in for a landing, the clatter of a train speeding down the track, or the sound of traffic when you first moved in. You probably also noticed that, after a while, the roar wasn't quite so deafening anymore and eventually you were able to ignore the sounds of the planes, trains, or automobiles in your vicinity. This welcome reduction in responding reflects the operation of habituation.

Habituation occurs even in the simplest organisms. For example, in the Memory chapter you learned about the sea slug *Aplysia*, studied in detail by Nobel Prize–winner Eric Kandel (2006). Kandel and his colleagues showed clearly that *Aplysia* exhibits habituation: When lightly touched, the sea slug initially withdraws its gill, but the response gradually weakens after repeated light touches. In addition, *Aplysia* exhibits another simple form of learning known as **sensitization,** which occurs when *presentation of a stimulus leads to an increased response to a later stimulus.* For example, Kandel found that after receiving a strong shock, *Aplysia* showed an increased gill-withdrawal response to a light touch. In a similar manner, people whose houses have been broken into may later become hypersensitive to late-night sounds that wouldn't have bothered them previously.

Although these simple kinds of learning are important, in this chapter we'll focus on more complex kinds of learning that psychologists have studied intensively. As you'll recall from the Evolution of Psychological Science chapter, a sizable chunk of psychology's history was devoted to behaviourism, with its insistence on measuring only observable, quantifiable behaviour and its dismissal of mental activity as

learning The acquisition, from experience, of new knowledge, skills, or responses that results in a relatively permanent change in the state of the learner.

habituation A general process in which repeated or prolonged exposure to a stimulus results in a gradual reduction in responding.

sensitization A simple form of learning that occurs when presentation of a stimulus leads to an increased response to a later stimulus.

irrelevant and unknowable. Behaviourism was the major outlook of most psychologists working from the 1930s through the 1950s, the period during which most of the fundamental work on learning theory took place.

You might find the intersection of behaviourism and learning theory a bit surprising. After all, at one level, learning seems abstract: Something intangible happens to you, and you think or behave differently thereafter. It seems logical that you'd need to explain this transformation in terms of a change in mental outlook. However, most behaviourists argued that learning's "permanent change in experience" could be demonstrated equally well in almost any organism: rats, dogs, pigeons, mice, pigs, or humans.

In many ways, the behaviourists were right and their approach moved the field forward. Much of what we know about how organisms learn comes directly from the behaviourists' observations of behaviours. However, they also overstated their case. We need to address some important cognitive considerations (i.e., elements of mental activity) in order to understand the learning process.

How might psychologists use the concept of habituation to explain the fact that today's action movies, like *Black Widow*, tend to show much more graphic violence than movies of the 1980s, which in turn tended to show more graphic violence than movies of the 1950s?

Classical Conditioning: One Thing Leads to Another

The American psychologist John B. Watson kick-started the behaviourist movement in the early 20th century, arguing that psychologists should "never use the terms *consciousness, mental states, mind, content, introspectively verifiable, imagery*, and the like" (Watson, 1913, p. 166). Watson's firebrand stance was fuelled in large part by the work of a Russian physiologist, Ivan Pavlov (1849–1936). Ironically, however, although Pavlov respected the behaviourist approach, he did not deny the importance of subjective experience and in fact was deeply interested in understanding consciousness and related mental states (Todes, 2014).

Pavlov was awarded the Nobel Prize in Physiology in 1904 for his work on the salivation of dogs. He studied the digestive processes of laboratory animals by surgically implanting test tubes into the cheeks of dogs to measure their salivary responses to different kinds of foods. Serendipitously, his explorations into spit and drool revealed the mechanics of one form of learning, which came to be called classical conditioning. **Classical conditioning** is *a type of learning that occurs when a neutral stimulus produces a response after being paired with a stimulus that naturally produces a response*. In his classic experiments, Pavlov showed that dogs learned to salivate to neutral stimuli such as a buzzer or a metronome after the dogs had associated that stimulus with another stimulus that naturally evokes salivation, such as food.

When Pavlov's findings first appeared in the scientific and popular literature (Pavlov, 1923a, 1923b), they produced a flurry of excitement because psychologists now had demonstrable evidence of how conditioning produced learned behaviours. This was the kind of behaviourist psychology John B. Watson was proposing: An organism experiences events or stimuli that are observable and measurable, and scientists can directly observe and measure changes in that organism. Dogs learned to salivate to the sound of a buzzer or metronome, and there was no need to resort to explanations about what the dog wanted, or how the animal thought about the situation. In other words, there was no need to consider the mind in this classical conditioning paradigm, which appealed to Watson and the behaviourists. Pavlov also appreciated the significance of his discovery, and he embarked on a systematic investigation of the mechanisms of classical conditioning. Let's take a closer look at some of these principles. (As The Real World: Understanding Drug Overdoses shows, these principles help explain how drug overdoses occur.)

Learning Outcomes

WHAT YOU NEED TO KNOW

- Describe the process of classical conditioning.

- Explain how cognitive, neural, and evolutionary aspects influence our understanding of classical conditioning.

classical conditioning A type of learning that occurs when a neutral stimulus produces a response after being paired with a stimulus that naturally produces a response.

The Basic Principles of Classical Conditioning

Pavlov's basic experimental setup involved cradling dogs in a harness to administer the foods and to measure the salivary response, as shown in **FIGURE 7.1**. He noticed that dogs that had previously been in the experiment began to produce a kind of "anticipatory" salivary response as soon as they were put in the harness, even before any food was presented. Pavlov and his colleagues regarded these responses as annoyances at first because they interfered with collecting naturally occurring salivary secretions. In reality, the dogs were behaving in line with the basic elements of classical conditioning:

- When the dogs were initially presented with a plate of food, they began to salivate. No surprise here—placing food in front of most animals will launch the salivary process. Pavlov called the presentation of food an **unconditioned stimulus (US),** *something that reliably produces a naturally occurring reaction in an organism* (see **FIGURE 7.2a**). He called the dogs' salivation an **unconditioned response (UR),** *a reflexive reaction that is reliably produced by an unconditioned stimulus.*

- Then Pavlov paired the presentation of food with the sound of the ticking of a metronome, a buzzer, the humming of a tuning fork, or the flash of a light (Pavlov, 1927). This period is called **acquisition,** *the phase of classical conditioning when the CS and the US are presented together* (see Figure 7.2b).

- Nothing in nature would make a dog salivate to the sound of a metronome or a buzzer. However, when the CS (the sound of the metronome) is paired over time with the US (the food), the animal will learn to associate food with the sound, and eventually the CS is sufficient to produce a response, or salivation. Sure enough, Pavlov found that the dogs ultimately salivated to these sounds and flashes, each of which had become a **conditioned stimulus (CS),** *a previously neutral stimulus that produces a reliable response in an organism after being paired with a US.* This response resembles the UR, but Pavlov called it the **conditioned response (CR),** *a reaction that resembles an unconditioned response but is produced by a conditioned stimulus.* In this example, the dogs' salivation (CR) was eventually prompted by the sound of the metronome (CS) alone because the sound of the metronome and the food (US) had been associated so often in the past (see Figure 7.2c). The CR reflects learning, whereas the UR does not.

Consider your own dog (or cat). Does your dog always know when dinner's coming, preparing just short of pulling up a chair and tucking a napkin into her collar?

unconditioned stimulus (US)
Something that reliably produces a naturally occurring reaction in an organism.

unconditioned response (UR)
A reflexive reaction that is reliably produced by an unconditioned stimulus.

acquisition The phase of classical conditioning when the CS and the US are presented together.

conditioned stimulus (CS)
A previously neutral stimulus that produces a reliable response in an organism after being paired with a US.

conditioned response (CR)
A reaction that resembles an unconditioned response but is produced by a conditioned stimulus.

Figure 7.1
Pavlov's Apparatus for Studying Classical Conditioning Using a metronome or a buzzer, Pavlov presented auditory stimuli to the dogs. Visual stimuli could be presented on the screen.

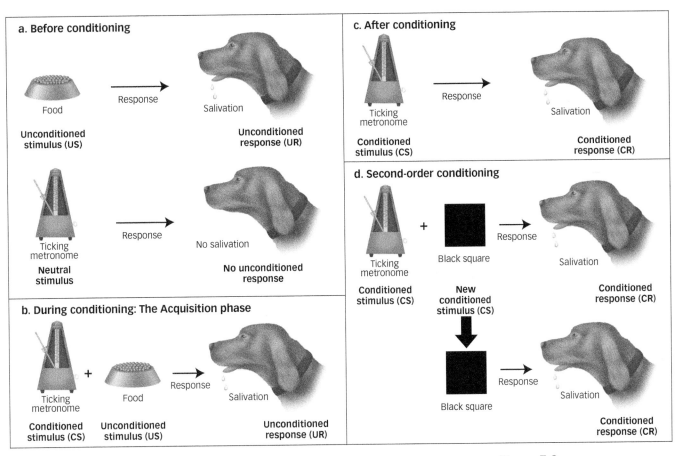

Figure 7.2
The Elements of Classical Conditioning (a) Before conditioning, the dog salivates in response to food, the unconditioned stimulus (US), but not to the ticking of a metronome. (b) During conditioning, the food is paired with the ticking metronome, which becomes a conditioned stimulus (CS). (c) After conditioning, the ticking metronome, now a conditioned stimulus (CS), can produce salivation. (d) In second-order conditioning, the ticking metronome can be used to condition a new stimulus, such as a black square.

It's as though she has one eye on the clock every day, waiting for the dinner hour. Alas, your dog is no clock-watching wonder hound. Instead, for the dog the presentation of food (the US) has become associated with a complex CS—your getting up, moving into the kitchen, opening the cabinet, working the can opener—such that the CS alone signals to your dog that food is on the way, therefore initiating the CR of the dog getting ready to eat. And classical conditioning isn't just for dogs. When you hear your smartphone ring announcing the arrival of a new text, you may not salivate but you probably feel like you've got to check it right away—and you might even experience anxiety if you are in a situation in which you can't. Socially important information from friends and others contained in prior texts (the US) has become associated with the text message sound on your phone (the CS), so that the CS alone signals that important information may be on the way, thus initiating the phone-checking CR.

After conditioning has been established, a phenomenon called **second-order conditioning,** which is *a type of learning in which a CS is paired with a stimulus that became associated with the US in an earlier procedure,* can be demonstrated. For instance, in an early study, Pavlov repeatedly paired a new CS, a black square, with the now reliable tone. After a number of training trials, his dogs produced a salivary response to the black square, even though the square itself had never been directly associated with the food (see Figure 7.2d).

Acquisition, Extinction, and Spontaneous Recovery

Remember when you first got your dog? Chances are the dog didn't seem too smart, especially with the vacant stares at you as you went into the kitchen, not anticipating that food was on the way. During the initial phase of the acquisition

second-order conditioning A type of learning in which a CS is paired with a stimulus that became associated with the US in an earlier procedure.

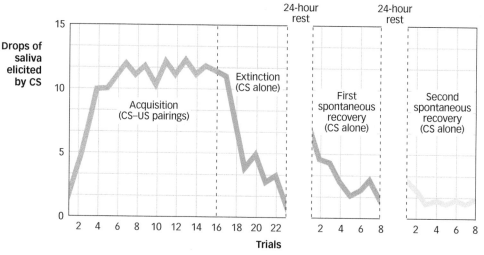

Figure 7.3

Acquisition, Extinction, and Spontaneous Recovery In classical conditioning, the CS is originally neutral and elicits no specific response. As an example, after several trials pairing the CS with the US, the CS alone comes to elicit the salivary response (the CR). Learning tends to take place fairly rapidly and then levels off as stable responding develops. In extinction, the CR diminishes quickly until it no longer occurs. A rest period, however, is typically followed by spontaneous recovery of the CR. In fact, a well-learned CR may show spontaneous recovery after more than one rest period even without any additional learning trials.

Second-order conditioning helps explain why some people desire money to the point that they hoard it and value it even more than the objects it purchases. Money is initially used to purchase objects that produce gratifying outcomes, such as an expensive car. Although money is not directly associated with the thrill of driving a new sports car, through second-order conditioning, money can become linked with this type of desirable reward.

extinction The gradual elimination of a learned response that occurs when the CS is repeatedly presented without the US.

spontaneous recovery The tendency of a learned behaviour to recover from extinction after a rest period.

period of classical conditioning, typically there is a gradual increase in learning: It starts low, rises rapidly, and then decreases, as shown on the left side of the first panel of **FIGURE 7.3**. Pavlov's dogs gradually increased their amount of salivation over several trials of pairing a tone with the presentation of food; similarly, your dog eventually learned to associate your kitchen preparations with the subsequent appearance of food. After learning has been established, the CS by itself will reliably elicit the CR.

After Pavlov and his colleagues had explored the process of acquisition extensively, they turned to the next logical question: What would happen if they continued to present the CS (metronome ticking) but stopped presenting the US (food)? Repeatedly presenting the CS without the US produces exactly the result you might imagine. As shown on the right side of the first panel in Figure 7.3, behaviour declines abruptly and continues to drop until eventually the dog ceases to salivate to the sound of the tone. This process is called **extinction,** *the gradual elimination of a learned response that occurs when the CS is repeatedly presented without the US.* This term was introduced because the conditioned response is "extinguished" and no longer observed. Having established that he could produce learning through conditioning and then extinguish it, Pavlov wondered if this elimination of conditioned behaviour was permanent. Is a single session of extinction sufficient to knock out the CR completely? Or is there some residual change in the dog's behaviour such that the CR might reappear?

To explore this question, Pavlov extinguished the classically conditioned salivation response and then allowed the dogs to have a short rest period. When they were brought back to the lab and presented with the CS again, they displayed **spontaneous recovery,** *the tendency of a learned behaviour to recover from extinction after a rest period.* This phenomenon is shown in the middle panel in Figure 7.3. Notice that this recovery takes place even though there have not been any additional associations between the CS and US. Some spontaneous recovery of the conditioned response even takes place in what is essentially a second extinction session after another period of rest (see the right-hand panel in Figure 7.3). Clearly, extinction had not completely erased the learning that had been acquired. The ability of the CS to elicit the CR was weakened, but it was not eliminated.

Generalization and Discrimination

Do you think your dog will be stumped, unable to anticipate the presentation of food, if you get a new can opener? Will you need to establish a whole new round of conditioning with this modified CS?

Probably not. It wouldn't be very adaptive for an organism if each little change in the CS–US pairing required an extensive regimen of new learning. Rather, the phenomenon of **generalization** tends to take place: *The CR is observed even though the CS is slightly different from the CS used during acquisition.* In other words, the conditioning generalizes to stimuli that are similar to the CS used during the original training. As you might expect, the more the new stimulus changes, the less conditioned responding is observed—which means that if you replaced a manual can opener with an electric can opener, your dog would probably show a much weaker conditioned response (Pearce, 1987; Rescorla, 2006).

When an organism generalizes to a new stimulus, two things are happening. First, by responding to the new stimulus used during generalization testing, the organism demonstrates that it recognizes the similarity between the original CS and the new stimulus. Second, by displaying a *diminished* response to that new stimulus, it also tells us that it notices a difference between the two stimuli. In the second case, the organism shows **discrimination,** *the capacity to distinguish between similar but distinct stimuli.* Generalization and discrimination are two sides of the same coin. The more organisms show one, the less they show the other, and training can modify the balance between the two.

Conditioned Emotional Responses: The Case of Little Albert

Before you conclude that classical conditioning is merely a sophisticated way to train your dog, let's revisit the larger principles of Pavlov's work. Classical conditioning demonstrates that scientists can achieve durable, substantial changes in behaviour simply by setting up the proper conditions. It was this kind of simplicity that appealed to behaviourists. In fact, Watson and his followers thought that it was possible to develop general explanations of pretty much *any* behaviour of *any* organism, based on classical conditioning principles. As a step in that direction, Watson embarked on a controversial study with his research assistant Rosalie Rayner (Watson & Rayner, 1920).

To support his contention that even complex behaviours were the result of conditioning, Watson enlisted the assistance of 9-month-old "Little Albert." Albert was a healthy, well-developed child and, by Watson's assessment, was "stolid and unemotional" (Watson & Rayner, 1920, p. 1). Watson wanted to see if such a child could be classically conditioned to experience a strong emotional reaction—namely, fear. Here's how he proceeded:

John Watson and Rosalie Rayner show Little Albert an unusual bunny mask. Why isn't the mere presence of these experimenters a conditioned stimulus in itself?

- Watson presented Little Albert with a variety of stimuli: a white rat, a dog, a rabbit, various masks, and a burning newspaper. Albert reacted in most cases with curiosity or indifference, and he showed no fear of any of the items.
- Watson also established that an unconditioned stimulus *could* make Albert afraid. While Albert was watching Rayner, Watson unexpectedly struck a large steel bar with a hammer, producing a loud noise. Predictably, this caused Albert to cry, tremble, and be generally displeased.

generalization The CR is observed even though the CS is slightly different from the CS used during acquisition.

discrimination The capacity to distinguish between similar but distinct stimuli.

- Watson and Rayner then led Little Albert through the acquisition phase of classical conditioning. Albert was presented with a white rat. As soon as he reached out to touch it, the steel bar was struck. This pairing occurred again and again over several trials. Eventually, the sight of the rat alone caused Albert to recoil in terror, crying and clamoring to get away from it. In this situation, a US (the loud sound) was paired with a CS (the presence of the rat) such that the CS all by itself was sufficient to produce the CR (a fearful reaction).

- Little Albert also showed stimulus generalization. The sight of a white rabbit, a seal-fur coat, and a Santa Claus mask produced the same kinds of fear reactions in the infant.

What was Watson's goal in all this? First, he wanted to show that a relatively complex reaction could be conditioned using Pavlovian techniques. Second, he wanted to show that emotional responses such as fear and anxiety could be produced by classical conditioning and therefore need not be the product of deeper unconscious processes or early life experiences as Freud and his followers had argued (see the Evolution of Psychological Science chapter). Instead, Watson proposed that fears could be learned, just like any other behaviour. Third, Watson wanted to confirm that conditioning could be applied to humans as well as to other animals. This study was controversial in its cavalier treatment of a young child, especially given that Watson and Rayner did not follow up with Albert or his mother during the ensuing years (Harris, 1979). Modern ethical guidelines that govern the treatment of research participants ensure that this kind of study could not be conducted today.

The kind of conditioned fear responses that were at work in Little Albert's case were also important in the chapter-opening case of Jennifer, who experienced fear and anxiety when hearing the previously innocent sound of an approaching helicopter as a result of her experiences in Iraq. Indeed, a therapy that has proven effective in dealing with such trauma-induced fears is based directly on principles of classical conditioning: Individuals are repeatedly exposed to conditioned stimuli associated with their trauma in a safe setting, in an attempt to extinguish the conditioned fear response (Bouton, 1988; Rothbaum & Schwartz, 2002). However, conditioned emotional responses include much more than just fear and anxiety responses.

Advertisers, for example, understand that conditioned emotional responses can include various positive emotions that they would like potential customers to associate with their products, which may be why attractive women are commonly involved in ads for products geared towards young males, including beer and sports cars. Even the warm and fuzzy feelings that envelop you when hearing a song that you used to listen to with a former boyfriend or girlfriend are a type of conditioned emotional response.

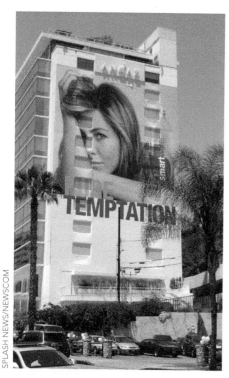

What response do you think the advertisers of Smart Water are looking for when they feature Jennifer Aniston in an ad?

A Deeper Understanding of Classical Conditioning

As a form of learning, classical conditioning could be reliably produced: It had a simple set of principles and applications to real-life situations. In short, classical conditioning offered a good deal of utility for psychologists who sought to understand the mechanisms that underlie learning, and it continues to do so today.

Like a lot of strong starters, though, classical conditioning has been subjected to deeper scrutiny in order to understand exactly how, when, and why it works. Let's examine three approaches that zero in on the mechanisms of classical conditioning: the cognitive, neural, and evolutionary elements.

The Cognitive Elements of Classical Conditioning

As we've seen, Pavlov's work was a behaviourist's dream come true. In this view, conditioning is something that *happens* to a dog, a rat, or a person, apart from what the organism thinks about the conditioning situation. However, although the dogs salivated when their feeders approached (see the Evolution of Psychological Science chapter), they did not salivate when Pavlov approached. Eventually, someone was bound to ask an important question: *Why not?* After all, Pavlov also delivered the food to the dogs, so why didn't *he* become a CS? Indeed, if Watson was present whenever the unpleasant US was sounded, why didn't Little Albert come to fear *him?*

Somehow, Pavlov's dogs were sensitive to the fact that Pavlov was not a *reliable* indicator of the arrival of food. Pavlov was linked with the arrival of food, but he was also linked with other activities that had nothing to do with food, including checking on the apparatus, bringing the dog from the kennel to the laboratory, and standing around talking with his assistants.

Robert Rescorla and Allan Wagner (1972) were the first to theorize that classical conditioning occurs when an animal has learned to set up an *expectation*. The sound of a metronome, because of its systematic pairing with food, set up this cognitive state for the laboratory dogs; Pavlov, because of the lack of any reliable link with food, did not. In fact, in situations such as this, many responses are actually being conditioned. When the metronome ticks, the dogs also wag their tails, make begging sounds, and look towards the food source (Jenkins et al., 1978). In short, what is really happening is something like the situation shown in **FIGURE 7.4**.

The Rescorla–Wagner model introduced a cognitive component that accounted for a variety of classical conditioning phenomena that were difficult to understand from a simple behaviourist point of view. For example, the model predicted that conditioning would be easier when the CS was an *unfamiliar* event than when it was familiar. The reason is that familiar events, being familiar, already have expectations associated with them, making new conditioning difficult. In short, classical conditioning might appear to be a primitive process, but it is actually quite sophisticated and incorporates a significant cognitive element.

The Neural Elements of Classical Conditioning

Pavlov saw his research as providing insights into how the brain works. After all, he was trained in medicine, not psychology, and was a bit surprised when psychologists became excited by his findings. Recent research has clarified some of what Pavlov hoped to understand about conditioning and the brain.

A series of pioneering experiments conducted across several decades by Richard Thompson and his colleagues focused on classical conditioning of eyeblink responses in rabbits. In the most basic type of eyeblink conditioning, the CS (a tone) is immediately followed by the US (a puff of air), which elicits a reflexive eyeblink response. After many CS–US pairings, the eyeblink response occurs in response to the CS alone. Thompson and colleagues showed convincingly that the cerebellum is critical

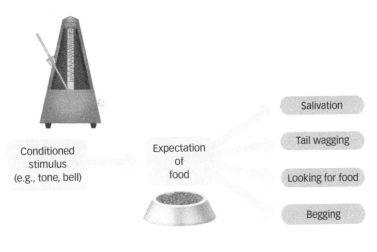

Conditioned stimulus (e.g., tone, bell)

Expectation of food

Salivation

Tail wagging

Looking for food

Begging

Figure 7.4
Expectation in Classical Conditioning In the Rescorla–Wagner model of classical conditioning, a CS sets up an expectation. The expectation in turn leads to an array of behaviours associated with the presence of the CS.

DON MASON/GETTY IMAGES

for the occurrence of eyeblink conditioning (Thompson, 2005). Studies of people with lesions to the cerebellum supported these findings by demonstrating impaired eyeblink conditioning (Daum et al., 1993). Rounding out the picture, more recent neuroimaging findings in healthy young adults show activation in the cerebellum during eyeblink conditioning (Cheng et al., 2008). As you learned in the Neuroscience and Behaviour chapter, the cerebellum is part of the hindbrain and plays an important role in motor skills and learning.

In addition to eyeblink conditioning, fear conditioning has been extensively studied. Also in the Neuroscience and Behaviour chapter, you saw that the amygdala plays an important role in the experience of emotion, including fear and anxiety. So it should come as no surprise that the amygdala, particularly an area known as the *central nucleus,* is also critical for emotional conditioning.

Consider a rat that is conditioned to a series of CS–US pairings in which the CS is a tone and the US is a mild electric shock. When rats experience sudden painful stimuli, they show a defensive reaction, known as *freezing,* in which they crouch down and sit motionless. In addition, their autonomic nervous systems go to work: Heart rate and blood pressure increase, and various hormones associated with stress are released. When fear conditioning takes place, these two components—one behavioural and one physiological—occur, except that now they are elicited by the CS.

The central nucleus of the amygdala plays a role in producing both of these outcomes through two distinct connections with other parts of the brain. If connections linking the amygdala to the midbrain are disrupted, the rat does not exhibit the behavioural freezing response. If the connections between the amygdala and the hypothalamus are severed, the autonomic responses associated with fear cease (LeDoux et al., 1988). Hence, the action of the amygdala is an essential element in fear conditioning, and its links with other areas of the brain are responsible for producing specific features of conditioning (Bentz & Schiller, 2015). The amygdala is involved in fear conditioning in people as well as in rats and other animals (Olsson & Phelps, 2007; Phelps & LeDoux, 2005).

The Evolutionary Elements of Classical Conditioning

In addition to this cognitive component, evolutionary mechanisms also play an important role in classical conditioning. As you learned in the Evolution of Psychological Science chapter, evolution and natural selection go hand in hand with adaptiveness: Behaviours that are adaptive allow an organism to survive and thrive in its environment. In the case of classical conditioning, psychologists began to appreciate how this type of learning could have adaptive value. Much research exploring this adaptiveness has focused on conditioned food aversions, primarily taste aversions.

Consider this example: A psychology professor was once on a job interview in Southern California, and his hosts took him to lunch at a Middle Eastern restaurant. Suffering from a case of bad hummus, he was up all night long and developed a lifelong aversion to hummus.

This looks like a case of classical conditioning, but there are several peculiar aspects to this case. The hummus was the CS, a bacterium or some other source of toxicity was the US, and the resulting nausea was the UR. The UR (the nausea) became linked to the once-neutral CS (the hummus) and became a CR (an aversion to hummus). However, all of the psychologist's hosts also ate the hummus, yet none of them reported feeling ill. It's not clear, then, what the US was; it couldn't have been anything that was actually in the food. What's more, the time between the hummus and the distress was several hours; usually, a response follows a stimulus fairly quickly. Most baffling, this aversion was cemented with a single acquisition trial. It usually takes several pairings of a CS and US to establish learning.

Under certain conditions, people may develop taste aversions. This serving of hummus looks inviting and probably tastes delicious, but at least one psychologist avoids all hummus like the plague.

These peculiarities are not so peculiar from an evolutionary perspective. Any species that forages or consumes a variety of foods needs to develop a mechanism by which it can learn to avoid any food that once made it ill. To have adaptive value, this mechanism should have several properties:

- Rapid learning should occur in perhaps one or two trials. If learning takes more trials than this, the animal could die from eating a toxic substance.

- Conditioning should be able to take place over very long intervals, perhaps up to several hours. Toxic substances often don't cause illness immediately, so the organism would need to form an association between the food and the illness over a longer term.

- The organism should develop the aversion to the smell or taste of the food rather than its ingestion. It's more adaptive to reject a potentially toxic substance based on smell alone than it is to ingest it.

- Learned aversions should occur more often with novel foods than with familiar ones. It is not adaptive for an animal to develop an aversion to everything it has eaten on the particular day it got sick. Our psychologist friend didn't develop an aversion to the Coke he drank with lunch or the scrambled eggs he had for breakfast that day; however, the sight and smell of hummus do make him uneasy.

A Modern Application

John Garcia and his colleagues illustrated the adaptiveness of classical conditioning in a series of studies with rats (Garcia & Koelling, 1966). They used a variety of CSs (visual, auditory, tactile, taste, and smell) and several different USs (injection of a toxic substance, radiation) that caused nausea and vomiting hours later. The researchers found weak or no conditioning when the CS was a visual, auditory, or tactile stimulus, but a strong food aversion developed with stimuli that had a distinct taste and smell.

This research had an interesting application. It led to the development of a technique for dealing with an unanticipated side effect of radiation and chemotherapy: Cancer patients who experience nausea from their treatments often develop aversions to foods they ate before the therapy. Broberg and Bernstein (1987) reasoned that, if the findings with rats generalized to humans, a simple technique should minimize the negative consequences of this effect. They gave their patients an unusual food (coconut- or root-beer-flavoured candy) at the end of the last meal before undergoing treatment. Sure enough, the conditioned food aversions that the patients developed were overwhelmingly for one of the unusual flavours and not for any of the other foods in the meal. Other than any root beer or coconut fanatics among the sample, patients were spared from developing aversions to common foods that they were more likely to eat.

Studies such as these suggest that evolution has provided each species with a kind of **biological preparedness,** *a propensity for learning particular kinds of associations over other kinds,* such that some behaviours are relatively easy to condition in some species but not others. For example, the taste and smell stimuli that produce food aversions in rats do not work with most species of birds. Birds depend primarily on visual cues for finding food and are relatively insensitive to taste and smell. However, as you might guess, it is relatively easy to produce a food aversion in birds using an unfamiliar visual stimulus as the CS, such as a brightly coloured food (Wilcoxon et al., 1971). Indeed, most researchers agree that conditioning works best with stimuli that are biologically relevant to the organism (Domjan, 2005).

biological preparedness A propensity for learning particular kinds of associations over other kinds.

The Real World • Understanding Drug Overdoses

All too often, police are confronted with a perplexing problem: the sudden death of addicts from a drug overdose. The problem exists worldwide, has increased substantially over the last several years (Martins et al., 2015), and is receiving increasing attention because of the opioid epidemic in the United States and Canada (Lyden & Binswanger, 2019; Volkow & Blanco, 2021). These deaths are puzzling for at least three reasons: The victims are often people who are experienced at using drugs; the dose taken is usually not larger than what they usually take; and the deaths tend to occur in unusual settings. People who are experienced at using drugs are just that: experienced! So you'd think that the chances of an overdose would be lower than usual.

McMaster University neuroscientist Shepard Siegel realized that classical conditioning provides some insight into how these deaths occur (Siegel, 2016). First, when classical conditioning takes place, the conditioned stimulus (CS) is more than a simple buzzer or tone: It also includes the overall *context* within which the conditioning takes place. Indeed, Pavlov's dogs often began to salivate even as they approached the experimental apparatus. Second, many conditioned responses (CRs) are compensatory reactions to the unconditioned stimulus (US). Heroin, for example, slows down a person's breathing rate, so the body responds with a compensatory reaction that speeds up breathing in order to maintain a state of balance, or homeostasis, a critically important CR.

These two finer points of classical conditioning help explain the seeming paradox of fatal heroin overdoses in people who are experienced with using drugs (Siegel, 1984, 2016). When the drug is injected, the entire setting (the drug paraphernalia, the room, the lighting, the addict's usual companions) functions as the CS, and the addict's brain reacts to the heroin by secreting neurotransmitters that counteract its effects. Over time, this protective physiological response becomes part of the CR, and like all CRs, it occurs in the presence of the CS but prior to the actual administration of the drug. These compensatory physiological reactions are also what make drug abusers take increasingly larger doses

Supervised drug consumption facilities provide a safe, clean space for people to bring their own drugs to use in the presence of trained staff. In addition to providing clean needles and access to a variety of evidence-based harm reduction services, like drug checking, the consistent environment becomes part of the addict's CS. Without such legal sites, addicts may be pushed to use drugs in new situations when illegal sites are closed down, contributing to overdoses and fatalities.

to achieve the same effect. Ultimately, these reactions produce *drug tolerance*, discussed in the Consciousness chapter.

On the basis of these principles of classical conditioning, taking drugs in a new environment can be fatal for those who have been using drugs for a long time. If an addict injects the usual dose in a setting that is sufficiently novel or where they have never taken heroin before, the CS is now altered, such that the physiological compensatory CR that usually has a protective function either does not occur or is substantially decreased (Siegel et al., 2000). As a result, the addict's usual dose becomes an overdose, and death often results. Addicts intuitively may stick with the crack houses, drug dens, or "shooting galleries" with which they're familiar for just this reason. Tragically, similar effects also occur in cancer patients who take prescription opiates for pain relief, and are vulnerable to overdoses that result in visits to the emergency room (Jairam et al., 2020). Siegel (2017) describes a cancer patient who usually received his morphine injection in a dimly lit bedroom. On a day when he received the same injection for the first time in a brightly lit living room, he overdosed and died.

This effect has also been shown experimentally: Rats that have had extensive experience with morphine in one setting were much more likely to survive dose increases in that same setting than in a novel one (Siegel, 1976; Siegel et al., 2000). This same basic effect occurs with a variety of drugs. For example, university students show less tolerance for the intoxicating effects of alcohol when they consume it in the presence of a novel cue (a peppermint-flavoured drink) than a familiar one (a beer-flavoured drink) (Siegel, 2005).

Understanding these principles has also led to treatments for drug addiction. For instance, the addict can experience the brain's compensatory response to a drug—when elicited by the familiar contextual cues ordinarily associated with drug taking that constitute the CS—as withdrawal symptoms. In *cue exposure therapies,* an addict is exposed to drug-related cues without being given the usual dose of the drug itself, eventually resulting in extinction of the association between the contextual cues and the effects of the drug. After such treatment, encountering familiar drug-related cues will no longer result in the compensatory response linked to withdrawal symptoms, thereby making it easier for a recovering addict to remain abstinent (Siegel, 2005).

Operant Conditioning: Reinforcements from the Environment

The study of classical conditioning is the study of behaviours that are *reactive*. Most animals don't voluntarily salivate or feel spasms of anxiety; rather, they exhibit these responses involuntarily during the conditioning process. Involuntary behaviours make up only a small portion of our behavioural repertoires. The remainder are behaviours that we voluntarily perform. We engage in these voluntary behaviours in order to obtain rewards and avoid punishment; understanding them is essential to developing a complete picture of learning. Because classical conditioning has little to say about these voluntary behaviours, we turn now to a different form of learning, **operant conditioning,** *a type of learning in which the consequences of an organism's behaviour determine whether it will repeat that behaviour in the future.* The study of operant conditioning is the exploration of behaviours that are *active*.

Learning Outcomes

WHAT YOU NEED TO KNOW

- Describe the process of operant conditioning.

- Explain how behavioural, cognitive, neural, and evolutionary aspects influence our understanding of operant conditioning.

The Development of Operant Conditioning: The Law of Effect

The study of how active behaviour affects the environment began at about the same time as classical conditioning. In fact, Edward L. Thorndike (1874–1949) first examined active behaviours back in the 1890s, before Pavlov published his findings. Thorndike's research focused on *instrumental behaviours*, that is, behaviour that required an organism to *do* something, such as solve a problem or otherwise manipulate elements of its environment (Thorndike, 1898). For example, Thorndike completed several experiments using a puzzle box, which was a wooden crate with a door that would open when a concealed lever was moved in the right way (see **FIGURE 7.5**). A hungry cat placed in a puzzle box would try various behaviours to get out — scratching at the door, meowing loudly, sniffing the inside of the box,

operant conditioning A type of learning in which the consequences of an organism's behaviour determine whether it will repeat that behaviour in the future.

Figure 7.5
Thorndike's Puzzle Box In Thorndike's original experiments, food was placed just outside the door of the puzzle box, where the cat could see it. If the cat triggered the appropriate lever, the door would open and the cat could get out.

Figure 7.6

The Law of Effect Thorndike's cats displayed trial-and-error behaviour when trying to escape from the puzzle box. For example, they made lots of irrelevant movements and actions until, over time, they discovered the solution. Once they figured out which behaviour was instrumental in opening the latch, they stopped all other ineffective behaviours and escaped from the box faster and faster.

putting its paw through the openings—but only one behaviour opened the door and led to food: tripping the lever in just the right way. After the cat earned its reward, Thorndike placed it back in the puzzle box for another round. Don't get the wrong idea. Thorndike probably *really liked* cats. Far from teasing them, he was after an important behavioural principle.

Eventually, the cats became quite skilled at triggering the lever for their release. Notice what's going on. At first, the cat enacts any number of likely (yet ultimately ineffective) behaviours, but only one behaviour leads to freedom and food. Over time, the ineffective behaviours occur less and less frequently, and the one instrumental behaviour (going right for the latch) becomes more frequent (see **FIGURE 7.6**). From these observations, Thorndike developed the **law of effect,** *the principle that behaviours that are followed by a "satisfying state of affairs" tend to be repeated, and those that produce an "unpleasant state of affairs" are less likely to be repeated.*

The circumstances that Thorndike used to study learning were very different from those used in classical conditioning research. Remember that in classical conditioning experiments, the US occurred on every training trial, no matter what the animal did. Pavlov delivered food to the dog whether it salivated or not. But in Thorndike's work, the behaviour of the animal determined what happened next. If the behaviour was "correct" (i.e., the animal triggered the latch), the animal was rewarded with food. Incorrect behaviours produced no results, and the animal was stuck in the box until it performed the correct behaviour. Although different from classical conditioning, Thorndike's work resonated with most behaviourists at the time: It was still observable, quantifiable, and free from explanations involving the mind (Galef, 1998).

B. F. Skinner: The Role of Reinforcement and Punishment

Several decades after Thorndike's work, B. F. Skinner (1904–1990) coined the term **operant behaviour** to refer to *behaviour that an organism performs that has some impact on the environment.* In Skinner's system, all of these emitted behaviours "operated" on the environment in some manner, and the environment responded by providing events that either strengthened those behaviours (i.e., they *reinforced* them) or made them less likely to occur (i.e., they *punished* them). Skinner's elegantly simple observation was that most organisms do *not* behave like a dog in a harness, passively waiting to receive food no matter what the circumstances. Rather, most organisms are like cats in a box, actively engaging the environment in which they find themselves to reap rewards (Skinner, 1938, 1953).

law of effect The principle that behaviours that are followed by a "satisfying state of affairs" tend to be repeated, and those that produce an "unpleasant state of affairs" are less likely to be repeated.

operant behaviour Behaviour that an organism performs that has some impact on the environment.

In order to study operant behaviour scientifically, Skinner developed a variation on Thorndike's puzzle box. The *operant conditioning chamber,* or *Skinner box,* as it is commonly called (shown in **FIGURE 7.7**), allows a researcher to study the behaviour of small organisms in a controlled environment.

Skinner's approach to the study of learning focused on *reinforcement* and *punishment.* These terms, which have commonsense connotations, turned out to be rather difficult to define. For example, some people love roller coasters, whereas others find them horrifying; the chance to go on one will be reinforcing for one group but punishing for another. Dogs can be trained with praise and a good belly rub—procedures that are nearly useless for most cats. Skinner settled on a neutral definition that would characterize each term by its effect on behaviour. Therefore, a **reinforcer** is *any stimulus or event that increases the likelihood of the behaviour that led to it,* whereas a **punisher** is *any stimulus or event that decreases the likelihood of the behaviour that led to it.*

Whether a particular stimulus acts as a reinforcer or a punisher depends in part on whether it increases or decreases the likelihood of a behaviour. Presenting food is usually reinforcing and it produces an increase in the behaviour that led to it; removing food is often punishing and leads to a decrease in the behaviour. Turning on an electric shock is typically punishing (and decreases the behaviour that led to it); turning it off is rewarding (and increases the behaviour that led to it).

To keep these possibilities distinct, Skinner used the term *positive* for situations in which a stimulus was presented and *negative* for situations in which it was removed. Consequently, as shown in **TABLE 7.1**, there is *positive reinforcement* (a stimulus is presented, and its presentation increases the likelihood of a behaviour) and a *negative reinforcement* (a stimulus is removed, and its removal increases the likelihood of a behaviour), as well as *positive punishment* (a stimulus is administered, and its administration reduces the likelihood of a behaviour) and a *negative punishment* (a stimulus is removed, and its removal decreases the likelihood of a behaviour). Here the words *positive* and *negative* mean, respectively, something that is *added* or something that is *taken away*; they do not mean "good" or "bad" as they do in everyday speech.

These distinctions can be confusing at first; after all, "negative reinforcement" and "punishment" both sound like they should be "bad" and produce the same type of behaviour. However, negative reinforcement, for example, does not involve administering something that decreases the likelihood of a behaviour; it's the *removal* of something, such as a shock, that increases the likelihood of a behaviour. For example, new parents are highly trainable by their babies, and quickly learn to repeat behaviours (such as bouncing a certain way; swinging the baby in their car seat at a certain rate; pulling goofy faces) that the baby either positively reinforces (by smiling or cooing) or negatively reinforces (by stopping crying). The baby's reinforcing feedback encourages these behaviours.

Figure 7.7

Skinner Box This is a typical Skinner box, or operant conditioning chamber. A rat, pigeon, or other suitably sized animal is placed in this environment and observed during learning trials that apply operant conditioning principles.

reinforcer Any stimulus or event that increases the likelihood of the behaviour that led to it.

punisher Any stimulus or event that decreases the likelihood of the behaviour that led to it.

TABLE 7.1

REINFORCEMENT AND PUNISHMENT

	Reinforcement: Increases the Likelihood of Behaviour	Punishment: Decreases the Likelihood of Behaviour
Stimulus is presented	***Positive reinforcement:*** Parents buy teen a new car as a reward for safe driving.	***Positive punishment:*** Parents assign difficult new chores after teen is stopped for speeding.
Stimulus is removed	***Negative reinforcement:*** Parents reduce restrictions on where teen can drive as a reward for safe driving.	***Negative punishment:*** Parents suspend driving privileges after teen is stopped for speeding.

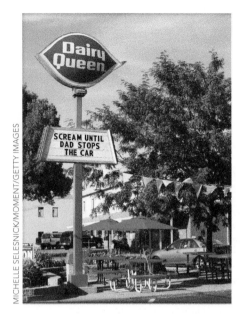

Negative reinforcement involves the removal of something unpleasant from the environment. When Daddy stops the car, he gets a reward: His little monster stops screaming. However, from the perspective of the child, this is positive reinforcement. The child's tantrum results in something positive added to the environment—stopping for a snack.

Reinforcement is generally more effective than punishment in promoting learning, for many reasons (Gershoff, 2002). One reason is that punishment signals that an unacceptable behaviour has occurred, but it doesn't specify what should be done instead. Scolding a young child for starting to run into a busy street certainly stops the behaviour, but it doesn't promote any kind of learning about the *desired* behaviour.

Primary and Secondary Reinforcement and Punishment

Reinforcers and punishers often gain their functions from basic biological mechanisms. A pigeon that pecks at a target in a Skinner box is usually reinforced with food pellets, just as an animal that learns to escape a mild electric shock has avoided the punishment of tingly paws. Food, comfort, shelter, and warmth are examples of *primary reinforcers* because they help satisfy biological needs or desires. However, the vast majority of reinforcers or punishers in our daily lives have little to do with biology: Verbal approval, a bronze trophy, or money all serve powerful reinforcing functions, yet none of them taste very good or help keep you warm at night. The point is, we learn to perform a lot of behaviours on the basis of reinforcements that have little or nothing to do with biological satisfaction.

These *secondary reinforcers* derive their effectiveness from their associations with primary reinforcers through classical conditioning. For example, money starts out as a neutral CS that, through its association with primary USs such as acquiring food or shelter, takes on a conditioned emotional element. Flashing lights, originally a neutral CS, acquire powerful negative elements through association with a speeding ticket and a fine, or as an indicator of a dangerous situation.

Immediate Versus Delayed Reinforcement and Punishment

A key determinant of the effectiveness of a reinforcer is the amount of time between the occurrence of a behaviour and the reinforcer: The more time elapses, the less effective the reinforcer (Lattal, 2010; Renner, 1964). This was dramatically illustrated in experiments with hungry rats in which food reinforcers were given at varying times after a rat pressed a lever (Dickinson et al., 1992). Delaying reinforcement by even a few seconds led to a reduction in the number of times the rat subsequently pressed the lever, and extending the delay to a minute rendered the food reinforcer completely ineffective (see **FIGURE 7.8**). The most likely explanation for this effect is that delaying the reinforcer made it difficult for the rats to figure out exactly what behaviour they needed to perform in order to obtain it. In the same way, parents who wish to use a piece of candy to reinforce their children for playing quietly should provide the candy while the child is still playing quietly; waiting until later, when the child may be engaging in other behaviours—perhaps making a racket with pots and pans—will make it more difficult for the child to link the reinforcer with the behaviour of playing quietly (Powell et al., 2009).

Figure 7.8

Delay of Reinforcement Rats pressed a lever in order to obtain a food reward. Researchers varied the amount of time between the lever press and the delivery of food reinforcement. The number of lever presses declined substantially with longer delays.

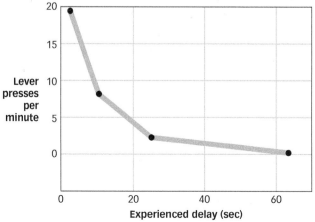

The greater potency of immediate versus delayed reinforcers may help us appreciate why it can be difficult to engage in behaviours that have long-term benefits. The smoker who desperately wants to quit smoking will be reinforced immediately by the feeling of relaxation that results from lighting up, but they may have to wait years to be reinforced with the better health that results from quitting; the dieter who sincerely wants to lose weight may easily succumb to the temptation of a chocolate sundae that provides reinforcement now, rather than waiting weeks or months for the reinforcement (looking and feeling better) that would be associated with losing weight.

Similar considerations apply to punishment: As a general rule, the longer the delay between a behaviour and the administration of punishment, the less effective the punishment will be in suppressing the targeted behaviour (Kamin, 1959; Lerman & Vorndran, 2002). The reduced effectiveness of delayed punishment can be a serious problem in nonlaboratory settings because in everyday life, it is often difficult to administer punishment immediately or even soon after a problem behaviour has occurred (Meindl & Casey, 2012). For example, a parent whose child misbehaves at a shopping mall may be unable to punish the child immediately with a time-out because it is impractical in the mall setting. Some problem behaviours, such as cheating, can be difficult to detect immediately, therefore punishment is necessarily delayed. Research in both the laboratory and everyday settings suggests several strategies for increasing the effectiveness of delayed punishment, including increasing the severity of the punishment or attempting to bridge the gap between the behaviour and the punishment with verbal instructions (Meindl & Casey, 2012). The parent in the shopping mall, for instance, might tell the misbehaving child exactly when and where a later time-out will occur.

Suppose you are the mayor of a suburban town, and you want to institute some new policies to decrease the number of drivers who speed on residential streets. How might you use punishment to decrease the undesirable behaviour (speeding)? How might you use reinforcement to increase the desirable behaviour (safe driving)? Thinking about the principles of operant conditioning you read about in this section, which approach do you think might be most fruitful?

The Basic Principles of Operant Conditioning

After establishing how reinforcement and punishment produced learned behaviour, Skinner and other scientists began to expand the parameters of operant conditioning. This took the form of investigating some phenomena that were well known in classical conditioning—such as discrimination, generalization, and extinction—as well as some practical applications, such as how best to administer reinforcement or how to produce complex learned behaviours in an organism. Let's look at some of these basic principles of operant conditioning.

Discrimination, Generalization, and the Importance of Context

We all take off our clothes at least once a day, but usually not in public. We scream at rock concerts, but not in libraries. We say, "Please pass the gravy," at the dinner table, but not in a classroom. Although these observations may seem like nothing more than common sense, Thorndike was the first to recognize the underlying message: Learning takes place *in contexts*, not in the free range of any plausible situation. As Skinner rephrased it later, most behaviour is under *stimulus control*, which develops when a particular response occurs only when an appropriate *discriminative stimulus* (one that indicates that a response will be reinforced) is present.

Skinner (1972) discussed this process in terms of a "three-term contingency": In the presence of a *discriminative stimulus* (classmates drinking coffee together in Starbucks), a *response* (joking comments about a psychology professor's increasing waistline and receding hairline) produces a *reinforcer* (laughter among classmates). The same response in a different context—say, the professor's office—would most likely produce a very different outcome.

Stimulus control, perhaps not surprisingly, shows both discrimination and generalization effects similar to those we saw with classical conditioning. To demonstrate

In research on stimulus control, participants trained with Picasso paintings, such as the one on the left, responded to other paintings by Picasso or even to paintings by other cubists. Participants trained with Monet paintings, such as the one on the right, responded to other paintings by Monet or by other French impressionists. An interesting detail: The participants in this study were pigeons.

this, researchers used either a painting by the French impressionist Claude Monet or one of Pablo Picasso's paintings from his cubist period for the discriminative stimulus (Watanabe et al., 1995). Participants in the experiment were reinforced only if they responded when the appropriate painting was presented.

After training, the participants discriminated appropriately: Those trained with the Monet painting responded when other paintings by Monet were presented, and those trained with a Picasso painting reacted when other cubist paintings by Picasso were shown. And as you might expect, Monet-trained participants did not react to Picassos, and Picasso-trained participants did not respond to Monets. What's more, the research participants showed that they could generalize *across* painters as long as they were from the same artistic tradition. Those trained with Monet responded appropriately when shown paintings by Auguste Renoir (another French impressionist), and the Picasso-trained participants responded to artwork by the cubist painter Henri Matisse, despite never having seen those paintings before.

If these results don't seem particularly startling to you, it might help to know that the research participants were pigeons that were trained to key-peck to these various works of art. Stimulus control, and its ability to foster stimulus discrimination and stimulus generalization, is effective even if the stimulus has no meaning to the respondent.

Extinction

As in classical conditioning, operant behaviour undergoes extinction when the reinforcements stop. Pigeons cease pecking at a key if food is no longer presented following that behaviour. You wouldn't put more money into a vending machine if it failed to give you its promised candy bar or soda. On the surface, extinction of operant behaviour looks like that of classical conditioning: The response rate drops off fairly rapidly and, if a rest period is provided, spontaneous recovery is typically seen.

However, there is an important difference. As noted, in classical conditioning, the US occurs on *every* trial, no matter what the organism does. In operant conditioning, the reinforcements occur *only* when the proper response has been made, and they don't always occur even then. Not every trip into the forest produces nuts for a squirrel, auto salespeople don't sell to everyone who takes a test drive, and researchers run many experiments that do not work out and thus never get published. Yet these behaviours don't weaken and gradually extinguish. In fact, they typically become stronger and more resilient. Curiously, then, extinction is a bit more complicated in operant conditioning than in classical conditioning because it depends, in part, on how often reinforcement is received. In fact, this principle is an important cornerstone of operant conditioning that we'll examine next.

Schedules of Reinforcement

Skinner was intrigued by the apparent paradox surrounding extinction, and in his autobiography, he described how he began studying it (Skinner, 1979). He had been laboriously rolling ground rat meal and water to make food pellets to reinforce the rats in his early experiments. It occurred to him that perhaps he could save time and effort by not giving his rats a pellet for every bar press but instead delivering food on some intermittent schedule. The results of this hunch were dramatic. Not only did the rats continue bar pressing, but they also shifted the rate and pattern of bar pressing depending on the timing and frequency of the presentation of the reinforcers. Unlike in classical conditioning, where the sheer *number* of learning trials was important, the *pattern* with which reinforcements appeared was crucial in operant conditioning.

Skinner explored dozens of what came to be known as *schedules of reinforcement* (Ferster & Skinner, 1957) (see **FIGURE 7.9**). The two most important are *interval schedules,* based on the time intervals between reinforcements, and *ratio schedules,* based on the ratio of responses to reinforcements.

Interval Schedules Under a **fixed-interval (FI) schedule,** *reinforcers are presented at fixed time periods, provided that the appropriate response is made.* For example, on a 2-minute fixed-interval schedule, a response will be reinforced, but only after 2 minutes have expired since the last reinforcement. Rats and pigeons in Skinner boxes produce predictable patterns of behaviour under these schedules. They show little responding right after the presentation of the reinforcement, but as the next time interval draws to a close, they show a burst of responding. Many undergraduates behave exactly like this. They do relatively little work until just before the upcoming exam, then engage in a burst of reading and studying.

Under a **variable-interval (VI) schedule,** *a behaviour is reinforced on the basis of an average time that has expired since the last reinforcement.* For instance, on a 2-minute variable-interval schedule, responses will be reinforced every 2 minutes, *on average,* but not after each 2-minute period. Variable-interval schedules typically produce steady, consistent responding because the time until the next reinforcement is less

Interval Schedules Students cramming at the last minute for an exam often show the same kind of behaviour as pigeons being reinforced under a fixed-interval schedule. Radio stations offer tickets to hopeful concert goers on a less predictable, variable-interval schedule of reinforcement.

Figure 7.9
Reinforcement Schedules Different schedules of reinforcement produce different rates of response. These lines represent the number of responses that occur under each type of reinforcement. The black slash marks indicate when reinforcement was administered. Notice that ratio schedules tend to produce higher rates of responding than do interval schedules, as shown by the steeper lines for fixed-ratio and variable-ratio reinforcement.

fixed-interval (FI) schedule An operant conditioning principle whereby reinforcers are presented at fixed time periods, provided that the appropriate response is made.

variable-interval (VI) schedule An operant conditioning principle whereby behaviour is reinforced on the basis of an average time that has expired since the last reinforcement, although the exact time to the next reinforcement is not predictable.

predictable. Such schedules are not encountered that often in real life, although one example might be radio promotional giveaways, such as tickets to rock concerts. The reinforcement—getting the tickets—might average out to once an hour across the span of the broadcasting day, but the presentation of the reinforcement is variable: It might come early in the 10:00 o'clock hour, later in the 11:00 o'clock hour, immediately into the 12:00 o'clock hour, and so on.

Both fixed-interval schedules and variable-interval schedules tend to produce slow, methodical responding because the reinforcements follow a time scale that is independent of how many responses occur. It doesn't matter if a rat on a fixed-interval schedule presses a bar 1 time during a 2-minute period or 100 times: The reinforcing food pellet won't drop out of the chute until 2 minutes have elapsed, regardless of the number of responses.

Ratio Schedules Under a **fixed-ratio (FR) schedule,** *reinforcement is delivered after a specific number of responses have been made.* One schedule might present reinforcement after every fourth response, and a different schedule might present reinforcement after every 20 responses; the special case of presenting reinforcement after each response is called *continuous reinforcement,* and it's what drove Skinner to investigate these schedules in the first place. Notice that, in each example, the ratio of reinforcements to responses, once set, remains fixed.

There are many situations in which people, sometimes unknowingly, find themselves being reinforced on a fixed-ratio schedule: Pieceworkers get paid after making a fixed number of products, and some credit card companies return to their customers a percentage of the amount charged. When a fixed-ratio schedule is operating, it is possible, in principle, to know exactly when the next reinforcer is due.

Under a **variable-ratio (VR) schedule,** *the delivery of reinforcement is based on a particular average number of responses, although the ratio of responses to reinforcements is variable.* Slot machines in a modern casino pay off on variable-ratio schedules that are determined by the random number generator controlling the play of the machines. A casino might advertise that its machines pay off on "every 100 pulls, on average," which could be true. However, one player might hit a jackpot after 3 pulls on a slot machine, whereas another player might not hit a jackpot until after 200 pulls. The ratio of responses to reinforcements is variable, which probably helps casinos stay in business.

It should come as no surprise that variable-ratio schedules produce slightly higher rates of responding than fixed-ratio schedules, primarily because the organism never knows when the next reinforcement is going to appear. What's more, the higher the ratio, the higher the response rate tends to be: A 20-response variable-ratio schedule will produce considerably more responding than a 2-response variable-ratio schedule will. When schedules of reinforcement provide **intermittent reinforcement,** *whereby only some of the responses made are followed by reinforcement,* they produce behaviour that is much more resistant to extinction than does a continuous reinforcement schedule. One way to think about this effect is to recognize that the more irregular and intermittent a schedule is, the more difficult it becomes for an organism to detect when it has actually been placed on extinction.

fixed-ratio (FR) schedule An operant conditioning principle whereby reinforcement is delivered after a specific number of responses have been made.

variable-ratio (VR) schedule An operant conditioning principle whereby the delivery of reinforcement is based on a particular average number of responses, although the ratio of responses to reinforcements is variable.

intermittent reinforcement An operant conditioning principle whereby only some of the responses made are followed by reinforcement.

Ratio Schedules These pieceworkers in a textile factory get paid according to a fixed-ratio schedule: They receive payment after sewing some set number of shirts. Slot machines in casinos pay out following a variable-ratio schedule. This helps explain why some gamblers feel incredibly lucky, whereas others can't believe they can play a machine for so long without winning a thing.

For instance, if you've just put a toonie into a vending machine that, unknown to you, is broken, no snacks come out. Because you're used to getting your potato chips on a continuous reinforcement schedule—one toonie produces one bag of chips—this abrupt change in the environment is easy to notice, and you are unlikely to put additional money into the machine: You'd quickly show extinction. However, if you've put your toonie into a slot machine that, unknown to you, is broken, do you stop after one or two plays? Almost certainly not. If you're a regular slot player, you're used to going for many plays in a row without winning anything, so it's difficult to tell that anything is out of the ordinary. Under conditions of intermittent reinforcement, all organisms will show considerable resistance to extinction and continue for many trials before they stop responding. This effect has been observed even in infants (Weir et al., 2005).

This relationship between intermittent reinforcement schedules and the robustness of the behaviour they produce is called the **intermittent reinforcement effect,** *the fact that operant behaviours that are maintained under intermittent reinforcement schedules resist extinction better than those maintained under continuous reinforcement.* In one extreme case, Skinner gradually extended a variable-ratio schedule until he managed to get a pigeon to make an astonishing 10,000 pecks at an illuminated key for one food reinforcer! Behaviour maintained under a schedule like this is virtually immune to extinction.

Imagine you own an insurance company, and you want to encourage your salespeople to sell as many policies as possible. You decide to give them bonuses according to the number of policies they sell. How might you set up a system of bonuses using a fixed-ratio schedule? Using a variable-ratio schedule? Which system do you think would encourage your salespeople to work harder, in terms of making more sales?

Shaping Through Successive Approximations

Have you ever been to a dolphin show at an aquarium and wondered how the dolphins learn to jump up in the air, twist around, splash back down, do a somersault, and then jump through a hoop, all in one smooth motion? Well, they don't. Wait—of course they do—you've seen them. It's just that they don't learn to do all those complex aquabatics in *one* smooth motion. Rather, elements of their behaviour are shaped over time until the final product looks like one smooth motion.

Skinner noted that the trial-by-trial experiments of Pavlov and Thorndike were rather artificial. Behaviour rarely occurs in fixed frameworks where a stimulus is presented and then an organism has to engage in some activity or another. We are continuously acting and behaving, and the world around us reacts in response to our actions. Most of our behaviours, then, are the result of **shaping,** *learning that results from the reinforcement of successive steps to a final desired behaviour.* The outcomes of one set of behaviours shape the next set of behaviours, whose outcomes shape the next set of behaviours, and so on. For example, parents use shaping to teach young children skills such as riding a bike by reinforcing successive behaviours that are needed to attain the complex goal behaviour.

Skinner realized the potential power of shaping when, one day in 1943, he was working on a wartime project sponsored by General Mills in a lab on the top floor of a flour mill where pigeons frequently visited (Peterson, 2004). In a lighthearted moment, Skinner and his colleagues decided to see whether they could teach the pigeons to "bowl" by swiping with their beaks at a ball that Skinner had placed in a box along with some pins. Nothing worked until Skinner decided to reinforce any response even remotely related to a swipe, such as merely looking at the ball. "The result amazed us," Skinner recalled. "In a few minutes the ball was caroming off the walls of the box as if the pigeon had been a champion squash player" (Skinner, 1958, p. 974).

Skinner applied this insight in his later laboratory research. For instance, he noted that if you put a rat in a Skinner box and wait for it to press the bar, you could end up waiting a very long time: Bar pressing just isn't very high in a rat's natural hierarchy of responses. However, it is relatively easy to shape bar pressing. Watch the rat closely: If it turns in the direction of the bar, deliver a food reward. This will reinforce turning

intermittent reinforcement effect The fact that operant behaviours that are maintained under intermittent reinforcement schedules resist extinction better than those maintained under continuous reinforcement.

shaping Learning that results from the reinforcement of successive steps to a final desired behaviour.

towards the bar, making such a movement more likely. Now wait for the rat to take a step towards the bar before delivering food; this will reinforce moving towards the bar. After the rat walks closer to the bar, wait until it touches the bar before presenting the food. Notice that none of these behaviours is the final desired behaviour (reliably pressing the bar). Rather, each behaviour is a *successive approximation* to the final product, or a behaviour that gets incrementally closer to the overall desired behaviour. In the dolphin example—and indeed, in many instances of animal training in which relatively simple animals seem to perform astoundingly complex behaviours—you can think through how each smaller behaviour is reinforced until the overall sequence of behaviour is performed reliably.

Superstitious Behaviour

Everything we've discussed so far suggests that one of the keys to establishing reliable operant behaviours is the correlation between an organism's response and the occurrence of reinforcement. In the case of continuous reinforcement, when every response is followed by the presentation of a reinforcer, there is a one-to-one, or perfect, correlation. In the case of intermittent reinforcement, the correlation is weaker (i.e., not every response is met with the delivery of reinforcement), but it's not zero. As you read in the Methods in Psychology chapter, however, just because two things are correlated (i.e., they tend to occur together in time and space) doesn't imply that there is causality (i.e., the presence of one reliably causes the other to occur).

Skinner (1948) designed an experiment that illustrates this distinction. He put several pigeons in Skinner boxes, set the food dispenser to deliver food every 15 seconds, and left the birds to their own devices. Later he returned and found the birds engaging in odd, idiosyncratic behaviours, such as pecking aimlessly in a corner or turning in circles. He referred to these behaviours as "superstitious" and offered a behaviourist analysis of their occurrence. The pigeons, he argued, were simply repeating behaviours that had been accidentally reinforced. That is, a pigeon that just happened to have

B. F. Skinner shaping a dog named Agnes. By reinforcing Agnes for touching successively higher lines on the wall, Skinner taught Agnes a pretty neat trick: After 20 minutes of shaping, Agnes wandered in, stood on her hind legs, and jumped straight to the top line.

pecked randomly in the corner when the food showed up had connected the delivery of food to that behaviour. Because this pecking behaviour was reinforced by the delivery of food, the pigeon was likely to repeat it. Now pecking in the corner was more likely to occur, and it was more likely to be reinforced 15 seconds later when the food appeared again. For each pigeon, the behaviour that is reinforced would most likely be whatever the pigeon happened to be doing when the food was first delivered. Skinner's pigeons acted as though there was a causal relationship between their behaviours and the appearance of food when it was merely an accidental correlation.

Although some researchers questioned Skinner's characterization of these behaviours as superstitious (Staddon & Simmelhag, 1971), later studies have shown that reinforcing adults or children using schedules in which reinforcement is not contingent on their responses can produce seemingly superstitious behaviour. It seems that people, like pigeons, behave as though there's a correlation between their responses and reward when in fact the connection is merely accidental (Bloom et al., 2007; Mellon, 2009; Ono, 1987; Wagner & Morris, 1987).

Baseball players who play well on days they happened not to have showered may continue that tradition, mistaking the accidental correlation between poor personal hygiene and a good day at bat as somehow causal. This "stench causes home runs" hypothesis is just one of many examples of human superstitions (Gilbert et al., 2000; Radford & Radford, 1949).

A Deeper Understanding of Operant Conditioning

Like classical conditioning, operant conditioning also quickly proved to be a powerful approach to learning. But Skinner, like Watson before him, was satisfied to observe an organism perform a learned behaviour; he didn't look for a deeper explanation of mental processes (Skinner, 1950). In this view, an organism behaved in a certain way in response to stimuli in the environment, not because the animal in question wanted, wished, or willed anything. However, some research on operant conditioning digs deeper into the underlying mechanisms that produce the familiar outcomes of reinforcement. As we did with classical conditioning earlier in this chapter, let's examine three elements that expand our view of operant conditioning: the cognitive, neural, and evolutionary elements of operant conditioning.

The Cognitive Elements of Operant Conditioning

Edward Chace Tolman (1886–1959) was one of the first researchers to question Skinner's strictly behaviourist interpretation of learning and was the strongest early advocate of a cognitive approach to operant learning. Tolman argued that there was more to learning than just knowing the circumstances in the environment (the properties of the stimulus) and being able to observe a particular outcome (the reinforced response). Instead, Tolman proposed that an animal established a means–ends relationship. That is, the conditioning experience produced knowledge or a belief that in this particular situation, a specific reward (the end state) will appear if a specific response (the means to that end) is made.

Tolman's means–ends relationship may remind you of the Rescorla–Wagner model of classical conditioning. Rescorla argued that the CS functions by setting up an expectation about the arrival of a US, and expectations most certainly involve cognitive processes. In both Rescorla's and Tolman's theories, the stimulus does not directly evoke a response; rather, it establishes an internal cognitive state that then produces the behaviour. These cognitive theories of learning focus less on the stimulus–response (SR) connection and more on what happens in the organism's mind when faced with the stimulus. During the 1930s and 1940s, Tolman and his students conducted studies that focused on *latent learning* and *cognitive maps*, two phenomena that strongly suggest that simple S–R interpretations of operant learning behaviour are inadequate.

Latent Learning and Cognitive Maps In **latent learning,** *something is learned, but it is not manifested as a behavioural change until sometime in the future.* Latent learning

latent learning A process in which something is learned, but it is not manifested as a behavioural change until sometime in the future.

Figure 7.10

Latent Learning Rats in a control group that never received any reinforcement (green curve) improved at finding their way through the maze over 17 days, but not by much. Rats that received regular reinforcements (blue curve) showed fairly clear learning; their error rate decreased steadily over time. Rats in the latent learning group (orange curve) were treated exactly like the control group rats for the first 10 days and then like the regularly rewarded group for the last 7 days. Their dramatic improvement on day 12 shows that these rats had learned a lot about the maze and the location of the goal box even though they had never received reinforcements.

can easily be established in rats and it occurs without any obvious reinforcement, a finding that posed a direct challenge to the then-dominant behaviourist position that all learning required some form of reinforcement (Tolman & Honzik, 1930a).

Tolman gave three groups of rats access to a complex maze every day over a span of 17 days. The control group never received any reinforcement for navigating the maze. They were simply allowed to run around until they reached the goal box at the end of the maze. In **FIGURE 7.10**, you can see that over the 17 days of the study, the control group (in green) got a little better at finding their way through the maze, but not by much. A second group of rats received regular reinforcements; when they reached the goal box, they found a small food reward there. Not surprisingly, these rats showed clear learning, as can be seen in blue in Figure 7.10. A third group was treated exactly like the control group for the first 10 days and then rewarded for the last 7 days. This group's behaviour (in orange) was quite striking. For the first 10 days, they behaved like the rats in the control group. However, during the final 7 days, their learning curve shifted abruptly; now they showed substantial learning, behaving a lot like the rats in the second group, which had been reinforced every day. Clearly, the rats in this third group had learned a lot about the maze and the location of the goal box during those first 10 days even though they had not received any reinforcements for their behaviour. In other words, they showed evidence of latent learning.

These results suggested to Tolman that beyond simply learning "start here, end here," his rats had developed a sophisticated mental picture of the maze. Tolman called this a **cognitive map,** *a mental representation of the physical features of the environment.* Tolman thought that the rats had developed a mental picture of the maze that allowed them to navigate it, and he devised several experiments to test that idea (Tolman & Honzik, 1930b; Tolman et al., 1946).

Further Support for Cognitive Explanations One simple experiment provided support for Tolman's theories and wreaked havoc with the noncognitive explanations offered by staunch behaviourists. Tolman trained a group of rats in the maze shown in **FIGURE 7.11a**. As you can see, rats run down a straightaway, take a left, a right, a long right, ending up in the goal box at the end of the maze. Because we're looking at it from above, we can see that the rat's position at the end of the maze, relative to the starting point, is diagonal to the upper right. Of course, all that the rat in the maze sees is the next set of walls and turns until it eventually reaches the goal box. Nonetheless, rats learned to navigate this maze without error or hesitation after about four nights. Clever rats. But they were cleverer than you think.

After the rats had mastered the maze, Tolman changed things around a bit and put them in the maze shown in Figure 7.11b. The goal box was still in the same place relative to the start box. However, many alternative paths now spoked off

cognitive map A mental representation of the physical features of the environment.

(a) Apparatus used in preliminary training   (b) Apparatus used in test trial

Figure 7.11
Cognitive Maps (a) Rats trained to run from a start box to a goal box in the maze on the left mastered the task quite readily. When those rats were then placed in the maze on the right (b), in which the main straightaway had been blocked, they did something unusual. Rather than simply backtracking and trying the next closest runway (i.e., one of those labelled 8 or 9 in the figure), which would be predicted by stimulus generalization, the rats typically chose runway 5, which led most directly to where the goal box had been during their training. The rats had formed a cognitive map of their environment and knew where they needed to end up spatially, relative to where they began.

the main platform, and the main straightaway that the rats had learned to use was blocked. Most behaviourists would predict that the rats in this situation — running down a familiar path only to find it blocked — would show stimulus generalization and pick the next closest path, such as one immediately adjacent to the straightaway. This is not what Tolman observed. When faced with the blocked path, the rats instead ran all the way down the path that led directly to the goal box. The rats had formed a sophisticated cognitive map of their environment and behaved in a way that suggested they were successfully following that map after the conditions had changed. Latent learning and cognitive maps suggest that operant conditioning involves an animal's doing much more than responding to a stimulus. Tolman's experiments strongly suggest that there is a cognitive component, even in rats, to operant learning.

The Neural Elements of Operant Conditioning

Soon after psychologists came to appreciate the range and variety of things that could function as reinforcers, they began looking for underlying brain mechanisms that might account for these effects. The first hint of how specific brain structures might contribute to the process of reinforcement arose from the discovery of what came to be called *pleasure centres*. McGill researchers James Olds and Peter Milner inserted tiny electrodes into different parts of a rat's brain and allowed the animal to control electric stimulation of its own brain by pressing a bar. They discovered that some brain areas, particularly those in the limbic system (see the Neuroscience and Behaviour chapter), produced what appeared to be intensely positive experiences: The rats would press the bar repeatedly to stimulate these structures. The researchers observed that these rats would ignore food, water, and other life-sustaining

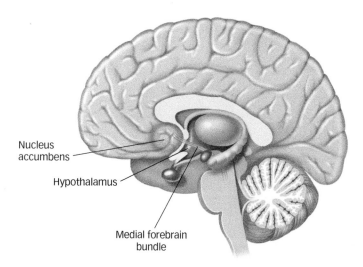

Figure 7.12
Pleasure Centres in the Brain The nucleus accumbens, medial forebrain bundle, and hypothalamus are all major pleasure centres in the brain.

Nucleus accumbens

Hypothalamus

Medial forebrain bundle

necessities for hours on end simply to receive stimulation directly in the brain. They then called these parts of the brain *pleasure centres* (Olds, 1956) (see **FIGURE 7.12**).

In the years since these early studies, researchers have identified a number of structures and pathways in the brain that deliver rewards through stimulation (Wise, 1989, 2005). The neurons in the *medial forebrain bundle,* a pathway that meanders its way from the midbrain through the *hypothalamus* into the *nucleus accumbens,* are the most susceptible to stimulation that produces pleasure. This is not surprising because psychologists have identified this bundle of cells as crucial to behaviours that clearly involve pleasure, such as eating, drinking, and engaging in sexual activity. Second, the neurons all along this pathway and especially those in the nucleus accumbens itself are all *dopaminergic* (i.e., they secrete the neurotransmitter *dopamine*). Remember from the Neuroscience and Behaviour chapter that higher levels of dopamine in the brain are usually associated with positive emotions. Several competing hypotheses about the precise role of dopamine have emerged, including the idea that dopamine is more closely linked with the expectation of reward than with reward itself (Fiorillo et al., 2008; Schultz, 2016) or that dopamine is more closely associated with wanting or even *craving* something rather than simply liking it (Berridge, 2007).

Whichever view turns out to be correct, researchers have found good support for a reward centre in which dopamine plays a key role. First, as you've just seen, rats will work to stimulate this pathway at the expense of other basic needs (Olds & Fobes, 1981). However, if drugs that block the action of dopamine are administered to the rats, they cease stimulating the pleasure centres (Stellar et al., 1983). Second, drugs such as cocaine, amphetamine, and opiates activate these pathways and centres (Moghaddam & Bunney, 1989), but dopamine-blocking drugs dramatically diminish their reinforcing effects (White & Milner, 1992). Third, fMRI studies show increased activity in the nucleus accumbens in heterosexual men looking at pictures of attractive women (Aharon et al., 2001) and in individuals who believe they are about to receive money (Cooper et al., 2009; Knutson et al., 2001). Finally, rats that are given primary reinforcers (e.g., food or water) or that are allowed to engage in sexual activity show increased dopamine secretion in the nucleus accumbens—but only if they are hungry, thirsty, or sexually aroused (Damsma et al., 1992).

This last finding is exactly what we might expect, given our earlier discussion of the complexities of reinforcement. After all, food tastes a lot better when we are hungry, and sexual activity is more pleasurable when we are aroused. The biological structures that underlie rewards and reinforcements probably evolved to ensure that species engaged in activities to help their survival and reproduction. (For more on the relationship between dopamine and Parkinson's, see Hot Science: Dopamine and Reward Learning: From Parkinson's Disease to Gambling.)

Learning to Trust: For Better or Worse Research using fMRI also illustrates a contribution of cognitive factors to reward-related learning in people who played a "trust" game with a fictional partner (Delgado et al., 2005). On each trial, a participant could either keep a $1 reward or transfer the reward to a partner, who would receive $3. The partner could then either keep the $3 or share half of it with the participant. When playing with a partner who was willing to share the reward, the participant would be better off transferring the money, but when playing with a partner who did not share, the participant would be better off keeping the reward in the first place. Participants in such experiments typically find out who is trustworthy on the basis of trial-and-error learning during the game, transferring more money to partners who reinforce them by sharing.

In the study by Delgado and colleagues, participants were given detailed descriptions of their partners as either trustworthy, neutral, or suspect. Even though, during the game itself, the sharing behaviour of the three types of partners did not differ—they each reinforced participants to the same extent through sharing—the participants' cognitions about their partners had powerful effects. Participants transferred more money to the trustworthy partner than to the others, essentially ignoring the trial-by-trial feedback that would ordinarily shape their playing behaviour, thus reducing the amount of reward they received. Highlighting the power of the cognitive effect, signals in a part of the brain that ordinarily distinguishes between positive and negative feedback were evident only when participants played with the neutral partner; these feedback signals were absent when participants played with the trustworthy partner and decreased when participants played with the suspect partner.

These kinds of effects might help us understand otherwise perplexing real-life cases such as that of the American con artist Bernard Madoff, who in March 2009 pleaded guilty to swindling numerous investors out of billions of dollars in a highly publicized case that attracted worldwide attention. Madoff had been the chairman of the American NASDAQ stock exchange and seemed to his investors an extremely trustworthy figure with whom they could safely invest their money. Those powerful cognitions might have caused investors to miss danger signals that otherwise would have led them to learn about the true nature of Madoff's operation. If so, the result was one of the most expensive failures of learning in modern history.

Bernard Madoff, shown here leaving a court hearing in March 2009, pleaded guilty to fraud after swindling billions of dollars from investors who trusted him.

The Evolutionary Elements of Operant Conditioning

As you'll recall, classical conditioning has an adaptive value that has been fine-tuned by evolution. Not surprisingly, we can also view operant conditioning from an evolutionary perspective. This viewpoint grew out of a set of curious observations from the early days of conditioning experiments. Several behaviourists who were using simple T mazes, such as the one shown in **FIGURE 7.13**, to study learning in rats discovered that if a rat found food in one arm of the maze on the first trial of the day, it typically ran down the *other* arm on the very next trial. A staunch behaviourist wouldn't expect the rats to behave this way. After all, the rats in these experiments were hungry, and they had just been reinforced for turning in a particular direction. According to operant conditioning, this should *increase* the likelihood of their turning in that same direction, not reduce it. With additional trials, the rats eventually learned to go to the arm with the food, but they had to learn to overcome this initial tendency to go the wrong way. How can we explain this?

What was puzzling from a behaviourist perspective makes sense when viewed from an evolutionary perspective. Rats are foragers, and like all foraging species, they have evolved a highly adaptive strategy for survival. They move around in their environment, looking for food. If they find it somewhere, they eat it (or store it) and then go look somewhere else for more. If they do not find food, they forage in another part of the environment. So if the rat just found food in the *right* arm of a T maze, the obvious place to look next time is the *left* arm. The rat knows that there isn't any more food in the right arm because it just ate the food it found there! Indeed, foraging animals such as rats have well-developed spatial representations that allow them to search their environment efficiently. If given the opportunity to explore a complex environment such as the multiarm maze shown in **FIGURE 7.14**, rats will systematically go from arm to arm collecting food, rarely returning to an arm they have previously visited (Olton & Samuelson, 1976).

Two of Skinner's former students, Keller Breland and Marian Breland, were among the first researchers to discover that it wasn't just rats in T mazes that presented a problem for behaviourists (Breland & Breland, 1961). The Brelands pointed out that psychologists and the organisms they study often seemed to "disagree" on what the organisms should be doing. Their argument was simple: When this kind of dispute develops, the animals are always right, and the psychologists had better rethink their theories.

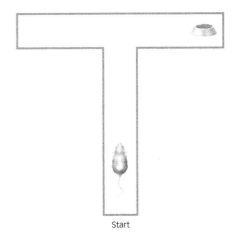

Start

Figure 7.13

A Simple T Maze When rats find food in the right arm of a typical T maze, on the next trial, they will often run to the left arm of the maze. This contradicts basic principles of operant conditioning: If the behaviour of running to the right arm is reinforced, it should be more likely to occur again in the future. However, this behaviour is perfectly consistent with a rat's evolutionary preparedness. Like most foraging animals, rats explore their environments in search of food and seldom return to where food has already been found. If the rat already has found food in the right arm of the T maze, it quite sensibly will search the left arm next to see if more food is there.

Figure 7.14

A Complex T Maze Like many other foraging species, rats placed in a complex T maze such as this one show evidence of their evolutionary preparedness. These rats will systematically travel from arm to arm in search of food, never returning to arms they have already visited.

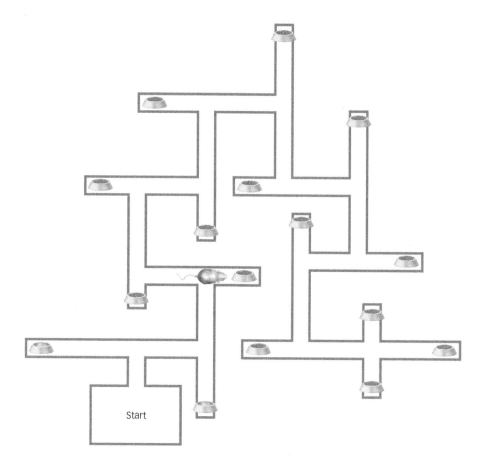

Start

The Brelands, who made a career out of training animals for commercials and movies, often used pigs because pigs are surprisingly good at learning all sorts of tricks. However, they discovered that it was extremely difficult to teach a pig the simple task of dropping coins in a box. Instead of depositing the coins, the pigs persisted in rooting with them as if they were digging them up in soil, tossing them in the air with their snouts and pushing them around. The Brelands tried to train raccoons at the same task, with different but equally dismal results. The raccoons spent their time rubbing the coins between their paws instead of dropping them in the box.

Having learned the association between the coins and food, the animals began to treat the coins as stand-ins for food. Pigs are biologically predisposed to root out their food, and raccoons have evolved to clean their food by rubbing it with their paws. That is exactly what each species of animal did with the coins.

The Brelands' work shows that all species, including humans, are biologically predisposed to learn some things more readily than others and to respond to stimuli

The misbehaviour of organisms: Pigs are biologically predisposed to root out their food, just as raccoons are predisposed to wash their food. Trying to train either species to behave differently can prove to be an exercise in futility.

in ways that are consistent with their evolutionary history (Gallistel, 2000). Such adaptive behaviours, however, evolved over extraordinarily long periods and in particular environmental contexts. If those circumstances change, some of the behavioural mechanisms that support learning can lead an organism astray. Raccoons that associated coins with food failed to follow the simple route to obtaining food by dropping the coins in the box; "nature" took over and they wasted time rubbing the coins together. The point is that, although much of every organism's behaviour results from predispositions sharpened by evolutionary mechanisms, these mechanisms sometimes can have ironic consequences.

Hot Science • Dopamine and Reward Learning: From Parkinson's Disease to Gambling

The neurotransmitter dopamine plays an important role in reward-based learning, especially *reward prediction error,* the difference between the actual reward received and the amount of predicted or expected reward. For example, when an animal presses a lever and receives an unexpected food reward, a *positive* prediction error occurs (a better-than-expected outcome), and the animal learns to press the lever again. By contrast, when an animal expects to receive a reward from pressing a lever but does not receive it, a *negative* prediction error occurs (a worse-than-expected outcome), and the animal subsequently will be less likely to press the lever again. Reward prediction error can thus be a kind of "teaching signal" that helps the animal learn to behave in a way that maximizes reward.

In pioneering studies linking reward prediction error to dopamine, Wolfram Schultz and his colleagues recorded activity in dopamine neurons located in the reward centres of a monkey's brain. They found that those neurons showed increased activity when the monkey received unexpected juice rewards but showed decreased activity when the monkey did not receive expected juice rewards. This suggests that dopamine neurons play an important role in generating the reward prediction error (Schultz, 2016; Schultz et al., 1997). Schultz and his colleagues' observations have been backed up by studies that use neuroimaging techniques to show that human brain regions involved in reward-related learning also produce reward prediction error signals and that dopamine is involved in generating those signals (Howard & Kahnt, 2018; Pessiglione et al., 2006). These and related studies support the idea that dopamine-related prediction errors

play a critical role in learning (Diederen & Fletcher, 2021).

Recent research has shown that these findings have important implications for people with Parkinson's disease, which involves movement disorders and loss of neurons that produce dopamine. As you learned in the Neuroscience and Behaviour chapter, the drug L-dopa is often used to treat Parkinson's disease because it spurs surviving neurons to produce more dopamine.

Several studies report that reward-related learning can be impaired in individuals with Parkinson's (Dagher & Robbins, 2009; Skvortsova et al., 2017), and others provide evidence that when individuals with Parkinson's perform reward-related learning tasks, the reward prediction error signal is disrupted (Meder et al., 2018; Schonberg et al., 2009). There is also evidence that Parkinson's treatment drugs can interfere with reward-related learning and the reward prediction error signal (García-García et al., 2017; Rutledge et al., 2009).

These results may relate to another intriguing feature of Parkinson's disease: Some individuals with the disease develop serious problems with compulsive gambling, shopping, and related impulsive behaviours. Such problems seem to be largely the consequence of Parkinson's drugs that stimulate dopamine receptors (Baig et al., 2019; Napier et al., 2020). Indeed, neuroimaging studies have provided evidence of increased dopamine responses to reward cues in Parkinson's patients who develop problems with compulsive gambling as a consequence of drugs that stimulate dopamine receptors (Clark & Dagher, 2014).

Recent findings suggest that boosting dopamine levels increases propensity to gamble.

These findings linking dopamine and risk-taking behaviours such as gambling may have more general implications. In a study by Rigoli and colleagues (2016), healthy adults performed a task in which they could either choose a guaranteed monetary reward or take a gamble by choosing an option in which they would receive double the guaranteed reward or nothing at all. The researchers examined the effect of boosting dopamine levels on performance of this task by administering L-dopa to the participants in one experimental session, versus administering a placebo to the same participants in a separate session. Importantly, administering L-dopa increased participants' overall propensity to gamble when performing the choice task.

Although much remains to be learned about how dopamine impacts reward learning and cognition more generally (Webber et al., 2021; Westbrook & Frank, 2018), future studies that combine drug manipulations, neuroimaging, and controlled learning paradigms should have important scientific and practical implications.

Observational Learning: Look at Me

Learning Outcomes

WHAT YOU NEED TO KNOW

- Explain the social, cultural, and evolutionary aspects of observational learning.

- Compare evidence of observational learning in animals raised among humans with that in animals raised in the wild.

- Explain the neural elements of observational learning.

Four-year-old Rodney and his 2-year-old sister Margie had always been told to keep away from the stove, which is good advice for any child and many an adult. Being a mischievous imp, however, Rodney decided one day to heat up a burner and place his hand over it until the singeing of his flesh led him to recoil, shrieking in pain. Rodney was more scared than hurt, really—and no one hearing this story doubts that he learned something important that day. But little Margie, who stood by watching these events unfold, *also* learned the same lesson. Rodney's story is a behaviourist's textbook example: The administration of punishment led to a learned change in his behaviour. But how can we explain Margie's learning? She received neither punishment nor reinforcement—indeed, she didn't even have direct experience with the wicked appliance—yet it's arguable that she's just as likely to keep her hands away from stoves in the future as Rodney is.

Margie's is a case of **observational learning,** *a process in which an organism learns by watching the actions of others.* In all societies, appropriate social behaviour is passed on from generation to generation largely through observation (Bandura, 1965). The rituals and behaviours that are a part of our culture are acquired by each new generation, not only through deliberate training of the young but also through young people observing the patterns of behaviours of their elders and each other (Flynn & Whiten, 2008).

Tasks such as using chopsticks or operating a TV's remote control are more easily acquired if we watch these activities being carried out before we try them ourselves. Even complex motor tasks, such as performing surgery, are learned in part through extensive observation and imitation of models. And anyone who is about to undergo surgery is grateful for observational learning. Just the thought of a generation of surgeons acquiring their surgical techniques through the trial-and-error methods that Thorndike studied, or the shaping of successive approximations that captivated Skinner, would make any of us very nervous.

CARSTEN KOALL/GETTY IMAGES

Happily, recent research on observational learning in surgeons and other medical professionals is providing useful new information about how to optimize learning from watching others (Cordovani & Cordovani, 2016; Harris et al., 2018).

Observational Learning in Humans

In a series of studies that have become landmarks in psychology, Canadian psychologist Albert Bandura and his colleagues investigated the parameters of observational learning (Bandura et al., 1961; for additional discussion of Bandura's work, see the Social Psychology chapter). The researchers escorted individual preschoolers into a play area, where they found a number of desirable toys that 4-year-olds typically like. An adult *model*—someone whose behaviour might be a guide for others—was then led into the room and seated in the opposite corner, where among other toys was a Bobo doll, which is a large, inflatable plastic toy with a weighted bottom that allows it to bounce back upright when knocked down. The adult played quietly for a bit but then started aggressing towards the Bobo doll, knocking it down, jumping on it, hitting it with a toy mallet, kicking it around the room, and yelling "Pow!" and "Kick him!" When the children who observed these actions were later allowed to play with a variety of toys, including a child-size Bobo doll, they were more than twice as likely to interact with it in an aggressive manner as a group of children who hadn't observed the aggressive model.

So what? Kids like to break stuff, and after all, Bobo dolls are made to be punched. Also, children in both groups had been to some extent biased towards aggressive behaviour just before being given the opportunity to play with the Bobo doll: The experimenter had stopped them from playing with some especially attractive toys, which she said were reserved for other children. As **FIGURE 7.15** shows, the degree of

observational learning A process in which an organism learns by watching the actions of others.

Figure 7.15

Beating Up Bobo Children who were exposed to an adult model who behaved aggressively towards a Bobo doll were likely to behave aggressively towards the doll themselves. This behaviour occurred in the absence of any direct reinforcement. Observational learning was responsible for producing the children's behaviours.

imitation displayed by the children who had initially observed the aggressive model was startling. In fact, the adult model purposely used novel behaviours such as hitting the doll with the toy mallet or throwing it up in the air, so that the researchers could distinguish aggressive acts that were clearly the result of observational learning.

The children in these studies also showed that they were sensitive to the consequences of the actions they observed. When they saw the adult models being punished for behaving aggressively, the children showed considerably less aggression. When the children observed a model being rewarded and praised for aggressive behaviour, they displayed an increase in aggression (Bandura et al., 1963). The observational learning seen in Bandura's studies has implications for social learning and cultural transmission of behaviours, norms, and values (Bandura, 1977, 1994). For example, research conducted across several decades has revealed that exposure to media violence is linked with an increased likelihood of aggressive or hostile thoughts and behaviours among youth (Anderson et al., 2017; Bushman, 2016), and observational learning has been implicated as one of the mechanisms responsible for this association (Anderson et al., 2003). An important question concerns whether interventions aimed at reducing exposure to media violence are effective, and if so, whether they also reduce aggression (Krahé, 2020). Results of a large study involving over 600 German 7th and 8th graders provide positive evidence: A school-based intervention produced less use of violent media (compared with a no-intervention control group) that persisted for 2 years after the intervention concluded, and this effect was associated with a reduction in self-reported aggressive behaviour (Krahé & Busching, 2015; Möller et al., 2012).

Research with children has also shown that observational learning is well suited to seeding behaviours that can spread widely across a culture through a process called a **diffusion chain,** *a process in which individuals initially learn a behaviour by observing another individual perform that behaviour, and then become models from which other*

diffusion chain A process in which individuals initially learn a behaviour by observing another individual perform that behaviour; they themselves then become models from which other individuals learn the behaviour.

individuals learn the behaviour (Flynn, 2008; Flynn & Whiten, 2008). Experiments investigating the operation of diffusion chains in preschool-age children have used a procedure in which a child (B) observes an adult model (A) performing a target act, such as using a novel tool to obtain a reward. Then, B becomes a model for another child, C, who watches B perform the target act, followed by child D observing C perform the target act, and so forth. The evidence to date indicates that children can learn how to use a novel tool by observing an adult model use that tool; more importantly, they can then become effective models for other children to learn how to use that tool.

Initial studies of diffusion chains showed that behaviours such as novel tool use could be spread accurately across 10 children (Flynn & Whiten, 2008; Horner et al., 2006). Subsequent work indicated faithful transmission of tool use across a diffusion chain comprising 20 children (Hopper et al., 2010). These findings of transmission across multiple "cultural generations" underscore that observational learning is well suited for transmission through a diffusion chain and thus a potentially powerful means of influencing a culture (Legare & Nielsen, 2015).

Coaches rely on observational learning when they demonstrate techniques to athletes.

Observational learning is important in many domains of everyday life. Sports provide a good example. Coaches in just about all sports rely on observational learning when demonstrating critical techniques and skills for their players, and athletes also have numerous opportunities to observe other athletes perform. Studies of varsity- and recreational-level athletes in both team and individual sports indicate that they all report relying heavily on observational learning to improve their performance of critical skills in their respective sports, with varsity athletes reporting an even greater reliance on observational learning than recreational athletes (Wesch et al., 2007). But can merely observing a skill result in an improvement in performing that skill without actually practicing it? A number of studies have shown that observing someone else perform a motor task, ranging from reaching for a target to pressing a sequence of keys, can produce robust learning in the observer. In fact, observational learning sometimes results in just as much learning as practicing the task itself (Heyes & Foster, 2002; Mattar & Gribble, 2005; Vinter & Perruchet, 2002).

Observational learning is especially effective when people can observe both experts and novices perform a task, because they can learn to avoid making the same errors the novices made (Andrieux & Prouteau, 2014). Additional research has also shown that although interrupting performance of a motor task impairs learning during physical practice, it has no impact on observational learning of the interrupted task (Badets et al., 2018), suggesting that observational learning can be more flexible than physical motor learning.

Observational Learning in Animals

Humans aren't the only creatures capable of learning through observing. A wide variety of species learn by observing. In one study, for example, pigeons watched other pigeons get reinforced for either pecking at the feeder or stepping on a bar. When placed in the box later, the pigeons tended to use whatever technique they had observed the other pigeons use earlier (Zentall et al., 1996).

In an interesting series of studies, researchers showed that laboratory-raised rhesus monkeys that had never seen a snake would develop a fear of snakes simply by observing the fear reactions of other monkeys (Cook & Mineka, 1990; Mineka & Cook, 1988). In fact, the fear reactions of these lab-raised monkeys were so authentic and pronounced that they could be models for still *other* lab-raised monkeys, creating a kind of observational learning "chain" that resembles the diffusion chains seen in young children that we discussed earlier. Indeed, more recent studies have provided evidence that other behaviours acquired through observational learning among chimpanzees can be transmitted along such diffusion chains, such as ways to search for food (Horner et al., 2006; Whiten, 2017). These findings highlight that diffusion chains are not unique to humans and indeed contribute to behaviours that are critical for survival (Whiten, 2021; Whiten & van de Waal, 2018).

The results on fear learning also support our earlier discussion of how each species has evolved particular biological predispositions for specific behaviours. Virtually every rhesus monkey raised in the wild has a fear of snakes, which strongly suggests that such a fear is one of this species' predispositions. This research also helps explain why some phobias that humans suffer from, such as fear of heights (acrophobia) or of enclosed spaces (claustrophobia), are so common, even in people who have never had unpleasant experiences in these contexts (Mineka & Ohman, 2002). The fears may emerge not from specific conditioning experiences but from observing and learning from the reactions of others.

Monkeys and Chimpanzees Can Learn to Use Tools Through Observation

One of the most important questions about observational learning in animals concerns whether monkeys and chimpanzees can learn to use tools by observing tool use in others, which we've already seen that young children can accomplish. In one study (Nagell et al., 1993), some chimpanzees saw the experimenter using a rake in its normal position (with the teeth pointed towards the ground) to drag a food reward into reach; this method was rather inefficient because the teeth were widely spaced, and the food sometimes slipped between them. Other chimpanzees saw the experimenter using the rake more efficiently, with the teeth pointing up and the flat edge of the rake touching the ground. Both groups of chimpanzees later used the rake when trying to obtain the food themselves, indicating observational learning. But those chimpanzees who observed the more efficient "teeth up" procedure did not use it any more often than did those who observed the less efficient "teeth down" procedure. By contrast, 2-year-old children exposed to the same conditions used the rake in the exact same way that they had seen the experimenter use it. The chimpanzees seemed only to be learning that the tool could be used to obtain food, whereas the children learned something specific about how to use the tool.

Chimpanzees Raised with Humans Learn to Imitate Exact Actions

The chimpanzees in these studies had been raised by their mothers in the wild. However, the researchers showed that chimpanzees who had been raised in environments that also included human contact could learn to imitate the exact actions performed by the experimenter, and performed similarly to human children on the task (Tomasello et al., 1993). This finding led Tomasello and colleagues (1993) to put forth what they termed the *enculturation hypothesis:* Being raised in a human culture has a profound effect on the cognitive abilities of chimpanzees, especially their ability to understand the intentions of others when performing tasks such as using tools, which in turn increases their observational learning capacities.

Other research has found something similar in capuchin monkeys, who are known for their tool use in the wild, such as employing branches or stone hammers to crack open nuts (Boinski et al., 2000; Fragaszy et al., 2004) or using stones to dig up buried roots (Moura & Lee, 2004). In one study, the experimenter demonstrated two ways of using a screwdriver to gain access to a food reward hidden in a box (Fredman & Whiten, 2008). Some monkeys observed the experimenter poke through a hole in the centre of the box, whereas others watched him pry open the lid at the rim of the box (see **FIGURE 7.16**). A control group did not observe any use of the tool. Both mother-reared and human-reared monkeys showed evidence

Monkeys can learn to fear snakes through observational learning if they see another monkey reacting with fear to the sight of a snake. But monkeys cannot be trained to fear flowers through observational learning—no matter how many times they watch another monkey who has been conditioned to fear the same flower. How does the principle of biological preparedness account for this finding?

Figure 7.16

Observational Learning Monkeys who had been reared in the wild by their mothers or reared by human families watched a model either (top) poke a screwdriver through a hole in the centre of a box to obtain a food reward or (bottom) pry open the lid to obtain the reward. Both groups showed some evidence of observational learning, but the human-reared monkeys were more likely to carry out the exact action they had watched.

of observational learning compared with those in the control group, but the human-reared monkeys carried out the exact action they had observed more often than did the mother-reared monkeys.

Although this and related evidence supports the idea that there is a cultural influence on the cognitive processes that support observational learning (Whiten, 2021), more work is needed to understand the exact nature of those processes (Damerius et al., 2017; Mesoudi et al., 2015; Tomasello & Call, 2004).

Neural Elements of Observational Learning

Studies of the neural components of observational learning have yielded some important findings. As you read in the Neuroscience and Behaviour chapter, *mirror neurons* are a type of cell found in the brains of primates (including humans). They fire when an animal performs an action, as when a monkey reaches for a food item. More important, however, mirror neurons also fire when an animal watches someone *else* perform the same specific task (Rizzolatti & Craighero, 2004). Although this "someone else" is usually a fellow member of the same species, some research suggests that mirror neurons in monkeys also fire when they observe humans performing an action (Fogassi et al., 2005). For example, monkeys' mirror neurons fired when they observed humans grasping for a piece of food, either to eat it or to place it in a container.

Mirror neurons, then, may play a critical role in the imitation of behaviour as well as the prediction of future behaviour (Rizzolatti, 2004). Mirror neurons are thought to be located in specific subregions in the frontal and parietal lobes, and there is evidence that individual subregions respond most strongly to observing certain kinds of actions (see **FIGURE 7.17**). If appropriate neurons fire when an animal sees another animal performing an action, it could indicate an awareness of intentionality or that the animal is anticipating a likely course of future actions. Although the exact functions of mirror neurons continue to be debated (Hickok, 2009, 2014; Rizzolatti & Rozzi, 2018), both of these elements — rote imitation of well-understood behaviours and an awareness of how behaviour is likely to unfold — contribute to observational learning.

Studies of observational learning in healthy adults have shown that watching someone else perform a task engages some of the same brain regions that are activated when people actually perform the task themselves. Do you consider yourself a good dancer? Have you ever watched someone who is a good dancer—a friend or maybe a celebrity on *Dancing with the Stars*—in the hopes of improving your own dance-floor moves? In one fMRI study, participants performed two tasks for several days prior to scanning: practicing dance sequences to unfamiliar techno-dance songs and watching music videos of other dance sequences accompanied by unfamiliar techno-dance songs (Cross et al., 2009). The participants were then scanned while viewing videos of sequences that they had previously danced or watched, as well as videos of sequences they had not danced or watched (untrained sequences).

Analysis of the fMRI data revealed that in comparison with the untrained sequences, viewing the previously danced or watched sequences recruited largely similar brain networks, including regions considered part of the mirror neuron system, as well as a couple of brain regions that showed more activity for previously danced than watched videos. The results of a surprise dancing test given to participants after the conclusion of scanning showed that performance was better on sequences previously watched than on the untrained sequences, demonstrating significant observational learning; but performance was best of all on the previously danced sequences (Cross et al., 2009). So although watching *Dancing with the Stars* might indeed improve your dancing skills, practicing on the dance floor should help even more.

Figure 7.17
Mirror Neuron System Regions in the frontal lobe (area 44) and parietal lobe (area 40) are thought to be part of the mirror neuron system in humans.

ABC/PHOTOFEST

Observing skilled dancers, such as this energetic pair on *Dancing with the Stars,* engages many of the same brain regions as does actual dance practice, and can produce significant learning.

Related evidence indicates that observational learning of some motor skills relies on the motor cortex, which is known to be critical for motor learning. For example, work by Western University researcher Paul Gribble and colleagues has demonstrated that significant observational learning occurs when participants watch another individual engage in a task that involves making a complex reaching movement (Mattar & Gribble, 2005). To examine whether the observational learning depends on the motor cortex, the researchers applied transcranial magnetic stimulation (TMS) to the motor cortex just after participants observed performance of the reaching movement. (As you learned in the Neuroscience and Behaviour chapter, TMS results in a temporary disruption in the function of the brain region to which it is applied.) In a striking finding, applying TMS to the motor cortex greatly reduced the amount of observational learning, whereas applying TMS to a control region outside the motor cortex had no effect on observational learning (Brown et al., 2009).

These findings indicate that some kinds of observational learning are grounded in brain regions that are essential for action. When one organism patterns its actions on another organism's behaviours, learning is speeded up, and potentially dangerous errors are prevented. (Think of Margie, who won't burn her hand on the stove.)

Observational Learning and Intergenerational Trauma So far, we've shown how observational learning is a powerful means of transmitting knowledge and behaviour among people and other animals, for good (hot stoves and dance moves) and for ill (beating up Bobo). Observational learning is one of the mechanisms that perpetuates intergenerational trauma experienced by First Nations and other equity-deserving groups in Canada (see, in the chapter on Social Psychology, Other Voices: The Intergenerational Trauma of First Nations Still Runs Deep).

Implicit Learning: Under the Radar

It's safe to assume that people are sensitive to the patterns of events that occur in the world around them. Most people don't stumble through life, thoroughly unaware of what's going on. Okay, maybe your roommate does. But people usually are attuned to linguistic, social, emotional, or sensorimotor events in the world around them—so much so that they gradually build up internal representations of those patterns that they acquired without explicit awareness. This process is often called **implicit learning,** or *learning that takes place largely independent of awareness of both the process and the products of information acquisition.* Because it occurs without our awareness, implicit learning is knowledge that sneaks in "under the radar."

Habituation, which we discussed at the outset of this chapter, is a very simple kind of implicit learning in which repeated exposure to a stimulus results in a reduced response. Habituation occurs even in a simple organism such as *Aplysia,* which probably lacks the brain structures necessary for explicit learning, such as the hippocampus (Eichenbaum, 2008; Squire & Kandel, 1999). In contrast, some forms of learning start out explicitly, but as one continues to learn, become more implicit over time. When you first learned to drive a car, for example, you probably devoted a lot of attention to the many movements and sequences that you needed to carry out simultaneously. ("Step lightly on the accelerator while you push the turn indicator, and look in the rearview mirror while you turn the steering wheel.") That complex interplay of motions is now probably quite effortless and automatic for you. Explicit learning has become implicit over time.

These distinctions in learning might remind you of similar distinctions in memory, and for good reason. In the Memory chapter, you read about the differences between *implicit* and *explicit* memories. Do implicit and explicit learning mirror implicit and explicit memory? Not entirely. Both distinctions refer

Learning Outcomes

WHAT YOU NEED TO KNOW

- Explain why language studies led to studies of implicit learning.

- Outline the number of ways that implicit and explicit learning differ.

implicit learning Learning that takes place largely independent of awareness of both the process and the products of information acquisition.

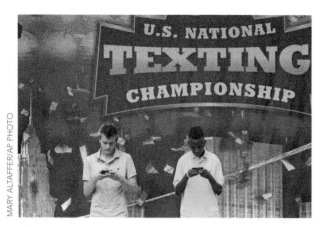

Fifteen years ago, no one knew how to type using their thumbs; now just about all teenagers do it automatically.

Grammatical Strings	Nongrammatical Strings
VXJJ	VXTJJ
XXVT	XVTVVJ
VJTVXJ	VJTTVTV
VJTVTV	VJTXXVJ
XXXXVX	XXXVTJJ

Figure 7.18

Artificial Grammar and Implicit Learning These are examples of letter strings formed by an artificial grammar. Research participants are exposed to the rules of the grammar and are later tested on new letter strings. Participants show reliable accuracy at distinguishing the valid, grammatical strings from the invalid, nongrammatical strings—even though they usually can't explicitly state the rule they are following when making such judgements. Using an artificial grammar is one way of studying implicit learning (Reber, 1996).

to memory or learning without awareness versus learning with awareness; but implicit and explicit memory typically refer to the retrieval of information about a single past event, whereas implicit and explicit learning typically refers to gradually acquiring knowledge and skills over time. More importantly, however, learning and memory are inextricably linked. Learning produces memories, and, conversely, the existence of memories implies that knowledge was acquired, that experience was registered and recorded in the brain, or that learning has taken place.

Cognitive Approaches to Implicit Learning

Most children, by the time they are 6 or 7 years old, are fairly sophisticated in terms of linguistics and social behaviour. Yet most children reach this state with very little explicit awareness that they have learned something, and with equally little awareness of what it was they actually learned. For example, although children are often given explicit rules of social conduct ("Don't chew with your mouth open"), they learn through experience how to behave in a civilized way. They're probably not aware of when or how they learned a particular course of action and may not even be able to state the general principle underlying their behaviour. Yet most kids have learned not to eat with their feet, to listen when they are spoken to, and not to kick the dog.

Lab Studies Reveal Basic Properties of Implicit Learning

To investigate implicit learning in the laboratory, researchers, in early studies, showed participants 15- or 20-letter strings and asked them to memorize them. The letter strings, which at first glance look like nonsense syllables, were actually formed using a complex set of rules called an *artificial grammar* (see **FIGURE 7.18**). Participants were not told anything about the rules, but, with experience, they gradually developed a vague, intuitive sense of the "correctness" of particular letter groupings. Once these letter groups became familiar to the participants, they processed them more rapidly and efficiently than the "incorrect" letter groupings (Reber, 1967, 1996).

Take a look at the letter strings shown in Figure 7.18. Those on the left are correct and follow the rules of the artificial grammar; those on the right all violate the rules. The differences are pretty subtle, and if you haven't been through the learning phase of the experiment, both sets look a lot alike. In fact, each nongrammatical string has only a single letter violation. Research participants were asked to classify new letter strings according to whether they follow the rules of the grammar. People perform this task reasonably well (usually they get 60–70% correct), but they are unable to provide much in the way of explicit awareness of the rules and regularities that they are using. The experience is similar to coming across a sentence with a grammatical error. You are immediately aware that something is wrong, and you can certainly make the sentence grammatical, but unless you are a trained linguist, you'll probably find it difficult to articulate which rules of English grammar were violated or which rules you used to repair the sentence.

Other studies of implicit learning have used a *serial reaction time* task (Nissen & Bullemer, 1987). Here, research participants are presented with five small boxes on a computer screen. Each box lights up briefly; when that happens the participant is asked to press the button just beneath that box as quickly as possible. Like the artificial grammar task, the sequence of lights appears to be random but in fact follows a pattern. Research participants eventually get faster with practice as they learn to anticipate which box is most likely to light up next. But if asked, they are generally unaware that there is a pattern to the lights.

Implicit learning has some characteristics that distinguish it from explicit learning. For example, when asked to carry out implicit tasks, people differ relatively little from one another; but on explicit tasks (e.g., conscious problem solving), they show large differences among individuals (Reber et al., 1991). Implicit learning also seems to be unrelated to IQ. People with high scores on standard intelligence tests are no better at implicit learning tasks, on average, than those whose scores are more modest (Reber & Allen, 2000). Implicit learning, in contrast to explicit learning, changes little across the life span. Researchers discovered well-developed implicit learning of complex, rule-governed auditory patterns in 8-month-old infants (Saffran et al., 1996). Infants listened to streams of speech that contained experimenter-defined nonsense words. For instance, the infants might hear a sequence such as "bidak-upadotigolabubidaku," which contains the nonsense word *bida*. The infants weren't given any explicit clues as to which sounds were "words" and which were not, but after several repetitions, the infants showed signs that they had learned the novel words. Infants tend to prefer novel information, and they spent more time listening to novel nonsense words that had not been presented earlier than to the nonsense words such as *bida* that had been presented. It was remarkable that the infants in this study were as good at learning these sequences as university students.

At the other end of the life span, researchers have found that implicit learning abilities also tend to be less affected by aging than are explicit learning abilities (Howard & Howard, 1997), although implicit learning is not completely preserved in older adults (Stillman et al., 2016). There is, however, mounting evidence that implicit learning is influenced by culture (see A World of Difference: Cultural Influences on Implicit Learning).

Implicit Learning Is Resistant to Some Disorders That Affect Explicit Learning

Implicit learning is remarkably resistant to various disorders that are known to affect explicit learning (Reber, 2013). A group of patients suffering from various psychoses were so severely impaired that they could not solve simple problems that university students had little difficulty with. Yet those patients were able to solve an artificial grammar learning task about as well as university students (Abrams & Reber, 1988). Other studies have found that profoundly amnesic patients not only show normal implicit memories but also display virtually normal implicit learning of artificial grammar (Knowlton et al., 1992). In fact, they made accurate judgements about novel letter strings even though they had essentially no explicit memory of having been in the learning phase of the experiment!

In contrast, several studies have shown that dyslexic children who fail to acquire reading skills despite normal intelligence and good educational opportunities exhibit deficits in implicit learning of artificial grammars (Pavlidou et al., 2009) as well as motor and spatial sequences on the serial reaction time task (Bennett et al., 2008; Orban et al., 2008; Stoodley et al., 2008). These findings suggest that problems with implicit learning play an important role in developmental dyslexia and need to be taken into account in the development of remedial programs (Stoodley et al., 2008).

Implicit learning, which is involved in acquiring and retaining the skills needed to ride a bicycle, tends to decline less in old age than explicit learning.

MIKE KEMP/GETTY IMAGES

Implicit and Explicit Learning Use Distinct Neural Pathways

The fact that individuals suffering amnesia show intact implicit learning strongly suggests that the brain structures that underlie implicit learning are distinct from those that underlie explicit learning. As we learned in the Memory chapter, amnesic individuals are characterized by lesions to the hippocampus and nearby structures in the medial temporal lobe; thus, researchers have concluded that these regions are not necessary for implicit learning (Bayley et al., 2005). What's more, it appears that distinct regions of the brain may be activated depending on how people approach a task (Reber, 2013).

For example, in one study, participants saw a series of dot patterns, each of which looked like an array of stars in the night sky (Reber et al., 2003). Actually, all the stimuli were constructed to conform to an underlying prototypical dot pattern. The dots, however, varied so much that it was virtually impossible for a viewer to guess that they all had this common structure. Before the experiment began, half of the participants were told about the existence of the prototype; in other words, they were given instructions that encouraged explicit processing. The others were given standard implicit learning instructions: They were told nothing other than to attend to the dot patterns.

The participants were then scanned as they made decisions about new dot patterns, attempting to categorize them according to whether or not they conformed to the prototype. Interestingly, both groups performed equally well on this task, correctly classifying about 65% of the new dot patterns. However, the brain scans revealed that the two groups made these decisions using very different parts of their brains (see **FIGURE 7.19**). Participants who were given the explicit instructions showed *increased* brain activity in the prefrontal cortex, parietal cortex, hippocampus, and a variety of other areas known to be associated with the processing of explicit memories. Those given the implicit instructions showed *decreased* brain activation primarily in the occipital region, which is involved in visual processing. This finding suggests that participants recruited distinct brain structures in different ways, depending on whether they were approaching the task using explicit or implicit learning.

Other studies have begun to pinpoint the brain regions that are involved in two of the most commonly tested implicit learning tasks: artificial grammar learning and sequence learning on the serial reaction time task. Several fMRI studies have shown that Broca's area — which, as you learned in the Neuroscience and Behaviour chapter, plays a key role in language production — is turned on during

Figure 7.19

Implicit and Explicit Learning Activate Different Brain Areas Research participants were scanned with fMRI while engaged in either implicit learning or explicit learning about the categorization of dot patterns. The occipital region (in blue) showed decreased brain activity after implicit learning. The areas in yellow, orange, and red showed increased brain activity during explicit learning, including the left temporal lobe (far left), the right frontal lobe (second from left and second from right), and the parietal lobe (second from right and far right) (Reber et al., 2003).

REBER, P. J., GITELMAN, D. R., PARRISH, T. B., & MESULAM, M. M. (2003). DISSOCIATING EXPLICIT AND IMPLICIT CATEGORY KNOWLEDGE WITH FMRI. *JOURNAL OF COGNITIVE NEUROSCIENCE, 15*, 574–583. PERMISSION CONVEYED THROUGH COPYRIGHT CLEARANCE CENTER.

Implicit Learning

Occipital lobe

Explicit Learning

Right frontal lobe

Parietal lobe

Left temporal lobe

artificial grammar learning (Forkstam et al., 2006; Petersson et al., 2004). Furthermore, activating Broca's area by applying electrical stimulation to the overlying scalp enhances implicit learning of artificial grammar, most likely by facilitating acquisition of grammatical rules (De Vries et al., 2010). In contrast, the motor cortex appears critical for sequence learning on the serial reaction time task. When the motor cortex was temporarily disabled by the application of a recently developed type of TMS that lasts for a long time (so that participants can perform the task without having TMS constantly applied while they are doing the task), sequence learning was abolished (Wilkinson et al., 2010).

A World of Difference · Cultural Influences on Implicit Learning

As you learned, implicit learning isn't much affected by various kinds of individual differences, including age and intelligence. That might create the impression that implicit learning occurs in the same way for pretty much everyone, regardless of their cultural background. But evidence from studies that have compared implicit learning in individuals from different cultures suggests that this impression is mistaken.

These studies emerged from earlier research indicating that Westerners (usually from North America, Europe, or Australia) tend to engage in *analytic* perceptual processing, focusing on an object independently of its context, whereas Easterners (typically Japanese, Chinese, and other Asians), tend to engage in *holistic* perceptual processing, focusing on the relationship between an object and its context (Nisbett & Miyamoto, 2005). The distinction between analytic and holistic processing is closely related to a distinction between *local* and *global* processing that has been investigated in studies of implicit learning. Consider the string of letters shown in the accompanying figure, referred to as a "GLOCAL" string because it contains letters at both global and local levels. If you focus on the global level, you will see the string as "NVJTVJ," but if you attend to the local level, you will see the string as "BYYFLB."

To study possible cultural differences in implicit learning, researchers instructed Japanese and British undergraduates to attend to patterns similar to the one in the figure, without any further instruction to focus on the global or local level; each string was repeated six times (Kiyokawa et al., 2012). Unknown to the participants, both the global and local strings were formed by a set of rules, just like the artificial grammars you learned about earlier (see Figure 7.18). On a later test, participants were told that the training strings at both the global and local levels had followed a set of rules. They were shown pairs of regular letter strings (i.e., normal text, not the GLOCAL strings depicted in the figure) and were asked to judge which member of the pair followed a grammatical rule and which did not.

Previous studies had shown that when participants are *instructed* to focus on the global pattern during the study phase, they later show implicit learning of grammatical rules that apply to the global strings but not the local strings; by contrast, participants who are instructed to focus on the local patterns later show implicit learning of grammatical rules that apply to the local but not the global strings (Tanaka et al., 2008). In the study by Kiyokawa et al. (2012), even though participants were not specifically instructed to focus on the global or local patterns, Japanese participants showed implicit learning of grammatical rules that apply to the global but not the local strings, whereas the British undergraduates performed similarly for the global and local strings. In a later study that also used GLOCAL strings along with a slightly different implicit learning task, Chinese undergraduates showed greater implicit learning than British undergraduates for global strings but not for local strings (Fu et al., 2013). Taken together, the results suggest that during the study phase, Easterners spontaneously focused on the global patterns to a greater extent than Westerners, thus producing the subsequent cultural difference in implicit learning.

The evidence we've considered so far comes from studies of visual implicit learning. Are the observed cultural differences specific to the visual modality or are they more general? To investigate the issue, researchers examined auditory implicit learning of global and local patterns embedded in Chinese tones and syllables (Ling et al., 2018). Chinese participants once again showed a significant advantage over Westerners in acquiring implicit knowledge of the global patterns, but not the local patterns, that were contained in the tones and the syllables. Putting together these results with the earlier findings from studies using GLOCAL strings, it seems clear that the kind of knowledge that supports implicit learning—even though it operates "under the radar" of our awareness—is not immune from cultural influences.

Learning in the Classroom

Learning Outcomes

WHAT YOU NEED TO KNOW

- Explain why distributed practice and practice testing are effective study techniques.
- Describe how judgements of learning (JOLs) impact learning.

In this chapter, we've considered several different types of learning from behavioural, cognitive, evolutionary, and neural perspectives. Yet it may seem strange to you that we haven't discussed the kind of learning to which you are currently devoting much of your life: learning in educational settings such as the classroom. During the past several years, psychologists have published a great deal of work specifically focused on enhancing learning in educational settings. Let's consider what some of this research says about learning techniques and then turn to the equally important topic of exerting control over learning processes.

Techniques for Learning

Students use a wide variety of study techniques in attempts to improve their learning. Popular techniques—ones that you might use yourself—include highlighting and underlining, rereading, summarizing, and visual imagery mnemonics (Annis & Annis, 1982; Wade et al., 1990). How effective are these and other techniques? A team of psychologists who specialize in learning published a comprehensive analysis of research concerning 10 learning techniques that students use (Dunlosky et al., 2013). They considered the usefulness of each technique across four main variables: learning conditions (e.g., how often and in what context the technique is used), materials to be learned (e.g., texts, math problems, concepts), student characteristics (e.g., age and ability level), and outcome measures (e.g., rote retention, comprehension, problem solving). On the basis of the picture that emerged across these four variables, Dunlosky and colleagues evaluated the overall usefulness of each technique and classified it as high, moderate, or low utility (**TABLE 7.2**).

Despite their popularity, highlighting, rereading, summarizing, and visual imagery mnemonics (which encompasses keyword mnemonic and imagery for the text) all received a low utility assessment. That doesn't mean these techniques have no value whatsoever for improving learning, but it does indicate that each one has significant limitations and that students could better spend their time using other approaches—a reason that none of these techniques appeared in the Six Tips for Reading This Textbook section of the Preface. We also discussed some material related to these techniques in the Memory chapter. Because distributed practice, interleaved practice, and practice testing are the most successful techniques, let's take a deeper look at them now (see also Other Voices: The Dangers of Learning Loss).

Distributed Practice

Cramming for exams—that is, neglecting to study for an extended period of time and then studying intensively just before an exam (Vacha & McBride, 1993)—is a common occurrence in educational life. Surveys of undergraduates across a range of colleges and universities indicate that anywhere from about 25% to as many as 50% of students report

TABLE 7.2		
EFFECTIVENESS OF STUDY TECHNIQUES		
High Effectiveness	**Moderate Effectiveness**	**Low Effectiveness**
Practice testing	Elaborative interrogation	Summarization
Distributed practice	Interleaved practice	Highlighting/underlining
		Keyword mnemonic
		Imagery for text
		Rereading

that they rely on cramming (McIntyre & Munson, 2008). Although cramming is better than not studying at all, when students cram for an exam, they repeatedly study the information to be learned with little or no time between repetitions, a procedure known as *massed practice.* Such students are thus denying themselves the benefits of *distributed practice,* which involves spreading out study activities so that more time intervenes between repetitions of the information to be learned. (Furthermore, students who rely on cramming are also inviting some of the health and performance problems associated with procrastination that we will address in the Stress and Health chapter).

The benefits of distributed practice relative to massed practice have been known for a long time; in fact, Ebbinghaus (1885/1964) first reported them in his classic studies concerning retention of nonsense syllables (see the Memory chapter). What's most impressive is just how widespread the benefits of distributed practice are: They have been observed for numerous different kinds of materials, including foreign vocabulary, definitions, and face–name pairs, and they have been demonstrated not only in undergraduates but also in children, older adults, and individuals with memory problems due to brain damage (Dunlosky et al., 2013). A review of 254 separate studies involving more than 14,000 participants concluded that, on average, participants retained 47% of studied information after distributed practice, compared with 37% after massed practice (Cepeda et al., 2006). Several other studies have also shown that distributed practice can improve long-term retention of actual classroom learning in student populations, including 8th graders and university students (Lyle et al., 2020; Rohrer, 2015). Although research on distributed practice has focused on explicit learning, recent evidence shows that it can also benefit implicit learning (Schiff et al., 2021).

Despite all the evidence indicating that distributed practice is an effective learning strategy, we still don't fully understand why that is so. One promising idea is that when we engage in massed practice, retrieving recently studied information is relatively easy, whereas during distributed practice, it is more difficult to retrieve information that we studied less recently. More difficult retrievals benefit subsequent learning more than easy retrievals, what psychologists call "desirable difficulties" (Bjork & Bjork, 2011). Whatever the explanation for the effects of distributed practice, there is no denying its benefits for students.

Interleaved Practice

Researchers have also discovered some novel benefits of the closely related technique of *interleaved practice,* a practice schedule that mixes different kinds of problems or materials within a single study session. Dunlosky and colleagues (2013) assigned interleaved practice a moderate utility assessment, but other research suggests that it may be particularly effective for learning mathematics. Rohrer and colleagues (2015) gave 7th-grade students practice math problems over a three-month period. The first group of students were given problems in the traditional blocked form; they practiced a set of similar problems that all required the same solution. The second group of students received problems in interleaved form; they practiced a mixture of different kinds of problems that each required distinct strategies.

The interleaved practice group scored higher than the blocked practice group on surprise tests given 1 day or 30 days after the conclusion of practice. The researchers suggested that interleaved practice was more effective because it requires students to choose a strategy according to the nature of individual problems (as students must do on a test), whereas during blocked practice, students could repeatedly apply the same strategy without having to select among possible strategies.

The benefits of interleaving have also been documented for social science concepts and various kinds of visual patterns, and they can be observed after delays of several minutes or several days (Firth et al., 2021). However, the vast majority of studies on interleaving have been conducted in the laboratory, so we don't yet know whether the same benefits will be seen in the classroom, so more school-based research is clearly needed (Firth et al., 2021).

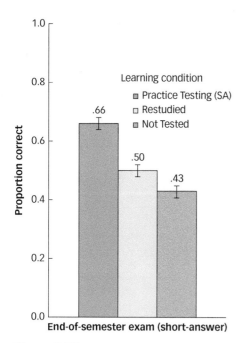

Figure 7.20
Practice Testing Improved Performance on an End-of-Semester Exam In a classroom study, 7th-grade science students received short-answer practice tests for some learning units, restudied other learning units, and received no practice tests or restudy for other units. On a short-answer exam at the end of the semester, practice testing produced significantly higher scores than either of the other two conditions (McDermott et al., 2014).

Practice Testing

Practice testing, like distributed practice, has proven useful across a wide range of materials, including learning of stories, facts, vocabulary, and lectures (Karpicke & Aue, 2015; Roediger & Karpicke, 2018). As you learned in the Memory chapter, practice testing is effective, in part, because actively retrieving an item from memory during a test improves subsequent retention of that item more efficiently than simply studying it again (Roediger & Karpicke, 2006). Yet when asked about their preferred study strategies, students indicated by a wide margin that they prefer rereading materials to testing themselves (Karpicke, 2012).

The benefits of testing tend to be greatest when the test is difficult and requires considerable retrieval effort (Pyc & Rawson, 2009), also consistent with the desirable difficulties hypothesis (Bjork & Bjork, 2011). Not only does testing increase verbatim learning of the exact material that is tested but it can also enhance the *transfer* of learning from one situation to another (Carpenter, 2012; Pan & Rickard, 2018). For example, if you are given practice tests with short-answer questions, such testing improves later performance on both short-answer and multiple-choice questions more than restudying does (Kang et al., 2007). Testing also improves the ability to draw conclusions from the studied material, which is an important part of learning and often critical to performing well in the classroom (Karpicke & Blunt, 2011). Importantly, students with different personality traits and working memory capacities benefit similarly from practice testing (Bertilsson et al., 2021).

Also important, studies of students' performance in actual classrooms reveal benefits of practice testing that are similar to those observed in the laboratory (McDaniel et al., 2013; McDermott et al., 2014) (see **FIGURE 7.20**). These findings have turned out to be extremely robust. A recent review and analysis of 222 independent studies that pulled together findings from over 48,000 students in actual classrooms revealed that practice testing, compared with restudying and several other strategies, significantly boosts both fact learning and knowledge comprehension in each of 18 different academic subject categories (Yang et al., 2021). These benefits occurred across a range of test formats, equally for males and females, and at all educational levels examined, ranging from elementary school all the way to college and university. So, if you haven't been testing yourself when studying, now would be a good time to begin!

Testing Aids Attention

Research conducted in the laboratory of one of your textbook authors highlights yet another benefit of testing: Including brief tests during a lecture can improve learning by reducing the mind's tendency to wander (Szpunar et al., 2013). How often have you found your mind wandering—thinking about your evening plans, recalling a scene from a movie, or texting a friend—in the midst of a lecture that you know you ought to be paying close attention to? It's probably happened more than once. Research indicates that students' minds wander frequently during classroom lectures (Bunce et al., 2011; Lindquist & McLean, 2011; Wilson & Korn, 2007). Such mind wandering critically impairs learning of the lecture material (Risko et al., 2012; Wammes et al., 2016). In the study by Szpunar and colleagues (2013), participants watched a videotaped statistics lecture that was divided into four segments. All of the participants were told they might or might not be tested after each segment; they were also encouraged to take notes during the lectures.

- Participants in the *tested* group received brief tests on each segment.
- Participants in the *nontested* group did not receive a test until after the final segment. (They worked on arithmetic problems after each of the earlier segments.)
- Participants in a *restudy* group were shown, but not tested on, the same material as the tested group after each segment.

At random times during the lectures, participants in all groups were asked about whether they were paying attention to the lecture or whether their minds were wandering off to other topics. Participants in the nontested and restudy groups indicated that their minds wandered in response to about 40% of the inquiries, but, in the tested group, the incidence of mind wandering was cut in half, to about 20%. Participants in the tested group took significantly more notes during the lectures and retained significantly more information from the lecture on a final test than did participants in the other two groups, who performed similarly on this test. Participants in the tested group were also less anxious about the final test than those in the other groups.

These results indicate that part of the value of testing comes from encouraging people to sustain attention to a lecture in a way that discourages task-irrelevant activities such as mind wandering, and encourages task-relevant activities such as note taking. A subsequent study using a similar design (Jing et al., 2016) showed that when participants in the tested group did mind wander, they tended to think about other parts of the lecture, whereas participants in the restudy group mind wandered about topics that were unrelated to the lecture (i.e., day-to-day happenings in their own lives). The tested group not only showed enhanced verbatim recall of lecture material but also showed an increased ability to integrate information from different parts of the lecture.

Because these benefits of testing were observed in response to a videotaped lecture, they apply most directly to online learning, where taped lectures are the norm (Breslow et al., 2013; Schacter & Szpunar, 2015), but recent evidence indicates that similar benefits are observed with live classroom lectures in an introductory psychology course (Shobe, 2021).

Control of Learning

It's the night before the final exam in your introductory psychology course. You've put in a lot of time reviewing your course notes and the material in this textbook, and you feel that you have learned most of it pretty well. You are in the home stretch with little time left, and you've got to decide whether to devote those precious remaining minutes to studying psychological disorders or social psychology. How do you make that decision? What are its potential consequences? An important part of learning involves assessing how well we know something and how much more time we need to devote to studying it.

Experimental evidence shows that people's judgements about what they have learned play a critical role in guiding further study and learning (Dunlosky & Thiede, 2013; Metcalfe, 2009). These subjective assessments, which psychologists refer to as *judgements of learning* (JOLs), have a causal influence on learning: People typically devote more time to studying items that they judge they have not learned well (Metcalfe & Finn, 2008; Son & Metcalfe, 2000).

The finding that JOLs are causally related to decisions about how much to study a particular item is important because JOLs are sometimes inaccurate (Castel et al., 2007). For example, after you read and reread a chapter or article in preparation for a test, the material will likely feel quite familiar, and that feeling may convince you that you've learned the material well enough that you don't need to study it further. However, the feeling of familiarity can be misleading: It may be the result of a low-level process such as perceptual priming (see the Memory chapter) and not the kind of learning that will be necessary to perform well on an exam (Bjork & Bjork, 2011).

Similarly, research has shown that students are sometimes overconfident in judging how well they have learned definitions of new terms and thus fail to study them effectively (Dunlosky & Rawson, 2012). Practice testing can help reduce this kind of overconfidence (Soderstrom & Bjork, 2014), but students underuse practice testing, suggesting that they are not aware of its benefits (Rivers, 2020). Therefore, one way to avoid being fooled by misleading subjective impressions when studying for an exam is to test yourself from time to time under exam-like conditions; in the case of learning definitions, carefully compare your answers to the actual definitions.

So if you are preparing for the final exam in this course and need to decide whether to devote more time to studying psychological disorders or social psychology, try to exert control over your learning by testing yourself on material from those two chapters; you can use the results of those tests to help you decide which chapter requires further work. Heed the conclusion from researchers (Bjork et al., 2013) that becoming a more sophisticated and effective learner requires understanding: (1) key features of learning and memory; (2) effective learning techniques; (3) how to monitor and control one's own learning; and (4) biases that can undermine judgements of learning.

Other Voices ┊ The Dangers of Learning Loss

One of the most impactful consequences of the COVID-19 pandemic resulted from the need to shift from live class-room learning to remote learning. You have no doubt experienced this shift yourself in high school, university, or both. Recent research in the United States, United Kingdom, Belgium, and the Netherlands (e.g., Engzell et al., 2021) indicates significant learning loss in schools as a result of pandemic-related suspension of face-to-face teaching. Learning loss is the decay in knowledge and skills over time that students experience when they are not in school. Before the pandemic, learning loss was chiefly associated with the long summer break.

Wendy Cukier is the founder of the Diversity Institute at Ryerson University and academic research lead for the Future Skills Centre. Kelly Gallagher-Mackay is an assistant professor in the Faculty of Liberal Arts at Wilfrid Laurier University. Karen Mundy is a professor of international and comparative education at the Ontario Institute for Studies in Education, and director of the UNESCO International Institute for Educational Planning.

Canada prides itself on a strong system of public primary and secondary education. But when it comes to the impact of COVID-19 on student learning and educational equity, we have fallen far short.

Little has been done to ensure that students do not face lasting educational and social harms from pandemic disruptions — even as we face the next round of challenges associated with the Omicron variant. The pandemic has disproportionately worsened already significant disparities in educational outcomes for racialized and Indigenous students, as well as those living in poverty or with disabilities. This neglect is setting the stage for a generation with depressed lifetime incomes, increased social inequality and national productivity losses estimated at $1.6-trillion.

These effects are preventable. There is good evidence that social and educational interventions — including early childhood education and wraparound supports — can improve outcomes, especially for students facing barriers. Tutoring in particular, compared with almost all other alternatives, stands out for its ability to close the gaps in learning that COVID-19 has widened.

One-on-one or small-group tutoring is designed to support — not replace — the more complex work of classroom teachers. Our forthcoming Future Skills Centre report highlights how other countries, such as the United Kingdom and United States, have made investments in tutoring central to their pandemic recovery. But rather than investing in

system-level educational recovery, Canada has relied on unsupported front-line educators to meet students' growing needs while grappling with new technologies and delivery modes, pandemic outbreaks and their own individual struggles, stress and burnout. Teachers recognize students are falling behind and won't catch up, but they have limited capacity to intervene.

A recent review and policy brief for the Nobel-Prize-winning Poverty Action Lab highlights key lessons for effective tutoring programs that support public education. Tutoring that uses paraprofessionals — trained educational assistants or full-time youth-service program members — has positive results at a much lower cost than teacher-led tutoring. More frequent tutoring (three or more times a week) has almost twice the effect of tutoring that occurs only once or twice a week. Most studies focus on literacy in the early years, but there are strong results throughout kindergarten to Grade 12: One study showed that disadvantaged students working with a college-grad tutor three times a week gained 2.5 years of learning in one year.

While the pandemic has triggered major growth in private tutoring, the relatively high upfront cost — one report estimated an annual cost of US$1,462 a student for high-frequency tutoring by college grads in U.S. public schools—represents an obstacle to providing support for those who need it most.

But we must not let sticker shock overshadow the evidence that investing now will pay back later with measurable benefits—which even outstrip the gains associated with early childhood education. Tutoring delivered through a youth service/work-integrated learning initiative may provide an additional 4:1 return on investment in terms of economic benefits.

In Canada, Alberta has committed $45-million to support students who are falling behind during the pandemic. Ontario and Quebec are offering some free tutoring on demand, but our forthcoming ecosystem map of community tutoring in Toronto highlights the fragmented nature of public support for these initiatives.

All of us have been advocating for ambitious and innovative responses to the devastating educational disruptions of the pandemic since it began, pointing to the need for supports to be directed towards students facing the greatest educational challenges and inequities.

Large-scale, targeted, school-based tutoring should be a key point of leverage to accelerate learning recovery and improve equity. Although education is primarily the responsibility of provincial governments, the federal government could support tutoring as a part of its significant investments in the inclusive-skills agenda, youth employment and work-integrated learning.

For example, Ottawa could fund work-integrated learning that sees diverse recent graduates assist students with the greatest needs. This targeted, high-dosage approach would support both students and teachers. An infusion of recent grads would also help jump-start badly needed diversity into the teaching profession pipeline.

Well-designed tutoring programs are powerful interventions that can accelerate learning, especially for students facing barriers. Canada needs to develop an ambitious educational recovery strategy that has evidence-based tutoring models at its heart. If we do not invest in student success, we should not be surprised at the lack of diversity in the work force and leadership in the years to come.

In addition, incorporating the kinds of effective learning techniques discussed, such as distributed practice, interleaved practice, and practice testing, into such interventions would be an important step to help overcome the learning loss that has been so devastating for too many students and families.

From "Canada needs to invest in tutoring for students falling behind during the pandemic." Used with permission of Wendy Cukier, Kelly Gallagher-Mackay, and Karen Mundy.

Chapter Review

What Is Learning?

- Learning involves the acquisition of new knowledge, skills, and responses. It is based on experience and produces a change in the organism, and that change is relatively permanent.

- Even the simplest organisms exhibit simple forms of learning known as habituation and sensitization.

Classical Conditioning: One Thing Leads to Another

- Classical conditioning can be thought of as an exercise in pairing a neutral stimulus with a meaningful event or stimulus. Ivan Pavlov's initial work paired a neutral tone (a conditioned stimulus, CS) with a meaningful act: the presentation of food to a hungry animal (an unconditioned stimulus, US). As he and others demonstrated, the pairing of a CS and a US during the acquisition phase of classical conditioning eventually allows the CS, all by itself, to elicit a response called a conditioned response (CR).

  - *In second-order conditioning, the CS can be paired with a new neutral stimulus to elicit a response.*

  - *The conditioned response will decline in a process called extinction if the CS is repeatedly presented without the US, although spontaneous recovery can occur after a rest period.*

  - *Conditioning generalizes to similar stimuli, which indicates an ability to discriminate between them.*

- Classical conditioning was embraced by behaviourists such as John B. Watson, who believed that higher-level functions, such as thinking or awareness, did not need to be invoked to understand behaviour. Later researchers showed, however, that the underlying mechanism of classical conditioning is more complex (and more interesting) than the simple association between a CS and a US.

- Classical conditioning involves setting up expectations and is sensitive to the degree to which the CS is a genuine predictor of the US, indicating that classical conditioning can involve some degree of cognition. The cerebellum plays an important role in eyeblink conditioning, whereas the amygdala is important for fear conditioning.

- The evolutionary aspects of classical conditioning show that each species is biologically predisposed to acquire particular CS–US associations on the basis of its evolutionary history. In short, classical conditioning is not an arbitrary mechanism that merely forms associations. Rather, it is a sophisticated mechanism that evolved precisely because it has adaptive value.

Operant Conditioning: Reinforcements from the Environment

- Operant conditioning has at its root the law of effect and is a process by which behaviours are reinforced and therefore become more likely to occur. Positive and negative reinforcement increase the likelihood of behaviour; positive and negative punishment decrease the likelihood of behaviour.

  ○ *Secondary reinforcers can derive their effectiveness from associations with primary reinforcers.*

  ○ *Delayed reinforcement or punishment is less effective than immediate reinforcement or punishment.*

  ○ *Reinforcements occur only when the proper response has been made, but not every time, as evidenced by varying schedules of reinforcement.*

  ○ *Complex behaviours are shaped through reinforcement of successive steps.*

- Like John B. Watson, B. F. Skinner tried to explain behaviour without considering cognitive, neural, or evolutionary mechanisms. However, as with classical conditioning, this approach turned out to be incomplete.

  ○ *Operant conditioning has clear cognitive components: Organisms behave as though they have expectations about the outcomes of their actions and adjust their actions accordingly. Cognitive influences can sometimes override the trial-by-trial feedback that usually influences learning.*

  ○ *Studies with both animals and people highlight the operation of a neural reward centre that affects learning.*

  ○ *The associative mechanisms that underlie operant conditioning have their roots in evolutionary biology. Some things are relatively easy to learn, whereas others are difficult; the history of the species is usually the best clue as to which will be which.*

Observational Learning: Look at Me

- Observational learning is based on cognitive mechanisms such as attention, perception, memory, and reasoning. But observational learning also has roots in evolutionary biology

and for the most basic of reasons: It has survival value. Observational learning is an important process by which species gather information about the world around them.

- Observational learning has important social and cultural consequences because it appears to be well suited to transmission of novel behaviours across individuals.

- Chimpanzees and monkeys can benefit from observational learning, supporting the idea that each species evolved particular biological predispositions.

- The mirror neuron system becomes active during observational learning, and many of the same brain regions are active during both observation and performance of a skill. Observational learning is closely tied to parts of the brain that are involved in action.

Implicit Learning: Under the Radar

- In general, children are linguistically and socially sophisticated by age 6 or 7, but without awareness of how they have learned.

- Implicit learning is a process that detects, learns, and stores patterns without the application of explicit awareness by the learner. Simple behaviours such as habituation can reflect implicit learning, but complex behaviours, such as language use or socialization, can also be learned through an implicit process.

- Tasks that have been used to document implicit learning include artificial grammar and serial reaction time tasks.

- Implicit and explicit learning differ from each other in a number of ways: There are fewer individual differences in implicit than explicit learning; psychotic and amnesic patients with explicit learning problems can exhibit intact implicit learning; and neuroimaging studies indicate that implicit and explicit learning recruit different brain structures, sometimes in different ways.

Learning in the Classroom

- Research on learning techniques indicates that some popular study methods, such as highlighting, underlining, and rereading, have low utility, whereas other techniques, such as practice testing and distributed practice, have high utility.

- Practice testing improves retention and transfer of learning and can also enhance learning and reduce mind wandering during lectures.

- Judgements of learning play a causal role in determining what material to study, but they can be misleading.

Changing Minds

1. A friend is taking a class in childhood education. "Back in the old days," your friend says, "teachers used physical punishment, but of course that's not allowed anymore. Now, a good teacher should only use reinforcement. When children behave, teachers should provide positive reinforcement, like praise. When children misbehave, teachers should provide negative reinforcement, like scolding or withholding privileges." What is your friend

misunderstanding about reinforcement? Can you give better examples of how negative reinforcement could be applied productively in an elementary school classroom?

2. A friend of your family is trying to train her daughter to make her bed every morning. You suggest trying positive reinforcement. A month later, the woman reports back to you. "It's not working very well," she says. "Every time Vicky

makes her bed, I put a gold star on the calendar, and at the end of the week, if there are seven gold stars, I give her a reward—a piece of licorice. But so far, she's earned the licorice only twice." How could you explain why the desired behaviour—bed making—might not increase as a result of this reinforcement procedure?

3. While studying for the psych exam, you ask your study partner to provide a definition of classical conditioning. "In classical conditioning," your study partner says, "there's a stimulus, the CS, that predicts an upcoming event, the US. Usually it's something bad, like an electric shock, nausea, or a loud, frightening noise. The learner makes a response, the CR, in order to prevent the US. Sometimes, the US is good, like food for Pavlov's dogs, and then the learner makes the response in order to earn the US." What's wrong with this definition?

4. One of your classmates announces that they liked the last chapter (on memory) better than the current chapter on learning. "I want to be a psychiatrist," he says, "so I mostly care about human learning. Conditioning might be a really powerful way to train animals to push levers or perform tricks, but it really doesn't have much relevance to how humans learn things." How similar is learning in humans and other animals? What real-world examples can you provide to show that conditioning does occur in humans?

5.
Visualizing Data

A friend says, "I have so many classes and so much homework to do, I just can't take much time to sleep." Using the DATA, convince your friend whether or not this is a good way to think.

Key Terms

learning (p. 246)

habituation (p. 246)

sensitization (p. 246)

classical conditioning (p. 247)

unconditioned stimulus (US) (p. 248)

unconditioned response (UR) (p. 248)

acquisition (p. 248)

conditioned stimulus (CS) (p. 248)

conditioned response (CR) (p. 248)

second-order conditioning (p. 249)

extinction (p. 250)

spontaneous recovery (p. 250)

generalization (p. 251)

discrimination (p. 251)

biological preparedness (p. 255)

operant conditioning (p. 257)

law of effect (p. 258)

operant behaviour (p. 258)

reinforcer (p. 259)

punisher (p. 259)

fixed-interval (FI) schedule (p. 263)

variable-interval (VI) schedule (p. 263)

fixed-ratio (FR) schedule (p. 264)

variable-ratio (VR) schedule (p. 264)

intermittent reinforcement (p. 264)

intermittent reinforcement effect (p. 265)

shaping (p. 265)

latent learning (p. 267)

cognitive map (p. 268)

observational learning (p. 274)

diffusion chain (p. 275)

implicit learning (p. 279)

Emotion and Motivation

LEONARDO DOES WHAT YOU'D EXPECT A 5-YEAR-OLD CHILD TO DO. He builds towers of blocks, does puzzles, and plays guessing games. But unlike most children, Leonardo isn't proud when he solves a puzzle or angry when he loses a game. That's because Leonardo has an unusual condition that has made him incapable of experiencing normal human emotions. He does not feel joy or sorrow, delight or despair, shame, envy, annoyance, excitement, gratitude, or regret. Never once has he laughed or cried.

Leonardo's condition has had profound consequences. For instance, interacting with people is quite challenging, and to do it, Leonardo has had to learn how to make just the right facial expression at just the right time—to pull his mouth into a smile when his interaction partner says something nice to him, or to raise his eyebrow once in a while to signal his interest in what they are saying. When his mother comes into the room, Leonardo knows that he is supposed to smile at her, and so he does. She's proud that he has mastered this trick, but she is also keenly aware of the fact that when Leonardo smiles he is simply "making faces" and that he is not actually *feeling* happy to see her. Most mothers would be bothered by this, but not Cynthia Breazeal. In fact, she's delighted. Because despite Leonardo's limitations, she still thinks he is the cutest robot she ever designed.

Leonardo and his "mom," robot designer and MIT professor Cynthia Breazeal.

THAT'S RIGHT. LEONARDO IS A ROBOT. He can see and hear, he can remember and reason. But despite his loveable smile and knowing wink, he can't feel a thing—and that makes him infinitely different from us. Our ability to love and to hate, to be amused and annoyed, to feel elated and devastated, is a defining feature of our humanity, and a person who couldn't feel these emotions would seem a lot like a robot to the rest of us. But what exactly are emotions? And why are they so essential? In this chapter, we'll explore these questions. We'll start by discussing the nature of emotions and seeing how they relate to the states of our bodies and our brains. Next, we'll see how people express their emotions and how they use those expressions to communicate with each other. We'll then examine the essential role that emotions play in motivation—how they inform us and how they compel us to do everything from making war to making love. Finally, we'll discuss a few of our most powerful motivations—those we share with other animals and those that make us uniquely human.

SAM OGDEN/SCIENCE SOURCE

The Nature of Emotion

Are you alive? You probably answered that question quickly and in the affirmative. At least we hope so. But what exactly does the word *alive* mean? Alive is not a *thing* you can point to. Rather, it is a *state* that an entity may or may not be in—a state that is defined by many features, such as the capacity for reproduction, growth, metabolic activity, and so on. Some entities (such as you) have all these features and so are clearly alive; other entities (such as rocks) have none of these features and so are clearly not alive; and some entities (such as viruses) have a few of these features but not others, which makes it a bit more difficult to say whether they are alive or not.

An emotion is also not a thing. There is no place in the brain where it resides and no single way to measure it (Mauss & Robinson, 2009). Rather, an **emotion** is *a temporary state that includes unique subjective experiences and physiological activity, and that prepares people for action*. An emotion has many distinct features (Mauss et al., 2005). Its mental features include what a person thinks, feels, and is prepared to do; and its physical features include the activity of both the body and the brain. When a person's state at a particular moment in time has most or all of these features, we say that person is "experiencing an emotion." What are these features? Let's start by examining the mental ones.

The Emotional Mind

People all over the planet experience an emotion for which the English language has no word. In Sanskrit it is called *kama muta* (Zickfeld et al., 2019). When people experience this emotion, they say they are feeling "moved to tears" or "touched." They describe the experience as "stirring" or "heart-warming." You've probably felt this emotion yourself, but how would you describe it to someone who hasn't felt it? You might start by telling them about the circumstances that trigger this emotion (e.g., seeing someone do something that bonds them to others, such as making a sacrifice or giving a gift), and you might try telling them about what happens to your body when you experience it (e.g., your eyes get moist, your chest gets warm, and your throat gets tight). But in the end, these descriptions would fall a bit flat because one of the essential features of kama muta—like any emotion—is the *feeling* of it, and trying to explain a feeling to someone who hasn't had it is a bit like trying to explain *green* to a person who was born blind. It *feels* like something to be moved to tears, and what it feels like is one of kama muta's defining features (Heavey et al., 2012).

Feelings

If we can't easily describe a feeling, then how can we study it scientifically? One way is by capitalizing on the fact that even though we can't always say *what* we are feeling, we usually can say how *close* one feeling is to another ("Kama muta is more like happiness than like anger"). That's good news, because knowing how close a bunch of things are allows scientists to map them! Consider the table in **FIGURE 8.1** that lists the distance between—or "closeness" of—six Canadian cities. If you tried to draw a map using the numbers in the table, you would have to draw a map of Canada, just like the one beneath the table. If you don't believe it, just try moving Winnipeg. You can't. If you move Winnipeg even a hair to the right, it will suddenly be too close to Ottawa and too far from Victoria. Winnipeg is in the *one and only spot* that allows it to be exactly 2,146 kilometres from Ottawa and 2,378 kilometres from Victoria, while still being 3,292 kilometres from Whitehorse—and the same is true of every other city on the map. What does this have to do with feelings? When people say how close two feelings

It is almost impossible not to feel something when you look at this photograph, but it is almost impossible to say exactly what you are feeling.

emotion A temporary state that includes unique subjective experiences and physiological activity, and that prepares people for action.

Figure 8.1

From Distances to Maps Knowing the distances between things—like cities, for example—allows us to draw a map that reveals the dimensions on which they vary.

	St John's	Halifax	Ottawa	Winnipeg	Whitehorse	Victoria
St John's	0	1,484	2,727	4,802	8,109	7,506
Halifax	1,484	0	1,435	3,510	6,814	6,214
Ottawa	2,727	1,435	0	2,146	5,385	4,429
Winnipeg	4,802	3,510	2,146	0	3,292	2,378
Whitehorse	8,109	6,814	5,385	3,292	0	2,484
Victoria	7,506	6,214	4,429	2,378	2,484	0

are, they are essentially estimating the "distance" between them, which allows psychologists to draw a map of the feeling-scape. As it turns out, the map of emotions shown in **FIGURE 8.2** is the one that people's "closeness ratings" most commonly produce (Kuppens et al., 2013).

So what? No one spends their summer vacation driving from Glad to Excited, so why do we need a map of the feeling-scape? Because maps don't merely show us where things are located; they also reveal the *dimensions* on which those locations vary. For example, the map in Figure 8.1 reveals that cities' locations vary on exactly two dimensions, which we call longitude (the east–west dimension) and latitude (the north–south dimension). Now look at Figure 8.2. You can see that feelings vary on two dimensions as well: *valence* (how positive the feeling is) and *arousal* (how energetic the feeling is). Although some researchers have produced more complex maps of the feeling-scape (Cowen & Keltner, 2017), decades of research suggest that the feelings of people all over the world can be fairly well described by each feeling's unique location on this simple two-dimensional map (Russell, 1980; Watson & Tellegen, 1985; Yik et al., 2011).

Appraisals and Action Tendencies

Emotions rarely come out of nowhere; rather, they are typically triggered by events in the world. If you see a person with a gun running towards you, your emotional reaction is called fear. If you see a small child bending down to pick a flower for their mother, your emotional reaction is called kama muta. But if the person is a police officer who is coming to your rescue, your emotional reaction is called relief, and if the small child is visiting their mother's grave, your reaction is called sorrow.

Emotions may be triggered by events in the world but they are not *determined* by events in the world. Rather, they are determined by our interpretation of those events. If you interpret a policeman with a gun as a rescuer, you feel relief, but if you interpret them as a threat, you feel fear. Psychologists use the word **appraisal** to refer to *conscious or unconscious evaluations and interpretations of the emotion-relevant aspects of a stimulus or event* (Arnold, 1960; Blascovich & Mendes, 2000; Ellsworth & Scherer, 2003; Lazarus, 1984; Roseman, 1984; Roseman & Smith, 2001; Scherer, 1999, 2001). Research suggests that we naturally appraise events on a number of dimensions, such as the event's self-relevance ("Does this

appraisal Conscious or unconscious evaluation and interpretations of the emotion-relevant aspects of a stimulus or event.

Figure 8.2
Two Dimensions of Emotion Just as the locations of cities vary on two dimensions called longitude and latitude, emotional experiences vary on two dimensions called valence and arousal.

affect me?") and importance ("Does this matter?"), our ability to cope with the event ("Can I handle this?") and to control it ("Can I change this?"), and others. How we answer these questions—that is, how we appraise the events—influences the emotions we experience.

Because emotions are responses to interpretations of events, different people may have different emotional reactions to precisely the same event. For instance, in one study (Siemer et al., 2007), participants were asked to perform a demanding task ("Count backwards in steps of 7 from 18,652"), and each time they tried, the experimenter gave them increasingly snarky feedback about their performance ("You aren't speaking loudly enough" or "Stop moving around so much"). After they had attempted the task three times, the experimenter explained with great annoyance that the participant's performance had been worthless and that they were terminating the task. How did participants respond to this event? It depended on how they appraised it. Those who thought the problem was the experimenter's fault ("They didn't *tell* me I was supposed to sit still") felt amused or angry, whereas those who thought the problem was their own fault ("I should know better than to wiggle in my chair") felt guilty, ashamed, or sad.

Emotions follow from appraisals and produce **action tendencies,** which are *a readiness to engage in a specific set of emotion-relevant behaviours* (Frijda et al., 1989). For example, have you ever noticed that when you are frightened by a sudden loud noise, you instantly stop moving? Why? Because the emotion called fear produces an action tendency called "freezing" (Roelofs, 2017). Similarly, if you've ever gotten into a heated argument with someone, you may have noticed yourself inching

action tendencies A readiness to engage in a specific set of emotion-relevant behaviours.

towards that person rather than away, because the emotional state called anger produces an action tendency called "approach" (Carver & Harmon-Jones, 2009). And when you are surfing the Web and accidentally come across a picture that is vile and repulsive, you probably lean back, close your eyes, and turn your head to the side, because the emotion called disgust produces an action tendency called "avoidance" (Chapman et al., 2009). Each of these action tendencies makes a good deal of evolutionary sense: When a bear growls at you, you *should* stand still; when an enemy threatens you, you *should* move forwards to stop him; and when you see a festering wound covered with maggots, you *should* move away before you get infected. Action tendencies remind us that emotions are adaptive states that nature designed to ensure our survival—and perhaps the survival of other species (see Other Voices: Do Dogs Feel Emotions Like Hope and Guilt?).

The Emotional Body

Speaking of bears, what do you think would happen if you walked into your kitchen right now and saw one nosing through the garbage can? You'd feel afraid, of course. Really very highly afraid. Then your heart would start pounding, you'd begin to breathe heavily, and the muscles in your legs would tense as they prepared you to do some of that fleeing you've heard so much about. In short, you *first* would feel fear and *then* your body would respond. Right?

Not according to William James. In the late 19th century, James suggested that the feeling of fear does not cause these bodily responses, but, rather, these bodily responses cause the feeling of fear:

> Our natural way of thinking about these coarser emotions is that the mental perception of some fact excites the mental affection called the emotion, and that this latter state of mind gives rise to the bodily expression. My theory, on the contrary, is that the bodily changes follow directly the perception of the exciting fact, and that our feeling of the same changes as they occur *is* the emotion. Common-sense says, we lose our fortune, are sorry and weep; we meet a bear, are frightened and run; we are insulted by a rival, are angry and strike. The hypothesis here to be defended says that this order of sequence is incorrect . . . and that the more rational statement is that we feel sorry because we cry, angry because we strike, afraid because we tremble (James, 1890, Vol. 2, p. 449).

According to James, first you see the bear (the "exciting fact"), which instantly causes your heart to start pounding (the "bodily changes"), and *then* you have the feeling called fear, which is nothing more than *your perception of your body's response*. The psychologist Carl Lange suggested something similar at about the same time, so this idea became known as the **James–Lange theory** of emotion, which states that *feelings are simply the perception of one's own physiological responses to a stimulus*. According to this theory, our feelings are the consequence—and not the cause—of our body's reactions to events in the world, such as the sudden appearance of bears in our kitchens.

This theory is original, elegant, and provocative—but as the physiologists Walter Cannon and Philip Bard noted, it can't possibly be right. Although Cannon and Bard had their own incorrect ideas about emotions (which they thought occurred at the same time as, but independently of, physiological activity), they correctly noted that the James–Lange theory was at odds with three basic facts.

James–Lange theory The theory that feelings are simply the perception of one's own physiological responses to a stimulus.

- First, some of our emotional experiences happen *before* our bodily responses do. People *feel* embarrassed at precisely the moment their pants fall down in public, but the bodily response called "blushing" takes a full 15 to 30 seconds to occur. How could embarrassment simply be "the perception of blushing" if the feeling happens first?

- Second, all sorts of things can cause bodily responses without also causing emotions. When your bedroom gets hot, your heart naturally starts to beat a bit faster, yet you don't feel afraid of your pillow. At least we hope not. If fear were merely "the perception of a rapid heartbeat," then why wouldn't you be scared every time your roommate cranked the thermostat?

- Third, for the James–Lange theory to work, every human emotion would have to be associated with a unique set of bodily responses — that is, every emotion would have to have a unique "physiological fingerprint," so to speak (Clark-Polner et al., 2017; Siegel et al., 2018). And they don't! Different emotional experiences are sometimes associated with the same set of bodily responses, and different bodily responses are sometimes associated with the same emotional experience.

The James–Lange theory was broken from the start, and nearly a century later, psychologists Stanley Schachter and Jerome Singer (1962) tried to repair it. Like James and Lange, Schachter and Singer believed that our emotional experiences are based on our perceptions of our body's reactions. But instead of suggesting that a specific set of bodily responses correspond to each and every unique emotional experience, they proposed that there is just one bodily response (which they called "undifferentiated physiological arousal") and that the way people interpret this response determines which emotion they experience (**FIGURE 8.3**). Their **two-factor theory of emotion** stated that *stimuli trigger a general state of physiological arousal, which is then interpreted as a specific emotion.*

According to this theory, when you see a bear in your kitchen, your body instantly goes on red alert—your heart pounds, your muscles tense, and you start breathing like a marathon runner. Your mind notices this heightened physiological arousal and instantly tries to interpret it. It looks around the room, sees a bear, and, knowing something about how much bears like to eat people, it concludes the bear is causing you to feel *fear*. But, according to the two-factor theory, if you had looked around and seen a pair of cute kittens instead of a bear, your mind would have drawn a completely different conclusion—namely, that you were feeling *delight*. The two-factor theory suggests that we have just one bodily response to all emotionally relevant stimuli, but that we interpret that response differently on different occasions. Different emotions are simply different interpretations of the same physiological reaction.

How has the two-factor theory fared? Although Schachter and Singer's experiments were disastrously flawed by modern standards (Cotton, 1981), at least one of their theory's key claims has been largely supported by more rigorous testing: Under some circumstances, people make inferences about the causes of their physiological

two-factor theory of emotion The theory that stimuli trigger a general state of physiological arousal, which is then interpreted as a specific emotion.

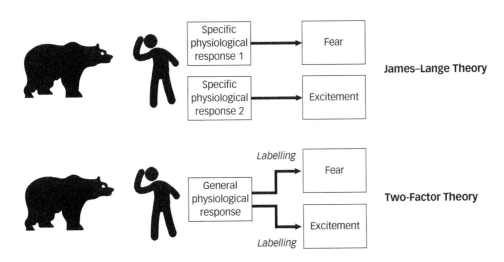

James–Lange Theory

Two-Factor Theory

Figure 8.3

Classic Theories of Emotion The James–Lange theory suggests that different stimuli (e.g., your favourite singer and a growling bear) trigger different physiological responses that are then experienced as different emotions. The two-factor theory suggests that different stimuli trigger the same general physiological response, which is interpreted or "labelled" differently under different circumstances. Research suggests that neither of these classic theories is quite right.

arousal, and those inferences can determine which emotions they experience. For instance, after exercising, people are more sexually attracted to potential romantic partners, as though they were interpreting their exercise-induced arousal as lust (Cantor et al., 1975; Dutton & Aron, 1974; White et al., 1981; White & Kight, 1984). Is it possible that exercise just makes people horny? No, because after exercising, the same people behave more aggressively towards potential enemies, as though under these circumstances they were interpreting their exercise-induced arousal as anger (Zillmann & Bryant, 1974). In one study (Lindquist & Barrett, 2008), participants either were or were not led to think about fear, and then either were or were not exposed to highly arousing music. The experimenters then measured how fearful the participants themselves felt by asking whether they'd be willing to do a whole bunch of scary things. Results showed that participants felt afraid only when they had thought about fear *and* been aroused by music, presumably because under those conditions they interpreted their arousal as fear (see also Sinclair et al., 1994).

Although research suggests that a single bodily response can sometimes give rise to different emotional experiences, research has not been so kind to the two-factor theory's claim that different emotional experiences are *nothing but* different interpretations of a single bodily response. For example, research shows that anger, fear, and sadness all produce a higher heart rate than disgust does; fear and disgust produce higher galvanic skin response (sweating) than sadness or anger do; and anger produces a larger increase in finger temperature than fear does (Christie & Friedman, 2004; Ekman et al., 1983; Kreibig, 2010; Levenson et al., 1990, 1991, 1992; Shiota et al., 2011; Stemmler et al., 2007). It seems rather unlikely (as James and Lange maintained) that every human emotion has its own unique "physiological fingerprint," but it seems even more unlikely (as Schacter and Singer maintained) that every human emotion has precisely the same physiological fingerprint. The truth is probably somewhere in the middle, and modern researchers continue working to determine exactly where in the middle it lies.

The Emotional Brain

In the late 1930s, two researchers made an accidental discovery (Klüver & Bucy, 1937, 1939). A few days after performing brain surgery on a monkey named Aurora, they noticed that she was acting strangely. First, she would eat just about anything and have sex with just about anyone—as though she could no longer distinguish between good and bad food, or between good and bad mates. Second, she was absolutely fearless and unflappable, remaining perfectly calm when she was handled by researchers or even when confronted by snakes, both of which monkeys generally don't much like. What had happened to Aurora?

As it turned out, during the surgery the researchers had accidentally damaged a structure in Aurora's brain called the *amygdala*. (There are two of these structures in every mammalian brain, and the pair is called the *amygdalae*.) Subsequent studies have confirmed that the amygdalae often play an important role in producing emotions (Cunningham & Brosch, 2012). For example, in the 1960s, researchers surgically altered a monkey's brain so that visual information entering the monkey's left eye was transmitted to its amygdalae, but visual information entering its right eye was not (Downer, 1961). When the monkey saw a threatening stimulus with only its left eye, it responded with fear and alarm; but when it saw a threatening stimulus with only its right eye, it remained calm and unruffled. Nonsurgical studies of human beings have shown similar effects. For instance, when shown words in the laboratory, most people have better memory for the

DAVID LONGSTREATH/AP PHOTO

The tourist and the tiger have something in common: Each has amygdalae that are working at lightning speed to decide whether the other is a threat. Let's hope the tourist's amygdalae are working a little faster.

emotionally evocative words such as *death* or *vomit* than for the ordinary words such as *box* or *chair*. But this is not true of people whose amygdalae have been damaged (LaBar & Phelps, 1998) or who have been given drugs that temporarily impair neurotransmission in the amygdalae (van Stegeren et al., 1998). Interestingly, people with damage to their amygdalae do not feel fear when they *see* a threat, but they do feel fear when they *experience* a threat—for example, when they suddenly can't breathe (Feinstein et al., 2013).

Together, these findings provide clues about what the amygdalae do. Before an animal feels fear, it must know that there is something to be afraid of—in other words, it must generate an appraisal. The amygdalae seem to play a part in that, helping to determine whether stimuli are emotionally relevant. In his work on rats, psychologist Joseph LeDoux discovered that information about a stimulus enters the eye and is then simultaneously transmitted along two different routes: a "fast pathway" that goes from the eye to the thalamus and then directly to the amygdalae (shown in green in **FIGURE 8.4**), and a "slow pathway" that goes from the eye to the thalamus and then *to the cortex* and *then* to the amygdalae (shown in red in Figure 8.4). As such, when you see a bear in your kitchen, information about the bear arrives at your amygdalae and at your cortex at about the same time. While your cortex conducts a relatively slow, full-scale investigation of the information ("This seems to be an animal, probably a mammal, maybe a member of the genus *Ursus* . . ."), your amygdalae use the information quickly to answer a simple question: "Is this stimulus relevant to my survival?" If your amygdalae's answer to that question is yes, they help produce the bodily responses that, when your cortex is finally done with its investigation, you will come to call *fear*.

LeDoux's research shows how fear gets started. So how does it stop? As Figure 8.4 shows, your amygdalae receive information directly from your thalamus via the fast pathway (shown in green), but they also receive information from your cortex via the slow pathway (shown in red). This latter connection allows your cortex to "talk" to your amygdalae—and one of the things it sometimes tells them is: "Chill out!" Once the cortex has finished its full-scale investigation of the information it has received, this connection allows the cortex to *downregulate* the amygdalae, which is a fancy way of saying that the cortex tells the amygdalae to reduce their activity. In a sense, the amygdalae's job is to hit the emotional gas pedal and the cortex's job is to hit the emotional brakes. That's why both adults who have cortical damage and children (whose cortices are not yet well developed) often have trouble inhibiting their emotional responses (Cohen et al., 2016; Stuss & Benson, 1986). When people are asked to make themselves feel sad, afraid, or angry, they show increased activity in the amygdalae and decreased activity in the cortex (Damasio et al., 2000); but when they are asked to make themselves *not* feel these emotions, they show increased cortical activity and decreased amygdala activity (Ochsner et al., 2002).

Does all of this mean that the amygdalae are the brain's "fear centre"? If only the brain were that simple! Although specific areas of the brain do seem to play special roles in the production of specific emotions—the anterior insula in disgust, the orbitofrontal cortex in anger, the anterior cingulate cortex in sadness—the fact is that the brain doesn't have different "centres" for different emotions (Lindquist et al., 2012). The amygdalae's precise role in producing fear is complicated and still not well understood (Phelps & LeDoux, 2005). There are times when the amygdalae are highly active and people do not report feeling afraid, just as there are times when the amygdalae are not highly active and people do report feeling afraid (Feinstein et al., 2013). What's more, the amygdalae appear to play a role in emotions other than fear (Phelps, 2006). The bottom line is that we don't yet know exactly what the amygdalae do, but we do know that the cortex, the amygdalae, and other limbic and non-limbic structures all work together in complex ways to produce the state of mind, brain, and body that we call an emotion.

Stimulus　　　　Experience of fear

Figure 8.4
The Fast and Slow Pathways of Fear Information about a stimulus takes two routes simultaneously through the brain: the "fast pathway" (shown in green), which runs from the thalamus directly to the amygdala, and the "slow pathway" (shown in red), which runs from the thalamus to the cortex and then to the amygdala. Because the amygdala receives information from the thalamus before it receives information from the cortex, a person can be afraid of something before they know what it is.
BEAR: JIM ZUCKERMAN/GETTY IMAGES; WOMAN: SNAP/SHUTTERSTOCK

Other Voices | Do Dogs Feel Emotions Like Hope and Guilt?

This chapter is about emotions in people, but we are not alone in experiencing emotions. Dr. Frans de Waal, a primatologist, has spent his career studying our primate relations and other animals, and he thinks that we should consider emotions not just across cultures, but across species. Here's what he has to say:

Like organs, the emotions evolved over millions of years to serve essential functions. Their usefulness has been tested again and again, giving them the wisdom of ages. They nudge us to do what is best for us. Some emotions may be more developed in humans, or apply to a wider range of circumstances, but none is fundamentally new.

. . .

Open your front door and tell your dog that you are going out for a walk, then close the door and return to your seat. Your dog, who had been barking and wriggling with excitement, now slinks back to his basket and puts his head down on his paws. You have just witnessed both hope and disappointment in another species. . . .

You may say that it is impossible to know what a dog feels. True, yet his behaviour clearly reflects an abrupt change in his emotional state. Expressed in the body, these states are perfectly observable and measurable even if the associated private experiences are not.

In fact, the possibility of animal hope was experimented upon nearly a century ago by the psychologist Otto Tinklepaugh. He first let a monkey watch a banana being hidden under a cup, then allowed her into the room where this had been done. If she found the banana, everything proceeded smoothly. But if the experimenter had surreptitiously replaced the banana with a piece of lettuce, the monkey would frantically look around, lifting up the cup, while shrieking at the experimenter. Her expectations had been violated, for which she rightly blamed the sneaky experimenter.

We share so many so-called secondary emotions with other species that the whole concept is questionable. There is one exception, though, which keeps being proposed as definitely cultural: guilt.

This is despite the many dog owners who seem to recognize it in their pets when they hide under the table after a transgression. One expert in animal cognition at Barnard, Alexandra Horowitz, tested this out by having dogs meet an angry owner both when they had not broken any rules and when they had; she also had them meet a relaxed owner in the same two situations. Dr. Horowitz concluded that whether dogs take on a guilty look—lowered gaze, ears pressed back, tail rapidly beating between the legs—is unrelated to whether or not they followed orders. If the owner scolds them, they look extremely guilty. If the owner doesn't, they still sometimes look like this, but less often.

One problem, however, is that our rules are of our own making, such as "Don't jump on that couch!" or "Keep your nails off my leather chair!" It must be as tough for our pets to grasp these prohibitions as it was for me to understand why I couldn't chew gum in Singapore.

It would be better to test behaviour that is wrong by almost any standard, including that of their own species. The Austrian ethologist Konrad Lorenz gave one of my favourite examples, about his dog, Bully, who broke the fundamental rule never to bite your superior.

Humans don't need to teach this rule, and indeed Bully had never been punished for it. The dog bit his master's hand when Dr. Lorenz tried to break up a dogfight. Even though Dr. Lorenz petted him right away, Bully suffered a complete nervous breakdown. For days, he was virtually paralyzed and ignored his food. He would lie on the rug breathing shallowly, occasionally interrupted by a deep sigh. He had violated a natural taboo, which among ancestral canines could have had the worst imaginable consequences, such as expulsion from the pack.

Among the primates, the most suggestive cases of remorse concern bonobos. These apes are as close to us as chimpanzees, but far more peaceful and gentle, which means that they almost never hurt one another. Whereas in most primates reconciliation after a fight is typically sought by the subordinate party, in bonobos it is the dominant animal that seeks to make amends, especially if he has inflicted an injury. He may return to his victim and unerringly reach for the exact same toe that he has bitten and carefully inspect the damage. He obviously knows precisely what he has done and where. Then he spends half an hour or more licking and cleaning the wound that he himself inflicted.

. . .

For the longest time, science has depicted animals as stimulus–response machines while declaring their inner lives barren. This has helped us sustain our customary "anthropodenial": the denial that we are animals. We like to see ourselves as special, but whatever the difference between humans and animals may be, it is unlikely to be found in the emotional domain.

Dr. Frans de Waal is a Dutch/American biologist. He is a professor at Emory University in Georgia, United States, and the author of numerous books on primate social behaviour.

AGENCE OPALE/ALAMY STOCK PHOTO

Emotional Communication

Leonardo is a robot, so he can't experience emotions, but he can smile and frown, and wink and nod. Indeed, humans who interact with Leonardo quickly forget that he is a machine precisely because he is so good at *expressing* emotions that he isn't actually experiencing. An **emotional expression** is *an observable sign of an emotional state,* and, although robots can be taught to exhibit them, human beings do so naturally. Our emotions influence the way we talk—from our intonation and inflection to the volume and duration of our speech—which is why observers can guess our emotional state from our voice alone (Banse & Scherer, 1996; Cordaro et al., 2016; Frick, 1985; Sauter et al., 2010). They can also guess our emotional state from the direction of our gaze, the rhythm of our gait, or the way we touch them on the arm (Dael et al., 2012; Dittrich et al., 1996; Hertenstein et al., 2009; Parkinson et al., 2017; Wallbott, 1998). In some sense, we are all walking, talking advertisements for what's going on inside us.

Of course, no part of our bodies is more exquisitely designed for communicating our emotional state than is our face (Jack & Schyns, 2017). Beneath the skin of your face lie 43 muscles that are capable of creating more than 10,000 unique configurations that enable you to convey information about your emotional state with an astonishing degree of subtlety and specificity (Campos et al., 2013; Ekman, 1965) (see **FIGURE 8.5**). The psychologists Paul Ekman and Wallace Friesen (1971) identified 46 unique muscle configurations or "action units" whose names (e.g., cheek puffer, chin raiser, lip corner puller) pretty much say it all. Research shows that some (though not all) of these action units are reliably associated with specific emotional states (Davidson et al., 1990; Mehu & Scherer, 2015). For example, when you feel happy, your *zygomaticus major* (a muscle that pulls your lip corners up) and your *orbicularis oculi* (a muscle that crinkles the outside edges of your eyes) produce a unique facial expression that psychologists describe as "action units 6 and 12" but that you probably just call smiling (Ekman & Friesen, 1982; Martin et al., 2017).

Communicative Expression

Why are our emotions written all over our faces? In 1872, Charles Darwin published *The Expression of the Emotions in Man and Animals,* in which he speculated about the evolutionary significance of emotional expression. Darwin noticed that human and nonhuman animals share certain postures and facial expressions, and he suggested that these "displays" were meant to communicate information about internal states. It isn't hard to see how such communications might be useful (Shariff & Tracy, 2011; Tracy et al., 2015). If a dominant animal can bare its teeth and communicate the message "I am angry," and if a subordinate animal can lower its head and communicate the message "I am afraid," then the two can establish a pecking order without any actual pecking. Darwin suggested that emotional expressions are a convenient way for one animal to let another animal know how it is feeling and how it is prepared to act. Darwin thought that emotional expressions were a bit like the words of a nonverbal language.

The Universality of Expression

But a language doesn't work unless everybody speaks the same one, and that's what led Darwin to advance the **universality hypothesis,** which suggests that *all emotional expressions mean the same thing to all people in all places at all times.* Darwin believed that every human being naturally expresses happiness with a smile, for instance, and that as a result, every human being naturally understands that a smile signifies happiness. Emotional expression is a language that is universally spoken and universally understood.

<h2>Learning Outcomes</h2>

WHAT YOU NEED TO KNOW

- Describe evidence for and against the universality hypothesis.
- Explain the facial feedback hypothesis.
- Describe how people deceive and how they detect deception.

Nobuyuki Tsujii is a classical pianist who won the prestigious Van Cliburn International Piano Competition. Although he was born blind and has never seen a facial expression, winning a million-dollar prize immediately gave rise to a million-dollar smile.

emotional expression An observable sign of an emotional state.

universality hypothesis The theory that all emotional expressions mean the same thing to all people in all places at all times.

Figure 8.5

Facial Expressions of Emotion Human observers can identify at least 20 distinct facial expressions of emotion, such as those indicated here.

Happy   Sad   Fearful   Angry   Surprised

Disgusted   Happily surprised   Happily disgusted   Sadly fearful   Sadly angry

Sadly surprised   Sadly disgusted   Fearfully angry   Fearfully surprised   Fearfully disgusted

Angrily surprised   Angrily disgusted   Disgustedly surprised   Hatred   Awed

DU, S., TAO, Y., & MARTINEZ, A. M. (2014). COMPOUND FACIAL EXPRESSIONS OF EMOTION. PROCEEDINGS OF THE NATIONAL ACADEMY OF SCIENCES, 111(15). E1454-E1462. IMAGE COURTESY OF ALEIX M. MARTINEZ.

Evidence suggests that Darwin was not entirely right. Some facial expressions do seem to be universal. For instance, people who have never seen a human face make many of the same facial expressions as those who have. For example, congenitally blind people smile when they are happy (Galati et al., 1997; Matsumoto & Willingham, 2009), and 2-day-old infants make a disgust face when bitter chemicals are put in their mouths (Steiner, 1973, 1979). People are quite good at identifying the meaning of the emotional expressions made by members of their own cultures, but they are also pretty good (though not as good) at identifying the meaning of the emotional expressions made by members of other cultures (Ekman & Friesen, 1971; Elfenbein & Ambady, 2002; Frank & Stennet, 2001; Haidt & Keltner, 1999). Recently, researchers used artificial intelligence to analyze the facial expressions of people in 6 million videos and they found that when people from 144 different countries were in the same situation—at a wedding, for example, or at a sporting event—they made the same facial expressions (Cowen et al., 2021). This and other evidence has convinced the majority of psychologists that the facial expressions of at least five emotions—*anger, disgust, fear, happiness,* and *sadness*—are universal (Ekman, 2016) and that the expressions of a few other emotions—such as *embarrassment, surprise, amusement, guilt, shame,* and *pride*—may be universal as well (Keltner, 1995; Keltner & Buswell, 1996; Keltner & Haidt, 1999; Keltner & Harker, 1998; Tracy et al., 2013).

Pain (Western)   Pain (East Asian)   Pleasure (Western)   Pleasure (East Asian)

Figure 8.6
The Faces of Pain and Pleasure Westerners and East Asians agree about how the face expresses the experience of intense physical pain, but they disagree about how it expresses the experience of intense physical pleasure. For instance, East Asians expect the physical pleasure of orgasm to produce an expression that is a lot like the expression of happiness, but Westerners expect it to produce an expression that is a lot like the expression of surprise. DISTINCT FACIAL EXPRESSIONS REPRESENT PAIN AND PLEASURE ACROSS CULTURES. CHAONA CHEN, ET AL. PNAS OCT 2018, 115 (43) E10013-E10021. COPYRIGHT 2018, NATIONAL ACADEMY OF SCIENCES.

But not all psychologists agree. In the 1950s, researchers took photographs of Westerners expressing anger, disgust, fear, happiness, sadness, and surprise and showed them to members of the South Fore, a people who lived a Stone Age existence in the highlands of Papua New Guinea and who at that point had had little contact with the modern world. When the researchers asked these participants to match each photograph to a word (such as *happy* or *afraid*), they found that the South Fore made matches that were very similar to those made by Americans, and for decades psychologists took this as powerful evidence for Darwin's universality hypothesis. More recently, researchers asked members of another isolated tribe, the Himba people of Namibia and Angola, to match faces to emotion words, and they found what previous researchers had found: The Himba made the same matches that Americans do. But when the researchers asked Himba participants to match faces to other faces that are "feeling the same way," the participants produced matches that were quite *unlike* those produced by their American counterparts (Gendron et al., 2014). Other research suggests that some emotional expressions—such as shame, happiness, and sadness—are similar across cultures but still have distinct cultural "accents" (Elfenbein, Beaupré et al., 2007) (see **FIGURE 8.6**). All of this suggests that Darwin's universality hypothesis was on the right track, but was probably overstated (Gendron et al., 2018). Human beings show some agreement about the meaning of many emotional expressions, but that agreement is short of being universal (Cordaro et al., 2018).

The Cause and Effect of Expression

Emotions cause emotional expressions. For instance, the emotion called happiness causes the contraction of the zygomatic major muscle in the face, which most of us refer to as "a smile." But every emotion doesn't have its own unique expression. Look at the face of the man in **FIGURE 8.7**. Is he experiencing great joy or great sorrow? It's hard to tell because although these emotions are polar opposites, they often produce precisely the same facial expression! And yet, in everyday life we rarely confuse sorrow and joy—so how do we normally use facial expressions to figure out what people are feeling? The answer is that we normally see facial expressions in the *context of the body* and in the *context of the situation* (Aviezer et al., 2008; Barrett et al., 2011; Kayyal et al., 2015; Reschke et al., 2019). It is hard to tell whether the man in Figure 8.7 is feeling sorrow or joy when you look only at his face, but if you go to **FIGURE 8.8** and look at his face in the context of his body and in the context of the things going on around him, you will instantly recognize his emotion. Indeed, when you return to Figure 8.7 (and please do come back soon because we already miss you), you will look at his face and wonder how you could ever have been unsure about his feelings.

Figure 8.7
Two Emotions, One Expression Without any context, it is difficult to know if this man is feeling sorrow or joy.

Figure 8.8
What Do You Think Now? This Pakistani man is being led away from the scene of the suicide bombing that killed his father. Now that you see the sorrow in his face, is it hard to imagine how you could ever have thought he might be feeling joy?

FAYAZ AZIZ/REUTERS/NEWSCOM

facial feedback hypothesis The theory that emotional expressions can cause the emotional experiences they typically signify.

JONATHAN KALB

Jonathan Kalb is a theatre professor who contracted Bell's palsy and lost the ability to make a smile. "For the past thirteen years, my smile has been an incoherent tug-of-war between a grin on one side and a frown on the other: an expression of joy spliced to an expression of horror. . . . The worst effect of my damaged smile is that it can dampen my experience of joy . . . my brain doesn't receive the same feedback messages that normal people receive from their smiles, which reinforce their happy feelings as well as relaying them. I've been devastated by the loss" (Kalb, 2015).

So emotions cause emotional expressions. But it can also work the other way around. The **facial feedback hypothesis** (Adelmann & Zajonc, 1989; Izard, 1971; Tomkins, 1981) suggests that *emotional expressions can cause the emotional experiences they typically signify*. For instance, studies show that under the right circumstances, people feel happier when they are asked to hold a pencil in their teeth (which puts their mouths in the "smiling" position) than when they are asked to hold a pencil in their lips (which puts their mouths in the "frowning" position) (Coles et al., 2019; Marsh et al., 2018; Noah et al., 2018; Strack, 2016; Strack et al., 1988). Similarly, when people are instructed to arch their brows (which is typically an expression of surprise), they find the facts they hear more surprising; and when people are instructed to wrinkle their noses (which is typically an expression of disgust), they find the odours to which they are exposed less pleasant (Lewis, 2012). These things happen because facial expressions and emotional states are strongly associated with each other (ding! Remember Pavlov?), and therefore each has the power to bring the other about. By the way, these expression-causes-emotion effects are not limited to the face: People feel more assertive when instructed to make a fist (Schubert & Koole, 2009) and feel more confident when instructed to stand with their legs spread and their hands on their hips (Carney et al., 2010). And when Americans are instructed to extend their middle fingers (which is an expression of . . . well, you know) they tend to rate other people more negatively (Chandler & Schwarz, 2009).

The fact that emotional expressions can cause the emotional experiences they signify may help explain why people are so good at recognizing the emotional expressions of others (but not groups of others; see Hot Science: The Unhappy Audience Illusion). When you interact with a friend, you unconsciously mimic each other's body postures and facial expressions (Chartrand & Bargh, 1999; Dimberg, 1982). Indeed, the tendency to ape the facial expressions of our interaction partners is so natural that even apes do it (Davila Ross et al., 2008). So when your friend smiles, you smile too—just a teeny tiny bit, so you probably don't even realize you are doing it (Foroni & Semin, 2009). Because your facial expressions can cause you to experience the emotions they ordinarily signify, mimicking your friend's expression can cause you to *feel* what your friend is feeling—which makes it easy for you to identify your friend's emotion. If your friend's frown makes you frown, and your frown makes you feel a teeny tiny bit sad, then you don't have to work very hard to know that your friend must be down in the dumps.

Is there any evidence to suggest that people do, in fact, use their own emotions to identify the emotions of others? There is. People who are naturally good at reading facial expressions tend to be natural mimics (Sonnby-Borgstrom et al., 2003), and that mimicry pays off: Negotiators who mimic the facial expressions of their opponents earn more money than those who don't (Maddux et al., 2008). Conversely, people who are bad at mimicry are also bad at reading facial expressions. For instance, people who cannot make

A World of Difference · **Say Cheese**

Canada is one of the most culturally diverse countries in the world. About one in five Canadians was born elsewhere, and those born here can also belong to different distinct cultures. Different cultures have different display rules—different ways of nonverbally expressing emotions—which suggests that Canadians with different backgrounds should have trouble "reading" their neighbours. And yet, they don't seem to. How come?

Wood, Rychlowska, and Niedenthal (2016) analyzed data from 92 scientific papers that had measured the accuracy with which people from 82 different cultures could recognize the emotional expressions of people from other cultures. First, the researchers used historical, genetic, and sociological data to compute the cultural diversity of each of the 82 cultures. Nations such as Brazil and the United States scored high in diversity, whereas nations such as Japan and Ethiopia scored low (see the map above). Second, they computed how easily the facial expressions of people from each of these cultures could be recognized by people from other cultures. When they compared these two measures, they found a positive correlation (see the graph to the right). The more diverse a culture is, the more easily the facial expressions of its members can be understood by members of other cultures. Why might that be the case?

The researchers suggest that in nations with little cultural diversity, people can communicate with subtle expressions—a slightly raised eyebrow or the fleeting flare of a nostril—because everyone knows and follows the same display rules. But in diverse nations, people of different backgrounds follow different sets of rules, so to communicate with each other, they have learned to use expressions that are so perfectly clear that they can be accurately recognized by any human on the planet.

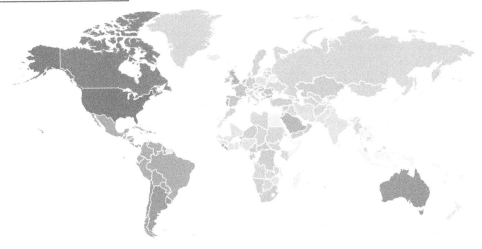

The diversity of cultures: Darker colours indicate greater cultural diversity.

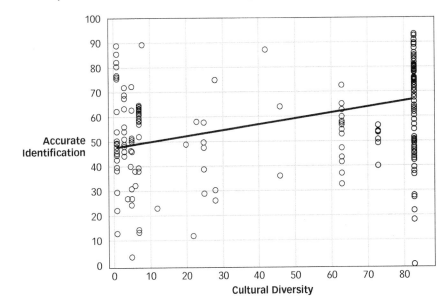

Diversity and accuracy: Each circle in this figure represents one of the 82 cultures.

facial expressions because their facial muscles have been paralyzed with Botox find it hard to identify the emotions of others (Niedenthal et al., 2005). People also find it hard to identify the emotions of others when they themselves are unable to *experience* emotions (Hussey & Safford, 2009; Pitcher et al., 2008). For example, some people with damaged amygdalae don't feel anger, and as a result, are typically quite poor at recognizing the expressions of that emotion in others (Adolphs et al., 1999). Similarly, people with psychopathy typically don't feel fear, and they find it difficult to identify fear in another person's face. As a prisoner with psychopathy told a researcher who had just shown him a photo of a fearful face, "I don't know what that expression is called, but I know that's what people look like right before you stab them" (Marsh, 2017).

Hot Science | **The Unhappy Audience Illusion**

If you've ever had to stand up and give a presentation to a roomful of people, you may have come away with the unpleasant suspicion that they didn't really like it very much. Yes, the woman in the third row was smiling a lot and the man in the fifth row was scowling a lot, but in general there seemed to be a whole lot more scowls than smiles. Afterwards, your friends probably tried to console you by telling you that your presentation actually went quite well and that the audience really enjoyed it—and you probably thought that your friends were just being kind. After all, *you* were standing right there, and you could see for yourself that most of the audience members looked out of sorts.

But recent research suggests that your friends were probably not just kind, but

right. Amit Goldenberg and colleagues (2021) showed participants faces on a computer screen for 1 second each. Sometimes the faces looked angry and sometimes they did not. On some trials, participants saw a single face (panel A), and on other trials they saw a crowd of faces (panel B). On each trial, participants were asked to estimate how angry the single face was or how angry the crowd of faces was on average.

What the researchers found was quite remarkable: When participants saw a crowd of faces, their ratings of the crowd's average emotional expression were considerably more extreme than the average of the ratings of the individual faces that constituted that crowd. This effect was stronger when the crowd was larger, and it occurred

for positive emotions, such as happiness, as well as for negative emotions, such as anger.

Why did this happen? Apparently, when we look at a sea of faces, our attention is automatically drawn to those faces that have the most extreme emotional expressions, and this leads us to overestimate the average extremity of the crowd's emotions. Every time you looked up, your eyes automatically found the scowling guy in the fifth row, and so came away with the sense that the audience didn't like you when on average, they liked you just fine. This study seems to provide experimental support for a little trick that many professional speakers use to overcome stage fright and build confidence: Once you start talking, locate the biggest smiler in the entire room and give the rest of your talk to them!

Panel A

Panel B

GOLDENBERG, A., WEISZ, E., SWEENY, T. D., CIKARA, M., & GROSS, J. J. (2021). THE CROWD-EMOTION-AMPLIFICATION EFFECT. PSYCHOLOGICAL SCIENCE, 32(3), PAGE 9. REPRINTED BY PERMISSION OF SAGE PUBLICATIONS.

Deceptive Expression

Our emotional expressions can communicate what we are feeling—or they can communicate what we want people to *think* we are feeling. When a friend makes a sarcastic remark about your taste in music, you may express your contempt with an arched brow or an exaggerated eye roll; but when your grandmother makes the same remark, you probably swallow hard and fake a smile. That's because you believe it is permissible to show contempt for a friend but not for a grandparent, and this knowledge is called a **display rule,** which is *a norm for the appropriate expression of emotion* (Ekman, 1972; Ekman & Friesen, 1968). Obeying display rules requires using several techniques, which by your age, most people have mastered:

display rule A norm for the appropriate expression of emotion.

- *Intensification* involves exaggerating the expression of emotion, as people do when pretending to be delighted by an unwanted gift. ("Leggings with little pictures of tropical fruit! Thanks, Dad. They're just what I always wanted!")

- *Deintensification* involves muting the expression of one's emotion, as athletes do when they lose their events but try not to look too disappointed ("No, really, I'm perfectly fine with the silver medal. It matches my belt buckle.")

- *Masking* involves expressing one emotion while feeling another, as judges do when they try to seem interested in, rather than contemptuous of, a lawyer's argument. ("So if I understand correctly, counselor, you are arguing that your client simply didn't realize that the bank belonged to someone else?")

- *Neutralizing* involves showing no expression of the emotion one is feeling, as card players do when they try to maintain a "poker face" despite having been dealt a winning hand. ("Four aces. Ho hum. Nice weather we're having.")

Although people in different cultures use the same techniques, they use them in the service of different display rules. In one study, Japanese and American university students watched an unpleasant video of car accidents and amputations (Ekman, 1972; Friesen, 1972). When the students didn't know the experimenters were observing them, Japanese and American students made similar facial expressions of disgust; but when they knew the experimenters were observing them, the Japanese students masked their disgust with pleasant expressions and the American students did not. Why? Because in Japan it is considered rude to display negative emotions in public, so Japanese people tend to mask or neutralize such expressions when being observed. In the United States, on the other hand, expressing disgust in public is a national pastime. The fact that different cultures have different display rules may be one of the reasons that people are generally better at recognizing the facial expressions of members of their own cultures (Elfenbein & Ambady, 2002) (see A World of Difference: Say Cheese).

Of course, even when we try to obey our culture's display rules, it doesn't always work out so well. Anyone who has ever watched the Olympic silver medalist congratulate the Olympic gold medalist knows that voices, bodies, and faces often betray a person's true emotional state (Medvec et al., 1995). Darwin noted that "those muscles of the face which are least obedient to the will, will sometimes alone betray a slight and passing emotion" (1899/2007, p. 64), and Darwin was right. The so-called reliable muscles are those that people cannot easily control, and they do provide clues to the sincerity of an expression. For instance, most people can easily control the *zygomaticus major* muscles that raise the corners of the mouth but not the *orbicularis oculi* muscles that crinkle the corners of the eyes, which is why eye crinkles are a better clue to the sincerity of a smile than is the mouth (see **FIGURE 8.9**). Sincere expressions also tend to be symmetrical, to last between a half second and 5 seconds, and to start and end smoothly. That's why asymmetrical expressions that are too short or too long and that have abrupt onsets or offsets are likely to be insincere (Ekman, 2003).

Lying

Sometimes people lie with their smiles, but just as often they lie with their words. Research shows that telling a lie can change both our verbal behaviour and nonverbal expressions (DePaulo et al., 2003). Given this, you might think that we would be pretty good at distinguishing between people who are telling the truth and people who are not, but you'd be wrong. In most cases, participants in lie-detection experiments don't perform much better than chance (Bond & DePaulo, 2006; cf. ten Brinke et al., 2016). One reason is that although there are indeed some differences between people who are telling the truth and people who are telling lies on average, those differences tend to be small, variable, idiosyncratic, and difficult to observe, which

Can you tell what this woman is feeling? She hopes not. Jiyoung Kim is a professional poker player who does not want other players to know how she feels about her cards. Given all the money she's won, she seems to be doing a pretty good job.

Figure 8.9
How Reliable Are the Reliable Muscles? Real smiles (*left*) are often accompanied by a crinkling of the eye corners, and fake smiles (*right*) are not. Eye crinkles are reliable signs—but not perfectly reliable signs—of happiness. Happy people don't always crinkle their eyes (Crivelli et al., 2015), and although most people can't fake the crinkle, some can (Gunnery et al., 2013).

According to Kang Lee, a professor at the Ontario Institute for Studies in Education (OISE), by the age of 2, about 30% of kids are able to pull off a convincing lie. By age 3, about 50% can lie successfully. And by age 4, about 80% can do it (Evans & Lee, 2013). Honesty isn't always the best policy: We are social animals, and to get along with others, sometimes we have to lie (remember the tropical-fruit leggings).

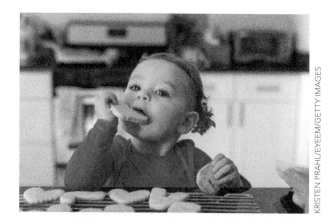

is to say that lie-detection is just plain hard (Vrij et al., 2019). A second reason is that people are simply predisposed to believe that others are telling the truth, which explains why they tend to mistake lie-tellers for truth-tellers much more often than they mistake truth-tellers for lie-tellers (Gilbert, 1991). A third reason is that people typically don't know what to look for when they try to detect lies (Vrij et al., 2011). For instance, people think that averting one's gaze is a sign of lying when in fact it isn't, and they don't think that the use of "illustrators" (which are hand and arm movements designed to supplement or modify what the person is saying) is a sign of lying when in fact it is (see **TABLE 8.1**). To make matters worse, people are not just

TABLE 8.1		
ACTUAL AND ASSUMED RELATIONSHIPS BETWEEN VERBAL/NONVERBAL CUES AND LYING		
Cues	**Actual Relationship?**	**Assumed Relationship?**
Vocal		
Hesitations (use of speech fillers, e.g., *ah, um, er, uh,* and *hmmm*)	NO	YES
Speech errors (grammatical errors, word or sentence repetition, false starts, sentence change, sentence incompletions, slips of the tongue, etc.)	NO	YES
High-pitched voice	YES	YES
Speech rate (number of spoken words in a certain period of time)	NO	NO
Latency period (period of silence between question and answer)	NO	NO
Pauses (silent, filled, or mixed)	NO	YES
Visual		
Gaze aversion (looking away from the conversation partner)	NO	YES
Smiles (smiling and laughing)	NO	NO
Facial fidgeting (face touching or rubbing hair)	NO	YES
Self-fidgeting (touching, rubbing, or scratching body or face)	NO	YES
Fidgeting (undifferentiated)	YES	YES
Illustrators (hand and arm movements designed to modify or supplement what is being said verbally)	YES	NO
Leg and foot movements	NO	YES
Posture shifts (movements made to change seating position)	NO	YES
Head movements (head nods and head shakes)	NO	YES
Eye blinks (blinking of the eyes)	NO	YES

Information from: Vrij, A., Hartwig, M., & Granhag, P. A. (2019). Reading lies: Nonverbal communication and deception. *Annual Review of Psychology, 70*(1), 295–317.

bad lie detectors, but bad lie detectors who don't *know* they are bad lie detectors: The correlation between a person's ability to detect lies and the person's confidence in that ability is essentially zero (DePaulo et al., 1997).

When we humans can't do something very easily—such as adding huge numbers or lifting huge rocks—we often turn the job over to a machine. Can machines detect lies better than we can? Although several companies claim that they can use brain scans to detect lies, the scientific evidence suggests that they may not . . . um, be telling the truth. At present, at least, brain scans cannot tell us with much accuracy whether or not a person is lying (Farah et al., 2014). But what about the traditional lie-detecting machine—the polygraph? As you probably know, a polygraph measures a variety of physiological responses that are associated with stress, which people often feel when they are afraid of being caught in a lie. So can it actually detect lies? Well, yes, a polygraph can detect lies with better-than-chance accuracy, but its error rate is far too high to be useful.

To understand why, imagine that 10 of the 10,000 people coming through an airport are terrorists. The authorities decide to hook every one of them up to a polygraph and ask them, "Are you a terrorist?" to which all of them naturally say, "No." If the polygraph were set to *maximum* sensitivity, it would catch 8 of the 10 terrorists in a lie. Not bad, huh? Yes—*very* bad! Because it would also mistakenly "catch" 1,598 innocent people! Okay, so what if we set the polygraph to *minimum* sensitivity? If we did that then the polygraph would mistakenly "catch" 39 innocent people, and it would also catch just 2 of the 10 terrorists. The Supreme Court of Canada has ruled repeatedly that polygraph evidence is inadmissible in court. "The history of polygraphy offers tragic reminders of the cost, in national security and human life, of overreliance on an apparently high-tech but inaccurate method for detecting deception" (Farah et al., 2014, p. 23). In short, neither people nor machines are particularly good at lie detection, which is probably why lying remains such a popular human sport.

MARK WILSON/GETTY IMAGES

The polygraph was invented in 1921 by a police officer named John Augustus Larson, and it has been in widespread use ever since. The machine measures a person's blood pressure, pulse, respiration rate, and skin conductivity during questioning. Does it work? "Like most junk science that just won't die (graphology, astrology, and homeopathy come to mind), because of the usefulness or profit their practitioners enjoy, the polygraph stays with us." Those words were written by Aldrich Ames (shown above), a former CIA agent who is currently serving a life sentence in prison for selling state secrets to the Russian government. Ames passed several polygraph exams before he was caught, and claimed that fooling the machine was easy.

The Nature of Motivation

Because Leonardo is a robot, he does what he is commanded to do and nothing more. He doesn't have wants and urges of his own—he doesn't crave friendship or desire chocolate or hate homework—and so he doesn't initiate his own behaviour. He is reactive rather than proactive, a responder rather than an originator. The activating spark that Leonardo lacks and that you have is called **motivation,** which refers to *the internal causes of purposeful behaviour.* You eat because you feel hungry and you sleep because you feel tired. You find friends because you think they will lend you money and you ditch friends because they won't. Everything you do, you do for a reason—but what are those reasons? And where do they come from? And how do they get you to act on them?

A Little History

Psychologists have been studying motivation for a rather long time. Two of the most historically important concepts to emerge from their work are the concepts of *instinct* and *drive.* Although neither of these terms is much used today, both have something important to teach us about motivation, so let's explore them in turn.

Instinct

When a newborn baby is given a drop of sugar water, they smile, and when given a check for $10,000, they act like they couldn't care less. By the time that baby goes to

Learning Outcomes

WHAT YOU NEED TO KNOW

- Explain what's right and what's wrong with the concept of instinct.

- Describe the concept of drive and the role it plays in homeostasis.

- Explain the hedonic principle and how it influences emotion regulation.

motivation The internal causes of purposeful behaviour.

LALO R. VILLAR/AP PHOTO

All animals are born with instincts. In the annual running of the bulls in Pamplona, Spain, no one has to teach the bulls to chase the runners, and no one has to teach the runners to flee.

university, these responses pretty much reverse. It seems clear that nature endows us with certain motivations and that experience endows us with others. William James (1890) called the natural motivation to seek a particular goal an *instinct,* which he defined as "the faculty of acting in such a way as to produce certain ends, without foresight of the ends, and without previous education in the performance" (p. 383). According to James, nature hard-wired people, penguins, parrots, and puppies to want certain things without being taught to want them, and to execute the behaviours that produce these things without ever thinking about it. He and other psychologists of his time tried to make a list of what those things were.

They were a little too successful. In just a few decades, their list of instincts contained nearly 6,000 entries, including some rather exotic ones such as "the instinct to be secretive" and "the instinct to grind one's teeth." Some researchers complained that the term suffered from "a great variety of usage and the almost universal lack of critical standards" (Bernard, 1924, p. 21), and others worried that attributing the tendency for people to affiliate to an "affiliation instinct" was not really saying much—that it was more of a description than an explanation (Ayres, 1921; Dunlap, 1919; Field, 1921). By 1930, the term had fallen out of fashion, in part because it didn't really seem to explain anything, but also because it flew in the face of Western psychology's hot new trend—behaviourism—which you learned about in The Evolution of Psychological Science chapter and the Learning chapter.

Behaviourists rejected the concept of instinct on two grounds. First, behaviourists believed that complex behaviours were learned, not hard-wired by nature. Second, behaviourists believed that all behaviours could be fully explained by the *external* stimuli that elicited them and that there was no need to talk about hypothetical internal states such as instincts. As James had noted, instincts are inborn and internal, and therefore behaviourists found them of little theoretical value. By the 1930s, behaviourists were running the show in American psychology, and so the concept of instinct fell out of the conversation.

Drive

Behaviourists didn't like to talk about internal states, but that made it difficult for them to explain certain phenomena. For example, if all behaviour is simply a response to an external stimulus, then why does a rat that is sitting quietly in its cage suddenly get up and start wandering around, looking for food? Nothing in the environment has changed, so why has the rat's behaviour changed? What visible, measurable, external stimulus is the wandering rat responding to? The obvious answer (obvious at least to you and to us) is that the rat is not responding to something happening in the world, but to something happening inside it. So how could behaviourists explain the rat's behaviour without talking about unobservable internal states?

By talking about thermostats. When a thermostat senses that the room is too cold, it sends a signal to the furnace to take corrective action—that is, to fire itself up and start blowing heat into the room. Later, when the thermostat senses that the room has reached the optimal temperature, it sends a signal to the furnace to terminate its action—that is, to turn itself off and stop blowing heat. When a room is at the optimal temperature, a thermostat is said to be in *equilibrium* (from the Latin words for "equal" and "balance"). It isn't telling the furnace to turn itself on or to shut itself off. It's just hanging out there on the wall, happily doing nothing. **Homeostasis** is *the tendency for a system to take action to keep itself in equilibrium,* which is why a thermostat is said to be a "homeostatic device."

The brain and body work the same way. The brain monitors states of the body—its hydration, its glucose levels, its temperature, and so on. When it senses that the body is in disequilibrium, it sends a signal to initiate a corrective action such as drinking, eating, shivering, and so on. When later it senses that equilibrium has been restored, it sends a signal to terminate those actions. The language of equilibrium

homeostasis The tendency for a system to take action to keep itself in equilibrium.

and homeostasis provided a convenient way for behaviourists to talk about the inside of a rat without talking about things like its hopes and dreams and desires. According to Clark Hull, one of the most influential behaviourists of his day, disequilibrium produces a "need," which Hull called a "drive." Hull's **drive-reduction theory** suggested that *the primary motivation of all organisms is to reduce their drives.* According to this theory, animals are not actually motivated to eat and don't actually find food rewarding. Rather, they are motivated to reduce their drive for food, and it is the reduction of this drive that they find rewarding. A reinforcement is simply any "substance or commodity in the environment which satisfies a need, that is, which reduces a drive" (Hull, 1943, p. 131).

Although the words *instinct* and *drive* are no longer widely used in psychology, both concepts have something to teach us. The concept of instinct reminds us that nature endows us with certain desires, and the concept of drive reminds us that our actions are often attempts to fulfill them. So what *kinds* of desires do we have?

The Hedonic Principle

It is no coincidence that the words *emotion* and *motivation* share a common Latin root: *movere*, which means "to move." Of all the many things that people are moved to do, or motivated to do, or driven to do, or want to do, experiencing positive emotion and avoiding negative emotion is chief among them. The **hedonic principle** is the idea that *people are primarily motivated to experience pleasure and avoid pain,* and that idea has a very long history (which happily, has nothing to do with thermostats). The ancient Greek philosopher Aristotle thought the hedonic principle explained everything there was to explain about human motivation: "It is for the sake of this that we all do all that we do," he wrote. Although we want many things, from peace and prosperity to health and security, we want them for just one reason: They make us happy. "Are these things good for any other reason except that they end in pleasure, and get rid of and avert pain?" asked Plato, Aristotle's favourite student. "Are you looking to any other standard but pleasure and pain when you call them good?" In other words, feeling good is our *raison d'être* — our reason for being (though it is a stronger reason for being in some cultures than others; see Hornsey et al., 2018). Even when we purposefully do things that feel bad, such as paying the dentist to drill our teeth or waking up early for a boring class, we are doing these things because we believe they will make us feel even better later (Michaela et al., 2009; Miyamoto et al., 2014; Tamir & Ford, 2012; Tamir et al., 2015).

If our primary motivation is to feel good rather than bad, how do we accomplish that goal? **Emotion regulation** refers to *the strategies people use to influence their own emotional experience.* Nine out of 10 people report that they attempt to regulate their emotional experience at least once a day (Gross, 1998), and they report more than a thousand different strategies for doing so (Parkinson & Totterdell, 1999). Some of these strategies are behavioural (e.g., avoiding situations that trigger unwanted emotions) and some are cognitive (e.g., recruiting memories that trigger the desired emotion or talking about events in the third person) (Orvell et al., 2019; Webb et al., 2012), but regardless of how they work, research suggests that ordinary people have a poor understanding of which are most effective (Heiy & Cheavens, 2014; Troy et al., 2018).

For example, most people think that the emotion-regulation strategy called *suppression,* which involves inhibiting the outward signs of an emotion, is an effective way to make themselves feel good. *Just don't frown and you won't feel down!* That's a lovely tweet, but it generally isn't true (Gross, 2002; Kalokerinos et al., 2015). Not only is suppression a relatively ineffective way to regulate emotions, but it also requires a lot of effort and therefore makes it harder for people to function successfully in their everyday lives (Franchow & Suchy, 2015). On the other hand, most

C'mon. This has got to be an ad. In all of human history, no one has ever actually *enjoyed* flossing. So why do we do it? According to the hedonic principle, people are often willing to feel slightly bad in the present if it will make them feel very good in the future — for instance, when they get to keep their teeth.

drive-reduction theory A theory suggesting that the primary motivation of all organisms is to reduce their drives.

hedonic principle The claim that people are motivated to experience pleasure and avoid pain.

emotion regulation The strategies people use to influence their own emotional experiences.

Figure 8.10
Labelling Affect with 140 Characters Fan et al. (2019) analyzed the emotional content of the tweets of nearly 75,000 Twitter users over time and discovered that when a user's tweet contains the sentence "I feel _____" followed by a negative emotion word, within an hour their tweets begin to contain much more positive emotion words. One interpretation of this finding is that labelling their negative emotions helped users overcome them.

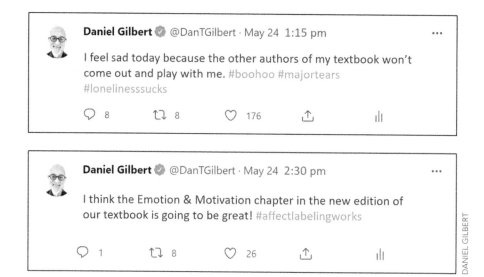

people think that *affect labelling,* which involves putting one's feelings into words, is an ineffective way to regulate their emotions. In fact, affect labelling turns out to be an excellent way to reduce the intensity of negative emotional states (Lieberman et al., 2011; Torre & Lieberman, 2018) (see **FIGURE 8.10**).

Perhaps the best strategy for regulating one's emotions is **reappraisal,** which is the process of *changing one's emotional experience by changing the way one thinks about the emotion-eliciting stimulus* (Gross, 1998). In one study, participants who watched a video of a circumcision that was described as a joyous religious ritual had slower heart rates and reported less distress than did participants who watched the same video but did not hear that description (Lazarus & Alfert, 1964). In another study, participants' brains were scanned as they saw photos that induced negative emotions, such as a photo of a woman crying during a funeral. Some participants were then asked to reappraise the picture, for example, by imagining that the woman in the photo was at a wedding rather than a funeral. The results showed that when participants initially saw the photo, their amygdalae were activated; but when they reappraised the picture, their cortex was activated and then moments later their amygdalae were deactivated (Ochsner et al., 2002). In other words, participants were able to downregulate the activity of their own amygdalae simply by thinking about the photo in a different way.

Reappraisal is a skill. Like most skills, it can be learned (Denny & Ochsner, 2014; Smith et al., 2018), and like most skills, some people are naturally better at it than others (Malooly et al., 2013). People who are especially good at reappraisal tend to be both mentally and physically healthier (Davidson et al., 2000; Gross & Muñoz, 1995), and to have better relationships with their parents (Cooke et al., 2018) and romantic partners (Bloch et al., 2014). This should not be surprising given that reappraisal is one of the skills that therapists commonly try to teach people who are dealing with emotional problems (Jamieson et al., 2013). Given how effective reappraisal is, you might expect people to do it all the time, but you'd be wrong (Heiy & Cheavens, 2014). People tend to underutilize reappraisal in part because it is a strategy that requires some effort to implement (Milyavsky et al., 2018), which may also explain why people are even less inclined to use reappraisal as they age (Scheibe et al., 2015). It is worth noting that reappraisal can occasionally have a dark side (Ford & Troy, 2019). For example, people who are good at changing how they see things in order to feel better about the things they see are sometimes less compassionate towards those who are suffering (Cameron & Payne, 2011).

reappraisal The process of changing one's emotional experience by changing the way one thinks about the emotion-eliciting stimulus.

The Motivated Body

People feel good when their needs are met—so what do people need? The psychologist Abraham Maslow (1954) suggested that the list of human needs could be organized by how "pressing" each of them was. Maslow designed a hierarchy (see **FIGURE 8.11**) with the most pressing human needs at the bottom and the least pressing needs at the top, and suggested that as a rule, people do not experience a need until the needs below it are met. According to Maslow, people are motivated to experience things like intellectual satisfaction and moral clarity, but they do not experience such "high level" needs until their more basic "low level" needs for food, water, and sleep have been met. In Maslow's hierarchy, the most pressing needs are those we share with other animals, such as the need to eat and the need to mate (Kenrick et al., 2010), so let's begin our exploration of these needs at the bottom of the pyramid and then work our way up. Let's start by examining one of the most basic of all needs—a need you had recently and will have again soon.

Hunger: The Need to Eat

Animals convert matter into energy by eating, and the need to eat is called *hunger*. But what exactly is hunger and how is it produced? At every moment, your body is sending reports to your brain about its current energy state. If your body has insufficient energy (i.e., if it is in disequilibrium), it sends an *orexigenic* signal to your brain telling it to switch hunger on, and if your body has sufficient energy, it sends an *anorexigenic* signal to your brain telling it to switch hunger off (Gropp et al., 2005). No one knows precisely what these signals are or how they are sent and received, but research has identified a few candidates.

Ghrelin is a hormone that is produced in the stomach and appears to be one of the orexigenic signals that tells the brain to switch hunger on (Inui, 2001; Nakazato et al., 2001). When people are injected with ghrelin, they become intensely hungry and eat about 30% more than usual (Wren et al., 2001). Interestingly, ghrelin also binds to neurons in the hippocampus and temporarily improves learning and memory (Diano et al., 2006), perhaps so that we become just a little bit better at locating food when our bodies need it most. *Leptin* is a chemical secreted by fat cells, and it is an anorexigenic signal that tells the brain to switch hunger off, which makes food less appealing (Farooqi et al., 2007). People who are born with a leptin deficiency have trouble controlling their appetites (Montague et al., 1997). For example, in 2002, medical researchers reported on the case of a 9-year-old girl who weighed 200 pounds, but after just a few leptin injections, she reduced her food intake by 84% and attained normal weight (Farooqi et al., 2002). Some researchers think the idea that chemicals turn hunger on and off is far too simple. In fact, they argue, there is no general need called *hunger*, but rather, there are many different kinds of hunger, each of which is a response to a unique nutritional deficit and each of which is switched on by a unique chemical messenger (Rozin & Kalat, 1971). For example, rats that are deprived of protein will seek proteins while turning down fats and carbohydrates, suggesting that they are experiencing a specific "protein hunger" and not a general hunger (Rozin, 1968).

We do not know whether hunger is one signal or many, but we do know that the primary receiver of these signals is the hypothalamus. Different parts of the hypothalamus receive different signals (see **FIGURE 8.12**). The *lateral hypothalamus* receives orexigenic signals, and when it is destroyed, animals sitting in a cage full of food will starve themselves to death. The *ventromedial hypothalamus* receives anorexigenic signals, and when it is destroyed, animals will gorge themselves to the point of illness and obesity (Miller, 1960; Steinbaum & Miller, 1965). These two structures were once thought to be the "hunger centre" and the "satiety centre" of the brain, respectively, but that view turned out to be

Learning Outcomes

WHAT YOU NEED TO KNOW

- Describe Maslow's hierarchy of needs.
- Explain how hunger signals get turned on and off.
- Identify the common eating disorders.
- Understand what causes obesity and how it can be prevented.
- Describe the role that hormones play in sexual interest.
- Describe the human sexual response cycle.

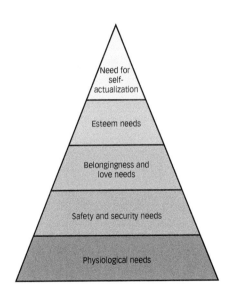

Figure 8.11
Maslow's Hierarchy of Needs The psychologist Abraham Maslow believed that needs form a hierarchy, with physiological needs at the bottom and self-actualization needs at the top.

Figure 8.12

Hunger, Satiety, and the Hypothalamus
The hypothalamus comprises many parts.
In general, the lateral hypothalamus
receives the signals that turn hunger
on and the ventromedial hypothalamus
receives the signals that turn hunger off.

Lateral
hypothalamus

Ventromedial
hypothalamus

far too simple (Woods et al., 1998). Hypothalamic structures clearly play an important role
in turning hunger on and off, but the precise way in which they execute these functions
remains poorly understood (Stellar & Stellar, 1985).

Eating Disorders

Feelings of hunger tell most of us when to start and stop eating. But for people with
an eating disorder, eating is a much more complicated affair.

- The most common eating disorder is **binge eating disorder** (or **BED**), which
  is *an eating disorder characterized by recurrent and uncontrolled episodes of con-
  suming a large number of calories in a short time*. People with BED quickly consume large quantities of food over a period of just a few hours, often at night.
  They frequently report feeling a lack of control over their own behaviour—a
  sense that they "just can't stop eating."

- The second most common eating disorder is **bulimia nervosa,** which is *an
  eating disorder characterized by binge eating followed by compensatory behaviour*.
  People with bulimia also binge, but then they take actions to compensate for
  their binging such as fasting, excessive exercising, taking diuretics or laxatives,
  or even inducing vomiting to purge the food from their bodies. People with
  BED or bulimia are caught in a cycle: They eat to ease negative emotions such
  as sadness and anxiety, but then concern about weight gain leads them to experience negative emotions such as guilt and self-loathing (Sherry & Hall, 2009;
  cf. Haedt-Matt & Keel, 2011).

- The third most common eating disorder is **anorexia nervosa,** which is *an
  eating disorder characterized by an intense fear of being overweight and a severe
  restriction of food intake*. People with anorexia tend to have a distorted body
  image that leads them to believe they are overweight when they may actually
  be emaciated. They tend to be high-achieving perfectionists who see their
  severe control of eating as a triumph of will over impulse. Anorexia is one of the
  most common diagnoses in young women, affecting about 1 in 50 females aged
  15–22 (Eating Disorder Support Network of Alberta, 2022). In 100 people
  with anorexia, about 10 are males, and about 10 will die. In fact, eating disorders have the highest mortality rate of any mental disorder (National Initiative
  on Eating Disorders, 2022).

What causes these eating disorders? Many things, from the genetic (Zerwas &
Bulik, 2011) to the environmental (Inniss et al., 2011) to the psychological (Klump
et al., 2004). Culture may play a role as well (Hogan & Strasburger, 2008).

binge eating disorder (BED) An
eating disorder characterized by
recurrent and uncontrolled episodes of
eating a large number of calories in a
short time.

bulimia nervosa An eating disorder
characterized by binge eating followed
by compensatory behaviour.

anorexia nervosa An eating
disorder characterized by an intense
fear of being overweight and a severe
restriction of food intake.

For example, women with anorexia typically believe that thinness equals beauty, and it isn't hard to understand where that idea comes from. The average Canadian woman is 164 centimetres tall (5′4″) and weighs 70 kilograms (169 pounds) (Fryar et al., 2016; Statistics Canada, 2008), but the average fashion model is 180 centimetres (5′10″) and weighs 53 kilograms (119 pounds) (Rosenbaum, 2016) (see **FIGURE 8.13**). Most university-age women report wanting to be thinner than they are (Rozin et al., 2001) and nearly 20% report being *embarrassed* to be seen buying chocolate (Rozin et al., 2003). Tellingly, the more attractive their dinner date is, the fewer calories they consume at the restaurant (Baker et al., 2019). Although North American women's satisfaction with their bodies has increased in the last 30 years (Karazsia et al., 2017), the pressure to be thin remains strong. That's why we talk about "fat shaming" but not "skinny shaming."

But anorexia is not just "vanity run amok" (Striegel-Moore & Bulik, 2007). Most researchers believe that there are biological and genetic components to this illness as well. For example, although anorexia primarily affects women, men have a sharply increased risk of becoming anorexic if they have a female twin who has the disorder (Procopio & Marriott, 2007), suggesting that anorexia may have something to do with prenatal exposure to female hormones.

Obesity

Bulimia and anorexia are serious problems that thankfully affect just a small fraction of the world's population. A more pervasive eating-related problem is obesity. In 2018, 63% of Canadians 18 years of age or older were overweight or obese: 36% are overweight, 27% obese (Statistics Canada, 2019). To give you a sense of what this means, "overweight" for a person who is 170 centimetres tall (5′6″) would be 73 kilograms (161 pounds), and "obese" would be 87 kilograms (192 pounds) or more. Rates of obesity across the country vary substantially, but are increasing everywhere (see **FIGURE 8.14**). Rates of unhealthy weight are increasing among children and adolescents as well. In 1978, fewer than 15% of adolescents were overweight or obese — by 2007, 29% were (Statistics Canada, 2010). The problem is not unique to North America: Nearly 30% of the world's population is overweight or obese, and no country has reduced its obesity rate in the last three decades (Ng et al., 2016).

Obesity is defined as having a body mass index (BMI) of 30 or greater. (You can compute your BMI simply by searching "BMI Calculator" on the Internet.) Some researchers think BMI is a very rough and not very useful indicator of obesity, and indeed, BMI predicts mortality for some people much better than for others (Romero-Corral et al., 2006; van Dis et al., 2009). But most researchers agree that an *extremely* high BMI is generally unhealthy.

The model Yityish Aynaw was crowned Miss Israel in 2013, the same year that Israel became the first nation to ban advertisements showing models whose body mass index is below 18.5. In the years since, Italy, Spain, and France have all passed similar laws.

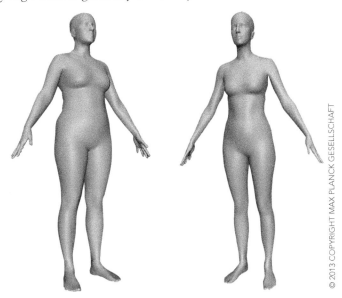

Figure 8.13

The Real and the Ideal These body simulations were made using the BMI Visualizer (http://www.bmivisualizer .com/), and, as you can see, the average North American woman (*left*) and the average fashion model (*right*) don't look very much alike.

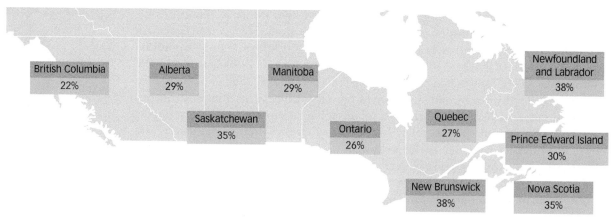

Figure 8.14

The Geography of Obesity The map shows the proportion of the adult population who were obese in the 10 provinces of Canada in 2016–2017. Obesity rates are particularly high in the Atlantic provinces. DATA FROM STATISTICS CANADA, 2018A.

When sea turtles hatch at night, they naturally move towards the light. This behaviour was once adaptive because moonlight makes oceans bright. But today, well-lit human habitats lure hatchlings away from the ocean, where they inevitably die. That's evolutionary mismatch.

evolutionary mismatch The idea that traits that were adaptive in an ancestral environment may be maladaptive in a modern environment.

Obesity and related illnesses cost the Canadian health care system about $4 billion annually (Eisenberg et al., 2011; Public Health Agency of Canada, 2009). Arguably more important is the cost in lives: Affected adults appear to die 3 to 7 years earlier than individuals at a healthy weight (Peeters et al., 2003).

In addition to the health risks, obese people tend to have lower psychological well-being, lower self-esteem, lower quality of life, and are viewed more negatively by others (Gallup, 2014a; Hebl & Heatherton, 1997; Kolotkin et al., 2001; Sutin et al., 2015). Obese women earn about 7% less than their nonobese counterparts (Lempert, 2007), and the stigma of obesity is so powerful that average-weight people are viewed negatively if they have a relationship with someone who is obese (Hebl & Mannix, 2003). All of this is true, but sad. As one scientist noted, we need "a war on obesity, not the obese" (Friedman, 2003).

Obesity's Causes Obesity seems to have many causes. It is highly heritable (Allison et al., 1996), which may explain why a disproportionate amount of the weight gained by Canadians in the past few decades has been gained by those who were already the heaviest (Flegal & Troiano, 2000) and by those who score high on heritable personality traits such as impulsivity (Stevenson, 2017). Some studies suggest that toxins in the environment can disrupt the functioning of the endocrine system and predispose people to obesity (Grün & Blumberg, 2006; Newbold et al., 2005), some suggest that obesity can be caused by a dearth of "good bacteria" in the gut (Liou et al., 2013), some suggest that obesity can result from everyday wear-and-tear on the hippocampus (Stevenson & Francis, 2017), and some suggest that the brains of obese people are simply more sensitive to rewards (Stice & Yokum, 2016). Whatever the causes, obese people are often leptin-resistant (i.e., their brains do not respond to the chemical signal that tells the brain to shut hunger off), and even leptin injections don't seem to help (Friedman & Halaas, 1998; Heymsfield et al., 1999).

But in many cases, the cause of obesity isn't much of a mystery: We simply exercise too little and eat too much (Rosenheck, 2008). We eat when we are hungry, but we also eat when we are sad or anxious, when it is convenient, when we just happen to think about food, or when everyone else is eating (Altheimer & Urry, 2019; Herman et al., 2003; Papies et al., 2020) (see The Real World: Get It While You Can). Sometimes we eat simply because the clock tells us to do so, which is why people with amnesia will happily eat a second lunch shortly after finishing an unremembered first one (Rozin et al., 1998).

Why do we overeat? After all, we don't breathe ourselves sick or sleep ourselves sick, so why do we eat ourselves sick? **Evolutionary mismatch** refers to *the idea that traits that were adaptive in an ancestral environment may be maladaptive* *in a modern environment* (Mayr, 1942; Riggs, 1993). Hundreds of thousands of years ago, the main food-related problem facing our ancestors was starvation, and humans evolved two strategies to avoid it. First, we developed a strong attraction to foods that provide large amounts of energy per bite, which is why most of us prefer cheeseburgers and milkshakes to spinach and green tea. Second, we developed an ability to store excess food energy in the form of fat, which enabled us to eat more than we needed when food was plentiful and then live off our reserves when food was scarce. These two adaptations allowed our species to survive in a world in which calorie-rich food was rarely available, but the problem is that we don't live in that world anymore (Li et al., 2018). Instead, we live in a world in which the calorie bombs of modern technology—from chocolate cupcakes to sausage pizzas—are inexpensive and abundant (Simpson & Raubenheimer, 2014). As one research team noted, "We evolved on the savannahs of Africa; we now live in Candyland" (Power & Schulkin, 2009). To make matters worse, many of Candyland's foods tend to be high not only in calories but also in saturated fat, which has the paradoxical effect of making the brain *less* sensitive to some of the chemical messengers that tell it to shut hunger off (Benoit et al., 2009).

Conquering Obesity Our brains and bodies evolved for a very different world than this one, which is why it is so easy for us to bulk up and so hard for us to slim down. Just as our bodies seek weight gain, they resist weight loss, and they do this in two ways.

- First, when we gain weight, we experience an increase in both the size and the number of fat cells in our bodies (usually in our abdomens if we are male and in our thighs and buttocks if we are female). When we lose weight, the *size* of our fat cells decreases, but the *number* of fat cells does not. Once our bodies have added a fat cell, that cell is with us pretty much forever. It may become smaller when we lose weight, but it is unlikely to die. It's always there, just waiting for an opportunity to be re-enlarged.
- Second, our bodies respond to dieting by decreasing our **metabolism,** which is *the rate at which the body uses energy.* When our brain concludes that there is a famine (which is what it concludes when we refuse to feed our bodies), it decreases our caloric requirements by finding more efficient ways to turn food into fat. This was a great trick for our ancestors, but it is a real problem for us. When rats are overfed, then put on diets, then overfed again, then put on diets again, they gain weight faster and lose weight more slowly the second time around, which suggests that with each round of dieting, their bodies become increasingly efficient at converting food to fat (Brownell et al., 1986). This is why "yo-yo dieting" generally doesn't work.

All of this explains why avoiding obesity is easier than overcoming it (Casazza et al., 2013). And avoiding it is exactly what some psychologists are trying to help people do by using small interventions that have a big impact—interventions commonly known as *nudges* (Thaler & Sunstein, 2008). For instance, one study showed that placing hard-boiled eggs just a few inches away from the more healthful ingredients in a salad bar rather than smack dab in the middle of them led people to eat 10% fewer eggs (Rozin et al., 2011). Ten percent of an egg may not sound like much to you, but if you are a person who eats two eggs every day, cutting that amount by just 10% would allow you to lose about 1.5 pounds every year, which would make you the slimmest person at your 25th high school reunion.

Other nudges have been shown to be equally successful: People are less likely to order a sugary soft drink when it appears in the middle of the menu than at the top or bottom (Dayan & Bar-Hillel, 2011); they eat less when they are given a large fork than a small one (Mishra et al., 2012); they take less cake when they have to

Actor and comedian Jonah Hill (*left*, in 2007; *right*, in 2018) has lost and gained weight many times in his career. In an interview with Ellen DeGeneres, he said, "I spent most of my young adult life listening to people say I was fat, gross, and unattractive, and it's only in the last four years . . . that I've started to understand how much that hurt and got into my head."

One reason obesity rates are rising is that "normal portions" keep getting larger. When researchers analyzed 52 depictions of the Last Supper that were painted between the years 1000 and 1800, they found that the average plate size had increased by 66% (Wansink & Wansink, 2010).

metabolism The rate at which the body uses energy.

The Real World | Get It While You Can

Scientists have known for some time that children who grow up in low-SES (socioeconomic status) households are at increased risk of becoming obese adults. But why? The typical explanation is that these children have limited access to healthy foods and so they eat the unhealthy foods that are available to them, which eventually cause them to become obese. But recent research suggests that this isn't the whole story: Growing up in poverty doesn't just influence what people eat, but when.

A team of psychologists (Hill et al., 2016) invited university students to their laboratory and asked them to drink either sparkling water or a high-calorie soft drink that raised their blood sugar levels and reduced their hunger. Then they asked the students to rate the taste of some cookies and told them they could sample as many cookies as they wished in order to make their ratings. How many cookies did the two groups of students sample?

That depended on whether the students had grown up in a high-SES or low-SES household. Students who had grown up in high-SES households ate far fewer cookies after drinking soda than after drinking water, suggesting that their decisions about how many cookies to eat were based on how hungry they felt at the moment. But students who had grown up in low-SES households ate just as many cookies when they were not hungry as when they were hungry. Interestingly, the students' *current* SES had no effect on the number of cookies they ate; only their *childhood* SES did.

What do these results mean? Children who grow up in poverty cannot always count on having steady access to food, so they may learn to eat when food is available and not to wait until they are hungry. *The cookies are here now and there is no guarantee there will be more later, so get them while you can.* The lessons of childhood do not simply disappear when we become adults, and this research suggests that the relationships we establish with food early on may have enduring consequences for our health.

---

cut it themselves (Hagen et al., 2016); and when they mix foods — such as granola and yogurt — they use more of the ingredient they put in the bowl first and less of the ingredient they put on top of it (Bschaden et al., 2019). These and many other studies show that small changes to the environment can make big differences to our waistlines (Cadario & Chandon, 2019).

Sexual Desire: The Need to Mate

Food motivates us because without it we die. Although sex is not essential to our personal survival, it is essential to the survival of our DNA, and that's why evolution has wired sexual desire into almost everybody's brain. The general wiring scheme is simple: Glands secrete hormones that travel through the blood to the brain and stimulate our sexual interest. But the details of the wiring scheme are complicated: Which hormones trigger which parts of the brain, and what triggers the launch in the first place?

The Hormonal Basis of Sexual Desire

Three hormones appear to play key roles. The hormone *dehydroepiandrosterone* (DHEA) seems to be involved in the initial onset of sexual desire. Both boys and girls begin producing this slow-acting hormone at about the age of 6, which may help to explain why boys and girls both experience their initial sexual interest at about the age of 10, despite the fact that boys reach puberty much later than girls do. Two other hormones have more sex-specific effects. Both males and females produce *testosterone* and *estrogen,* but males produce more of the former and females produce more of the latter. As you will learn in the Development chapter, these two hormones are largely responsible for the physical and psychological changes that characterize puberty. But are they also responsible for sexual desire in adults?

The answer is yes — as long as those adults are mice. Testosterone regulates sexual desire in male mice and estrogen regulates both sexual desire and fertility in female mice, and the same is true for most mammals. That's why most female mammals have little or no interest in sex except when their estrogen levels are high, which happens when they are ovulating or "in estrus." Like other female mammals, human females often experience a diminished interest in sex after menopause (when the production of estrogen ceases), and research suggests that estrogen replacement therapy can resurrect that interest (Cappelletti & Wallen, 2016). But unlike other female mammals, the normal fluctuations in estrogen levels associated with the monthly cycle do not seem to regulate sexual desire in human females. It appears that somewhere in the course of our evolution, female sexual desire became independent of the ovulatory cycle, and some scientists believe this happened because having full-time sexual interest gave females an evolutionary advantage by making it difficult for males to know whether a female was ovulating.

Why was this an advantage? Most male mammals guard their mates jealously when their mates are receptive and ovulating, but then go off in search of other receptive females when their mates are not. If a male cannot use his mate's sexual receptivity as information about when she is ovulating, then he has no choice but to hang around and guard her all the time. This is a considerable advantage for females who are trying to keep their mates at home so that they will contribute to the rearing of young. No one knows if this is the reason why female humans—unlike all other female mammals—are interested in sex even when they are not ovulating, but it is a reasonable guess about why this unusual tendency evolved.

Hormonally, then, female humans are a lot more complicated than female rats. But if estrogen is not the hormonal basis of a woman's sex drive, then what is? Two pieces of evidence suggest that the answer is testosterone—the same hormone that drives male sexuality. First, men naturally have more testosterone than women do, and they generally have stronger sex drives. Men are more likely than women to think about sex, have sexual fantasies, seek sex and sexual variety (whether positions or partners), masturbate, want sex at an early point in a relationship, sacrifice other things for sex, have permissive attitudes towards sex, and complain about low sex drive in their partners (Baumeister et al., 2001). Second, when women are given testosterone, their sex drives increase. These facts suggest that testosterone may be the hormonal basis of sexual motivation in both human males and human females.

The Consequences of Sexual Desire

Sexual desire has consequences, one of which is sex. As the old song says, "Birds do it, bees do it, even educated fleas do it," and people, it turns out, do it too. What do we know about "it"? Prior to the 1960s, the answer was "Not much" because data on human sexual behaviour consisted primarily of people's answers to questions about their sex lives, and as you may have noticed, this is a topic about which people don't always tell the truth. William Masters and Virginia Johnson changed all that by conducting groundbreaking studies in which they actually measured the physical responses of hundreds of volunteers as they masturbated or had sex in a laboratory (Masters & Johnson, 1966). Their work was controversial at the time, but it led to a much deeper scientific understanding of the **human sexual response cycle,** which comprises *the stages of physiological arousal during sexual activity* (see **FIGURE 8.15**). The human sexual response cycle has four phases:

- During the *excitement phase,* muscle tension and blood flow increase in and around the sexual organs, heart and respiration rates increase, and blood pressure rises. Both males and females may experience erect nipples and a "sex flush" on the skin of the upper body and face. A male's penis typically becomes erect or partially erect and his testicles draw upward, while a female's vagina typically becomes lubricated and her clitoris becomes swollen.
- During the *plateau phase,* heart rate and muscle tension increase further. A male's urinary bladder closes to prevent urine from mixing with semen, and muscles at the base of his penis begin a steady rhythmic contraction. A male's Cowper gland may secrete a small amount of lubricating fluid (which, by the way, often contains

The red colouration on the female gelada's chest (*top*) indicates that she is ovulating and amenable to sex. Her mate therefore knows exactly when to guard her (to make sure that other males do not inseminate her) and when to go off in search of other mating opportunities. In contrast, the sexual interest of a female human (*bottom*) is not limited to a particular time in her ovulatory cycle, therefore her behaviour does not provide a clue to her fertility.

human sexual response cycle The stages of physiological arousal during sexual activity.

Figure 8.15

The Human Sexual Response Cycle
The pattern of the sexual response cycle is quite similar for males and for females. Both go through the excitement, plateau, orgasm, and resolution phases, although the timing of their responses may differ.

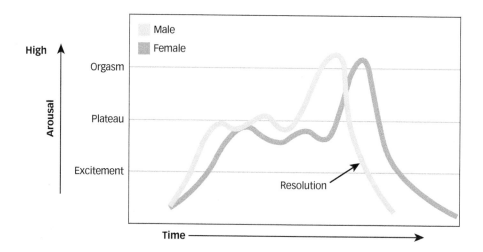

enough sperm to cause pregnancy). A female's clitoris may withdraw slightly, and her vagina may become more lubricated. Her outer vagina may swell, and her muscles may tighten and reduce the diameter of the opening of the vagina.

- During the *orgasm phase,* people's breathing becomes extremely rapid and their pelvic muscles begin a series of rhythmic contractions. Both males and females experience quick cycles of muscle contraction of the anus and lower pelvic muscles, and females often experience uterine and vaginal contractions as well. During this phase, males ejaculate about 2 to 5 milliliters of semen (depending on how long it has been since their last orgasm and how long they were aroused prior to ejaculation). Ninety-five percent of heterosexual males and 69% of heterosexual females reported having an orgasm during their last sexual encounter (Richters et al., 2006). However, roughly 15% of females never experience orgasm, fewer than half experience orgasm from intercourse alone, and roughly half report having "faked" an orgasm at least once (Wiederman, 1997). The frequency with which females have orgasms seems to be heritable because their orgasm frequency generally resembles their mother's (Dawood et al., 2005). It probably goes without saying that when males and females have orgasms, they typically experience them as intensely pleasurable.

- During the *resolution phase,* a person's muscles relax, their blood pressure drops, and their body returns to its resting state. Most people experience a *refractory period* during which further stimulation does not produce excitement. This period may last from minutes to days and is typically longer for males than for females.

Why do people do all this? Although sex is generally a prerequisite for reproduction, the vast majority of sexual acts are not intended to produce babies. University students, for example, are rarely aiming to get pregnant, but they are often aiming to have sex—and when they get what they are aiming for, they feel happier and find life to be more meaningful in the following days (Kashdan et al., 2018). Students report a wide variety of reasons for having sex. They have it because they are *physically attracted* to a partner ("Alex has beautiful eyes"), to increase *emotional connection* ("I wanted to communicate at a deeper level"), to *alleviate insecurity* ("It was the only way Alex would spend time with me"), as a *means to an end* ("I wanted to be popular"), or for more than one of these reasons (Meston & Buss, 2007). Although men are more likely than women to report having sex for purely physical reasons, **TABLE 8.2** shows that men and women don't differ dramatically in their most frequent reasons. It is important to note that not all sex or sexualized behaviour on Canadian postsecondary campuses is consensual: In 2019, 7 out of 10 postsecondary students in Canada either witnessed unwanted sexualized behaviours (jokes, touching, sexual

TABLE 8.2

TOP 10 REASONS WHY WOMEN AND MEN REPORT HAVING SEX

	Women	Men
1	I was attracted to the person.	I was attracted to the person.
2	I wanted to experience the physical pleasure.	It feels good.
3	It feels good.	I wanted to experience the physical pleasure.
4	I wanted to show my affection to the person.	It's fun.
5	I wanted to express my love for the person.	I wanted to show my affection to the person.
6	I was sexually aroused and wanted the release.	I was sexually aroused and wanted the release.
7	I was "horny."	I was "horny."
8	It's fun.	I wanted to express my love for the person.
9	I realized I was in love.	I wanted to achieve an orgasm.
10	I was "in the heat of the moment."	I wanted to please my partner.

Information from Meston and Buss (2007).

attention) or experienced it themselves, and 1 in 10 women were sexually assaulted (most commonly, unwanted sexual touching) (Statistics Canada, 2020). We will have much more to say about sexual attraction and relationships in the Social Psychology chapter.

The Motivated Mind

Survival and reproduction are every animal's first order of business, so it is no surprise that we are strongly motivated by food and sex. But humans are motivated by other things, too. Yes, we crave kisses of both the chocolate and romantic variety, but we also crave friendship and respect, security and certainty, wisdom and meaning, and a whole lot more. Our psychological motivations can be every bit as powerful as our biological motivations, but they differ in two important ways.

First, although we share our biological motivations with most other animals, our psychological motivations appear to be relatively unique. Chimps and rabbits and robins and turtles are all motivated to have sex, but only human beings seem motivated to imbue the act with deeper meaning. Second, although our biological motivations are of a few basic kinds—food, sex, oxygen, sleep, and a handful of other things—our psychological motivations are virtually limitless. The things we care about feeling and thinking, knowing and believing, having and being are just so numerous and varied that no psychologist has ever been able to make a complete list of them (Hofmann et al., 2012). Nonetheless, even if you looked at an incomplete list, you'd quickly notice that psychological motivations vary on three key dimensions: Some are extrinsic and others are intrinsic, some are conscious and others are unconscious, and some lead us to approach while others lead us to avoid. Let's examine each of these dimensions in turn.

Intrinsic Versus Extrinsic

Eating a potato chip and taking a psychology exam are different in many ways. One makes you chubby while the other makes you crabby, one requires that you move your lips while the other requires that you don't, and one is so pleasant that you'd pay to have it while the other is so unpleasant that you'd pay not to. But the most significant difference between these activities is that one is a means to an end and

Learning Outcomes

WHAT YOU NEED TO KNOW

- Explain the advantages of intrinsic and extrinsic motivations.

- Explain how rewards and threats can backfire.

- Explain when people become conscious of their motivations.

- Explain how we know that avoidance motivation is more powerful than approach motivation.

Mohammed Bouazizi was a fruit seller. In 2010, he set himself on fire to protest his treatment by the Tunisian government, and his dramatic suicide ignited the revolution that came to be known as the Arab Spring. Clearly, psychological needs—such as the need for justice—can be even more powerful than biological needs.

the other is an end in itself. An **intrinsic motivation** is *a motivation to take actions that are themselves rewarding.* When we eat a potato chip because it tastes good, ride a bicycle because it feels good, or listen to music because it sounds good, we are intrinsically motivated. These activities don't *have* a payoff because they *are* a payoff.

Conversely, an **extrinsic motivation** is *a motivation to take actions that are not themselves rewarding but that lead to reward.* When we floss our teeth so we can avoid gum disease, when we work hard for money so we can pay our rent, and when we take a psychology exam so we can get a university degree that will allow us to earn enough money to buy dental floss and pay rent, we are extrinsically motivated. None of these things is a source of pleasure in and of itself, but all can increase pleasure in the long run.

Extrinsic Motivation

Extrinsic motivation has a bad reputation. Canadians tend to believe that people should "follow their hearts" and "do what they love," and we feel sorry for students who choose courses just to please their parents and for parents who choose jobs just to earn a pile of money. But the fact is that our ability to engage in behaviours that are unrewarding in the present because we believe they will bring greater rewards in the future is one of our species' most significant talents—and no other species can do it quite as well as we can (Gilbert, 2006). Researchers who study how well people can put off pleasure, or "delay gratification" (Ayduk et al., 2007; Mischel et al., 2004), typically give participants a choice between getting something they want right now (e.g., a scoop of ice cream today) or getting more of what they want later (e.g., two scoops of ice cream tomorrow). Waiting for ice cream in a study like this is a lot like taking an exam or flossing: It isn't much fun, but you might do it because you know that if you are patient, you will reap greater rewards in the end. Studies show that 4-year-old children who can delay gratification are judged to be more intelligent and socially competent 10 years later and have higher university admission scores when they enter university (Mischel et al., 1989). In fact, some research suggests that the ability to delay gratification is as good a predictor of a child's grades in school as is the child's IQ (Duckworth & Seligman, 2005). Apparently, there is something to be said for extrinsic motivation.

Intrinsic Motivation

There is a lot to be said for intrinsic motivation too (Patall et al., 2008). People work harder when they are intrinsically motivated, they enjoy what they do more, and they do it more creatively. Both kinds of motivation have advantages, which is why many of us try to build lives in which we are both intrinsically and extrinsically motivated by the same activity—lives in which we are paid the big bucks for doing exactly what we like to do best. Who hasn't fantasized about becoming an artist or an athlete or Cardi B's personal party planner?

Alas, research suggests that it is difficult to get paid for doing what you love and still end up loving what you do because rewards can undermine intrinsic motivation (Deci et al., 1999; Henderlong & Lepper, 2002). The **overjustification effect** is *a phenomenon whereby people who are rewarded for a behaviour become less intrinsically motivated to repeat it.* For example, in one study, university students who were intrinsically motivated to complete a puzzle either were paid to complete it or completed it for free. Those who received money were less likely to play with the puzzle later on (Deci, 1971). In a similar study, children who were intrinsically motivated to draw with coloured markers were either promised or not promised a reward. Those who were promised the reward were less likely to use the markers later when the reward was absent (Lepper et al., 1973). It appears that under some circumstances, people interpret rewards as information about the intrinsic goodness of an activity ("If they had to pay me to do that puzzle, it couldn't have been a very fun one"), which means that rewards can sometimes undermine intrinsic motivation.

intrinsic motivation A motivation to take actions that are themselves rewarding.

extrinsic motivation A motivation to take actions that are not themselves rewarding but that lead to reward.

overjustification effect A phenomenon whereby people who are rewarded for a behaviour become less intrinsically motivated to repeat it.

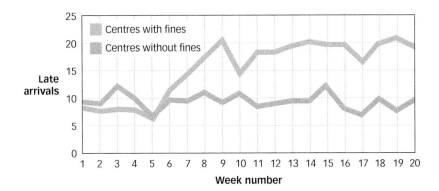

Figure 8.16
When Threats Backfire Threats can cause behaviours that were once intrinsically motivated to become extrinsically motivated. Day care centres that instituted fines for late-arriving parents saw an increase in the number of parents who arrived late.

Threats can have the same effect. For example, when a group of day care centres got fed up with parents who picked up their children late, some instituted a small financial penalty for tardiness. As **FIGURE 8.16** shows, the financial penalty did not decrease tardiness — it *increased* it (Gneezy & Rustichini, 2000). Why? Because most parents were already intrinsically motivated to pick up their kids on time. But when the day care centres started punishing them for their tardiness, the parents became *extrinsically* motivated to pick up their children on time — and because the price of tardiness wasn't particularly high, they decided to pay a small financial penalty in order to leave their children in day care for an extra hour. When threats and rewards change intrinsic motivation into extrinsic motivation, unexpected consequences can follow.

Conscious Versus Unconscious

When prizewinning artists and scientists are asked to explain how they achieved greatness, they typically say things like "I wanted to liberate colour from form" or "I wanted to discover a vaccine that prevented COVID-19." They almost never say things like "I wanted to exceed my father's accomplishments, thereby proving to my mother that I was worthy of her love." Prizewinners can articulate their **conscious motivations,** which are *motivations of which people are aware,* but by definition they have trouble articulating their **unconscious motivations,** which are *motivations of which people are not aware* (Aarts et al., 2008; Bargh et al., 2001; Hassin et al., 2009).

We all have conscious motivations, of course. We want to impress a first date so we consciously choose an especially flattering outfit, or we want to lose a few pounds so we consciously walk the long way around to avoid the dessert bar. But research suggests that we have unconscious motivations as well. For instance, **achievement motivation** is *the desire to experience a sense of accomplishment by meeting one's goals* (McClelland et al., 1953), and this basic motive sometimes operates unconsciously. In one study (Bargh et al., 2001), participants were given a word-search puzzle. Some participants were told to find a bunch of ordinary words such as *carpet, river,* and *shampoo,* and other participants were asked to find a bunch of achievement-related words, such as *compete, win,* and *succeed.* After completing the puzzle, participants were given a second word-search puzzle — only this time they were not told which words they should find. Rather, they were simply instructed to find as many words as possible. What happened? The group that had previously looked for achievement-related words found an average of 26 words in the new puzzle, whereas the group that had previously looked for ordinary words found just 21. It appears that simply *reading* words related to achievement while working on the first puzzle had caused participants to work harder (and achieve more!) on the second puzzle. Importantly, these participants had no idea that reading achievement-related words had impacted their performance. As the researchers reported, "They did not recognize the connection between the priming and experimental task, and most appeared perplexed by the suggestion during debriefing that the priming task might have influenced their behaviour and were surprised when they

conscious motivations Motivations of which people are aware.

unconscious motivations Motivations of which people are not aware.

achievement motivation The desire to experience a sense of accomplishment by meeting one's goals.

It seems fair to speculate that Zhong Huijuan is high in the need for achievement. She and her husband started a pharmaceutical company in 1995 with just 10 employees, and Zhong decided to quit her job as a teacher to run it. Today she is the world's richest self-made female billionaire.

learned of the experimental hypotheses." In other words, these participants were not consciously *trying* to "compete, win, and succeed"; rather, their achievement motive had been primed and was operating unconsciously (see Weingarten et al., 2016 for confirmation of the replicability of this finding).

What determines whether we are or are not conscious of our motivations to act? Many things, but one is the ease or difficulty of performing the action (Vallacher & Wegner, 1985, 1987). When actions are easy (e.g., screwing in a light bulb), we tend to be aware of our *general motivations* (e.g., to be helpful), but when actions are difficult (e.g., wrestling with a light bulb that is stuck in its socket), we become aware of our more specific motivations (e.g., to get the threads aligned). In general, we are aware of our general motivations for acting and become aware of our more specific motivations only when we encounter problems. For example, participants in one study (Wegner et al., 1984) drank coffee from a normal mug or from a mug that had a heavy weight attached to the bottom, which made the mug difficult to manipulate. When asked what they were doing, those who were drinking from the normal mug explained that they were "satisfying needs," whereas those who were drinking from the weighted mug explained that they were "swallowing." The ease with which we can execute an action is one of many factors that determine which of our motivations we are conscious of.

Approach Versus Avoidance

The poet James Thurber (1956) wrote: "All men should strive to learn before they die / What they are running from, and to, and why." As these lines remind us, the hedonic principle actually describes two distinct motivations: one that makes us "run to" pleasure and another that makes us "run from" pain. Psychologists—being a bit less poetic and a lot more precise—call these **approach motivation,** which is *the motivation to experience positive outcomes*, and **avoidance motivation,** which is *the motivation to avoid experiencing negative outcomes*. Pleasure and pain may be two sides of the same coin, but they *are* two sides. Pleasure is not just the lack of pain, and pain is not just the lack of pleasure. Pleasure and pain are distinct experiences, each of which is associated with distinct patterns of activity in different regions of the brain (Davidson et al., 1990; Gray, 1990).

But which is more powerful? Research suggests that, all else being equal, avoidance motivation tends to be the stronger of the two. This is easy to illustrate: Would you bet on a coin flip that will pay you $100 if it comes up heads but will require you to pay $80 if it comes up tails? Mathematically speaking, this should be an extremely attractive wager, because the potential gain is larger than the equally likely potential loss. And yet, most people refuse this bet because they expect the pain of losing $80 to be stronger than the pleasure of winning $100. **Loss aversion** is *the tendency to care more about avoiding losses than about achieving equal-size gains* (Kahneman & Tversky, 1979, 1984), and its effects can be dramatic.

Some grocery stores in the United States tried to motivate their customers to reuse their shopping bags by giving them a 5-cent bonus whenever they did (a financial gain), or by taxing them whenever they didn't (a financial loss), or by doing neither or both of these things. As **FIGURE 8.17** shows, the prospect of losing money had a large impact on shoppers' behaviour, but the prospect of gaining the same amount of money had no impact at all (Homonoff, 2013). People, it seems, are unusually anxious about losing what they have, which is why they display a reduction in loss aversion after taking drugs that reduce fear and anxiety (Sokol-Hessner et al., 2015), and an increase in loss aversion after being exposed to stimuli that increase fear and anxiety (Schulreich et al., 2016).

approach motivation The motivation to experience positive outcomes.

avoidance motivation The motivation to avoid experiencing negative outcomes.

loss aversion The tendency to care more about avoiding losses than about achieving equal-size gains.

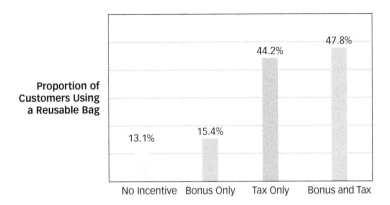

Figure 8.17
The Power of Loss Avoidance motivation is typically more powerful than approach motivation. Shoppers were highly motivated to reuse their bags to avoid a 5-cent tax, but they were entirely unmotivated to reuse their bags to get a 5-cent bonus (Homonoff, 2013).

Because people expect the pain of a loss to outweigh the pleasure of a gain, they typically take more risks to avoid the former than to achieve the latter. For instance, what would you do if you knew that a pandemic was going to kill 600 students at your school, and you were the one who was in charge of deciding whether to administer Vaccine A (which would save exactly 200 students) or Vaccine B (which has a one-third chance of saving everybody and a two-thirds chance of saving nobody)? When people are asked this question, about three-quarters of them decide to play it safe and select Vaccine A. And yet, when people are given a choice between Vaccine C (which would allow exactly 400 students to die) and Vaccine D (which has a one-third chance of allowing no one to die and a two-thirds chance of allowing everyone to die), about three-quarters of them decide to take the risk and select Vaccine D (Tversky & Kahneman, 1981). As **FIGURE 8.18** shows, Vaccines A and C are actually identical, as are Vaccines B and D. Indeed, the only difference is that A and B are *described* in terms of lives gained, whereas C and D are *described* in terms of lives lost. Those descriptions matter a lot, leading people to take risks in one case but not in another. It is worth noting that monkeys are also more likely to take risks to avoid losses than to achieve gains (Lakshminarayanan et al., 2011), which suggests that we probably should not put one in charge of national health policy.

Although avoidance motivation is stronger than approach motivation on average, the relative strength of these two tendencies does differ from person to person. A person's

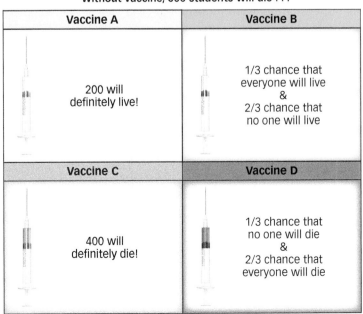

Figure 8.18
When Do We Take Risks? Loss aversion leads people to take risks and to avoid losses (most people choose Vaccine D over C) but not to achieve gains (most people choose Vaccine A over B).

TABLE 8.3

MEASURING APPROACH AND AVOIDANCE TENDENCIES

If you agree with these statements, you probably have a strong approach motivation, and if you disagree you probably have a strong avoidance motivation.

I go out of my way to get things I want.
When I'm doing well at something, I love to keep at it.
I'm always willing to try something new if I think it will be fun.
When I get something I want, I feel excited and energized.
When I want something, I usually go all out to get it.
I will often do things for no other reason than that they might be fun.
If I see a chance to get something I want, I move on it right away.
When I see an opportunity for something I like, I get excited right away.
I often act on the spur of the moment.
When good things happen to me, it affects me strongly.
If something bad is about to happen to me, I usually experience fear or nervousness.
Criticism or scolding hurts me quite a bit.
I feel pretty worried or upset when I think or know somebody is angry at me.
If I think something unpleasant is going to happen, I usually get pretty "worked up."
I feel worried when I think I have done poorly at something important.
I have quite a few fears compared to my friends.
I worry about making mistakes.

Information from Carver and White (1994).

agreement or disagreement with each of the statements shown in **TABLE 8.3** turns out to be a pretty good measure of that person's approach and avoidance tendencies (Carver & White, 1994). Research shows that people who tend to agree with the statements are happier when rewarded than those who disagree, and that those who tend to disagree with the statements are more anxious when threatened than are those who disagree (Carver, 2006).

Just as some people seem to be more responsive to rewards than to punishments (and vice versa), some people tend to think about their behaviours as attempts to get rewards rather than to avoid punishment (and vice versa). People who have a *promotion focus* tend to think in terms of achieving gains, whereas people who have a *prevention focus* tend to think in terms of avoiding losses (Higgins, 1997). In one study, participants were given an anagram task. Some were told that they would be paid $4 for the experiment, but they could earn an extra dollar by finding 90% or more of all the possible words. Others were told that they would be paid $5 for the experiment, and that they could avoid losing a dollar by not missing more than 10% of all the possible words. People who had a promotion focus performed better in the first case than in the second, but people who had a prevention focus performed better in the second case than in the first (Shah et al., 1998).

So what is the one thing that virtually every human being wants to avoid? Death, of course. All animals strive to stay alive, but only human beings know that all that striving is ultimately in vain, because no matter what you do, eventually you will die. Some psychologists have suggested that this knowledge of our inevitable demise creates a uniquely human "existential terror" that much of human behaviour is an attempt to manage. **Terror management theory** is *a theory about how people respond to knowledge of their own mortality* and it suggests that one way in which people cope with this knowledge is by developing a *cultural worldview,* which is a shared set of beliefs about what is good and right and true (Greenberg et al., 2008; Solomon et al., 2004).

terror management theory A theory about how people respond to the knowledge of their own mortality.

These beliefs allow people to see themselves as more than mortal animals because they inhabit a world of meaning in which they can achieve symbolic immortality (e.g., by leaving a great legacy or having children) and perhaps even literal immortality (e.g., by being pious and earning a prime spot in the afterlife). According to this theory, a cultural worldview is a kind of shield that buffers people against the overwhelming anxiety that certain knowledge of their own mortality elicits.

If that's true, then people who are reminded of their mortality should be especially motivated to hang on to their cultural worldviews. And they are. In the last 20 years, more than 400 studies have shown that when people are reminded of death (often in very subtle ways, such as by flashing the word *death* for just a few milliseconds in a laboratory, or by stopping people on a street corner that happens to be near a graveyard), they are more likely to praise and reward those who share their cultural worldviews, derogate and punish those who don't, value their spouses and defend their countries, and so on. All of these responses are presumably ways of shoring up their cultural worldviews, thereby protecting themselves from the existential terror that knowledge of their own mortality creates.

Chapter Review

The Nature of Emotion

- Feelings are difficult to describe, but psychologists have identified two underlying dimensions: arousal and valence.

- Emotions are reactions to the person's interpretation or appraisal of an event, and they give rise to action tendencies, which prepare people to act in particular ways that make evolutionary sense.

- Psychologists have spent more than a century trying to understand how emotional experience and physiological activity are related. The James–Lange theory suggests that a stimulus triggers a specific bodily reaction that produces an emotional experience, and the two-factor theory suggests that a stimulus triggers general physiological arousal that is then interpreted as a specific emotion. Neither of these theories is entirely right, but each has elements that are supported by research.

- Emotions are produced by the complex interaction of many brain areas, including the cortex and limbic structures such as the amygdalae. Information about a stimulus is sent simultaneously to the amygdala (which play a role in the rapid appraisal of the stimulus) and the cortex (which conducts a slower and more comprehensive analysis of the stimulus). Depending on the results of that analysis, the cortex may downregulate the amygdalae.

Emotional Communication

- The voice, the body, and the face all communicate information about a person's emotional state. Research suggests that some emotional expressions may be universal.

- Emotions cause expressions, but expressions can also cause emotions. Emotional mimicry allows people to experience and hence identify the emotions of others.

- People follow display rules that tell them when and how to express emotion. Different cultures have different display rules, but people follow them by using the same basic techniques.

- There are reliable differences between sincere and insincere expressions, but people are generally poor at telling them apart. The same is true of verbal lies. The polygraph detects lies at a better-than-chance rate, but its error rate is far too high to make it useful.

The Nature of Motivation

- All organisms are born with some motivations and acquire others through experience, but calling these motivations "instincts" describes them without explaining how they operate. Drive-reduction theory explains how they operate by suggesting that disequilibrium of the body produces drives that organisms are motivated to reduce. Neither instinct nor drive are widely used concepts in modern psychology, but both have something useful to teach us.

- The hedonic principle suggests that people are motivated to experience pleasure and avoid pain and that this basic motivation underlies all others. One of the ways people achieve this goal is by using different strategies to regulate their emotions. Research shows that people don't always use the most effective strategies—for example, affect labelling (which involves naming and describing one's emotions) and reappraisal (which involves changing the way one thinks about the emotion-eliciting event) are both effective but underutilized.

The Motivated Body

- Physiological motivations generally take precedence over psychological motivations in Maslow's hierarchy of needs. One of the most basic physiological motivations is hunger, which is the result of the complex interplay between different kinds of chemical messengers.

- Eating disorders and obesity have genetic, experiential, environmental, psychological, and cultural origins — all of which are difficult to overcome. Obesity is the most common eating-related problem in the world, and it is easier to prevent than to remedy. Dieting is generally ineffective because our bodies store excess food energy as fat as a defense against times of food scarcity, and our metabolism slows as a response to reduced calories.

- Unlike most other mammals, the sex drives of male and female humans are both regulated by testosterone. Males and females experience roughly the same sequence of physiological events during sex, and they engage in consensual sex for many of the same reasons.

The Motivated Mind

- People have many psychological motivations that vary on three key dimensions, one of which is the intrinsic-extrinsic dimension. Research shows that intrinsic motivations can be undermined by extrinsic rewards and punishments.

- People are not always conscious of their motivations. They tend to be conscious of their most general motivations and become conscious of their more specific motivations only when they encounter difficulty carrying out their actions.

- The fact that avoidance motivation is generally more powerful than approach motivation leads people to be loss-averse. Death is the ultimate loss, and people develop cultural worldviews to protect themselves against the anxiety that knowledge of their mortality produces.

Changing Minds

1. While watching the news, you and a friend hear about a celebrity who punched a fan in a restaurant. "I just lost it," the celebrity said. "I saw what I was doing, but I just couldn't control myself." According to the news, the celebrity was sentenced to anger management classes. "I'm not excusing the violence," your friend says, "but I'm not sure anger management classes are very useful. I mean, you can't *control* your emotions. They just *happen*." What evidence would you use to explain to your friend why they are wrong?

2. One of your friends has just been dumped by his boyfriend, and he's devastated. He's spent days in his room, refusing to go out. You and your roommate decide to keep a close eye on him during this tough time. "Negative emotions are so destructive," your roommate says. "We'd all be better off without them." How would you convince your roommate that negative emotions are actually critical for our survival?

3. A friend is majoring in education. "We learned today about several schoolboards that tried giving cash rewards to students who passed their classes or did well on achievement tests. That's bribing kids to get good grades, and as soon as you stop paying them, they'll stop studying." Your friend is assuming that extrinsic motivation undermines intrinsic motivation. In what ways is the picture more complicated?

4. One of your friends is a gym rat who spends all his free time working out and is very proud of his ripped abs. His roommate is obese. "I keep telling him to diet and exercise," your friend says, "but he never loses any weight. If he just had a little more willpower, he could slim down." What would you tell your friend? What makes it so hard for people to lose weight?

5. **Visualizing Data** You'd like to lose weight, and have heard that the relationship between cutting calories and BMI is simple and direct. Review the DATA to confirm whether or not that is the correct information.

Key Terms

emotion (p. 293)

appraisal (p. 294)

action tendencies (p. 295)

James–Lange theory (p. 296)

two-factor theory of emotion (p. 297)

emotional expression (p. 301)

universality hypothesis (p. 301)

facial feedback hypothesis (p. 304)

display rule (p. 306)

motivation (p. 309)

homeostasis (p. 310)

drive-reduction theory (p. 311)

hedonic principle (p. 311)

emotion regulation (p. 311)

reappraisal (p. 312)

binge eating disorder (BED) (p. 314)

bulimia nervosa (p. 314)

anorexia nervosa (p. 314)

evolutionary mismatch (p. 316)

metabolism (p. 317)

human sexual response cycle (p. 319)

intrinsic motivation (p. 322)

extrinsic motivation (p. 322)

overjustification effect (p. 322)

conscious motivations (p. 323)

unconscious motivations (p. 323)

achievement motivation (p. 323)

approach motivation (p. 324)

avoidance motivation (p. 324)

loss aversion (p. 324)

terror management theory (p. 326)

Language and Thought

A**N ENGLISH BOY NAMED CHRISTOPHER** showed an amazing talent for languages. By the age of 6, he had learned French from his sister's schoolbooks; he acquired Greek from a textbook in only 3 months. His talent was so prodigious that grown-up Christopher could converse fluently in 16 languages. When tested on English–French translations, he scored as well as a native French speaker. Presented with a made-up language, he figured out the complex rules easily, even though advanced language students found them virtually impossible to decipher. Christopher's abilities were sufficiently extraordinary that two prominent linguists devoted an entire book to documenting them (Smith & Tsimpli, 1995).

If you've concluded that Christopher is extremely smart, perhaps even a genius, you're wrong. His scores on standard intelligence tests are far below normal. He fails simple cognitive tests that 4-year-old children pass with ease, and he cannot even learn the rules for simple games like tic-tac-toe. Despite his dazzling talent, Christopher lives in a halfway house because he does not have the cognitive capacity to make decisions, reason, or solve problems in a way that would allow him to live independently.

- Language and Communication: From Rules to Meaning

- Language and the Brain

- Language and Thought: How Are They Related?

- Concepts and Categories: How We Think

- Decision Making: Rational and Otherwise

- Problem Solving: Working It Out

- Reasoning: Truth and Validity

THE IDEA THAT COGNITION IS COMPOSED OF DISTINCT ABILITIES receives compelling support from the evidence regarding Christopher's strengths and weaknesses. People who learn languages with lightning speed are not necessarily gifted at decision making or problem solving. People who excel at reasoning may have no special ability to master languages. In this chapter, you will learn about five key higher cognitive functions: acquiring and using language, forming concepts and categories, making decisions, solving problems, and reasoning. We excel at these functions compared with other animals, and they help define who we are as a species. We'll learn about each of these abilities by examining evidence that reveals their unique psychological characteristics, and we'll learn about their distinct neural underpinnings by considering individuals with brain lesions, as well as neuroimaging studies. But despite clear differences among them, these five cognitive abilities have something important in common: They are critical to our functioning in just about all aspects of our everyday existence—including work, school, and personal relationships—and as we've just seen with Christopher, impairment of these cognitive abilities can result in major and lasting disruptions to our lives.

Christopher absorbed languages quickly from textbooks, yet he completely failed simple tests of other cognitive abilities.

B.O'KANE/ALAMY STOCK PHOTO

Language and Communication: From Rules to Meaning

Learning Outcomes

WHAT YOU NEED TO KNOW

- Describe the basic characteristics of language.
- Explain the milestones of language development.
- Compare the behaviourist, nativist, and interactionist theories of language development.

Most social species have systems of communication that allow them to transmit messages to each other. Honeybees communicate the location of food sources by means of a "waggle dance" that indicates both the direction and distance of the food source from the hive (Kirchner & Towne, 1994; Von Frisch, 1974). Vervet monkeys have three different warning calls that uniquely signal the presence of their main predators: a leopard, an eagle, and a snake (Cheney & Seyfarth, 1990). A leopard call provokes monkeys to climb higher into a tree; an eagle call makes them look up into the sky; and a snake signal makes them look down. Each different warning call conveys a particular meaning and functions like a word in a simple language.

Language is *a system for communicating with others using signals that are combined according to rules of grammar and that convey meaning*. **Grammar** is *a set of rules that specify how the units of language can be combined to produce meaningful messages*. Language allows individuals to exchange information about the world, coordinate group action, and form strong social bonds.

Human language may have evolved from signaling systems used by other species. However, three striking differences distinguish human language from vervet monkey yelps, for example. First, the complex structure of human language distinguishes it from simpler signaling systems. Most humans can express a wide range of ideas and concepts, as well as generate an essentially infinite number of novel sentences. Second, humans use words to refer to intangible things, such as *unicorn* or *democracy*. These words could not have originated as simple alarm calls. Third, we use language to name, categorize, and describe things to ourselves when we think, which influences how knowledge is organized in our brains. It's doubtful that honeybees consciously think, "I'll fly north today to find more honey so the queen will be impressed!"

In this section, we'll examine the elements of human language that contribute to its complex structure. We'll consider the ease with which we acquire language despite this complexity, and how both biological and environmental influences shape language acquisition and use.

language A system for communicating with others using signals that are combined according to rules of grammar and that convey meaning.

grammar A set of rules that specify how the units of language can be combined to produce meaningful messages.

Honeybees communicate with each other about the location of food by doing a waggle dance that indicates the direction and distance of food from the hive.

The Complex Structure of Human Language

Compared with other forms of communication, human language is a relatively recent evolutionary phenomenon, emerging as a spoken system no more than 1 to 3 million years ago and as a written system as recently as 6,000 years ago. According to recent estimates, there are over 7,100 human languages, which linguists have grouped into about 140 language families (Simons, 2021). Despite their differences, all of these languages share a basic structure involving a set of sounds and rules for combining those sounds to produce meanings.

Basic Characteristics

The smallest units of speech that distinguish one word from another are called **phonemes.** These building blocks of spoken language differ in how they are produced. For example, when you say *ba,* your vocal cords start to vibrate as soon as you begin the sound, but when you say *pa,* there is a 60-millisecond lag between the time you start the *p* sound and the time your vocal cords start to vibrate. *B* and *p* are classified as separate phonemes in English because they differ in the way they are produced by the human speaker.

Every language has **phonological rules** that *indicate how phonemes can be combined to form words.* For example, the initial sound *ts* is acceptable in German but not in English. Typically, people learn these phonological rules without instruction, and if the rules are violated, the resulting speech sounds odd.

Phonemes are combined to make **morphemes,** *the smallest meaningful units of language* (see **FIGURE 9.1**). For example, your brain recognizes the *d* sound you make at the beginning of *dog* as a speech *sound,* but it carries no particular meaning. The morpheme *dog,* on the other hand, is recognized as an element of speech that carries meaning. Adding *s* to *dog (dogs)* changes the meaning of the word, so here *s* functions as a morpheme.

All languages have grammar rules that generally fall into two categories: rules of morphology and rules of syntax. **Morphological rules** *indicate how morphemes can be combined to form words.* Some morphemes—content morphemes and function morphemes—can stand alone as words. *Content morphemes* refer to things and events (e.g., "cat," "dog," "take"). *Function morphemes* serve grammatical functions, such as tying sentences together ("and," "or," "but"). About half of the morphemes in a particular sentence are function morphemes, and it is the function morphemes that make human language grammatically complex enough to permit us to express abstract ideas rather than simply to point verbally to real objects in the here and now. Many function morphemes are not words on their own—they get added to content morphemes (as a prefix or suffix) to change meaning. One example is the suffix *-s* to make plurals (e.g., "dogs"). Another example is adding the prefix *re-* to the beginning of many verbs to create the idea of a second attempt (e.g., "redo," "retake," "relive," "relearn").

phoneme The smallest units of speech that distinguish one word from another.

phonological rules A set of rules that indicate how phonemes can be combined to produce words.

morphemes The smallest meaningful units of language.

morphological rules A set of rules that indicate how morphemes can be combined to form words.

Figure 9.1

Units of Language A sentence—the largest unit of language—can be broken down into progressively smaller units: phrases, morphemes, and phonemes. In all languages, phonemes and morphemes form words, which can be combined into phrases and ultimately into sentences.

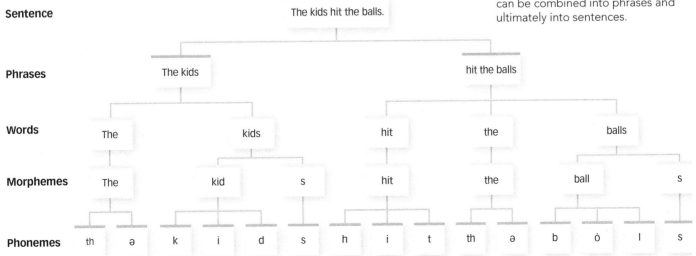

Sentence	The kids hit the balls.				
Phrases	The kids		hit the balls		
Words	The	kids	hit	the	balls
Morphemes	The	kid s	hit	the	ball s
Phonemes	th ə	k i d s	h i t	th ə	b ȯ l s

Figure 9.2

Syntactic Rules Syntactic rules indicate how words can be combined to form sentences. Every sentence must contain one or more nouns, which can be combined with adjectives or articles to create a noun phrase. A sentence also must contain one or more verbs, which can be combined with noun phrases, adverbs, or articles to create a verb phrase.

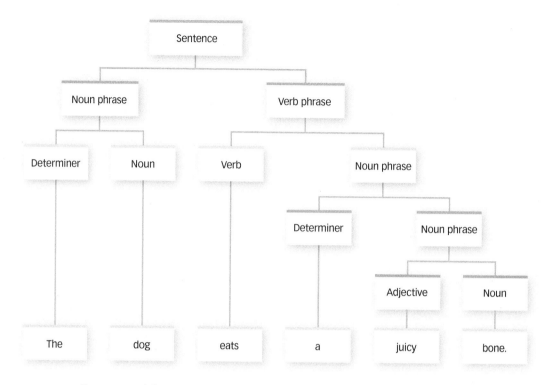

Content and function morphemes can be combined and recombined to form an infinite number of new sentences, which are governed by syntax. **Syntactic rules** *indicate how words can be combined to form phrases and sentences.* A simple syntactic rule in English is that every sentence must contain one or more nouns, which may be combined with adjectives or articles to create noun phrases (see **FIGURE 9.2**). A sentence also must contain one or more verbs, which may be combined with adverbs or articles to create verb phrases. So, the utterance "dogs bark" is a full sentence, but "the big grey dog over by the building" is not.

Language Development

Language is a complex cognitive skill, yet we can carry on complex conversations with playmates and family even before we begin school. Three characteristics of language development are worth bearing in mind. First, children learn language at an astonishingly rapid rate. The average 1-year-old has a vocabulary of 10 words. This tiny vocabulary expands to over *10,000* words in the next 4 years, requiring the child to learn, on average, about 6 or 7 new words *every day*. Second, children make few errors while learning to speak, and as we'll see shortly, the errors they do make usually result from applying, but *overregularizing*, grammatical rules they've learned. This is an extraordinary feat. There are over 3 *million* ways to rearrange the words in any 10-word sentence, but only a few of these arrangements will be both grammatically correct and meaningful (Bickerton, 1990). Third, children's *comprehension* of language develops faster than their *production*. At every stage of language development, children understand language better than they speak it.

Distinguishing Speech Sounds

At birth, infants can distinguish among all of the contrasting sounds that occur in all human languages. But within the first 6 months of life, like their parents, they can only distinguish among the contrasting sounds in the language they hear being spoken around them. For example, two distinct sounds in English are the *l* sound and the *r* sound, as in *lead* and *read*. These sounds are not distinguished in Japanese; instead, the *l* and *r* sounds fall within the same phoneme. Japanese adults cannot hear the difference between these two phonemes, but American adults can distinguish between them easily—and so can Japanese infants. By the same token, American speakers do not hear many of the contrasts that are common in Japanese.

syntactic rules A set of rules that indicate how words can be combined to form phrases and sentences.

In one study, researchers played computer synthesized sounds of "la" or "ra" syllables to American and Japanese infants aged approximately 6–8 months and 10–12 months (Kuhl et al., 2006). The infants sat on their mothers' laps in a set-up similar to the one in the accompanying photo, and learned that when they heard a specific target sound after they heard a specific background sound, they could turn their heads and see a pleasing, novel visual display. Half of the infants learned that "ra" was the target sound and "la" was the background sound, whereas the other half of the infants learned that "la" was the target sound and "ra" was the background sound. So, each infant needed to be able to distinguish "ra" from "la" in order to check out the fun visual display by turning their head when the background sound changed to the target sound. The researchers found that at age 6–8 months, Japanese and American infants performed similarly well. But by 10–12 months, the performance of the American infants improved, whereas the performance of the Japanese infants declined, reflecting their different linguistic experiences as development continued.

Infants can distinguish among speech sounds, but they cannot produce them dependably and so must rely mainly on cooing (i.e., simple vowel-like sounds, such as *ah-ah*), cries, laughs, and other vocalizations to communicate. Between the ages of about 4 and 6 months, they begin to babble speech sounds. Babbling involves combinations of vowels and consonants that sound like real syllables but are meaningless. Regardless of the language they hear spoken, all infants go through the same babbling sequence. For example, *d* and *t* appear in infant babbling before *m* and *n*. Even deaf infants babble sounds they've never heard, and they do so in the same order as hearing infants do (Ollers & Eilers, 1988). This is evidence that infants aren't simply imitating the sounds they hear; rather, it suggests that babbling is a natural part of the language development process. Deaf infants don't babble as much, however, and their babbling starts later than that of hearing infants (at 11 months rather than 6 months).

For vocal babbling to continue, though, infants must be able to hear themselves. In fact, delayed babbling or the cessation of babbling merits testing for possible hearing difficulties. McGill University researchers discovered that deaf infants whose parents communicate using American Sign Language (ASL) begin to babble with their hands at the same age that hearing children begin to babble vocally—between 4 and 6 months (Petitto & Marentette, 1991). Their babbling consists of sign language syllables that are the fundamental components of ASL.

Language Milestones

At about 10 to 12 months of age, infants begin to utter (or sign) their first words. By 18 months, they can say about 50 words and can understand several times more than that. Toddlers generally learn nouns before verbs, and the nouns they learn first are names for everyday, concrete objects (e.g., chair, table, milk) (see **TABLE 9.1**). At about this time, their vocabularies undergo explosive growth. By the time the average child begins school, a vocabulary of 10,000 words is not unusual. (These averages may differ for children in low- and high-income families, as discussed in The Real World: Exploring the 30-Million-Word Gap). By fifth grade, the average child knows the meanings of 40,000 words. By university, the average student's vocabulary is about 200,000 words. This astonishingly easy process contrasts dramatically with the effort required later to learn other concepts and skills, such as arithmetic or writing.

Around 24 months, children begin to form two-word sentences, such as "More milk" or "Throw ball." Such sentences are referred to as **telegraphic speech** because they are *devoid of function morphemes and consist mostly of content words*. Yet despite the absence of function words, such as prepositions or articles, these two-word sentences tend to be grammatical; the words are ordered in a manner consistent with the syntactic rules of the language the children are learning to speak. So, for example, toddlers will say "Throw ball" rather than "Ball throw" when they want you to throw the ball to them, and they will say "More milk" rather than "Milk more" when they want you to give them more milk. With these seemingly primitive expressions, 2-year-olds show that they have already acquired an appreciation of the syntactic rules of the language they are learning.

In this videotaped test, the infant watches an animated toy animal while a single speech sound is repeated. After a few repetitions, the sound changes and then the display changes, and then they both change again. If the infant switches her attention when the sound changes, she is anticipating the new display, which demonstrates that she can discriminate between the sounds.

Deaf infants who learn sign language from their parents start babbling with their hands around the same time that hearing infants babble vocally.

telegraphic speech Speech that is devoid of function morphemes and consists mostly of content words.

TABLE 9.1

LANGUAGE MILESTONES

Average Age	Language Milestones
0–4 months	Can tell the difference between all possible speech sounds (phonemes); coos, especially in response to speech
4–6 months	Babbles consonants
6–10 months	Understands some words and simple requests
10–12 months	Begins to use single words; can no longer reliably distinguish sounds that are not used in their native language
12–18 months	Has vocabulary of 30–50 words (simple nouns, adjectives, and action words)
18–24 months	Two-word phrases are ordered according to syntactic rules; vocabulary consists of 50–200 words; understands rules
24–36 months	Has vocabulary of about 1,000 words; produces phrases and incomplete sentences
36–60 months	Vocabulary grows to more than 10,000 words; produces full sentences; shows mastery of grammatical morphemes (such as -ed for past tense) and function words (such as *the, and, but*); can form questions and negations

The Emergence of Grammatical Rules

Evidence of the ease with which children acquire grammatical rules comes from some interesting errors that children make while forming sentences. If you listen to average 2- or 3-year-old children speaking, you may notice that they use the correct past-tense versions of common verbs, as in the expressions "I ran" and "You ate." By the age of 4 or 5, the same children will be using incorrect forms of these verbs, saying such things as "I runned" or "You eated," forms most children are unlikely ever to have heard (Prasada & Pinker, 1993). The reason is that very young children memorize the particular sounds (i.e., words) that express what they want to communicate. But as children acquire the grammatical rules of their language, they tend to *overregularize*. For example, if a child *overregularizes* the rule that past tense is indicated by *-ed*, then *run* becomes *runned* or even *ranned* instead of *ran*.

These errors show that language acquisition is not simply a matter of imitating adult speech. Instead, children acquire grammatical rules by listening to the speech around them and using those rules to create verbal forms they've never heard. They manage this without explicit awareness of the grammatical rules they've learned. In fact, few children or adults can articulate the grammatical rules of their native language, yet the speech they produce obeys these rules.

By about 3 years of age, children begin to generate complete simple sentences that include function words (e.g., "Give me *the* ball" and "That belongs *to* me"). The sentences increase in complexity over the next 2 years. By the time children are 4 to 5 years of age, many aspects of the language acquisition process are complete. As children continue to mature, their language skills become more refined, with added appreciation of subtler communicative uses of language, such as humour, sarcasm, or irony.

Language Development and Cognitive Development

Language development typically unfolds as a sequence of steps in which children achieve one milestone before moving on to the next. Nearly all infants begin with one-word utterances before progressing to telegraphic speech and then to simple sentences that include function morphemes. It's hard to find solid evidence of infants launching immediately into speaking in sentences — even though you may occasionally hear reports of such feats from proud parents, including possibly your own! There are two possible explanations for this:

- The orderly progression could result from general cognitive development that is unrelated to experience with a specific language (Shore, 1986; Wexler, 1999). For example, perhaps infants begin with one- and then two-word utterances because their short-term memories are so limited that initially they can hold in mind only a word or two; additional cognitive development might be necessary before they have the capacity to put together a simple sentence.

- By contrast, the orderly progression might depend on experience with a specific language, reflecting a child's emerging knowledge of that language (Bates & Goodman, 1997; Gillette et al., 1999).

These two possibilities are difficult to tease apart, but researchers have done so using a novel strategy: examining the acquisition of English by internationally adopted children who did not know any English prior to adoption (Snedeker et al., 2007, 2012). Although most of those adoptees were infants or toddlers, a significant proportion were preschoolers. Studying the acquisition of English in such an older adoptee provides a unique opportunity to explore the relationship between language development and cognitive development. If the orderly sequence of milestones that characterizes the acquisition of English by non-adopted infants is a by-product of general cognitive development, then different patterns should be observed in older internationally adopted children, who are more advanced cognitively than infants. However, if the milestones of language development are critically dependent on experience with a specific language — English — then language learning in older adopted children should show the same orderly progression as seen in infants.

Snedeker and colleagues (2007) examined preschoolers ranging from 2½ to 5½ years old, 3 to 18 months after they were adopted from China. They did so by mailing materials to parents, who periodically recorded language samples in their homes and also completed questionnaires concerning specific features of language observed in their children. These data were compared with similar data obtained from monolingual infants. The main result was clear-cut: Language acquisition in preschool-age adopted children showed the same orderly progression of milestones that characterizes infants' language learning. These children began with one-word utterances before moving on to simple word combinations. Furthermore, their vocabulary, just like that of infants, was initially dominated by nouns, and they produced few function morphemes.

These results indicate that some of the key milestones of language development depend on experience with English. However, the adopted children did add new words to their vocabularies more quickly than infants did, perhaps reflecting an influence of general cognitive development. Overall, though, the main message from this study is that observed shifts in early language development reflect specific characteristics of language learning rather than general limitations of cognitive development. A later study by Snedeker and colleagues (2012) provided additional support for this general conclusion, but also produced new evidence for a role of cognitive development in specific aspects of language. For example, adopted preschoolers acquire words that refer to the past or the future — such as *tomorrow, yesterday, before,* or *after* — much more quickly than do infants, perhaps reflecting that infants have difficulty representing these abstract concepts and therefore take longer to learn the words than more cognitively sophisticated preschoolers.

Chinese preschoolers who are adopted by English-speaking parents progress through the same sequence of linguistic milestones as do infants born into English-speaking families, suggesting that these milestones reflect experience with English in particular rather than general cognitive development.

Theories of Language Development

We know a good deal about how language develops, but what underlies the process? The language acquisition process has been the subject of considerable controversy and (at times) angry exchanges among scientists coming from three different approaches: behaviourist, nativist, and interactionist.

Behaviourist Explanations

According to B. F. Skinner's behaviourist explanation of language learning, we learn to talk in the same way we learn any other skill: through reinforcement, shaping, extinction, and the other basic principles of operant conditioning that you read about in the Learning chapter (Skinner, 1957). As infants mature, they begin to vocalize. Those vocalizations that are not reinforced gradually diminish, and those

Though behaviourist explanations are widely discredited, parents do indeed reinforce the sounds "da-da" and "ma-ma."

that are reinforced remain in the developing child's repertoire. So, for example, when an infant gurgles "prah," most parents are pretty indifferent. However, a sound that even remotely resembles "da-da" is likely to be reinforced with smiles, whoops, and cackles of "Goooood baaaaaby!" by doting parents. Maturing children also imitate the speech patterns they hear. Then parents or other adults shape the children's speech patterns by reinforcing those that are grammatical and ignoring or punishing those that are ungrammatical. "I no want milk" is likely to be squelched by parental clucks and titters, whereas "No milk for me, thanks" will probably be reinforced.

The behavioural explanation is attractive because it offers a simple account of language development, but this theory cannot account for many fundamental characteristics of language development (Chomsky, 1986; Pinker, 1994; Pinker & Bloom, 1990).

Nativist Explanations

The study of language and cognition underwent an enormous change in the 1950s, when the linguist Noam Chomsky (1957, 1959) published a blistering reply to the behaviourist approach. According to Chomsky, language-learning capacities are built into the brain, which is specialized to acquire language rapidly through simple exposure to speech. This **nativist theory** holds that *language development is best explained as an innate, biological capacity.* According to Chomsky, the human brain is equipped with a **universal grammar,** *a collection of processes that facilitate language learning.* Language processes naturally emerge as the infant matures, provided the infant receives adequate input to maintain the acquisition process.

Language Ability Is Partly Separate from General Intelligence Christopher's story is consistent with the nativist view of language development: His genius for language acquisition, despite his low overall intelligence, indicates that language capacity can be somewhat distinct from other mental capacities. Other individuals show the opposite pattern: Some people with normal or nearly normal intelligence have severe problems with certain aspects of human language. One particularly striking example of this pattern comes from a single family, known as the KE family, in which about half of the members of the family across three generations are characterized by problems primarily with language production. A single dominant gene has been implicated in transmission of the condition (Gontier, 2008; Gopnik, 1990a, 1990b; Vargha-Khadem et al., 2005). Several interpretations have been advanced to explain the problems seen in these family members, ranging from a specific deficit in learning grammatical rules (Gopnik, 1990a, 1990b) to a problem articulating specific components of words (Vargha-Khadem et al., 2005). Recent evidence is consistent with the latter view, and also indicates that the articulatory problem in affected members of the KE family produces an impairment in the phonological loop component of working memory in these individuals (Schulze et al., 2018; for the phonological loop and working memory, see the Memory chapter).

Language Is Harder to Learn after Puberty Sets In Also consistent with the nativist view is evidence that language can be fully acquired only during a restricted period of development, as has been observed with songbirds. If young songbirds are prevented from hearing adult birds sing during a particular period in their early lives, they do not learn to sing. A similar mechanism seems to affect human language learning, as illustrated by the tragic case of Genie (Curtiss, 1977). At the age of 20 months, Genie was tied to a chair by her parents and kept in virtual isolation. Her father forbade Genie's mother and brother to speak to her, and he himself only growled and barked at her. She remained in this brutal state until the age of 13 when her mother finally sought help for Genie. Genie's life improved substantially, and she received years of language instruction, but it was too late. Her language skills remained extremely primitive. She developed a basic vocabulary and could communicate her ideas, but she could not grasp the grammatical rules of English.

SIDNEY HARRIS/CARTOON STOCK

"GOT IDEA. TALK BETTER. COMBINE WORDS. MAKE SENTENCES."

nativist theory The view that language development is best explained as an innate, biological capacity.

universal grammar A collection of processes that facilitate language learning.

Similar cases have been reported, with a common theme: Once puberty is reached, acquiring language becomes extremely difficult (Brown, 1958). Data from studies of language acquisition in immigrants support this conclusion. In one study, researchers found that the proficiency with which immigrants spoke English depended not on how long they'd lived in the United States but on their age at immigration (Johnson & Newport, 1989). Those who arrived as children were the most proficient, whereas among those who immigrated after puberty, proficiency showed a significant decline regardless of the number of years immigrants were in their new country. More recent work using fMRI shows that acquiring a second language early in childhood (between 1 and 5 years of age) results in very different representation of that language in the brain than does acquiring that language much later (after 9 years of age; Bloch et al., 2009). Furthermore, a child's first language appears to leave lasting traces in the brain, even when that language is no longer used after infancy. McGill researchers used fMRI to study teenagers in Quebec who had been adopted from China as infants by French-speaking parents. These teens were French-speaking and did not consciously remember any Chinese at all. Activation in the brains of these teens to Chinese speech sounds was more similar to that of native Chinese-speaking teens who continued to use the language than it was to French-speaking teens who had never been exposed to Chinese (Pierce et al., 2014). Early language exposure appears to leave lasting traces on brain organization.

Immigrants who learn English as a second language are more proficient if they start to learn English before puberty rather than after.

Interactionist Explanations

Nativist theories are often criticized because they do not explain *how* language develops; they merely explain why. A complete theory of language acquisition requires an explanation of the processes by which the innate, biological capacity for language combines with environmental experience. The interactionist approach holds that although infants are born with an innate ability to acquire language, social interactions play a crucial role in language. Interactionists point out that parents tailor their verbal interactions with children in ways that simplify the language acquisition process: They speak slowly, enunciate clearly, and use simpler sentences than they do when speaking with adults (Bruner, 1983; Farrar, 1990).

Further evidence of the interaction of biology and experience comes from a fascinating study of the creation of a new language by deaf children (Senghas et al., 2004). Prior to about 1980, deaf children in Nicaragua stayed at home and usually had little contact with other deaf individuals. In 1981, some deaf children began to attend a new vocational school. At first, the school did not teach a formal sign language, and none of the children had learned to sign at home, but the children gradually began to communicate using hand signals they themselves invented.

Over the past 30 years, their sign language has developed considerably (Pyers et al., 2010), and researchers have studied this new language for the telltale characteristics of languages that have evolved over much longer periods. For instance, mature languages typically break down experience into separate components. When we describe something in motion, such as a rock rolling down a hill, our language separates the type of movement (rolling) and the direction of movement (down). If we simply made a gesture, however, we would use a single continuous downward movement to indicate this motion. This is exactly what the first children to develop the Nicaraguan sign language did. But younger groups of children, who have developed the sign language further, use separate signs to describe the direction and the type of movement—a defining characteristic of mature languages. That the younger children did not merely copy the signs from the older users suggests that a predisposition exists to use language to dissect our experiences. Thus, their acts of creation nicely illustrate the interplay of nativism (the predisposition to use language) and experience (growing up in an insulated deaf culture).

How does the evolution of the Nicaraguan deaf children's sign language support the interactionist explanation of language development?

The Real World • Exploring the 30-Million-Word Gap

An early study of the language development of 1- to 2-year-old children in American families at different levels of socioeconomic status (SES)—ranging from families on welfare (low SES) to working class (middle SES) to professional (high SES)—produced stunning results: By the time they reached age 3, children in high-SES families were exposed to millions more words than were children in lower-SES families (Hart & Risley, 1995). This came to be widely known as the "30-million-word gap." The researchers also found that these early language differences were highly predictive of how these children performed as third graders on various language and cognitive tests.

Since that time, the 30-million-word gap has become widely known and somewhat controversial. For example, a more recent study suggests that the gap may be much smaller than initially claimed, perhaps closer to a 4-million-word gap (Gilkerson et al., 2017). The authors of another recent study (Sperry et al., 2019) have questioned the basis for concluding that a gap exists, but other researchers have criticized their argument (Golinkoff et al., 2019). Despite the controversy, concern about the consequences of a gap has led to increased appreciation of the importance of SES differences in early language development, as well as attempts to increase language exposure in low-SES children. Learning more about the origins and nature of the gap is critical to devising effective methods to reduce it, and psychologists have made some important discoveries during the past decade. For example, Fernald and colleagues (2013) found significant differences between low- and high-SES children as young as 18 months of age: Low-SES children had smaller vocabularies than high-SES children, and they were also slower and less accurate in moving their eyes to the object named by the speaker than were high-SES children. By the age of 24 months, language

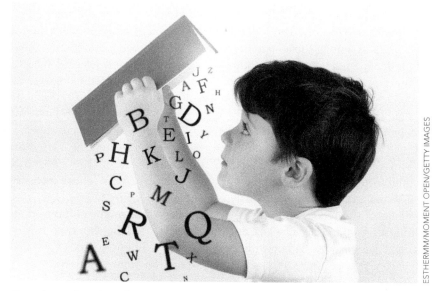

Quantity and quality of communication between a parent and a child is an essential factor in language development.

abilities in the low-SES children were already about 6 months behind those in the high-SES children.

What exactly produces these troubling lags in low-SES children? A study by American researcher Kathy Hirsh-Pasek and colleagues (2015) provides evidence that in addition to the sheer number of words that low-SES children are exposed to, the *quality* of early communications makes an important contribution. Hirsh-Pasek and her associates focused on 24-month-old children from low-SES families, using video records of mother–child interactions while they played with items from three different boxes (a storybook, toy stove/cooking accessories, and a dollhouse). The researchers assessed the quantity of words used during these interactions and also the quality of the communications, such as how coordinated the mother–child interactions were (e.g., taking turns), and how often they were jointly engaged in a task (e.g., when playing with the dollhouse, the child produced the word "baby" with a gesture indicating sleep, and the mother placed the figure on the bed).

A year later, the researchers assessed the children's language abilities using scales that were developed to detect changes in language development in young children. Consistent with earlier studies, Hirsh-Pasek and colleagues found that the quantity of words used by the mother during the play task was associated with her child's language performance a year later. (More words from the mother predicted higher performance by the child.) Importantly, though, they also found that the rated quality of communication during the play task was an even stronger predictor of language performance a year later. In a more recent study, Masek et al. (2021) reported similar findings in toddlers from low- and high-income backgrounds, but not in toddlers from middle-income backgrounds. Although the reasons for the latter finding remain to be determined, the findings from the studies by Hirsh-Pasek et al. and Masek et al. suggest that it will be important to take into account and improve the quality of communications between parents and children in low-SES families.

Language and the Brain

As the brain matures, specific neurological structures become specialized, which allows language to develop (Kuhl, 2010; Kuhl & Rivera-Gaxiola, 2008). Where, then, are the brain regions that support language?

Broca's Area and Wernicke's Area of the Brain

Historically, language processing has been linked primarily with two brain areas: Broca's area and Wernicke's area, which are sometimes referred to as the language centres of the brain. (For recent evidence that brain regions not traditionally viewed as language centres can support language acquisition, see A World of Difference: Language without Sight: A Role for Visual Cortex.) These areas are connected to one another by a pathway known as the arcuate fasciculus; they are also interconnected with many other brain regions, as language is a complex process that cannot be simply localized to these two parts of the brain (Fedorenko et al., 2011; Price, 2012). Nonetheless, damage to Broca's and Wernicke's areas is often associated with a serious condition called **aphasia,** *difficulty in producing or comprehending language.*

Broca's area is located in the left frontal cortex and is involved in the production of the sequential patterns in vocal and sign languages (see **FIGURE 9.3**). As you saw in The Evolution of Psychological Science chapter, Broca's area is named after the French physician Paul Broca, who first reported on speech problems resulting from damage to a specific area of the left frontal cortex (Broca, 1861, 1863). Individuals with damage that includes this area exhibit *Broca's aphasia*: they understand language relatively well, but they have increasing comprehension difficulty as grammatical structures get more complex. Their real struggle, though, is with speech production. Typically, they speak in short, staccato phrases that consist mostly of content morphemes (e.g., *cat, dog*). Function morphemes (e.g., *and, but*) are usually missing, and grammatical structure is impaired. A person with Broca's aphasia might say something like "Ah, Monday, uh, Casey park. Two, uh, friends, and, uh, 30 minutes." Although it was once believed that damage to Broca's area alone is sufficient to cause Broca's aphasia, the location of lesions that produce these striking symptoms varies across patients, often extending outside Broca's area (Fridriksson et al., 2015). In fact, a study that used high-resolution structural MRI to examine the brains of the two patients initially described by Broca back in the 1860s revealed that their damage extended from the surface area of the left frontal cortex that we call Broca's area deeper into the left hemisphere than was previously realized (Dronkers et al., 2007).

Wernicke's area, located in the left temporal cortex, is involved in language comprehension (whether spoken or signed). The German neurologist Carl Wernicke first described the area that bears his name after observing speech difficulty in patients who had sustained damage to the left posterior temporal cortex (Wernicke, 1874). Individuals with *Wernicke's aphasia* differ from those with Broca's aphasia in two ways: They can produce grammatical speech, but it tends to be meaningless, and they have considerable difficulty comprehending language. A person suffering from Wernicke's aphasia might say something like "Feel very well. In other words, I used to be able to work cigarettes. I don't know how. Things I couldn't hear from are here." Modern research has revealed that individuals with Wernicke's aphasia typically have brain lesions that extend beyond just Wernicke's area (Dronkers & Baldo, 2010). Moreover, neuroimaging studies of people with normal language processing abilities have implicated middle and lower regions of the left temporal cortex rather than Wernicke's area in processing the meaning of words (Binder et al., 2009; Visser et al., 2012).

Learning Outcomes

WHAT YOU NEED TO KNOW

- Describe brain regions associated with language production and comprehension.

- Identify cognitive advantages and disadvantages for bilingual children.

- Explain what has been learned from language studies with nonhuman primates.

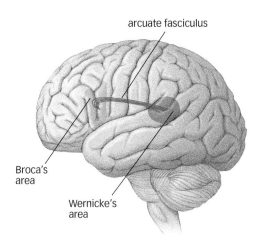

arcuate fasciculus

Broca's area

Wernicke's area

Figure 9.3
Broca's and Wernicke's Areas
Neuroscientists study people who have brain damage in order to better understand how the brain normally operates. When Broca's area and nearby regions are damaged, people have a hard time producing sentences, but speech, when produced, is meaningful. When Wernicke's area and other nearby regions are damaged, people can produce sentences, but the sentences tend to be meaningless. The arcuate fasciculus connects the two areas.

aphasia Difficulty in producing or comprehending language.

Thus, the contribution of Wernicke's area to language comprehension is more limited than was once believed.

Rather than just focusing on Broca's area and Wernicke's area, researchers attempting to understand the neural basis of language are examining a broader network of brain areas in the left hemisphere that contribute to language, and are studying how those regions interact with one another to support language production and comprehension (Braga et al., 2020; Price, 2012).

Involvement of the Right Cerebral Hemisphere

Although we tend to focus on the left cerebral hemisphere when thinking about language, four kinds of evidence indicate that the right cerebral hemisphere also contributes to language processing, especially to language comprehension (Jung-Beeman, 2005). First, when words are presented to the right hemisphere of healthy participants using divided visual field techniques (see the Neuroscience and Behaviour chapter), the right hemisphere shows some capacity for processing meaning. Second, individuals with damage to the right hemisphere sometimes have subtle problems with language comprehension, such as drawing inferences from text and understanding humour (Blake, 2003). Third, a number of neuroimaging studies have revealed evidence of right-hemisphere activation during language tasks (Walenski et al., 2019). Fourth, some children who have had their entire left hemispheres removed as a treatment for brain abnormalities can recover many of their language abilities (Bulteau et al., 2015; Vargha-Khadem et al., 1997).

Bilingualism and the Brain

In most parts of the world, speaking more than one language is the norm, not the exception as it is here in North America. How does speaking two (or more) languages affect the brain and cognitive abilities? Early studies of bilingual children seemed to suggest that bilingualism slows or interferes with normal cognitive development. When compared with monolingual children, bilingual children performed more slowly when processing language, and their IQ scores were lower. A reexamination of these studies, however, revealed several crucial flaws. First, the tests were given in English even when that was not the children's primary language. Second, the bilingual participants were often first- or second-generation immigrants whose parents were not proficient in English. Finally, the bilingual children came from lower socio-economic backgrounds than the monolingual children (Andrews, 1982).

Later studies controlled for these factors and revealed a very different picture, indicating that bilingual and monolingual children in Montreal, where bilingualism is common, do not differ significantly in the course and rate of many aspects of their language development (Nicoladis & Genesee, 1997). In fact, several studies showed that middle-class children who are fluent in two languages score higher than monolingual children on several measures of cognitive functioning, including executive control capacities such as the ability to prioritize information and flexibly focus attention (Bialystok, 1999, 2009; Bialystok et al., 2012). The idea here is that bilingual individuals benefit from exerting executive control in their daily lives when they attempt to suppress the language that they don't want to use. However, a number of recent studies have failed to replicate the beneficial effects of bilingualism on these cognitive tasks. Replication failures have been reported for children (Duñabeitia et al., 2014), young adults (Paap & Sawi, 2014; von Bastian et al., 2016), and old adults (Kirk et al., 2014), although the evidence for a bilingual advantage in executive functioning appears to be stronger in old adults and children than in young adults (Bialystok, 2017). However, a comprehensive analysis of both published and unpublished studies revealed little to no evidence of a bilingual advantage in executive function (Lehtonen et al., 2018).

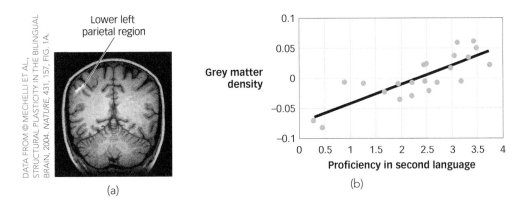

DATA FROM © MECHELLI ET AL., STRUCTURAL PLASTICITY IN THE BILINGUAL BRAIN, 2004. *NATURE*, 431, 157, FIG. 1A.

Lower left parietal region

(a)

Grey matter density

Proficiency in second language

(b)

Figure 9.4
Bilingualism Alters Brain Structure
Learning a second language early in life increases the density of grey matter in the brain. Panel (*a*) shows a view of the lower left parietal region, which has denser grey matter in bilingual individuals relative to monolingual individuals. (*b*) As proficiency in a second language increases, so does the density of grey matter in the lower parietal region. People who acquired a second language earlier in life were also found to have denser grey matter in this region. Interestingly, this area corresponds to the same area that is activated during verbal fluency tasks (Mechelli et al., 2004).

Nonetheless, bilingualism may have benefits much later in life: Evidence indicates that bilingual individuals tend to have a later onset of Alzheimer's disease than monolingual individuals do, perhaps reflecting the fact that during their lives they have built up a greater amount of back-up cognitive ability, or "cognitive reserve" (Bak et al., 2014; Woumans et al., 2015). These benefits are more consistently supported by research (Bialystok, 2021; Guzmán-Vélez & Tranel, 2015; Klein et al., 2016). Furthermore, these findings are consistent with research showing that learning a second language produces lasting changes in the brain (Mechelli et al., 2004; Stein et al., 2009). For example, the grey matter in a part of the left parietal lobe that is involved in language is denser in bilingual than in monolingual individuals, and the increased density is most pronounced in those who are most proficient in using their second language (Mechelli et al., 2004; see **FIGURE 9.4**). More recent studies have also shown significant effects of bilingualism on both brain structure and function (Tao et al., 2021).

Failures to replicate beneficial effects of bilingualism on some cognitive tasks have led to a fierce but as yet unresolved debate about why a bilingual advantage that initially appeared to be robust has been cast in doubt by more recent studies (Antoniou, 2019; Bialystok, 2017; Lehtonen et al., 2018). Given the theoretical and practical importance of understanding if and why any type of bilingual advantage exists, it seems certain that researchers will continue to try to pin down which cognitive benefits are real and which are not. Of course, the ability to converse with people in another language is a clear and uncontroversial benefit of bilingualism!

Can Other Species Learn Human Language?

The human vocal tract and the extremely nimble human hand are better suited to human language than are the throats and paws of other species. Nonetheless, attempts have been made to teach nonhuman animals, particularly apes, to communicate using human language.

Early attempts to teach apes to speak failed dismally because their vocal tracts cannot accommodate the sounds used in human languages (Hayes & Hayes, 1951). Later attempts to teach apes human language have met with more success, including teaching them to use American Sign Language and computer-monitored keyboards that display geometric symbols that represent words. Allen and Beatrix Gardner were the first to use ASL with apes (Gardner & Gardner, 1969). The Gardners worked with a young female chimpanzee named Washoe as though she were a deaf child, signing to her regularly, rewarding her correct efforts at signing, and assisting her acquisition of signs by manipulating her hands in a process referred to as *molding*. In 4 years, Washoe learned approximately 160 words and could construct simple sentences, such as "More fruit." She also formed novel word constructions such as "water bird" for "duck." After a fight with a rhesus monkey, she signed,

©FRIENDS OF WASHOE, CHIMPANZEE & HUMAN COMMUNICATION INSTITUTE, CENTRAL WASHINGTON UNIVERSITY

Allen and Beatrix Gardner used sign language to teach the female chimpanzee Washoe about 160 words. Washoe could also construct simple sentences and combine words in novel ways.

"dirty monkey!" This constituted a creative use of the term because she had only been taught the use of *dirty* to refer to soiled objects.

Other chimpanzees were immersed in ASL in a similar fashion, and Washoe and her companions were soon signing to each other, creating a learning environment conducive to language acquisition. One of Washoe's cohorts, a chimpanzee named Lucy, learned to sign "drink fruit" for watermelon. When Washoe's second infant died, her caretakers arranged for her to adopt an infant chimpanzee named Loulis.

In a few months, young Loulis, who was not exposed to human signers, learned 68 signs simply by watching Washoe communicate with the other chimpanzees. People who have observed these interactions and are themselves fluent in ASL report little difficulty in following the conversations (Fouts & Bodamer, 1987). One such observer, a *New York Times* reporter who spent some time with Washoe, reported, "Suddenly I realized I was conversing with a member of another species in my native tongue."

Other researchers have taught bonobo chimpanzees to communicate using a geometric keyboard system (Savage-Rumbaugh et al., 1998). Their star pupil, Kanzi, learned the keyboard system by watching researchers try to teach his mother. Like Loulis, young Kanzi picked up the language relatively easily (his mother never did learn the system), suggesting that like humans, birds, and other species, apes experience a critical period for acquiring communicative systems.

Kanzi, a young male bonobo chimpanzee, learned hundreds of words and word combinations through a keyboard system as he watched researchers try to teach his mother.

Kanzi has learned hundreds of words and has combined them to form thousands of word combinations. Also, as in human children, his passive mastery of language appears to exceed his ability to produce language. In one study, researchers tested 9-year-old Kanzi's understanding of 660 spoken sentences. These grammatically complex sentences asked him to perform simple actions, such as "Go get the balloon that's in the microwave" and "Pour the Perrier into the Coke." Some sentences were also potentially misleading, such as "Get the pine needles that are in the refrigerator," when there were pine needles in clear view on the floor. Impressively, Kanzi correctly carried out 72% of the 660 requests (Savage-Rumbaugh & Lewin, 1996).

These results indicate that apes can acquire sizable vocabularies, string words together to form short sentences, and process sentences that are grammatically complex. Their skills are especially impressive because human language is hardly their normal means of communication. Research with apes also suggests that the neurological "wiring" that allows us to learn language overlaps to some degree with theirs (and perhaps with that of other species).

Equally informative are the limitations apes exhibit when learning, comprehending, and using human language:

- *Limited vocabularies.* As mentioned, Washoe's and Kanzi's vocabularies number in the hundreds, but an average 4-year-old human child has a vocabulary of approximately 10,000 words.

- *Limited conceptual repertoire.* Apes primarily sign and respond to names for concrete objects and simple actions. Apes (and several other species) have the ability to map arbitrary sounds or symbols onto objects and actions, but learning, say, the meaning of the word *economics* would be difficult for Washoe or Kanzi. In other words, apes can learn signs for concepts they understand, but the words they can master are smaller and simpler than those that humans understand.

- *Limited understanding of grammar.* The third and perhaps most important limitation is the complexity of grammar that apes can use and comprehend. Apes can string signs together, but their constructions rarely exceed three or four words, and when they do, they are rarely grammatical. Comparing the grammatical structures produced by apes with those produced by human children highlights the complexity of human language as well as the ease and speed with which we generate and comprehend it.

A World of Difference · Language without Sight: A Role for Visual Cortex

As discussed in the main text, researchers interested in understanding the neural basis of language have explored a variety of brain regions, including Broca's area, Wernicke's area, other left temporal and frontal regions, and even some areas in the right hemisphere. Notably absent from this discussion is any mention of visual cortex, which as you learned in the chapters on Neuroscience and Behaviour as well as Sensation and Perception, is linked most strongly to the occipital lobe. This omission isn't too surprising because the visual cortex does not figure prominently in language comprehension and production—at least for most of us. But for others—people who are congenitally blind—the situation is very different.

Studies of people who have been blind from birth have established that on language tasks spanning both comprehension and production, individuals who are congenitally blind recruit areas within the occipital lobe that we typically think of as performing exclusively visual functions, and that are not recruited during language tasks in those who are not blind (Bedny et al., 2011; Lane et al., 2015). Two prominent ideas have been advanced to explain these striking results, the *developmental specialization hypothesis* and the *unmasking hypothesis* (Pant et al., 2020). The developmental specialization hypothesis states that being blind from birth alters the typical development of brain specialization, which allows regions that are normally devoted to

vision to be co-opted for language processing. The unmasking hypothesis, in contrast, states that the absence of visual input at any time of life "unmasks" the hidden ability of what are typically visual regions to become involved in language processing, even in individuals who first became blind as adults.

Evidence from fMRI has shown that visual cortex does become active in individuals with adult-onset blindness in response to spoken language, but this activation was stronger and more extensive in congenitally blind individuals (Burton et al., 2002, 2003). A more recent fMRI study examined whether visual cortex activation in adult-onset blind individuals responds to high-level features of language such as the meaning and the grammatical complexity of sentences to the same extent as in congenitally blind individuals (Pant et al., 2020). The researchers scanned three groups: individuals who were (1) blind from birth, (2) became blind at age 17 yrs. or later, or (3) not blind but wearing a blindfold. All participants listened to sentences and made judgements about who did what to whom. In grammatically complex sentences (e.g., "The accountant that the corrupt detective in the organized crime division dislikes advises the Sicilian mob"), it was more difficult to determine who did what to whom than in less grammatically complex sentences (e.g., "The corrupt detective in the organized crime division dislikes that the accountant advises the Sicilian mob"). In a control task, participants listened to and held in mind a

series of nonsense words. Both congenitally blind and adult-onset blind participants showed visual cortex activation during the sentence comprehension task compared to the control task, whereas the blindfolded /not blind participants did not, but this meaning-related activation was much larger in the congenitally blind group than in the adult-onset group. Moreover, the congenitally blind group—but not the adult-onset group—showed a stronger response in visual cortex to more grammatically complex versus less grammatically complex sentences.

Taken together, these results mainly support the developmental specialization account of visual cortex involvement in language processing, which holds that blindness from birth alters the development of brain specialization. One caveat that Pant et al. (2020) noted, however, is that the congenitally blind participants were blind for longer than the adult-onset participants, raising the possibility that the observed differences between the two groups occurred because visual cortex had longer to become involved in language processing in the congenitally blind participants. They tested this hypothesis by examining the relationship between blindness duration and responses of visual cortex to language in adult-onset participants. There was no consistent relationship, and so the authors could conclude that there is a sensitive period in brain development during which visual cortex can be most effectively co-opted to perform language functions.

Language and Thought: How Are They Related?

Language is such a dominant feature of our mental world that it is tempting to equate language with thought. Some theorists have even argued that language is only a means of expressing thought. However, Benjamin Whorf (1956), who was an engineer who studied language in his spare time and was especially interested in Native American languages, studied the Inuit language which has various terms for frozen white flakes of precipitation, for which we use the word *snow*. Whorf believed that because they have more than one term for snow, the

Learning Outcome

WHAT YOU NEED TO KNOW

- Describe the evidence that both supports and discounts the linguistic relativity hypothesis.

The Inuit of Canada use many different terms for snow, leading Benjamin Whorf (1956) to propose that the Inuit think about snow differently than do English speakers.

Inuit perceive and think about snow differently than do English speakers. Whorf championed this **linguistic relativity hypothesis,** *the idea that language shapes the nature of thought.* However, Whorf has been criticized for the anecdotal nature of his observations (Pinker, 1994).

Language and Colour Processing: Differing Results

Eleanor Rosch (1973) cast doubt on Whorf's hypothesis with studies of the Dani, an isolated agricultural tribe living in New Guinea. They have only two terms for colours, which roughly refer to "dark" and "light." If Whorf's hypothesis were correct, you would expect the Dani to have problems perceiving and learning different shades of colour (hues). But in Rosch's experiments, they learned hues just as well as people who have many more colour terms in their first language.

However, more recent evidence shows that language may indeed influence colour processing (Roberson et al., 2004). Researchers compared English children with African children from a cattle-herding tribe in Namibia known as the Himba. The English have 11 basic colour terms, but the Himba, who are largely isolated from the outside world, have only 5. For example, they use the term *serandu* to refer to what English speakers would call red, pink, or orange. Researchers showed a series of coloured tiles to each child and then asked the child to choose one colour from an array of 22 different colours. The youngest children, both English and Himba, who knew few or no colour names, tended to confuse similar colours. But as the children grew and acquired more names for colours, their choices increasingly reflected the colour terms they had learned. English children made fewer errors matching tiles that had English colour names; Himba children made fewer errors for tiles with colour names in Himba. These results reveal that language can indeed influence how children think about colours.

Similar effects have been observed in adults. Consider the row of 20 blue rectangles shown in **FIGURE 9.5**, which you'll easily see change gradually from lightest blue on the left to darkest blue on the right. What you might not know is that in Russian, there are different words for light blue (*goluboy*) and dark blue (*siniy*). Researchers investigated whether Russian speakers would respond differently to patches of blue when they fell into different linguistic categories rather than into the same linguistic category (Winawer et al., 2007). Russian speakers as well as English speakers, on

linguistic relativity hypothesis The idea that language shapes the nature of thought.

Figure 9.5
Language Affects How We Think about Colour Unlike English, the Russian language has different words for light blue and dark blue. Russian speakers who were asked to pick which of the two bottom squares matched the colour of the single square above responded more quickly when one of the bottom squares was called goluboy (light blue) and the other was called siniy (dark blue) than when both were referred to by the same name. English speakers took about the same amount of time.

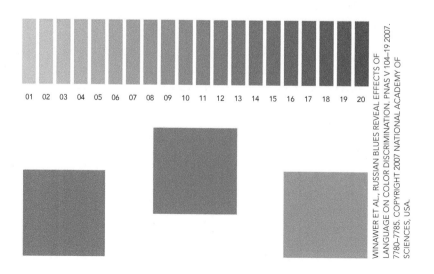

WINAWER ET AL, RUSSIAN BLUES REVEAL EFFECTS OF LANGUAGE ON COLOR DISCRIMINATION. PNAS V 104-19 2007. 7780-7785. COPYRIGHT 2007 NATIONAL ACADEMY OF SCIENCES, USA.

average, classified rectangles 1 through 8 as light blue and 9 through 20 as dark blue, but only Russian speakers used different words to refer to the two classes of blue. In the same experimental task, participants were shown three blue squares, as in the lower part of Figure 9.5, and were asked to pick which of the two bottom blue squares among the three matched the colours of the top square. Russian speakers responded more quickly when one of the bottom squares was *goluboy* and the other was *siniy* than when both bottom squares were *goluboy* or both were *siniy*, whereas English speakers took about the same amount of time to respond in the two conditions (Winawer et al., 2007). As with children, language can affect how adults think about colours.

Was Whorf "Half Right"?

Bear in mind, however, that either thought or language ability can be severely impaired while the capacity for the other is spared, as illustrated by the dramatic case of Christopher, which you read about earlier in this chapter—and as we'll see again in the next section. These kinds of observations have led some researchers to suggest that Whorf was only "half right" in his claims about the effect of language on thought (Regier & Kay, 2009). Others suggest that, consistent with this idea, it is overly simplistic to talk in general terms about whether language influences thought and that researchers need to be more specific about the exact ways in which language influences thought. For example, Wolff and Holmes (2011) rejected the idea that language entirely determines thought. But they also pointed out that there is considerable evidence that language can *influence* thought both by highlighting specific properties of concepts and by allowing us to formulate verbal rules that help solve problems. Thus, recent research has started to clarify the ways in which the linguistic relativity hypothesis is right and the ways in which it is wrong.

Concepts and Categories: How We Think

In October 2000, a 69-year-old man known by the initials JB went for a neurological assessment because he was having difficulty understanding the meaning of words, even though he still performed well on many other perceptual and cognitive tasks. In 2002, as his problems worsened, he began participating in a research project concerning the role of language in naming, recognizing, and classifying colours (Haslam et al., 2007). As the researchers observed JB over the next 15 months, they documented that his colour language deteriorated dramatically; he had great difficulty naming colours and could not even match objects with their typical colours (e.g., strawberry and red, banana and yellow). Yet even as his language deteriorated, JB could still classify colours normally, sorting colour patches into groups of green, yellow, red, and blue in the exact same manner that healthy participants did. JB retained an intact *concept* of colours despite the decline of his language ability—a finding that suggests we need to look at factors in addition to language in order to understand concepts (Haslam et al., 2007).

Concept refers to *a mental representation that groups or categorizes shared features of related objects, events, or other stimuli.* A concept is an abstract representation, description, or definition that designates a class or category of things. The brain organizes our concepts about the world, classifying them into categories based on shared similarities. Our category for *dog* may be something like "small, four-footed animal with fur that wags its tail and barks." Our category for *bird* may be something like

Learning Outcomes

WHAT YOU NEED TO KNOW

- Identify why concepts are fundamental to our ability to think.

- Compare the family prototype and exemplar theories of concepts.

- Describe the involvement of the brain in organizing and processing concepts.

concept A mental representation that groups or categorizes shared features of related objects, events, or other stimuli.

There is family resemblance between family members despite the fact that there is no defining feature that they all have in common. Instead, there are shared common features. Someone who also shares some of those features may be categorized as belonging to the family.

"small winged, beaked creature that flies." We form these categories in large part by noticing similarities among objects and events that we experience in everyday life. For example, your concept of a chair might include such features as sturdiness, relative flatness, and an object that you can sit on. That set of attributes defines a category of objects in the world—desk chairs, recliner chairs, flat rocks, bar stools, and so on—that can all be described in that way.

Concepts are fundamental to our ability to think and make sense of the world. We'll first compare various theories that explain the formation of concepts and then consider studies that link the formation and organization of concepts to the brain. As with other aspects of cognition, we can gain insight into how concepts are organized by looking at some instances in which they are rather disorganized. We'll encounter some unusual disorders that help us understand how concepts are organized in the brain.

Psychological Theories of Concepts and Categories

Early psychological theories described concepts as rules that specify the necessary and sufficient conditions for membership in a particular category. A *necessary condition* is something that must be true of the object in order for it to belong to the category. For instance, suppose you were trying to determine whether an unfamiliar animal was a dog. It is necessary that the creature be a mammal; otherwise it doesn't belong to the category *dog* because all dogs are mammals. A *sufficient condition* is something that, if it is true of the object, proves that it belongs to the category. Suppose someone told you that the creature was a German shepherd and you know that a German shepherd is a type of dog. *German shepherd* is a sufficient condition for membership in the category *dog*.

Most natural categories, however, cannot be so easily defined in terms of this classical approach of necessary and sufficient conditions. For example, what is your definition of *dog*? Can you come up with a rule of "dogship" that includes all dogs and excludes all non-dogs? Most people can't, but they still use the term *dog* intelligently, easily classifying objects as dogs or non-dogs. Two major theories seek to explain how people perform these acts of categorization.

Prototype theory, which can be traced to the pioneering experimental studies of Eleanor Rosch and her colleagues (Rosch, 1973, 1975; Rosch & Mervis, 1975), is *the concept that we classify new objects by comparing them to the "best" or "most typical" member of a category.* A prototype possesses many (or all) of the most characteristic features of the category. For North Americans, the prototype of the *bird* category would be something like a wren: a small animal with feathers and wings that flies through the air, lays eggs, and migrates (see **FIGURE 9.6**).

prototype theory The concept that we classify new objects by comparing them to the "best" or "most typical" member (the *prototype*) of a category.

Figure 9.6
Critical Features of a Category We tend to think of a generic bird as possessing a number of critical features, but not every bird possesses all of those features. In North America, a wren is a better example of a bird than a penguin or an ostrich.

Properties	Generic bird	Wren	Blue heron	Golden eagle	Domestic goose	Penguin
Flies regularly	✔	✔	✔	✔		
Sings	✔	✔	✔			
Lays eggs	✔	✔	✔	✔	✔	✔
Is small	✔	✔				
Nests in trees	✔	✔				

If you lived in Antarctica, your prototype of a bird might be a penguin: a small animal that has flippers, swims, and lays eggs. According to *prototype theory,* if your prototypical bird is a robin, then a canary would be considered a better example of a bird than would an ostrich, because a canary has more features in common with a robin than an ostrich does. People make category judgements by comparing new instances with the category's prototype. This contrasts with the classical approach to concepts in which something either is or is not an example of a concept (i.e., it either does or does not belong in the category *dog* or *bird*).

Exemplar theory holds that *we make category judgements by comparing a new instance with stored memories of other instances of the category* (Medin & Schaffer, 1978). Imagine that you're out walking in the woods, and from the corner of your eye you spot a four-legged animal that might be a wolf or a coyote but that reminds you of your cousin's German shepherd. You figure it must be a dog and continue to enjoy your walk rather than fleeing in a panic. You probably categorized this new animal as a dog because it bore a striking resemblance to other dogs you've encountered; in other words, it was a good example (or an *exemplar*) of the category *dog*. Exemplar theory does a better job than prototype theory of accounting for certain aspects of categorization (Ashby & Rosedahl, 2017; Nosofsky et al., 2018), especially in that we recall not only what a *prototypical* dog looks like but also what *specific* dogs look like. **FIGURE 9.7** illustrates the difference between prototype theory and exemplar theory.

exemplar theory The concept that we make category judgements by comparing a new instance with stored memories of other instances of the category.

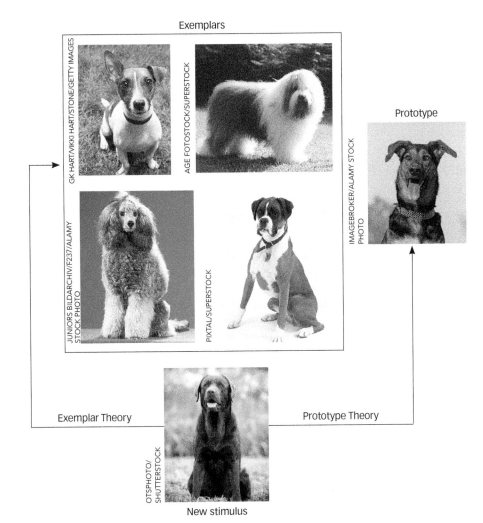

Figure 9.7
Prototype Theory and Exemplar Theory According to prototype theory, we classify new objects by comparing them to the "prototype" (or most typical) member of a category. According to exemplar theory, we classify new objects by comparing them with all category members.

Concepts, Categories, and the Brain

Studies that have attempted to link concepts and categories to the brain have helped make sense of the theories we have just considered. For example, in one set of studies (Marsolek, 1995), participants classified prototypes faster when the stimuli were presented to the right visual field, meaning that the left hemisphere received the input first. (See the Neuroscience and Behaviour chapter for a discussion of how the two hemispheres of the brain receive input from the outside world.) In contrast, participants classified previously seen exemplars faster when images were presented to the left visual field (meaning that the right hemisphere received the input first). These results suggest a role for both exemplars and prototypes: The left hemisphere is primarily involved in forming prototypes, and the right hemisphere is mainly active in recognizing exemplars.

More recently, researchers using neuroimaging techniques have also concluded that we use both prototypes and exemplars when forming concepts and categories. The visual cortex is involved in forming prototypes, whereas the prefrontal cortex and basal ganglia are involved in learning exemplars (Ashby & Ell, 2001; Ashby & O'Brien, 2005). This evidence suggests that exemplar-based learning involves analysis and decision making (prefrontal cortex), whereas prototype formation is a more holistic activity involving image processing (visual cortex).

Category-Specific Deficit

Some of the most striking evidence linking concepts and categories with the brain originated in a pioneering study of an odd case. Two neuropsychologists (Warrington & McCarthy, 1983) described a man with brain damage who could not recognize a variety of human-made objects or retrieve any information about them, but whose knowledge of living things and foods was perfectly normal. In the following year, neuropsychologists (Warrington & Shallice, 1984) reported on four individuals with brain damage who exhibited the reverse pattern: They could recognize information about human-made objects, but their ability to recognize information about living things and foods was severely impaired. Over 100 similar cases have since been reported (Martin & Caramazza, 2003). These unusual cases became the basis for a syndrome called **category-specific deficit,** *a neurological syndrome characterized by an inability to recognize objects that belong to a particular category, even when the ability to recognize objects outside the category is undisturbed.*

Category-specific deficits like these have been observed even when the brain trauma that produces them occurs shortly after birth. Two researchers reported the case of Adam, a 16-year-old boy who suffered a stroke a day after he was born (Farah & Rabinowitz, 2003). Adam has severe difficulty recognizing faces and other biological objects. When shown a picture of a cherry, he identified it as "a Chinese yo-yo." When shown a picture of a mouse, he identified it as an owl. He made errors like these on 79% of the animal pictures and 54% of the plant pictures he was shown. In contrast, he made errors only 15% of the time when identifying pictures of nonliving things, such as spatulas, brooms, and cigars. What's so important about this case? The fact that 16-year-old Adam exhibited category-specific deficits despite suffering a stroke when he was only 1 day old strongly suggests that the brain is "prewired" to organize perceptual and sensory inputs into broad-based categories, such as living and nonliving things.

The type of category-specific deficit suffered depends on where the brain is damaged. Deficits usually result when an individual suffers a stroke or other trauma to areas in the left hemisphere of the cerebral cortex (Mahon & Caramazza, 2009). Damage to the front part of the left temporal lobe results

category-specific deficit
A neurological syndrome characterized by an inability to recognize objects that belong to a particular category, even when the ability to recognize objects outside the category is undisturbed.

Figure 9.8

Brain Areas Involved in Category-Specific Processing Participants were asked to silently name pictures of animals and tools while they underwent fMRI scanning. The fMRIs revealed greater activity in the areas in yellow when participants named animals, and areas in purple showed greater activity when participants named tools. Specific regions indicated by numbers include areas within the visual cortex (1, 2), parts of the temporal lobe (3, 4), and the motor cortex (5). Note that the images are left/right reversed. DATA FROM ALEX MARTIN AND LINDA CHAO, CURRENT OPINIONS NEUROBIOLOGY 2001, 11.

in difficulty identifying humans; damage to the lower left temporal lobe results in difficulty identifying animals; damage to the region where the temporal lobe meets the occipital and parietal lobes impairs the ability to retrieve names of tools (Damasio et al., 1996). Similarly, when healthy people undertake the same task, imaging studies have demonstrated that the same regions of the brain are more active during naming of tools than during naming of animals and vice versa, as shown in **FIGURE 9.8** (Martin, 2007; Martin & Chao, 2001).

Are Our Brains Prewired?

How do particular brain regions develop category preferences for objects such as tools or animals? One possibility is that these preferences develop from the specific visual experiences that individuals have during the course of their lives. An alternative possibility is suggested by the study of Adam that we just considered: The brain may be prewired such that particular regions respond more strongly to some categories than to others. An fMRI study tested these ideas by examining the activity of category-preferential regions in adults who have been blind since birth (Mahon et al., 2009). While in the scanner, blind and sighted individuals each heard a series of words, including some words that referred to animals and others that referred to tools. For each word, participants made a judgement about the size of the corresponding object. The critical finding was that category-preferential regions showed highly similar patterns of activity in the blind and sighted individuals. In both groups, for example, regions in the visual cortex and temporal lobe responded to animals and tools in much the same manner as shown in Figure 9.8.

More recent research has reported similar findings concerning a region of the temporal lobe, which you learned about in the Sensation and Perception chapter, that responds more strongly to faces than to any other object category. When congenitally blind individuals explored three-dimensional printed faces and other kinds of objects haptically (i.e., by touch), the same temporal lobe region that responds selectively to faces in sighted individuals also responded selectively to faces in the congenitally blind (Murty et al., 2020). These results provide compelling evidence that category-specific organization of visual regions does not depend on an individual's visual experience. The category-specific organization conceivably could have arisen from interactions with objects that blind individuals have had that involved senses other than vision, such as touch (Peelen & Kastner, 2009). However, when these results are combined with the observations of Adam, the simplest explanation may be that category-specific brain organization is innately determined (Bedny & Saxe, 2012; Mahon et al., 2009; Murty et al., 2020).

Touch is one way that blind individuals could develop category-preferential brain responses.

Decision Making: Rational and Otherwise

Learning Outcomes

WHAT YOU NEED TO KNOW

- Explain why people sometimes fail to make rational decisions.
- Summarize the ideas underlying prospect theory.
- Describe the role of the brain in decision making.

We use categories and concepts to guide the hundreds of decisions and judgements we make during the course of an average day. Some decisions are easy (what to wear; what to eat for breakfast; whether to walk, ride a bicycle, or drive to class) and some are more difficult (which car to buy, which apartment to rent, who to hang out with on Friday night, and even which job to take after graduation). Some decisions are based on sound judgements. Others are not.

The Rational Ideal

Economists contend that if we are rational thinkers, free to make our own decisions, we will behave as predicted by **rational choice theory:** *the classical view that we make decisions by determining how likely something is to happen, judging the value of the outcome, and then multiplying the two* (Edwards, 1955). This means that our judgements will vary depending on the value we assign to the possible outcomes. Suppose, for example, you were asked to choose between a 10% chance of gaining $500 and a 20% chance of gaining $2,000. The rational person would choose the second alternative because the expected payoff is $400 ($2,000 × 20%), whereas the first offers an expected gain of only $50 ($500 × 10%). Selecting the option with the highest expected value seems so straightforward that many economists accept the basic ideas in rational choice theory. But how well does this theory describe decision making in our everyday lives? In many cases, the answer is: not very well.

The Irrational Reality

Is the ability to classify new events and objects into categories always a useful skill? Alas, no. These strengths of human decision making can turn into weaknesses when certain tasks inadvertently activate these skills. In other words, the same principles that allow cognition to occur easily and accurately can pop up to bedevil our decision making.

Judging Frequencies and Probabilities

Consider the following list of words:

> *block, table, block, pen, telephone, block, disk, glass, table, block, telephone, block, watch, table, candy*

You probably noticed that the words *block* and *table* occur more frequently than the other words do. In fact, studies have shown that people are quite good at estimating *frequency,* simply the number of times something will happen. Adults judge frequency accurately and nearly automatically, and young children perform just as well on similar tasks (Gallistel & Gelman, 1992; Hasher & Zacks, 1984). All of this suggests that processing frequencies is "natural" and easy for most humans to accomplish, perhaps because we encode frequencies through direct experience in our daily lives (Gigerenzer & Hoffrage, 1995; Todd & Gigerenzer, 2012). This skill matters quite a bit when it comes to decision making. In contrast, we perform poorly on tasks that require us to think in terms of *probabilities,* or the likelihood that something will happen. Probabilities are more abstract and less familiar based on everyday experience.

Even with probabilities, however, performance varies depending on how the problem is described. In one experiment, 100 physicians were asked to predict the incidence of breast cancer among women whose mammogram screening tests showed possible evidence of breast cancer. The physicians were told to take into consideration the rarity of breast cancer (1% of the population at the time the study was done) and radiologists' record in diagnosing the condition (correctly recognized only 80% of the time and falsely diagnosed almost 10% of the time). Of the 100 physicians, 95 estimated the probability that cancer

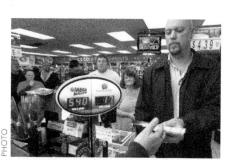

People don't always make rational choices. When a lottery jackpot is larger than usual, more people will buy lottery tickets, thinking that they might well win big. However, more people buying lottery tickets reduces the likelihood of any one person winning the lottery. Ironically, people have a better chance at winning a lottery with a relatively small jackpot.

rational choice theory

The classical view that we make decisions by determining how likely something is to happen, judging the value of the outcome, and then multiplying the two.

was present to be about 75%! The correct answer is 8%*. The physicians apparently had difficulty taking into account that much information when making their decision (Eddy, 1982). Similar dismal results have been reported with a number of medical screening tests (Hoffrage & Gigerenzer, 1996; Windeler & Kobberling, 1986).

However, dramatically different results were obtained when the study was repeated using *frequency* information instead of *probability* information. Stating the problem as "10 out of every 1,000 women actually have breast cancer. Of these 10 women with breast cancer, 8 will have a positive mammogram. Of the remaining 990 women without cancer, 99 will have a positive mammogram" instead of using probabilities, as above, which led 46% of the physicians to derive the right answer (Hoffrage & Gigerenzer, 1998). The difference between 8% correct (with probabilities) and 46% correct (with frequencies) suggests, at a minimum, that when seeking advice (even from a highly skilled decision maker), make sure your problem is described using frequencies rather than probabilities.

Availability Heuristic

Take a look at the list of names in **FIGURE 9.9**. Now look away from the book and estimate the number of male names and female names in the figure. Did you notice that some of the women on the list are famous and none of the men are? Was your estimate off because you thought the list contained more women's names than men's names (Tversky & Kahneman, 1973, 1974)? People often rely on an **availability heuristic:** *A rule of thumb that items that are more readily available in memory are judged as having occurred more frequently.* If the list contained the names of famous men and unknown women, your estimates probably would have been reversed.

More generally, a **heuristic** is a *fast and efficient strategy that may facilitate decision making but does not guarantee that a solution will be reached.*

The availability heuristic affects our estimates because memory strength and frequency of occurrence are directly related. Frequently occurring items are remembered more easily than *in*frequently occurring items, so you naturally conclude that items for which you have better memory must also have been more frequent. Unfortunately, better memory in this case was due not to greater *frequency* but to greater *familiarity*.

Heuristics are mental shortcuts that are often—but not always—effective when approaching a problem (Swinkels, 2003). In contrast, an **algorithm** is *a well-defined sequence of procedures or rules that guarantees a solution to a problem.* Consider, for example, two approaches to constructing a PowerPoint presentation involving features you rarely use, such as inserting movies and complex animations: (1) You try to remember what you did the last time you tried to do a similar presentation; and (2) you follow a set of step-by-step directions that you wrote down the last time you did something similar, which tells you exactly how to insert movies and build complex animations.

The first procedure is an intelligent heuristic that may be successful, but you could continue searching your memory until you finally run out of time or patience. The second strategy is a series of well-defined steps that, if properly executed, will guarantee a solution.

Representativeness Heuristic

Think about the following situation: A panel of psychologists wrote 100 descriptions based on interviews with engineers and lawyers. The descriptions were of 70 engineers and 30 lawyers. You will be shown a random selection of these descriptions. Read each one and then pause and decide if it is more likely that the person is an engineer or a lawyer. Note your decision and read on.

1. Jack enjoys reading books on social and political issues. During the interview, he displayed particular skill at argument.

Jennifer Aniston	Robert Kingston
Judy Smith	Gilbert Chapman
Frank Carson	Gwyneth Paltrow
Elizabeth Taylor	Martin Mitchell
Daniel Hunt	Thomas Hughes
Henry Vaughan	Michael Drayton
Agatha Christie	Julia Roberts
Arthur Hutchinson	Hillary Clinton
Jennifer Lopez	Jack Lindsay
Allen Nevins	Richard Gilder
Jane Austen	George Nathan
Joseph Litton	Britney Spears

Figure 9.9

Availability Heuristic Looking at this list of names, estimate the number of women's and men's names.

availability heuristic A rule of thumb that items that are more readily available in memory are judged as having occurred more frequently.

heuristic A fast and efficient strategy that may facilitate decision making but does not guarantee that a solution will be reached.

algorithm A well-defined sequence of procedures or rules that guarantees a solution to a problem.

---

*For those who want to know where this number comes from, the actual *probability* that breast cancer is accurately diagnosed from the test depends on the number who are truly positive (1% × 79%) expressed as a proportion of all who test positive (true positives: 1% × 79%, plus false positives: 99% × 10%). The numerator of this proportion is 0.79%, and the denominator is 10.69%, so the proportion we're after—the probability of cancer given a positive test—is 7.4%.

representativeness heuristic
A mental shortcut that involves making a probability judgement by comparing an object or event with a prototype of the object or event.

conjunction fallacy Thinking that two events are more likely to occur together than either individual event alone.

2. Tom is a loner who enjoys working on mathematical puzzles during his spare time. During the interview, his speech remained fairly abstract and his emotions were well controlled.

3. Harry is a bright man and an avid racquetball player. During the interview, he asked many insightful questions and was very well spoken.

Research participants read a series of descriptions like these and were then asked to judge the likelihood that the person described was a lawyer or an engineer (Kahneman & Tversky, 1973). Remember, of the descriptions, 70 were engineers and 30 were lawyers. If participants took this proportion into consideration, their judgements should have reflected the fact that there were more than twice as many engineers as lawyers. But researchers found that, instead of using this information, people based their judgements solely on how closely the description matched their own concepts of lawyers and engineers. So the majority of participants thought descriptions such as #1 were more likely to be lawyers, whereas descriptions such as #2 were more likely to be engineers and that descriptions such as #3 could be either.

Consider participants' judgements about Harry. His description doesn't sound like a lawyer's or an engineer's, so most people said he was *equally likely* to hold either occupation. But the pool contains more than twice as many engineers as lawyers, so it is far *more* likely that Harry is an engineer. People seem to ignore information about *base rate*, or the existing probability of an event, basing their judgements on similarities to categories. Researchers call this the **representativeness heuristic:** *a mental shortcut that involves making a probability judgement by comparing an object or event with a prototype of the object or event* (Kahneman & Tversky, 1973). Thus, the probability judgements were skewed towards the participants' prototypes of lawyer and engineer. The greater the similarity, the more likely the people in the descriptions were judged to be members of that category despite the existence of much more useful base rates.

The Conjunction Fallacy

Consider the following description:

> Linda is 31 years old, single, outspoken, and very bright. At university, she majored in philosophy. As a student, she was deeply concerned with issues of discrimination and social justice and also participated in antinuclear demonstrations.

Which state of affairs is more probable?

a. Linda is a bank teller.

b. Linda is a bank teller and is active in the feminist movement.

In one study, 89% of participants rated option b as more probable than option a (Tversky & Kahneman, 1983), although that's logically impossible. The combined probability of multiple events is always less than the independent probability of each event; therefore, it's always *more* probable that any one state of affairs is true (here, bank teller) than that multiple states would simultaneously be true (bank teller *and* activist). This situation is called the **conjunction fallacy** because *people think that two events are more likely to occur together than either individual event.* The fallacy is that when people are given more and more pieces of information, they think there's a higher probability that all are true. In actuality, the probability diminishes rapidly. Here, people are misled because they rely on the representativeness heuristic: The description of Linda makes it seem like she is very likely to be a feminist, but that doesn't change the fact that it isn't more likely that she is both a bank teller and active in the feminist movement than just a bank teller. Judging by her description, do you think Linda also voted for the liberal candidate in the last election? Do you think she also writes poetry? Do you think she's also signed her name to fair-housing petitions? With each additional bit of information, you probably think you're getting a better and better description of Linda, but as you can see in **FIGURE 9.10**, the likelihood of *all* those events being true *at the same time* is very small.

Heuristics such as availability and representativeness, and related phenomena such as the conjunction fallacy highlight both the strengths and weaknesses of the

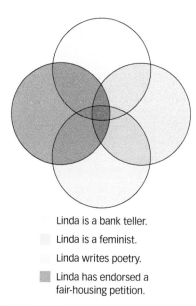

Linda is a bank teller.

Linda is a feminist.

Linda writes poetry.

Linda has endorsed a fair-housing petition.

Figure 9.10

The Conjunction Fallacy People often think that with each additional bit of information, the probability that all the facts are simultaneously true of a person increases. In fact, the probability decreases dramatically. Notice how the intersection of all these possibilities is much smaller than the area of any one possibility alone.

way we think. We are very good at forming categories based on prototypes and making classification judgements on the basis of similarity to prototypes. Judging probabilities is not our strong suit. As we saw earlier in this chapter, the human brain easily processes frequency information, so decision-making performance can usually be improved if probability problems are reframed using frequencies.

Framing Effects and the Sunk-Cost Fallacy

You've seen that, according to rational choice theory, our judgements will vary depending on the value we place on the expected outcome. So how effective are we at assigning value to our choices? Studies show that **framing effects,** which occur when *people give different answers to the same problem depending on how the problem is framed,* can influence the assignment of value.

For example, if people are told that a particular drug has a 70% effectiveness rate, they're usually pretty impressed: Getting what ails you cured 70% of the time by using the drug sounds like a good deal. Tell them instead that a drug has a 30% failure rate — that 30% of the time the drug does no good — and they typically perceive it as risky, potentially harmful, and something to be avoided. Notice that the information is the same: A 70% effectiveness rate means that 30% of the time, it's ineffective. The way the information is framed, however, leads to substantially different conclusions (Tversky & Kahneman, 1981).

A phenomenon related to framing effects is the **sunk-cost fallacy,** *a framing effect in which people make decisions about a current situation on the basis of what they have previously invested in the situation.* Imagine waiting in line for 3 hours, paying $100 for a ticket to the Warped Tour to see your favourite bands, and waking on the day of the outdoor concert to find that it's bitterly cold and rainy. If you go, you'll feel miserable. But you go anyway, reasoning that the $100 you paid for the ticket and the time you spent in line will have been wasted if you stay home.

Notice that you have two choices: (1) Spend $100 and stay comfortably at home; or (2) spend $100 and endure many uncomfortable hours in the rain. The $100 is gone in either case: It's a sunk cost, irretrievable at the moment of your decision. But the way you framed the problem created a problem: Because you invested time and money, you feel obligated to follow through, even though it's something you no longer want. If you can turn off this feeling and ask yourself if you'd rather spend $100 to be comfortable or spend it to be miserable, the smart choice is clear: Stay home and listen to the live stream!

Even the National Basketball Association (NBA) is guilty of a sunk-cost fallacy. Coaches should play their most productive players and keep them on the team longer, but they don't. The most *expensive* players are given more time on court and are kept on the team longer than cheaper players, even if the costly players are not performing up to par (Staw & Hoang, 1995). Coaches act to justify their team's investment in an expensive player rather than recognize the loss.

Framing a problem in a way that produces the sunk-cost fallacy can result in financial loss, but framing effects can also be exploited to increase wealth (Hershfield et al., 2020). Based on findings suggesting that people find it more painful to part with a large sum of money than the same amount of money meted out in smaller amounts, Hershfield and colleagues conducted a study in collaboration with an actual company, Acorns, which allows people to invest spare change or larger amounts of money to an online account (for details, go to www.acorns.com). They found that more users signed up to deposit $150 each month when the deposit was framed as $5/day than when it was framed as $35/week or $150/month. This is one framing effect that many of us could benefit from incorporating into our everyday lives.

Optimism Bias

In addition to heuristics and the biases we've just considered, human decision making often reflects the effects of **optimism bias:** *People believe that, compared with other individuals, they are more likely to experience positive events and less likely to experience negative events in the future* (Sharot, 2011). For example, people believe they are

framing effects A bias whereby people give different answers to the same problem depending on how the problem is framed.

sunk-cost fallacy A framing effect in which people make decisions about a current situation on the basis of what they have previously invested in the situation.

optimism bias A bias whereby people believe that, compared with other individuals, they are more likely to experience positive events and less likely to experience negative events in the future.

Different cultures show different levels of optimism bias, which may be a clue to understanding its origins.

more likely than others to own their own homes and live a long life and that they are less likely to have a heart attack or a drinking problem (Weinstein, 1980). Although optimism about the future is often a good thing for our mental and physical health—optimistic individuals are usually well adjusted psychologically and are able to handle stress well (Nes & Sergerstrom, 2006)—too much optimism can be detrimental because it may prevent us from taking the necessary steps to achieve our goals. Thus, overly optimistic individuals may think that they can attain a goal even when they lack the ability to achieve it, as exemplified by the finding that higher levels of optimism can be associated with lower levels of academic achievement (Sweeny et al., 2006).

Optimism bias occurs for a variety of reasons: We want good things to happen in the future, tend to more vividly imagine positive than negative future events, and are more likely to incorporate new positive information into our beliefs than new negative information (Garrett & Sharot, 2017; Sharot et al., 2007, 2011). Optimism bias can also be influenced by culture. Several studies have found that optimism bias is greater in North Americans than in individuals from Eastern cultures such as Japan (Heine & Lehman, 1995; Klein & Helweg-Larsen, 2002). One study examined optimism bias concerning the risk of natural disasters and terrorist attacks in American, Japanese, and Argentinean mental health workers who had received training in responding to such events (Gierlach et al., 2010). Although participants in all three countries judged that they were at lower risk of experiencing a disaster than others in their country, optimism bias was strongest in the American sample. These findings highlight the pervasiveness of optimism bias while also indicating that cultural factors play a role in shaping it.

Why Do We Make Decision-Making Errors?

As you have seen, everyday decision making seems riddled with errors and shortcomings (for an example related to risk assessment, see Hot Science: Aligning Perceived and Actual Risk During the COVID-19 Pandemic). Our decisions vary wildly, depending on how a problem is presented (e.g., framed in terms of frequencies versus probabilities or in terms of losses rather than savings). We also seem to be prone to fallacies, such as the sunk-cost fallacy, the conjunction fallacy, or optimism bias. Psychologists have developed several theories to explain why everyday decision making suffers from these failings. We'll review the most influential theory, known as *prospect theory*.

According to a totally rational model of inference, people should make decisions that maximize value; in other words, they should seek to increase what psychologists and economists call *expected utility*. We face decisions like this every day. If you are making a decision that involves money, and if money is what you value, then you should choose the outcome that is likely to bring you the most money. For instance, when deciding which of two apartments to rent, you'd compare the monthly expenses for each and choose the one that leaves more money in your pocket.

As you have seen, however, people often make decisions that are inconsistent with this simple principle. The question is, why? To explain these effects, Amos Tversky and Daniel Kahneman (1992) developed **prospect theory,** which proposes that *people choose to take on risks when evaluating potential losses and to avoid risks when evaluating potential gains*. These decision processes take place in two phases:

- First, people simplify available information. So in a task such as choosing an apartment, they tend to ignore a lot of potentially useful information because apartments differ in so many ways (the closeness of restaurants, the presence of a swimming pool, the colour of the carpet, and so forth). Comparing each apartment on each factor is simply too much work; focusing only on differences that matter is more efficient.

- In the second phase, people choose the prospect that they believe offers the best value. This value is personal and may differ from an objective measure of "best value." For example, you might choose the apartment with higher rent because you can walk to eight great bars and restaurants.

prospect theory The theory that people choose to take on risk when evaluating potential losses and avoid risks when evaluating potential gains.

Prospect theory makes other assumptions that account for people's choice patterns. One assumption, called the *certainty effect,* suggests that when making decisions, people give greater weight to outcomes that are a sure thing. When deciding between playing a lottery with an 80% chance of winning $4,000 or receiving $3,000 outright, most people choose the $3,000, even though the expected value of the first choice is $200 more ($4,000 × 80% = $3,200)! Apparently, people weigh certainty much more heavily than expected payoffs when making choices.

Prospect theory also assumes that, in evaluating choices, people compare them with a reference point. For instance, suppose you're still torn between two apartments. The $400 monthly rent for apartment A is discounted $10 if you pay before the fifth of the month. A $10 surcharge is tacked onto the $390 per month rent for apartment B if you pay after the fifth of the month. Although the apartments are objectively identical in terms of cost, different reference points may make apartment A seem psychologically more appealing than apartment B. The reference point for apartment A is $400, and the offer describes a change in terms of a potential gain (money saved), whereas the reference point for apartment B is $390, and the change involves a potential loss (money penalized).

Furthermore, prospect theory also assumes that people are more willing to take risks to avoid losses than to achieve gains. Given a choice between a definite $300 rebate on your first month's rent or spinning a wheel that offers an 80% chance of getting a $400 rebate, you'll most likely choose the lower sure payoff over the higher potential payoff ($400 × 80% = $320). However, given a choice between a sure fine of $300 for damaging an apartment or spinning a wheel that has an 80% chance of a $400 fine, most people will choose the higher potential loss over the sure loss. This asymmetry in risk preferences shows that we are willing to take on risk if we think it will ward off a loss, but we're risk averse if we expect to lose some benefits. (For further elaboration, see the discussion of loss aversion in the chapter on Emotion and Motivation.)

Decision Making and the Brain

A man identified as Elliot was a successful businessman, husband, and father prior to developing a brain tumour. After surgery, his intellectual abilities seemed intact, but he was unable to differentiate between important and unimportant activities and would spend hours doing mundane tasks. He lost his job and got involved in several risky financial ventures that bankrupted him. He had no difficulty discussing what had happened, but his descriptions were so detached and dispassionate that it seemed as though his abstract intellectual functions had become dissociated from his social and emotional abilities.

Research confirms that this interpretation of Elliot's downfall is right on track in terms of the effects of his brain tumour. In one study, researchers looked at how healthy volunteers differed from people with prefrontal lobe damage on a gambling task that involves risky decision making (Bechara et al., 1994, 1997). Four decks of cards were placed face down, and participants were required to make 100 selections of cards that specified an amount of play money they could win or lose. Two of the decks usually provided large payoffs or large losses, whereas the other two provided smaller payoffs and losses. While playing the game, the participants' skin conductance responses (SCRs) were recorded to measure heightened emotional reactions.

The performance of players with prefrontal lobe damage mirrored Elliot's real-life problems: They selected cards equally from the riskier and the safer decks, leading most players to eventually go bankrupt. At first, the healthy volunteers also selected from each deck equally, but they gradually shifted to choosing primarily from the safer decks. This difference in strategy occurred even though both groups showed strong emotional reactions to big gains and losses, as measured by their comparable GSR scores. The two groups differed in one important way, however. As the game progressed, the healthy participants began to show anticipatory emotional reactions when they even *considered* choosing a card from the risky deck. Their GSR scores jumped dramatically even before they were able to say that some decks were riskier

Figure 9.11

The Neuroscience of Risky Decision Making In a study of risky decision making, researchers compared healthy participants' (the control group) choices to those made by people with damage to the prefrontal cortex. Participants played a game in which they selected a card from one of four decks. Two of the decks were made up of riskier cards, that is, cards that provided large payoffs or large losses. The other two decks contained safer cards—those with much smaller payoffs and losses. At the beginning of the game, both groups chose cards from the two decks with equal frequency. Over the course of the game, however, the healthy controls avoided the bad decks and showed large emotional responses (SCRs, or skin conductance responses) when they even considered choosing a card from a risky deck. Participants with prefrontal brain damage, on the other hand, continued to choose cards from the two decks with equal frequency and showed no evidence of emotional learning; they eventually went bankrupt (data from Bechara et al., 1997).

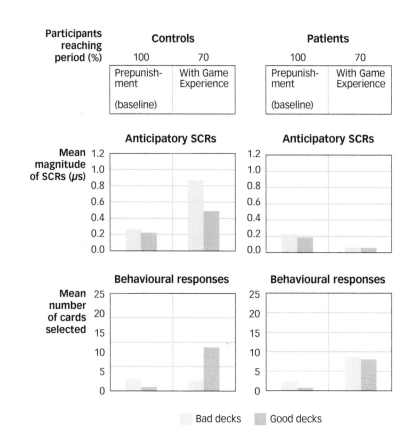

than others (Bechara et al., 1997). The participants with prefrontal damage didn't show these anticipatory feelings when they were thinking about selecting a card from the risky deck. Apparently, their emotional reactions did not guide their thinking, so they continued to make risky decisions, as shown in **FIGURE 9.11**.

Further studies of the participants with prefrontal damage suggest that their risky decision making grows out of insensitivity to the future consequences of their behaviour (Naqvi et al., 2006). Unable to think beyond immediate consequences, they could not shift their choices in response to a rising rate of losses or a declining rate of rewards (Bechara et al., 2000). Interestingly, substance-dependent individuals, such as alcoholics and cocaine addicts, act the same way. Most perform as poorly on the gambling task as do individuals with prefrontal damage (Bechara et al., 2001). More work has extended these impairments on the gambling task across cultures to Chinese adolescents with binge-drinking problems (Johnson et al., 2008).

These findings have potentially important implications for such everyday issues as road safety. A recent study focused on people who had been convicted of driving while under the influence of alcohol (DUI). Offenders who performed poorly on the gambling task were much more likely to commit repeated DUI offenses than those who performed well on the gambling task (Bouchard et al., 2012). Related work has documented gambling-task impairments in binge eaters, another group who demonstrate an insensitivity to the future consequences of behaviour (Danner et al., 2012).

Neuroimaging studies of healthy individuals have provided evidence that fits well with the earlier studies of individuals with damage to the prefrontal cortex: During the gambling task, an area in the prefrontal cortex is activated when participants make risky decisions as compared to safe decisions. Indeed, the activated region is in the part of the prefrontal cortex that is typically damaged in participants who perform poorly on the gambling task; greater activation in this region is correlated with better task performance in healthy individuals (Fukui et al., 2005; Lawrence et al., 2009). Taken together, the neuroimaging and lesion studies show clearly that aspects of risky decision making depend critically on the contributions of the prefrontal cortex.

Hot Science · Aligning Perceived and Actual Risk During the COVID-19 Pandemic

A challenge we've all faced during the COVID-19 pandemic is to assess the risk associated with various activities and make decisions about what to do or not to do based on our risk assessments. No doubt you've thought about some or all of the following scenarios since the pandemic began: How risky is it to go for a walk outside, eat inside a restaurant, shop in a grocery store, or meet with a small group of friends? How about travelling within the province where you live, or travelling outside your province? The list goes on and on.

It's difficult to determine exactly the level of risk associated with each of these and other activities. In a recent study, researchers attempted to assess the accuracy of COVID-19-related risk perceptions by asking a nationally representative online sample of U.S. residents in May 2020 to judge the level of risk associated with each of the six activities just mentioned (Sinclair et al., 2021). To obtain an estimate of actual risk, the researchers used the number of active COVID-19 cases in the county where each participant lived on the day that the participant completed the survey, and then converted that number to a probability that at least one person in a hypothetical gathering of 10 individuals would be infected with the virus that causes COVID-19. The researchers reasoned that if people have a reasonably accurate assessment of COVID-19-related risk, there should be a positive correlation between participants' subjective risk perceptions and the actual risk in their county of residence. However, they found no correlation between perceived and actual risk, with a general tendency for participants to underestimate actual risk. In addition, the researchers asked participants about their willingness to engage in risky activities, and found that this, too, was uncorrelated with

actual risk. In light of our discussion of biases in judgement and decision making, these findings should not be too surprising, because subjective perception of risk is influenced by some of the same processes that result in decision-making errors, such as the availability heuristic (Lunn et al., 2020). But these findings are nonetheless disturbing, because if people don't accurately perceive risk, they may engage in overly risky activities, or refrain from engaging in activities that aren't that risky or are useful in reducing risk, such as social distancing. The findings also raise an important question: Can anything be done to improve the accuracy of risk assessments?

Sinclair and colleagues designed an intervention to increase the alignment between perceived and actual risk that involves an imagination exercise where participants play out in their mind's eye a scenario related to COVID-19. In the Memory chapter, you learned that people draw on episodic memory to imagine or simulate future experiences, a process known as *episodic simulation* (Schacter et al., 2008). Previous studies had revealed that engaging in episodic simulation can impact subsequent decision making. For example, episodic simulations focused on future health goals helped obese individuals focus dietary decisions away from immediate food rewards and on health-related outcomes, resulting in consumption of fewer calories (O'Neill et al., 2016). Sinclair and colleagues examined whether episodic simulation of a COVID-19 scenario, combined with facts about the actual risk of COVID-19 in their area, could help people to better align perceived and actual risk.

To assess the intervention, the researchers recruited a new nationally representative online sample of U.S. residents. In a

baseline session, they assessed participants' perceived risk of engaging in 15 potentially risky COVID-19-related behaviours. Next, they divided the sample into separate groups, each given a different intervention. In the *personal episodic simulation* group, participants imagined hosting a dinner party where a guest shows COVID-19 symptoms, leaves the dinner party, and later confirms going to the hospital with a COVID-19 diagnosis; finally, participants imagine that they, too, come down with COVID-19 after the dinner party. In the *impersonal episodic simulation* group, participants imagined the same events happening to a fictional character. In the *unrelated episodic simulation* group, participants imagined a story about an animal getting sick after eating. Following each intervention, participants completed a task in which they estimated the risk associated with various activities in their location, and were then given numerical feedback about the actual risk of these activities. Finally, participants completed once again the same risk assessment task that they had done prior to the intervention.

Providing the numerical feedback increased the alignment between perceived and actual risk. Importantly, the amount of learning about actual risk from the numerical feedback was significantly enhanced by both the personal and impersonal episodic simulation interventions, but not by the unrelated simulation. These results highlight that pairing a situationally relevant episodic simulation with numerical feedback about actual risk can be an effective strategy for better aligning perceived and actual risk perception related to the COVID-19 pandemic, and also suggest possible avenues for improving risk assessment in other situations where perceived and actual risk are misaligned.

A Perceived Risk Rating

Rate how risky it is to do each of the following activities in your current location.

- Picking up takeout food
- Grocery shopping indoors, wearing a mask
- Dining indoors at a restaurant
- Going to an indoor nightclub
  ... etc. (15 items)

B Episodic Simulation

In the next part of the study, you will imagine an event that could happen in your own life.

- Visualize a dinner party
- A guest shows COVID-19 symptoms, then later confirms a diagnosis and goes to the hospital
- The host informs the other guests, then also falls ill

C Risk Estimation

Think about a hypothetical event in your location. Try to guess the probability that *at least one* person is infected with COVID-19.

Estimate the probability (out of 100%) that in a **group of 25 people**, someone is infected.

Impossible ———————— Definitely
0 10 20 30 40 50 60 70 80 90 100

D Feedback

Next, we'll give you feedback about each of your predictions.

For an event in your location with **25 people,** you guessed that there was a **19% chance** that at least one person was infected.

The actual risk probability is **33%.**

PAIRING FACTS WITH IMAGINED CONSEQUENCES IMPROVES PANDEMIC-RELATED RISK PERCEPTION ALYSSA H. SINCLAIR, SHABNAM HAKIMI, MATTHEW L. STANLEY, R. ALISON ADCOCK, GREGORY R. SAMANEZ-LARKIN PROCEEDINGS OF THE NATIONAL ACADEMY OF SCIENCES AUG 2021, 118 (32) E2100970118; DOI:10.1073/PNAS.2100970118.

Problem Solving: Working It Out

Learning Outcomes

WHAT YOU NEED TO KNOW

- Compare the means–ends analysis and analogical problem-solving approaches.

- Explain the factors that lead to, or inhibit, creativity and insight.

Even though it may not be easy to put together this model, having instructions for assembly makes it a well-defined problem.

You have a problem when you find yourself in a place where you don't want to be. In such circumstances, you try to find a way to change the situation so that you end up in a situation you *do* want. Let's say that it's the night before a test, and you are trying to study but just can't settle down and focus on the material. This is a situation you don't want, so you try to think of ways to help yourself focus. You might begin with the material that most interests you, or provide yourself with rewards, such as a music break or a trip to the refrigerator. If these activities enable you to get down to work, your problem is solved.

Two major types of problems complicate our daily lives. The first and most frequent is the *ill-defined problem,* one that does not have a clear goal or well-defined path(s) to a solution. Your study block is an ill-defined problem: Your goal isn't clearly defined (i.e., somehow get focused), and the solution path for achieving the goal is even less clear (i.e., there are many ways to gain focus). Most everyday problems (being a better person, finding that special someone, achieving success) are ill defined. In contrast, a *well-defined problem* is one with clearly specified goals and clearly defined solution paths. Examples include following a clear set of directions to get to school, solving simple algebra problems, or playing a game of chess.

Means–Ends Analysis

In 1945, the German psychologist Karl Duncker reported some important studies of the problem-solving process. He presented people with ill-defined problems and asked them to "think aloud" while solving them (Duncker, 1945). On the basis of what people said about how they solve problems, Duncker described problem solving in terms of **means–ends analysis,** *a process of searching for the means or steps to reduce the differences between the current situation and the desired goal.* This process usually took the following steps:

1. Analyze the goal state (i.e., the desired outcome you want to attain).
2. Analyze the current state (i.e., your starting point, or the current situation).
3. List the differences between the current state and the goal state.
4. Reduce the list of differences by
   a. Direct means (a procedure that solves the problem without intermediate steps).
   b. Generating a subgoal (an intermediate step on the way to solving the problem).
   c. Finding a similar problem that has a known solution.

Consider, for example, one of Duncker's problems:

A patient has an inoperable tumour in his abdomen. The tumour is inoperable because it is surrounded by healthy but fragile tissue that would be severely damaged during surgery. How can the patient be saved?

The *goal state* is a patient without the tumour and with undamaged surrounding tissue. The *current state* is a patient with an inoperable tumour surrounded by fragile tissue. The *difference* between these two states is the tumour. A *direct-means solution* would be to destroy the tumour with X-rays, but the required X-ray dose would destroy the fragile surrounding tissue and possibly kill the patient. A *subgoal* would be to modify the X-ray machine to deliver a weaker dose. After this subgoal is achieved, a direct-means solution could be to deliver the weaker dose to the patient's abdomen. But this solution won't work either: The weaker dose wouldn't damage the healthy tissue but also wouldn't kill the tumour. So, what to do? Find a similar problem that has a known solution. Let's see how this can be done.

means–ends analysis A process of searching for the means or steps to reduce differences between the current situation and the desired goal.

SERGEY RYZHOV/SHUTTERSTOCK

Analogical Problem Solving

When we engage in **analogical problem solving,** we attempt to *solve a problem by finding a similar problem with a known solution and applying that solution to the current problem.* Consider the following story:

> An island surrounded by bridges is the site of an enemy fortress. The massive fortification is so strongly defended that only a very large army could capture it. Unfortunately, the bridges would collapse under the weight of such a huge force. So a clever general divides the army into several smaller units and sends the units over different bridges, timing the crossings so that the many streams of soldiers converge on the fortress at the same time, and the fortress is taken.

Does this story suggest a solution to the tumour problem? It should. Removing a tumour and attacking a fortress are very different problems, but the two problems are analogous because they share a common structure: The *goal state* is a conquered fortress with undamaged surrounding bridges. The *current state* is an occupied fortress surrounded by fragile bridges. The *difference* between the two states is the occupying enemy. The *solution* is to divide the required force into smaller units that are light enough to spare the fragile bridges and send them down the bridges simultaneously so that they converge on the fortress. The combined units will form an army strong enough to take the fortress (see **FIGURE 9.12**).

This analogous problem of the island fortress suggests the following direct-means solution to the tumour problem:

> Surround the patient with X-ray machines and simultaneously send weaker doses that converge on the tumour. The combined strength of the weaker X-ray doses will be sufficient to destroy the tumour, but the individual doses will be weak enough to spare the surrounding healthy tissue.

Why was the fortress problem so ineffective by itself? Problem solving is strongly affected by superficial similarities between problems, and the relationship between the tumour and fortress problems lies deep in their structure (Catrambone, 2002).

analogical problem solving
The process of solving a problem by finding a similar problem with a known solution and applying that solution to the current problem.

Figure 9.12
Analogical Problem Solving Just as smaller, lighter battalions can reach the fortress without damaging the bridges, many small X-ray doses can destroy the tumour without harming the delicate surrounding tissue. In both cases, the additive strength achieves the objective. Did this solution occur to you after reading the fortress story? In studies that have used the tumour problem, only 10% of participants spontaneously generated the correct solution. This percentage rose to 30% if participants read the island fortress problem or another analogous story. However, the success rate climbed dramatically to 75% among participants who had a chance to read more than one analogous problem or were given a deliberate hint to use the solution to the fortress story (Gick & Holyoak, 1980).

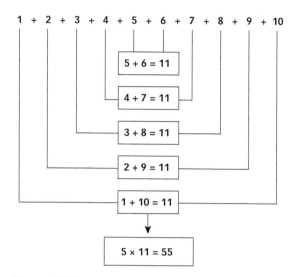

Figure 9.13

Genius and Insight Young Friedrich Gauss imagined the scheme shown here and quickly reduced a laborious addition problem to an easy multiplication task. Gauss's early insight later led him to realize an intriguing truth: This simple solution generalizes to number series of any length (information from Wertheimer, 1945/1982).

Coherent	Incoherent
Playing	Still
Credit	Pages
Report	Music
Blank	Light
White	Folk
Lines	Head
Ticket	Town
Shop	Root
Broker	Car
Magic	House
Plush	Lion
Floor	Butter
Base	Swan
Snow	Army
Dance	Mask
Gold	Noise
Stool	Foam
Tender	Shade

INFORMATION FROM BOWERS ET AL., 1990.

Figure 9.14

Insightful Solutions Are Really Incremental Participants were asked to find a fourth word that was associated with the other three words in each series. Even if they couldn't find a solution, they could reliably choose which series of three words were solvable and which were not. Try to solve these. See page 362 for answers.

Creativity and Insight

Analogical problem solving shows us that successfully solving a problem often depends on learning the principles that underlie a particular type of problem and also that solving lots of problems improves our ability to recognize certain problem types and generate effective solutions. Some problem solving, however, seems to involve brilliant flashes of insight and creative solutions that have never before been tried. Creative and insightful solutions often rely on restructuring a problem so that it turns into a problem you already know how to solve (Cummins, 2012).

Genius and Insight

Consider the exceptional mind of the mathematician Friedrich Gauss (1777–1855). One day, Gauss's elementary schoolteacher asked the class to add up the numbers 1 through 10. While his classmates laboriously worked their sums, Gauss had a flash of insight that caused the answer to occur to him immediately. Gauss imagined the numbers 1 through 10 as weights lined up on a balance beam, as shown in **FIGURE 9.13**. Starting at the left, each "weight" increases by 1. For the beam to balance, each weight on the left must be paired with a weight on the right. You can see this by starting at the middle and noticing that $5 + 6 = 11$, then moving outward, $4 + 7 = 11$, $3 + 8 = 11$, and so on. This produces five number pairs that add up to 11. Now the problem is easy: multiply. Gauss's genius lay in restructuring the problem in a way that allowed him to notice a very simple and elegant solution to an otherwise tedious task—a procedure, by the way, that generalizes to series of any length.

According to Gestalt psychologists, insights such as these reflect a spontaneous restructuring of a problem. A sudden flash of insight contrasts with non-insight, incremental problem-solving procedures whereby one gradually gets closer and closer to a solution. Early researchers studying insight found that people were more likely to solve a non-insight problem if they felt they were gradually getting "warmer" (incrementally closer to the solution). But whether someone felt "warm" did not predict the likelihood of their solving an insight problem (Metcalfe & Wiebe, 1987). The solution for an insight problem seemed to appear out of the blue, regardless of what the participant felt.

Later research suggested that unconscious processes contribute to performance on insight problem-solving tasks (Bowers et al., 1990). In one study, research participants were shown paired, three-word series like those in **FIGURE 9.14** and asked to find a fourth word that was associated with the three words in each series. However, only one series in each pair had a common associate. Solvable series were termed *coherent*, whereas those with no solution were called *incoherent*.

Even if participants couldn't find a solution, they could reliably decide, more than by chance alone, which of the pairs was coherent. However, if insightful solutions only occur in a sudden, all-or-nothing manner, their performance should have been no better than chance. Thus, the findings suggest that insight problem solving may be impacted by processing that occurs outside of conscious awareness. The process works something like this: The pattern of clues that constitute a problem unconsciously activates relevant information in memory. Activation then spreads through the memory network, recruiting additional relevant information (Bowers et al., 1990). When sufficient information has been activated, it crosses the threshold of awareness, and we experience a sudden flash of insight into the problem's solution.

Finding a connection between the words *strawberry* and *traffic* might take some time, even for someone motivated to figure out how they are related. But if the word *strawberry* activates *jam* in long-term memory (see the Memory chapter), and the activation spreads from *strawberry* to *traffic*, the solution to the puzzle may suddenly spring into awareness without the thinker's knowing how it got there.

Sudden Insight and the Brain

The "aha!" moment that accompanies a sudden flash of insight highlights that solving a problem based on insight *feels* radically different from solving it through step-by-step analysis or trial and error. This difference in subjective experience suggests that something different is going on in the brain when we solve a problem using insight instead of analytic strategies (Kounios & Beeman, 2009).

To examine brain activity associated with insight, researchers used a procedure called *compound remote associates* that is similar in some respects to the three-word problems displayed in Figure 9.14. Each compound remote associates problem consists of three words, such as *crab, pine*, and *sauce*. Sometimes people solve these problems with a flash of insight: The solution word (*apple!*) suddenly pops into their minds, seemingly out of nowhere. Other times, people solve the problem by using analytic strategies that involve trying out different alternatives by generating a compound word for *crab* and then assessing whether that word fits *pine* and *sauce*. *Crabgrass* works, but *grass* doesn't work with *pine* and *sauce*. *Crabapple*? Problem solved.

Participants are instructed to press a button the moment a solution comes to mind, then describe whether they arrived at the solution via insight or through an analytic strategy. In an initial study, researchers used the electroencephalograph (EEG; see the Neuroscience and Behaviour chapter) to measure brain electrical activity as participants attempted to solve the problems. What they observed was striking: Beginning about one-third of a second before participants came up with a solution, there was a sudden and dramatic burst of high-frequency electrical activity (40 cycles per second, or gamma band) for problems solved via insight, but not for problems solved via analytic strategies (Jung-Beeman et al., 2004). This activity was centred over the front part of the right temporal lobe, slightly above the right ear. When the researchers performed a similar study using fMRI to measure brain activity, they found that this right temporal area was the only region in the entire brain that showed greater activity for insight solutions than for solutions based on analytic strategies.

The great French scientist Louis Pasteur once stated "Le hasard ne favorise que les esprits préparés" ("Chance favours only the prepared mind."). Inspired by this observation, researchers asked whether brain activity occurring just before presentation of a problem influenced whether that problem was solved via insight or analytic strategies (Kounios et al., 2006). It did. In the moments before a problem was solved with an insight solution, there was increased activity deep in the frontal lobes, in a part of the brain known as the anterior cingulate, which controls cognitive processes, such as the ability to switch attention from one thing to another. The researchers suggested that this increased activity in the anterior cingulate enabled participants to attend to and detect associations that were only weakly activated, perhaps at a subconscious level, and that facilitated sudden insight.

The results of these studies suggest that the familiar image of a lightbulb turning on in your head when you experience an "aha!" moment is on the mark. Those moments are accompanied by something like an electrical power surge in the brain, and the increasing amount of research on creative insight and the brain (Beaty et al., 2016; Kounios & Beeman, 2015) should tell us much more about how to turn on the mental lightbulb and keep it burning bright.

Functional Fixedness

Sudden insights occur relatively infrequently. One reason for their rarity is that problem solving (like decision making) suffers from framing effects. In problem solving, framing tends to limit the types of solutions that occur to us. **Functional fixedness**—*the tendency to perceive the functions of objects as unchanging*—is a process that constricts our thinking. Look at **FIGURES 9.15** and **9.16** and see if you can solve the problems before reading on. In Figure 9.15, your task is to illuminate a dark room using the following objects: some thumbtacks, a box of matches, and a candle. In Figure 9.16, your task is to

functional fixedness The tendency to perceive the functions of objects as unchanging.

Figure 9.15
Functional Fixedness and the Candle Problem How can you use these objects—a box of matches, thumbtacks, and a candle—to mount the candle on the wall so that it illuminates the room? Give this problem some thought before you check the answer in Figure 9.18 on page 364.

Figure 9.16
Functional Fixedness and the String Problem The strings hanging from hooks on either side of the ceiling are long enough to be tied together, but they are positioned too far apart to reach one while holding on to the other. Using the tools shown on the table (nails, matches, and a hammer), how can you accomplish the task? Compare your answer with that in Figure 9.19 on page 364.

Figure 9.17
The Nine-Dot Problem Connect all nine dots with four straight lines without lifting your pencil from the paper. Compare your answer with those in Figure 9.20 on page 364.

Answers to Figure 9.14
Solutions:
Card, paper, pawn, carpet, ball, bar

use the items on the table to find a way to hold on to a string hanging from the ceiling and at the same time reach a second string that is too far away to grasp.

Difficulty with solving these problems derives from our tendency to think of the objects only in terms of their normal, typical, or "fixed" functions. We don't think to use the matchbox for a candleholder because boxes typically hold matches, not candles. Similarly, using the hammer as a pendulum weight doesn't spring to mind because hammers are typically used to pound things. Did functional fixedness prevent you from solving these problems? (The solutions are shown in **FIGURES 9.18** and **9.19**.)

Sometimes framing limits our ability to generate a solution. Before reading on, look at **FIGURE 9.17**. Without lifting your pencil from the page, try to connect all nine dots with only four straight lines. To solve this problem, you must allow the lines you draw to extend outside the imaginary box that surrounds the dots (see **FIGURE 9.20**). This constraint resides not in the problem but in the mind of the problem solver (Kershaw & Ohlsson, 2004). Despite the apparent sudden flash of insight that seems to yield a solution to problems of this type, research indicates that the thought processes people apply when solving even this type of insight problem are best described as an incremental, means–ends analysis (MacGregor et al., 2001).

Reasoning: Truth and Validity

Learning Outcome

WHAT YOU NEED TO KNOW

• Explain the distinction between truth and validity in reasoning, as well as how it links to belief biases, illusions of truth, and the illusion of explanatory depth in the lab and in everyday life.

Reasoning is *a mental activity that consists of organizing information or beliefs into a series of steps in order to reach conclusions.* We rely on logic to assess the results of the reasoning process. Logic is a system of rules that specifies which conclusions follow from a set of statements. To put it another way, if you know that a given set of statements is true, logic will tell you which other statements *must* also be true. If the statement "Jack and Jill went up the hill" is true, then according to the rules of logic, the statement "Jill went up the hill" must also be true. Accepting the truth of the first statement while denying the truth of the second statement would be a contradiction. Logic is a tool for evaluating reasoning, but it should not be confused with the process of reasoning itself. Equating logic and reasoning would be like equating carpenter's tools (logic) with building a house (reasoning).

These considerations highlight that there is a fundamental distinction in reasoning between the *truth* of statements and the *validity* of an argument. If statements are true and an argument is valid (i.e., logical), then sound conclusions will be reached. But even if statements are true, a faulty argument will produce invalid conclusions. For example, the statements that "All football players are athletes" and "LeBron James is an athlete" are true, but the conclusion that "LeBron James is a football player" is not true because the argument relating the two statements is invalid.

Belief Bias

The distinction between truth and validity can help us understand why people are sometimes prone to failures in reasoning, as illustrated by **belief bias,** *the idea that people's judgements about whether to accept conclusions depend more on how believable the conclusions are than on whether the arguments are logically valid* (Evans et al., 1983). For example, **syllogistic reasoning** assesses *whether a conclusion follows from two statements that are assumed to be true,* as in the LeBron James example. Consider the two following syllogisms, evaluate the argument, and ask yourself whether or not the conclusions must be true if the statements are true:

Syllogism 1

Statement 1: No cigarettes are inexpensive.

Statement 2: Some addictive things are inexpensive.

Conclusion: Some addictive things are not cigarettes.

Syllogism 2

Statement 1: No addictive things are inexpensive.

Statement 2: Some cigarettes are inexpensive.

Conclusion: Some cigarettes are not addictive.

If you're like most people, you probably concluded that the argument is valid in Syllogism 1 but flawed in Syllogism 2. Indeed, researchers found that nearly 100% of participants accepted the first conclusion as valid, but fewer than half accepted the second (Evans et al., 1983). But notice that the syllogisms are in exactly the same form. This form of syllogism is valid, so both conclusions are valid given that the two statements are true. Evidently, the believability of the conclusions influences people's judgements.

These findings suggest that it is difficult for people to inhibit their preexisting knowledge and beliefs when reasoning about syllogisms. Children and older adults are known to have difficulties inhibiting knowledge and beliefs that are activated by a task even when they are not needed for performing the task (Bédard et al., 2002; Christ et al., 2001). Consistent with a role for inhibitory processing in overcoming belief bias, 12-year-old children and older adults (65+ years) performed worse than young adults (20 years old) when they reasoned about syllogisms that require inhibition of preexisting beliefs to come to a correct conclusion; on the other hand, there was no effect of age on reasoning about syllogisms that do not require such inhibitory processing (De Neys & Van Gelder, 2009).

Research using fMRI provides additional insights into how preexisting knowledge and inhibitory processes impact belief biases on reasoning tasks (Goel & Dolan, 2003; Goel, 2007). In *belief-laden* trials, participants' brains were scanned while they reasoned about syllogisms that could be influenced by knowledge that affected the believability of the conclusions. In *belief-neutral* trials, syllogisms contained obscure terms whose meaning was unknown to participants, as in the following example:

Syllogism 3

Statement 1: No codes are highly complex.

Statement 2: Some quipu are highly complex.

Conclusion: No quipu are codes.

Battling the causes of climate change could be undermined by belief bias.

reasoning A mental activity that consists of organizing information or beliefs into a series of steps in order to reach conclusions.

belief bias The idea that people's judgements about whether to accept conclusions depend more on how believable the conclusions are than on whether the arguments are logically valid.

syllogistic reasoning Determining whether a conclusion follows from two statements that are assumed to be true.

Figure 9.18
The Solution to the Candle Problem What makes this problem difficult is that the usual function of the box (to hold matches) interferes with recognizing that it can be tacked to the wall to serve as a candleholder.

Figure 9.19
The Solution to the String Problem The usual function of the hammer (to pound things) interferes with recognizing that it can also serve as a weighted pendulum to swing the string into the person's grasp.

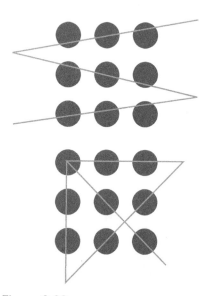

Figure 9.20
Two Solutions to the Nine-Dot Problem Solving this problem requires "thinking outside the box"—that is, going outside the imaginary box implied by the dot arrangement. The limiting box isn't really there; it is imposed by the problem solver's perceptual set.

illusory truth effect An error in reasoning that occurs when repeated exposure to a statement increases the likelihood that people will judge that statement to be true.

Belief-neutral reasoning activated different brain regions than did belief-laden reasoning. Activity in a part of the left temporal lobe that's involved in retrieving and selecting facts from long-term memory increased during belief-laden reasoning. In contrast, during belief-neutral reasoning, that part of the brain showed little activity while parts of the parietal lobe that are involved in mathematical reasoning and spatial representation showed greater activity. Critically, in belief-laden reasoning trials in which conclusions conflicted with people's preexisting knowledge (as in Syllogism 2 above), the right prefrontal cortex—a region known to be involved in inhibitory processing—showed increased activity. This finding is consistent with the evidence from children and older adults that indicates that inhibitory processing is critically important for resisting belief bias.

Although the evidence we've considered regarding belief bias comes from controlled laboratory tasks, the phenomenon has important real-world implications. For example, despite a near-universal scientific consensus that climate change is a genuine phenomenon, a significant minority of the population (around 20% in the United States) deny the existence of climate change (Lewandowsky et al., 2013). Denial of climate change, in turn, is linked to a strong belief in free markets (whose operation could be threatened by steps taken to counter climate change) and in conspiracy theories (e.g., the Apollo moon landing never happened—it was staged in a Hollywood film studio). These findings highlight that belief biases can impact assessment of critically important scientific findings.

The Illusion of Truth

People sometimes are misled regarding the truth of a statement because they reason about truth on the basis of influences other than a valid argument. This is illustrated by the **illusory truth effect,** *an error in reasoning that occurs when repeated exposure to a statement increases the likelihood that people will judge the statement to be true* (Hasher et al., 1977). Repeated exposure increases the familiarity of a statement, which is mistakenly accepted as evidence that the statement is true (Begg et al., 1992; Fazio et al., 2015).

A striking everyday example of the illusory truth effect comes from recent research on "fake news"—made-up news stories that are presented as factual. Fake news became a topic of intense concern during the 2016 presidential election because planted fake stories appeared frequently on social media sites such as Facebook and attracted at least as much attention as did real news stories (Silverman et al., 2016). Researchers Pennycook and colleagues (2018) asked participants to judge the accuracy of fake news stories that had actually been posted on Facebook. They found that just a single prior exposure to one of these stories increased participants' estimates of their accuracy, even when they were implausible and flagged as contested by fact checkers. The only stories that were not affected by this illusory truth effect were completely implausible ones that could be easily judged as false (e.g., "The Earth is a perfect square"). Here, we can see the danger of assessing truth without relying on a valid argument: Simply repeating a statement does not make it so.

More recent research indicates that susceptibility to sharing fake news and misinformation on social media often occurs because people do not focus enough attention on whether the information is accurate (Pennycook et al., 2021). However, reminders to focus on accuracy can significantly reduce sharing of fake political headlines (Pennycook et al., 2021) and misinformation about COVID-19 (Pennycook et al., 2020b). Related research shows that providing a fact check (i.e., a tag that a headline is true or false) just after people see a real or fake news headline significantly boosts their ability to distinguish between the two one week later, and is more effective than presenting a fact check before people see a headline or at the same time they see the headline—perhaps because providing the fact check right after seeing a headline is particularly memorable (Brashier et al., 2021). The spread of fake news and misinformation is especially rampant on social media, so strategies for countering the disruptive and dangerous transmissions that occur online are urgently needed (see Other Voices: The Right Way to Fight Fake News).

The Illusion of Explanatory Depth

Reasoning and truth assessment may also be undermined because people are sometimes prone to the **illusion of explanatory depth,** *an illusion that occurs when people overestimate the depth of their understanding.* Researchers discovered this illusion in studies where participants initially rated the depth of their understanding regarding the workings of various everyday objects (e.g., zippers, flush toilets, sewing machines) or procedures (e.g., how to make chocolate cookies from scratch), then tried to provide detailed, step-by-step explanations, viewed expert descriptions and diagrams, and after that re-rated their depth of understanding. The second set of ratings was significantly lower than the first. Attempting to explain the workings of the objects and procedures, and then seeing the much more detailed expert description, led participants to realize that they had greatly overestimated the depth of their understanding (Rozenblit & Keil, 2002).

This illusion has potentially broad relevance to important everyday issues because research has also revealed that it applies to a problem of great contemporary importance: political extremism (Sloman & Fernbach, 2017). Many pressing issues of our times, such as climate change and health-related policies, often generate extreme views at either end of the political spectrum. In one study, researchers asked whether political views become polarized because people think that they understand the relevant policies in greater depth than they actually do (Fernbach et al., 2013). The researchers asked American participants to rate their positions regarding six political policies (e.g., sanctions on Iran for its nuclear program, or single-payer health care system) on a seven-point scale ranging from strongly against to strongly in favour. Next, the participants rated their understanding of each of the six policies. Participants were then asked to generate detailed explanations of two of the six policies, followed in each case by a second set of ratings concerning their positions and their level of understanding of all the policies. After attempting to generate detailed explanations, participants provided lower ratings of understanding and less extreme positions concerning all six policies than they had expressed previously. Furthermore, those participants who exhibited the largest decreases in their pre- versus post-explanation understanding ratings also exhibited the greatest moderation of their positions as a result of explaining them.

Although it is troubling that extreme political views are enabled, at least in part, by an illusion of explanatory depth, it is also encouraging that once people realize that they don't understand the relevant policy issues in as much depth as they had thought, their views moderate.

illusion of explanatory depth
An illusion that occurs when people overestimate the depth of their understanding.

Other Voices : The Right Way to Fight Fake News

The spread of misinformation is now widely recognized as a significant problem for society—and the dangers of misinformation have been particularly clear during the COVID-19 pandemic. In our discussion of the illusion of truth, we briefly sketched some ways to reduce the spread of misinformation. Gordon Pennycook is assistant professor at the University of Regina, and the lead researcher behind much of the work discussed. Here, he makes the case that social media companies must use scientific methods to verify that the strategies introduced to reduce the spread of fake news actually work.

Social media companies have been under tremendous pressure since the 2016 presidential election to do something—anything—about the proliferation of misinformation on their platforms.

Companies like Facebook and YouTube have responded by applying anti-fake-news strategies that seem as if they would be effective. As a public-relations move, this is smart: The companies demonstrate that they are willing to take action, and the policies sound reasonable to the public.

But just because a strategy sounds reasonable doesn't mean it works. Although the platforms are making some progress in their fight against misinformation, recent research by us and other scholars suggests that many of their tactics may be ineffective—and can even make matters worse, leading to confusion, not clarity, about the truth. Social media companies need to empirically investigate whether the concerns raised in these experiments are relevant to how their users are processing information on their platforms.

One strategy that platforms have used is to provide more information about the news' source. YouTube has "information panels" that tell users when content was produced by government-funded organizations, and Facebook has a "context" option that provides background information for the sources of articles in its News Feed. This sort of tactic makes intuitive sense because well-established mainstream news sources, though far from perfect, have higher editing and reporting standards than, say, obscure websites that produce fabricated content with no author attribution.

But recent research of ours raises questions about the effectiveness of this approach. We conducted a series of experiments with nearly 7,000 Americans and found that emphasizing sources had virtually no impact on whether people believed news headlines or considered sharing them (Dias et al., 2020)

People in these experiments were shown a series of headlines that had circulated widely on social media—some of which came from mainstream outlets such as NPR and some from disreputable fringe outlets like the now-defunct newsbreakshere.com. Some participants were provided no information about the publishers, others were shown the domain of the publisher's website, and still others were shown a large banner with the publisher's logo. Perhaps surprisingly, providing the additional information did not make people much less likely to believe misinformation.

. . .

Consider another anti-misinformation tactic used by social media platforms: enlisting professional fact checkers to identify false content. An early Facebook strategy for combating fake news, for example, was to flag false headlines with a "disputed by third-party fact checkers" warning. . . .

UNIVERSITY OF REGINA PHOTO DEPARTMENT

Gordon Pennycook is assistant professor in the Department of Psychology, and in the Hill and Levene Schools of Business, at the University of Regina in Saskatchewan.

Unfortunately, this is also an example of an intuitive approach that research suggests may not work as expected. We and our colleagues conducted experiments that found that though people were less likely to believe and share headlines that had been labeled false—common sense was right about that—people also sometimes mistook the absence of a warning label to mean that the false headlines may have been verified by fact checkers (Pennycook et al, 2020). This is a problem because only a small percentage of false headlines ever get checked and marked: Fact-checking is a painstaking, time-consuming process, whereas troll farms and internet bots can create and distribute misinformation with alarming speed.

In other words, a system of sparsely supplied warnings could be less helpful than a system of no warnings, since the former can seem to imply that anything without a warning is true.

Another seemingly promising strategy is to provide general warnings about the existence of fake news and to offer tips about spotting misinformation. In 2017, Facebook began a public-relations campaign along those lines that included billboards and subway signage informing people that "Fake news is not your friend." Here, too, research suggests that such tactics can be counterproductive, since they often reduce confidence in all news (Clayton et al, 2020), regardless of veracity (which, as it happens, is the goal of many disinformation campaigns).

Of course, sometimes ideas that make intuitive sense do work. Getting people to slow down and engage in more critical thinking, for example, has been shown to reduce belief in fake news and to reduce the sharing of it (Bago et al, 2020).

Likewise, sometimes ideas that seem terrible turn out to be effective. In 2018, Facebook proposed surveying its users about how much they trusted various news sources and then using that information to selectively promote content from sources rated as trustworthy. That proposal was greeted with widespread condemnation and ridicule, but empirical tests that we conducted indicated that this crowdsourcing approach was highly effective at identifying sources of misinformation (Pennycook & Rand, 2019).

The obvious conclusion to draw from all this evidence is that social media platforms should rigorously test their ideas for combating fake news and not just rely on common sense or intuition about what will work. . . .

Put Pennycook's advice into action in your own life by keeping in mind the lessons you've learned about why people are prone to belief biases and the illusions of truth and ways to combat false beliefs due to misinformation.

Chapter Review

Language and Communication: From Rules to Meaning

- Human language is characterized by a complex organization—from phonemes to morphemes to phrases and finally to sentences.

- Children can distinguish between all contrasting sounds of human language, but they lose that ability within the first year. Vocal babbling occurs at about 4 to 6 months, and first words are uttered or signed by 10 to 12 months. Sentences emerge around 24 months.

- Children acquire grammatical rules in development, even without being taught explicitly.

- The behaviourist explanation for language learning is based on operant conditioning, whereas nativists hold that humans are biologically predisposed to process language. Interactionists explain it as both a biological and a social process.

Language and the Brain

- Our abilities to produce and comprehend language depend on distinct but interacting regions of the brain.

- Broca's area plays a role in language production and Wernicke's area plays a role in comprehension, but recent research has highlighted that other brain regions make important contributions to these functions.

- Bilingual and monolingual children show similar rates of language development. Some bilingual children show greater executive control capacities, such as the ability to prioritize information and flexibly focus attention, but this finding has proven difficult to replicate in recent research. Bilinguals do tend to have a later onset of Alzheimer's disease.

- Nonhuman primates can learn new vocabulary and construct simple sentences, but there are significant limitations on the size of their vocabularies and the grammatical complexity they can handle.

Language and Thought: How Are They Related?

- The linguistic relativity hypothesis maintains that language shapes the nature of thought.

- Recent studies on colour processing point to an influence of language on thought.

- However, either language or thought may be impaired while the other is not, suggesting that language and thought are to some extent separate.

Concepts and Categories: How We Think

- We organize knowledge about objects, events, or other stimuli by creating concepts, prototypes, and exemplars.

- We acquire concepts using processes suggested by two theories: Prototype theory uses the most typical member of a category to assess new items; exemplar theory states that we compare new items with stored memories of other members of the category.

- Neuroimaging studies have shown that prototypes and exemplars are processed in different parts of the brain.

- Studies of people with cognitive and visual deficits have shown that the brain organizes concepts into distinct categories, such as living things and human-made things; the studies also suggest that visual experience is not necessary for the development of such categories.

Decision Making: Rational and Otherwise

- Human decision making often departs from a completely rational process. The mistakes that accompany this departure tell us a lot about how the human mind works.

- The values we place on outcomes weigh so heavily in our judgements that they sometimes overshadow objective evidence. When people are asked to make probability judgements, they will turn the problem into something they know how to solve, such as judging memory strength, judging similarity to prototypes, or estimating frequencies. This can lead to errors of judgement.

- When a problem fits our mental algorithms, we show considerable skill at making appropriate judgements. In making a judgement about the probability of an event, performance can vary dramatically.

- Because we feel that avoiding losses is more important than achieving gains, framing effects can affect our choices. Emotional information also strongly influences our decision making, even when we are not aware of it. Although this influence can lead us astray, it often is crucial for making decisions in everyday life.

- The prefrontal cortex plays an important role in decision making, and patients with prefrontal damage make more risky decisions than do individuals without brain damage.

Problem Solving: Working It Out

- Like concept formation and decision making, problem solving is a process in which new inputs (in this case, problems) are interpreted in terms of old knowledge. Problems may be ill defined or well defined, leading to less obvious or more obvious solutions.

- The solutions we generate depend as much on the organization of our knowledge as on the objective characteristics of the problems we face. Means–ends analysis and analogical problem solving offer pathways to effective solutions, although we often frame things in terms of what we already know and already understand.

- Sometimes, as in the case of functional fixedness, that knowledge can restrict our problem-solving processes, making it difficult to reach solutions that should be easy to find.

Reasoning: Truth and Validity

- A fundamental distinction in human reasoning concerns the *truth* of statements and the *validity* of an argument. The success of human reasoning requires both true statements and valid arguments about them in order to reach sound conclusions.

- Belief bias describes a distortion of judgements about conclusions of arguments, causing people to focus on the believability of the conclusions rather than on the logical connections between the premises. This bias is exaggerated when people fail to inhibit preexisting knowledge and beliefs.

- The illusory truth effect occurs when repeated exposure to a statement increases the likelihood that people will judge the statement to be true, even when it is false.

- The illusion of explanatory depth occurs when people overestimate the depth of their understanding of a process or issue.

- Belief bias, the illusory truth effect, and the illusion of explanatory depth all have potentially important real-world implications, as illustrated by how beliefs impact assessments of climate change, how exposure to fake news stories impacts assessment of their accuracy, and how the illusion of explanatory depth may contribute to political extremism.

Changing Minds

1. You mention to a friend that you've just learned that the primary language we learn can shape the way that we think. Your friend says that people are people everywhere and that this can't be true. What evidence could you describe to support your point?

2. In September 2011, *Wired* magazine ran an article discussing the fourth-down decisions of National Football League coaches. On fourth down, a coach can choose to play aggressively and go for a first down (or even a touchdown), or the coach can settle for a punt or a field goal, which are safer options but result in fewer points than a touchdown. Statistically, the riskier play results in greater point gain, on average, than playing it safe. But in reality, coaches choose the safer plays over 90% of the time. Reading this article, one of your friends is incredulous. "Coaches aren't stupid, and they want to win," he says. "Why would they always make the wrong decision?" Your friend is assuming that humans are rational decision makers. In what ways is your friend wrong? What might be causing the football coaches to make irrational decisions?

3.
Visualizing Data A friend who is studying to be a lawyer says, "I'll present the facts of the case. It won't matter what I say, since facts are facts." Review the DATA and respond to your friend.

Key Terms

language (p. 330)

grammar (p. 330)

phoneme (p. 331)

phonological rules (p. 331)

morphemes (p. 331)

morphological rules (p. 331)

syntactic rules (p. 332)

telegraphic speech (p. 333)

nativist theory (p. 336)

universal grammar (p. 336)

aphasia (p. 339)

linguistic relativity hypothesis (p. 344)

concept (p. 345)

prototype theory (p. 346)

exemplar theory (p. 347)

category-specific deficit (p. 348)

rational choice theory (p. 350)

availability heuristic (p. 351)

heuristic (p. 351)

algorithm (p. 351)

representativeness heuristic (p. 352)

conjunction fallacy (p. 352)

framing effects (p. 353)

sunk-cost fallacy (p. 353)

optimism bias (p. 353)

prospect theory (p. 354)

means–ends analysis (p. 358)

analogical problem solving (p. 359)

functional fixedness (p. 361)

reasoning (p. 362)

belief bias (p. 363)

syllogistic reasoning (p. 363)

illusory truth effect (p. 364)

illusion of explanatory depth (p. 365)

Intelligence

WHEN ANNE MCGARRAH DIED at the age of 57, she had lived more years than she could count. That's because Anne couldn't count at all. Like most people with Williams syndrome, she couldn't add 3 and 7, couldn't make change for a dollar, and couldn't distinguish right from left. Her cognitive ability was so impaired that she was unable to care for herself or hold a full-time job. So what did she do with her time?

- How Can Intelligence Be Measured?
- What Is Intelligence?
- Where Does Intelligence Come From?
- Who Is Most Intelligent?

> I love to read. Biographies, fiction, novels, different articles in newspapers, articles in magazines, just about anything. I just read a book about a young girl—she was born in Scotland—and her family who lived on a farm. . . . I love listening to music. I like a little bit of Beethoven, but I specifically like Mozart and Chopin and Bach. I like the way they develop their music—it's very light, it's very airy, and it's very cheerful music. I find Beethoven depressing. (Finn, 1991, p. 54)

People with Williams syndrome may not be able to tie their own shoes or make change for a dollar, but as Anne's beautiful prose suggests, they often have an unusual flair for language and for music. Williams syndrome is caused by the absence of just a few genes on a single chromosome, and no one knows why this tiny genetic glitch so profoundly impairs people's general cognitive abilities while at the same time gifting them with special talents.

SO HERE'S THE QUESTION: WAS ANNE MCGARRAH INTELLIGENT? That's a tough one. It seems odd to say that someone is intelligent when they can't do simple addition, but it seems equally odd to say that someone is not intelligent when they can tell the difference between baroque counterpoint and 19th-century romanticism. In a world of Albert Einsteins and Homer Simpsons, we'd have no trouble distinguishing the geniuses from the dullards. But ours is a world of people like Anne McGarrah and people like us: people who are sometimes brilliant, often bright, usually competent, and occasionally dimmer than broccoli. So what is this thing called intelligence?

Gabrielle Marion-Rivard, who has Williams syndrome, won the Canadian Screen Award for Best Actress in 2014.

GEORGE PIMENTEL/WIREIMAGE/GETTY IMAGES

More than 25 years ago, a large group of scientific experts came together to answer this question. They concluded that intelligence involves . . .

the ability to reason, plan, solve problems, think abstractly, comprehend complex ideas, learn quickly, and learn from experience. It is not merely book learning, a narrow academic skill, or test-taking smarts. Rather it reflects a broader and deeper capability for comprehending our surroundings—"catching on," "making sense" of things, or "figuring out" what to do. (Gottfredson, 1997, p. 13)

In short, **intelligence** is *the ability to use one's mind to solve novel problems and learn from experience,* and for more than a century, psychologists have been asking four questions about this remarkable ability: *How* can intelligence be measured? *What* exactly is intelligence? *Where* does intelligence come from? *Why* are some people more intelligent than others? As you will see, psychologists now have solid answers to all of these questions.

How Can Intelligence Be Measured?

Learning Outcomes

WHAT YOU NEED TO KNOW

- Define intelligence.
- Explain how and why intelligence tests were developed.
- Explain why intelligence matters.

intelligence The ability to use one's mind to solve novel problems and learn from experience.

Towards the end of the 19th century, France instituted a sweeping set of social reforms that for the first time required all children between the ages of 6 and 13 to attend school. This was nice in theory but difficult in practice because, as it turned out, not all children of the same age were equally prepared to learn. So the government appointed a small group of experts to figure out how mandatory public education might actually work. Some of the experts argued that psychiatrists should examine every French child and that the government should build special schools for the "slow-witted" ones—or better yet, send them to asylums. But one of the experts, a psychologist named Alfred Binet, disagreed. He believed that the government should rely not on the subjective evaluations of parents, teachers, or psychiatrists, but rather, that it should use an objective method to determine the learning capabilities of each child. Those who needed extra help, he argued, should not be put in asylums, but placed in special classrooms alongside their peers (Nicolas et al., 2013).

To make proper placement possible, Binet and colleague Theodore Simon created a series of tasks that "quick" children could perform well and that "slow" children could not. These tasks included solving logic problems, remembering words, copying pictures, distinguishing edible and inedible foods, making rhymes, and answering questions such as "Before deciding something important, what should you do?" Binet and Simon assembled 30 of these tasks into a test that they hoped would measure a child's "aptitude for learning" rather than the child's prior educational achievement. A child's score on this test could be used to estimate that child's "mental level" simply by computing the average test score of many children in different age groups, and then finding the age group whose average test score best matched the test score of the particular child. For example, if 10-year-old Henri's score was about the same as the average test score of all 8-year-old children, then Henri was said to have the mental level of an 8-year-old, and therefore to need remedial education.

The Intelligence Test

About a decade later, the German psychologist William Stern (1914) suggested that a child's mental level was better thought of as the child's *mental age* ("Henri may be 10, but mentally he's 8"), and that the best way to determine whether a child was developing normally was simply to compute the ratio of their mental and physical ages. This metric was called the *intelligence quotient,* which most of us now abbreviate as IQ. In the early days, psychologists computed a specific form of this metric called **ratio IQ,** which is *a metric obtained by dividing a child's mental age by the child's physical age and then multiplying the quotient by 100.* According to this formula, if 10-year-old Marianne's test score is about the same as the average 10-year-old child's test score, then she has a ratio IQ of 100 because $(10/10) \times 100 = 100$. But her twin brother Henri—a 10-year-old child whose test score is about the same as the average 8-year-old child's test score—has a ratio IQ of 80 because $(8/10) \times 100 = 80$.

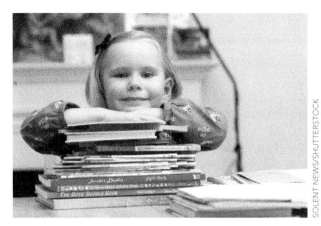

At 4 years old, Heidi Hankins became one of the youngest people ever admitted to Mensa, an organization for people with unusually high IQs. Heidi's IQ is 159—which makes her smarter than 99.99% of her fellow humans.

This computation sounds simple, and it is, but there's a problem with it. Intelligence increases dramatically in the first decade or so of life and then levels off. As you probably know from your own experience, the intellectual difference between a 10-year-old and a 5-year-old is quite dramatic, but the intellectual difference between a 40-year-old and a 35-year-old is not. This fact is a problem for the ratio IQ metric. For example, a 7-year-old who performs as well on an intelligence test as a 14-year-old does will have a whopping ratio IQ score of 200—and that's okay, because any 7-year-old who can do linear algebra is probably pretty smart. But a 20-year-old who performs like a 40-year-old isn't necessarily super smart; and yet, they will also have a ratio IQ of 200, which clearly doesn't make any sense at all.

Psychologists quickly realized that comparing mental age to chronological age works well enough for kids, but not for adults because adults of different ages don't have remarkably different intellectual capacities (Ackerman, 2017). To solve this problem, psychologists began calculating a different metric called **deviation IQ,** which is *a metric obtained by dividing a person's test score by the average test score for people that age and then multiplying the quotient by 100.* So, instead of comparing a person's mental age to their own physical age, the deviation IQ score compares their performance to the performance of others. A 20-year-old who scores the same as the average adult has a deviation IQ of 100. The nice thing about the deviation IQ is that a 20-year-old whose test performance is similar to that of the average 40-year-old is no longer mistakenly labelled a genius, since average performance by 20- and 40-year-olds is quite similar. When you hear people talk about IQ scores today, they are almost always talking about deviation IQ.

Most modern intelligence tests have their roots in the test that Binet and Simon developed more than a century ago. For instance, the *Stanford–Binet Intelligence Scale* is based on Binet and Simon's original test, updated by Stanford University professor Lewis Terman (whom we'll encounter again later in this chapter). The most widely used modern intelligence tests are the *Wechsler Adult Intelligence Scale* (WAIS) and the *Wechsler Intelligence Scale for Children* (WISC), developed by the psychologist David Wechsler, who worked with the U.S. army during World War I to develop tests to screen new recruits. Like Binet and Simon's original test, the WAIS and the WISC measure intelligence by asking people to answer questions and solve problems. Test takers are required to see the similarities and differences between ideas and objects, to draw inferences from evidence, to work out and apply rules, to remember and manipulate material, to construct shapes, to articulate the meaning of words, to recall general knowledge, to explain practical actions in everyday life, to use numbers, to attend to details, and so forth. Some sample problems from the WAIS are shown in **TABLE 10.1**.

ratio IQ A metric obtained by dividing a child's mental age by the child's physical age and then multiplying the quotient by 100.

deviation IQ A metric obtained by dividing a person's test score by the average test score for people that age and then multiplying the quotient by 100.

TABLE 10.1

THE TESTS AND CORE SUBTESTS OF THE WECHSLER ADULT INTELLIGENCE SCALE IV

WAIS-IV Test	Core Subtest	Questions and Tasks
Verbal comprehension test	Vocabulary	The test taker is asked to tell the examiner what certain words mean. For example: *chair* (easy), *hesitant* (medium), and *presumptuous* (hard).
	Similarities	The test taker is asked what 19 pairs of words have in common. For example: In what way are an apple and a pear alike? In what way are a painting and a symphony alike?
	Information	The test taker is asked several general knowledge questions. These cover people, places, and events. For example: How many days are in a week? What is the capital of France? Name three oceans. Who wrote *The Inferno*?
Perceptual reasoning test	Block design	The test taker is shown 2-D patterns made up of red and white squares and triangles and is asked to reproduce these patterns using cubes with red and white faces.
	Matrix reasoning	The test taker is asked to add a missing element to a pattern so that it progresses logically. For example: Which of the four symbols at the bottom goes in the empty cell of the table?
	Visual puzzles	The test taker is asked to complete visual puzzles like this one: "Which three of these pictures go together to make this puzzle?"
Working memory test	Digit span	The test taker is asked to repeat a sequence of numbers. Sequences run from two to nine numbers in length. In the second part of this test, the sequences must be repeated in reversed order. An easy example is to repeat 3-7-4. A harder one is 3-9-1-7-4-5-3-9.
	Arithmetic	The test taker is asked to solve arithmetic problems, progressing from easy to difficult ones.
Processing speed test	Symbol search	The test taker is asked to indicate whether one of a pair of abstract symbols is contained in a list of abstract symbols. There are many of these lists, and the test taker does as many as they can in 2 minutes.
	Coding	The test taker is asked to write down the number that corresponds to a code for a given symbol (e.g., a cross, a circle, and an upside-down T) and does as many as they can in 90 seconds.

Intelligence Matters

The problems on intelligence tests may look like fun and games (perhaps without the fun part), but decades of research show that a person's score on these tests can predict an astonishing variety of important life outcomes (Brown et al., 2021). For instance, one study compared siblings who had significantly different IQs and found that the less intelligent sibling earned roughly half of what the more intelligent sibling earned over the course of their lifetimes (Murray, 2002; see **FIGURE 10.1**). One reason for this is that intelligent people are more patient, better at calculating risk, and better at predicting how other people will act and how they should respond, all of which makes them more successful financially (Burks et al., 2009). But another reason intelligent people earn more money is that they get more education (Deary et al., 2005; Nyborg & Jensen, 2001). Indeed, a person's IQ is a better predictor of the amount of education they will receive than is that person's social class (Deary, 2012; Deary et al., 2005). Intelligent people not only spend more time in school but also perform better when they're there (Roth et al., 2015). The relationship between IQ and performance continues when school ends: Intelligent people perform so much better at their jobs that one pair of researchers concluded that "for hiring employees without previous experience in the job, the most valid measure of future performance and learning is general mental ability" (Schmidt & Hunter, 1998, p. 262).

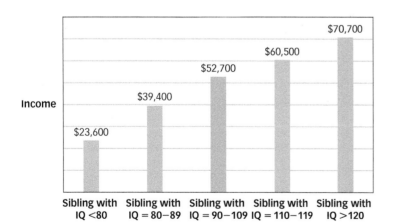

Figure 10.1

Income and Intelligence Among Siblings This graph shows the average annual salary of a person who has an IQ of 90–109 (shown in pink) and of their siblings who have higher or lower IQs (shown in blue). (These incomes are in USD, averaged for the years 1993 and 1995.)

Intelligence is also a good predictor of health and longevity (Calvin et al., 2011; Wraw et al., 2015). In fact, every 15-point increase in a young person's IQ is associated with a 24% decrease in their risk of death from a wide variety of causes, including cardiovascular disease, suicide, homicide, and accidents (Calvin et al., 2011). In part that's because intelligent people are less likely to smoke and drink alcohol and are more likely to exercise and eat well (Batty et al., 2007; Ciarrochi et al., 2012; Weiser et al., 2010), but it's also because intelligent people are more likely to succeed in school—which allows them to get better jobs, which allows them to earn more money, which allows them to avoid illnesses such as cardiovascular disease (Deary et al., 2011; Jokela et al., 2009). Intelligent people are healthier and wealthier, and not surprisingly, they are happier too (Gonzalez-Mule et al., 2017; Nikolaev & McGee, 2016). In short, intelligence tests may look to you like a list of random questions, but a person's ability to answer those questions is a very good predictor of almost everything people value in life (see A World of Difference: Equality in Smartland).

A World of Difference · Equality in Smartland

Being smart and being happy are pretty nice things, so it doesn't seem fair that the people who have a whole lot of one should also have more than their fair share of the other. But (sigh) they do. Smart people have better health, better jobs, and better relationships; so, predictably, they tend to be happier as well. What's true at the individual level is also true at the national level. Scientists have long known that a nation's average IQ scores and average happiness scores are positively correlated: Happy nations have smart citizens and smart nations have happy citizens. Go, Denmark!

But recently, scientists have discovered that the relationship between national happiness and national intelligence is more interesting than anyone had realized. Nikolaev and Salahodjaev (2016) gathered data on the intelligence and happiness of the citizens of 81 countries. As expected, they found a positive correlation between a nation's average IQ and its average happiness. But in addition to calculating the mean of each nation's happiness scores, they also calculated the standard deviation, which (as you know from the Methods in Psychology chapter) measures the dispersion of scores around a mean. Just as the mean of a set of happiness scores provides a rough

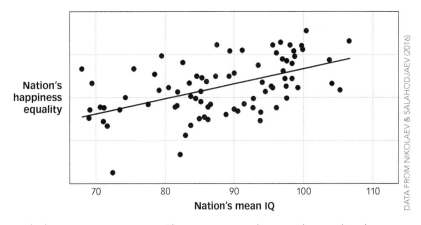

DATA FROM NIKOLAEV & SALAHODJAEV (2016)

Each dot represents a nation. The positive correlation indicates that the smarter a nation is, the more "happiness equality" it has.

index of a nation's happiness, the standard deviation provides a rough index of a nation's "happiness equality." If most citizens are about equally happy, then the standard deviation is low and happiness equality is high. But if many citizens are ecstatic and many are despondent, then the standard deviation is high and happiness equality is low.

When the researchers computed the correlation between IQ and happiness equality, they discovered something that no one had noticed before: Nations with smart citizens do not just have more happiness, they also have more happiness equality (see the accompanying graph). In other words, if two nations have the same average happiness, the smarter one tends to distribute that happiness more equally among its citizens. Correlations must always be interpreted with caution, of course, but this one is intriguing and begs for explanation. One explanation is that intelligent people spread happiness to others. Another explanation is that the social policies that give rise to happiness equality also foster intelligence. Whether either, both, or neither of these explanations turns out to be right, it seems clear that smart people are about as happy as their neighbours.

What Is Intelligence?

Learning Outcomes

WHAT YOU NEED TO KNOW

- Explain how the three-level hierarchy of intelligence confirms both Spearman and Thurstone's conclusions.

- Identify the strengths and weaknesses of the data-based and theory-based approaches to measuring abilities.

- Describe how the concept of intelligence differs across cultures.

Sean Penn is a very talented actor but not a particularly talented writer. So does he or doesn't he have "artistic talent"?

two-factor theory of intelligence
Spearman's theory suggesting that a person's performance on a test is due to a combination of general cognitive ability and specific abilities that are unique to the test.

Sean Penn is, by any measure, a remarkably talented artist, which is why he won Academy Awards for his riveting performances in *Mystic River* (2003) and *Milk* (2008). So when Penn released his first novel in 2018, he may have been a bit surprised to learn from critics that his writing was…well, um, under-appreciated. The *New York Times* said his prose was "conspicuously un-fun." The *Guardian* called the book "repellent on one level, but stupid on so many others," and the *Huffington Post* said, "it's nonsensical, unpleasant and left me sweaty with mingled horror and confusion." Other critics were less kind.

Penn's excellence on the silver screen and mediocrity on the printed page would make sense if acting and writing were entirely separate abilities. But if they are separate abilities, then what does it mean to say that Penn—or anyone else for that matter—has "artistic talent"? After all, acting and writing are both forms of art, so shouldn't someone with artistic talent be good at both of them? The science of intelligence has grappled with a similar question for more than a century. Intelligence test scores predict important outcomes such as health and financial success, but do they measure a single underlying ability that deserves to be called intelligence, or do they measure a collection of distinct and unrelated abilities? Is intelligence one thing or many?

A Hierarchy of Abilities

Let's puzzle this one out. If there is a single ability called intelligence that enables people to perform a wide variety of intelligent behaviours, then those who have this ability should do well at just about everything, and those who lack it should do well at just about nothing. In other words, if intelligence is a single ability, then there should be a very strong positive correlation between people's performances on many different kinds of tests. Is there? This is precisely the question that psychologist Charles Spearman (1904) sought to answer at the start of the 20th century. He began by measuring how well school-age children could perform a variety of tasks such as discriminating small differences in colour, auditory pitch, and weight, and he then computed the correlation between their performances on these tasks and their grades in various academic subjects. He immediately noticed two things.

- First, Spearman noticed that children's grades and test performances were positively correlated, which is to say that the kid who got an A+ in algebra class was also pretty good at distinguishing between moss green and seaweed green. The fact that a person's performances on a variety of tests tend to be positively correlated is called *the positive manifold*, and it may well be "the most replicated result in all of psychology" (Deary, 2000, p. 6; Lubinski, 2004). Indeed, the positive manifold has been documented among test takers in 31 nations (Warne & Burningham, 2019) and even appears when the "test takers" are dogs or mice (Arden & Adams, 2016; Matzel et al., 2003).

- The second thing Spearman noticed was that although children's grades and test performances were positively correlated, they were not *perfectly* correlated. In other words, the kid who got the top mark in algebra class was also a *pretty good* colour distinguisher (that's the positive manifold), but not necessarily *the best* colour distinguisher.

These two facts led Spearman to develop his **two-factor theory of intelligence,** which suggests that *a person's performance on a test is due to a combination of general cognitive ability and specific abilities that are unique to the test.* Spearman referred to this general cognitive ability as *g* and to these specific abilities as *s*.

Spearman's theory was sensible, but not everyone bought it. Louis Thurstone (1938) noticed that although the correlations between performances on different tests were all *positive*, they were much *stronger* when the tests had something in common. For example, a child's score on a verbal test was more strongly correlated with their score on another verbal test than with their score on a mathematical test. Thurstone took this to mean that, contrary to Spearman's claims, there was no single general ability called intelligence (Kovacs & Conway, 2019). Rather, there were a few "primary mental abilities" such as perceptual ability, verbal ability, and numerical ability. These were not as general as Spearman's g (e.g., a child could have strong verbal abilities and weak numerical abilities) nor as specific as Spearman's s (e.g., a child who had strong verbal abilities tended both to speak well and read well).

Of course, Spearman did not give up. Nor did Thurstone. Nor did any of their followers. And so, for more than half a century, psychologists debated the existence of g. That debate might still be raging if it weren't for a mathematical technique called *confirmatory factor analysis* that provided a clear and decisive answer to the question everyone had been arguing about. The answer suggested that Spearman and Thurstone had both been right in their own ways. Specifically, this mathematical technique showed that the correlations between scores on different tests are best described not by Spearman's g and s, and not by Thurstone's primary mental abilities, but by a three-level hierarchy (see **FIGURE 10.2**) with a *general factor* (like Spearman's g) at the top, some *specific factors* (like Spearman's s) at the bottom, and a set of so-called *group factors* (like Thurstone's *primary mental abilities*) in the middle (Gustafsson, 1984). Indeed, a reanalysis of massive amounts of data collected over 60 years from more than 130,000 people showed that almost every study done since the early 1900s can be described by a three-level hierarchy of this kind (Carroll, 1993). This hierarchy suggests that people do indeed have a general ability called intelligence, but that it is made up of a small number of middle-level abilities, each of which enables a large number of specific abilities that are unique to particular tasks.

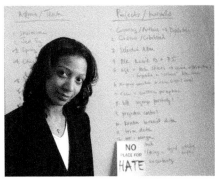

Social psychologist Jennifer Richeson received a so-called genius award from the MacArthur Foundation for her research on the dynamics of interracial interaction. Spearman's notion of g suggests that because she's really good at psychology, she's probably pretty good at most other things too.

The Middle-Level Abilities

But what *are* those middle-level abilities? Some psychologists have taken a *data-based approach* to answering this question: They start by examining people's responses to questions on intelligence tests and then they try to see how those responses correlate with each other. Other psychologists have taken a *theory-based approach* to answering this question: They start by considering the broad range of human abilities and then try to determine which of them intelligence tests measure, and which of them are not measured by these tests. As you will see, these different approaches to the same question yield rather different answers (Deary & Sternberg, 2021).

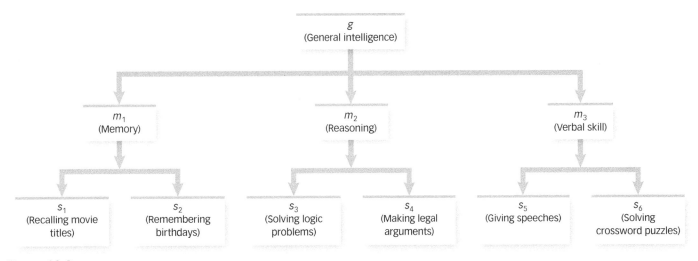

Figure 10.2

A Three-Level Hierarchy Most intelligence test data are best described by a three-level hierarchy with general intelligence (g) at the top, specific abilities (s) at the bottom, and a small number of middle-level abilities (m) in the middle.

The Data-Based Approach

One way to determine the number and nature of the middle-level abilities is to start with the data and go where they take us. Just as Spearman and Thurstone did, we could compute the correlations between people's performances on a large number of tests and then observe the pattern those correlations create. For example, imagine that we gave a group of people four tests that measured their respective abilities to (1) balance teacups, (2) recite Shakespeare, (3) swat flies, and (4) sum the numbers between one and a thousand. Now imagine that we computed the correlations between their scores on these four tests and that we observed a pattern of correlations like the one shown in **FIGURE 10.3a**. What would this pattern of correlations tell us?

This pattern suggests that people who are good at fly swatting are also good at teacup balancing ($r = .91$), and that people who are good at Shakespeare reciting are also good at number summing ($r = .94$). But it also suggests that people who are good at fly swatting are not necessarily good at Shakespeare reciting ($r = .05$) or number summing ($r = .01$), and that people who are good at teacup balancing are also not necessarily good at Shakespeare reciting ($r = .03$) or number summing ($r = .05$). This complex pattern of correlations contains a lot of information. Specifically, it suggests that there are two distinct middle-level abilities (shown in **FIGURE 10.3b**), one of which we might call *physical coordination* (the ability that allows people both to swat flies and balance teacups) and the other of which we might call *academic skill* (the ability that allows people both to recite Shakespeare and sum numbers). In other words, some people are really good at the specific tasks of fly swatting and teacup balancing *because* they have a middle-level ability called physical coordination — but this middle-level ability is unrelated to the other middle-level ability, academic skill, which is why these people are not necessarily good at summing numbers or reciting Shakespeare. The point of this example is that simply by examining the pattern of correlations between different tests, we can discover the nature and number of the middle-level abilities. And *that* is the data-based approach.

So what happens when we use this approach with real intelligence tests? In 1993, the psychologist John Carroll answered this question by computing the pattern of correlations between the intelligence test scores from nearly 500 studies conducted over a half century. And what he discovered was that there are eight middle-level abilities which he called *memory and learning, visual perception, auditory perception, retrieval ability, cognitive speediness, processing speed, crystallized intelligence,* and *fluid intelligence.* Most of these abilities are self-explanatory but the last two deserve

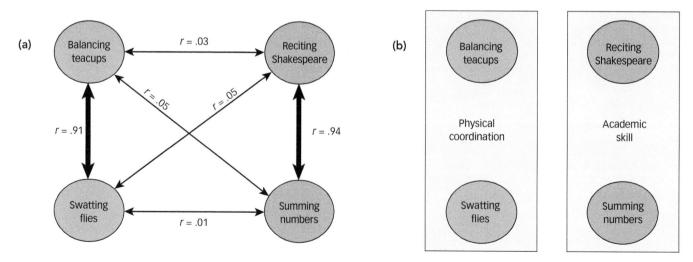

Figure 10.3

Patterns of Correlation Can Reveal Middle-Level Abilities The pattern of correlations (*a*) suggests that these four specific abilities can be thought of as instances of the two middle-level abilities, physical coordination and academic skill (*b*).

some comment. **Crystallized intelligence** refers to the *ability to apply knowledge that was acquired through experience* and is generally measured by tests of vocabulary and factual information (Horn & Cattell, 1966), and **fluid intelligence** refers to the *ability to solve and reason about novel problems* and is generally measured by tests that present people with abstract problems in new domains that must be solved under time pressure (see **FIGURE 10.4**). This distinction is more than semantic. Problems that require crystallized or fluid intelligence activate different networks in the brain (Barbey, 2018), which is why impairment of one kind of intelligence does not always lead to impairment of the other. For example, autism and Alzheimer's disease impair crystallized intelligence more than fluid intelligence, but damage to the prefrontal cortex impairs fluid intelligence more than crystallized intelligence (Blair, 2006).

The Theory-Based Approach

The data-based approach discovers middle-level abilities by observing the pattern of correlations between people's performances on different tests. The problem with this approach is that it cannot tell us about middle-level abilities that the tests themselves don't require (Stanovich, 2009). For example, if intelligence tests never ask people to, oh, say, find three new uses for an origami fish or to answer the question "What is the question you thought you'd be asked but weren't?" then no data-based analysis of those test scores can ever reveal the existence of a middle-level ability called *imagination* (Zabelina, in press). In short, the data from intelligence tests are useful, but they can't tell us about abilities that the tests don't measure.

Are there such abilities? The psychologist Robert Sternberg (1999, 2006) thinks so. He has argued that because standard intelligence tests present clearly defined problems that have one right answer, and then supply all the information needed to solve them, they are good measures of *analytic intelligence,* which is the ability to identify and define problems and to find strategies for solving them. But in everyday life, people find themselves in situations in which they must formulate the problem themselves, find the information needed to solve it, and then choose among multiple right answers. According to Sternberg, these situations require *creative intelligence,* which is the ability to generate solutions that other people do not, as well as *practical intelligence,* which is the ability to implement these solutions in everyday settings. For instance, in one study, workers at milk-processing plants developed complex strategies for efficiently combining partially filled cases of milk. Not only did they outperform highly educated white-collar workers, but their performances were unrelated to their scores on standard intelligence tests, suggesting that those tests don't measure practical intelligence (Scribner, 1984). Sternberg has argued that tests of practical intelligence are better than tests of analytic intelligence at predicting a person's job performance (though his critics

crystallized intelligence The ability to apply knowledge that was acquired through experience.

fluid intelligence The ability to solve and reason about novel problems.

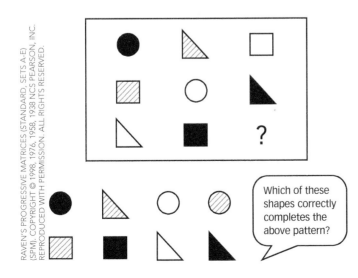

Which of these shapes correctly completes the above pattern?

Figure 10.4
Measuring Fluid Intelligence Problems like this one from Raven's Progressive Matrices Test (Raven et al., 2004) measure fluid intelligence rather than crystallized intelligence.

argue that even Sternberg's own data demonstrate the importance of *g* to job performance; Brody, 2003; Gottfredson, 2003).

Of course, not all the problems that intelligence enables us to solve are analytical, practical, or creative. For instance, how do you tell a friend that she talks too much without hurting her feelings? How do you cheer yourself up after failing a test? How do you know whether you are feeling anxious or angry? The psychologists John Mayer and Peter Salovey define **emotional intelligence** as *the ability to reason about emotions and to use emotions to enhance reasoning* (Mayer et al., 2008; Salovey & Grewal, 2005). Emotionally intelligent people know what kinds of emotions a particular event will trigger; they can identify, describe, and manage their emotions; they know how to use their emotions to improve their decisions; and they can identify other people's emotions from facial expressions and tones of voice. Furthermore, they do all this quite easily, which is why emotionally intelligent people show *less* neural activity when solving emotional problems than emotionally unintelligent people do (Jausovec & Jausovec, 2005; Jausovec et al., 2001).

Emotional intelligence is also quite important for social relationships. Emotionally intelligent people have better social skills and more friends (Eisenberg et al., 2000; Mestre et al., 2006; Schultz et al., 2004), they are judged to be more competent in their interactions (Brackett et al., 2006), and they have better romantic relationships (Brackett et al., 2005) and workplace relationships (Elfenbein et al., 2007; Lopes et al., 2006). Given all this, it isn't surprising that emotionally intelligent people tend to be happier (Brackett & Mayer, 2003; Brackett et al., 2006), healthier (Mikolajczak et al., 2015), and more satisfied with their lives (Ciarrochi et al., 2000; Mayer et al., 1999). Accumulating evidence suggests that emotional intelligence may be one of the middle-level abilities that the data-based approach misses (MacCann et al., 2014).

emotional intelligence The ability to reason about emotions and to use emotions to enhance reasoning.

1.

2.

Tom felt worried when he thought about all the work he needed to do. He believed he could handle it—if only he had the time. When his supervisor brought him an additional project, he felt _____. (Select the best choice.)

Emotion	Select one:
a. Happy	○
b. Angry	○
c. Fearful	○
d. Sad	○

Emotion	Select one:
a. Frustrated and anxious	○
b. Content and calm	○
c. Ashamed and accepting	○
d. Sad and guilty	○

Shown here are two items from a test of emotional intelligence (Mayer et al., 2008). Item 1 measures the accuracy with which a person can read emotional expressions (*left*). Item 2 measures the ability to predict emotional responses to events (*right*). The correct answer on both items is *a*.

Intelligence Across Cultures

Intelligence tests were developed and perfected in Europe and the United States so it is only natural that they reflect a Western conceptualization of intelligence. Are there others? Do non-Westerners think of intelligence differently than we do? In some cases, yes. For instance, Westerners tend to regard people as intelligent when they speak up and speak quickly, but Africans tend to regard people as intelligent when they are deliberative and quiet (Irvine, 1978). The Confucian tradition's conception of intelligence emphasizes flexibility in thinking, as well as the ability to spot wisdom in others (Pang et al., 2017); the Taoist tradition equates intelligence with humility and self-knowledge; and the Buddhist tradition associates it with determination and mental effort (Yang & Sternberg, 1997). Unlike people in Western societies, people in some African and Asian societies conceive of intelligence as including social responsibility and cooperativeness (Azuma & Kashiwagi, 1987; Serpell, 1974; White & Kirkpatrick, 1985). Indeed, in Zimbabwe, the word for intelligence is *ngware,* which means to be wise and cautious in one's social relationships (Sternberg & Grigorenko, 2004).

What does all this mean? Some researchers take it to mean that different cultures have radically different conceptualizations of intelligence of which the Western conceptualization we've discussed is just one—and not a particularly special one at that. Other researchers think that's an extreme position. They argue that every human culture

The Hungarian chess grandmaster Judit Polgar (*left*) and the Korean actress Ryu Si-Hyeon (*right*) both have genius-level IQs. But their cultures construe intelligence differently. Westerners tend to think of intelligence as an individual's ability to engage in rational thinking, but Easterners tend to think of it as the ability to recognize contradictions and complexities.

values the ability to solve important problems, and what distinguishes cultures is the *kinds* of problems that the people who live in them consider important. What's clear is that our traditional understanding of intelligence is being broadened by increased attention to those aspects of intelligence that traditional IQ tests don't measure.

Where Does Intelligence Come From?

No one is born knowing how to do calculus, and no one has to be taught how to blink. Some things are learned and others are not. But almost all the really *interesting* things about people are a joint product of their innate characteristics and their unique experiences. Intelligence is one of those interesting things, and as you are about see, it is indeed influenced both by nature and by nurture. Let's look at each of these influences in turn.

Genetic Influences on Intelligence

The notion that intelligence is "in the blood" has been with us for a very long time. As early as 380 BCE, the philosopher Plato suggested that people are born with innate aptitudes that make them good rulers, good soldiers, or good tradesmen. But it wasn't until late in the 19th century that this idea became the subject of serious scientific inquiry. Sir Francis Galton was a half cousin of Charles Darwin, and his contributions to science ranged from meteorology to fingerprinting. He was also the father of eugenics—the idea that humankind should be improved by controlled breeding—which was adopted by the Nazis as a rationale for exterminating millions of people during World War II. Despite the horrors that his work inspired, Galton did careful genealogical studies of eminent families, collected measurements from over 12,000 people, and concluded that intelligence "runs in families" and therefore must be largely inherited. Was he right?

Learning Outcomes

WHAT YOU NEED TO KNOW

- Describe the influence of genes on intelligence.

- Explain how environmental factors influence intelligence.

BOTH: ULRIC COLLETTE

These photos, taken from the "Genetic Portraits" series by Quebec City artist Ulric Collette, were made by blending the face of a 32-year-old woman with the face of her mother (*left*) and the face of her father (*right*). Because physical appearance is highly heritable, the resemblance between family members can often be quite striking. Intelligence is also highly heritable, which is why people tend to be about as intelligent as their parents.

fraternal (dizygotic) twins Siblings who develop from two different eggs that were fertilized by two different sperm.

identical (monozygotic) twins Siblings who develop from the splitting of a single egg that was fertilized by a single sperm.

© ANGEL FRANCO/THE NEW YORK TIMES/REDUX PICTURES

Tamara Rabi and Adriana Scott were 20 years old when they met for the first time in a McDonald's parking lot in New York. "I'm just standing there looking at her," Adriana recalled. "It was a shock. I saw me" (Gootman, 2003). It turned out that the two women were identical twins who had been separated at birth and adopted by different families. By coincidence, both families lived in the New York area and sent their daughters to universities just a few miles apart.

Genetic Relatedness

Intelligence certainly does appear to "run in families," which is to say that smart parents do indeed tend to have smart kids. But that doesn't mean intelligence is inherited because, after all, family members share experiences as well as genes. Parents and children typically live in the same house and get the same nutrition; siblings often go to the same schools and watch the same movies. And so on. Family members may have similar levels of intelligence because they share genes (as Galton thought) or because they share environments, or because they share both. So how can we tell which of these is responsible for their similar levels of intelligence?

The answer is: We can compare the intelligence test scores of people who share genes, environments, both, or neither, and use those data to figure out which of these factors is most influential. For example, adopted children who are raised together share environments but do not share genes; siblings who are raised together share both environments and genes; and siblings who are separated at birth and raised by different families share genes but not environments. To make matters a bit more complicated, different *kinds* of siblings share different *amounts* of their genes. Siblings who were born at different times share, on average, about 50% of their genes, as do **fraternal** (or **dizygotic**) **twins,** who are *siblings who develop from two different eggs that were fertilized by two different sperm.* On the other hand, **identical** (or **monozygotic**) **twins** are *siblings who develop from the splitting of a single egg that was fertilized by a single sperm,* and they share 100% of their genes.

By comparing people who have different amounts of shared genes and shared environments, psychologists have been able to estimate the role that genes play in producing intelligence. And it turns out that Galton was right: That role is quite large. As **TABLE 10.2** shows, the IQs of genetically identical twins who were raised in different households are more similar to each other than the IQs of biologically unrelated children who were raised in the same household—and are even more similar to each other than are the IQs of fraternal twins who were raised in the same household (Bouchard & McGue, 2003). These patterns of correlation suggest that genes play an important role in determining a person's intelligence—and that really shouldn't surprise you. After all, intelligence is influenced by the structure and function of the brain, and the structure and function of the brain are influenced by the genes that provide the blueprint for it. Indeed, given that genes influence just about every other human trait (Polderman et al., 2015), it would be rather remarkable if they *didn't* influence intelligence.

TABLE 10.2

INTELLIGENCE TEST CORRELATIONS BETWEEN PEOPLE WITH
DIFFERENT RELATIONSHIPS

Relationship	Shared Environment	Shared Genes (%)	Correlation Between Intelligence Test Scores (r)
Twins			
Identical twins (n = 4,672)	yes	100	.86
Identical twins (n = 93)	no	100	.78
Fraternal twins (n = 5,533)	yes	50	.60
Parents and Children			
Parent–biological child (n = 8,433)	yes	50	.42
Parent–biological child (n = 720)	no	50	.24
Nonbiological parent–adopted child (n = 1,491)	yes	0	.19
Siblings			
Biological siblings (2 parents in common) (n = 26,473)	yes	50	.47
Nonbiological siblings (no parents in common) (n = 714)	yes	0	.32
Biological siblings (2 parents in common) (n = 203)	no	50	.24

Information from Plomin et al. (2001), p. 168.

Measuring the Influence of Genes on IQ

So yes, genes exert a powerful influence on intelligence—but exactly how powerful? There's an answer to that! The **heritability coefficient** (commonly denoted as h^2) is *a statistic that describes the proportion of the difference between two or more people's IQ scores that can be explained by differences in their genes.* When the data from numerous studies of children and adults are analyzed together, the heritability coefficient is usually somewhere between .5 and .7, which is to say that roughly 50% to 70% of the differences between people's IQ scores is due to the genetic differences between those people (Plomin & Spinath, 2004; Plomin et al., 2013; cf. Chabris et al., 2012).

What the Heritability Coefficient *Doesn't* Tell Us Most people misunderstand the heritability coefficient and we want to be sure you aren't one of them. So let's get a few things straight. First, the heritability coefficient h^2 is *not* the same as the correlation coefficient *r*. Yes, both are quite efficient, but that's where the similarity ends. Second, many people who hear that "the heritability of intelligence is roughly .5" think this means that roughly half of *an individual's* intelligence is due to their genes and half is due to their experiences. That is totally wrong—and to understand why, consider the rectangles in **FIGURE 10.5**. These rectangles have the same heights but different widths, which means they have different areas because Area = Height ×Width. Now, if you were asked how much of the difference in their areas was due to differences in their widths, you would say 100%; and if you were asked how much of the difference in their areas was due to differences in their heights, you would say 0%. Bravo. Your answers about the *differences between the rectangles* are 100% right and 0% wrong!

Now let's try a different question: How much of rectangle A's area is due to its height, and how much is due to its width? If you are confused, then congratulations. This is a nonsense question to which "I'm confused" is the only right response.

heritability coefficient
A statistic (commonly denoted as h^2) that describes the proportion of the difference between people's IQ scores that can be explained by differences in their genes.

Small genetic differences can matter a lot. A single gene on chromosome 15 determines whether a dog will be too small for your pocket or too large for your garage.

Figure 10.5

Questions With and Without Answers These rectangles differ in area. The question "How much of the difference in their areas is due to differences in their widths, and how much is due to differences in their heights?" has an answer. But the question "How much of rectangle A's area is due to width and how much is due to height?" does not.

The reason you're confused is that an *individual* rectangle's area is a product of *both* its height and its width, so it can't be "due to" one of these things more or less than it is "due to" the other. You can sensibly ask how much of *the difference between the areas of two rectangles* is due to differences in their heights and widths, but you can't sensibly ask how much of *the area of an individual rectangle* is due to its height or its width. Got it?

Okay, now let's apply this deep wisdom to questions about genes and intelligence. If you measured the intelligence of every person at a hockey game and were then asked to say how much of the *difference in their IQs* was due to differences in their genes, the fact that h^2 is between .5 and .7 would allow you to guess correctly that the answer is between 50% and 70%. But if someone pointed to the guy in Row 17 with the really stupid hat, and asked how much of *that individual's* intelligence was due to his genes, the right answer would be, "You didn't read all that stuff about rectangles very carefully, did you?" This is a nonsense question because the intelligence of an individual is a joint product of both their genes and their experience—just as the area of a particular rectangle is a joint product of its height and width—and so it cannot be "due to" one of these things or the other.

What the Heritability Coefficient *Does* Tell Us The heritability coefficient, then, tells us how big an influence genes have on the *differences* in a particular group of people's IQ scores. Naturally, then, the value of the heritability coefficient is different when we measure different groups. For instance, the heritability of intelligence among high-income children in the United States is about .72, but among low-income children it is only about .10 (Turkheimer et al., 2003; cf. Figlio et al., 2017; Grasby et al., 2019). Wait. Why would that be? Because high-income children in the United States tend to have fairly similar environments—they all have nice homes with fast Internet connections, plenty of free time, and ample nutrition—and so the differences in their IQ scores must be due to the one and only factor that differs among them: their genes. But poor children in America have very dissimilar environments—some have Internet access and free time and ample nutrition, while others have little or none of these things—and so differences in their IQ scores could be due to differences in their environments as well as to differences in their genes (Tucker-Drob et al., 2010). This may explain why intelligence is more heritable among high-income than low-income children in America, as we already noted, but it is equally heritable among high-income and low-income children in Western Europe and Australia where most children have roughly the same resources, regardless of their family incomes (Bates et al., 2016; Tucker-Drob & Bates, 2016).

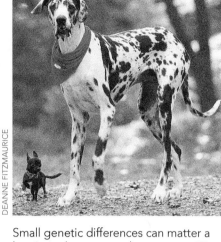

Some research suggests that IQ is more heritable among higher-income children, perhaps because their environments are so similar. If there are fewer differences in their environments, then differences in their IQs are more likely to be due to differences in their genes.

This same logic explains why the value of the heritability coefficient also varies depending on the age of the people being measured. For example, the heritability of intelligence is higher among adults than among children (see **FIGURE 10.6**), and higher among older children than among younger children. Indeed, genes account for less than 25% of the differences in the intelligence of infants, but they account for about 70% of the differences in the intelligence of adolescents (Haworth et al., 2010).

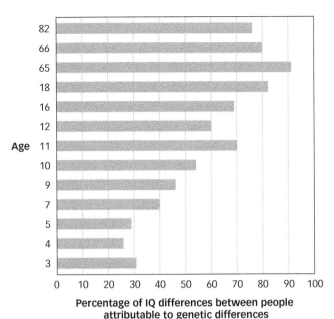

Figure 10.6
Age and Heritability of Intelligence The heritability of intelligence generally increases with the age of the people measured.

Why might that be? The environments of older people are more similar than the environments of younger people, and when environments don't differ much across people, then any differences in their IQs must be due to the one thing that does differ between them: their genes. It may seem paradoxical, but in a science-fiction world of clones (i.e., humans who are genetically identical), the heritability coefficient for intelligence would be zero. After all, in a world of genetic duplicates, environments would be the only thing that distinguished one clone from another, and therefore their environments would have to be the source of all the differences in their IQs.

So does that mean that in a science-fiction world in which humans were genetically different but lived in identical houses and ate identical meals and had identical educations and so on, the heritability coefficient for intelligence would be 1.00? Probably not, and that's because people who live in the same household share *some* of their experiences, but not *all* of their experiences. The **shared environment** refers to *features of the environment that are experienced by all relevant members of a household.* For example, siblings raised in the same household usually get roughly the same nutrition, have roughly the same Internet connections, and so on. The **nonshared environment** refers to *features of the environment that are not experienced by all relevant members of a household.* Siblings raised in the same household usually have different friends and different teachers, they contract different illnesses, and so on. The distinction between shared and nonshared environments helps explain why the correlation between the IQ scores of siblings is greater when the siblings are similar in age (Sundet et al., 2008). Similar-aged siblings have more shared environment—they are more likely to have the same teachers, hang out with the same friends, watch the same shows, and so on—so it makes sense that their IQ scores would be more similar.

shared environment Features of the environment that are experienced by all relevant members of a household.

nonshared environment Features of the environment that are not experienced by all relevant members of a household.

First-born children tend to be more intelligent than their later-born siblings. But when a first-born child dies in infancy and the second-born child becomes the oldest child in the family, that second-born child ends up being just as intelligent as the average first-born child (Kristensen & Bjerkedal, 2007). This suggests that first-borns are smarter than their siblings not for biological reasons but because they experience a different family environment.

Environmental Influences on Intelligence

Americans believe that every individual should have an equal chance to succeed in life, and one of the reasons that people get nervous when they hear about genetic influences on intelligence is that they mistakenly think that genes are destiny—that *genetic* is a synonym for *unchangeable* (Pinker, 2003). But that simply isn't true. Some traits that are strongly influenced by genes are also strongly influenced by the environment. For example, height is a highly heritable trait, which is why tall parents tend to have tall children. But that doesn't mean that height is unchangeable. In 1848, 25% of all Dutch men were rejected by the military because they were less than 1.6 m (5′ 2″) tall, but because of changes in nutrition after World War II, the average Dutch man today is 1.8 m (over 6′) tall (Max, 2006). For the same reason, the average height of Korean boys has increased by more than 7 inches in the last 50 years alone (Nisbett, 2009). Genes may explain why two people who have the same diet differ in height—that is, why Chang-sun is taller than Kwan-ho or why Thijs is taller than Daan—but they do not *dictate* how tall any of these boys will grow up to be.

Like height, intelligence is influenced by genes, but it is also influenced by the environment. For instance, as **FIGURE 10.7** shows, intelligence changes considerably over the life span (Owens, 1966; Schaie, 1996, 2005; Schwartzman et al., 1987). For most people, the direction of this change is upwards between adolescence and middle age and then downwards thereafter (cf. Ackerman, 2014). The sharpest decline occurs in old age (Kaufman, 2001; Salthouse, 1996a, 2000; Schaie, 2005) and may be due to a general decrease in the brain's processing speed (Salthouse, 1996b; Zimprich & Martin, 2002). These age-related declines are more evident in some domains than in others. For example, on tests that measure vocabulary, general information, and verbal reasoning, people show only small changes from age 18 to 70; but on tests that are timed, have abstract material, involve making new memories, or require reasoning about spatial relationships, most people show marked declines in performance after middle age (Avolio & Waldman, 1994; Lindenberger & Baltes, 1997; Rabbitt et al., 2004; Salthouse, 2001).

The brain is still growing and changing during adolescence, and intelligence also can change quite dynamically in this time period. Figure 10.7 shows central tendency (see the Methods in Psychology chapter) across a large group. The apparent stability in average IQ from 16 to 19 years of age (two leftmost bins in Figure 10.7) masks the fact that IQ can change quite a lot in individuals over this approximate time period, and changes in IQ within individuals over this time are also linked to structural changes in the brain (Ramsden et al., 2011) (see The Real World: Is IQ Stable in Adolescence?).

Intelligence not only changes over the life span, but it also changes over generations (see **FIGURE 10.8**). The *Flynn effect* refers to the fact that the average IQ score today is roughly 30 points higher than it was a century ago (Dickens & Flynn, 2001; Flynn, 2012; cf. Lynn, 2013). This is a striking number. It means that the average person today is smarter than 95% of the people who were alive in 1900! Why is each generation outscoring the one before it? Some researchers credit improved nutrition, schooling, and parenting (Baker et al., 2015; Lynn, 2009; Neisser, 1998),

Figure 10.7

Intelligence Changes Over Time
Intelligence changes over the life span, rising early, peaking in middle age, and declining thereafter.

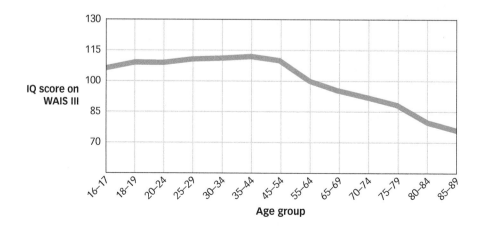

The Real World • **Is IQ Stable in Adolescence?**

Now, Albert Einstein is revered for his intellect. As a young child, however, he was slow to learn to talk, and his family nickname was "the dopey one." Clearly, something changed between his childhood and his 40s, when he was awarded the Nobel Prize in Physics.

Figure 10.7 shows that IQ changes over the adult life span, but only very slowly. And, in general, IQ seems to be pretty stable. IQ measurements made at different points in a person's life tend to correlate well, and, as discussed in the text, can predict life outcomes such as life span and wealth. But even quite strong correlations may mask a lot of individual variability. As discussed in the Methods in Psychology chapter, a reasonably strong correlation, like .5, can be obtained even if there are exceptions to the "rule" (in this case, that IQ is constant).

In an important study (Ramsden et al., 2011), Ramsden and colleagues studied variation in IQ over time in a group of British teenagers aged 12–20. The researchers used standardized tests to measure IQ twice, about 3 years apart, and they found that the teenagers' scores were surprisingly variable. The scatter plot in part a of the accompanying figure shows how IQ measured at Time 1 (on the *x* axis) relates to IQ measured at Time 2 (on the *y* axis). If the scores are identical, they fall on the red line; but, most of the data are not on the red line. The two time points correlate at .6, which is reasonably strong, but there is still much individual variability.

The same data are shown in a different way in part b of the accompanying figure. Each coloured line shows measured IQ for an individual at a young age (Time 1), and then about 3 years later (Time 2). As you can see, on average, IQ rises slightly over time, which is consistent with known increases in IQ with maturation. However, IQ dropped in some participants and increased in others. In 11 of the 33 participants, scores changed quite dramatically;

for example, someone with an IQ in the Very High range (scores of 120–129) at Time 1 may have had an IQ in the Average range (scores of 90–109) at Time 2, or vice versa.

You might wonder (and you'd be right to wonder!) whether this variation is just random. As you learned in the Methods in Psychology chapter, if a test is used to measure the same property at different times and gives similar results each time, it is reliable. If repeating the test yields a different measurement (assuming the property has not changed), the test is not reliable. Maybe IQ tests are just not perfectly reliable. After all, people are generally brighter when they are rested and relaxed, as compared to when they are tired, hungry, distracted, or stressed. Situational differences are undoubtedly part of the reason why scores vary, but they don't explain the variation entirely. Why not? *Because brain structure also changed between Time 1 and Time 2, in ways that related systematically to the changes in IQ.*

As you've learned, IQ is a composite measure of performance across many domains, including verbal and nonverbal (spatial and sensorimotor) domains. The researchers found that changes in grey matter volume in a region of the left frontal lobe

were important for speech production, which is correlated with the verbal subscale score. If verbal IQ increased over time, so had the grey matter volume in this area; if verbal IQ decreased over time, so had the grey matter volume. Because the amount of grey matter in a region is thought to reflect, at least in part, the number and density of neurons in a region, the presence of more grey matter suggests that more neurons are present. The implication is that, even in adolescence, local brain regions are growing (or shrinking) over time.

Changes on the nonverbal subscale of the IQ test from Time 1 to Time 2 also correlated with grey matter volume, but in a motor region of the brain. Again, increases in nonverbal IQ were associated with increases in volume in this region, and decreases in nonverbal IQ were associated with decreases in volume.

The work by Ramsden and colleagues suggests that the brain is surprisingly plastic in adolescence. People's intelligence, relative to that of their peers, can increase or decrease in the teenage years. Perhaps the class smarty-pants you remember from grade 7 has since sunk back into the crowd, and the dopey kid in the back row has since become a rocket scientist.

(a)

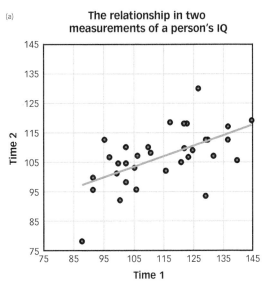

The relationship in two measurements of a person's IQ

(b)

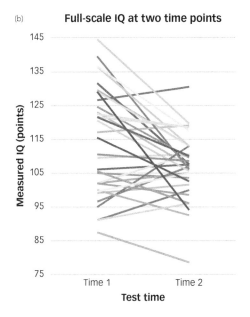

Full-scale IQ at two time points

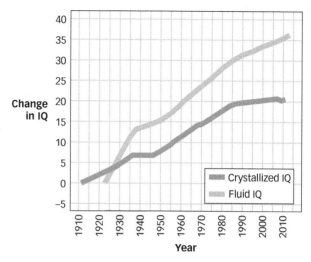

SOLSTOCK/E+/GETTY IMAGES

Figure 10.8

The Flynn Effect As the graph shows, human intelligence has been increasing across generations for at least the last century. If you've ever tried to help your grandparents use a computer, this news may not surprise you. (Data from Pietschnig et al., 2015.)

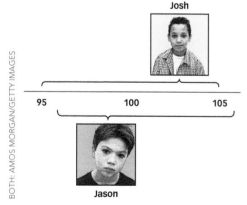

BOTH: AMOS MORGAN/GETTY IMAGES

Figure 10.9

Genes and Environment Genes establish the range in which a person's intelligence *may* fall, but environment determines the point in that range at which the person's intelligence *will* fall. Although Jason's genes give him a better chance to be smart than Josh's genes do, differences in their diets could easily cause Josh to have a higher IQ than Jason.

some suggest that the least intelligent people are increasingly excluded from the mating game (Mingroni, 2007), and some aren't sure the Flynn effect exists at all (Wicherts et al., 2004). But most seem to think that the industrial and technological revolutions of the 20th century have changed the nature of daily life so that ordinary people now spend more and more time solving precisely the kinds of abstract problems that intelligence tests include (Gordon, 1997), and as we all know, practice makes perfect (Bordone et al., 2015; Bratsberg & Rogeberg, 2018; Flynn, 2012). This could explain why these generational increases are nearly twice as large for fluid intelligence as they are for crystallized intelligence (Pietschnig et al., 2015). It is worth noting that some recent evidence suggests that the increase in IQ across generations has recently come to a halt (Dutton et al., 2016).

Intelligence doesn't just change across generations or over the life span: It changes over the course of months, weeks, days, and even hours. For instance, one study (Könen et al., 2015) showed that the amount and quality of a child's sleep influences their cognitive performance the next day. Indeed, as the school day wears on, children show a nearly 1 standard deviation decrement in cognitive performance with each passing hour (Sievertsen et al., 2016), and giving children a 20- to 30-minute break every hour improves their performance as much as giving them an extra 19 days of schooling! Even momentary emotions such as anxiety and frustration can impair children's performance on cognitive tasks (Pnevmatikos & Trikkaliotis, 2013). All of this suggests that while our genes determine the range in which our IQ will fall, our environments determine the point in that range at which it actually does fall (Hunt, 2011; see **FIGURE 10.9**). As you are about to see, two of the most powerful environmental influences on intelligence involve economics and education.

Poverty Lowers Intelligence

Money can't buy love, or so they say. But it sure can buy intelligence. One of the best predictors of a person's intelligence is the material well-being of the family in which they were raised—what social scientists call SES or *socioeconomic status* (Lubinski, 2009). Studies suggest that being raised in a high-SES family rather than a low-SES family is worth between 12 and 18 IQ points (Nisbett, 2009; van IJzendoorn et al., 2005). For instance, one study compared pairs of siblings who were born to low-SES parents. In each case, one of the siblings was raised by their low-SES parents, and the other was adopted and raised by a high-SES family. On average, the child who had been raised by high-SES parents had an IQ that was 14 points higher than their sibling (Schiff et al., 1978). Although these siblings had similar genes, they ended up with dramatically different IQs simply because one was raised in a wealthier household. High-SES and low-SES children have different IQs at the age of 2, and by the age of 16 the size of the difference between them nearly triples (von Stumm & Plomin, 2015).

Exactly how does SES influence intelligence? One way is by influencing the brain itself. Low-SES children have poorer nutrition and medical care, they experience greater daily stress, and they are more likely to be exposed to environmental toxins such as air pollution and lead—all of which can impair brain development (Ash & Boyce, 2018; Chen et al., 2010; Evans, 2006; Hackman & Farah, 2008). The fact that low SES can impair a child's brain development may explain why children who experience poverty in early childhood are less intelligent than those who experience poverty in middle or late childhood (Duncan et al., 1998). No doubt about it: Poverty is bad for the health of both the body and the brain (Evans & Kim, 2012).

School Raises Intelligence

If poverty is the enemy of intelligence, education is its best friend. The correlation between the amount of formal education a person receives and their intelligence is somewhere in the range of $r = .55$ to $.90$ (Ceci, 1991; Neisser et al., 1996). One reason this correlation is so large is that smart people tend to stay in school (Lee et al., 2018; Malanchini et al., 2020), but the other reason is that staying in school makes people smart (Ceci & Williams, 1997). When schooling is delayed because of war, political strife, economic crisis, or the simple lack of qualified teachers, children show a measurable decline in intelligence (Bisharat et al., 2020; Nisbett, 2009). The best estimate to date suggests that each additional year of education raises a person's IQ by about 1 to 5 points (Ritchie & Tucker-Drob, 2018).

Does this mean that anyone can become a genius just by showing up for class? Unfortunately not. Although education does have positive effects on intelligence, those effects tend to dissipate when education ends (Protzko, 2015, 2016; see **FIGURE 10.10**). For example, highly enriched pre-kindergarten programs for low-SES children tend to raise their IQs, but the effects generally fade once the children leave these intellectually enriched environments and go to normal elementary schools. On the other hand, a few intensive education programs have managed to produce longer-lasting gains. For instance, an experiment conducted in the 1970s in the United States allowed low-SES children to enroll in a full-time preschool program that focused on developing their cognitive, linguistic, and social skills in small classes of about six students (Campbell et al., 2002). Compared with a control group in the same community, those children showed IQ gains that were still measurable at the age of 21 (though it appears that girls benefited far more than boys) (Anderson, 2008). It is worth noting that even when education does not produce long-lasting increases in intelligence, it does produce long-lasting increases in other critical skills such as reading—and when it comes to life outcomes such as health, wealth, and happiness, the difference between a person with an IQ of 100 who can't read and a person with an IQ of 101 who can is much larger than a single IQ point would suggest.

The Malleability of Intelligence

In 1909, Alfred Binet wrote:

> A few modern philosophers ... assert that an individual's intelligence is a fixed quantity that cannot be increased. We must protest and react against this brutal pessimism. ... With practice, training, and above all method, we manage to increase our attention, our memory, our judgment, and literally to become more intelligent than we were before. (p. 141)

Research on the effects of poverty and education clearly show that Binet was right: Intelligence is malleable. But he was also right when he said that the opposite belief

To encourage low-SES parents to talk more to their children, the city of Providence, on the East Coast of the United States, created a program called Providence Talks. Once a month, a child wears a small recording device for the day, which allows a computer to calculate how many words they spoke, how many were spoken by adults in their vicinity, and how many conversational exchanges they experienced. A caseworker then visits the child's parents and provides a progress report.

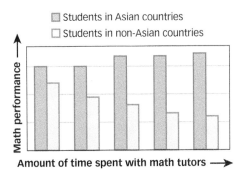

Figure 10.10

Can Education Hurt? In Asian countries, the majority of students spend time getting extra tutoring in math, and as this graph shows, the more time they spend, the better their math performance. Is that because the tutoring helps? Probably so. But in non-Asian countries, the majority of students get no extra tutoring in math, and the more time they spend with tutors, the *worse* their math performance. Is that because the tutoring hurts? Probably not. Rather, it's because in non-Asian countries, only weak students get tutoring. DATA FROM HUNT, 2012.

is a form of "brutal pessimism," and research shows that such pessimism has consequences. In one study (Blackwell et al., 2007), a group of seventh graders learned about the malleability of intelligence. Specifically, they saw demonstrations of how neurons make new connections during learning and read an essay called "You Can Grow Your Intelligence." A control group of other seventh graders learned about different topics. Seventh grade is typically a time when students' grades decline over the course of the year, and that's just what happened to the students in the control group. But the seventh graders in the experimental group, who had been taught that intelligence is malleable, showed no such decline. Why? They believed that their intelligence could be improved, and so they worked hard to improve it! Their math teacher's notes about two of these students document this motivational shift:

> L., who never puts in any extra effort and doesn't turn in homework on time, actually stayed up late working for hours to finish an assignment early so I could review it and give him a chance to revise it. ... M. was [performing] far below grade level. During the past several weeks, she has voluntarily asked for extra help from me during her lunch period in order to improve her test-taking performance. Her grades drastically improved from failing to an 84 on her recent exam.

Simply knowing that intelligence is malleable seems to increase it. In case you are wondering, the same thing happens to university students who are taught about the malleability of intelligence (Aronson et al., 2002; Good et al., 2003). Luckily, you are now such a student.

Gene–Environment Interactions

Both genes and environments, then, can have a direct impact on intelligence. For instance, most embryos have 23 pairs of chromosomes—one of each pair inherited from their mother and one of each pair inherited from their father. But about 1 in every 700 embryos has an extra 21st chromosome, and these embryos become children with "trisomy 21," which is also known as Down syndrome. That extra 21st chromosome holds about 250 genes, and one or more of those genes directly impairs the development of the embryos' brains and lowers intelligence. Environments can have a similarly direct impact on intelligence: For instance, mercury is an environmental toxin that can kill brain cells, or alter a cell's ability to migrate and proliferate, which is why children who live in places where they are exposed to mercury end up being less intelligent (Lanphear, 2015). Trisomy 21 and mercury poisoning are just two examples of the ways in which genes and environments can directly and independently influence intelligence.

But in addition to their direct and independent effects, genes and environments can also *interact* to influence intelligence. Consider two examples:

Roundworms that have the NPR-1 gene get fewer infections than those that don't. But this gene does not directly influence the functioning of the immune system. Rather, it causes roundworms to "dislike" the kinds of environments where bacteria hang out. Similarly, genes may influence intelligence not by directly influencing the functioning of the brain, but by causing people to gravitate towards or away from particular environments.

- A person may *have* a gene, but that person's environment may determine whether the gene will or will not play an active role in producing proteins. You can think of a gene as a little switch that the environment can turn to the *on* or *off* position. If the environment turns it on, then the gene plays a role in the production of proteins that influence both the development and function of the brain; but if the environment turns it off, then the gene is silent and does nothing—as if it weren't even there. Scientists have discovered more than 50 genes that can influence intelligence (Sniekers et al., 2017), and whether a person *has* these genes depends on their parents, but whether these genes are activated may depend on their environment.

- Genes can cause people to be "pulled towards" or "pushed away from" particular environments (Dickens & Flynn, 2001; Nisbett, 2009; Plomin et al., 2001; Tucker-Drob et al., 2013). For example, we know that personality traits such as extraversion are heritable (Polderman et al., 2015). If a particular set of genes makes people more outgoing and more sociable, then the people who have those genes may be especially likely to enjoy the company of their peers, and therefore especially likely to stay in school, and therefore especially likely to gain in intelligence. Those "extraversion genes" would not be playing a direct role in promoting intelligence, but rather, they would be playing an indirect role by "pushing" people towards the environments that promote intelligence.

The fact that genes and environments can interact in these and other ways challenges the way most of us think about them. For example, imagine a gene that can impair brain function and is normally switched off, but that can be switched on by the stress of an impoverished environment. If a poor child has this gene, should we attribute their low intelligence to their genes or to their environment? Or imagine a gene that makes people extraverted. A student who has that gene may be especially likely to join school clubs, study with groups, attend extracurricular lectures, and so on. Should we attribute that student's high intelligence to their extraversion gene or to their extra educational experiences? These questions are difficult to answer because they ask us to choose between genes and environments, and as you've just learned, genes and environments often interact in complex ways to influence intelligence. As science progresses, the obvious distinction between nature and nurture is becoming less and less obvious (see Hot Science: Brains Wide Open).

Hot Science ⫶ **Brains Wide Open**

One of the things that makes our species so smart is that our brains are designed to be programmed by our environments. Turtles, lizards, and houseflies are all prewired by evolution to react in very specific ways to very specific stimuli. But mammalian brains—and especially human brains — are built to be *environmentally sensitive*, which means that humans are born with the minimal amount of hardwiring and are instead wired by their experiences in the world in which they find themselves. This is one of the things that allows human beings to function so effectively in a wide variety of physical and cultural environments.

But the brain's remarkable openness to experience doesn't last forever. The brain in adulthood is not as environmentally sensitive as it was in childhood. If the brain's environmental sensitivity is one of the things that makes our species so smart, it stands to reason that the smartest people among us might have brains that remain environmentally sensitive for longer than usual. Is that true?

That's what Brant and colleagues (2013) set out to discover. They examined data from nearly 11,000 sets of monozygotic (MZ) and dizygotic (DZ) twins who had taken IQ tests sometime between infancy and adulthood. Using sophisticated mathematical techniques, they computed the extent to which differences in IQ scores at each age had been influenced by genes or by the environment. What they found was fascinating. Children's brains were relatively open to environmental influence, while adult's brains were relatively closed—but the point at which the closing happened was different for high-IQ people than for low-IQ people. Whereas the brains of low-IQ people closed by early adolescence, the brains of high-IQ people remained open to influence well into adolescence.

The accompanying graph shows the magnitude of both environmental and genetic influences at different ages. As indicated, the brains of high-IQ adolescents remained as sensitive as the brains of children, but the brains of low-IQ adolescents were as insensitive as the brains of adults. Whether you look at the effect of genes (in orange) or the effect of environment (in purple), you'll notice that the high- and low-IQ people start in the same place and end in the same place, but they get there at different speeds—specifically, low-IQ people get there faster.

No one knows why the brains of high-IQ people remain sensitive to the environment for longer, and no one knows if this is a cause or a consequence of their intelligence. All we know is that the longer the brain retains its childlike openness to experience, the more effectively it functions for the rest of its life.

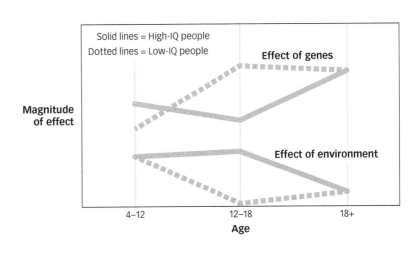

Who Is Most Intelligent?

Learning Outcomes

WHAT YOU NEED TO KNOW

- Describe myths about the intellectually gifted and the intellectually disabled.

- Explain what is and is not known about between-group differences in intelligence.

- Identify ways in which intelligence can be enhanced.

Intelligence is a human characteristic, and like every other human characteristic, different humans have different amounts. Everyone you know isn't equally tall or extraverted or musically inclined, and so it makes sense that they are not equally intelligent. But how exactly does intelligence vary? We'll answer that question by first considering variations in the intelligence of individuals, and then considering variations in the average intelligence of groups.

Individual Differences in Intelligence

The average IQ is 100, and about 85% of us have IQs between 85 and 115 (see **FIGURE 10.11**). Those who score well above this large middle range are said to be *intellectually gifted,* and those who score well below it are said to be *intellectually disabled.* Although the people in these two categories live at opposite ends of the intelligence continuum, they have one thing in common: They are more likely to be male than female. Males and females have the same average IQ, but the distribution of males' IQ scores is wider and more variable than the distribution of females' IQ scores, which means that there are more males than females at both the very top and the very bottom of the IQ range (Hedges & Nowell, 1995; Lakin, 2013; Wai et al., 2012). Some of this difference is due to the different ways in which boys and girls are socialized, of course. Whether any of this difference is due to innate biological differences remains a hotly debated issue in psychology (Ceci et al., 2009; Nisbett et al., 2012; Spelke, 2005).

Those of us who occupy the large middle of the intelligence distribution tend to have several misconceptions about those who live at the extremes. For example, movies often portray the "tortured genius" as a person (usually a male person) who is brilliant, creative, misunderstood, despondent, and more than a little weird (Brown et al., 2021). Although some psychologists believe there is a link between creative genius and certain forms of psychopathology (Gale et al., 2012; Jamison, 1993; cf. Schlesinger, 2012; Simonton, 2014), for the most part, Hollywood has the relationship between intelligence and mental illness backwards. The fact is that people with very high intelligence are *less* susceptible to mental illness than are people with very low intelligence (Dekker & Koot, 2003; Didden et al., 2012; Walker et al., 2002). Indeed, a 15-point *decrease* in IQ at age 20 is associated with a 50% *increase* in the risk of later hospitalization for schizophrenia, mood disorder, and alcohol-related disorders (Gale et al., 2010), as well as for personality disorders (Moran et al., 2009). Just as intelligence seems to buffer people against physical illness, so it seems to buffer people against mental illness.

Another thing that Hollywood often gets wrong is that its geniuses tend to be super brainiacs who are good at everything. And yet, in real life, genius tends to be specialized. For example, gifted children are usually gifted in math or language or music, but not in all three (Achter et al., 1996; Makel et al., 2016). Because gifted children

The artist Vincent van Gogh was the iconic "tortured genius." But data suggest that low intelligence, not high intelligence, is most strongly associated with mental illness.

Figure 10.11

The Normal Curve of Intelligence Deviation IQ scores produce a normal curve. This graph shows the percentage of people who score in each range of IQ.

tend to be single-gifted, they also tend to be single-minded, displaying a "rage to master" the domain in which they excel. As one psychologist noted, "One cannot tear these children away from activities in their area of giftedness, whether they involve an instrument, a computer, a sketch pad, or a math book. These children ...can focus so intently on work in this domain that they lose sense of the outside world" (Winner, 2000, p. 162). Some research suggests that what most clearly distinguishes gifted children from their less gifted peers is the sheer amount of time they spend engaged in their domain of excellence (Ericsson & Charness, 1999; Lubinski & Benbow, 2021), which suggests that a part of nature's gift may simply be the capacity for passionate devotion to a single activity (cf. Hambrick et al., 2013; Mayer et al., 1989). This passionate devotion may explain why gifted children are much more likely to become high-achieving adults (Lubinski, 2016).

On the other end of the intelligence spectrum are people with intellectual disabilities, which can range from mild ($50 < IQ < 69$) to moderate ($35 < IQ < 49$) to severe ($20 < IQ < 34$) to profound ($IQ < 20$). About 70% of people with IQs in this range are male. Two of the most common causes of intellectual disability are Down syndrome (or trisomy 21, caused by the presence of a third copy of chromosome 21) and fetal alcohol syndrome (caused by a mother's excessive alcohol use during pregnancy). Unlike intellectual gifts, intellectual disabilities tend to be general rather than specific, and people who have them typically show impaired performance on a wide range of cognitive tasks. (Williams syndrome, which you learned about at the beginning of this chapter, is an exception to this rule.) There are many myths about intellectually disabled people, but perhaps the most pervasive is that they are unhappy. Just. Not. True. In fact, almost all people with Down syndrome report being happy with their lives, liking who they are, and liking how they look (Skotko et al., 2011b). Their families feel the same way. For instance, siblings of people with Down syndrome are proud of them, feel that their relationships with their intellectually disabled siblings have made them "better people," and do not wish that their siblings were different (Skotko et al., 2011a). People with intellectual disabilities face many challenges and being misunderstood by those who don't know them is one of the most difficult.

Group Differences in Intelligence

As you learned earlier, eugenics is the idea that the intelligence of humankind should be increased by controlled breeding, which often involves limiting the rights of the least intelligent people to reproduce. The Nobel laureate George Bernard Shaw; U.S. presidents Theodore Roosevelt and Calvin Coolidge; the feminist icon Margaret Sanger; and the father of socialized medicine in Canada, Tommy Douglas, were just some of the enthusiastic proponents of eugenics, which was "hugely popular in America and Europe among the 'better sort' before Hitler gave it a bad name" (Lemann, 1999).

The Stanford University professor Lewis Terman (whom you encountered earlier in this chapter) was also a proponent of eugenics. In the early 1900s, he improved on Binet and Simon's work and produced the intelligence test that today is known as the Stanford–Binet Intelligence Scale. One of the things Terman discovered when he gave people his intelligence test was that American white people performed better than American non-white people. "Are the inferior races really inferior, or are they merely unfortunate in their lack of opportunity to learn?" Terman asked, and then quickly answered, "Their dullness seems to be racial, or at least inherent in the family stocks from which they come" (1916, pp. 91–92).

A century later, Terman's words make most of us cringe. But exactly which of those words are the cringe-worthy ones? Terman claimed that (1) intelligence is influenced by genes, (2) members of some racial groups score better than others on intelligence tests, and (3) the reason members of some racial groups score better than others is that they have superior genes. Virtually all modern scientists who

Isabella Springmuhl Tejada is a fashion designer who has Down syndrome. Her work has been showcased during London Fashion Week, and the British Broadcasting Corporation (BBC) voted her one of the 100 most inspiring and innovative women of 2016.

study intelligence consider Terman's first two claims to be well-established facts: Intelligence *is* influenced by genes, and some groups *do* perform better than others on intelligence tests. On the other hand, Terman's third claim—that differences in their genes is the *reason* some groups outperform others—is not an established fact, but a highly charged conjecture that has been the subject of acrimonious debate in both science and society. There is no shortage of opinions on this issue, but what are the facts?

Before answering that question, let's be clear about one thing: Group differences in intelligence are not inherently problematic. No one is troubled by the possibility that this year's winners of the Nobel Prize in Physics are on average more intelligent than this year's winners of the Super Bowl, or that people who graduate from university are on average more intelligent than people who never attended school. On the other hand, most of us *are* troubled by the possibility that groups defined by gender, race, religion, or nationality are more or less intelligent than others. Intelligence is a valuable trait, and it doesn't seem fair for some groups to have more of it simply because of an accident of birth or geography.

But fair or not, they do. Women routinely outscore men on tests that require rapid access to and use of semantic information, production and comprehension of complex prose, fine motor skills, and perceptual speed of verbal intelligence. Men routinely outscore women on tests that require transformations in visual or spatial memory, certain motor skills, spatiotemporal responding, and fluid reasoning in abstract mathematical and scientific domains (Halpern et al., 2007; Nisbett et al., 2012). In North America, Asian people routinely outscore white people who routinely outscore Black people on standard intelligence tests (Mendoza-Denton, 2014; Nisbett et al., 2012). Although the average difference between groups is not large—usually less than the average difference between people within a group—there is no doubt that some groups outperform others on average. The important question is: Why?

Tests and Test Takers

One possibility is that the tests are biased. And in fact, the earliest intelligence tests did indeed ask questions whose answers were more likely to be known by members of one group (usually white Europeans) than by members of another. For example, one of Binet and Simon's questions was this: "When anyone has offended you and asks you to excuse him, what ought you to do?" Binet and Simon were looking for answers such as "accept the apology like a gentleman or explain why it is insufficient." Answers such as "challenge him to a fight" or "demand three goats" would have been counted as wrong despite the fact that in some cultures or subcultures those answers would have been spot on. Early intelligence tests were clearly culturally biased. But intelligence tests have come a long way in a century, and there is no evidence to suggest that modern intelligence tests are biased in this way (Sackett et al., 2008). Moreover, group differences emerge even on those portions of intelligence tests that don't ask potentially biased questions but instead present people with nonverbal problems, such as the item from Raven's Progressive Matrices Test shown in Figure 10.4.

Of course, even when test *questions* are unbiased, testing *situations* may not be. For example, studies show that African American students (but not European American students) perform more poorly on tests if they are asked to report their race at the top of the answer sheet, presumably because doing so leads them to feel anxious about confirming negative racial stereotypes about their group (Steele & Aronson, 1995), and anxiety naturally interferes with test performance (Reeve et al., 2009). **Stereotype threat** is *the anxiety associated with the possibility of confirming other people's stereotypes about one's group* (Aronson & Steele, 2004; Schmader et al., 2008; Walton & Spencer, 2009), and it understandably impairs people's performances on tests.

stereotype threat The anxiety associated with the possibility of confirming other people's stereotypes about one's group.

These students are writing the Medical College Admission Test (MCAT). When people are asked about their race before taking a test, their performance can be affected.

FUSE/GETTY IMAGES

Consider two common stereotypes: Women are bad at math and Asians are good at math. In one study, Asian American women were reminded either of their gender or their ethnicity before taking a math test, and guess what? When reminded of their gender they performed worse, but when reminded of their ethnicity they performed better (Gibson et al., 2014; Shih et al., 1999). One of the things that reminds us of our social identities is the presence of people who do not share them, which may help explain why women perform better on math tests when all their fellow test takers are women than when some of them are men (Inzlicht & Ben-Zeev, 2000). Findings such as these suggest that the situations in which intelligence tests are administered can affect members of different groups differently and may lead to group differences in *performance* that do not reflect group differences in *ability*. As Mendoza-Denton (2014) concludes, "the underestimation of performance among stigmatized groups does not result from test bias per se... as much as from the threatening contexts in which such tests are administered and taken."

Environments and Genes

Biases in the testing situation may explain some of the between-group differences in intelligence test scores, but probably not all. If we assume that some of these differences reflect real differences in the abilities that intelligence tests are meant to measure, then what accounts for these ability differences? Is it environment, genes, or both?

There is broad agreement among scientists that environment plays a major role. For example, Black children in America have lower birth weights, poorer diets, higher rates of chronic illness, and poorer medical care; they attend worse schools; and they are three times more likely than European American children to live in single-parent households (Acevedo-Garcia et al., 2007; National Center for Health Statistics, 2016a). Black U.S. households have lower incomes, and studies show that children in families earning more than $100,000 per year are nearly 50% more likely to be in excellent health than are children in families earning less than $35,000 per year (National Center for Health Statistics, 2016b). In the United States, Black, Indigenous and Latino/Latina people are several times more likely to be exposed through air pollution to toxic chemicals (Tessum et al., 2021), which is one of the reasons they "age faster," showing more marked age-related declines in physical capability, sensory functioning, physiological functioning, and cognitive performance (Steptoe & Zaninotto, 2020). Black, Indigenous and Latino/Latina people are not just exposed to more toxic chemicals but also to more toxic messages about their innate abilities, which may cause them to minimize the importance of academic achievement in order to preserve their self-esteem (Major et al., 1998; Steele, 1997). Given all the extraordinary differences between the physical, economic, and social environments of people high and low in SES, it is hardly surprising that Black Americans score, on average, 10 points lower on IQ tests than white Americans do. Poverty affects the brain, the body, and the mind, and it would be quite remarkable if differences in poverty did *not* result in differences in cognitive test performance.

What does this suggest about the question that has caused so much controversy over the last century, namely, whether genes play any role in group differences? There are ignorant people on every side of this issue and most of them seem to have Twitter accounts, but the simple fact is that *scientists have not found any facts about group differences that require a genetic explanation.* They have, however, found several facts that make such an explanation unlikely. For example, the average Black American has about 20% European genes; and yet, those who have more of these genes are no smarter than those who have fewer, which is not what we'd expect if European genes made people smart (Loehlin, 1973; Nisbett et al., 2012; Scarr et al., 1977). Similarly, Black children and biracial children have different amounts of European genes, and yet, when they are adopted into middle-class families, their IQs don't differ (Moore, 1986), which is once again not what we'd expect if European genes made people smart. The absence of evidence is not evidence of absence and so these facts do not prove that there is no genetic basis for between-group differences in intelligence; but they sure do make that possibility less plausible.

What would it take to prove that intelligence differences — or any other psychological differences — between groups have a genetic origin? It would take the kind of evidence that scientists often find when they study the *physical* differences between groups. For instance, people who have hepatitis C are often given a prescription for antiviral drugs, and studies show that European American patients typically benefit more from this treatment than African American patients do. Physicians once thought this was because European Americans were "better patients" who were more likely to *take* the medicines they were given. But recently, scientists have discovered a gene that makes people unresponsive to these antiviral drugs — and guess what? African Americans are *more* likely than European Americans to have that gene for unresponsiveness (Ge et al., 2009). This kind of evidence of genetic differences between groups is exactly what's lacking in the debate on group differences in intelligence. The best research suggests that intelligence is not strongly influenced by a single gene but is instead weakly influenced by a very large number of genes (Davies et al., 2011; von Stumm & Plomin, 2021). Unless researchers isolate those genes and show that they are more prevalent in one group than another, most scientists are unlikely to embrace a genetic explanation of between-group differences in intelligence. In other words, the best science to date suggests that there is no evidence to support Terman's contentious conclusion.

Improving Intelligence

Intelligence can be improved — by money, for example, and by education. But most people can't just snap their fingers and become wealthier, and education takes time. Is there anything that average parents can do to raise their child's IQ? Researchers analyzed the data from a large number of high-quality scientific studies on this question (Protzko et al., 2013), and they found four things that

Other Voices ┆ **Not By Intelligence Alone**

Intelligence matters. But is it all that matters? Professor Barry Schwartz thinks not. He believes that intelligence alone cannot make us happy, productive, and successful citizens unless it is combined with a list of "intellectual virtues" that enable us to *use* our intelligence properly. In his view, universities should focus less on teaching students *what* to think and focus more on teaching students *how* to think by demonstrating and instilling nine key intellectual virtues. What are they?

Knowing how to think demands a set of cognitive skills— quantitative ability, conceptual flexibility, analytical acumen, expressive clarity. But beyond those skills, learning how to think requires the development of a set of intellectual virtues that make good students, good professionals, and good citizens ...

Love of truth. Students need to love the truth to be good students . . . It has become intellectually fashionable to attack the very notion of truth. You have your truth, and I have mine. You have one truth today, but you may have a different one tomorrow. Everything is relative, a matter of perspective. People who claim to know the "truth," it is argued, are in reality just using their positions of power and privilege to shove their truth down other people's throats.

This turn to relativism is in part a reflection of something good and important that has happened to intellectual inquiry. People have caught on to the fact that much of what the intellectual elite thought was the truth *was* distorted by limitations of perspective. Slowly the voices of the excluded have been welcomed into the conversation. And their perspectives have enriched our understanding. But the reason they have enriched our understanding is that they have given the rest of us an important piece of the truth that was previously invisible to us. Not *their* truth, but *the* truth. It is troubling to see how quickly an appreciation that each of us can attain only a partial grasp of the truth degrades into a view that there really isn't any truth out there to be grasped . . .

Honesty. Honesty enables students to face the limits of what they themselves know; it encourages them to own up to their mistakes. And it allows them to acknowledge uncongenial truths about the world . . .

Fair-mindedness. Students need to be fair-minded in evaluating the arguments of others . . .

Humility. Humility allows students to face up to their own limitations and mistakes and to seek help from others . . .

Perseverance. Students need perseverance, since little that is worth knowing or doing comes easily . . .

Courage. Students need intellectual courage to stand up for what they believe is true, sometimes in the face of disagreement from others, including people in authority, like their professors. And they need courage to take risks, to pursue intellectual paths that might not pan out.

Good listening. Students can't learn from others, or from their professors, without listening. It takes courage to be a good listener, because good listeners know that their own views of the world, along with their plans for how to live in it, may be at stake whenever they have a serious conversation.

Perspective-taking and empathy. It may seem odd to list perspective-taking and empathy as intellectual virtues, but it takes a great deal of intellectual sophistication to get perspective-taking right. Young children "feel" for a peer who is upset but are clueless about how to comfort her. They try to make a crying child feel better by doing what would make them feel better. And teachers, at all levels, must overcome "the curse of knowledge." If they can't remind themselves of what they were like before they understood something well, they will be at a loss to explain it to their students. Everything is obvious once you know it . . .

© TOBY MADDEN/EYEVINE/ REDUX PICTURES

Barry Schwartz is the Dorwin Cartwright Professor of Social Theory and Social Action at Swarthmore College. He is the author of numerous books including *The Paradox of Choice* (2004) and *Practical Wisdom: The Right Way to Do the Right Thing* (2010).

Wisdom. Finally, students need what Aristotle called practical wisdom. Any of the intellectual virtues I've mentioned can be carried to an extreme. Wisdom is what enables us to find the balance (Aristotle called it the "mean") between timidity and recklessness, carelessness and obsessiveness, flightiness and stubbornness, speaking up and listening up, trust and skepticism, empathy and detachment. Wisdom is also what enables us to make difficult decisions when intellectual virtues conflict. Being empathetic, fair, and open-minded often rubs up against fidelity to the truth. Practical wisdom is the master virtue . . .

Cultivation of intellectual virtues is not in conflict with training in specific occupations. On the contrary, intellectual virtues will help to create a work force that is flexible, able to admit to and learn from mistakes, and open to change. People with intellectual virtues will be persistent, ask for help when they need it, provide help when others need it, and not settle for expedient but inaccurate solutions to tough problems . . . Workplaces need people who have intellectual virtues, but workplaces are not in a good position to instill them. Colleges and universities should be doing this training for them.

Schwartz believes that without a love of truth, honesty, fair-mindedness, and the rest, intelligence itself just can't get us very far. Is he right? And if so, can these virtues be taught? How? Is his list complete, and if not, what's missing? These are difficult but important questions which, if you believe Schwartz, will never be answered by intelligence alone.

Used with permission of The Chronicle of Higher Education, excerpt from Barry Schwartz, "What Learning How to Think Really Means," ©2015 The Chronicle of Higher Education; permission conveyed through Copyright Clearance Center, Inc.

seem to reliably raise a child's intelligence. First, supplementing the diets of pregnant women and neonates with long-chain polyunsaturated fatty acids (substances found in breast milk) appears to raise children's IQ by up to 4 points (Boutwell et al., 2018). Second, enrolling low-SES infants in so-called early educational interventions tends to raise their IQ by about 6 points. Third, reading to children in an interactive manner raises their IQ by about 6 points. Fourth, sending children to preschool raises their IQ by about 6 points. In short, there do seem to be some things parents can do to make their kids smarter.

There are also some simpler ways to improve intelligence. **Cognitive enhancers** are *drugs that improve the psychological processes that underlie intelligent performance.* Stimulants such as Ritalin and Adderall can enhance cognitive performance (Elliott et al., 1997; Halliday et al., 1994; McKetin et al., 1999), temporarily improving people's ability to focus attention, manipulate information in working memory, and flexibly control their responses (Sahakian & Morein-Zamir, 2007). Cognitive performance can also be enhanced by drugs such as Modafinil (Ingvar et al., 1997), which has been shown to improve short-term memory and planning abilities (Turner et al., 2003). All these drugs enhance cognitive performance, but they can also have damaging side effects and lead to abuse, which is one of the reasons smart people don't use them.

In the near future, cognitive enhancement may be achieved not with chemicals that alter the brain's function, but with techniques that alter its actual structure. By manipulating the genes that guide hippocampal development, for instance, scientists have created a strain of "smart mice" that have extraordinary memory and learning abilities, (Tang et al., 1999, p. 64), and new "gene-editing" techniques such as CRISPR (which stands for *clustered regularly interspaced short palindromic repeats*) may allow these animals to pass their genetic modifications on to their young. Although no one has yet developed a safe and powerful "smart pill" or a gene-editing technique that enhances intelligence in mammals, many experts believe that both things will happen in the not-too-distant future (Farah et al., 2004; Rose, 2002; Turner & Sahakian, 2006).

It is hard to know what to think about these technologies because there is no bright line between technological enhancers and the more traditional kinds. As one group of scientists concluded, "Drugs may seem distinctive among enhancements in that they bring about their effects by altering brain function, but in reality so does any intervention that enhances cognition." If Adderall and good nutrition both enhance cognition by altering brain function, then what's the difference between them? Some think the answer is more ethical than biological: Both drugs and diet can enhance intelligence, but one requires willpower and commitment while the other just requires a prescription. Do we want to live in a world in which a highly prized human attribute such as intelligence can be purchased rather than earned or endowed by nature? That's a question we will all soon be asking—and we will need a whole lot of intelligence and other qualities to answer it (see Other Voices: Not by Intelligence Alone).

cognitive enhancers Drugs that improve the psychological processes that underlie intelligent performance.

Chapter Review

How Can Intelligence Be Measured?

- *Intelligence* is the ability to use one's mind to solve problems and learn from experience. Binet and Simon developed a test that was meant to measure a child's natural aptitude for learning, independent of previous experience.

- Intelligence tests produce a score known as an *intelligence quotient*, or IQ. *Ratio IQ* is the ratio of a person's mental to physical age. *Deviation IQ* is the deviation of an adult's test score from the average adult's test score. Deviation IQ is the more common method for estimating intelligence.

- Intelligence test scores predict many important life outcomes, such as scholastic performance, job performance, health, and wealth.

What Is Intelligence?

- People who score well on one test of mental ability tend to score well on others, which suggests that each person has a particular level of general intelligence (*g*). Yet the person who scores highest on one test doesn't necessarily score highest on every other test, which suggests that different people have different specific abilities (*s*).

- Most intelligence test data can be described by a three-level hierarchy that has several *middle-level abilities* between *g* and *s*.

- The *data-based approach* suggests that there are eight middle-level abilities.

- The *theory-based approach* suggests that there may be middle-level abilities that standard intelligence tests don't measure, such as practical, creative, and emotional intelligence.

- While all cultures value the intellectual ability to solve problems, non-Western cultures sometimes include social responsibility and cooperation in their definitions of intelligence.

Where Does Intelligence Come From?

- The IQs of MZ twins (who share 100% of their genes) are more highly correlated than are the IQs of DZ twins (who share 50% of their genes), suggesting that genes have a powerful influence on intelligence.

- The heritability coefficient (h^2) tells us how much of the difference between the IQ scores of different people is due to differences in their genes, but it does not tell us anything about individuals.

- Environments can influence intelligence. SES and education can both be powerful influences on IQ, though the effects of education are sometimes short-lived.

- Whether or not a person has a specific gene depends on that person's parents, but environmental factors can determine whether that gene is activated.

Who Is Most Intelligent?

- Intelligence is correlated with mental health, and gifted children are as well-adjusted as their peers. Despite the myth, people with intellectual disabilities are typically happy with themselves and their lives.

- Some groups outscore others on intelligence tests. This may happen in part because testing situations can impair the performance of some groups more than others, and in part because low-SES environments have an adverse impact on intelligence. There is no compelling evidence to suggest that this is due to genetic differences between the groups.

- Human intelligence can be increased by a variety of means, from preschool to pharmaceuticals. Some of these methods carry greater risks, and raise more difficult ethical questions, than others.

Changing Minds

1. In biology class, the topic turns to genetics. The professor describes how scientists used gene editing to make a smarter mouse. Your classmate turns to you. "I knew it," they say. "There's a 'smart gene' after all. Some people have it, and some people don't, and that's why some people are intelligent and others aren't." What would you tell your friend about the role genetics plays in intelligence and about the way in which genes affect it?

2. One of your friends tells you about his sister. "We're very competitive," he says. "But she's smarter. We both took IQ tests when we were kids, and she scored 104, but I only scored 102." What would you tell your friend about the relationship between IQ scores and intelligence?

3. A new survey shows that in mathematics departments all over the country, tenured male professors outnumber tenured female professors by about 9 to 1. One of your friends says, "But it's a fact—girls just don't do as well as boys at math, so it's not surprising that fewer girls choose math-related careers." Considering what you've read in this chapter about group differences in intelligence, how might you explain this fact to your friend?

4. One of your cousins has a young son, and she's very proud of the boy's accomplishments. "He's very smart," she says. "I know this because he has a great memory: He gets 100% on all his vocabulary tests." What kind of intelligence do vocabulary tests measure? Although these skills are important for intelligence, what other abilities contribute to an individual's overall intelligence?

5.
Visualizing Data Talking about one of your roommates, a friend says, "I can't believe Pat is doing so poorly in school. Their brother gets straight A's." Review the DATA and explain possible reasons why Pat and their brother perform so differently.

Key Terms

intelligence (p. 370)

ratio IQ (p. 371)

deviation IQ (p. 371)

two-factor theory of intelligence (p. 374)

crystallized intelligence (p. 377)

fluid intelligence (p. 377)

emotional intelligence (p. 378)

fraternal (dizygotic) twins (p. 380)

identical (monozygotic) twins (p. 380)

heritability coefficient (p. 381)

shared environment (p. 383)

nonshared environment (p. 383)

stereotype threat (p. 392)

cognitive enhancers (p. 396)

Development

HIS MOTHER CALLED HIM ADI and showered him with affection, but his father was not so kind. According to his sister, Adi "got his sound thrashing every day. . . . How often on the other hand did my mother caress him and try to obtain with her kindness what my father could not obtain with his harshness." Although Adi's father wanted him to become a civil servant, Adi's true love was art, and his mother quietly encouraged that gentle interest. But when Adi was 18 years old, his mother was diagnosed with terminal cancer, and Adi was bereft. His sister wrote that Adi "spoiled my mother during this time of her life with overflowing tenderness. He was indefatigable in his care for her, wanted to comply with any desire she could possibly have and did all to demonstrate his great love for her."

Adi was heartbroken when his mother died, but he had little time for grieving. As he later wrote, "Poverty and hard reality compelled me to make a quick decision. I was faced with the problem of somehow making my own living." In defiance of his father, Adi decided to make his living as an artist. He applied to art school but was rejected, and so—motherless, homeless, and penniless—Adi wandered the streets for years, sleeping on park benches, living in shelters, and eating in soup kitchens, all the while trying desperately to sell his sketches and watercolours, and more often trading them for food.

But this is not the story of a forgotten artist. Indeed, just 10 years after his mother died, Adi had achieved a degree of fame that few artists have ever known. Today, collectors from all over the world compete at auctions to buy his paintings, which rarely come up for sale. The largest collection of his work is not in the hands of any private citizen or museum but is instead owned by the U.S. government, which keeps the collection under lock and key, in a windowless room in Washington, DC, where few people have ever been allowed to visit. Marylou Gjernes, the longtime curator of this collection, once remarked, "I often looked at them and wondered, 'What if? What if he had been accepted into art school? Would World War II have happened?'" Why would the curator ask such a question? Because the artist's mother called him Adi, but the rest of the world knew him as Adolf Hitler.

In 2014, Adi's painting of Munich's Civil Registry Office (shown here) sold for more than $160,000.

WHY IS IT SO DIFFICULT TO IMAGINE THE ARCHITECT OF THE HOLOCAUST as a gentle child who loved to draw, as a compassionate adolescent who cared for his ailing mother,

Throughout the life span, human beings show both continuity and change in how they look, think, feel, and behave.

or as a dedicated young adult who suffered for the sake of his art? After all, *you* didn't start out as the person you are today. You are utterly different from the baby you once were and utterly different from the elderly person you will someday become—so different, in fact, that people who saw just one of these versions of you would probably be unable to recognize the other. From birth to infancy, from childhood to adolescence, from young adulthood to old age, human beings are transformed by time. They experience dramatic changes in the way they look, think, feel, and act, but they also display some surprising consistencies. **Developmental psychology** is *the study of continuity and change across the life span,* and in the last century, developmental psychologists have discovered some truly amazing things about our metamorphosis.

The story of our development starts where we do: at conception. First we'll examine the 9-month period between conception and birth and see how prenatal events set the stage for much of what's to come. Then we'll examine infancy and childhood, the periods during which children learn how to think about the world and their relationship to it, understand and bond with others, and tell the difference between right and wrong. Next, we'll examine a relatively new invention called adolescence, which is the stage at which children become both independent and sexual creatures. Finally, we'll examine adulthood, the stage at which people typically leave their parents, find mates, and have children of their own.

developmental psychology The study of continuity and change across the life span.

Prenatality: A Womb with a View

Most of us calculate our age by counting our birthdays, but the fact is that on the day we are born we are already 9 months old. The *prenatal stage* of development ends with birth, but it begins 9 months earlier when the egg from a woman and the sperm from a man join together—usually in a fallopian tube, but it could be in a culture medium in a fertility clinic (i.e., *in vitro* fertilization). In either case, the genetic material of both biological parents combines in the fertilized egg.

Prenatal Development

The fertilized egg is called a *zygote,* and its brief existence is known as the **germinal stage,** which is *the period from conception to 2 weeks after conception* (see the timeline in **FIGURE 11.1**, which shows the first three stages of development). During this stage, the one-celled zygote divides into two cells that then divide

Learning Outcomes

WHAT YOU NEED TO KNOW

- Describe the three prenatal stages of development.
- Give reasons why it is advantageous for humans to be born with underdeveloped brains.
- Explain how the prenatal environment influences fetal development.

germinal stage The period from conception to 2 weeks after conception.

embryonic stage The period of prenatal development that lasts from about the 2nd week until about the 8th week.

fetal stage The period of prenatal development that lasts from about the 9th week until birth.

myelination The formation of a fatty sheath around the axons of a neuron.

EYE OF SCIENCE/SCIENCE SOURCE

This electron micrograph shows several human sperm, one of which is fertilizing an egg. Contrary to what many people think, fertilization does not happen right away. It typically happens 1 to 2 days after intercourse but can happen as many as 5 days later.

into four cells that then divide into eight cells, and so on. By the time an infant is born, its body contains trillions of cells, each of which came from the original zygote. During the germinal stage, the zygote migrates down the fallopian tube and implants itself in the wall of the uterus. This is a difficult journey, and about half of zygotes don't complete it, either because they are defective or because they implant themselves in an inhospitable part of the uterus.

The moment the zygote successfully implants itself in the uterine wall, it gives up its old name and takes on a new one: *embryo*. The **embryonic stage** is *a period that starts at about the 2nd week after conception and lasts until about the 8th week after conception*. During this stage, the implanted embryo continues to divide, and its cells begin to differentiate. Although it is only an inch long, the embryo already has arms, legs, and a beating heart. It also has the beginnings of female reproductive organs. If it is a male embryo, it begins to produce a hormone called testosterone that will ultimately masculinize those organs.

At about 9 weeks, the embryo gets a new name: *fetus*. The **fetal stage** is *a period that lasts from about the 9th week after conception until birth*. The fetus has a skeleton and muscles that make it capable of movement. It develops a layer of insulating fat beneath its skin, and its digestive and respiratory systems mature. During the fetal stage, brain cells begin to generate axons and dendrites that allow them to communicate with other brain cells. These cells also begin to undergo a process (described in the Neuroscience and Behaviour chapter) known as **myelination,** which is *the formation of a fatty sheath around the axons of a neuron*. Just as plastic sheathing insulates the wires in a kitchen appliance, myelin insulates the neurons in the brain, preventing the leakage of the signals that travel along the axon.

The human brain grows rapidly during the fetal period, but unlike the brains of other primates, it does not come close to achieving its adult size. A newborn chimpanzee's brain is nearly 60% of its adult size, but a newborn human's brain is only 25% of its adult size, which is to say that 75% of a human's brain development occurs after birth. Why are humans born with such underdeveloped brains? First, humans have really big heads, and if a newborn baby's head were anywhere close to its adult size, then the baby could never pass through its mother's birth canal. So there's that. Second, one of our species' greatest talents is its ability to adapt to a wide range of novel environments that differ in climate, social structure, and so on. Rather than arriving in the world with a highly developed brain that may or may not meet the requirements of its environment, human beings arrive with underdeveloped brains that do much of their developing *within* the very environments in which they ultimately must function, thereby gaining the unique capacities that each environment requires.

Figure 11.1
Developmental Timeline—Germinal, Embryonic, and Fetal Stages This developmental timeline shows the first three stages of development. We'll continue adding to this timeline as the chapter goes on with extra information about the first three stages that we are currently discussing, as well as additional stages. (PHOTO CREDIT FROM LEFT TO RIGHT: BSIP/NEWSCOM; CLAUDE EDELMANN/SCIENCE SOURCE; KATERYNA KON/SCIENCE PHOTO LIBRARY/ ALAMY STOCK PHOTO)

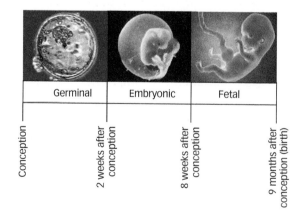

Prenatal Environment

The word *environment* probably makes you think of green fields and blue skies. But the womb is also an environment, and it has a powerful impact on development (Coe & Lubach, 2008; Glynn & Sandman, 2011; Wadhwa et al., 2001; Walsh et al., 2019). Although a woman's bloodstream is separated from the bloodstream of her unborn child by the placenta, many substances can pass through the placenta. A **teratogen** is *any substance that passes from mother to unborn child and impairs development.*

Teratogens include mercury in fish, lead in water, and radon in air (in enclosed spaces like basements), but the most common teratogens are substances that have their very own advertising campaigns. **Fetal alcohol syndrome (FAS)** is *a developmental disorder that stems from heavy alcohol use by the mother during pregnancy* and children born with FAS have a variety of brain abnormalities and cognitive deficits (Carmichael Olson et al., 1997; Streissguth et al., 1999). One study that followed children born with FAS for 25 years found that by the age of 14, a stunning 60% had been suspended or expelled from school (Streissguth, 2007). Although some studies suggest that light drinking does not harm the fetus, there is little consensus about how much drinking is "light" (Warren & Hewitt, 2009). On the other hand, everyone agrees that "none" is a perfectly safe amount.

Tobacco is the other common teratogen, and there is no debate about its effects. Rates of smoking among pregnant women vary dramatically around the globe— ranging from 10 to 11 for every 100 mothers in several European nations (Lange et al., 2018), to 7 or 8 per 100 in Canada and the United States (Drake et al., 2018), to fewer than 1 per 100 in many African nations (Lange et al., 2018). Babies born to mothers who smoke are smaller, more likely to be born prematurely, and more likely to have perceptual and attentional problems in both infancy (Wiebe et al., 2014) and childhood (Espy et al., 2011; Fried & Watkinson, 2000). Even second-hand smoke can lead to reduced birth weight and deficits in attention and learning (Makin et al., 1991; Windham et al., 1999). Exactly how dangerous is smoking during pregnancy? Very! Research suggests that smoking during pregnancy increases a woman's odds of having a stillborn child by a whopping 47% (Marufu et al., 2015).

The things a pregnant woman ingests can harm her unborn child, but so too can the things she *fails* to ingest. Women who receive insufficient nutrition during pregnancy often have babies who have *intrauterine growth restriction* or IUGR. These newborns are extremely small and underweight, and have a greatly increased chance of becoming physically or mentally ill adults (Levine et al., 2015). Nearly 15% of the world's newborns suffer from IUGR (Blencowe et al., 2019), which is a particular problem in developing countries (see **FIGURE 11.2**). It is worth noting that the embryo is more vulnerable to the effects of malnutrition and teratogens than is the fetus, but structures such as the central nervous system are vulnerable throughout the entire prenatal period.

The prenatal environment is rich with chemicals that affect the unborn child, but it is also rich with information. The fetus can hear its mother's heartbeat, the gastrointestinal sounds associated with her digestion, and her voice. Fetuses show more elevated heart rates when they hear their mother's voice than the voice of a female stranger (Kisilevsky et al., 2003). Newborns who listen to strangers speaking two languages will suck more vigorously when they hear words from their mother's native language, indicating that they are already familiar with the tempo and rhythm of their mother's speech (Byers-Heinlein et al., 2010). What unborn children hear in the womb even influences the sounds they make themselves. French newborns cry with a rising pitch and German newborns cry with a falling pitch, mimicking the cadence of their mother's native tongue (Mampe et al., 2009). Clearly, the fetus is listening.

This chimp and boy share a deep interest in dirt, bugs, and leaves. But one difference between them is that a newborn chimp's brain will not quite double in size while a newborn human's brain will quadruple!

teratogen Any substance that passes from mother to unborn child and impairs development.

fetal alcohol syndrome (FAS) A developmental disorder that stems from heavy alcohol use by the mother during pregnancy.

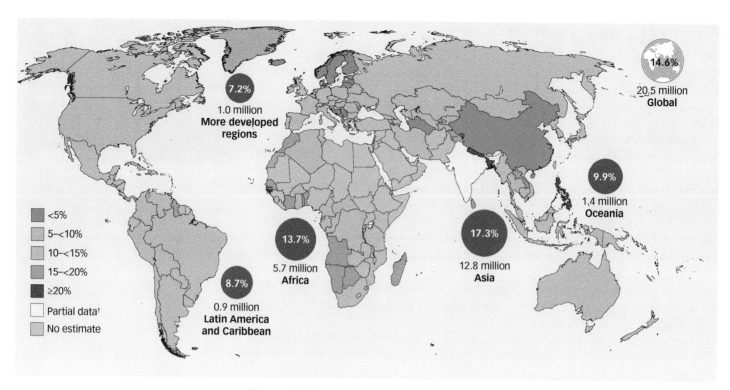

Figure 11.2
Worldwide Prevalence of Newborns Suffering from Intrauterine Growth Restriction
IUGR is a problem everywhere, but particularly in developing nations.

Infancy and Childhood: Perceiving, Doing, and Thinking

Learning Outcomes

WHAT YOU NEED TO KNOW

- Describe the evidence suggesting that newborns can see.

- Explain the two rules of motor development.

- Outline the stages of Piaget's theory of cognitive development.

- Differentiate between egocentrism and theory of mind.

- Describe the key skills that allow infants to learn from others.

infancy The stage of development that begins at birth and lasts between 18 and 24 months.

Newborn babies don't look like they can do much more than poop, burp, sleep, and cry. But looks can be deceiving. **Infancy** is *the stage of development that begins at birth and lasts between 18 and 24 months,* and in the last few decades, researchers have discovered that much more is going on inside the infant than meets the untrained eye.

Perceptual Development

New parents might not stand around the crib and make goofy faces if they realized that their babies can't see them. Newborns have a limited range of vision, and the amount of detail they can see from 6 metres away is roughly equivalent to the amount of detail that you can see from 183 metres away (Banks & Salapatek, 1983). On the other hand, newborns can see things that are about 20 to 30 centimetres away, which just so happens to be the distance between a mother's face and their nursing infant's eyes.

But wait. How do psychologists know what a newborn can and can't see? Recall from the Learning chapter that *habituation* is the tendency for organisms to respond less intensely to a stimulus each time it is presented. So if a newborn habituates to a visual stimulus, that means they must have been able to see it. If newborns are shown an object over and over again, they will stare a lot at first and then less and less each time the object is presented. If the object is then rotated 90°, the newborns will begin staring at it again (Slater et al., 1988). So yes, newborns can see objects.

As it turns out, the objects to which newborns are especially attentive are those that look like faces (Biro et al., 2014; Jayaraman et al., 2015). For example, newborns in

(a)

(b)

Figure 11.3

Infants Attend to Social Stimuli When newborns are shown the stimuli in panel A, they look longer at the one with facial features. And when three lights are shined through a mother's belly in the configurations shown in panel B, fetuses are more likely to turn their heads towards the lights in the face-like configuration on the left. (A) FROM MORTON, J., & JOHNSON, M. H. (1991). CONSPEC AND CONLERN: A TWO-PROCESS THEORY OF INFANT FACE RECOGNITION. COPYRIGHT © 1991 BY AMERICAN PSYCHOLOGICAL ASSOCIATION. REPRODUCED AND ADAPTED WITH PERMISSION ALL RIGHTS RESERVED.; (B) THE HUMAN FETUS PREFERENTIALLY ENGAGES WITH FACE-LIKE VISUAL STIMULI, REID, ET AL. CURRENT BIOLOGY 27, PAGE 1826, JUNE 19, 2017 © 2017. PUBLISHED BY ELSEVIER LTD. OPEN ACCESS ARTICLE UNDER THE CC BY LICENSE (HTTP://CREATIVECOMMONS.ORG /LICENSES/BY/4.0/).

Newborns have a limited range of vision. They can see just far enough to make eye contact with the person cuddling them.

one study were shown a shape that either had facial features, scrambled facial features, or no facial features (see **FIGURE 11.3A**). When the shape was moved across their fields of vision, the newborns tracked the movement with their eyes—but they tracked the moving shape that had facial features longer than they tracked either of the others (Johnson et al., 1991; cf. Kwon et al., 2016). Some studies suggest that even the fetus attends to facial features (see **FIGURE 11.3B**). When lights were shined through pregnant women's abdomens, their fetuses were more likely to turn towards the lights that were configured like a human face (Reid et al., 2017; Reid & Dunn, 2021).

Infants don't just attend to human objects—they also respond to them. In one study, researchers got very close to two groups of newborn infants. They stuck out their tongues in front of one group and pursed their lips in front of the other. Did the newborns see them? Yes, and not only that, but the newborns in the first group stuck out their own tongues more often than did the newborns in the second group; and the newborns in the second group pursed their lips more often than did the newborns in the first group (Davis et al., 2021; Meltzoff & Moore, 1977; cf. Meltzoff et al., 2018; Oostenbroek et al., 2016; Slaughter, 2021). It doesn't take newborns long to learn this trick: They have been shown to mimic facial expressions in their very first *hour* of life (Reissland, 1988). Clearly, babies are watching—and what they are watching most closely is us!

Motor Development

Infants can use their eyes and ears right away, but they have to spend some time learning to use their other parts. **Motor development** is *the emergence of the ability to execute physical actions* such as reaching, grasping, crawling, and walking. Infants can do a bit of this at birth because they are born with a small set of **motor reflexes,** which are *motor responses that are triggered by specific patterns of sensory stimulation.* For example, the *rooting reflex* causes infants to move their mouths towards any object that touches their cheek, and the *sucking reflex* causes them to suck any object that enters their mouth. Together, these two reflexes allow newborn infants to find their mother's nipple and begin feeding—a behaviour so vitally important that nature took no chances and hard-wired it into every one of us. Interestingly, these and other reflexes that are present at birth seem to disappear in the first few months as infants learn to execute more sophisticated motor behaviour.

The development of these more sophisticated behaviours tends to follow two general principles. The first is the **cephalocaudal principle** (or the "top-to-bottom" principle), which describes *the tendency for motor skills to emerge in sequence from the head to the feet.* Infants tend to gain control over their heads first, their arms and trunks next, and their legs last. Young infants who are placed on their stomachs may

Infants mimic the facial expressions of adults—and vice versa, of course!

motor development The emergence of the ability to execute physical actions.

motor reflexes Motor responses that are triggered by specific patterns of sensory stimulation.

cephalocaudal principle The "top-to-bottom" principle that describes the tendency for motor skills to emerge in sequence from the head to the feet.

Motor skills develop through practice. In just 1 hour in a playroom, the average 12- to 19-month-old infant takes 2,368 steps; travels 600 metres; and falls 17 times (Adolph et al., 2012).

lift their heads and chests by using their arms for support, but they typically have little control over their legs. The second principle is the **proximodistal principle** (or the "inside-to-outside" principle), which describes *the tendency for motor skills to emerge in sequence from the centre to the periphery*. Infants learn to control their trunks before their elbows and knees, which they learn to control before their hands and feet (see **FIGURE 11.4**). Although motor skills develop in an orderly sequence, they do not develop on a strict timetable. Rather, the timing of these skills is influenced by many factors, such as the infant's incentive for reaching, body weight, muscular development, and general level of activity. Some evidence suggests that the early emergence of certain motor skills is associated with greater intelligence in adulthood (Flensborg-Madsen & Mortensen, 2018).

For most adults, perceptual and motor skills work seamlessly together: You see your phone sitting on the table, you reach for it, and then you slide it into a pocket that is large enough to hold it. But children take a while to learn to coordinate their perceptions and their actions. When infants or young children are allowed to play with an object such as a slide or a car and are then given a miniature version of the object, they will often make a *scale error* by treating the miniature object as though it were the regular-sized one—for instance, they'll try to get inside the miniature car or slide down the miniature slide (DeLoache et al., 2004) (see **FIGURE 11.5**). Although the children can *see* that the miniature objects are small (which is why they bend down to touch them), their perceptual knowledge of the object's size is not yet coordinated with their motor behaviour so they try to do with the miniature object what they would normally do with the regular-sized object. The perceptual system that is responsible for the identification of objects is neurologically distinct from the motor system that is responsible for the control of movements, which is why certain kinds of brain damage can cause these two systems to become dis-coordinated in adults. The same two systems appear to be not-yet-coordinated in infants and young children.

proximodistal principle The "inside-to-outside" principle that describes the tendency for motor skills to emerge in sequence from the centre to the periphery.

Figure 11.4
Motor Development Motor skills do not emerge on a strict timetable, but they do emerge in a strict sequence.

Figure 11.5

Scale Errors The photo on the left shows a 21-month-old child making a "scale error" by attempting to slide down a miniature slide. The photo on the right shows a 24-month-old child trying to force their foot inside a miniature car. REPUBLISHED WITH PERMISSION OF AAAS FROM DELOACHE ET AL. SCALE ERRORS OFFER EVIDENCE FOR A PERCEPTION-ACTION DISSOCIATION EARLY IN LIFE, SCIENCE, 304, 1027 (2004). PERMISSION CONVEYED THROUGH COPYRIGHT CLEARANCE CENTER.

Cognitive Development

Infants can see and hear and move their bodies. But so can grasshoppers. Can infants do the things that make humans so special, such as thinking? In the first half of the 20th century, a Swiss biologist named Jean Piaget became interested in this question and began to study **cognitive development,** which is *the process by which infants and children gain the ability to think and understand.* Piaget's studies suggested that in the course of cognitive development, infants and children learn three essential lessons: how the physical world works, how their minds work, and how other people's minds work. Let's see how they achieve each of these understandings.

Discovering the World

Piaget (1954) suggested that cognitive development occurs in four stages: the sensorimotor stage, the preoperational stage, the concrete operational stage, and the formal operational stage (see **FIGURE 11.6** and **TABLE 11.1** and don't worry, we'll explain all the terms in quotes as we go). The **sensorimotor stage** is *a stage of cognitive development that begins at birth and lasts through infancy.* As the term *sensorimotor* suggests, infants at this stage are mainly busy using their ability to *sense* (their perceptual skills) and their ability to *move* (their motor skills) to acquire information about the world.

cognitive development The process by which infants and children gain the ability to think and understand.

sensorimotor stage A stage of cognitive development that begins at birth and lasts through infancy.

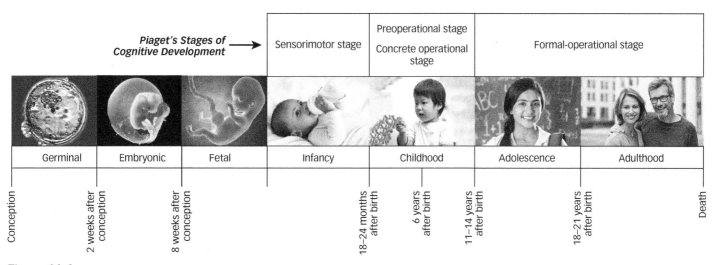

Figure 11.6

Developmental Timeline—Infancy and Childhood with Piaget's Stages of Cognitive Development
(PHOTO CREDIT FROM LEFT TO RIGHT: BSIP/NEWSCOM; CLAUDE EDELMANN/SCIENCE SOURCE; KATERYNA KON/SCIENCE PHOTO LIBRARY/ALAMY STOCK PHOTO; PROSTOCK-STUDIO/ISTOCK/GETTY IMAGES; RYULTSUKI/IMAGESOURCE/AGE FOTOSTOCK; ASISEEIT/E+/GETTY IMAGES; WESTEND61/GETTY IMAGES)

Jean Piaget (1896–1980) was the father of modern developmental psychology, as well as the last man who could actually get away with wearing a beret.

TABLE 11.1

PIAGET'S FOUR STAGES OF COGNITIVE DEVELOPMENT

Stage	Characteristic
Sensorimotor (Birth–2 years)	Infant experiences the world by sensing it and moving in it, develops "schemas," begins to act intentionally, and shows evidence of understanding "object permanence."
Preoperational (2–6 years)	Child acquires motor skills but does not understand "conservation." Child begins this stage by thinking egocentrically but ends with a basic understanding of other minds.
Concrete operational (6–11 years)	Child can think logically about physical objects and events and understands "conservation."
Formal operational (11 years and up)	Child can think logically about abstract propositions and hypotheticals.

By actively exploring their environments with their eyes, mouths, and fingers, infants begin to construct **schemas,** which are *theories about the way the world works.* If an infant tugs a stuffed animal with their hand and the toy moves closer, that fact is incorporated into the infant's theory about how physical objects respond to force ("Things come closer if I pull them"). Later, the infant can apply that theory to a novel stimulus, such as a rattle or a ball. Piaget called this process **assimilation,** which is *the process of applying a schema to novel stimuli.* Of course, infants' theories about the world are sometimes disconfirmed, which causes infants to take special notice (Stahl & Feigenson, 2015). If the infant applies their theory about how physical objects respond to force by tugging on the tail of the family cat, the cat is likely to sprint in the opposite direction, which will lead the infant to modify their theory ("Aha, inanimate things come closer when I pull them, but animate things just hiss and run"). Piaget called this process **accommodation,** which is *the process of adjusting a schema to incorporate new information.*

What kinds of schemas do infants develop, apply, and adjust? Piaget suggested that infants are surprisingly clueless about some of the most basic properties of the physical world and must acquire information about those properties through experience. For example, when you put your shoes in the closet, you know that they are still there even after you close the closet door, and you would be surprised if you opened the door a moment later and found the closet empty. But according to Piaget, this wouldn't surprise an infant at all because infants do not yet have **object permanence,** which refers to *the understanding that objects exist even when they are not visible.* Piaget noted that in the first few months of life, infants act as though objects stop existing the moment they are out of sight. For instance, a 2-month-old infant will track a moving object with her eyes, but once the object leaves her visual field, she will not search for it. Put the shoes in the closet and close the door and — poof! — the infant acts as if they no longer exist. As every babysitter knows, if the baby keeps reaching for your phone, just put it in your pocket, and as far as the baby is concerned, it no longer exists.

But does that really tell us that the baby doesn't yet have object permanence? To answer this question definitively, of course, we'd have to know what infants are thinking, which Piaget considered impossible: "The child's first year of life is unfortunately still an abyss of mysteries for the psychologist. If only we could know what is going on in a baby's mind while observing him in action, we could certainly understand everything there is to psychology" (Piaget, 1927/1977, p. 199). But there's nothing scientists love more than an abyss of mysteries, and in the 1960s, the psychologist Robert Fantz (1964) developed an ingenious technique for finding out what is "going on in a baby's mind." The logic of his *preferential looking time* technique is simple. Take a look at the objects in **FIGURE 11.7**. Chances are good that you looked longer

During the sensorimotor stage, infants explore with their hands and mouths, learning important lessons about the physical world such as "frosting sticks to your face whether you like it or not."

schemas Theories about the way the world works.

assimilation The process of applying a schema to novel stimuli.

accommodation The process of adjusting a schema to incorporate new information.

object permanence The understanding that objects exist even when they are not visible.

Figure 11.7
But . . . That's Impossible! Which of these pictures did you look at longer? What does that reveal about your theory of the physical world?

at the one on the left than the one on the right. Why? Because the object on the left is an "impossible object" that could not possibly exist in the real three-dimensional world. You found it interesting precisely because it violates your theory of how the physical world works. Now, here's the cool part: Because you naturally stare longer at things that violate your theories, psychologists can use the duration of your stare to figure out what your theories are! You must believe that when you look at a box, the bar that connects the back bottom corner to the right bottom corner cannot possibly pass in *front* of the vertical bar closest to you. But that's exactly what the figure on the left seems to do, which is exactly what made it stare-worthy.

When psychologists started using this simple technique with infants, they discovered that infants actually know more than Piaget suspected. For instance, in one study, infants were shown a miniature drawbridge that flipped up and down (see **FIGURE 11.8**). These were the "habituation trials." Once the infants got used to this, they watched as a solid box was placed behind the drawbridge—in the path of the drawbridge, but out of the infant's sight. Some infants then saw a *possible* event: The drawbridge began to flip and then it suddenly stopped, as if its motion were being impeded by the unseen solid box. Other infants saw an *impossible* event: The drawbridge began to flip—and then it didn't stop, as if its motion were unimpeded by the unseen solid box. So what did infants do? Four-month-old infants stared longer at the impossible event than at the possible event (Baillargeon et al., 1985). The only thing that made the impossible event impossible was the fact that an unseen box should have—but didn't—impede the motion of the drawbridge, which means that

Habituation

Possible event

Impossible event

Figure 11.8
The Impossible Event During the habituation trials, infants watch a drawbridge flip back and forth with nothing in its path until they grow bored. During the test trials, a box is placed behind the drawbridge, and the infants are shown either a possible event (in which the motion of the drawbridge is impeded) or an impossible event (in which the motion of the drawbridge is not impeded). The graph shows the infants' looking times during the habituation trials and the test trials. As you can see, during the test trials, the infants' interest was reawakened by the impossible event but not by the possible event (Baillargeon et al., 1985).

Looking time (seconds)

60
50
40
30
20
10
0

Impossible event

Possible event

Habituation trials   **Test trials**

childhood The period that begins at about 18 to 24 months and lasts until about 11 to 14 years.

preoperational stage The stage of cognitive development that begins at about 2 years and ends at about 6 years, during which children develop a preliminary understanding of the physical world.

concrete operational stage The stage of cognitive development that begins at about 6 years and ends at about 11 years, during which children learn how various actions, or *operations*, can transform the concrete objects of the physical world.

conservation The understanding that many of the physical properties of an object are conserved (i.e., not changed) by changes in the object's appearance.

formal operational stage The final stage of cognitive development that begins around the age of 11, during which children learn to reason about abstract concepts.

When preoperational children are shown two equal-size glasses filled with equal amounts of liquid, they correctly say that neither glass "has more." But when the contents of one glass are poured into a taller, thinner glass, they incorrectly say that the taller glass now "has more." Concrete operational children don't make this mistake, because they recognize that operations such as pouring change the appearance of the liquid but not its actual volume.

the infants must have realized that the box continued to exist even when it could no longer be seen. These and other studies suggest that infants acquire object permanence much earlier than Piaget realized (Shinskey & Munakata, 2005; Wang & Baillargeon, 2008).

Discovering the Mind

The long period following infancy is called **childhood,** which is *the period that begins at about 18 to 24 months and lasts until about 11 to 14 years.* According to Piaget, people enter childhood at one stage of cognitive development and leave at another. They enter at the **preoperational stage,** which is *the stage of cognitive development that begins at about 2 years and ends at about 6 years, during which children develop a preliminary understanding of the physical world.* They exit at the **concrete operational stage,** which is *the stage of cognitive development that begins at about 6 years and ends at about 11 years, during which children learn how actions, or operations, can transform the concrete objects of the physical world.*

The difference between these stages is nicely illustrated by one of Piaget's clever experiments, in which he showed children a row of cups and asked them to place an egg in each. Preoperational children were able to do this, and afterward they readily agreed that there were just as many eggs as there were cups. Then Piaget removed the eggs and spread them out in a long line that extended beyond the row of cups. Preoperational children incorrectly claimed that there were now more eggs than cups, pointing out that the row of eggs was longer than the row of cups and hence there must be more of them. Concrete operational children, on the other hand, correctly reported that the number of eggs did not change when they were merely spread out in a longer line. They understood that *quantity* is a property of a set of concrete objects that does not change when an operation such as *spreading out* alters the set's appearance (Piaget, 1954). Piaget called this insight **conservation,** which is *the understanding that many of the physical properties of an object are conserved (i.e., not changed) by changes in the object's appearance.*

Preoperational children, it seems, don't readily distinguish between appearances and reality—between the way things look and the way things are. You know that a wagon can *be* red but *look* gray at dusk, and that a highway can *be* dry but *look* wet in the heat. Adults are delighted by visual illusions precisely because they know that things can look one way and yet be another. Preoperational children don't yet have this understanding. They assume that things are as they seem, so when something *looks* gray or wet it must *be* gray or wet. As they move from the preoperational to the concrete operational stage, they come to realize that the way the world *appears* and the way the world *is* are sometimes very different things.

Once children have this epiphany, they can solve problems that require them to ignore an object's subjective appearance (cf. Deák, 2006; Lane et al., 2014). For example, they can understand that when a ball of clay is rolled, stretched, or flattened, it is still the same amount of clay despite the fact that it looks larger in one form than in another. They can understand that when water is poured from a short, wide beaker into a tall, thin cylinder, it is still the same amount of water despite the fact that the water level in the tall cylinder is higher. They can understand that when a sponge is painted gray to look like a rock, it is still a sponge despite its rocky appearance. In short, they can understand that certain operations—such as squishing, pouring, and spreading out—can change what an object *looks* like without changing what the object *is* like.

Children learn to solve physical problems at the concrete operational stage, and they learn to solve nonphysical problems at the **formal operational stage,** which is *the final stage of cognitive development that begins around the age of 11, during which children learn to reason about abstract concepts.* People who move on to this stage (and Piaget believed that some people never do) are able to reason systematically about abstract concepts such as *liberty* and *love* and about hypotheticals and counterfactuals—about events that have not yet happened and about events that might have happened but didn't. There are no concrete objects in the world to which the words *liberty* and *love* refer, yet people at the formal operational stage can think and reason about such concepts in the same way that a concrete operational child can think and reason about squishing and folding. The ability to generate, consider, reason about, or mentally "operate on" abstract concepts is the hallmark of formal operations.

Discovering Other Minds

As children develop, they discover their own minds. But they also discover the minds of others. Preoperational children don't fully grasp the fact that they have minds that mentally represent objects (which is why they think that things must be the way they look), and as a result, they also don't fully grasp the fact that different people have different minds that can mentally represent the same objects in different ways. As such, preoperational children typically expect others to see the world as they do: "If it looks like a rock then it is a rock, and if it is a rock, then it looks like a rock to everyone." When a 3-year-old child is seated so that they can see the front side of an object on a table, and is then asked what a person on the opposite side of the table is seeing, they typically claim that the other person is also seeing the front side—just as the child is (see **FIGURE 11.9**). **Egocentrism** is *the failure to understand that the world appears different to different people.* It is a hallmark of the preoperational stage, and it reveals itself in a variety of interesting ways.

Perceptions and Beliefs Just as 3-year-old children fail to realize that other people don't always see what they themselves see, they also fail to realize that other people don't always know what they themselves know. This fact has been demonstrated in numerous studies using the *false-belief task* (Wimmer & Perner, 1983). In the standard version of this task, children see a puppet named Maxi deposit some chocolate in a cupboard and then leave the room. A second puppet arrives a moment later, finds the chocolate, and moves it to a different cupboard. The children are then asked where Maxi will look for the chocolate when he returns: in the first cupboard where he initially put it, or in the second cupboard, where the children know it currently is?

Most 5-year-olds realize that Maxi will search the first cupboard because Maxi did not see what the children saw—namely, that the chocolate was moved. But 3-year-olds typically claim that Maxi will look in the second cupboard. Why? Because that's where *the children* know the chocolate is—and they assume that what they know, everyone knows! Children are able to give the right answer in the false-belief task somewhere between the ages of 4 and 6 (Callaghan et al., 2005), though children in some cultures are able to give it earlier than children in others (Liu et al., 2008).

According to Piaget, people cannot reason about abstract concepts such as freedom and justice until they reach the formal operational stage. But they can still hold signs!

egocentrism The failure to understand that the world appears different to different people.

Figure 11.9

Egocentrism Preoperational children mistakenly believe that others share their points of view. The child can see the tree on the table, but when asked what the adult sees, will say "A tree." The child doesn't seem to realize that although they can see the tree, the adult cannot.

Did you ever notice that when small children are told to hide, they sometimes cover their eyes? That's because if they can't see you, they assume that you can't see them either (Russell et al., 2012).

But some researchers think the false-belief task (like Piaget's test for object permanence) simply doesn't allow very young children to demonstrate their true abilities (Scott & Baillargeon, 2017), and several studies have shown that even infants can perform surprisingly well when given modified versions of the false-belief task that make it easier for them to respond (Baillargeon et al., 2010; Onishi & Baillargeon, 2005; Rubin-Fernandez & Geurts, 2012; Senju et al., 2011; Southgate et al., 2007; but see Kulke et al., 2018). Even chimpanzees, bonobos, and orangutans can perform well on the modified versions of this task (Krupenye et al., 2016). Of course, infants and great apes may not arrive at the right answer the same way older children do, namely, by truly understanding that others can have beliefs that differ from their own (Apperly & Butterfill, 2009; Low & Watts, 2013). Still, whatever it is they are doing, their performances are impressive, and it seems clear that the age at which children acquire some rudimentary understanding of other minds is lower than Piaget suspected.

Desires and Emotions Different people have different perceptions and beliefs, but they also have different desires and emotions. What do children understand about these things? Even infants seem to understand that desires guide behaviour (Liu et al., 2017) and that other people's desires can differ from their own. For example, a 2-year-old who likes dogs can understand that other children don't like dogs and can correctly predict that other children will avoid dogs that the child themselves would approach. When 18-month-old toddlers see an adult express disgust while eating a food that the toddlers enjoy, they hand the adult a different food, as if they understand that different people have different tastes (Repacholi & Gopnik, 1997). Interestingly, young children seem to understand other people's desires best when their own desires have been fulfilled and are not competing for their attention (Atance et al., 2010).

In contrast, children take a much longer time to understand that other people may have emotional reactions unlike their own. When 5-year-olds hear a story in which Little Red Riding Hood knocks on her grandmother's door, unaware that a wolf is inside waiting to devour her, they realize that Little Red Riding Hood does not know what they themselves know; nonetheless, they expect Little Red Riding Hood to feel what they themselves feel, namely, afraid (Bradmetz & Schneider, 2004; de Rosnay et al., 2004; Harris et al., 1989). When asked where Maxi will look for the chocolate that was moved while Maxi was out of the room, they correctly say that Maxi will look in the original location, but they incorrectly say that Maxi feels sad right now. It is only at about 6 years of age that children come to understand that because they and others have different knowledge, they and others may also experience different emotions in the same situation.

Theory of Mind Clearly, children have a whole lot to learn about how the mind works—and most of them eventually do. The vast majority of children ultimately come to understand that they and others have minds that can represent the world in different ways. Once children understand these things, they are said to have acquired a **theory of mind,** which is *the understanding that the mind produces representations of the world and that these representations guide behaviour.*

The age at which most children acquire a theory of mind appears to be influenced by a variety of factors, such as the number of siblings the child has, the frequency with which the child engages in pretend play, whether the child has an imaginary companion, the socioeconomic status of the child's family, and even the child's family's culture (see A World of Difference: That's the Dumbest Thing I Never Heard!). But of all the factors researchers have studied, language seems to be the most important in this regard (Astington & Baird, 2005). Children's language skills are an excellent predictor of how well they perform on false-belief tasks (Happé, 1995), as is the way caregivers talk to those children. Perhaps not surprisingly, children whose caregivers frequently talk about thoughts and feelings tend to be good at understanding beliefs and emotions. Some psychologists speculate that children benefit from hearing psychological words such as *think, know,* and *want* (Ruffman et al., 2018). Others suggest that children benefit

theory of mind The understanding that the mind produces representations of the world and that these representations guide behaviour.

from the grammatically complex sentences that typically contain these psychological words. And still others believe that caregivers who use psychological words are also more effective in getting children to reflect on their own mental states. Whatever the explanation, it is clear that language—and especially language about thoughts and feelings—is an important tool for helping children make sense of their own and others' minds (Harris et al., 2005). This fact also helps explain why deaf children whose parents do not know sign language are slow to acquire a theory of mind (DeVilliers, 2005; Peterson & Siegal, 1999; Peterson et al., 2016; Pyers & Senghas, 2009).

Another group of children who are slow to acquire a theory of mind are those with *autism,* a disorder we'll cover in more depth in the Disorders chapter. Children with autism often have difficulty communicating with other people and making friends, and some psychologists have suggested that this is because they have trouble acquiring a theory of mind (Frith, 2003). They often find it difficult to understand the inner lives of other people (Dawson et al., 2007; Peterson et al., 2016), are often slow to recognize that other people can believe what they don't believe themselves (Baron-Cohen et al., 1985; Senju et al., 2009), and often have trouble understanding belief-based emotions such as embarrassment and shame (Baron-Cohen, 1991; Heerey et al., 2003). Interestingly, children with autism (and other children who have not yet acquired a theory of mind) are less likely to experience "contagious yawning," which apparently requires that one be able to imagine what the yawner herself is experiencing (Platek et al., 2003; Senju et al., 2007).

Piaget Remixed Cognitive development is a long, strange trip, and Piaget's ideas about it were nothing short of groundbreaking. Few psychologists have had such a profound and enduring impact. But while some of his ideas have held up quite well, in the last few decades psychologists have discovered two general ways in which Piaget got it wrong. First, Piaget thought that children graduated from one stage to another in the same way that they graduated from kindergarten to first grade: A child is in kindergarten *or* first grade, they are never in both, and there is an exact moment of transition to which anyone can point. Modern psychologists see development as a more fluid, continuous, and less step-like progression than Piaget believed it to be. Children who are making the transition between stages may perform more mature behaviours one day and less mature behaviours the next. In a sense, cognitive development is more like the gradual change of seasons than it is like graduation day.

The second thing about which Piaget was mistaken was the ages at which these transitions occur. By and large, as you've seen, they happen *earlier* than Piaget realized (Gopnik, 2012). For example, Piaget suggested that infants lacked object permanence because they did not actively search for objects that were moved out of their sight. But when researchers use experimental procedures that allow infants to "show what they know," even 4-month-olds display some object permanence. Piaget also suggested that it takes many years until children can overcome their egocentrism enough to realize that others do not know what they know, but new experimental procedures have detected some evidence of this understanding in infants as young as 13 months (Baillargeon et al., 2010). Every year, ingenious researchers find new ways of testing infants and children, and every year, textbook authors must lower the age at which cognitive milestones are achieved. Don't be too surprised if in the coming years, someone discovers that zygotes can do algebra.

Discovering Our Cultures

Piaget saw the child as a lone scientist who goes out into the world and makes observations, develops and applies theories, and then revises those theories in light of disconfirming evidence. But scientists rarely go it alone. Rather, they receive training from more experienced scientists, inherit the theories and methods of their forebears, and seek each other's opinions. According to the Russian psychologist Lev Vygotsky, children do the same thing. Vygotsky was born in 1896—the same year as

Some people with autism have an unusual ability to concentrate on small details, words, and numbers for extended periods of time. Thorkil Sonne (*right*) started a company called Specialisterne.com, which places people who have autism—such as his son Lars (*left*)—at jobs that they can do better than more "neurotypical" people can.

A World of Difference • That's the Dumbest Thing I Never Heard!

Everyone sees the world a bit differently. That's obvious to you. But it isn't obvious to a 2-year-old child, who naturally assumes that her view is everyone else's view as well. As children develop, they acquire a theory of mind, and one component of that theory is the realization that other people may believe things that the child doesn't, and may not believe things that the child does.

But where does that realization come from? Does a lightbulb just switch on at some point, leaving the child permanently illuminated? Piaget didn't think so. He thought children came to this realization in the course of their social interactions, where they inevitably encountered disagreement. A child says, "That dog is mean," and their father replies, "No, he's very nice." A playmate says, "My house is red," and another responds, "You're wrong. It's blue!" All of the disagreements that children hear eventually lead them to understand that different people have different beliefs about the world.

Although being disagreeable is a popular pastime in Western societies, not all cultures appreciate a good argument as much as Americans do. For instance, many Eastern cultures encourage respect for one's elders and family harmony, and they encourage people to avoid interpersonal conflict. In such cultures, if a person doesn't have something agreeable to say, they often say nothing at all. Thus, children who grow up in these cultures do not regularly hear people challenging each other's beliefs. So how do they come to understand that different people *have* different beliefs?

Slowly! For example, in one study, 77% of Australian preschoolers understood that different people have different beliefs, but only 47% of Iranian preschoolers understood the same (Shahaeian et al., 2011). Were the Iranian children just slow learners? Nope. In fact, they were just as likely as the Australian children to have acquired other components of a theory of mind—for instance, the realization that different people *like* different things—and they were even *more* likely than the Australian children to realize that people know what they see and not what they don't. Iranian preschoolers appear to learn just as fast as Australian preschoolers do, but it takes them a bit longer to understand that people have different beliefs because they are exposed to fewer debates about them. The pattern seen in Australia is also seen in the United States, and the pattern seen in Iran is also seen in China, suggesting that this may be a stable difference between Western and Eastern cultures (Wellman et al., 2006).

In the end, of course, everyone comes to realize that human beings don't always see eye to eye. But people who live in places where they are encouraged to speak their minds and air their differences in public seem to figure that out a bit earlier than most. At least that's what research suggests.

When parents debate the best way to get a bike into a car, their children learn that people have different beliefs. For example, Mom believes that Dad should shut up, and Dad doesn't. But he will. Probably soon.

PHOTOALTO/LAURENCE MOUTON/GETTY IMAGES

Piaget—but unlike Piaget, he believed that cognitive development was largely the result of the child's interaction with members of their own culture rather than their interaction with rocks, paper, scissors, and other concrete objects. Vygotsky didn't think it made sense to divide the universe of skills into those that a child has and has not yet acquired. He noted that between the things a child can do and the things a child cannot do lies a *zone of proximal development,* which refers to the range of things children cannot do by themselves but can do with guidance and instruction. For example, most infants cannot open a jar on their own, but they can learn to open a jar if an adult shows them how.

Vygotsky also noted that *cultural tools,* such as language and counting systems, exert a strong influence on cognitive development (Vygotsky, 1978). For instance, in both English and Chinese, the numbers beyond 20 are named by a decade (twenty) that is followed by a digit (one), and their names follow a logical pattern (twenty-one, twenty-two, twenty-three, etc.). In Chinese, the numbers from 11 to 19 are constructed the same way (ten-one, ten-two, ten-three . . .). But in English, the names of the numbers between 11 and 19 either reverse the order of the decade and the digit (sixteen, seventeen) or are just plain arbitrary (eleven, twelve). The difference in the regularity of these two systems makes a big difference to the children who must learn them. The fact that 12 is a 10 plus a 2 is obvious to the Chinese-speaking child, who actually calls the number "ten-two," but not so obvious to the English-speaking child, who calls it "twelve."

In one study, children from many countries were asked to hand an experimenter a certain number of bricks. Some of the bricks were single, and some were glued together in strips of 10. When Asian children were asked to hand the experimenter 26 bricks, they tended to hand over two strips of 10 plus six singles. Non-Asian children used the clumsier strategy of counting out 26 single bricks (Miura et al., 1994). Results such as these suggest that the regularity of the counting system that children inherit can promote or discourage their discovery of basic mathematical facts (Gordon, 2004; Imbo & LeFevre, 2009).

Human children can take advantage of the accumulated wisdom of their species because unlike most other animals, they have three essential skills that allow them to learn from others (Meltzoff et al., 2009; Striano & Reid, 2006; Whiten, 2017):

1. If an adult turns their head to the left, both 3-month-old infants and 9-month-old infants will look to the left. But if the adult first closes their eyes and then looks to the left, the 3-month old infant will still look to the left, but the 9-month-old infant will not (Brooks & Meltzoff, 2002; see **FIGURE 11.10**). This suggests that younger infants are following the adult's head movements but that older infants are following the adult's gaze. That is, the older infants are trying to see what they think the adult is seeing (Rossano et al., 2012). The ability to focus on what another person is focused on, known as *joint attention,* is a prerequisite for learning what others have to teach us (Sodian & Kristen-Antonow, 2015).

2. Infants are natural mimics who often do what they see adults do (Jones, 2007). This tendency is known as *imitation*. Children imitate adults so precisely that they even copy parts of their actions that they know to be unimportant (e.g., saying "Here goes" before opening a jar), a phenomenon called *overimitation* (Lyons et al., 2007; Simpson & Riggs, 2011). But they don't copy parts of the adult's actions that they know to be wrong. When an 18-month-old sees an adult's hand slip as the adult tries to pull the lid off a jar, the child won't copy the slip but will instead perform the *intended* action of removing the lid (Meltzoff, 1995, 2007; Yu & Kushnir, 2014).

3. An infant who approaches a new toy will often stop and look back to examine their caregiver's face for cues about whether the caregiver thinks the toy is or isn't dangerous. The infant's ability to use another person's reactions as information about how they should think about the world is known as *social referencing* (Kim et al., 2010; Walden & Ogan, 1988). This is just one of the many instances in which children rely on adults to tell them what they should and shouldn't fear.

These three abilities—joint attention ("I see what you see"), imitation ("I do what you do"), and social referencing ("I think what you think")—allow infants to learn from other members of their species and discover things about the world that they might never discover alone (Heyes, 2016).

As Vygotsky pointed out, children are not lone explorers who discover the world for themselves; rather, they are members of families, communities, and societies that teach them much of what they need to know.

Figure 11.10

Joint Attention Joint attention allows children to learn from others. When a 9-month-old infant interacts with an adult (*a*) who then looks at an object (*b*), the infant will typically look at the same object (*c*)—but only when the adult's eyes are open (Meltzoff et al., 2009).

(a)

(b)

(c)

Infancy and Childhood: Bonding and Helping

Infants and children learn how to think about the world, about their minds, and about other minds. But there is more to life than thinking. Children also learn to form relationships and establish emotional bonds with these other people, as well as to reason about right and wrong and behave accordingly. Social development and moral development are among the most important projects of infancy and childhood, so let's take a look at how each of them is accomplished.

Social Development

When Konrad Lorenz was a child, his neighbour gave him a day-old duckling that soon began to follow Lorenz wherever he went. A few decades later, Lorenz was awarded the Nobel Prize in physiology for explaining how and why that had happened (Lorenz, 1952). Everyone who had ever raised a duckling already knew that it would follow its mother, and they assumed that ducklings did this because some sort of "mother-following" instinct was hard-wired into their brains. But Lorenz realized that evolution had not designed ducklings to follow their mothers per se; rather, it had designed them to follow the first noisy moving object they saw upon hatching. In most cases, that object was indeed their mother, but if it just so happened to be a little boy destined to win a Nobel Prize, then the duckling would ignore its mother and follow the boy instead. Ducklings, it seems, are not specifically prepared to follow their mothers; they are generally prepared to form a bond.

Becoming Attached

Like ducklings, human infants need adults of their species to survive, and therefore they too come into the world prepared to form a bond. Because they cannot waddle after an adult, they instead do things to make adults waddle after them: They cry, gurgle, coo, and smile, and these signals cause adults to move towards them, pick them up, comfort them, change them, and feed them (Schaller, 2018). At first, newborns will send these signals to any adult within range, but they seem to keep a "mental tally" of how different adults respond to their signals, and at about 6 months they begin to direct those signals towards the adult who responds first, best, fastest, and most often.

That person is known as the *primary caregiver,* and they quickly become the emotional centre of the infant's universe. Infants feel safe in the primary caregiver's presence and will happily crawl around and explore the environment. If their primary caregiver gets a little too far away, the infant will begin to feel unsafe and will take action to close the gap, either by moving towards the primary caregiver or by crying until the primary caregiver moves towards them. The *emotional bond with a primary caregiver* is called an **attachment** (Bowlby, 1969, 1973, 1980). This bond is so important that infants who, by unfortunate circumstances, are deprived of the opportunity to form one, are at serious risk for a wide range of physical, mental, and emotional impairments (Gillespie & Nemeroff, 2007; Kessler et al., 2008; O'Connor & Rutter, 2000; Rutter et al., 2004).

Attachment Styles

Infants form attachments, but not all of these attachments are of the same quality (Ainsworth et al., 1978). A common method for measuring the quality of an attachment involves bringing an infant and their primary caregiver to a laboratory room and then staging a series of episodes in which the primary caregiver briefly leaves the room and then returns. Infants tend to react to these episodes in one of four ways,

Like hatchlings, human infants need to stay close to their caregiver to survive. Unlike hatchlings, human infants know how to get their caregivers to come to them rather than the other way around.

attachment The emotional bond with a primary caregiver.

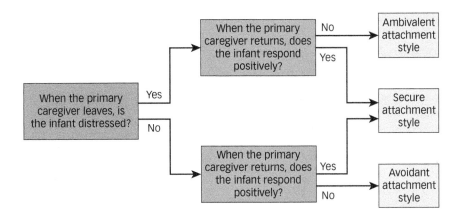

Figure 11.11
Attachment Styles How an infant responds when the primary caregiver leaves and returns allows researchers to identify the infant's attachment style. If the infant does not consistently show one of these three patterns, then the infant's attachment style is said to be disorganized.

which are known as **attachment styles,** or *characteristic patterns of reacting to the presence and absence of one's primary caregiver* (**FIGURE 11.11**).

- Infants with a *secure* attachment style may or may not be distressed when their caregiver leaves the room, but they respond positively to them when they return—either by acknowledging them with a glance or a smile (if the infant was not distressed) or by going to them for calming (if the infant was distressed). The majority of infants in all cultures have a secure attachment style.

- Infants with an *ambivalent* attachment style are distressed when their caregiver leaves the room, but when their caregiver returns they respond negatively to them—either by rebuffing them, or by refusing their attempts at calming.

- Infants with an *avoidant* attachment style are not distressed when their caregiver leaves the room, and they don't respond positively or negatively when their caregiver returns—they mainly just ignore them.

- Infants with a *disorganized* attachment style show no consistent pattern of response to either their caregiver's absence or return.

What makes infants react in these different ways? A bit of nature and a bit of nurture. Infants are born with a **temperament,** or a *biologically based pattern of attentional and emotional reactivity* (Kagan, 1997; Rothbart & Bates, 2006; Thomas & Chess, 1977). About 40% of infants are *easy babies* who adjust quickly to new situations, quickly establish routines, and are generally cheerful and easy to calm; about 10% are *difficult babies* who are slow to adjust to new experiences and are likely to react negatively and intensely to novel stimuli and events; about 15% are *slow-to-warm-up babies* who are somewhat difficult at first but then become easier over time; and the remaining 35% cannot be easily classified (Thomas & Chess, 1977; but see Gartstein et al., 2017). Not only are these differences present at birth, but they are quite stable over time (Baker et al., 2013). For example, difficult babies who react fearfully to novel stimuli—such

attachment styles Characteristic patterns of reacting to the presence and absence of one's primary caregiver.

temperament A biologically based pattern of attentional and emotional reactivity.

In a series of classic studies, psychologist Harry Harlow (1958) raised baby rhesus monkeys in isolation and then put them in a cage with two "artificial mothers." One was made of wire and dispensed food while the other was made of cloth and did not. The baby monkeys spent most of their time clinging to the cloth mother, leading Harlow to conclude that even monkeys are "born to bond."

Some parents worry that placing their child in day care may impair the attachment process. But a massive long-term study by the American National Institute for Child Health and Human Development showed that while attachment style is strongly influenced by maternal sensitivity and responsiveness, the quality, amount, stability, or type of day care have little or no influence (Friedman & Boyle, 2008; Waters et al., 2021).

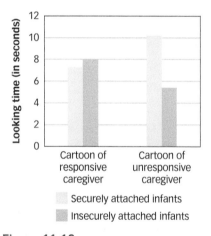

Figure 11.12

Internal Working Models Do infants really have internal working models? It appears they do. Infants stare longer when they see something they don't expect, and securely attached infants will stare longer at a cartoon of a mother ignoring rather than comforting her child. Infants who are not securely attached do just the opposite (Johnson et al., 2007).

internal working model A set of beliefs about the way relationships work.

as sudden movements, loud sounds, or unfamiliar people—tend to become quiet, cautious, and shy adults who avoid unfamiliar people and novel situations (Schwartz et al., 2003; Tang et al., 2020). Nature clearly plays a role in how infants react to situations, including the absence and return of their primary caregiver.

But nurture seems to play an even bigger role. How caregivers think, feel, and act has a strong influence on an infant's attachment style. For instance, mothers of securely attached infants tend to be especially sensitive to signs of their child's emotional state, especially good at detecting their infant's "requests" for reassurance, and especially responsive to those requests (Ainsworth et al., 1978; De Wolff & van IJzendoorn, 1997; van IJzendoorn & Sagi, 1999). Mothers of securely attached infants also tend to be "mind-minded," which is to say that they think of their infants as unique individuals with mental and emotional lives, not just as creatures with urgent physical needs (Meins, 2003; Meins et al., 2001; McMahon & Bernier, 2017).

A mother's behaviour is correlated with her infant's attachment style—but is it actually a cause of her infant's attachment style? It appears so. Researchers studied a group of young mothers whose infants were particularly irritable or difficult. When the infants were about 6 months old, half the mothers participated in a training program designed to sensitize them to their infants' emotional signals and to encourage them to be more responsive. A year later, infants whose mothers had received the training were more likely to be securely attached than were infants whose mothers did not (van den Boom, 1994, 1995). Clearly, it takes two to make a bond.

The Consequences of Attachment Styles

As a result of interactions with their primary caregivers, infants develop an **internal working model,** which is *a set of beliefs about the way relationships work* (Bretherton & Munholland, 1999). Infants with different attachment styles appear to have different internal working models (see **FIGURE 11.12).** Infants with a secure attachment style seem to be confident that their primary caregivers will respond when they feel insecure, whereas infants with an avoidant attachment style seem to be confident that they won't. Both sets of infants have clear expectations about what will happen when they feel insecure. On the other hand, infants with an ambivalent attachment style do not have a clear expectation: They seem to be uncertain about whether or not their primary caregiver will respond on any particular occasion. Finally, infants with a disorganized attachment style seem to be confused about their relationships with their primary caregivers, which has led some psychologists to speculate that this style primarily characterizes children who have been abused (Carolson, 1998; Cicchetti & Toth, 1998).

Some psychologists believe that an infant's attachment style, and the internal working model that goes with it, have a long-lasting influence (Waters et al., 2015; cf. Fraley, 2019; Fraley & Roisman, 2019). For example, adults who were securely attached as infants have greater academic success (Jacobson & Hoffman, 1997), superior cognitive functioning (Bernier et al., 2015), and higher psychological well-being (Madigan et al., 2013). They also have more successful social relationships (McElwain et al., 2011; Schneider et al., 2001; Simpson et al., 2011; Sroufe et al., 1990; Steele et al., 1999; Vondra et al., 2001). One study that tracked participants over two decades showed that 1-year-old infants who are securely attached are less likely to experience negative emotions when trying to resolve major relationship conflicts with their romantic partners *twenty* years later! (Simpson et al., 2007). They are also more likely to rebound from conflicts with their romantic partners (Salvatore et al., 2011) and make the transition to parenthood more easily (Simpson & Rholes, 2018). The bond we form with that first noisy moving object—the one that most of us call Mom or Dad—is a powerful force that impacts our development for years to come. See Other Voices: For Indigenous Kids' Welfare, Our Government Knows Better; It Just Needs to Do Better for an illustration of how social welfare policies in Canada are damaging the social development of First Nations youth, contributing to intergenerational trauma.

Other Voices | For Indigenous Kids' Welfare, Our Government Knows Better; It Just Needs to Do Better

This week, the story of a newborn baby removed from her family in Manitoba added to a litany of reports about the over-representation of First Nations children in child-welfare care. The number and persistence of these stories lead many to believe this is a problem without a solution. But real answers have been on the books for decades—governments just need to implement them.

In 1967, social worker George Caldwell observed that 80 percent of the children placed in residential schools in Saskatchewan were there as child-welfare placements. He called upon Indian Affairs to put more emphasis on services to support families and to ensure services were culturally appropriate.

In the succeeding decades, his recommendations were never properly implemented and a plethora of provincial and federal reports followed, finding the same problem and recommending the same solutions. These reports suffered the same fate as Mr. Caldwell's recommendations: piecemeal government implementation or being flat out ignored.

It has been a year since outgoing Indigenous Services Minister Jane Philpott called the over-representation of First Nations children in child welfare a "humanitarian crisis."

As the Truth and Reconciliation Commission noted in its 2015 report, First Nations children are placed in child-welfare care at 12 times the rate of other children, due largely to poverty, poor housing, parental addictions and mental-health issues. Yet, despite all of the discussion, the public knows very little about First Nations child welfare and what can be done to tackle the heartbreaking pace at which these children and youth are separated from their families. First Nations have always had ways to address child well-being in their communities; however, these systems were displaced and, in some cases, fractured by the imposition of the residential-school system in the late 1800s.

While residential schools slowly began to close in the 1940s, with the last one in Saskatchewan shuttering its doors in 1996, the ones that remained gradually morphed into child-welfare placements.

Meanwhile, the federal government amended the Indian Act in the 1950s to allow "laws of general application," including provincial child welfare laws, to apply on reserves. Services resulting from these laws are federally funded. The amendment created an overlap between residential schools operating as child-welfare placements and the provincial child-welfare system. As a result, social workers who knew little of the trauma of residential schools removed large numbers of First Nations children and placed them, often permanently, with non-Indigenous families in what is now known as the Sixties Scoop.

Beginning in the 1970s, First Nations urgently called on the federal government to create First Nations child-welfare agencies on reserves. And although Canada agreed, the implementation fell far short of perfect.

Provincial and territorial child-welfare laws would be enforced despite the fact they were not tailored to the needs of First Nations children and families, who by this point had suffered generations of colonial trauma. The agencies could only serve on reserve and although the federal government would fund them, it would be at a far lesser level than other children received off-reserve.

Today, there are more than 105 First Nations child-welfare agencies across Canada that serve clients both on- and off-reserve, but the legislative and funding constraints persist. On a positive note, despite the barriers, First Nations children served by these agencies are more likely to be able to stay safely at home than those served by provincial agencies off-reserve.

The on-reserve funding deficit for child welfare is being addressed thanks to the five orders issued by the Canadian Human Rights Tribunal that require the federal government to properly fund the agencies and family-support programs, paying due account to the unique cultures and contexts of First Nations children. While there are persistent concerns with the federal government's compliance with the tribunal's orders, the funding relief is already paying dividends for families who are now able to access basic support services available to other Canadian families.

Cindy Blackstock is the executive director of the First Nations Child and Family Caring Society of Canada. She is a professor at the School of Social Work at McGill University.

However, federal funding shortfalls on reserve for basics such as water, sanitation, early childhood and education programs continue, undermining the ability of First Nations families to care for their children.

Off-reserve, provincial legislation and funding apply, but few programs answer Mr. Caldwell's call—now more than 50 years old—for culturally based services that target the reasons why First Nations children end up in care at such high rates. The expansion of First Nations agency services off reserve would provide some much-needed assistance, as would bolstering culturally based family supports.

First Nations youth in care have repeatedly called for more programs to promote healthy connections to family and culture, improved supports to address issues stemming from childhood trauma, youth addictions and turnover in service providers, as well as supports so they are not just left on their own when they turn 18. These are basics a compassionate and rich country such as ours should provide without question, but doesn't.

The over-representation of First Nations children in care is a problem with a solution.

There have been numerous reports over the years calling for the same things: First, to ensure child-welfare programs are based on the unique cultures of First Nations with the affirmation of First Nations jurisdiction; secondly, that family supports are put in place to address the reasons why children are at risk; third, to end the shortfalls in child welfare and other services First Nations children need and to provide higher quality care for children and youth who cannot live at home; lastly, to institute culturally based alternative justice approaches to replace or augment the current role of the provincial courts and provide a check system when children are removed.

While we do all of this, we need to ensure child-welfare policy is driven by facts, instead of exceptional cases or social-media exposure of vulnerable children and youth.

More than a decade ago, I sat with children and youth—some of whom were in care—to talk about ethical engagement. They told me we need to be very careful with their stories. Videos and photos of their most tragic moments will endure a lifetime and should only be shared with those in a position to do something to ensure their safety, dignity and well-being—not the public. While public scrutiny of child welfare is needed, it can be done without violating the privacy of children, youth and families.

After more than 30 years of seeing the over-representation of First Nations children and youth in child welfare, I know one thing for sure: Unless the public puts pressure on provincial, territorial and federal governments, the good solutions on the books will not be implemented. We must tell our politicians: literally thousands of children need our help.

Cindy Blackstock, "For Indigenous Kids' welfare, our government knows better; it just needs to do better," *The Globe and Mail*, January 16, 2019.

Moral Development

Infants can make one distinction quickly and well, and that's the distinction between plea-sure and pain. Before their bottoms hit their very first diaper, infants can tell when some-thing feels good or bad and can demonstrate to anyone within earshot that they strongly prefer the former. But over the next few years, they begin to notice that their pleasures ("Throwing food is fun") can be someone else's pains ("Throwing food makes Mom mad"), which is a problem because infants need those other people to survive, and making them mad is not a winning strategy. Infants care what adults think about them (Botto & Rochat, 2018), so they learn to balance their needs with the needs of those around them, and they do this in part by developing a distinction between *right* and *wrong*. How does this happen?

Moral Reasoning

Piaget spent time playing games with children and quizzing them about how they came to know the rules of those games and what they thought should happen to children who broke those rules. By listening carefully to what children said, Piaget concluded that as they develop, children's thinking about right and wrong—that is, their moral reasoning—changes in three ways (Piaget, 1932/1965).

- First, Piaget noticed that children's moral reasoning tends to shift *from real-ism to relativism.* Very young children regard moral rules as real, inviolable truths about the world. For the young child, the rightness or wrongness of an action is like the height and weight of an object: They have an actual exis-tence in the world and do not depend on what people think or say. That's why young children generally don't believe that a bad action such as hitting some-one can ever be good, even if everyone agrees to allow it. But as they mature, children begin to realize that some moral rules are human inventions and that people can agree to adopt them, change them, or abandon them entirely.

- Second, Piaget noticed that children's moral reasoning tends to shift *from prescriptions to principles.* Young children think of moral rules as guidelines for specific actions in specific situations. ("Each child can play with the iPad for 5 minutes and must then pass it to the child sitting to their left.") As they mature, children come to see that these rules are expressions of more general principles, such as fairness and equity, which means that specific rules can be abandoned or modified when they fail to uphold the general principle. ("If Jason missed his turn with the iPad, then he should get two turns now.")

- Third, Piaget noticed that children's moral reasoning tends to shift *from outcomes to intentions.* For the young child, an unintentional action that causes great harm

Most Indians consider it immoral to eat cows, but Canadians eat more than 31 million kilograms of beef each year at McDonald's alone! According to Piaget, young children from each nation should find the behaviour of people in the other nation puzzling because young children do not realize that moral rules can vary across people and cultures.

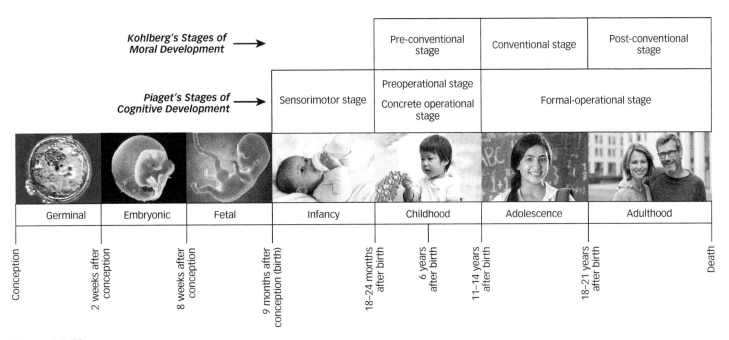

Figure 11.13
Developmental Timeline—Infancy and Childhood with Kohlberg's Stages
(PHOTO CREDIT FROM LEFT TO RIGHT: BSIP/NEWSCOM; CLAUDE EDELMANN/SCIENCE SOURCE; KATERYNA KON/SCIENCE PHOTO LIBRARY/ALAMY STOCK PHOTO; PROSTOCK-STUDIO/ISTOCK/GETTY IMAGES; RYULTSUKI/IMAGESOURCE/AGE FOTOSTOCK; ASISEEIT/E+/GETTY IMAGES; WESTEND61/GETTY IMAGES)

("Reiko accidentally broke the iPad") seems "more wrong" than an intentional action that causes slight harm ("Reiko got mad and broke the pencil") because young children tend to judge the morality of an action by its outcome rather than by the actor's intentions. As they mature, children begin to see that the morality of an action is critically dependent on the actor's state of mind (Cushman et al., 2013; Nobes et al., 2017).

The psychologist Lawrence Kohlberg used Piaget's insights as the basis of a detailed theory of the development of moral reasoning (Kohlberg, 1958, 1963, 1986). Kohlberg asked both children and adults how they would resolve a series of "moral dilemmas" (e.g., should a poor husband steal a drug from a pharmacy to save his dying wife?). On the basis of their responses, he concluded that there are three distinct stages of moral development (see **FIGURE 11.13**). According to Kohlberg:

- Most children are at the **preconventional stage,** which is *a stage of moral development in which the morality of an action is primarily determined by its consequences for the actor.* A person at this stage might reason: "If the husband steals the drug he could end up in jail, so he shouldn't."

- Most adolescents are at the **conventional stage,** which is *a stage of moral development in which the morality of an action is primarily determined by the extent to which it conforms to social rules.* A person at this stage might reason: "Stealing is against the law, so the husband shouldn't steal the drug."

- Most adults are at the **postconventional stage,** which is *a stage of moral development in which the morality of an action is determined by a set of general principles that reflect core values.* A person at this stage might reason: "Saving a person is more important than being honest, so the husband should steal the drug."

Beyond Moral Reasoning

Although Kohlberg got many things right, we now know that he also got a few things wrong. First, although the development of moral reasoning does seem to follow the basic trajectory described by his theory, the three stages are not

preconventional stage A stage of moral development in which the morality of an action is primarily determined by its consequences for the actor.

conventional stage A stage of moral development in which the morality of an action is primarily determined by the extent to which it conforms to social rules.

postconventional stage A stage of moral development in which the morality of an action is determined by a set of general principles that reflect core values.

At the postconventional stage of moral development, people act on principle, regardless of laws or personal consequences. During World War II, Albanian Muslims such as Baba Haxhi Dede Reshatbardhi (pictured) shielded their Jewish neighbours from the Nazis.

Most people are upset by the suffering of others, and research suggests that even young children have this response, which may be the basis of their emerging morality.

as discrete as Kohlberg thought (which is the same mistake Piaget made). For instance, a person might apply preconventional, conventional, and postconventional thinking in different circumstances, which suggests that the person did not "reach a stage" so much as "acquire a skill" that they may or may not use on a particular occasion. Second, Kohlberg's theory does a better job of describing the development of moral reasoning in Western societies than in non-Western societies (McNamara et al., 2019). For example, some non-Western societies value obedience and community more than liberty and individuality; thus, the moral reasoning of people in such societies may *appear* to reflect a conventional devotion to social norms when it actually reflects a postconventional consideration of deeply held ethical principles. Third, moral reasoning turns out to be just a piece of the story of moral development. What are the other pieces?

Research on moral reasoning portrays people as deliberating judges who use rational analysis — sometimes simple and sometimes sophisticated — to decide what's right and what's wrong. But recent studies show that long before children are capable of deliberation or rational analysis, they display a surprising amount of "moral sense" (Blake et al., 2014; Dahl & Brownell, 2019; Warneken, 2018). For instance, when 16-month-olds watch a puppet show in which one puppet helps others and another puppet hinders others, they are more likely to reach out and touch the puppet who helped (Hamlin et al., 2007; Margoni & Surian, 2018). Even 3-month-old infants who can't yet reach out will tend to look at the helper longer than at the hinderer (Hamlin et al., 2011; cf. Scarf et al., 2012; Hamlin, 2014). When 16-month-olds watch toys being distributed, they are surprised when one person gets more than another (Bian et al., 2018; Sloan et al., 2012; Sommerville et al., 2013), and they prefer those who distribute the toys fairly to those who don't (Geraci & Surian, 2011). One-year-olds will helpfully point towards an object that they can see an adult is searching for (Liszkowski et al., 2006), and 2-year-olds smile more after giving someone else a tasty treat than after receiving one themselves (Aknin et al., 2012). In short, infants and young children seem to have many of the moral sensibilities of adults.

They also seem to have many of the same moral limitations: They favour people who have been kind to them in the past (Paulus, 2016), they favour familiar people over strangers, they favour members of their own group over members of other groups, and so on (Wynn et al., 2018). Studies such as these suggest that morality is not simply the result of reasoning, but also of basic psychological tendencies — such as a sense of fairness or a desire to help and cooperate — whose roots may be part of our evolutionary heritage.

Adolescence: Minding the Gap

Learning Outcomes

WHAT YOU NEED TO KNOW

- Explain why the protraction of adolescence matters.

- Describe the determinants of sexual orientation and behaviour.

- Explain how adolescents are influenced by their peers.

Between childhood and adulthood is an extended developmental stage that may not qualify for a hood of its own, but that is clearly distinct from the stages that come before and after. **Adolescence** is *the period of development that begins with the onset of sexual maturity (about 11 to 14 years of age) and lasts until the beginning of adulthood (about 18 to 21 years of age).* Unlike the transition from embryo to fetus or from infant to child, this transition is abrupt and well-marked. In just 3 or 4 years, the average adolescent gains about 18 kilograms and grows about 25 centimetres. For females, all this growing starts at about the age of 10 and ends when they reach their full heights at about the age of 16; for males, it starts and ends about 2 years later.

The beginning of this growth spurt signals the onset of **puberty,** which is *the onset of bodily changes associated with sexual maturity.* These changes involve the **primary sex characteristics,** which are *bodily structures that change at puberty and are directly involved in reproduction* (e.g., females begin to menstruate and males begin to ejaculate), as well as the **secondary sex characteristics,** which are *bodily structures that change at puberty but are not directly involved in reproduction* (e.g., females develop breasts and males develop facial hair). All of these changes are caused by the increased production of hormones—specifically, estrogen in females and testosterone in males.

Just as the body changes during adolescence, so too does the brain. For example, just before puberty there is a marked increase in the growth rate of the tissue that connects different regions of the brain (Thompson et al., 2000). The Czech Canadian researcher Tomáš Paus and his colleagues have demonstrated that the connections between two regions essential for language function—Broca's area in the frontal lobe, and Wernicke's area in the parietal lobe—become stronger and denser between the ages of 4 and 17 (Paus et al., 2005). These connections presumably allow brain areas to share information faster and more efficiently. The most significant neural changes occur in the prefrontal cortex, the part of the brain associated with the ability to regulate emotions, and to control attention and behaviour. Infants' brains form many more new synapses than they actually need, and by the time they are 2-year-old children, they have about 15,000 synapses per neuron, which is roughly twice as many as the average adult (Huttenlocher, 1979). This early period of *synaptic proliferation* is followed by a period of *synaptic pruning,* in which the connections that are not frequently used are eliminated. Scientists used to think that proliferation and pruning happened only during infancy, but we now know that the prefrontal cortex undergoes a second wave of proliferation just before puberty, and a second wave of pruning during adolescence (Giedd et al., 1999). During this period, the prefrontal cortex also seems to be forming faster, more efficient connections with the rest of the brain (Paus et al., 2005). The adolescent brain is a true work in progress.

The Protraction of Adolescence

The age at which puberty begins varies across individuals (e.g., people tend to reach puberty at about the same age as their same-sex parent did) and across racial groups (e.g., in the United States, Black females tend to reach puberty before white females do). It also varies across generations (Malina et al., 1988; Sawyer et al., 2018). For example, in the 19th century, females in Scandinavia, the United Kingdom, and the United States tended to have their first menstrual periods when they were about 17 years old, but by 1960, that age had fallen to about 13 years (Patton & Viner, 2007). In newly industrialized countries like China, the age at which females have their first menstrual period has decreased by almost 5 months every decade for the past 25 years (Song et al., 2014). Similarly, the average age at which American males show early signs of puberty has fallen to between 9 and 10 years old (Herman-Giddens et al., 2012).

Puberty is happening much earlier today than it did just a few decades ago—but why? For females at least, the main reason appears to be diet (Ellis & Garber, 2000). Young females have more body fat today than ever before, and body fat secretes estrogen, which hastens puberty. Some evidence suggests that exposure to environmental toxins that mimic estrogen may also play a role (Buck Louis et al., 2008). Stress appears to be another cause of early puberty in females (Belsky, 2019). Studies show that females reach puberty earlier if they grow up in unpredictable households with high levels of conflict, if they grow

adolescence The period of development that begins with the onset of sexual maturity (about 11 to 14 years of age) and lasts until the beginning of adulthood (about 18 to 21 years of age).

puberty The onset of bodily changes associated with sexual maturity.

primary sex characteristics Bodily structures that change at puberty and are directly involved in reproduction.

secondary sex characteristics Bodily structures that change at puberty but are not directly involved in reproduction.

WOLFGANG KLUGE/AP IMAGES

The famous Leipzig Boy's Choir is in trouble. Boys enter the choir at the age of 9 and sing soprano until their voices change. Back in 1723, when Johann Sebastian Bach was the choirmaster, that change happened at about the age of 17. But today it happens at about the age of 12, and as a result, by the time a soprano learns to sing, he isn't a soprano anymore. As a result, the choir is struggling.

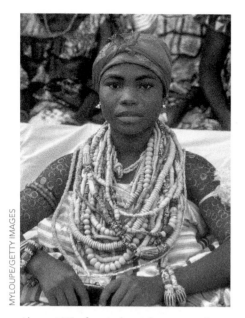

About 60% of preindustrial societies don't have a word for adolescence because there is no such stage. When a Krobo girl menstruates for the first time, older women take her into seclusion for 2 weeks and teach her about sex, birth control, and marriage. Afterward, a public ceremony is held, and the young woman who was regarded as a child just days earlier is thereafter regarded as an adult.

up in households without a biological father, or if they are victims of early sexual abuse (Greenspan & Deardorff, 2014).

Whatever its causes, early puberty has important psychological consequences. Just two centuries ago, the gap between childhood and adulthood was relatively brief because people became physically mature at roughly the same time that they were ready to accept adult roles in society — that is, to marry and get a job. But today, people typically spend 3 to 10 more years in school, and they take jobs and get married much later than they once did (Fitch & Ruggles, 2000). So while the age at which people become physically adult has gone down, the age at which they take on adult roles and responsibilities has gone up, resulting in a *protracted* period of adolescence. Some researchers argue that in the Western world, adolescence now lasts for a full 15 years (Sawyer et al., 2018).

What are the consequences of protracted adolescence? Adolescence is often characterized as a time of internal turmoil and external recklessness, and some psychologists have speculated that the protraction of adolescence is partly to blame for its sorry reputation (Moffitt, 1993). According to these theorists, adolescents are essentially adults who have been denied a place in adult society. Teenagers in the United States and Canada are often subjected to a lot of restrictions — even more than people in the military on active duty, or incarcerated felons (Epstein, 2007a). They often feel compelled to protest these restrictions and demonstrate their adulthood by doing things such as smoking, drinking, using drugs, having sex, and committing crimes. In a sense, adolescents are forced to live in a strange gap between two worlds — childhood and adulthood — and the pathologies of adolescence are at least in part a response to that predicament. As one researcher noted, "Isolated from adults and wrongly treated like children, it is no wonder that some teens behave, by adult standards, recklessly or irresponsibly" (Epstein, 2007b).

With that said, the storm and stress of adolescence is not quite as intense or prevalent as "Degrassi" would have you believe (Steinberg & Morris, 2001). Research suggests that the "moody adolescent" who is a victim of "raging hormones" is largely a myth. Adolescents are no moodier than children (Buchanan et al., 1992), and fluctuations in their hormone levels have a very small impact on their moods (Brooks-Gunn et al., 1994). Although they can be more impulsive and susceptible to peer influence than essentially adults (see **FIGURE 11.14**), they are just as capable of making wise decisions based on good information (Steinberg, 2007). Canadian adolescents do some fairly questionable stuff — about 10% have tried vaping, about 19% have tried cannabis, and about 42% try alcohol — but few go farther than that (Boak et al., 2017). Those who do these things generally don't develop problems that impair their academic success or personal relationships (Hughes et al., 1992; Johnston et al., 1997). Adolescents may minor in misbehaviour, but they don't seem to major in it, and on average, little of what they do ends up having long-term consequences (Warren et al., 2016). The fact is that adolescence is not a terribly troubled time for most people, and most adolescents "age out" of whatever troubles they manage to get themselves into (Epstein, 2007b; Martin et al., 2014; Sampson & Laub, 1995).

Adolescents who experiment with reckless behaviour generally don't become reckless adults—if they live that long. This is the text that 17-year-old Maria Droesch was sending to her mother when she crashed the car she was driving and died. Her mother now hauls the wreckage of Maria's car from town to town to persuade people not to text while driving. In 2017, in a large survey of Ontario high school students, about 1 in 3 students with a driver's license admitted to texting while driving (Boak et al., 2018). Whether texting is to blame or not, about 1 in 12 high school–aged drivers is involved in a car collision every year.

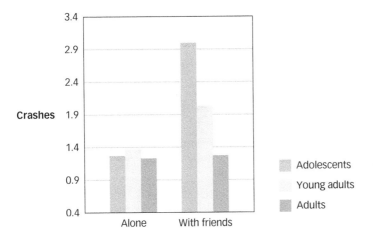

Figure 11.14
How Do Peers Affect Decision Making?
Adolescents make better decisions when no one is around. Participants in one study played a video driving game with or without their peers in the room. The presence of peers greatly increased the number of risks taken and crashes experienced by adolescents but had little or no effect on adults (Gardner & Steinberg, 2005).

Emerging Sexuality

Puberty can be a difficult time, but it is especially difficult for females who reach puberty before the majority of their peers. These early bloomers are at elevated risk for a wide range of negative consequences, from distress and depression to delinquency and disease (Mendle et al., 2007, 2018). This happens for several reasons (Ge & Natsuaki, 2009). First, early blooming females don't have as much time as their peers do to develop the skills necessary to cope with adolescence (Petersen & Grockett, 1985). And yet, because they look so mature, people expect them to act like adults. In other words, early puberty creates unrealistic expectations that female adolescents may have trouble fulfilling. Second, older males may draw these adolescent females into activities that they are simply not ready to engage in, from drinking to sex (Ge et al., 1996). Some research suggests that for females, the *timing* of puberty has a greater influence on emotional and behavioural problems than does the occurrence of puberty itself (Buchanan et al., 1992).

The timing of puberty does not have such a consistent effect on males. Some studies suggest that early maturing males do better than their peers, some suggest they do worse, and some suggest that it makes no difference at all (Ge et al., 2001). Interestingly, research suggests that for males, the *tempo* or speed with which they make the transition from the first to the last stages of puberty may be a better predictor of negative outcomes than is the timing (Mendle et al., 2010; Mendle, 2014).

Adolescents are often described as gawky because different parts of their faces and bodies mature at different rates. But as the actress Rashida Jones can attest, the gawkiness generally clears up.

PAUL BRUINOOGE/PATRICK MCMULLAN VIA GETTY IMAGES

Figure 11.15
Attitudes Towards Homosexuality Vary Dramatically Around the World
A 2019 survey of attitudes of nearly 38,500 adults in 34 countries revealed huge variability from region to region in the percentage of people who said that homosexuality should be accepted by society (Pew Research Center, 2020).

The global divide on acceptance of homosexuality
% who say homosexuality should be accepted by society

Sexual Orientation: A Matter of Biology

For some adolescents, puberty is further complicated by the fact that they identify with a gender different from that which corresponds to their sex at birth, and/or they are attracted to members of the same sex. Why does this make puberty complicated? In 2018, approximately 1 out of every 25 people over the age of 15 in Canada identified themselves as homosexual or bisexual and/or with a gender that does not correspond with their birth sex (Statistics Canada, 2021). Rates were lowest in those over age 65, and highest in the 15–24 age range. These adolescents are different from the majority of their peers, and as you probably know, adolescents care a whole lot about "fitting in" (Somerville et al., 2013). Not only are these adolescents a minority, but they are a minority that is often subject to the disdain and disapproval of family, friends, and community. Engaging in sexual activity with members of the same sex is illegal in many nations and punishable by death in some (Bailey et al., 2016). The overwhelming majority of Canadians (85%) believe that society should accept homosexuality (Pew Research Center, 2020), and Canada is much more accepting of homosexuality than are many other nations (see **FIGURE 11.15**), but some still disapprove. Social Disapproval naturally makes an adolescent's life difficult. The happiness and well-being of adolescents with non-normative sexual orientations are a great concern to mental-health professionals. Several provincial legislatures have enacted laws to reduce gender-based violence and acts of homophobia in primary and secondary schools. For example, in Ontario, students at any school can set up clubs called Gay Straight Alliances. The hope is that this will promote tolerance of all people, regardless of sexual orientation.

What determines a person's sexual orientation? For a long time, psychologists thought the answer was upbringing. For example, during the 1940s and 1950s, psychoanalytic theorists suggested that males who grew up with domineering mothers and cold, distant fathers were less likely to identify with their fathers and therefore more likely to become gay. The only trouble with this theory is that it is wrong: Scientific research to date has failed to identify *any* aspect of parenting that has a significant impact on a child's ultimate sexual orientation. Indeed, researchers have not even been able to find evidence that a parent's own sexual orientation has any influence on the sexual orientation of their children (Patterson, 2013). And while peers have a measurable influence on both the decision to engage in sexual activity and the desire for romantic relationships, they seem to have little or no influence on an adolescent's sexual orientation (Brakefield et al., 2014).

So what *does* determine a person's sexual orientation? Considerable evidence suggests that biology and genetics play major roles. First, same-sex sexual activity is nothing new: It predates civilization itself and is observed in almost all mammals (Nash, 2001). Second, sexual orientation varies in the same way that many other heritable traits do. For instance, the fraternal twin of a gay man (with whom he shares 50% of his genes) has a 15% chance of being gay, but the identical twin of a gay man (with whom he shares 100% of his genes) has about a 50% chance (Bailey & Pillard, 1991; Gladue, 1994). A similar pattern characterizes women (Bailey et al., 1993). Third, the brains of gay and lesbian people look in some ways like the brains of opposite-sexed straight people (Savic & Lindström, 2008). For example, the cerebral hemispheres of straight men and gay women (both of whom are *gynephilic,* or attracted to females) tend to be of different sizes, whereas the hemispheres of straight women and gay men (both of whom are *androphilic,* or attracted to males) tend to be the same size.

On January 14, 2001, two same-sex couples made history by being legally married in Toronto.

REUTERS/ALAMY STOCK PHOTO

The fourth striking piece of evidence for the role of biology and genetics in determining sexual orientation is the fact that a signs of it emerge very early. Indeed, child's behaviour is a surprisingly good predictor of their adult sexual orientation (Bailey & Zucker, 1995). Most children go through a period in which they adamantly refuse to do anything that is stereotypically associated with the opposite gender (Halim et al., 2014). But a few children are eager to engage in what researchers call "gender nonconforming behaviour," which for boys includes dressing like a girl and playing with dolls, and for girls includes dressing like a boy and engaging in rough play. These behaviours usually emerge by the time the child is 2 to 4 years old, despite the fact that parents typically discourage them (Cohen-Kettenis & Pfäfflin, 2003). As it turns out, children who engage in gender nonconforming behaviour are significantly more likely to become gay, lesbian, or bisexual adults (Li et al., 2017), and are more likely to experience prejudice once they do (Thoma et al., 2021). Experimental participants who are shown family videos or photos of children are able to predict the child's ultimate sexual orientation with better-than-chance accuracy (Rieger et al., 2010; Watts et al., 2018). This does not mean that every boy who likes mermaid costumes will eventually be gay or that every girl who likes footballs will eventually become a lesbian, but it does mean that some signs of adult sexual orientation are observable long before people begin to experience sexual attraction around the age of 10.

Although men and women both *have* a sexual orientation, they seem to *experience* them differently. For example, men's sexual orientations are good predictors of their physiological arousal to erotic stimuli: Straight men are aroused by erotic pictures of women but not of men, and gay men are aroused by erotic pictures of men but not of women. But women's sexual orientations are not such good predictors of their physiological arousal to erotic stimuli. For instance, Queen's University researcher Meredith Chivers has found that straight women are equally aroused by erotic pictures of women and men, and lesbians are only slightly more aroused by erotic pictures of women than men (Chivers et al., 2004, 2007). Interestingly, transgender men's sexual arousal shows both male-typical and female-typical patterns: Like straight men, they respond more strongly to their preferred gender, but like straight women, they respond to some degree to both genders (Raines et al., 2021). Men's sexual orientations also appear to be more rigid and less fluid than women's. For example, men are more likely than women to report being either exclusively straight or exclusively gay, whereas women are more likely than men to report being either "mostly straight" or bisexual (Savin-Williams & Vrangalova, 2013). Women's sexual orientations are also more likely to depend on circumstances and to shift over time (Bailey et al., 2016; Baumeister, 2000). It is important to note that just because people's sexual orientations *can* change does not mean that they can *be* changed: There is no evidence to suggest that "conversion" or "reparative" therapies can transform gay, lesbian, or bisexual people into straight people (American Psychological Association, 2009).

The science of sexual orientation is still young and fraught with conflicting findings, but at least two conclusions are noncontroversial. First, whatever the complete story of its determinants turns out to be, sexual orientation clearly has biological and genetic components. People don't just *decide* to whom they will be attracted, and their environments and experiences seem to have little to do with their sexual orientations. Second, human sexual orientation is far more complex and diverse than one-word labels like "straight" and "gay" would suggest. Physiological arousal, psychological attraction, sexual behaviour, biological sex, and gender identity are different things that combine in seemingly endless variations that defy the simple categorization that language imparts (see The Real World: Coming to Terms with Ourselves). Indeed, the variety of acronyms—such as LGBTQ2S+, LGBT, LGBTQ, LGBTQA, and TBLG that refer to lesbian, gay, bisexual, transgender, transsexual, queer, questioning, two-spirit, asexual, and ally—attests to the poverty of language, to the remarkable diversity of human sexuality, and to our growing understanding of it. Human beings are highly varied sexual creatures who still have a great deal to learn about themselves.

Sexual Behaviour: A Matter of Choice

Sexual orientation may not be a matter of choice, but sexual activity typically is—and many teenagers choose it. Although the percentage of Canadian high school students who are sexually active has been declining in recent years (see **FIGURE 11.16**), it is still close to a third. Sex is a positive and rewarding experience for many teenagers (Vasilenko et al., 2015), but it is a problem for others—especially for those who start having it too early. Teenagers who begin having sex before the age of 15, for instance, have a lower sense of self-worth and higher rates of anxiety, depression, aggressiveness, and substance abuse (Golden et al., 2016), though of course it is not easy to tell whether these problems are the causes or the effects of early *sexual debut* (which is the term psychologists use to indicate a person's first experience of sexual intercourse). Condom use is fairly widespread among high school students in Canada. A Canadian survey revealed that 80% of 15- to 17-year-olds used a condom the last time they had sex, and 72% reported using oral contraception and a condom (Rotermann & McKay, 2020). However, barely more than half of sexually active adolescents always use contraceptives when engaging in sexual relations (Amialchuk & Gerhardinger, 2015). Sexually transmitted infections such as chlamydia, gonorrhea, and syphilis are increasingly common in Canada, particularly among young people aged 15 to 29 (Public Health Agency of Canada, 2019).

What can be done to help teenagers make wise choices about their sexual behaviour? Comprehensive sex education is a powerful tool. Research shows that it leads teens to delay having sex for the first time, decreases the number of partners they have, increases the likelihood they will use condoms and other forms of birth control when they do have sex, and lowers the likelihood that they will get pregnant or get a sexually transmitted infection (Chin et al., 2012; Mueller et al., 2008; Satcher, 2001). As in almost every other domain, open and honest education has positive consequences.

Percentage of 15- to 17-year-olds reporting having had sex in the past year

Figure 11.16
Teenagers Are Having Less Sex The percentage of Canadians aged 15 to 17 who have had sex in the past year is dropping and has been dropping over the last 25 years.

And yet, despite its well-documented benefits, sex education in some countries, notably the United States, is often absent, sketchy, or based entirely on the goal of abstinence. This is unfortunate. Abstinence-only programs turn out to be largely ineffective (Kohler et al., 2008; Santelli et al., 2017), and some studies even suggest that teens who take abstinence pledges are just as likely to have sex as those who don't but are less likely to use birth control when they do (Rosenbaum, 2009). That's unfortunate too, because teenage mothers fare more poorly than teenage women without children on almost every measure of academic and economic achievement, and their children fare more poorly on most measures of educational success and emotional well-being than do the children of older mothers (Olausson et al., 2001).

From Parents to Peers

Children's views of themselves and their world are tightly tied to the views of their parents, but puberty creates a new set of needs that snip away at those bonds by orienting adolescents towards peers rather than parents. The psychologist Erik Erikson (1959) characterized each stage of life by the major task confronting the individual at that stage. His *stages of psychosocial development* (shown in **TABLE 11.2**) suggest that the adolescent's major task is to develop a new, unique adult identity (Becht et al., 2017). Adolescents do this in different ways: Some explore a variety of identities before finally committing to one of them, while others do little personal exploration and instead adopt the identities prescribed for them by family, religion, or culture (Kroger, 2017; Marcia, 1966, 1993). Regardless of how and when they find them, adolescent identities all have one thing in common: An expanded focus on peers (Roisman et al., 2004).

This shift from parents to peers can be difficult for several reasons. First, adolescents cannot choose their parents, but they can choose their peers, and therefore

The human papilloma virus is a sexually transmitted infection that can lead to cervical cancer. Luckily, there is a vaccine that can prevent it. Studies show that young women who have been vaccinated do not have sex any earlier than those who have not been vaccinated (Cook et al., 2018).

TABLE 11.2

ERIKSON'S STAGES OF PSYCHOSOCIAL DEVELOPMENT

According to Erikson, at each "stage" of development a "key event" creates a challenge or "crisis" that a person can resolve positively or negatively.

Ages	Key Event	Crisis	Positive Resolution
1. Birth to 12–18 months	Feeding	Trust vs. mistrust	Child develops a belief that the environment can be counted on to meet their basic physiological and social needs.
2. 18 months to 3 years	Toilet training	Autonomy vs. shame/doubt	Child learns what they can control and develops a sense of free will and a corresponding sense of regret and sorrow for inappropriate use of self-control.
3. 3–6 years	Independence	Initiative vs. guilt	Child learns to begin action, to explore, to imagine, and to feel remorse for their actions.
4. 6–12 years	School	Industry vs. inferiority	Child learns to do things well or correctly in comparison to a standard or to others.
5. 12–18 years	Peer relationships	Identity vs. role confusion	Adolescent develops a sense of self in relation to others and to their own thoughts and desires.
6. 19–40 years	Love relationships	Intimacy vs. isolation	Person develops the ability to give and receive love; begins to make long-term commitment to relationships.
7. 40–65 years	Parenting	Generativity vs. stagnation	Person develops interest in guiding the development of the next generation.
8. 65 to death	Reflection on and acceptance of one's life	Ego integrity vs. despair	Person develops a sense of acceptance of life as it was lived and the importance of the people and relationships that the individual developed over the life span.

"You're free-range when I say you're free-range."

they have the power to shape themselves by joining groups that will lead them to develop new values, attitudes, beliefs, and perspectives (Shin & Ryan, 2014). In a sense, adolescents are in the business of inventing the adults they will soon become, and that can be an overwhelming responsibility (Tarantino et al., 2014). Second, as adolescents strive for greater autonomy, their parents naturally rebel. For instance, parents and adolescents tend to disagree about the age at which certain adult behaviours—such as staying out late or having sex—are permissible, and you don't need us to tell you which position each party in this conflict typically holds (Deković et al., 1997; Holmbeck & O'Donnell, 1991).

Because adolescents and parents often have different ideas about who should control the adolescent's behaviour, their relationships become more conflictive and less close, their interactions become briefer and less frequent (Larson & Richards, 1991), and the parents become less happy (Luthar & Ciciolla, 2016). Even so, most adolescents don't have an unusually large number of conflicts with their parents (Chung et al., 2009), and when they do, they tend to be conflicts over relatively minor issues, such as dress and language (which may explain why teenagers argue more with their mothers, who are more often in charge of such issues than are fathers; Caspi et al., 1993).

When adolescents pull away from their parents, they move towards their peers. Across a wide range of cultures, historical epochs, and even species, these peer relations evolve in a similar way (Dunphy, 1963; Weisfeld, 1999). Most young adolescents initially form groups or "cliques" with same-gender peers, many of whom were friends during childhood (Brown et al., 1994). Next, the cliques of men and the cliques of women begin to meet in public places, such as town squares or shopping malls, and they begin to interact—but only in groups and only in public. After a few years, the older members of these same-gender cliques peel off and form smaller, mixed-gender cliques, which may assemble in private as well as in public, but they usually assemble as a group (Molloy et al., 2014). Finally, couples peel off from the small, mixed-gender clique and begin romantic relationships.

Studies show that throughout adolescence, people spend increasing amounts of time with opposite-gender peers while maintaining the amount of time they spend with same-gender peers (Richards et al., 1998), and they accomplish this by spending less time with their parents (Larson & Richards, 1991). Although peers

Adolescents form same-gender cliques that meet opposite-gender cliques in public places. Eventually, most of them will form mixed-gender cliques, pair off into long-term romantic relationships, have children, and then worry about those kids when they do all the same things.

exert considerable influence on adolescents' beliefs and behaviours, this influence generally occurs because adolescents like their peers and want to impress them, and not because the peers exert pressure (Smith et al., 2014; Susman et al., 1994). As they age, adolescents show an increasing tendency to resist whatever peer pressure they do experience (Steinberg & Monahan, 2007). Acceptance by peers is tremendously important to adolescents, and those who are rejected by their peers tend to be withdrawn, lonely, and depressed (Pope & Bierman, 1999), in part because adolescents take negative feedback from their peers much more seriously than adults do (Rodman et al., 2017). Fortunately for those of us for whom seventh-grade was a special form of torture, people who are unpopular in early adolescence can become popular in later adolescence as their peers become less rigid and more tolerant (Kinney, 1993).

The Real World • **Coming to Terms with Ourselves**

Sexuality involves both the body and the mind. But people's bodies are hidden beneath their clothes, and people's minds are hidden behind their eyes, so the complexity and diversity of sexuality in the real world is all too easy to miss. Understanding it requires understanding three distinct but related concepts.

Sex refers to the bodies we are born with. Most (though not all) human bodies are either male (i.e., they have XY chromosomes and a penis) or female (i.e., they have XX chromosomes and a vagina). *Gender* refers to our identities—how we see ourselves, how we want others to see us, and how it feels to be inside our own skins. Most (though not all) adults identify themselves as men or women. Last, *sexual orientation* refers to the kinds of people to whom we find ourselves attracted. Most (though not all) adults are attracted to people of the opposite sex and opposite gender. These three dimensions don't capture every important aspect of human sexuality, of course, but they do allow us to build a classification scheme that helps us understand and talk to each other. The accompanying table shows the terms that are typically used to refer to people who differ on these dimensions. (For more on this topic, go to http://www.glaad.org/reference/transgender.)

In Latin, the prefix *trans* means "on the other side of," and the prefix *cis* means "on this side of." So the term *transgender* refers to anyone whose gender and sex do not match, and the term *cisgender* refers to anyone whose gender and sex do match. Notice also that the terms *male* and *female*

		SEX			
		Male		Female	
		Gender		**Gender**	
		Man	Woman	Man	Woman
Sexual Orientation Towards . . .	Males	Cisgender gay man	Transgender straight woman	Transgender gay man	Cisgender straight woman
	Females	Cisgender straight man	Transgender lesbian	Transgender straight man	Cisgender lesbian
	Males & Females	Cisgender bisexual man	Transgender bisexual woman	Transgender bisexual man	Cisgender bisexual woman

refer to a person's sex, whereas the terms *man* and *woman* refer to a person's gender. Most people prefer to be described in terms of their gender rather than their sex, so both transgender and cisgender women typically prefer to be called *she,* and both cisgender and transgender men typically prefer to be called *he.* There are some people who feel that none of these adjectives or pronouns properly describe them. In general, it makes sense to think about other people's sex, gender, and orientation the way they think about it themselves.

It also makes sense to talk about them that way. Over time, descriptors of marginalized groups often take on pejorative connotations. The word *homosexual,* for example, has traditionally been used as a neutral description of people with same-sex orientations, but lately it has become an unflattering way to refer to gay and lesbian people. Conversely, terms that were once pejorative are occasionally reclaimed

by the people whom they were initially meant to demean. For example, for many people, *queer* is now a positive description of anyone who is not cisgender and straight.

The term *two-spirit* is used by some equity-deserving groups to describe their sexual, gender, and/or spiritual identity, and refers to someone who identifies as having both a feminine and a masculine spirit.

The vast majority of humans are cisgender and straight, and all these other terms and categories make some of them wistful for simpler times. But the truth is that there never were simpler times—just times in which the complexity of human sexuality was a secret, hidden from our view. In most of North America, those times have now passed, and the full range of our diversity is proudly on display. For those who hope to understand human behaviour scientifically, this is a welcome change.

Adulthood: Change We Can't Believe In

Learning Outcomes

WHAT YOU NEED TO KNOW

- Specify the physical and socioemotional changes that occur in adulthood.
- Describe how marriage and children affect adults' happiness.

Adulthood is *the stage of development that begins around 18 to 21 years and lasts for the remainder of life.* Many of us think of adulthood as the destination to which the process of development finally delivers us, and that once we've arrived, our journey is pretty much complete: Middle-aged adults are just young adults with the addition of kids, and older adults are just middle-aged adults with the addition of wrinkles. But this conception of development is utterly wrong. Although they are a bit more difficult to see, a whole host of physical, cognitive, and emotional changes take place between our first legal beer and our last legal breath.

Changing Abilities

The early 20s are the peak years for health, stamina, vigor, and prowess, and because our psychology is so closely tied to our biology, these are also the years during which many of our cognitive abilities are at their sharpest. If you are a typical university student, then at this very moment you see farther, hear better, remember more, and weigh less than you ever will again. Take pictures now, because this glorious moment at your physical peak will be over in just a few dozen months. That's right: *months.* Somewhere between the ages of 26 and 30, your body will start the slow process of breaking down in every way. Your muscles will slowly be replaced by fat, your skin will slowly become less elastic, your hair will start to thin and your bones will start to weaken. Your sensory abilities will become less acute and your brain cells will die at an accelerated rate. Other than becoming more resistant to colds and less sensitive to pain, your older body just won't work as well as your current one does. Older doesn't just mean 70. It also means 30. Yikes!

These physical changes will have measurable psychological consequences (Hartshorne & Germine, 2015; Salthouse, 2006). For instance, as your brain ages, your prefrontal cortex and its associated subcortical connections will deteriorate more quickly than the other areas of your brain (Raz, 2000), and you will experience a noticeable decline in many cognitive tasks that require effort, initiative, or strategy. Your memory will get worse overall, though some kinds of memory will get worse faster than others (Spreng & Turner, 2019). For example, you will experience a greater decline in working memory (the ability to hold information "in mind") than in long-term memory (the ability to retrieve information), a greater decline in episodic memory (the ability to remember particular past events) than in semantic memory (the ability to remember general information such as the meanings of words), and a greater decline in retrieval accuracy ("Who was the U.S. president in 1962?") than in recognition accuracy ("Was Kennedy the president in 1962?"). Also, your memory will get worse overall, and some kinds of memory will get worse faster than others. Wait. Did we say that already? Anyway, as **FIGURE 11.17** shows, performance on most (but not all) cognitive tasks peaks when people are young.

Older adults may experience declines in their ability to attend and remember, but they do come up with ways to compensate (Bäckman & Dixon, 1992; Park & McDonough, 2013; Salthouse, 1987). For example, older chess players *remember* chess positions more poorly than younger players do, but they *play* just as well because they learn to search the board more efficiently (Charness, 1981). Older typists *react* more slowly than younger typists do, but they *type* just as quickly and accurately because they are better at anticipating the next word in spoken or written

adulthood The stage of development that begins around 18 to 21 years and lasts for the remainder of life.

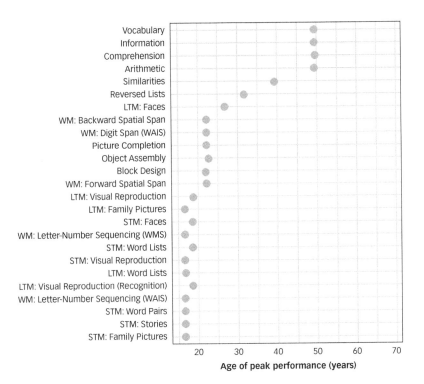

Figure 11.17
Age-Related Changes in Cognitive Performance This chart shows the age of peak performances on a wide variety of cognitive tests, some of which measure working memory (WM), short-term memory (STM), and long-term memory (LTM).
DATA FROM HARTSHORNE & GERMINE (2015).

text (Salthouse, 1984). Older airline pilots are worse than younger pilots when it comes to remembering a list of nonsense words, but they are just as good at remembering the heading commands that pilots receive from the control tower every flight (Morrow et al., 1994).

Even the brain itself learns to compensate for time's inevitable toll. As you know from the Neuroscience chapter, young brains are highly differentiated—that is, they have different parts that do different things. But as the brain ages, it becomes *de-differentiated* (Lindenberger & Baltes, 1994; Koen & Rugg, 2019). For example, regions of the visual cortex that specialize in face and scene perception in younger people are much less specialized in older people (Grady et al., 1992; Park et al., 2004). The brain is like a bunch of specialists who work independently when they are young and able, but who pull together as a team when each specialist gets older and slower (Park & McDonough, 2013). For instance, when young adults try to keep verbal information in working memory, the left prefrontal cortex is more strongly activated than the right, and when they try to keep spatial information in working memory, the right prefrontal cortex is more strongly activated than the left (Smith & Jonides, 1997). But this *bilateral asymmetry* pretty much disappears in older adults, which suggests that the older brain is compensating for the declining

One week before his 58th birthday, commercial airline pilot Chesley "Sully" Sullenberger made a perfect emergency landing in the Hudson River in New York City and saved the lives of everyone on board. None of the passengers wished they'd had a younger pilot.

Figure 11.18

Bilateral Asymmetry in Younger and Older Brains Across a variety of tasks, young brains show more bilateral asymmetry in their patterns of activation than do older brains. One explanation is that older brains compensate for the declining abilities of one neural structure by calling on other neural structures for help.

Young Adult   Older Adult

ROBERTO CABEZA, CENTER FOR COGNITIVE NEUROSCIENCE, DUKE UNIVERSITY. RESEARCH FROM CABEZA ET AL (1997) AND MADDEN ET AL (1999).

abilities of each individual neural structure by calling on its other neural structures to help out (Cabeza, 2002) (see **FIGURE 11.18**). The physical machinery breaks down as time passes, and one of the ways in which the brain meets that challenge is by changing its division of labor.

Changing Goals

So one reason that Grandpa can't remember where he left his socks is that his prefrontal cortex doesn't work as well as it used to. But another reason is that the location of socks just isn't the sort of thing that grandpas care much about remembering (Haase et al., 2013). According to *socioemotional selectivity theory* (Carstensen & Turk-Charles, 1994), younger adults are mainly motivated to acquire information that will be useful to them in the future (which is why they spend their time reading political news and learning new languages), whereas older adults are mainly motivated to acquire information that brings them emotional satisfaction in the present (which is why they spend their time reading novels and learning to paint). Young people *invest* their time by attending to, thinking about, and remembering information that will have practical benefits tomorrow, while older people *spend* their time attending to, thinking about, and remembering information that has emotional benefits today.

For example, younger adults show equal amounts of amygdala activation when they see very pleasant or very unpleasant pictures, but older adults show much more activation when they see very pleasant than very unpleasant pictures, suggesting that older adults just aren't attending closely to information that doesn't make them happy (Mather et al., 2004; Mikels & Shuster, 2016). Indeed, compared with younger adults, older adults are generally better at sustaining positive emotions and curtailing negative ones (Ford et al., 2018; Isaacowitz, 2012; Isaacowitz & Blanchard-Fields, 2012; Mather & Carstensen, 2005; Verstaen et al., 2018). They experience fewer negative emotions in their daily lives (Carstensen et al., 2000; Charles et al., 2001; Mroczek & Spiro, 2005; Schilling et al., 2013; Stone et al., 2010) and are more accepting of them when they do (Shallcross et al., 2013). They are more emotionally stable and better at regulating their emotions (Burr et al., 2021). Even their daydreams seem to be more pleasant (Maillet et al., 2018)!

Because they are not concerned about "saving for tomorrow," older adults are also more willing than younger people to forego personal gains and instead contribute to the public good (Freund & Blanchard-Fields, 2014; see Hot Science: There's No Time Like the Present). And because they care more about the emotional benefits of experience than the practical benefits, older adults become more selective about their interaction partners, choosing to communicate and spend time with family and a few close friends rather than with a large circle of acquaintances (Chui et al., 2014; David-Barrett et al., 2016). One

Hot Science • There's No Time Like the Present

It is often said that children and their grandparents get along so well because they share a common enemy. Kidding aside, there do seem to be ways in which younger and older people are more like each other than either group is like the folks in the middle, and recent research suggests that one of those ways is patience. We all know people who just "have to have it now" and others who are able to wait patiently until later. Researchers can measure these differences using an "intertemporal discounting task." The idea behind the task is simple: Give people a choice between receiving some amount of money today or receiving more money in the future, and then see how *much* more money it takes to get them to wait. The smallest amount required to convince a person to wait is a measure of their patience: The more money they require, the less patient they are.

Richter and Mata (2018) gave this task to more than 1,500 people ranging in age from 18 to 96. Would they rather receive $230 right now or wait and receive $235 in a year? How about $240? How about

$245? The researchers went all the way up to $360 and found something that you probably would have guessed yourself: Adolescents and young adults were less patient than their parents. What you might not have guessed is that elderly people were nearly as impatient as adolescents. Yes, young people were more likely than their parents to say, "Forget about tomorrow, I want it *now*." But so were their grandparents! When the researchers

controlled for variables such as cognitive ability, education, health, and financial security, the results did not change.

Exactly why this happened is anyone's guess, but one possibility is that younger people have not yet learned to think about the future, and older people don't have all that much future to think about. Both of them care more about today than tomorrow, and so they like to get together—and eat dessert first!

Adolescents and older adults have something in common: They don't like to wait for the things they want!

---

study monitored a group of people from the 1930s to the 1990s and found that their rate of interaction with acquaintances declined from early to middle adulthood, but that their rate of interaction with spouses, parents, and siblings remained stable or increased (Carstensen, 1992; Sander et al., 2017; see **FIGURE 11.19**). A study of older adults who ranged in age from 69 to 104 found that the oldest adults had fewer peripheral social partners than the younger adults did, but they had just as many emotionally close partners whom they identified as members of their "inner circle" (Lang & Carstensen, 1994; Zhaoyang et al., 2018). "Let's go meet some new people" isn't something that most 60-year-olds tend to say, but "Let's go hang out with some old friends" is. It is sad but informative to note that many of these same cognitive and emotional changes can be observed among younger people who have discovered that their futures will be short because of a terminal illness (Carstensen & Fredrickson, 1998; Sullivan-Singh et al., 2015).

Given that older adults mainly focus on positive experiences and meaningful social interactions, you shouldn't be surprised to learn that late adulthood is one of the happiest and most satisfying stages of life. You *shouldn't* be surprised, but you probably

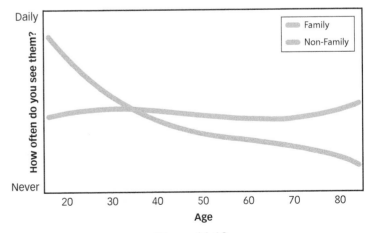

Figure 11.19

Friends but Not Family Become Less Important as We Age The amount of time people spend with their families doesn't change much over the course of their lives, but the amount of time they spend with friends diminishes dramatically.
ADAPTED FROM SANDER ET AL. (2017).

"Things they do look awfully cold, I hope I die before I get old." That's a line from The Who's 1965 hit song, "My Generation," which *Rolling Stone* magazine declared the 11th greatest rock song of all time. Although old age may *look* "awfully cold" to you, research suggests that young adults vastly overestimate the problems of aging. Pete Townshend, who wrote the song, is 76 years old and is still touring and making records, which suggests that he has reconsidered his position.

are because research shows that young adults vastly overestimate the problems of aging (Pew Research Center for People & the Press, 2009; Sneed, 2005). Young adults predict that they will be happier at the age of 30 than at the age of 70, but 70-year-olds typically report greater happiness than 30-year-olds do (Lacey et al., 2006; cf. Twenge et al., 2016; Globe and Mail, Survey of Canadians' Happiness, 2018).

Changing Roles

The psychological separation from parents that begins in adolescence usually becomes a physical separation in adulthood. In almost all human societies, young adults leave home, pair off with another person, and have children of their own. Being in a committed long-term relationship and parenthood are two of the most significant milestones of adult life. If you are a university-age Canadian, then you are likely to settle down with a special someone around the age of 30 and have an average of 1.7 children, and you will do these things not because someone told you to, but because you believe they will make you happy. Will they?

According to an Ipsos poll, in 2018 half of Canadians over age 18 were married or living common law, 3 in 10 were single, 1 in 10 were divorced and not in a relationship, 1 in 20 were dating, and 1 in 20 were widowed (Ipsos, 2018). Two in 10 people in committed long-term relationships (married or living common law) say that they are on their second (or higher) such relationship. Mixed-orientation relationships (in which one partner is straight while the other identifies as LGBTQ2S+) are quite common in Canada, accounting for 1 in 50 relationships among those age 35 and older, and 1 in 10 relationships for those under age 35. Arranged marriages are also quite common, again accounting for 1 in 50 relationships for people age 35 and older, and 1 in 20 for people under age 35 (Ipsos, 2018). Over half of Canadians who report a previous long-term relationship, or who are in arranged marriages, report that their bond with their current partner is stronger as a result (Ipsos, 2018).

More generally, people in committed relationships are generally happier than those who are single. This is particularly true for men, for older people, for those with more education, and for those in worse health (Oh et al., 2021). Nevertheless, many single people seem to be happy and are able to meet their relationship needs through nonromantic relationships with friends and family (Oh et al., 2021). The importance of friendships for health and well-being was recently highlighted in a large study of over 320,000 adult participants in 99 different countries (Lu et al., 2021). Placing importance on friendships was strongly associated with better health, greater happiness, and higher levels of subjective well-being across cultures. The association between prioritizing friendships and health and happiness was particularly strong among older adults; women; and those living in individualistic cultures, such as Canada and the United States (Lu et al., 2021).

Children are another story — not because the happiness boost lasts longer, but because there isn't one. Research shows that children do not increase their parents' happiness; indeed, more often than not, they decrease it by a small amount (Stanca, 2016). Parents typically report lower satisfaction with their partner than do nonparents — and the more children they have, the less satisfaction they report (Twenge et al., 2003). Although the proportion of stay-at-home fathers in Canada has increased dramatically in the last 40 years (see **FIGURE 11.20**), mothers still generally do more child care than fathers do, and so it is not surprising that the negative impact of parenthood on overall happiness and life satisfaction is stronger for women than for men. Mothers of young children experience role conflicts ("How am I supposed to manage being a full-time lawyer and a full-time mother?") and restrictions of freedom ("I never get to play tennis anymore") that fathers often side-step. A study that measured the moment-to-moment happiness of American women as they went about their daily activities found that women were less happy when taking care of their children than when eating, exercising, shopping, napping, or watching television — and

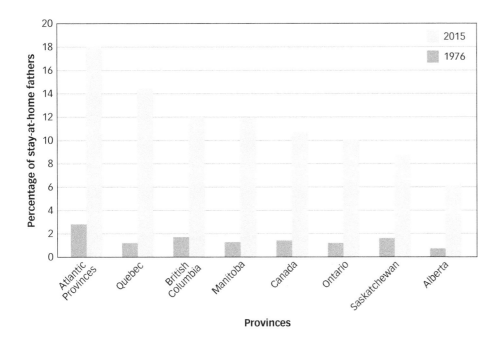

only slightly happier than when they were doing housework (Kahneman et al., 2004). The relationship between children and happiness seems to change after children leave home: A survey of 200,000 older people in 86 countries has shown that, independent of sex, income, or partnership status, parents of adult children are happier the more children they have (Margolis & Myrskylä, 2011).

Does all this mean that people would be happier if they didn't have children? Not necessarily. Because researchers cannot randomly assign people to be parents or nonparents, studies of the effects of parenthood on happiness are necessarily correlational. When controlling for other factors, people who want children and have children may be somewhat less happy than people who neither want them nor have them, but it is possible that people who want children

On average, children lower their parents' happiness. But this effect is stronger in some countries than in others—and in about a third of all countries, children raise their parents' happiness. In 2015, parents in Macedonia (*left*) experienced the largest "happiness penalty" and parents in Montenegro (*right*) experienced the largest "happiness premium" (Stanca, 2016).

would be even less happy if they *didn't* have them. What does seem clear is that raising children is a challenging job that people find most rewarding when they're not in the middle of doing it.

Chapter Review

Prenatality: A Womb with a View

- Developmental psychology studies continuity and change across the life span.

- The prenatal stage of development begins when a sperm fertilizes an egg, producing a zygote. The zygote, which contains chromosomes from both the egg and the sperm, develops into an embryo at 2 weeks and then into a fetus at 8 weeks.

- Humans are born with underdeveloped brains, which is essential to the birth process and allows for adaptation to the social and physical environment after birth.

- The fetal environment has important physical and psychological effects. In addition to the food a pregnant person eats, teratogens — agents that impair fetal development — can affect the fetus. The most common teratogens are tobacco and alcohol.

- The fetus can hear and becomes familiar with its mother's voice.

Infancy and Childhood: Perceiving, Doing, and Thinking

- Infants have a limited range of vision, but they can see and remember objects that appear within it. They learn to control their bodies from the top down and from the centre out.

- Infants slowly develop theories about how the world works. Piaget believed that these theories developed through four stages in which children learn basic facts about the world, such as the fact that objects continue to exist even when they are out of sight and the fact that objects have enduring properties that are not changed by superficial transformations. Children also learn that their minds represent objects; hence objects may not be as they appear, and others may not see them as the child does.

- Language helps children acquire a theory of mind.

- Cognitive development depends on social interactions and infants have three key abilities that allow them to learn from others.

Infancy and Childhood: Bonding and Helping

- At a very early age, human beings develop strong emotional ties to their primary caregivers. The quality of these ties — which are indexed by either secure, avoidant, ambivalent, or disorganized attachment styles — is determined both by the caregiver's behaviour and the child's temperament.

- Piaget concluded that children's reasoning about right and wrong develops in three ways. It is initially based on inviolable truths about the world, but expands to include concepts of fairness and equity. As they mature, children begin to consider the actor's intentions as well as the extent to which the action obeys abstract moral principles. Kohlberg outlined a theory of morality that progresses from evaluation of an action's consequences, to determination of whether it obeys social rules, and finally to how it aligns with core values.

- Infants seem to have some "moral sense," such as an affinity towards kind people and a concern with fairness.

Adolescence: Minding the Gap

- Adolescence begins with puberty, the onset of sexual maturity of the human body. Puberty now occurs earlier than ever before, and the entrance of young people into adult society occurs later.

- Adolescents are more likely to do things that are risky or illegal, but they rarely inflict serious or enduring harm on themselves or others.

- Research suggests that biology and genetics play key roles in determining a person's sexual orientation. Sex education has been shown to reduce risky sexual behaviour.

- As adolescents develop their adult identities, they seek increasing autonomy from their parents and become more peer oriented, forming single-sex cliques, followed by mixed-sex cliques. Finally, they pair off as couples.

Adulthood: Change We Can't Believe In

- Performance on most cognitive tasks peaks when people are in their 20s, but older people develop a variety of strategies to compensate for their cognitive declines.

- Older adults are more oriented towards emotional satisfaction, which influences the way they attend to and remember information, the size and structure of their social networks, and their happiness.

- For most people, adulthood means leaving home, getting married, and having children. The responsibilities that parenthood entails present a significant challenge to people's happiness.

Changing Minds

1. One of your female friends recently got married, and says that she is planning to have children. You mention that once this happens she will have to stop drinking. She scoffs. "They make it sound as though a pregnant person who drinks alcohol is murdering their baby. But my mom drank wine every weekend when she was pregnant with me, and I'm just fine." What is your friend failing to understand about the effects of alcohol on prenatal development? What other teratogens might you tell her about?

2. You are at the grocery store when you see a father reprimanding his 5-year-old child for eating candy while the father wasn't looking. "I've told you before that it's wrong to eat food you haven't paid for. Why can't you understand that?" Are the father's expectations realistic? What would you tell him about moral development?

3. You and your roommate are watching a movie in which a young man tells his parents that he's gay. The parents react badly and decide that they should send him to a "camp" where he can learn to change his sexual orientation. Your roommate turns to you: "Do you know anything about this? Can people really be changed from gay to straight?" What would you tell your friend about "conversion therapy" and about the factors that determine sexual orientation?

4.
Visualizing Data
One of your cousins has just turned 30 and, to their horror, has discovered a grey hair. "This is the end," your cousin says. "Soon I'll start losing my eyesight, growing new chins, and forgetting how to use a cell phone. Aging is just one long, slow, agonizing decline." Review the DATA. What could you tell your cousin to cheer them up? Does everything in life get worse with age?

Key Terms

developmental psychology (p. 399)

germinal stage (p. 399)

embryonic stage (p. 400)

fetal stage (p. 400)

myelination (p. 400)

teratogen (p. 401)

fetal alcohol syndrome (FAS) (p. 401)

infancy (p. 402)

motor development (p. 403)

motor reflexes (p. 403)

cephalocaudal principle (p. 403)

proximodistal principle (p. 404)

cognitive development (p. 405)

sensorimotor stage (p. 405)

schemas (p. 406)

assimilation (p. 406)

accommodation (p. 406)

object permanence (p. 406)

childhood (p. 408)

preoperational stage (p. 408)

concrete operational stage (p. 408)

conservation (p. 408)

formal operational stage (p. 408)

egocentrism (p. 409)

theory of mind (p. 410)

attachment (p. 414)

attachment styles (p. 415)

temperament (p. 415)

internal working model (p. 416)

preconventional stage (p. 419)

conventional stage (p. 419)

postconventional stage (p. 419)

adolescence (p. 420)

puberty (p. 421)

primary sex characteristics (p. 421)

secondary sex characteristics (p. 421)

adulthood (p. 430)

Personality

GROWING UP, STEFANI JOANNE ANGELINA GERMANOTTA seemed to have personality. As a child, she was said to have shown up at the occasional family gathering naked. As the pop star now known as Lady Gaga, she continues the tradition of being different. Her first albums, *The Fame* and *The Fame Monster,* as well as the fact that she calls her fans "Little Monsters" and herself the "Mother Monster," hinted she might have issues. But she, like most of us, is not one-dimensional. Yes, her style is eccentric (sometimes a dress made of meat, sometimes feathers), but she also is a serious supporter of humanitarian and personal causes, including equality for people who are gay, bisexual, lesbian, or transgender (as in her song "Born This Way"). Lady Gaga is one of a kind. She has personality in an important sense—she is similar to other people in many ways, but also has qualities that make her psychologically different from other people.

THE FORCES THAT CREATE ANY ONE PERSONALITY ARE ALWAYS something of a mystery. Your personality is different from anyone else's and expresses itself pretty consistently across settings—at home, in the classroom, and elsewhere. But how and why do people differ psychologically? By studying many unique individuals, psychologists seek to gather enough information to answer these central questions of personality psychology scientifically.

Personality is *an individual's characteristic style of behaving, thinking, and feeling.* Whether Lady Gaga's quirks are real or merely part of a persona she performs for entertainment value, they certainly are identifiably hers and they show her distinct personality. In this chapter, we will explore personality, first by looking at what it is and how it is measured, and then by focusing on each of four main approaches to understanding personality: trait–biological, psychodynamic, humanistic–existential, and social–cognitive. Psychologists have personalities, too (well, *most* of them), so their different approaches, even to the topic of personality, shouldn't be that surprising. At the end of the chapter, we discuss the psychology of self to see how our views of what we are like can shape and define our personality.

The singer Lady Gaga in her meat dress at the MTV Video Music Awards (2010) and her feather dress at the Golden Globes (2019).

Personality: What It Is and How It Is Measured

If someone said, "You have no personality," how would you feel? Like a cookie-cutter person, a boring, grayish lump who should go out and get a personality as soon as possible? As a rule, people don't strive for a personality—one seems to develop naturally as we travel through life. As psychologists have tried to understand the process of personality development, they have pondered questions of description (*how* do people differ?), explanation (*why* do people differ?), and the more quantitative question of measurement (how can personality be *assessed*?).

Learning Outcomes

WHAT YOU NEED TO KNOW

- Explain how prior and anticipated events explain personality differences.

- Compare personality inventories and projective techniques.

Describing and Explaining Personality

As the first biologists earnestly attempted to classify all plants and animals (whether lichens or ants or fossilized lions), personality psychologists began by labelling and describing different personalities. And just as biology came of age with Darwin's theory of evolution, which *explained* how biological differences among species arose, the maturing study of personality also has developed explanations of the basis for psychological differences among people.

What leads Lady Gaga to all of her entertaining extremes? Many psychologists attempt to study and explain personality differences by thinking about them in terms of *prior events* that may have shaped an individual's personality or *anticipated events* that motivate the person to reveal particular personality characteristics. In a biological prior event, Stefani Germanotta inherited genes from her parents that may have led her to develop into the sort of person who loves putting on a display (not to mention putting on meat and feathers) and stirring up controversy. Researchers interested in events that happen prior to our behaviour study our genes, brains, and other aspects of our biological makeup; they also delve into our subconscious, as well as into our circumstances and interpersonal surroundings. The consideration of *anticipated events* emphasizes the person's own, subjective perspective and often seems intimate and personal in its reflection of the person's inner life (hopes, fears, and aspirations).

Of course, our understanding of how the baby named Stefani Germanotta grew into the adult Lady Gaga (or of the life of any person) also depends on insights into the interaction between the prior and anticipated events: We need to know how her history may have shaped her motivations.

Donald Trump   Megan, Duchess of Sussex

Drake   Justin Trudeau

How would you describe each of these personalities?

Measuring Personality

Of all the things psychologists have set out to measure, personality may be one of the toughest. How do you capture the uniqueness of a person? What aspects of people's personalities are important to know about? How should we quantify them? The general personality measures can be classified broadly into personality inventories and projective techniques.

Personality Inventories Rely on Self-Reporting

To learn about an individual's personality, you could follow the person around, clipboard in hand, and record every single thing the person does, says, thinks, and feels (including how long this goes on before the person calls the police). Some observations might involve your own impressions (Day 5: seems to be getting irritable);

personality An individual's characteristic style of behaving, thinking, and feeling.

TABLE 12.1

TEN-ITEM PERSONALITY INVENTORY (TIPI)

Here are a number of personality traits that may or may not apply to you. Please write a number next to each statement to indicate the extent to which *you agree or disagree with that statement.* You should rate the extent to which the pair of traits applies to you, even if one characteristic applies more strongly than the other.

1 = Disagree strongly
2 = Disagree moderately
3 = Disagree a little
4 = Neither agree nor disagree
5 = Agree a little
6 = Agree moderately
7 = Agree strongly

I see myself as:

____ Extraverted, enthusiastic
____ Critical, quarrelsome
____ Dependable, self-disciplined
____ Anxious, easily upset
____ Open to new experiences, complex
____ Reserved, quiet
____ Sympathetic, warm
____ Disorganized, careless
____ Calm, emotionally stable
____ Conventional, uncreative

TIPI scale scoring (R = reverse-scored items): Extraversion (1, 6R); Agreeableness (2R, 7); Conscientiousness (3, 8R); Emotional Stability (4R, 9); Openness to Experience (5, 10R).

Information from Gosling et al., 2003.

Personality inventories ask people to report what traits they possess. Think about how you would rate yourself according to the items in TABLE 12.1. Can we rely on people to accurately report on their personality?

self-report A method in which people provide subjective information about their own thoughts, feelings, or behaviours, typically via questionnaire or interview.

Minnesota Multiphasic Personality Inventory (MMPI) A well-researched clinical questionnaire used to assess personality and psychological problems.

others would involve objectively observable events that anyone could verify (Day 7: grabbed my pencil and broke it in half, then bit my hand).

Psychologists have figured out ways to obtain objective data on personality without driving their subjects to violence. The most popular technique is **self-report,** *a method in which people provide subjective information about their own thoughts, feelings, or behaviours, typically via questionnaire or interview.* In most self-report measures, respondents are asked to circle a number on a scale indicating the degree to which they endorse that item as being self-descriptive (e.g., reporting on a scale of 0–5 to what extent they believe they are a "worrier") or to indicate whether an item is true or false in describing them. The researcher then combines the answers to get a general sense of the individual's personality with respect to a particular domain. **TABLE 12.1** shows the 10 items from a self-report test of different personality traits (Gosling et al., 2003). In this case, the respondent is asked to indicate whether each personality trait applies to them. To score the measure, simply add up the two items for each of the five traits listed at the bottom of the table.

How is a self-report scale created? The usual strategy is to collect sets of self-descriptive statements that indicate different degrees of a personality characteristic. To measure friendliness, for example, you could ask people to rate their agreement with statements ranging from "I am somewhat friendly" to "I am very outgoing," or even to "I love being around people." Adding up the number of statements the person endorses that indicate friendliness (and subtracting endorsements of those that indicate unfriendliness) yields a measure of the person's self-reported friendliness. Scales based on the content of self-reports have been devised to assess a whole range of personality characteristics, all the way from general tendencies such as overall happiness (Lyubomirsky, 2008) and mental toughness (Kawabata et al., 2021) to specific ones such as responding rapidly to insults (Swann & Rentfrow, 2001) or complaining about poor service (Lerman, 2006).

One of the most commonly used personality tests is the **Minnesota Multiphasic Personality Inventory (MMPI),** *a well-researched clinical questionnaire used to assess personality and psychological problems.* The MMPI was developed in 1939 and has been revised several times over the years, leading up to the current version, the MMPI–2–RF (restructured form) (Ben-Porath & Tellegen, 2008). The MMPI–2–RF consists of 338 self-descriptive statements to which the respondent answers "true," "false," or "cannot say." The MMPI–2–RF measures a wide range of psychological constructs: clinical problems (e.g., antisocial behaviour, thought dysfunction), somatic problems (e.g., head pain, cognitive complaints), internalizing problems (e.g., anxiety, self-doubt), externalizing problems (e.g., aggression, substance abuse), and interpersonal problems (e.g., family problems, avoidance). The MMPI–2–RF also includes *validity scales* that assess a person's attitudes towards test taking and any tendency to try to distort the results by faking answers.

Personality inventories such as the MMPI–2–RF are easy to administer: All that is needed is the test and a pencil (or a computer-based version). The respondent's scores are then calculated and compared with the average ratings of thousands of other test takers. Because no human interpretation of the responses is needed (i.e., "true" means true, "false" means false, and so on), any potential biases of the person giving the test are minimized. Of course, an accurate measurement of personality will occur only if people provide accurate responses. Although self-report test results are easy to obtain, critics of this approach highlight several limitations. One problem is that many people have a tendency to respond in a socially desirable way, such that they underreport things that are unflattering or embarrassing. Perhaps even more problematic is that there are many things we don't know about ourselves and are thus unable to report them! Studies show that people often are inaccurate in their self-report about what they have experienced in the past, what factors motivate their behaviours in the present, or how they will feel or behave in the future (Wilson, 2009).

Projective Techniques Rely on Analysis of Ambiguous Information

A second, somewhat controversial, class of tools for evaluating personality, known as **projective tests,** are designed to circumvent the limitations of self-report just described. These tests are *designed to reveal inner aspects of individuals' personalities by analysis of their responses to a standard series of ambiguous stimuli.* The developers of projective tests assume that people will project personality factors that are below awareness—wishes, concerns, impulses, and ways of seeing the world—onto the ambiguous stimuli and will not censor these responses.

Probably the best known of these tests is the **Rorschach Inkblot Test,** *a projective technique in which respondents' inner thoughts and feelings are believed to be revealed by analysis of their responses to a set of unstructured inkblots.* An sample inkblot is shown in **FIGURE 12.1**. Responses are scored according to complicated systems (derived in part from research involving people with psychological disorders) that classify what people see (Exner, 1993; Rapaport, 1946). For instance, most people who look at Figure 12.1 report seeing birds or people. Someone who reports seeing something very unusual (e.g., "I see two purple tigers eating a velvet cheeseburger") may be experiencing thoughts and feelings that are very different from those of most other people.

The **Thematic Apperception Test (TAT)** is *a projective technique in which respondents' underlying motives, concerns, and the way they see the social world are believed to be revealed through analysis of the stories they make up about ambiguous pictures of people.* To get a sense of the test, look at **FIGURE 12.2**. The test administrator shows the respondent the card and asks them to tell a story about the picture, asking questions such as: Who is the person shown on the card? What is happening? What led them to this moment? What will happen next? Many of the TAT drawings tend to elicit a consistent set of themes, such as successes and failures, competition and jealousy, conflict with parents and siblings, feelings about intimate relationships, aggression, and sexuality. Different people tell very different stories about the images. In creating the stories, the respondent is thought to identify with the main characters and to project their view of others and the world onto the other details in the drawing. Thus, any details that are not obviously drawn from the picture are believed to be projected onto the story from the respondent's own desires and internal conflicts.

The value of projective tests is debated by psychologists. Although they continue to be used by practicing clinicians, critics argue that tests such as the Rorschach and the TAT are open to the biases of the examiner. A TAT story may *seem* revealing; however, the examiner must always add an interpretation (was this about the respondent's actual father, about his own concerns about his academic failures, or about trying to be funny or provocative?), and that interpretation could well be the scorer's *own* projection into the mind of the test taker. Thus, despite the rich picture of a personality and the insights into an individual's motives that these tests may appear to offer, we should understand projective tests primarily as a way in which a psychologist can try to get to better know someone personally and intuitively (McClelland et al., 1953). When measured by rigorous scientific criteria, projective tests such as the TAT and the Rorschach have not been found to be reliable or valid in predicting behaviour (Lilienfeld et al., 2003).

Methods Using Technology

Newer personality measurement methods are moving beyond both self-report inventories and projective tests (Robins et al., 2007). Higher-tech methods such as smartphones, wearable devices, and real-time analysis of social media posts open the door to personality measurements that are leaps beyond asking people to make up stories about old pictures—and can lead to surprising findings. The stereotype that women are more talkative than men, for example, was challenged by research that involved 396 university students in the United States and Mexico who each

Figure 12.1
Sample Rorschach Inkblot Test takers are shown a card such as this sample and asked, "What might this be?" What they perceive, where they see it, and why they believe it looks that way are assumed to reflect unconscious aspects of their personality.

Figure 12.2
Sample TAT Card Test takers are shown cards that display ambiguous scenes such as the one shown in this sample and are asked to tell a story about what is happening in the picture. The main themes of the story, the thoughts and feelings of the characters, and how the story develops and resolves are considered useful indices of unconscious aspects of an individual's personality (Murray, 1943).

projective tests Tests designed to reveal inner aspects of individuals' personalities by analysis of their responses to a standard series of ambiguous stimuli.

Rorschach Inkblot Test A projective technique in which respondents' inner thoughts and feelings are believed to be revealed by analysis of their responses to a set of unstructured inkblots.

Thematic Apperception Test (TAT) A projective technique in which respondents' underlying motives, concerns, and the way they see the social world are believed to be revealed through analysis of the stories they make up about ambiguous pictures of people.

As the technologies we use in our day-to-day lives have evolved and advanced, from tape recorders to smartphones to social media platforms to the new metaverse described by Mark Zuckerberg, so too have our opportunities for studying people's personalities in their natural (and virtual) environment.

spent several days wearing an EAR (electronically activated recorder) that captured random snippets of their talk (Mehl et al., 2007). The result? Women and men were *equally* talkative, each averaging about 16,000 words per day. The advanced measurement of how people differ (and how they do not) is a key step in understanding personality. More recently, the EAR technology has been converted into a smartphone app that can be installed on a person's phone (with their permission of course) and randomly record real-world interactions to better understand their personality and a range of other aspects of human interaction patterns (Kaplan et al., 2020).

Psychologists are also using social media to better understand personality traits and how people express themselves in different ways. An important advantage of this approach, as with the EAR findings, is that it allows psychologists to study people as they actually behave out in the world while interacting with others (as opposed to in the lab under experimental conditions). For example, one study analyzed more than 700 million words and phrases that 75,000 people posted on their Facebook pages and compared them to the results from personality tests given to the same people (Schwartz et al., 2013). The results revealed significant differences in how people who self-identified as males and females express themselves, as well as differences by age and personality. For instance, females use more words about emotions, whereas males use more words about objects and more swear words. People who posted about going out and partying scored high on extraversion; people who posted about being "sick of" things scored high on neuroticism; and people who posted about computers and Pokémon cards scored high on introversion. As the world creates newer forms of communicating, psychologists benefit by having newer ways of studying personality.

The Trait Approach: Identifying Patterns of Behaviour

Learning Outcomes

WHAT YOU NEED TO KNOW

- Describe how the trait approach to personality has changed over time.

- Describe the traits in the Big Five Factor Model.

- Explain the biological basis for personality traits.

Imagine writing a story about the people you know. To capture their special qualities, you might describe their traits: Ayesha is *friendly, assertive,* and *contemplative;* Andy is *flaky, humourous,* and *superficial.* With a thesaurus and a free afternoon, you might even be able to describe Madison as *perspicacious, flagitious,* and *callipygian.* The trait approach to personality uses such trait terms to characterize differences among individuals. In attempting to create manageable and meaningful sets of descriptors, trait theorists face two significant challenges: narrowing down an almost infinite set of adjectives and answering the more basic question of why people have particular traits and whether those traits arise from biological or hereditary foundations.

Traits as Behavioural Dispositions and Motives

One way to think about personality is as a combination of traits. This was the approach of Gordon Allport (1937), one of the first trait theorists, who believed people could be described in terms of traits just as an object could be described in terms of its properties. He saw a **trait** as *a relatively stable disposition to behave in a particular and consistent way.* For example, a person who keeps their books organized alphabetically in bookshelves, hangs their clothing neatly in the closet, knows the schedule for the local bus, keeps a clear agenda in a smartphone or daily planner, and lists birthdays of friends and family in their calendar can be

trait A relatively stable disposition to behave in a particular and consistent way.

said to have the trait of *orderliness*. This trait consistently manifests itself in a variety of settings.

The orderliness trait *describes* a person but doesn't *explain* their behaviour. Why does the person behave in this way? A trait might provide an explanation for behaviour in two basic ways: The trait may be a preexisting disposition of the person that causes the person's behaviour, or it may be a motivation that guides the person's behaviour. Allport saw traits as preexisting dispositions, causes of behaviour that reliably trigger that behaviour. The person's orderliness, for example, is an inner property of the person that will cause the person to straighten things up and be tidy in a wide array of situations. Other personality theorists, such as Henry Murray (the creator of the TAT), suggested instead that traits reflect motives. Just as a hunger motive might explain someone's many trips to the snack bar, a need for orderliness might explain the neat closet, organized calendar, and familiarity with the bus schedule (Murray & Kluckhohn, 1953). Researchers examining traits as causes have used personality inventories to measure them, whereas those examining traits as motives have more often used projective tests.

Researchers have described and measured hundreds of different personality traits over the past several decades. Back in the late 1940s, in the wake of World War II, psychologists were very interested in right-wing *authoritarianism*, the tendency towards political conservatism, obedience to authority, and conformity. At that time, researchers were trying to understand what had made people support the rise of Nazi Germany and fascism (Adorno et al., 1950). Although research on the personality traits that lead to authoritarianism continues (Strosberg, 2021; Womick et al., 2019), the topic became less focal for researchers once World War II receded into history. Other traits that have come into vogue over the years include cognitive complexity, defensiveness, sensation seeking, and optimism. Like television shows and hairstyles, fashions in trait dimensions come and go over time.

By many accounts, Bashar al-Assad of Syria is a despotic ruler who imprisons, tortures, and kills those who oppose him. Why would anyone want to be a follower of such a dictator? The study of the authoritarian personality was inspired by the idea that some people might follow most anyone because their personalities make them adhere to hierarchies of authority, submitting to those above them and dominating those below them.

The Search for Core Traits

Picking a fashionable trait and studying it in depth doesn't get us very far in the search for the core of human character: the basic set of traits that defines how humans differ from each other. People may differ strongly in their choice of Coke versus Pepsi, or dogs versus cats, but are these differences important? Researchers have used several different approaches in an effort to discover the core personality traits.

Early Research Focused on Adjectives That Describe Personality

The study of core traits began with an exploration of how personality is represented in the store of wisdom we call *language*. Generation after generation, people have described people with words, so early psychologists proposed that core traits could be discerned by finding the main themes in all the adjectives used to describe personality. In one such analysis, a painstaking count of relevant words in a dictionary of English resulted in a list of more than 18,000 potential traits (Allport & Odbert, 1936)! Attempts to narrow down the list to a more manageable set depend on the idea that traits might be related in a hierarchical pattern (see **FIGURE 12.3**), with more general or abstract traits at higher levels than more specific or concrete traits. Perhaps the more abstract traits represent the core of personality.

To identify this core, researchers have used the computational procedure called *factor analysis*, described in the Intelligence chapter, which sorts trait terms or self-descriptions into a small number of underlying dimensions, or *factors*, based on how people use the traits to rate themselves. In a typical study using factor

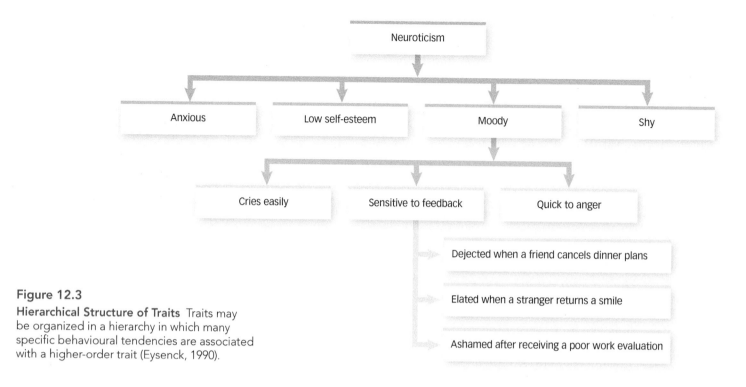

Figure 12.3

Hierarchical Structure of Traits Traits may be organized in a hierarchy in which many specific behavioural tendencies are associated with a higher-order trait (Eysenck, 1990).

analysis, hundreds of people rate themselves on hundreds of adjectives, indicating how accurately each one describes their personality. The researcher then performs calculations to determine similarities in the raters' usage, such as whether people who describe themselves as *ambitious* also describe themselves as *active* but not *laid-back* or *contented*. Factor analysis can also reveal which adjectives are unrelated. For example, if people who describe themselves as *ambitious* are neither more nor less likely to describe themselves as *creative* or *innovative,* the factor analysis would reveal that *ambitiousness* and *creativity/innovativeness* represent different factors. Each factor is typically presented as a continuum, ranging from one extreme trait (such as *ambitious*) to its opposite (in this case, *laid-back*).

Different factor analysis techniques have yielded different views of personality structure. Cattell (1950) proposed a 16-factor theory of personality (way down from 18,000, but still a lot), whereas others proposed theories with far fewer basic dimensions (John et al., 2008). Hans Eysenck (1967) simplified things nicely with a model of personality with only two major traits (although he later expanded it to three). Eysenck's two-factor analysis identified one dimension that distinguished people who are sociable and active (extraverts) from those who are quiet and introspective (introverts). His analysis also identified a second dimension ranging from the tendency to be very neurotic or emotionally unstable to the tendency to be more emotionally stable. He believed that many behavioural tendencies could be understood in terms of their relation to the core traits of extraversion and neuroticism. The third factor he proposed was psychoticism, which refers to the extent to which a person is impulsive or hostile. (Note that nowadays, the term *psychotic* refers to an abnormal mental state marked by detachment from reality. This is discussed further in the Disorders chapter.)

A Consensus Is Reached: The Big Five Dimensions of Personality

Big Five The traits of the five-factor model: openness to experience, conscientiousness, extraversion, agreeableness, and neuroticism.

Today most researchers agree that personality is best captured by 5 factors rather than 2, 3, 16, or 18,000 (Denissen et al., 2019; John & Srivastava, 1999). The **Big Five,** as they are affectionately called, are *the traits of the five-factor personality model: openness to experience, conscientiousness, extraversion, agreeableness, and neuroticism* (see **TABLE 12.2**) (remember them by the initials O.C.E.A.N.). The five-factor model, which overlaps with the pioneering work of Cattell and Eysenck, is now widely preferred for several reasons. First, modern factor analysis techniques confirm that this set of five factors strikes the right balance between accounting for as much variation in personality as possible while avoiding overlapping traits. Second, in a large number of studies using different kinds of data (people's descriptions of their own personalities, other people's descriptions of their personalities, interviewer checklists, and behavioural observation), the same five factors have emerged. Third, and perhaps most important, the basic five-factor structure seems to show up across a wide range of participants, including children, adults in other cultures, and even among those who use other languages, suggesting that the Big Five may be universal (Denissen et al., 2019; Kajonius & Giolla, 2017) (see Other Voices: How Accurate Are Personality Tests?).

The reality of these traits has been clearly established in research showing that self-reports on the Big Five are associated with predictable patterns of behaviour and social outcomes. People identified as high in extraversion, for example, tend to spend time with lots of other people and are more likely than introverts to look people in the eye. People high in conscientiousness generally perform well at work and tend to live longer. People low on conscientiousness and low in agreeableness are more likely than average to be juvenile delinquents (John & Srivastava, 1999). It turns out that the Big Five personality traits also predict people's online behaviour on social networking sites such as Facebook (see Hot Science: Personality on the Surface).

Research on the Big Five indicates the rather interesting finding that people's personalities tend to remain fairly stable through their lifetime: Scores at one time in life correlate strongly with scores at later dates, even decades later (Caspi et al., 2005). William James offered the opinion that "in most of us, by the age of 30, the character has set like plaster, and will never soften again" (James, 1890, p. 121), but this turns out to be too strong a view. Some variability is typical in childhood, and, though there is less in adolescence, some personality change can even occur in adulthood for some people (Srivastava et al., 2003). In general, people become slightly more conscientious in their 20s (got to keep that job!) and a bit more agreeable in their 30s (got to keep those friends!). Neuroticism decreases with age, but only among women (Srivastava et al., 2003). So enjoy the personality you have now, because it may be changing soon.

Traits as Biological Building Blocks

Can we explain *why* a person has a stable set of personality traits? Many trait theorists have argued that unchangeable brain and biological processes produce the remarkable stability of traits over the life span. Allport viewed traits as characteristics of the brain that influence the way people respond to their environment. And, as you will see, Eysenck searched for a connection between his trait dimensions and specific individual differences in the workings of the brain.

Brain damage certainly can produce personality change, as the classic case of Phineas Gage so vividly demonstrates (see the Neuroscience and Behaviour chapter). You may recall that after the blasting accident that blew a steel rod through his frontal lobes, Gage showed a dramatic loss of social appropriateness and conscientiousness (Damasio, 1994). In fact, when someone experiences a profound change in personality, testing often reveals the presence of such brain pathologies as Alzheimer's disease, stroke, or brain tumour (Boyle, 2018). The administration of pharmaceutical treatments that change brain chemistry can also trigger personality changes, such as making people somewhat more extraverted and less neurotic (Bagby et al., 1999).

TABLE 12.2

THE BIG FIVE FACTOR MODEL

	High on Trait . . . Low on Trait
Openness to experience	imaginative............ down-to-earth
	variety .... routine
	independent .... conforming
Conscientiousness	organized .... disorganized
	careful .... careless
	self-disciplined ...... weak-willed
Extraversion	social .... retiring
	fun loving .... sober
	affectionate .... reserved
Agreeableness	softhearted............ ruthless
	trusting .... suspicious
	helpful................... uncooperative
Neuroticism	worried .... calm
	insecure .... secure
	self-pitying .... self-satisfied

Other Voices | How Accurate Are Personality Tests?

As described in this chapter, psychologists have developed a range of methods to quantify different aspects of your personality. Some assessments ask you to report on your own characteristics (how would you rate yourself on the following traits?: neuroticism, extraversion…) and tell you how you compare to others, whereas others might ask you a series of questions and use that information to tell you what kind of life partner or career path is your best match. How accurate are these different approaches? This brief article by Angus Chen tackles this question by talking with some of the experts in this kind of research.

If you're looking for insight into the true you, there's a buffet of personality questionnaires available. Some are silly—like the internet quiz that tells everyone who takes it that they are procrastinators at the core. Other questionnaires, developed and sold as tools to help people hire the right candidate or find love, take themselves more seriously.

The trouble is, if you ask the experts, most of these might not be worth the money. "You should be skeptical," says Simine Vazire, a personality researcher at the University of California, Davis. "Until we test them scientifically we can't tell the difference between that and pseudoscience like astrology."

One famous example of a popular but dubious commercial personality test is the Myers–Briggs Type Indicator. This questionnaire divides people into 16 different "types" and, often, the assessment will suggest certain career or romantic pairings. It costs $15 to $40 for an individual, but psychologists say the questionnaire is one of the worst personality tests in existence for a wide range of reasons. It is unreliable because a person's type may change from day to day. It gives false information ("bogus stuff," one researcher puts it). The questions are confusing and poorly worded. Vazire sums it up as "shockingly bad."

Personality questionnaires began evolving about a century ago, says Jim Butcher, an emeritus psychologist at the University of Minnesota. "They started asking questions about an individual's thinking and behavior during World War I," he says. "These were to study personality problems and mental health problems." And importantly, he adds, the U.S. military wanted the questionnaires to help weed out soldiers who weren't fit to fly military aircraft.

The problem with practically all of the assessments at the time was they were a built on the creators' subjective feelings about personality, he notes. "Then people started to raise questions about do they really measure what they think

they're measuring? How reliable are those conclusions, and are they valid?"

Butcher describes what followed as a mass culling of personality systems and questionnaires by the scientific method. There is one personality model that did survive the 20th century, though. It is popular among academics today, and is what Vazire uses in her research. It's called the Big 5 Personality Traits (aka 5-Factor Model), and it was developed over three decades beginning in 1961 at Brooks Air Force Base [in San Antonio, Texas].

Vazire says in developing the Big 5 Personality model, psychologists tried to avoid pitfalls that plagued early personality researchers—like selecting criteria based primarily on intuition. Instead, the Big 5 model took a holistic tack by compiling every word that could be considered a personality trait and creating simple, straightforward questions about them. For example, on a scale of 1 to 5, are you outgoing, sociable? Based on how people answered initial surveys, researchers used statistical methods to group traits that seemed to cluster together (like "talkative" and "sociable") into five basic categories: extraversion, conscientiousness, agreeableness, neuroticism and openness to experience.

The key to the Big 5 model is its simplicity. It doesn't sort anybody into a "type," just informs them where they fall on a continuum of personality traits. There are no tricks and no surprises to be revealed, Vazire says. "In a way, it's disappointing. It just means that personality tests can only tell you what you tell it." You won't learn anything that you didn't already know about yourself, she adds, and its accuracy comes entirely from how honest and self-reflective you were with your answers.

Angus Chen is a freelance journalist specializing in drugs, addiction, and mental health. He has has worked with National Public Radio, WNYC Radio, *Scientific American* magazine, and other publications.

JENNIFER WANG

Although straightforward and non-mysterious, personality tests based on the Big 5 model can provide valuable information about a person's personality structure based on decades of rigorous research. Beware of any personality test that promises to tell you much more about yourself than you have told it. If it does, how can you examine the evidence supporting the claims being made by those who developed it?

Genes, Traits, and Personality

Some of the most compelling evidence for the importance of biological factors in personality comes from the domain of behavioural genetics. Like researchers studying genetic influences on intelligence (see the Intelligence chapter), personality psychologists have looked at correlations between the traits in monozygotic (or identical) twins, who share the same genes, and dizygotic (or fraternal) twins, who on average share only half of their genes. Simply put, the more genes you have in common with someone, the more similar your personalities are likely to be. Genes seem to influence most personality traits, and current estimates, based on a recent study of more than 100,000 participants, place the average genetic component of personality at about 0.40 (Vukasović & Bratko, 2015). These heritability coefficients, as you learned in the Intelligence chapter, indicate that roughly 40% of the variability among individuals results from genetic factors, with the number appearing fairly stable across personality domains (see **TABLE 12.3**). Of course, genetic factors do not account for everything; the remaining 60% of the variability in personality remains to be explained by differences in life experiences and other factors.

Twin Studies Underscore the Importance of Genetics

Studies of twins suggest that the extent to which the Big Five traits derive from genetic differences ranges from 0.44 to 0.54 (Vukasović & Bratko, 2015). As in the study of intelligence, potential confounding factors must be ruled out to ensure that effects are truly due to genetics and not to environmental experiences. Are identical twins treated more similarly, and do they have a greater *shared environment,* than fraternal twins do? As children, were they dressed in the same snappy outfits and placed on the same competitive dance teams? Could this somehow have produced similarities in their personalities? Studies of identical twins reared far apart in adoptive families—an experience that pretty much eliminates the potential effect of shared environmental factors—suggest that shared environments have little impact: Reared-apart identical twins end up just as similar in personality as those who grow up together (McGue & Bouchard, 1998).

Indeed, one provocative related finding is that such shared environmental factors as parental divorce or parenting style may have little direct impact on personality (Plomin & Caspi, 1999). According to these researchers, simply growing up in the same family does not make people very similar. In fact, when two siblings are similar, this is thought to be due primarily to genetic similarities.

Researchers also have assessed specific behavioural and attitudinal similarities in twins, and the evidence for heritability in these studies is often striking. One such study examined the DNA of 13,000 people and measured the extent to which they reported conservative versus liberal attitudes. The researchers found associations between conservatism–liberalism and chromosomal regions linked to mental flexibility, or the extent to which people change their thinking in response to shifts in their environment, which could be one of the factors influencing our views on social and

TABLE 12.3	
HERITABILITY ESTIMATES FOR THE BIG FIVE PERSONALITY TRAITS	
Trait Dimension	**Heritability**
Openness	0.41
Conscientiousness	0.31
Extraversion	0.36
Agreeableness	0.35
Neuroticism	0.37

Information from Vukasović & Bratko, 2015.

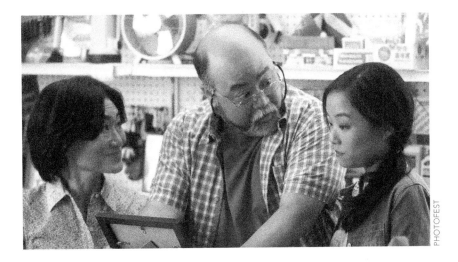

Our genes influence our personality in various ways, such as affecting how rigidly versus flexibly we think about things. This causes family members to share such traits, but not enough to prevent all disagreements.

Research has shown that there are small differences in the personalities of men versus women; however, these differences are largely absent during childhood and don't emerge until adolescence, suggesting that they may be learned based on cultural expectations. This brother and sister seem to have the same personality. Their dog looks happy though.

political issues (Hatemi et al., 2011). Current research by psychological scientists is aimed at better understanding how variations in our genetic code may contribute to the development of personality.

Gender Differences: Biology or Culture?

Do you think there is a typical female personality or a typical male personality? On a variety of personality characteristics, including helpfulness, men and women on average show no reliable differences. Overall, men and women seem to be far more similar in personality than they are different (Hyde, 2005). However, researchers have found some reliable differences between men and women with respect to their traits, attitudes, and behaviours. For example, males report having greater assertiveness, self-esteem, and sensation seeking, whereas women are higher on neuroticism, agreeableness, and conscientiousness (Costa et al., 2001; Schmitt et al., 2008).

Interestingly, many of the gender differences that do exist among adults seem to have developed over time. For instance, a review of more than 150 previous studies that included more than 20,000 participants found gender differences in the expression of emotion (with boys showing more externalizing emotions like anger and girls showing more internalizing emotions such as sadness and anxiety—consistent with the study noted in the last paragraph) (Chaplin & Aldao, 2013). However, these differences were much more pronounced as children aged into adolescence, suggesting that cultural factors play a role in how children learn to express their emotions. The finding that gender differences in personality do not begin to emerge until adolescence also has been reported in studies conducted across dozens of different cultures around the world, suggesting that this is a universal phenomenon (De Bolle et al., 2015) (see A World of Difference: Do People of Different Genders Have Different Personality Traits?).

Another factor that may contribute to the emergence of personality differences in adolescence is the simultaneous emergence of differences in sex hormones during puberty. As you know, a lot of things change during adolescence (e.g., more hormones, more interactions with friends, less time spent with parents), and it can be difficult to know what changes are causing what other changes. Interestingly, however, the effect of hormones on personality can be studied experimentally. One study followed a sample of transgender men over a three-month period during which they were undergoing testosterone treatment. Personality tests administered before and after testosterone treatment revealed that significant changes occurred, with the transgender men viewing themselves as being more masculine and their scores more closely matching those of cisgender men (Keo-Meier et al., 2015).

Traits Are Wired in the Brain

What neurophysiological mechanisms might influence the development of personality traits? Much of the thinking on this topic has focused on the extraversion–introversion dimension. In his personality model, Eysenck (1967) speculated that extraversion and introversion might arise from individual differences in cortical arousal. Eysenck suggested that extraverts pursue stimulation because their *reticular formation* (the part of the brain that regulates arousal or alertness, as described in the Neuroscience and Behaviour chapter) is not easily stimulated. To achieve greater cortical arousal and feel fully alert, Eysenck argued, extraverts seek out social interaction, parties, and other activities to achieve mental stimulation. In contrast, introverts may prefer reading or quiet activities because their cortex is very easily stimulated to a point higher than optimal alertness.

Behavioural and physiological research generally supports Eysenck's view. When introverts and extraverts are presented with a range of intense stimuli, introverts respond more strongly, including salivating more when a drop of lemon juice

A World of Difference • Do People of Different Genders Have Different Personality Traits?

Although the gender differences in personality are quite small, they tend to get a lot of attention. The debate about the origins of gender differences in personality often involves contrasting an evolutionary biological perspective with a social–cognitive perspective known as *social role theory*. The evolutionary perspective holds that men and women have evolved different personality characteristics, in part because their reproductive success depends on different behaviours. For instance, aggressiveness in men may have an adaptive value in intimidating sexual rivals, whereas being agreeable and nurturing may have evolved more among women to protect and ensure the survival of their offspring (Campbell, 1999). Cross-cultural analyses have supported the presence of some consistent gender differences between those identifying as men and women. For instance, in one study of personality including people from 22 different countries, women scored higher on agreeableness in every country (Kajonius & Giolla, 2017). In terms of evolution, however, science has yet to reveal conclusive and replicable differences between the brains of men and women (Rippon, 2019).

According to social role theory, personality characteristics and behavioural differences between men and women result from cultural standards and expectations that assign them: socially permissible jobs, activities, and family positions (Eagly & Wood, 1999). Because of their physical size and their lack of childbearing, men historically have taken roles of greater power — but most of these roles, in our postindustrial society, no longer require great physical strength. These differences then snowball, with men more likely to be granted roles that require assertiveness and aggression (e.g., executive, school

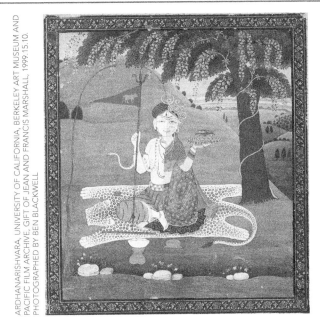

ARDHANARISHVARA, UNIVERSITY OF CALIFORNIA, BERKELEY ART MUSEUM AND PACIFIC FILM ARCHIVE, GIFT OF JEAN AND FRANCIS MARSHALL, 1999.15.10. PHOTOGRAPHED BY BEN BLACKWELL

Cultures differ in their appreciation of male and female characteristics, but the Hindu deity Ardhanarishvara represents the value of combining both parts of human nature. Male on one side and female on the other, this god is symbolic of the dual nature of the sacred. The only real problem with such side-by-side androgyny comes in finding clothes that fit.

principal, surgeon) and women more likely granted roles that emphasize greater supportiveness and nurturance (e.g., nurse, day care worker, teacher).

Regardless of the source of gender differences in personality, the degree to which people identify personally with masculine and feminine stereotypes may tell us about important personality differences between individuals. Sandra Bem (1974) designed a scale (the Bem Sex Role Inventory) that assesses the degree of identification with stereotypically masculine and feminine traits. Bem suggested that psychologically *androgynous* people (those who adopt the best of both worlds and identify with positive feminine traits and positive masculine traits; perhaps similar to those identifying as gender nonbinary or gender neutral) might be better adjusted than people who identify strongly with only one sex role or who don't identify much with either one. So far, the data seem to support this

idea. For instance, those who endorse an androgynous sex role report fewer symptoms of depression than those with a masculine or feminine role, regardless of their biological sex (Vafaei et al., 2016).

Bem Sex Role Inventory Sample Items

Respondents taking the Bem Sex Role Inventory rate themselves on each of the items without seeing the gender categorization. Then the scale is scored for masculinity (use of stereotypically masculine items), femininity (use of stereotypically feminine items), and androgyny (the tendency to use both the stereotypically masculine and feminine adjectives to describe oneself) (Bem, 1974).

Masculine Items	Feminine Items
Self-reliant	Yielding
Defends own beliefs	Affectionate
Independent	Flatterable
Assertive	Sympathetic
Forceful	Sensitive to the needs of others

is placed on their tongues and reacting more negatively to electric shocks or loud noises (Bartol & Costello, 1976; Stelmack, 1990). This reactivity has an impact on the ability to concentrate: Extraverts tend to perform well at tasks that are done in a noisy, arousing context (such as bartending or teaching), whereas introverts are

PAUL SMITH/ALAMY STOCK PHOTO

Extraverts pursue stimulation in the form of people, loud noise, and bright colours. Introverts tend to prefer softer, quieter settings. Pop quiz: Lil Nas X—introvert or extravert?

better at tasks that require concentration in tranquil contexts (such as the work of a librarian or nighttime security guard) (Lieberman & Rosenthal, 2001; Matthews & Gilliland, 1999).

In a refined version of Eysenck's ideas about arousability, Jeffrey Gray (1970) proposed that the dimensions of extraversion–introversion and neuroticism reflect two basic brain systems. The *behavioural activation system (BAS)*, essentially a "go" system, activates approach behaviour in response to the anticipation of reward. The extravert has a highly reactive BAS and will actively engage the environment, seeking social reinforcement and being on the go. The *behavioural inhibition system (BIS)*, a "stop" system, inhibits behaviour in response to stimuli signaling punishment. The anxious or introverted person, in turn, has a highly reactive BIS and will focus on negative outcomes and be on the lookout for stop signs. Because these two systems operate independently, it is possible for someone to be both a go and a stop person (simultaneously activated and inhibited), caught in a constant conflict between these two traits. An introverted person might be low on BAS (less motivated to seek out potentially rewarding social situations) and high on BIS (more likely to steer clear of others for fear of some form of punishment, such as outside criticism).

Studies of brain electrical activity (EEG) and functional brain imaging (fMRI) suggest that individual differences in activation and inhibition arise through the operation of distinct brain systems underlying these tendencies (DeYoung & Gray, 2009). Studies have suggested that the core personality traits described earlier may arise from individual variations in the volume of the different brain regions associated with each trait. For instance, self-reported neuroticism is correlated with the volume of brain regions involved in sensitivity to threat; agreeableness with areas associated with processing information about the mental states of other people; conscientiousness with regions involved in self-regulation; and extraversion with areas associated with processing information about reward (DeYoung et al., 2010). Research aimed at understanding how the structure and activity of our brains can contribute to the formation of our personality traits is still in its early stages, but it is a growing area of the field that many believe holds great promise for helping us better understand how we each develop into the unique humans that we are.

Do Animals Have Personalities?

Another source of evidence for the biological basis of human personality comes from the study of nonhuman animals. Any dog owner, cat owner, or cattle farmer can tell you that individual animals have characteristic patterns of behaviour. One Missouri woman who reportedly enjoyed raising chickens in her suburban home said that the "best part" was "knowing them as individuals" (Tucker, 2003). As far as we know, this pet owner did not give her feathered companions a personality test, though the researcher Sam Gosling (1998) used this approach in a study of a group of spotted hyenas. Well, not exactly. He recruited four human observers to use personality scales to rate the different hyenas in the group. When he examined ratings on the scales, he found five dimensions; three closely resembled the Big Five traits of neuroticism (i.e., fearfulness, emotional reactivity), openness to experience (i.e., curiosity), and agreeableness (i.e., absence of aggression).

In similar studies of mammals, fish, birds, reptiles, and other animals, individual differences in traits resembling extraversion, neuroticism, and agreeableness are the most commonly observed across different species (Gosling, 2008). For instance, one study asked pet owners of 4,300 cats to rate their personalities on various dimensions, with three of the most prominent traits emerging as neuroticism (fearfulness), extraversion (sociability towards cats and humans), and agreeableness (aggression) (Mikkola et al., 2021).

PHOTOLIBRARY/GETTY IMAGES

How would you rate this honey badger? Is it antagonistic or agreeable? Neurotic or emotionally stable? Researchers have found that even animals appear to have personalities. Or should they be called "animalities"?

Not only do animal personalities generalize across species, but personalities within animals show consistency over time. For instance, one recent study examined 31 prior studies that measured the consistency of personality traits in dogs over time. It turns out that personality characteristics present during puppyhood tend to persist into dogs' adult years (Fratkin et al., 2013), with evidence of a genetic basis for a number of these traits (Ilska et al., 2017). Consistency in dog personality is important for working dogs (e.g., bomb-sniffing dogs, service dogs, etc.), as well as for pet owners who sometimes select their pets for their apparent personality. Beyond that, studying personality in nonhuman animals offers several serious benefits: improved ability to measure physiology, more opportunities for naturalistic observation (e.g., observing aggression and social hierarchies), and an accelerated lifespan (e.g., making longitudinal and lifespan studies much more efficient) (Gosling, 2008).

Hot Science | **Personality on the Surface**

When you judge someone as friend or foe, interesting or boring, or potential life partner, how do you do it? It's nice to think that your impressions of personality are based on something deep. You wouldn't judge personality based on something as shallow as someone's looks, would you? You wouldn't form an impression of them from looking at what pops up on their Instagram or Twitter feed, would you? These criteria may seem to be flimsy bases for understanding personality, but it turns out that some valid personality judgements can be made from exactly such superficial cues. And in certain cases, such judgements are remarkably accurate.

It turns out that you *can* get some accurate information about a book by judging its cover. Researchers are increasingly using advances in computer science to study people's *digital footprints* — or the electronic information that they post online about themselves, including their written posts, photos, and videos — and examining the extent to which such information can tell us about people's personalities. It turns out that digital footprints can tell us quite a bit. One meta-analysis examined data from 14 different studies showing that the content of a person's social media posts (e.g., Instagram, Twitter, Facebook) correlate pretty well (0.29 to 0.40) with self-reported ratings of Big Five

personality traits (Azucar et al., 2018). The signs of personality that appear on the surface may be more than skin deep.

Beyond social media use, studies of personality also have shown that smartphone use and behaviour correlates with personality in expected ways. For instance, one recent analysis of smartphone data including over 25 million pieces of data collected from 624 people over a 30-day period revealed that smartphone use and behaviour patterns significantly predict Big Five personality traits in expected ways (Stachl et al., 2020). The researchers used behaviours like call and text logs, mobility, music consumption, and time-of-day phone usage to predict each person's personality scores and found that smartphones best predicted personality characteristics related to extraversion. For instance, how sociable you report being can best be predicted using information about your volume of outgoing calls (especially at night), whereas how adventurous you are is best predicted by factors like the irregularity of your outgoing and incoming calls. Conscientiousness, in contrast, is best predicted by your checking of your weather apps and self-monitoring apps. We can hope that those conscientious people are using the time they save to do other important things, such as their assigned Intro Psych reading.

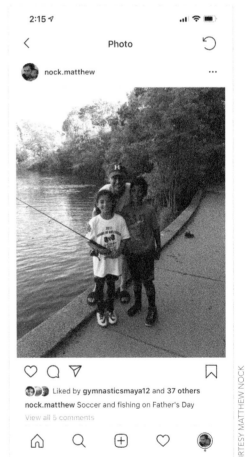

They say you can't judge a book by its cover, but some new research suggests you can judge a person by their Instagram feed.

COURTESY MATTHEW NOCK

The Psychodynamic Approach: Forces That Lie Beneath Awareness

Learning Outcomes

WHAT YOU NEED TO KNOW

- Differentiate the id, ego, and superego.
- Explain how defense mechanisms reduce anxiety.

psychodynamic approach An approach that regards personality as formed by needs, strivings, and desires largely operating outside of awareness—motives that also can produce emotional disorders.

id The part of the mind containing the drives present at birth; it is the source of our bodily needs, wants, desires, and impulses, particularly our sexual and aggressive drives.

superego The mental system that reflects the internalization of cultural rules, mainly learned as parents exercise their authority.

ego The component of personality, developed through contact with the external world, that enables us to deal with life's practical demands.

Rather than trying to understand personality in terms of broad theories for describing individual differences, Freud looked for personality in the details: the meanings and insights revealed by careful analysis of the tiniest blemishes in a person's thought and behaviour. Working with patients who came to him with disorders that did not seem to have any physical basis, he began by interpreting the origins of their everyday mistakes and memory lapses, errors that have come to be called *Freudian slips.*

Freud used the term *psychoanalysis* to refer to both his theory of personality and his method of treating patients. Freud's ideas were the first of many theories building on his basic idea that personality is a mystery to the person who "owns" it because we can't know our own deepest motives. The theories of Freud and his followers (discussed in the Treatment chapter) are referred to as the **psychodynamic approach,** which *regards personality as formed by needs, strivings, and desires largely operating outside of awareness—motives that can produce emotional disorders.* The real engines of personality, in this view, are forces of which we are largely unaware.

The Structure of the Mind: Id, Ego, and Superego

To explain the emotional difficulties that beset his patients, Freud proposed that the mind consists of three independent, interacting, and often conflicting systems: the id, the superego, and the ego.

The most basic system, the **id,** is *the part of the mind containing the drives present at birth; it is the source of our bodily needs, wants, desires, and impulses, particularly our sexual and aggressive drives.* The id operates according to the *pleasure principle,* the psychic force that motivates the tendency to seek immediate gratification of any impulse. If governed by the id alone, you would never be able to tolerate the buildup of hunger while waiting to be served at a restaurant but would simply grab food from tables nearby.

Opposite the id is the **superego,** *the mental system that reflects the internalization of cultural rules, mainly learned as parents exercise their authority.* The superego consists of a set of guidelines, internal standards, and other codes of conduct that regulate and control our behaviours, thoughts, and fantasies. It acts as a kind of conscience, developing around age 5, punishing us when it finds we are doing or thinking something wrong (by producing guilt or other painful feelings) and rewarding us (with feelings of pride or self-congratulation) for living up to ideal standards.

The final system of the mind, according to psychoanalytic theory, is the **ego,** *the component of personality, developed through contact with the external world, that enables us to deal with life's practical demands.* The ego, thought to develop within the first 3 years of life, operates according to the *reality principle,* the regulating mechanism that enables us to delay gratifying immediate needs and function effectively in the real world. It is the mediator between the id and the superego. The ego helps you resist the impulse to snatch others' food and also finds the restaurant and pays the check.

Freud believed that the relative strength of the interactions among the three systems of mind (i.e., which system is usually dominant) determines an individual's basic personality structure. Together, the id force of personal needs, the superego force of pressures to quell those needs, and the ego force of reality's demands are

TABLE 12.4

DEFENSE MECHANISMS

Defense Mechanism	Description	Example
Repression	Removing painful experiences and unacceptable impulses from the conscious mind: "motivated forgetting"	Not lashing out physically in anger; putting a bad experience out of your mind
Rationalization	Supplying a reasonable-sounding explanation for unacceptable feelings and behaviour to conceal (mostly from oneself) one's underlying motives or feelings	Dropping calculus, allegedly because of poor ventilation in the classroom
Reaction formation	Unconsciously replacing threatening inner wishes and fantasies with an exaggerated version of their opposite	Being rude to someone you're attracted to
Projection	Attributing one's own threatening feelings, motives, or impulses to another person or group	Judging others as being dishonest because you believe that you are dishonest
Regression	Reverting to an immature behaviour or earlier stage of development, a time when things felt more secure, to deal with internal conflict and perceived threat	Using baby talk, even though able to use appropriate speech, in response to distress
Displacement	Shifting unacceptable wishes or drives to a neutral or less threatening alternative	Slamming a door; yelling at someone other than the person you're mad at
Identification	Dealing with feelings of threat and anxiety by unconsciously taking on the characteristics of another person who seems more powerful or better able to cope	A bullied child becoming a bully
Sublimation	Channelling unacceptable sexual or aggressive drives into socially acceptable and culturally enhancing activities	Diverting anger to the football or rugby field, or other contact sport

in constant internal conflict. Freud believed that the dynamics among the id, superego, and ego are largely governed by *anxiety*, an unpleasant feeling that arises when unwanted thoughts or feelings occur, such as when the id seeks a gratification that the ego thinks will lead to real-world dangers or that the superego sees as leading to punishment.

When the ego receives an "alert" signal in the form of anxiety, it launches into a defensive position in an attempt to ward off the anxiety. According to Freud, it does so using one of several different **defense mechanisms,** *unconscious coping mechanisms that reduce the anxiety generated by threats from unacceptable impulses* (see **TABLE 12.4**). Psychodynamically oriented psychologists believe that defense mechanisms help us overcome anxiety and engage effectively with the outside world and that our characteristic style of defense becomes our signature in dealing with the world—and an essential aspect of our personality.

Freud also proposed that a person's basic personality is formed before 6 years of age during a series of sensitive periods, or life stages, when experiences influence all that will follow. Freud called these periods *psychosexual stages,* distinct early life stages through which personality is formed as children experience sexual pleasures from specific body areas and as caregivers redirect or interfere with those pleasures (see **TABLE 12.5**). He argued that, as a result of adult interference with pleasure-seeking, the child experiences conflict. At each stage, a different bodily region dominates the child's subjective experience. Problems and conflicts encountered at any psychosexual stage, Freud believed, will influence personality in adulthood.

What should we make of all this? Critics argue that psychodynamic explanations lack any real evidence and tend to focus on provocative after-the-fact interpretation rather than testable prediction. The psychosexual stage theory offers a compelling set of story lines for interpreting lives once they have unfolded, but it has not generated clear-cut predictions supported by research findings.

THE PHOTO WORKS

Sigmund Freud was the first psychology theorist to be honoured with his own bobblehead doll. Let's hope he's not the last.

defense mechanisms Unconscious coping mechanisms that reduce the anxiety generated by threats from unacceptable impulses.

TABLE 12.5

FREUD'S PSYCHOSEXUAL STAGES

Stage	Description
Oral	The stage in which experience centres on the pleasures and frustrations associated with the mouth, sucking, and being fed
Anal	The stage in which experience is dominated by the pleasures and frustrations associated with the anus, retention and expulsion of feces and urine, and toilet training
Phallic	The stage in which experience is dominated by the pleasure, conflict, and frustration associated with the phallic–genital region, as well as coping with powerful incestuous feelings of love, hate, jealousy, and conflict
Latency	The stage in which the primary focus is on the further development of intellectual, creative, interpersonal, and athletic skills
Genital	The time for the coming together of the mature adult personality with a capacity to love, work, and relate to others in a mutually satisfying and reciprocal manner

The Humanistic–Existential Approach: Personality as Choice

Learning Outcomes

WHAT YOU NEED TO KNOW

- Describe the humanistic–existential approach to personality.

- Explain the role of self-actualization and angst in personality development.

During the 1950s and 1960s, psychologists began trying to understand personality from a viewpoint quite different from trait theory's biological determinism and Freud's focus on unconscious drives. These new humanistic and existential theorists turned attention to how humans make *healthy choices* that create their personalities. *Humanistic psychologists* emphasized a positive, optimistic view of human nature that highlights people's inherent goodness and their potential for personal growth. *Existentialist psychologists* focused on the individual as a responsible agent who is free to create and live their life while negotiating the issue of meaning and the reality of death. The *humanistic–existential approach* integrates these insights with a focus on how a personality can become optimal.

Human Needs and Self-Actualization

Humanists see the **self-actualizing tendency,** *the human motive towards realizing our inner potential,* as a major factor in personality. The pursuit of knowledge, the expression of one's creativity, the quest for spiritual enlightenment, and the desire to give to society are all examples of self-actualization. As you saw in the Emotion and Motivation chapter, the noted humanistic theorist Abraham Maslow (1943) proposed a *hierarchy of needs,* a model of essential human needs arranged according to their priority, in which basic physiological and safety needs must be satisfied before a person can afford to focus on higher-level psychological needs. Only when these basic needs are met can one pursue higher needs, culminating in *self-actualization*: the need to be good, to be fully alive, and to find meaning in life.

Humanist psychologists explain individual personality differences as arising from the various ways that the environment facilitates—or blocks—attempts to satisfy psychological needs. For example, someone with the inherent potential to be a great scientist, artist, parent, or teacher might never realize these talents if

self-actualizing tendency The human motive towards realizing our inner potential.

their energies and resources are instead directed towards meeting basic needs of security, belongingness, and the like. Research indicates that when people shape their lives around goals that do not match their true nature and capabilities, they are less likely to be happy than those whose lives and goals do match (Ryan & Deci, 2000).

It feels great to be doing exactly what you are capable of doing. Hungarian-American psychologist Mihaly Csikszentmihalyi (pronounced *me-high CHEEK-sent-me-high*) (1990) found that engagement in tasks that exactly match one's abilities creates a mental state of energized focus that he called *flow* (see **FIGURE 12.4**). Tasks that are below our abilities cause boredom, those that are too challenging cause anxiety, and those that are "just right" lead to the experience of flow. If you know how to play the piano, for example, and are playing a Chopin prelude that you know well enough that it just matches your abilities, you are likely to experience this optimal state. People report being happier at these times than at any other times. Humanists believe that such peak experiences, or states of flow, reflect the realization of one's human potential and represent the height of personality development.

Personality as Existence

Existentialists agree with humanists about many of the features of personality but focus on challenges to the human condition that are more profound than the lack of a nurturing environment. Rollo May (1983) and Victor Frankl (2000), for example, argued that specific aspects of the human condition, such as awareness of our own existence and the ability to make choices about how to behave, have a double-edged quality: They bring an extraordinary richness and dignity to human life, but they also force us to confront realities that are difficult to face, such as the prospect of our own death. The **existential approach** is *a school of thought that regards personality as governed by an individual's ongoing choices and decisions in the context of the realities of life and death.*

According to the existential perspective, the difficulties we face in finding meaning in life and in accepting the responsibility of making free choices provoke a type of anxiety that existentialists call *angst* (the anxiety of fully being). The human ability to consider limitless numbers of goals and actions is exhilarating, but it can also open the door to profound questions such as "Why am I here?" and "What is the meaning of my life?"

Thinking about the meaning of existence also can evoke an awareness of the inevitability of death. What, then, should we do with each moment? What is the purpose of living if life as we know it will end one day, perhaps even today? Alternatively, does life have *more* meaning, given that it is so temporary? Existential theorists do not suggest that people consider these profound existential issues on a day-to-day and moment-to-moment basis. Rather than ruminating about death and meaning, people typically pursue superficial answers that help them deal with the angst and dread they experience, and the defenses they construct form the basis of their personalities (May, 1983). Some people organize their lives around obtaining material possessions; others may immerse themselves in drugs or addictive behaviours such as compulsive Tik Tok scrolling, video gaming, or television watching to numb the mind to existential realities.

For existentialists, a healthier solution is to face the issues head on and learn to accept and tolerate the pain of existence. Indeed, being fully human means confronting existential realities rather than denying them or embracing comforting illusions. This requires the courage to accept the inherent anxiety and the dread of nonbeing that is part of being alive. Such courage may be bolstered by developing supportive relationships with others who can supply unconditional positive regard. Something about being loved helps relieve the angst.

Decades of research have shown that growing up in a distressed neighbourhood is associated with worse educational, occupational, and health outcomes than growing up in wealthier neighbourhoods. Humanistic psychologists would suggest that people in such settings must struggle to meet their basic daily needs and so do not have opportunities for self-actualization.

Challenge

ANXIETY

BOREDOM

Abilities

Figure 12.4

Flow Experience It feels good to do things that challenge your abilities but that don't challenge them too much. Mihaly Csikszentmihalyi (1990) described this feeling between boredom and anxiety as the "flow experience."

existential approach A school of thought that regards personality as being governed by an individual's ongoing choices and decisions in the context of the realities of life and death.

The Social–Cognitive Approach: Personalities in Situations

Learning Outcomes

WHAT YOU NEED TO KNOW

- Describe the social–cognitive approach to personality.

- Explain how personal constructs are key to personality differences.

- Identify how one's perception of control influences behaviour.

What is it like to be a person? The **social–cognitive approach** *views personality in terms of how a person thinks about the situations encountered in daily life and behaves in response to them.* Bringing together insights from social psychology, cognitive psychology, and learning theory, this approach emphasizes how the person experiences and interprets situations (Bandura, 1986; Mischel & Shoda, 1999; Wegner & Gilbert, 2000).

Researchers in social cognition believe that both the current situation and learning history are key determinants of behaviour, and focus on how people *perceive* their environments. People think about their goals, the consequences of their behaviour, and how they might achieve certain objectives in different situations (Lewin, 1951). The social–cognitive approach looks at how personality and situation interact to cause behaviour, how personality contributes to the way people construct situations in their own minds, and how people's goals and expectancies influence their responses to situations.

Consistency of Personality Across Situations

Although social–cognitive psychologists attribute behaviour both to the individual's personality and to their situation, situation can often trump personality. For example, a person would have to be pretty strange to act exactly the same way at a memorial service as at a keg party. In their belief that the strong push and pull of situations can influence almost everyone, social–cognitive psychologists are somewhat at odds with the basic assumptions of classic personality psychology; that is, that personality characteristics (e.g., traits, needs, unconscious drives) cause people to behave in the same way across situations and over time. At the core of the social–cognitive approach is a natural puzzle, the **person–situation controversy,** which focuses on *the question of whether behaviour is caused more by personality or by situational factors.*

This controversy began in earnest when Walter Mischel (1968) argued that measured personality traits often do a poor job of predicting individuals' behaviour in everyday life. He reviewed decades of research that compared scores on standard personality tests with actual behaviour, looking at evidence from studies that asked questions such as "Does a person with a high score on a test of introversion actually spend more time alone than someone with a low score?" Mischel's disturbing conclusion: The average correlation between trait and behaviour is only about 0.30. This is certainly better than zero (i.e., no relation at all) but not very good when you remember that a perfect prediction is represented by a correlation of 1.0.

Mischel also noted that knowing how a person will behave in one situation is not particularly helpful in predicting that person's behaviour in another situation. For example, in classic studies, Hugh Hartshorne and M. A. May (1928) assessed children's honesty by examining their willingness to cheat on a test and found that such dishonesty was not consistent from one situation to another. The assessment of a child's trait of honesty in a cheating situation was of almost no use in predicting whether that child would act honestly in a different situation, such as when given the opportunity to steal money. Mischel proposed that measured traits do not predict behaviours very well because behaviours are determined more by situational factors than personality theorists were willing to acknowledge.

"It's great things are back to normal, except that there are people everywhere."

AMY HWANG/CARTOON STOCK

social–cognitive approach An approach that views personality in terms of how the person thinks about the situations encountered in daily life and behaves in response to them.

person–situation controversy The question of whether behaviour is caused more by personality or by situational factors.

Is there no personality, then? Do we all just do what situations require? The person–situation controversy has inspired many studies in the years since Mischel's critique, and it turns out that information about both personality and situation best predict behaviour when they are considered together (Horstmann et al., in press). Some situations are particularly powerful, leading most everyone to behave similarly regardless of personality (Cooper & Withey, 2009). At a funeral, almost everyone looks somber, and during an earthquake, almost everyone shakes. But in more moderate situations, personality can come to the fore to influence behaviour (Funder, 2001). Among the children in Hartshorne and May's (1928) studies, cheating versus not cheating on a test was actually a fairly good predictor of cheating on a test later—as long as the situation was similar. Personality consistency, then, appears to be a matter of when and where a certain kind of behaviour tends to be shown (see The Real World: Does Your Personality Change Depending on Who You're With?). Social–cognitive theorists believe these patterns of personality consistency arise from the way different people interpret situations and from how different people pursue goals within situations.

Personal Constructs: The Key to the Perceiver's Personality

How can we understand differences in how situations are interpreted? Recall our notion that personality often exists in the eye of the beholder. Situations may exist in the eye of the beholder as well. One person's gold mine may be another person's useless hole in the ground. George Kelly (1955) long ago realized that these differences in perspective could be used to understand the *perceiver's* personality. He suggested that people view the social world from differing perspectives and that these different views arise through the application of **personal constructs,** *dimensions people use in making sense of their experiences.* Consider, for example, different individuals' personal constructs of a clown: One person may see a clown as a source of fun, another as a tragic figure, and yet another as so frightening that McDonald's must be avoided at all costs.

Kelly assessed personal constructs about social relationships by asking people to (1) list the people in their life; (2) consider three of the people and state a way in which two of them are similar to each other and different from the third; and (3) repeat this for other triads of people in their lives to produce a list of the dimensions that

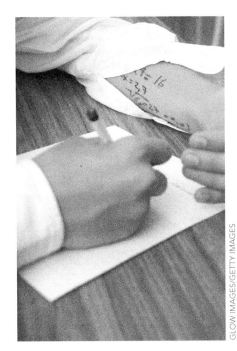

Is a student who cheats on a test more likely than others to steal candy or lie to their grandmother? Social–cognitive research indicates that behaviour in one situation does not necessarily predict behaviour in a different situation.

personal constructs Dimensions people use in making sense of their experiences.

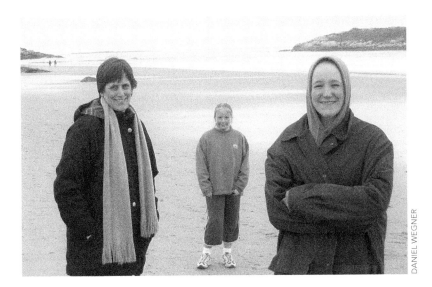

Are two of these people taller and one shorter? Are two bareheaded while one wears a hood? Or are two the daughters and one the mom? George Kelly held that the personal constructs we use to distinguish among people in our lives are basic elements of our own personalities.

respondents use to classify friends and family. One respondent might focus on the degree to which people are lazy or hardworking, for example, whereas, someone else might attend to the degree to which people are sociable or unfriendly.

Kelly proposed that different personal constructs (*construals*) are the key to personality differences; that is, different construals lead people to engage in different behaviours. Taking a long break from work for a leisurely lunch might seem lazy to you. To your friend, the break might seem an ideal opportunity for catching up with friends and wondering why *you* always choose to eat at your desk. Social–cognitive theory explains different responses to situations with the idea that people experience and interpret the world in different ways.

Personal Goals and Expectancies Lead to a Characteristic Style of Behaviour

Social–cognitive theories also recognize that a person's unique perspective on situations is reflected in their personal goals, which are often conscious. In fact, people can usually tell you their goals, whether to find a date for this weekend, get a good grade in psych, establish a fulfilling career, or just get this darn bag of chips open. These goals often reflect the tasks that are appropriate to the person's situation and, in a larger sense, fit the person's role and stage of life (Vallacher & Wegner, 1985). For instance, common goals for adolescents include being popular, achieving greater independence from parents and family, and getting into a good university. Common goals for adults include developing a meaningful career, finding a mate, securing financial stability, and starting a family.

People translate goals into behaviour in part through **outcome expectancies,** *a person's assumptions about the likely consequences of a future behaviour.* Just as a laboratory rat learns that pressing a bar releases a food pellet, we learn that "if I am friendly towards people, they will be friendly in return," and "if I ask people to pull my finger, they will withdraw from me." We learn to perform behaviours that we expect will have the outcome of moving us closer to our goals. We learn outcome expectancies through direct experience, both bitter and sweet, and through merely observing other people's actions and the resulting consequences.

People differ in their generalized expectancy for achieving goals. Some people seem to feel that they are fully in control of what happens to them in life, whereas others feel that the world doles out rewards and punishments to them irrespective of their actions. Julian Rotter (1966) developed a questionnaire (see **TABLE 12.6**) to measure *a*

Some days you feel like a puppet on a string. If you have an external locus of control and believe you are at the mercy of other people, or of fate, you may feel that way most days.

TABLE 12.6

ROTTER'S LOCUS-OF-CONTROL SCALE

For each pair of items, choose the option that most closely reflects your personal belief. Then check the answer key below to see if you have more of an internal or external locus of control.

1. (a) Many of the unhappy things in people's lives are partly due to bad luck.
   (b) People's misfortunes result from the mistakes they make.

2. (a) I have often found that what is going to happen will happen.
   (b) Trusting to fate has never turned out as well for me as making a decision to take a definite course of action.

3. (a) Becoming a success is a matter of hard work; luck has little or nothing to do with it.
   (b) Getting a good job depends mainly on being in the right place at the right time.

4. (a) When I make plans, I am almost certain that I can make them work.
   (b) It is not always wise to plan too far ahead because many things turn out to be a matter of good or bad fortune anyhow.

Information from Rotter, 1966.

Answers: A more internal locus of control would be reflected in choosing options 1b, 2b, 3a, and 4a.

outcome expectancies

A person's assumptions about the likely consequences of a future behaviour.

The Real World | Does Your Personality Change Depending on Who You're With?

Social–cognitive psychologists suggest that how you behave is influenced by both your personality and the situations you are in. For instance, you act differently when sitting in a classroom than you do when dancing at a club (unless it's a really fun class). But do your personality and behaviour also change when you're talking to different people regardless of context? For instance, do things such as your language, tone of voice, and level of warmth change depending on whom you are talking to?

For most people, the answer is yes. For example, we speak and act differently when interacting with our parents ("*Hello mother, hello father*") than with our friends ("*Yo! Sup, punk?!*"). Many people change their language and personality when interacting with people from their own race or cultural group as opposed to those from other groups (e.g., Coates, 2015). And there is evidence from studies of bilingual speakers that people's personality traits shift slightly when they are speaking in one language versus another (Ramirez-Esparza et al., 2004). These are notably subtle shifts rather than complete personality transplants.

Why would our personality characteristics change when we are interacting with one person versus another? One possibility is that we shift our personality and language to match the people with whom we are interacting to signal closeness or affiliation with them. Another possibility is that we do this to influence what other people think about us. For instance, one recent study found that people in positions of power tend to downplay their competence when interacting with subordinates to appear warmer and more likeable, whereas subordinates tend to conceal their warmth to appear more competent (Swencionis & Fiske, 2016). The authors suggest that in both situations, the participants are attempting to increase the perceived similarity between them and the person with whom they are interacting. The fact that things such as personality, similarity, and perceived competence can influence decisions about hiring and promotions (Rivera, 2012; Tews et al., 2011) means that personality actually has a huge impact on the experiences you have in the real world.

person's tendency to perceive the control of rewards as internal to the self or external in the environment, a disposition he called **locus of control.** People whose answers suggest that they believe they control their own destiny are said to have an *internal* locus of control, whereas those who believe that outcomes are random, determined by luck, or controlled by other people are described as having an *external* locus of control. These beliefs translate into individual differences in emotion and behaviour. For example, people with an internal locus of control tend to be less anxious, achieve more, and cope better with stress than do people with an external orientation (Lefcourt, 1982). To get a sense of your standing on this trait dimension, choose one of the options for each of the sample items from the locus-of-control scale in Table 12.6.

locus of control A person's tendency to perceive the control of rewards as internal to the self or external in the environment.

The Self: Personality in the Mirror

Imagine that you wake up tomorrow morning, drag yourself to the bathroom, look in the mirror, and don't recognize the face looking back at you. This was the plight of a patient studied by the neurologist Todd Feinberg (2001). The woman, married for 30 years and the mother of two grown children, one day began to respond to her mirror image as if it were a different person. She talked to and challenged the person in the mirror. When she got no response, she tried to attack it as if it were an intruder. Her husband, shaken by this bizarre behaviour, brought her to the neurologist, who was gradually able to convince her that the image in the mirror was in fact herself.

Most of us are pretty familiar with the face that looks back at us from every mirror. We develop the ability to recognize ourselves in mirrors by 18 months of age (as discussed in the Consciousness chapter), and we share this skill with chimpanzees and other apes that have been raised in the presence of mirrors. Self-recognition

Learning Outcomes

WHAT YOU NEED TO KNOW

- Describe the features that make up the self-concept.
- Identify how self-esteem develops.
- Identify the motivations for self-esteem.

signals our amazing capacity for reflexive thinking, for directing attention to our own thoughts, feelings, and actions—an ability that enables us to construct ideas about our own personality. Unlike a cow, which will never know that it has a poor sense of humour, or a cat, which will never know that it is awfully friendly, humans have rich and detailed self-knowledge.

Admittedly, none of us knows all there is to know about our own personality. In fact, sometimes others may know us better than we know ourselves (Vazire & Mehl, 2008). But we do have enough self-knowledge to respond reliably to personality inventories and report on our traits and behaviours. These observations draw on what we think about ourselves (our *self-concept*) and on how we feel about ourselves (our *self-esteem*). Self-concept and self-esteem are critically important facets of personality, not just because they reveal how people see their own personalities but because they also guide how people think others will see them.

Self-Concept

In his renowned psychology textbook, William James (1890) included a theory of self in which he pointed to the self's two facets, the *I* and the *Me*. The *I* is the self that thinks, experiences, and acts in the world; it is the self as a *knower*. The *Me* is the self that is an object in the world; it is the self that is *known*. The *I* is much like consciousness, then, a perspective on all of experience (see the Consciousness chapter), but the *Me* is less mysterious: It is just a concept of a person.

If asked to describe your *Me,* you might mention your physical characteristics (tall or short, light or dark hair); your activities (listening to hip-hop, pop, or classical music); your personality traits (extraverted or introverted, agreeable or independent); or your social roles (student, best friend, sibling). These features make up the **self-concept,** *a person's explicit knowledge of their own behaviours, traits, and other personal characteristics*. A person's self-concept is an organized body of knowledge that develops from social experiences and has a profound effect on a person's behaviour throughout life.

Self-Concept Organization

Almost everyone has a way to preserve their memories, whether it's via a photo and video storing app, printed photo albums, or maybe that old stuffed animal or first blanket—all memories of "life as *Me*." Perhaps you've wanted to organize these things sometime but have never gotten around to it. Fortunately, the knowledge of ourselves that we store in our *autobiographical memory* seems to be organized naturally in two ways: as narratives about episodes in our lives and in terms of traits (as would be suggested by the distinction between episodic memory and semantic memory discussed in the Memory chapter).

self-concept A person's explicit knowledge of their own behaviours, traits, and other personal characteristics.

What do these self-portraits of Vincent van Gogh, Wanda Wulz, and Jean-Michel Basquiat reveal about each artist's self-concept?

DEA/M. CARRIERI/GETTY IMAGES

ALINARI ARCHIVES/AGE FOTOSTOCK

© ESTATE OF JEAN-MICHEL BASQUIAT. LICENSED BY ARTESTAR, NEW YORK/MANUEL LAGOS CID/PARIS MATCH/GETTY IMAGES

Self-Narratives Are Stories We Tell About Ourselves The aspect of the self-concept that is a *self-narrative* (a story that we tell about ourselves) can be brief or very lengthy. Your life story could start with your birth and upbringing, describe a series of defining moments, and end where you are today. You could select specific events and experiences, goals and life tasks, and memories of places and people that have influenced you. Self-narratives organize the highlights (and low blows) of your life into a story in which you are the leading character and binds them together into your self-concept (McLean, 2008).

Self-Schemas Are Sets of Traits We Use to Define Ourselves Self-concept is also organized in a more abstract way, in terms of personality traits. Just as you can judge an object on its attributes (is this apple green?), you can judge yourself on any number of traits — whether you are considerate or smart or lazy or impulsive — and do so quite reliably, making the same rating on multiple occasions. Hazel Markus (1977) observed that each person finds certain unique personality traits particularly important for conceptualizing the self. One person might define themselves as independent, for example, whereas another might not care much about their level of independence but instead emphasize their sense of style. Markus called the traits people use to define themselves *self-schemas*, emphasizing that they draw information about the self into a coherent scheme. She asked people to indicate whether they had a trait by pressing response buttons labelled *me* or *not me*. She found that participants' judgement reaction times were faster for self-schemas than for other traits. It's as though some facets of the self-concept have almost a knee-jerk quality — letting us tell quickly who we are and who we are not.

Think about your own self-narrative (what you have done) and self-concept (how you view yourself). Are there areas that don't match up? Are there things that you've done, good or bad, that are not part of your self-concept? How might you explain that?

Research also shows that the traits people use to judge the self tend to stick in memory. When people make judgements of themselves on traits, they later recall the traits better than when they judge other people on the same traits (Rogers et al., 1977). For example, answering a question such as "Are you generous?" — no matter what your answer — is likely to enhance your memory for the trait generous. In studies of this effect of *self-relevance* on memory, researchers using brain-imaging technologies have found that the simple activity of making judgements about the trait self-concept is accompanied by activation of the medial prefrontal cortex (mPFC), a brain area involved in understanding people (Mitchell et al., 2002).

This activation is stronger when people are judging their own standing on traits than when they are judging the standing of others (Kelley et al., 2002). But of course, not all others are the same — and these differences appear to map onto activation patterns in the mPFC. The pattern of activation in the mPFC is most similar when rating the self and members of our social network, and most different when rating the self versus those outside of our network (e.g., celebrities) (Courtney & Meyer, 2020) (see **FIGURE 12.5**).

Self-Narratives, Traits, and Behaviour Don't Always Match Up How do our behaviour self-narratives and trait self-concepts compare? These two methods of self-conceptualization don't always match up. You may think of yourself as an honest person, for example, but also recall that time you nabbed a handful of change from your parents' dresser and conveniently forgot to replace it. The traits we use to describe ourselves are generalizations, and not every episode in our life stories may fit them. In fact, research suggests that the stores of knowledge about our behaviours and traits are not very well integrated (Kihlstrom et al., 2002). In people who develop amnesia, for example, memory for behaviours can be lost even though the trait self-concept remains stable (Klein, 2004). People can have a pretty strong sense of who they are even though they may not remember a single example of when they acted that way.

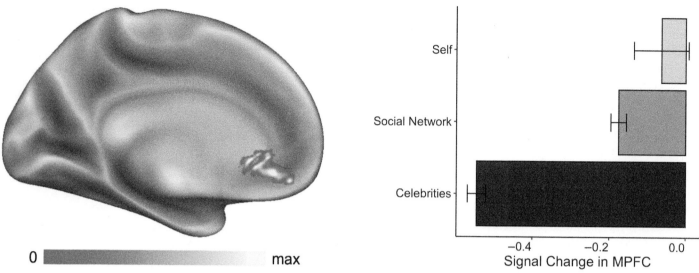

Figure 12.5

Self-Concept in the Brain fMRI scans reveal that the medial prefrontal cortex (MPFC) is activated (shown here in red and yellow) when people make judgements about themselves, respond similarly when making judgements about those close to them (in their own social networks), and respond much less similarly when making judgements about those not close to them (celebrities)—suggesting one way our brains keep track of our connections with others.

Causes and Effects of Self-Concept

How do self-concepts arise, and how do they affect us? In some sense, you learn something about yourself every day. Although we can gain self-knowledge in private moments of insight, we more often arrive at our self-concepts through interacting with others. Young children in particular receive plenty of feedback from their parents, teachers, siblings, and friends about their characteristics, which helps them form an idea of who they are. Even adults would find it difficult to hold a view of the self as "kind" or "smart" if no one else ever shared this impression. The sense of self, then, is largely developed and maintained in relationships with others.

Over the course of a lifetime, however, we become less and less impressed with what others have to say about us. The social theorist George Herbert Mead (1934) observed that all the things people have said about us accumulate after a while into what we see as a kind of consensus held by the "generalized other." We typically adopt this general view of ourselves and hold onto it stubbornly. As a result, the person who says you're a jerk may upset you momentarily, but you bounce back, secure in the knowledge that you actually are not a jerk. And just as we might argue vehemently with someone who tried to tell us a refrigerator is a penguin, we are likely to defend our self-concept against anyone whose view of us departs from our own.

Because it is so stable, a major effect of the self-concept is to promote consistency in behaviour across situations (Lecky, 1945). We tend to engage in what William Swann (1983, 2012) called **self-verification,** *the tendency to seek evidence to confirm the self-concept,* and we find it disconcerting if someone sees us quite differently from the way we see ourselves. In one study, Swann (1983) gave people who considered themselves submissive feedback that they seemed very dominant and forceful. Rather than accepting this discrepant information, they went out of their way to act in an extremely submissive manner. As existential theorists emphasize, people derive a comforting sense of familiarity and stability from knowing who they are.

Self-Esteem

When you think about yourself, do you feel good and worthy? Do you like yourself? Or do you feel bad and have negative, self-critical thoughts? **Self-esteem** is *the extent to which an individual likes, values, and accepts the self.* Thousands of studies have examined differences between people with high self-esteem (who generally like themselves) and those with relatively low self-esteem (who are less keen on, and may actively dislike, themselves). Researchers who study self-esteem typically ask participants to fill

self-verification The tendency to seek evidence to confirm the self-concept.

self-esteem The extent to which an individual likes, values, and accepts the self.

TABLE 12.7

ROSENBERG SELF-ESTEEM SCALE

Consider each statement and circle SA for strongly agree, A for agree, D for disagree, and SD for strongly disagree.

1. On the whole, I am satisfied with myself.	SA	A	D	SD
2. At times, I think I am no good at all.	SA	A	D	SD
3. I feel that I have a number of good qualities.	SA	A	D	SD
4. I am able to do things as well as most other people.	SA	A	D	SD
5. I feel I do not have much to be proud of.	SA	A	D	SD
6. I certainly feel useless at times.	SA	A	D	SD
7. I feel that I'm a person of worth, at least on an equal plane with others.	SA	A	D	SD
8. I wish I could have more respect for myself.	SA	A	D	SD
9. All in all, I am inclined to feel that I am a failure.	SA	A	D	SD
10. I take a positive attitude towards myself.	SA	A	D	SD

Information from Rosenberg, 1965.

Scoring: For items 1, 3, 4, 7, and 10, SA = 3, A = 2, D = 1, SD = 0; for items 2, 5, 6, 8, and 9, the scoring is reversed, with SA = 0, A = 1, D = 2, SD = 3. The higher the total score, the higher one's self-esteem.

out a self-esteem questionnaire such as the one shown in **TABLE 12.7** (Rosenberg, 1965). This widely used measure of self-esteem asks people to evaluate themselves in terms of each statement. People who strongly agree with the positive statements about themselves and strongly disagree with the negative statements are considered to have high self-esteem.

Although some personality psychologists have argued that self-esteem determines virtually everything about a person's life (from a tendency to engage in criminal activity and violence to professional success), the accumulated evidence shows that the benefits of high self-esteem are less striking and all-encompassing but still significant. In general, compared with people with low self-esteem, those with high self-esteem tend to live happier and healthier lives, cope better with stress, and are more likely to persist at difficult tasks. In contrast, individuals with low self-esteem are more likely, for example, to perceive rejection in ambiguous feedback from others and to develop eating disorders than those with high self-esteem (Baumeister et al., 2003). How does this aspect of personality develop? And why does everyone—whether high or low in self-esteem—seem to *want* high self-esteem?

"I don't want to be defined by who I am."

P.C. VEY/CARTOON STOCK

Sources of Self-Esteem

Some psychologists contend that high self-esteem arises primarily from being accepted and valued by significant others (Brown, 1993). Other psychologists focus on the influence of specific self-evaluations: judgements about one's value or competence in specific domains such as appearance, athletics, or scholastics.

An important factor is whom people choose for comparison. For example, James (1890) noted that an accomplished athlete who is the second best in the world should feel pretty proud, but this athlete might not feel that way if the standard of comparison involves being best in the world. In fact, athletes in the 1992 Olympics who had won silver medals looked less happy during the medal ceremony than those who had

JULIAN FINNEY/GETTY IMAGES

These are the men's fencing medalists at the 2020 Olympics. From left, Daniele Garozzo of Team Italy (silver), Ka Long Cheung of Team Hong Kong (gold), and Alexander Choupenitch of Team Czech Republic (bronze), pose with their medals. Notice Garozzo's facial expression and body language compared with those of the gold and bronze medal winners.

won bronze medals (Medvec et al., 1995). A potential explanation for this effect is that the silver medalist may be upset because they came so close to winning gold (but fell short), whereas the bronze medalist may be happier because they came so close to not earning a medal at all (but achieved that goal). If people see the actual self as falling short of the ideal self (the person that they would like to be), they tend to feel sad or dejected. When they become aware that the actual self is inconsistent with the self they have a duty to be, they are likely to feel anxious or agitated (Higgins, 1987).

The Desire for Self-Esteem

What's so great about self-esteem? Why do people want to see themselves in a positive light and avoid seeing themselves negatively?

Self-Esteem May Reflect High Social Status Does self-esteem feel good because it reflects our degree of social dominance or status? People with high self-esteem seem to carry themselves in a way that is similar to how high-status animals of other social species carry themselves. Dominant male gorillas, for example, appear confident and comfortable, not anxious or withdrawn. Perhaps high self-esteem in humans reflects high social status or suggests that the person is worthy of respect, and this perception triggers natural affective responses (Barkow, 1980; Maslow, 1937).

Self-Esteem May Have Played a Role in Evolution Could the desire for self-esteem come from a basic need to belong or to be related to others? Evolutionary theory holds that early humans who managed to survive and pass on their genes were those able to maintain good relations with others rather than being cast out to fend for themselves. Clearly, belonging to groups is adaptive, as is knowing whether you are accepted. Thus, self-esteem could be a kind of "sociometer," an inner gauge of how much a person feels included by others at any given moment (Leary & Baumeister, 2000). According to evolutionary theory, then, we seek higher self-esteem because we have evolved to seek out belongingness in our families, work groups, and culture, and higher self-esteem indicates that we are being accepted.

Self-Esteem Provides a Sense of Security Consistent with the existential and psychodynamic approaches to personality, self-esteem can be a matter of security. The studies of mortality salience discussed in the Emotion and Motivation chapter suggest that the source of distress underlying negative self-esteem is ultimately the fear of death (Solomon et al., 1991). In this view, humans find it anxiety-provoking—in fact, terrifying—to contemplate their own mortality, so they try to defend against this awareness by immersing themselves in activities (e.g., earning money or dressing up to appear attractive) that their culture defines as meaningful and valuable. The desire for self-esteem may stem from a need to find value in ourselves as a way of escaping the anxiety associated with recognizing our mortality. The higher our self-esteem, the less anxious we feel with the knowledge that someday we will no longer exist.

But Can We All Be Above Average? Whatever the reason that low self-esteem feels so bad and high self-esteem feels so good, people are generally motivated to see themselves positively. In fact, we often process information in a biased manner in order to feel good about the self. Research on the **self-serving bias** shows that *people tend to take credit for their successes but downplay responsibility for their failures.* You may have noticed this tendency in yourself, particularly in terms of the attributions you make about exams when you get a good grade ("I studied really intensely, and I'm good at that subject") or a bad grade ("The test was ridiculously tricky, and the professor is unfair").

On the whole, most people satisfy the desire for high self-esteem and maintain a reasonably positive view of self by engaging in the self-serving bias (Miller &

Survivor, The Bachelor, Big Brother. Why are shows in which everyone is fighting to remain a part of the group so popular today? Is it because these shows exploit the evolutionary desire to belong? (Or do people just like to see other people get kicked out of the club?)

self-serving bias People's tendency to take credit for their successes but downplay responsibility for their failures.

narcissism A trait that reflects a grandiose view of the self, combined with a tendency to seek admiration from and exploit others.

Ross, 1975; Shepperd et al., 2008). In fact, if people are asked to rate themselves across a range of characteristics, they tend to see themselves as better than the average person in most domains (Alicke et al., 1995). For example, 90% of drivers describe their driving skills as better than average, and 86% of workers rate their performance on the job as above average. Even among university professors, 94% feel they are above average in teaching ability compared with other professors (Cross, 1977). These kinds of judgements simply cannot be accurate, statistically speaking, because the average of a group of people has to be the average, not better than average! This particular error may be adaptive, however. People who do not engage in this self-serving bias to boost their self-esteem tend to be more at risk for depression, anxiety, and related health problems (Taylor & Brown, 1988).

On the other hand, a few people take positive self-esteem to the extreme. Unfortunately, seeing yourself as way, way better than average—a trait called **narcissism,** *a grandiose view of the self, combined with a tendency to seek admiration from and exploit others*—brings some costs. In fact, at its extreme, narcissism is considered a personality disorder (see the Psychological Disorders chapter). Research has documented disadvantages of an overinflated view of self, most of which arise from the need to defend that grandiose view at all costs. For example, when highly narcissistic adolescents were given reason to be ashamed of their performance on a task, their aggressiveness increased in the form of willingness to deliver loud blasts of noise to punish their opponents in a laboratory game (Thomaes et al., 2008).

Implicit Egotism

What's your favourite letter of the alphabet? About 30% of people answer by picking what just happens to be the first letter of their first name. Could this choice indicate that some people think so highly of themselves that they base judgements of seemingly unrelated topics on how much those topics remind them of themselves?

This *name-letter effect* was discovered some years ago (Nuttin, 1985), but more recently researchers have gone on to discover how broad the egotistic bias in preferences can be. Brett Pelham and his colleagues have found subtle yet systematic biases towards this effect when people choose their home cities, streets, and even occupations (Pelham et al., 2002). People whose last name is Street seem biased towards addresses ending in *street,* whereas Lanes like to live on lanes. The name effect seems to work for occupations as well: Slightly more people named Dennis and Denise chose dentistry, and Lauras and Lawrences chose law, compared with other occupations. Although the biases are small, they are consistent across many tests of this hypothesis.

These biases have been called expressions of *implicit egotism* because people are not typically aware that they are influenced by the wonderful sound of their own names (Pelham et al., 2005). Most participants in research experiments who show these biases do not report that the reason for doing so has to do with similarity between their name and some related fact (Pelham et al., 2020). These biases are, well, implicit. When Otto moves to Ottawa, he is not likely to volunteer that he did so because it matched his name.

At some level, a bit of egotism is probably good for us, yet implicit egotism is a curiously subtle error: a tendency to make biased judgements of what we will do and where we will go in life just because we happen to have a certain name.

The self is the part of personality that the person knows and can report about. Some of the personality measures we have seen in this chapter (such as personality inventories based on self-reports) are really no different from measures of self-concept. Both depend on the person's perceptions and memories of the self's behaviour and traits. But personality runs deeper than this as well. The unconscious forces identified in psychodynamic approaches provide themes for behaviour and

"I suffer from accurate self-esteem."

Henry Head (1861–1940; top) and Walter Russell Brain (1895–1966; bottom) were British neurologists ("brain doctors"). Dr. Brain was also Lord Brain, Baron Brain of Eynsham, and editor of the journal *Brain*. Head preceded Brain as head of *Brain*. Head was much admired by Brain, who wrote an essay in *Brain* about Head. Lord Brain's *Brain* tribute to Head suggests that Dr. Head had no lack of self esteem: Brain writes "Some men . . . feel impelled to impart information to others. Head was one of those." Brain doesn't look like he suffers from a lack of self-esteem, either, does he? (Abrahams, 2011)

sources of mental disorder that are not accessible for self-report. The humanistic and existential approaches remind us of the profound concerns we humans face and the difficulties we may have in understanding all the forces that shape our self-views. Finally, in emphasizing how personality shapes our perceptions of social life, the social–cognitive approach brings the self back to centre stage. The self, after all, is the hub of each person's social world.

Chapter Review

Personality: What It Is and How It Is Measured

- In psychology, *personality* refers to a person's characteristic style of behaving, thinking, and feeling. Personality differences can be studied from two points of view: *prior events*, such as biological makeup, life circumstances, and culture; and *anticipated events*, as reflected in a person's hopes, dreams, and fears.

- Personality inventories, such as the MMPI–2–RF, are easy to administer, but people are often inaccurate in their self-reporting. Projective techniques, such as the Rorschach Inkblot Test and the TAT, provide richer information for a one-to-one relationship but are subject to interpreter bias.

- Newer, high-tech methods are proving to be even more effective in measuring personality.

The Trait Approach: Identifying Patterns of Behaviour

- The trait approach tries to identify personality dimensions that can be used to characterize an individual's behaviour. Researchers have attempted to boil down the potentially huge array of things people do, think, and feel into some core personality dimensions.

- Researchers use factor analysis to study relationships between the adjectives that people use to self-report traits.

- Many personality psychologists currently focus on the Big Five personality factors: openness to experience, conscientiousness, extraversion, agreeableness, and neuroticism. These traits account for variations in personality and appear universal, on the basis of results from many different studies and cultures.

- Twin studies indicate that the more genes you have in common with someone else, the more similar your personalities will be. Studies with animals further support the idea that biological mechanisms underlie personality traits.

- Research indicates that the part of the brain that regulates arousal and alertness (the reticular formation) is more easily stimulated in introverts than in extraverts, who may need to seek out more interaction and activity to achieve mental stimulation.

The Psychodynamic Approach: Forces That Lie Beneath Awareness

- Freud believed that the personality results from forces that are largely unconscious, shaped by the interplay among id, superego, and ego.

- Defense mechanisms are techniques the mind may use to reduce anxiety generated by unacceptable impulses.

- Freud also believed that the developing person passes through a series of psychosexual stages and that failing to progress beyond one of the stages results in fixation, which is associated with corresponding personality traits.

- Critics argue that psychodynamic explanations lack real evidence and are after-the-fact interpretations.

The Humanistic–Existential Approach: Personality as Choice

- The humanistic–existential approach to personality grew out of philosophical traditions that are at odds with most of the assumptions of the trait and psychoanalytic approaches. It focuses on how people make healthy choices that form their personalities.

- Humanists see personality as directed by an inherent striving towards self-actualization and development of our unique human potentials.

- Existentialists focus on angst and the defensive response people often have to questions about the meaning of life and the inevitability of death.

The Social–Cognitive Approach: Personalities in Situations

- The social–cognitive approach focuses on personality as arising from individuals' behaviour in situations. According to social–cognitive personality theorists, the same person may behave differently in different situations but should behave consistently in similar situations.

- Personal constructs are dimensions people use to make sense of their experiences and that reveal the perceiver's personality.

- People translate their goals into behaviour through outcome expectancies. People differ in whether they believe they control their own destiny (internal locus of control) or are at the mercy of fate or of other people (external locus of control). Those with an internal locus of control tend to be better able to cope with stress and to achieve more.

The Self: Personality in the Mirror

- The self-concept is a person's knowledge of self, including both specific self-narratives and more abstract personality traits or self-schemas. People's self-concept develops through social feedback, and people often act to try to confirm these views through a process of self-verification.

- Self-esteem is a person's evaluation of self; it is derived from being accepted by others, as well as by how we evaluate ourselves in comparison to others. Theories of why we seek positive self-esteem suggest that we do so to achieve perceptions of status, or belonging, or of being symbolically protected against mortality.

- People strive for positive self-views through self-serving biases and implicit egotism.

Changing Minds

1. A political candidate makes a Freudian slip on live TV, calling his mother "petty"; he corrects himself quickly and says he meant to say "pretty." The next day, the video has gone viral, and the morning talk shows discuss the possibility that the candidate has an unresolved Oedipal conflict. If so, he's stuck in the phallic stage and is likely a relatively unstable person preoccupied with issues of seduction, power, and authority (which may be why he wants to be president). Your roommate knows you're taking a psychology class and asks for your opinion: "Can we really tell that a person is sexually repressed, and maybe in love with his own mother, just because he stumbled over a single word?" How would you reply? How widely are Freud's ideas about personality accepted by modern psychologists?

2. While reading a magazine, you come across an article on the nature–nurture controversy in personality. The magazine describes several adoption studies in which adopted children (who share no genes with each other but grow up in the same household) are no more like each other than complete strangers. This suggests that family environment—and the influence of parental behaviour—on personality is very weak. You show the article to a friend, who has trouble believing the results: "I always thought parents who don't show affection produce kids who have trouble forming lasting relationships." How would you explain to your friend the relationship between nature, nurture, and personality?

3. One of your friends has found an online site that offers personality testing. They take the test and report that the results prove they are an "intuitive" rather than a "sensing" personality, who likes to look at the big picture rather than focusing on tangible here-and-now experiences. "This explains a lot," your friend says, "like why I have trouble remembering details like other people's birthdays, and why it's hard for me to finish projects before the deadline." Aside from warning your friend about the dangers of self-diagnosis via Internet quizzes, what would you tell them about the relationship between personality types and behaviour? How well do scores on personality tests predict a person's actual behaviour?

4. One of your friends tells you that their boyfriend cheated on them, so they will never date him again or date anyone who has ever been unfaithful because "once a cheat, always a cheat." Your friend goes on to explain that personality and character are stable over time, so people will always make the same decisions and repeat the same mistakes over time. What do we know about the interaction between personality and situations that might confirm or deny her statements?

5. **Visualizing Data** Your close friend worries that as you age, your personality will change drastically and that you won't be friends any more due to any personality changes. Review the DATA and determine if your friend is right to be concerned.

Key Terms

personality (p. 438)
self-report (p. 440)
Minnesota Multiphasic Personality Inventory (MMPI) (p. 440)
projective tests (p. 441)
Rorschach Inkblot Test (p. 441)
Thematic Apperception Test (TAT) (p. 441)

trait (p. 442)
Big Five (p. 444)
psychodynamic approach (p. 452)
id (p. 452)
superego (p. 452)
ego (p. 452)
defense mechanisms (p. 453)

self-actualizing tendency (p. 454)
existential approach (p. 455)
social–cognitive approach (p. 456)
person–situation controversy (p. 456)
personal constructs (p. 457)

outcome expectancies (p. 458)
locus of control (p. 459)
self-concept (p. 460)
self-verification (p. 462)
self-esteem (p. 462)
self-serving bias (p. 464)
narcissism (p. 465)

Social Psychology

- Interpersonal Behaviour
- Interpersonal Attraction
- Interpersonal Perception
- Interpersonal Influence

TERRY, NELSON, AND JOHN have something in common: They have all been tortured. Terry was a British hostage negotiator working in Lebanon when he was kidnapped by Hezbollah guerrillas; Nelson was a political activist whose protests against the apartheid regime in South Africa earned him 27 years in prison; and John was an American naval aviator when he was shot down and captured during the Vietnam War. All three men experienced a variety of tortures, and all agree on which was the worst.

> **Terry:** I soon realized that if I was to survive, it was essential to maintain a strong inner life . . . because the threat of dissolving into madness was ever present.
>
> **Nelson:** Nothing is more dehumanizing.
>
> **John:** It is an awful thing. It crushes your spirit and weakens your resistance more effectively than any other form of mistreatment.

The cruel technique that these three men describe has nothing to do with electric shock or waterboarding. It does not require wax, rope, or razor blades. It is a remarkably simple technique that has been used for millennia to break the body and destroy the mind. That technique is called solitary confinement. Terry Waite spent 4 years in a cell by himself, Nelson Mandela spent 6, and John McCain spent 2.

Torture involves depriving people of something they desperately need, such as oxygen, water, food, or sleep, and as torturers have known for ages, the need for social interaction is every bit as vital. "I found solitary confinement the most forbidding aspect of prison life," Mandela wrote. "I have known men who took half a dozen lashes in preference to being locked up alone." Studies of prisoners show that

Terry Waite (left), John McCain (middle), and Nelson Mandela (right) each spent years in isolation and described it as the worst form of torture. John McCain was a U.S. senator (1987–2018), and Nelson Mandela was president of South Africa (1994–1999).

extensive periods of isolation can induce symptoms of psychosis (Grassian, 2006; see Other Voices: We Should Not Tolerate the Torture of Prisoners in Canada). But even in smaller doses, social isolation takes a toll. Ordinary people who are socially isolated are more likely to become depressed, to become ill, and to die prematurely. Indeed, being socially isolated is as dangerous to your health as is smoking or being obese (Cacioppo & Patrick, 2008; Holt-Lunstad, 2021). Social contact—even with strangers—is so important to health and well-being that some researchers refer to it as Vitamin S (Van Lange & Columbus, 2021).

Human beings are the most social animal on our planet and connecting to each other is nearly as important as breathing. But why are we built that way? Snails and centipedes aren't social. Neither are skunks, moose, badgers, or aardvarks. In fact, the majority of the earth's animals are loners that lead a solitary existence and rely on only themselves. Why are we so different? And how much do these differences matter? **Social psychology** is *the study of the causes and consequences of sociality*, and it attempts to answer these questions. Here's the approach to social psychology that we'll take in this chapter:

- All animals must solve the twin problems of survival and reproduction, and human beings are no exception. In the first two sections ("Interpersonal Behaviour" and "Interpersonal Attraction"), you will see that sociality is nature's most ingenious solution to both of these problems.

- But this ingenious solution requires two things of us. First, it requires that we be able to understand each other—that is, that we have the ability to predict what others will do, to determine whether others can be trusted, and so on. In the third section ("Interpersonal Perception"), you'll see how and how well human beings do this, using information to form impressions of each other that sometimes are spot-on and sometimes are tragically mistaken.

- The second thing the ingenious solution requires is that we be able to influence each other—that is, that we have the ability to convince others to accept us as mates, do favours for us as friends, and so on. In the final section ("Interpersonal Influence"), you'll learn about some of the clever techniques that human beings have developed to get other people to do what they want.

social psychology The study of the causes and consequences of sociality.

Interpersonal Behaviour

All species need food and water, some need mates and shelter, and one appears to need the limited-edition iPhone on the day it is released. All these things are resources, and the problem with resources is that there's rarely enough of them to go around. So if somebody gets them, then somebody else doesn't. We'd all rather be the one who gets them, of course, and human beings have developed two tactics to make sure that happens: *Hurting* and *helping*. Although these words are antonyms, they turn out to be mirror-image solutions to the same problem. Let's start with hurting.

Aggression

Whether the scarce resource is a carrot, a cave, or an iPhone, the simplest way to make sure you get one is just to take it, and kick the stuffing out of anyone who tries

Learning Outcomes

WHAT YOU NEED TO KNOW

- Identify biological and cultural influences on aggression.
- Explain why cooperation is risky.
- Describe the costs and benefits of groups.
- Distinguish between apparent and genuine altruism.

Other Voices ⏐ We Should Not Tolerate the Torture of Prisoners in Canada

In 2015, the United Nations General Assembly unanimously adopted a revised set of rules representing best practices for the treatment of prisoners. The "Nelson Mandela Rules" (United Nations Office on Drugs and Crime, 2015) define solitary confinement as spending 22 hours or more without meaningful human contact. Solitary confinement with no clear end date, or which lasts for more than 15 days, or which takes place in a dark or persistently lit cell is considered "torture or other cruel, inhuman or degrading treatment." Solitary confinement cannot be used against women or children, or the mentally or physically disabled if it would make their conditions worse. For adult men, the rules say that it should be used only in exceptional cases, as a last resort, for as short a time as possible and each case should undergo independent review. Finally, each country needs to have a law governing the use of solitary confinement. Doob and Sprott are Canadian criminologists who think that Canada is not following these rules.

Correctional Service Canada (CSC) states on its website that administrative and disciplinary segregation—solitary confinement—no longer exists in Canadian federal penitentiaries. This is true only because Parliament changed the name to Structured Intervention Units (SIUs). CSC has ensured that the practice still exists, notwithstanding court decisions prohibiting it and Parliament's rebranding.

Solitary confinement is a practice, not a place. It has been defined internationally in the so-called Mandela Rules to which Canada is signatory. In a report we released in February [2021] using that definition, we examined the implementation of CSC's new SIUs and found that 556 (28 percent) stays in these SIUs clearly fell within the international definition of solitary confinement. Using these same international definitions, we identified 195 SIU stays (10 percent) that constitute what is internationally described as "torture or other cruel, inhuman or degrading treatment." CSC's response? Crickets.

But wait, isn't there oversight of these SIUs? CSC suggests on its website that its SIUs receive effective oversight from two independent bodies to ensure that prisoners do not experience solitary confinement or torture. First, "Independent External Decision Makers" (IEDMs) are described as making binding decisions on some aspects of a prisoner's life, including release from the SIU. Second, CSC mentions the "Implementation Advisory Panel" (IAP).

Our fourth report—using CSC's data—demonstrated that the IEDM system does not provide adequate oversight. To give just two examples: Some people do not receive their legislated reviews by IEDMs and some of those whom the IEDMs "order" released from the SIU simply aren't released for many weeks.

The second oversight body, the IAP, ceased to exist about a year ago.* Furthermore, publicly available reports demonstrated that CSC did not allow this oversight body to do its work. In May [2021], we brought this error—and the oversight problems—to CSC's attention. Its response? You guessed it: Crickets.

Change represents a political challenge. Many Canadians do not care how our prisoners are treated. They are seen simply as people who committed offences. But Canadians should care if they care about human rights; or if they care that a government organization is being allowed to operate outside of the law. Eventually, most of these prisoners will be back in our communities and we know that reintegration into Canadian society is hard enough without making it even harder by damaging people further in solitary confinement and by subjecting them to torture. A government that purports to care about the rule of law and human rights should act.

Anthony N. Doob is a Canadian criminologist and Professor Emeritus of Criminology at the University of Toronto. In 2019, he chaired the "Structured Intervention Units—Implementation Advisory Committee" for Public Safety Canada.

We are not suggesting that "fixing" our solitary confinement system would be easy. But a first step would be if CSC management would engage with the issue. You might think that, when a "torture rate" was calculated for the penitentiaries in each of Canada's five regions, CSC or the government might have shown some concern. Using CSC's own data, we calculated that B.C.'s torture rate was about 22 times higher than Ontario's. The response to these findings? You guessed it again: Crickets, followed by the same old song—we take it very seriously and are working on it.

Our prime minister seems to enjoy apologizing for terrible things previous Canadian governments have done (usually when the recipients of inhumane treatment are dead). But he doesn't seem very concerned when yesterday, today, and tomorrow—all on his watch—Canadian citizens in our federal penitentiaries are being mistreated.

Jane B. Sprott is Professor in the Department of Criminology at Toronto Metropolitan University.

Indigenous people constitute about five percent of Canada's population. But about 30 percent of our federal prisoners are Indigenous and 39 percent of the stays in SIUs involve Indigenous prisoners. These figures should alarm him and start him thinking about his own legacy. The government's response so far? You guessed it: Crickets.

Fixing the SIUs will not be easy. Ignoring the issue is not the solution. We need to start the work necessary to address this very serious problem.

SOURCE: *Ottawa Citizen*, https://ottawacitizen.com/opinion/doob-and-sprott-trudeau-should-not-tolerate-the-torture-of-prisoners-in-canada

Anthony N. Doob and Jane B. Sprott, excerpt from Trudeau should not tolerate the torture of prisoners in Canada, Ottawa Citizen, June 14 2021. Reproduced with permission of Anthony N. Doob and Jane B. Sprott.

*This was originally published in June 2021. The panel being referred to ceased to exist in July 2020. One year later, in July 2021, a new panel was appointed, chaired by Howard Sapers, the former Correctional Investigator of Canada (the Ombudsman for Correctional Service Canada). Anthony Doob was appointed as a member of that panel. Jane Sprott is the panel's head of research.

to stop you. **Aggression** is *behaviour whose purpose is to harm another* (Anderson & Bushman, 2002; Bushman & Huesmann, 2010), and it is a strategy used by virtually all animals to achieve their goals. The **frustration–aggression hypothesis** suggests that *animals aggress when their goals are frustrated* (Berkowitz, 1989; Dollard et al., 1939). The word "frustration" here refers not to a feeling, but rather to the obstruction of a goal. A chimp who wants a banana (*goal*) that is in the hands of another chimp (*frustration*) may attack in order to get that banana (*aggression*), just as a person who wants money (*goal*) that is in the hands of another person (*frustration*) may attack (*aggression*) to get that money.

Aggression comes in two flavours. **Proactive aggression** is *aggression that is planned and purposeful* (Wrangham, 2017). The mafia hit man who executes a rival gangster in cold blood is engaging in proactive aggression. Because this kind of aggression is a means to an end, it tends to be specifically directed towards a relevant target (the hit man's task is to kill the gangster and not just anybody who happens to be eating in the restaurant that day), it tends to occur only when the aggressor believes that the benefits will outweigh the costs (the hit man won't pull the trigger if he thinks there's a good chance he'll be caught), and it is not associated with a heightened state of arousal (hey, it's just a job).

The second kind of aggression is **reactive aggression,** which is *aggression that occurs spontaneously in response to a negative affective state*. The man who gets fired, gets angry, and then goes home and yells at his wife is engaging in reactive aggression. This kind of aggression is strongly associated with the experience of pain or anger and is not always directed towards a relevant target. When rats are given painful electric shocks, they will attack whatever happens to be in their cage, whether that's another rat or a tennis ball (Kruk et al., 2004), and when experimental participants are made to experience physical pain (which can safely be done by having people immerse their hands in ice water), they will hurt others who had nothing to do with their pain (Anderson, 1989; Anderson et al., 1997).

Unlike proactive aggression, reactive aggression occurs even when the costs outweigh the benefits: The angry man who screams at his wife has done nothing to get his job back, and he's probably just made his life worse instead of better. Reactive aggression is typically a response to the experience of negative affect (Berkowitz, 1990), which explains why so many acts of violence—from murders to brawls—are more likely to occur on hot days, when people are already feeling uncomfortable, irritated, and easily angered (Rinderu et al., 2018) (see **FIGURE 13.1**). Indeed, the relationship between temperature and violence is so reliable that scientists can predict with reasonable precision how much more violence will be experienced over the next few decades due to climate change (Burke et al., 2015). Hint: It's a lot.

aggression Behaviour whose purpose is to harm another.

frustration–aggression hypothesis A principle stating that animals aggress when their goals are frustrated.

proactive aggression Aggression that is planned and purposeful.

reactive aggression Aggression that occurs spontaneously in response to a negative affective state.

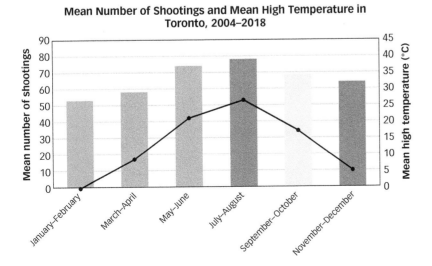

Figure 13.1

Heat and Aggression This graph shows the relationship between mean high temperature (in Celsius) and the mean number of shooting victims in Toronto, for six time points throughout the year, over a 14-year period. The number of victims is highest in the warmest months, and lowest in the coldest months. DATA FROM TORONTO POLICE SERVICE, 2019; CURRENT RESULTS, 2019.

How Biology Influences Aggression

If you want to know whether someone is likely to engage in reactive aggression and you can ask them just one question, it should be this: "Are you male?" The size of the sex difference in violent behaviour is nothing short of staggering. Crimes such as assault, battery, and murder are almost exclusively perpetrated by males (and especially by young males), who are responsible for all of the mass murder events in Canada, going back to the 1960s. In Canada, in 2020, 619 people were accused of homicide—of these, 87% were men (Statistics Canada, 2021). Although socialization practices all over the world encourage males to be more aggressive than females (more on that shortly), male aggressiveness is not merely the product of playing with toy soldiers or watching hockey. Studies show that aggression is associated with the presence of a hormone called *testosterone,* which is typically much higher in males than in females, and much higher in younger males than in older males (Carré & Archer, 2018; Hooven, 2021).

How does testosterone promote aggression? Testosterone isn't "bad mood juice" so much as it is "bad ass juice." A male's testosterone levels wax and wane, and when those levels wax, males tend to feel more powerful and confident in their ability to prevail in interpersonal conflicts (Eisenegger et al., 2010, 2011). Males with high levels of testosterone in their bloodstream tend to walk more purposefully, focus more directly on the people they are talking to, and speak in a more forward and independent manner (Dabbs et al., 2001). What's more, testosterone makes males more sensitive to provocations (Ronay & Galinsky, 2011) and less sensitive to signs of retaliation. For example, participants in one experiment watched a face as its expression changed from neutral to threatening and were asked to respond as soon as the expression became threatening (see **FIGURE 13.2**). Participants who were given a small dose of testosterone were slower to recognize the threatening expression (van Honk & Schutter, 2007; see also Olsson et al., 2016). As you can imagine, feeling powerful while simultaneously failing to realize that the person whose parking space you just stole looks really, really mad is a good way to end up in a fist fight.

One of the most reliable methods for raising a male's testosterone levels and provoking an aggressive response is to challenge their beliefs about their own status or dominance. Indeed, three-quarters of all murders can be classified as "status competitions" or "contests to save face" (Daly & Wilson, 1988). Contrary to popular wisdom, it isn't males with unusually low self-esteem who are most prone to this sort of aggression, but males with unusually *high* self-esteem, because those males are especially likely to perceive other people's actions as a challenge to their inflated sense of self-worth (Baumeister et al., 1996). Males seem especially sensitive to such challenges when they are competing for the attention of females (Ainsworth & Maner, 2012), and losing those competitions can be deadly—especially for the females. The rate at which women in their reproductive years die at the hands of

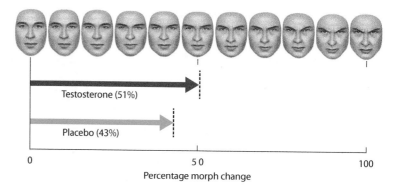

Figure 13.2

I Spy Threat Subjects who were given testosterone needed to see a more objectively threatening expression before they were able to recognize it as such.
RESEARCH FROM VAN HONK & SCHUTTER (2007).

a current or former partner is about as high as the rate at which they die of cancer (Garcia-Moreno et al., 2006).

So that's males. Are females, by contrast, all sweetness and light? Hardly. Females can be just as aggressive as males, but their aggression tends to be proactive rather than reactive. Although women are considerably less likely than men to engage in physical aggression, they are just as likely to engage in verbal aggression (Denson et al., 2018) and cyber-bullying (Barlett & Coyne, 2014). Indeed, women may even be *more* likely than men to aggress by causing social harm—for example, by ostracizing others (Benenson et al., 2011) or by spreading malicious rumors about them (Bjorkqvist, 2018; Card et al., 2008; Richardson, 2014). Several studies suggest that women tend to use rumors to damage the reputations of other women whom they see as romantic rivals (Keys & Bhogal, 2018; Muggleton et al., 2019; Reynolds et al., 2018; Wyckoff et al., 2019). It seems that men and women both use aggression as a tool, but they use it in different ways.

How Culture Influences Aggression

"Our ancestors have bred pugnacity into our bone and marrow," wrote William James (1911, p. 272) "and thousands of years of peace won't breed it out of us." Is that true? It depends. If James was saying that aggression is part of our biological heritage and that humans will always be capable of it, then yes, he was surely right. But if he was saying that our biological heritage means that we are destined to rape, pillage, and plunder our way through the rest of history, then he was surely wrong. Two pieces of evidence make that clear.

First, human beings have become remarkably less aggressive in just the last century alone. As the psychologist Steven Pinker (2007) noted:

> We have been getting kinder and gentler. Cruelty as entertainment, human sacrifice to indulge superstition, slavery as a labor-saving device, conquest as the mission statement of government, genocide as a means of acquiring real estate, torture and mutilation as routine punishment, the death penalty for misdemeanors and differences of opinion, assassination as the mechanism of political succession, rape as the spoils of war, pogroms as outlets for frustration, homicide as the major form of conflict resolution—all were unexceptionable features of life for most of human history. But, today, they are rare to nonexistent in the West, far less common elsewhere than they used to be, concealed when they do occur, and widely condemned when they are brought to light.

So the first piece of evidence is that people have gotten a whole lot nicer lately, which must mean that their biology doesn't *force* them to be aggressive. The second piece of evidence is this: Just as the prevalence of aggression has changed over time, so too does it vary across locations. For example, violent crime in the United States is more prevalent in the South, where men are taught to react aggressively when they feel their status has been challenged, than in the North, where men are taught to resolve conflicts by appealing to authority (Brown et al., 2009; Nisbett & Cohen, 1996). In one set of experiments (Cohen et al., 1996), researchers insulted American men from northern and southern states. As the participants were leaving the laboratory via a narrow hallway, a large man (who was a trained actor) came walking towards them. What happened? The previously insulted Southerners got right up in the man's face before letting him pass, whereas the previously insulted Northerners simply stepped aside. Are Northern men just less aggressive? Do they just have less testosterone? Nope. Because in another condition of the study in which the participants were *not* insulted, Southern men stepped aside *before* Northern men did. Southern men, it seems, are more aggressive when insulted but more polite otherwise.

Male aggression is often a response to a status threat. In 2017, the 17-year-old Mexican YouTube star Juan Luis Lagunas Rosales posted a video in which he insulted a local drug lord. Shortly thereafter, a group of armed men found Rosales at a bar and shot the teenager to death. Over. Some. Words.

Major League Baseball pitchers have extremely good aim, so when they hit a batter with the ball (a "bean ball"), you can assume they meant it. Statistics show that pitchers born in southern U.S. states are 40% more likely to throw a bean ball than are pitchers born in northern U.S. states (Timmerman, 2007).

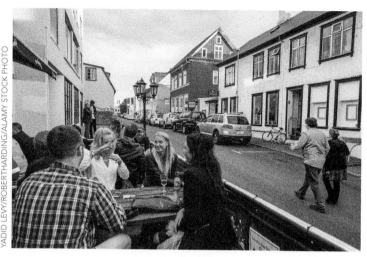

For more than a decade, the Global Peace Index has rated Iceland the least violent nation on Earth. The average number of murders each year is less than one. What's Iceland's secret? According to the U.S. State Department's Overseas Security Advisory Council, Iceland's "very low level of violent crime is due to a high-standard of living, lack of tension between social and economic classes, small population, strong social attitudes against criminality, high level of trust in law enforcement, and a well-trained, highly-educated police force."

These variations over time and across locations tell us that the cultural environment plays an important role in determining whether our innate capacity for aggression will result in aggressive behaviour (Leung & Cohen, 2011). For example, some cultural environments just make aggression easy. The U.S. murder rate is three times higher than the murder rate in Canada, and one reason is that while Americans are just 4% of the world's population, they own about half the world's guns. Like everything else, aggression is more likely to happen when it is easy to accomplish. It is also more likely to happen when it is easy to imagine (Labella & Masten, 2017). Research suggests that watching violent movies and playing violent video games may make people (and especially children) behave more aggressively (Mathur & VanderWeele, 2019; cf. Ferguson et al., 2020) and less cooperatively (cf. Ferguson, 2010; Sheese & Graziano, 2005). As one researcher noted, "Violence can be viewed as a contagious disease which can be caught simply through its observation" (Huesmann, 2017, p. 119).

That's the bad news. The good news is that just as a culture can accidentally encourage aggression, so too can it purposefully discourage it (Fry, 2012). For example, the Inuit people of the Canadian Arctic do not resolve conflicts with guns or knives, but with song contests in which the person who delivers the most effective musical put-down of their opponent is declared the winner (Briggs, 2000). Replacing war with *American Idol* sounds like a remarkably sane idea.

Cooperation

Two wolves can fight over a dead rabbit, or they can work together to bring down a gazelle. Aggression may be the simplest way to solve the problem of scarce resources, but it is rarely the most effective way, because when individuals work together, each of them can often get more resources per capita than either could get alone. **Cooperation** is *behaviour by two or more individuals that leads to mutual benefit* (Rand & Nowak, 2016), and it is one of our species' greatest achievements—right up there with language, fire, and free two-day delivery (Axelrod, 1984; Henrich, 2018; Nowak, 2006; Rand, 2016). Every roadway and supermarket, every toothbrush and cell phone, every ballet and surgery is the result of cooperation, and it is hard to think of any important human accomplishment that could possibly have happened without it. But if the benefits of cooperation are clear, why don't we cooperate all the time?

Why Cooperation Is Risky

Although cooperation is beneficial, it is also risky, as demonstrated by a well-studied game called the *prisoner's dilemma*. Here's how it works. Imagine that you and your friend Tucker have been arrested for hacking into a bank's mainframe and directing a few million dollars to your personal accounts. The police have found some stolen bank codes on your laptops, but they don't know which of you actually did the hacking. You and Tucker are now being interrogated in separate rooms, and the detectives ask each of you to sign a statement saying that the other was the actual hacker. They explain that if you both sign, then you'll both get 2 years in prison for hacking, and if you both refuse to sign, then you'll both get 1 year in prison for possession of the stolen codes. However, if one of you signs and the other refuses, then the one who signs will go free, and the one who refuses will get 3 years in prison. What should

cooperation Behaviour by two or more individuals that leads to mutual benefit.

	Tucker refuses to sign (i.e., he cooperates with you)	Tucker signs (i.e., he does not cooperate with you)
You refuse to sign (i.e., **you cooperate** with Tucker)	You both serve 1 year	You serve 3 years Tucker goes free
You sign (i.e., **you do not cooperate** with Tucker)	You go free Tucker serves 3 years	You both serve 2 years

Figure 13.3

The Prisoner's Dilemma Game The prisoner's dilemma game illustrates the risk of cooperation. Mutual cooperation leads to a moderate benefit to both players, but if one player cooperates and the other one doesn't, the cooperator gets no benefit and the noncooperator gets a large benefit. (And in case you were wondering, the game was not devised by a prisoner, but by the mathematician Albert Tucker.)

you do (other than math)? As **FIGURE 13.3** shows, it would be best if you and Tucker cooperated and refused to implicate each other, because you'd both get off with a very light sentence. But if you agree to cooperate and then Tucker gets sneaky and decides to sign, you'll serve a long sentence while Tucker goes free. So should you cooperate with Tucker or not? Oh my. What a dilemma!

The prisoner's dilemma is not just a game (which is good, because compared with *Cards Against Humanity* it pretty much sucks). It is also a metaphor for the potential costs and benefits of cooperation in everyday life. For example, consider the dilemma taxpayers face at tax time. If everyone pays their taxes, then the government can afford to maintain the roads and bridges that everyone needs; and if no one pays their taxes, then the roads buckle and the bridges fall down. So there is benefit to everyone if everyone cooperates and pays their fair share; but there is a much *bigger* benefit to the sneaky cheater who avoids paying their own taxes because they get to use all the roads and bridges for free. So, should you pay your fair share and risk being taken advantage of by a sneaky cheater, or should you *be* a sneaky cheater and risk the possibility that everyone will do the same, which will cause the bridges to collapse? If you are like most citizens, you'd be more than happy to cooperate in this situation if you knew that everyone else would too, but you aren't sure that everyone else will—and *that's* the dilemma that cooperation so often produces.

Much of social life is essentially a prisoner's dilemma game, and so it isn't surprising that people in every culture value and reward those who play the game honourably, and despise and sanction those who don't (Feinberg et al., 2014). When people are asked what single quality they most want those around them to have, the answer is *trustworthiness* (Cottrell et al., 2007), and when those around us fail to demonstrate that quality, we respond with disappointment, anger, and even retribution (unless they are on our side; see Hot Science: Partners in Crime).

For example, the *ultimatum game* requires one player (the divider) to divide a monetary prize into two parts and offer one of the parts to a second player (the decider) who can either accept or reject the offer. If the decider rejects the offer, then both players get nothing and the game is over. If deciders were economically rational, they would accept any offer: After all, something is always better than nothing. But human deciders are not economically rational and they typically reject offers that are much less than half the prize (Fehr & Gaechter, 2002; Thaler, 1988). People apparently dislike unfairness so much that they are willing to get nothing in order to make sure that someone who has treated them unfairly gets nothing too. The same goes for nonhumans, by the way. In one study, monkeys were willing to work for a slice of cucumber until they saw the experimenter

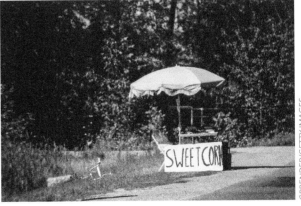

At roadside farm stands, customers select what they want, put money in a box, and leave. If a few people cheat, it won't matter much; but if a lot of people cheat, then the farmer will have to close the stand. "Honour systems" such as these are real-world versions of the prisoner's dilemma.

Hot Science | Partners in Crime

Chances are good that most of your friends think of you as a fair, trustworthy, and honest person, because if they didn't, they probably wouldn't be your friends. The upside of having a reputation for honesty is that others will befriend you, work with you, share with you, and cooperate with you; but the downside is that you miss all the illicit benefits that dishonesty provides, such as free movies from pirate Web sites and free sodas from machines with a "no refills" sign. Is there any way to have the best of both worlds—to reap the reputational rewards of honesty while also reaping the material benefits of dishonesty?

There is: Be honest, but team up with dishonest people who will do your dirty work. For example, you can honestly report every penny of your income to your accountant, but you can choose an accountant who is known to bend the rules when tax time rolls around. That way, your hands are clean, but you still get a major tax rebate! Can anyone say win-win? This strategy is devilishly sneaky and sounds too clever by half. Do honest people really do such things?

That's what Gross and colleagues (2018) wanted to know when they brought pairs of female participants into their laboratory to play a potentially lucrative game. The two participants sat in separate rooms that were electronically interconnected so that

they and the experimenter could hear each other speak. Each participant rolled a die in the privacy of their own room, and their job was simply to announce the outcome of that die roll aloud so that the experimenter and the other participant could hear them. One participant was assigned to announce their outcome first (let's call them the First Mover), and the other participant was assigned to announce their outcome second (let's call them the Second Mover). Participants were told that they would receive a cash payment that corresponded to the number shown on their die. So if the participant reported that the outcome of their die roll was 1, they received a small payment; but if they reported that the outcome was 6, they received a large payment. Furthermore, participants were told that whenever they both reported the same outcome, their payments would be doubled.

Now, if you think about it for a moment, you'll realize that this game was designed so that it was easy for participants to cheat. The First Mover could cheat by claiming that their die showed a 6 even when it didn't (which gave them a large payment), and the Second Mover could cheat by claiming that their die also showed a 6 even when it didn't (which gave them a large payment *and* which then doubled both their payment and the First Mover's

payment). Were participants honest? Some were and some weren't, of course, but the really interesting part of the study was what happened next.

After playing a few rounds of the game, participants were allowed to choose new partners or keep their old ones. The results showed that when dishonest First Movers were paired with dishonest Second Movers, they almost never chose to switch partners; but when they were paired with honest Second Movers, they chose to switch about 40% of the time. In other words, dishonest participants were more likely to dump an honest partner than a dishonest one. So, what about honest participants? What did they do when offered the chance to switch? When honest First Movers were paired with honest Second Movers, they chose to switch about 40% of the time; but when they were paired with dishonest Second Movers, they chose to switch only 15% of the time! In other words, just like the dishonest participants, *honest participants were more likely to dump an honest partner than a dishonest one.*

One way to protect our own reputations for honesty while still benefiting from dishonesty is to team up with people who will do the sketchy stuff that we won't do ourselves. This study suggests that you don't have to be a criminal to want a partner in crime.

---

give another monkey a more delicious food for doing less work, at which point the first set of monkeys went on strike and refused to participate further (Brosnan & DeWaal, 2003).

How Groups Minimize the Risks of Cooperation

Cooperation requires that we take a risk by benefiting others, and then trusting that they will do the same for us. How do we know whom to trust? A **group** is *a collection of people who have something in common that distinguishes them from others.* Every one of us is a member of many groups—from families and teams to religions and nations. Although these groups are all quite different, they do have one thing in common, which is that the members of each group generally trust that other members will treat them fairly and well (Cruwys et al., 2021). **In-group favouritism** is *the tendency to treat people better when they are members of one's own group than when they are not.* Research suggests that people aren't necessarily unkind to members of out-groups, but that they are especially kind to members of their in-groups

group A collection of people who have something in common that distinguishes them from others.

in-group favouritism Tendency to treat people better when they are members of one's own group than when they are not.

(Brewer, 1999; DiDonato et al., 2011; Balliet et al., 2014). Groups don't necessarily make us hate, but they sure do make us love.

In-group favouritism is evolutionarily ancient (Fu et al., 2012; Mahajan et al., 2011), arises early in development (Dunham et al., 2013), and is remarkably easy to elicit (Efferson et al., 2008). When researchers randomly assign participants to be members of utterly meaningless groups such as "Group A" or "Group B," the participants still tend to favour members of their in-group over members of the out-group (Hodson & Sorrentino, 2001; Locksley et al., 1980). Simply knowing that "You are one of *us* and not one of *them*" is sufficient to create in-group favouritism (Tajfel et al., 1971), even when the words "us" and "them" mean pretty much nothing at all.

Group membership creates in-group favouritism which makes cooperation less risky, and that's one of the reasons why our species became the groupist animal on earth. But groups can also have costs. For example, you've probably heard that two heads are better than one, but research shows that when groups try to make decisions, they rarely do better than the best member would have done alone—and they often do much worse (Baumeister et al., 2016; Minson & Mueller, 2012). When a school board meets to solve its budget crisis, for example, it will probably end up approving a plan that is not nearly as good as the plan the most qualified member would have developed on their own. Why?

- Most groups do not fully capitalize on the expertise of their members (Hackman & Katz, 2010; Silver et al., 2021). For instance, groups (such as a school board) often give too little weight to the opinions of members who are experts (the financial advisor) and too much weight to the opinions of members who happen to be high in status (the mayor) or especially talkative (the mayor).

- The **common knowledge effect** is *the tendency for group discussions to focus on information that all members share* (Gigone & Hastie, 1993; Kerr & Tindale, 2004). When chatting with a group of friends, it's nice to choose topics that allow everyone to be included in the conversation. But that's not the best way for a group to make a decision, because the information everyone shares (the cost of running the cafeteria) is often relatively unimportant, whereas the truly important information (how a school in Sweden solved a similar budget crisis) may be known to just a few.

- A group whose members come to the table with moderate opinions ("We probably shouldn't renovate the gym this year") can end up making an extreme decision ("Let's shut down the gym and fire the entire athletic staff") simply because, in the course of discussion, each member was exposed to many different arguments in favour of a single position (Isenberg, 1986). **Group polarization** is *the tendency of groups to make decisions that are more extreme than any member would have made alone* (Myers & Lamm, 1975).

- Group members usually care about how other members feel and are sometimes reluctant to "rock the boat" even when it needs a good rocking. **Groupthink** is *the tendency for groups to reach consensus in order to facilitate interpersonal harmony* (Janis, 1982). Harmony is important (especially if the group is a choir), but studies show that groups often sacrifice the soundness of their decisions in order to achieve it (Turner & Pratkanis, 1998).

For all these reasons, then, groups typically underperform individuals in a wide variety of tasks. But the costs of groups go beyond making suboptimal decisions. People in groups sometimes do truly terrible things that none of their members would do alone (Yzerbyt & Demoulin, 2010). Lynching, looting, rioting, gang-raping—why do human beings sometimes behave so badly when they assemble? One reason is that when assembled in groups, people's attention is drawn towards others and away from themselves, and they become momentarily less likely to consider their

common knowledge effect
The tendency for group discussions to focus on information that all members share.

group polarization The tendency of groups to make decisions that are more extreme than any member would have made alone.

groupthink The tendency of groups to reach consensus in order to facilitate interpersonal harmony.

When are people most and least likely to cheat? Researchers posted a picture above an office coffee pot and found that people were less likely to take coffee without paying when the picture showed eyes than when it showed flowers (Bateson et al., 2006). Other researchers paid people to sit alone in a room and complete puzzles for cash and found that people were less likely to cheat when the lights were bright than when the lights were low (Zhong et al., 2010). People behave better when they think they are being observed, and both watchful eyes and bright lights make them feel like they are.

personal values before taking action (Wicklund, 1975). **Deindividuation** occurs *when immersion in a group causes people to become less attentive to their personal values* (Postmes & Spears, 1998) and this can lead people in groups to do things that they would not do on their own (Baumeister et al., 2016). When you walk by a jewelry store, you probably don't consider smashing the window and grabbing a Rolex because stealing conflicts with your personal values; but if you're pressed tightly into a big crowd and someone suddenly breaks a jewelry store window, you may be so busy attending to what others are saying and doing (and stealing) that you don't even stop to consider what you personally believe.

A second reason for the bad behaviour of people in groups is **diffusion of responsibility,** which refers to *the tendency to feel diminished responsibility for one's actions when surrounded by others who are acting the same way.* Diffusion of responsibility is the main culprit behind **social loafing,** which is *the tendency to contribute less when in a group than when alone* (Karau & Williams, 1993). For example, individuals in large groups are less likely than individuals in small groups to clap loudly after a performance (Latané et al., 1979), exert effort in a team sport (Williams et al., 1989), donate money to charity (Wiesenthal et al., 1983), or say hello to passersby (Jones & Foshay, 1984). And if you've ever worked as a server in a restaurant, you already know that large groups are least likely to leave good tips (Freeman et al., 1975).

But social loafing is by no means the worst consequence of the diffusion of responsibility. The **bystander effect** is *the tendency for people to be less likely to help a stranger in an emergency situation when other bystanders are present* (Darley & Latane, 1968; cf. Philpot et al., 2020). There are several reasons for this (Hortensius & de Gelder, 2018; Havlik et al., 2022), one of which is that people in a large group often feel that the other bystanders are collectively more responsible than they are (Fischer et al., 2011). If you saw someone fall off their bicycle in the middle of campus, you'd probably feel more responsible for stopping to help if you were the only witness than if a hundred other students witnessed it too, because with a hundred other witnesses, you'd own a smaller share of the moral responsibility to help (see **FIGURE 13.4**).

So groups make bad decisions and foster bad behaviour. Might we be better off without them? Not likely. Groups not only minimize the risks of cooperation (which makes human civilization possible), but they also contribute to our general health, happiness, and well-being (which makes human civilization worthwhile). Being excluded from groups is one of the most painful experiences people can have (Eisenberger et al., 2003; Uskul & Over, 2014; Williams, 2007), so it isn't any wonder that people who are routinely excluded (or who just feel excluded) are anxious, lonely, depressed, and at increased risk for illness and premature death (Cacioppo & Cacioppo, 2018; Leary, 1990; Bzdok & Dunbar, 2020). Belonging to groups is not just a source of psychological and physical well-being but also a source of identity

deindividuation A phenomenon in which immersion in a group causes people to become less concerned with their personal values.

diffusion of responsibility The tendency of individuals to feel diminished responsibility for their actions when surrounded by others who are acting the same way.

social loafing The tendency of people to expend less effort when in a group than when alone.

bystander effect The tendency for people to be less likely to help a stranger in an emergency situation when other bystanders are present.

Figure 13.4
Mob Size and Level of Atrocity These two men were rescued by police just as residents of their town prepared to lynch them for stealing a car. Because larger mobs provide more opportunity for diffusion of responsibility, they also commit more atrocious crimes. When researchers divide the number of mob victims by the number of mob members, they find that this ratio predicts the atrociousness of the mob's actions (Leader et al., 2007; Ritchey & Ruback, 2018). Small mobs with many victims do bad things, and large mobs with few victims do even worse things.

(Ellemers, 2012; Leary, 2010; Tajfel & Turner, 1986), which is why when you ask individuals to tell you about themselves, they typically describe the groups of which they are members ("I'm a young white lesbian Canadian architect"). Groups sometimes cause us to misjudge and to misbehave, but they are essential to our cooperativeness, our health, and our happiness.

Altruism

Cooperation solves the problem of scarce resources: We can do better by cooperating than we can by competing. But is "doing better" the only reason we cooperate with others? Aren't we ever just . . . well, *nice*? **Altruism** is *intentional behaviour that benefits another at a potential cost to oneself,* and for centuries, scientists and philosophers have argued about whether people are ever truly altruistic. That may seem like an odd argument for a bunch of smart folks to be having. After all, people give their blood to those who are injured and their food to those who are homeless. We volunteer, donate, contribute, and tithe. People do nice things all the time—so why is there any debate about whether people are altruistic?

Because behaviours that appear to be altruistic often have hidden benefits for those who do them. Consider some examples from the world of nonhuman animals. Squirrels emit alarm calls when they see a predator, which puts them at increased risk of being eaten (because the hawks can hear them as well as see them) but which also allows their fellow squirrels to hide. Honeybees spend their lives caring for the offspring of their queen rather than producing offspring of their own. These behaviours appear to be altruistic because the animals that engage in them clearly pay a large cost and appear to receive no benefits. But don't be fooled by appearances: There *are* benefits, because squirrels and honeybees are *genetically related* to the individuals they help. Squirrels emit alarm calls, but only when they are closely related to the other squirrels in the den (Maynard-Smith, 1965); and by an odd genetic quirk, honeybees are more closely related to the queen's offspring whom they are helping than they would be to their own offspring. When an animal promotes the survival of its relatives it is actually benefitting itself by promoting the survival of its own genes (Hamilton, 1964). **Kin selection** is *the process by which evolution selects for individuals who cooperate with their relatives,* and although cooperating with relatives may look like altruism, scientists generally think of it as selfishness in disguise.

What about cooperation among unrelated individuals? That happens, of course, but it isn't necessarily altruistic either. Male baboons will sometimes risk injury to help an unrelated male baboon win a fight, and monkeys will spend time grooming

In 2013, a customer at a Tim Horton's drive-through in Winnipeg, decided to perform a random act of kindness and pay for the order of the car behind him. This caused a chain reaction of altruism as 228 consecutive cars received free orders and, in turn, decided to pay for the order of the folks in the next car. The cascade ended when a customer who received four free coffees refused to pay for the three coffees ordered by the car behind them. There's always *that* person.

altruism Intentional behaviour that benefits another at a potential cost to oneself.

kin selection The process by which evolution selects for individuals who cooperate with their relatives.

Wesley Autrey jumped onto the subway tracks to save a stranger's life. "I had a split-second decision to make . . . I don't feel like I did something spectacular; I just saw someone who needed help. I did what I felt was right" (Buckley, 2007). Said no raccoon ever.

reciprocal altruism Behaviour that benefits another with the expectation that those benefits will be returned in the future.

unrelated monkeys when they could be eating or resting instead. Are these examples of altruism? Not necessarily, because as it turns out, baboons and monkeys are pretty good at keeping score, and the ones that *do* favours today are the ones that *get* favours tomorrow. **Reciprocal altruism** is *behaviour that benefits another with the expectation that those benefits will be returned in the future,* and despite the second word in this term, scientists don't think there is anything altruistic about it (Trivers, 1972). In many ways, reciprocal altruism is merely cooperation extended over time—and cooperating is one of the most selfish things a smart animal can do!

The behaviour of nonhuman animals does not provide clear evidence of genuine altruism (cf. Bartal et al., 2011). But what about us? Are we any different? Yes and no. Like squirrels and honeybees, we are *much* more likely to help our kin than to help strangers (Burnstein et al., 1994; Komter, 2010); and like baboons and monkeys, we are *much* more likely to help those who have helped us (Burger et al., 2009). But unlike these other animals, humans clearly do provide benefits to unrelated strangers who have absolutely no chance of repaying them (Batson, 2002; Warneken & Tomasello, 2009). Just think about it. We hold the door for people who share precisely none of our genes and we tip servers in restaurants in foreign cities to which we know we will never return. We give strangers directions, advice, and free coffee and even go out of our way to return their misdelivered packages and lost wallets (see The Real World: Where Are All the Altruists?). And that's the least of it. When Wesley Autrey saw a student stumble and fall on the subway tracks just as a train was approaching, he didn't ask whether they shared his genes or how he would be repaid in the future. He just jumped onto the tracks and lay on top of the student, holding him down while the train passed over both of them—with less than an inch to spare (see **FIGURE 13.5**). If *that* doesn't qualify as altruism, it's hard to imagine what would.

Clearly, then, humans do help other humans, sometimes at a staggering cost to themselves. We are not only capable of genuine altruism, but we may be more capable than we realize (Gerbasi & Prentice, 2013; Miller & Ratner, 1998). Some scientists even argue that our altruistic orientation is the single essential characteristic that gave our species' dominion over all others (Hare, 2017). It is worth noting that although altruistic people do not help others in order to benefit themselves, they may benefit nonetheless. People who are oriented towards helping others have better psychological well-being, physical health, and social relationships (Crocker et al., 2017). And it might surprise Darwin to learn that they also have more children (Eriksson et al., 2020)!

Figure 13.5

Organ Donation and Altruism Canada's rate of organ donation by living donors in 2016 was 15.0 donors per million population (dpmp), slightly down from 15.7 dpmp the previous year. Every year, hundreds of living Canadians donate a liver or a kidney. Although many of these donations are for family and friends, fully 2 in 3 kidneys are donated anonymously by altruistic strangers (Canadian Blood Services, 2019). Another type of altruism in Canada is gestational surrogacy—the carrying of a child for people who cannot have a child on their own. In Canada, surrogates cannot be paid—only their expenses can be reimbursed, making this an altruistic act. In 2013, in Ontario alone, 145 babies were born to gestational surrogates (White, 2016). DATA FROM CANADIAN BLOOD SERVICES, 2017.

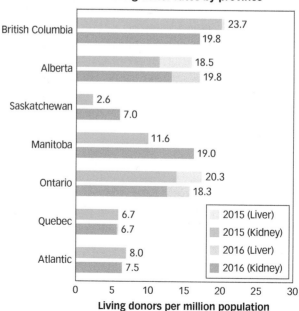

Living donor rates by province

Province	Value 1	Value 2
British Columbia	23.7	19.8
Alberta	18.5	19.8
Saskatchewan	2.6	7.0
Manitoba	11.6	19.0
Ontario	20.3	18.3
Quebec	6.7	6.7
Atlantic	8.0	7.5

Legend:
- 2015 (Liver)
- 2015 (Kidney)
- 2016 (Liver)
- 2016 (Kidney)

Living donors per million population

The Real World • Where Are All the Altruists?

"The art of losing isn't hard to master," wrote the poet Elizabeth Bishop. Lately, some social scientists have been testing that assertion by losing things all over the world—and in the process, discovering what makes people behave altruistically.

In a recent study (Cohn et al., 2019), a researcher walked into a public or private institution such as a bank, a post office, or a police station, and placed a wallet on the counter. "Hi," the researcher said. "I found this on the street around the corner. Somebody must have lost it. I'm in a hurry and have to go. Can you please take care of it?" Then the researcher turned and left. Inside the wallet was some money, as well as a

business card with contact information that presumably belonged to the wallet's owner but that actually belonged to the researcher, which allowed them to count the number of people who behaved altruistically by trying to contact the wallet's owner. The researcher turned in an astounding 17,000 wallets in 355 cities in 40 different countries. What did they discover?

One surprising finding was that the more money the wallet contained, the *more* likely people were to try to contact its owner. But the biggest differences were not between amounts of money, but between nations. In Peru, for example, fewer than 15% of the institutions attempted to contact the wallet's owner,

but in Denmark, more than 80% did. These findings suggest that some cultures are more altruistic than others.

But why? There are a nearly infinite number of differences between Peru and Denmark—different languages, different religions, different customs, foods, literature, and so on. Which of these many factors accounts for the differences in altruism?

To answer that question, another researcher (Baldassarri, 2020) also went out and lost something—not a wallet this time, but a letter—and they did it in different regions of a single nation. Specifically, the researcher dropped self-addressed stamped letters all over Italy—on streets and sidewalks, on benches and at bus stops—and then waited

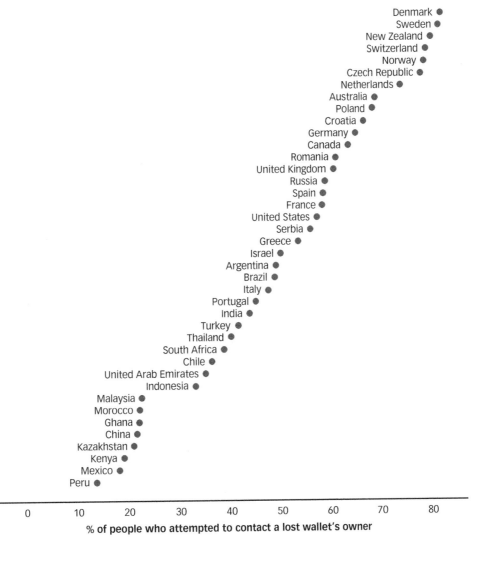

% of people who attempted to contact a lost wallet's owner

to see how many altruistic Italians picked them up and mailed them as a favour to the stranger who had apparently dropped them. The researcher dropped an astounding 5,980 letters in 188 Italian communities. As the map here shows, the favour-doing rates in different regions were remarkably different: 53.3% of the residents of Marche mailed a lost letter, but only 10.3% of the residents of Calabria did the same.

Unlike Peru and Denmark, the regions of Italy all have the same language, the same religion, the same major traditions, and so on. So what distinguishes them? As it turned out, the highest letter-mailing rates were in regions that were also high in "market integration," which is a measure of the extent to which everyday life forces people to have economic transactions with strangers (Henrich et al., 2004). If you have to buy groceries from someone who isn't your cousin, or sell hats to someone who isn't your aunt's best friend, then you have to learn to deal with strangers, to trust strangers, to treat strangers fairly and kindly. Apparently, once that habit is acquired, the kindness even extends to strangers you've never met who seem to have left a letter on the sidewalk.

All of us are capable of behaving altruistically, but as these studies suggest, our social environments play an important role in determining whether and when we will exercise that option. These studies also suggest that even if the art of losing isn't hard to master, it is still an art from which we can learn a lot.

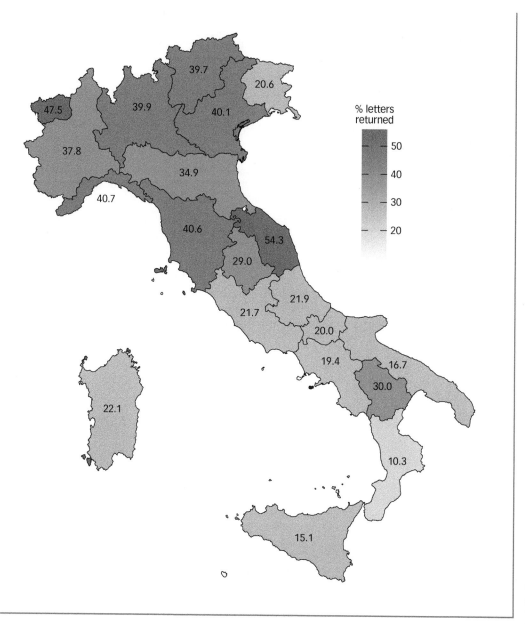

% letters returned

Interpersonal Attraction

Social behaviour is useful for survival, but it is absolutely essential for reproduction, which generally doesn't happen unless two fertile people get extremely social. The first step on the road to reproduction is finding someone who wants to travel that road with us, and psychologists know a lot about how people do that.

Learning Outcomes

WHAT YOU NEED TO KNOW

- Explain the biological and cultural factors that influence selectivity in mate choice.
- Describe the situational, physical, and psychological factors that determine feelings of attraction.
- Describe the factors that cause people to get married and divorced.

Selectivity

Outside of Hollywood, people don't mate randomly. Rather, they *select* their sexual partners, and women tend to be more selective than men (Feingold, 1992a; Fiore et al., 2010). When researchers arranged for a trained actor to approach opposite-gender strangers on a campus and ask, "Would you go out with me?" they found that roughly half of both the men and the women who were approached agreed to the request. On the other hand, when the actor asked the stranger, "Would you go to bed with me?" precisely *none* of the women said yes, but *three-quarters* of the men did (Clark & Hatfield, 1989). There are many reasons other than "being selective" that a woman might turn down a sexual offer from a strange man who approaches her in a public place (Conley, 2011), but research suggests that women tend to be choosier than men under most ordinary circumstances as well (Buss & Schmitt, 1993; Schmitt et al., 2012).

Why? One reason is biology. Females produce a small number of eggs in their lifetimes, conception eliminates their ability to conceive for at least 9 months, and pregnancy increases their nutritional requirements and puts them at risk of illness and maybe even death. When females have sex with males, they are taking a serious risk. Males, on the other hand, produce billions of sperm in their lifetimes, and their ability to conceive a child tomorrow is not inhibited by having conceived one today. When males have sex with females, they are risking a few minutes of their time and roughly a teaspoon of bodily fluid. Basic biology makes sex a much riskier proposition for females than for males, so it makes sense that females are much more selective about the people with whom they have it. After all, if one person bet $1,000,000 on a horse race and another bet $1, wouldn't you expect the first person to select their horse much more carefully?

Biology plays a role in determining how selective a person will be, but so does culture (Finkel & Eastwick, 2009; Petersen & Hyde, 2010; Zentner & Mitura, 2012). In virtually all human cultures, the reputational costs of not being selective—that is, of being promiscuous—are considerably higher for women than they are for men (Eagly & Wood, 1999; Kasser & Sharma, 1999; Krems et al., 2021). For more than a thousand years, the English language has had a long list of derogatory terms for promiscuous females (e.g., "slut" and "whore") but almost none for promiscuous males ("player" is not pejorative and "manslut" was invented about 5 minutes ago). So yes, biology does make sex a riskier proposition for females than for males, but cultural norms almost always exacerbate those risks. Interestingly, on those occasions when selecting a sexual partner does present a risk to men—for instance, when they are selecting a spouse instead of a date—they quickly become every bit as choosy as women ordinarily are (Kenrick et al., 1990).

Among sea horses, it is the male that carries the young, and, not coincidentally, males are more selective than are females.

Attraction

There is probably an extremely small number of people with whom you'd be willing to have sex, an even smaller number with whom you'd be willing to have children, and an astonishingly large number with whom you'd be unwilling to have either. So when you meet someone new, how do you decide which of these bins they will end up in? Many things go into choosing a date, and even more go into choosing a lover or a life partner, but few are as important as the simple feeling called *attraction* (Berscheid & Reis, 1998). Research suggests that this powerfully important feeling is the product of situational, physical, and psychological factors, so let's explore all three in turn.

How Situational Factors Influence Attraction

We tend to think that we select our romantic partners based on their personalities, their appearances, and so on—and we do. But we can only select from the pool of people we've met, and the likelihood of meeting a potential partner is largely determined by *proximity*. Before you ever start ruling out potential romantic partners, geography has already ruled out more than 99.9999% of the world's population for you (Festinger et al., 1950). For most of human history, two people who were separated by mountains or even just a few dozen kilometres had virtually no chance of coming into contact, and although the Internet has changed that (Finkel et al., 2012; Okdie et al., 2014; Rosenfeld et al., 2019), online dating becomes offline mating only when the people live in relatively close proximity. Tinder is fairly useless if you are "swiping right" on someone who lives an ocean away.

When actress Tallia Storm looks at herself in the mirror, she probably likes what she sees, as do her fans. But she and her fans aren't seeing or liking the same thing. Tallia's fans usually see her face on a screen, so they probably prefer the image on the left; but Tallia usually sees her face in a mirror, so she probably prefers the "reversed image" on the right. Research on the mere exposure effect shows that people do indeed prefer mirror-reversed images of themselves, but not of others (Mita et al., 1977).

Proximity makes attraction possible, but it also facilitates it directly. How? The more proximal people are, the more likely we are to see them, and the more often we see them, the more familiar they become—and research shows that humans (and other animals) generally prefer familiar to unfamiliar stimuli. The **mere exposure effect** is *the tendency for liking of a stimulus to increase with the amount of exposure to that stimulus* (Bornstein, 1989; Van Dessel et al., 2019; Zajonc, 1968). For instance, in one experiment, participants stared at a computer screen while faces were flashed at "subliminal speed" (which means they appeared and disappeared so quickly that participants were unaware of seeing anything more than a flash of light). Afterwards, participants were asked to examine some faces—some of which had been flashed and some of which had not—and report (a) whether they had seen the face before and (b) how much they liked it. The first finding was that participants could not reliably determine whether a face had or had not previously been shown. The second finding was that participants *liked* the face more if it had been shown (Monahan et al., 2000). Merely being exposed to the face at subliminal speed was enough to make them like it. Although there are some special circumstances under which mere exposure can decrease liking (Norton et al., 2007), for the most part, it increases it (Reis et al., 2011). Familiarity can sometimes breed contempt, but more often it breeds attraction.

Attraction can be the result of geographical accidents that put people in the same place at the same time—as neighbours or coworkers or fellow students—but as you might guess, some places and times are better than others. For instance, in one study at the University of British Columbia, researchers observed men as they crossed Capilano bridge, a swaying suspension bridge in North Vancouver. They arranged for an attractive woman to approach the men—either when the men were in the middle of the bridge or after they had finished crossing it—and to ask them to complete a survey. After the men completed the survey, the woman gave them her phone number and offered to "explain her project in greater detail" if they called. Did they? Many did, but they were more likely to call when they had met the woman in the middle of the swaying bridge than when they had met her at the end of it (Dutton & Aron, 1974). Why? As you learned in the Emotion and Motivation chapter, people sometimes misinterpret their physiological arousal as a sign of attraction (Byrne et al., 1975; Schachter & Singer, 1962). The men were presumably more aroused when they were in the middle of a swaying bridge, and some of those men mistook their bridge-induced arousal for woman-induced attraction. (And in case you are wondering, the fact that some of the men may have been gay, happily married, celibate, or otherwise uninterested in the woman may explain why they didn't call, but it does not explain why more men called in one condition than in the other.) The fact that arousing circumstances can promote attraction may be one reason roller coasters and horror movies continue to be popular locations for first dates.

How Physical Factors Influence Attraction

Once people are in the same place at the same time, they can begin to learn about each other's personal qualities, and the first personal quality they usually learn about is the other person's appearance. You probably can't tell whether the person who sits farthest from you in class likes sports, plays piano, or prefers dogs to cats, but you definitely know if they are hot or not. Does hotness matter?

Yes, it matters a lot. In one study, nearly 800 first-year university students bought a ticket to a dance whose organizers promised to use a computer algorithm to match them with an optimal opposite-gender partner (Walster et al., 1966). Students

mere exposure effect The tendency for liking of a stimulus to increase with the amount of exposure to that stimulus.

Ben Bostic and Laura Zych met when their plane crashed into the Hudson River in New York City in 2009. Then they fell in love. Being in highly arousing situations can lead to romantic attraction, as well as wet shoes.

submitted information about their academic performance and their interests, and took tests to measure their social skills, their extraversion, their self-esteem, and more. What they didn't know was that the organizers were a team of psychologists who did not even *have* a computer, and who instead *randomly* assigned each student to an opposite-gender partner. Midway through the dance, the researchers asked students to confidentially report how attracted they were to their partner and how much they would like to go out with them again. When the researchers later crunched the data (by hand!), they found that a student's physical appearance was the one and only factor that predicted their partner's attraction. In other words, appearance didn't just matter—it was the *only* thing that mattered! Other studies have confirmed the power of physical appearance. One study found that a man's height and a woman's weight are among the best predictors of how many responses their personal ads received (Lynn & Shurgot, 1984), and another study found that physical attractiveness is the *only* factor that predicts the online dating choices of both women and men (Green et al., 1984).

Physical attractiveness gets us more than dates (Etcoff, 1999; Langlois et al., 2000). It may not be fair, but physically attractive people have more sex, more friends, and more fun than the rest of us do (Curran & Lippold, 1975). A recent study in the United States documents that they even have more money (see **FIGURE 13.6**). People believe that physically attractive people have superior personal qualities (Dion et al., 1972; Eagly et al., 1991), and in some cases they do. For instance, because attractive people have more friends and more opportunities for social interaction, they tend to have better social skills than less attractive people do (Feingold, 1992b). Physical appearance is so powerful that it even influences non-romantic relationships: For example, mothers are more affectionate and playful when their children are cute than when they are not (Langlois et al., 1995). The only downside of being physically attractive is that other people sometimes feel threatened (Agthe et al., 2010) and can be unsympathetic to an attractive person's problems (Fisher & Ma, 2014). Research suggests that men and women are both powerfully and equally

Figure 13.6

It Pays to be Beautiful Jay Z and Beyonce have a combined net worth of roughly $1.5 billion and that's because they are wildly talented performers and savvy entrepreneurs. But the fact that they are also quite attractive surely hasn't hurt their finances. As the graph shows, attractive men and women of all races in the United States earn more money than less attractive people do—and in fact, racial disparities in income pretty much disappear at the highest levels of attractiveness. (Data from Monk et al., 2021)

Standards of beauty can vary across cultures. Mauritanian women long to be heavy (*left*), and Ghanaian men are grateful to be short (*right*).

influenced by the physical appearance of their partners in the early stages of a relationship (Eastwick et al., 2011) but that this influence may fade more quickly for women than for men (Li et al., 2013; Meltzer et al., 2014).

So yes, it pays to be beautiful. But what exactly constitutes beauty? The answer to that question varies across cultures. For example, most American women want to be slender; but in Mauritania, girls are encouraged to drink up to 5 gallons of high-fat milk every day so that someday they will be heavy enough to attract a husband. As one Mauritanian woman noted, "Men want women to be fat, and so they are fat" (LaFraniere, 2007). Similarly, most American men want to be tall; but in Ghana, men not only tend to be short, but they consider height a curse. "To be a tall person can be quite embarrassing," said one particularly altitudinous Ghanaian man. "When you are standing in a crowd, the short people start to jeer at you" (French, 1997). Tall and thin or short and fat, beauty, it seems, is in the eye of the beholder.

But not entirely. Although different cultures do have different standards of beauty, it turns out that those standards have a surprising amount in common (Cunningham et al., 1995). For example:

- *Symmetry.* People in all cultures seem to prefer faces and bodies that are *bilaterally symmetrical* — that is, faces and bodies whose left half is a mirror image of the right half (Perilloux et al., 2010; Perrett et al., 1999). People not only prefer symmetry, but are also excellent at detecting it: In a blind "sniff test," women prefer the smell of t-shirts that were worn by symmetrical men more than the smell of t-shirts that were worn by asymmetrical men (Thornhill & Gangestad, 1999).

- *Body shape.* In most cultures, male bodies are considered attractive when they are shaped like a triangle (i.e., broad shoulders with a narrow waist and hips), and female bodies are considered attractive when they are shaped like an hourglass (i.e., broad shoulders and hips with a narrow waist; Deady & Law Smith, 2015; Singh, 1993). Culture may determine whether straight men prefer women who are slender or heavy, but in all cultures, straight men seem to prefer women with hourglass figures whose waists are about 60–70% the size of their hips (Bovet, 2019).

- *Age.* Characteristics such as large eyes, high eyebrows, and a small chin make people look immature or "baby faced" (Berry & McArthur, 1985). As a rule, female faces are considered more attractive when they have immature features, whereas male faces are considered more attractive when they have mature features (Cunningham et al., 1990; Zebrowitz & Montepare, 1992). In every culture that psychologists have studied, straight women tend to prefer older men, and straight men tend to prefer younger women (Walter et al., 2020).

© EMOTIONWISE GROUP/DR. LENNY KRISTAL

There are many gender differences in attraction. For example, straight women think men are sexier when they look proud rather than happy, but straight men think women are sexier when they look happy rather than proud (Tracy & Beall, 2011).

Is there any rhyme or reason to this list of scenic attractions? Why would people in so many different and diverse cultures share these particular preferences? Because no matter what culture you live in, evolution designed you to be attracted to people who have good genes and who will be good parents (Gallup & Frederick, 2010; Neuberg et al., 2010), and the features that all human beings seem to find attractive turn out to be fairly reliable signals for one or both of these things. Consider the three features just mentioned:

- *Symmetry.* Asymmetry is sometimes caused by disease or by genetic mutation, so asymmetry is a signal that a person's genes may be likely to produce unhealthy offspring (Jones et al., 2001; Thornhill & Gangestad, 1993).

- *Body shape.* Estrogen causes female bodies to become "hourglasses," and females who are high in estrogen tend to be especially fertile and may have more offspring (Jasienska et al., 2004). Testosterone causes male bodies to become "triangles," and males who are high in testosterone tend to be socially dominant and therefore have more resources to devote to their offspring (Hughes & Kumari, 2019). So body shape is a signal of how many offspring a female can produce, and how well a male can provide for them.

- *Age.* Younger females are generally more fertile than older females, so a youthful appearance is a signal of a female's ability to produce offspring. Conversely, older males generally command more resources than younger males do, so a mature appearance is a signal of a male's ability to provide for offspring (Pelham, 2021).

The feeling we call *attraction* isn't based on whimsy. It is, at least in part, nature's way of telling us that we have met a fertile person with good genes and the ability to provide for children.

These ideas explain why straight people the world over prefer so many of the same features in the opposite sex (Thomas et al., 2020). But what about everyone else? America's closet has only recently opened and research on everyone else is still sparse (Amos & McCabe, 2015), but at least some studies suggest that gay, lesbian, and straight people share many of the same basic preferences (Legenbauer et al., 2009; Swami & Tovée, 2008). For example, gay men and straight women agree to a remarkable extent on which male faces are attractive (Valentová et al., 2013), both straight men and gay men have a strong preference for youthful faces in their potential partners (Teuscher & Teuscher, 2007), and both straight women and lesbians care more about physical features when choosing a short-term partner than a long-term partner (Lucas et al., 2011). On the other hand, there are some differences. For example, some research suggests that lesbians are more accepting of heavier female body types than straight men are (Cohen & Tannenbaum, 2001; Swami & Tovée, 2006).

Whatever elicits the feeling of attraction, it is important to remember that it *is* a feeling and not a behaviour (Montoya et al., 2018). Everyone may *desire* the most attractive person in the room, but studies suggest that most people tend to approach, date, and marry people who are about as attractive as they are (Berscheid et al., 1971; Lee et al., 2008). In a study that simulated human dating (Kalick & Hamilton, 1986), researchers assigned robots different "attractiveness scores" and then programmed them to pair up by asking other robots on "dates." If both robots agreed to the date, they became a couple and left the dating game; if not, they both kept trying to pair up with other robots. In one version of the game, the robots were programmed to try pairing with the most attractive robot they could find, and in another version, the robots were programmed to try pairing with a robot that was about as attractive as they were. Paradoxically, when the robots were programmed to find the most beautiful robot, the resulting couples were extremely similar in attractiveness ($r = .85$), but when the robots were programmed to seek a partner who was about as attractive as they were, the resulting couples were only moderately similar in attractiveness ($r = .5$). What's interesting about this particular number is that $r = .5$ is the correlation commonly observed between the attractiveness ratings of real human couples, suggesting that most humans may be seeking similar models rather than supermodels.

Psychological Factors Influence Attraction

If attraction is all about big biceps and high cheekbones, then why don't we just skip the small talk and pick our life partners from their Insta profiles? Because for human beings, attraction is about more than skin and teeth. Physical appearance is assessed easily, early, and from across a crowded room (Lenton & Francesconi, 2010), and it definitely determines who draws our attention and quickens our pulse. But once people begin interacting, they start to move beyond appearances (Cramer et al., 1996; Regan, 1998), which is why physical attractiveness matters less when people have known each other for a long time (Hunt et al., 2015). People's *inner* qualities—their personalities, points of view, attitudes, beliefs, values, ambitions, and abilities—play an important role in determining their sustained interest in each other, and there isn't much mystery about the kinds of inner qualities most people find attractive. Intelligence, loyalty, trustworthiness, and kindness are high on just about everybody's list (Daniel et al., 1985; Farrelly et al., 2007; Fletcher et al., 1999).

But exactly how much of those qualities do we want our mates to have? You might think the answer is "As much as possible!" but research suggests that people are most attracted to those who are *similar* to them on these dimensions—and on almost every other dimension as well (Iyengar et al., 2018; Montoya & Horton, 2013). We marry people of a similar age who have similar levels of education, similar religious backgrounds, similar ethnicities, similar socioeconomic statuses, similar personalities, similar political beliefs, and so on (Botwin et al., 1997; Buss, 1985; Caspi & Herbener, 1990). When researchers measured the distinct characteristics of 1,000 couples, they found that the couples were more similar than one would expect by chance on 75% of those characteristics, and less similar than one would expect by chance on precisely none (Burgess & Wallin, 1953). **Homophily** is *the tendency for people to like others who are similar to themselves*, and human beings turn out to be remarkably homophilous. Indeed, of all the characteristics psychologists have measured, the only one for which the vast majority of people have a consistent preference for dissimilarity is sex.

Why is similarity so attractive? There are at least three reasons. First, it's easy to interact with people who are similar to us because we can easily agree on a wide range of issues, such as what to eat, where to live, how to raise children, and how to spend money. Second, when someone shares our attitudes and beliefs, we feel

homophily The tendency for people to like others who are similar to themselves.

validated and become more confident that those attitudes and beliefs are the right ones (Byrne & Clore, 1970). Indeed, research shows that when a person's attitudes or beliefs are challenged, they momentarily become even more attracted to similar others (Greenberg et al., 1990; Hirschberger et al., 2002). Third, because we like people who share our attitudes and beliefs, we expect them to like us back for the same reason—and *being liked* is a powerful source of attraction (Aronson & Worchel, 1966; Backman & Secord, 1959; Condon & Crano, 1988), especially when the people who like us don't seem to like everyone (Eastwick et al., 2007).

Our preference for similarity goes beyond attitudes and beliefs, and extends to abilities as well. For example, we may admire extraordinary skill in quarterbacks and saxophone players, but when it comes to friends and lovers, extraordinary people can threaten our self-esteem and make us worry about our own competence (Tesser, 1991). This is especially likely when the extraordinary person is a woman and the worried person is a man (Ratliff & Oishi, 2013). The fact that other people's competence can threaten us may explain why truly amazing people are often considered more attractive when they display a minor incompetence, such as the brilliant scientist who can't seem to scramble an egg or the award-winning poet whose socks never match (Aronson et al., 1966; Ein-Gar et al., 2012). A minor flaw makes highly competent people seem a bit more human, a bit more like the rest of us, and a bit less threatening (see **FIGURE 13.7**).

Relationships

Attraction is a feeling that can have important consequences, one of which is a relationship (Finkel et al., 2017). Most nonhuman animals have relationships that end about 10 seconds after sex is over, some have relationships that last through a breeding season, and a few have relationships that endure for years. The last group includes grey wolves, beavers, pigeons, and us. Human beings often have relationships that endure for a lifetime, or at least that they thought would endure for a lifetime when they signed up for them (Clark & Lemay, 2010). Why are we one of the animal kingdom's gold-medalists in the long-term relationships contest?

One slightly weird answer is that we have unusually large heads to house our unusually large brains. A fully developed human infant could not pass through its mother's birth canal, and so human mothers must give birth while their fetuses are still relatively underdeveloped—and underdeveloped newborns need a lot more care than one parent can easily provide. If newborn humans were more like newborn tadpoles—instantly ready to take off, find food, and escape predators—then their parents might not need to form enduring relationships (Eastwick, 2009). But human infants are just about the most helpless creatures on the planet and they require

Figure 13.7
To Err Is Human Participants in a study (Mirnig et al., 2017) worked with a robot to build a Lego tower. Sometimes the robot performed perfectly and sometimes it made minor mistakes, such as failing to grasp a block, or repeating a word too many times ("Let's build something from the yellow, yellow, yellow blocks"). Can you guess which of the robots participants liked best? That's right—the one that made mistakes. Minor flaws, it seems, can even humanize things that aren't.

Figure 13.8

Big Brain Baby Smart animals tend to have helpless infants. This figure shows the relationship between the intelligence of different primate species and the age at which their offspring stop nursing. As you can see, the smarter a species is, the longer its infants remain reliant on their parents, which means their parents need to stick together and stick around. DATA FROM PIANTADOSI & KIDD, 2016

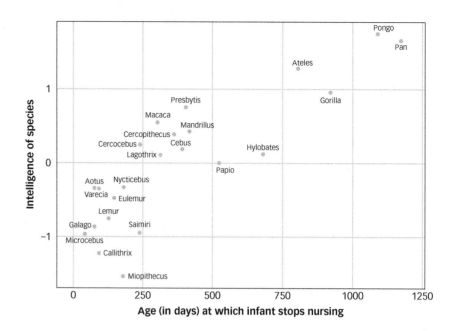

years of nurturing and protection before they can fend for themselves. And that's one reason humans tend to do their parenting in the context of committed, long-term relationships (see **FIGURE 13.8**).

Love and Commitment

In most cultures, adults settle into committed long-term relationships in which they live together, and often have children. Although such relationships have traditionally been celebrated with marriage, rates of marriage are declining in Canada—yet rates of enduring relationships are not. In 2017 (the most recent data), almost 3 in 4 Canadians aged 25–64 lived with a partner, and nearly 4 in 5 of these couples were married, with the rest living in common law. The rate of common-law unions has increased dramatically in Canada in the last few decades, from 6 in 100 couples in 1981, to 1 in 5 couples in 2017 (Statistics Canada, 2019).

Throughout history, marriage has traditionally served a variety of economic, practical, and decidedly unromantic functions, ranging from cementing agreements between clans to paying back debts. In North America, marriage was traditionally regarded as an alliance that helped people fulfill basic needs, such as growing food, building shelter, and protecting each other from violence. The fact is that people have been falling in love forever, but it wasn't until the 20th century in Western countries that they began thinking of love as a reason to marry (Finkel, 2017).

So what is romantic love? Psychologists distinguish two basic kinds: **passionate love,** which is *an experience involving feelings of euphoria, intimacy, and intense sexual attraction,* and **companionate love,** which is *an experience involving affection, trust, and concern for a partner's well-being* (Acevedo & Aron, 2009; Hatfield, 1988; Rubin, 1973; Sternberg, 1986). The ideal romantic relationship gives rise to both types of love, but the speeds, trajectories, and durations of the two experiences are markedly different (see **FIGURE 13.9**). Passionate love is what brings people together: It has a rapid onset, reaches its peak quickly, and generally begins to diminish within just a few months (Aron et al., 2005). Companionate love is what keeps people together: It takes some time to get started, grows slowly, and need never stop growing (Gonzaga et al., 2001). Companionate love is more strongly associated with marital satisfaction than is passionate love (Sprecher & Regan, 1998), which may explain why the people who get the greatest happiness from their marriages are those who say their

passionate love An experience involving feelings of euphoria, intimacy, and intense sexual attraction.

companionate love An experience involving affection, trust, and concern for a partner's well-being.

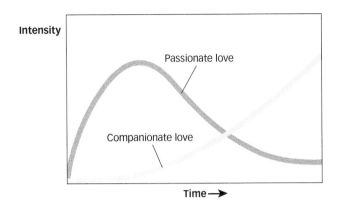

Figure 13.9
Passionate and Companionate Love
Passionate and companionate love have different time courses and trajectories. Passionate love begins to cool within just a few months, but companionate love can grow slowly yet steadily over years.

spouse is their best friend (Grover & Helliwell, 2019). But don't dismiss passionate love. Yes, it tends to decline over time, but that decline is not inevitable (Carswell et al., 2019), and research suggests that if it declines too quickly or too much, marriages suffer (Carswell & Finkel, 2018). Indeed, sexual satisfaction is one of the best predictors of marital satisfaction (Joel et al., 2020). It appears that both the friends part and the benefits part matter.

Divorce: Unmaking the Commitment

In 2017, there were 20 million Canadians aged 25–64, and 2.9 million of them (or almost 3 in every 20) had experienced at least one termination of a marriage or common-law relationship (Statistics Canada, 2017). A committed relationship offers benefits (such as love, regular sex, and financial security), but it also imposes costs (such as additional responsibility, loss of personal freedom, and the potential for interpersonal conflict). According to *interdependence theory* (Kelley & Thibaut, 1978), people tend to remain in relationships only as long as they perceive a favourable ratio of costs to benefits. What exactly does "favourable" mean?

Whether a person considers a particular cost–benefit ratio to be favourable depends on at least two things (Le & Agnew, 2003; Lemay, 2016; Rusbult & Van Lange, 2003). First, it depends on the person's **comparison level for alternatives,** which is *the cost/benefit ratio that a person believes they could attain in another relationship.* A cost/benefit ratio that seems favourable to two people stranded on a desert island may seem unfavourable to two people who live in a large city filled with other potential partners. And indeed, research shows that the better a person's imagined alternatives are, the more likely that person is to break up with their current partner (Simpson, 1987).

Second, the favourability of a cost/benefit ratio depends on how much the person has already invested in the relationship. A ratio that seems favourable to people who have been in a committed relationship for many years may seem unfavourable to people who have been in a committed relationship for just a few months, which is one of the reasons new committed relationships are more likely to end than old ones are (Bramlett & Mosher, 2002; Cherlin, 1992). Indeed, people have to be very unhappy to end a very long-term committed relationship, but only moderately unhappy to end a new one (White & Booth, 1991). It is also worth noting that people care about their partners' cost/benefit ratio as well as their own. **Equity** is *a state of affairs in which the cost/benefit ratios of two partners are roughly equally favourable* (Bolton & Ockenfels, 2000; Messick & Cook, 1983; Walster et al., 1978), and research suggests that while people are naturally distressed when their own ratio is less favourable than their partner's ratio, they are also distressed when it is *more* favourable (Schafer & Keith, 1980).

comparison level for alternatives The cost–benefit ratio that a person believes they could attain in another relationship.

equity A state of affairs in which the cost/benefit ratios of two partners are roughly equally favourable.

Interpersonal Perception

Learning Outcomes

WHAT YOU NEED TO KNOW

- Explain how stereotypes cause people to draw inaccurate conclusions about others.

- Explain why stereotypes are so difficult to overcome.

- Explain what an attribution is and what kinds of errors attributions entail.

Kanye West is a creative genius—or at least that's what he tells anyone who will listen. Whether or not you agree with his self-assessment, just reading that sentence probably activated your medial prefrontal cortex, an area of your brain that becomes especially active when you think about other people but not when you think about inanimate objects such as houses or tools (Mitchell et al., 2002). Although most of your brain shows diminished activity when you are at rest, this area remains active all the time (Buckner et al., 2008; Spunt et al., 2015). Now, that's odd. The world has more rocks and trees and ants than humans, so why should your brain have a special area devoted to processing information about one particular mammal? And why is that area active all the time?

The answer is that we are the most social species on Earth, and our survival and reproduction depends much more on other humans than on rocks or trees or ants. **Social cognition** is *the processes by which people understand others,* and your brain is busy doing it all day long. Whether you know it or not, your brain is constantly making inferences about other people's thoughts and feelings, beliefs and desires, abilities and aspirations, intentions, needs, and characters. These inferences are of two general kinds: **Category-based inferences** are *inferences based on information about the categories to which a person belongs,* and **target-based inferences** are *inferences based on information about an individual's behaviour.* As you are about to see, both kinds of information are essential, but both can be misused.

Stereotyping: The Problem with Category-Based Inferences

One of the mind's best tricks is that it can put new things into old categories. As soon as you categorize a novel stimulus ("That's a textbook"), you can use your knowledge of the category to make educated guesses about the stimulus ("It's probably expensive") and then act accordingly towards it ("I think I'll borrow my friend's copy").

What the mind does with textbooks it also does with people. **Stereotyping** is *the process of drawing inferences about individuals based on their category membership.* The moment we categorize a person as a male baseball player from Japan, we can use our knowledge of those categories to make some educated guesses about him—for example, that he shaves his face but not his legs, that he understands the infield fly rule, and that he knows more about Tokyo than we do. When we give an older person our seat instead of our phone number, quiz our server about the fried zucchini instead of Fermat's Last Theorem, or comfort a lost child with candy instead of a martini, we are making inferences about people whom we have never met based solely on their category membership. As these examples suggest, stereotyping is not just useful—it is essential (Allport, 1954; Liberman et al., 2017). Without it, the world would be filled with perplexed seniors, irritated waiters, and children hoping to get lost more often.

And yet, ever since the journalist Walter Lippmann coined the word "stereotype" in 1936, it has had an unpleasant connotation, and that's because stereotyping is a helpful process that often produces harmful results. **Prejudice** is *a negative evaluation of another person based solely on their category membership* and **discrimination** is *negative behaviour towards another person based solely on their category membership* (Dovidio & Gaertner, 2010), and stereotyping can lead to both. Stereotypes have four properties that make them subject to misuse, and we will examine each of those properties in turn.

social cognition The processes by which people come to understand others.

category-based inferences Inferences based on information about the categories to which a person belongs.

target-based inferences Inferences based on information about an individual's behaviour.

stereotyping The process of drawing inferences about individuals based on their category membership.

prejudice A negative evaluation of another person based solely on their category membership

discrimination Negative behaviour towards another person based solely on their category membership.

Stereotypes Can Be Inaccurate

Canadians and Americans have a wide range of stereotypes that vary on two dimensions: warmth and competence (Cuddy et al., 2007; Fiske, 2012, 2018). When we say that someone is kind or unkind, honest or dishonest, we are talking about their warmth or about how much we like them; and when we say that someone is intelligent or unintelligent, powerful or powerless, we are talking about their competence or about their ability to accomplish their goals. As **FIGURE 13.10** shows, Canadians consider some categories of people to be warm and competent (women), others to be warm but incompetent (the elderly), others to be cold and competent (the rich), and others to be cold and incompetent (the poor). Some stereotypes are accurate: It seems highly likely that, on average, educated professionals have advantages that allow them to accomplish their goals more easily than impoverished people or people with intellectual disabilities can. But other stereotypes are inaccurate: Many Vancouverites are couch potatoes who do not spend their weekends hiking. So where do these inaccurate stereotypes come from?

Most of our inaccurate stereotypes are picked up from other people. We read tweets, watch shows, listen to songs, overhear our friends talking, and all of these can be sources of inaccurate stereotypes. When Jay Electronica rapped, "And I bet you a Rothschild I get a bang for my dollar / The synagogue of Satan want me to hang by my collar," it is not surprising that some listeners' inaccurate stereotypes of Jews were reinforced (Friedman, 2020). The transmission of stereotypes doesn't even require words. One study found that children can acquire inaccurate stereotypes simply by seeing adults smile or frown at members of the stereotyped group (Skinner et al., 2020).

Inaccurate stereotypes can also come from our own observation. For example, research participants in one study were shown a long series of positive and negative behaviours and were told that each behaviour had been performed by a member of one of two groups: Group A or Group B (see **FIGURE 13.11**). The behaviours were carefully arranged so that each group behaved negatively exactly one third of the time. They were also carefully arranged so that there were more positive than negative behaviours in the series, and more members of Group A than of Group B. As such, participants saw (1) more positive behaviours than negative behaviours, and (2) more Group A members than Group B members. After seeing all the behaviours, participants correctly reported that Group A had behaved negatively one third of the time—but

Gurdeep Pandher lives in Whitehorse Yukon, where he dances and teaches Bhangra. Stereotypes of Sikhs, or Yukoners, don't generally accommodate Gurdeep, and Gurdeep works every day to change that!

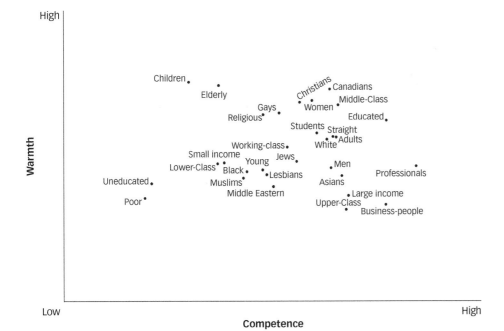

Figure 13.10

Stereotype Content Stereotypes tend to vary on the dimensions of warmth and competence. This figure shows how Canadians see Canadian groups in terms of these two dimensions. DATA FROM FISKE, 2012.

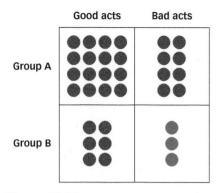

Figure 13.11
Seeing Correlations That Aren't Really There Both Group A and Group B engage in bad behaviour one third of the time, so there is no real difference in the average "badness" of the two groups. However, bad behaviour and Group B membership are both uncommon, and when two uncommon things happen at the same time, we tend to notice and remember. This tendency can lead us to see a relationship between group membership and bad behaviour that isn't really there.

they incorrectly reported that Group B had behaved negatively more than *half* the time (Hamilton & Gifford, 1976). Why? Both *bad behaviour* and *Group B membership* were uncommon, and when two uncommon things happen at the same time, people pay special attention ("Look! There's one of those Group B people doing something terrible"). That's one reason why members of majority groups often overestimate the number of violent crimes (which are relatively uncommon events) committed by members of minority groups (who are relatively uncommon people, hence the word *m-i-n-o-r-i-t-y*). The bottom line is that even when we directly observe people, we can still end up with inaccurate beliefs about the groups to which they belong.

Stereotypes Can Be Overused

Because all thumbtacks are pretty much alike, we are rarely mistaken when we use our stereotypes (small, cheap, and painful when chewed) to generalize from one thumbtack to another. But human categories are so variable that our stereotypes may offer only the vaguest of clues about the individuals who populate those categories. You probably believe that males have greater upper body strength than females do, and this belief is right—*on average*. But the upper body strength of the individuals *within* each of these gender categories is so varied that knowing a person's sex doesn't give you *a lot* of insight into how much weight they can lift. If you randomly selected males and females from a population and bet each time that the male could lift more weight, you'd be right more often than wrong—but you'd still be wrong *a lot*.

Stereotypes, then, are most useful when variability is low and least useful when variability is high—and in human categories, variability is almost always high. Why don't we recognize the high variability of human categories? One reason is that the mere act of categorizing a stimulus makes us believe that the category is less variable than it actually is, and that stereotypes are therefore more useful than they actually are. Participants in one study were shown a series of lines of different lengths (see **FIGURE 13.12**; McGarty & Turner, 1992; Tajfel & Wilkes, 1963). For one group of participants, the longest lines were labelled *Group A* and the shortest lines were labelled *Group B*, as shown on the right side of Figure 13.12. For the second group of participants, the lines were shown without these category labels, as they are on the left side of Figure 13.12. Did placing the lines in categories change the way participants saw them? Indeed, it did. When participants were later asked to remember the lengths of the lines, participants who had seen the category labels tended to underestimate the variability of the lines that shared a label. Simply placing lines of different lengths in the same category led participants to see them as more similar than they really were.

You have experienced this yourself if you've ever looked at a rainbow. (And if you haven't, then you're really missing out.) Because we think of colours by their category labels (e.g., blue or green), we tend to overestimate the similarity of colours that share a label. As such, we see discrete *bands* of colour when we look at rainbows, but—news alert!—rainbows do not have bands. The colours in a rainbow vary across a smooth chromatic continuum, and the apparently clear difference

Figure 13.12
Categorization Reduces Perceived Variability People see less variability among lines 1–3 (and also among lines 4–6) if they see them labelled as they are on the right (Group A and Group B boxes), than if they see them unlabelled as they are in the left box.

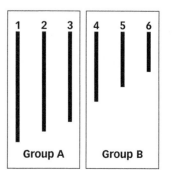

between the yellow band and the green band is just an effect of identifying colours by their category (see **FIGURE 13.13**). The same thing happens when we estimate distances. Memphis, Tennessee, is slightly closer to Toronto than to Pierre, South Dakota, and yet, people think Memphis is closer to Pierre than to Toronto. Why? Because Memphis and Pierre are both members of the category "American towns," but Toronto is not (Burris & Branscombe, 2005). Indeed, people are more likely to predict that they will feel an earthquake whose epicentre is exactly 230 miles away when that epicentre is in the same American state rather than in a neighbouring state (Mishra & Mishra, 2010).

What is true of colours and cities is true of people as well. The mere act of categorizing people as Asian or Indigenous, as Jewish or Sikh, as artists or accountants, can cause us to underestimate the variability within those categories, which naturally leads us to overestimate how useful our stereotypes about those categories will be (Park & Hastie, 1987; Rubin & Badea, 2012).

Stereotypes Can Be Self-Perpetuating

When we meet a linebacker who likes ballet more than wrestling, or a Newfoundlander who likes tacos more than fish and chips, why don't we revise or abandon our stereotypes of these groups? The answer is that stereotypes tend to be self-perpetuating. Like viruses and parasites, once they take up residence inside us, they resist even our most concerted efforts to eradicate them. When a person who holds a stereotype (the observer) interacts with a person about whom that stereotype is held (the target), three things can happen that may perpetuate that stereotype:

- **Behavioural confirmation** (also known as "self-fulfilling prophecy") is *the tendency of targets to behave as observers expect them to behave.* For instance, when targets know that observers have a negative stereotype about them, they may experience **stereotype threat,** which is *the anxiety associated with the possibility of confirming other people's stereotypes about one's group* (Aronson & Steele, 2004; Schmader et al., 2008; Spencer et al., 2016; Walton & Spencer, 2009). Ironically, this anxiety may cause targets to behave in ways that confirm the very stereotype that threatened them. In one study (Steele & Aronson, 1995), Black students and white students took a test, and half the students in each group were asked to list their race at the top of the exam. When students were not asked to list their race, the students all performed at their academic level; but when the students were asked to list their races, Black students became anxious about confirming a negative stereotype of their group, which caused them to perform below their academic level. Stereotypes perpetuate themselves in part by causing targets to behave in precisely the ways that observers expect, thereby confirming the observers' stereotypes (Klein & Snyder, 2003).

- Even when targets do *not* confirm observers' stereotypes, observers may mistakenly think that they have. **Perceptual confirmation** is *the tendency of observers to see what they expect to see,* which can perpetuate the observer's stereotypes. In one American study, participants listened to a radio broadcast of a men's varsity basketball game (Stone et al., 1997). Some participants were led to believe that a particular player was Black while others were led to believe that he was white. After listening to the game, participants evaluated the player's performance. When participants thought the player was Black, they reported that he had shown more athletic ability and played a better game; when they thought he was white, they reported that he had shown more basketball intelligence and hustle. Keep in mind that the participants who drew these disparate conclusions had all listened to *the same game!* Stereotypes perpetuate themselves in part by biasing our perception of individuals, leading us to believe that those individuals have confirmed our stereotypes even when they have not (Fiske, 1998).

GOODSHOOT/GETTY IMAGES

Figure 13.13
Perceiving Categories Categorization can influence how we see colours and estimate distances.

behavioural confirmation
The tendency of targets to behave as observers expect them to behave.

stereotype threat The anxiety associated with the possibility of confirming other people's stereotypes about one's group.

perceptual confirmation
The tendency of observers to see what they expect to see.

The Implicit Association Test measures how easily people can learn to associate two things (Greenwald et al., 1998). Studies using the test show that 70% of white Americans find it easier to associate white faces with positive concepts, such as "peace," and Black faces with negative concepts, such as "bomb," than the other way around. Surprisingly, 40% of Black Americans show this same pattern. You can take the IAT yourself at https://implicit.harvard.edu/implicit/

subtyping The tendency of observers to think of targets who disconfirm stereotypes as "exceptions to the rule."

• So what happens when targets clearly *disconfirm* an observer's stereotypes? **Subtyping** is *the tendency of observers to think of targets who disconfirm stereotypes as "exceptions to the rule"* (Weber & Crocker, 1983). For example, most of us think of people who work in public relations as sociable. In one study, participants learned about a PR agent who was *slightly* unsociable, and the results showed that their stereotypes about PR agents shifted a bit to accommodate this new information. So far, so good. But when participants learned about a PR agent who was *extremely* unsociable, their stereotypes did not change at all (Kunda & Oleson, 1997). Instead, they decided that the extremely unsociable PR agent was a rare "subtype" of PR agents — an "exception to the rule" — which allowed them to keep their stereotypes intact. Subtyping is a powerful method by which stereotypes preserve themselves in the face of clearly disconfirming evidence.

Stereotyping Can Be Unconscious and Automatic

Once we recognize that a stereotype is inaccurate and self-perpetuating, why don't we just make a firm resolution to stop using it? One reason is that we probably didn't realize we *were* using it in the first place! Stereotyping often happens *unconsciously* (which means that we don't always know we are doing it) and *automatically* (which means that we often cannot avoid doing it even when we try) (Banaji & Heiphetz, 2010; Greenwald et al., 1998; Greenwald & Nosek, 2001).

Almost all of the research on unconscious stereotyping comes from psychology laboratories in the United States. In Canada, very few researchers work on unconscious and automatic stereotyping, although all the evidence suggests that Canadians harbour just as much unconscious and automatic bias as Americans.

For example, a recent survey asked people whether in the last 5 years they had experienced "discrimination or been treated unfairly by others in Canada because of their sex, ethnicity or culture, race or skin colour, physical appearance, religion, sexual orientation, gender identity or expression, age, physical or mental disability, language, or another reason." The results for visible minorities are shown in **FIGURE 13.14**. One in 3 Indigenous people and 1 in 2 Black people living in Canada reported that they had experienced discrimination (Statistics Canada, 2022). For this reason, although the research reported below is American, do not think that it only applies in the United States.

In one American study, American participants played a video game in which photos of Black or white men holding either guns or cameras were flashed on the

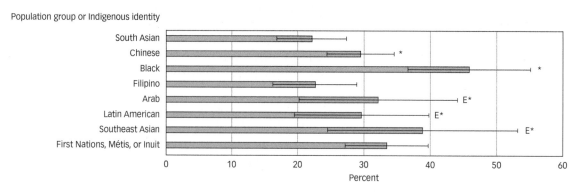

Figure 13.14

Experience of Discrimination by Population Group or Indigenous Identity The General Social Survey on Canadians' Safety (Victimization), 2019, was a national survey of 20,000 adults living in Canada. People self-identified as belonging to different groups, including the visible minority groups shown here. This graph shows the proportion of respondents from each visible minority group who reported experiencing discrimination in the years 2014–2019. DATA FROM STATISTICS CANADA, GENERAL SOCIAL SURVEY CANADIANS' SAFETY (VICTIMIZATION), 2019.

screen for less than 1 second each. Participants earned money by shooting men with guns and lost money by shooting men with cameras. The results showed that when participants made mistakes, they tended to be of two kinds: They shot Black men holding cameras and failed to shoot white men holding guns (Correll et al., 2002). The photos appeared on the screen so quickly that participants did not have enough time to consciously consider their stereotypes, but that didn't matter because their stereotypes were working unconsciously, causing them to mistake a camera for a gun when it was in the hands of a Black man and to mistake a gun for a camera when it was in the hands of a white man (Correll et al., 2015).

Were these white participants just a bunch of racists? Probably not, because Black participants showed this same pattern of errors. Stereotypes comprise all the information about human categories that we have encountered and absorbed over the years—information from friends and uncles, books and blogs, jokes and movies and late-night television. When we see Black men holding guns in crime dramas and rap videos, our minds naturally associate these two things, and although we know that we are seeing art and not news, our brains make and remember the association anyway because, as you saw in the Memory chapter and the Learning chapter, associating things that co-occur is one of the tricks that our brains do best. Once our brains have made these associations, we can't just *decide* not to be influenced by them any more than Pavlov's dogs could *decide* not to salivate when they heard the tone that they had come to associate with the appearance of food. In fact, some research suggests that consciously trying not to use a stereotype can cause us to use it even more (Macrae et al., 1994).

The effects of implicit bias can be devastating. In Canada, for example, race-based legislation has normalized serious inequities in health funding, resources, and services that systematically disadvantage Indigenous groups (Allan & Smylie, 2015). Indigenous individuals also experience and anticipate racist treatment by health care providers: Anticipation of racist treatment in Canada is at least a barrier to care and prevents some Indigenous individuals from seeking treatment altogether (Browne et al., 2011). In the United States, it is well established that minorities receive fewer procedures and poorer quality medical care (Williams & Wyatt, 2015). Although systematic research has not been done, it seems reasonable to assume that this is the case in Canada as well. Unconscious bias can literally be a matter of life and death.

Are the Undesirable Consequences of Stereotyping Inevitable?

Although stereotyping is unconscious and automatic, its undesirable consequences are not inevitable (Blair, 2002; Kawakami et al., 2000; Milne & Grafman, 2001; Rudman et al., 2001). For instance, American police officers who receive special training before playing the camera-or-gun video game described earlier do not show the same biases that ordinary people do (Correll et al., 2007; Johnson et al., 2018). Like most people, they take a few milliseconds longer to decide not to shoot a Black man than a white man, indicating that their stereotypes are still unconsciously and automatically influencing their perception; but they don't actually *shoot* Black men more often than white men, indicating that they have learned how to keep their stereotypes from influencing their behaviour (Phills et al., 2011; Todd et al., 2011). Other studies suggest that because stereotypes reflect all the information to which people are exposed through videos, advertisements, newscasts, and social media, changing that information can change the stereotypes. In laboratory experiments, for example, white participants who are exposed to pictures of Black people whom everyone admires (e.g., Michael Jordan and Denzel Washington) show a reduction in automatic anti-Black bias (Dasgupta, 2013).

Which techniques are most effective? In 2014, a team of American psychologists held a contest in which they invited researchers to submit techniques for reducing unconscious stereotyping of Blacks, and then tested each of the techniques against the other. As **FIGURE 13.15** shows, about half the techniques had some effect, and these tended to be techniques that exposed whites to examples of Blacks who defied their stereotypes. For example, the most effective technique asked participants to

Figure 13.15
Stereotype Reduction Contest Results of a study that compared 18 techniques for reducing unconscious stereotyping of Blacks by whites in the United States (Lai et al., 2014).

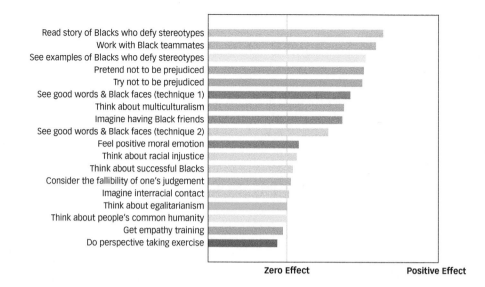

imagine in gory detail that they were being assaulted by a white man and then to imagine being rescued by a Black man. The least effective techniques were those that simply encouraged people to feel compassion towards or to take the perspective of a Black person (see A World of Difference: What's It Like to Be You?). Alas, even the best techniques were not very good: They tended to produce small and short-lived changes in unconscious bias, and those changes were not associated with any changes in people's conscious beliefs or actual behaviour (Forscher et al., 2019).

These findings are troubling for many reasons, not the least of which is that many of the failed techniques look a lot like the programs commonly used in schools, businesses, and other organizations to reduce unconscious stereotyping or "implicit bias." Today, most large American companies have some form of diversity training, as do the vast majority of colleges and universities, and yet "two-thirds of human resources specialists report that diversity training does not have positive effects, and several field studies have found no effect of diversity training on women's or minorities' careers or on managerial diversity" (Dobbin & Kalev, 2018, p. 48). Indeed, one recent large-scale study found that diversity training changes the behaviour of only the most egalitarian people—that is, the people who needed it the least (Chang et al., 2019). A team of psychologists who conducted a thorough review of the scientific literature on "multicultural education, anti-bias instruction more generally, workplace diversity initiatives, dialogue groups, cooperative learning, moral and values education, inter-group contact, peace education, media interventions, reading interventions, intercultural and sensitivity training, cognitive training, and a host of miscellaneous techniques and interventions" reluctantly concluded that "we currently do not know whether a wide range of programs and policies tend to work on average, and we are quite far from having an empirically grounded understanding of the conditions under which these programs work best" (Paluck & Green, 2009, p. 357). The fact is that psychologists do not yet have a powerful way to eliminate the pernicious effects of stereotyping.

Attribution: The Problem with Target-Based Inferences

In 1963, Dr. Martin Luther King Jr. gave a speech in which he described his vision for America: "I have a dream that my four children will one day live in a nation where they will not be judged by the colour of their skin but by the content of their character." Research on stereotyping suggests that Dr. King's concern continues to be well-justified. We do judge others by the colour of their skin—as well as by their

A World of Difference · What's It Like to Be You?

In order to encourage diversity and inclusion, many organizations ask their members to participate in "perspective-taking exercises" that are meant to help them understand the world from other people's points of view. On the face of it, this seems like a promising idea. Maybe it works and maybe it doesn't, but what could possibly be the harm of taking some time to think about what it's like to live inside another person's skin?

That's what Silverman et al. (2014) wondered when they gave sighted people the opportunity to experience blindness and then measured how well the participants really understood what it's like to be a blind person. Participants reported to the laboratory, were blindfolded, and were then asked to perform a variety of ordinary tasks, ranging from filling a glass with water to finding the stairwell in a hallway. Participants in a control condition merely watched the first group perform these tasks. After either performing these tasks or watching others perform them, all participants reported their feelings towards blind people and then estimated how capable blind people are of working and living independently.

Wearing the blindfold did precisely what we might have hoped it would do: It made participants feel more compassionate—more empathetic, friendly, open, sympathetic, and warm towards blind people. So, was the exercise a success? Not exactly. Because compared with observers, participants who wore the blindfold also came to believe that blind people are much *less* competent and capable—less able to get around a city, to cook, to own their own business, to teach school or become an accountant, and so on. In other words, taking a blind person's perspective for a few minutes led participants to conclude that blind people were not capable of doing most of the tasks that daily life requires.

And that's just not true. Most blind people are perfectly capable of performing ordinary tasks, such as pouring water and finding a stairwell, and perfectly capable of performing jobs from schoolteacher to accountant. Blindness is a disability to which people adapt extraordinarily well over time, and although there are a few things that blind people can't do as well as sighted people can (e.g., driving a car on the street), there are other things they can do even better (e.g., hearing a car on the street). Participants in this study had enough time to experience blindness but not enough time to adapt to it. Being blindfolded for a few minutes made them more compassionate towards blind people, but it also led them to mistakenly believe that they understood what a lifetime of blindness was like when they'd only experienced a few minutes of it. Rather than becoming more accurate about what it is like to be disabled, they became less accurate.

All of us are trapped inside our own skins and we can never really know what another person's experience of the world is like. Well-meaning exercises that are designed to expand our perspectives can sometimes do the opposite, suggesting that organizations would do well to consult with psychologists before implementing remedies that can make problems worse instead of better.

Paul Scruggs is blind, but that doesn't prevent him from working as a machine operator in a factory that makes military uniforms. You too could probably run this machine with your eyes closed—but not in the first hour of trying.

gender, nationality, religion, age, sexual orientation, and occupation—and in so doing, we often make consequential errors. But are we any better at judging people by the content of their characters? If we could magically "turn off" our stereotypes and treat each person as a unique individual, would we judge them accurately?

Dispositions Versus Situations

The clear answer is no. Treating people as individuals means judging them by their own words and deeds, but this is more difficult than it sounds because what a person says and does is not necessarily a good indicator of what that person is actually like. Honest people sometimes lie to save a friend from embarrassment and dishonest people sometimes tell the truth to bolster their credibility. Happy people sometimes weep at funerals and polite people are sometimes rude in traffic. The fact is that an individual's behaviour can sometimes tell us about the kind of person they are, but

Figure 13.16
Three Attributional Questions To determine whether we should attribute a person's behaviour to the situation or to that person's dispositions, we simply need to ask whether the behaviour is consistent, consensual, and distinctive.

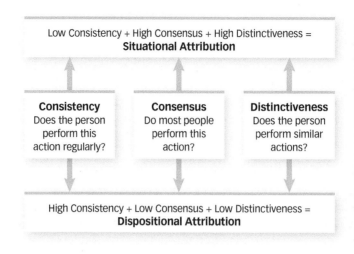

Low Consistency + High Consensus + High Distinctiveness =
Situational Attribution

Consistency
Does the person perform this action regularly?

Consensus
Do most people perform this action?

Distinctiveness
Does the person perform similar actions?

High Consistency + Low Consensus + Low Distinctiveness =
Dispositional Attribution

sometimes it just tells us about the kinds of situations they're in. To know a person, we need to know not only *what* they said and did but also *why* they said and did it. Is the politician who gave the pro-life speech really opposed to abortion or were they just trying to win the conservative vote? Is the batter who hit the home run a talented slugger or was the wind blowing in just the right direction?

When we try to answer questions such as these, we are making an **attribution,** which is *an inference about the cause of a person's behaviour* (Epley & Waytz, 2010; Gilbert, 1998). We make *situational attributions* when we decide that a person's behaviour was caused by some temporary aspect of the situation in which it happened ("The batter was lucky that the wind carried the ball into the stands"), and we make *dispositional attributions* when we decide that a person's behaviour was caused by a relatively enduring tendency to think, feel, or act in a particular way ("The batter has a great eye and a powerful swing"). Deciding which of these attributions to make requires answering three questions (Kelley, 1967). For example, why do you think the man in **FIGURE 13.16** is wearing a watermelon helmet? Is it because he has a goofy personality (a dispositional attribution) or because he's a perfectly normal guy who just happens to be on his way to a Saskatchewan football game (a situational attribution)? To answer that question, you should first answer these:

- Is his behaviour consistent (i.e., does he usually wear a watermelon helmet?)
- Is his behaviour consensual (i.e., are other people wearing watermelon helmets?)
- Is his behaviour distinctive (i.e., is this the only goofy thing he does?).

If you can answer these three questions, then you will know whether you should make a dispositional or situational attribution for his behaviour. For instance, if he wears this helmet every day (his behaviour is consistent), and if no one else wears this helmet (his behaviour is not consensual), and if he does lots of other goofy things (his behaviour is not distinctive), then you should make a dispositional attribution ("He's an eccentric"). On the other hand, if he rarely wears a watermelon helmet (his behaviour is not consistent), and if lots of other people are wearing watermelon helmets (his behaviour is consensual), and if he doesn't tend to do other goofy things (his behaviour is distinctive), then you should make a situational attribution ("He's a Roughriders fan on game day"). As Figure 13.16 shows, patterns of consistency, consensus, and distinctiveness provide the information we need to determine the true cause of the man's behaviour.

Attribution Errors

As sensible as this analysis may seem, research suggests that people don't always do it, and as a result, often make the wrong attribution. And when they make the wrong attribution, it is typically the dispositional one! The **fundamental attribution error** is *the*

attribution An inference about the cause of a person's behaviour.

fundamental attribution error The tendency to make a dispositional attribution even when we should instead make a situational attribution.

tendency to make a dispositional attribution when we should instead make a situational attribution (Gilbert & Malone, 1995; Jones & Harris, 1967; Ross, 1977), and it is an error to which people are extraordinarily prone. In one experiment (Ross et al., 1977), participants played a trivia game in which one participant played the role of the quizmaster and made up a list of unusual questions, a second participant played the role of the contestant and tried to answer those questions, and a third participant played the role of the observer and simply watched the game. The quizmasters had a stupendous advantage, of course, because they could ask any tricky question they wished based on their own idiosyncratic knowledge ("What store sells the shoes I am wearing?"). So it wasn't too surprising that contestants were unable to answer most of them.

After watching the game, the observers were asked to estimate how smart the quizmaster and the contestant were. Although the quizmasters had asked good questions and the contestants had given bad answers, it should have been clear to the observers that this discrepancy was merely a product of the roles to which they had been assigned. Quizmasters had been given an easy job, contestants had been given a hard one, and if their roles had been reversed, the participant who had played the role of contestant would have asked impossible questions and the participant who played the role of quizmaster would have given terrible answers. It should have been clear, but it wasn't. Instead, observers mistakenly attributed the other participants' performances to their dispositions, concluding that the quizmasters were genuinely *smarter* than the contestants. It seems that even when we know that a successful athlete had a home-field advantage or that a successful entrepreneur had family connections, we tend to attribute their success to talent and tenacity.

What causes the fundamental attribution error? At least two things:

"I think success is all perspiration. You make your own luck," said Robert Herjavec, a successful businessman and a judge on "Shark Tank." But research on the fundamental attribution error suggests that it is all too easy to credit success to intelligence and tenacity, and all too easy to blame failure on stupidity and laziness.

- First, people don't consider the situational causes of behaviour because those causes are often invisible (Ichheiser, 1949). Professors tend to think that fawning students really do admire them despite the strong incentive for students to kiss up to those who control their grades—and they think this because professors can *see* their students laughing at witless jokes and applauding after boring lectures, but they cannot *see* "control over grades." Situations are not as palpable, tangible, or salient as behaviours, so it is all too easy to ignore them (Taylor & Fiske, 1975).

- Second, situational attributions are more difficult to make. In one study (Gilbert et al., 1988), participants were asked to make attributions while simultaneously performing a mentally demanding task (i.e., keeping a seven-digit number in short-term memory). They had no trouble making dispositional attributions, but they found it nearly impossible to make situational attributions simply because the former took less concentration than the latter.

In short, information about situations is hard to get and hard to use, so we tend to believe that other peoples' actions are caused by their dispositions even when there is a perfectly reasonable situational explanation for them.

The fundamental attribution error is stronger in some cultures than in others (Choi et al., 1999) and among some people than others (D'Agostino & Fincher-Kiefer, 1992; Li et al., 2012). It is also stronger under some circumstances than others. For example, people are more likely to make the fundamental attribution error when they make attributions for other people's behaviour than when they make attributions for their own behaviour. The **actor–observer effect** is *the tendency to make situational attributions for our own behaviours while making dispositional attributions for the identical behaviour of others* (Jones & Nisbett, 1972). When university students are asked to explain why they and their friends chose their majors, they tend to make situational attributions for their own choices ("I chose economics because my parents told me I have to support myself as soon as I'm done with school") and dispositional attributions for their friends' choices ("Leah chose economics because she's materialistic") (Nisbett et al., 1973).

actor–observer effect The tendency to make situational attributions for our own behaviours while making dispositional attributions for the identical behaviour of others.

The actor–observer effect occurs because people typically have more information about the situations that caused their own behaviour than about the situations that caused other people's behaviour. We will always remember getting the please-major-in-something-practical lecture from our parents, but we weren't at our friend's house to see them get the same lecture. As observers, our eyes are focused on other people's behaviour, but as actors, our eyes are quite literally focused on the situations to which our own behaviour is a response. That's why when people are allowed to see themselves on video, and therefore to see their own behaviour as observers see it, they suddenly make dispositional attributions about themselves (Storms, 1973; Taylor & Fiske, 1975).

What are we to make of these attribution errors? Are they just technical fouls, mistakes around the margin, or do they really matter? Gustav Ichheiser was the first psychologist to describe the fundamental attribution error, and he thought it mattered a lot. Ichheiser was a Jew whose entire family was murdered in the Nazi invasion of Austria. He fled to America, but things didn't go well for him there. He was poor, often unemployed, and ultimately took his own life in despair. But his writings about attribution were prescient. In 1949, he wrote:

> We all have in everyday life the tendency to interpret and evaluate the behaviour of other people in terms of specific personality characteristics rather than in terms of specific social situations in which those people are placed. . . . Many things which happened between the two world wars would not have happened if social blindness had not prevented the privileged from understanding the predicament of those who were living in an invisible jail. (p. 47)

Ichheiser thought the fundamental attribution error was a kind of "social blindness" that keeps us from seeing the "invisible jails" that shape the behaviour of those who are marginalized, or raised in poverty, or the victims of pogroms, and more. Instead of recognizing that these people are profoundly affected by situations beyond their control, we mistakenly attribute their life outcomes to their dispositions—to their choices and abilities and personalities and work ethics—and mistakenly conclude that they basically deserve what they've gotten (Lerner, 1980). The fundamental attribution error is not a mistake around the margin, but a significant source of human misunderstanding.

Interpersonal Influence

Learning Outcomes

WHAT YOU NEED TO KNOW

- Describe the hedonic motive and explain how appeals to it can backfire.
- Describe the approval motive and distinguish normative influence, conformity, and obedience.
- Describe the accuracy motive and distinguish informational influence, persuasion, and consistency.

If you grew up on superhero movies, you've probably thought a bit about which of the standard superpowers you'd most like to have. Super strength and super speed have obvious benefits, invisibility and X-ray vision could be interesting as well as lucrative, and there's a lot to be said for flying. But when it comes down to it, the ability to control other people would surely be the super-est of all powers. Why get in a death match with an alien overlord or rescue baby elephants from a burning zoo if you can convince someone else to do those jobs for you? The things we want from life—gourmet food, interesting jobs, big houses, fancy cars—can all be given to us by others, and the things we want most—loving families, loyal friends, admiring children, appreciative employers—cannot be acquired any other way. This super-power has a name: **social influence,** which is *the ability to change or direct another person's behaviour* (Cialdini & Goldstein, 2004).

How does social influence work? If you want someone's time, money, allegiance, or affection, you'd be wise to consider first what it is *they* want. People have three basic motivations that turn out to be the levers for almost all attempts at social influence. First, people are motivated to experience pleasure and to avoid experiencing pain (the *hedonic motive*). Second, people are motivated to be accepted and to avoid

hudabeauty Follow

1,388 posts   48.8m followers   884 following

HUDA KATTAN
Makeup Artist & Blogger @huda
Founder of @wishfulskin
Products are tested on Huda, NOT animals 🐾
#GloWish IS FINALLY HERE!!👇
bit.ly/34DbD7S

Huda Kattan is a social media influencer with nearly 50 million followers on Instagram alone. That's roughly the population of Canada, Finland, and Costa Rica combined. Although her posts may change people's choices of skin care products, they probably have less impact on people's choices of careers, political candidates, and investments. Is Huda influential? That depends on whether you think influence should be defined more by its scope or by its depth.

being rejected (the *approval motive*). Third, people are motivated to believe what is true and to avoid believing what is false (the *accuracy motive*). As you are about to see, most attempts at social influence appeal to one or more of these three basic motives (Bargh et al., 2010; Fiske, 2010).

The Hedonic Motive

Pleasure seeking is the most basic of all motives, and social influence often involves creating situations in which others can achieve more pleasure by doing what we want them to do than by doing something else. Parents, teachers, governments, and businesses influence our behaviour by offering rewards and threatening punishments. There's nothing mysterious about how these influence attempts work, and they are often quite effective. When the Republic of Singapore warned its citizens that anyone caught chewing gum in public would face a year in prison and a $5,500 fine, gum chewing in Singapore fell to an all-time low. The threat of incarceration really gets your attention.

Rewards and punishments can be effective, but they can also backfire. The **overjustification effect** occurs *when a reward decreases a person's intrinsic motivation to perform a behaviour* (Deci et al., 1999). In one study (Lepper et al., 1973), children were allowed to play with coloured markers, and some of the children received a Good Player Award for doing so. When the children were given markers the next day, those who had received an award the previous day were *less* likely to play with the markers than were those who had not received an award. Why? Because children who had received an award the first day came to think of drawing as something one does to win a reward, not as something one does because it's fun. If no one was going to give them a reward on the second day, then why should they waste their time playing with those stupid markers?

Rewards and punishments can also backfire simply because people resent being bribed with rewards or threatened with punishments. **Reactance** is *an unpleasant feeling that arises when people feel they are being coerced,* and when people experience reactance, they often try to alleviate it by doing the very thing they were being coerced *not* to do—just to prove to themselves that they can (Brehm, 1966). In one study (Pennebaker & Sanders, 1976), researchers placed signs in two washrooms on a university campus. One sign read "Please don't write on these walls" and the other read "Do not write on these walls under any circumstances." Two weeks later, the researchers returned to find that the walls in the second washroom had more graffiti than the walls in the first, presumably because students didn't appreciate the threatening tone of the second sign and wrote on the walls in defiance. No wonder the latest review of research on reactance is titled "Do not read this article" (Rosenberg & Siegel, 2018).

social influence The ability to change or direct another person's behaviour.

overjustification effect An effect that occurs when a reward decreases a person's intrinsic motivation to perform a behaviour.

reactance An unpleasant feeling that arises when people feel they are being coerced.

The Approval Motive

Other people are the only thing standing between us and starvation, predation, loneliness, and all the other things that make getting shipwrecked such a bad idea. We depend on others for safety, sustenance, and solidarity, which is why being rejected or excluded by others is one of the most painful of all human experiences (Chen et al., 2020; Eisenberger et al., 2003; Uskul & Over, 2014; Williams, 2007). We are powerfully motivated to have others accept us, like us, and approve of us (Baumeister & Leary, 1995; Leary, 2010)—a noble motive to be sure, but one that leaves us vulnerable to several forms of social influence.

Normative Influence: We Do What We Think Is Appropriate

To see this vulnerability in action, just consider this rule of elevator etiquette:

> *When you get on an elevator you are supposed to face forward and not talk to the person next to you even if you were talking to that person before you got on the elevator unless you are the only two people on the elevator in which case it's okay to talk and face sideways but still not backwards.*

Although no one ever taught you this long-winded rule, you probably picked it up somewhere along the way. The unwritten rules that govern social behaviour are called **norms,** which are *customary standards for behaviour that are widely shared by members of a culture* (Cialdini, 2013; Miller & Prentice, 1996; Hawkins et al., 2019). We learn norms with exceptional ease and we obey them with exceptional fidelity because we know that if we don't, others won't approve of us (Centola & Baronchelli, 2015). For example, every human culture has a **norm of reciprocity,** which is *the unwritten rule that people should benefit those who have benefited them* (Gouldner, 1960). When a friend buys you lunch, you eventually return the favour, and if you don't, your friend will have a variety of new names for you, none of them good. The norm of reciprocity is so strong that when researchers randomly selected the names of strangers from a database and sent them holiday cards, they received holiday cards back from most of them (Kunz & Woolcott, 1976).

Norms are a powerful weapon in the game of social influence (Miller & Prentice, 2016). **Normative influence** occurs when *another person's behaviour provides information about what is appropriate* (see **FIGURE 13.17**). For example, restaurant servers sometimes give customers a piece of candy along with the bill because they

norms Customary standards for behaviour that are widely shared by members of a culture.

norm of reciprocity The unwritten rule that people should benefit those who have benefited them.

normative influence A phenomenon in which another person's behaviour provides information about what is appropriate.

Figure 13.17

The Perils of Connection Other people's behaviour defines what is normal, so we tend to do the things we see others doing. Overeating is one of those things. Research shows that if someone you know becomes obese, your chances of becoming obese can increase dramatically (Christakis & Fowler, 2007).

On average, your risk of becoming obese increases by ...

... **57%** if someone you consider a friend becomes obese.

... **171%** if a very close friend becomes obese.

... **100%** if you are a man and your male friend becomes obese.

... **38%** if you are a woman and your female friend becomes obese.

... **37%** if your spouse becomes obese.

... **40%** if one of your siblings becomes obese.

... **67%** if you are a woman and your sister becomes obese.

... **44%** if you are a man and your brother becomes obese.

FRANCIS DEAN/DEAN PICTURES/TOPFOTO

know about the norm of reciprocity, and indeed, studies show that customers who receive a candy feel obligated to do "a little extra" for the server who did "a little extra" for them and leave bigger tips (Strohmetz et al., 2002). People sometimes refuse gifts precisely because they don't want to feel indebted to the gift giver (Shen et al., 2011). Grocery stores offer free samples because customers who accept the gift of a sample often feel obligated to buy the product; and some customers refuse the sample precisely because they don't want to feel obligated to buy the product.

The norm of reciprocity involves swapping favours (e.g., candy for tips, or product samples for product purchases). But the thing being swapped doesn't have to be a favour. It can also be a concession. The **door-in-the-face technique** is *an influence strategy that involves getting someone to accept a small request by first getting them to refuse a large request.* Here's how it works: You ask someone for something more valuable than you really want, you wait for that person to refuse (to "slam the door in your face"), and then you ask the person for what you really wanted in the first place. For example, in one study (Cialdini et al., 1975), researchers asked some university students to volunteer to supervise adolescents who were going on a field trip. Only 17% of them said yes. Then the researchers asked a new group of students to commit to spending 2 hours per week for 2 years working at a youth detention centre (to which 100% of them said no — or probably something more like "no freaking way") and *then* asked the students to supervise the field trip. Fifty percent of the students said yes. Why was this group nearly three times as likely to say yes? The researchers began by asking for a large favour that the students naturally refused, and then the researchers "made a concession" by asking for a smaller favour. Because the researchers had made a concession, the norm of reciprocity demanded that the students make a concession too — by saying yes. When researchers repeated this study almost a half century later, they got nearly identical results (Genschow et al., 2021).

Conformity: We Do What We See Others Do

People can influence us by invoking familiar norms, such as the norm of reciprocity. But if you've ever found yourself at a fancy dinner, sneaking a peek at the person next to you in the hopes of discovering whether the little fork is supposed to be used for the shrimp or the salad, then you know that other people can also influence us by defining *new* norms in ambiguous, confusing, or novel situations. **Conformity** is *the tendency to do what others do,* and it results in part from normative influence.

In a classic study, the psychologist Solomon Asch (1951, 1956) had participants sit in a room with seven other people who appeared to be ordinary participants but who were actually trained actors. An experimenter explained that the participants would be shown cards with three printed lines, and their job was simply to say which of the three lines matched a "standard line" that was printed on another card (see **FIGURE 13.18**). The experimenter held up a card and then asked each person to answer in turn. The real participant was among the last to be called on. Everything went well

Have you ever wondered which big spenders left bills for a tip? In fact, the bills are often put there by the very people you are tipping because they know that the presence of paper money will suggest to you that others are leaving big tips and that it would be appropriate for you to do the same. By the way, the customary gratuity for someone who writes a textbook for you is 15%. But most students send us more.

door-in-the-face technique
An influence strategy that involves getting someone to accept a small request by first getting them to refuse a large request.

conformity The tendency to do what others do.

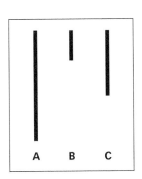

Figure 13.18
Asch's Conformity Study If you were asked which of the lines on the right (A, B, or C) matches the standard line on the left, what would you say? Research on conformity suggests that your answer would depend, in part, on how other people in the room answered the same question.

Standard

A   B   C

on the first two trials, but then on the third trial, something weird happened: The actors all began giving the same wrong answers! What did the real participants do? Although most participants continued to give the right answer on most trials, 75% of them conformed and gave the patently wrong answer on at least one trial. Subsequent research has shown that these participants didn't actually misperceive the length of the lines but were instead succumbing to normative influence (Asch, 1955; Nemeth & Chiles, 1988). Giving the wrong answer was apparently the "right thing to do" in this confusing, novel, and ambiguous situation, so participants did it.

The behaviour of others can tell us what is proper, appropriate, expected, and accepted—in other words, it can define a norm—and once a norm is defined, we feel obliged to honour it. The managers of a Holiday Inn in Tempe, Arizona, allowed researchers to leave a variety of different "message cards" in guests' bathrooms in the hope of convincing those guests to reuse their towels rather than having them laundered every day. The researchers discovered that the single most effective message was the one that defined a norm. It simply read: "Seventy-five percent of our guests use their towels more than once" (Cialdini, 2005). When the Sacramento Municipal Utility District in Sacramento, California, randomly selected 35,000 customers and sent them electric bills showing how their energy consumption compared with that of their neighbours, consumption fell by 2% (Kaufman, 2009; see also Jachimowicz et al., 2018). In another study (Yoeli et al., 2013), utility customers were much more likely to participate in an energy-conservation program when they could see that their neighbours had signed up, and this information was even more effective than a cash incentive of $25. Clearly, normative influence can be a force for good.

Obedience: We Do What We're Told to Do

Other people's behaviour can provide information about existing norms or it can establish new ones. But in many situations, there are a few people whom we all recognize as having special authority both to define norms and to enforce them. The person who works at the movie theatre may be a high-school kid with a 10:00 p.m. curfew, but in the context of the theatre, they are the authority. So when they ask you to stop texting in the middle of the movie, you do as you are asked. **Obedience** is *the tendency to do what authorities tell us to do.*

Why do we obey authorities? Well, okay, yes, sometimes they have guns. But while authorities are often capable of rewarding and punishing us, research shows that much of their influence is *normative* (Tyler, 1990). The psychologist Stanley Milgram (1963) demonstrated this in one of psychology's most infamous experiments. The participants in this experiment reported to a laboratory at Yale University where they met a man who was introduced as another participant but who was actually a trained actor. An experimenter in a lab coat (the authority) explained that the

obedience The tendency to do what authorities tell us to do.

How would you feel if you received a bill showing that you used about three times as much electricity as your neighbours did? The word "proud" doesn't come quickly to mind, does it?

participant would play the role of *teacher* and the actor would play the role of *learner*. The teacher and the learner would sit in different rooms, the teacher would read words to the learner over an intercom (the 1960s version of a cell phone on speaker), and the learner would then repeat the words back to the teacher. If the learner made a mistake, the teacher would press a button on a machine that would deliver an electric shock to the learner (see **FIGURE 13.19**). The shock machine was fake, but the teachers didn't know that. Its switches appeared to allow teachers to deliver 30 different levels of shock, ranging from 15 volts (labelled *slight shock*) to 450 volts (labelled *Danger: severe shock*).

After the learner was strapped into their chair, the experiment began. When the learner made their first mistake, the participant dutifully delivered a 15-volt shock. As the learner made more mistakes, they received more shocks, each stronger than the one before it. When the teacher delivered the 75-volt shock, the learner cried out in pain. At 150 volts, the learner screamed, "Get me out of here . . . I refuse to go on. Let me out!" With every shock, the learner's screams became more agonized as they pleaded pitifully for their freedom. Then, after receiving the 330-volt shock, the learner stopped responding altogether. Participants were naturally upset by all this and typically asked the experimenter to stop, but the experimenter simply replied, "You have no choice. You must go on." The experimenter never threatened the participant with punishment of any kind. Rather, they just stood there with a clipboard in hand, looking very authoritative, and calmly instructed the participant to continue.

Did the participants obey? Indeed, they did: A stunning 80% of participants continued to shock the learner even after they screamed, complained, pleaded, and then fell silent—and an even more stunning 62% of participants went all the way, delivering the highest possible voltage. Although Milgram's study was conducted nearly half a century ago, more recent replications reveal about the same rates of obedience (Burger, 2009; Grzyb et al., 2017).

Were these participants psychopathic sadists? Would normal people electrocute a stranger just because some guy in a lab coat told them to? The answer, it seems, is yes—as long as *normal* means being sensitive to social norms (Zimbardo, 2007). Like you, the participants in this experiment knew that hurting others is *usually* wrong but not *always* wrong: Doctors give painful injections, teachers give painful exams, and in these and many other situations, it is permissible to cause someone to suffer in the service of a higher goal. The experimenter's calm demeanor and persistent instruction suggested that they, and not the participants, knew the norms of this particular situation, so the participants typically did what they were told. Subsequent research confirmed that participants' obedience was due to normative pressure. For instance, when the experimenter's authority to define the norm was undermined (e.g., when a second experimenter appeared to disagree with the first or when the instructions were given by a person who wasn't wearing a lab coat), the participants rarely obeyed the instructions (Milgram, 1974; Miller, 1986). Obedience, it seems, is not just for soldiers and Golden Retrievers.

The Accuracy Motive

When you are hungry, you open the refrigerator and grab an apple because you know that apples (a) taste good and (b) are in the refrigerator. This action, like most actions, relies on both an **attitude,** which is *an enduring positive or negative evaluation of a stimulus* ("Apples taste good") and a **belief,** which is *an enduring piece of knowledge about a stimulus* ("Apples are in the fridge"). In a sense, our attitudes tell us what to do (eat an apple) and our beliefs tell us how to do it (open the fridge). So if our attitudes or beliefs are inaccurate—that is, if we can't tell what's good from what's bad, or what's true from what's false—then our actions are likely to be . . . um, fruitless. Because we rely so much on our attitudes and beliefs, it isn't surprising that we are motivated to have accurate ones, and that motivation leaves us vulnerable to social influence. Here's how.

Why do publishers and booksellers go out of their way to remind people that a book is a "best seller"? Because they know that people are more inclined to buy books when they think that others are buying them, too.

attitude An enduring positive or negative evaluation of a stimulus.

belief An enduring piece of knowledge about a stimulus.

informational influence A phenomenon that occurs when another person's behaviour provides information about what is good or true.

Informational Influence: We Do What We Think Is Correct

If everyone in the mall suddenly ran screaming for the exit, you'd probably join them—not because you were afraid that they would disapprove of you if you didn't, but because their behaviour would suggest to you that there was something worth running from, such as a fire, an active shooter, or a sale on dad jeans. **Informational influence** occurs when *another person's behaviour provides information about what is good or true.* You can observe the power of informational influence yourself just by standing in the middle of the sidewalk, tilting back your head, and staring at the top of a tall building. Research shows that within just a few minutes, other people will stop and stare too (Milgram et al., 1969). Why? Because they will assume that if you are looking, then there must be something worth looking at.

You are the constant target of informational influence. When a salesperson tells you that "most people buy the laptop with extra memory," they are artfully suggesting that you should take other people's behaviour as information about which product is best. Advertisements that refer to soft drinks as "popular" or books as "best sellers" remind you that other people are buying these particular drinks and books, which suggests that they know something you don't and that you'd be wise to follow their example. Restaurants and clubs sometimes make people stand in line outside even when there is room to stand inside because they know that passersby will see the line and assume there is something worth waiting for. In short, the world is full of objects and situations about which we know little, and we often cure our ignorance by watching how others act. Alas, the very thing that makes us open to information leaves us open to manipulation as well.

Persuasion: We Do What We Believe In

When the next provincial or federal election rolls around, two things are likely to happen. First, the candidates are likely to promise that they will earn your vote by making solid arguments that focus on the issues. Second, the candidates will likely avoid arguments, ignore issues, and attempt to win your vote by attending pancake breakfasts and other homespun community events with lots of smiling children and honest-looking next-door-neighbour types, and other clever tricks (Unkelback & Hogden, 2019). What the candidates promise to do and what they actually do reflect two basic forms of **persuasion,** which occurs when *a person's attitudes or beliefs are*

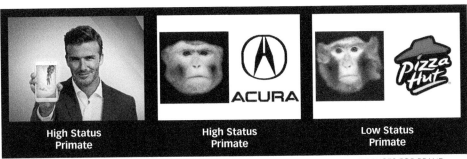

High Status Primate | High Status Primate | Low Status Primate

ACIKALIN MY, WATSON KK, FITZSIMONS GJ, PLATT ML (2018) RHESUS MACAQUES FORM PREFERENCES FOR BRAND LOGOS THROUGH SEX AND SOCIAL STATUS BASED ADVERTISING. PLOS ONE 13(2): E0193055. HTTPS://DOI.ORG/10.1371/JOURNAL.PONE.0193055

Peripheral-route persuasion can be powerful. Samsung hopes that pairing soccer star David Beckham with their phone (*left*) will make you prefer it—and it might. After all, it works with monkeys. When rhesus monkeys were shown various corporate logos paired with pictures of high-status monkeys (*middle*) and low-status monkeys (*right*), they came to prefer the former logos to the latter (Acikalin et al., 2018).

influenced by a communication from another person (Albarracín & Shavitt, 2018; Berger, 2014; Petty & Wegener, 1998). According to the *elaboration likelihood model* of persuasion, there are two basic kinds of persuasion, or two "routes" to being persuaded (Petty & Cacioppo, 1986). **Central-route persuasion** is *the process by which attitudes or beliefs are changed by appeals to reason* and **peripheral-route persuasion** is *the process by which attitudes or beliefs are changed by appeals to habit or emotion.* The candidates will promise to persuade you by the central route, using logic and reason to directly change your attitudes or beliefs, but they will actually try to persuade you by the peripheral route, using words and images that attempt to make an end run around logic and reason and appeal to your habits and emotions instead.

How do these two forms of persuasion work? Because central-route persuasion appeals to logic and reason, it works best when the evidence and arguments a person presents are strong rather than weak. Because peripheral-route persuasion appeals to habit and emotion, it works best when people are not particularly motivated to weigh evidence and analyze arguments. For example, in one study, students heard a speech in favour of instituting comprehensive exams at their school (Petty et al., 1981). The experimenters manipulated three things:

- First, some students heard a speech that contained very strong arguments in favour of the new exams, and some heard a speech that contained only weak arguments.

- Second, some students were told that the speaker was a high-status university professor, and others were told that the speaker was a low-status high school student.

- Third, some students were told that their university was considering implementing these exams right away while others were told that their university was considering implementing these exams long after they had graduated.

The strength of a speaker's argument appeals to reason ("If the data show that most students take classes more seriously when they have comprehensive exams, then I must agree that they're a good idea"), while a speaker's status appeals to habit ("She's some sort of fancy professor so she must know what she's talking about"). The researchers assumed that students who would be personally affected by the exams would be motivated to analyze the arguments and would therefore be persuaded via the central route; and indeed, as **FIGURE 13.20** shows, those students were more persuaded when the arguments were strong rather than weak. The researchers also assumed that students who would not be personally affected by the exams would be persuaded via the peripheral route; and indeed, those students were more persuaded when the speaker was high status rather than low status.

persuasion A phenomenon that occurs when a person's attitudes or beliefs are influenced by a communication from another person.

central-route persuasion The process by which attitudes or beliefs are changed by appeals to reason.

peripheral-route persuasion The process by which attitudes or beliefs are changed by appeals to habit or emotion.

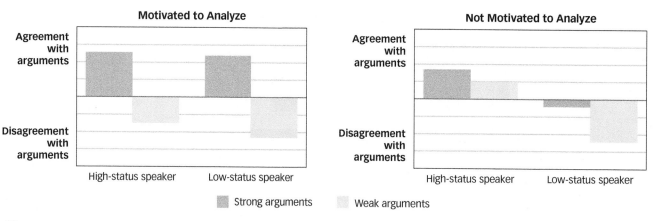

Strong arguments   Weak arguments

Figure 13.20

Two Types of Persuasion The graph on the left shows central-route persuasion and the graph on the right shows peripheral-route persuasion (Petty et al., 1981). Notice how, when motivation to analyze the evidence was high (at left), strong arguments (in orange) were convincing, but weak arguments from either speaker were not. However, when motivation was low, students found weak arguments from the high- (but not low-) status speaker somewhat convincing.

Consistency: We Believe in What We Do

If a friend told you that rabbits had just staged a coup in Antarctica and were halting all carrot exports, you wouldn't go online to check. You'd know that your friend was either joking or stoned because their statement is logically inconsistent with so many other things you know to be true—for example, that rabbits do not foment revolution and that Antarctica does not export carrots. People evaluate the accuracy of new beliefs by assessing their *consistency* with old beliefs, and although this is not a foolproof method for determining whether something is true, it provides a pretty good approximation (Kruglanski et al., 2018). We are motivated to be accurate, and, because consistency is a rough indicator of accuracy, we are motivated to be consistent as well (Cialdini et al., 1995).

Like other motivations, this one leaves us vulnerable to social influence. For example, the **foot-in-the-door technique** (which is not to be confused with the door-in-the face technique described earlier) involves *making a small request and then following it with a larger request* (Burger, 1999). In one study (Freedman & Fraser, 1966), experimenters went to a neighbourhood and knocked on doors to see if they could convince homeowners to install a big ugly "Drive Carefully" sign in their front yards. One group of homeowners was simply asked to install the sign, and only 17% said yes. A second group of homeowners was first asked to sign a petition urging the state legislature to promote safe driving (which almost all agreed to do) and was *then* asked to install the ugly sign. A full 55% said yes. Why would homeowners—or anyone else, for that matter—be more likely to grant two requests than one?

Well, just imagine how the homeowners in the second group felt. They were happy to sign a petition but not to install an ugly yard sign. But wait—that's inconsistent! If you really care about safe driving, then you should do both of these things, and if you don't care, then you should do neither. As the homeowners wrestled with this inconsistency, they probably began to experience **cognitive dissonance,** which is *an unpleasant state that arises when a person recognizes the inconsistency of their actions, attitudes, or beliefs* (Festinger, 1957). When people experience cognitive dissonance, they naturally try to alleviate it, and while there are many ways to do this (Randles et al., 2015), a very simple one is just to eliminate the inconsistency (Aronson, 1969; Cooper & Fazio, 1984; Harmon-Jones et al., 2015). Homeowners couldn't "unsign" the petition that they'd already signed, so they eliminated the inconsistency by "signing" their yards. The lesson for any would-be social influencer is clear: You can often get people to take an action by first getting them to express an attitude with which that action is consistent. For example, if hotel guests are subtly induced at check-in to tick a box saying they are "Friends of the Earth," they are subsequently 25% more likely to reuse their towels during their stay (Baca-Motes et al., 2013). After all, what kind of friend of the earth would use more towels than necessary?

foot-in-the-door technique
A technique that involves making a small request and following it with a larger request.

cognitive dissonance An unpleasant state that arises when a person recognizes the inconsistency of their actions, attitudes, or beliefs.

Just as people take actions that are consistent with their previously expressed attitudes, so too do they adopt attitudes that are consistent with their previous actions. In a classic study (Aronson & Mills, 1958), women university students applied to join a weekly discussion on the "psychology of sex." Women in the control group were allowed to join the discussion, but women in the experimental group were allowed to join the discussion only after first taking an embarrassing test that involved reading sexy fiction to a strange man (which was even more embarrassing for most women in 1958 than it might be today). After either taking or not taking the embarrassing test, the women took part in a carefully scripted discussion that was deliberately extremely dull. Afterwards, the women were asked how much they had enjoyed the discussion, and those who had taken the embarrassing test reported that it was much more interesting than did those who hadn't. Why? Women who took the embarrassing test knew that they had paid a steep price to join the discussion group, and that belief was inconsistent with the belief that the discussion group was

University of Toronto engineering students engage in one of the many (probably unpleasant, certainly inconvenient) rituals associated with Frosh Week. Rituals like these foster group loyalty.

dull. This inconsistency caused the women to experience cognitive dissonance, which they alleviated by changing their beliefs about the value of the discussion.

We normally think that people pay for things because they value them, but as this study shows, people sometimes value things because they've paid for them—with money, time, attention, blood, sweat, tears, or embarrassment. It is little wonder that some university groups use hazing to instill loyalty, that some religions require their adherents to make large personal or monetary sacrifices to create commitment, that some gourmet restaurants charge outrageous amounts to keep their patrons coming back, or that some people "play hard to get" to stimulate a potential romantic partner's interest. Making people suffer for something is a powerful way to make them like it.

Although we are all motivated to behave in ways that are consistent with our beliefs, there are times when we simply can't. A friend's new hairstyle may resemble a wet skunk after an unfortunate encounter with a snow blower, but when they ask us, "What do you think of my do?" we swallow hard and say we like it. And yet, we don't come to believe our own words. Why doesn't the inconsistency between our private belief ("Very wet skunk") and our public action ("Hey, that's a great look for you!") lead us to experience cognitive dissonance, which we alleviate by changing our private belief? Because while complementing our friend's hairstyle is inconsistent with our belief that it is actually quite hideous, our actions in this case seem *justified* by the strong incentive we have to maintain our friendship. And when an inconsistency feels justified, it does not cause people to experience cognitive dissonance.

In a classic study (Festinger & Carlsmith, 1959), students were asked to perform a dull task that involved turning knobs one way, then the other way, and then back again. After the students were sufficiently bored, the researcher explained that they desperately needed a few more participants and asked the students to go into the hallway, find another student, and untruthfully tell them to sign up for the knob-turning task because it was loads of fun. The experimenter offered some participants $1 to tell this lie, and offered other participants $20. All participants gave in to the social pressure to help the researcher by telling a lie, and after they did so, they were asked to report their true enjoyment of the knob-turning task.

The results showed that participants liked the task *more* when they were paid $1 than $20 to lie about it. Why? Because $20 is a whole lot of money (and it was a whole more in 1959!), and getting that kind of money seemed to justify telling a little lie. But $1 is not a lot of money—not nearly enough to justify lying to a fellow student—so participants in this condition experienced cognitive dissonance ("I said the task was fun, but I actually thought it was boring"), which they then alleviated by changing their beliefs about the task ("Now that I think about it, the task *was* kind of fun"). Getting people to behave in ways that they cannot justify is one of the most powerful ways to influence their beliefs.

Chapter Review

Interpersonal Behaviour

- Both survival and reproduction require scarce resources, and aggression and cooperation are two ways to get them.

- Aggressions can be proactive or reactive. Proactive aggression is planned and purposeful. Reactive aggression typically results from negative affect, and the likelihood that people will engage in it is influenced both by biological and cultural factors.

- Cooperation is an excellent strategy for attaining resources, but it entails the risk that others will take advantage of us. One way to reduce that risk is to cooperate with members of one's own groups, who are likely to show in-group favouritism.

- Groups reduce the risk of cooperation, but they also have costs. They can promote unethical behaviour by causing people to lose sight of their personal values, and they often make decisions that are worse than the decisions their best members would have made on their own.

- Many behaviours that appear to be altruistic have hidden benefits for the person who performs them. Human beings, however, do appear to exhibit genuine altruism.

Interpersonal Attraction

- Both biology and culture make the costs of reproduction higher for women than for men, which is one reason that women tend to be choosier when selecting mates.

- Attraction is determined by situational, physical, and psychological factors.

- Most people participate in one or more long-term romantic relationships, which are often signified by marriage. People usually remain in these relationships as long as they believe the benefits outweigh the costs.

Interpersonal Perception

- We make inferences about people on the basis of the categories to which they belong, as well as on the basis of their individual behaviours.

- Category-based inferences can be mistaken because our stereotypes about categories are often inaccurate, overused, self-perpetuating, and unconscious and automatic.

- Target-based inferences can also be mistaken. People tend to attribute behaviour to the actor's dispositions rather than to the situation in which the behaviour was performed.

Interpersonal Influence

- People are motivated to experience pleasure and avoid pain (the hedonic motive), and thus can be influenced by rewards and punishments. These influence attempts can sometimes backfire by changing how people think about their own behaviour or by making them feel as though they are being manipulated.

- People are motivated to attain the approval of others (the approval motive), and thus can be influenced by social norms, such as the norm of reciprocity. People often look to the behaviour of others to determine what kinds of behaviour are normative. People tend to obey authorities even when they should not.

- People are motivated to know what is true (the accuracy motive). People often look to the behaviour of others to determine what is true.

- People can be persuaded by appeals to reason or emotion. Each is effective under different circumstances.

- People feel bad when they notice inconsistency among their attitudes, beliefs, and actions, and they will often change one of these things in order to alleviate this feeling of "cognitive dissonance" and achieve consistency.

Changing Minds

1. Your local MPP is supporting legislation that would impose heavy fines on aggressive drivers who run red lights. One of your classmates thinks this is a good idea. "The textbook taught us a lot about punishment and reward. It's simple. If we punish aggressive driving, its frequency will decline." Is your classmate right? Might the new law backfire? Might another policy be more effective in promoting safe driving?

2. One of your friends is outgoing, funny, and a star athlete on the men's varsity basketball team. They have started to date someone who is introverted and prefers playing computer games to attending parties. You tease your friend about the contrast in personalities, and they reply, "Well, opposites attract." Is your friend right?

3. A large law firm is found guilty of discriminatory hiring practices. Your father reads about the case and scoffs, "People are always so quick to claim racial discrimination. Sure, there are still a few racists out there, but when survey researchers ask people how they feel about people of other races, they generally say they like them just fine." What would you tell your father?

4. One of your friends wears a neon orange track suit and a battered fedora. Every. Single. Day. "Most people follow the crowd," your friend says. "But not me. I'm an individual, and I'm just not influenced by other people." Could your friend be right? What examples might you provide for or against your friend's claim?

5. A classmate learns about Stanley Milgram's 1963 study in which participants were willing to obey orders to administer painful electric shocks to a learner who begged them to

stop. "Some people are such sheep!" they say. "I would never have done that." Are they right? What evidence would you give to support or oppose their claim?

6. Your family gathers for a holiday dinner, and your cousin Wendy brings her fiancée, Amanda. It's the first time Amanda has met the whole family, and she seems nervous. She talks too much, laughs too loud, and rubs everyone the wrong way. Later, one of your uncles says to you, "It's hard to imagine Wendy wanting to spend the rest of her life married to someone so annoying." Has your uncle fallen prey to the fundamental attribution error? How could you know?

7. **Visualizing Data** After studying neuroscience and the brain, a friend says the human brain grew in size to adapt to larger social groups. Review the DATA to see if your friend is correct.

Key Terms

social psychology (p. 469)

aggression (p. 471)

frustration–aggression hypothesis (p. 471)

proactive aggression (p. 471)

reactive aggression (p. 471)

cooperation (p. 474)

group (p. 476)

In-group favouritism (p. 476)

common knowledge effect (p. 477)

group polarization (p. 477)

groupthink (p. 477)

deindividuation (p. 478)

diffusion of responsibility (p. 478)

social loafing (p. 478)

bystander effect (p. 478)

altruism (p. 479)

kin selection (p. 479)

reciprocal altruism (p. 480)

mere exposure effect (p. 484)

homophily (p. 488)

passionate love (p. 490)

companionate love (p. 490)

comparison level for alternatives (p. 491)

equity (p. 491)

social cognition (p. 492)

category-based inferences (p. 492)

target-based inferences (p. 492)

stereotyping (p. 492)

prejudice (p. 492)

discrimination (p. 492)

behavioural confirmation (p. 495)

stereotype threat (p. 495)

perceptual confirmation (p. 495)

subtyping (p. 496)

attributions (p. 500)

fundamental attribution error (p. 500)

actor–observer effect (p. 501)

social influence (p. 502)

overjustification effect (p. 503)

reactance (p. 503)

norms (p. 504)

norm of reciprocity (p. 504)

normative influence (p. 504)

door-in-the-face technique (p. 505)

conformity (p. 505)

obedience (p. 506)

attitude (p. 508)

belief (p. 508)

informational influence (p. 508)

persuasion (p. 508)

central-route persuasion (p. 509)

peripheral-route persuasion (p. 509)

foot-in-the-door technique (p. 510)

cognitive dissonance (p. 510)

CHAPTER

14

Stress and Health

"**I HAVE A KNIFE TO YOUR NECK.** Don't make a sound. Get out of bed and come with me or I will kill you and your family." These are the words that awoke 14-year-old Elizabeth Smart in the middle of the night on June 5, 2002, while she was sleeping in her bedroom next to her 9-year-old sister Mary Katherine. Fearing for her life, and the lives of her family, she kept quiet and left with her abductor. Her little sister, terrified, hid in her bedroom for several hours before waking the girls' parents, who awoke to their daughter saying, "She's gone. Elizabeth is gone." Elizabeth was kidnapped by Brian David Mitchell, a man Elizabeth's parents had hired previously to do some roof work on their home. Mitchell broke into the family's home in Salt Lake City, Utah, through an open window and abducted Elizabeth. He and his wife, Wanda Ileen Barzee, held her in captivity for 9 months, during which time Mitchell repeatedly raped her and threatened to kill her and her entire family. Mitchell, Barzee, and Smart were spotted walking down the street by a couple who recognized them from a recent episode of the television show *America's Most Wanted* and called the police. Mitchell and Barzee were apprehended, and Elizabeth was returned to her family.

Elizabeth suffered under unimaginable circumstances for a prolonged period of time in what can be thought of as one of the most stressful situations possible. So what became of Elizabeth? Fortunately, she is now safe and sound, happily married, and working as an activist. She endured life-threatening stressors for months, and those experiences undoubtedly affected her in ways that will last her entire lifetime. At the same time, hers is a story of resilience. Despite the very difficult hand she was dealt, she appears to have bounced back and to be leading a happy, productive, and rewarding life. Hers is a story of both stress and health.

This smiling young face is that of Elizabeth Smart, who, between the times of these two photographs, was kidnapped, raped, and tortured for nearly a year. Stressful life events often affect us in ways that cannot be seen from the outside. Fortunately, there are things that we can do in response to even the most stressful of life events that can get us smiling again.

FORTUNATELY, FEW OF US WILL EVER HAVE TO ENDURE the type of stress that Elizabeth Smart lived through. But life can present a welter of frights, bothers, and looming disasters that can be difficult to manage. A reckless driver may nearly run you over; you may be discriminated against, threatened, or intimidated in some way; or a fire may leave you out on the street. Life has its **stressors**, *specific events or chronic pressures that place demands on a person or threaten a* *person's well-being.* Although such stressors rarely involve threats of death, they do have both immediate and cumulative effects that can influence health.

In this chapter, we'll look at what psychologists have learned about the kinds of life events that produce **stress**, *the physical and psychological response to internal or external stressors;* typical responses to such stressors; and ways to manage stress. Stress has such a profound influence on health that we consider stress and health together in this chapter. And because sickness and health are not merely features of the physical body, we then consider the more general topic of **health psychology**, *the subfield of psychology concerned with how psychological factors influence the causes and treatment of physical illness and the maintenance of health.* You will see how perceptions of illness can affect its course and how health-promoting behaviours can improve the quality of people's lives.

Sources of Stress: What Gets to You

What are the sources of stress in our lives? A natural catastrophe, such as a hurricane, earthquake, or volcanic eruption, is an obvious source. But for most of us, stressors are personal events that affect the comfortable pattern of our lives and the little annoyances that bug us day after day. Let's look at the life events that can cause stress, chronic sources of stress, and the relationship between lack of perceived control and the impact of stressors.

Stressful Events

People often seem to get sick after major life events. In pioneering work, Thomas Holmes and Richard Rahe (1967) followed up on this observation, proposing that major life changes cause stress and that increased stress causes illness. To test their idea, they asked people to rate the magnitude of readjustment required by each of many events found to be associated with the onset of illness (Rahe et al., 1964). The resulting list of life events is remarkably predictive: Simply adding up the stress ratings of each life change experienced is a significant indicator of a person's likelihood of future illness (Miller, 1996). Someone who gets divorced, loses a job, and has a friend die all in the same year, for example, is more likely to get sick than someone who escapes the year with only a divorce.

A version of this list adapted for the life events of university students (and sporting the snappy acronym CUSS, for College Undergraduate Stress Scale) is shown in **TABLE 14.1**. To assess your stressful events, check off any events that have happened to you in the past year and sum your point total. In a large sample of students in an introductory psychology class, the average was 1,247 points, ranging from 182 to 2,571 (Renner & Mackin, 1998).

Looking at the list, you may wonder why positive events are included. Stressful life events are unpleasant, right? Why would getting married be stressful? Isn't a wedding supposed to be fun? Research has shown that, compared with negative events, positive events produce less psychological distress and fewer physical symptoms (McFarlane et al., 1980), and that happiness can sometimes even counteract the effects of negative events (Fredrickson, 2000). However, because positive events often require readjustment and preparedness that many people find extremely stressful (Brown & McGill, 1989), these events are included in computing life-change scores.

Learning Outcomes

WHAT YOU NEED TO KNOW

- Compare the impact of stressful events and chronic stress.

- Identify the importance of perceived control.

stressors Specific events or chronic pressures that place demands on a person or threaten a person's well-being.

stress The physical and psychological response to internal or external stressors.

health psychology The subfield of psychology concerned with how psychological factors influence the causes and treatment of physical illness and the maintenance of health.

TABLE 14.1

COLLEGE UNDERGRADUATE STRESS SCALE

Event	Stress Rating	Event	Stress Rating
Being raped	100	Lack of sleep	69
Finding out that you are HIV positive	100	Change in housing situation (hassles, moves)	69
Being accused of rape	98	Competing or performing in public	69
Death of a close friend	97	Getting in a physical fight	66
Death of a close family member	96	Difficulties with a roommate	66
Contracting a sexually transmitted disease (other than AIDS)	94	Job changes (applying, new job, work hassles)	65
Concerns about being pregnant	91	Declaring a major or concerns about future plans	65
Finals week	90	A class you hate	62
Concerns about your partner being pregnant	90	Drinking or use of drugs	61
Oversleeping for an exam	89	Confrontations with professors	60
Flunking a class	89	Starting a new semester	58
Having a boyfriend or girlfriend cheat on you	85	Going on a first date	57
Ending a steady dating relationship	85	Registration	55
Serious illness in a close friend or family member	85	Maintaining a steady dating relationship	55
Financial difficulties	84	Commuting to campus or work or both	54
Writing a major term paper	83	Peer pressures	53
Being caught cheating on a test	83	Being away from home for the first time	53
Drunk driving	82	Getting sick	52
Sense of overload in school or work	82	Concerns about your appearance	52
Two exams in one day	80	Getting straight A's	51
Cheating on your boyfriend or girlfriend	77	A difficult class that you love	48
Getting married	76	Making new friends; getting along with friends	47
Negative consequences of drinking or drug use	75	Fraternity or sorority rush	47
Depression or crisis in your best friend	73	Falling asleep in class	40
Difficulties with parents	73	Attending an athletic event	20
Talking in front of class	72		

Note: To compute your personal life change score, sum the stress ratings for all events that have happened to you in the last year.
Information from Renner & Mackin (1998).

Chronic Stressors

Life would be simpler if an occasional stressful event such as a wedding or a lost job were the only pressures we faced. At least each event would be limited in scope, with a beginning, a middle, and, ideally, an end. But unfortunately, life brings with it continued exposure to **chronic stressors**, *sources of stress that occur continuously or repeatedly.* Strained relationships, discrimination, bullying, overwork, money troubles—small stressors that may be easy to ignore if they happen only occasionally—can accumulate to produce distress and illness. People who report being affected by daily hassles also report more psychological symptoms (LaPierre et al., 2012) and physical symptoms (Piazza et al., 2013), and these effects often have a greater and longer-lasting impact than major life events.

Many chronic stressors are linked to social relationships. For instance, as described in the Social Psychology chapter, people often form different social groups based on race, culture, interests, popularity, and so on. Being outside the in-group can be stressful. Being actively targeted by members of the in-group can be even more stressful, especially if this happens repeatedly over time (see A World of Difference: Can

chronic stressors Sources of stress that occur continuously or repeatedly.

Discrimination Cause Stress and Illness?). Chronic stressors also can be linked to particular environments. For example, features of city life—noise, traffic, crowding, pollution, and even the threat of violence—provide particularly insistent sources of chronic stress (Evans, 2006). More recent research has started to identify potential pathways through which this may occur. For instance, people who live in cities show significantly greater amygdala activity in response to stressors than do those who live in towns (slightly less activity) and in rural regions (much less activity) (Lederbogen et al., 2011). The realization that chronic stressors are linked to environments has spawned the subfield of *environmental psychology,* the scientific study of environmental effects on behaviour and health.

In a classic study of the influence of noise on children, environmental psychologists looked at the impact of attending schools under the flight path to Heathrow Airport in London, England. Did the noise of more than 1,250 jets flying overhead each day have an influence beyond making kids yell to be heard? Compared with children from matched control schools in low-noise areas, children who attended school under the flight path reported higher levels of noise annoyance and showed poorer reading comprehension (Haines et al., 2001).

In addition to chronic stress being distributed differently across neighbourhoods, it also is distributed unevenly across people of different races and ethnicities. For instance, in Canada, Black, Indigenous and other people of colour (BIPOC) experience significantly more chronic stressors than do non-BIPOC people (Williams et al., 2022)—especially chronic stress related to financial and housing-related issues and racial discrimination (Williams et al., 2022). This differential exposure to chronic stress has negative downstream consequences through multiple pathways that include higher likelihood of engaging in unhealthy coping behaviours (e.g., eating, smoking, gambling), elevated physiological stress response (e.g., see Physical Reactions section), and higher rates of chronic physical conditions (e.g., cancer, heart disease, diabetes) (Jackson et al., 2010).

As the movie *Crazy Rich Asians* showcased, although weddings are positive events, they also can be stressful due to the often overwhelming amount of planning and decision making involved (and occasionally because of the difficulties in managing the interactions of friends and family).

COLLECTION CHRISTOPHEL/© COLOR FORCE/ SK GLOBAL/WARNER BROS/ALAMY STOCK PHOTO

Perceived Control Over Stressful Events

What do catastrophes, stressful life changes, and daily hassles have in common? Right off the bat, of course, their threat to the person or the status quo is easy to see. Stressors challenge you to *do something*—to take some action to eliminate or overcome the stressors.

Paradoxically, events are most stressful when there is *nothing to do*—no way to deal with the challenge. Expecting that you will have control over what happens to you is associated with effectiveness in dealing with stress. The researchers David Glass and Jerome Singer (1972), in classic studies of *perceived control,* looked at the aftereffects of loud noise on people who could or could not control it. Participants were asked to solve puzzles and proofread in a quiet room or in a room filled with loud noise. Glass and Singer found that bursts of such noise hurt people's performance on the tasks after the noise was over. However, this dramatic decline in performance did not occur among participants who were told during the noise period that they could stop the noise just by pushing a button. They didn't actually take this option, but just having access to the "panic button" shielded them from the detrimental effects of the noise. In another classic study (Hanson et al., 1976), one group of monkeys was taught to press a lever to turn off a loud noise, whereas individuals in the "yoked group" were exposed to the identical amount of noise but couldn't turn it off. The yoked monkeys had higher levels of cortisol (a stress hormone) and were more aggressive than monkeys who could control the noise. Interestingly, when control was removed from the first group, their cortisol and aggression levels were even higher than those in

A common feature of most of the stressors we experience is the lack of perceived control. Whether it's a global pandemic involving a deadly virus, a natural disaster, or threat of injury or death to us or our loved ones, things that we perceive to be potentially harmful and outside of our control reliably engage our stress response.

J. CONRAD WILLIAMS, JR./NEWSDAY LLC/ GETTY IMAGES

A World of Difference | Can Discrimination Cause Stress and Illness?

Have you ever been discriminated against because of your race, gender, sexual orientation, or some other characteristic? If so, then you know that this can be a stressful experience. Discrimination that occurs repeatedly over time can be an especially powerful stressor. But what exactly does it *do* to people?

There are a number of ways in which discrimination can lead to elevated stress and negative health outcomes. People from equity-seeking groups who experience higher levels of stress as a result of discrimination often engage more frequently in maladaptive behaviours (e.g., drinking, smoking, gambling, drug use, and overeating) in efforts to cope with stress. Also, a history of discrimination by health care providers against equity-seeking groups in Canada has resulted in people from those groups fearing and mistrusting health care providers (Williams et al., 2022); thereby, they tend to avoid seeking health care at all. Thus, although such groups have significantly higher rates of health problems, they have lower rates of treatment than do members of socially advantaged groups (Penner et al., 2010; Roy-Byrne et al., 2009; Spence et al., 2016; Williams et al., 2022).

Research has begun to reveal how discrimination can literally "get under the skin" to cause negative health outcomes. One American study by Wendy Mendes and colleagues (Jamieson et al., 2013) exposed Black and white participants to social rejection by a person of the same race or by a person of a different race to test whether there is something particularly harmful about discrimination, compared with social rejection in general. To test this hypothesis, research participants delivered a speech to two confederates in different rooms via a video chat program, after which the confederates provided negative feedback about the participant's speech. The confederates were not seen by the participant but were represented by computer avatars that either matched the participant's race or did not. In an interesting finding, although the nature of the rejection was the same in all cases, participants responded very differently if the people rejecting them were of a different race than if they were of the same race. Specifically, whereas being rejected by people of your own race was associated with greater displays of shame and physiological changes associated with an avoidance state (increased cortisol), being rejected by members of a different race was associated with displays of anger, greater vigilance for danger, physiological changes associated with an approach state (i.e., higher cardiac output and lower vascular resistance), and higher risk taking. The results suggest that discrimination can lead to physiological, cognitive, and behavioural changes that in the short term prepare a person for action, but that in the long term could lead to negative health outcomes.

Studies such as this one help explain some of the health disparities that currently exist across different social groups. For example, in a 2011–2014 survey (Statistics Canada, 2016), 60% of Canada's non-Indigenous population rated their health as good or excellent. In stark contrast, only 48.5%, 51.3%, and 44.9% of First Nations, Métis, and Inuit people, respectively, reported their health as such—and life expectancy is 5–10 years shorter for Indigenous people compared to other Canadians (Statistics Canada, 2017). Although Indigenous peoples in Canada suffer poorer health than others for many reasons, chronic stress due to prejudice, discrimination, and systemic racism are among them.

the yoked group! This tells us that history and perceived control are both very important for understanding how we respond to stress.

Subsequent studies have found that a lack of perceived control underlies the body's response to other stressors, too. The stressful effects of crowding, for example, appear to stem from the feeling that you can't control getting away from the crowded conditions (Evans & Stecker, 2004). Being jammed into a crowded dormitory room may be easier to handle once you realize you could take a walk and get away from it all.

Stress Reactions: All Shook Up

Learning Outcomes

WHAT YOU NEED TO KNOW

- Explain physical responses to stress.
- Identify possible psychological responses to stress.

It was a regular Tuesday morning in New York City. University students were sitting in their morning classes. People were arriving at work and the streets were beginning to fill with shoppers and tourists. Then, at 8:46 a.m., American Airlines Flight 11 crashed into the North Tower of the World Trade Center. People watched in horror. How could this have happened? This seemed like a terrible accident. Then at 9:03 a.m., United Airlines Flight 175 crashed into the South Tower of the World Trade Center. There were then reports of a plane crashing into the Pentagon, the headquarters of the American Department of Defense in Washington, D.C. And another somewhere in Pennsylvania.

The terrorist attacks on the World Trade Center on September 11, 2001, were an enormous stressor that had a lasting impact on many people, physically and psychologically. Research done several years after this event revealed that people who lived in close proximity to the World Trade Center (within 2 kilometres) on 9/11 now had less grey matter in the amygdala, hippocampus, insula, anterior cingulate, and medial prefrontal cortex than did those who lived more than 200 miles away during the attacks; this suggested that the stress associated with the attacks may have reduced the size of these parts of the brain that play an important role in emotion, memory, and decision making (Ganzel et al., 2008). The brain measurements were taken more than 3 years after 9/11: This tells us that the event had long-term consequences on brain structure. Children who watched more television coverage of 9/11 had higher symptoms of posttraumatic stress disorder than did children who watched less coverage (Otto et al., 2007). People around the United States who had a stronger acute stress response to the events of 9/11 had a 53% increased incidence of heart problems over the next 3 years (Holman et al., 2008). Stress can produce changes in every system of the body and mind, stimulating both physical reactions and psychological reactions. Let's consider each in turn.

The threat of death or injury, such as many in New York City experienced at the time of the 9/11 attacks, can cause significant and lasting physical and psychological stress reactions.

Physical Reactions

You are at a party, and a guy jumps in front of you with his fists up ready to punch you in the face. What do you do?! Walter Cannon (1929) coined a phrase to describe the body's response to any threatening stimulus: the **fight-or-flight response**, *an emotional and physiological reaction to an emergency that increases readiness for action.* The mind asks, "Should I stay and fight this guy? Or should I flee this situation?" And the body prepares to react. Cannon recognized this common response across species and suspected that it might be the body's first mobilization to any threat.

Research conducted since Cannon's discovery has revealed what is happening in the brain and body during this reaction. Brain activation in response to threat occurs in the hypothalamus, stimulating the nearby pituitary gland, which in turn releases a hormone known as ACTH (short for adrenocorticotropic hormone). ACTH travels through the bloodstream and stimulates the adrenal glands atop the kidneys (see **FIGURE 14.1**).

fight-or-flight response An emotional and physiological reaction to an emergency that increases readiness for action.

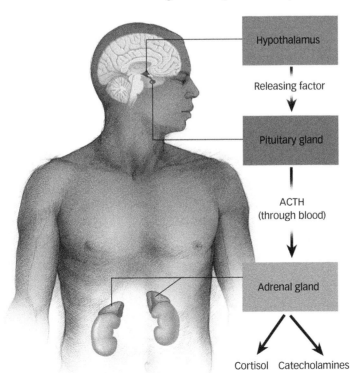

Figure 14.1

HPA Axis Just a few seconds after a fearful stimulus is perceived, the hypothalamus activates the pituitary gland to release adrenocorticotropic hormone (ACTH). The ACTH then travels through the bloodstream to activate the adrenal glands to release catecholamines and cortisol, which energize the fight-or-flight response.

In this cascading response of the HPA (hypothalamic–pituitary–adrenocortical) axis, the adrenal glands are stimulated to release hormones, including the *catecholamines* (epinephrine and norepinephrine), which increase sympathetic nervous system activation (and therefore increase heart rate, blood pressure, and respiration rate) and decrease parasympathetic activation (see the Neuroscience and Behaviour chapter). The increased respiration and blood pressure make more oxygen available to the muscles to energize attack or to initiate escape. The adrenal glands also release *cortisol*, a hormone that increases the concentration of glucose in the blood to make fuel available to the muscles. Everything is prepared for a full-tilt response to the threat.

General Adaptation Syndrome

What might have happened if the terrorist attacks of 9/11 were spaced out over a period of days or weeks? Starting in the 1930s, Hans Selye, a Canadian physician working in Montreal, undertook a variety of experiments that looked at the physiological consequences of severe threats to well-being. He subjected rats to heat, cold, infection, trauma, hemorrhage, and other prolonged stressors, making few friends among the rats or their sympathizers, but learning a lot about stress. His stressed-out rats developed physiological responses that included enlargement of the adrenal cortex, shrinking of the lymph glands, and ulceration of the stomach. Noting that many different kinds of stressors caused similar patterns of physiological change, he called the reaction the **general adaptation syndrome (GAS)**, which he defined as a *three-stage physiological stress response that appears regardless of the stressor that is encountered.* The GAS is *nonspecific;* that is, the response doesn't vary, no matter what the source of the repeated stress.

None of this is very good news. Although Friedrich Nietzsche once said, "What does not kill me makes me stronger," Selye found that severe stress takes a toll on the body. He saw the GAS as occurring in three phases (see **FIGURE 14.2**):

Hans Selye with rat. Given all the stress Selye put rats under, this one looks surprisingly calm.

general adaptation syndrome (GAS) A three-stage physiological stress response that appears regardless of the stressor that is encountered.

- First comes the *alarm phase,* in which the body rapidly mobilizes its resources to respond to the threat. Energy is required, and the body calls on its stored fat and muscle. The alarm phase is equivalent to Cannon's fight-or-flight response.

- Next, in the *resistance phase,* the body adapts to its high state of arousal as it tries to cope with the stressor. Continuing to draw on resources of fat and muscle, it shuts down unnecessary processes: Digestion, growth, and sex drive stall; menstruation stops; production of testosterone and sperm decreases. The body is being taxed to generate resistance, and all the fun stuff is put on hold.

Figure 14.2
Selye's Three Phases of Stress Response In Selye's theory, resistance to stress builds over time, but then can only last so long before exhaustion sets in.

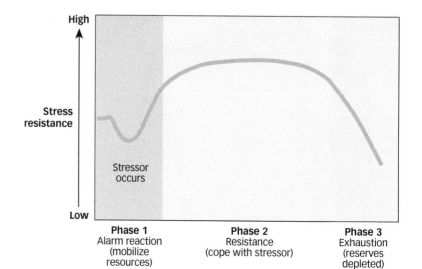

- If the GAS continues long enough, the *exhaustion phase* sets in. The body's resistance collapses. Many of the resistance-phase defenses cause gradual damage as they operate, leading to costs for the body that can include susceptibility to infection, tumour growth, aging, irreversible organ damage, or death.

Stress Negatively Affects Health and Speeds Aging

Right now, you are (we hope!) enjoying years of healthy living. Unfortunately, as people age, the body slowly begins to break down. (Just ask any of the authors of this textbook.) Interestingly, recent research has revealed that stress significantly accelerates the aging process. Elizabeth Smart's parents noted that, on being reunited with her after 9 months of separation, they almost did not recognize her because she appeared to have aged so much (Smart et al., 2003). Theirs is an extreme example; you can see examples of the effects of stress on aging around you in everyday life. People exposed to chronic stress, whether due to their relationships or jobs, or something else, experience actual wear and tear on their bodies and accelerated aging. Take a look at the pairs of pictures of three past world leaders. As you can see, they appear to have aged much more than the 8 years that passed between their first and second photographs. How exactly can stressors in the environment speed up the aging process?

Understanding this process requires knowing a little bit about how aging occurs. The cells in our bodies are constantly dividing, and as part of this process, our chromosomes are repeatedly copied so that our genetic information is carried into the new cells. This process is facilitated by the presence of **telomeres**, *caps at the ends of the chromosomes that prevent the chromosomes from sticking to each other*. They are analogous to the metal or plastic sheaths at the end of your shoelaces that keep them from fraying and not working as efficiently. Each time a cell divides, the telomeres become slightly shorter. If they become too short, cells can no longer divide, which can lead to the development of tumours and a range of diseases.

Fortunately, our bodies fix this problem by producing a substance called **telomerase**, *an enzyme that rebuilds telomeres at the tips of chromosomes*. As cells repeatedly divide over the course of our lives, telomerase does its best to recap our chromosomes with telomeres. Ultimately, though, telomerase cannot keep up telomere repair at a sufficient pace, and over time cells lose their ability to divide, causing aging and, in the end, cell death. The discovery of the function of telomeres and telomerase and their relation to aging and disease by Elizabeth Blackburn and colleagues has been one of the most exciting advances in science in the past several decades (earning Dr. Blackburn a Nobel Prize in 2009).

Interestingly, social stressors can play an important role in this process. People exposed to chronic stress have shorter telomere length and lower telomerase activity (Epel et al., 2004). Laboratory studies suggest that cortisol can reduce the activity of telomerase, which in turn leads to shortened telomeres, with downstream negative effects in the form of accelerated aging and increased risk of a wide range of diseases

telomeres Caps at the ends of the chromosomes that prevent the chromosomes from sticking to each other.

telomerase An enzyme that rebuilds telomeres at the tips of chromosomes.

Chronic stress can actually speed the aging process. Just look at how much political leaders age after 8 years in office.

Dr. Elizabeth Blackburn was awarded a Nobel Prize in Physiology or Medicine in 2009 for her groundbreaking discoveries on the functions of telomeres (shown here in yellow) and telomerase.

including cancer, cardiovascular disease, diabetes, and depression (Blackburn et al., 2015). This sounds dire, but there are things you can do to combat this process and potentially live a healthier and longer life! Activities such as exercise and meditation seem to prevent chronic stress from shortening telomere length, providing a potential explanation of how these activities may convey health benefits such as longer life and lower risk of disease (Epel et al., 2009; Puterman et al., 2010) (see Hot Science: Stress, Health, and Money).

Chronic Stress Affects the Immune Response

The **immune system** is *a complex response system that protects the body from bacteria, viruses, and other foreign substances.* You can observe the operation of your immune system directly when you experience a bug bite or cut on your skin. When any foreign particles (e.g., splinter) or pathogens (e.g., germs) get under your skin, your immune system activates the *inflammatory response*, in which white blood cells are sent to the site of the injury to fight off potential infection. You often will observe swelling and redness at the site of injury, which means your immune system is at work. This system includes **lymphocytes**, *white blood cells that produce antibodies that fight infection, including T cells and B cells.* The immune system is remarkably responsive to psychological influences. *Psychoneuroimmunology* is the study of how the immune system responds to psychological variables, such as the presence of stressors. Stressors can cause hormones known as *glucocorticoids* (e.g., cortisol) to flood the brain (described in the Neuroscience and Behaviour chapter), wearing down the immune system and making it less able to fight invaders (Webster Marketon & Glaser, 2009; Marketon & Glaser, 2008).

For example, in one study, medical student volunteers agreed to receive small wounds to the roof of the mouth. Researchers observed that these wounds healed more slowly during exam periods than during summer vacation (Marucha et al., 1998). In another series of studies, a set of selfless, healthy volunteers permitted researchers to swab the common cold virus into their noses (Cohen et al., 2012). You might think that a direct application of the virus would be like exposure to a massive full-facial sneeze and that all the participants would catch colds. The researchers observed, however, that some people got colds, but others didn't—and stress helped account for the difference. Volunteers who had experienced chronic stressors (lasting a month or longer) were especially likely to suffer from colds. In particular, participants who had lost a job or who were going through extended interpersonal problems with family or friends were most susceptible to the virus. Brief stressful life events (those lasting less than a month) had no impact. So if you're fighting with

immune system A complex response system that protects the body from bacteria, viruses, and other foreign substances.

lymphocytes White blood cells that produce antibodies that fight infection, including T cells and B cells.

your friends or family, best to get it over with quickly; it's better for your health.

The effect of stress on immune response may help explain why social status is related to health. Several decades of research have suggested that whereas short bursts of immune system activity are needed to fight foreign pathogens entering the body, chronic and exaggerated immune responses can lead to significantly worse health outcomes, such as increased risk of cancer and heart disease (Chen et al., 2018). Chronic stress, such as that experienced by members of equity-seeking groups such as those who are Black, Indigenous, and/or people of colour (BIPOC) can lead to dysfunctional immune responses, and this may help to explain why such individuals have higher risk of adverse health outcomes.

The links between social status, immune function, and illness are of course complex and difficult to tease apart. However, one clever study showed clearly that being of lower social status disrupts immune functioning. In this study, the researchers experimentally decreased the social status of 45 female rhesus monkeys, one at a time, and observed that doing so increased the harassment and decreased the social support (i.e., grooming behaviour) they experience, which in turn was associated with a pro-inflammatory immune response of the type associated with increased risk of chronic health conditions (Snyder-Mackler et al., 2016). Although this study was performed in monkeys, it helps us to understand just one of the many ways that stress can "get under the skin" to increase the risk of health problems.

Chris Rock's joke that "rich 50 is like poor 35!" matches up with data suggesting that wealthier people tend to be healthier and younger looking than poorer people.

Stress Affects Cardiovascular Health

The heart and circulatory system are also sensitive to stress. For example, one study of more than 60,000 U.S. military veterans found that among those who had been deployed during wartime, the ones who experienced combat had 93% higher odds of developing coronary heart disease (CHD) over the next few years than did those who did not experience combat (Crum-Cianflone et al., 2014). The association between major stressors and later heart disease also has been found in large (>1 million people) and rigorous studies of the general population (Song et al., 2019). The full story of how stress affects the cardiovascular system starts earlier than the actual occurrence of a heart attack: Chronic stress creates changes in the body that increase later vulnerability.

The main cause of CHD is *atherosclerosis,* a gradual narrowing of the arteries that occurs as fatty deposits, or plaque, build up on the inner walls of the arteries. Narrowed arteries reduce blood supply and, eventually, when an artery is blocked by a blood clot or detached plaque, result in a heart attack. Although smoking, a sedentary lifestyle, and a diet high in fat and cholesterol can cause CHD, chronic stress also is a major contributor (Silvani et al., 2016). As a result of stress-activated arousal of the sympathetic nervous system, blood pressure goes up and stays up, gradually damaging the blood vessels. The damaged vessels accumulate plaque, and the more plaque, the greater the likelihood of CHD.

During the 1950s, the cardiologists Meyer Friedman and Ray Rosenman (1974) conducted a revolutionary study that demonstrated a link between work-related stress and CHD. They interviewed and tested 3,000 healthy middle-aged men and then tracked their subsequent cardiovascular health. From their research, Friedman and Rosenman developed the concept of the **Type A behaviour pattern**, which is characterized by *a tendency towards easily aroused hostility, impatience, a sense of time urgency, and competitive achievement strivings.* They compared Type A individuals with those who have a less-driven behaviour pattern (sometimes called *Type B*). The Type A men were identified not only by their answers to questions in the interview

Type A behaviour pattern
The tendency towards easily aroused hostility, impatience, a sense of time urgency, and competitive achievement strivings.

(agreeing that they walk and talk fast, work late, set goals for themselves, work hard to win, and easily get frustrated and angry at others) but also by the pushy and impatient way in which they answered the questions. They watched the clock, barked back answers, and interrupted the interviewer, at some points even slapping him with a fish. Okay, the part about the fish is wrong, but you get the idea: These people were intense. The researchers found that of the 258 men who had heart attacks in the 9 years following the interview, more than two-thirds had been classified as Type A, and only one-third had been classified as Type B.

A later study of stress and anger tracked medical students for up to 48 years to see how their behaviour during their youth related to their later susceptibility to coronary problems (Chang et al., 2002). Students who responded to stress with anger and hostility were found to be three times more likely to later develop premature heart disease and six times more likely to have an early heart attack than were students who did not respond with anger. Hostility, particularly in men, predicts heart disease better than any other major causal factor, such as smoking, high caloric intake, or even high levels of LDL cholesterol (Niaura et al., 2002; see also **FIGURE 14.3**). Stress affects the cardiovascular system to some degree in everyone, but it is particularly harmful in those people who respond to stressful events with hostility.

Psychological Reactions

The body's response to stress is intertwined with responses of the mind. Perhaps the first thing the mind does is try to sort things out — to interpret whether an event is threatening or not — and if it is, whether something can be done about it.

Stress Interpretation Is a Two-step Process

The interpretation of a stimulus as being stressful or not is called *primary appraisal* (Lazarus & Folkman, 1984). Primary appraisal allows you to realize that a small, dark spot on your shirt is a stressor (spider!) or that a 120-kilometre-per-hour drop from a great height in a small car full of screaming people may not be (roller coaster!). In a demonstration of the importance of interpretation, researchers used a gruesome film of a subincision of the penis (a kind of genital surgery that is part of some tribal initiation rites) to severely stress volunteer participants (Speisman et al., 1964). Self-reports and participants' autonomic arousal (heart rate and skin conductance level) were used as measures of stress. Before viewing the film, one group heard

Figure 14.3

Hostility and Coronary Heart Disease Of 2,280 men studied over the course of 3 years, 45 suffered CHD incidents, such as heart attack. Many more of these incidents occurred in the men who had initially scored above the 80th percentile in hostility (Niaura et al., 2002).

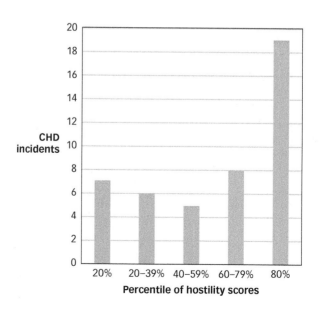

an introduction that downplayed the pain and emphasized the coming-of-age aspect of the initiation. This interpretation markedly reduced the film viewers' stress compared with the stress of another group whose viewing was preceded by a lecture accentuating the pain and trauma.

The next step in interpretation is *secondary appraisal,* determining whether the stressor is something you can handle or not; that is, whether you have control over the event (Lazarus & Folkman, 1984). Interestingly, the body responds differently depending on whether the stressor is perceived as a *threat* (a stressor you believe you might *not* be able to overcome) or a *challenge* (a stressor you feel fairly confident you can control) (Blascovich & Tomaka, 1996). The same midterm exam is seen as a challenge if you are well prepared, but a threat if you didn't study.

Fortunately, interpretations of stressors can change threats into challenges. One study (Jamieson et al., 2010) showed that instructing students to reframe their anxiety about an upcoming exam as arousal that would help them on the test actually boosted their sympathetic arousal (signaling a challenge orientation) and improved test performance. Remember this technique next time you are feeling anxious about a test or presentation: Increased arousal can improve your performance!

Although both threats and challenges raise the heart rate, threats increase vascular reactivity (such as constriction of the blood vessels, which can lead to high blood pressure) (see A World of Difference: Can Discrimination Cause Stress and Illness?). In one study, researchers found that even interactions as innocuous as conversations can produce threat or challenge responses, depending on the race of the conversation partner. Asked to talk with another, unfamiliar student, American white students showed a challenge reaction when the student was white and a threat reaction when the student was Black (Mendes et al., 2002). Similar threat responses were found when American white students interacted with an unexpected partner, such as an Asian student with an accent typical of the American South (Mendes et al., 2007). It's as if social unfamiliarity creates the same kind of stress as lack of preparedness for an exam. Interestingly, previous interaction with members of an unfamiliar group tempers the threat reaction (Blascovich et al., 2001).

Chronic Stress Can Lead to Burnout

Did you ever take a class from a teacher who had lost interest in the job? The syndrome is easy to spot: The teacher looks distant and blank, almost robotic, giving predictable and humdrum lessons each day, as if it doesn't matter whether

Is there anything worse than taking a horribly boring class? How about being the teacher of that class? What techniques would prevent burnout from stress in people in helping professions (teachers, doctors, nurses, and so on)?

STOCK4B GMBH/ALAMY STOCK PHOTO

anyone is listening. Now imagine being this teacher. You decided to teach because you wanted to shape young minds. You worked hard, and for a while things were great. But one day, you looked up to see a room full of students who were bored and didn't care about anything you had to say. They scrolled Instagram and Tik-Tok while you talked and started shuffling papers and putting things away long before the end of class. You're happy at work only when you're not in class. When people feel this way, especially about their jobs or careers, they are suffering from **burnout**, *a state of physical, emotional, and mental exhaustion resulting from long-term involvement in an emotionally demanding situation and accompanied by lowered performance and motivation.*

Burnout is a particular problem in the helping professions (Fernandez Nievas & Thaver, 2015; Nieves & Thaver, 2015). Teachers, nurses, clergy, doctors, dentists, psychologists, social workers, police officers, and others who repeatedly encounter emotional turmoil on the job may be able to work productively only for a limited time. Eventually, many succumb to symptoms of burnout: overwhelming exhaustion, a deep cynicism and detachment from the job, and a sense of ineffectiveness and lack of accomplishment (Maslach, 2003). Those experiencing burnout have higher rates of depression and anxiety, with the exhaustion component of burnout showing the strongest link with increased depression and anxiety symptoms (Koutsimani et al., 2019). Their unhappiness can even spread to others; people with burnout tend to become disgruntled employees who revel in their coworkers' failures and ignore their coworkers' successes (Brenninkmeijer et al., 2001).

burnout A state of physical, emotional, and mental exhaustion resulting from long-term involvement in an emotionally demanding situation and accompanied by lowered performance and motivation.

Hot Science | **Stress, Health, and Money**

Many of us are motivated by money. But why? There has always been a general assumption that money will bring happiness. But does it? In a landmark study of 450,000 survey responses, Daniel Kahneman and Angus Deaton (2010), a pair of Nobel Prize winners, showed that as your income increases, your self-reported happiness goes up, and stress goes down. But this is true only up to a point—and that point was about $80,000 Canadian dollars in 2010, equivalent to about $105,000 today. Beyond that point, higher income is not associated with happiness *or* stress.

More research has shown more alarmingly that those with less money also are at risk for the most serious outcome: death. Using data from 1.4 billion U.S. tax and death records, researchers found that people with higher incomes live significantly longer than those with lower incomes (Chetty et al., 2016). How much longer? It turns out that the difference between the wealthiest 1% and the poorest 1% is approximately 15 years for men and 10 years for women, as shown in the accompanying figure. Even more

concerning is that the difference in life expectancy has been increasing over time, with life expectancy rising 2 to 3 years for the wealthiest, but only <.5 years for the poorest from 2001 to 2014.

But income is not destiny, and even among the poorest in society, behavioural and environmental factors can make a huge difference. For instance, Chetty and Hendren (2018) found that among children growing up in poor families, each year of life they spend living in a nicer neighbourhood (e.g., better schools, lower crime) is associated with a significant increase in the amount of money they will earn as an adult later in life. Chetty and colleagues (2016) found that smoking and obesity are associated with a significantly higher death rate, whereas exercise is associated with a significantly lower rate of death. Moreover, if you are poor but live in a place with higher population density, a higher percentage of immigrants and university graduates, higher government expenditures, and higher home values, you will live significantly longer.

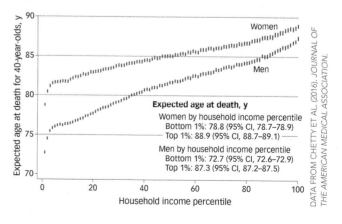

DATA FROM CHETTY ET AL. (2016). JOURNAL OF THE AMERICAN MEDICAL ASSOCIATION.

What causes burnout? One theory suggests that the culprit is using your job to give meaning to your life (Pines, 1993). If you define yourself only by your career and gauge your self-worth by success at work, you risk having nothing left when work fails. For example, a teacher in danger of burnout might do well to invest time in family, hobbies, or other self-expressions. Others argue that some emotionally stressful jobs lead to burnout no matter how they are approached and that active efforts to overcome the stress before burnout occurs are important. The stress management techniques discussed in the next section may be lifesavers for people in such jobs.

Stress Management: Dealing with It

Most undergraduate students (92%) say they occasionally feel overwhelmed by the tasks they face, and over a third say they have dropped courses or received low grades in response to severe stress (Duenwald, 2002). No doubt you are among the lucky 8% who are entirely cool and report no stress. But just in case you're not, you may be interested in our exploration of stress management techniques: ways to counteract psychological and physical stress reactions directly by managing your mind and body, as well as ways to sidestep stress altogether by managing your situation early on.

Mind Management

A significant part of stress management is control of the mind. Changing the way you think about potentially stressful events can change how you respond to them. Three ways of changing your thinking about stressors are the use of repression, rationalization, and reframing.

Repressive Coping: Holding an Artificially Positive Viewpoint

Controlling your thoughts is not easy, but some people do seem to be able to banish unpleasant thoughts from the mind. This style of dealing with stress, called **repressive coping**, is characterized by *avoiding feelings, thoughts, or situations that are reminders of a stressor and maintaining an artificially positive viewpoint.* Everyone has some problems, of course, but repressors are good at deliberately ignoring them (Barnier et al., 2004). So, for example, when repressors suffer a heart attack, they are less likely than other people to report intrusive thoughts of their heart problems in the days and weeks that follow (Ginzburg et al., 2002).

Like Elizabeth Smart, who for years after her rescue focused in interviews on what was happening in her life now, rather than repeatedly discussing her past in captivity, people often rearrange their lives to avoid stressful situations. Many victims of rape, for example, not only avoid the place where the rape occurred but may move away from their home or neighbourhood (Ellis, 1983). Anticipating and attempting to avoid reminders of the traumatic experience, they become wary of strangers, especially men who resemble the assailant, and they check doors, locks, and windows more frequently than before. It may make sense to try to avoid stressful thoughts and situations if you're the kind of person who is good at putting unpleasant thoughts and emotions out of mind (Coifman et al., 2007). For some people, however, the avoidance of unpleasant thoughts and situations is so difficult that it can turn into a grim preoccupation (Parker & McNally, 2008; Wegner & Zanakos, 1994). For those who can't avoid negative emotions effectively, it may be better to come to grips with them. This is the basic idea of rational coping.

Learning Outcomes

WHAT YOU NEED TO KNOW

- Explain techniques for coping with psychological stress.

- Identify physical activities that reduce stress.

- Define and give examples of situation management.

On April 23, 2018, a 25-year-old man intentionally drove his van into pedestrians on Yonge Street in Toronto, killing 10 and injuring 15 others. People deal with major stressful life events such as this in different ways. Repressive copers use avoidance; rational copers use acceptance, exposure, and understanding; and reframers try to think about the situation in more positive ways.

repressive coping Avoiding feelings, thoughts, or situations that are reminders of a stressor and maintaining an artificially positive viewpoint.

Rational Coping: Working to Overcome

Rational coping involves *facing a stressor and working to overcome it.* This strategy is the opposite of repressive coping, so it may seem to be the most unpleasant and unnerving thing you could do when faced with stress. It requires approaching, rather than avoiding, a stressor in order to diminish its longer-term negative impact (Hayes et al., 1999). Rational coping is a three-step process: *acceptance,* coming to realize that the stressor exists and cannot be wished away; *exposure,* attending to the stressor, thinking about it, and even seeking it out; and *understanding,* working to find the meaning of the stressor in your life.

When the trauma is particularly intense, rational coping may be difficult to undertake. In rape trauma, for example, even accepting that the rape happened takes time and effort; the initial impulse is to deny the event and try to live as though it had never occurred. Psychological treatment may help during the exposure step by aiding victims in confronting and thinking about what happened. Using a technique called *prolonged exposure,* rape survivors relive the traumatic event in their imaginations by recording a verbal account of the event and then listening to the recording daily. In one study, rape survivors were instructed to seek out objectively safe situations that caused them anxiety or that they had avoided. This sounds like bitter medicine indeed, but it is remarkably effective, producing significant reductions in anxiety and symptoms of posttraumatic stress disorder compared with no therapy and compared with other therapies that promote more gradual and subtle forms of exposure (Foa & McLean, 2016).

The third element of rational coping involves coming to an understanding of the meaning of the stressful events. A trauma victim may wonder again and again: Why me? How did it happen? Why? Survivors of incest frequently voice the desire to make sense of their trauma (Weiss & Curcio Alexander, 2013), a process that is difficult, even impossible, during bouts of suppression and avoidance.

Reframing: Changing Your Thinking

Changing the way you think is another way to cope with stressful thoughts. **Reframing** involves *finding a new or creative way to think about a stressor that reduces its threat.* If you experience anxiety at the thought of public speaking, for example, you might reframe by shifting from thinking of an audience as evaluating you to thinking of yourself as evaluating them, which might make speech giving easier.

rational coping Facing a stressor and working to overcome it.

reframing Finding a new or creative way to think about a stressor that reduces its threat.

Nervous about a class presentation or performance? Reframing that anxiety as arousal, which can help you perform better, can actually improve your performance. Get out there and reframe!

Reframing can be an effective way to prepare for a moderately stressful situation, but if something like public speaking is so stressful that you can't bear to think about it until you absolutely must, you may not be able to apply this technique. **Stress-inoculation training (SIT)** is *a reframing technique that helps people cope with stressful situations by developing positive ways to think about the situations.* For example, in one study, people who had difficulty controlling their anger were trained to rehearse and reframe their thoughts with phrases such as these: "You don't need to prove yourself"; "I'm not going to let him get to me"; and "I'll just let him make a fool of himself." Anger-prone people who practiced these thoughts were less likely to become physiologically aroused in response to laboratory-based provocations, both imaginary and real. Subsequent research on SIT has revealed that it can also be useful for people who have suffered prior traumatic events, helping them become more comfortable living with those events (Foa & Meadows, 1997).

Reframing can take place spontaneously if people are given the opportunity to spend time thinking and writing about stressful events. In an important series of studies, Jamie Pennebaker (1989) found that the physical health of undergraduate students improved after they spent a few hours writing about their deepest thoughts and feelings. Compared with students who had written about something else, members of the self-disclosure group were less likely in subsequent months to visit the student health centre; they also used less aspirin and achieved better grades (Pennebaker & Chung, 2007). In fact, engaging in such expressive writing was found to improve immune function as well (Pennebaker et al., 1988), whereas suppressing emotional topics weakened it (Petrie et al., 1998). The positive effect of self-disclosing writing may reflect its usefulness in reframing trauma and reducing stress.

Body Management

Stress can express itself as tension in your neck, back pain, a knot in your stomach, sweaty hands, or that distressed face you may glimpse in the mirror. Because stress often manifests itself through bodily symptoms, bodily techniques such as meditation, relaxation therapy, biofeedback, and aerobic exercise can be useful in managing it.

Meditation: Turning Inward

Meditation is *the practice of intentional contemplation.* Techniques of meditation are associated with a variety of religious traditions and are increasingly being practiced outside religious contexts. The techniques vary widely. Some forms of meditation call for attempts to clear the mind of thought; others involve focusing on a single thought (e.g., thinking about a candle flame); still others involve concentration on breathing or on a *mantra* (a repetitive sound, such as *om*). At a minimum, these techniques have in common a period of quiet.

Time spent meditating can be restful and revitalizing. Beyond these immediate benefits, many people also meditate in an effort to experience deeper or transformed consciousness. Whatever the reason, meditation appears to have positive psychological effects (Hölzel et al., 2011). Many believe it does so, in part, by improving control over attention. The focus of many forms of meditation, such as mindfulness meditation, is on teaching ourselves how to remain focused on, and to accept, our immediate experience. Interestingly, experienced meditators show deactivation in the default mode network (which is associated with mind wandering; see Figure 5.7 in the Consciousness chapter) during meditation relative to nonmeditators (Brewer et al., 2011). Even short-term meditation training administered to undergraduates has been shown to improve the connectivity between parts of the brain involved in conflict monitoring and cognitive and emotional control, and to do so via increased myelination (perhaps due to increased neuron firing) and other axonal changes (Tang et al., 2012).

stress-inoculation training (SIT) A reframing technique that helps people cope with stressful situations by developing positive ways to think about the situations.

meditation The practice of intentional contemplation.

Prince Harry, a member of the British royal family, has been a prominent advocate for mental health and wellness. He recently shared that he is among the increasing number of people who engages in daily meditation, which has been shown to reduce stress and improve health.

Moreover, recent research suggests that those who engage in several weeks of intensive meditation show lengthening of their telomeres, which suggests a slight reversal of the effects of stress and aging as described earlier (Conklin et al., 2015). Taken together, these findings indicate that meditators may be better able to regulate their thoughts and emotions, which may translate to a better ability to manage interpersonal relations, anxiety, and a range of other activities that require conscious effort (Sedlmeier et al., 2012).

Relaxation: Picturing Peace

Imagine for a moment that you are scratching your chin. Don't actually do it; just think about it and notice that your body participates by moving ever so slightly, tensing and relaxing in the sequence of the imagined action. Edmund Jacobson (1932) discovered these effects with *electromyography* (EMG), a technique used to measure the subtle activity of muscles. A person asked to imagine rowing a boat or plucking a flower from a bush would produce slight levels of tension in the muscles involved in performing the act. Jacobson also found that thoughts of relaxing the muscles sometimes reduced EMG readings when people didn't even report feeling tense. Our bodies respond to all the things we think about doing every day. These thoughts create muscle tension even when we think we're doing nothing at all.

These observations led Jacobson to develop **relaxation therapy,** *a technique for reducing tension by consciously relaxing muscles of the body.* A person in relaxation therapy may be asked to relax specific muscle groups one at a time or to imagine warmth flowing through the body or to think about a relaxing situation. This activity draws on a **relaxation response**, *a condition of reduced muscle tension, cortical activity, heart rate, breathing rate, and blood pressure* (Benson, 1990). Basically, as soon as you get in a comfortable position, quiet down, and focus on something repetitive or soothing that holds your attention, you relax.

Setting aside time (e.g., 45 minutes) to relax on a regular basis can reduce symptoms of stress and even reduce blood levels of cortisol, the biochemical marker of the stress response (Cruess et al., 2000). How can you use this in your daily life? Quite simply: Take a break. Go for a walk and take in nature. Experimental studies have shown that going for short walks in the park during workers' lunch breaks decreased their feelings of stress (de Bloom et al., 2017) and that 90-minute walks in nature (versus those in urban settings) decrease rumination and activity in parts of the brain associated with increased risk for mental disorders (Bratman et al., 2015).

Biofeedback: Enlisting the Help of an External Monitor

Wouldn't it be nice if, instead of having to learn to relax, you could just flip a switch and relax as fast as possible? **Biofeedback**, *the use of an external monitoring device to obtain information about a bodily function and then to possibly gain control over that function,* was developed with the goal of high-tech relaxation in mind. You might not be aware right now of whether your fingers are warm or cold, for example, but with an electronic thermometer displayed before you, the ability to sense your temperature might allow you (with a bit of practice) to make your hands warmer or cooler at will (e.g., Roberts & McGrady, 1996)

Biofeedback can help people control physiological functions they are not likely to become aware of in other ways. For instance, you probably have no idea what brain-wave patterns you are producing right now. In the late 1950s, Joe Kamiya (1969), a psychologist using the electroencephalograph (also called the EEG and discussed in the Neuroscience and Behaviour chapter), initiated a brain-wave biofeedback revolution when he found that people could change their brain waves from alert beta patterns to relaxed alpha patterns and back again when permitted to monitor their own EEG readings.

relaxation therapy A technique for reducing tension by consciously relaxing muscles of the body.

relaxation response A condition of reduced muscle tension, cortical activity, heart rate, breathing rate, and blood pressure.

biofeedback The use of an external monitoring device to obtain information about a bodily function and then to possibly gain control over that function.

More recent studies suggest that EEG biofeedback (or neurofeedback) is moderately successful in treating brain-wave abnormalities in disorders such as epilepsy (Yucha & Gilbert, 2004) and in teaching people to downregulate activity in regions of the brain that are involved in the strong emotional responses seen in some forms of psychopathology (Hamilton et al., 2010). Often, however, the use of biofeedback to produce relaxation in the brain turns out to be a bit of technological overkill and may not be much more effective than simply having the person stretch out in a hammock and hum a happy tune. Although biofeedback is not a magic bullet that gives people control over stress-induced health troubles, it has proven to be a useful technique for increasing relaxation and decreasing chronic pain (Palermo et al., 2011). People who do not benefit from relaxation therapy may find that biofeedback provides a useful alternative.

Aerobic Exercise: Boosting Mood

A jogger nicely decked out in fresh new lululemon running gear bounces in place at the crosswalk and then springs away when the signal changes. It is tempting to assume that this jogger is the picture of psychological health: happy, unstressed, and even downright exuberant. As it turns out, this stereotype is true: Studies indicate that *aerobic exercise* (exercise that increases heart rate and oxygen intake for a sustained period) is associated with psychological well-being (Hassmen et al., 2000). But does exercise *cause* psychological well-being, or does psychological well-being cause people to exercise? Perhaps general happiness is what inspires the jogger's bounce. Or could some unknown third factor (wearing lululemon?) cause both the need to exercise and the sense of well-being? As we've mentioned many times, correlation does not always imply causation.

To try to tease apart causal factors, researchers have randomly assigned people to aerobic exercise activities and no-exercise comparison groups and have found that exercise actually does promote stress relief and happiness. One meta-analysis (a quantitative review of existing studies) compiled data from 90 studies that involved more than 10,000 people with chronic illness who were randomly assigned either to an exercise or a no-exercise condition. People assigned to the aerobic exercise condition experienced a significant reduction in depressive symptoms (Herring et al., 2012). Other meta-analyses have come to similar conclusions, showing, for instance, that exercise is as effective as the strongest psychological interventions for depression (Rimer et al., 2012) and that exercise even shows positive physical and mental health benefits for individuals with schizophrenia (Gorczynski & Faulkner, 2011). Pretty good effects for a simple, timeless intervention with no side effects!

The reasons for these positive effects are unclear. Researchers have suggested that the effects result from increases in the body's production of neurotransmitters such as serotonin, which can have a positive effect on mood (as discussed in the Neuroscience and Behaviour chapter) or from increases in the production of endorphins (the endogenous opioids discussed in the Neuroscience and Behaviour and Consciousness chapters).

Beyond boosting positive mood, exercise also stands to keep you healthy into the future. Recent research has shown that engaging in bouts of aerobic exercise helps you to recover more quickly from future stressors (Bernstein & McNally, 2017). Perhaps the simplest thing you can do to improve your happiness and health, then, is to participate regularly in an aerobic activity. Pick something you find fun: Sign up for a dance class, get into a regular basketball game, or start paddling a canoe—just not all at once.

Biofeedback gives people access to visual or audio feedback showing levels of psychophysiological functions—such as heart rate, breathing, brain electrical activity, or skin temperature—that they would otherwise be unable to sense directly.

Exercise helps reduce stress—unless, as for John Stibbard, your exercise involves carrying the Olympic torch on Vancouver's wobbly Capilano Suspension Bridge, 70 metres above the Capilano River.

Situation Management

After you have tried to manage stress by managing your mind and managing your body, what's left to manage? Look around and you'll notice a whole world out there. Perhaps that could be managed as well. Situation management involves changing your life situation as a way of reducing the impact of stress on your mind and body. Ways to manage your situation can include seeking out social support, religious or spiritual practice, and finding a place for humour in your life.

Social Support: "Swimming with a Buddy"

The wisdom of the National Safety Council's first rule — "Always swim with a buddy" — is obvious when you're in water over your head, but people often don't realize that the same principle applies whenever danger threatens. Other people can offer help in times of stress. **Social support** is *aid gained through interacting with others.* One of the more self-defeating things you can do in life is fail to connect to people in this way. Just failing to find a life partner, for example, is bad for your health. Single people have an elevated risk of mortality from cardiovascular disease, cancer, pneumonia and influenza, chronic obstructive pulmonary disease, and liver disease and cirrhosis (Johnson et al., 2000). More generally, good ongoing relationships with friends and family and participation in social activities and religious groups can be as healthy for you as exercising and not smoking (Umberson et al., 2006). Social support is helpful on many levels:

- An intimate partner can help you remember to exercise and follow your doctor's orders, and together you'll probably follow a healthier diet than you would all alone with your snacks.
- Talking about problems with friends and family can offer many of the benefits of professional psychotherapy, usually without the hourly fees.
- Sharing tasks and helping each other when times get tough can reduce the amount of work and worry in each other's lives.

Many first-year undergraduate students experience something of a crisis of social support. No matter how outgoing and popular they were in high school, newcomers typically find the task of developing satisfying new social relationships quite daunting. New friendships can seem shallow, connections with teachers may be perfunctory and even threatening, and social groups that are encountered can seem like islands of lost souls. ("Hey, we're forming a club to investigate the lack of clubs on campus—want to join?") It's not surprising that research shows that students who report the greatest feelings of isolation also show reduced immune responses to flu vaccinations (Pressman et al., 2005). Time spent getting to know people in new social situations can be an investment in your own health.

The value of social support in protecting against stress may be very different for women and men: Whereas women seek support under stress, men are less likely to do so. The fight-or-flight response to stress may be largely a male reaction, according to research on sex differences by Shelley Taylor (2002). Taylor suggested that the female response to stress is to *tend-and-befriend* by taking care of people and bringing them together. This is believed by some to be due at least in part to the release of *oxytocin,* a hormone secreted by the pituitary gland when women are pregnant or nursing, as well as in a range of other contexts. In the presence of estrogen, oxytocin triggers social responses: a tendency to seek out social contacts, nurture others, and create and maintain cooperative groups. After a hard day at work, a man may come home frustrated and worried about his job and end up drinking a beer and fuming alone. A woman under the same type of stress may be more likely to instead play with her kids or talk to friends on the phone. The tend-and-befriend response to stress may help explain why women are healthier and have a longer life span than men.

social support The aid gained through interacting with others.

Women are more likely than men to seek support when under stress.

The typical male response amplifies the unhealthy effects of stress, whereas the female response takes less of a toll on a woman's mind and body and provides social support for the people around her as well.

Religious Experiences: Reaping Earthly Rewards

In 2019, about 2 in 3 Canadians reported having a religious affiliation, and just over 1 in 2 said their religious or spiritual beliefs were somewhat or very important to how they live their lives (Cornelissen, 2021). Although many who believe in a higher power believe that their faith will be rewarded in an afterlife, it turns out that there may be some benefits here on earth as well. An enormous body of research has examined the associations between *religiosity* (affiliation with or engagement in the practices of a particular religion) and *spirituality* (having a belief in and engagement with some higher power, not necessarily linked to any particular religion) and positive health outcomes. The helpful effects of religiosity and spirituality have been observed in a wide range of areas, including lower rates of heart disease, decreases in chronic pain, and improved psychological health (Seybold & Hill, 2001).

Why do people who endorse religiosity or spirituality have better mental and physical health? Is it divine intervention? Several testable ideas have been proposed. Engagement in religious or spiritual practices, such as attendance at weekly religious services, may lead to the development of a stronger and more extensive social network, which has well-known health benefits. Those who are religious or spiritual also may fare better psychologically and physically as a result of following the healthy recommendations offered in many religious or spiritual teachings. That is, they may be more likely to observe dietary restrictions, abstain from the use of drugs or alcohol, or endorse a more hopeful and optimistic perspective of daily life events, all of which can lead to more positive health outcomes (Seeman et al., 2003; Seybold & Hill, 2001). However, many claims made by some religious groups have not been supported, such as the beneficial effects of intercessory prayer (see **FIGURE 14.4**).

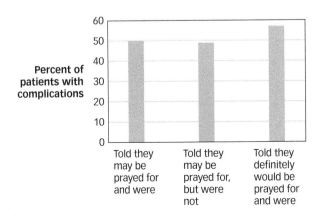

Figure 14.4

Pray for Me? To test whether praying for someone in their time of need actually helped, researchers randomly assigned 1,802 patients about to undergo cardiac bypass surgery to one of three conditions: those who were told they might be prayed for and were; those who were told they might be prayed for and weren't; and those who were told they definitely would be prayed for and were. Unfortunately, there were no differences in the presence of complications between those who were or were not prayed for. To make matters worse, those who were told they definitely would be prayed for and were (the bar on the far left) experienced significantly more complications than the other two groups (Benson et al., 2006).

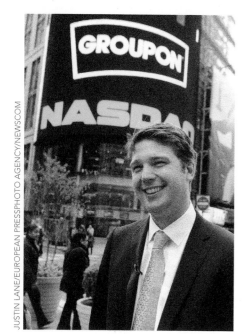

When Andrew Mason, CEO of the Internet company Groupon, left his position, his resignation letter read: "After four and a half intense and wonderful years as CEO of Groupon, I've decided that I'd like to spend more time with my family. Just kidding—I was fired today." He went on to add, "I am so lucky to have had the opportunity to take the company this far with all of you. I'll now take some time to decompress (FYI I'm looking for a good fat camp to lose my Groupon 40, if anyone has a suggestion), and then maybe I'll figure out how to channel this experience into something productive." This seems like a textbook case of using humour to mitigate stress, which is why we put it, um, you know where.

Psychologists are actively testing the effectiveness of various religious and spiritual practices with the goal of better understanding how they might help explain, and improve, the human condition.

Humour: Laughing It Off

Wouldn't it be nice to laugh at your troubles and move on? Most of us recognize that humour can defuse unpleasant situations and bad feelings, and it makes sense that bringing some fun into your life could help reduce stress. The extreme point of view on this topic is staked out in self-help books with titles such as *Health, Healing, and the Amuse System* and *How Serious Is This? Seeing Humor in Daily Stress*. Is laughter truly the best medicine? Should we close down the hospitals and send in the clowns?

There is a kernel of truth to the theory that humour can help us cope with stress. For example, humour can reduce sensitivity to pain and distress, as researchers found when they subjected volunteers to an overinflated blood pressure cuff. Participants were more tolerant of the pain during a laughter-inducing comedy audiotape than during a neutral tape or guided relaxation (Cogan et al., 1987).

Humour can also reduce the time needed to calm down after a stressful event. For instance, men viewing a highly stressful film about industrial accidents were asked to narrate the film aloud, either by describing the events seriously or by making their commentary as funny as possible. Although men in both groups reported feeling tense while watching the film and showed increased levels of sympathetic nervous arousal (increased heart rate and skin conductance, decreased skin temperature), those looking for humour in the experience bounced back to normal arousal levels more quickly than did those in the serious story group (Newman & Stone, 1996).

If laughter and fun can alleviate stress quickly in the short term, do the effects accumulate to improve health and longevity? Sadly, the evidence suggests not (Provine, 2000). A study titled "Do Comics Have the Last Laugh?" tracked the longevity of comedians in comparison to other entertainers and non-entertainers (Rotton, 1992). It was found that the comedians died younger—perhaps after too many nights on stage thinking, *I'm dying out here*.

Scheduling and Activating: Getting It Done

At one time or another, most of us have avoided carrying out a task or put it off to a later time. The task may be unpleasant, difficult, or just less entertaining than other things we could be doing at the moment. For undergraduates, procrastination can affect a range of academic activities, such as writing a term paper or preparing for an exam. Academic procrastination is not uncommon: University students report engaging in academic procrastination between 30 and 60% of the time (Rabin et al., 2011). Although it's fun to hang out with your friends at night, it's not so much fun to worry for 3 days about your impending history exam or try to study at 4:00 a.m. the day of the test. Studying now, or at least a little bit each day, robs procrastination of its power over you.

Some procrastinators defend this practice by claiming that they tend to work best under pressure or by noting that as long as a task gets done, it doesn't matter all that much if it is completed just before the deadline. Is there any merit to such claims? Or are they just feeble excuses for counterproductive behaviour?

Among students, higher levels of procrastination are associated with poorer academic performance (Moon & Illingworth, 2005) and higher levels of psychological distress (Rice et al., 2012). In fact, recent evidence indicates that habitual procrastinators show higher levels of self-reported hypertension and cardiovascular disease, even when controlling for other personality traits associated with these health problems (Sirois, 2015). Although there is no proven method of eliminating procrastination, there is some evidence that procrastination in undergraduate students can be reduced by interventions that use training in time management or behavioural methods that target the processes that are believed to be responsible for procrastination (Glick & Orsillo, 2015). If you tend towards procrastination, we hope that the research discussed here can alert you to its pitfalls.

The Psychology of Illness: Mind Over Matter

One of the mind's most important influences on the body's health and illness is the mind's sensitivity to bodily symptoms. Noticing what is wrong with the body can be helpful when it motivates a search for treatment, but sensitivity can also lead to further problems when it snowballs into a preoccupation with illness that itself can cause harm.

Learning Outcome

WHAT YOU NEED TO KNOW

- Describe the interrelationship between the mind and body relating to illness.

Psychological Effects of Illness

Why does it feel so bad to be sick? You notice scratchiness in your throat or the start of sniffles, and you think you might be coming down with something. And in just a few short hours, you're achy all over, energy gone, no appetite, feverish, feeling dull and listless. You're sick. The question is, why does it have to be like this? Why couldn't it feel good? As long as you're going to have to stay at home and miss out on things anyway, couldn't sickness be less of a pain?

Sickness makes you miserable for good reason. Misery is part of the *sickness response,* a coordinated, adaptive set of reactions to illness organized by the brain (Hart, 1988; Watkins & Maier, 2005). The sickness response makes you withdraw from activity and lie still, conserving the energy for fighting illness that you'd normally expend on other behaviour. Appetite loss is similarly helpful: The energy spent on digestion is conserved. Thus, the behavioural changes that accompany illness are not random side effects; they help the body fight disease. These responses become prolonged and exaggerated with aging—subtle signs that we are losing the fight (Barrientos et al., 2009).

How does the brain know it should do this? The immune response to an infection begins with the activation of white blood cells that "eat" microbes and release *cytokines,* proteins that circulate through the body and communicate with the other white blood cells and also communicate the sickness response to the brain (Maier & Watkins, 1998). Administering cytokines to an animal can artificially induce the sickness response, and administering drugs that oppose the action of cytokines can block the sickness response even during an ongoing infection. Cytokines do not enter the brain, but they activate the vagus nerve, which runs from the intestines, stomach, and chest to the brain and convey the "I am infected" message (Goehler et al., 2000; Klarer et al., 2014). This may be why we often feel sickness in the "gut," a gnawing discomfort in the very centre of the body.

Interestingly, the sickness response can be prompted without any infection at all, merely by the introduction of stress. The stressful presence of a predator's odour, for instance, can trigger the sickness response of lethargy in an animal, along with symptoms of infection such as fever and increased white blood cell count (Maier & Watkins, 2000). In humans, the connection among sickness response, immune

If you have been reading this very exciting textbook, there is no chance you have been yawning. However, seeing this guy yawning may cause your brain to initiate a yawn response as well.

reaction, and stress is illustrated in depression, a condition in which all the sickness machinery runs at full speed. In addition to fatigue and malaise, depressed people show signs characteristic of infection, including high levels of cytokines circulating in the blood (Maes, 1995). Just as illness can make you feel a bit depressed, severe depression seems to recruit the brain's sickness response and make you feel ill (Watkins & Maier, 2005).

Recognizing Illness and Seeking Treatment

You probably weren't thinking about your breathing a minute ago, but now that you're reading this sentence, you notice it. Sometimes we are very attentive to our bodies. At other times, the body seems to be on "automatic," running along unnoticed until specific symptoms announce themselves or are pointed out by an annoying textbook writer.

People differ substantially in the degree to which they attend to and report bodily symptoms. Do people with many symptom complaints truly have a lot of problems? Or are they just more sensitive to the experience of any bodily changes? To answer this question, researchers used fMRI brain scans to compare the severity of reported sensation of pain with the degree of activation in brain areas usually associated with pain experience. Volunteers underwent several applications of a thermal stimulus (43.3–48.9°C) to the leg; and as you might expect, some of the participants found it more painful than did others. Scans during the painful events revealed that the anterior cingulate cortex, somatosensory cortex, and prefrontal cortex (brain areas known to respond to painful body stimulation) were particularly active in those participants who reported higher levels of pain experience (see **FIGURE 14.5**), suggesting that people can report accurately on the extent to which they experience pain (Coghill et al., 2003) (see The Real World: This Is Your Brain on Placebos).

Some people are particularly slow at recognizing illness, which can come with costs: It can delay the search for treatment, sometimes with serious repercussions. Of 2,404 patients in one study who had been treated for a heart attack, 40% had delayed going to the hospital for more than 6 hours from the time they first noticed

Figure 14.5

The Brain in Pain These fMRI scans show brain activation in high- (*left*) and low-pain-sensitive (*right*) individuals during painful stimulation. The anterior cingulate cortex and primary somatosensory areas show greater activation in high-pain-sensitive individuals. Levels of activation are highest in yellow and red, then light blue and dark blue (Coghill et al., 2003).

suspicious symptoms (Gurwitz et al., 1997). Severe chest pain or a history of prior heart surgery did send people to the hospital in a hurry. Those with more subtle symptoms often waited around for hours, however, not calling an ambulance or their doctor, just hoping the problem would go away. This is not a good idea, because many of the treatments that can reduce the damage of a heart attack are most useful when provided early. When it comes to your own health, protecting your mind from distress through the denial of illness can result in exposing your body to great danger.

On Being a Patient

Getting sick is more than a change in physical state; it can involve a—transformation of identity. This change can be particularly profound with a serious illness: A kind of cloud settles over you, a feeling that you are now different, and this transformation can influence everything you feel and do in this new world of illness. You even take on a new role in life, a **sick role,** *a socially recognized set of rights and obligations linked with illness* (Parsons, 1975). The sick person often is absolved of responsibility for many daily obligations and enjoys exemption from normal activities. For example, in addition to skipping school and homework and staying on the couch all day, a sick child can watch TV and avoid eating anything unpleasant at dinner. In return for these exemptions, the sick role also incurs obligations. The properly "sick" individual cannot appear to enjoy the illness or reveal signs of wanting to be sick and must also take care to pursue treatment to end this "undesirable" condition. Parsons (1975) observed that illness has psychological, social, and even moral components. You may recall times when you have felt the conflict between sickness and health as though it were a moral decision: Should you drag yourself out of bed and try to make it to the chemistry exam or just slump back under the covers and wallow in your "pain"?

Historically, many people have argued that if a person is "healthy enough" to get out of bed and attend school or work, then they should do so. Ideas about this are likely to change due to the COVID-19 pandemic. Given that the *sick role* is based on social norms, it can change as societal norms shift over time.

Some people feign medical or psychological symptoms to achieve something they want, a type of behaviour called *malingering.* Because many symptoms of illness cannot be faked (even facial expressions of pain are difficult to simulate) (Williams, 2002), malingering is possible only with a small number of illnesses. Faking illness is suspected when the secondary gains of illness outweigh the costs. Such gains can be very subtle, as when a child stays in bed because of the comfort provided by an otherwise distant parent, or they can be obvious, as when insurance benefits turn out to be a cash award for Best Actor. Some behaviours that may lead to illness may not be under the patient's control; for example, self-starvation may be part of an uncontrollable eating disorder (see the Emotion and Motivation chapter). For this reason, malingering can be difficult to diagnose and treat (Bass & Halligan, 2014).

Patient–Practitioner Interaction

Medical care usually occurs through a strange interaction. On one side is a patient who expects to be questioned and examined and possibly prodded or given bad news. On the other side is a health care provider, who comes in knowing nothing about what brings the patient in but who hopes to quickly obtain information from the patient by asking lots of extremely personal questions (and examining extremely personal parts of the body); to identify the problem and a potential solution; to help in some way; and to achieve all of this as efficiently as possible because more patients are waiting. It seems less like a time for healing than an occasion for major awkwardness.

One of the keys to an effective medical care interaction is physician empathy (Kelm et al., 2014). To offer successful treatment, the clinician must simultaneously

sick role A socially recognized set of rights and obligations linked with illness.

Doctor and patient have two modes of interaction, the technical and the interpersonal. Medical training with robot patients may help doctors learn the technical side of health care, but it is likely to do little to improve the interpersonal side.

understand the patient's physical state *and* psychological state. Physicians often err on the side of failing to acknowledge patients' emotions, focusing instead on technical issues of the case (Suchman et al., 1997). This is particularly unfortunate, because a substantial percentage of patients who seek medical care do so for treatment of psychological and emotional problems (Wiegner et al., 2015). As the Greek physician Hippocrates wrote in the 4th century BCE: "Some patients, though conscious that their condition is perilous, recover their health simply through their contentment with the goodness of the physician." The best physician treats the patient's mind as well as the patient's body.

Another important part of the medical care interaction is motivating the patient to follow the prescribed regimen of care (Miller & Rollnick, 2012). When researchers check compliance by counting the pills remaining in a patient's bottle after a prescription has been started, they find that patients often do an astonishingly poor job of following doctors' orders (see **FIGURE 14.6**). Compliance deteriorates when the treatment must be frequent, as when eye drops for glaucoma are required every few hours, or is inconvenient or painful, such as drawing blood or performing injections in managing diabetes. Finally, compliance decreases as the number of treatments increases. This is a worrisome problem, especially for older patients, who may have difficulty remembering when to take which pill. Failures in medical care may stem from the failure of health care providers to recognize the psychological challenges that are involved in self-care. Helping people follow doctors' orders involves psychology and is an essential part of promoting health.

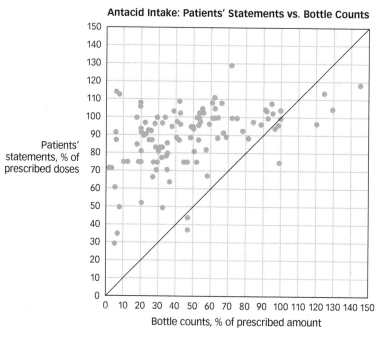

Figure 14.6

Antacid Intake A scatterplot of antacid intake measured by bottle count plotted against patient's stated intake for 116 patients. When the actual and stated intakes are the same, the point lies on the diagonal line; when stated intake is greater than actual, the point lies above the line. Most patients exaggerated their intake (Roth & Caron, 1978).

The Real World • **This Is Your Brain on Placebos**

There is something miraculous about Band-Aids. Your standard household toddler typically requires one for any injury at all, expecting and often achieving immediate relief. It is not unusual to find a child who reports that aches or pains are "cured" if a Band-Aid has been applied by a helpful adult. Of course, the Band-Aid is not really helping the pain—or is it?

Physicians and psychologists have long puzzled over the *placebo effect*, a clinically significant psychological or physiological response to a therapeutically inert substance or procedure. The classic placebo is the sugar pill, but Band-Aids, injections, heating pads, neck rubs, homeopathic remedies, and kind words can have placebo effects (Diederich & Goetz, 2008).

How do placebos operate? Do people being treated for pain really feel the pain but distort their report of the experience to make it fit their beliefs about treatment? Or does the placebo actually reduce the pain a patient experiences? Howard Fields and Jon Levine (1984) discovered that placebos trigger the release of endorphins (or *endogenous opioids*), painkilling chemicals similar to morphine that are produced by the brain (see the Consciousness chapter).

Placebos also have been found to lower the activation of specific brain areas associated with pain. One set of fMRI studies examined brain activation as volunteers

Can a Band-Aid cure all of your aches and pains? Many children, like this little guy, report immediate pain relief following application of a Band-Aid to whatever spot hurts. Although most adults know that Band-Aids don't treat pain, the placebo effect remains powerful throughout the life span.

were exposed to electric shock or heat (Wager et al., 2004). In preparation for some exposures to these painful stimuli, a placebo cream was applied to the skin, and the participant was told it was an analgesic that would reduce the pain. Other participants merely experienced the pain. As you can see in the accompanying images, the fMRI scans showed decreased activation during placebo analgesia in the *thalamus, anterior cingulate cortex,* and *insula,* pain-sensitive brain regions that were activated during untreated pain. These findings suggest that placebos do not lead people to misreport their pain experience, but, rather, they reduce brain activity in areas that normally are active during pain experiences.

The Brain's Response to Placebo These fMRI scans reveal that some brain regions that are normally activated when individuals report pain in response to shocks are deactivated when those individuals are given a placebo analgesic during the shock. These regions include (a) the anterior cingulate cortex and (b) the insula and thalamus (Wager et al., 2004).

The Psychology of Health: Feeling Good

Two kinds of psychological factors influence personal health: health-relevant personality traits and health behaviour. Personality can influence health through relatively enduring traits that make some people particularly susceptible to health problems or stress while sparing or protecting others. The Type A behaviour pattern is an example. Because personality is not typically something we choose ("I'd like a bit of that sense of humour and extraversion over there, please, but hold the whininess"), this source of health can be beyond personal control. In contrast, engaging in positive health behaviours is something anyone can do, at least in principle.

Learning Outcome

WHAT YOU NEED TO KNOW

- Explain the attitudes and behaviours that lead to good health.

"Whoa—*way* too much information."

ALEX GREGORY/CARTOON STOCK

Personality and Health

Different health problems seem to plague different social groups. For example, South Asian people in Canada have higher rates of heart disease, have double the rate of diabetes, and are more prone to becoming overweight compared to white people (Rana et al., 2014). Indigenous people in Canada also have a much higher rate of heart disease (Reading, 2015) and First Nations people on reserves have 3 to 5 times the rate of diabetes (Public Health Agency of Canada, 2011).

Personality is another factor that turns out to matter for wellness, with individual differences in optimism and hardiness being important influences.

Optimism

Pollyanna is one of literature's most famous optimists. Eleanor H. Porter's 1913 novel *Pollyanna* portrayed her as a girl who greeted life with boundless good cheer, even when she was orphaned and sent to live with her cruel aunt. Her response to a sunny day was to remark on the good weather, of course, but her response to a gloomy day was to point out how lucky it is that not every day is gloomy! Her crotchety Aunt Polly had exactly the opposite attitude, somehow managing to turn every happy moment into an opportunity for strict correction. A person's level of optimism or pessimism tends to be fairly stable over time, and research comparing the personalities of twins reared together with those of twins reared apart suggests that this stability arises because these traits are moderately heritable (Plomin et al., 1992). Perhaps Pollyanna and Aunt Polly were each "born that way."

An optimist who believes that "in uncertain times, I usually expect the best" is likely to be healthier than a pessimist who believes that "if something can go wrong for me, it will." One recent review of dozens of studies that included tens of thousands of participants concluded that of all the measures of psychological well-being examined, optimism is the one that most strongly predicted a positive outcome for cardiovascular health (Boehm & Kubzansky, 2012). It is important to note that the association between optimism and cardiovascular health remains even after statistically controlling for traditional risk factors for heart disease, including depression and anxiety, suggesting that it is not merely the absence of psychopathology but the presence of positive expectancies for the future that predicts positive health outcomes. Does just having positive thoughts about the future make it so? Unfortunately not.

Rather than improving physical health directly, optimism seems to aid in the maintenance of *psychological* health in the face of physical health problems. When sick, optimists are more likely than pessimists to maintain positive emotions, avoid negative emotions such as anxiety and depression, stick to the medical regimens their caregivers have prescribed, and keep up their relationships with others. Among women who have surgery for breast cancer, for example, optimists are less likely to experience distress and fatigue after treatment than are pessimists, largely because they keep up social contacts and recreational activities during their treatment (Carver et al., 2003).

Optimism also seems to aid in the maintenance of physical health. For instance, optimism appears to be associated with cardiovascular health because optimistic people tend to engage in healthier behaviours such as eating a balanced diet and exercising, which in turn leads to a healthier lipid profile, which decreases the risk of heart disease (Boehm et al., 2013). (Higher levels of high-density lipoprotein cholesterol help to prevent buildup in your arteries and lower triglycerides, which are the chemical form of fat storage in the body.) So being optimistic is a positive asset, but it takes more than just hope to obtain positive health benefits.

The benefits of optimism raise an important question: If the traits of optimism and pessimism are stable over time—even resistant to change—can pessimists ever hope to gain any of the advantages of optimism? Research has shown that even die-hard pessimists can be trained to become significantly more optimistic and that this training can improve their psychosocial health outcomes. For example, pessimistic breast cancer patients who received 10 weeks of training in stress management techniques became

Adrianne Haslet was approximately 1.3 metres from one of the bombs that exploded at the Boston Marathon in 2013. Although the explosion caused her to lose her left foot, Adrianne (centre) vowed that she would continue her career as a dancer—and she actually ran in the Boston Marathon in 2016. She is an optimist, and optimism can lead to positive health outcomes.

BILL GREENE/THE BOSTON GLOBE/ GETTY IMAGES

more optimistic and were less likely than those who received only relaxation exercises to suffer distress and fatigue during their cancer treatments (Antoni et al., 2001).

Hardiness

Some people seem to be thick-skinned, somehow able to take stress or abuse that could be devastating to others. Are there personality traits that contribute to such resilience and offer protection from stress-induced illness? To identify such traits, Suzanne Kobasa (1979) studied a group of stress-resistant business executives. These individuals reported high levels of stressful life events but had histories of relatively few illnesses compared with a similar group who succumbed to stress by getting sick. The stress-resistant group (Kobasa labelled them *hardy*) shared several traits, all conveniently beginning with the letter C. They showed a sense of *commitment*, an ability to become involved in life's tasks and encounters rather than just dabbling. They exhibited a belief in *control,* the expectation that their actions and words have a causal influence over their lives and environment. And they were willing to accept *challenge,* undertaking change and accepting opportunities for growth.

Can anyone develop hardiness? Researchers have attempted to teach hardiness and they have achieved some success. In one such attempt, participants attended 10 weekly hardiness-training sessions, in which they were encouraged to examine their stresses, develop action plans for dealing with them, explore their bodily reactions to stress, and find ways to compensate for unchangeable situations without falling into self-pity. Compared with control groups (who engaged in relaxation and meditation training or in group discussions about stress), the hardiness-training group reported greater reductions in their perceived personal stress, as well as fewer symptoms of illness (Maddi et al.,1998). Hardiness training can have similar positive effects in undergraduates, for some even boosting their grades (Maddi et al., 2009).

Sometimes hardiness tips over the edge into foolhardiness. Here, participants in a polar bear dip in Charlottetown, Prince Edward Island, take the plunge into freezing cold water during the winter.

Health-Promoting Behaviours and Self-Regulation

Even without changing our personalities at all, we can do certain things to be healthy. The importance of healthy eating, safe sex, and giving up smoking are common knowledge. But we don't seem to be acting on the basis of this knowledge. Over 40% of Americans over age 20 are obese (Hales et al., 2020). The prevalence of unsafe sex is difficult to estimate, but 1 in 5 people in the United States suffer from a sexually transmitted infection (STI), most of which are initially transmitted in those aged 15 to 24 years old (Kreisel et al., 2021). Another million people live with human immunodeficiency virus/acquired immune deficiency syndrome (HIV/AIDS). Of these, many are unaware of their infection, which is most often contracted through unprotected sex with an infected partner (Centers for Disease Control and Prevention [CDC], 2021b). And despite endless warnings, 14% of U.S. adults still smoke cigarettes (Cornelius et al., 2020). What's going on?

Self-Regulation

Doing what is good for you is not necessarily easy. Mark Twain once remarked, "The only way to keep your health is to eat what you don't want, drink what you don't like, and do what you'd rather not." Engaging in health-promoting behaviours involves **self-regulation**, *the exercise of voluntary control over the self to bring the self into line with preferred standards.* When you decide on a salad rather than a cheeseburger, for instance, you control your impulse and behave in a way that will help make you the kind of person you would prefer to be—a healthy one. Self-regulation often involves putting off immediate gratification for longer-term gains.

Sometimes self-regulation is less a matter of brute force than of strategy. Martial artists claim that anyone can easily overcome a large attacker with the right moves, and overcoming our own unhealthy impulses may also be a matter of finesse. Let's

Nobody ever said self-control was easy. Probably the only reason you're able to keep yourself from eating this cookie is that it's just a picture of a cookie. Really. Don't eat it.

self-regulation The exercise of voluntary control over the self to bring the self into line with preferred standards.

look carefully at healthy approaches to some key challenges for self-regulation—eating, safe sex, and smoking—to learn which "smart moves" can aid us in our struggles.

In addition to using self-regulation to manage your behaviour, such strategies also can help you to cope more adaptively with stress. For instance, there is growing evidence for the "shift-and-persist" strategy being protective against the effects of chronic stressors, such as those in equity-deserving groups (Chen & Miller, 2012). This model suggests that developing an ability to accept and adjust to chronic stressors, such as by reframing them as situations that one can learn from (i.e., shifting) combined with an ability to develop a purpose in life and remaining optimistic about one's future (i.e., persisting), one can decrease the biological impact of stressors. Adolescents from more disadvantaged backgrounds who report using shift-and-persist strategies show lower levels of inflammation than those without such a perspective (Chen et al., 2015).

Eating Wisely In many Western cultures, the weight of the average citizen is increasing alarmingly. One explanation is based on our evolutionary history: In order to ensure their survival, our ancestors found it useful to eat well in times of plenty to store calories for leaner times. In 21st-century postindustrial societies, however, there are no leaner times, and people can't burn all of the calories they consume (Pinel et al., 2000). But why, then, isn't obesity endemic throughout the Western world? Why are people in France leaner on average than North Americans, even though their foods are high in fat? One reason has to do with the fact that activity level in France is higher. Research by Paul Rozin and his colleagues also finds that portion sizes in France are significantly smaller than in the United States, but at the same time, people in France take longer to finish their smaller meals. At a McDonald's in France, diners take an average of 22 minutes to consume a meal, whereas in the United States, people take less than 15 minutes (Rozin et al., 2003). The fact that people in France are eating less food more slowly may lead them to be more conscious of what they are eating. This, ironically, probably leads to lower French fry consumption.

One of the reasons that people in France are leaner than people in the United States is that the average French diner spends 22 minutes to consume a fast-food meal, whereas the average American diner spends only 15 minutes. How could the length of the average meal influence an individual's body weight?

Short of moving to France, what can you do? Studies indicate that dieting doesn't always work because the process of conscious self-regulation can easily be undermined by stress, causing people who are trying to control themselves to lose control by overindulging in the very behaviour they had been trying to overcome. This may remind you of a general principle we discussed in the Consciousness chapter: Trying hard not to do something can often directly result in the unwanted behaviour (Wegner, 1994a, 1994b, 2009).

The restraint problem may be inherent in the very act of self-control. Rather than dieting, then, heading towards normal weight should involve a new emphasis on exercise and nutrition (Prochaska & Sallis, 2004). In emphasizing what is good to eat, a person can think freely about food rather than trying to suppress thoughts about it. A focus on increasing activity rather than reducing food intake, in turn, gives people another positive and active goal to pursue. Self-regulation is more effective when it focuses on what to do rather than on what *not* to do (Molden et al., 2009; Wegner & Wenzlaff, 1996).

Avoiding Sexual Risks People put themselves at risk when they have unprotected vaginal, oral, or anal intercourse. Sexually active adolescents and adults are usually aware of such risks, not to mention the risk of unwanted pregnancy, yet many behave in risky ways nonetheless. Why doesn't awareness translate into avoidance? Risk takers harbour an *illusion of unique invulnerability,* a systematic bias towards believing that they are less likely to fall victim to the problem than are others (Perloff & Fetzer, 1986). For example, a classic study of female undergraduates found that sexually active respondents judged their own likelihood of getting pregnant in the next year as less than 10%, but estimated the average for other women at the university to be 27% (Burger & Burns, 1988). Paradoxically, this illusion was even stronger among women in the sample who reported using inadequate or no contraceptive techniques. The tendency to think "It won't happen to me" may be most pronounced when it probably will.

Unprotected sex often is the impulsive result of last-minute emotions. When thought is further blurred by alcohol or drugs, people often fail to use the condoms that can reduce their exposure to the risks of pregnancy, HIV, and many other STIs. Like other forms of self-regulation, the avoidance of sexual risk requires the kind of planning that can easily be undone by circumstances that hamper the ability to think ahead. One approach to reducing sexual risk taking, then, is simply finding ways to help people plan ahead. Sex education programs offer adolescents just such a chance by encouraging them, at a time when they have not had much sexual experience, to think about what they might do when they need to make decisions. Although sex education is sometimes criticized as increasing adolescents' awareness of and interest in sex, the research evidence is clear: Sex education reduces the likelihood that undergraduate students will engage in unprotected sexual activity and it benefits their health (Li et al., 2017).

Not Smoking One in two smokers dies prematurely from smoking-related diseases such as lung cancer, heart disease, emphysema, and cancer of the mouth and throat. Lung cancer alone kills more people than any other form of cancer, and smoking causes 80% of lung cancers. Although the rate of cigarette smoking had been declining in Canada for years, new users of nicotine abound. For example, in a 2020 survey, about 1 in 7 young people aged 15–24 reported vaping in the last 30 days (Statistics Canada, 2021). In the face of all the devastating health consequences, why don't people quit?

Nicotine, the active ingredient in cigarettes, is addictive, so smoking and vaping are difficult to stop once the habit is established (as discussed in the Consciousness chapter). As with other forms of self-regulation, the resolve to quit smoking is fragile and seems to break down under stress. And for some time after quitting, ex-smokers remain sensitive to cues in the environment: Eating or drinking, a bad mood, anxiety, or just seeing someone else smoking is enough to make them want a cigarette (Shiffman et al., 1996). The good news is that the urge diminishes, and people become less likely to relapse the longer they've been away from nicotine.

Psychological programs and techniques to help people kick the habit include nicotine replacement systems such as gum and skin patches, counselling programs, and hypnosis, but these programs are not always successful. Some of the best predictors of quitting smoking are having lower levels of nicotine dependence to begin with and having the motivation and confidence in your own ability to quit (Pardavila-Belio et al., 2019). Keeping yourself healthy by behaving in healthy ways is one of the great challenges of life—and hopefully one that you have learned, or soon will (see Other Voices: The Dangers of Overparenting).

"*Boy, I'm going to pay for this tomorrow at yoga class.*"

Other Voices • The Dangers of Overparenting

Many parents want to protect their children from experiencing any stress or hardship. This is only natural; we want to protect the ones we love from being hurt, and we want to ensure that they have the best life possible. But is there a downside to doing so? Julie Lythcott-Haims, who for a decade served as Stanford University's Dean of Freshman, believes that "overparenting" can cause significant harm by depriving children of opportunities to learn creativity, competence, and confidence, and to develop a true sense of who they really are. In her book, *How to Raise an Adult,* Lythcott-Haims describes how overbearing "helicopter parenting" can backfire among university undergraduate students.

I became a university dean because I'm interested in supporting humans in growing to become who they're meant to become, unfettered by circumstances or other people's expectations. I expected that the kids who would need my help would be first-generation college students or low-income kids, and these populations certainly benefited from the mentorship and support that a dean could provide. But it was my solidly middle- or upper-middle-class students who had the most bewildered looks on their faces, looks that turned to relief when Mom or Dad handled the situation, whatever it was. These parents seemed involved in their college students' lives in ways that held their kids back instead of propelling them forward.

In 2013 the news was filled with worrisome statistics about the mental health crisis on college campuses, particularly the number of students medicated for depression. Charlie Gofen, the retired chairman of the board at the Latin School of Chicago, a private school serving about 1,100 students, emailed the statistics off to a colleague at another school and asked, "Do you think parents at your school would rather their kid be depressed at Yale or happy at University of Arizona?" The colleague quickly replied, "My guess is 75 percent of the parents would rather see their kids depressed at Yale. They figure that the kid can straighten the emotional stuff out in their 20's, but no one can go back and get the Yale undergrad degree."

In 2013 the American College Health Association surveyed close to 100,000 college students from 153 different campuses about their health. When asked about their experiences, at some point over the past 12 months:

- 84.3 percent felt overwhelmed by all they had to do
- 60.5 percent felt very sad
- 57.0 percent felt very lonely
- 51.3 percent felt overwhelming anxiety
- 8.0 percent seriously considered suicide

You're right to be thinking *Yes, but do we know whether overparenting causes this rise in mental health problems?* The answer is that we don't have studies proving causation, but a number of recent studies show *correlation.*

In 2010, psychology professor Neil Montgomery of Keene State College in New Hampshire surveyed 300 college freshmen nationwide and found that students with helicopter parents were less open to new ideas and actions and more vulnerable, anxious, and self-conscious. "[In s]tudents who were given responsibility and not constantly monitored by their parents—so-called 'free rangers'—the effects were reversed," Montgomery's study found. A 2011 study by Terri LeMoyne and Tom Buchanan at the University of Tennessee at Chattanooga looking at more than 300 students found that students with "hovering" or "helicopter" parents are more likely to be medicated for anxiety and/or depression.

When parents have tended to do the stuff of life for kids—the waking up, the transporting, the reminding about deadlines and obligations, the bill-paying, the question-asking, the decision-making, the responsibility-taking, the talking to strangers, and the confronting of authorities, kids may be in for quite a shock when parents turn them loose in the world of college or work. They will experience setbacks, which will feel to them like failure. Lurking beneath the problem of whatever thing needs to be handled is the student's inability to differentiate the self from the parent.

Here's the point—and this is so much more important than I realized until rather recently when the data started coming in: The research shows that figuring out for themselves is a critical element to people's mental health. Your kids have to be there for *themselves.* That's a harder truth to swallow when your kid is in the midst of a problem or worse, a crisis, but taking the long view, it's the best medicine for them.

Is being exposed to stressful situations necessarily a bad thing? How else will we learn how to cope with difficult situations? If we never learn to do so, we may be more likely to experience some of the bad outcomes that Lythcott-Haims writes about. So get out there, get stressed, and manage it!

Julie Lythcott-Haims served as Stanford University's Dean of Freshman for a decade and is a best-selling author.

Courtesy of Julie Lythcott-Haims.

Chapter Review

Sources of Stress: What Gets to You

- Stressors are events and threats that place specific demands on a person or threaten well-being.

- Sources of stress include negative life events, but even happy ones require readjustment and preparedness. Chronic stress involves triggers that occur repeatedly, some that are social and some that can be traced to a particular environment.

- Events are most stressful when we perceive that there is no way to control or deal with the challenge.

Stress Reactions: All Shook Up

- The body responds to stress with an initial fight-or-flight reaction, which activates the hypothalamic–pituitary–adrenocortical (HPA) axis and prepares the body to face the threat or run away from it.

- The general adaptation syndrome (GAS) outlines three phases of stress response that occur regardless of the type of stressor: alarm, resistance, and exhaustion.

- Chronic stress can wear down the immune system, causing susceptibility to infection, aging, tumour growth, organ damage, and death. People who respond to stress with anger are most at risk of heart disease.

- The response to stress will vary depending on whether it's interpreted as something that can be overcome or not.

- If prolonged, the psychological response to stress can lead to burnout. It is a particular problem in professions in which emotional turmoil is part of the job.

Stress Management: Dealing with It

- The management of stress involves strategies for influencing the mind, the body, and the situation.

- People try to manage their minds by suppressing stressful thoughts or avoiding the situations that produce them, by rationally coping with the stressor, and by reframing.

- Body management strategies involve attempting to reduce stress symptoms through meditation, relaxation, biofeedback, and aerobic exercise.

- Overcoming stress by managing your situation can involve seeking out social support, engaging in religious experiences, or attempting to find humour in stressful events.

- The Learning chapter details reasons why it's important to avoid procrastinating when studying for a test, and there are health reasons as well.

The Psychology of Illness: Mind Over Matter

- The psychology of illness concerns how sensitivity to the body leads people to recognize illness and seek treatment.

- The sick role is a set of rights and obligations linked with illness; some people fake illness in order to accrue those rights.

- Successful health care providers interact with their patients to understand both the physical state and the psychological state.

The Psychology of Health: Feeling Good

- The connection between mind and body can be revealed through the influences of personality and self-regulation of behaviour on health.

- The personality traits of optimism and hardiness are associated with reduced risk for illnesses, perhaps because people with these traits can fend off stress.

- The self-regulation of behaviours such as eating, sexuality, and smoking is difficult for many people because self-regulation is easily disrupted by stress; strategies for maintaining self-control can pay off with significant improvements in health and quality of life.

Changing Minds

1. In 2002, researchers compared severe acne in undergraduate students during a relatively stress-free period with acne during a highly stressful exam period. After adjusting for other variables such as changes in sleep or diet, the researchers concluded that increased acne severity was strongly correlated with increased levels of stress. Learning about the study, your roommate is surprised. "Acne is a skin disease," your roommate says. "I don't see how it could have anything to do with your mental state." How would you weigh in on the role of stress in medical diseases? What other examples could you give of ways in which stress can affect health?

2. A friend of yours who is taking a heavy course load confides that they are feeling overwhelmed. "I can't take the stress," your friend says. "Sometimes I daydream of living on an island somewhere, where I can just lie in the sun and have no stress at all." What would you tell your friend about stress? Is all stress bad? What would a life with no stress really be like?

3. **Visualizing Data** A friend says, "Regardless of gender, *all* people binge eat when they're stressed." Review the DATA and respond to your friend.

Key Terms

stressors (p. 514)

stress (p. 515)

health psychology (p. 515)

chronic stressors (p. 516)

fight-or-flight response (p. 519)

general adaptation
    syndrome (GAS) (p. 520)

telomeres (p. 521)

telomerase (p. 521)

immune system (p. 522)

lymphocytes (p. 522)

Type A behaviour pattern
    (p. 523)

burnout (p. 526)

repressive coping (p. 527)

rational coping (p. 528)

reframing (p. 528)

stress-inoculation training
    (SIT) (p. 529)

meditation (p. 529)

relaxation therapy (p. 530)

relaxation response (p. 530)

biofeedback (p. 530)

social support (p. 532)

sick role (p. 537)

self-regulation (p. 541)

CHAPTER 15

Psychological Disorders

ROBIN WILLIAMS WAS ONE OF THE FUNNIEST and most beloved comedians in history. Over the course of his nearly 40-year career, Williams was an amazingly successful stand-up comedian, television and movie star, and philanthropist. He was best known for his fun and zany improvisational style and his ability to consistently make others laugh. He appeared as an actor in over 100 films and television shows, including four major movies released in 2014. Then, on August 11, 2014, Williams locked himself in his bedroom and hanged himself with his belt, dying by suicide. Why would a person who appeared to be so happy, and who was so successful, active, and beloved, purposely end his life?

Many people familiar with Robin Williams's professional career did not know that he had suffered from mental illness for years. Throughout his life, Williams struggled with drug- and alcohol-use disorders that impaired his ability to function and led to multiple hospitalizations. Williams also suffered from major depressive disorder, a condition characterized by long periods of depressed mood, diminished interest in pleasurable activities, feelings of worthlessness, and problems with eating and sleeping. Shortly before his death, he was also diagnosed with Parkinson's disease and dementia, conditions associated with a progressive decline of physical and mental abilities. Many people who have thoughts of suicide say that their motivation is not necessarily to be dead, but rather to escape from some seemingly intolerable situation, such as a long-term struggle with mental illness. That may have been the reason for Williams's suicide, although we will never know for sure.

Williams's case highlights several important facts about mental disorders. They can affect anyone, regardless of their apparent happiness or success. They are characterized by extreme distress and impairment, often limiting a person's ability to carry out daily activities. At the same time, however, many people suffer silently; even their closest friends and family members may not know. And finally, in extreme cases, mental disorders can be lethal, leading to severe self-injury or death by suicide. What are mental disorders, and what causes them?

WE FIRST CONSIDER THE QUESTION, "WHAT IS A MENTAL DISORDER?" The enormously complicated human mind can produce a wide range of behaviours, thoughts, and emotions that change radically from moment to moment. How do psychologists decide when a person's thoughts, emotions, and behaviours are

- **Defining Mental Disorders: What Is Psychopathology?**

- **Anxiety Disorders: Excessive Fear, Anxiety, and Avoidance**

- **Obsessive-Compulsive Disorder: Persistent Thoughts and Repetitive Behaviours**

- **Posttraumatic Stress Disorder: Distress and Avoidance After a Trauma**

- **Depressive and Bipolar Disorders: Extreme Highs and Lows**

- **Schizophrenia and Other Psychotic Disorders: Losing the Grasp on Reality**

- **Disorders of Childhood and Adolescence**

- **Personality Disorders: Extreme Traits and Characteristics**

- **Self-Harm Behaviours: Intentionally Injuring Oneself**

The actor and comedian Robin Williams (1951–2014) was a brilliant performer who had audiences laughing for over 40 years. In his personal life, however, he suffered with bouts of addiction, depression, and dementia, ending with his suicide.

"disordered"? We will first examine the key factors that must be weighed in making such a decision. We'll then focus on several major forms of *mental disorder*: depressive and bipolar disorders; anxiety, obsessive-compulsive, and trauma-related disorders; schizophrenia; disorders that begin in childhood and adolescence; personality disorders; and self-harm behaviours. As we view each type of disorder, we will examine how they manifest and what is known about their prevalence and causes.

The disorders explored in this chapter represent a tragic loss of human potential. The contentment, peace, and productivity that people could be enjoying are crowded out by pain, suffering, and impairment. The current scientific approach to mental disorders considers the biological, psychological, and social factors that combine to cause disorders. Appropriately called the *biopsychosocial perspective*, this approach begins to sort out the symptoms and causes of mental disorders. As we will see in the next chapter, this approach already offers remarkably effective treatments for some disorders; for other disorders, it offers hope that pain and suffering can be alleviated in the future.

Defining Mental Disorders: What Is Psychopathology?

Learning Outcomes

WHAT YOU NEED TO KNOW

- Explain why the *Diagnostic and Statistical Manual of Mental Disorders (DSM)* has become a more credible diagnostic tool over the course of revisions to each edition.

- Identify the fundamental ideas behind the medical model, the biopsychosocial perspective, and the diathesis–stress model.

- Relate how the Research Domain Criteria (RDoC) expands on the *DSM*.

- Explain why labelling someone with a disorder can be problematic.

mental disorder A persistent disturbance or dysfunction in behaviour, thoughts, or emotions that causes significant distress or impairment.

The concept of a mental disorder may seem simple at first glance, but it turns out to be very complex and quite a tricky thing to define (similar to clearly defining "consciousness," "stress," or "personality"). Any extreme variation in your thoughts, feelings, or behaviours is not a mental disorder. For instance, severe anxiety before a test, sadness after the loss of a loved one, or a night of excessive alcohol consumption—although unpleasant—is not necessarily pathological. Similarly, a persistent pattern of deviating from the norm does not qualify as a mental disorder. If it did, we would diagnose mental disorders in the most creative and visionary people—anyone whose ideas deviate from those of people around them.

So what *is* a mental disorder? Perhaps surprisingly, there is no universal agreement on a precise definition of the term *mental disorder*. However, there is general agreement that a **mental disorder** (also referred to as "psychopathology") can be broadly defined as *a persistent disturbance or dysfunction in behaviour, thoughts, or emotions that causes significant distress or impairment* (Stein et al., 2010; Wakefield, 2007). One way to think about mental disorders is as dysfunctions or deficits in the normal human psychological processes you have learned about throughout this textbook. People with mental disorders have problems with their perception, memory, learning, emotions, motivation, thinking, and social processes. Of course, this definition leaves many questions unanswered. What kinds of disturbances count as mental disorders? How long must they last to be considered "persistent?" And how much distress or impairment is required? These are all still hotly debated questions in the field.

Conceptualizing Mental Disorders

Since ancient times, there have been reports of people acting strangely or reporting bizarre thoughts or emotions. Until fairly recently, such difficulties were conceptualized as the result of religious or supernatural forces. In some cultures,

Although mental disorders are deviations from normal behaviour, not all deviations from the norm are disordered. Indeed, people thinking differently about the world, and behaving in ways that deviated from the norm, have encouraged us all to think differently about ourselves and our place in the world. Pandemonia (left), an anonymous London-based conceptual artist characterized by an inflatable full-head mask, started their career by crashing fashion and social events. Juliana Huxtable (middle), a transgender artist, DJ, and poet, founded Shock Value, a New York City–based nightlife collective aimed at elevating women performers. Tina Guo (right), a Chinese American cellist, takes her cello performance outside of the classical realm and into the cinematic, video game, and metal music genres.

psychopathology is still interpreted as possession by spirits or demons, as enchantment by a witch or shaman, or as God's punishment for wrongdoing. In many societies, including our own, people with psychological disorders have been feared and ridiculed, and often treated as criminals: punished, imprisoned, or put to death for their "crime" of deviating from what is considered to be normal. However, focusing solely on deviating from the norm is problematic, as deviations from the norm can be extremely helpful to society—such as the case with creativity, athleticism, and entertainment.

Over the past 200 years, these ways of looking at psychological abnormalities have largely been replaced in most parts of the world by a **medical model**, an *approach that conceptualizes abnormal psychological experiences as illnesses that, like physical illnesses, have biological and environmental causes, defined symptoms, and possible cures.* Conceptualizing abnormal thoughts and behaviours as illness suggests that a first step is to determine the nature of the problem through *diagnosis*.

In diagnosis, clinicians seek to determine the nature of a person's mental disorder by assessing *signs* (objectively observed indicators of a disorder) and *symptoms* (subjectively reported behaviours, thoughts, and emotions) that suggest an underlying illness. So, for example, just as self-reported sniffles and a cough are symptoms of a cold, Robin Williams's depressed mood and struggles to control his use of mind-altering substances can be seen as symptoms of his depressive and substance-use disorders. Clinicians distinguish among three related general medical and classification terms:

- A *disorder* is a common set of signs and symptoms.
- A *disease* is a known pathological process affecting the body.
- A *diagnosis* is a determination as to whether a disorder or disease is present (Kraemer et al., 2007).

Bear in mind that knowing that a disorder is present (i.e., diagnosed) does not necessarily mean that we know the underlying disease process in the body that gives rise to the signs and symptoms of the disorder.

medical model An approach that conceptualizes abnormal psychological experiences as illnesses that, like physical illnesses, have biological and environmental causes, defined symptoms, and possible cures.

According to the theory of physiognomy, mental disorders could be diagnosed from facial features. This fanciful theory is now considered superstition, but it was popular from antiquity until the early 20th century.

Some critics of the medical model of mental disorders suggest that such an approach "pathologizes" normal human behaviour, such as calling shyness social phobia. However, proponents are quick to note that conditions such as social phobia are not merely normal shyness, but serious problems that can impair a person's functioning and ability to carry out a normal life. Here's just one example: The professional baseball player Zack Greinke was unable to play baseball in 2006, early in his professional career, due to social phobia. Fortunately, through effective treatment, he was able to return to the game and has gone on to a very successful professional career.

Diagnostic and Statistical Manual of Mental Disorders (DSM)

A classification system that describes the symptoms used to diagnose each recognized mental disorder and indicates how that disorder can be distinguished from other, similar problems.

Viewing mental disorders as medical problems reminds us that people who are suffering deserve care and treatment, not condemnation. Nevertheless, the medical model of mental disorders has been criticized. Some psychologists argue that it is inappropriate to use people's subjective self-reports, rather than physical tests of pathology (as in other areas of medical diagnostics), to determine underlying illness. Others argue that the model often "medicalizes" or "pathologizes" normal human behaviour. For instance, extreme sadness can be considered to be an illness called *major depressive disorder*; extreme shyness can be diagnosed as an illness called *social anxiety disorder*; and trouble concentrating in school is called *attention-deficit/hyperactivity disorder*. Although there are some valid concerns about the current method of defining and classifying mental disorders, it is a huge advance over older alternatives, such as viewing mental disorders as the product of witchcraft or as punishment for sin. Moreover, psychologists keep these concerns in mind as they work to improve the diagnostic procedures.

Classifying Disorders: The *DSM*

So how is the medical model used to determine which types of experiences and behaviours should be classified as mental disorders? Psychologists, psychiatrists (physicians concerned with the study and treatment of mental disorders), and other mental health professionals use a standardized system for classifying mental disorders. In fact, there are currently two established systems for classifying mental disorders: The *International Classification of Diseases* (ICD-10), produced by the World Health Organization, and the **Diagnostic and Statistical Manual of Mental Disorders (DSM)**, produced by the American Psychiatric Association (APA). Since the DSM tends to be the classification used most widely in North America, it is the one we shall focus on. The *DSM* is *a classification system that describes the symptoms used to diagnose each recognized mental disorder and indicates how the disorder can be distinguished from other, similar problems*. Each disorder is named and classified as a distinct illness. The initial version of the *DSM*, published in 1952, and its 1968 revision, *DSM–II*, provided a common language for talking about disorders. This was a major advance in the study of mental disorders; however, the diagnostic criteria listed in these early volumes were quite vague and based on thin theoretical assumptions. For instance, people who were extremely depressed or anxious for long periods of time might be given the general diagnosis of "neurosis reaction."

The next two editions of the *DSM* (*DSM–III*, published in 1980, and *DSM–IV*, published in 1994) moved from vague descriptions of disorders to very detailed lists of symptoms (or *diagnostic criteria*) that had to be present for a disorder to be diagnosed. For instance, in addition to being extremely sad or depressed (for at least 2 weeks), a person must have at least five of nine agreed-on symptoms of depression—for example, diminished interest in usually enjoyable activities, significant weight loss or gain, significantly increased or decreased sleep, loss of energy, feelings of worthlessness or guilt, trouble concentrating. The use of these detailed lists of symptoms for each of more than 200 disorders described in the *DSM* led to a dramatic increase in the reliability, or consistency, of diagnoses of mental disorders. Two clinicians interviewing the same individual were now much more likely to agree on what mental disorders were present, greatly increasing the credibility of the diagnostic process (and the fields of psychiatry and clinical psychology) and improving psychologists' ability to talk to each other, as well as talk to people suffering from these conditions, about the disorders being experienced.

In May 2013, the American Psychiatric Association released the current version of the manual, the *DSM–5*, followed by a text revision (TR) in 2022, which is referred to as *DSM–5–TR* (American Psychiatric Association, 2022). The *DSM–5–TR* describes 22 major categories containing more than 200 different mental disorders (see **TABLE 15.1**). Along with the disorders listed in these 22 categories, the *DSM–5–TR*

TABLE 15.1

MAIN *DSM–5–TR* CATEGORIES OF MENTAL DISORDERS

1. **Neurodevelopmental Disorders:** These conditions begin early in development and cause significant impairments in functioning, such as intellectual disability, autism spectrum disorder (ASD), and attention-deficit/hyperactivity disorder (ADHD).

2. **Schizophrenia Spectrum and Other Psychotic Disorders:** This group of disorders is characterized by major disturbances in perception, thought, language, emotion, and behaviour.

3. **Bipolar and Related Disorders:** These disorders include major fluctuations in mood—from mania to depression—and also can include psychotic experiences, which is why they are placed between the psychotic and depressive disorders in *DSM–5–TR*.

4. **Depressive Disorders:** These conditions are characterized by extreme and persistent periods of depressed mood.

5. **Anxiety Disorders:** These disorders are characterized by excessive fear and anxiety that are extreme enough to impair a person's functioning, such as panic disorder, generalized anxiety disorder, and specific phobias.

6. **Obsessive-Compulsive and Related Disorders:** These conditions are characterized by the presence of obsessive thinking followed by compulsive behaviour in response to that thinking.

7. **Trauma- and Stressor-Related Disorders:** These disorders develop in response to a traumatic event, such as posttraumatic stress disorder.

8. **Dissociative Disorders:** These conditions are characterized by disruptions or discontinuity in consciousness, memory, or identity, such as dissociative identity disorder (formerly called "multiple personality disorder").

9. **Somatic Symptom and Related Disorders:** These are conditions in which a person experiences bodily symptoms (e.g., pain, fatigue) associated with significant distress or impairment.

10. **Feeding and Eating Disorders:** These are problems with eating that impair health or functioning, such as anorexia nervosa and bulimia nervosa.

11. **Elimination Disorders:** These involve inappropriate elimination of urine or feces (e.g., bedwetting).

12. **Sleep–Wake Disorders:** These are problems with the sleep–wake cycle, such as insomnia, narcolepsy, and sleep apnea.

13. **Sexual Dysfunctions:** These are problems related to unsatisfactory sexual activity, such as erectile disorder and premature ejaculation.

14. **Gender Dysphoria:** This is a single disorder characterized by incongruence between a person's experienced/expressed gender and assigned gender.

15. **Disruptive, Impulse-Control, and Conduct Disorders:** These conditions involve problems controlling emotions and behaviours, such as conduct disorder, intermittent explosive disorder, and kleptomania.

16. **Substance-Related and Addictive Disorders:** This collection of disorders involves persistent use of substances or some other behaviour (e.g., gambling) despite the fact that it leads to significant problems.

17. **Neurocognitive Disorders:** These are disorders of thinking caused by conditions such as Alzheimer's disease or traumatic brain injury.

18. **Personality Disorders:** These are enduring patterns of thinking, feeling, and behaving that lead to significant life problems.

19. **Paraphilic Disorders:** These conditions are characterized by inappropriate sexual activity, such as pedophilic disorder.

20. **Other Mental Disorders:** This is a residual category for conditions that do not fit into one of the above categories but are associated with significant distress or impairment, such as an unspecified mental disorder due to a medical condition.

21. **Medication-Induced Movement Disorders and Other Adverse Effects of Medication:** These are problems with physical movement (e.g., tremors, rigidity) that are caused by medication.

22. **Other Conditions That May Be the Focus of Clinical Attention:** These include disorders related to abuse, neglect, relationship, and other problems.

Information from *DSM–5–TR* (American Psychiatric Association, 2022).

describes conditions that could be included as formal disorders but that, for now, require additional research. Furthermore, one section is devoted to cultural considerations in diagnosing mental disorders. Why the switch from Roman to Arabic numerals? The hope is that with more rapid advances in our understanding of mental disorders, rather than waiting another 20 years to update the *DSM*, we can make revisions as we learn more (e.g., *DSM–5.1*, *5.2*, *5.3*, and so on). The 2022 text revision includes more minor changes (not big enough to warrant a change in edition number), such as the addition of one new disorder (Prolonged Grief Disorder), modifications to more than 70 existing disorders, and new codes to note the presence of suicidal behaviour.

Each of the 22 chapters in the main body of the *DSM–5–TR* lists the specific criteria that must be met for a person to be diagnosed with each disorder. According to the Canadian Mental Health Association, by age 40, one in every two

Canadians will have experienced a mental disorder (Canadian Mental Health Association, 2021). Many individuals with a mental disorder (greater than 80%) experience **comorbidity**, *the co-occurrence of two or more disorders in a single individual* (Gadermann et al., 2012).

Disorders Appear in All Cultures

Are mental disorders experienced by people around the world the same way? To better understand the *epidemiology* (the study of the distribution and causes of health and disease) of mental disorders, Ronald Kessler and colleagues launched the World Health Organization World Mental Health Survey Initiative, a large-scale study in which people from over two dozen countries around the world were assessed for the presence of mental disorders (Kessler & Üstün, 2008). The results of this study (see **FIGURE 15.1**) revealed that the major mental disorders seen in North America are similar to those that appear in countries and cultures all around the world. For instance, depression, anxiety, attention-deficit/hyperactivity disorder, and substance-use disorders occur all over the globe. They are reported at different rates in different countries, but depression and anxiety are always the most common, followed by impulse-control and substance-use disorders (Kessler et al., 2007).

Although the common mental disorders described above are universal, cultural context can influence how mental disorders are experienced, described, assessed, and treated (see A World of Difference: The Impact of Culture on Mental Disorders). To address this issue, the *DSM–5–TR* includes a section containing a Cultural Formulation Interview (CFI). The CFI includes 16 questions that the clinician asks a client during a mental health assessment to help the clinician understand how the client's culture might influence the experience, expression, and explanation of their mental disorder.

Although the *DSM* is the preferred diagnostic system in Canada and the United States, many other countries use the World Health Organization's *International Classification of Diseases (ICD)*, which is similar to the *DSM* in many ways. In fact, hospitals and insurance companies use *ICD* codes (i.e., each disorder is assigned a specific number) rather than *DSM* codes in documenting which medical or psychological disorder a patient may be experiencing. The reason for this is that it allows all countries to work together to track the incidence and treatment of various conditions around the world.

comorbidity The co-occurrence of two or more disorders in a single individual.

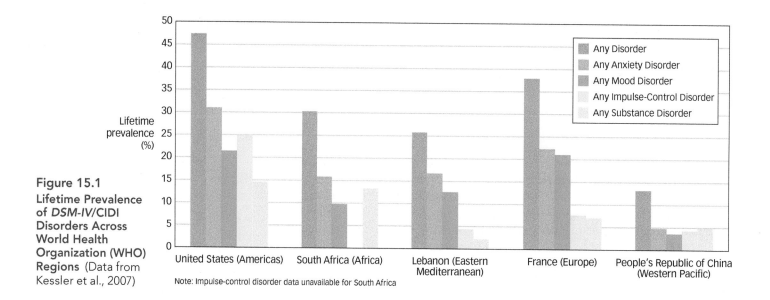

Figure 15.1
Lifetime Prevalence of *DSM-IV*/CIDI Disorders Across World Health Organization (WHO) Regions (Data from Kessler et al., 2007)

Note: Impulse-control disorder data unavailable for South Africa

A World of Difference • The Impact of Culture on Mental Disorders

Just as language, traditions, customs, and other factors differ across cultures, so does the manifestation of mental disorders. The disorders you learn about in this chapter (anxiety disorders, depressive disorders, psychotic disorders, and so on) appear in every culture, but cultural factors often influence the way these disorders are experienced, talked about, and explained. The *DSM–5–TR* provides a framework for thinking about differences in cultural concepts of distress. It distinguishes among three important concepts:

- *Cultural syndromes* are groups of symptoms that tend to cluster together in specific cultures. For instance, *taijin kyofusho* is a cultural syndrome seen in Japan that is a combination of two *DSM–5–TR* conditions: social anxiety disorder (in which a person fears negative feedback from others) and body dysmorphic disorder (in which a person is preoccupied with perceived flaws in their own physical appearance).

- *Cultural idioms of distress* are ways of talking about or expressing distress that can differ across cultures. For instance, *kufungisisa,* or "thinking too much," is an idiom of distress in Zimbabwe (and many other countries/cultures, but by different names) that is associated

Taijin kyofusho is a Japanese syndrome in which a person fears and avoids contact with others due to the belief that they are inadequate or offensive in some way. This syndrome appears to be a combination of two *DSM–5–TR* conditions: social anxiety disorder and body dysmorphic disorder.

with a number of depressive and anxiety disorders.

- *Cultural explanations* are culturally recognized descriptions of what causes the symptoms, distress, or disorder. For example, in many South Asian cultures, mental disorder is believed to be caused by the loss of *dhat* or *dhatu,* a white substance believed to be in the body and essential for health that can exit the body in the form of semen or during urination or defecation.

So in addition to individual differences (across all people) in how we think, feel, and behave, the cultural context in which we are living can have an impact on how we experience, talk about, and explain mental disorders. This is important to keep in mind when trying to understand mental disorders within your own cultures, and also when trying to understand mental disorders in people from other cultures.

Causation of Disorders

The medical model of mental disorder suggests that knowing a person's diagnosis is useful because any given category of mental illness is likely to have a distinctive cause. In other words, just as different viruses, bacteria, or genetic abnormalities cause different physical illnesses, a specifiable pattern of causes (or *etiology*) may exist for different psychological disorders. The medical model also suggests that each category of mental disorder is likely to have a common *prognosis,* a typical course over time and susceptibility to treatment and cure. Unfortunately, this basic medical model is usually an oversimplification; it is rarely useful to focus on a *single cause* that is *internal* to the person and that suggests a *single cure.*

To understand what factors might cause mental disorders, most psychologists take an integrated **biopsychosocial perspective** that *explains mental disorders as the result of interactions among biological, psychological, and social factors* (see **FIGURE 15.2a**). On the biological side, the focus is on genetic and epigenetic influences (see Figure 3.18), biochemical imbalances, and abnormalities in brain

biopsychosocial perspective
Explains mental disorders as the result of interactions among biological, psychological, and social factors.

Figure 15.2

Proposed Models of How Disorders Develop (a) The biopsychosocial model suggests that biological, psychological, and social factors all interact to produce mental health or mental illness. (b) The diathesis–stress model suggests that mental illness develops when a person who has some predisposition or vulnerability to mental illness (the "diathesis") experiences a major life stressor (the "stress").

(a)

(b)

Suppose that identical twins (with the same genetic profile) grow up in the same household (sharing the same parents, the same basic diet, the same access to television, and so on). When they are teenagers, one twin but not the other develops a mental disorder such as schizophrenia. How might this happen? Mental disorders can be caused by biological, psychological, and environmental factors. The diathesis–stress model suggests that a person may be predisposed for a psychological disorder that remains unexpressed until triggered by stress.

diathesis–stress model Suggests that a person may be predisposed to a psychological disorder that remains unexpressed until triggered by stress.

structure and function. The psychological perspective focuses on maladaptive learning and coping, cognitive biases, dysfunctional attitudes, and interpersonal problems. Social factors include poor socialization, stressful life experiences, and cultural and social inequities. The complexity of causation suggests that different individuals can experience a similar psychological disorder (e.g., depression) for different reasons. A person might fall into a depression as a result of biological causes (e.g., genetics, hormones), psychological causes (e.g., faulty beliefs, hopelessness, poor strategies for coping with loss), environmental causes (e.g., stress or loneliness), or more likely as a result of some combination of these factors. And, of course, multiple causes mean there may not be a single cure.

The observation that most disorders have both internal (biological/psychological) *and* external (environmental) causes has given rise to a theory known as the **diathesis–stress model**, which suggests that *a person may be predisposed to a psychological disorder that remains unexpressed until triggered by stress* (see Figure 15.2b). The diathesis is the internal predisposition, and the stress is the external trigger. For example, going away to university is a major change that can disrupt the equilibrium of a person's life. This is a stressor that may precipitate a psychological disorder in people who are susceptible (i.e., who have a diathesis). Although diatheses can be inherited, it's important to remember that heritability is not destiny. A person who inherits a diathesis may never encounter the precipitating stress, whereas someone with little genetic propensity to a disorder may come to suffer from it, given the right pattern of stress.

The issue of intergenerational trauma to equity-deserving groups in Canada, resulting from Indian Residential School experiences, illustrates the complexity of tracing the cause of a psychological disorder. The Indian Residential School system was established in the 1880s, to assimilate equity-deserving groups based on the assumption that white European culture was inherently superior to others (Royal Commission on Aboriginal Peoples [RCAP], 1996). Approximately 150,000 equity-deserving children attended residential schools over the 100 or so years that the schools were in existence. Children as young as 3 years were forced by law to leave their families and communities to attend these schools, which systematically attempted to eliminate equity-deserving groups' languages, traditions, and beliefs.

For many children, the trauma of losing family, culture, and community was compounded by woeful mistreatment, neglect, and abuse (RCAP, 1996). This damage resulted in many of the children suffering from psychological disorders such as depressive and anxiety disorders, substance-related and addictive disorders, and trauma and stressor-related disorders (see Table 15.1; Elias et al., 2012; Wilk et al., 2017). These traumatized children went on to become parents and grandparents of other children.

As discussed later in this chapter, rates of suicide amongst equity-deserving groups in Canada are at least three times as high as they are in the general population (Kumar & Tjepkema, 2019). If a First Nations adult living on-reserve has a parent or grandparent who attended an Indian Residential School, the chance of them thinking about suicide, and attempting suicide, is higher than it would otherwise be (McQuaid et al., 2017). If they have both a parent *and* a grandparent who attended a residential school, the chance is higher still (McQuaid et al., 2017). This is an example of how severe stressors can be passed down through generations, affecting the mental health and quality of life of even those with potentially little genetic predisposition towards a disorder.

The example of intergenerational trauma in residential schools illustrates how incorrect it would be to oversimplify mental disorders by attributing them to single internal causes. Such oversimplification is nowhere more evident than in the interpretation of the role of the brain in psychological disorders. Brain scans of people with and without disorders can give rise to an unusually strong impression that psychological problems are internal and permanent, inevitable, and even untreatable. But changes in brain activity or brain structure may simply reflect (not cause) a disorder, much as behavioural symptoms do. Furthermore, brains adapt and change, just as behaviour does. Comparing brain activity patterns and brain structure of people with mental disorders to people without mental disorders can be a useful way to study those disorders, but it is only one of several approaches.

A New Approach to Understanding Mental Disorders: RDoC

Although the *DSM* and *ICD* provide a useful framework for classifying disorders, concern has been growing over the fact that the findings from scientific research on the biopsychosocial factors that appear to cause psychopathology do not map neatly onto individual *DSM/ICD* diagnoses. Succinctly characterizing the current state of affairs, one mental-health leader has noted that although many people describe the *DSM* as a bible, it is more accurate to think of it as a dictionary that provides labels and current definitions: "People think that everything has to match *DSM* criteria, but you know what? Biology never read that book" (Thomas R. Insel, quoted in Belluck & Carey, 2013, p. A13).

To better understand what actually causes mental disorders, researchers have proposed a newer framework for thinking about mental disorders, focused not on the currently defined *DSM/ICD* categories of disorders but on the more basic biological, cognitive, and behavioural constructs that are believed to be the building blocks of mental disorders. This new system is called the **Research Domain Criteria Project (RDoC)**, *a new initiative that aims to guide the classification and understanding of mental disorders by revealing the basic processes that give rise to them.* The RDoC is not intended to immediately replace the

Research Domain Criteria Project (RDoC) A new initiative that aims to guide the classification and understanding of mental disorders by revealing the basic processes that give rise to them.

DSM/ICD but to inform future revisions to it in the coming years (see The Real World: How Are Mental Disorders Defined and Diagnosed?).

Using the RDoC, researchers study the causes of abnormal functioning by focusing on units (or levels) of analysis that include biological factors from genes to cells to brain circuits; psychological domains, such as learning, attention, memory; and various social processes and behaviour (see **TABLE 15.2** for a list of domains). The hope is that the RDoC approach will shift researchers away from studying currently defined *DSM/ICD* categories and towards the study of the dimensional biopsychosocial processes believed, at the extreme end of the continuum, to lead to mental disorders. These processes (e.g., fear, anxiety, attention, perception) are referred to as *constructs*, which are themselves grouped into broader categories referred to as *domains*. The six domains included in the RDoC are Negative Valence Systems, Positive Valence Systems, Cognitive Systems, Systems for Social Processes, Arousal/Regulatory Systems, and Sensorimotor Systems. The long-term goal is to better understand which abnormalities cause different disorders and to classify disorders on the basis of those underlying causes rather than on observed symptoms.

This approach would bring the study of mental disorders in line with the study of other medical disorders. For example, if you are experiencing chest pain, severe headaches, fatigue, and difficulty breathing, it is unlikely that you are experiencing four separate disorders (*chest pain disorder, headache disorder,* and so on). Instead, we now know that these are all symptoms of an underlying disease process called hypertension. The RDoC approach similarly aims to shift the focus away from classifications based on surface symptoms and towards an understanding of the processes that give rise to disordered behaviour. For instance, rather than studying cocaine addiction as a distinct disorder, from the RDoC perspective researchers might try to understand what causes abnormalities in "responsiveness to reward," a

---

TABLE 15.2

RESEARCH DOMAIN CRITERIA (RDoC)

Domains/Constructs					
Negative Valence Systems	**Positive Valence Systems**	**Cognitive Systems**	**Systems for Social Processes**	**Arousal/Regulatory Systems**	**Sensorimotor Systems**
acute threat ("fear")	approach motivation	attention	affiliation and attachment	arousal	motor actions
potential threat ("anxiety")	initial responsiveness to reward	perception	social communication	circadian rhythms	agency and ownership
sustained threat	sustained responsiveness to reward	working memory	perception and understanding of self	sleep and wakefulness	habit-sensorimotor
loss	reward learning	declarative memory	perception and understanding of others		innate motor patterns
frustrative nonreward		habit	language behaviour cognitive (effortful) control		

Units of Analysis							
genes	molecules	cells	circuits	physiology	behaviour	self-reports	paradigms

factor seen in those with excessive cocaine use as well as in those with other addictive behaviours.

Indeed, research has shown that variations in a gene (*DRD2*) that codes for dopamine D2 receptors are associated with abnormal connections between two parts of the brain: the frontal lobe and the striatum (described in the Neuroscience and Behaviour chapter). This atypical connectivity is, in turn, related to the impulsiveness and responsiveness to rewards associated with a range of addictive behaviour disorders (Buckholtz & Meyer-Lindenberg, 2012), which may help explain why some people seem to have addictive personalities and have trouble inhibiting their reward-seeking behaviour. Importantly, understanding what processes cause problems such as addiction will help us to develop more effective treatments, a topic we address in more detail in the next chapter.

You might have noticed that the list of domains in Table 15.2 looks like a slightly more detailed version of the table of contents for this textbook! The RDoC approach has an overall emphasis on neuroscience (Chapter 3), and specific focuses on abnormalities in emotional and motivational systems (Chapter 8), cognitive systems such as memory (Chapter 6), learning (Chapter 7), language and cognition (Chapter 9), social processes (Chapter 13), and stress and arousal (Chapter 14). From the RDoC perspective, mental disorders can be thought of as the result of abnormalities or dysfunctions in normal psychological processes. By learning about many of these processes in this textbook, you will likely have a good understanding of new definitions of mental disorders as they are developed in the years ahead.

Dangers of Labelling

An important complication in the diagnosis and classification of psychological disorders is the effect of labelling. Psychiatric labels can have negative consequences because of their association with negative stereotypes and stigma, such as the idea that a mental disorder is a sign of personal weakness or that those with a mental disorder are dangerous. The stigma associated with mental disorders may explain why most people with diagnosable psychological disorders (approximately 60%) do not seek treatment (Kessler et al., 2005b; Wang et al., 2005).

Labelling may even affect how labelled individuals view themselves. Persons given a label may come to view themselves not just as having a mental disorder, but as hopeless or worthless. Among those with a mental disorder, those who believe that others hold negative views of them because of their mental disorder, and who hold negative views of themselves because of their mental disorder, report lower self-esteem, lower self-efficacy, and higher levels of depressive symptoms (Marcussen et al., 2019). As one small step towards counteracting such consequences, clinicians have adopted the important practice of applying labels to the *disorder* and not to the *person* with the disorder. For example, an individual might be described as "a person with schizophrenia," not as "a schizophrenic." You'll notice that we follow this convention in this text.

These effects of labelling are particularly disturbing in light of evidence that hospitalizing people with mental disorders is seldom necessary. One set of studies followed the lives of patients who were thought to be too dangerous to release and therefore had been kept in the back wards of institutions for years. Their release resulted in no harm to the community (Harding et al., 1987), and more recent studies have shown that those with a mental disorder are no more likely to be violent than those without a disorder (Elbogen & Johnson, 2009).

The new Research Domain Criteria (RDoC) are intended to help us better understand why some people seem to have addictive personalities and have trouble limiting their engagement in pleasurable experiences.

Although we label mental disorders, we should not apply those labels to people. For instance, rather than saying someone "is ADHD," we would say that the person currently meets diagnostic criteria for ADHD.

The Real World | How Are Mental Disorders Defined and Diagnosed?

Who decides what goes in the *DSM*? How are these decisions made? In psychology and psychiatry, as in the early days of most areas of the study of human health and behaviour, these decisions currently are made by consensus among leaders in the research field. These leaders meet repeatedly over several years to make decisions about which disorders should be included in the new revision of the *DSM* and how they should be defined. Over the years, these decisions have been based on descriptive research reporting in which clinical symptoms tend to cluster together.

Everyone agrees that we need a system for classifying and defining mental disorders; however, as the currently available body of knowledge about mental disorders grows, the field is moving beyond simple descriptive diagnostic categories towards others based on underlying biopsycho-social processes, such as the Research Domain Criteria Project. Future decisions about how mental disorders are defined will likely continue to be reached by consensus among leaders in the field but will be driven more directly by research on the underlying causes of these disorders.

Who decides whether someone actually has a diagnosable disorder? And how are these decisions made? Over the years, researchers have developed structured clinical interviews that convert the lists of symptoms included in the *DSM* into sets of interview questions through which the clinician (psychologist, psychiatrist, social worker) makes a determination about whether or not a given person meets the criteria for a given disorder (Nock et al., 2007). For instance, according to *DSM–5–TR*, a person must have at least five of the nine symptoms of major depressive disorder in order to meet the criteria for this disorder. Structured clinical interviews typically include nine questions about depression (one per symptom), and if the person reports having at least five of these symptoms, the clinician may conclude that this person is suffering from major depression. Right now, diagnoses are determined primarily by a patient's self-reporting of symptoms. With increasing attention to the underlying causes of mental disorders, many hope that in the future we will have biological and behavioural tests to help us make decisions about who has a mental illness and who does not.

Anxiety Disorders: Excessive Fear, Anxiety, and Avoidance

Learning Outcomes

WHAT YOU NEED TO KNOW

- Explain the major symptoms of anxiety disorders, including phobias, panic disorder, and GAD.

- Describe factors that contribute to phobias, panic disorder, and GAD.

"Okay, time for a pop quiz that will count for half your grade in this class." If your instructor had actually said that, you would probably have experienced a wave of anxiety. Your reaction would be appropriate and—no matter how intense the feeling—would not be a sign that you have a mental disorder. In fact, situation-related anxiety is normal and adaptive: in this case, perhaps by reminding you to keep up with your assignments so you are prepared for pop quizzes. When anxiety arises that is out of proportion to real threats and challenges, however, it is maladaptive: It can take hold of people's lives, stealing their peace of mind and undermining their ability to function normally. Pathological anxiety is expressed as an **anxiety disorder**, *the class of mental disorders in which anxiety is the predominant feature.* People commonly experience more than one type of anxiety disorder at a given time, and there is significant comorbidity between anxiety and depression (Brown & Barlow, 2002; Jacobson & Newman, 2017). Among the anxiety disorders recognized in the *DSM–5–TR* are phobic disorders, panic disorder, and generalized anxiety disorder.

Phobic Disorders

Consider Mary, a 47-year-old mother of three, who sought treatment for *claustrophobia*—an intense fear of enclosed spaces. She traced her fear to her childhood, when her older siblings would scare her by locking her in closets and confining her under blankets. With her own children grown, she wanted to find a job but could not

anxiety disorder The class of mental disorders in which anxiety is the predominant feature.

because of a terror of elevators and other confined places that, she felt, shackled her to her home (Carson et al., 2000). Many people feel a little anxious in enclosed spaces, but Mary's fears were dysfunctional because they were disproportionate to any actual risk and impaired her ability to function in daily life. The *DSM–5–TR* describes **phobic disorders** as *characterized by marked, persistent, and excessive fear and avoidance of specific objects, activities, or situations*. An individual with a phobic disorder recognizes that the fear is irrational but cannot prevent it from interfering with everyday functioning.

A **specific phobia** is *an irrational fear of a particular object or situation that markedly interferes with an individual's ability to function*. Specific phobias fall into five categories: (1) animals (e.g., dogs, cats, rats, snakes, spiders); (2) natural environments (e.g., heights, darkness, water, storms); (3) situations (e.g., bridges, elevators, tunnels, enclosed places); (4) blood, injections, and injury; and (5) other phobias, including choking or vomiting; and in children, loud noises or costumed characters. Approximately 12% of people in Canada and the United States will develop a specific phobia during their lives (AnxietyBC, 2016; Kessler et al., 2005a), with rates slightly higher among women than men (Kessler et al., 2012).

Social phobia involves *an irrational fear of being publicly humiliated or embarrassed*. Social phobia can be restricted to situations—such as public speaking, eating in public, or urinating in a public bathroom—or can be generalized to a variety of social situations that involve being observed or interacting with unfamiliar people. Individuals with social phobia try to avoid situations where unfamiliar people might evaluate them, and they experience intense anxiety and distress when public exposure is unavoidable. Social phobia can develop in childhood, but it typically emerges between early adolescence and early adulthood (Kessler et al., 2005a). Many people experience social phobia, with about 4% of people around the world qualifying for a diagnosis at some time in their lives, with women experiencing the disorder at slightly higher rates than men (Stein et al., 2017).

Why are phobias so common? The high rates of both specific and social phobias suggest a predisposition to be fearful of certain objects and situations. Indeed, most of the situations and objects of people's phobias could pose a real threat, such as falling from a high place or being attacked by a vicious dog or a poisonous snake or spider. Social situations have their own dangers. A roomful of strangers may not attack or bite, but they could form impressions that affect your prospects for friends, jobs, or marriage.

Observations such as these are the basis for the **preparedness theory** of phobias, which maintains that *people are instinctively predisposed towards certain fears*. The preparedness theory, proposed by Martin E. P. Seligman (1971), is supported by research showing that both humans and monkeys can quickly be conditioned to have a fear response for stimuli such as snakes and spiders, but not for neutral stimuli such as flowers or toy rabbits (Cook & Mineka, 1989). Phobias are particularly likely to form for objects that evolution has predisposed us to avoid. This idea is also supported by studies of the heritability of phobias. Family studies of specific phobias indicate greater concordance rates for identical than for fraternal twins (Kendler et al., 2002; O'Laughlin & Malle, 2002).

Temperament may also play a role in vulnerability to phobias. Researchers have found that infants who display excessive shyness and inhibition are at an increased risk for developing a phobic behaviour later in life (Morris, 2001; Stein et al., 2001). Neurobiological factors may also play a role. Abnormalities in the neurotransmitters serotonin and dopamine are more common in individuals who report phobias than among people who don't (Frick et al., 2015; Plavén-Sigray et al., 2017). In addition, individuals with phobias sometimes show abnormally high levels of activity in the amygdala, an area of the brain linked with the development of emotional associations (discussed in the chapter on Emotion and Motivation). Interestingly, although

MATHEW NOCK

Phobias are anxiety disorders that involve excessive and persistent fear of a specific object, activity, or situation. Some phobias may be learned through classical conditioning, in which a conditioned stimulus (CS) that is paired with an anxiety-evoking unconditioned stimulus (US) itself comes to elicit a conditioned fear response (CR). Suppose your friend has a phobia of dogs that is so intense that he is afraid to go outside in case one of his neighbours' dogs barks at him. Applying the principles of classical conditioning you studied in the Learning chapter, how might you help him overcome his fear?

phobic disorders Disorders characterized by marked, persistent, and excessive fear and avoidance of specific objects, activities, or situations.

specific phobia A disorder that involves an irrational fear of a particular object or situation that markedly interferes with an individual's ability to function.

social phobia A disorder that involves an irrational fear of being publicly humiliated or embarrassed.

preparedness theory The idea that people are instinctively predisposed towards certain fears.

The preparedness theory explains why most merry-go-rounds carry children on beautiful horses. This mom might have some trouble getting her daughter to ride on a big spider or snake.

COURTESY OF DANIEL WEGNER

people with social phobia report feeling much more distressed than those without social phobia during tasks involving social evaluation (such as giving a speech), they are actually no more physiologically aroused than others (Jamieson et al., 2013). This suggests that social phobia may be due to a person's subjective experience of the situation, rather than an abnormal physiological stress response to such situations.

This evidence does not rule out the influence of environments and upbringing on the development of phobic overreactions. As the learning theorist John Watson (1924) demonstrated many years ago, phobias can be classically conditioned (see the discussion of Little Albert and the white rat in the Learning chapter). Similarly, the discomfort of a dog bite could create a conditioned association between dogs and pain, resulting in an irrational fear of all dogs. The idea that phobias are learned from emotional experiences with feared objects, however, is not a complete explanation for the occurrence of phobias. Most studies find that people with phobias are no more likely than people without phobias to recall personal experiences with the feared object that could have provided the basis for classical conditioning (Craske, 1999). Moreover, many people are bitten by dogs, but few develop phobias. Despite its shortcomings, however, the idea that this is a matter of learning provides a useful model for therapy (see the Treatment chapter).

Panic Disorder and Agoraphobia

If you suddenly found yourself in danger of death (that lion is headed straight for us!), a wave of panic might wash over you. People who suffer panic attacks are frequently overwhelmed by such intense fears and by powerful physical symptoms of anxiety, even in the complete absence of actual danger. Wesley, a 20-year-old college student, began having panic attacks with increasing frequency, often two or three times a day, so he finally sought help at a clinic. The attacks would begin with a sudden wave of "intense, terrifying fear" that seemed to come out of nowhere, often accompanied by dizziness, a tightening of the chest, and the thought that he was going to pass out or possibly die. Wesley's attacks had started a few years earlier and had occurred intermittently ever since. He decided to seek treatment because he had begun to avoid buses, trains, and public places for fear that he would have an attack and not be able to escape.

Wesley's condition, called **panic disorder**, is characterized by *the sudden occurrence of multiple psychological and physiological symptoms that contribute to a*

panic disorder A disorder characterized by the sudden occurrence of multiple psychological and physiological symptoms that contribute to a feeling of stark terror.

feeling of stark terror. The acute symptoms of a panic attack typically last only a few minutes and include shortness of breath, heart palpitations, sweating, dizziness, depersonalization (a feeling of being detached from one's body) or derealization (a feeling that the external world is strange or unreal), and a fear that one is going crazy or about to die. Not surprisingly, panic attacks often send people rushing to emergency rooms or to their physicians' offices for what they believe are heart attacks. Unfortunately, because many of the symptoms mimic various medical disorders, a correct diagnosis may take years in spite of costly medical tests that produce normal results (Meuret et al., 2017). According to the *DSM–5–TR* diagnostic criteria, a person has panic disorder only if they experience recurrent unexpected attacks and report significant anxiety about having another attack.

A disorder that sometimes co-occurs with panic disorder is **agoraphobia**, *a specific phobia involving a fear of public places.* Many people with agoraphobia, including Wesley, are not frightened of public places in themselves; instead, they are afraid that something terrible will happen (e.g., panic symptoms) while they are in a public place and that they will not be able to escape or get help. In severe cases, people who have agoraphobia are unable to leave home, sometimes for years.

Approximately 13% of adults around the world report having had at least one panic attack (de Jonge et al., 2016). An occasional episode is not sufficient for a diagnosis of panic disorder: The individual also has to experience significant dread and anxiety about having another attack, and such attacks must cause significant impairment in the person's life. When these criteria are applied, approximately 2% of people will have a diagnosable panic disorder sometime in their lives (de Jonge et al., 2016). Panic disorder is approximately twice as prevalent among women than men (Kessler et al., 2012). Family studies suggest some hereditary component to panic disorder, with 30 to 40% of the variance in liability for developing panic disorder attributed to genetic influence (Hettema et al., 2001).

In an effort to understand the role that physiological arousal plays in panic attacks, researchers have compared the responses of experimental participants with and without panic disorder to *sodium lactate,* a chemical that produces rapid, shallow breathing and heart palpitations. Those with panic disorder were found to be acutely sensitive to the chemical; within a few minutes after its being administered, 60 to 90% experienced a panic attack. Participants without the disorder rarely responded to this substance with a panic attack (Liebowitz et al., 1985).

The difference in responses to this chemical may be due to differing interpretations of physiological signs of anxiety; that is, people who experience panic attacks may be hypersensitive to physiological signs of anxiety, which they interpret as having disastrous consequences for their well-being. Supporting this cognitive explanation is research showing that people who are high in anxiety sensitivity (i.e., they believe that bodily arousal and other symptoms of anxiety can have dire consequences) have an elevated risk for experiencing panic attacks (Olatunji & Wolitzky-Taylor, 2009). Thus, panic attacks may be conceptualized as a "fear of fear" itself.

Generalized Anxiety Disorder

Gina, a 24-year-old woman, began to experience debilitating anxiety during her first year of graduate school for clinical psychology. At first, she worried about whether she was sufficiently completing all of her assignments; then she worried about whether her clients were improving or if she was actually making them worse. Soon her concerns spread to focus on her own health (did she have an undiagnosed medical problem?) as well as that of her boyfriend (he smokes cigarettes . . . perhaps he is currently giving himself cancer?). She worried incessantly for a year and ultimately

WESTEND61/GETTY IMAGES

We were all in lockdown during the height of the COVID-19 pandemic, but agoraphobia is something different. Agoraphobia is the fear of being in public because of an unfounded fear that something bad is going to happen and escape will not be possible. It can greatly reduce people's time outside their home or prevent them from going outside at all.

agoraphobia A specific phobia involving a fear of public places.

took time off from school to get treatment for her worries, extreme agitation, fatigue, and feelings of sadness and depression.

Gina's symptoms are typical of **generalized anxiety disorder (GAD)**—called *generalized* because the unrelenting worries are not focused on any particular threat; they are, in fact, often exaggerated and irrational. GAD is *chronic excessive worry accompanied by three or more of the following symptoms: restlessness, fatigue, concentration problems, irritability, muscle tension, and sleep disturbance.* In people suffering from GAD, the uncontrollable worrying produces a sense of loss of control that can so erode self-confidence that simple decisions seem fraught with dire consequences. For example, Gina struggled to make everyday decisions as basic as which vegetables to buy at the market and how to prepare her dinner.

Approximately 1 in 16 people in Canada and the United States suffer from GAD at some time in their lives (Canadian Psychological Association, 2020; Kessler et al., 2005a), with women experiencing GAD at higher rates (1 in 12) than men (1 in 20) (Kessler et al., 2012). Research suggests that both biological and psychological factors contribute to the risk of GAD. Family studies indicate a mild to modest level of heritability (Norrholm & Ressler, 2009). Although identical twin studies of GAD are rare, some evidence suggests that, compared with fraternal twins, identical twins have modestly higher *concordance rates* (the percentage of pairs that share the characteristic) (Hettema et al., 2001). Moreover, teasing out environmental versus personality influences on concordance rates is quite difficult.

Biological explanations of GAD suggest that neurotransmitter imbalances may play a role in the disorder. The precise nature of this imbalance is not clear. *Benzodiazepines* (a class of sedative drugs such as Valium and Librium, discussed in the Treatment chapter) that appear to stimulate the neurotransmitter *gamma-aminobutyric acid (GABA)* can sometimes reduce the symptoms of GAD, suggesting a potential role for this neurotransmitter in the occurrence of GAD. However, other drugs that do not directly affect GABA levels (e.g., buspirone and antidepressants such as Prozac) can also be helpful in the treatment of GAD (Strawn et al., 2018). To complicate matters, these different prescription drugs do not help all individuals and, in some cases, can produce serious side effects and dependency.

Psychological explanations focus on anxiety-provoking situations in explaining high levels of GAD. The condition is especially prevalent among people who have low incomes, live in large cities, and/or face environments that are rendered unpredictable by political and economic strife. The relatively high rates of GAD among women may also be related to stress because women are more likely than men to

generalized anxiety disorder (GAD) A disorder characterized by chronic excessive worry accompanied by three or more of the following symptoms: restlessness, fatigue, concentration problems, irritability, muscle tension, and sleep disturbance.

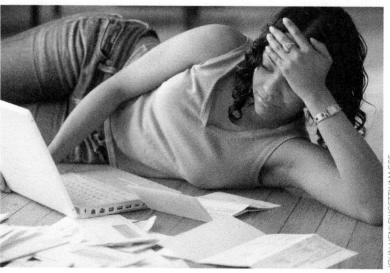

The experience of major stressful life events, such as losing a job or a home, can lead to generalized anxiety disorder, a condition characterized by chronic, excessive worry.

JOHN HENLEY/GETTY IMAGES

live in poverty, experience discrimination, or be subjected to sexual or physical abuse (e.g., Dworkin et al., 2017). Research shows that unpredictable traumatic experiences in childhood increase the risk of developing GAD, and this evidence also supports the idea that stressful experiences play a role (Bandoli et al., 2017). Risk of GAD also increases following the experience of a loss or situation associated with future perceived danger (Kendler et al., 2003), such as loss of a home due to foreclosure (McLaughlin et al., 2012). Still, many people who might be expected to develop GAD don't, supporting the diathesis–stress model that personal vulnerability must also be a key factor in this disorder.

Obsessive-Compulsive Disorder: Persistent Thoughts and Repetitive Behaviours

Learning Outcome

WHAT YOU NEED TO KNOW

- Describe the symptoms and potential causes of OCD.

You may have had an irresistible urge to go back to check whether you actually locked the door or turned off the oven, even when you're pretty sure that you did. Or you may have been unable to resist engaging in some superstitious behaviour, such as not walking under a ladder or stepping on a crack. For some people, such thoughts and actions spiral out of control and become a serious problem.

Ling, a 34-year-old with four children, sought treatment after several months of experiencing intrusive, repetitive thoughts in which she imagined that one or more of her children was having a serious accident. In addition, an extensive series of protective counting rituals hampered her daily routine. For example, when grocery shopping, Ling had the feeling that if she selected the first item (say, a box of cereal) on a shelf, something terrible would happen to her oldest child. If she selected the second item, some unknown disaster would befall her second child, and so on for all four children. The children's ages were also important. The sixth item in a row, for example, was associated with her youngest child, who was 6 years old.

Ling's preoccupation with numbers extended to other activities, most notably the pattern in which she smoked cigarettes and drank coffee. If she had one cigarette, she felt that she had to smoke at least four in a row or one of her children would be harmed in some way. If she drank one cup of coffee, she felt compelled to drink four more to protect her children from harm. She acknowledged that her counting rituals were irrational, but she became extremely anxious when she tried to stop (Oltmanns et al., 1991).

Ling's symptoms are typical of **obsessive-compulsive disorder (OCD)**, in which *repetitive, intrusive thoughts (obsessions) and ritualistic behaviours (compulsions) designed to fend off those thoughts interfere significantly with an individual's functioning.* Anxiety plays a role in this disorder because the obsessive thoughts typically produce anxiety, and the compulsive behaviours are performed to reduce it. In OCD, these obsessions and compulsions are intense, frequent, and experienced as irrational and excessive. Attempts to cope with the obsessive thoughts by trying to suppress or ignore them are of little or no benefit. In fact (as discussed in the Consciousness chapter), thought suppression can backfire, increasing the frequency and intensity of the obsessive thoughts (Wegner, 1989; Wenzlaff & Wegner, 2000). Despite anxiety's role, *DSM–5–TR* classifies OCD separately from anxiety disorders, because researchers believe that this disorder has a distinct cause and is maintained via different neural circuitry in the brain than anxiety disorders.

About 1 in 100 Canadians has had an episode of OCD. It is perhaps slightly more common in women than in men, and almost always begins before middle age

obsessive-compulsive disorder (OCD) A disorder in which repetitive, intrusive thoughts (obsessions) and ritualistic behaviours (compulsions) designed to fend off those thoughts interfere significantly with an individual's functioning.

Howie Mandel is a successful Canadian comedian, but his struggle with OCD is no laughing matter. Like approximately 2% of people in Canada and the United States, Mandel struggles with extreme fears of being contaminated by germs and engages in repeated checking and cleaning behaviours that often interfere with his daily life. He has spoken publicly about his struggles with OCD and about the importance of seeking effective treatment for this condition.

(Canadian Psychological Association, 2021). Among those with OCD, the most common obsessions and compulsions involve checking (79% of those with OCD), ordering (57%), moral concerns (43%), and contamination (26%) (Ruscio et al., 2010). Although compulsive behaviour is always excessive, it can vary considerably in intensity and frequency. For example, fear of contamination may lead to 15 minutes of hand washing in some individuals, whereas others may need to spend hours with disinfectants and extremely hot water, scrubbing their hands until they bleed.

The obsessions that plague individuals with OCD typically derive from concerns that could pose a real threat (such as contamination or disease), which supports preparedness theory. Thinking repeatedly about whether we've left a stove burner on when we leave the house makes sense, after all, if we want to return to a house that is not "well done." The concept of preparedness places OCD in the same evolutionary context as phobias (Szechtman & Woody, 2006). However, as with phobias, we need to consider other factors to explain why fears that may have served an evolutionary purpose can become so distorted and maladaptive.

OCD has been recognized by clinicians for more than 200 years, but the precise biological mechanisms driving this behaviour have eluded scientific understanding (Stone, 1997). Recent family and twin studies indicate a moderate to strong genetic heritability for OCD (~50%), which is even stronger for OCD traits (~70%) (Burston et al., 2018). But what exactly is passed on genetically that contributes to the behaviours observed in those with OCD? Brain-imaging research over the past few decades suggests that one key component of this disorder is abnormally high activity or connectedness between a specific brain circuit involved in habitual behaviour: the cortico-striato-thalamo-cortical loop (which connects parts of the cortex with the striatum and thalamus) (Dougherty et al., 2018; Milad & Rauch, 2012). Treatments for OCD that decrease the activity of this specific brain circuit using brain surgery or brain stimulation have shown some promise, but they are still being developed and tested. The most effective treatment remains behavioural therapy: 3 in 4 individuals with OCD who complete treatment will show a long-term, meaningful reduction in obsessive thoughts and compulsive behaviours (Canadian Psychological Association, 2021; see the Treatment chapter for more on these approaches).

Posttraumatic Stress Disorder: Distress and Avoidance After a Trauma

Learning Outcome

WHAT YOU NEED TO KNOW

- Describe the symptoms and potential causes of PTSD.

posttraumatic stress disorder (PTSD) A disorder characterized by chronic physiological arousal, recurrent unwanted thoughts or images of the trauma, and avoidance of things that call the traumatic event to mind.

Psychological reactions to traumatic or stressful events can lead to stressor-related disorders. For example, a person who lives through a terrifying and uncontrollable experience may develop **posttraumatic stress disorder (PTSD)**, which is characterized by *chronic physiological arousal, recurrent unwanted thoughts or images of the trauma, and avoidance of things that call the traumatic event to mind.*

Psychological disorders following exposure to traumatic events are perhaps nowhere more apparent than in war. Many soldiers returning from combat experience symptoms of PTSD, including flashbacks of battle, exaggerated anxiety and startle reactions, and even medical conditions that do not arise from physical damage (e.g., paralysis or chronic fatigue). Most of these symptoms are appropriate responses to horrifying events, and for most people, the symptoms subside with time. In PTSD, however, the symptoms can last much longer. For example, more than 40,000 Canadian Armed Forces members served in Afghanistan between 2001 and 2014, and approximately 1 in 6 of these subsequently received support for PTSD (The Canadian Press, 2019). The effects of PTSD are recognized not only among victims, witnesses, and perpetrators of war but also among people who are traumatized by terrible events in civilian life. Approximately 3 out of every 4 Canadians are, at some point in their lives, involved in an event that could trigger PTSD (e.g., been in combat, a victim of assault, or in a serious accident). Most individuals exposed to such events do not develop PTSD. How do they differ from those who do?

Research using brain-imaging techniques to examine brain structure and function has identified important neural correlates of PTSD. Specifically, those with PTSD show heightened activity in the amygdala (a region associated with the evaluation of threatening information and fear conditioning), decreased activity in the medial prefrontal cortex (a region important in the extinction of fear conditioning), and a smaller-size hippocampus (the part of the brain most linked with memory, as described in the Neuroscience and Behaviour and Memory chapters) (Shin et al., 2006).

Of course, an important question is whether people whose brains have these characteristics are at greater risk for PTSD if traumatized, or if these characteristics are the consequences of trauma in some people. For instance, does reduced hippocampal volume reflect a preexisting condition that makes the brain sensitive to stress? Or does the traumatic stress itself somehow kill nerve cells? One important study suggests that although a group of combat veterans with PTSD showed reduced hippocampal volume, so did the identical (monozygotic) twins of those men (see **FIGURE 15.3**), even though the twins had never had any combat exposure or developed PTSD (Gilbertson et al., 2002). This suggests that the veterans' reduced hippocampal volumes weren't caused by the combat exposure; instead, both these veterans and their twin brothers might have had a smaller hippocampus to begin with, a preexisting condition that made them susceptible to developing PTSD when they were later exposed to trauma.

PTSD may become a big problem in Ukraine when the current war there ends. Good preparation for deployment during military training can reduce PTSD prevalence and severity (Iversen et al., 2008); but many soldiers in the war did not have military training. Furthermore, after the war, the soldiers will return to a country that, given the damage war caused, may lack resources for therapeutic interventions. However, Ukrainian soldiers believe that they are behaving ethically when they fight Russia's invasion, and they have high morale—these factors protect against PTSD (Barnes et al., 2019; Iversen et al., 2008).

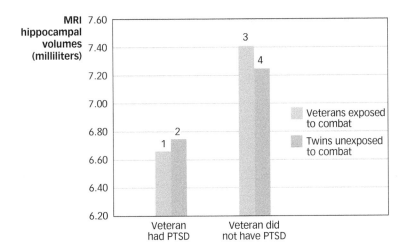

Figure 15.3

Hippocampal Volumes in American veterans of the Vietnam War, and Their Identical Twins Average hippocampal volumes for four groups of participants: (1) combat-exposed veterans who developed PTSD; (2) their combat-unexposed twins with no PTSD themselves; (3) combat-exposed veterans who never developed PTSD; and (4) their unexposed twins, also with no PTSD. Smaller hippocampal volumes were found for both the combat-exposed veterans with PTSD (Group 1) and their twins who had not been exposed to combat (Group 2), in contrast to veterans without PTSD (Group 3) and their twins (Group 4). This pattern of findings suggests that an inherited smaller hippocampus may make some people sensitive to conditions that cause PTSD (Gilbertson et al., 2002).

Depressive and Bipolar Disorders: Extreme Highs and Lows

You're probably experiencing a mood state right now. Maybe you're happy that it's almost time to get a snack or saddened by something you heard from a friend—or you may feel good or bad without having a clue why. As you learned in the Emotion and Motivation chapter, moods are relatively long-lasting, nonspecific emotional states—and *nonspecific* means we often may have no idea what has caused a mood. Changing moods lend variety to our experiences, like different-coloured lights shining on the stage as we play out our lives. However, for people like Robin Williams and others with mood disorders, moods can become so intense that they are pulled or pushed into life-threatening actions. **Mood disorders** are *mental disorders that have mood disturbance as their predominant feature* and take two main forms: *depression* (also called *unipolar depression*) and *bipolar disorder* (so named because people go from one end of the emotional pole [extreme depression] to the other [extreme mania]).

Depressive Disorders

Everyone feels sad, pessimistic, and unmotivated from time to time. For most people, these periods are relatively short lived and mild, but depression is much more than typical sadness. The experience of Darren, a 34-year-old man who visited his primary-care physician complaining of chronic fatigue, is fairly typical. During the visit, he mentioned difficulties falling asleep and staying asleep that left him chronically tired, so much so that he feared that maybe he had some kind of medical problem. He complained that over the past 6 months, he no longer had the energy to exercise and had gained 10 pounds. He also lost all interest in going out with his friends or even talking to other people. Nothing he usually enjoyed, even sexual activity, gave him pleasure anymore; he had trouble concentrating and was forgetful, irritable, impatient, and frustrated. Darren's change in mood and behaviour, and the sense of hopelessness and weariness he felt, goes far beyond normal sadness. Instead, depressive disorders are dysfunctional and chronic, and they fall outside the range of socially or culturally expected responses.

mood disorders Mental disorders that have mood disturbance as their predominant feature.

Depression is among the most common, and most impairing, mental disorder. Despite this, there continues to be a lot of stigma about depression. Public figures are increasingly speaking out about their own struggles with depression to try to decrease stigma and encourage people to seek treatment. For example, actress Taraji P. Henson has spoken out about her own struggles with depression and has created a non-profit foundation focused on decreasing the stigma about mental illness in the Black community.

KEVIN DIETSCH/UPI/ALAMY STOCK PHOTO

Seasonal affective disorder is not merely having the blues because of the weather. It appears to be due to reduced exposure to light in the winter months.

Major depressive disorder (or **unipolar depression**), which we refer to here simply as "depression," is characterized by *a severely depressed mood and/or inability to experience pleasure that lasts 2 or more weeks and is accompanied by feelings of worthlessness, lethargy, and sleep and appetite disturbance.* In a related condition called **persistent depressive disorder**, *the same cognitive and bodily problems as in depression are present, but they are less severe and last longer, persisting for at least 2 years.* When both types co-occur, the resulting condition is called **double depression**, defined as *a moderately depressed mood that persists for at least 2 years and is punctuated by periods of major depression.*

Some people experience *recurrent depressive episodes in a seasonal pattern* that is commonly known as **seasonal affective disorder (SAD)**. In most cases, SAD episodes begin in fall or winter and remit in spring, in a pattern that is due to reduced levels of light over the colder seasons (Westrin & Lam, 2007). Nevertheless, recurrent summer depressive episodes have been reported. A winter-related pattern of depression appears to be more prevalent in higher latitudes.

Who Is at Risk?

Approximately 1 in 9 people in Canada and the United States meet the criteria for depression at some point in their lives (Kessler et al., 2012; Pearson, Janz, & Ali, 2013). On average, major depression lasts about 12 weeks (Eaton et al., 2008). However, without treatment, approximately 80% of individuals with an initial depressive episode will experience at least one recurrence of the disorder (Judd, 1997; Mueller et al., 1999). Compared with people who have a single episode, individuals with recurrent depression have more severe symptoms, higher rates of depression in their families, more suicide attempts, and higher rates of divorce (Merikangas et al., 1994).

Similar to that of anxiety disorders, the rate of depression is much higher in women (22%) than in men (14%) (Kessler et al., 2012). Socioeconomic standing has been invoked as an explanation for women's heightened risk: Their incomes are lower than those of men, and poverty could cause depression. Sex differences in hormones are another possibility: Estrogen, androgen, and progesterone influence depression; some women experience *postpartum depression* (depression following

major depressive disorder (unipolar depression) A disorder characterized by a severely depressed mood and/or inability to experience pleasure that lasts 2 or more weeks and is accompanied by feelings of worthlessness, lethargy, and sleep and appetite disturbance.

persistent depressive disorder The same cognitive and bodily problems as in depression are present, but they are less severe and last longer, persisting for at least 2 years.

double depression A moderately depressed mood that persists for at least 2 years and is punctuated by periods of major depression.

seasonal affective disorder (SAD) Recurrent depressive episodes in a seasonal pattern.

Postpartum depression can strike women out of nowhere, often causing new mothers to feel extreme sadness, guilt, and disconnection, and even to experience serious thoughts of suicide. The actress Brooke Shields wrote about her experience with postpartum depression in a popular book on this condition.

childbirth) due to changing hormone balances. It is also possible that the higher rate of depression in women reflects their greater willingness to face their depression and seek help, leading to higher rates of diagnosis (Nolen-Hoeksema, 2012). Significant research has shown that in the aggregate, women have a greater tendency to accept, disclose, and ruminate on their negative emotions, whereas men are more likely to deny negative emotions and engage in self-distractions such as work and drinking alcohol.

Neurotransmitters and Genes Play a Role, and So Does Stress

Beginning in the 1950s, researchers noticed that drugs that increased levels of the neurotransmitters norepinephrine and serotonin could sometimes reduce depression. This observation suggested that depression might be caused by an absolute or relative depletion of these neurotransmitters, which sparked a revolution in the pharmacological treatment of depression (Schildkraut, 1965) and led to the development and widespread use of popular prescription drugs such as Prozac and Zoloft, which increase the availability of serotonin in the brain. Further research has shown, however, that reduced levels of these neurotransmitters cannot be the whole story regarding the causes of depression. For example, some studies have found *increases* in norepinephrine activity among depressed individuals (Thase & Howland, 1995). Moreover, even though these antidepressant medications change neurochemical transmission in less than a day, they typically take at least 2 weeks to relieve depressive symptoms. In many cases, they are not effective in decreasing depressive symptoms. A biochemical model of depression has yet to be developed that accounts for all the evidence.

As with many other types of mental disorders, depression shows moderate heritability, with heritability estimates increasing as a function of severity. For instance, a relatively large study of nearly 500,000 people found that the heritability estimate for less severe depression was approximately 35%, whereas for severe depression it was close to 50% (Corfield et al., 2017).

Newer biological models of depression have tried to understand depression using a diathesis–stress model. For example, Avshalom Caspi and his colleagues (2003) proposed, and reported, that a certain genetic diathesis related to the activity of the neurotransmitter serotonin is much more likely to lead to depression among those with major stressful life events. This appeared to be evidence that nature and nurture interact to influence brain structure, function, and chemistry in depression and was widely celebrated by the field. However, subsequent larger studies and meta-analyses (which are a quantitative synthesis of the results of many individual studies) combining such studies have failed to support such a finding (Culverhouse et al., 2017). Of course, this is how science works: initial discoveries must be consistently replicated in follow-up studies before they become accepted pieces of our scientific understanding.

Research also has begun to tell us what parts of the brain show differences in depression. For instance, some important findings came out of a meta-analysis of 24 brain-imaging studies. Results showed that when viewing negative stimuli (words or images), people suffering from depression showed both increased activity in regions of the brain associated with processing emotional information and decreased activity in areas associated with cognitive control (see **FIGURE 15.4**) (Hamilton et al., 2012).

Of course, this is not the whole picture; these findings don't explain all of the symptoms seen in depression, why and when depression comes and goes, or how treatment works. Given that depression arises not from a single gene or brain region, but rather from the interactions of different biological systems that each

COURTESY PAUL HAMILTON

Structure	Direction of Effect
A) amygdala	increased in MDD
B) dorsal anterior cingulate cortex	increased in MDD
C) insula and superior temporal gyrus	increased in MDD
D) dorsolateral prefrontal cortex	decreased in MDD
E) caudate body	decreased in MDD

Figure 15.4

The Brain and Depression When presented with negative information, people with depression show increased activation in regions of the brain associated with emotional processing, such as the amygdala, insula, and dorsal anterior cingulate cortex (ACC), and decreased activity in regions associated with cognitive control such as the dorsal striatum and dorsolateral prefrontal cortex (DLPFC) (Hamilton et al., 2012).

give rise to the different psychological traits seen in depression, it will likely be many years before we fully understand the biological causes of this disorder (Young et al., 2016).

Negative Thoughts Contribute to Depression

If optimists see the world through rose-coloured glasses, people who suffer from depression tend to view the world through dark grey lenses. Their negative cognitive style is remarkably consistent and, some argue, begins in childhood with experiences that create a pattern of negative self-thoughts (Gibb et al., 2001) that help to convert negative life events into depressive episodes (Mac Giollabhui et al., 2018). One of the first theorists to emphasize the role of thought in depression, Aaron T. Beck (1967), noted that his depressed patients distorted perceptions of their experiences and embraced dysfunctional attitudes that promoted and maintained negative mood states. His observations led him to develop a *cognitive model of depression,* which states that biases in how information is attended to, processed, and remembered lead to and maintain depression.

Elaborating on this initial idea, researchers proposed a theory of depression that emphasizes the role of people's negative inferences about the causes of their experiences (Abramson et al., 1978). **Helplessness theory**, which is a part of the cognitive model of depression, maintains that *individuals who are prone to depression automatically attribute negative experiences to causes that are internal (i.e., their own fault), stable (i.e., unlikely to change), and global (i.e., widespread).* For example, a student at risk for depression might view a bad grade on a math test as a sign of low intelligence (internal) that will never change (stable) and that will lead to failure in all their future endeavors (global). In contrast, a student without this tendency might have the opposite response, attributing the grade to something external (poor teaching), unstable (a missed study session), and/or specific (boring subject).

The relationship between one's perceptions and depression has been further developed and supported over the past several decades. The update to Beck's cognitive model suggests that due to a combination of a genetic vulnerability

MARY EVANS PICTURE LIBRARY/ALAMY STOCK PHOTO

The cognitive model of depression is based on approaches to thinking developed by the Stoic philosophers of ancient Greece and Rome. Epictetus's famous quote, "Men are disturbed not by things, but by the principles and notions which they form concerning things," is commonly cited by cognitive theorists as a guiding principle of the cognitive model of depression.

helplessness theory The idea that individuals who are prone to depression automatically attribute negative experiences to causes that are internal (i.e., their own fault), stable (i.e., unlikely to change), and global (i.e., widespread).

and negative early life events, people with depression have developed a negative *schema* (described in the Development chapter). This negative schema is characterized by biases in:

- interpretations of information (a tendency to interpret neutral information negatively—seeing the world through grey glasses)
- attention (trouble disengaging from negative information)
- memory (better recall of negative information) (Gotlib & Joormann, 2010)

For example, a student at risk for depression who gets a bad grade on a test might interpret a well-intentioned comment from the teacher ("Good job on the test") negatively ("The teacher's being sarcastic!"); might have trouble forgetting about both the test score and the perceived negative comment; and might have better memory about this test in the future ("Sure, I did well on my English exam, but don't forget about that bad math test last month"). The presence of these biases may help to explain the internal, stable, and global attributions seen in depression. In addition, recent research suggests that some of the differences in brain structure and function seen in those with depression can help to explain some of these cognitive biases. For instance, people with depression show abnormalities in parts of the brain that are involved in attention and memory, especially when presented with negative information (Disner et al., 2011). Although we don't fully understand the causes of depression, pieces of the puzzle are being discovered and fit together even as you read this.

Bipolar Disorder

If depression is distressing and painful, would the opposite extreme be better? Not for Lateefah, a 20-year-old second-year undergraduate. When first seen by a clinician, Lateefah had gone 5 days without sleep and was extremely active and expressing bizarre thoughts and ideas. She proclaimed to friends that she did not menstruate because she was "of a third sex, a gender above the two human sexes." She claimed to be a "superwoman," capable of avoiding human sexuality and yet still able to give birth. Preoccupied with the politics of global disarmament, she felt that she had switched souls with the premier of her province, had tapped into his thoughts and memories, and could save the world from nuclear destruction. She began to campaign for an elected position in federal Parliament (even though no elections were scheduled at that time). Worried that she would forget some of her thoughts, she had been leaving hundreds of notes about her ideas and activities everywhere, including on the walls and furniture of her residence room (Vitkus, 1999).

In addition to her manic episodes, Lateefah had a history of depression. The diagnostic label for this constellation of symptoms is **bipolar disorder**, *a condition characterized by cycles of abnormal, persistent high mood (mania) and low mood (depression)*. The lifetime risk for bipolar disorder is about 1 in 40 people and does not differ between men and women (Kessler et al., 2012). The depressive phase of bipolar disorder is often clinically indistinguishable from major depression (Johnson et al., 2009). In the manic phase, which must last at least 1 week to meet *DSM* requirements, mood can be elevated, expansive, or irritable. Other prominent symptoms include grandiosity, decreased need for sleep, talkativeness, racing thoughts, distractibility, and reckless behaviour (such as compulsive gambling, sexual indiscretions, and unrestrained spending sprees). Psychotic features such as hallucinations (erroneous perceptions) and delusions (erroneous beliefs) may be present, so the disorder can be misdiagnosed as schizophrenia (described in a later section of this chapter).

bipolar disorder A condition characterized by cycles of abnormal, persistent high mood (mania) and low mood (depression).

Here's how Kay Redfield Jamison (1993, p. 67), in *An Unquiet Mind: A Memoir of Madness,* described her own experience with bipolar disorder.

There is a particular kind of pain, elation, loneliness, and terror involved in this kind of madness. When you're high it's tremendous. The ideas and feelings are fast and frequent like shooting stars, and you follow them until you find better and brighter ones. . . . But, somewhere, this changes. The fast ideas are far too fast, and there are far too many; overwhelming confusion replaces clarity. Memory goes. Humor and absorption on friends' faces are replaced by fear and concern. Everything previously moving with the grain is now against — you are irritable, angry, frightened, uncontrollable, and enmeshed totally in the blackest caves of the mind. You never knew those caves were there. It will never end, for madness carves its own reality.

Subtypes of Bipolar Disorder

The psychologist Kay Redfield Jamison has written several best-selling books about her own struggles with bipolar disorder.

The experience of bipolar disorder is not the same for all people; there are general subtypes of this condition. Those with bipolar disorder, by definition, will experience a major depressive episode, which occurs before an episode of elevated mood in 45–90% of people with bipolar disorder (Kupka et al., 2021). *Bipolar I Disorder* refers to instances of this disorder in which a person experiences at least one depressive episode and at least one manic episode. *Bipolar II Disorder* refers to instances in which a person experiences a depressive episode accompanied by a *hypomanic* episode, which is an elevation of mood similar to mania but of lower intensity. Depressive episodes tend to last much longer than manic/hypomanic episodes for most people (5 months vs. 3 months, respectively) (Tondo et al., 2017). Approximately 1 in 10 people with bipolar disorder have *rapid cycling bipolar disorder,* characterized by at least four mood episodes (either manic/hypomanic or depressive) every year. This form of the disorder is particularly difficult to treat (Post et al., 2008).

Some researchers have suggested that people with psychotic and mood (especially bipolar) disorders have higher creativity and intellectual ability (Andreasen, 2011). In bipolar disorder, this suggestion goes, before the mania becomes too pronounced, the energy, grandiosity, and ambition that it supplies may help people achieve great things. Notable individuals thought to have had the disorder include Isaac Newton, Vincent van Gogh, Abraham Lincoln, Virginia Woolf, Ernest Hemingway, Winston Churchill, Mariah Carey, and Demi Lovato.

Genetics and Life Situation Play a Role

Among the various mental disorders, bipolar disorder has one of the highest rates of heritability, with concordance from 40 to 70% for identical twins and 10% for fraternal twins (Craddock & Jones, 1999). Like most other disorders, bipolar disorder is likely *polygenic,* arising from the interaction of multiple genes that combine to create the symptoms observed in those with this disorder; however, these genes have been difficult to identify. Adding to the complexity, there also is evidence of *pleiotropic effects,* in which one gene influences a person's susceptibility to multiple disorders. For instance, one study revealed a shared genetic vulnerability for bipolar disorder and schizophrenia. The genes linked to both disorders are associated with compromised abilities both in filtering unnecessary information and in recognition memory, as well as problems with dopamine and serotonin transmission — factors present in both types of disorders (Huang et al., 2010).

A follow-up study examining more than 60,000 people revealed that common genetic risk factors are associated with bipolar disorder and schizophrenia, as well as major depression, autism spectrum disorder, and attention-deficit/hyperactivity disorder. These disorders share overlapping symptoms such as problems with mood regulation, cognitive impairments, and social withdrawal (Cross-Disorder Group of the Psychiatric Genomics Consortium, 2013). Findings like these are exciting because they help us begin to understand why we see similar symptoms in people with what we previously thought were unrelated disorders. Although some genetic links have been made, we currently lack an understanding of how different biological factors work together to cause the symptoms observed in bipolar and other disorders.

There is growing evidence that the epigenetic changes you learned about in the Neuroscience and Behaviour chapter can help explain how genetic risk factors influence the development of bipolar and related disorders. Remember how rat pups whose moms spent less time licking and grooming them experienced epigenetic changes (decreased DNA methylation) that led to a poorer stress response? As you might expect, these same kinds of epigenetic effects seem to help explain who develops symptoms of mental disorders and who doesn't. For instance, studies examining monozygotic twin pairs (identical twins, who share 100% of their DNA) in which one develops bipolar disorder or schizophrenia and one doesn't, reveal significant epigenetic differences between the two, with decreased methylation at genetic locations known to be important in brain development and the occurrence of bipolar disorders and schizophrenia (Dempster et al., 2011; Labrie et al., 2012).

Stressful life experiences often precede manic and depressive episodes (S. L. Johnson et al., 2008). In fact, people with bipolar disorder experience significantly more negative life events just before a mood episode than they do before a euthymic (or more balanced) episode, suggesting that negative life events may push people with bipolar disorder into one of their more extreme mood states (Lex et al., 2017). Interestingly, people living with family members who are high in **expressed emotion**, which in this context is *a measure of how much hostility, criticism, and emotional overinvolvement people communicate when speaking about a family member with a mental disorder,* are more likely to relapse than are people with supportive families (Miklowitz & Johnson, 2006). This is true not just of those with bipolar disorder: Expressed emotion is associated with higher rates of relapse across a wide range of mental disorders (Hooley, 2007).

expressed emotion A measure of how much hostility, criticism, and emotional overinvolvement people communicate when speaking about a family member with a mental disorder.

Schizophrenia and Other Psychotic Disorders: Losing the Grasp on Reality

Learning Outcomes

WHAT YOU NEED TO KNOW

- Compare the negative, positive, and cognitive symptoms of schizophrenia.
- Describe the biological factors contributing to schizophrenia.
- Explain the evidence for the influence of environmental factors.

Maggie, a 39-year-old wife and mother, believed that God was punishing her for marrying a man she did not love and bringing two children into the world. As her punishment, God had made her and her children immortal so that they would have to suffer in their unhappy home life forever—a realization that came to her one evening when she was washing dishes and saw a fork lying across a knife in the shape of a cross. Maggie found further support for her belief in two pieces of evidence: First, a local television station was rerunning old episodes of *The Honeymooners*, a 1950s situation comedy in which the main characters often argue and shout at each other. She saw this as a sign from God that her own marital conflict would go on forever. Second, she believed (falsely) that the pupils of her children's eyes were fixed in size and would neither dilate nor constrict—a sign of their immortality.

At home, she would lock herself in her room for hours and sometimes days. The week before her diagnosis, she kept her 7-year-old son home from school so that he could join her and his 4-year-old sister in reading aloud from the Bible (Oltmanns et al., 1991). Maggie was suffering from the best-known, most widely studied psychotic disorder: schizophrenia, one of the most mystifying and devastating of all the mental disorders. Many people with this disorder experience a lifetime of suffering and impairment, but see Other Voices: Successful and Schizophrenic for a discussion of the fact that many with this disorder have very successful careers and fulfilling lives. A review of the symptoms of this disorder make clear why this condition can be so distressing and impairing.

Symptoms and Types of Schizophrenia

Schizophrenia is a psychotic disorder (*psychosis* is a break from reality) characterized by *the profound disruption of basic psychological processes; a distorted perception of reality; altered or blunted emotion; and disturbances in thought, motivation, and behaviour.* Traditionally, schizophrenia was regarded primarily as a disturbance of thought and perception, in which the sense of reality becomes severely distorted and confused. However, this condition is now understood to take different forms affecting a wide range of functions. According to the *DSM–5–TR,* schizophrenia is diagnosed when two or more symptoms emerge during a continuous period of at least 1 month, with signs of the disorder persisting for at least 6 months. The symptoms of schizophrenia often are separated into *positive, negative,* and *disorganized symptoms.*

Positive symptoms of schizophrenia can be thought of as things that weren't there before but are added when the disease is present, including *thoughts and behaviours, such as hallucinations and delusions, not seen in those without the disorder:*

- **Hallucinations** are *false perceptual experiences that have a compelling sense of being real despite the absence of external stimulation.* The perceptual disturbances associated with schizophrenia can include hearing, seeing, smelling, or having a tactile sensation of things that are not there. Schizophrenic hallucinations are often auditory (e.g., hearing voices that no one else can hear). Among people with schizophrenia, some 65% report hearing voices repeatedly (Frith & Fletcher, 1995). The British psychiatrist Henry Maudsley (1886) long ago proposed that these voices are in fact produced in the mind of the person with schizophrenia, and recent research substantiates his idea. In a PET imaging study (conducted appropriately enough in the hospital named for Maudsley in London, UK) researchers found that Broca's area, a part of the brain involved in speaking (see the Neuroscience and Behaviour chapter), was active during auditory hallucinations (McGuire et al., 1993). Unfortunately, the voices heard in schizophrenia seldom sound like the self or like a kindly uncle offering advice. They command, scold, suggest bizarre actions, or offer snide comments. One individual reported a voice saying, "He's getting up now. He's going to wash. It's about time" (Frith & Fletcher, 1995).

- **Delusions** are *false beliefs, often bizarre and grandiose, that are maintained in spite of their irrationality.* For example, an individual with schizophrenia may believe that they are Jesus Christ, Napoleon, Joan of Arc, or some other well-known person. Such delusions of identity have helped foster the misconception that schizophrenia involves multiple personalities. However, adopted identities in schizophrenia do not alternate, exhibit amnesia for each other, or otherwise "split." Delusions of persecution are also common. Some individuals believe that demons, extraterrestrials, or other malevolent forces are conspiring to harm them or control their minds, which may represent an attempt to make sense of the tormenting delusions (Roberts, 1991). People with schizophrenia have little or no insight into their disordered perceptual and thought processes (Karow et al., 2007). Without understanding that they

Those suffering from schizophrenia often experience hallucinations and delusions, unable to determine what is real and what their own minds have created. The experience of John Nash, a Nobel Prize–winning economist with schizophrenia, was depicted in the book and movie *A Beautiful Mind.*

schizophrenia A disorder characterized by the profound disruption of basic psychological processes; a distorted perception of reality; altered or blunted emotion; and disturbances in thought, motivation, and behaviour.

positive symptoms Thoughts and behaviours, such as hallucinations and delusions, not seen in those without the disorder.

hallucination A false perceptual experience that has a compelling sense of being real despite the absence of external stimulation.

delusion A false belief, often bizarre and grandiose, that is maintained in spite of its irrationality.

GRUNNITUS STUDIO/SCIENCE SOURCE

A person suffering from catatonic schizophrenia may assume an unusual posture and fail to move for hours.

negative symptoms Deficits in or disruptions of emotions and behaviours (e.g., emotional and social withdrawal; apathy; poverty of speech; and other indications of the absence or insufficiency of normal behaviour, motivation, and emotion) that are missing in those with schizophrenia.

disorganized symptoms Disruptions or deficits in abilities of speech, movement, and cognition in those with schizophrenia.

disorganized speech A severe disruption of verbal communication in which ideas shift rapidly and incoherently among unrelated topics.

grossly disorganized behaviour Behaviour that is inappropriate for the situation or ineffective in attaining goals, often with specific motor disturbances.

catatonic behaviour A marked decrease in all movement or an increase in muscular rigidity and overactivity.

cognitive symptoms Deficits in cognitive abilities, specifically executive functioning, attention, and working memory, present in those with schizophrenia.

have lost control of their own minds, they may develop unusual beliefs and theories that attribute control to external agents.

Negative symptoms are things that were present before the disorder but have now gone away. These are *deficits in or disruptions of emotions and behaviours.* They include emotional and social withdrawal; apathy; poverty of speech; and other indications of the absence or insufficiency of normal behaviour, motivation, and emotion. These symptoms refer to things that are missing in those with schizophrenia. Negative symptoms may rob people of emotion, for example, leaving them with flat, deadpan responses; their interest in people or events may be undermined, or their capacity to focus attention may be impaired.

Disorganized symptoms refer to *disruptions or deficits in abilities of speech, movement, and cognition.* They often take the form of:

- **Disorganized speech** is *a severe disruption of verbal communication in which ideas shift rapidly and incoherently among unrelated topics.* The abnormal speech patterns in schizophrenia reflect difficulties in organizing thoughts and focusing attention. Individuals often make irrelevant responses to questions, associate ideas loosely, and use words in peculiar ways. For example, asked by a doctor, "Can you tell me the name of this place?" one patient with schizophrenia responded, "I have not been a drinker for 16 years. I am taking a mental rest after a 'carter' assignment of 'quill.' You know, a 'penwrap.' I had contracts with Warner Brothers Studios and Eugene broke phonograph records but Mike protested. I have been with the police department for 35 years. I am made of flesh and blood—see, Doctor" [pulling up clothing] (Carson et al., 2000, p. 474).

- **Grossly disorganized behaviour** is *behaviour that is inappropriate for the situation or ineffective in attaining goals,* often with specific motor disturbances. An individual might exhibit constant childlike silliness, improper sexual behaviour (such as masturbating in public), disheveled appearance, or loud shouting or swearing. Specific motor disturbances might include strange movements, rigid posturing, odd mannerisms, bizarre grimacing, or hyperactivity.

- **Catatonic behaviour** is *a marked decrease in all movement or an increase in muscular rigidity and overactivity.* Individuals with catatonia may actively resist movement (when someone is trying to move them) or become completely unresponsive and unaware of their surroundings, in a stupor. In addition, individuals receiving drug therapy may exhibit motor symptoms (such as rigidity or spasm) as a side effect of the medication. Indeed, the *DSM–5–TR* includes a diagnostic category labelled "medication-induced movement disorders" that identifies motor disturbances arising from medications of the sort commonly used to treat schizophrenia.

Cognitive symptoms are *deficits in cognitive abilities, specifically in executive functioning, attention, and working memory, present in those with schizophrenia.* These are the least noticeable symptoms because they are much less bizarre and public than the positive and negative symptoms. However, these cognitive deficits often play a large role in preventing people with schizophrenia from achieving a high level of functioning, such as maintaining friendships and holding down a job (Green et al., 2000).

Schizophrenia occurs in about 1 of every 200 people (Simeone et al., 2015) and is slightly more common in men than in women (McGrath et al., 2008). Early versions of the *DSM* suggested that schizophrenia might have a very early onset—in the form of infantile autism—but more recent studies suggest that these disorders are distinct and that schizophrenia rarely develops before early adolescence and most often has an onset between ages 20–29 years (Miettunen et al., 2018). The first episode typically occurs in late adolescence or early adulthood. Despite its relatively low frequency, people with schizophrenia are over-represented among psychiatric inpatients and have inpatient hospital stays that are significantly longer than those for other psychiatric patients (Chen et al., 2017). The disproportionate rate and length of hospitalization for schizophrenia is a testament to the devastation it causes in people's lives.

Biological Factors

In 1899, when the German psychiatrist Emil Kraepelin first described the syndrome we now know as schizophrenia, he remarked that the disorder was so severe that it suggested "organic," or biological, origins. Over the years, accumulating evidence for the role of biology in schizophrenia has come from studies of genetic factors, biochemical factors, and neuroanatomy.

Genetic Factors and Environment Play a Role

Family studies indicate that the closer a person's genetic relatedness is to someone with schizophrenia, the greater their likelihood of developing the disorder (Gottesman, 1991). As shown in **FIGURE 15.5**, concordance rates increase dramatically with biological relatedness. These rates are estimates and vary considerably from study to study, but almost every study over the years has found the average concordance rates to be much higher for monozygotic twins (33%) than for dizygotic twins (7%), which suggests a genetic component to the disorder (Hilker et al., 2018).

Although genetics clearly has a strong predisposing role in schizophrenia, considerable evidence suggests that environmental factors, such as prenatal and perinatal environments, also affect concordance rates (Jurewicz et al., 2001; Thaker, 2002). For example, because approximately 70% of identical twins share the same prenatal blood supply, toxins in the mother's blood could contribute to the high concordance rate. More recent studies (discussed in the earlier section on bipolar disorder) are contributing to a better understanding of how environmental stressors can trigger epigenetic changes that increase susceptibility to this disorder.

The Precise Role of Neurotransmitters Has Yet to Be Fully Understood

During the 1950s, researchers discovered major tranquilizers that could reduce the symptoms of schizophrenia by lowering levels of the neurotransmitter dopamine. The

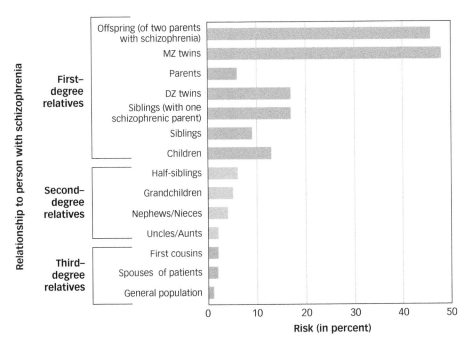

Figure 15.5
Average Risk of Developing Schizophrenia The risk of schizophrenia among biological relatives is greater for those with greater degrees of relatedness. An identical (MZ) twin of a person with schizophrenia has a 48% risk of developing schizophrenia, for example. Offspring of two parents with schizophrenia have a 46% risk of developing this disorder (data from Gottesman, 1991).

effectiveness of many drugs in alleviating symptoms of schizophrenia is related to the drugs' capacity to reduce dopamine's role in neurotransmission in certain brain tracts. This finding suggested the **dopamine hypothesis,** *the idea that schizophrenia involves an excess of dopamine activity.* The hypothesis has been invoked to explain why amphetamines, which increase dopamine levels, often exacerbate symptoms of schizophrenia (Harro, 2015).

If only things were so simple. Considerable evidence suggests that this hypothesis is inadequate (Moncrieff, 2009). For example, many individuals with schizophrenia do not respond favourably to dopamine-blocking drugs (e.g., major tranquilizers), and those who do respond seldom show a complete remission of symptoms. Moreover, the drugs block dopamine receptors very rapidly, yet individuals with schizophrenia typically do not show a beneficial response for weeks. Finally, research has implicated other neurotransmitters in schizophrenia, suggesting that the disorder may involve a complex interaction among a host of different biochemicals (Risman et al., 2008; Sawa & Snyder, 2002). In sum, the precise role of neurotransmitters in schizophrenia has yet to be determined.

Research Has Identified Structural Changes in the Brain

When neuroimaging techniques became available, researchers immediately started looking for distinctive anatomical features of the brain in individuals with schizophrenia. The earliest observations revealed enlargement of the *ventricles,* hollow areas filled with cerebrospinal fluid, lying deep within the core of the brain (see **FIGURE 15.6**) (Johnstone et al., 1976). In some individuals (primarily those with chronic, negative symptoms), the ventricles were unusually enlarged, suggesting a loss of brain-tissue mass that could arise from an anomaly in prenatal development (Arnold et al., 1998).

Understanding the significance of this brain abnormality for schizophrenia is complicated by several factors, however. First, such enlarged ventricles are found in only a minority of individuals with schizophrenia. Second, some individuals who do not have schizophrenia also show evidence of enlarged ventricles. Finally, this type of brain abnormality can be caused by the long-term use of some types of antipsychotic medications commonly prescribed for schizophrenia (Jørgensen et al., 2016).

Neuroimaging studies provide evidence of a variety of brain abnormalities associated with schizophrenia. Paul Thompson and his colleagues (2001) examined changes in the brains of adolescents whose MRI scans could be traced sequentially from the onset of schizophrenia. By superimposing the scans onto an image of a standardized brain, the researchers were able to detect progressive tissue loss beginning in the parietal lobe and eventually encompassing much of the brain

dopamine hypothesis The idea that schizophrenia involves an excess of dopamine activity.

Figure 15.6

Enlarged Ventricles in Schizophrenia These MRI scans of monozygotic twins reveal that (a) the twin affected by schizophrenia shows enlarged ventricles (all the central white space), compared with (b) the unaffected twin (Kunugi et al., 2003).

(a)   (b)

DR. KUNUGI

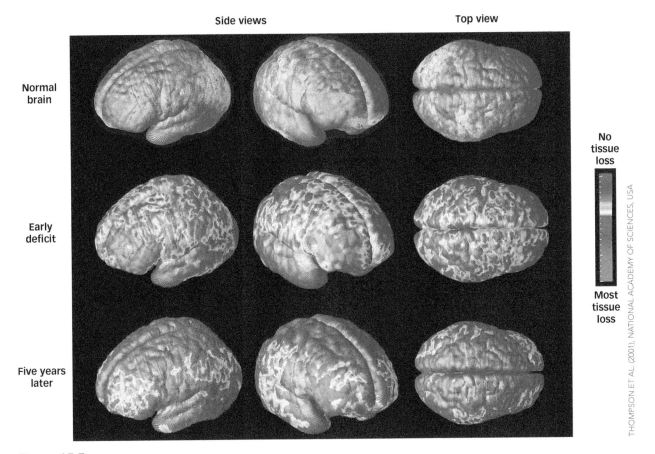

Figure 15.7

Brain Tissue Loss in Adolescent Schizophrenia MRI scan composites reveal brain tissue loss in adolescents diagnosed with schizophrenia. Normal brains show minimal loss due to "pruning" (*top*). Early-deficit scans reveal loss in the parietal areas (*middle*); individuals at this stage may experience symptoms such as hallucinations or bizarre thoughts. Scans 5 years later reveal extensive tissue loss over much of the cortex (*bottom*); individuals at this stage are likely to suffer from delusions, disorganized speech and behaviour, and negative symptoms such as social withdrawal (Thompson et al., 2001).

(see **FIGURE 15.7**). All adolescents lose some grey matter over time in a kind of normal "pruning" of the brain, but in those developing schizophrenia, the loss was dramatic enough to seem pathological. A variety of specific brain changes found in other studies suggests a clear relationship between biological changes in the brain and the progression of schizophrenia (Cannon, 2015).

Social/Psychological Factors

With all these potential biological contributors to schizophrenia, you might think there would be few psychological or social causes of this disorder. However, several studies suggest that family environment plays a role in the development of and recovery from the condition. One large-scale study compared the risk of schizophrenia in children adopted into healthy families to those adopted into severely disturbed families (Tienari et al., 2004). (Disturbed families were defined as those with extreme conflict, lack of communication, or chaotic relationships.) Among children whose biological mothers had schizophrenia, the disturbed environment increased their likelihood of developing schizophrenia—an outcome that was not found among children who were also reared in disturbed families but whose biological mothers did *not* have schizophrenia. This finding provides support for the diathesis–stress model described earlier.

Other Voices • Successful and Schizophrenic

This chapter describes what we know about the characteristics and causes of mental disorders, and the next chapter describes how these disorders are commonly treated. For some of the more severe disorders, such as schizophrenia, the picture does not look good. People diagnosed with schizophrenia often are informed that it is a lifelong condition; and although current treatments show some effectiveness in decreasing the delusional thinking and hallucinations often associated with schizophrenia, people with this disorder often are unable to hold down a full-time job, maintain healthy relationships, or achieve a high quality of life.

Elyn Saks is one such person. She received a diagnosis of schizophrenia and was informed of this prognosis. She described what happened next in a longer version of the following article, which appeared in the *New York Times*.

Thirty years ago, I was given a diagnosis of schizophrenia. My prognosis was "grave": I would never live independently, hold a job, find a loving partner, get married. My home would be a board-and-care facility, my days spent watching TV in a day room with other people debilitated by mental illness. . . .

Then I made a decision. I would write the narrative of my life. Today I am a chaired professor at the University of Southern California Gould School of Law. I have an adjunct appointment in the department of psychiatry at the medical school of the University of California, San Diego. The MacArthur Foundation gave me a genius grant.

Although I fought my diagnosis for many years, I came to accept that I have schizophrenia and will be in treatment the rest of my life. . . . What I refused to accept was my prognosis.

Conventional psychiatric thinking and its diagnostic categories say that people like me don't exist. Either I don't have schizophrenia (please tell that to the delusions crowding my mind), or I couldn't have accomplished what I have (please tell that to U.S.C.'s committee on faculty affairs). But I do, and I have. And I have undertaken research with colleagues at U.S.C. and U.C.L.A. to show that I am not alone. There are others with schizophrenia and such active symptoms as delusions and hallucinations who have significant academic and professional achievements.

Over the last few years, my colleagues . . . and I have gathered 20 research subjects with high-functioning schizophrenia in Los Angeles. They suffered from symptoms like mild delusions or hallucinatory behavior. Their average age was 40. Half were male, half female, and more than half were minorities. All had high school diplomas, and a majority either had or were working towards college or graduate degrees. They were graduate students, managers, technicians and professionals, including a doctor, lawyer, psychologist and chief executive of a nonprofit group. At the same time, most were unmarried and childless, which is consistent with their diagnoses. . . . More than three-quarters had been hospitalized between two and five times because of their illness, while three had never been admitted.

How had these people with schizophrenia managed to succeed in their studies and at such high-level jobs? We learned that, in addition to medication and therapy, all the participants had developed techniques to keep their schizophrenia at bay. For some, these techniques were cognitive. An educator with a master's degree said he had learned to face his hallucinations and ask, "What's the evidence for that? Or is it just a perception problem?" Another participant said, "I hear derogatory voices all the time. . . . You just gotta blow them off. . . ."

Other techniques that our participants cited included controlling sensory inputs. For some, this meant keeping their living space simple (bare walls, no TV, only quiet music), while for others, it meant distracting music. "I'll listen to loud music if I don't want to hear things," said a participant who is a certified nurse's assistant. Still others mentioned exercise, a healthy diet, avoiding alcohol and getting enough sleep. . . .

One of the most frequently mentioned techniques that helped our research participants manage their symptoms was work. "Work has been an important part of who I am," said an educator in our group. "When you become useful to an organization and feel respected in that organization, there's a certain value in belonging there." This person works on the weekends too because of "the distraction factor." In other words, by engaging in work, the crazy stuff often recedes to the sidelines. . . .

That is why it is so distressing when doctors tell their patients not to expect or pursue fulfilling careers. Far too often, the conventional psychiatric approach to mental illness is to see clusters of symptoms that characterize people. Accordingly, many psychiatrists hold the view that treating symptoms with medication is treating mental illness. But this fails to take into account individuals' strengths and capabilities, leading mental health professionals to underestimate what their patients can hope to achieve in the world. . . . A recent *New York Times Magazine* article described a new company that hires high-functioning adults with autism, taking advantage of their unusual memory skills and attention to detail. . . .

An approach that looks for individual strengths, in addition to considering symptoms, could help dispel the pessimism surrounding mental illness. Finding "the wellness within the illness," as one person with schizophrenia said, should be a therapeutic goal. Doctors should urge their patients to develop relationships and engage in meaningful work. They should encourage patients to find their own repertory of techniques to manage their symptoms and aim for a quality of life as they define it. And they should provide patients with the resources — therapy, medication and support — to make these things happen.

Elyn Saks's story is amazing and inspiring. It is also quite unusual. How should we incorporate stories like hers and the people in the research study she described? Are these people outliers — simply a carefully selected collection of people who had unusually favourable outcomes? (Given that Los Angeles is such a large city, it is reasonable to think one could amass a small sample of such cases.) Or has Professor Saks touched on an important limitation to the way in which the field currently conceptualizes, classifies, and treats mental disorders? Do we focus too much on what is wrong and on how professionalized health care can treat the pathology and not enough on what inherent strengths people have that can help them overcome their challenges, function at a high level, and achieve a high quality of life? These are all questions that are testable with the methods of psychological science, and the answers may help to improve the lives of many people.

Elyn R. Saks is a law professor at the University of Southern California and the author of the memoir *The Center Cannot Hold: My Journey Through Madness.*

Elyn R. Saks, excerpt from "Successful and Schizophrenic," The New York Times, January 25, 2013. From The New York Times. ©2013 The New York Times Company. https://www.nytimes.com

Disorders of Childhood and Adolescence

Most of the disorders described thus far can have their onset during childhood, adolescence, or adulthood. In fact, half of all disorders begin by age 14 and three-quarters by age 24 (Kessler et al., 2005a). Several of the disorders you have learned about, such as bipolar disorder and schizophrenia, tend not to begin until early adulthood. However, other disorders *always,* by definition, begin in childhood or adolescence—and if they don't, they will never manifest. These include autism spectrum disorder, attention-deficit/hyperactivity disorder, conduct disorder, intellectual disability, learning disorders, communication disorders, and motor skill disorders, in addition to many others. The first three are among the most common and best known, so we will review them briefly here.

Autism Spectrum Disorder

Marco is a 4-year-old only child. His parents have become worried because, although his mother stays home with him all day and tries to talk with him and play with him, he still has not spoken a single word and he shows little interest in trying. He spends much of his time playing with his toy trains, which seem to be the thing he enjoys most in life. He often sits for hours staring at spinning train wheels or pushing a single train back and forth, seeming completely in his own world, uninterested in playing with anyone else. Marco's parents have become concerned about his apparent inability to speak, lack of interest in others, and development of some peculiar mannerisms, such as flapping his arms repeatedly for no apparent reason.

Autism spectrum disorder (ASD) is *a condition beginning in early childhood in which a person shows persistent communication deficits, as well as restricted and repetitive patterns of behaviours, interests, or activities.* In *DSM–5–TR,* ASD now subsumes multiple disorders that were considered separate in *DSM–IV:* autistic disorder, Asperger's disorder, childhood disintegrative disorder, and pervasive developmental disorder not otherwise specified (i.e., these disorders are no longer recognized in the *DSM*).

The true rate of ASD is difficult to pinpoint, especially given the recent change in diagnostic definition. Estimates from the 1960s indicated that autism was a rare diagnosis, occurring in 4 per 10,000 children. Estimates have been increasing over time and now stand at approximately 230 per 10,000 (1 in 44) children if one considers the full range of disorders that now fall under the ASD umbrella in the *DSM–5–TR* (Maenner et al., 2021). It is unclear whether this increased rate is due to increased awareness and recognition of ASD, better screening and diagnostic tools, or to some other factor. Boys have higher rates of ASD than girls by a ratio of about 4:1.

Early theories of autism described it as "childhood schizophrenia," but it is now understood to be separate from schizophrenia, which is rarely diagnosed in children (emerging mainly in adolescence or young adulthood) (Kessler & Wang, 2008). ASD is currently viewed as a heterogeneous set of traits that cluster together in some families (heritability estimates for ASD are as high as 90%), leaving some children with just a few mild ASD traits and others with a more severe form of the disorder (Geschwind, 2009). Although the causes of ASD are not yet fully understood, one thing that is now clear is that despite a great deal of research examining the question, there is no evidence that ASD is caused by vaccinations (Mandy & Lai, 2016).

One current model suggested that ASD can be understood as an impaired capacity for *empathizing,* or knowing the mental states of others, combined with a superior ability for *systematizing,* or understanding the rules that organize the structure and function of objects (Baron-Cohen & Belmonte, 2005). Consistent with this model,

Learning Outcomes

WHAT YOU NEED TO KNOW

- Describe the characteristic indications of autism.
- Define the difference between normal problems with inattention and ADHD.
- Explain why it is difficult to pin down the causes of conduct disorder.

autism spectrum disorder (ASD) A condition beginning in early childhood in which a person shows persistent communication deficits as well as restricted and repetitive patterns of behaviours, interests, or activities.

Temple Grandin, a professor of animal sciences at Colorado State University, is living proof that people with autism spectrum disorder can have very successful professional careers.

brain-imaging studies show that people with autism have comparatively decreased activity in regions associated with understanding the minds of others and greater activation in regions related to basic object perception (Sigman et al., 2006).

Although many people with ASD experience impairments throughout their lives that prevent them from having relationships and holding down a job, many go on to very successful careers. This is often due to the unique strengths that some people with ASD have, such as the abilities to perceive or remember details or to master symbol systems such as mathematics or music (Happé & Vital, 2009). The renowned behavioural scientist and author Temple Grandin has written of her personal experience with autism. She was diagnosed with autism at age 3, started learning to talk late, and then suffered teasing for odd habits and "nerdy" behaviour. Fortunately, she developed ways to cope and found a niche through her special talent—the ability to understand animal behaviour (Sacks, 1996).

She is now a Professor of Animal Sciences at Colorado State University; celebrated author of books such as *Animals in Translation;* designer of animal handling systems used widely in ranching, farming, and zoos; and the central character in an HBO movie starring Claire Danes based on her life. Temple Grandin's story lets us know that there are happy endings. Overall, those diagnosed with ASD as children have highly variable trajectories, with some achieving normal or better-than-normal functioning and others struggling with profound disorder. Autism is a childhood disorder that in adulthood can have many outcomes (see Hot Science: Optimal Outcome in Autism Spectrum Disorder).

Attention-Deficit/Hyperactivity Disorder

Chances are you have had the experience of being distracted during a lecture or while reading one of your *other* textbooks. We all have trouble focusing from time to time. Far beyond normal distraction, however, **attention-deficit/hyperactivity disorder (ADHD)** is *a persistent pattern of severe problems with inattention and/or hyperactivity or impulsiveness that cause significant impairments in functioning.* This is quite different from occasional mind-wandering or bursts of activity. Meeting the criteria for ADHD requires having multiple symptoms of inattention (e.g., persistent problems with sustained attention, organization, memory, following instructions), hyperactivity–impulsiveness (e.g., persistent difficulties with remaining still, waiting for a turn, interrupting others), or both. Most children experience some of these behaviours at some point, but to meet the criteria for ADHD, a child has to have many of these behaviours for at least 6 months in at least two settings (e.g., home and school)—to the point where they impair the child's ability to perform at school or get along at home. Note that a person can meet *DSM–5–TR* criteria for a diagnosis of ADHD three different ways: predominantly inattentive symptoms, predominantly hyperactive/impulsive symptoms, or with a combined presentation.

Approximately 1 in 10 boys and 1 in 23 girls meet criteria for ADHD (Polanczyk et al., 2007). The *DSM–5–TR* requires that symptoms of ADHD be present before the age of 12 to meet the criteria for this disorder. As you can imagine, children and adolescents with ADHD often struggle in the classroom. One recent study of 500 people with ADHD found that about half had a C average or lower, and about one-third were in special classes (Biederman et al., 2006). For a long time, ADHD was thought of as a disorder that affects only children and adolescents and that people "age out" of it. However, we now know that in many instances, this disorder persists into adulthood. The same symptoms are used to diagnose both children and adults. (e.g., children with ADHD may struggle with attention and concentration in the classroom, whereas adults may experience the same problems in meetings.)

Approximately 1 in 23 adults meets the criteria for ADHD; they are more likely to be male, divorced, and unemployed—and most did not receive any treatment for their ADHD (Kessler et al., 2006). Unfortunately, most people still think of ADHD as a disorder of childhood and don't realize that adults can suffer from it as well.

attention deficit/hyperactivity disorder (ADHD) A persistent pattern of severe problems with inattention and/or hyperactivity or impulsiveness that cause significant impairments in functioning.

This could be why so few adults with ADHD receive treatment and why the disorder often wreaks havoc on job performance and relationships.

Because ADHD, like most disorders, is defined by the presence of a wide range of symptoms, it is unlikely that it emerges from one single cause or dysfunction. The exact cause of ADHD is not known, but there are some promising leads. Genetic studies suggest that there is a strong biological influence and they estimate that the heritability of ADHD is 76% (Faraone et al., 2005). Brain-imaging studies suggest that those with ADHD have smaller brain volumes (Castellanos et al., 2002) as well as structural and functional abnormalities in frontosubcortical networks associated with attention and behavioural inhibition (Makris et al., 2009). The good news is that drug treatments for ADHD are effective and appear to decrease the risk of later psychological and academic problems (Biederman et al., 2009).

Conduct Disorder

Michael is an 8-year-old boy whose mother brought him into a local clinic because his behaviour had been getting progressively out of control, and his parents and teachers could no longer handle him. Although Michael's two older brothers and little sisters got along perfectly fine at home and at school, Michael had always gotten into trouble. At home, he routinely bullied his siblings, threw glasses and dishes at family members, and on numerous occasions punched and kicked his parents. Outside of the house, Michael had been getting into trouble for stealing from the local store, yelling at his teacher, and spitting at the principal of his school. The last straw came when Michael's parents found him trying to set fire to his bedspread one night. They tried punishing him by taking away his toys, restricting his privileges, and trying to encourage him with a sticker chart, but nothing seemed to change his behaviour.

Conduct disorder is a condition in which a child or adolescent engages in a *persistent pattern of deviant behaviour involving aggression to people or animals, destruction of property, deceitfulness or theft, or serious rule violations.* In Canada, a large study of 12- to 13-year-olds in the late 1990s indicated that about 7 out of every 40 children exhibited symptoms of conduct disorder (Lacourse et al., 2010). About 4 in 10 people with conduct disorder have, on average, only three symptoms that cluster into one of three areas: rule breaking, theft/deceit, or aggression towards others. The other 60% have more symptoms, on average 6 to 8 of the 15 defined symptoms, with problems in many more areas and a much higher risk of having other mental disorders later in life (Nock et al., 2006).

Meeting the criteria for conduct disorder requires having any 3 of the 15 symptoms of conduct disorder. This means that approximately 32,000 different combinations of symptoms could lead to a diagnosis, which makes those with conduct disorder a pretty diverse group. This diversity makes it difficult to pin down the causes of conduct disorder. One thing that seems clear is that a wide range of genetic, biological, and environmental factors interact to produce this disorder. Indeed, risk factors for conduct disorder include maternal smoking during pregnancy, exposure to abuse and family violence during childhood, affiliation with deviant peer groups, and the presence of deficits in executive functioning (e.g., decision making, impulsiveness) (Boden et al., 2010).

Researchers are currently attempting to better understand the pathways through which inherited genetic factors interact with environmental stressors (e.g., childhood adversities) to create characteristics in brain structure and function (e.g., reduced activity in brain regions associated with planning and decision making) that interact with environmental factors (e.g., affiliation with deviant peers) to lead to the behaviours that are characteristic of conduct disorder. Not surprisingly, conduct disorder tends to co-occur with other disorders characterized by problems with decision making and impulsiveness, such as ADHD, substance use disorders, and antisocial personality disorder, which is described in more detail in the next section.

RAWPIXEL LTD/ALAMY STOCK PHOTO

Psychologists are attempting to identify the causes of conduct disorder in the hope of being able to decrease the harmful behaviours, such as bullying, that often accompany it.

conduct disorder A persistent pattern of deviant behaviour involving aggression towards people or animals, destruction of property, deceitfulness or theft, or serious rule violations.

Hot Science : Optimal Outcome in Autism Spectrum Disorder

What comes to mind when you think of the word *autism*? What kind of person do you imagine? If that person is an adult, what do you imagine that they do for a living? Can they hold a job? Can they care for themselves? Many people consider autism spectrum disorder (ASD) a lifelong condition and believe that those affected will forever experience significant difficulties and disabilities in their interpersonal, educational, and occupational functioning. However, recent studies are helping to change this outlook.

For decades, autism was considered a disorder that begins in early childhood and persists throughout a person's life. However, more recent research has revealed that many people diagnosed with autism as children no longer meet the criteria for ASD (Howlin, 2021). How could this be? Researchers have begun to document many instances in which some portion of children diagnosed with autism who are followed over time later fail to meet diagnostic criteria. For instance, in one study of children diagnosed with ASD followed over time starting at age 6, 2 in 7 no longer met diagnostic criteria by age 12 and more than 1 in 4 no longer met criteria by age 16 (May et al., 2021). There are several potential explanations for this change. The most obvious is that some portion of children diagnosed with ASD are misdiagnosed and don't really have this disorder. Perhaps they are overly shy or quiet, or develop speech later than other children, which in turn is misinterpreted as ASD. Another possibility is that children who lose their ASD diagnosis had a milder form of the disorder and/or were identified and treated earlier. There is some support for this idea, as one study found that 7 in every 40 children diagnosed with ASD at age 2 no longer met the criteria for this disorder at age 4. The strongest predictors of this optimal outcome were less severe symptoms, fewer repetitive behaviours,

and stronger adaptive skills (Moulton et al., 2016).

The possibility of effectively treating ASD was first raised in a landmark study by Ivar Lovaas back in 1987. Lovaas assigned 19 children with autism to an intensive behavioural intervention, in which they received over 40 hours per week of one-on-one behaviour therapy for 2 years; another 40 children were assigned to control conditions, in which they received fewer than 10 hours per week of treatment. Amazingly, the follow-up of the treated children revealed that nearly half (47%) of those in the intensive behaviour therapy condition obtained a normal level of intellectual and educational functioning — passing through a normal first-grade class — compared with only 2% of those in the control conditions.

Extending this earlier work, Geraldine Dawson and colleagues tested a program called the Early Start Denver Model (ESDM), an intensive behavioural intervention (20 hours per week for 2 years) similarly designed to improve outcomes among those with ASD. Using randomized, controlled trials, Dawson and her colleagues found that, compared with those receiving standard community treatment, toddlers with ASD who received ESDM showed significant improvements in IQ (a 17-point rise!), language, adaptive and social functioning, and ASD diagnosis (Dawson et al., 2010). Many of these gains persisted when the children were 6 years old, two years after the treatment ended (Estes et al., 2015). Interestingly, children in the ESDM showed normalized brain activity after treatment (i.e., greater brain activation when viewing faces), which was in turn associated with improved social behaviour; those in the control condition showed the opposite pattern (Dawson et al., 2012). A more recent multi-site randomized controlled trial of ESDM replicated some of the exciting

findings from the 2010 study, such as those showing significantly improved language ability among those receiving the ESDM intervention (Rogers et al., 2019)! These treatments historically have been delivered via intensive in-person sessions, which were largely disrupted during the COVID-19 pandemic. However, adapting to the times, autism researchers have shown that intensive interventions for children with ASD can be delivered virtually — a finding that may help increase the availability of these treatments in the future (White et al., 2021).

Given that early detection and treatment can lead to such positive outcomes for those with ASD, should we be screening all young children for ASD so we can catch it early and intervene? This is an area of intense debate. Dawson and others (e.g., Dawson & Sapiro, 2019) argue that because we have methods for accurately detecting and effectively treating ASD in young children, including new digital screening tools that can be widely and efficiently disseminated, we should screen all children for this disorder to maximize their chances of optimal outcomes. Researchers and policy makers will be working actively on this issue in the years ahead.

COURTESY UC DAVIS MIND INSTITUTE

Autism was once viewed as a condition with lifelong impairments. New research suggests that early intervention, such as the Early Start Denver Model, can help many of those in whom ASD is diagnosed to achieve normal levels of functioning.

Personality Disorders: Extreme Traits and Characteristics

As discussed in the chapter on Personalities, we all have one, and we all differ in the extent to which we have various ways of behaving, thinking, and feeling. Sometimes, personality traits can become so extreme that they can be considered mental disorders. **Personality disorders** are *enduring patterns of thinking, feeling, or relating to others or controlling impulses that deviate from cultural expectations and cause distress or impaired functioning.* Personality disorders begin in adolescence or early adulthood and are relatively stable over time. Let's look at the types of personality disorders and then more closely examine one that sometimes lands people in jail: antisocial personality disorder.

Types of Personality Disorders

The *DSM–5–TR* lists 10 specific personality disorders (see **TABLE 15.3**). They fall into three clusters: (1) *odd/eccentric,* (2) *dramatic/erratic,* and (3) *anxious/inhibited.* Personality disorders have been a bit controversial for several reasons. First, critics question whether having a problematic personality is really a disorder; perhaps it might be better just to admit that a lot of people can be difficult to interact with and leave it at that.

Learning Outcomes

WHAT YOU NEED TO KNOW

- Identify the three types of personality disorders.
- Explain the diagnostic signs of APD.

personality disorders Enduring patterns of thinking, feeling, or relating to others or controlling impulses that deviate from cultural expectations and cause distress or impaired functioning.

TABLE 15.3

CLUSTERS OF PERSONALITY DISORDERS

Cluster	Personality Disorder	Characteristics
A. Odd/Eccentric	Paranoid	Distrust in others, suspicion that people have sinister motives; apt to challenge the loyalties of friends and read hostile intentions into others' actions; prone to anger and aggressive outbursts but otherwise emotionally cold; often jealous, guarded, secretive, overly serious.
	Schizoid	Extreme introversion and withdrawal from relationships; prefers to be alone, little interest in others; humourless, distant, often absorbed with own thoughts and feelings, a daydreamer; fearful of closeness, with poor social skills, often seen as a "loner."
	Schizotypal	Peculiar or eccentric manners of speaking or dressing; strange beliefs; "magical thinking," such as belief in ESP or telepathy; difficulty forming relationships; may react oddly in conversation, not respond, or talk to self; speech elaborate or difficult to follow. (Possibly a mild form of schizophrenia.)
B. Dramatic/Erratic	Antisocial	Impoverished moral sense or "conscience"; history of deception, crime, legal problems, impulsive and aggressive or violent behaviour; little emotional empathy or remorse for hurting others; manipulative, careless, callous; at high risk for substance abuse and alcoholism.
	Borderline	Unstable moods and intense, stormy personal relationships; frequent mood changes and anger, unpredictable impulses; self-mutilation or suicidal threats or gestures to get attention or manipulate others; self-image fluctuation and a tendency to see others as "all good" or "all bad."
	Histrionic	Constant attention seeking; grandiose language, provocative dress, exaggerated illnesses, all to gain attention; believes that everyone loves them; emotional, lively, overly dramatic, enthusiastic, and excessively flirtatious; shallow and labile emotions; "onstage."
	Narcissistic	Inflated sense of self-importance, absorbed by fantasies of self and success; exaggerates own achievements, assumes others will recognize they are superior; good first impressions but poor longer-term relationships; exploitative of others.
C. Anxious/Inhibited	Avoidant	Socially anxious and uncomfortable unless they are confident of being liked; in contrast with schizoid person, yearns for social contact; fears criticism and worries about being embarrassed in front of others; avoids social situations due to fear of rejection.
	Dependent	Submissive, dependent, requiring excessive approval, reassurance, and advice; clings to people and fears losing them; lacking self-confidence; uncomfortable when alone; may be devastated by end of close relationship or suicidal if breakup is threatened.
	Obsessive-compulsive	Conscientious, orderly, perfectionist; excessive need to do everything "right"; inflexibly high standards and caution can interfere with their productivity; fear of errors can make them strict and controlling; poor expression of emotions. (Not the same as obsessive-compulsive disorder.)

Information from *DSM–5–TR* (American Psychiatric Association, 2022).

Henri Desiré Landru (1869–1922) was a serial killer who met widows through ads he placed in newspapers' lonely-hearts columns. After obtaining enough information to embezzle money from them, he murdered 10 women and the son of one of the women. He was executed for serial murder in 1922.

antisocial personality disorder (APD) A pervasive pattern of disregard for and violation of the rights of others that begins in childhood or early adolescence and continues into adulthood.

Another question is whether personality problems correspond to "disorders" in that there are distinct *types,* or whether such problems might be better understood as extreme values on trait *dimensions* such as the Big Five traits discussed in the Personality chapter (Trull & Durrett, 2005). In *DSM–IV,* personality disorders appeared as a separate type of disorder from all other disorders described earlier. (Specifically, mood, anxiety, psychotic, substance, and other "major" disorders were all in a category called *Axis I,* and personality disorders were in *Axis II.*) However, in *DSM–5–TR,* personality disorders earned equal footing as full-fledged disorders. One of the most thoroughly studied of all the personality disorders is antisocial personality disorder.

Antisocial Personality Disorder

Henri Desiré Landru began using personal ads to attract a woman "interested in matrimony" in Paris in 1914, and he succeeded in seducing 10 of them. He bilked them of their savings, poisoned them, and cremated them in his stove, also disposing of a boy and two dogs along the way. He recorded his murders in a notebook and maintained a marriage and a mistress all the while. The gruesome actions of serial killers such as Landru leave us frightened and wondering; however, bullies, compulsive liars, and even drivers who regularly speed through a school zone share the same shocking blindness to human pain. The *DSM–5–TR* includes the category of **antisocial personality disorder (APD)**, defining it as *a pervasive pattern of disregard for and violation of the rights of others that begins in childhood or early adolescence and continues into adulthood.*

Adults with an APD diagnosis typically have a history of *conduct disorder* before the age of 15. In adulthood, a diagnosis of APD is given to individuals who show three or more of a set of seven diagnostic signs: illegal behaviour, deception, impulsivity, physical aggression, recklessness, irresponsibility, and a lack of remorse for wrongdoing. About 3.6% of the general population has APD, and the rate of occurrence in men is three times the rate in women (Grant et al., 2004).

The terms *sociopath* and *psychopath* describe people with APD who are especially cold-hearted, manipulative, and ruthless—yet may appear friendly and charming (Cleckley, 1976; Hare, 1998). Many people with APD commit crimes, and many are caught because of the frequency and flagrancy of their infractions. Evidence of brain abnormalities in people with APD is also accumulating (Blair et al., 2005). One line of investigation has looked at sensitivity to fear in psychopaths and individuals who show no such psychopathology. For example, criminal psychopaths who are shown negative emotional words such as *hate* or *corpse* exhibit less activity in the amygdala and hippocampus (two areas involved in fear conditioning) than do noncriminals (Kiehl et al., 2001). Research like this has suggested that psychopaths experience fear but appear to have decreased abilities for detecting and responding to threats in their environment (Hoppenbrouwers et al., 2016).

Self-Harm Behaviours: Intentionally Injuring Oneself

Learning Outcomes

WHAT YOU NEED TO KNOW

- Explain the factors that increase the risk of suicide.

- Explain what is currently known to be the motivation behind nonsuicidal self-injury.

We all have an innate drive to keep ourselves alive. We eat when we are hungry, get out of the way of fast-moving vehicles, and go to school so we can earn a living to keep ourselves, and our families, alive (see the discussion of evolutionary psychology in The Evolution of Psychological Science chapter). One of the most extreme manifestations of human behaviour is revealed when a person acts in direct opposition to this drive for self-preservation and engages in intentionally self-destructive behaviour. Accounts of people intentionally harming themselves date back to the beginning of recorded history. However, it is only over the past several decades that we have begun to gain an understanding of why people purposely do things to hurt themselves. *DSM–5–TR* includes two self-destructive behaviours in its Section III (disorders in need of further study): suicidal behaviour disorder and nonsuicidal self-injury disorder.

Suicidal Behaviour

Kareem, a 35-year-old accountant, had by all appearances been living a pretty happy, successful life. He was married to his high school sweetheart and had two young children. Over the past several years, though, his workload had increased, and he started to experience severe job-related stress. At around the same time, he and his wife began to experience some financial problems, and his alcohol consumption increased, all of which put significant strain on the family and began to affect his work. Kareem's coworkers noted that he had become pretty angry and agitated lately—even yelling at coworkers on a few occasions. One evening Kareem and his wife got into a heated argument about the family's finances and Kareem's excessive alcohol use; Kareem went into the bathroom and swallowed a bottle full of prescription medicine in an effort to end his life. He was taken to the hospital and kept there to be treated for suicidal behaviour.

Suicide, *intentional self-inflicted death,* is the second most common cause of death for people aged 15 to 34 in Canada, claiming 18 out of every 100,000 males and 5 out of every 100,000 females aged 10 and older (Statistics Canada, 2022). There are large demographic differences in the suicide rate. For instance, in Canada, 3 of every 4 suicides occur among men, and immigrants are only about half as likely as those born in Canada to commit suicide (Statistics Canada, 2022).

Rates of suicide in equity-deserving populations are much higher. Between 2011 and 2016, the suicide rate amongst First Nations people was 3 times higher than in people not in equity-deserving groups. Among Métis, it was twice as high, and among Inuit, a staggering 9 times higher. Suicide rates were particularly high amongst Inuit adolescents and young adults aged 15–24. In this group, suicide rates are more than 30 times higher than for their peers who are not in equity-deserving groups (Kumar & Tjepkema, 2019). The reasons for higher rates of suicide in equity-deserving groups are not fully understood, but probably include chronic and constant life stress such as poverty and unemployment, the effects of intergenerational trauma from forced resettlement and residential school attendance, the effects of historical and ongoing social inequities, and lack of access to health care (Kumar & Tjepkema, 2019).

Nonfatal **suicide attempts**, in which people engage in *potentially harmful behaviour with some intention of dying,* occur much more frequently than suicide deaths. Across a range of countries, approximately 9 of every 100 adults report that they have seriously considered suicide at some point in their lives, 3 in 100 have made a plan to kill themselves, and 3 in 100 have actually made a suicide attempt. As these numbers suggest, only one-third of those who think about suicide go on to make a suicide attempt.

Although many more men than women die by suicide, women experience suicidal thoughts and (nonfatal) suicide attempts at significantly higher rates than do men (Nock et al., 2008). Moreover, the rates of suicidal thoughts and attempts increase dramatically during adolescence and young adulthood. A study of a representative sample of approximately 10,000 American adolescents revealed that suicidal thoughts and behaviours are virtually nonexistent before age 10 but increase dramatically from ages 12 to 18 (see **FIGURE 15.8**) before leveling off during early adulthood (Nock et al., 2013).

Why do people try to kill themselves? The short answer is: We do not yet know, and it's complicated. When interviewed in the hospital following their suicide

We all have an innate desire to keep ourselves alive. So why do some people purposely do things to harm themselves?

suicide Intentional self-inflicted death.

suicide attempt Engagement in potentially harmful behaviour with some intention of dying.

Figure 15.8

Age of Onset of Suicidal Behaviour During Adolescence A survey of American adolescents shows that although suicidal thoughts and behaviours are quite rare among children (the rate was 0.0 for ages 1–4), they increase dramatically starting at age 12 and continue to climb throughout adolescence (data from Nock et al., 2013).

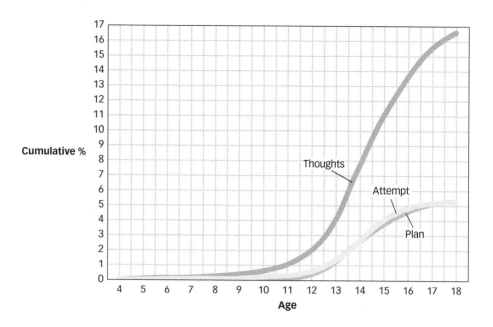

attempt, most people who have tried to kill themselves report that they did so to escape from an intolerable state of mind or impossible situation (Boergers et al., 1998). Consistent with this explanation, research has documented that the risk of suicidal behaviour is significantly increased if a person experiences factors that can create severely distressing states, such as the presence of multiple mental disorders (more than 90% of people who die by suicide have at least one mental disorder); the experience of significant negative life events during childhood and adulthood (e.g., physical or sexual assault); and the presence of severe medical problems (Nock et al., 2012). In addition, people experiencing suicidal thoughts show a greater tendency to try to escape from aversive situations in lab-based behavioural studies than to those without such thoughts (Millner et al., 2019). The search is ongoing for a more comprehensive understanding of how and why some people respond to negative life events with suicidal thoughts and behaviour, as well as for methods of how to better predict and prevent these devastating outcomes.

Nonsuicidal Self-Injury

Louisa, an 18-year-old undergraduate student, secretly cuts her lower abdomen and upper thighs about once per week, typically when she is feeling intense anger and hatred, either towards herself or someone else. She has always had a bit of a "hot streak," as she calls it, but it wasn't until she turned 14 that she started to use self-injury as a way to calm herself down. Louisa says that she feels a little ashamed after each episode of cutting, but she doesn't know how else to calm down when she gets really upset, so she has no plans to stop this behaviour.

Louisa is engaging in a behaviour called **nonsuicidal self-injury (NSSI)**, the *direct, deliberate destruction of body tissue in the absence of any intent to die*. NSSI has been reported since the beginning of recorded history; however, it is a behaviour that appears to be on the rise over the past few decades. Approximately 15 to 20% of adolescents and 3 to 6% of adults report engaging in NSSI at some point in their lifetime (Muehlenkamp et al., 2012). The rates appear to be even between males and females, and for people of different races and ethnicities. Though rates of NSSI

Although in Western cultures self-injury is considered pathological, in some parts of the world scarification of the skin is viewed as a rite of passage into adulthood and a symbol of one's tribe, as in the case of this young man from the Republic of Benin in West Africa.

nonsuicidal self-injury (NSSI) Direct, deliberate destruction of body tissue in the absence of any intent to die.

are much higher in those identifying as sexual (30%) and gender (47%) minorities (Liu et al., 2019). Like suicidal behaviour, NSSI is virtually absent during childhood, increases dramatically during adolescence, and then appears to decrease across adulthood.

In some parts of the world, cutting or scarification of the skin is socially accepted, and in some cases encouraged as a rite of passage (Favazza, 2011). In parts of the world where self-cutting is not socially encouraged, why would a person purposely hurt themselves if not to die? Recent studies suggest that people who engage in self-injury have very strong emotional and physiological responses to negative events, that they perceive this response as intolerable, and that NSSI serves to diminish the intensity of this response (Nock, 2009). There also is some evidence that in many instances, people engage in self-injury as a means to communicate distress or elicit help from others (Nock, 2010). Although we are beginning to get an understanding of why some people engage in NSSI, there are many aspects of this behaviour that we do not yet understand, and the study of NSSI is an increasingly active area of research.

Unfortunately, like suicidal behaviour, our understanding of the genetic and neurobiological influences on NSSI is limited, and there currently are no effective medications for these problems. There also is limited evidence for behavioural interventions or prevention programs (Mann et al., 2005; Zalsman et al., 2016). So, whereas suicidal behaviour and NSSI are some of the most disturbing and dangerous mental disorders, they also, unfortunately, are among the most perplexing. The field has made significant strides in our understanding of these behaviour problems in recent years, but there is a long way to go before we are able to predict and prevent them accurately and effectively.

Chapter Review

Defining Mental Disorders: What Is Psychopathology?

- The *DSM–5–TR* is a classification system that defines a mental disorder as occurring when a person experiences disturbances of thought, emotion, or behaviour that produce distress or impairment. The original volume provided a common language for talking about disorders, but diagnostic criteria were vague. The *DSM–5–TR* includes detailed lists of criteria, including cultural considerations, designed to increase the validity of the process.

- The medical model conceptualizes abnormal thought and behaviours as illnesses with defined symptoms and possible cures.

- According to the biopsychosocial model, mental disorders arise from an interaction of biological, psychological, and social factors, often thought of as a combination of a diathesis (internal predisposition) and a stressor (environmental life event). The diathesis–stress model suggests that a person

may be predisposed for a disorder that may or may not manifest, depending on whether it is triggered by stress.

- The RDoC is a new classification system that focuses on biological, cognitive, and behavioural aspects of mental disorders.

- Psychiatric labels may create negative stereotypes and may be one reason that many people do not seek help.

Anxiety Disorders: Excessive Fear, Anxiety, and Avoidance

- People with anxiety disorders have irrational worries and fears that undermine their ability to function.

- Phobic disorders are characterized by excessive fear and avoidance of specific objects, activities, or situations. The preparedness theory posits that people are instinctively predisposed towards certain fears, and heritability studies support this idea. Temperament and the influence of environment are additional factors.

- People who suffer from panic disorder experience a sudden, terrifying attack of intense anxiety. Agoraphobia can lead people to be housebound for fear of public humiliation. Panic disorder has a hereditary component, and people who experience panic attacks may be hypersensitive to physiological signs of anxiety.

- Generalized anxiety disorder (GAD) involves a chronic state of anxiety, whereas phobic disorders involve anxiety tied to a specific object or situation. Biological explanations of GAD suggest a role for neurotransmitters, but the evidence is unclear. Life situation and experience play a role as well, supporting the diathesis–stress model.

Obsessive-Compulsive Disorder: Persistent Thoughts and Repetitive Behaviours

- People with obsessive-compulsive disorder experience recurring, anxiety-provoking thoughts that compel them to engage in ritualistic, irrational behaviour. Attempts to suppress this behaviour have little or no benefit.

- OCD derives from concerns that could be real, supporting the preparedness theory. Studies indicate a moderate genetic link; one hypothesis implicates heightened neural activity in a portion of the basal ganglia.

Posttraumatic Stress Disorder: Distress and Avoidance After a Trauma

- Terrifying, life-threatening events, such as combat experience or rape, can lead to the development of posttraumatic stress disorder (PTSD), in which a person experiences chronic physiological arousal, unwanted thoughts or images of the event, and avoidance of things or situations that remind the person of the event.

- Research has identified neural correlates of PTSD.

Depressive and Bipolar Disorders: Extreme Highs and Lows

- Mood disorders are mental disorders in which a disturbance in mood is the predominant feature.

- Major depression (or unipolar depression) is characterized by a severely depressed mood and/or inability to experience pleasure lasting at least 2 weeks; symptoms include excessive self-criticism, guilt, difficulty concentrating, suicidal thoughts, sleep and appetite disturbances, and lethargy. Persistent depressive disorder, a related disorder, involves less severe symptoms that persist for at least 2 years. Some people experience depression in a seasonal pattern.

- Bipolar disorder is an unstable emotional condition involving extreme mood swings of depression and mania. The manic phase is characterized by periods of abnormally and persistently elevated, expansive, or irritable mood, lasting at least 1 week.

- Depression has at its roots socioecomonic, hormonal, genetic, and neural factors. Helplessness theory indicates that biases in how information is processed can lead to depression.

- Bipolar disorder has one of the highest rates of heritability. Epigenetics helps explain some of the genetic risk factors, a link to the influence of environment.

Schizophrenia and Other Psychotic Disorders: Losing the Grasp on Reality

- Schizophrenia is a severe psychological disorder involving hallucinations, disorganized thoughts and behaviour, and emotional and social withdrawal.

- Positive symptoms are thoughts and behaviours *not* seen in those without the disorder; negative symptoms indicate an absence of normal behaviour; cognitive symptoms are impairments in executive functioning, attention, and working memory.

- Schizophrenia affects only 1% of the population, but it accounts for a disproportionate share of psychiatric hospitalizations. The likelihood of getting the disorder increases with biological relatedness.

- The first drugs that reduced the availability of dopamine sometimes reduced the symptoms of schizophrenia, suggesting that the disorder involved an excess of dopamine activity; but recent research suggests that schizophrenia may involve a complex interaction among a variety of neurotransmitters.

- Brain changes are evident in people with schizophrenia, but evidence shows children whose biological mothers had schizophrenia are more likely to develop it if they are raised in an affected family.

Disorders of Childhood and Adolescence

- Some mental disorders always begin during childhood or adolescence, and in some cases (ASD, ADHD) persist into adulthood.

- Autism spectrum disorder (ASD) emerges in early childhood and is a condition in which a person has persistent communication deficits, including difficulty empathizing with others, as well as restricted and repetitive patterns of behaviour, interests, or activities.

- Attention-deficit/hyperactivity disorder (ADHD) begins by age 12 and involves a persistent pattern of severe problems with inattention and/or hyperactivity or impulsiveness that cause significant impairments in functioning.

- Conduct disorder begins in childhood or adolescence and involves a persistent pattern of deviant behaviour involving aggression towards people or animals, destruction of property, deceitfulness or theft, or serious rule violations. Because the diagnosis requires having any 3 of 15 symptoms, there are 32,000 different combinations. This suggests a wide diversity within the group of people who share this diagnosis.

Personality Disorders: Extreme Traits and Characteristics

- Personality disorders are enduring patterns of thinking, feeling, relating to others, or controlling impulses that cause distress or impaired functioning.
- They include three clusters: odd/eccentric, dramatic/erratic, and anxious/inhibited.
- Antisocial personality disorder (APD) is associated with a lack of moral emotions and behaviour. People with antisocial personality disorder can be manipulative, dangerous, and reckless, often hurting others and sometimes hurting themselves.

Self-Harm Behaviours: Intentionally Injuring Oneself

- Most people who die by suicide have a mental disorder. Suicide attempts most often are motivated by an attempt to escape intolerable mental states or situations.
- People in equity-deserving groups in Canada die from suicide at a rate that is 3 times higher than for people who are not in equity-deserving groups.
- Nonsuicidal self-injury (NSSI), like suicidal behaviour, increases dramatically during adolescence, but for many it is a persistent problem throughout adulthood. Although NSSI is performed without suicidal intent, like suicidal behaviour, it is most often motivated by an attempt to escape from painful mental states.

Changing Minds

1. You catch a TV interview with a celebrity who describes his difficult childhood, living with a mother who suffered from major depression. "Sometimes my mother stayed in her bed for days, not even getting up to eat," he says. "At the time, the family hushed it up. My parents were immigrants, and they came from a culture where it was considered shameful to have mental problems. You are supposed to have enough strength of will to overcome your problems, without help from anyone else. So my mother never got treatment." How might the idea of a medical model of psychiatric disorders have helped this woman and her family in the decision whether to seek treatment?

2. You're studying for your upcoming psychology exam when your roommate breezes in, saying: "I was just at the gym and I ran into Sue. She's totally schizophrenic: nice one minute, mean the next." You can't resist the opportunity to set the record straight. What psychiatric disorder is your roommate (incorrectly) attributing to Sue? How is the behaviour your roommate is describing different from schizophrenia?

3. A friend of yours has a family member who is experiencing severe mental problems, including delusions and loss of

motivation. "We went to one psychiatrist," your friend says, "and got a diagnosis of schizophrenia. We went for a second opinion, and the other doctor said it was probably bipolar disorder. They're both good doctors, and they're both using the same *DSM*—how can they come up with different diagnoses?"

4. After reading the chapter, one of your classmates turns to you with a sigh of relief. "I finally figured it out. I have a deadbeat brother who always gets himself into trouble and then blames other people for his problems. Even when he gets a ticket for speeding, he never thinks it's his fault—the police were picking on him, or his passengers were urging him to go too fast. I always thought he was just a loser, but now I realize he has a personality disorder!" Do you agree with your classmate's diagnosis of his brother? How would you caution your classmate about the dangers of self-diagnosis, or a diagnosis of friends and family?

5. **Visualizing Data** A friend is worried a diagnosis of PTSD means they'll be prone to abusing alcohol for their entire life. Review the DATA and give support to your friend.

Key Terms

mental disorder (p. 548)

medical model (p. 549)

Diagnostic and Statistical Manual of Mental Disorders (DSM) (p. 550)

comorbidity (p. 552)

biopsychosocial perspective (p. 553)

diathesis–stress model (p. 554)

Research Domain Criteria Project (RDoC) (p. 555)

anxiety disorder (p. 558)

phobic disorders (p. 559)

specific phobia (p. 559)

social phobia (p. 559)

preparedness theory (p. 559)

panic disorder (p. 560)

agoraphobia (p. 561)

generalized anxiety disorder (GAD) (p. 562)

obsessive-compulsive disorder (OCD) (p. 563)

posttraumatic stress disorder (PTSD) (p. 564)

mood disorders (p. 566)

major depressive disorder
    (or unipolar depression)
    (p. 567)

persistent depressive
    disorder (p. 567)

double depression (p. 567)

seasonal affective disorder
    (SAD) (p. 567)

helplessness theory (p. 569)

bipolar disorder (p. 570)

expressed emotion (p. 572)

schizophrenia (p. 573)

positive symptoms (p. 573)

hallucination (p. 573)

delusion (p. 573)

negative symptoms (p. 574)

disorganized symptoms
    (p. 574)

disorganized speech
    (p. 574)

grossly disorganized
    behaviour (p. 574)

catatonic behaviour (p. 574)

cognitive symptoms (p. 574)

dopamine hypothesis (p. 576)

autism spectrum disorder
    (ASD) (p. 579)

attention-deficit/
    hyperactivity disorder
    (ADHD) (p. 580)

conduct disorder (p. 581)

personality disorders (p. 583)

antisocial personality
    disorder (APD) (p. 584)

suicide (p. 585)

suicide attempt (p. 585)

nonsuicidal self-injury (NSSI)
    (p. 586)

Treatment of Psychological Disorders

"**TODAY WE'RE GOING TO BE TOUCHING A DEAD MOUSE** I found in the parking lot outside my office building this morning," Dr. Jenkins said. "Okay, let's do it, I'm ready," Christine responded. The pair walked down to the parking lot and spent the next 50 minutes touching, then stroking, the dead mouse. They then went back upstairs to plan out what other disgusting things Christine was going to touch over the next 7 days before coming back for her next therapy session. This is all part of the psychological treatment of Christine's obsessive-compulsive disorder (OCD). It is an approach called *exposure and response prevention* (ERP) in which people are gradually exposed to the content of their obsessions and prevented from engaging in their compulsions. Christine's obsessions include the fear that she is going to be contaminated by germs and die of cancer; her compulsive behaviour involves several hours per day of washing her body and scrubbing everything around her with alcohol wipes in order to decrease the possibility of her developing cancer. After dozens and dozens of exposures to the focus of their obsessions, without performing the compulsive behaviours that they believe have been keeping them safe, people undergoing ERP eventually learn that their obsessive thoughts are not accurate and that they don't have to act out their compulsions. ERP can be scary, but it has proven amazingly effective at decreasing obsessions and compulsions and helping people with OCD return to a high level of daily functioning. The condition was widely considered untreatable until the development of ERP, which is now considered to be the most effective way to treat it (Foa & McLean, 2016). Exposure and response prevention is just one of many approaches currently being used to help people overcome the mental disorders you learned about in the last chapter.

- **Treatment: Getting Help to Those Who Need It**
- **Psychological Treatments: Healing Through Human Interaction**
- **Biological Treatments: Healing Through Physical Alteration of the Brain**
- **Treatment Effectiveness: For Better or For Worse**

THERE ARE MANY DIFFERENT WAYS TO TREAT PSYCHOLOGICAL DISORDERS and to change the thoughts, behaviours, and emotions associated with them. In this chapter, we will explore the most common, and most effective, approaches to psychological treatment. We will examine why people seek psychological help in the first place, and then explore how psychological treatments are built on the major theories of the causes and cures of disorders, including psychoanalytic, humanistic, existential, behavioural, and cognitive theories. We will also consider biological treatment approaches that focus on directly modifying brain structure and function. We'll discuss which treatments are most effective and how we come to that conclusion. We'll also look to the future by exploring some exciting new directions in the assessment and treatment of disorders using innovative technologies.

Exposure-based treatments, in which a person learns to face the source of their fear and anxiety, have proven to be an effective way to treat anxiety disorders.

KEITH BINNS/GETTY IMAGES

Treatment: Getting Help to Those Who Need It

Learning Outcomes

WHAT YOU NEED TO KNOW

- Describe reasons people with mental disorders may fail to get treatment.
- Outline different approaches to treatment.

Many people avoid seeking psychological treatment because they don't know how or because of the stigma associated with help-seeking. Efforts to destigmatize help-seeking may change that. After the hip-hop artist Logic performed his song "1-800-273-8255," the number of the National Suicide Prevention Line, on the 2017 MTV Video Music Awards, the number of calls to that line increased by 50% and the number of suicides among adolescents in the United States decreased by 6% over the next month (Niederkrotenthaler et al., 2021).

In any given year, 1 in 5 Canadians suffers from a mental disorder (including addiction problems) (Smetanin et al., 2011). The personal costs of these disorders include the anguish of the sufferers as well as interference in their ability to carry on the activities of daily life. Think about Christine from the opening example. If she did not (or could not) seek treatment, she would continue to be crippled by her OCD, which was causing major problems in her life. She had to quit her job at the local coffee shop because she was no longer able to touch money or anything else that had been touched by other people without washing her hands immediately afterward. Her relationship with her boyfriend was in trouble because he was growing tired of her constantly seeking reassurance regarding cleanliness (hers and his). All of these problems in turn increased her anxiety and depression, making her obsessions even stronger. She desperately wanted and needed some way to break out of this vicious cycle. She needed an effective treatment.

The personal and social burdens of mental disorders are enormous. Such disorders typically have earlier ages of onset than physical disorders and are associated with significant impairments in the person's ability to carry out daily activities, such as causing days out of school or work or problems in family and personal relationships. Impairments associated with mental disorders are as severe, and in many cases more severe, than those associated with physical disorders such as cancer, chronic pain, and heart disease (Ormel et al., 2008). For instance, a person with severe depression may be unable to hold down a job or even get organized enough to collect a disability check; many disorders cause people to stop getting along with family, caring for their children, or trying to help others.

There are financial costs too. In any given week, at least half a million employed people in Canada are unable to work due to mental health problems, and the economic burden for all mental illness is estimated to be $51 billion per year (Dewa et al., 2010; Lim et al., 2008; Smetanin et al., 2011). Mental disorders are among the greatest contributors to the global disease burden, and depression is the mental disorder that contributes most to such a burden (Ferrari et al., 2022). People with severe depression often are unable to make it in to work due to their disorder, and even when they do make it to work they often perform poorly. In addition to the personal benefits of treatment, then, society also stands to benefit from the effective treatment of psychological disorders.

Do all people with a mental disorder receive treatment? Not by a long shot. Surveys of mental health provision in the year before the survey reveal that only about half of those requiring treatment for major depression received potentially adequate care, and mental health needs were not fully met for 1 in 3 who received treatment (Patten et al., 2016; Sunderland & Findlay, 2013). Three-quarters of children in Canada with mental disorders do not access specialized care (Waddell et al., 2005), and wait times for mental health services for children can be up to a year or more in some parts of the country (Children's Mental Health Ontario, 2016). Need has grown dramatically during the COVID-19 pandemic, but supports have not, thus exacerbating the problem.

Why Many People Fail to Seek Treatment

A physical symptom such as a toothache would send most people to the dentist—a trip that usually results in a successful treatment. The clear source of pain and the obvious solution make for a quick and effective response. In contrast, the path from a mental disorder to a successful treatment is often far less clear, and many people are less familiar with when they should seek treatment for a mental disorder or where they should go for it. Here are three of the most often reported reasons people fail to get treatment—which can affect everyone but may differ across cultures (see Other Voices: The Intergenerational Trauma of First Nations Still Runs Deep):

1. *People may not realize that they have a mental disorder that can be effectively treated.* Approximately 45% of those with a mental disorder who do not seek treatment report that they did not do so because they didn't think they

Other Voices | The Intergenerational Trauma of First Nations Still Runs Deep

For more than 100 years until the late 20th century, equity-deserving children were forcibly taken from their parents and communities and placed into government-funded, church-controlled, residential learning institutions among unfamiliar people, customs, and languages. Many children suffered horrific abuse and parents and communities were traumatized. After two to three generations of this, families were disconnected, parenting skills were lost, as was any sense of trust or feeling of belonging to family, community, and culture. Kevin Berube explains more.

Imagine a knock on your door. You open it and are met by strangers accompanied by a police officer. These people are speaking a different language so you don't understand what they're saying. Eventually, you come to the surreal realization that they've come for your children. There is some time given to pack clothes and say goodbye. Any resistance is met with the threat of arrest by the police. You're not sure where your children are going or if you will ever see them again. You're wondering what you did wrong. You have no idea what is happening as you helplessly watch this nightmare unfold before your eyes.

How does an event like this affect the child? The parents? The community?

This sounds like something that happened long ago, somewhere far away, but this was the reality only a half-century ago with the residential-school education project across Canada and the Sixties Scoop—the "scooping up" of First Nations children by the planeload for adoption, under the guise of protection, unbeknownst to their family and community across North America and Europe.

Can communities simply learn to move on, or will these two remarkable events in Canadian history reverberate through future generations—and for how long?

Many years after the last residential school closed its doors and most of the First Nations children taken from their homes through child welfare removal were returned, these events continue to have an impact on individuals, families and communities.

Intergenerational trauma, or transgenerational trauma, is what happens when untreated trauma-related stress experienced by survivors is passed on to second and subsequent generations. The trauma inflicted by residential schools and the Sixties Scoop was significant, and the scope of the damage these events wrought wouldn't be truly understood until years later.

Intergenerational trauma is usually seen within one family in which the parents or grandparents were traumatized, and each generation of that family continues to experience trauma in some form. In these cases, the source can usually be traced back to a devastating event, and the trauma is unique to that family.

What makes the intergenerational trauma in the case of First Nations people different is that it wasn't the result of a targeted event against an individual—it was a set of government policies that targeted and affected a whole generation. Children were traumatized when they were taken from their parents and placed into either government-funded, church-controlled, residential learning institutions or into foster homes. Many children suffered horrific abuse while in these homes and institutions. And parents and communities were traumatized when their children were taken away from them with little or no idea if or when they would return.

Direct survivors of these experiences often transmit the trauma they experienced to later generations when they don't recognize or have the opportunity to address their issues. Over time, these behaviours, often destructive, become normalized within the family and their community, leading to the next generation suffering the same problems.

Many self-destructive behaviours can result from unresolved trauma. Depression, anxiety, family violence, suicidal and homicidal thoughts, and addictions are some of the behaviours our mental health therapists see when working with clients who have experienced direct or intergenerational trauma. In most cases, the self-destructive behaviour exists because the client is having a difficult time dealing with the pain of remembering the past, or trying to survive an abusive situation now.

Talking with a mental-health therapist can help break the cycle of trauma. Family therapy may also be required to prevent behaviours continuing among the younger generation. The goals of the therapeutic relationship are to acknowledge the negative behaviour; help the individual and their family make the connection between the behaviour and the historical trauma; introduce healthy alternatives and coping mechanisms; and provide support and feedback to the individual and family as they carry on with their lives.

People reaching out for help may seek the support of traditional healers to assist them on their healing journey. Traditional healing, along with conventional therapeutic methods, have been effective tools in addressing intergenerational trauma. We must always be mindful to put the individual at the centre of the healing plan, critical not just in working with trauma survivors, but in the development of any patient plan that is going to yield the best outcomes. We need to recognize that patients know themselves better than anyone, and services should work together to consider their holistic needs.

Kevin Berube is a band member of Flying Post First Nation and has more than 20 years of experience in child welfare, mental health, and addictions working with equity-deserving groups.

From *The Globe and Mail*, February 16, 2015, www.theglobeandmail.com/life/health-and-fitness/health-advisor/the-intergenerational-trauma-of-first-nations-still-runs-deep/article23013789/. Reproduced with the permission of Kevin Berube.

The Real World | Types of Psychotherapists

What should you do if you're ready to seek the help of a mental health professional? To whom do you turn? Therapists have widely varying backgrounds and training, which affects the kinds of services they offer. Before you choose a therapist, it is useful to have a general understanding of a therapist's background, training, and areas of expertise. There are several major "flavours" of therapists.

- *Psychologist* A psychologist who practices psychotherapy holds a doctorate (a PhD or PsyD), with a specialization in clinical psychology. This degree takes about 6 years to complete after an undergraduate degree and includes extensive training in therapy, the assessment of psychological disorders, and research. In several provinces (Newfoundland and Labrador, Nova Scotia, New Brunswick, Saskatchewan, and Alberta) and in the Northwest Territories, only a master's degree is required for the designation "psychologist." This typically requires 2 years of study. The psychologist will sometimes have a specialty, such as working with adolescents or helping people overcome sleep disorders, and they will usually conduct therapy that involves talking. Psychologists must be registered with the provincial regulatory body, and most provinces require candidates to complete a period of supervised practical training and a competency exam. If you look for a *psychologist* on the Internet or through a clinic, you will usually find someone with this background.

- *Psychiatrist* A psychiatrist is a medical doctor who has completed a medical degree with specialized training in assessing and treating mental disorders. Psychiatrists can prescribe medications, and some also practice psychotherapy. General-practice physicians can also prescribe medications for mental disorders, and they are often the first to see people with such disorders because people consult them for a wide range of health problems. However, general-practice physicians do not typically receive much training in the diagnosis

or treatment of mental disorders, and they do not practice psychotherapy.

- *Clinical/psychiatric social worker* Social workers have a master's degree in social work and have training in working with people in dire life situations such as poverty, homelessness, or family conflict. Clinical or psychiatric social workers also receive special training to help people in these situations who have mental disorders. Social workers often work in government or private social service agencies and may also work in hospitals or have a private practice.

- *Counsellor* Counsellors have a wide range of training. Provinces and territories vary in how they define *counsellor*. In some cases, a counsellor must have a master's degree and extensive training in therapy, whereas in others, a counsellor may have minimal training or relevant education. Counsellors who work in schools usually have a master's degree and specific training in counselling in educational settings.

Some people offer therapy under made-up terms that sound professional— "mind/body healing therapist," for example, or "marital adjustment adviser." Often these are simply invented terms to mislead clients and avoid regulatory bodies—the "therapist" may have no training or expertise at all. And, of course, there are a few people who claim to be licensed practitioners who are not: Louise Wightman was convicted of fraud in 2007 after conducting psychotherapy as a psychologist with dozens of clients. She claimed she didn't know the PhD degree she had purchased over the Internet was bogus (Associated Press, 2007). People who offer therapy may be well-meaning and even helpful, but they might do harm, too. To be safe, it is important to shop wisely for a therapist whose training and credentials reflect expertise and inspire confidence.

How should you shop? One way is to start talking with people you know: your general-practice physician, a school counsellor, or a trusted friend or family member who might know of a good therapist. Or you can visit your university clinic or hospital or contact the Web site of an

MASKOT/GETTY IMAGES

organization, such as the Canadian Register of Health Service Psychologists (CRHSP) and the Canadian Counselling and Psychotherapy Association (CCPA), which provide contact details for registered mental health care providers. When you do contact someone, they will often be able to provide you with further advice about who would be just the right kind of therapist to consult.

Before you agree to see a therapist for treatment, you should ask questions (such as those below) to evaluate whether the therapist's style or background is a good match for your problem:

- What type of treatment do you provide?
- How effective is this type of therapy for the type of problem I'm having?
- How will you know if my problem is improving? What kind of measures do you use to evaluate this?

Not only will the therapist's answers to these questions tell you about their background and experience, but they will also tell you about their approach to treating clients. You can then make an informed decision about the type of service you need.

needed to be treated (Mojtabai et al., 2011). Mental disorders often are not taken nearly as seriously as physical illness, perhaps because the origin of mental illness is "hidden" and usually cannot be diagnosed by a blood test or X-ray.

2. *Barriers to treatment, such as beliefs and circumstances, may keep people from getting help.* Individuals may believe that they should be able to handle things themselves. In fact, this is the primary reason that people with a mental disorder give for not seeking treatment (72.6%) and for dropping out of treatment prematurely (42.2%) (Mojtabai et al., 2011). Other attitudinal barriers for not seeking treatment include the belief that the problem was not that severe (16.9% of people not seeking treatment), the belief that treatment would be ineffective (16.4%), and a perceived stigma from others (9.1%).

3. *Structural barriers prevent people from physically getting to treatment.* Like finding a good lawyer or plumber, finding the right psychologist can be more difficult than simply flipping through the yellow pages or searching online. This confusion is understandable given the plethora of different types of treatments available (see The Real World: Types of Psychotherapists). Once you find the therapist for you, you may encounter structural barriers related to not being able to afford treatment (15.3% of non-treatment seekers), lack of clinician availability (12.8%), the inconvenience of attending treatment (9.8%), and trouble finding transportation to the clinic (5.7%) (Mojtabai et al., 2011).

In Canada, evidence-based psychological services, delivered by psychologists and other professionals, are not typically publicly funded, and private coverage is generally only available to those with good employment. People in Canada who are poor, unemployed, or underemployed are not included. Low-income communities experience higher rates of mental disorders, but the provision of psychological and psychiatric services in such communities tends to be more limited than in large, affluent, urban centres. Canada's universal health care coverage tends to support "treatment for individuals with high socioeconomic status and comparatively milder [mental] disorders [more] than it supports care for disadvantaged groups or those with severe and persistent mental illness" (Steele et al., 2006, p. 322).

Clearly, Canada has work to do to ensure that people who seek help can find it, and get the most effective treatment. But this raises the question of what treatments are available, and which treatments are best for particular disorders.

Approaches to Treatment

Treatments can be divided broadly into two kinds: (1) *psychological* treatment, in which people interact with a clinician to use the environment to change their brain and behaviour; and (2) *biological* treatment, in which drugs, surgery, or some other direct intervention directly treat the brain. In some cases, people receive both psychological *and* biological treatments. Christine's OCD, for example, might be treated not only with ERP but also with medication that mitigates her obsessive thoughts and compulsive urges. For many years, psychological treatment was the main form of intervention for psychological disorders because few biological options were available. Folk remedies purporting to have a biological basis—such as hydrotherapy (pouring cold water on those with mental disorders), trephination (drilling holes in the skull to let the evil spirits escape), and bloodletting (the removal of blood from the body)—were once tried in efforts to cure psychological disorders. (*Note:* Do not try these at home. It turns out they don't work.) As we learn more about the biology and chemistry of the brain, approaches to mental health that begin with the brain are becoming increasingly effective and widespread.

Psychological Treatments: Healing Through Human Interaction

Figure 16.1

Approaches to Psychotherapy in the 21st Century This chart shows the percentage of 538 Canadian clinical psychologists and to which theoretical orientations they subscribed from 2009 to 2010 (Hunsley et al., 2013). The results of many studies conducted over the last 30 years demonstrate the efficacy of cognitive behavioural therapy over other forms of therapy for a wide range of mood, anxiety, substance abuse, personality, and psychotic disorders, and there is a strong emphasis on evidence-based treatment in Canadian clinical psychology training programs (Hunsley et al., 2013; Section on Clinical Psychology of the Canadian Psychological Association, 2016). It is not surprising, then, that a cognitive behavioural orientation is the most popular one.

psychotherapy An interaction between a socially sanctioned clinician and someone suffering from a psychological problem, with the goal of providing support or relief from the problem.

eclectic psychotherapy A form of psychotherapy that involves drawing on techniques from different forms of therapy, depending on the client and the problem.

psychodynamic psychotherapies Therapies that explore childhood events and encourage individuals to use this understanding to develop insight into their psychological problems.

Psychological treatment, or **psychotherapy**, *is an interaction between a socially sanctioned clinician and someone suffering from a psychological problem, with the goal of providing support or relief from the problem.* Over 500 different forms of psychotherapy exist. Although there are similarities among all the forms, there also are significant differences in their goals, aims, and methods. A survey of 538 psychologists registered with Canadian provincial regulatory bodies asked them to describe their theoretical orientation (Hunsley et al., 2013; see **FIGURE 16.1**). Many reported using **eclectic psychotherapy**, *a form of psychotherapy that involves drawing on techniques from different forms of therapy, depending on the client and the problem.* This approach allows therapists to apply an appropriate theoretical perspective suited to the problem at hand, rather than adhering to a single theoretical perspective for all clients and all types of problems. Nevertheless, as Figure 16.1 shows, the majority of practitioners relied on one of five orientations in their work. Cognitive behavioural therapy (CBT) was the most popular, reflecting the wealth of research demonstrating the efficacy of this approach for a wide range of disorders (Hunsley et al., 2013). Interpersonal therapy is a proven treatment for depression (Markowitz, 1999). It draws on both the cognitive and behavioural orientations as well as the psychodynamic orientation, and is discussed in the psychodynamic theory section. Family systems therapy is a form of group therapy used to treat issues involving both children and their parents (such as behavioural disorders that may be exacerbated by ineffective parenting). We will examine various popular approaches to psychotherapy in turn.

Psychodynamic Therapy

Psychodynamic psychotherapy has its roots in Freud's psychoanalytically oriented theory of personality. **Psychodynamic psychotherapies** *explore childhood events and encourage individuals to use the understanding gained from the exploration to develop insight into their psychological problems.* Psychoanalysis was the first psychodynamic therapy to be developed, but it has largely been replaced by modern psychodynamic therapies, such as interpersonal psychotherapy.

Psychoanalysis

As we saw in the Personality chapter, *psychoanalysis* assumes that people are born with aggressive and sexual urges that are repressed during childhood development through the use of defense mechanisms. Psychoanalysts encourage their clients to bring these repressed conflicts into consciousness so that the clients can understand them and reduce their unwanted influences. Psychoanalysts focus a great deal on early childhood events because they believe that urges and conflicts were likely repressed during this time.

Traditional psychoanalysis involves four or five sessions per week over an average of 3 to 6 years (Ursano & Silberman, 2003). During a session, the client reclines on a couch, facing away from the analyst, who asks the client to make *free associations*, in which the client expresses whatever thoughts and feelings come to mind. Occasionally, the therapist may comment on some information the client presents but does not express their values and judgements. The goal of psychoanalysis is for the client to understand the unconscious through a process Freud called *developing insight*.

Psychodynamic Therapy

Freud's original version of psychoanalysis is practiced by very few clinicians today (see Figure 16.1). However, many of his insights and techniques remain influential in a broader range of psychodynamic treatments that are used more frequently today. The new treatments differ from classic psychoanalysis in both their content and procedures. One of the most common psychodynamic treatments is **interpersonal psychotherapy (IPT)**, *a form of psychotherapy that focuses on helping clients improve current relationships* (Weissman et al., 2000). In terms of content, therapists using therapies such as IPT talk to clients about their interpersonal behaviours and feelings, rather than have them use free association. They pay particular attention to the client's grief (an exaggerated reaction to the loss of a loved one), role disputes (conflicts with a significant other), role transitions (changes in life status, such as starting a new job, getting married, or retiring), or interpersonal deficits (lack of the skills needed to start or maintain a relationship). The treatment focuses on interpersonal functioning, with the assumption that as interpersonal relations improve, symptoms will subside.

Modern psychodynamic psychotherapies such as IPT also differ from classical psychoanalysis in what procedures are used. For starters, in modern psychodynamic therapy the therapist and client typically sit face to face and meet only once a week over the course of months rather than years. In contrast to classical psychoanalysis, modern psychodynamic therapists are more likely to see relief from symptoms as a reasonable goal for therapy (in addition to the goal of facilitating insight), and they are more likely to offer support or advice in addition to interpretation (Barber et al., 2021). Therapists are also now less likely to interpret a client's statements as a sign of unconscious sexual or aggressive impulses, as was commonly the case in psychoanalysis. However, other concepts, such as fostering insight into unconscious processes, remain features of most psychodynamic therapies. Freud's couch casts a long shadow.

What Is the Evidence?

Although psychodynamic therapy has been around for a long time and continues to be widely practiced, there is limited evidence for its effectiveness. Some researchers suggest that there is evidence that psychodynamic therapies are effective (Shedler, 2010); however, data from randomized trials and meta-analyses report that IPT (just discussed) and cognitive behaviour (or behavioural) therapy (described below) are more effective than psychodynamic and other treatments, especially in the treatment of depressive and anxiety disorders (Tolin, 2010; Watzke et al., 2012; Zhou et al., 2015).

Humanistic and Existential Therapies

Humanistic and existential therapies emerged in the middle of the 20th century, in part as a reaction to the negative views that psychoanalysis holds about human nature (for instance, that we are focused primarily on sex and death). Humanistic and existential therapies assume that human nature is generally positive, and they emphasize the natural tendency of each individual to strive for personal improvement. Humanistic and existential therapies share the assumption that psychological problems stem from feelings of alienation and loneliness, and that those feelings can be traced to failure to reach one's potential (in the humanistic approach) or

In the classic movie *Good Will Hunting*, the lead character, played by Matt Damon, forms a strong bond with his therapist, played by Robin Williams. As in psychodynamic therapy, the therapist uses the doctor/patient relationship to help break down the patient's defense mechanisms and resolve an inner conflict. The amazing bond that was formed between therapist and patient and the life-changing treatment delivered are the stuff of therapists' dreams (and Hollywood scripts).

interpersonal psychotherapy (IPT)
A form of psychotherapy that focuses on helping clients improve current relationships.

Depictions of therapeutic interactions, such as those on shows like *Dr. Phil* and *Iyanla: Fix My Life*, while entertaining, are a far cry from what actually happens in psychological treatment sessions.

person-centred therapy (or client-centred therapy) A form of psychotherapy that assumes that all individuals have a tendency towards growth and that this growth can be facilitated by acceptance and genuine reactions from the therapist.

gestalt therapy A form of psychotherapy whose goal is helping the client become aware of their thoughts, behaviours, experiences, and feelings and to "own" or take responsibility for them.

from failure to find meaning in life (in the existential approach). Although interest in these approaches peaked in the 1960s and 1970s, some therapists continue to practice these approaches today. Two well-known types are person-centred therapy (a humanistic approach) and gestalt therapy (an existential approach).

Person-Centred Therapy

Person-centred therapy (or **client-centred therapy**) *assumes that all individuals have a tendency towards growth and that this growth can be facilitated by acceptance by and genuine reactions from the therapist.* The American psychologist Carl Rogers (1902–1987) developed person-centred therapy in the 1940s and 1950s (Rogers, 1951). This approach assumes that each person is qualified to determine their own goals for therapy, such as becoming more confident or making a career decision, and even the frequency and length of therapy. In this type of nondirective treatment, the therapist tends not to provide advice or suggestions about what the client should be doing, but instead paraphrases the client's words, mirroring the client's thoughts and sentiments (e.g., "I think I hear you saying . . ."). Person-centred therapists believe that with adequate support, the client will recognize the right things to do.

Rogers encouraged person-centred therapists to demonstrate three basic qualities: congruence, empathy, and unconditional positive regard. Congruence means openness and honesty in the therapeutic relationship and ensuring that the therapist communicates the same message at all levels. For example, the therapist must communicate the same message in words, in facial expressions, and in body language. Saying "I think your concerns are valid" while smirking simply will not do. Empathy is the continuous process of trying to understand the client by getting inside their way of thinking, feeling, and understanding the world. Interestingly, research has shown that the more empathic a client says the clinician is, the more similarity there is between the client's and therapist's levels of physiological arousal in that moment (Marci et al., 2007). This suggests that therapists who are being empathic may really be feeling some of what their clients are feeling. Seeing the world from the client's perspective enables the therapist to better appreciate the client's apprehensions, worries, or fears. Finally, the therapist must treat the client with unconditional positive regard by providing a nonjudgemental, warm, and accepting environment in which the client can feel safe expressing their thoughts and feelings.

The goal is not to uncover repressed conflicts, as in psychodynamic therapy, but instead to try to understand the client's experience and reflect that experience back to the client in a supportive way, encouraging the client's natural tendency towards growth. This style of therapy, however, is reminiscent of psychoanalysis in the way it encourages the client towards the free expression of thoughts and feelings.

Gestalt Therapy

Gestalt therapy was developed by Frederick "Fritz" Perls (1893–1970) and colleagues in the 1940s and 1950s (Perls et al., 1951). **Gestalt therapy** *has the goal of helping the client become aware of their thoughts, behaviours, experiences, and feelings and to "own" or take responsibility for them.* Gestalt therapists are encouraged to be enthusiastic and warm towards their clients, an approach they share with person-centred therapists. To help facilitate the client's awareness, gestalt therapists also reflect back to the client their impressions of the client.

Gestalt therapy emphasizes the experiences and behaviours that are occurring at that particular moment in the therapy session. For example, if a client is talking about something stressful that occurred during the previous week, the therapist might shift the attention to the client's current experience by asking, "How do you feel as you describe what happened to you?" This technique is known as focusing. Clients are also encouraged to put their feelings into action. One way to do this is the empty-chair technique, in which the client imagines that a person in their life (e.g., a spouse, a parent, a coworker) is in

As part of gestalt therapy, clients may be encouraged to imagine that another person is sitting across from them in a chair. The client then moves from chair to chair, role-playing what they would say to the imagined person and how that person would answer.

an empty chair sitting directly across from the client. The client then moves from chair to chair, alternating from role-playing what they would say to the other person and then role-playing how they imagine the other person would respond.

Behavioural and Cognitive Therapies

Unlike the older, more traditional talk therapies described above, behavioural and cognitive treatments emphasize actively changing a person's current thoughts and behaviours as a way to mitigate or eliminate their psychopathology. In the evolution of psychological treatments, clients started out lying down in psychoanalysis and then sitting in psychodynamic and related approaches, but in behavioural and cognitive therapies, they often stand and engage in behaviour-change homework assignments in their everyday life.

Behaviour Therapy: Changing Maladaptive Behaviour Patterns

Whereas Freud developed psychoanalysis as an offshoot of hypnosis and other clinical techniques that clinicians used before him, behaviour therapy was developed based on laboratory findings of behavioural psychologists. As you read in The Evolution of Psychological Science chapter, behaviourists rejected theories based on "invisible" mental properties that were difficult to test and impossible to observe directly. Behaviourists found psychoanalytic ideas particularly hard to test: How do you know whether a person has an unconscious conflict or whether insight has occurred? Behavioural principles, in contrast, focused solely on behaviours that could be observed (e.g., avoidance of a feared object, such as refusing to get on an airplane). **Behaviour therapy** assumes that *disordered behaviour is learned and that symptom relief is achieved through changing overt, maladaptive behaviours into more constructive behaviours.* A variety of behaviour therapy techniques have been developed for many disorders, based on the learning principles you encountered in the Learning chapter, including operant conditioning procedures (which focus on reinforcement and punishment) and classical conditioning procedures (which focus on extinction). Here are three examples of behaviour therapy techniques in action.

Eliminating Unwanted Behaviours How would you change a 3-year-old's habit of throwing tantrums at the grocery store? A behaviour therapist might investigate what happens immediately before and after the tantrum: Did the child get candy to "shut him up"? The study of operant conditioning shows that behaviour can be influenced by its *consequences* (the reinforcing or punishing events that follow). Adjusting these might help change the behaviour. Making the consequences less reinforcing (giving candy will only reinforce the tantrum!) and more punishing (a period of time-out facing the wall in the grocery store while the parent watches from nearby rather than providing a rush of attention) could eliminate the problem behaviour over time.

Promoting Desired Behaviours Candy and time-outs can have a strong influence on child behaviour, but they work less well with adults. How might you get an individual with schizophrenia to engage in activities of daily living? How would you get someone experiencing cocaine or opioid dependence to stop using these substances? A behaviour therapy technique that has proven to be quite effective in such cases is the **token economy**, which *involves giving clients "tokens" for desired behaviours that they can later trade for rewards.* In the case of cocaine dependence, for instance, the desired behaviour is not using cocaine. Programs that reward non-use (verified by clean urine samples) with vouchers that can be exchanged for rewards such as money, bus passes, clothes, and so on, have been shown to significantly reduce cocaine use and associated psychological problems (Miguel et al., 2022). Similar systems are used to promote abstinence from other drugs (Bolívar et al., 2021), as well as desired behaviours in classrooms, the workplace, and commercial advertising (e.g., airline and credit card rewards programs).

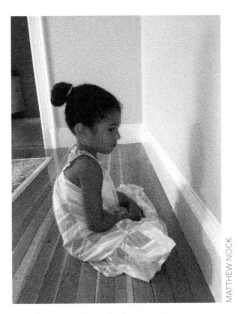

MATTHEW NOCK

A behavioural psychologist might treat a temper tantrum using time-out for reinforcement, a method that is based on the behavioural principle of operant conditioning and one that ensures that a child will not be rewarded for undesired behaviour.

behaviour therapy A type of therapy that assumes that disordered behaviour is learned and that symptom relief is achieved through changing overt, maladaptive behaviours into more constructive behaviours.

token economy A form of behaviour therapy that involves giving clients "tokens" for desired behaviours that they can later trade for rewards.

An exposure therapy client with obsessive-compulsive disorder who fears contamination in public restrooms might be given the "homework" of visiting three such restrooms in a week, touching the toilets, and then not washing up.

exposure therapy An approach to treatment of the client that involves confronting an emotion-arousing stimulus directly and repeatedly, ultimately leading to a decrease in the emotional response.

Reducing Unwanted Emotional Responses One of the most powerful ways to reduce anxious behaviour is by gradual exposure to the feared object or situation. **Exposure therapy** is an *approach to treatment of the client that involves confronting an emotion-arousing stimulus directly and repeatedly, ultimately leading to a decrease in the emotional response.* This technique depends on the processes of habituation and response extinction. For example, in Christine's case her clinician gradually exposed her to the content of her obsessions (dirt and germs), which became less and less distressing with repeated exposure (as she learned that she would not actually be harmed by coming into contact with the previously feared stimulus). Similarly, for clients who are afraid of social interaction and unable to function at school or work, a behavioural treatment might involve exposure first to imagined situations in which they talk briefly with one person, then talk a bit longer to a medium-sized group, and finally, give a speech to a large group. It's now known that *in vivo* (live) exposure is more effective than imaginary exposure (Choy et al., 2007). In other words, if a person fears social situations, it is better for that person to practice social interaction than merely to imagine it. And more recent research has shown that using virtual reality to conduct exposures works just as well as *in vivo* methods, making more difficult forms of exposure more easily practiced (e.g., exposure to heights or airplane flights) (Carl et al., 2019). Behavioural therapists use an exposure hierarchy to accustom the client gradually to the feared object or situation. Easier situations are practiced first, and as fear decreases, the client progresses to more difficult or frightening situations (see **TABLE 16.1**). It is vitally important that the person continue to be exposed to the feared stimulus until their anxiety decreases. If they leave the situation before that happens, their anxiety will be reinforced, because they fail to learn that the feared stimulus is not harmful and they also learn that avoiding it decreases their anxiety. So, if you have a fear of, say, public speaking, best to speak to increasingly large groups of people and to not leave each situation until your anxiety decreases!

Exposure therapy can also help people overcome unwanted emotional and behavioural responses through *exposure and response prevention*. Persons with OCD, for example, might have recurrent thoughts that their hands are dirty and need washing. Washing stops the uncomfortable feelings of contamination only briefly, though, and they wash again and again in search of relief. In exposure and response prevention, they might be asked in therapy to get their hands dirty on purpose (first by touching a coin picked up from the ground, then by touching a public toilet, and later by touching a dead mouse) and leave them dirty for hours. They may need to do this only a few times to break the cycle and be freed from the obsessive ritual (Foa et al., 2007).

TABLE 16.1

EXPOSURE HIERARCHY FOR SOCIAL PHOBIA

Item	Fear (0–100)
1. Have a party and invite everyone from work	99
2. Go to a holiday party for 1 hour without drinking	90
3. Invite Cindy to have dinner and see a movie	85
4. Go for a job interview	80
5. Ask boss for a day off work	65
6. Ask questions in a meeting at work	65
7. Eat lunch with coworkers	60
8. Talk to a stranger on the bus	50
9. Talk to cousin on the telephone for 10 minutes	40
10. Ask for directions at the gas station	35

Information from Ellis (1991).

Cognitive Therapy: Changing Distorted Thoughts

Whereas behaviour therapy focuses primarily on changing a person's behaviour, **cognitive therapy**, as the name suggests, *focuses on helping a client identify and correct any distorted thinking about self, others, or the world* (Beck, 2019). For example, behaviourists might explain a phobia as the outcome of a classical conditioning experience such as being bitten by a dog; the dog bite leads to the development of a dog phobia through the association of the dog with the experience of pain. Cognitive theorists might instead emphasize the *interpretation* of the event. It might not be the event itself that caused the fear, but rather the individual's beliefs and assumptions about the event and the feared stimulus. In the case of a dog bite, to explain the fear, cognitive theorists might focus on a person's new or strengthened belief that dogs are dangerous.

A principal technique of cognitive therapies is called **cognitive restructuring**, which *teaches clients to question the automatic beliefs, assumptions, and predictions that often lead to negative emotions and to replace negative thinking with more realistic and positive beliefs.* Specifically, clients are taught to examine the evidence for and against a particular belief or to be more accepting of outcomes that may be undesirable yet still manageable. For example, a depressed client may believe that they are stupid and will never pass their university courses—all on the basis of one poor grade. In this situation, the therapist would work with the client to examine the validity of this belief. The therapist would consider relevant evidence such as grades on previous exams, performance on other coursework, and examples of intelligence outside school. It may be that the client has never failed a course before and has achieved good grades in this particular course in the past. In this case, the therapist would encourage the client to consider all this information in determining whether they are truly "stupid." **TABLE 16.2** shows a variety of common, potentially irrational ideas that can unleash unwanted emotions such as anger, depression, or anxiety. Any of these irrational beliefs might bedevil a person with serious emotional problems if left unchallenged; for that reason, such beliefs are potential targets for cognitive restructuring. In therapy sessions, the cognitive therapist will help the client to identify evidence that either supports or fails to support each negative thought, in order to help the client generate more balanced thoughts that more accurately reflect the true state of affairs. In other words, the clinician tries to remove the dark lens through which the client views the world, not with the goal of replacing it with

The approach to psychotherapy developed by cognitive therapist Aaron Beck (1921–2021) employs a direct and rational approach to help people change maladaptive thinking patterns.

cognitive therapy Focuses on helping a client identify and correct any distorted thinking about self, others, or the world.

cognitive restructuring A therapeutic approach that teaches clients to question the automatic beliefs, assumptions, and predictions that often lead to negative emotions and to replace negative thinking with more realistic and positive beliefs.

TABLE 16.2

COMMON IRRATIONAL BELIEFS AND THE EMOTIONAL RESPONSES THEY CAN CAUSE

Belief	Emotional Response
I have to get this done immediately.	Anxiety, stress
I must be perfect.	
Something terrible will happen.	
Everyone is watching me.	Embarrassment, social anxiety
I won't be able to make friends.	
People know something is wrong with me.	
I'm a loser and will always be a loser.	Sadness, depression
Nobody will ever love me.	
She did that to me on purpose.	Anger, irritability
He is evil and should be punished.	

Information from Ellis (1991).

rose-coloured glasses, but instead with replacing it with clear glass. Here is a brief sample transcript of what part of a cognitive therapy session might sound like.

Clinician: Last week I asked you to keep a thought record of situations in which you felt very down and depressed, at least one per day, and the automatic thoughts that popped into your mind. Were you able to do that?

Client: Yes, here it is.

Clinician: Wonderful, I'm glad you were able to complete this assignment. Let's take a look at this together. What's the first situation that you recorded?

Client: Well . . . I went out on Friday night with my friends, which I thought would be fun and help me to feel better. But I was feeling kind of down about things and I ended up not really talking to anyone, which led me to just sit in the corner and drink all night, which caused me to get so drunk that I passed out at the party. I woke up the next day feeling embarrassed and more depressed than ever.

Clinician: Okay, sounds like a tough situation. So the situation is you had too much to drink and passed out. The resulting emotion you had was depression. How intense was your feeling of depression on a scale of 0 to 100?

Client: Ninety.

Clinician: Okay, and what thoughts automatically popped into your head?

Client: I can't control myself. I'll never be able to control myself. My friends think I'm a loser and will never want to hang out with me again.

Clinician: Okay, and which of these thoughts led you to feel most depressed?

Client: That my friends think I'm a loser and won't want to hang out with me anymore.

Clinician: All right, so let's focus on that one for a minute. What evidence can you think of that supports this thought?

Client: Well . . . um . . . I got really drunk and so they *have* to think I'm a loser. I mean, who does that?

Clinician: Okay, write that down on your thought record in this column here. Is there any other evidence you can think of that supports those thoughts?

Client: No.

Clinician: All right. Now let's take a moment to think about whether there is any evidence that doesn't support those thoughts. Did anything happen that suggests that your friends *don't* think you are a loser or that they do want to keep hanging out with you?

Client: Well . . . apparently some kids were making fun of me when I was passed out and my friends stopped them. And they also brought me home safely and then called the next day and my one friend Tommy said something like "we've all been there" and that he wants to hang out again this weekend.

Clinician: Okay, great, write that down in this next column. This is very interesting. So on one hand, you feel depressed and have thoughts that you are a loser and your friends don't like you. But on the other hand, you have some pretty real-world evidence that even though you drank too much, they were still there for you and they do in fact want to hang out with you again?

Client: Yeah, I guess you're right. I didn't think about it like that.

Clinician: So now if we were going to replace your first thoughts, which don't seem to have a lot of real-world evidence, with a more balanced thought based on the evidence, what would that more balanced thought be?

Client: Probably something like, "My friends probably weren't happy about the fact that I got so drunk because then they had to take care of me, but they are my friends and were there for me and want to keep hanging out with me."

Clinician: Excellent job. I think that sounds just right based on the evidence. Write that down in the next column. And how much do you believe in this new thought on a scale of 0 to 100?

Client: I think it's actually pretty accurate, so I would say 95.

Clinician: And thinking about this new more balanced thought rather than your first one, how would you rate your depression?

Client: Much lower than before. Probably a 40. I'm still not happy that I got so drunk, but I'm less depressed about my friends not liking me.

In addition to cognitive restructuring techniques, which try to change a person's thoughts to be more balanced or accurate, some forms of cognitive therapy also include techniques for coping with unwanted thoughts and feelings, techniques that resemble meditation (see the Consciousness chapter). Clients may be encouraged to attend to their troubling thoughts or emotions or be given meditative techniques that allow them to gain a new focus (Hofmann & Asmundson, 2008). One such technique, called **mindfulness meditation**, *teaches an individual to be fully present in each moment; to be aware of their thoughts, feelings, and sensations; and to detect symptoms before they become a problem.* Researchers found mindfulness meditation to be helpful for preventing relapse in people who have recovered from depression. People with depression who receive mindfulness meditation-based cognitive therapy show a decreased risk of having another depressive episode that is similar to that of people who continue taking antidepressant medication (Segal & Walsh, 2016). Cognitive and cognitive behavioural therapies (covered below) do well in preventing relapse because once a person learns the skills taught in these therapies, they can continue to use them in future situations all on their own, without guidance from a clinician (Hollon et al., 2021). This is in contrast to medications, which only work as long as they are present in the body.

Cognitive Behavioural Therapy: Blending Approaches

Historically, cognitive and behavioural therapies were considered distinct systems of therapy, and some people continue to follow this distinction, using solely behavioural *or* solely cognitive techniques. Today, the extent to which therapists use cognitive versus behavioural techniques depends on the individual therapist as well as the type of problem being treated. Most therapists working with anxiety and depression use **cognitive behavioural therapy (CBT)**, *a blend of cognitive and behavioural therapeutic strategies.* This technique acknowledges that there may be behaviours that people cannot control through rational thought, but also that there are ways of helping people think more rationally when thought does play a role. In contrast to traditional behaviour therapy and cognitive therapy, CBT is *problem-focused*, meaning that it is undertaken for specific problems (e.g., reducing the frequency of panic attacks or returning to work after a bout of depression), and *action-oriented*, meaning that the therapist tries to assist the client in selecting specific strategies that could help address those problems. The client is expected to *do* things, such as engage in exposure exercises, practice behaviour-change skills, or use a diary to monitor relevant symptoms (e.g., the severity of depressed mood, panic attack symptoms). This is in contrast to psychodynamic or other therapies in which goals may not be explicitly discussed or agreed on and the client's only necessary action is to attend the therapy session.

CBT also contrasts with psychodynamic approaches in its assumptions about what the client can know. CBT is *transparent* in that nothing is withheld from the client. By the end of the course of therapy, most clients have a very good understanding of the treatment they have received as well as the specific techniques that are used to make the desired changes. For example, clients with OCD who fear contamination would feel confident in knowing how to confront feared situations such as public washrooms and why confronting these situations is helpful.

Cognitive behavioural therapies have been found to be effective for a number of disorders (Hofmann et al., 2012) (see Hot Science: "Rebooting" Psychological

FILADENDRON/GETTY IMAGES

Whereas traditional forms of cognitive therapy focused largely on changing maladaptive thoughts, some newer forms incorporate meditation practices to help people become more aware of such thoughts and to simply let them pass on by—like clouds in the sky.

mindfulness meditation Teaches an individual to be fully present in each moment; to be aware of their thoughts, feelings, and sensations; and to detect symptoms before they become a problem.

cognitive behavioural therapy (CBT) A blend of cognitive and behavioural therapeutic strategies.

Treatment). Substantial positive effects of CBT have been found for clients with unipolar depression, generalized anxiety disorder, panic disorder, social phobia, posttraumatic stress disorder, and childhood depressive and anxiety disorders. CBT has moderate but less substantial positive effects for marital distress, anger, somatic disorders, and chronic pain.

Group Treatments: Healing Multiple Minds at the Same Time

It is natural to think of psychopathology as an illness that affects only one individual. A particular person "is depressed," for example, or "has anxiety." Yet each person lives in a world of other people, and interactions with others may intensify and even cause disorders. A depressed person may be lonely after moving away from friends and loved ones, or an anxious person could be worried about pressure from parents. These ideas suggest that people might be able to recover from disorders in the same way they got into them—not just as an individual effort, but through social processes.

Couples and Family Therapy

When a couple is "having problems," it may be that neither individual suffers from any psychopathology. Rather, it may be the relationship itself that is disordered. In *couple therapy*, a married, cohabiting, or dating couple is seen together in therapy to work on problems usually arising within the relationship. A traditional situation for couple therapy might involve a couple seeking help because they are unhappy with their relationship. In this scenario, both members of the couple are expected to attend therapy sessions because the problem is seen as arising from their interaction rather than from the problem(s) of one half of the couple. Treatment strategies would target changes in *both* parties, focusing on ways to break their repetitive dysfunctional pattern.

In some cases, therapy with even larger groups is warranted. An individual may be having a problem—say, an adolescent is abusing alcohol—but the source of the problem is the individual's relationships with family members; perhaps the mother is herself an alcoholic who subtly encourages the adolescent to drink, and the father travels and neglects the family. In this case, it could be useful for the therapist to work with the whole group at once in *family therapy*—psychotherapy involving members of a family. Family therapy can be particularly effective when adolescent children are having problems (Masten, 2004).

In family therapy, the "client" is the entire family. Family therapists believe that problem behaviours exhibited by a particular family member are the result of a dysfunctional family dynamic. For example, an adolescent girl suffering from bulimia might be treated in therapy with her mother, father, and older brother. The therapist would work to understand how the family members relate to one another, how the family is organized, and how it changes over time. In the discussions, the therapist might discover that the parents' excessive enthusiasm about her brother's athletic career led the daughter to try to gain their approval by controlling her weight to become "beautiful." Both couple and family therapy involve more than one person attending therapy together, since the problems and solutions are seen as arising from the *interactions* of these individuals rather than simply from any one individual.

Families enter therapy for many reasons, sometimes to help particular members and other times because there are problems in one or more of the relationships in the family.

ANNA GOLDBERG/AGEFOTOSTOCK

group therapy A type of therapy in which multiple participants (who often do not know each other at the outset) work on their individual problems in a group atmosphere.

Group Therapy

Taking these ideas one step further, if individuals (or families) can benefit from talking with a psychotherapist, perhaps they can also benefit from talking with other clients who are talking with the therapist. This is **group therapy**, *a type of therapy in which multiple participants (who often do not know one another at the outset) work on their individual problems in a group atmosphere.* The therapist in group therapy serves more as a group facilitator than as a personal therapist, conducting the sessions both by talking with individuals and by encouraging them to talk with each other. Group therapy is often useful for people who have a common problem, such as substance abuse, but it can also be beneficial for those with differing problems. It is important to note that group therapy is not an approach in itself but a mode of delivering treatment. That is, group therapy can be psychodynamic, cognitive, cognitive behavioural, and so on, in its approach.

Why do people choose group therapy? One advantage is that attending a group with others who have similar problems shows clients that they are not alone in their suffering. In addition, group members model appropriate behaviours for each other and share their insights about how to deal with their problems. Group therapy is often just as effective as individual therapy (e.g., Jonsson & Hougaard, 2008). From a societal perspective, then, group therapy is much more efficient.

Group therapy also has disadvantages. It may be difficult to assemble a group of individuals who have similar needs. This is particularly an issue with CBT, which tends to focus on specific problems such as depression or panic disorder. Group therapy may also become a problem if one or more members undermine the treatment of other group members. This can occur if some group members dominate the discussions, threaten other group members, or make others in the group uncomfortable (e.g., attempting to date other members). Finally, clients in group therapy get less attention than each might receive in individual psychotherapy.

Self-Help and Support Groups

Some important types of group therapy are *self-help groups* and *support groups,* which are discussion groups that focus on a particular disorder or difficult life experience; they are often run by peers (rather than a clinician) who have themselves struggled with the same issues. The most famous self-help and support groups are Alcoholics Anonymous (AA), Gamblers Anonymous, and Al-Anon (a program for families and friends of those with alcohol problems). Other self-help groups offer support to cancer survivors or to parents of children with autism or to people with mood disorders, eating disorders, and substance abuse problems. In fact, self-help and support groups exist for just about every psychological disorder. In addition to being cost effective, self-help and support groups allow people to realize that they are not the only ones with a particular problem, and the groups give them the opportunity to offer guidance and support to each other that has arisen from their own personal experiences of success.

In some cases, though, self-help and support groups can do more harm than good. Some members may be disruptive or aggressive or encourage each other to engage in behaviours that are countertherapeutic (e.g., continuing to avoid feared situations or using alcohol to cope). People with moderate problems who may be exposed to others with severe problems may become over-sensitized to symptoms they might not otherwise have found disturbing. Because self-help and support groups are usually not led by trained therapists, mechanisms to evaluate these groups or to ensure their quality are rarely in place.

AA has more than 123,000 groups in approximately 180 countries around the world, with their literature available in over 100 languages (Alcoholics Anonymous, 2022). Members are encouraged to follow *12 steps* to reach the goal of lifelong abstinence from all drinking; the steps include believing in a higher power, practicing prayer and meditation, and making amends for harm to others. Most members attend group meetings several times per week, and between meetings they receive additional support from their "sponsor." A few studies have examined the effectiveness of AA, and it appears that 12-step programs like AA can be as effective as cognitive and behavioural interventions at helping people to stop using addictive substances (Kelly et al., 2017).

Considered together, the many social approaches to psychotherapy reveal how important interpersonal relationships are for each of us. It may not always be clear how psychotherapy works, whether one approach is better than another, or what particular theory best explains how problems have developed. What *is* clear, however, is that social interactions among people—both in individual therapy and in all the different forms of group therapy—can be useful in treating psychological disorders.

STURTI/GETTY IMAGES

Self-help groups are a cost-effective, time-effective, and treatment-effective solution for dealing with some types of psychological problems. Many people like self-help groups, but are they effective? How could you test this?

Hot Science | "Rebooting" Psychological Treatment

Modern psychological treatments have advanced far beyond the days of Freud and his free-associating patients. However, most forms of psychological treatment are still pretty primitive in many ways. They usually involve a client meeting once per week with a clinician who attempts to talk them out of their psychological disorder—just as it did in the earliest days of psychological treatment. One of the world's leading researchers of traditional psychological treatments, Alan Kazdin, has called for a "rebooting" of psychotherapy research and practice (Kazdin, 2018; Kazdin & Blaise, 2011). What is needed, he argues, is a portfolio of treatment delivery approaches that take advantage of recent advances in technology.

In many cases, this involves using new technologies to deliver traditional interventions. For instance, the social distancing protocols instituted during the COVID-19 pandemic meant that in-person sessions were no longer possible. However, the availability of online conferencing apps meant that people could receive treatment remotely—and in many cases in groups (due in part to increased demand for treatment for anxiety and depression during the pandemic). Researchers from across several different countries showed that anxious and depressed university students could be reached via Facebook and provided group-based cognitive behavioural therapy (CBT) via Microsoft Teams, and that this treatment led to significant reductions in their anxiety and depression (Bantjes et al., 2021).

In an increasing number of cases, this also involves modifying both the content and delivery of interventions to make them more accessible to the person receiving treatment. That is, rather than going to see a therapist once per week, what if you had access to the skills you learn in treatment within your smartphone? One recent study delivered an abbreviated version of Dialectical Behaviour Therapy (DBT; a form of CBT) to university students aimed at decreasing student distress during the COVID-19 pandemic. Students were assigned to receive brief (2–5 minutes) videos via their smartphones (see youtube.com/dbtru) that taught them DBT skills and led to reductions in negative affect (Rizvi et al., 2022).

The development of computer- or smartphone-based interventions has been extremely exciting; however, although there are an increasing number of apps, very few can show data supporting their effectiveness (Wilks et al., 2021). So, although the development of computerized approaches has opened up lots of new opportunities for intervention, it is important that psychologists carefully evaluate which ones can help improve health outcomes and which are simply fancier ways of providing ineffective treatment.

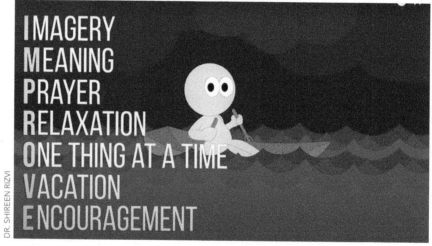

DR. SHIREEN RIZVI

In newly developed, smartphone-based interventions, clients are referred to online content—such as the videos depicted here (and available at youtube.com/dbtru)—which represents very brief versions of the content taught in traditional face-to-face sessions. Researchers are testing whether these brief but always-available interventions are as effective as traditional methods of delivering psychological treatments. If so, this would make treatments much more accessible to people all over the world, and to clients whenever and wherever they wanted to get a dose of treatment.

Biological Treatments: Healing Through Physical Alteration of the Brain

People have ingested foreign substances in an attempt to change or improve their mental state since the beginning of recorded history. Humans have been fermenting fruits and other natural substances to create alcohol since about 7000 BCE (McGovern et al., 2004). Over a period of more than 1,500 years, Greek physicians prescribed a substance called *theriac* to treat a wide range of ailments, including anxiety and depression. Theriac was composed of dozens of different ingredients (including red roses, carrots, and viper's flesh), although we now know that one ingredient in particular (opium) likely was responsible for its positive effects. In the more recent past, physicians found that another substance also worked wonders as a cure for depression, headaches, indigestion, and a range of other problems. That substance was cocaine, and it turns out that it has many negative side effects, which led to it falling out of favour as a sanctioned medicine (Markel, 2011). Since then, drug treatments have been developed that don't lead users to feel euphoric (as is the case with opium and cocaine). Instead they target specific neurotransmitters in the brain that researchers believe are involved in different mental disorders. These treatments have grown in variety, effectiveness, and popularity; they are now the most common medical approach in treating psychological disorders (see **FIGURE 16.2**).

Antipsychotic Medications

The story of drug treatments for severe psychological disorders starts in the 1950s, with chlorpromazine (brand-name Thorazine); it was originally developed as a sedative, but

Learning Outcomes

WHAT YOU NEED TO KNOW

- Explain how antipsychotic medications affect the brain.
- Identify the risks of antianxiety medications.
- Explain how modern antidepressants affect the brain.
- Identify which herbal supplements have been proven to be effective.
- Debate pros and cons of combining psychological therapy with drug therapy.
- Identify the more extreme treatment options when psychotherapy and medications are unsuccessful.

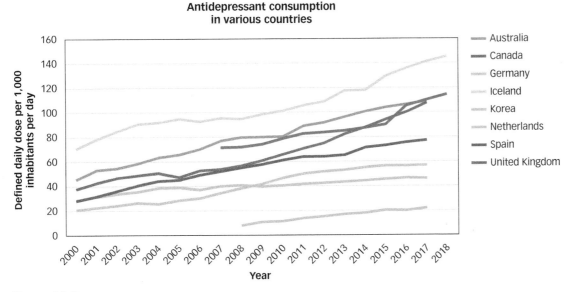

Antidepressant consumption in various countries

Legend: Australia, Canada, Germany, Iceland, Korea, Netherlands, Spain, United Kingdom

y-axis: Defined daily dose per 1,000 inhabitants per day
x-axis: Year (2000–2018)

Figure 16.2

Antidepressant Use The popularity of psychiatric medications has skyrocketed in recent years. A recent report from the Organisation for Economic Cooperation and Development (OECD) reveals that antidepressant use among Canadians is among the highest in the world. The OECD survey revealed that antidepressant consumption has been increasing across a range of OECD member countries, including Canada and the other seven shown here. The "defined daily dose" is the drug-specific standard maintenance dose for an adult—so, a value of 100 on the y-axis means that for every 1,000 people every day, the equivalent of 100 maintenance doses of antidepressant are taken (OECD, 2019).

when it was administered to agitated patients with schizophrenia they often became euphoric and docile (Barondes, 2003). The first in a series of **antipsychotic drugs**, which *treat schizophrenia and related psychotic disorders,* chlorpromazine completely changed the way schizophrenia was managed. Related medications, such as thioridazine (Mellaril) and haloperidol (Haldol), followed. Before antipsychotic drugs were introduced, people with schizophrenia often exhibited bizarre symptoms and were sometimes so disruptive and difficult to manage that the only way to protect them (and other people) was to keep them in hospitals for people with mental disorders; initially called *asylums,* these hospitals are now referred to as *psychiatric hospitals.* After the antipsychotic drugs were introduced, the number of people in psychiatric hospitals decreased by more than two-thirds. The drugs led to the deinstitutionalization of hundreds of thousands of people and gave a major boost to the field of **psychopharmacology**, *the study of drug effects on psychological states and symptoms.*

Researchers believe that antipsychotic medications exert their effect by blocking dopamine receptors in certain parts of the brain, such as the mesolimbic pathway—a pathway paved with dopamine neurons extending from the ventral tegmental area (VTA) to the nucleus accumbens in the basal ganglia (see the Neuroscience and Behaviour chapter). The effectiveness of these medications for schizophrenia led to the dopamine hypothesis (described in the Psychological Disorders chapter), which suggests that schizophrenia may be caused by excess dopamine in the synapse. Research has indeed found that dopamine overactivity in the mesolimbic pathway of the brain is related to the more bizarre positive symptoms of schizophrenia, such as hallucinations and delusions (Marangell et al., 2003).

Although antipsychotic drugs work well for positive symptoms, it turns out that the negative symptoms of schizophrenia, such as emotional numbing and social withdrawal, may be related to dopamine *under*activity in the mesocortical pathways of the brain (connections between parts of the VTA and the cerebral cortex), which may help explain why antipsychotic medications do not relieve negative symptoms well. Instead of a drug that blocks dopamine receptors, negative symptoms require one that *increases* the amount of dopamine available at the synapse. This is a good example of how medical treatments can have broad psychological effects but do not target specific psychological symptoms.

Over the past few decades, a new class of antipsychotic drugs has been introduced that includes clozapine (Clozaril), risperidone (Risperdal), and olanzapine (Zyprexa). These newer drugs are often referred to as *atypical* antipsychotics. (The older drugs are now often referred to as *conventional* or *typical* antipsychotics.) Unlike the older antipsychotic medications, these newer drugs appear to affect both the dopamine and serotonin systems, blocking both types of receptors. The ability to block serotonin receptors appears to be a useful addition, because enhanced serotonin activity in the brain has been implicated in some of the core difficulties in schizophrenia, such as cognitive and perceptual disruptions, as well as mood disturbances. This may explain why atypical antipsychotics work at least as well as older drugs for the positive symptoms of schizophrenia but also work fairly well for the negative symptoms, especially when the antipsychotic medication prescribed is augmented with a second antipsychotic (Galling et al., 2017).

Like most medications, antipsychotic drugs have side effects, which can be sufficiently unpleasant that some people "go off their meds," preferring their symptoms to the drug effects. A side effect that often occurs with long-term use of these drugs is *tardive dyskinesia,* a condition of involuntary movements of the face, mouth, and extremities. In fact, people often need to take another medication to treat the unwanted side effects of the conventional antipsychotic drugs. Side effects of the newer medications tend to be different from and are sometimes milder than those of the older ones. For that reason, the atypical antipsychotics are now usually the frontline treatments for schizophrenia (Meltzer, 2013).

"*The drug has, however, proved more effective than traditional psychoanalysis.*"

PAUL NOTH/CARTOON STOCK

antipsychotic drugs Medications that are used to treat schizophrenia and related psychotic disorders.

psychopharmacology The study of drug effects on psychological states and symptoms.

Antianxiety Medications

Antianxiety medications are *drugs that help reduce a person's experience of fear or anxiety.* The most commonly used antianxiety medications are the benzodiazepines, a type of tranquilizer that works by facilitating the action of the neurotransmitter gamma-aminobutyric acid (GABA). As you learned in the Neuroscience and Behaviour chapter, GABA inhibits certain neurons in the brain. This inhibitory action can produce a calming effect for the person. Commonly prescribed benzodiazepines include diazepam (Valium), lorazepam (Ativan), and alprazolam (Xanax). The benzodiazepines typically take effect in a matter of minutes and are extremely effective for reducing symptoms of anxiety disorders.

Nonetheless, doctors are relatively cautious when prescribing benzodiazepines since they have the potential for abuse (Bandelow et al., 2017). They are also often associated with the development of *drug tolerance,* which is the need for higher dosages over long-term use to achieve the same effects (see the Consciousness chapter). Furthermore, after people have become tolerant of the drug, they risk significant withdrawal symptoms when it's discontinued. Some withdrawal symptoms include increased heart rate, shakiness, insomnia, agitation, and anxiety—the very symptoms the drug was taken to eliminate! Therefore, people who take benzodiazepines for extended periods may have difficulty coming off these drugs; they should discontinue them gradually to minimize withdrawal symptoms (Bandelow et al., 2017). Another consideration when prescribing benzodiazepines is their side effects. The most common side effect is drowsiness, although they can also have negative effects on coordination and memory. And benzodiazepines combined with alcohol can depress respiration, potentially causing accidental death.

When anxiety leads to insomnia, drugs known as hypnotics may be useful as sleep aids. One such drug, zolpidem (Ambien), is widely used and is often effective, but there are some reports of sleepwalking, sleep-eating, and even sleep-driving (Hughes, 2007). Another alternative for anxiety is buspirone (Buspar), which has been shown to reduce anxiety among individuals who suffer from generalized anxiety disorder.

Antidepressants and Mood Stabilizers

Antidepressants are *a class of drugs that help lift people's moods.* They were first introduced in the 1950s, when iproniazid, a drug used to treat tuberculosis, was found to elevate mood (Selikoff et al., 1952). Iproniazid is a *monoamine oxidase inhibitor (MAOI),* a medication that prevents the enzyme monoamine oxidase from breaking down neurotransmitters such as norepinephrine, serotonin, and dopamine. A second category of antidepressants that were introduced in the 1950s are the tricyclic antidepressants, including drugs such as imipramine (Tofranil) and amitriptyline (Elavil), which block the reuptake of norepinephrine and serotonin, thereby increasing the amount of neurotransmitter in the synaptic space between neurons. The two classes of antidepressants are used sparingly due to their side effects, which include potentially dangerous increases in blood pressure, constipation, difficulty urinating, blurred vision, and a racing heart (Marangell et al., 2003).

Among the most commonly used antidepressants today are the *selective serotonin reuptake inhibitors,* or SSRIs, which include drugs such as fluoxetine (Prozac), citalopram (Celexa), and paroxetine (Paxil). The SSRIs work by blocking the reuptake of serotonin in the brain, which makes more serotonin available in the synaptic space between neurons. The greater availability of serotonin in the synapse gives the neuron a better chance of "recognizing" and using this neurotransmitter in sending the desired signal. The SSRIs were developed on the basis of the hypothesis that low levels of serotonin are a causal factor in depression. Supporting this hypothesis, SSRIs are effective for depression, as well as for a wide range of other problems. SSRIs are called *selective* because, unlike the tricyclic antidepressants, which work on the serotonin and norepinephrine systems, SSRIs work more specifically on the serotonin system (see **FIGURE 16.3**).

antianxiety medications Drugs that help reduce a person's experience of fear or anxiety.

antidepressants A class of drugs that help lift people's moods.

Figure 16.3

Antidepressant Drug Actions
Antidepressant drugs, such as MAOIs, SSRIs, and tricyclic antidepressants, act on neurotransmitters such as serotonin, dopamine, and norepinephrine by inhibiting their breakdown and blocking reuptake. These actions make more of the neurotransmitter available for release and leave more of the neurotransmitter in the synaptic gap to activate the receptor sites on the postsynaptic neuron. These drugs relieve depression and often alleviate anxiety and other disorders.

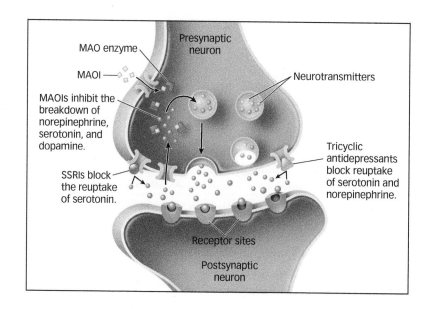

Finally, antidepressants such as venlafaxine (Effexor) and bupropion (Wellbutrin) offer other alternatives. Effexor is an example of a serotonin and norepinephrine reuptake inhibitor (SNRI). Whereas SSRIs act only on serotonin, SNRIs act on both serotonin and norepinephrine. Wellbutrin, in contrast, is a norepinephrine and dopamine reuptake inhibitor. These and other newly developed antidepressants appear to have fewer (or at least different) side effects than the tricyclic antidepressants and MAOIs.

Antidepressants and Anxiety Disorders

Most antidepressants can take up to a month before they start to have an effect on mood. Besides relieving symptoms of depression, almost all of the antidepressants effectively treat anxiety disorders, and many of them can resolve other problems, such as eating disorders. In fact, several companies that manufacture SSRIs have marketed their drugs as treatments for anxiety disorders rather than for their antidepressant effects.

How well do antidepressants work in treating these conditions? Although many studies supported by drug companies show positive results, there is evidence that drug companies are more likely to publish results of studies that suggest their drugs are effective and less likely to publish results that suggest their drugs don't work. In one meta-analysis, researchers found that 100% of studies of antidepressants that found positive results (i.e., results favouring the effectiveness of the drug) were transparently published, compared with only 47% of studies that found negative results (Turner et al., 2022). Researchers who obtained relevant unpublished data held by the U.S. Food and Drug Administration found that when combining *all* available data, antidepressants are only slightly more effective than a placebo (i.e., a sugar pill containing no active medicine) (Kirsch et al., 2008). These authors also found that antidepressants had stronger effects for some types of people. (Check out A World of Difference: Differences in People's Responses to Treatment to learn more.)

Mood Stabilizers Are Used for Bipolar Disorder

Although antidepressants are commonly used to treat major depression, they are not recommended for treating bipolar disorder, which is characterized by manic or hypomanic episodes (see the Psychological Disorders chapter). In this case, antidepressants are not prescribed because, in the process of lifting the person's mood, they might actually trigger a manic episode in a person with bipolar disorder. Instead, bipolar disorder is treated with *mood stabilizers,* which are medications used to suppress swings between mania and depression. Lithium and valproate are commonly used mood stabilizers. Even in unipolar depression, lithium is sometimes effective when combined with traditional antidepressants in people who do not respond to antidepressants alone.

Lithium has proven to be the most effective mood stabilizer currently available (Kessing et al., 2018); however, because it also has been associated with possible long-term kidney and thyroid problems, people taking lithium must monitor their blood levels of lithium on a regular basis. In sum, although antidepressants are effective for a wide variety of problems, mood stabilizers may be required when a person's symptoms include extreme swings between highs and lows, such as those experienced by people with bipolar disorder.

Herbal and Natural Products

A review of studies revealed that among people being treated at outpatient clinics for mental disorders, between 22 and 86% (depending on the study and population examined) reported using herbal or nutritional compounds as an alternative method of treating their condition (Solomon & Adams, 2015). Major reasons people use these products are that they are available over the counter, are less expensive, and are perceived as "natural" alternatives to synthetic or man-made "drugs." Are herbal and natural products effective in treating mental health problems? Or are they just "snake oil"?

The answer to this question isn't simple. Health Canada does not consider herbal and natural products to be drugs, but does consider them to belong to their own category—Natural Health Products—and does impose some regulations to ensure quality and to document side effects. In general, little is known about herbal products, including possible interactions with other medications, possible tolerance and withdrawal symptoms, side effects, appropriate dosages, how they work, or even *whether* they work—and the purity of the products often varies from brand to brand (Jordan et al., 2010).

There is research support for the effectiveness of some herbal and natural products, but the evidence is not overwhelming (Lake, 2009). Products such as inositol (a sugar alcohol), kava (an herb related to black pepper), omega-3 fatty acid (a fish oil), and SAM-e (an amino acid derivative) are sold as health foods and are described as having positive psychological effects of various kinds, but the evidence is mixed. For example, in the case of St. John's wort (a wort, it turns out, is an herb; not to be confused with a wart, which is a small bump on the skin caused by a virus), there was debate for many years about its effectiveness in treating depression, with some trials suggesting it is effective and others finding no effects. Subsequent meta-analyses that pooled and analyzed results from these trials concluded that St. John's wort does appear to be effective in the treatment of depression—about as much so as commonly prescribed antidepressants (Ng et al., 2017). Consumption of omega-3 fatty acids (i.e., fish oils) also have been linked with lower rates of depression and suicide, and several early treatment studies suggested that omega-3s are superior to a placebo at decreasing depression (Lewis et al., 2011; G. Parker et al., 2006). However, larger follow-up studies and meta-analyses reveal that taking omega-3s is no more effective than a placebo at preventing depressive symptoms (Okereke et al., 2021; Suradom et al., 2021) (see **FIGURE 16.4**). Overall, although herbal medications and treatments are worthy of continued research, these products should be closely monitored and used judiciously until more is known about their safety and effectiveness.

Phototherapy, *a therapy that involves repeated exposure to bright light,* is another natural treatment that may be helpful to people who have a seasonal pattern to their depression. This could include people suffering with seasonal affective disorder (SAD) (see the Psychological Disorders chapter), or those who experience depression

phototherapy A therapy that involves repeated exposure to bright light.

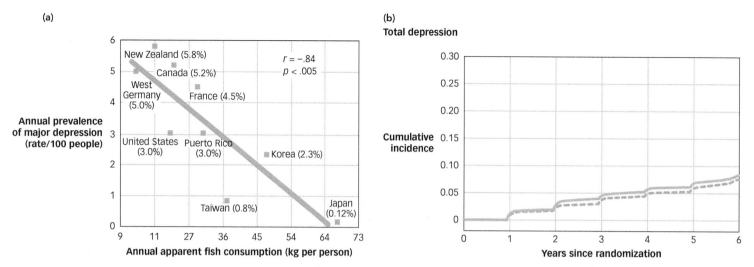

Figure 16.4

Omega-3 Fatty Acids and Depression
(*a*) Observational (correlational) studies have shown that countries that consume more fish (a main dietary source of omega-3s) have significantly lower rates of depression (Hibbeln, 1998). But remember, correlation does not mean causation! It could be that some other factor explains this association. For instance, it could be that living closer to the ocean or a greater focus on health overall predicts both greater omega-3 consumption and lower rates of depression. (*b*) Indeed, an experiment in which people were randomly assigned to receive omega-3s (orange line) or a placebo (dotted line) found that those receiving omega-3s did not have a lower incidence of depression over the next 6 years—they actually showed a slightly higher risk of depression (Okereke et al., 2021).

only in the winter months due to the lack of sunlight. Typically, people are exposed to bright light in the morning using a lamp designed for this purpose. Phototherapy has not been as well researched as psychological treatment or medication, but a recent review of 19 randomized controlled trials (many using dim light as a placebo) suggest that it is an effective treatment of SAD (Pjrek et al., 2020); it also has shown positive effects (and no side effects) in the treatment of nonseasonal depression as well (Perera et al., 2018; Tao et al., 2020).

Combining Medication and Psychotherapy

Given that psychological treatments and medications both have shown an ability to treat mental disorders effectively, some natural next questions are: Which is more effective? Is the combination of psychological and medicinal treatments better than either by itself?

Many studies have compared psychological treatments, medications, and combinations of these approaches for addressing psychological disorders. The studies' results often depend on the particular problem being considered. For example, in the cases of schizophrenia and bipolar disorder, researchers have found that medication is more effective than psychological treatment and so is considered a necessary part of treatment. Recent studies, however, have tended to examine whether adding psychotherapeutic treatments such as social skills training or cognitive behavioural treatment can be helpful. (They can.) In the case of mood and anxiety disorders, medication and psychological treatments are equally effective. One landmark study compared cognitive behaviour therapy (CBT), imipramine (the antidepressant also known as Tofranil), and the combination of these treatments (CBT plus imipramine) with a placebo (administration of an inert medication) for the treatment of panic disorder (Barlow et al., 2000). After 12 weeks of treatment, either CBT alone or imipramine alone was found to be superior to a placebo. For the CBT-plus-imipramine condition, the response rate also exceeded the rate for the placebo but was not significantly better than the rate for either CBT or imipramine alone. In other words, either treatment was better than nothing, but the combination of treatments was not significantly more effective than one or the other (see **FIGURE 16.5**). More is not always better.

Given that both therapy and medications are effective, one question is whether they work through similar mechanisms. A study of people with social phobia examined patterns of cerebral blood flow following treatment in which either citalopram (an SSRI) or CBT were used (Furmark et al., 2002). Participants in both groups were alerted to the possibility that they would soon have to speak in public. In both groups, those who responded to treatment showed decreased activation in the

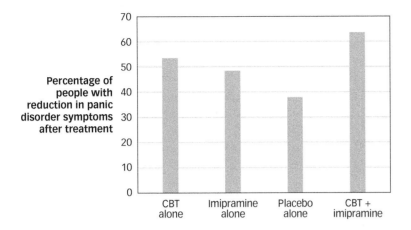

Figure 16.5
The Effectiveness of Medication and Psychotherapy for Panic Disorder One study of CBT and medication (imipramine) for panic disorder found that the effects of CBT, medication, and treatment that combined CBT and medication were not significantly different over the short term, although all three were superior to the placebo condition (Barlow et al., 2000).

amygdala, hippocampus, and neighbouring cortical areas during the public speaking challenge (see **FIGURE 16.6**); the amygdala, located next to the hippocampus (see Figure 6.18) plays a significant role in memory for emotional information. These findings suggest that both therapy and medication affect the brain in regions associated with a reaction to threat. Although we might expect that events that influence the brain should be physical—after all, the brain is a physical object—it is important to keep in mind that environmental learning experiences, such as psychological treatment, produce similar influences on the brain.

One problem in combining medication and psychotherapy is that the two treatments are often provided by different people. Psychiatrists are MDs trained in the administration of medication (although they may also provide psychological treatment), whereas psychologists provide psychological treatment but cannot prescribe medication. Thus, the coordination of treatment often requires cooperation between psychologists and psychiatrists.

The question of whether psychologists should be licensed to prescribe medications has long been a source of debate among psychologists and physicians. Opponents of prescription privileges argue that psychologists do not have the medical training to understand how medications interact with other drugs. Proponents argue that patient safety would not be compromised as long as rigorous training procedures were established. This issue remains a focus of debate, and at present, the coordination of medication and psychological treatment usually involves a team effort of psychiatry and psychology.

Biological Treatments Beyond Medication

Medication can be an effective biological treatment, but for some people medications do not work, or their side effects are intolerable. If these people don't respond to psychotherapy either, what other options do they have for symptom relief? There are additional avenues of help available but some are risky or poorly understood.

Figure 16.6
The Effects of Medication and Therapy in the Brain PET scans of individuals with social phobia showed similar reductions in activation of the amygdala–hippocampus region after they received treatment with CBT (*left*) and with citalopram (*right*), an SSRI (from Furmark et al., 2002).

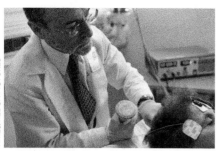

Electroconvulsive therapy (ECT) can be an effective treatment for severe depression. To reduce side effects, it is administered under general anesthesia.

One biological treatment sometimes used to treat severe mental disorders that do not respond to psychological treatment or medication is **electroconvulsive therapy (ECT)**, *a treatment that involves inducing a brief seizure by delivering an electrical shock to the brain;* it is also sometimes referred to as *shock therapy*. The shock is applied to the person's scalp for less than a second. ECT is used primarily to treat severe depression that has not responded to antidepressant medications, and also has been shown to be effective in the treatment of bipolar disorder (Bahji et al., 2019; Milev et al., 2016). People are pretreated with muscle relaxants and are under general anesthetic during treatment, so they are not conscious of the procedure. The main side effect of ECT is impaired short-term memory, which usually improves over the first month or two after the end of treatment. In addition, people sometimes report headaches and muscle aches afterward. Despite these side effects, the treatment can be helpful: It is more effective than simulated ECT, a placebo, and antidepressant drugs such as tricyclics and MAOIs (Pagnin et al., 2008).

Another biological approach that does not involve medication is **transcranial magnetic stimulation (TMS)**, *a treatment that involves placing a powerful pulsed magnet over a person's scalp to alter neuronal activity in the brain.* When TMS is used as a treatment for depression, the magnet is placed just above the right or left eyebrow in an effort to stimulate the right or left prefrontal cortex (areas of the brain implicated in depression). TMS is an exciting development because it is noninvasive and has fewer side effects than ECT (see the Neuroscience and Behaviour chapter). Side effects are minimal; they include mild headache and a small risk of seizure, but TMS has no impact on memory or concentration. TMS applied daily to the left prefrontal cortex for 4 to 6 weeks has been found to be effective in treating depression in people who have not responded to medication (Perera et al., 2016). In fact, a study comparing TMS with ECT found that both procedures were effective, with no significant differences between them (Janicak et al., 2002). Other studies have found that TMS can also be used to treat auditory hallucinations in people with schizophrenia (Aleman et al., 2007).

In very rare cases, **psychosurgery**, *the surgical destruction of specific brain areas,* may be used to treat severe and unresponsive psychological disorders. Psychosurgery has a controversial history, beginning in the 1930s with the invention of the lobotomy by the Portuguese physician Antonio Egas Moniz (1874–1955). After discovering that certain surgical procedures on animal brains calmed behaviour, Moniz began to use similar techniques on violent or agitated human patients. Lobotomies involved inserting an instrument into the brain through the patient's eye socket or through holes drilled in the side of the head. The objective was to sever connections between the frontal lobes and inner brain structures, such as the thalamus, known to be involved in emotion.

Although some lobotomies produced highly successful results and Moniz received the 1949 Nobel Prize for his work, significant side effects, such as extreme lethargy or childlike impulsiveness, detracted from these benefits. Lobotomy was used widely for years despite this, leaving many people devastated by these permanent side effects; because of this, for many years there was a movement challenging the awarding of the Nobel Prize to Moniz. (It was never revoked.) The development of antipsychotic drugs during the 1950s provided a safer way to treat violent individuals, and the practice of lobotomy was brought to an end (Swayze, 1995).

Psychosurgery is rarely used these days and is reserved for extremely severe cases for which no other interventions have been effective, and when the symptoms of the disorder are intolerable to the affected person. For instance, psychosurgery is sometimes used in severe cases of obsessive-compulsive disorder (OCD) in which the person is completely unable to function in daily life, and psychological treatment and medication are not effective. In contrast to the earlier days of lobotomy, when broad regions of brain tissue were destroyed, modern psychosurgery involves a very precise destruction of brain tissue in order to disrupt the brain circuits known to be involved in generating obsessions and compulsions. This increased precision has produced better results. For example, people suffering from OCD who fail to respond to treatment (including several trials of medication and cognitive

electroconvulsive therapy (ECT) A treatment that involves inducing a brief seizure by delivering an electrical shock to the brain.

transcranial magnetic stimulation (TMS) A treatment that involves placing a powerful pulsed magnet over a person's scalp to alter neuronal activity in the brain.

psychosurgery Surgical destruction of specific brain areas.

Transcranial magnetic stimulation (TMS) is a technique that allows researchers and clinicians to change brain activity using a magnetic wand—no surgery is required.

behavioural therapy) may benefit from specific surgical procedures called *cingulotomy* and *anterior capsulotomy*. Cingulotomy involves destroying part of the corpus callosum (see Figure 3.15) and the cingulate gyrus (the ridge just above the corpus callosum). Anterior capsulotomy involves creating small lesions to disrupt the pathway between the caudate nucleus and the putamen. Because of the relatively small number of cases of psychosurgery, there are not as many studies of these techniques as there are for other treatments. However, available studies have shown that psychosurgery typically leads to substantial improvements in both the short and long term for people with severe OCD (Csigó et al., 2010; van Vliet et al., 2013).

A final approach, called *deep brain stimulation* (DBS), combines the use of psychosurgery with electrical currents (as in ECT and TMS). In DBS, a treatment pioneered only recently, a small, battery-powered device is implanted in the person's body to deliver electrical stimulation to specific areas of the brain known to be involved in the disorder being targeted (**FIGURE 16.7**). This technique has been successful for OCD treatment (Abelson et al., 2009) and can also provide benefits for people with a variety of neurologic conditions. The tremor that accompanies Parkinson's disease has proven to be treatable in this way (Perlmutter & Mink, 2006), as have some cases of severe depression that were otherwise untreatable (Mayberg et al., 2005). Moreover,

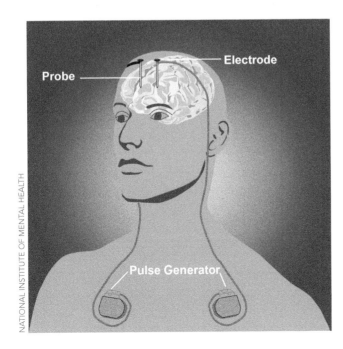

Figure 16.7

DBS Deep brain stimulation involves the insertion of battery-powered electrodes that deliver electrical pulses to specific areas of the brain believed to be causing a person's mental disorder.

A World of Difference | Differences in People's Responses to Treatment

We are all different. We like different foods, different music, different books, and so on. It turns out that we also differ in how we respond to treatments for psychological disorders. For instance, one recent study compared the decrease in symptoms of depression seen in 718 people randomly assigned to receive either antidepressant medication or a placebo pill (Fournier et al., 2010). Participants receiving the real medication showed a dramatic decrease in symptoms over the course of treatment. However, so did those taking a placebo. Closer examination of the data revealed that for those with mild or moderate depression, a placebo is just as effective as antidepressant medication at decreasing

a person's symptoms; it is only for people with severe depression that antidepressants seem to work better than a placebo (see figure).

More recent research is examining further what predicts which kind of people will respond best to which kind of treatment. For instance, one study by Robert DeRubeis and colleagues (2014) found that data collected before people are randomized to a given treatment (e.g., cognitive behavioural therapy vs. medication) could be used to predict accurately which treatment would benefit them most. A follow-up study by DeRubeis and colleagues found a similar result when they compared two other kinds of treatment (i.e., cognitive therapy and interpersonal

psychotherapy; Huibers et al., 2015). In this study, people who were randomly assigned to the treatment that was predicted to be more effective for them improved significantly more than those assigned to their nonoptimal treatment. Such findings suggest that in the future, psychologists will be able to collect information from new individuals with depression that will help them determine which of the many available treatments will benefit a particular individual the most. This personalized, or tailored, approach to treatment is likely to lead to much better outcomes for users of psychological services in the future, and in this way is expected to make a world of difference!

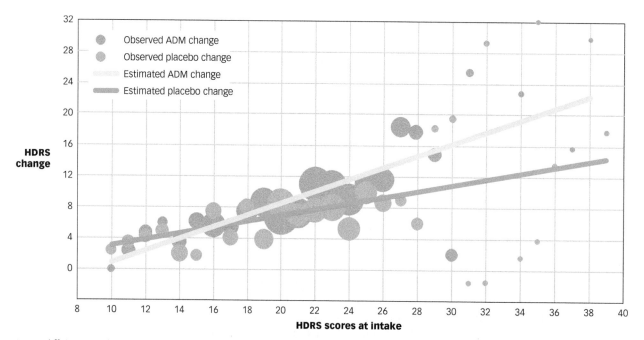

In six different studies, a total of 713 depressed individuals were given pills to treat their depression. Half were randomly assigned to receive an antidepressant medication (ADM) and half to receive a pill placebo. Importantly, the participants did not know if they were taking an antidepressant or simply a placebo. For those with mild or moderate depression, as measured by the Hamilton Depression Rating Scale (HDRS), antidepressants did not work any better than the placebo. However, those with severe depression showed much greater improvement on antidepressants than on the placebo. The circle size represents the number of people with data at each point (data from Fournier et al., 2010). The green and blue lines indicate the symptom severity (HDRS score) that would be predicted given a particular HDRS score when first assessed (at intake). A higher score indicates more severe depression. These lines are based on the observed data. As you can see, for an HDRS score of about 18 or greater at the time of intake, the antidepressant medication (line in green) is expected to result in a greater improvement than the placebo (line in blue).

the effects of DBS have been shown to persist across greater than 8 years of follow-up (Crowell et al., 2019). The early view of psychosurgery as a treatment of last resort is being replaced by a hope that newer, focused treatments that target brain circuits known to be functioning abnormally in those with certain mental disorders can have beneficial effects (Ramirez-Zamora et al., 2020).

Treatment Effectiveness: For Better or For Worse

Think back to Christine and the dead mouse at the beginning of this chapter. What if, instead of exposure and response prevention, Christine had been treated with psychoanalysis or psychosurgery? Would those alternatives have been just as effective for treating her OCD? Throughout this chapter, we have explored various psychological and biological treatments that might help people with psychological disorders. But do these treatments actually work? Which ones work better than the others?

As you learned in the Methods in Psychology chapter, pinning down a specific cause for an effect can be a difficult detective exercise. Detection is made even more difficult because clients and doctors may approach treatment evaluation very unscientifically, often by simply noticing an improvement (or no improvement, or even a worsening of symptoms) and reaching a conclusion based on that sole observation. Determining a treatment's effectiveness can be misdirected by illusions that can only be overcome by careful, scientific evaluation.

Learning Outcomes

WHAT YOU NEED TO KNOW

- Describe treatment illusions.
- Explain research methods used in treatment studies.
- Explain the criteria used to determine a treatment's effectiveness.

Treatment Illusions

Imagine you're sick and the doctor says, "Take this pill." You follow the doctor's orders and you get better. To what do you attribute your improvement? One possibility is that the pill cured you, but there are at least three other explanations: Maybe you would have gotten better naturally; maybe it was your expectation that the pill would be helpful is what led to your feeling better; or maybe you weren't really feeling that bad and after taking the pill you mistakenly remember being more ill than you really were. These possibilities point to three potential illusions of treatment: that improvements were produced by natural improvement, by placebo effects, and by reconstructive memory.

Natural Improvement

Natural improvement is the tendency of symptoms to return to their mean or average level. The illusion in this case happens when you conclude, mistakenly, that a treatment has made you better when you would have gotten better anyway. People typically turn to therapy or medication when their symptoms are at their worst. When this is the case, the client's symptoms will often improve regardless of whether there was any treatment at all; when you're at rock bottom, there's nowhere to move but up. In most cases, for example, depression that becomes severe enough to make individuals candidates for treatment will tend to lift in several months *no matter what they do*. A person who enters therapy for depression may develop the illusion that the therapy works because the therapy coincides with the typical course of the illness and the person's natural return to health. How can we know a treatment is effective, or if the change we observe following that treatment is caused by natural improvement? As discussed in the Methods in Psychology chapter, we could do an experiment in which we assign half of the people who are depressed to receive treatment and the other half to receive no treatment, and then monitor them over time to see if the ones who got treatment actually show greater improvement. This is precisely how researchers test out different interventions, as described in more detail below.

Placebo Effects

Recovery also could be the result of *nonspecific treatment effects* that are not related to the proposed active ingredient of the treatment. For example, the doctor prescribing the medication might simply be a pleasant and hopeful individual who gives the client a sense of hope or optimism that things will improve. Client and doctor alike might attribute the client's improvement to the effects of medication on the brain, whereas the true active ingredient was the warm relationship with the doctor or an improved outlook on life.

"If this doesn't help you don't worry, it's a placebo."

PETER C. VEY/CARTOON STOCK

Simply knowing that you are getting a treatment can be a nonspecific treatment effect. These instances include the positive influences that can be produced by a **placebo**, *an inert substance or procedure that has been applied with the expectation that it will produce a healing response.* For example, if you have a headache and take a sugar pill that does not contain any painkiller, thinking it is Tylenol or aspirin, the pill is a placebo if the headache goes away. Placebos can have profound effects in the case of psychological treatments. Research shows that a large percentage of individuals with anxiety, depression, and other emotional and medical problems experience significant improvement after a placebo treatment (see A World of Difference: Differences in People's Responses to Treatment).

Reconstructive Memory

A third treatment illusion can come about when the client's motivation to get well causes errors in *reconstructive memory* for the original symptoms. You might think that you've improved because of a treatment when in fact you're simply misremembering, mistakenly believing that your symptoms before treatment were worse than they actually were. This tendency was first observed in research that examined the effectiveness of a study skills class (Conway & Ross, 1984). Some students who wanted to take the class were enrolled, while others were randomly assigned to a waiting list until the class could be offered again. When their study abilities were measured afterward, those students who took the class were no better at studying than their wait-listed counterparts. However, those who took the class *said* that they had improved. How could this be? Those participants recalled their study skills before the class as being worse than they had actually been. Conway and Ross (1984) dubbed this motivated reconstruction of the past "Getting What You Want by Revising What You Had." Applying that kind of reconstructive memory to psychology, a client who forms a strong expectation of therapy success might later conclude that even a useless treatment had worked wonders by recalling past symptoms and troubles as worse than they had been, which would make the treatment seem effective.

Treatment Studies: Seeking Evidence

How can we make sure that we use treatments that actually work and not waste time with procedures that may be useless or even harmful? Research psychologists use approaches covered in the Methods in Psychology chapter to run experiments that

placebo An inert substance or procedure that has been applied with the expectation that it will produce a healing response.

test which treatments are effective for the different mental disorders described in the Psychological Disorders chapter.

Treatment outcome studies are designed to evaluate whether a particular treatment works to decrease a person's symptoms. For example, let's say that you have a new treatment for depression. How can you know if it works? One possibility is to recruit a sample of people with depression and administer your treatment. If after, say, 6 weeks, the people in your study report being less depressed, you might want to conclude that it was your treatment that caused changes in the experienced depression. However, how can you know that it was your treatment and not one of the treatment illusions described above, such as natural improvement or reconstructive memory, that were responsible? Indeed, we do know that people tend to come in for treatment when their symptoms are most severe, and that after some period of time symptoms of depression will often decrease naturally without any treatment.

Researchers use different types of control conditions to test the extent to which we can conclude that the observed changes in symptoms were due to the treatment rather than some alternative explanation. For example, we can rule out that the observed changes were due simply to the passage of time by randomly assigning half of our people with depression to 6 weeks of our preferred treatment and the other half to a 6-week no-treatment control condition. Comparing the change in the depressive symptoms of both groups, we can learn how much more of a change in depressive symptoms was caused by the treatment compared to the control condition.

On the other hand, we also know that receiving any treatment can cause a change in symptoms via the placebo effect. To rule out that the observed changes are due to such an effect, we can randomly assign half of our depressed group to our preferred treatment, and the other half to another condition that *appears* to be an effective treatment. Ideally, a treatment should be assessed in a *double-blind experiment*, a study in which neither the participant nor the researcher/therapist knows which treatment the participant is receiving. In drug studies, this isn't hard to arrange because active drugs and placebos can be made to look the same to both the participants and the researchers during the study. Keeping all involved "in the dark" is much harder in the study of psychological treatments. Nevertheless, by comparing treatments either with no treatment or with other active interventions (such as other psychological treatments or medications), researchers can determine which treatments work, and which are most effective for different disorders.

Which Treatments Work According to the Evidence?

Back in 1957, psychologist Hans Eysenck (1916–1997) reviewed the relatively few studies of psychotherapy's effectiveness available at the time and raised a furor among therapists by concluding that psychotherapy—particularly psychoanalysis—was not only ineffective but seemed to *impede* recovery (Eysenck, 1957). Much larger numbers of studies that have been examined statistically since then support a more optimistic conclusion: Studies have suggested for decades that the typical psychotherapy client is better off than three-quarters of untreated individuals (Seligman, 1995; Smith et al., 1980). Although critiques of psychotherapy research point out weaknesses in how clients are tested, diagnosed, and treated (Baker et al., 2009; Dawes, 1994), strong evidence generally supports the effectiveness of many different treatments (Hunsley et al., 2014). The key question then becomes: Which treatments are effective for which problems (Kessler & Luedtke, 2021)?

One of the most enduring debates in clinical psychology concerns how the various psychotherapies compare with each other. Some psychologists have argued for years that evidence supports the conclusion that most psychotherapies work about equally well. In this view, common factors shared by all forms of psychotherapy, such as contact with and empathy from a professional, contribute to change (Luborsky et al., 2002). In contrast, others have argued that there are important differences among therapies and that certain treatments are more effective than others, especially for treating particular types of problems. Studies of children, adolescents, and adults have revealed that for depression and anxiety, for example, cognitive behavioural therapy (CBT) and interpersonal psychotherapy (IPT) lead to significantly better outcomes than do other approaches (Tolin, 2010; Zhou et al., 2015). How can we make sense of these differing perspectives?

In 1995, the American Psychological Association (APA) published one of the first attempts to define criteria for determining whether a particular type of psychotherapy is effective for a particular problem (Task Force on Promotion and Dissemination of Psychological Procedures, 1995). The Canadian Psychological Association (CPA) followed, generally endorsing the APA guidelines, and elaborating upon them in a Canadian context ("Empirically Supported Treatments: Recommendations for Canadian Professional Psychology") in 1998. The official criteria for empirically validated treatments defined two levels of empirical support: *well-established treatments,* those with a high level of support (e.g., evidence from several randomized controlled trials); and *probably efficacious treatments,* those with preliminary support. After these criteria were established, the APA published a list of empirically supported treatments (Chambless et al., 1998; Woody & Sanderson, 1998). More recent reviews have highlighted several specific psychological treatments that have been shown to work as well as, or even better than, other available treatments, including medication (Barlow et al., 2013). **TABLE 16.3** lists several of these treatments.

Some researchers and clinicians have questioned whether treatments shown to work in well-controlled studies conducted at university clinics will work in the real world. For instance, some psychologists have noted that most treatment studies reported in the literature do not have large numbers of ethnic minority participants, and so it is unclear if these treatments will work with ethnically and culturally diverse groups. A review of available data suggests that despite gaps in the literature, current evidence-based psychological treatments work as well with ethnic minority clients as with white clients (Miranda et al., 2005; Pina et al., 2019).

TABLE 16.3

SELECTED LIST OF SPECIFIC PSYCHOLOGICAL TREATMENTS COMPARED WITH MEDICATION OR OTHER TREATMENTS

Disorder	Treatment	Results
Depression	CBT	PT = meds; PT + meds > either alone
Panic disorder	CBT	PT > meds at follow-up; PT = meds at end of treatment; both > placebo
Posttraumatic stress disorder	CBT	PT > present-centred therapy
Insomnia	CBT	PT > medication or placebo
Depression and physical health in Alzheimer's patients	Exercise and behavioural management	PT > routine medical care
Gulf War veterans' illnesses	CBT and exercise	PT > Usual care or alternative treatments

Note: CBT = cognitive behaviour therapy; PT = psychological treatment; Meds = medication.

Information from Barlow et al. (2013).

Treatments shown to be effective in research studies (which often include only a small percentage of individuals from equity-deserving groups) have been found to work equally well with people of different backgrounds and cultures (Miranda et al., 2005).

Even trickier than the question of establishing whether a treatment works is whether a form of psychotherapy or a medication might actually do harm. The dangers of drug treatment should be clear to anyone who has read a magazine ad for a drug and studied the fine print, with its list of side effects, potential drug interactions, and complications. Some drugs used in psychological treatment can be addictive, creating long-term dependency and serious withdrawal symptoms. The strongest critics of drug treatment claim that drugs do no more than trade one unwanted symptom for another: trading depression for lack of sexual interest, trading anxiety for intoxication, or trading agitation for lethargy and dulled emotion (Moncrieff, 2018).

The dangers of psychotherapy are more subtle, but one is clear enough in some cases that there is actually a name for it. **Iatrogenic illness** is *a disorder or symptom that occurs as a result of a medical or psychotherapeutic treatment itself* (Boisvert & Faust, 2002). Such an illness might arise, for instance, when a psychotherapist becomes convinced that a client has a disorder that in fact the client does not have. As a result, the therapist works to help the client accept that diagnosis and participate in psychotherapy to treat the disorder. Being treated for a disorder can, under certain conditions, make a person show signs of that very disorder—and so an iatrogenic illness is born.

In some cases, clients who have been influenced through hypnosis and/or repeated suggestions in therapy come to believe that they have dissociative identity disorder (even coming to express multiple personalities) or to believe that they were subjected to traumatic events as a child and then "recover" memories of such events when an investigation reveals no evidence for these problems prior to therapy (McNally, 2003). Some people enter therapy with a vague sense that something odd has happened to them; after hypnosis or other imagination-enhancing techniques they emerge with the conviction that their therapist's theory was right: They *were* abducted by space aliens (Clancy, 2005). Needless to say, a therapy that leads clients to develop such bizarre beliefs does more harm than good.

Just as psychologists have created lists of treatments that work, they have also begun to establish lists of treatments that *harm*. The purpose of doing so is to inform other researchers, clinicians, and the public which treatments they should avoid. Many people are under the impression that although every psychological treatment may not be effective, some treatment is better than no treatment. However, it turns out that a number of interventions intended to help alleviate people's symptoms actually make them worse! Did your high school have a D.A.R.E. (Drug Abuse and Resistance Education) program? Have you heard of critical-incident stress debriefing (CISD), Scared Straight, and boot-camp programs? They all sound as if they might work, but careful scientific experiments have determined that people who participate in these interventions are actually worse off afterward (see **TABLE 16.4**) (Lilienfeld, 2007)!

iatrogenic illness A disorder or symptom that occurs as a result of a medical or psychotherapeutic treatment itself.

TABLE 16.4

SOME PSYCHOLOGICAL TREATMENTS THAT CAUSE HARM

Type of Treatment	Potential Harm	Source of Evidence
CISD	Increased risk of PTSD	RCTs
Scared Straight	Worsening of conduct problems	RCTs
Boot-camp interventions for conduct problems	Worsening of conduct problems	Meta-analysis (review of studies)
DARE programs	Increased use of alcohol and drugs	RCTs

Note: CISD = critical-incident stress debriefing; PTSD = posttraumatic stress disorder; RCTs = randomized controlled trials.

Information from Lilienfeld (2007).

To regulate the potentially powerful influence of different therapies, psychologists hold themselves to a set of ethical standards for the treatment of people with mental disorders (American Psychological Association, 2017). Adherence to these standards is required for membership in the American and Canadian Psychological Associations, and provincial and territorial regulatory bodies also monitor adherence to ethical principles in therapy. The ethical standards in Canada are based on four principles: (1) respect for the dignity of persons, which includes protecting the welfare of vulnerable people and seeking fairness in treatment and avoiding biases; (2) responsible caring, which includes striving to benefit clients and taking care to do no harm; (3) integrity in relationships (promoting accuracy, honesty, and truthfulness); and (4) responsibility to society, which means that when psychological knowledge is used in the development of social policies, it will only be used for beneficial purposes (i.e., those that reflect the first three principles). When people suffering from mental disorders come to psychologists for help, adhering to these guidelines is the least that psychologists can do. Ideally, in the hope of relieving suffering, they can do much more.

Chapter Review

Treatment: Getting Help to Those Who Need It

- Mental illness is often misunderstood, and because of this, it too often goes untreated.

- Untreated mental illness can be extremely costly, not only affecting an individual's ability to function but also causing social and financial burdens.

- Many people who suffer from mental illness do not get the help they need: They may be unaware that they have a problem, they may be uninterested in getting help for their problem, or they may face structural barriers to getting treatment.

- Treatments include psychotherapy, which focuses on the mind; medical and biological methods, which focus on the brain and body; and the combination of the two approaches.

Psychological Treatments: Healing Through Human Interaction

- Psychodynamic therapies, including psychoanalysis, emphasize helping clients gain insight into their unconscious conflicts. Traditional psychoanalysis involves four to five treatment sessions per week, with the client lying on a couch and free-associating; modern psychodynamic therapies involve one session per week with face-to-face interactions in which therapists help clients solve interpersonal problems.

- Humanistic approaches (e.g., person-centred therapy) and existential approaches (e.g., gestalt therapy) focus on helping people develop a sense of personal worth.

- Behaviour therapy applies learning principles to specific behaviour problems.

- Cognitive therapy is focused on helping people change the way they think about events in their lives, and teaching them to challenge irrational thoughts.

- Cognitive behaviour therapy (CBT), which merges cognitive and behavioural approaches, has been shown to be effective for treating a wide range of psychological disorders.

- Group therapies target couples, families, or groups of clients brought together for the purpose of working together to solve their problems.

- Self-help and support groups, such as AA, are common in the United States and around the world but are not well studied.

Biological Treatments: Healing Through Physical Alteration of the Brain

- Antipsychotic medications block dopamine receptors in parts of the brain, thus reducing dopamine activity. They are used to treat the positive symptoms of schizophrenia.

- Antianxiety medications are used to treat anxiety disorders but have the potential for abuse, especially because of the development of drug tolerance.

- Antidepressants affect the level of serotonin in the brain and are used to treat depression and related disorders.

- Herbal and natural products are not considered medications by regulatory agencies and so are not subject to strict scrutiny. Although there is little scientific information on their effectiveness, some do seem to have mild positive effects.

- Medications are often combined with psychotherapy in treatment. Evidence from a study on social phobia suggests that both affect the brain in regions associated with threat.

- Other biomedical treatments include electroconvulsive therapy (ECT), transcranial magnetic stimulation (TMS), deep brain stimulation (DBS), and psychosurgery—this last used in extreme cases, when other methods of treatment have been exhausted.

Treatment Effectiveness: For Better or For Worse

- Observing improvement during treatment does not necessarily mean that the treatment was effective; it might instead reflect natural improvement, nonspecific treatment effects (e.g., the placebo effect), and reconstructive memory processes.

- Treatment studies focus on both treatment outcomes and processes, applying scientific research methods such as placebo controls and double-blind techniques.

- Treatments for psychological disorders are generally more effective than no treatment at all, but some (e.g., cognitive behaviour therapy and interpersonal psychotherapy) are more effective than others for certain disorders; both medication and psychotherapy have dangers that ethical practitioners must consider carefully.

Changing Minds

1. One of your friends recently lost a close family member in a tragic car accident, and they are devastated. Your friend hasn't been attending classes, and when you check up on them you learn that they are not sleeping well or eating regularly. You want to help your friend but feel out of your depth. You suggest your friend visit the campus counselling centre and talk to a therapist. "Only crazy people go to therapy," your friend says. What could you tell your friend to dispel this wrong assumption?

2. While you're talking to your bereaved friend, your friend's roommate comes in. The roommate agrees with your suggestion about therapy but takes it further. "I'll give you the name of my therapist. He helped me quit smoking—he'll be able to cure your depression in no time." Why is it dangerous to assume that a good therapist can cure anyone and anything?

3. In the Methods in Psychology chapter you read about Louise Hay, whose best-selling book, *You Can Heal Your Life,* promotes a kind of psychotherapy: teaching readers how to change their thoughts and thereby improve not only their inner lives but also their physical health. The chapter quotes Hay as saying that scientific evidence is unnecessary to validate her claims. Is her view correct? Is there a scientific basis for the major types of psychotherapy described in this chapter? How is scientific experimentation used to assess their effectiveness?

4. In June 2009, the pop icon Michael Jackson died from a fatal dose of the anesthetic propofol, which is sometimes used off-label as an antianxiety drug. An autopsy confirmed that his body contained a cocktail of prescription drugs, including the benzodiazepines lorazepam and diazepam. (Jackson's cardiologist, Dr. Conrad Murray, was later convicted of involuntary manslaughter for administering the fatal propofol dose.) Other celebrities whose deaths have been attributed to medications commonly prescribed for anxiety and depression include Prince in 2016, Mac Miller in 2018, and Juice WRLD in 2019. "These drugs are dangerous," your roommate notes. "People who have psychological problems should seek out talk therapy for their problems and stay away from the medications, even if they're prescribed by a responsible doctor." You agree that medications can be dangerous if misused, but how would you justify the use of drug treatment for serious mental disorders?

5. **Visualizing Data** A classmate says that after drugs are developed to treat certain disorders, the incidents of those disorders skyrockets as doctors find reasons to prescribe them. Review the DATA for ADHD and see if the results support that suggestion.

Key Terms

psychotherapy (p. 596)

eclectic psychotherapy
(p. 596)

psychodynamic
psychotherapies (p. 596)

interpersonal psychotherapy
(IPT) (p. 597)

person-centred therapy (or
client-centred therapy)
(p. 598

gestalt therapy (p. 598)

behaviour therapy (p. 599)

token economy (p. 599)

exposure therapy (p. 600)

cognitive therapy (p. 601)

cognitive restructuring
(p. 601)

mindfulness meditation
(p. 603)

cognitive behavioural
therapy (CBT) (p. 603)

group therapy (p. 604)

antipsychotic drugs (p. 608)

psychopharmacology
(p. 608)

antianxiety medications
(p. 609)

antidepressants (p. 609)

phototherapy (p. 611)

electroconvulsive therapy
(ECT) (p. 614)

transcranial magnetic
stimulation (TMS)
(p. 614)

psychosurgery (p. 614)

placebo (p. 618)

iatrogenic illness (p. 621)

GLOSSARY

absentmindedness A lapse in attention that results in memory failure.

absolute threshold The minimal intensity needed to just barely detect a stimulus in 50% of trials.

accommodation The process of adjusting a schema to incorporate new information.

accommodation The process whereby the eye maintains a clear image on the retina.

acetylcholine (ACh) A neurotransmitter involved in a number of functions, including voluntary motor control.

achievement motivation The desire to experience a sense of accomplishment by meeting one's goals.

acquisition The phase of classical conditioning when the CS and the US are presented together.

action potential An electric signal that is conducted along the length of a neuron's axon to a synapse.

action tendencies A readiness to engage in a specific set of emotion-relevant behaviours.

activation–synthesis model The theory that dreams are produced when the brain attempts to make sense of random neural activity that occurs during sleep.

actor–observer effect The tendency to make situational attributions for our own behaviours while making dispositional attributions for the identical behaviour of others.

acuity How well we can distinguish two very similar stimuli.

adolescence The period of development that begins with the onset of sexual maturity (about 11 to 14 years of age) and lasts until the beginning of adulthood (about 18 to 21 years of age).

adulthood The stage of development that begins around 18 to 21 years and lasts for the remainder of life.

aggression Behaviour whose purpose is to harm another.

agonists Drugs that increase the action of a neurotransmitter.

agoraphobia A specific phobia involving a fear of public places.

alcohol myopia A condition that results when alcohol hampers attention, leading people to respond in simple ways to complex situations.

algorithm A well-defined sequence of procedures or rules that guarantees a solution to a problem.

altered state of consciousness A form of experience that departs significantly from the normal subjective experience of the world and the mind.

altruism Intentional behaviour that benefits another at a potential cost to oneself.

amygdala Located at the tip of each horn of the hippocampus; plays a central role in many emotional processes, particularly the formation of emotional memories.

analogical problem solving The process of solving a problem by finding a similar problem with a known solution and applying that solution to the current problem.

anorexia nervosa An eating disorder characterized by an intense fear of being overweight and a severe restriction of food intake.

antagonists Drugs that diminish the function of a neurotransmitter.

anterograde amnesia The inability to transfer new information from the short-term store into the long-term store.

antianxiety medications Drugs that help reduce a person's experience of fear or anxiety.

antidepressants A class of drugs that help lift people's moods.

antipsychotic drugs Medications that are used to treat schizophrenia and related psychotic disorders.

antisocial personality disorder (APD) A pervasive pattern of disregard for and violation of the rights of others that begins in childhood or early adolescence and continues into adulthood.

anxiety disorder The class of mental disorders in which anxiety is the predominant feature.

aphasia Difficulty in producing or comprehending language.

apparent motion The perception of movement as a result of alternating signals appearing in rapid succession in different locations.

appraisal Conscious or unconscious evaluation and interpretations of the emotion-relevant aspects of a stimulus or event.

approach motivation The motivation to experience positive outcomes.

area A1 The primary auditory cortex in the temporal lobe.

area V1 The part of the occipital lobe that contains the primary visual cortex.

assimilation The process of applying a schema to novel stimuli.

association areas Composed of neurons that help provide sense and meaning to information registered in the cortex.

attachment The emotional bond with a primary caregiver.

attachment styles Characteristic patterns of reacting to the presence and absence of one's primary caregiver.

attention deficit/hyperactivity disorder (ADHD) A persistent pattern of severe problems with inattention and/or hyperactivity or impulsiveness that cause significant impairments in functioning.

attention The active and conscious processing of particular information.

attitude An enduring positive or negative evaluation of a stimulus.

attribution An inference about the cause of a person's behaviour.

autism spectrum disorder (ASD) A condition beginning in early childhood in which a person shows persistent communication deficits as well as restricted and repetitive patterns of behaviours, interests, or activities.

autonomic nervous system (ANS) A set of nerves that carries involuntary and automatic commands that control blood vessels, body organs, and glands.

availability heuristic A rule of thumb that items that are more readily available in memory are judged as having occurred more frequently.

avoidance motivation The motivation to avoid experiencing negative outcomes.

axon Carries information to other neurons, muscles, or glands.

balanced placebo design A study design in which behaviour is observed following the presence or absence of an actual stimulus and also following the presence or absence of a placebo stimulus.

basal ganglia A set of subcortical structures that directs intentional movements and plays a role in reward processing.

basilar membrane A structure in the inner ear that moves up and down in time with vibrations relayed from the ossicles, transmitted through the oval window.

behaviour therapy A type of therapy that assumes that disordered behaviour is learned and that symptom relief is achieved through changing overt, maladaptive behaviours into more constructive behaviours.

behavioural confirmation The tendency of targets to behave as observers expect them to behave.

behavioural neuroscience The study of the relationship between the brain and behaviour (especially in nonhuman animals).

behaviourism An approach to psychology that restricts scientific inquiry to observable behaviour.

belief An enduring piece of knowledge about a stimulus.

belief bias The idea that people's judgements about whether to accept conclusions depend more on how believable the conclusions are than on whether the arguments are logically valid.

bias The distorting influences of present knowledge, beliefs, and feelings on recollection of previous experiences.

Big Five The traits of the five-factor model: openness to experience, conscientiousness, extraversion, agreeableness, and neuroticism.

binding problem How the brain links features so that we see unified objects in our visual world rather than free-floating or miscombined features.

binge eating disorder (BED) An eating disorder characterized by recurrent and uncontrolled episodes of eating a large number of calories in a short time.

binocular disparity The difference in the retinal images of the two eyes that provides information about depth.

biofeedback The use of an external monitoring device to obtain information about a bodily function and then to possibly gain control over that function.

biological motion perception The ability to perceive biological motion critical for identifying individuals and various socially relevant features.

biological preparedness A propensity for learning particular kinds of associations over other kinds.

biopsychosocial perspective Explains mental disorders as the result of interactions among biological, psychological, and social factors.

bipolar disorder A condition characterized by cycles of abnormal, persistent high mood (mania) and low mood (depression).

blind spot A location in the visual field that produces no sensation on the retina.

blocking A failure to retrieve information that is available in memory even though you are trying to produce it.

bulimia nervosa An eating disorder characterized by binge eating followed by compensatory behaviour.

burnout A state of physical, emotional, and mental exhaustion resulting from long-term involvement in an emotionally demanding situation; accompanied by lowered performance and motivation.

bystander effect The tendency for people to be less likely to help a stranger in an emergency situation when other bystanders are present.

case method A procedure for gathering scientific information by studying a single individual.

catatonic behaviour A marked decrease in all movement or an increase in muscular rigidity and overactivity.

category-based inferences Inferences based on information about the categories to which a person belongs.

category-specific deficit A neurological syndrome characterized by an inability to recognize objects that belong to a particular category, even when the ability to recognize objects outside the category is undisturbed.

cell body (soma) Component of the neuron that coordinates information-processing tasks and keeps the cell alive.

central nervous system (CNS) Composed of the brain and spinal cord.

central-route persuasion The process by which attitudes or beliefs are changed by appeals to reason.

cephalocaudal principle The "top-to-bottom" principle that describes the tendency for motor skills to emerge in sequence from the head to the feet.

cerebellum A large structure of the hindbrain that controls fine motor skills.

cerebral cortex The outermost layer of the brain, visible to the naked eye and divided into two hemispheres.

change blindness Failure to detect changes to the visual details of a scene.

childhood The period that begins at about age 18 to 24 months and lasts until about age 11 to 14 years.

chromosomes Strands of DNA wound around each other in a double-helix configuration.

chronic stressors Sources of stress that occur continuously or repeatedly.

chunking Combining small pieces of information into larger clusters or chunks that are more easily held in short-term memory.

circadian rhythm A naturally occurring 24-hour cycle.

classical conditioning A type of learning that occurs when a neutral stimulus produces a response after being paired with a stimulus that naturally produces a response.

cochlea A fluid-filled tube that contains cells that transduce sound vibrations into neural impulses.

cocktail-party phenomenon A phenomenon in which people tune in one message even while they filter out others nearby.

cognitive behavioural therapy (CBT) A blend of cognitive and behavioural therapeutic strategies.

cognitive development The process by which infants and children gain the ability to think and understand.

cognitive dissonance An unpleasant state that arises when a person recognizes the inconsistency of their actions, attitudes, or beliefs.

cognitive enhancers Drugs that improve the psychological processes that underlie intelligent performance.

cognitive map A mental representation of the physical features of the environment.

cognitive neuroscience The study of the relationship between the brain and the mind (especially in humans).

cognitive psychology The study of human information processing.

cognitive restructuring A therapeutic approach that teaches clients to question the automatic beliefs, assumptions, and predictions that often lead to negative emotions and to replace negative thinking with more realistic and positive beliefs.

cognitive symptoms Deficits in cognitive abilities, specifically executive functioning, attention, and working memory, present in those with schizophrenia.

cognitive therapy Focuses on helping a client identify and correct any distorted thinking about self, others, or the world.

cognitive unconscious All the mental processes that give rise to a person's thoughts, choices, emotions, and behaviour even though they are not experienced by the person.

colour-opponent system Theory stating that pairs of cone types (channels) work in opposition.

common knowledge effect The tendency for group discussions to focus on information that all members share.

comorbidity The co-occurrence of two or more disorders in a single individual.

companionate love An experience involving affection, trust, and concern for a partner's well-being.

comparison level for alternatives The cost–benefit ratio that a person believes they could attain in another relationship.

concept A mental representation that groups or categorizes shared features of related objects, events, or other stimuli.

concrete operational stage The stage of cognitive development that begins at about age 6 years and ends at about age 11 years, during which children learn how various actions, or *operations*, can transform the concrete objects of the physical world.

conditioned response (CR) A reaction that resembles an unconditioned response but is produced by a conditioned stimulus.

conditioned stimulus (CS) A previously neutral stimulus that produces a reliable response in an organism after being paired with a US.

conduct disorder A persistent pattern of deviant behaviour involving aggression towards people or animals, destruction of property, deceitfulness or theft, or serious rule violations.

cones Photoreceptors that detect colour, operate under normal daylight conditions, and allow us to focus on fine detail.

conformity The tendency to do what others do.

conjunction fallacy Thinking that two events are more likely to occur together than either individual event alone.

conscious motivations Motivations of which people are aware.

consciousness A person's subjective experience of the world and the mind.

conservation The understanding that many of the physical properties of an object are conserved (i.e., not changed) by changes in the object's appearance.

consolidation The process by which memories become stable in the brain.

construct validity A feature of operational definitions whose specified operations are generally considered good indicators of the specified properties.

conventional stage A stage of moral development in which the morality of an action is primarily determined by the extent to which it conforms to social rules.

cooperation Behaviour by two or more individuals that leads to mutual benefit.

corpus callosum Connects large areas of the cerebral cortex on each side of the brain and supports communication of information across the hemispheres.

correlation A relationship between variables in which variations in the value of one variable are synchronized with variations in the value of the other.

correlation coefficient (r) A mathematical measure of both the direction and strength of a correlation, which is symbolized by the letter *r*.

crystallized intelligence The ability to apply knowledge that was acquired through experience.

cultural neuroscience The study of how culture and neurobiological processes influence one another.

cultural psychology The study of how culture influences mental life.

debriefing A verbal description of the true nature and purpose of a study.

defense mechanisms Unconscious coping mechanisms that reduce the anxiety generated by threats from unacceptable impulses.

deindividuation A phenomenon in which immersion in a group causes people to become less concerned with their personal values.

delusion A false belief, often bizarre and grandiose, that is maintained in spite of its irrationality.

demand characteristics Those aspects of an observational setting that cause people to behave as they think someone else wants or expects.

dendrite Receives information from other neurons and relays it to the cell body.

dependent variable The variable that is measured in an experiment.

depressants Substances that reduce the activity of the central nervous system.

developmental psychology The study of continuity and change across the life span.

deviation IQ A metric obtained by dividing a person's test score by the average test score for people that age and then multiplying the quotient by 100.

Diagnostic and Statistical Manual of Mental Disorders (DSM) A classification system that describes the symptoms used to diagnose each recognized mental disorder and indicates how that disorder can be distinguished from other, similar problems.

diathesis–stress model Suggests that a person may be predisposed to a psychological disorder that remains unexpressed until triggered by stress.

dichotic listening A task in which people wearing headphones hear different messages in each ear.

diffusion chain A process in which individuals initially learn a behaviour by observing another individual perform that behaviour; they themselves then become models from which other individuals learn the behaviour.

diffusion of responsibility The tendency of individuals to feel diminished responsibility for their actions when surrounded by others who are acting the same way.

discrimination Negative behaviour towards another person based solely on their category membership.

discrimination The capacity to distinguish between similar but distinct stimuli.

disorganized speech A severe disruption of verbal communication in which ideas shift rapidly and incoherently among unrelated topics.

disorganized symptoms Disruptions or deficits in abilities of speech, movement, and cognition in those with schizophrenia.

display rule A norm for the appropriate expression of emotion.

DNA methylation Adding a methyl group to DNA.

door-in-the-face technique An influence strategy that involves getting someone to accept a small request by first getting them to refuse a large request.

dopamine A neurotransmitter that regulates motor behaviour, motivation, pleasure, and emotional arousal.

dopamine hypothesis The idea that schizophrenia involves an excess of dopamine activity.

double depression A moderately depressed mood that persists for at least 2 years and is punctuated by periods of major depression.

double-blind study A study in which neither the researcher nor the participant knows how the participants are expected to behave.

drive-reduction theory A theory suggesting that the primary motivation of all organisms is to reduce their drives.

drug tolerance The tendency for larger doses of a drug to be required over time to achieve the same effect.

dual process theories Theories that suggest we have two different systems in our brains for processing information: one dedicated to fast, automatic, and unconscious processing, and the other dedicated to slow, effortful, and conscious processing.

dynamic unconscious An active system encompassing a lifetime of hidden memories, the person's deepest instincts and desires, and the person's inner struggle to control these forces.

echoic memory A fast-decaying store of auditory information.

eclectic psychotherapy A form of psychotherapy that involves drawing on techniques from different forms of therapy, depending on the client and the problem.

ego The component of personality, developed through contact with the external world, that enables us to deal with life's practical demands.

egocentrism The failure to understand that the world appears different to different people.

electroconvulsive therapy (ECT) A treatment that involves inducing a brief seizure by delivering an electrical shock to the brain.

electroencephalograph (EEG) A device used to record electrical activity in the brain.

electrooculograph (EOG) An instrument that measures eye movements.

embryonic stage The period of prenatal development that lasts from about the 2nd week until about the 8th week.

emotion A temporary state that includes unique subjective experiences and physiological activity, and that prepares people for action.

emotion regulation The strategies people use to influence their own emotional experiences.

emotional expression An observable sign of an emotional state.

emotional intelligence The ability to reason about emotions and to use emotions to enhance reasoning.

empirical method A set of rules and techniques for observation.

empiricism The conviction that accurate knowledge of the world can be acquired by observing it.

encoding The process of transforming what we perceive, think, or feel into an enduring memory.

encoding specificity principle The idea that a retrieval cue can be an effective reminder when it helps re-create the specific way in which information was initially encoded.

endocrine system A network of glands that produce and secrete into the bloodstream chemical messages known as hormones, which influence a wide variety of basic functions, including metabolism, growth, and sexual development.

endorphins Chemicals that act within the pain pathways and emotion centres of the brain.

epigenetic marks Chemical modifications to DNA that can turn genes on or off.

epigenetics The study of environmental influences that determine whether or not genes are expressed, or the degree to which they are expressed, without altering the basic DNA sequences that constitute the genes themselves.

episodic memory The collection of past personal experiences that occurred at a particular time and place.

equity A state of affairs in which the cost–benefit ratios of two partners are roughly equally favourable.

evolutionary mismatch The idea that traits that were adaptive in an ancestral environment may be maladaptive in a modern environment.

evolutionary psychology The study of the ways in which the human mind has been shaped by natural selection.

exemplar theory The concept that we make category judgements by comparing a new instance with stored memories of other instances of the category.

existential approach A school of thought that regards personality as being governed by an individual's ongoing choices and decisions in the context of the realities of life and death.

expectancy theory The idea that alcohol's effects can be produced by people's expectations of how it will influence them in particular situations.

experimentation A technique for establishing the causal relationship between variables.

explicit memory The act of consciously or intentionally retrieving past experiences.

exposure therapy An approach to treatment of the client that involves confronting an emotion-arousing stimulus directly and repeatedly, ultimately leading to a decrease in the emotional response.

expressed emotion A measure of how much hostility, criticism, and emotional overinvolvement people communicate when speaking about a family member with a mental disorder.

external validity An attribute of an experiment in which variables have been operationally defined in a representative way.

extinction The gradual elimination of a learned response that occurs when the CS is repeatedly presented without the US.

extrinsic motivation A motivation to take actions that are not themselves rewarding but that lead to reward.

facial feedback hypothesis The theory that emotional expressions can cause the emotional experiences they typically signify.

false recognition A feeling of familiarity about something that hasn't been encountered before.

feature-integration theory The idea that focused attention is not required to detect the individual features that make up a stimulus (e.g., the colour, shape, size, and location of letters), but it is required to bind those individual features together.

fetal alcohol syndrome (FAS) A developmental disorder that stems from heavy alcohol use by the mother during pregnancy.

fetal stage The period of prenatal development that lasts from about the 9th week until birth.

fight-or-flight response An emotional and physiological reaction to an emergency that increases readiness for action.

fixed-interval (FI) schedule An operant conditioning principle whereby reinforcers are presented at fixed time periods, provided that the appropriate response is made.

fixed-ratio (FR) schedule An operant conditioning principle whereby reinforcement is delivered after a specific number of responses have been made.

flashbulb memories Detailed recollections of when and where we heard about shocking events.

fluid intelligence The ability to solve and reason about novel problems.

foot-in-the-door technique A technique that involves making a small request then following it with a larger request.

formal operational stage The final stage of cognitive development that begins around the age of 11, during which children learn to reason about abstract concepts.

fovea An area of the retina where vision is clearest and there are no rods at all.

framing effects A bias whereby people give different answers to the same problem depending on how the problem is framed.

fraternal (dizygotic) twins Siblings who develop from two different eggs that were fertilized by two different sperm.

frequency distribution A graphic representation showing the number of times that the measurement of a property takes on each of its possible values.

frontal lobe Specialized areas for movement, abstract thinking, planning, memory, and judgement.

frustration–aggression hypothesis A principle stating that animals aggress when their goals are frustrated.

full consciousness A level of consciousness in which you know and are able to report your mental state.

functional fixedness The tendency to perceive the functions of objects as unchanging.

functionalism An approach to psychology that emphasized the adaptive significance of mental processes.

fundamental attribution error The tendency to make a dispositional attribution even when we should instead make a situational attribution.

GABA (gamma-aminobutyric acid) The primary inhibitory neurotransmitter in the brain.

gate-control theory A theory of pain perception based on the idea that signals arriving from pain receptors in the body can be stopped, or *gated*, by interneurons in the spinal cord via feedback from the skin or from the brain.

gateway drug A drug whose use increases the risk of the subsequent use of more harmful drugs.

gene The major unit of hereditary transmission.

general adaptation syndrome (GAS) A three-stage physiological stress response that appears regardless of the stressor that is encountered.

generalization The CR is observed even though the CS is slightly different from the CS used during acquisition.

generalized anxiety disorder (GAD) A disorder characterized by chronic excessive worry accompanied by three or more of the following symptoms: restlessness, fatigue, concentration problems, irritability, muscle tension, and sleep disturbance.

germinal stage The period from conception to 2 weeks after conception.

Gestalt psychology An approach to psychology that emphasized the way in which the mind creates perceptual experience.

gestalt therapy A form of psychotherapy whose goal is helping the client become aware of their thoughts, behaviours, experiences, and feelings and to "own" or take responsibility for them.

glial cells Support cells found in the nervous system.

glutamate The major excitatory neurotransmitter in the brain.

grammar A set of rules that specify how the units of language can be combined to produce meaningful messages.

grossly disorganized behaviour Behaviour that is inappropriate for the situation or ineffective in attaining goals, often with specific motor disturbances.

group A collection of people who have something in common that distinguishes them from others.

group polarization The tendency of groups to make decisions that are more extreme than any member would have made alone.

group therapy A type of therapy in which multiple participants (who often do not know each other at the outset) work on their individual problems in a group atmosphere.

groupthink The tendency of groups to reach consensus in order to facilitate interpersonal harmony.

habituation A general process in which repeated or prolonged exposure to a stimulus results in a gradual reduction in responding.

hallucination A false perceptual experience that has a compelling sense of being real despite the absence of external stimulation.

hallucinogens Drugs that alter sensation and perception and often cause visual and auditory hallucinations.

haptic perception The active exploration of the environment by touching and grasping objects with our hands.

health psychology The subfield of psychology concerned with how psychological factors influence the causes and treatment of physical illness and the maintenance of health.

hedonic principle The claim that people are motivated to experience pleasure and avoid pain.

helplessness theory The idea that individuals who are prone to depression automatically attribute negative experiences to causes that are internal (i.e., their own fault), stable (i.e., unlikely to change), and global (i.e., widespread).

heritability A measure of the variability of behavioural traits among individuals that can be accounted for by genetic factors.

heritability coefficient A statistic (commonly denoted as h^2) that describes the proportion of the difference between people's IQ scores that can be explained by differences in their genes.

heuristic A fast and efficient strategy that may facilitate decision making but does not guarantee that a solution will be reached.

hindbrain The area of the brain that coordinates information coming into and out of the spinal cord.

hippocampus Critical for creating new memories and integrating them into a network of knowledge so that they can be stored indefinitely in other parts of the cerebral cortex.

histone modification Adding chemical modifications to proteins called histones that are involved in packaging DNA.

homeostasis The tendency for a system to take action to keep itself in equilibrium.

homophily The tendency for people to like others who are similar to themselves.

human sexual response cycle The stages of physiological arousal during sexual activity.

hypnosis A social interaction in which one person (the hypnotist) makes suggestions that lead to a change in another person's (the participant's) subjective experience of the world.

hypnotic analgesia The reduction of pain through hypnosis in people who are susceptible to hypnosis.

hypothalamus Regulates body temperature, hunger, thirst, and sexual behaviour.

hypothesis A falsifiable prediction made by a theory.

hysteria A loss of function that has no obvious physical origin.

iatrogenic illness A disorder or symptom that occurs as a result of a medical or psychotherapeutic treatment itself.

iconic memory A fast-decaying store of visual information.

id The part of the mind containing the drives present at birth; it is the source of our bodily needs, wants, desires, and impulses, particularly our sexual and aggressive drives.

identical (monozygotic) twins Siblings who develop from the splitting of a single egg that was fertilized by a single sperm.

illusion of explanatory depth An illusion that occurs when people overestimate the depth of their understanding.

illusory conjunction A perceptual mistake whereby the brain incorrectly combines features from multiple objects.

illusory truth effect An error in reasoning that occurs when repeated exposure to a statement increases the likelihood that people will judge that statement to be true.

immune system A complex response system that protects the body from bacteria, viruses, and other foreign substances.

implicit learning Learning that takes place largely independent of awareness of both the process and the products of information acquisition.

implicit memory The influence of past experiences on later behaviour and performance, even without an effort to remember them or an awareness of the recollection.

inattentional blindness A failure to perceive objects that are not the focus of attention.

independent variable The variable that is manipulated in an experiment.

infancy The stage of development that begins at birth and lasts between 18 and 24 months.

informational influence A phenomenon that occurs when another person's behaviour provides information about what is good or true.

informed consent A verbal agreement to participate in a study made by an adult who has been informed of all the risks that participation may entail.

in-group favouritism Tendency to treat people better when they are members of one's own group than when they are not.

inner hair cells Specialized auditory receptor neurons embedded in the basilar membrane.

insomnia Difficulty in falling asleep or staying asleep.

intelligence The ability to use one's mind to solve novel problems and learn from experience.

intermittent reinforcement An operant conditioning principle whereby only some of the responses made are followed by reinforcement.

intermittent reinforcement effect The fact that operant behaviours that are maintained under intermittent reinforcement schedules resist extinction better than those maintained under continuous reinforcement.

internal validity An attribute of an experiment that allows it to establish causal relationships.

internal working model A set of beliefs about the way relationships work.

interneurons Connect sensory neurons, motor neurons, or other interneurons.

interpersonal psychotherapy (IPT) A form of psychotherapy that focuses on helping clients improve current relationships.

intrinsic motivation A motivation to take actions that are themselves rewarding.

introspection The analysis of subjective experience by trained observers.

ironic processes of mental control A mental process that can produce ironic errors because monitoring for errors can itself produce them.

James–Lange theory The theory that feelings are simply the perception of one's own physiological responses to a stimulus.

just noticeable difference (JND) The minimal change in a stimulus (e.g., its loudness or brightness) that can just barely be detected.

kin selection The process by which evolution selects for individuals who cooperate with their relatives.

language A system for communicating with others using signals that are combined according to rules of grammar and that convey meaning.

latent content A dream's true underlying meaning.

latent learning A process in which something is learned, but it is not manifested as a behavioural change until sometime in the future.

law of effect The principle that behaviours that are followed by a "satisfying state of affairs" tend to be repeated, and those that produce an "unpleasant state of affairs" are less likely to be repeated.

learning The acquisition, from experience, of new knowledge, skills, or responses that results in a relatively permanent change in the state of the learner.

linguistic relativity hypothesis The idea that language shapes the nature of thought.

locus of control A person's tendency to perceive the control of rewards as internal to the self or external in the environment.

long-term memory A type of storage that holds information for hours, days, weeks, or years.

long-term potentiation (LTP) A process whereby repeated communication across the synapse between neurons strengthens the connection, making further communication easier.

loss aversion The tendency to care more about avoiding losses than about achieving equal-size gains.

loudness Perception of a sound's intensity.

lymphocytes White blood cells that produce antibodies that fight infection, including T cells and B cells.

major depressive disorder (unipolar depression) A disorder characterized by a severely depressed mood and/or inability to experience pleasure that lasts 2 or more weeks and is accompanied by feelings of worthlessness, lethargy, and sleep as well as appetite disturbance.

manifest content A dream's apparent topic or superficial meaning.

manipulation A technique for determining the causal power of a variable by actively changing its value.

marijuana (cannabis) The leaves and buds of the hemp plant, which contain a psychoactive drug called tetrahydrocannabinol (THC).

mean The average value of all the measurements.

means–ends analysis A process of searching for the means or steps to reduce differences between the current situation and the desired goal.

median The value that is in the middle (i.e., greater than or equal to half the measurements and less than or equal to half the measurements).

medical model An approach that conceptualizes abnormal psychological experiences as illnesses that, like physical illnesses, have biological and environmental causes, defined symptoms, and possible cures.

meditation The practice of intentional contemplation.

medulla An extension of the spinal cord into the skull that coordinates heart rate, circulation, and respiration.

memory misattribution Assigning a recollection or an idea to the wrong source.

memory The ability to store and retrieve information over time.

mental control The attempt to change conscious states of mind.

mental disorder A persistent disturbance or dysfunction in behaviour, thoughts, or emotions that causes significant distress or impairment.

mere exposure effect The tendency for liking of a stimulus to increase with the amount of exposure to that stimulus.

metabolism The rate at which the body uses energy.

mind–body problem The issue of how the mind is related to the brain and body.

mindfulness meditation Teaches an individual to be fully present in each moment; to be aware of their thoughts, feelings, and sensations; and to detect symptoms before they become a problem.

minimal consciousness A low-level kind of sensory awareness and responsiveness that occurs when the mind inputs sensations and may output behaviour.

Minnesota Multiphasic Personality Inventory (MMPI) A well-researched clinical questionnaire used to assess personality and psychological problems.

mirror neurons Neurons that are active when an animal performs a behaviour, such as reaching for or manipulating an object, and are also activated when another animal observes that animal performing the same behaviour.

mnemonics Encoding strategies that improve subsequent retrieval.

mode The value of the most frequently observed measurement.

monocular depth cues Aspects of a scene that yield information about depth when viewed with only one eye.

mood disorders Mental disorders that have mood disturbance as their predominant feature.

morphemes The smallest meaningful units of language.

morphological rules A set of rules that indicate how morphemes can be combined to form words.

motivation The internal causes of purposeful behaviour.

motor development The emergence of the ability to execute physical actions.

motor neurons Carry signals from the spinal cord to the muscles to produce movement.

motor reflexes Motor responses that are triggered by specific patterns of sensory stimulation.

multisensory Events that stimulate multiple senses at the same time.

myelin sheath An insulating layer of fatty material.

myelination The formation of a fatty sheath around the axons of a neuron.

narcissism A trait that reflects a grandiose view of the self, combined with a tendency to seek admiration from and exploit others.

narcolepsy A disorder in which sudden sleep attacks occur in the middle of waking activities.

narcotics (opiates) Highly addictive drugs derived from opium that relieve pain.

nativist theory The view that language development is best explained as an innate, biological capacity.

natural correlation A correlation that is observed in the natural world.

natural selection The process by which the specific attributes that promote an organism's survival and reproduction become more prevalent in the population over time.

naturalistic observation A technique for gathering information by unobtrusively observing people in their natural environments.

negative symptoms Deficits in or disruptions of emotions and behaviours (e.g., emotional and social withdrawal; apathy; poverty of speech; and other indications of the absence or insufficiency of normal behaviour, motivation, and emotion) that are missing in those with schizophrenia.

nervous system An interacting network of neurons that conveys electrochemical information throughout the body.

neurons Cells in the nervous system that communicate with each other to perform information-processing tasks.

neurotransmitters Chemicals that transmit information across the synapse to a receiving neuron's dendrites.

nonshared environment Features of the environment that are not experienced by all relevant members of a household.

nonsuicidal self-injury (NSSI) Direct, deliberate destruction of body tissue in the absence of any intent to die.

norepinephrine Involved in states of vigilance or heightened awareness of dangers in the environment.

norm of reciprocity The unwritten rule that people should benefit those who have benefited them.

normal distribution A mathematically defined distribution in which the frequency of measurements is highest in the middle and decreases symmetrically in both directions.

normative influence A phenomenon in which another person's behaviour provides information about what is appropriate.

norms Customary standards for behaviour that are widely shared by members of a culture.

obedience The tendency to do what authorities tell us to do.

object permanence The understanding that objects exist even when they are not visible.

observational learning A process in which an organism learns by watching the actions of others.

observer bias The tendency for observers' expectations to influence both what they believe they observed and what they actually observed.

obsessive-compulsive disorder (OCD) A disorder in which repetitive, intrusive thoughts (obsessions) and ritualistic behaviours (compulsions) designed to fend off those thoughts interfere significantly with an individual's functioning.

occipital lobe Processes visual information.

olfactory bulb A brain structure located above the nasal cavity beneath the frontal lobes.

olfactory receptor neurons (ORNs) Receptor cells that transduce odourant molecules into neural impulses.

operant behaviour Behaviour that an organism performs that has some impact on the environment.

operant conditioning A type of learning in which the consequences of an organism's behaviour determine whether it will repeat that behaviour in the future.

operational definition A description of a property in measurable terms.

optimism bias A bias whereby people believe that, compared with other individuals, they are more likely to experience positive events and less likely to experience negative events in the future.

organizational encoding The process of categorizing information according to the relationships among a series of items.

outcome expectancies A person's assumptions about the likely consequences of a future behaviour.

overjustification effect A phenomenon whereby people who are rewarded for a behaviour become less intrinsically motivated to repeat it.

panic disorder A disorder characterized by the sudden occurrence of multiple psychological and physiological symptoms that contribute to a feeling of stark terror.

parallel processing The brain's capacity to perform multiple activities at the same time.

parasympathetic nervous system Helps the body return to a normal resting state.

parietal lobe Processes information about touch.

passionate love An experience involving feelings of euphoria, intimacy, and intense sexual attraction.

perception The organization, identification, and interpretation of a sensation in order to form a mental representation.

perceptual confirmation The tendency of observers to see what they expect to see.

perceptual constancy A perceptual principle stating that even as aspects of sensory signals change, perception remains consistent.

perceptual organization The process of grouping and segregating features to create whole objects organized in meaningful ways.

peripheral nervous system (PNS) Connects the central nervous system to the body's organs and muscles.

peripheral-route persuasion The process by which attitudes or beliefs are changed by appeals to habit or emotion.

persistence The intrusive recollection of events that we wish we could forget.

persistent depressive disorder The same cognitive and bodily problems as in depression are present, but they are less severe and last longer, persisting for at least 2 years.

personal constructs Dimensions people use in making sense of their experiences.

personality An individual's characteristic style of behaving, thinking, and feeling.

personality disorders Enduring patterns of thinking, feeling, or relating to others or controlling impulses that deviate from cultural expectations and cause distress or impaired functioning.

person-centred therapy (or client-centred therapy) A form of psychotherapy that assumes all individuals have a tendency towards growth and this growth can be facilitated by acceptance and genuine reactions from the therapist.

person–situation controversy The question of whether behaviour is caused more by personality or by situational factors.

persuasion A phenomenon that occurs when a person's attitudes or beliefs are influenced by a communication from another person.

phenomenology The study of how things seem to the conscious person.

pheromones Biochemical odourants emitted by other members of an animal's species that can affect its behaviour or physiology.

philosophical dualism The view that mind and body are fundamentally different things.

philosophical empiricism The view that all knowledge is acquired through experience.

philosophical idealism The view that our perceptions of the physical world are our brain's best interpretation of the information that enters through our sensory apparatus.

philosophical materialism The view that all mental phenomena are reducible to physical phenomena.

philosophical nativism The view that some knowledge is innate rather than acquired.

philosophical realism The view that our perceptions of the physical world are a faithful copy of information from the world that enters our brains through our sensory apparatus.

phobic disorders Disorders characterized by marked, persistent, and excessive fear and avoidance of specific objects, activities, or situations.

phoneme The smallest units of speech that distinguish one word from another.

phonological rules A set of rules that indicate how phonemes can be combined to produce words.

phototherapy A therapy that involves repeated exposure to bright light.

pitch How high or low a sound is.

pituitary gland The "master gland" of the body's hormone-producing system, which releases hormones that direct the functions of many other glands in the body.

place code The process by which the brain uses information about the relative activity of hair cells (e.g., which ones are more active and which are less active) across the whole basilar membrane to help determine the pitch you hear.

placebo An inert substance or procedure that has been applied with the expectation that it will produce a healing response.

pons A brain structure that relays information from the cerebellum to the rest of the brain.

population A complete collection of people.

positive symptoms Thoughts and behaviours, such as hallucinations and delusions, not seen in those without the disorder.

postconventional stage A stage of moral development in which the morality of an action is determined by a set of general principles that reflect core values.

posthypnotic amnesia The failure to retrieve memories following hypnotic suggestions to forget.

posttraumatic stress disorder (PTSD) A disorder characterized by chronic physiological arousal, recurrent unwanted thoughts or images of the trauma, and avoidance of things that call the traumatic event to mind.

power A detector's ability to detect the presence of differences or changes in the magnitude of a property.

preconventional stage A stage of moral development in which the morality of an action is primarily determined by its consequences for the actor.

prejudice A negative evaluation of another person based solely on their category membership.

preoperational stage The stage of cognitive development that begins at about age 2 years and ends at about age 6 years, during which children develop a preliminary understanding of the physical world.

preparedness theory The idea that people are instinctively predisposed towards certain fears.

primary sex characteristics Bodily structures that change at puberty and are directly involved in reproduction.

priming An enhanced ability to think of a stimulus, such as a word or an object, as a result of a recent exposure to that stimulus during an earlier study task.

principle of reinforcement A principle stating that any behaviour that is rewarded will be repeated and any behaviour that isn't rewarded won't be repeated.

proactive aggression Aggression that is planned and purposeful.

proactive interference Situations in which earlier learning impairs memory for information acquired later.

problem of other minds The fundamental difficulty we have in perceiving the consciousness of others.

procedural memory The gradual acquisition of skills as a result of practice, or "knowing how" to do things.

projective tests Tests designed to reveal inner aspects of individuals' personalities by analysis of their responses to a standard series of ambiguous stimuli.

proprioception Your sense of bodily position.

prospect theory The theory that people choose to take on risk when evaluating potential losses and avoid risks when evaluating potential gains.

prospective memory Remembering to do things in the future.

prototype theory The concept that we classify new objects by comparing them to the "best" or "most typical" member (the *prototype*) of a category.

proximodistal principle The "inside-to-outside" principle that describes the tendency for motor skills to emerge in sequence from the centre to the periphery.

psychoactive drugs Chemicals that influence consciousness or behaviour by altering the brain's chemical message system.

psychoanalysis A therapy that aims to give people insight into the contents of their unconscious minds.

psychoanalytic theory A general theory that emphasizes the influence of the unconscious on feelings, thoughts, and behaviours.

psychodynamic approach An approach that regards personality as formed by needs, strivings, and desires largely operating outside of awareness—motives that also can produce emotional disorders.

psychodynamic psychotherapies Therapies that explore childhood events and encourage individuals to use this understanding to develop insight into their psychological problems.

psychology The scientific study of mind and behaviour.

psychopharmacology The study of drug effects on psychological states and symptoms.

psychophysics Methods that systematically relate the physical characteristics of a stimulus to an observer's perception.

psychosurgery Surgical destruction of specific brain areas.

psychotherapy An interaction between a socially sanctioned clinician and someone suffering from a psychological problem, with the goal of providing support or relief from the problem.

puberty The onset of bodily changes associated with sexual maturity.

punisher Any stimulus or event that decreases the likelihood of the behaviour that led to it.

random assignment A procedure that assigns participants to conditions by chance.

random sampling A technique for selecting participants that ensures every member of a population has an equal chance of being included in the sample.

range The value of the largest measurement in a frequency distribution minus the value of the smallest measurement.

ratio IQ A metric obtained by dividing a child's mental age by the child's physical age and then multiplying the quotient by 100.

rational choice theory The classical view that we make decisions by determining how likely something is to happen, judging the value of the outcome, and then multiplying the two.

rational coping Facing a stressor and working to overcome it.

reactance An unpleasant feeling that arises when people feel they are being coerced.

reaction time The amount of time between the onset of a stimulus and a person's response to that stimulus.

reactive aggression Aggression that occurs spontaneously in response to a negative affective state.

reappraisal The process of changing one's emotional experience by changing the way one thinks about the emotion-eliciting stimulus.

reasoning A mental activity that consists of organizing information or beliefs into a series of steps in order to reach conclusions.

rebound effect of thought suppression The tendency of a thought to return to consciousness with greater frequency following suppression.

receptors Parts of the cell membrane that receive the neurotransmitter and either initiate or prevent a new electric signal.

reciprocal altruism Behaviour that benefits another with the expectation that those benefits will be returned in the future.

reconsolidation The process whereby memories can become vulnerable to disruption when they are recalled, thus requiring them to be consolidated again.

referred pain Feeling of pain on the surface of the body, but due to internal damage; occurs because sensory information from internal and external areas converges on the same nerve cells in the spinal cord.

reflex arc A neural pathway that controls reflex actions.

refractory period The time following an action potential during which a new action potential cannot be initiated.

reframing Finding a new or creative way to think about a stressor that reduces its threat.

rehearsal The process of keeping information in short-term memory by mentally repeating it.

reinforcer Any stimulus or event that increases the likelihood of the behaviour that led to it.

relaxation response A condition of reduced muscle tension, cortical activity, heart rate, breathing rate, and blood pressure.

relaxation therapy A technique for reducing tension by consciously relaxing muscles of the body.

reliability A detector's ability to detect the absence of differences or changes in the magnitude of a property.

REM sleep A stage of sleep characterized by rapid eye movements and a high level of brain activity.

replication An experiment that uses the same procedures as a previous experiment but with a new sample from the same population.

representativeness heuristic A mental shortcut that involves making a probability judgement by comparing an object or event with a prototype of the object or event.

repression A mental process that removes unacceptable thoughts and memories from consciousness and keeps them in the unconscious.

repressive coping Avoiding feelings, thoughts, or situations that are reminders of a stressor and maintaining an artificially positive viewpoint.

Research Domain Criteria Project (RDoC) A new initiative that aims to guide the classification and understanding of mental disorders by revealing the basic processes that give rise to them.

resting potential The difference in electric charge between the inside and outside of a neuron's cell membrane.

reticular formation Regulates sleep, wakefulness, and levels of arousal.

retina A layer of light-sensitive tissue lining the back of the eyeball.

retrieval The process of bringing to mind information that has been previously encoded and stored.

retrieval cue External information that is associated with stored information and helps bring it to mind.

retrieval-induced forgetting A process by which retrieving an item from long-term memory impairs subsequent recall of related items.

retroactive interference Situations in which later learning impairs memory for information acquired earlier.

retrograde amnesia The inability to retrieve information that was acquired before a particular date, usually the date of an injury or surgery.

rods Photoreceptors that become active under low-light conditions for night vision.

Rorschach Inkblot Test A projective technique in which respondents' inner thoughts and feelings are believed to be revealed by analysis of their responses to a set of unstructured inkblots.

sample A partial collection of people drawn from a population.

schemas Theories about the way the world works.

schizophrenia A disorder characterized by the profound disruption of basic psychological processes; a distorted perception of reality; altered or blunted emotion; and disturbances in thought, motivation, and behaviour.

scientific method A procedure for using empirical evidence to establish facts.

seasonal affective disorder (SAD) Recurrent depressive episodes in a seasonal pattern.

secondary sex characteristics Bodily structures that change at puberty but are not directly involved in reproduction.

second-order conditioning A type of learning in which a CS is paired with a stimulus that became associated with the US in an earlier procedure.

self-actualizing tendency The human motive towards realizing our inner potential.

self-concept A person's explicit knowledge of their own behaviours, traits, and other personal characteristics.

self-consciousness A distinct level of consciousness in which the person's attention is drawn to the self as an object.

self-esteem The extent to which an individual likes, values, and accepts the self.

self-regulation The exercise of voluntary control over the self to bring the self into line with preferred standards.

self-report A method in which people provide subjective information about their own thoughts, feelings, or behaviours, typically via questionnaire or interview.

self-selection A problem that occurs when anything about a participant determines the value of the independent variable to which the participant was exposed.

self-serving bias People's tendency to take credit for their successes but downplay responsibility for their failures.

self-verification The tendency to seek evidence to confirm the self-concept.

semantic encoding The process of relating new information in a meaningful way to knowledge that is already stored in memory.

semantic memory A network of associated facts and concepts that make up our general knowledge of the world.

sensation Simple stimulation of a sense organ.

sensitivity How responsive we are to faint stimuli.

sensitization A simple form of learning that occurs when presentation of a stimulus leads to an increased response to a later stimulus.

sensorimotor stage A stage of cognitive development that begins at birth and lasts through infancy.

sensory adaptation The process whereby sensitivity to prolonged stimulation tends to decline over time as an organism adapts to current (unchanging) conditions.

sensory memory A type of storage that holds sensory information for a few seconds or less.

sensory neurons Receive information from the external world and convey this information to the brain via the spinal cord.

serial position effect The observation that the first few and last few items in a series are more likely to be recalled than the items in the middle.

serotonin Involved in the regulation of sleep and wakefulness, eating, and aggressive behaviour.

shaping Learning that results from the reinforcement of successive steps to a final desired behaviour.

shared environment Features of the environment that are experienced by all relevant members of a household.

short-term memory A type of storage that holds nonsensory information for more than a few seconds but less than a minute.

sick role A socially recognized set of rights and obligations linked with illness.

signal detection theory An approach that holds that the response to a stimulus depends both on a person's sensitivity to the stimulus in the presence of noise and on a person's decision criterion.

sleep apnea A disorder in which the person stops breathing for brief periods while asleep.

sleep paralysis The experience of waking up unable to move.

sleep terrors (night terrors) Abrupt awakenings with panic and intense emotional arousal.

social cognition The processes by which people come to understand others.

social influence The ability to change or direct another person's behaviour.

social loafing The tendency of people to expend less effort when in a group than when alone.

social phobia A disorder that involves an irrational fear of being publicly humiliated or embarrassed.

social psychology The study of the causes and consequences of sociality.

social support The aid gained through interacting with others.

social–cognitive approach An approach that views personality in terms of how the person thinks about the situations encountered in daily life and behaves in response to them.

somatic nervous system A set of nerves that conveys information between skeletal muscles and the central nervous system.

somnambulism (sleepwalking) Occurs when a person arises and walks around while asleep.

sound waves Changes in air pressure unfolding over time.

source memory Recall of when, where, and how information was acquired.

spatial acuity The ability to distinguish two features that are very close together in space.

specific phobia A disorder that involves an irrational fear of a particular object or situation that markedly interferes with an individual's ability to function.

spinal reflexes Simple pathways in the nervous system that rapidly generate muscle contractions.

spontaneous recovery The tendency of a learned behaviour to recover from extinction after a rest period.

standard deviation A statistic that describes how each of the measurements in a frequency distribution differs from the mean.

state-dependent retrieval The process whereby information tends to be better recalled when the person is in the same state during encoding *and* retrieval.

stereotype threat The anxiety associated with the possibility of confirming other people's stereotypes about one's group.

stereotyping The process of drawing inferences about individuals based on their category membership.

stimulants Substances that excite the central nervous system, heightening arousal and activity levels.

storage The process of maintaining information in memory over time.

stress The physical and psychological response to internal or external stressors.

stress-inoculation training (SIT) A reframing technique that helps people cope with stressful situations by developing positive ways to think about the situations.

stressors Specific events or chronic pressures that place demands on a person or threaten a person's well-being.

structuralism An approach to psychology that attempted to isolate and analyze the mind's basic elements.

subcortical structures Areas of the forebrain housed under the cerebral cortex near the centre of the brain.

subtyping The tendency of observers to think of targets who disconfirm stereotypes as "exceptions to the rule."

suggestibility The tendency to incorporate misleading information from external sources into personal recollections.

suicide Intentional self-inflicted death.

suicide attempt Engagement in potentially harmful behaviour with some intention of dying.

sunk-cost fallacy A framing effect in which people make decisions about a current situation on the basis of what they have previously invested in the situation.

superego The mental system that reflects the internalization of cultural rules, mainly learned as parents exercise their authority.

syllogistic reasoning Determining whether a conclusion follows from two statements that are assumed to be true.

sympathetic nervous system A set of nerves that prepares the body for action in challenging or threatening situations.

synapse The junction or region between the axon of one neuron and the dendrites or cell body of another.

synesthesia When one attribute of a stimulus, such as its sound or shape, leads to the conscious experience of an additional attribute, often in a different sensory modality than the initiating stimulus.

syntactic rules A set of rules that indicate how words can be combined to form phrases and sentences.

tactile receptive field A small patch of skin that relates information about pain, pressure, texture, pattern, or vibration to a receptor.

target-based inferences Inferences based on information about an individual's behaviour.

taste buds The organs of taste transduction.

tectum Orients an organism in the environment.

tegmentum Involved in movement and arousal.

telegraphic speech Speech that is devoid of function morphemes and consists mostly of content words.

telomerase An enzyme that rebuilds telomeres at the tips of chromosomes.

telomeres Caps at the ends of the chromosomes that prevent the chromosomes from sticking to each other.

temperament A biologically based pattern of attentional and emotional reactivity.

temporal acuity The ability to distinguish two features that are very close together in time.

temporal code The process whereby the brain uses the timing of the action potentials in the auditory nerve to help determine the pitch you hear.

temporal lobe Responsible for hearing and language.

teratogen Any substance that passes from mother to unborn child and impairs development.

terminal buttons Knoblike structures that branch out from an axon.

terror management theory A theory about how people respond to the knowledge of their own mortality.

thalamus Relays and filters information from the senses and transmits the information to the cerebral cortex.

Thematic Apperception Test (TAT) A projective technique in which respondents' underlying motives, concerns, and the way they see the social world are believed to be revealed through analysis of the stories they make up about ambiguous pictures of people.

theory An explanation of a natural phenomenon.

theory of mind The understanding that the mind produces representations of the world and that these representations guide behaviour.

third-variable problem The fact that the natural correlation between two variables cannot be taken as evidence of a causal relationship between them because a third variable might be causing them both.

thought suppression The conscious avoidance of a thought.

timbre The quality of sound that allows you to distinguish two sources with the same pitch and loudness.

token economy A form of behaviour therapy that involves giving clients "tokens" for desired behaviours that they can later trade for rewards.

trait A relatively stable disposition to behave in a particular and consistent way.

transcranial magnetic stimulation (TMS) A treatment that involves placing a powerful pulsed magnet over a person's scalp to alter neuronal activity in the brain.

transduction The process whereby sense receptors convert physical signals from the environment into neural signals that are sent to the central nervous system.

transfer-appropriate processing The idea that memory is likely to transfer from one situation to another when the encoding and retrieval contexts of the situations match.

transience Forgetting what occurs with the passage of time.

travelling wave The up-and-down movement that sound causes in the basilar membrane.

two-factor theory of emotion The theory that stimuli trigger a general state of physiological arousal, which is then interpreted as a specific emotion.

two-factor theory of intelligence Spearman's theory suggesting that a person's performance on a test is due to a combination of general cognitive ability and specific abilities that are unique to the test.

Type A behaviour pattern The tendency towards easily aroused hostility, impatience, a sense of time urgency, and competitive achievement strivings.

Type I error An error that occurs when researchers conclude that there is a causal relationship between two variables when in fact there is not.

Type II error An error that occurs when researchers conclude that there is not a causal relationship between two variables when in fact there is.

unconditioned response (UR) A reflexive reaction that is reliably produced by an unconditioned stimulus.

unconditioned stimulus (US) Something that reliably produces a naturally occurring reaction in an organism.

unconscious The part of the mind that contains information of which people are not aware.

unconscious motivations Motivations of which people are not aware.

universal grammar A collection of processes that facilitate language learning.

universality hypothesis The theory that all emotional expressions mean the same thing to all people in all places at all times.

variable A property that can have more than one value.

variable-interval (VI) schedule An operant conditioning principle whereby behaviour is reinforced on the basis of an average time that has expired since the last reinforcement, although the exact time to the next reinforcement is not predictable.

variable-ratio (VR) schedule An operant conditioning principle whereby the delivery of reinforcement is based on a particular average number of responses, although the ratio of responses to reinforcements is variable.

ventriloquist illusion The fact that you depend on your visual system for reliable information about spatial location.

vestibular system The three fluid-filled semicircular canals and adjacent organs located next to the cochlea in each inner ear.

visual form agnosia The inability to recognize objects by sight.

visual imagery encoding The process of storing new information by converting it into mental pictures.

visual receptive field The region of the visual field to which each neuron responds.

Weber's law For every sense domain, the change in a stimulus that is just noticeable is a constant proportion despite variation in intensities.

working memory Active maintenance of information in short-term storage.

COMBINED REFERENCES

Aarts, H., Custers, R., & Marien, H. (2008). Preparing and motivating behavior outside of awareness. *Science, 319,* 1639.

Abel, T., Alberini, C., Ghirardi, M., Huang, Y.-Y., Nguyen, P., & Kandel, E. R. (1995). Steps toward a molecular definition of memory consolidation. In D. L. Schacter (Ed.), *Memory distortion: How minds, brains and societies reconstruct the past* (pp. 298–328). Harvard University Press.

Abelson, J., Curtis, G., Sagher, O., Albucher, R., Harrigan, M., Taylor, S., ... Giordani, B. (2009). Deep brain stimulation for refractory obsessive-compulsive disorder. *Biological Psychiatry, 57,* 510–516.

Abrams, M., & Reber, A. S. (1988). Implicit learning: Robustness in the face of psychiatric disorders. *Journal of Psycholinguistic Research, 17,* 425–439.

Abramson, L. Y., Seligman, M. E. P., & Teasdale, J. D. (1978). Learned helplessness in humans: Critique and reformulation. *Journal of Abnormal Psychology, 87,* 49–74.

Acevedo, B. P., & Aron, A. (2009). Does a long-term relationship kill romantic love? *Review of General Psychology, 13,* 59–65.

Acevedo-Garcia, D., McArdle, N., Osypuk, T. L., Lefkowitz, B., & Krimgold, B. K. (2007). *Children left behind: How metropolitan areas are failing America's children.* Harvard School of Public Health.

Achter, J. A., Lubinski, D., & Benbow, C. P. (1996). Multipotentiality among the intellectually gifted: "It was never there and already it's vanishing." *Journal of Counseling Psychology, 43,* 65–76.

Acikalin, M. Y., Watson, K. K., Fitzsimons, G. J., & Platt, M. L. (2018). Rhesus macaques form preferences for brand logos through sex and social status based advertising. *PLoS ONE, 13*(3), e0193055. https://doi.org/10.1371/journal.pone.0194055

Ackerman, P. L. (2014). Adolescent and adult intellectual development. *Current Directions in Psychological Science, 23*(4), 246–251. https://doi.org/10.1177/0963721414534960

Ackerman, P. L. (2017). Adult intelligence: The construct and the criterion problem. *Perspectives on Psychological Science, 12*(6), 987–998. https://doi.org/10.1177/1745691617703437

Addis, D. R., Wong, A. T., & Schacter, D. L. (2007). Remembering the past and imagining the future: Common and distinct neural substrates during event construction and elaboration. *Neuropsychologia, 45,* 1363–1377.

Addis, D. R., Wong, A. T., & Schacter, D. L. (2008). Age-related changes in the episodic simulation of future events. *Psychological Science, 19,* 33–41.

Adelmann, P. K., & Zajonc, R. B. (1989). Facial efference and the experience of emotion. *Annual Review of Psychology, 40,* 249–280.

Adolph, K. E., Cole, W. G., Komati, M., Garciaguirre, J. S., Badaly, D., Lingeman, J. M., ... Sotsky, R. B. (2012). How do you learn to walk? Thousands of steps and dozens of falls per day. *Psychological Science, 23*(11), 1387–1394. https://doi.org/10.1177/0956797612446346

Adolphs, R., Russell, J. A., & Tranel, D. (1999). A role for the human amygdala in recognizing emotional arousal from unpleasant stimuli. *Psychological Science, 10,* 167–171.

Adolphs, R., Tranel, D., Damasio, H., & Damasio, A. R. (1995). Fear and the human amygdala. *Journal of Neuroscience, 15,* 5879–5891.

Adorno, T. W., Frenkel-Brunswik, E., Levinson, D. J., & Sanford, R. N. (1950). *The authoritarian personality.* Harper & Row.

Aernout, E., Benradia, I., Hazo, J-B., Sy, A., Askevis-Leherpeux, F., Sebbane, D., & Roelandt, J-L. (2021). International study of the prevalence and factors associated with insomnia in the general population. *Sleep Medicine, 82,* 186–192. https://doi.org/10.1016/j.sleep.2021.03.028

Agbafe, V., & Juthani, P. (2021, July 22). The answer to medical misinformation on social media might be more information. *STAT.* https://www.statnews.com/2021/07/22/answer-medical-misinformation-social-media-more-information/

Aggleton, J. (Ed.). (1992). *The amygdala: Neurobiological aspects of emotion, memory and mental dysfunction.* Wiley-Liss.

Agin, D. (2007). *Junk science: An overdue indictment of government, industry, and faith groups that twist science for their own gain.* Macmillan.

Agren, T., Engman, J., Frick, A., Björkstrand, J., Larsson, E. M., Furmark, T., & Fredrikson, M. (2012). Disruption of reconsolidation erases a fear memory trace in the human amygdala. *Science, 337,* 1550–1552.

Agthe, M., Spörrle, M., & Maner, J. K. (2010). Don't hate me because I'm beautiful: Anti-attractiveness bias in organizational evaluation and decision making. *Journal of Experimental Social Psychology, 46*(6), 1151–1154. https://doi.org/10.1016/j.jesp.2010.05.007

Aharon, I., Etcoff, N., Ariely, D., Chabris, C. F., O'Conner, E., & Breiter, H. C. (2001). Beautiful faces have variable reward value: fMRI and behavioral evidence. *Neuron, 32,* 537–551.

Ainsworth, M. D. S., Blehar, M. C., Waters, E., & Wall, S. (1978). *Patterns of attachment: A psychological study of the strange situation.* Erlbaum.

Ainsworth, S. E., & Maner, J. K. (2012). Sex begets violence: Mating motives, social dominance, and physical aggression in men. *Journal of Personality and Social Psychology, 103*(5), 819–829. https://doi.org/10.1037/a0029428

Aknin, L. B., Hamlin, J. K., & Dunn, E. W. (2012). Giving leads to happiness in young children. *PLoS ONE, 7*(6), e39211. https://doi.org/10.1371/journal.pone.0039211

Alasaari, J. S., Lagus, M., Ollila, H. M., Toivola, A., Kivimaki, M., Vahterra, J., ... Paunio, T. (2012). Environmental stress affects DNA methylation of a CpG rich promoter region of serotonin transporter gene in a nurse cohort. *PLoS ONE, 7,* e45813. https://doi.org/10.1371/journal.pone.0045813

Albarracín, D., & Shavitt, S. (2018). Attitudes and attitude change. *Annual Review of Psychology, 69*(1), 299–327.

Alcoholics Anonymous. (2022). A.A. around the world. https://www.aa.org/aa-around-the-world

Aleman, A., Sommer, I. E., & Kahn, R. S. (2007). Efficacy of slow repetitive transcranial magnetic stimulation in the treatment of resistant auditory hallucinations in schizophrenia: A meta-analysis. *Journal of Clinical Psychiatry, 68,* 416–421.

Alicke, M. D., Klotz, M. L., Breitenbecher, D. L., Yurak, T. J., & Vredenburg, D. S. (1995). Personal contact, individuation, and the better-than-average effect. *Journal of Personality and Social Psychology, 68,* 804–824.

Allen, J. G., Flanigan, S. S., LeBlanc, M., Vallarino, J., MacNaughton, P., Stewart, J. H., & Christiani, D. C. (2016).

Flavoring chemicals in e-cigarettes: Diacetyl, 2,3-pentanedione, and acetoin in a sample of 51 products, including fruit-, candy-, and cocktail-flavored e-cigarettes. *Environmental Health Perspectives, 124*(6), 733–739.

Allison, D. B., Kaprio, J., Korkeila, M., Koskenvuo, M., Neale, M. C., & Hayakawa, K. (1996). The heritability of body mass index among an international sample of monozygotic twins reared apart. *International Journal of Obesity, 20*(6), 501–506.

Alloway, T. P. (Ed.) (2018). *Working memory and clinical developmental disorders.* Routledge.

Alloway, T. P., Gathercole, S. E., Kirkwood, H., & Elliott, J. (2009). The cognitive and behavioral characteristics of children with low working memory. *Child Development, 80,* 606–621.

Allport, G. W. (1937). *Personality: A psychological interpretation.* Holt.

Allport, G. W. (1954). *The nature of prejudice.* Addison-Wesley.

Allport, G. W., & Odbert, H. S. (1936). Trait-names: A psycholexical study. *Psychological Monographs, 47,* 592.

Altheimer, G., & Urry, H. L. (2019). Do emotions cause eating? The role of previous experiences and social context in emotional eating. *Current Directions in Psychological Science, 28*(3), 234–240. https://doi.org/10.1177/0963721419837685

Alvarez, L. W. (1965). A pseudo experience in parapsychology. *Science, 148,* 1541.

American Diabetes Association [ADA]. (2018). Economic costs of diabetes in the U.S. in 2017. *Diabetes Care, 41*(5), 917, LP-928. https://doi.org/10.2337/dci18-0007

American Psychiatric Association. (2022). *Diagnostic and Statistical Manual of Mental Disorders, Fifth Edition, Text Revision (DSM-5-TR™).* American Psychiatric Publishing.

American Psychiatric Association. (2013). *Diagnostic and Statistical Manual of Mental Disorders (DSM-5)* (5th ed.). American Psychiatric Publishing.

American Psychological Association. (2002). *Ethical principles of psychologists and code of conduct.* Author. apa.org/code/ethics/index .aspx [includes 2010 amendments].

American Psychological Association. (2009). *Report of the American Psychological Association task force on appropriate therapeutic responses to sexual orientation.* Author.

Amos, N., & McCabe, M. P. (2015). Conceptualizing and measuring perceptions of sexual attractiveness: Are there differences across gender and sexual orientation? *Personality and Individual Differences, 76,* 111–122. https://doi.org/10.1016/j.paid.2014.11.057

Amos, T. B., Tandon, N., Lefebvre, P., Pilon, D., Kamstra, R. L., Pivneva, I., & Greenberg, P. E. (2018). Direct and indirect cost burden and change of employment status in treatment-resistant depression: A matched-cohort study using a US commercial claims database. *Journal of Clinical Psychiatry, 79*(2), 17m11725. https://doi .org/10.4088/JCP.17m11725

Anand, S., & Hotson, J. (2002). Transcranial magnetic stimulation: Neurophysiological applications and safety. *Brain and Cognition, 50,* 366–386.

Anderson, C. A. (1989). Temperature and aggression: Ubiquitous effects of heat on occurrence of human violence. *Psychological Bulletin, 106,* 74–96.

Anderson, C. A., & Bushman, B. J. (2002). Human aggression. *Annual Review of Psychology, 53,* 27–51.

Anderson, C. A., Berkowitz, L., Donnerstein, E., Huesmann, L. R., Johnson, J. D., Linz, D., ... Wartella, E. (2003). The influence of media violence on youth. *Psychological Science in the Public Interest, 4,* 81–110.

Anderson, C. A., Bushman, B. J., & Groom, R. W. (1997). Hot years and serious and deadly assault: Empirical tests of the heat hypothesis. *Journal of Personality and Social Psychology, 73,* 1213–1223.

Anderson, C. A., Bushman, B. J., Cantor, J., Christakis, D., Coyne, S. M., Donnerstein, E., ... Ybarra, M. (2017). Screen violence and youth behavior. *Pediatrics, 140*(Suppl. 2), S142–S147. https://doi.org/10.1542/peds.2016-1758T

Anderson, C. A., Suzuki, K., Swing, E. L., Groves, C. L., Gentile, D. A., Prot, S., ... & Petrescu, P. (2017). Media violence and other aggression risk factors in seven nations. *Personality and Social Psychology Bulletin, 43*(7), 986–998. https://doi.org/10.1177 /0146167217703064

Anderson, J. R., & Schooler, L. J. (1991). Reflections of the environment in memory. *Psychological Science, 2,* 396–408.

Anderson, J. R., & Schooler, L. J. (2000). The adaptive nature of memory. In E. Tulving & F. I. M. Craik (Eds.), *Handbook of memory* (pp. 557–570). Oxford University Press.

Anderson, M. C. (2003). Rethinking interference theory: Executive control and the mechanisms of forgetting. *Journal of Memory and Language, 49,* 415–445.

Anderson, M. C., Bjork, R. A., & Bjork, E. L. (1994). Remembering can cause forgetting: Retrieval dynamics in long-term memory. *Journal of Experimental Psychology: Learning, Memory, and Cognition, 20,* 1063–1087.

Anderson, M. C., Ochsner, K. N., Kuhl, B., Cooper, J., Robertson, E., Gabrieli, S. W., ... Gabrieli, J. D. E. (2004). Neural systems underlying the suppression of unwanted memories. *Science, 303,* 232–235.

Anderson, M. L. (2008). Multiple inference and gender differences in the effects of early intervention: A reevaluation of the Abecedarian, Perry Preschool, and Early Training Projects. *Journal of the American Statistical Association, 103*(484), 1481–1495. https://doi.org/10.1198 /016214508000000841

Anderson, R. C., Pichert, J. W., Goetz, E. T., Schallert, D. L., Stevens, K. V., & Trollip, S. R. (1976). Instantiation of general terms. *Journal of Verbal Learning and Verbal Behavior, 15,* 667–679.

Anderson, T. (2021, June 2). Waze app and poor visibility lead SUV onto Newton golf course, driver tells police. *Boston Globe.* https:// www.bostonglobe.com/2021/06/02/metro/waze-app-poor-visibility -leads-suv-onto-newton-golf-course-driver-tells-police/

Andreasen, N. C. (2011). A journey into chaos: Creativity and the unconscious. *Mens Sana Monographs, 9,* 42–53.

Andrewes, D. (2001). *Neuropsychology: From theory to practice.* Psychology Press.

Andrews, I. (1982). Bilinguals out of focus: A critical discussion. *International Review of Applied Linguistics in Language Teaching, 20,* 297–305.

Andrieux, M., & Proteau, L. (2014). Mixed observation favors motor learning through better estimation of the model's performance. *Experimental Brain Research, 232,* 3121–3132.

Annis, L. F., & Annis, D. B. (1982). A normative study of students' reported preferred study techniques. *Literacy Research and Instruction, 21,* 201–207.

Ansfield, M., Wegner, D. M., & Bowser, R. (1996). Ironic effects of sleep urgency. *Behavior Research and Therapy, 34,* 523–531.

Anstis, S. (2010). Visual filling in. *Current Biology, 20*(16), R664–R666. https://doi.org/10.1016/j.cub.2010.06.029

Antoni, M. H., Lehman, J. M., Klibourn, K. M., Boyers, A. E., Culver, J. L., Alferi, S. M., ... Carver, C. S. (2001). Cognitive-behavioral stress management intervention decreases the prevalence of depression and enhances benefit finding among women under treatment for early-stage breast cancer. *Health Psychology, 20,* 20–32.

Apperly, I. A., & Butterfill, S. A. (2009). Do humans have two systems to track beliefs and belief-like states? *Psychological Review, 116,* 953–970.

Ardekani, B. A., Convit, A., & Bachman, A. H. (2016). Analysis of the MIRIAD data shows sex differences in hippocampal atrophy progression. *Journal of Alzheimer's Disease. 50,* 847–857.

Arden, R., & Adams, M. J. (2016). A general intelligence factor in dogs. *Intelligence, 55,* 79–85. https://doi.org/10.1016/j.intell.2016.01.008

Ariel, R., & Karpicke, J. D. (2018). Improving self-regulated learning with a retrieval practice intervention. *Journal of Experimental Psychology: Applied, 24,* 43–56.

Armstrong, D. M. (1980). *The nature of mind.* Cornell University Press.

Armstrong, T. (2015). The myth of the normal brain: Embracing neurodiversity. *AMA Journal of Ethics, 17*(4), 348–352. https://doi.org/10.1001/journalofethics.2015.17.4.msoc1-1504

Arnold, M. B. (Ed.). (1960). *Emotion and personality: Psychological aspects* (Vol. 1). Columbia University Press.

Arnold, S. E., Trojanowski, J. Q., Gur, R. E., Blackwell, P., Han, L., & Choi, C. (1998). Absence of neurodegeneration and neural injury in the cerebral cortex in a sample of elderly patients with schizophrenia. *Archives of General Psychiatry, 55,* 225–232.

Aron, A., Fisher, H., Mashek, D., Strong, G., Li, H., & Brown, L. (2005). Reward, motivation, and emotion systems associated with early-stage intense romantic love. *Journal of Neurophysiology, 93,* 327–337.

Aronson, E. (1969). The theory of cognitive dissonance: A current perspective. In L. Berkowitz (Ed.), *Advances in experimental social psychology* (Vol. 4, pp. 1–34). Academic Press.

Aronson, E., & Mills, J. (1958). The effect of severity of initiation on liking for a group. *Journal of Abnormal and Social Psychology, 59,* 177–181.

Aronson, E., & Worchel, P. (1966). Similarity versus liking as determinants of interpersonal attractiveness. *Psychonomic Science, 5,* 157–158.

Aronson, E., Willerman, B., & Floyd, J. (1966). The effect of a pratfall on increasing interpersonal attractiveness. *Psychonomic Science, 4,* 227–228.

Aronson, J., & Steele, C. M. (2004). Stereotypes and the fragility of academic competence, motivation, and self-concept. In A. J. Elliot & C. S. Dweck (Eds.), *Handbook of competence and motivation* (pp. 436–456). Guilford Press.

Aronson, J., Fried, C. B., & Good, C. (2002). Reducing stereotype threat and boosting academic achievement of African-American students: The role of conceptions of intelligence. *Journal of Experimental Social Psychology, 38*(2), 113–125. https://doi.org/10.1006/jesp.2001.1491

Asch, S. E. (1951). Effects of group pressure on the modification and distortion of judgments. In H. Guetzkow (Ed.), *Groups, leadership, and men* (pp. 177–190). Carnegie Press.

Asch, S. E. (1955). Opinions and social pressure. *Scientific American, 193,* 31–35.

Asch, S. E. (1956). Studies of independence and conformity: 1. A minority of one against a unanimous majority. *Psychological Monographs: General and Applied, 70,* 1–70.

Aschoff, J. (1965). Circadian rhythms in man. *Science, 148,* 1427–1432.

Aserinsky, E., & Kleitman, N. (1953). Regularly occurring periods of eye motility, and concomitant phenomena, during sleep. *Science, 118,* 273–274.

Ash, M., & Boyce, J. K. (2018). Racial disparities in pollution exposure and employment at U.S. industrial facilities. *Proceedings of the National Academy of Sciences, USA, 115,* 10636–10641.

Ashby, F. G., & Ell, S. W. (2001). The neurobiology of human category learning. *Trends in Cognitive Sciences, 5,* 204–210.

Ashby, F. G., & O'Brien, J. B. (2005). Category learning and multiple memory systems. *Trends in Cognitive Sciences, 9,* 83–89.

Ashby, F. G., & Rosedahl, L. (2017). A neural interpretation of exemplar theory. *Psychological Review, 124,* 472–482.

Asher, J. (2018, September 21). A rise in murder? Let's talk about the weather. *New York Times.* http://www.nytimes.com/2018/09/21/upshot/a-rise-in-murder-5lets-talk-about-the-weather.html

Associated Press. (2007). Former stripper guilty of posing as psychologist. *Boston Herald.* http://www.bostonherald.com

Astington, J. W., & Baird, J. (2005). *Why language matters for theory of mind.* Oxford University Press.

Atance, C. M., Bélanger, M., & Meltzoff, A. N. (2010). Preschoolers' understanding of others' desires: Fulfilling mine enhances my understanding of yours. *Developmental Psychology, 46*(6), 1505–1513. https://doi.org/10.1037/a0020374

Atkinson, R. C., & Shiffrin, R. M. (1968). Human memory: A proposed system and its control processes. In K. W. Spence & J. T. Spence (Eds.), *The psychology of learning and motivation* (Vol. 2, pp. 89–195). Academic Press.

Au, J., Sheehan, E., Tsai, N., Duncan, G. J., Buschkuehl, M., & Jaeggi, S. (2015). Improving fluid intelligence with training on working memory: A meta-analysis. *Psychonomic Bulletin & Review, 22,* 366–377.

Avena-Koenigsberger, A., Misic, B., & Sporns, O. (2018). Communication dynamics in complex brain networks. *Nature Reviews Neuroscience, 19,* 17–33.

Aviezer, H., Hassin, R. R., Ryan, J., Grady, C., Susskind, J., Anderson, A., … Bentin, S. (2008). Angry, disgusted, or afraid? Studies on the malleability of emotion perception. *Psychological Science, 19,* 724–732.

Avolio, B. J., & Waldman, D. A. (1994). Variations in cognitive, perceptual, and psychomotor abilities across the working life span: Examining the effects of race, sex, experience, education, and occupational type. *Psychology and Aging, 9,* 430–442.

Axelrod, R. (1984). *The evolution of cooperation.* Basic Books.

Ayduk, O., Shoda, Y., Cervone, D., & Downey, G. (2007). Delay of gratification in children: Contributions to social-personality psychology. In G. Downey, Y. Shoda, & C. Cervone (Eds.), *Persons in context: Building a science of the individual* (pp. 97–109). Guilford Press.

Ayres, C. E. (1921). Instinct and capacity. 1. The instinct of belief-in-instincts. *Journal of Philosophy, 18,* 561–565.

Azucar, D., Marengo, D., & Settanni, M. (2018). Predicting the Big 5 personality traits from digital footprints on social media: A meta-analysis. *Personality and Individual Differences, 124,* 150–159.

Azuma, H., & Kashiwagi, K. (1987). Descriptors for an intelligent person: A Japanese study. *Japanese Psychological Research, 29,* 17–26.

Baars, B. J. (1986). *The cognitive revolution in psychology.* Guilford Press.

Baca-Motes, K., Brown, A., Gneezy, A., Keenan, E. A., & Nelson, L. D. (2013). Commitment and behavior change: Evidence from the field. *Journal of Consumer Research, 39*(5), 1070–1084. https://doi.org/10.1086/667226

Backman, C. W., & Secord, P. F. (1959). The effect of perceived liking on interpersonal attraction. *Human Relations, 12,* 379–384.

Bäckman, L., & Dixon, R. A. (1992). Psychological compensation: A theoretical framework. *Psychological Bulletin, 112,* 259–283.

Baddeley, A. D. (2001). Is working memory still working? *American Psychologist, 56,* 851–864.

Baddeley, A. D. (2012). Working memory: Theories, models, and controversies. *Annual Review of Psychology, 63,* 1–29.

Baddeley, A. D., & Hitch, G. J. (1974). Working memory. In S. Dornic (Ed.), *Attention and performance* (Vol. 6, pp. 647–667). Erlbaum.

Baddeley, A. D., & Hitch, G. J. (2019). The phonological loop as a buffer store: An update. *Cortex, 112,* 91–106.

Baddeley, A. D., Allen, R. J., & Hitch, G. J. (2011). Binding in visual working memory: The role of the episodic buffer. *Neuropsychologia, 49,* 1393–1400.

Badets, A., Boutin, A., & Michelet, T. (2018). A safety mechanism for observational learning. *Psychonomic Bulletin & Review, 25,* 643–650.

Bagby, R. M., Levitan, R. D., Kennedy, S. H., Levitt, A. J., & Joffe, R. T. (1999). Selective alteration of personality in response to noradrenergic and serotonergic antidepressant medication in depressed sample: Evidence of non-specificity. *Psychiatry Research, 86,* 211–216.

Bahji, A., Hawken, E. R., Sepehry, A. A., Cabrera, C. A., & Vazquez, G. (2019). ECT beyond unipolar major depression: Systematic review and meta-analysis of electroconvulsive therapy in bipolar depression. *Acta Psychiatrica Scandanavica, 139*(3), 214–226. https://doi.org/10.1111/acps.12994

Bahrick, H. P. (1984). Semantic memory content in permastore: 50 years of memory for Spanish learned in school. *Journal of Experimental Psychology: General, 113,* 1–29.

Bahrick, H. P. (2000). Long-term maintenance of knowledge. In E. Tulving & F. I. M. Craik (Eds.), *The Oxford handbook of memory* (pp. 347–362). Oxford University Press.

Bahrick, H. P., Hall, L. K., & Berger, S. A. (1996). Accuracy and distortion in memory for high school grades. *Psychological Science, 7,* 265–271.

Bahrick, H. P., Hall, L. K., & DaCosta, L. A. (2008). Fifty years of college grades: Accuracy and distortions. *Emotion, 8,* 13–22.

Baig, F., Kelly, M. J., Lawton, M. A., Ruffman, C., Rolinski, M., Klein, J. C., ... Hu, M. T. (2019). Impulse control disorders in Parkinson disease and RBD: A longitudinal study of severity. *Neurology, 93*(7), e675–e687. https://doi.org/10.1212/WNL.0000000000007942

Bailey, J. M., & Pillard, R. C. (1991). A genetic study of male sexual orientation. *Archives of General Psychiatry, 48,* 1089–1096.

Bailey, J. M., & Zucker, K. J. (1995). Childhood sex-typed behavior and sexual orientation: A conceptual analysis and quantitative review. *Developmental Psychology, 31,* 43–55.

Bailey, J. M., Pillard, R. C., Neale, M. C., & Agyes, Y. (1993). Heritable factors influence sexual orientation in women. *Archives of General Psychiatry, 50,* 217–223.

Bailey, J. M., Vasey, P. L., Diamond, L. M., Breedlove, S. M., Vilain, E., & Epprecht, M. (2016). Sexual orientation, controversy, and science. *Psychological Science in the Public Interest, 17*(2), 45–101. https://doi.org/10.1177/1529100616637616

Baillargeon, R., Scott, R. M., & He, Z. (2010). False-belief understanding in infants. *Trends in Cognitive Sciences, 14*(3), 110–118.

Baillargeon, R., Spelke, E. S., & Wasserman, S. (1985). Object permanence in 5-month-old infants. *Cognition, 20,* 191–208.

Baird, B., Castelnovo, A., Gosseries, O., & Tononi, G. (2018). Frequent lucid dreaming associated with increased functional connectivity between frontopolar cortex and temporoparietal association areas. *Scientific Reports, 8,* 17798. https://doi.org/10.1038/s41598-018-36190-w

Baker, E., Shelton, K. H., Baibazarova, E., Hay, D. F., & van Goozen, S. H. M. (2013). Low skin conductance activity in infancy predicts aggression in toddlers 2 years later. *Psychological Science, 24*(6), 1051–1056. https://doi.org/10.1177/0956797612465198

Baker, M., Strickland, A., & Fox, N. D. (2019). Choosing a meal to increase your appeal: How relationship status, sexual orientation, dining partner sex, and attractiveness impact nutritional choices in social dining scenarios. *Appetite, 133,* 262–269. https://doi.org/10.1016/j.appet.2018.11.023

Baker, P. (2015, June 10). Michelle Obama talks about race and success, and makes it personal. *New York Times.* http://www.nytimes.com/2015/06/11/us/michelle-obama-king-college-prep-and-tuskegee-graduation-speeches.html

Baker, T. B., Brandon, T. H., & Chassin, L. (2004). Motivational influences on cigarette smoking. *Annual Review of Psychology, 55,* 463–491.

Baker, T. B., McFall, R. M., & Shoham, V. (2009). Current status and future prospects of clinical psychology: Toward a scientifically principled approach to mental and behavioral health care. *Psychological Science in the Public Interest, 9,* 67–103.

Baldassarri, D. (2020). Market integration accounts for local variation in generalized altruism in a nationwide lost-letter experiment. *Proceedings of the National Academy of Sciences, 117*(6), 2858–2863. https://doi.org/10.1073/pnas.1819934117

Baldwin, V. N., & Powell, T. (2015). Google Calendar: A single case experimental design study of a man with severe memory problems. *Neuropsychological Rehabilitation, 25,* 617–636.

Baler, R. D., & Volkow, N. D. (2006). Drug addiction: The neurobiology of disrupted self-control. *Trends in Molecular Medicine, 12,* 559–566.

Balliet, D., Wu, J., & De Dreu, C. K. (2014). Ingroup favoritism in cooperation: A meta-analysis. *Psychological Bulletin, 140*(6), 1556–1581. https://doi.org/10.1037/a0037737

Baltes, P. B., & Reinert, G. (1969). Cohort effects in cognitive development of children as revealed by cross-sectional sequences. *Developmental Psychology, 1,* 169–177.

Balthazart, J. (2018). Fraternal birth order effect on sexual orientation explained. *Proceedings of the National Academy of Sciences, USA, 115,* 234–236.

Banaji, M. R., & Heiphetz, L. (2010). Attitudes. In S. T. Fiske, D. T. Gilbert, & G. Lindzey (Eds.), *The handbook of social psychology* (5th ed., Vol. 1, pp. 348–388). Wiley.

Bandelow, B., Michaelis, S. S., & Wedekind, D. (2017). Treatment of anxiety disorders. *Dialogues in Clinical Neuroscience, 19,* 93–107.

Bandoli, G., Campbell-Sills, L., Kessler, R. C., Heeringa, S. G., Nock, M. K., Rosellini, A. J., ... Stein, M. B. (2017). Childhood adversity, adult stress, and the risk of major depression or generalized anxiety disorder in U.S. soldiers: A test of the stress sensitization hypothesis. *Psychological Medicine, 47,* 2379–2392.

Bandura, A. (1965). Influence of models' reinforcement contingencies on the acquisition of imitative responses. *Journal of Social and Personality Psychology, 1,* 589–595.

Bandura, A. (1977). *Social learning theory.* Prentice Hall.

Bandura, A. (1986). *Social foundations of thought and action: A social cognitive theory.* Prentice Hall.

Bandura, A. (1994). Social cognitive theory of mass communication. In J. Bryant & D. Zillmann (Eds.), *Media effects: Advances in theory and research* (pp. 61–90). Erlbaum.

Bandura, A., Ross, D., & Ross, S. (1961). Transmission of aggression through imitation of adult models. *Journal of Abnormal and Social Psychology, 63,* 575–582.

Bandura, A., Ross, D., & Ross, S. (1963). Vicarious reinforcement and imitative learning. *Journal of Abnormal and Social Psychology, 67,* 601–607.

Banissy, M. J., Walsh, V., & Ward, J. (2009). Enhanced sensory perception in synaesthesia. *Experimental Brain Research, 196*(4), 565–571. https://doi.org/10.1007/s00221-009-1888-0

Banks, M. S., & Salapatek, P. (1983). Infant visual perception. In M. Haith & J. Campos (Eds.), *Handbook of child psychology: Biology and infancy* (pp. 435–572). Wiley.

Banse, R., & Scherer, K. R. (1996). Acoustic profiles in vocal emotion expression. *Journal of Personality and Social Psychology, 70,* 614–636.

Bantjes, J., Kazdin, A. E., Cuijpers, P., Breet, E., Dunn-Coetzee, M., Davids, C., … Kessler, R. C. (2021). A web-based group cognitive behavioral therapy intervention for symptoms of anxiety and depression among university students: Open-label, pragmatic trial. *JMIR Mental Health, 8*(5), e27400. https://doi.org/10.2196/27400

Barber, J., Muran, J. C., McCarthy, K. S., Keefe, J. R., & Zilcha-Mano, S. (2021). Research on dynamic therapies. In M. Barkham, W. Lutz, & L. G. Castonguay (Eds.), *Bergin and Garfield's handbook of psychotherapy and behavior change: 50th anniversary edition* (pp. 387–420). John Wiley & Sons.

Barber, S. J., Harris, C. B., & Rajaram, S. (2015). Why two heads apart are better than two heads together: Multiple mechanisms underlie the collaborative inhibition effect in memory. *Journal of Experimental Psychology: Learning, Memory, and Cognition, 41,* 559–566.

Barber, S. J., Rajaram, S., & Fox, E. B. (2012). Learning and remembering with others: The key role of retrieval in shaping group recall and collective memory. *Social Cognition, 30,* 121–132.

Barbey, A. K. (2018). Network neuroscience theory of human intelligence. *Trends in Cognitive Sciences, 22*(1), 8–20. https://doi.org/10.1016/j.tics.2017.10.001

Bareš, M., Apps, R., Avanzino, L., Breska, A., D'Angelo, E., Filip, P., . . . Lusk, N. A. (2019). Consensus paper: Decoding the contributions of the cerebellum as a time machine. From neurons to clinical applications. *The Cerebellum, 18*(2), 266–286.

Bargh, J. A., Gollwitzer, P. M., & Oettingen, G. (2010). Motivation. In S. T. Fiske, D. T. Gilbert, & G. Lindzey (Eds.), *The handbook of social psychology* (5th ed., Vol. 1, pp. 263–311). Wiley.

Bargh, J. A., Gollwitzer, P. M., Lee-Chai, A., Barndollar, K., & Trötschel, R. (2001). The automated will: Nonconscious activation and pursuit of behavioral goals. *Journal of Personality and Social Psychology, 81,* 1014–1027.

Barker, A. T., Jalinous, R., & Freeston, I. L. (1985). Noninvasive magnetic stimulation of the human motor cortex. *Lancet, 2,* 1106–1107.

Barkow, J. (1980). Prestige and self-esteem: A biosocial interpretation. In D. R. Omark, F. F. Stayer, & D. G. Freedman (Eds.), *Dominance relations* (pp. 319–322). Garland.

Barlett, C., & Coyne, S. M. (2014). A meta-analysis of sex differences in cyber-bullying behavior: The moderating role of age. *Aggressive Behavior, 40,* 474–488. https://doi.org/10.1002/ab.21555

Barlow, D. H., Bullis, J. R., Comer, J. S., & Ametaj, A. A. (2013). Evidence-based psychological treatments: An update and a way forward. *Annual Review of Clinical Psychology, 9,* 1–27.

Barlow, D. H., Gorman, J. M., Shear, M. K., & Woods, S. W. (2000). Cognitive-behavioral therapy, imipramine, or their combination for panic disorder: A randomized controlled trial. *Journal of the American Medical Association, 283*(19), 2529–2536.

Barnett, A., & Spence, C. (2016). Assessing the effect of changing a bottled beer label on taste ratings. *Nutrition and Food Technology Open Access, 2*(4). https://doi.org/10.16966/2470-6086.132

Barnier, A. J., Levin, K., & Maher, A. (2004). Suppressing thoughts of past events: Are repressive copers good suppressors? *Cognition and Emotion, 18,* 457–477.

Baron-Cohen, S. (1991). Do people with autism understand what causes emotion? *Child Development, 62,* 385–395.

Baron-Cohen, S. (2017). Editorial perspective: Neurodiversity. A revolutionary concept for autism and psychiatry. *Journal of Child Psychology and Psychiatry, 58*(6), 744–747. https://doi.org/10.1111/jcpp.12703

Baron-Cohen, S., & Belmonte, M. K. (2005). Autism: A window onto the development of the social and analytic brain. *Annual Review of Neuroscience, 28,* 109–126.

Baron-Cohen, S., Leslie, A., & Frith, U. (1985). Does the autistic child have a "theory of mind"? *Cognition, 21,* 37–46.

Barondes, S. (2003). *Better than Prozac.* Oxford University Press.

Barr, W. B., & Karantzoulis, S. (2019). Chronic traumatic encephalopathy. In L. D. Ravdin, & H. L. Katzen (Eds.), *Handbook on the neuropsychology of aging and dementia* (pp. 727–745). Springer.

Barragán, R., Coltell, O., Portolés, O., Asensio, E. M., Sorlí, J. V., Ortega-Azorín, C., … Corella, D. (2018). Bitter, sweet, salty, sour and umami taste perception decreases with age: Sex-specific analysis, modulation by genetic variants and taste-preference associations in 18- to 80-year-old subjects. *Nutrients, 10*(10), E1539. https://doi.org/10.3390/nu10101539

Barrett, L. F., Mesquita, B., & Gendron, M. (2011). Context in emotion perception. *Current Directions in Psychological Science, 20*(5), 286–290. https://doi.org/10.1177/0963721411422522

Barrientos, R. M., Watkins, L. R., Rudy, J. W., & Maier, S. F. (2009). Characterization of the sickness response in young and aging rats following *E. coli* infection. *Brain, Behavior, and Immunity, 23,* 450–454.

Bartal, I. B.-A., Decety, J., & Mason, P. (2011). Empathy and pro-social behavior in rats. *Science, 334*(6061), 1427–1430.

Bartol, C. R., & Costello, N. (1976). Extraversion as a function of temporal duration of electric shock: An exploratory study. *Perceptual and Motor Skills, 42,* 1174.

Bartoshuk, L. M. (2000). Comparing sensory experiences across individuals: Recent psychophysical advances illuminate genetic variation in taste perception. *Chemical Senses, 25,* 447–460.

Bartoshuk, L. M., & Beauchamp, G. K. (1994). Chemical senses. *Annual Review of Psychology, 45,* 419–445.

Basden, B. H., Basden, D. R., Bryner, S., & Thomas, R. L. (1997). A comparison of group and individual remembering: Does collaboration disrupt retrieval strategies? *Journal of Experimental Psychology: Learning, Memory, and Cognition, 23,* 1176–1191.

Basile, K. C., Chen, J., Black, M. C., & Saltzman, L. E. (2007). Prevalence and characteristics of sexual violence victimization among U.S. adults, 2001–2003. *Violence and Victims, 22*(4), 437–448.

Bass, C. & Halligan, P. (2014) Factitious disorders and malingering: Challenges for clinical assessment and management. *Lancet, 383,* 1422–1432.

Bates, E., & Goodman, J. C. (1997). On the inseparability of grammar and the lexicon: Evidence from acquisition, aphasia, and real-time processing. *Language and Cognitive Processes, 12,* 507–584.

Bates, T. C., Hansell, N. K., Martin, N. G., & Wright, M. J. (2016). When does socioeconomic status (SES) moderate the heritability of IQ? No evidence for g × SES interaction for IQ in a representative sample of 1176 Australian adolescent twin pairs. *Intelligence, 56,* 10–15. https://doi.org/10.1016/j.intell.2016.02.003

Bateson, M., Nettle, D., & Roberts, G. (2006). Cues of being watched enhance cooperation in a real-world setting. *Biology Letters, 2*(3), 412–414.

Batson, C. D. (2002). Addressing the altruism question experimentally. In S. G. Post & L. G. Underwood (Eds.), *Altruism & altruistic love: Science, philosophy, & religion in dialogue* (pp. 89–105). Oxford University Press.

Baumeister, R. F. (2000). Gender differences in erotic plasticity: The female sex drive as socially flexible and responsive. *Psychological Bulletin, 126,* 347–374.

Baumeister, R. F., Ainsworth, S., & Vohs, K. (2016). Are groups more or less than the sum of their members? The moderating role of individual identification. *Behavioral and Brain Sciences, 39,* e137. https://doi.org/10.1017/S0140525X15000618

Baumeister, R. F., Campbell, J. D., Krueger, J. I., & Vohs, K. D. (2003). Does high self-esteem cause better performance, interpersonal success, happiness, or healthier lifestyles? *Psychological Science in the Public Interest, 4,* 1–44.

Baumeister, R. F., Cantanese, K. R., & Vohs, K. D. (2001). Is there a gender difference in strength of sex drive? Theoretical views, conceptual distinctions, and a review of relevant evidence. *Personality and Social Psychology Review, 5,* 242–273.

Baumeister, R. F., & Leary, M. R. (1995). The need to belong: Desire for interpersonal attachments as a fundamental human motivation. *Psychological Bulletin, 117,* 497–529.

Baumeister, R. F., Smart, L., & Boden, J. M. (1996). Relation of threatened egotism to violence and aggression: The dark side of high self-esteem. *Psychological Review, 103,* 5–33.

Baumer, Y., Farmer, N., Premeaux, T. A., Wallen, G. R., & Powell-Wiley, T. M. (2020). Health disparities in COVID-19: Addressing the role of social determinants of health in immune system dysfunction to turn the tide. *Frontiers in Public Health, 8,* 559312. https://doi.org/10.3389/fpubh.2020.559312

Bayley, P. J., Frascino, J. C., & Squire, L. R. (2005). Robust habit learning in the absence of awareness and independent of the medial temporal lobe. *Nature, 436,* 550–553.

Beaty, R. E., Benedek, M., Silvia, P. J., & Schacter, D. L. (2016). Creative cognition and brain network dynamics. *Trends in Cognitive Sciences, 20,* 87–95.

Beaty, R. E., Thakral, P. P., Madore, K. P., Benedek, M., & Schacter, D. L. (2018). Core network contributions to remembering the past, imagining the future, and thinking creatively. *Journal of Cognitive Neuroscience, 30*(12), 1939–1951.

Bechara, A., Damasio, A. R., Damasio, H., & Anderson, S. W. (1994). Insensitivity to future consequences following damage to human prefrontal cortex. *Cognition, 50,* 7–15.

Bechara, A., Damasio, H., Tranel, D., & Damasio, A. R. (1997). Deciding advantageously before knowing the advantageous strategy. *Science, 275,* 1293–1295.

Bechara, A., Dolan, S., Denburg, N., Hindes, A., & Anderson, S. W. (2001). Decision-making deficits, linked to a dysfunctional ventromedial prefrontal cortex, revealed in alcohol and stimulant abusers. *Neuropsychologia, 39,* 376–389.

Bechara, A., Tranel, D., & Damasio, H. (2000). Characterization of the decision-making deficit of patients with ventromedial prefrontal cortex lesions. *Brain, 123,* 2189–2202.

Becht, A. I., Nelemans, S. A., Branje, S. T., Vollebergh, W. M., Koot, H. M., & Meeus, W. J. (2017). Identity uncertainty and commitment making across adolescence: Five-year within-person associations using daily identity reports. *Developmental Psychology,* 53(11), 2103–2112. https://doi.org/10.1037/dev0000374

Beck, A. T. (1967). *Depression: Causes and treatment.* University of Pennsylvania Press.

Beck, A. T. (2019). A 60-year evolution of cognitive theory and therapy. *Perspectives on Psychological Science, 14*(1), 16–20.

Becker, D. V., Neel, R., & Anderson, U. S. (2010). Illusory conjunctions of angry facial expressions follow intergroup bias. *Psychological Science, 21,* 938–940.

Bédard, A.-C., Nichols, S., Barbosa, J. A., Schachar, R., Logan, G. D., & Tannock, R. (2002). The development of selective inhibitory control across the life span. *Developmental Neuropsychology, 21,* 93–111.

Bedny, M., & Saxe, R. (2012). Insights into the origins of knowledge from the cognitive neuroscience of blindness. *Cognitive Neuropsychology, 29,* 56–84.

Bedny, M., Pascual-Leone, A., Dodell-Feder, D., Fedorenko, E., & Saxe, R. (2011). Language processing in the occipital cortex of congenitally blind adults. *Proceedings of the National Academy of Sciences, 108*(11), 4429–4434. https://doi.org/10.1073/pnas.1014818108

Beek, M. R., Levin, D. T., & Angelone, B. (2007). Change blindness: Beliefs about the roles of intention and scene complexity in change detection. *Consciousness and Cognition, 16,* 31–51.

Begg, I. M., Anas, A., & Farinacci, S. (1992). Dissociation of processes in belief: Source recollection, statement familiarity, and the illusion of truth. *Journal of Experimental Psychology: General, 121,* 446–458.

Bell, R., Roer, J. P., & Buchner, A. (2015). Adaptive memory: Thinking about function. *Journal of Experimental Psychology: Learning, Memory, & Cognition, 41,* 1038–1048.

Bellot, E., Abassi, E., & Papeo, L. (2021). Moving toward versus away from another: How motion direction changes the representation of bodies and actions in the visual cortex. *Cerebral Cortex, 31*(5), 2670–2685. https://doi.org/10.1093/cercor/bhaa382

Belluck, P., & Carey, B. (2013, May 7). Psychiatry's guide is out of touch with science, experts say. *New York Times.* http://www.nytimes.com/2013/05/07/psychiatrys-new-guide-falls-short-experts-say.html

Belsky, J. (2019). Early-life adversity accelerates child and adolescent development. *Current Directions in Psychological Science, 28*(3), 241–246. https://doi.org/10.1177/0963721419837670

Bem, S. L. (1974). The measure of psychological androgyny. *Journal of Consulting and Clinical Psychology, 42,* 155–162.

Bender, J., O'Connor, A. M., & Evans, A. D. (2018). Mirror, mirror on the wall: Increasing young children's honesty through inducing self-awareness. *Journal of Experimental Child Psychology, 167,* 414–422. https://doi.org/10.1016/j.jecp.2017.12.001

Benedek, M., Jauk, E., Fink, A., Koschutnig, K., Reishofer, G., Ebner, F., & Neubauer, A. C. (2014). To create or to recall? Neural mechanisms underlying the generation of creative new ideas. *NeuroImage, 88,* 125–133.

Benenson, J. F., Markovits, H., Thompson, M. E., & Wrangham, R. W. (2011). Under threat of social exclusion, females exclude more than males. *Psychological Science, 22*(4), 538–544. https://doi.org/10.1177/0956797611402511

Bennett, I. J., Romano, J. C., Howard, J. H., & Howard, D. V. (2008). Two forms of implicit learning in young adults with dyslexia. *Annals of the New York Academy of Sciences, 1145,* 184–198.

Benoit, R. G., & Anderson, M. C. (2012). Opposing mechanisms support the voluntary forgetting of unwanted memories. *Neuron, 76,* 450–460.

Benoit, R. G., & Schacter, D. L. (2015). Specifying the core network supporting episodic simulation and episodic memory by activation likelihood estimation. *Neuropsychologia, 75,* 450–457.

Benoit, S. C., Kemp, C. J., Elias, C. F., Abplanalp, W., Herman, J. P., Migrenne, S., … Clegg, D. J. (2009). Palmitic acid mediates hypothalamic insulin resistance by altering PKC-theta subcellular localization in rodents. *Journal of Clinical Investigation, 119*(9), 2577–2589.

Ben-Porath, Y. S., & Tellegen, A. (2008). *Minnesota Multiphasic Personality Inventory–2–Restructured Form: Manual for administration, scoring, and interpretation.* University of Minnesota Press.

Benson, H. (Ed.). (1990). *The relaxation response.* Harper Torch.

Benson, H., Dusek, J. A., Sherwood, J. B., Lam, P., Bethea, C. F., Carpenter, W., ... Hibberd, P. L. (2006). Study of the therapeutic effects of intercessory prayer (STEP) in cardiac bypass patients: A multicenter randomized trial of uncertainty and certainty of receiving intercessory prayer. *American Heart Journal, 151,* 934–942.

Bentz, D., & Schiller, D. (2015). Threat processing: Models and mechanisms. *WIREs Cognitive Science, 6,* 427–439.

Berger, H. (1929). Über das Elektrenkephalogramm des Menschen [Electroencephalogram of man]. *Archiv für Psychiatrie und Nervenkrankheiten, 87,* 527–570.

Berger, J. (2014). Word of mouth and interpersonal communication: A review and directions for future research. *Journal of Consumer Psychology, 24*(4), 586–607.

Berkowitz, L. (1989). Frustration-aggression hypothesis: Examination and reformulation. *Psychological Bulletin, 106*(1), 59–73. https://doi.org/10.1037/0033-2909.106.1.59

Berkowitz, L. (1990). On the formation and regulation of anger and aggression: A cognitive-neoassociationistic analysis. *American Psychologist, 45,* 494–503.

Bernard, L. L. (1924). *Instinct: A study in social psychology.* Holt.

Bernstein, E. E., & McNally, R. J. (2017). Acute aerobic exercise hastens emotional recovery from a subsequent stressor. *Health Psychology, 36,* 560–567.

Berntsen, D. (2010). The unbidden past: Involuntary autobiographical memories as a basic mode of remembering. *Current Directions in Psychological Science, 19,* 138–142.

Berridge, K. C. (2007). The debate over dopamine's role in reward: The case for incentive salience. *Psychopharmacology, 191,* 391–431.

Berry, D. S., & McArthur, L. Z. (1985). Some components and consequences of a babyface. *Journal of Personality and Social Psychology, 48,* 312–323.

Berscheid, E., Dion, K., Walster, E., & Walster, G. W. (1971). Physical attractiveness and dating choice: A test of the matching hypothesis. *Journal of Experimental Social Psychology, 7*(2), 173–189.

Berscheid, E., & Reis, H. T. (1998). Interpersonal attraction and close relationships. In D. T. Gilbert, S. T. Fiske, & G. Lindzey (Eds.), *The handbook of social psychology* (4th ed., Vol. 2, pp. 193–281). McGraw-Hill.

Bertenthal, B. I., Rose, J. L., & Bai, D. L. (1997). Perception–action coupling in the development of visual control of posture. *Journal of Experimental Psychology: Human Perception & Performance, 23,* 1631–1643.

Berthoud, H.-R., & Morrison, C. (2008). The brain, appetite, and obesity. *Annual Review of Psychology, 59,* 55–92.

Bertilsson, F., Stenlund, T., Wiklund-Hörnquist, C., & Jonsson, B. (2021). Retrieval practice: Beneficial for all students or moderated by individual differences? *Psychology Learning & Teaching, 20*(1), 21–39. https://doi.org/10.1177/1475725720973494

Bialystok, E. (1999). Cognitive complexity and attentional control in the bilingual mind. *Child Development, 70,* 636–644.

Bialystok, E. (2009). Bilingualism: The good, the bad, and the indifference. *Bilingualism: Language and Cognitive Processes, 12,* 3–11.

Bialystok, E. (2017). The bilingual adaptation: How minds accommodate experience. *Psychological Bulletin, 143,* 233–262.

Bialystok, E. (2021). Bilingualism: Pathway to cognitive reserve. *Trends in Cognitive Sciences, 25*(5), 355–364. https://doi.org/10.1016/j.tics.2021.02.003

Bialystok, E., Craik, F. I. M., & Luk, G. (2012). Bilingualism: Consequences for mind and brain. *Trends in Cognitive Sciences, 16,* 240–250.

Bian, L., Sloane, S., & Baillargeon, R. (2018). Infants expect ingroup support to override fairness when resources are limited. *Proceedings of the National Academy of Sciences, USA, 115*(11), 2705–2710.

Bickerton, D. (1990). *Language and species.* University of Chicago Press.

Biederman, J., Faraone, S. V., Spencer, T. J., Mick, E., Monuteaux, M. C., & Aleardi, M. (2006). Functional impairments in adults with self-reports of diagnosed ADHD: A controlled study of 1001 adults in the community. *Journal of Clinical Psychiatry, 67,* 524–540.

Biederman, J., Monuteaux, M. C., Spencer, T., Wilens, T. E., & Faraone, S. V. (2009). Do stimulants protect against psychiatric disorders in youth with ADHD? A 10-year follow-up study. *Pediatrics, 124,* 71–78.

Bierer, L. M., Bader, H. N., Daskalakis, N. P., Lehrener, A., Provencal, N., Wiechmann, T., ... & Yehuda, R. (2020). Intergenerational effects of maternal Holocaust exposure on FKBP5 methylation. *American Journal of Psychiatry, 177*(8), 744–753. https://doi.org/10.1176/appi.ajp.2019.19060618

Binder, J. R., Desai, R. H., Graves, W. W., & Conant, L. L. (2009). Where is the semantic system? A critical review and meta-analysis of 120 functional neuroimaging studies. *Cerebral Cortex, 19,* 2767–2796.

Biro, S., Alink, L. R., van IJzendoorn, M. H., & Bakermans-Kranenburg, M. J. (2014). Infants' monitoring of social interactions: The effect of emotional cues. *Emotion, 14*(2), 263–271. https://doi.org/10.1037/a0035589

Bisharat, K., Christ, A., & Kröner, S. (2020). Detrimental effects of an economic crisis on student cognitive achievement: A natural experiment from Palestine. *Intelligence, 79,* 101435. https://doi.org/10.1016/j.intell.2020.101435

Biswal, B., Yetkin, F. Z., Haughton, V. M., & Hyde, J. S. (1995). Functional connectivity in the motor cortex of resting human brain using echo-planar MRI. *Magnetic Resonance in Medicine, 34*(4), 537–541. https://doi.org/10.1002/mrm.1910340409

Bjork, E. L., & Bjork, R. A. (2011). Making things hard on yourself, but in a good way: Creating desirable difficulties to enhance learning. In M. A. Gernsbacher, R. W. Pewe, L. M. Hough, & J. R. Pomerantz (Eds.), *Psychology and the real world: Essays illustrating fundamental contributions to society* (pp. 56–64). Worth Publishers.

Bjork, R. A. (1975). Retrieval as a memory modifier. In R. Solso (Ed.), *Information processing and cognition: The Loyola Symposium* (pp. 123–144). Erlbaum.

Bjork, R. A. (2011). On the symbiosis of remembering, forgetting, and learning. In A. S. Benjamin (Ed.), *Successful remembering and successful forgetting: A festschrift in honor of Robert A. Bjork* (pp. 1–22). Psychology Press.

Bjork, R. A., & Bjork, E. L. (1988). On the adaptive aspects of retrieval failure in autobiographical memory. In M. M. Gruneberg, P. E. Morris, & R. N. Sykes (Eds.), *Practical aspects of memory: Current research and issues* (pp. 283–288). Wiley.

Bjork, R. A., Dunlosky, J., & Kornell, N. (2013). Self-regulated learning: Beliefs, techniques, and illusions. *Annual Review of Psychology, 64,* 417–444.

Bjorkqvist, K. (2018). Gender differences in aggression. *Current Opinion in Psychology, 19,* 39–42.

Blackburn, E. H., Epel, E. S., & Lin, J. (2015). Human telomere biology: A contributory and interactive factor in aging, disease risks, and protection. *Science, 350,* 1193–1198.

Blackwell, L. S., Trzesniewski, K. H., & Dweck, C. S. (2007). Implicit theories of intelligence predict achievement across an adolescent transition: A longitudinal study and an intervention. *Child Development, 78*(1), 246–263. https://doi.org/10.1111/j.1467-8624 .2007.00995.x

Blair, C. (2006). How similar are fluid cognition and general intelligence? A developmental neuroscience perspective on fluid cognition as an aspect of human cognitive ability. *Behavioral and Brain Sciences, 29*(2), 109–125 (article), 125–160 (discussion). https://doi.org/10.1017/S0140525X06009034

Blair, I. V. (2002). The malleability of automatic stereotypes and prejudice. *Personality and Social Psychology Review, 6,* 242–261.

Blair, J., Peschardt, K., & Mitchell, D. R. (2005). *Psychopath: Emotion and the brain.* Blackwell.

Blake, M. J., Trinder, J. A., & Allen, N. B. (2018). Mechanisms underlying the association between insomnia, anxiety, and depression in adolescence: Implications for behavioral sleep interventions. *Clinical Psychology Review, 63,* 25–40.

Blake, M. L. (2003). Affective language and humor appreciation after right hemisphere brain damage. *Seminars in Speech and Language, 24*(2), 107–120. https://doi.org/ 10.1055/s-2003-38902

Blake, P. R., McAuliffe, K., & Warneken, F. (2014). The developmental origins of fairness: The knowledge-behavior gap. *Trends in Cognitive Sciences, 18*(11), 559–561. https://doi.org/10.1016/j.tics .2014.08.003

Blake, R., & Shiffrar, M. (2007). Perception of human motion. *Annual Review of Psychology, 58,* 47–73. https://doi.org/10.1146 /annurev.psych.57.102904.190152

Blascovich, J., & Mendes, W. B. (2000). Challenge and threat appraisals: The role of affective cues. In J. P. Forgas (Ed.), *Studies in emotion and social interaction, Second Series. Feeling and thinking: The role of affect in social cognition* (pp. 59–82). Cambridge University Press.

Blascovich, J., Mendes, W. B., Hunter, S. B., Lickel, B., & Kowai-Bell, N. (2001). Perceiver threat in social interactions with stigmatized others. *Journal of Personality and Social Psychology, 80,* 253–267.

Blascovich, J., & Tomaka, J. (1996). The biopsychosocial model of arousal regulation. In M. P. Zanna (Ed.), *Advances in experimental social psychology* (Vol. 28, pp. 1–51). Academic Press.

Blencowe, H., Krasevec, J., de Onis, M., Black, R. E., An, X., Stevens, G. A., Borghi, E., Hayashi, C., Estevez, D., Cegolon, L., Shiekh, S., Ponce Hardy, V., Lawn, J. E., & Cousens, S. (2019). National, regional, and worldwide estimates of low birthweight in 2015, with trends from 2000: A systematic analysis. *The Lancet Global Health, 7*(7), e849–e860. https://doi.org/10.1016/S2214-109X (18)30565-5

Blesch, A., & Tuszynski, M. H. (2009). Spinal cord injury: Plasticity, regeneration and the challenge of translational drug development. *Trends in Neurosciences, 32,* 41–47.

Bliss, T. V. P. (1999). Young receptors make smart mice. *Nature, 401,* 25–27.

Bliss, T. V. P., & Lømo, W. T. (1973). Long-lasting potentiation of synaptic transmission in the dentate area of the anesthetized rabbit following stimulation of the perforant path. *Journal of Physiology, 232,* 331–356.

Bloch, C., Kaiser, A., Kuenzli, E., Zappatore, D., Haller, S., Franceschini, R., ... Nitsch, C. (2009). The age of second language acquisition determines the variability in activation elicited by narration in three languages in Broca's and Wernicke's area. *Neuropsychologia, 47,* 625–633.

Bloch, L., Haase, C. M., & Levenson, R. W. (2014). Emotion regulation predicts marital satisfaction: More than a wives' tale. *Emotion, 14*(1), 130–144. https://doi:10.1037/a0034272

Bloom, C. M., Venard, J., Harden, M., & Seetharaman, S. (2007). Non-contingent positive and negative reinforcement schedules of superstitious behaviors. *Behavioural Process, 75,* 8–13.

Blumen, H. M., & Rajaram, S. (2008). Influence of re-exposure and retrieval disruption during group collaboration on later individual recall. *Memory, 16,* 231–244.

Boden, J. M., Fergusson, D. M., & Horwood, L. J. (2010). Risk factors for conduct disorder and oppositional/defiant disorder: Evidence from a New Zealand birth cohort. *Journal of the American Academy of Child and Adolescent Psychiatry, 49,* 1125–1133.

Boecker, H., Sprenger, T., Spilker, M. E., Henriksen, G., Koppenhoefer, M., Wagner, K. J., ... Tolle, T. R. (2008). The runner's high: Opioidergic mechanisms in the human brain. *Cerebral Cortex, 18,* 2523–2531.

Boehm, J. K., & Kubzansky, L. D. (2012). The heart's content: The association between positive psychological well-being and cardiovascular health. *Psychological Bulletin, 138,* 655–691.

Boehm, J. K., Williams, D. R., Rimm, E. B., Ryff, C., & Kubzansky, L. D. (2013). Relation between optimism and lipids in midlife. *American Journal of Cardiology, 111,* 1425–1431.

Boergers, J., Spirito, A., & Donaldson, D. (1998). Reasons for adolescent suicide attempts: Associations with psychological functioning. *Journal of the American Academy of Child and Adolescent Psychiatry, 37,* 1287–1293.

Boinski, S., Quatrone, R. P., & Swartz, H. (2000). Substrate and tool use by brown capuchins in Suriname: Ecological contexts and cognitive bases. *American Anthropologist, 102,* 741–761.

Boisvert, C. M., & Faust, D. (2002). Iatrogenic symptoms in psychotherapy: A theoretical exploration of the potential impact of labels, language, and belief systems. *American Journal of Psychotherapy, 56,* 244–259.

Bolívar, H. A., Klemperer, E. M., Coleman, S. R. M., DeSarno, M., Skelly, J. M., & Higgins, S. T. (2021). Contingency management for patients receiving medication for opioid use disorder: A systematic review and meta-analysis. *JAMA Psychiatry, 78*(10), 1092–1102. https://doi.org/10.1001/jamapsychiatry.2021.1969

Bolton, G. E., & Ockenfels, A. (2000). ERC: A theory of equity, reciprocity, and competition. *American Economic Review, 90,* 166–193.

Bond, C. F., & DePaulo, B. M. (2006). Accuracy of deception judgments. *Personality and Social Psychology Review, 10,* 214–234.

Bonfiglio, N. (2021, July 12). The Delta variant of COVID has different symptoms than other coronavirus versions. *Nautilus.* https: //coronavirus.nautil.us/delta-variant-symptoms/

Bonnici, H. M., Cheke, L. G., Green, D. A. E., FitzGerald, T. H. M. B., & Simons, J. S. (2018). Specifying a causal role for angular gyrus in episodic memory. *Journal of Neuroscience, 38,* 10438–10443.

Boomsma, D., Busjahn, A., & Peltonen, L. (2002). Classical twin studies and beyond. *Nature Reviews Genetics, 3,* 872–882.

Bordone, V., Scherbov, S., & Steiber, N. (2015). Smarter every day: The deceleration of population ageing in terms of cognition. *Intelligence, 52,* 90–96. https://doi.org/10.1016/j.intell.2015.07.005

Boring, E. G. (1929). *A history of experimental psychology* (p. 624). The Century Company.

Born, R. T., & Bradley, D. C. (2005). Structure and function of visual area MT. *Annual Review of Neuroscience, 28,* 157–189.

Bornstein, R. F. (1989). Exposure and affect: Overview and meta-analysis of research, 1968–1987. *Psychological Bulletin, 106,* 265–289.

Botto, S. V., & Rochat, P. (2018). Sensitivity to the evaluation of others emerges by 24 months. *Developmental Psychology, 54,* 1723–1734.

Botwin, M. D., Buss, D. M., & Shackelford, T. K. (1997). Personality and mate preferences: Five factors in mate selection and marital satisfaction. *Journal of Personality, 65,* 107–136.

Bouchard, S. M., Brown, T. G., & Nadeau, L. (2012). Decision making capacities and affective reward anticipation in DWI recidivists compared to non-offenders: A preliminary study. *Accident Analysis and Prevention, 45,* 580–587.

Bouchard, T. J., & McGue, M. (2003). Genetic and environmental influences on human psychological differences. *Journal of Neurobiology, 54,* 4–45.

Bouton, M. E. (1988). Context and ambiguity in the extinction of emotional learning: Implications for exposure therapy. *Behaviour Research and Therapy, 26,* 137–149.

Boutwell, B. B., Young, J. T. N., & Meldrum, R. C. (2018). On the positive relationship between breastfeeding & intelligence. *Developmental Psychology, 54*(8), 1426–1433. https://doi.org/10.1037/dev0000537

Bovet, J. (2019). Evolutionary theories and men's preferences for women's waist-to-hip ratio: Which hypotheses remain? A systematic review. *Frontiers in Psychology, 10,* 1221. https://www.frontiersin.org/article/10.3389/fpsyg.2019.01221

Bower, G. H. (1981). Mood and memory. *American Psychologist, 36,* 129–148.

Bower, G. H., Clark, M. C., Lesgold, A. M., & Winzenz, D. (1969). Hierarchical retrieval schemes in recall of categorical word lists. *Journal of Verbal Learning and Verbal Behavior, 8,* 323–343.

Bowers, K. S., Regehr, G., Balthazard, C., & Parker, D. (1990). Intuition in the context of discovery. *Cognitive Psychology, 22,* 72–110.

Bowers, K. S., Regehr, G., Balthazard, C., & Parker, D. (1990). Intuition in the context of discovery. *Cognitive Psychology, 22,* 72–110.

Bowlby, J. (1969). *Attachment and loss: Vol. 1. Attachment.* Basic Books.

Bowlby, J. (1973). *Attachment and loss: Vol. 2. Separation.* Basic Books.

Bowlby, J. (1980). *Attachment and loss: Vol. 3. Loss: Sadness and depression.* Basic Books.

Boyd, R. (2008, February 7). Do people use only 10 percent of their brains? *Scientific American.* http://www.scientificamerican.com/article.cfm?id=people-only-use-10-percent-of-brain&page=2

Boyle, L. L. (2018). Psychological and neuropsychological testing. In R. R. Tampi, D. J. Tampi, & L. L. Boyle (Eds.), *Psychiatric disorders late in life: A comprehensive review* (pp. 81–90). Springer International Publishing.

Bozarth, M. A. (Ed.). (1987). *Methods of assessing the reinforcing properties of abused drugs.* Springer-Verlag.

Bozarth, M. A., & Wise, R. A. (1985). Toxicity associated with long-term intravenous heroin and cocaine self-administration in the rat. *Journal of the American Medical Association, 254,* 81–83.

Brackett, M. A., & Mayer, J. D. (2003). Convergent, discriminant, and incremental validity of competing measures of emotional intelligence. *Personality and Social Psychology Bulletin, 29,* 1147.

Brackett, M. A., Rivers, S. E., Shiffman, S., Lerner, N., & Salovey, P. (2006). Relating emotional abilities to social functioning: A comparison of self-report and performance measures of emotional intelligence. *Journal of Personality and Social Psychology, 91,* 780.

Brackett, M. A., Warner, R. M., & Bosco, J. (2005). Emotional intelligence and relationship quality among couples. *Personal Relationships, 12*(2), 197–212.

Bradmetz, J., & Schneider, R. (2004). The role of the counterfactually satisfied desire in the lag between false-belief and false-emotion attributions in children aged 4–7. *British Journal of Developmental Psychology, 22,* 185–196.

Braga, R. M., DiNicola, L. M., Becker, H. C., & Buckner, R. L. (2020). Situating the left-lateralized language network in the broader organization of multiple specialized large-scale distributed networks. *Journal of Neurophysiology, 124*(5), 1415–1448. https://doi.org/10.1152/jn.00753.2019

Brakefield, T. A., Mednick, S. C., Wilson, H. W., De Neve, J. E., Christakis, N. A., & Fowler, J. H. (2014). Same-sex sexual attraction does not spread in adolescent social networks. *Archives of Sexual Behavior, 43*(2), 335–344. https://doi.org/10.1007/s10508-013-0142-9

Bramlett, M. D., & Mosher, W. D. (2002). *Cohabitation, marriage, divorce, and remarriage in the United States* (Vital and Health Statistics Series 23, No. 22). National Center for Health Statistics.

Brandt, K. R., Gardiner, J. M., Vargha-Khadem, F., Baddeley, A. D., & Mishkin, M. (2009). Impairment of recollection but not familiarity in a case of developmental amnesia. *Neurocase, 15,* 60–65.

Brant, A. M., Munakata, Y., Boomsma, D. I., Defries, J. C., Haworth, C. M. A., Keller, M. C., ... Hewitt, J. K. (2013). The nature and nurture of high IQ: An extended sensitive period for intellectual development. *Psychological Science, 24*(8), 1487–1495. https://doi.org/10.1177/0956797612473119

Brashier, N. M., Pennycook, G., Berinsky, A. J., & Rand, D. G. (2021). Timing matters when correcting fake news. *Proceedings of the National Academy of Sciences, 118*(5), e2020043118. https://doi.org/10.1073/pnas.2020043118

Bratman, G. N., Hamilton, J. P., Hahn, K. S., Daily, G. C., & Gross, J. J. (2015). Nature experience reduces rumination and subgenual prefrontal cortex activation. *Proceedings of the National Academy of Science, USA, 112,* 8567–8572.

Bratsberg, B., & Rogeberg, O. (2018). Flynn effect and its reversal are both environmentally caused. *Proceedings of the National Academy of Sciences, USA, 115*(26), 6674–6678. https://doi.org/10.1073/pnas.1718793115

Braun, A. R., Balkin, T. J., Wesensten, N. J., Gwadry, F., Carson, R. E., Varga, M., ... Herskovitch, P. (1998). Dissociated pattern of activity in visual cortices and their projections during rapid eye movement sleep. *Science, 279,* 91–95.

Bravo-Moncayo, L., Reinoso-Carvalho, F., & Velasco, C. (2020). The effects of noise control in coffee tasting experiences. *Food Quality and Preference, 86,* 104020. https://doi.org/10.1016/j.foodqual.2020.104020

Breckler, S. J. (1994). Memory for the experiment of donating blood: Just how bad was it? *Basic and Applied Social Psychology, 15,* 467–488.

Brédart, S., & Valentine, T. (1998). Descriptiveness and proper name retrieval. *Memory, 6,* 199–206.

Bredy, T. W., Wu, H., Crego, C., Zellhoefer, J., Sun, Y. E., & Barad, M. (2007). Histone modifications around individual BDNF gene promoters in prefrontal cortex are associated with extinction of conditioned fear. *Learning and Memory, 14,* 268–276.

Brehm, J. W. (1966). *A theory of psychological reactance.* Academic Press.

Breland, K., & Breland, M. (1961). The misbehavior of organisms. *American Psychologist, 16,* 681–684.

Brennan, P. A., & Zufall, F. (2006). Pheromonal communication in vertebrates. *Nature, 444,* 308–315.

Brenninkmeijer, V., Vanyperen, N. W., & Buunk, B. P. (2001). I am not a better teacher, but others are doing worse: Burnout and perceptions of superiority among teachers. *Social Psychology of Education, 4*(3–4), 259–274.

Breslow, L., Pritchard, D. E., DeBoer, J., Stump, G. S., Ho, A. D., & Seaton, D. T. (2013). Studying learning in the worldwide classroom: Research into edX's first MOOC. *Research & Practice in Assessment, 8*, 13–25.

Brethel-Haurwitz, K. M., & Marsh, A. A. (2014). Geographical differences in subjective well-being predict extraordinary altruism. *Psychological Science, 25*(3), 762–771. https://doi.org/10.1177/0956797613516148

Bretherton, I., & Munholland, K. A. (1999). Internal working models in attachment relationships: A construct revisited. In J. Cassidy & P. R. Shaver (Eds.), *Handbook of attachment: Theory, research and clinical applications* (pp. 89–114). Guilford Press.

Brewer, J. A., Worhunsky, P. D., Gray, J. R., Tang, Y.-Y., Weber, J., & Kober, H. (2011). Meditation experience is associated with differences in default mode network activity and connectivity. *Proceedings of the National Academy of Sciences, 108*, 20254–20259.

Brewer, M. B. (1999). The psychology of prejudice: Ingroup love or outgroup hate? *Journal of Social Issues, 55*(3), 429–444. https://doi.org/10.1111/0022-4537.00126

Brewer, W. F. (1996). What is recollective memory? In D. C. Rubin (Ed.), *Remembering our past: Studies in autobiographical memory* (pp. 19–66). Cambridge University Press.

Briggs, J. (2000). Conflict management in a modern Inuit community. In P. P. Schweitzer, M. Biesele, & R. K. Hitchcock (Eds.), *Hunters and gatherers in the modern world: Conflict, resistance, and self-determination* (pp. 110–124). Berghahn Books.

Broberg, D. J., & Bernstein, I. L. (1987). Candy as a scapegoat in the prevention of food aversions in children receiving chemotherapy. *Cancer, 60*, 2344–2347.

Broca, P. (1861). Remarques sur le siège de la faculté du langage articulé; suivies d'une observation d'aphémie (perte de la parole) [Remarks on the seat of the faculty of articulated language, following an observation of aphemia (loss of speech)]. *Bulletin de la Société Anatomique de Paris, 36*, 330–357.

Broca, P. (1863). Localisation des fonctions cérébrales: Siège du langage articulé [Localization of brain functions: Seat of the faculty of articulated language]. *Bulletin de la Société d'Anthropologie de Paris, 4*, 200–202.

Brody, D. J., & Gu, Q. (2020). Antidepressant use among adults: United States, 2015–2018. *NCHS Data Brief, no. 377*. National Center for Health Statistics.

Brody, N. (2003). Construct validation of the Sternberg Triarchic Abilities Test: Comment and reanalysis. *Intelligence, 31*(4), 319–329.

Brooks, R., & Meltzoff, A. N. (2002). The importance of eyes: How infants interpret adult looking behavior. *Developmental Psychology, 38*, 958–966.

Brooks-Gunn, J., Graber, J. A., & Paikoff, R. L. (1994). Studying links between hormones and negative affect: Models and measures. *Journal of Research on Adolescence, 4*, 469–486.

Brosnan, S. F., & DeWaal, F. B. M. (2003). Monkeys reject unequal pay. *Nature, 425*, 297–299.

Brown, B. B., Mory, M., & Kinney, D. (1994). Casting crowds in a relational perspective: Caricature, channel, and context. In G. A. R. Montemayor & T. Gullotta (Eds.), *Advances in adolescent development: Personal relationships during adolescence* (Vol. 5, pp. 123–167). Sage.

Brown, J. D. (1993). Self-esteem and self-evaluation: Feeling is believing. In J. M. Suls (Ed.), *The self in social perspective: Psychological perspectives on the self* (Vol. 4, pp. 27–58). Erlbaum.

Brown, J. D., & McGill, K. L. (1989). The cost of good fortune: When positive life events produce negative health consequences. *Journal of Personality and Social Psychology, 57*, 1103–1110.

Brown, L. L., Mitchell, U. A., & Ailshire, J. A. (2020). Disentangling the stress process: Race/ethnic differences in the exposure and appraisal of chronic stressor among older adults. *The Journals of Gerontology: Series B, 75*(3), 650–660. https://doi.org/10.1093/geronb/gby072

Brown, M. I., Wai, J., & Chabris, C. F. (2021). Can you ever be too smart for your own good? Comparing linear and nonlinear effects of cognitive ability on life outcomes. *Perspectives on Psychological Science, 16*(6), 1337–1359. https://doi.org/10.1177/1745691620964122

Brown, R. P., Osterman, L. L., & Barnes, C. D. (2009). School violence and the culture of honor. *Psychological Science, 20*(11), 1400–1405.

Brown, R. (1958). *Words and things*. Free Press.

Brown, R., & Kulik, J. (1977). Flashbulb memories. *Cognition, 5*, 73–99.

Brown, R., & McNeill, D. (1966). The "tip-of-the-tongue" phenomenon. *Journal of Verbal Learning and Verbal Behavior, 5*, 325–337.

Brown, S. C., & Craik, F. I. M. (2000). Encoding and retrieval of information. In E. Tulving & F. I. M. Craik (Eds.), *The Oxford handbook of memory* (pp. 93–107). Oxford University Press.

Brown, T. A., & Barlow, D. H. (2002). Classification of anxiety and mood disorders. In D. H. Barlow (Ed.), *Anxiety and its disorders: The nature and treatment of anxiety and panic* (2nd ed.). Guilford Press.

Brownell, K. D., Greenwood, M. R. C., Stellar, E., & Shrager, E. E. (1986). The effects of repeated cycles of weight loss and regain in rats. *Physiology and Behavior, 38*, 459–464.

Bruneau, E. G., Jacoby, N., & Saxe, R. (2015). Empathic control through coordinated interaction of amygdala, theory of mind and extended pain matrix brain regions. *Neuroimage, 114*, 105–119. https://doi.org/10.1016/j.neuroimage.2015.04.034

Bruner, J. S. (1983). Education as social invention. *Journal of Social Issues, 39*, 129–141.

Brunet, A., Orr, S. P., Tremblay, J., Robertson, K., Nader, K., & Pitman, R. K. (2008). Effects of post-retrieval propranolol on psychophysiologic responding during subsequent script-driven traumatic imagery in posttraumatic stress disorder. *Journal of Psychiatric Research, 42*, 503–506.

Brunet, A., Saumier, D., Liu, A., Streiner, D. L., Tremblay, J., & Pitman, R. K. (2018). Reduction of PTSD symptoms with pre-reactivation propranolol therapy: A randomized controlled trial. *American Journal of Psychiatry, 175*, 427–433. https://doi.org/10.1176/appi.ajp.2017.17050481

Brunetti, P., Pirani, F., Carlier, J., Giorgetti, R., Busardò, F. P., & Lo Faro, A. F. (2021). A 2017–2019 update on acute intoxications and fatalities from illicit fentanyl and analogs. *Journal of Analytical Toxicology, 45*(6), 537–554. https://doi.org/10.1093/jat/bkaa115

Brunner, D. P., Dijk, D. J., Tobler, I., & Borbely, A. A. (1990). Effect of partial sleep deprivation on sleep stages and EEG power spectra. *Electroencephalography and Clinical Neurophysiology, 75*, 492–499.

Bryck, R. L., & Fisher, P. A. (2012). Training the brain: Practical applications of neural plasticity from the intersection of cognitive neuroscience, developmental psychology, and prevention science. *American Psychologist, 67*, 87–100.

Bschaden, A., Pietrynik, K., Schulenberg, I., Dieze, A., Rack, I., & Stroebele-Benschop, N. (2019). Preparation sequence of two snack components influences snack composition and calorie intake. *Appetite, 133*, 199–203. https://doi.org/10.1016/j.appet.2018.11.010

Buchanan, C. M., Eccles, J. S., & Becker, J. B. (1992). Are adolescents the victims of raging hormones? Evidence for activational effects of hormones on moods and behavior at adolescence. *Psychological Bulletin, 111*, 62–107.

Buchanan, T. W. (2007). Retrieval of emotional memories. *Psychological Bulletin, 133*, 761–779.

Buck Louis, G. M., Gray, L. E., Marcus, M., Ojeda, S. R., Pescovitz, O. H., Witchel, S. F., ... Euling, S. Y. (2008). Environmental factors and puberty timing: Expert panel research. *Pediatrics, 121*(Suppl. 3), S192–S207. https://doi.org/10.1542/peds1813E

Buckholtz, J. W., & Meyer-Lindenberg, A. (2012). Psychopathology and the human connectome: Toward a transdiagnostic model of risk for mental illness. *Neuron, 74*, 990–1003.

Buckley, C. (2007, January 3). Man is rescued by stranger on subway tracks. *New York Times.* http://www.nytimes.com/2007/01/03/nyregion/03life.html

Buckner, R. L., & DiNicola, L. M. (2019). The brain's default network: Updated anatomy, physiology and evolving insights. *Nature Reviews Neuroscience, 20*(10), 593–608. https://doi.org/10.1038/s41583-019-0212-7

Buckner, R. L., Andrews-Hanna, J. R., & Schacter, D. L. (2008). The brain's default network: Anatomy, function, and relevance to disease. *Annals of the New York Academy of Sciences, 1124*, 1–38.

Buckner, R. L., Petersen, S. E., Ojemann, J. G., Miezin, F. M., Squire, L. R., & Raichle, M. E. (1995). Functional anatomical studies of explicit and implicit memory retrieval tasks. *The Journal of Neuroscience, 15*, 12–29.

Bunce, D. M., Flens, E. A., & Neiles, K. Y. (2011). How long can students pay attention in class? A study of student attention decline using clickers. *Journal of Chemical Education, 87*, 1438–1443.

Burger, J. M. (1999). The foot-in-the-door compliance procedure: A multiple-process analysis and review. *Personality and Social Psychology Review, 3*, 303–325.

Burger, J. M. (2009). Replicating Milgram: Would people still obey today? *American Psychologist, 64*, 1–11.

Burger, J. M., & Burns, L. (1988). The illusion of unique invulnerability and the use of effective contraception. *Personality and Social Psychology Bulletin, 14*, 264–270.

Burgess, E. W., & Wallin, P. (1953). *Engagement and marriage.* J. B. Lippincott.

Burke, D., MacKay, D. G., Worthley, J. S., & Wade, E. (1991). On the tip of the tongue: What causes word failure in young and older adults? *Journal of Memory and Language, 30*, 237–246.

Burke, M., Hsiang, S. M., & Miguel, E. (2015). Climate and conflict. *Annual Review of Economics, 7*(1), 577–617.

Burks, S. V., Carpenter, J. P., Goette, L., & Rustichini, A. (2009). Cognitive skills affect economic preferences, strategic behavior, and job attachment. *Proceedings of the National Academy of Sciences, 106*(19), 7745–7750. https://doi.org/10.1073/pnas. 0812360106

Burns, D. J., Hwang, A. J., & Burns, S. A. (2011). Adaptive memory: Determining the proximate mechanisms responsible for the memorial advantages of survival processing. *Journal of Experimental Psychology: Learning, Memory, and Cognition, 37*, 206–218.

Burnstein, E., Crandall, C., & Kitayama, S. (1994). Some neo-Darwinian decision rules for altruism: Weighing cues for inclusive fitness as a function of the biological importance of the decision. *Journal of Personality and Social Psychology, 67*, 773–789.

Burr, D. A., Castrellon, J. J., Zald, D. H., & Samanez-Larkin, G. R. (2021). Emotion dynamics across adulthood in everyday life: Older adults are more emotionally stable and better at regulating desires. *Emotion, 21*(3), 453–464. https://doi.org/10.1037/emo0000734

Burris, C. T., & Branscombe, N. R. (2005). Distorted distance estimation induced by a self-relevant national boundary. *Journal of Experimental Social Psychology, 41*, 305–312.

Burston, C. L., Park, L. S., Corfield, E. C., Forget-Dubois, N., Dupuis, A., Sinopoli, V. M., ... Arnold, P. D. (2018). Heritability of obsessive-compulsive trait dimensions in youth from the general population. *Translational Psychiatry, 8*, 191.

Burton, H., Snyder, A. Z., Conturon, T. E., Akbudak, E., Ollinger, J. M., & Raichle, M. E. (2002). Adaptive changes in early and late blind: a fMRI study of braille reading. *Journal of Neurophysiology, 87*, 589–607.

Bushdid, C., Magnasco, M. O., Vosshall, L. B., & Keller, A. (2014). Humans can discriminate more than one trillion olfactory stimuli. *Science, 343*(6177), 1370–1372. https://doi.org/10.1126/science.1249168

Burton, H., Diamond, J. B., & McDermott, K. B. (2003). Dissociating cortical regions activated by semantic and phonological tasks: A fMRI study in blind and sighted people. *Journal of Neurophysiology, 90*, 1965–1982.

Bushman, B. J. (2016). Violent media and hostile appraisals: A meta-analytic review. *Aggressive Behavior, 42*(6), 605–613. https://doi.org/10.1002/ab.21655

Bushman, B. J., & Huesmann, L. R. (2010). Aggression. In S. T. Fiske, D. T. Gilbert, & G. Lindzey (Eds.), *The handbook of social psychology* (5th ed., Vol. 2, pp. 833–863). Wiley.

Buss, D. M. (1985). Human mate selection. *American Scientist, 73*, 47–51.

Buss, D. M., & Schmitt, D. P. (1993). Sexual strategies theory: An evolutionary perspective on human mating. *Psychological Review, 100*, 204–232.

Butler, M. A., Corboy, J. R., & Filley, C. M. (2009). How the conflict between American psychiatry and neurology delayed the appreciation of cognitive dysfunction in multiple sclerosis. *Neuropsychology Review, 19*, 399–410.

Byers-Heinlein, K., Burns, T. C., & Werker, J. F. (2010). The roots of bilingualism in newborns. *Psychological Science, 21*(3), 343–348. https://doi.org/10.1177/0956797609360758

Byrne, D., & Clore, G. L. (1970). A reinforcement model of evaluative responses. *Personality: An International Journal, 1*, 103–128.

Byrne, D., Allgeier, A. R., Winslow, L., & Buckman, J. (1975). The situational facilitation of interpersonal attraction: A three-factor hypothesis. *Journal of Applied Social Psychology, 5*, 1–15.

Byrne, D., Ervin, C. R., & Lamberth, J. (1970). Continuity between the experimental study of attraction and real-life computer dating. *Journal of Personality and Social Psychology, 16*, 157–165.

Bzdok, D., & Dunbar, R. (2020). The neurobiology of social distance. *Trends in Cognitive Sciences, 24*(9), 717–733. https://doi.org/10.1016/j.tics.2020.05.016

Cabeza, R. (2002). Hemispheric asymmetry reduction in older adults: The HAROLD model. *Psychology and Aging, 17*, 85–100.

Cabeza, R., McIntosh, A. R., Tulving, E., Nyberg, L., & Grady, C. L. (1997). Age-related differences in effective neural connectivity during encoding and recall. *Neuroreport, 8*, 3479–3483.

Cabeza, R., Rao, S., Wagner, A. D., Mayer, A., & Schacter, D. L. (2001). Can medial temporal lobe regions distinguish true from false? An event-related fMRI study of veridical and illusory recognition memory. *Proceedings of the National Academy of Sciences, USA, 98*, 4805–4810.

Cacioppo, J. T., & Cacioppo, S. (2018). The growing problem of loneliness. *The Lancet, 391*(10119), 426. https://doi.org/10.1016/S0140-6736(18)30142-9

Cacioppo, J. T., & Patrick, B. (2008). *Loneliness: Human nature and the need for social connection.* Norton.

Cadario, R., & Chandon, P. (2020). Which healthy eating nudges work best? A meta-analysis of field experiments. *Marketing Science, 39*(3), 459-665. https://doi.org/10.2139/ssrn.3090829

Cahill, L., & McGaugh, J. L. (1998). Mechanisms of emotional arousal and lasting declarative memory. *Trends in Neurosciences, 21,* 294–299.

Cahill, L., Haier, R. J., Fallon, J., Alkire, M. T., Tang, C., Keator, D., ... McGaugh, J. L. (1996). Amygdala activity at encoding correlated with long-term, free recall of emotional information. *Proceedings of the National Academy of Sciences, USA, 93,* 8016–8021.

Caird, J. K., Simmons, S. M., Wiley, K., Johnston, K. A., & Horrey, W. J. (2018). Does talking on a cell phone, with a passenger, or dialing affect driving performance? An updated systematic review and meta-analysis of experimental studies. *Human Factors, 60*(1), 101–133. https://doi.org/10.1177/0018720817748145

Callaghan, T., Rochat, P., Lillard, A., Claux, M. L., Odden, H., Itakura, S., ... Singh, S. (2005). Synchrony in the onset of mental-state reasoning: Evidence from five cultures. *Psychological Science, 16,* 378–384.

Calvin, C. M., Deary, I. J., Fenton, C., Roberts, B. A., Der, G., Leckenby, N., & Batty, G. D. (2011). Intelligence in youth and all-cause-mortality: Systematic review with meta-analysis. *International Journal of Epidemiology, 40*(3), 626–644. https://doi.org /10.1093/ije/dyq190

Cameron, C. D., & Payne, B. K. (2011). Escaping affect: How motivated emotion regulation creates insensitivity to mass suffering. *Journal of Personality and Social Psychology, 100*(1), 1–15.

Campbell, A. (1999). Staying alive: Evolution, culture, and women's intra-sexual aggression. *Behavioral & Brain Sciences, 22,* 203–252.

Campbell, F. A., Ramey, C. T., Pungello, E., Sparling, J., & Miller-Johnson, S. (2002). Early childhood education: Young adult outcomes from the Abecedarian Project. *Applied Developmental Science, 6*(1), 42–57. https://doi.org/10.1207/S1532480XADS0601_05

Campos, B., Shiota, M. N., Keltner, D., Gonzaga, G. C., & Goetz, J. L. (2013). What is shared, what is different? Core relational themes and expressive displays of eight positive emotions. *Cognition & Emotion, 27*(1), 37–52. https://doi.org/10.1080/02699931.2012.683852

Cannon, T. D. (2015). How schizophrenia develops: Cognitive and brain mechanisms underlying onset of psychosis. *Trends in Cognitive Science, 19,* 744–756.

Cannon, W. B. (1929). *Bodily changes in pain, hunger, fear, and rage: An account of recent research into the function of emotional excitement* (2nd ed.). Appleton-Century-Crofts.

Cantor, J. R., Zillmann, D., & Bryant, J. (1975). Enhancement of experienced sexual arousal in response to erotic stimuli through mis-attribution of unrelated residual excitation. *Journal of Personality and Social Psychology, 32*(1), 69–75. https://doi.org/10.1037/h0076784

Cappelletti, M., & Wallen, K. (2016). Increasing women's sexual desire: The comparative effectiveness of estrogens and androgens. *Hormones and Behavior, 78,* 178–193. https://doi.org/10.1016/j .yhbeh.2015.11.003

Card, D., & Giuliano, L. (2016). Can tracking raise the test scores of high-ability minority students? *American Economic Review, 106*(10), 2783–2816.

Card, N. A., Stucky, B. D., Sawalani, G. M., & Little, T. D. (2008). Direct and indirect aggression during childhood and adolescence: A meta-analytic review of gender differences, intercorrelations, and relations to maladjustment. *Child Development, 79,* 1185–1229. https://doi.org/10.1111/j.1467-8624.2008.01184.x

Carey, N. (2012). *The epigenetics revolution: How modern biology is rewriting our understanding of genetics, disease, and inheritance.* Columbia University Press.

Carhart-Harris, R., Giribaldi, B., Watts, R., Baker-Jones, M., Murphy-Beiner, A., Murphy, R., ... Nutt, D. J. (2021). Trial of psilocybin versus escitalopram for depression. *New England Journal of Medicine, 384*(15), 1402–1411. https://doi.org/10.1056 /NEJMoa2032994

Carl, E., Stein, A. T., Levihn-Coon, A., Pogue, J. R., Rothbaum, B., Emmelkamp, P., ... Powers, M. B. (2019). Virtual reality exposure therapy for anxiety and related disorders: A meta-analysis of randomized controlled trials. *Journal of Anxiety Disorders, 61,* 27–36. https://doi.org/10.1016/j.janxdis.2018.08.003

Carmena, J. M., Lebedev, M. A., Crist, R. E., O'Doherty, J. E., Santucci, D. M., Dimitrov, D. F., ... Nicolelis, M. A. (2003). Learning to control a brain-machine interface for reaching and grasping by primates. *Public Library of Science Biology, 1,* 193–208.

Carmichael, D. A., Down M. P., Shillcock R. C., Eagleman D. M., & Simner J. (2015). Validating a standardised test battery for synesthesia: Does the Synesthesia Battery reliably detect synesthesia? *Consciousness and Cognition, 33,* 375–385. https://doi.org/10.1016/j .concog.2015.02.001

Carmichael Olson, H., Streissguth, A. P., Sampson, P. D., Barr, H. M., Bookstein, F. L., & Thiede, K. (1997). Association of prenatal alcohol exposure with behavioral and learning problems in early adolescence. *Journal of the American Academy of Child & Adolescent Psychiatry, 36*(9), 1187–1194.

Carney, D. R., Cuddy, A. J. C., & Yap, A. J. (2010). Power posing: Brief nonverbal displays affect neuroendocrine levels and risk tolerance. *Psychological Science, 21*(10), 1363–1368. https://doi.org /10.1177/0956797610383437

Carolson, E. A. (1998). A prospective longitudinal study of attachment disorganization/disorientation. *Child Development, 69,* 1107–1128.

Carpenter, A. C., & Schacter, D. L. (2017). Flexible retrieval: When true inferences produce false memories. *Journal of Experimental Psychology: Learning, Memory, and Cognition, 43,* 335–349.

Carpenter, A. C., Thakral, P. P., Preston, A. R., & Schacter, D. L. (2021). Reinstatement of item-specific contextual details during retrieval supports recombination-related false memories. *NeuroImage, 236,* 118033. https://doi.org/10.1016/j.neuroimage.2021.118033

Carpenter, S. K. (2012). Testing enhances the transfer of learning. *Current Directions in Psychological Science, 21,* 279–283.

Carré, J. M., & Archer, J. (2018). Testosterone and human behavior: The role of individual and contextual variables. *Current Opinion in Psychology, 19,* 149–153. https://doi.org/10.1016/j.copsyc.2017.03.021

Carroll, J. B. (1993). *Human cognitive abilities.* Cambridge University Press.

Carson, R. C., Butcher, J. N., & Mineka, S. (2000). *Abnormal psychology and modern life* (11th ed.). Allyn & Bacon.

Carstensen, L. L. (1992). Social and emotional patterns in adulthood: Support for socioemotional selectivity theory. *Psychology and Aging, 7,* 331–338.

Carstensen, L. L., & Fredrickson, B. L. (1998). Influence of HIV status and age on cognitive representations of others. *Health Psychology, 17,* 1–10.

Carstensen, L. L., & Turk-Charles, S. (1994). The salience of emotion across the adult life span. *Psychology and Aging, 9,* 259–264.

Carstensen, L. L., Pasupathi, M., Mayr, U., & Nesselroade, J. R. (2000). Emotional experience in everyday life across the adult life span. *Journal of Personality and Social Psychology, 79,* 644–655.

Carswell, K. L., & Finkel, E. J. (2018). Can you get the magic back? The moderating effect of passion decay beliefs on relationship commitment. *Journal of Personality and Social Psychology, 115*(6), 1002–1033.

Carswell, K. L., Finkel, E. J., & Kumashiro, M. (2019). Creativity and romantic passion. *Journal of Personality and Social Psychology*, *116*(6), 919–941. https://doi.org/10.1037/pspi0000162

Carver, C. S. (2006). Approach, avoidance, and the self-regulation of affect and action. *Motivation and Emotion, 30,* 105–110.

Carver, C. S., & Harmon-Jones, E. (2009). Anger is an approach-related affect: Evidence and implications. *Psychological Bulletin, 135*(2), 183–204.

Carver, C. S., & White, T. L. (1994). Behavioral inhibition, behavioral activation, and affective responses to impending reward and punishment: The bis/bas scales. *Journal of Personality and Social Psychology, 67*(2), 319–333.

Carver, C. S., Lehman, J. M., & Antoni, M. H. (2003). Dispositional pessimism predicts illness-related disruption of social and recreational activities among breast cancer patients. *Journal of Personality and Social Psychology, 84,* 813–821.

Casazza, K., Fontaine, K. R., Astrup, A., Birch, L. L., Brown, A. W., Bohan Brown, M. M., ... Allison, D. B. (2013). Myths, presumptions, and facts about obesity. *New England Journal of Medicine, 368*(5), 446–454.

Caselli, N., Pyers, J., & Lieberman, A. M. (2021). Deaf children of hearing parents have age-level vocabulary growth when exposed to American Sign Language by 6 months of age. *The Journal of Pediatrics, 232,* 229–236. https://doi.org/10.1016/j.jpeds.2021.01.029

Caspi, A., & Herbener, E. S. (1990). Continuity and change: Assortative marriage and the consistency of personality in adulthood. *Journal of Personality and Social Psychology, 58,* 250–258.

Caspi, A., Lynam, D., Moffitt, T. E., & Silva, P. A. (1993). Unraveling girls' delinquency: Biological, dispositional, and contextual contributions to adolescent misbehavior. *Developmental Psychology, 29,* 19–30.

Caspi, A., Roberts, B. W., & Shiner, R. L. (2005). Personality development: Stability and change. *Annual Review of Psychology, 56,* 453–484.

Caspi, A., Sugden, K., Moffitt, T. E., Taylor, A., Craig, I. W., Harrington, H., ... Poulton, R. (2003). Influence of life stress on depression: Moderation by a polymorphism in the 5-HTT gene. *Science, 301*(5631), 386–389.

Castel, A. D., McCabe, D. P., & Roediger, H. L., III. (2007). Illusions of competence and overestimation of associate memory for identical items: Evidence from judgments of learning. *Psychonomic Bulletin & Review, 14,* 197–111.

Castellani, R. J., Perry, G., & Iverson, G. L. (2015). Chronic effects of mild neurotrauma: Putting the cart before the horse? *Journal of Neuropathology & Experimental Neurology, 74,* 493–499.

Castellanos, F. X., Patti, P. L., Sharp, W., Jeffries, N. O., Greenstein, D. K., Clasen, L. S., ... Rapoport, J. L. (2002). Developmental trajectories of brain volume abnormalities in children and adolescents with attention-deficit/hyperactivity disorder. *Journal of the American Medical Association, 288,* 1740–1748. https://doi.org/10.1001/jama.288.14.1740

Catrambone, R. (2002). The effects of surface and structural feature matches on the access of story analogs. *Journal of Experimental Psychology: Learning, Memory, & Cognition, 28,* 318–334.

Cattell, R. B. (1950). *Personality: A systematic, theoretical, and factual study.* McGraw-Hill.

Ceci, S. J. (1991). How much does schooling influence general intelligence and its cognitive components? A reassessment of the evidence. *Developmental Psychology, 27,* 703–722.

Ceci, S. J., & Williams, W. M. (1997). Schooling, intelligence, and income. *American Psychologist, 52,* 1051–1058.

Ceci, S. J., DeSimone, M., & Johnson, S. (1992). Memory in context: A case study of "Bubbles P.," a gifted but uneven memorizer. In D. J. Herrmann, H. Weingartner, A. Searleman, & C. McEvoy (Eds.), *Memory improvement: Implications for memory theory* (pp. 169–186). Springer-Verlag.

Ceci, S. J., Ginther, D. K., Kahn, S., & Williams, W. M. (2014). Women in academic science: A changing landscape. *Psychological Science in the Public Interest, 15*(3), 75–141. https://doi.org/10.1177/1529100614541236

Ceci, S. J., Williams, W. M., & Barnett, S. M. (2009). Women's underrepresentation in science: Sociocultural and biological considerations. *Psychological Bulletin, 135*(2), 218–261. https://doi.org/10.1037/a0014412

Cellini, N., & Capuozzo, A. (2018). Shaping memory consolidation via targeted memory reactivation during sleep. *Annals of the New York Academy of Sciences, 1426,* 52–71.

Centers for Disease Control and Prevention [CDC]. (2021a). *Drug overdose deaths.* https://www.cdc.gov/drugoverdose/deaths/index.html

Centers for Disease Control and Prevention [CDC]. (2021b). Estimated HIV incidence and prevalence in the United States, 2015–2019. *HIV Surveillance Supplemental Report 2021, 26*(1), 1-81.

Centers for Disease Control and Prevention [CDC]. (2022). *Web-based injury statistics query and reporting system.* https://www.cdc.gov/injury/wisqars/index.html

Centola, D., & Baronchelli, A. (2015). The spontaneous emergence of conventions: An experimental study of cultural evolution. *Proceedings of the National Academy of Sciences, USA, 112*(7), 1989–1994. https://doi.org/10.1073/pnas.1418838112

Cepeda, N. J., Pashler, H., Vul, E., Wixted, J. T., & Rohrer, D. (2006). Distributed practice in verbal recall tests: A review and quantitative synthesis. *Psychological Bulletin, 132,* 354–380.

Cerf-Ducastel, B., & Murphy, C. (2001). fMRI activation in response to odorants orally delivered in aqueous solutions. *Chemical Senses, 26*(6), 625–637.

Chabris, C. F., Hebert, B. M., Benjamin, D. J., Beauchamp, J., Cesarini, D., van der Loos, M., & Laibson, D. (2012). Most reported genetic associations with general intelligence are probably false positives. *Psychological Science, 23*(11), 1314–1323. https://doi.org/10.1177/0956797611435528

Chabris, C., & Simons, D. (2012, November 16). Using just 10% of your brains? Think again. *Wall Street Journal Online.* Retrieved from https://www.wsj.com/articles/SB10001424127887324556304578119351875421218.

Chalmers, D. (1996). *The conscious mind: In search of a fundamental theory.* Oxford University Press.

Chambless, D. L., Baker, M. J., Baucom, D. H., Beutler, L. E., Calhoun, K. S., Crits-Christoph, P., ... Woody, S. R. (1998). Update on empirically validated therapies, II. *Clinical Psychologist, 51*(1), 3–14.

Chandler, J., & Schwarz, N. (2009). How extending your middle finger affects your perception of others: Learned movements influence concept accessibility. *Journal of Experimental Social Psychology, 45,* 123–128.

Chang, E. H., Milkman, K. L., Gromet, D. M., Rebele, R. W., Massey, C., Duckworth, A. L., & Grant, A. M. (2019). The mixed effects of online diversity training. *Proceedings of the National Academy of Sciences, 116*(16), 7778–7783. https://doi.org/10.1073/pnas.1816076116

Chang, L., Zhang, S., Poo, M-M., & Gong, N. (2017). Spontaneous expression of mirror self-recognition in monkeys after learning precise visual-proprioceptive association for mirror images. *Proceedings of the National Academy of Science, 114*(12), 3258–3263. https://doi.org/10.1073/pnas.1620764114/-/DCSupplemental

Chang, P. P., Ford, D. E., Meoni, L. A., Wang, N., & Klag, M. J. (2002). Anger in young men and subsequent premature cardiovascular disease. *Archives of Internal Medicine, 162,* 901–906.

Chaplin, T. M., & Aldao, A. (2013). Gender differences in emotion expression in children: A meta-analytic review. *Psychological Bulletin, 139,* 735–765.

Chapman, H. A., Kim, D. A., Susskind, J. M., & Anderson, A. K. (2009). In bad taste: Evidence for the oral origins of moral disgust. *Science, 27,* 1222–1226.

Charles, S. T., Reynolds, C. A., & Gatz, M. (2001). Age-related differences and change in positive and negative affect over 23 years. *Journal of Personality and Social Psychology, 80,* 136–151.

Charness, N. (1981). Aging and skilled problem solving. *Journal of Experimental Psychology: General, 110,* 21–38.

Charpak, G., & Broch, H. (2004). *Debunked! ESP, telekinesis, and other pseudoscience* (B. K. Holland, Trans.). Johns Hopkins University Press.

Chartrand, T. L., & Bargh, J. A. (1999). The chameleon effect: The perception-behavior link and social interaction. *Journal of Personality and Social Psychology, 76,* 893–910.

Chen, E., Cohen, S., & Miller, G. E. (2010). How low socioeconomic status affects 2-year hormonal trajectories in children. *Psychological Science, 21*(1), 31–37.

Chen, E., McLean, K. C., & Miller, G. E. (2015). Shift-and-persist strategies: Associations with socioeconomic status and the regulation of inflammation among adolescents and their parents. *Psychosomatic Medicine, 77*(4), 371–382. https://doi.org/10.1097/psy.0000000000000157

Chen, E., & Miller, G. E. (2012). "Shift-and-persist" strategies: Why being low in socioeconomic status isn't always bad for health. *Perspectives on Psychological Science, 7*(2), 135–158. https://doi.org/10.1177/1745691612436694

Chen, L., Deng, H., Cui, H., Fang, J., Zuo, Z. … Zhao, L. (2018). Inflammatory responses and inflammation-associated diseases in organs. *Oncotarget, 9*(6), 7204–7218. https://doi.org/10.18632/oncotarget.23208

Chen, Q. & Yan, Z. (2015). Does multitasking with mobile phones affect learning? A review. *Computers in Human Behavior, 54,* 34–42.

Chen, S., Collins, A., Anderson, K., McKenzie, K., & Kidd, S. (2017). Patient characteristics, length of stay, and functional improvement for schizophrenia spectrum disorders: A population study of inpatient care in Ontario, 2005–2015. *Canadian Journal of Psychiatry, 62,* 854–863.

Chen, Z., Poon, K.-T., DeWall, C. N., & Jiang, T. (2020). Life lacks meaning without acceptance: Ostracism triggers suicidal thoughts. *Journal of Personality and Social Psychology, 119*(6), 1423–1443. https://doi.org/10.1037/pspi0000238

Cheney, D. L., & Seyfarth, R. M. (1990). *How monkeys see the world.* University of Chicago Press.

Cheng, D. T., Disterhoft, J. F., Power, J. M., Ellis, D. A., & Desmond, J. E. (2008). Neural substrates underlying human delay and trace eyeblink conditioning. *Proceedings of the National Academy of Sciences, USA, 105,* 8108–8113.

Cherlin, A. J. (Ed.). (1992). *Marriage, divorce, remarriage* (2nd ed.). Harvard University Press.

Cherry, C. (1953). Some experiments on the recognition of speech with one and two ears. *Journal of the Acoustical Society of America, 25,* 275–279.

Chetty, R. (2021). Improving equality of opportunity: New insights from big data. *Contemporary Economic Policy, 39*(1), 7–41. https://doi.org/10.1111/coep.12478

Chetty, R., & Hendren, N. (2018). The impacts of neighborhoods on intergenerational mobility. II: County-level estimates. *Quarterly Journal of Economics, 133*(3), 1163–1228.

Chetty, R., Stepner, M., Abraham, S., Lin, S., Scuderi, B., Turner, N., … Cutler, D. (2016). The association between income and life expectancy in the United States, 2001–2014. *Journal of the American Medical Association, 315*(16), 1750–1766.

Chiao, J. Y., & Ambady, N. (2007). Cultural neuroscience: Parsing universality and diversity across levels of analysis. In S. Kitayama & D. Cohen (Eds.), *Handbook of cultural psychology* (pp. 237–254). Guilford Press.

Chin, A., Markey, A., Bhargava, S., Kassam, K. S., & Loewenstein, G. (2017). Bored in the USA: Experience sampling and boredom in everyday life. *Emotion, 17*(2), 359–368. https://doi.org/10.1037/emo0000232

Chin, H. B., Sipe, T. A., Elder, R., Mercer, S. L., Chattopadhyay, S. K., Jacob, V., … Santelli, J. (2012). The effectiveness of group-based comprehensive risk-reduction and abstinence education interventions to prevent or reduce the risk of adolescent pregnancy, human immunodeficiency virus, and sexually transmitted infections: Two systematic reviews for the Guide to Community Preventive Services. *American Journal of Preventive Medicine, 42,* 272–294.

Chivers, M. L., Rieger, G., Latty, E., & Bailey, J. M. (2004). A sex difference in the specificity of sexual arousal. *Psychological Science, 15,* 736–744.

Chivers, M. L., Seto, M. C., & Blanchard, R. (2007). Gender and sexual orientation differences in sexual response to sexual activities versus gender of actors in sexual films. *Journal of Personality and Social Psychology, 93,* 1108–1121.

Choi, I., Nisbett, R. E., & Norenzayan, A. (1999). Causal attribution across cultures: Variation and universality. *Psychological Bulletin, 125,* 47–63.

Chomsky, N. (1957). *Syntactic structures.* Mouton.

Chomsky, N. (1959). A review of *Verbal Behavior* by B. F. Skinner. *Language, 35,* 26–58.

Chomsky, N. (1986). *Knowledge of language: Its nature, origin, and use.* Praeger.

Choy, Y., Fyer, A. J., & Lipsitz, J. D. (2007). Treatment of specific phobia in adults. *Clinical Psychology Review, 27,* 266–286.

Christ, S. E., White, D. A., Mandernach, T., & Keys, B. A. (2001). Inhibitory control across the life span. *Developmental Neuropsychology, 20*(3), 653–669.

Christakis, N. A., & Fowler, J. H. (2007). The spread of obesity in a large social network over 32 years. *New England Journal of Medicine, 357*(4), 370–379.

Christianson, S.-Å., & Loftus, E. F. (1987). Memory for traumatic events. *Applied Cognitive Psychology, 1,* 225–239.

Christie, I. C., & Friedman, B. H. (2004). Autonomic specificity of discrete emotion and dimensions of affective space: A multivariate approach. *International Journal of Psychophysiology, 51,* 143–153. https://doi.org/10.1016/j.ijpsycho.2003.08.002

Chui, H., Hoppmann, C. A., Gerstorf, D., Walker, R., & Luszcz, M. A. (2014). Social partners and momentary affect in the oldest-old: The presence of others benefits affect depending on who we are and who we are with. *Developmental Psychology, 50*(3), 728–740. https://doi.org/10.1037/a0033896

Chung, G. H., Flook, L., & Fuligni, A. J. (2009). Daily family conflict and emotional distress among adolescents from Latin American, Asian, and European backgrounds. *Developmental Psychology, 45,* 1406–1415.

Cialdini, R. B. (2005). Don't throw in the towel: Use social influence research. *American Psychological Society, 18,* 33–34.

Cialdini, R. B. (2013). The focus theory of normative conduct. In P. A. M. van Lange, A. W. Kruglanski, & E. T. Higgins (Eds.), *Handbook of theories of social psychology* (Vol. 3, pp. 295–312). Sage.

Cialdini, R. B., & Goldstein, N. J. (2004). Social influence: Compliance and conformity. *Annual Review of Psychology, 55*(1), 591–621. https://doi.org/10.1146/annurev.psych.55.090902.142015

Cialdini, R. B., Trost, M. R., & Newsom, J. T. (1995). Preference for consistency: The development of a valid measure and the discovery of surprising behavioral implications. *Journal of Personality and Social Psychology, 69*, 318–328.

Cialdini, R. B., Vincent, J. E., Lewis, S. K., Catalan, J., Wheeler, D., & Darby, B. L. (1975). Reciprocal concessions procedure for inducing compliance: The door-in-the-face technique. *Journal of Personality and Social Psychology, 31*, 206–215.

Ciarrochi, J. V., Chan, A. Y., & Caputi, P. (2000). A critical evaluation of the emotional intelligence concept. *Personality & Individual Differences, 28*, 539.

Ciarrochi, J., Heaven, P. C. L., & Skinner, T. (2012). Cognitive ability and health-related behaviors during adolescence: A prospective study across five years. *Intelligence, 40*(4), 317–324. https://doi.org/10.1016/j.intell.2012.03.003

Cicchetti, D., & Toth, S. L. (1998). Perspectives on research and practice in developmental psychopathology. In I. E. Sigel & K. A. Renninger (Eds.), *Handbook of child psychology: Vol. 4. Child psychology in practice* (5th ed., pp. 479–583). Wiley.

Cicero, T. J., Ellis, M. S., Surratt, H. L., & Kurtz, S. P. (2014). The changing face of heroin use in the United States: A retrospective analysis of the past 50 years. *Journal of the American Medical Association Psychiatry, 71*, 821–826.

Clancy, S. A. (2005). *Abducted: How people come to believe they were kidnapped by aliens.* Harvard University Press.

Clark, C. A., & Dagher, A. (2014). The role of dopamine in risk taking: A specific look at Parkinson's disease and gambling. *Frontiers in Behavioral Neuroscience, 8*, 196. https://doi.org/10.3389/fnbeh.2014.00196

Clark, I. A., & Maguire, E. A. (2016). Remembering preservation in hippocampal amnesia. *Annual Review of Psychology, 67*, 51–82.

Clark, M. S., & Lemay, E. P. (2010). Close relationships. In S. T. Fiske, D. T. Gilbert, & G. Lindzey (Eds.), *The handbook of social psychology* (5th ed., Vol. 2). Wiley.

Clark, R. D., & Hatfield, E. (1989). Gender differences in receptivity to sexual offers. *Journal of Psychology and Human Sexuality, 2*, 39–55.

Clarke, A., & Tyler, L. K. (2015). Understanding what we see: How we derive meaning from vision. *Trends in Cognitive Sciences, 19*(11), 677–687. https://doi.org/10.1016/j.tics.2015.08.008

Clark-Polner, E., Johnson, T., & Barrett, L. F. (2017). Multivoxel pattern analysis does not provide evidence to support the existence of basic emotions. *Cerebral Cortex, 27*, 1944–1948. https://doi.org/10.1093/cercor/bhw028

Cleckley, H. M. (1976). *The mask of sanity* (5th ed.). Mosby.

Coates, T. (2015). *Between the world and me.* Spiegel & Grau.

Coe, C. L., & Lubach, G. R. (2008). Fetal programming prenatal origins of health and illness. *Current Directions in Psychological Science, 17*, 36–41.

Cogan, R., Cogan, D., Waltz, W., & McCue, M. (1987). Effects of laughter and relaxation on discomfort thresholds. *Journal of Behavioral Medicine, 10*, 139–144.

Coghill, R. C., McHaffie, J. G., & Yen, Y. (2003). Neural correlates of individual differences in the subjective experience of pain. *Proceedings of the National Academy of Sciences, USA, 100*, 8538–8542.

Cohen, A. B., & Tannenbaum, I. J. (2001). Lesbian and bisexual women's judgments of the attractiveness of different body types. *Journal of Sex Research, 38*(3), 226–232. https://doi.org/10.1080/00224490109552091

Cohen, A. O., Breiner, K., Steinberg, L., Bonnie, R. J., Scott, E. S., Taylor-Thompson, K. A., … Casey, B. J. (2016). When is an adolescent an adult? Assessing cognitive control in emotional and nonemotional contexts. *Psychological Science, 27*(4), 549–562.

Cohen, D., Nisbett, R. E., Bowdle, B. F., & Schwarz, N. (1996). Insult, aggression, and the southern culture of honor: An "experimental ethnography." *Journal of Personality and Social Psychology, 70*, 945–960.

Cohen, G. (1990). Why is it difficult to put names to faces? *British Journal of Psychology, 81*, 287–297.

Cohen, L., Lehéricy, S., Henry, C., Bourgeois, M., Larroque, C., Sainte-Rose, C., … Hertz-Pannier, L. (2004). Learning to read without a left occipital lobe: Right-hemispheric shift of visual word form area. *Annals of Neurology, 56*(6), 890–894. https://doi.org/10.1002/ana.20326

Cohen, S., Janicki-Deverts, D., Doyle, W. J., Miller, G. E., Frank, E., Rabin, B. S., & Turner, R. B. (2012). Chronic stress, glucocorticoid receptor resistance, inflammation, and disease risk. *Proceedings of the National Academy of Sciences, USA, 109*, 5995–5999.

Cohen-Kettenis, P. T., & Pfäfflin, F. (2003). *Transgenderism and intersexuality in childhood and adolescence: Making choices.* SAGE.

Cohn, A., Maréchal, M. A., Tannenbaum, D., & Zünd, C. L. (2019). Civic honesty around the globe. *Science, 365*(6448), 70–73. https://doi.org/10.1126/science.aau8712

Coifman, K. G., Bonanno, G. A., Ray, R. D., & Gross, J. J. (2007). Does repressive coping promote resilience? Affective-autonomic response discrepancy during bereavement. *Journal of Personality and Social Psychology, 92*, 745–758.

Colcombe, S. J., Erickson, K. I., Scalf, P. E., Kim, J. S., Prakesh, R., McAuley, E., … Kramer, A. F. (2006). Aerobic exercise training increases brain volume in aging humans. *Journals of Gerontology Series A: Biological Sciences and Medical Sciences, 61*, 1166–1170.

Colcombe, S. J., Kramer, A. F., Erickson, K. I., Scalf, P., McAuley, E., Cohen, N. J., … Elavsky, S. (2004). Cardiovascular fitness, cortical plasticity, and aging. *Proceedings of the National Academy of Sciences, USA, 101*, 3316–3321.

Coles, N. A., Larsen, J. T., & Lench, H. C. (2019). A meta-analysis of the facial feedback literature: Effects of facial feedback on emotional experience are small and variable. *Psychological Bulletin, 145*(6), 610–651. https://doi.org/10.1037/bul0000194

Coman, A., Manier, D., & Hirst, W. (2009). Forgetting the unforgettable through conversation: Social shared retrieval-induced forgetting of September 11 memories. *Psychological Science, 20*, 627–633.

Condon, J. W., & Crano, W. D. (1988). Inferred evaluation and the relation between attitude similarity and interpersonal attraction. *Journal of Personality and Social Psychology, 54*, 789–797.

Conklin, Q., King, B., Zanesco, A., Pokorny, J., Hamidi, A., Lin, J., … Saron, C. (2015). Telomere lengthening after three weeks of an intensive insight meditation retreat. *Psychoneuroendocrinology, 61*, 26–27.

Conley, T. D. (2011). Perceived proposer personality characteristics and gender differences in acceptance of casual sex offers. *Journal of Personality and Social Psychology, 100*(2), 309–329. https://doi.org/10.1037/a0022152

Conway, M., & Ross, M. (1984). Getting what you want by revising what you had. *Journal of Personality and Social Psychology, 47*, 738–748.

Cook, E. E., Venkataramani, A. S., Kim, J. J., Tamimi, R. M., & Holmes, M. D. (2018). Legislation to increase uptake of HPV vaccination and adolescent sexual behaviors. *Pediatrics, 142*(3), e20180458. https://doi.org/10.1542/peds.2018-0458

Cook, M., & Mineka, S. (1989). Observational conditioning of fear to fear-relevant versus fear-irrelevant stimuli in rhesus monkeys. *Journal of Abnormal Psychology, 98*(4), 448–459.

Cook, M., & Mineka, S. (1990). Selective associations in the observational conditioning of fear in rhesus monkeys. *Journal of Experimental Psychology: Animal Behavior Process, 16,* 372–389.

Cooke, J. E., Kochendorfer, L. B., Stuart-Parrigon, K. L., Koehn, A. J., & Kerns, K. A. (2018). Parent–child attachment and children's experience and regulation of emotion: A meta-analytic review. *Emotion.* https://doi.org/10.1037/emo0000504

Cooper, J., & Fazio, R. H. (1984). A new look at dissonance theory. In L. Berkowitz (Ed.), *Advances in experimental social psychology* (Vol. 17, pp. 229–266). Academic Press.

Cooper, J. C., Hollon, N. G., Wimmer, G. E., & Knutson, B. (2009). Available alternative incentives modulate anticipatory nucleus accumbens activation. *Social Cognitive and Affective Neuroscience, 4,* 409–416.

Cooper, J. M., & Strayer, D. L. (2008). Effects of simulator practice and real-world experience on cell-phone-related driver distraction. *Human Factors, 50,* 893–902.

Cooper, J. R., Bloom, F. E., & Roth, R. H. (2003). *Biochemical basis of neuropharmacology.* Oxford University Press.

Cooper, M. L. (2006). Does drinking promote risky sexual behavior? A complex answer to a simple question. *Current Directions in Psychological Science, 15,* 19–23.

Cordaro, D. T., Keltner, D., Tshering, S., Wangchuk, D., & Flynn, L. M. (2016). The voice conveys emotion in ten globalized cultures and one remote village in Bhutan. *Emotion, 16*(1), 117–128. https://doi.org/10.1037/emo0000100

Cordaro, D. T., Sun, R., Keltner, D., Kamble, S., Huddar, N., & McNeil, G. (2018). Universals and cultural variations in 22 emotional expressions across five cultures. *Emotion, 18*(1), 75–93. https://doi.org/10.1037/emo0000302

Cordi, M. J., & Rasch, B. (2021). How robust are sleep-mediated memory benefits? *Current Opinion in Neurobiology, 67,* 1–7. https://doi.org/10.1016/j.conb.2020.06.002

Cordovani, L., & Cordovani, D. (2016). A literature review on observational learning for medical motor skills and anesthesia teaching. *Advances in Health Sciences Education: Theory and Practice, 21,* 1113–1121.

Coren, S. (1997). *Sleep thieves.* Free Press.

Corfield, E. C., Yang, Y., Martin, N. G., & Nyholt, D. R. (2017). A continuum of genetic liability for minor and major depression. *Translational Psychiatry, 7,* e1131.

Corkin, S. (2002). What's new with the amnesic patient HM? *Nature Reviews Neuroscience, 3,* 153–160.

Corkin, S. (2013). *Permanent present tense: The unforgettable life of the amnesic patient, H.M.* Basic Books.

Corneliessen, L. (2021). Religiosity in Canada and its evolution from 1985–2019. Statistics Canada: Insights on Canadian Society (75-006-X).

Cornelius, M. E., Wang, T. W., Jamal, A., Loretan, C., & Neff, L. (2020). Tobacco product use among adults: United States, 2019. *Morbidity and Mortality Weekly Report, 69*(46), 1736–1742.

Correll, J., Park, B., Judd, C. M., & Wittenbrink, B. (2002). The police officer's dilemma: Using ethnicity to disambiguate potentially threatening individuals. *Journal of Personality and Social Psychology, 83,* 1314–1329.

Correll, J., Wittenbrink, B., Crawford, M. T., & Sadler, M. S. (2015). Stereotypic vision: How stereotypes disambiguate visual stimuli. *Journal of Personality and Social Psychology, 108*(2), 219–233. https://doi.org/10.1037/pspa0000015

Corsi, P. (Ed.). (1991). *The enchanted loom: Chapters in the history of neuroscience.* Oxford University Press.

Corti, E. (1931). *A history of smoking* (P. England, Trans.). Harrap.

Cosmides, L., & Tooby, J. (2000). The evolutionary psychology of the emotions and their relationship to internal regulatory variables. In M. Lewis, J. M. Haviland-Jones, & L. Feldman Barrett (Eds.), *Handbook of emotions* (3rd ed.), pp. 114–137. Guilford Press.

Costa, P. T., Terracciano, A., & McCrae, R. R. (2001). Gender differences in personality traits across cultures: Robust and surprising findings. *Journal of Personality and Social Psychology, 81,* 322–331.

Costanza, A., Weber, K., Gandy, S., Bouras, C., Hof, P. R., Giannakopoulos, G., & Canuto, A. (2011). Contact sport–related chronic traumatic encephalopathy in the elderly: Clinical expression and structural substrates. *Neuropathology and Applied Neurobiology, 37,* 570–584.

Cotton, J. L. (1981). A review of research on Schachter's theory of emotion and the misattribution of arousal. *European Journal of Social Psychology, 11*(4), 365–397.

Cottrell, C. A., Neuberg, S. L., & Li, N. P. (2007). What do people desire in others? A sociofunctional perspective on the importance of different valued characteristics. *Journal of Personality and Social Psychology, 92,* 208–231.

Courtney, A. L., & Meyer, M. L. (2020, July 15) Self–other representation in the social brain reflects social connection. *Journal of Neuroscience, 40*(29), 5616–5627. https://doi.org/10.1523/JNEUROSCI.2826-19.2020

Cowen, A. S., & Keltner, D. (2017). Self-report captures 27 distinct categories of emotion bridged by continuous gradients. *Proceedings of the National Academy of Sciences, USA, 114*(38), E7900–LPE7909. https://doi.org/10.1073/pnas.1702247114

Cowen, A. S., Keltner, D., Schroff, F., Jou, B., Adam, H., & Prasad, G. (2021). Sixteen facial expressions occur in similar contexts worldwide. *Nature, 589*(7841), 251–257. https://doi.org/10.1038/s41586-020-3037-7

Cox, S. R., Ritchie, S. J., Faws-Ritchie, C., Tucker-Drob, E. M., & Deary, I. J. (2019). Structural brain imaging correlates of general intelligence in UK Biobank. *Intelligence, 76,* 101376. https://doi.org/10.1016/j.intell.2019.101376

Craddock, N., & Jones, I. (1999). Genetics of bipolar disorder. *Journal of Medical Genetics, 36,* 585–594.

Craik, F. I. M., & Tulving, E. (1975). Depth of processing and the retention of words in episodic memory. *Journal of Experimental Psychology: General, 104,* 268–294.

Craik, F. I. M., Govoni, R., Naveh-Benjamin, M., & Anderson, N. D. (1996). The effects of divided attention on encoding and retrieval processes in human memory. *Journal of Experimental Psychology: General, 125,* 159–180.

Cramer, R. E., Schaefer, J. T., & Reid, S. (1996). Identifying the ideal mate: More evidence for male–female convergence. *Current Psychology, 15,* 157–166.

Crane, C. A., Godleski, S. A., Przybyla, S. M., Schlauch, R. C., & Testa, M. (2015). The proximal effects of acute alcohol consumption on male-to-female aggression: A meta-analytic review of the experimental literature. *Trauma, Violence, & Abuse.* https://doi.org/10.1177/1524838015584374

Craske, M. G. (1999). *Anxiety disorders: Psychological approaches to theory and treatment.* Westview Press.

Creery, J. D., Oudiette, D., Antony, J. W., & Paller, K. A. (2015). Targeted memory reactivation during sleep depends on prior learning. *Sleep, 38,* 755–763.

Crivelli, C., Carrera, P., & Fernández-Dols, J.-M. (2015). Are smiles a sign of happiness? Spontaneous expressions of judo winners. *Evolution and Human Behavior, 36*(1), 52–58.

Crocker, J., Canevello, A., & Brown, A. A. (2017). Social motivation: Costs and benefits of selfishness and otherishness. *Annual Review of Psychology, 68*, 299–325. https://doi.org/10.1146/annurev-psych-010416-044145

Crocq, M.-A. (2007). Historical and cultural aspects of man's relationship with addictive drugs. *Dialogues in Clinical Neuroscience, 9*, 355–361.

Crombag, H. F. M., Wagenaar, W. A., & Van Koppen, P. J. (1996). Crashing memories and the problem of "source monitoring." *Applied Cognitive Psychology, 10*, 95–104.

Crone, E. A., & Kronjin, E. A. (2018). Media use and brain development during adolescence. *Nature Communications, 9*, 588. https://doi.org/10.1038/s41467-018-03126-x

Cross, E. S., Kraemer, D. J. M., Hamilton, A. F. de C., Kelley, W. M., & Grafton, S. T. (2009). Sensitivity of the action observation network to physical and observational learning. *Cerebral Cortex, 19*, 315–326.

Cross, P. (1977). Not can but will college teachers be improved? *New Directions for Higher Education, 17*, 1–15.

Cross-Disorder Group of the Psychiatric Genomics Consortium. (2013). Identification of risk loci with shared effects on five major psychiatric disorders: A genome-wide analysis. *Lancet, 381*, 1371–1379.

Crowell, A. L., Riva-Posse, P., Holtzheimer, P. E., Garlow, S. J., Kelley, M. E., … Maybarg, H. S. (2019). Long-term outcomes of subcallosal cingulate deep brain stimulation for treatment-resistant depression. *American Journal of Psychiatry, 176*(11), 949–956. https://doi.org/10.1176/appi.ajp.2019.18121427

Cruess, D. G., Antoni, M. H., Kumar, M., & Schneiderman, N. (2000). Reductions in salivary cortisol are associated with mood improvement during relaxation training among HIV-seropositive men. *Journal of Behavioral Medicine, 23*, 107–122.

Crum-Cianflone, N. F., Bagnell, M. E., Schaller, E., Boyko, E. J., Smith, B., … Smith, T. C. (2014). Impact of combat deployment and posttraumatic stress disorder on newly reported coronary heart disease among U.S. active duty and reserve forces. *Circulation, 129*, 1813–1820.

Cruwys, T., Greenaway, K. H., Ferris, L. J., Rathbone, J. A., Saeri, A. K., Williams, E., … Grace, L. (2021). When trust goes wrong: A social identity model of risk taking. *Journal of Personality and Social Psychology, 120*(1), 57–83. https://doi.org/10.1037/pspi0000243

Csigó, K., Harsányi, A., Demeter, G., Rajkai, C., Németh, A., & Racsmány, M. (2010). Long-term follow-up of patients with obsessive-compulsive disorder treated by anterior capsulotomy: A neuropsychological study. *Journal of Affective Disorders, 126*, 198–205.

Csikszentmihalyi, M. (1990). *Flow: The psychology of optimal experience*. Harper & Row.

Cuc, A., Koppel, J., & Hirst, W. (2007). Silence is not golden: A case of socially shared retrieval-induced forgetting. *Psychological Science, 18*, 727–733.

Cuddy, A. J. C., Fiske, S. T., & Glick, P. (2007). The BIAS map: Behaviors from intergroup affect and stereotypes. *Journal of Personality and Social Psychology, 92*(4), 631–648. https://doi.org/10.1037/0022-3514.92.4.631

Culverhouse, R. C., Saccone, N. L., Horton, A. C., Ma, Y., Antsey, K. J., … Bierut, L. J. (2017). Collaborative meta-analysis finds no evidence of a strong interaction between stress and 5-HTTLPR genotype contributing to the development of depression. *Molecular Psychiatry, 23*, 133–142.

Cummins, D. D. (2012). *Good thinking: Seven powerful ideas that influence the way we think.* Cambridge University Press.

Cunningham, M. R., Barbee, A. P., & Pike, C. L. (1990). What do women want? Facial metric assessment of multiple motives in the perception of male facial physical attractiveness. *Journal of Personality and Social Psychology, 59*, 61–72.

Cunningham, M. R., Roberts, A. R., Barbee, A. P., Druen, P. B., & Wu, C.-H. (1995). "Their ideas of beauty are, on the whole, the same as ours": Consistency and variability in the cross-cultural perception of female physical attractiveness. *Journal of Personality and Social Psychology, 68*, 261–279.

Cunningham, W. A., & Brosch, T. (2012). Motivational salience: Amygdala tuning from traits, needs, values, and goals. *Current Directions in Psychological Science, 21*(1), 54–59.

Curran, J. P., & Lippold, S. (1975). The effects of physical attraction and attitude similarity on attraction in dating dyads. *Journal of Personality, 43*, 528–539.

Curtiss, S. (1977). *Genie: A psycholinguistic study of a modern-day "wildchild."* Academic Press.

Cushman, F., Sheketoff, R., Wharton, S., & Carey, S. (2013). The development of intent-based moral judgment. *Cognition, 127*, 6–21.

Dabbs, J. M., Bernieri, F. J., Strong, R. K., Campo, R., & Milun, R. (2001). Going on stage: Testosterone in greetings and meetings. *Journal of Research in Personality, 35*, 27–40.

Dael, N., Mortillaro, M., & Scherer, K. R. (2012). Emotion expression in body action and posture. *Emotion, 12*, 1085–1101.

Dagher, A., & Robbins, T. W. (2009). Personality, addiction, dopamine: Insights from Parkinson's disease. *Neuron, 61*, 502–510.

Dahl, A., & Brownell, C. A. (2019). The social origins of human prosociality. *Current Directions in Psychological Science, 28*(3), 274–279. https://doi.org/10.1177/0963721419830386

Dahmani, L., & Bohbot, V. D. (2020). Habitual use of GPS negatively impacts spatial memory during self-guided navigation. *Scientific Reports, 10*(1), 6310. https://doi.org/10.1038/s41598-020-62877-0

Dalton, P. (2003). Olfaction. In H. Pashler & S. Yantis (Eds.), *Stevens' handbook of experimental psychology: Vol. 1. Sensation and perception* (3rd ed., pp. 691–746). Wiley.

Daly, M., & Wilson, M. (1988). Evolutionary social psychology and family homicide. *Science, 242*, 519–524.

Damasio, A. R. (1989). Time-locked multiregional retroactivation: A systems-level proposal for the neural substrates of recall and recognition. *Cognition, 33*, 25–62.

Damasio, A. R. (1994). *Descartes' error: Emotion, reason, and the human brain*. Putnam.

Damasio, A. R. (2005). *Descartes' error: Emotion, reason, and the human brain*. Penguin.

Damasio, A. R., Grabowski, T. J., Bechara, A., Damasio, H., Ponto, L. L. B., Parvisi, J., & Hichwa, R. D. (2000). Subcortical and cortical brain activity during the feeling of self-generated emotions. *Nature Neuroscience, 3*, 1049–1056.

Damasio, H., Grabowski, T. J., Tranel, D., Hichwa, R. D., & Damasio, A. R. (1996). A neural basis for lexical retrieval. *Nature, 380*, 499–505.

Damerius, L. A., Forss, S. I. F., Kosonen, Z. K., Willems, E. P., Burkhart, J. M., Call, J., … van Schaik, C. P. (2017). Orientation toward humans predicts cognitive performance in orang-utans. *Scientific Reports, 7*, Art. No.: 40052.

Damsma, G., Pfaus, J. G., Wenkstern, D., Phillips, A. G., & Fibiger, H. C. (1992). Sexual behavior increases dopamine transmission in the nucleus accumbens and striatum of male rats:

Comparison with novelty and locomotion. *Behavioral Neurosciences, 106*, 181–191.

Daneshvar, D. H., Nowinski, C. J., McKee, A. C., & Cantu, R. C. (2011). The epidemiology of sport-related concussion. *Clinical Sports Medicine, 30*, 1–17.

Daniel, H. J., O'Brien, K. F., McCabe, R. B., & Quinter, V. E. (1985). Values in mate selection: A 1984 campus survey. *College Student Journal, 19*, 44–50.

Daniel, K. (2015, June 16). Pixar movie teaches future jurors wrong lesson on memory. *Chicago Sun-Times.*

Danner, U. N., Ouwehand, C., van Haastert, N. L., Homsveld, H., & de Ridder, D. T. (2012). Decision-making impairments in women with binge eating disorder in comparison with obese and normal weight women. *European Eating Disorders Review, 20*, e56–e62.

Darley, J. M., & Gross, P. H. (1983). A hypothesis-confirming bias in labeling effects. *Journal of Personality and Social Psychology, 44*, 20–33.

Darley, J. M., & Latané, B. (1968). Bystander intervention in emergencies: Diffusion of responsibility. *Journal of Personality and Social Psychology, 8*, 377–383.

Darwin, C. (2007). *The expression of the emotions in man and animals.* Bibliobazaar. (Original work published 1899)

Darwin, C. J., Turvey, M. T., & Crowder, R. G. (1972). An auditory analogue of the Sperling partial report procedure: Evidence for brief auditory storage. *Cognitive Psychology, 3*, 255–267.

Dasgupta, N. (2013). Implicit attitudes and beliefs adapt to situations: A decade of research on the malleability of implicit prejudice, stereotypes, and the self-concept. *Advances in Experimental Social Psychology, 47*, 233–279. https://doi.org/10.1016/B978-0-12-407236-7.00005-X

Dauer, W., & Przedborski, S. (2003). Parkinson's disease: Mechanisms and models. *Neuron, 39*, 889–909.

Daum, I., Schugens, M. M., Ackermann, H., Lutzenberger, W., Dichgans, J., & Birbaumer, N. (1993). Classical conditioning after cerebellar lesions in humans. *Behavioral Neuroscience, 107*, 748–756.

David-Barrett, T., Kertesz, J., Rotkirch, A., Ghosh, A., Bhattacharya, K., Monsivais, D., & Kaski, K. (2016). Communication with family and friends across the life course. *PLoS ONE, 11*(11), 1–15. https://doi.org/10.1371/journal.pone.0165687

Davidson, R. J., Ekman, P., Saron, C., Senulis, J., & Friesen, W. V. (1990). Emotional expression and brain physiology: I. Approach/withdrawal and cerebral asymmetry. *Journal of Personality and Social Psychology, 58*, 330–341.

Davidson, R. J., Putnam, K. M., & Larson, C. L. (2000). Dysfunction in the neural circuitry of emotion regulation: A possible prelude to violence. *Science, 289*, 591–594.

Davies, G, Tenesa, A., Payton, A., Yang, J., Harris, S. E., Liewald, D., ... Deary, I. J. (2011). Genome-wide association studies establish that human intelligence is highly heritable and polygenic. *Molecular Psychiatry, 16*(10), 996–1005. https://doi.org/10.1038/mp2011.85

Davila Ross, M., Menzler, S., & Zimmermann, E. (2008). Rapid facial mimicry in orangutan play. *Biology Letters, 4*(1), 27–30.

Davis, J., Redshaw, J., Suddendorf, T., Nielson, M., Kennedy-Costantini, S., Oostenbroek, J., & Slaughter, V. (2021, February). Does neonatal imitation exist? Insights from a meta-analysis of 336 effect sizes. *Perspectives on Psychological Science.* https://doi.org/10.1177/1745691620959834

Davis, S., & Wahlin-Jacobsen, S. (2015). Testosterone in women: The clinical significance. *Lancet Diabetes & Endocrinology, 3*, 980–992.

Dawes, A. J., Keogh, R., Andrillon, T., & Pearson, J. (2020). A cognitive profile of multi-sensory imagery, memory and dreaming in aphantasia. *Scientific Reports, 10*, 10022. https://doi.org/10.1038/s41598-020-65705-7

Dawes, R. M. (1994). *House of cards: Psychology and psychotherapy built on myth.* Free Press.

Dawood, K., Kirk, K. M., Bailey, J. M., Andrews, P. W., & Martin, N. G. (2005). Genetic and environmental influences on the frequency of orgasm in women. *Twin Research, 8*, 27–33.

Dawson, G., & Sapiro, G. (2019). Potential for digital behavioral measurement tools to transform the detection and diagnosis of autism spectrum disorder. *Journal of the American Medical Association Pediatrics, 173*, 305–306.

Dawson, G., Jones, E. J. H., Merkle, K., Venema, K., Lowry, R., Faja, S., ... Webb, S. J. (2012). Early behavioral intervention is associated with normalized brain activity in young children with autism. *Journal of the American Academy of Child and Adolescent Psychiatry, 51*, 1150–1159.

Dawson, G., Rogers, S., Munson, J., Smith, M., Winter, J., Greenson, J., ... Varley, J. (2010). Randomized, controlled trial of an intervention for toddlers with autism: The Early Start Denver Model. *Pediatrics, 125*, e17–e23.

Dawson, M., Soulieres, I., Gernsbacher, M. A., & Mottron, L. (2007). The level and nature of autistic intelligence. *Psychological Science, 18*, 657–662.

Day, J. J., & Sweatt, J. D. (2011). Epigenetic mechanisms in cognition. *Neuron, 70*, 813–829.

Dayan, E., & Bar-Hillel, M. (2011). Nudge to obesity. II: Menu positions influence food orders. *Judgment and Decision Making, 6*(4), 333.

Dayan, P., & Huys, Q. J. M. (2009). Serotonin in affective control. *Annual Review of Neuroscience, 32*, 95–126.

de Araujo, I. E., Rolls, E. T., Velazco, M. I., Margot, C., & Cayeux, I. (2005). Cognitive modulation of olfactory processing. *Neuron, 46*, 671–679.

De Bloom, J., Sianoja, M., Korpela, K., Tuomisto, M., Lilja, A., Geurts, S., & Kinnunen, U. (2017). Effects of park walks and relaxation exercises during lunch breaks on recovery from job stress: Two randomized controlled trials. *Journal of Environmental Psychology, 51*, 14–30.

De Bolle, M., De Fryut, F., McCrae, R. R., Löckenhoff, C. E., Costa, P. T., Jr., Aguilar-Valfae, M. E., ... Terracciano, A. (2015). The emergence of sex differences in personality traits in early adolescence: A cross-sectional, cross-cultural study. *Journal of Personality and Social Psychology, 108*, 171–185.

de Jonge, P., Roest, A. M., Lim, C. C. W., Florescu, S., Bromet, E. J., Stein, D. J., ... Scott, K. M. (2016). Cross-national epidemiology of panic disorder and panic attacks in the World Mental Health Surveys. *Depression and Anxiety, 33*(12), 1155–1177. https://doi.org/10.1002/da.22572

De Marco, M., Mazzoni, G., Manca, R., & Venneri, A. (2021). Functional neural architecture supporting highly superior autobiographical memory. *Brain Connectivity, 11*(4), 297–307. https://doi.org/10.1089/brain.2020.0858

De Neys, W., & Van Gelder, E. (2009). Logic and belief across the lifespan: The rise and fall of belief inhibition during syllogistic reasoning. *Developmental Science, 12*, 123–130.

de Rosnay, M., Pons, F., Harris, P. L., & Morrell, J. M. B. (2004). A lag between understanding false belief and emotion attribution in young children: Relationships with linguistic ability and mothers' mental-state language. *British Journal of Developmental Psychology, 24*(1), 197–218.

De Simoni, C., & von Bastian, C. C. (2018). Working memory updating and binding training: Bayesian evidence supporting the absence of transfer. *Journal of Experimental Psychology: General, 147,* 829–858.

De Vries, M. H., Barth, A. C. R., Maiworm, S., Knecht, S., Zwitserlood, P., & Flöel, A. (2010). Electrical stimulation of Broca's area enhances implicit learning of an artificial grammar. *Journal of Cognitive Neuroscience, 22,* 2427–2436.

De Wolff, M., & van IJzendoorn, M. H. (1997). Sensitivity and attachment: A meta-analysis on parental antecedents of infant attachment. *Child Development, 68,* 571–591.

Deady, D. K., & Law Smith, M. J. (2015) Changing male preferences for female body type in the U.S.: An adaptive response to a changing socioeconomic climate. *Journal of Behavioral and Brain Science, 5,* 570–577. http://dx.doi.org/10.4236/jbbs.2015.513054

Deák, G. O. (2006). Do children really confuse appearance and reality? *Trends in Cognitive Sciences, 10*(12), 546–550.

Deary, I. J. (2000). *Looking down on human intelligence: From psychometrics to the brain.* Oxford University Press.

Deary, I. J., & Sternberg, R. J. (2021). Ian Deary and Robert Sternberg answer five self-inflicted questions about human intelligence. *Intelligence, 86,* 101539. https://doi.org/10.1016/j.intell.2021.101539

Deary, I. J., Taylor, M. D., Hart, C. L., Wilson, V., Smith, G. D., Blane, D., & Starr, J. M. (2005). Intergenerational social mobility and mid-life status attainment: Influences of childhood intelligence, childhood social factors, and education. *Intelligence, 33*(5), 455–472. https://doi.org/10.1016/j.intell.2005.06.003

Deary, I. J., Weiss, A., & Batty, G. D. (2011). Intelligence and personality as predictors of illness and death: How researchers in differential psychology and chronic disease epidemiology are collaborating to understand and address health inequalities. *Psychological Science in the Public Interest, 11*(2), 53–79. https://doi.org/10.1177/1529100610387081

Deci, E. L. (1971). Effects of externally mediated rewards on intrinsic motivation. *Journal of Personality and Social Psychology, 18,* 105–115.

Deci, E. L., Koestner, R., & Ryan, R. M. (1999). A meta-analytic review of experiments examining the effects of extrinsic rewards on intrinsic motivation. *Psychological Bulletin, 125,* 627–668.

Deese, J. (1959). On the prediction of occurrence of particular verbal intrusions in immediate recall. *Journal of Experimental Psychology, 58,* 17–22.

DeFelipe, J., & Jones, E. G. (1988). *Cajal on the cerebral cortex: An annotated translation of the complete writings.* Oxford University Press.

Degenhardt, L., Chiu, W. T., Sampson, N., Kessler, R. C., Anthony, J. C., Angermeyer, M., … Wells, J. E. (2008). Toward a global view of alcohol, tobacco, cannabis, and cocaine use: Findings from the WHO World Mental Health surveys. *PLoS Medicine, 5,* e141.

Dekker, M. C., & Koot, H. M. (2003). *DSM–IV* disorders in children with borderline to moderate intellectual disability: I. Prevalence and impact. *Journal of the American Academy of Child and Adolescent Psychiatry, 42*(8), 915–922. https://doi.org/10.1097/01.CHI.0000046892.27264.1A

Dekker, S., Lee, N. C., Howard-Jones, P., & Jolles, J. (2012). Neuromyths in education: Prevalence and predictors of misconceptions among teachers. *Frontiers in Psychology, 3,* 429. doi:10.3389/fpsyg.2012.00429

Deković, M., Noom, M. J., & Meeus, W. (1997). Expectations regarding development during adolescence: Parental and adolescent perceptions. *Journal of Youth and Adolescence, 26,* 253–272. http://doi.org/10.1007/s10964-005-0001-7

Del Vicario, M., Bessi, A., Zollo, F., Petroni, F., Scalåa, A., Caldarelli, G., … Quattrociocchi, W. (2016). The spreading of misinformation online. *Proceedings of the National Academy of Sciences, PNAS, 113*(3), 554–559. https://doi.org/10.1073/pnas.1517441113

Delgado, M. R., Frank, R. H., & Phelps, E. A. (2005). Perceptions of moral character modulate the neural systems of reward during the trust game. *Nature Neuroscience, 8,* 1611–1618.

DeLoache, J. S., Uttal, D. H., & Rosengren, K. S. (2004). Scale errors offer evidence for a perception–action dissociation early in life. *Science, 304*(5673), 1027–1029.

Demb, J. B., Desmond, J. E., Wagner, A. D., Vaidya, C. J., Glover, G. H., & Gabrieli, J. D. E. (1995). Semantic encoding and retrieval in the left inferior prefrontal cortex: A functional MRI study of task difficulty and process specificity. *Journal of Neuroscience, 15,* 5870–5878.

Dement, W. C. (1959, November 30). Dreams. *Newsweek.*

Dement, W. C. (1978). *Some must watch while some must sleep.* W. W. Norton.

Dement, W. C. (1999). *The promise of sleep.* Delacorte Press.

Dement, W. C., & Kleitman, N. (1957). The relation of eye movements during sleep to dream activity: An objective method for the study of dreaming. *Journal of Experimental Psychology, 53,* 339–346.

Dement, W. C., & Wolpert, E. (1958). Relation of eye movements, body motility, and external stimuli to dream content. *Journal of Experimental Psychology, 55,* 543–553.

Dempster, E. L., Pidsley, R., Schalkwyk, L. C., Owens, S., Georgiades, A., Kane, F., … Mill, J. (2011). Disease-associated epigenetic changes in monozygotic twins discordant for schizophrenia and bipolar disorder. *Human Molecular Genetics, 20,* 4786–4796.

Denault, V., Plusquellec, P., Jupe, L. M., St-Yves, M., Dunbar, N. E., Hartwig, M., … van Koppen, P. J. (2020). The analysis of nonverbal communication: The dangers of pseudoscience in security and justice contexts. *Anuario de Psicología Jurídica, 30*(1), 1–12. https://doi.org/10.5093/apj2019a9

Denissen, J. J., Geenen, R., Soto, C. J., John, O. P., & van Aken, M. A. G. (2019). The Big Five Inventory–2: Replication of psychometric properties in a Dutch adaptation and first evidence for the discriminant predictive validity of the facet scales. *Journal of Personality Assessment.* https://doi.org/10.1080/00223891.2018.1539004

Dennett, D. (1991). *Consciousness explained.* Basic Books.

Denny, B. T., & Ochsner, K. N. (2014). Behavioral effects of longitudinal training in cognitive reappraisal. *Emotion, 14*(2), 425–433. https://doi.org/10.1037/a0035276

Denson, T. F., O'Dean, S. M., Blake, K. R., & Beames, K. R. (2018). Aggression in women: Behavior, brain and hormones. *Frontiers in Behavioral Neuroscience, 12.* https://doi.org/ezp-prod1.hul.harvard.edu/10.3389/fnbeh.2018.00081

DePaulo, B. M., Charlton, K., Cooper, H., Lindsay, J. J., & Muhlenbruck, L. (1997). The accuracy–confidence correlation in the detection of deception. *Personality and Social Psychology Review, 1,* 346–357.

DePaulo, B. M., Lindsay, J. J., Malone, B. E., Muhlenbruck, L., Charlton, K., & Cooper, H. (2003). Cues to deception. *Psychological Bulletin, 129,* 74–118.

DePaulo, B. M., & Morris, W. L. (2006). The unrecognized stereotyping and discrimination against singles. *Current Directions in Psychological Science, 15,* 251–254.

DeRubeis, R. J., Cohen, Z. D., Forand, N. R., Fournier, J. C., Gelfand, L. A., & Lorenzo-Luaces, L. (2014). The personalized advantage index: Translating research on prediction into individualized treatment recommendations: A demonstration. *PLoS ONE, 9,* e83875.

D'Esposito, M., & Postle, B. R. (2015). The cognitive neuroscience of working memory. *Annual Review of Psychology, 66,* 115–142.

DeSantis, A. D., Webb, E. M., & Noar, S. M. (2008). Illicit use of prescription ADHD medications on a college campus: A multi-methodological approach. *Journal of American College Health, 57*(3), 315–324. https://doi.org/10.3200/JACH.57.3.315-324

DeVilliers, P. (2005). The role of language in theory-of-mind development: What deaf children tell us. In J. W. Astington & J. A. Baird (Eds.), *Why language matters for theory of mind* (pp. 266–297). Oxford University Press.

Dewhurst, S. A., Anderson, R. J., Grace, L., & van Esch, L. (2016). Adaptive false memories: Imagining future scenarios increases false memories in the DRM paradigm. *Memory & Cognition, 44,* 1076–1084.

DeYoung, C. G., & Gray, J. R. (2009). Personality neuroscience: Explaining individual differences in affect, behavior, and cognition. In P. J. Corr & G. Matthews (Eds.), *The Cambridge handbook of personality psychology* (pp. 323–346). Cambridge University Press.

DeYoung, C. G., Hirsh, J. B., Shane, M. S., Papademetris, X., Rajeevan, N., & Gray, J. R. (2010). Testing predictions from personality neuroscience: Brain structure and the Big Five. *Psychological Science, 21,* 820–828.

Diaconis, P., & Mosteller, F. (1989). Methods for studying coincidences. *Journal of the American Statistical Association, 84,* 853–861.

Diamond, K. (2020, September 6). The strange grief of losing my sense of taste. *New York Times.* https://www.nytimes.com/2020/09/06/opinion/coronavirus-covid-symptoms-taste.html

Diano, S., Farr, S. A., Benoit, S. C., McNay, E. C., da Silva, I., Horvath, B., … Horvath, T. L. (2006). Ghrelin controls hippocampal spine synapse density and memory performance. *Nature Neuroscience, 9*(3), 381–388.

Dickens, W. T., & Flynn, J. R. (2001). Heritability estimates versus large environmental effects: The IQ paradox resolved. *Psychological Review, 108,* 346–369.

Dickinson, A., Watt, A., & Griffiths, J. H. (1992). Free-operant acquisition with delayed reinforcement. *Quarterly Journal of Experimental Psychology Section B: Comparative and Physiological Psychology, 45,* 241–258.

Didden, R., Sigafoos, J., Lang, R., O'Reilly, M., Drieschner, K., & Lancioni, G. E. (2012). Intellectual disabilities. In P. Sturmey & M. Hersen (Eds.), *Handbook of evidence-based practice in clinical psychology.* Wiley. https://doi.org/10.1002/9781118156391.ebcp001006

DiDonato, T. E., Ullrich, J., & Krueger, J. I. (2011). Social perception as induction and inference: An integrative model of intergroup differentiation, ingroup favoritism, and differential accuracy. *Journal of Personality and Social Psychology, 100*(1), 66–83. https://doi.org/10.1037/a0021051

Diederen, K. M. J., & Fletcher, P. C. (2021). Dopamine, prediction error and beyond. *The Neuroscientist, 27*(1), 30–46. https://doi.org/10.1177/1073858420907591

Diederich, N. J., & Goetz, C. G. (2008). The placebo treatments in neurosciences: New insights from clinical and neuroimaging studies. *Neurology, 71,* 677–684.

Diekelmann, S., & Born, J. (2010). The memory function of sleep. *Nature Reviews Neuroscience, 11,* 114–126.

Dimberg, U. (1982). Facial reactions to facial expressions. *Psychophysiology, 19,* 643–647.

Dion, K. L. (2005). Marital status as stimulus variable and subject variable. *Psychological Inquiry, 16,* 104–110.

Dion, K., Berscheid, E., & Walster, E. (1972). What is beautiful is good. *Journal of Personality and Social Psychology, 24,* 285–290.

Dismukes, R. K. (2012). Prospective memory in workplace and everyday situations. *Current Directions in Psychological Science, 21,* 215–220.

Disner, S. G., Beevers, C. G., Haigh, E. A., & Beck, A. T. (2011). Neural mechanisms of the cognitive model of depression. *Nature Reviews Neuroscience, 12,* 467–477.

Dittrich, W. H., Troscianko, T., Lea, S., & Morgan, D. (1996). Perception of emotion from dynamic point-light displays represented in dance. *Perception, 25,* 727–738. https://doi.org/10.3389/fpsyg.2011.00337

Dobbin, F., & Kalev, A. (2018). Why doesn't diversity training work? The challenge for industry and academia. *Anthropology Now, 10*(2), 48–55. https://doi.org/10.1080/19428200.2018.1493182

Dollard, J., Doob, L. W., Miller, N. E., Mowrer, O. H., & Sears, R. R. (1939). *Frustration and aggression.* Yale University Press.

Domhoff, G. W. (2001). A new neurocognitive theory of dreams. *Dreaming, 11*(1), 13–33. https://doi.org/10.1023/A:1009464416649

Domhoff, G. W. (2019). The neurocognitive theory of dreams at age 20: As assessment and a comparison with four other theories of dreaming. *Dreaming, 29*(4), 265–302. https://doi.org/10.1037/drm0000119

Domjan, M. (2005). Pavlovian conditioning: A functional perspective. *Annual Review of Psychology, 56,* 179–206.

Doucet, S., Soussignan, R., Sagot, P., & Schaal, B. (2009). The secretion of areolar (Montgomery's) glands from lactating women elicits selective, unconditional responses in neonates. *PLoS ONE, 4,* e7579. https://doi.org/10.1371/journal.pone.0007579

Doucet, S., Soussignan, R., Sagot, P., & Schaal, B. (2012). An overlooked aspect of the human breast: Areolar glands in relation with breastfeeding pattern, neonatal weight gain, and the dynamics of lactation. *Early Human Development, 88,* 119–128. https://doi.org/10.1016/j.earlhumdev.2011.07.020

Dougherty, D. D., Brennan, B. P., Stewart, S. E., Wilhelm, S., Widge, A. S., & Rauch, S. L. (2018). Neuroscientifically informed formulation and treatment planning for patients with obsessive-compulsive disorder: A review. *Journal of the American Medical Association Psychiatry, 75,* 1081–1087.

Dovidio, J. F., & Gaertner, S. L. (2010). Intergroup bias. In S. T. Fiske, D. T. Gilbert, & G. Lindzey (Eds.), *The handbook of social psychology* (5th ed., Vol. 2, pp. 1085–1121). Wiley.

Downer, J. D. C. (1961). Changes in visual gnostic function and emotional behavior following unilateral temporal damage in the "split-brain" monkey. *Nature, 191,* 50–51.

Drake, P., Driscoll, A. K., & Mathews, T. J. (2018). Cigarette smoking during pregnancy: United States, 2016. *NCHS Data Brief, no. 305.* National Center for Health Statistics.

Dresler, M., Shirer, W. R., Konrad, B. N., Müller, N. C. J., Wagner, I. C., Fernández, G., … Greicius, M. D. (2017). Mnemonic training reshapes brain networks to support superior memory. *Neuron, 93*(5), 1227–1235.

Dronkers, N. F., & Baldo, J. V. (2010). Aphasia. In L.R. Squire (Ed.), *Encyclopedia of neuroscience* (pp. 343–348). Elsevier.

Dronkers, N. F., Plaisant, O., Iba-Zizen, M. T., & Cabanis, E. A. (2007). Paul Broca's historic cases: High resolution MR imaging of the brains of Leborgne and Lelong. *Brain, 130*(5), 1432–1441. https://doi.org/10.1093/brain/awm042

Duchaine, B. & Yovel, G. (2015). A revised neural framework for face processing. *Annual Review of Vision Science, 1,* 393–416.

Duckworth, A. L., Kautz, T., Defnet, A., Satlof-Bedrick, E., Talamas, S., … Steinberg, L. (2021). Students attending school remote suffer socially, emotionally, and academically. *Educational Researcher, 50*(7), 479–482. https://doi.org/10.3102/0013189X211031551

Duckworth, A. L., & Seligman, M. E. P. (2005). Self-discipline outdoes IQ in predicting academic performance of adolescents. *Psychological Science, 16,* 939–944.

Dudai, Y. (2012). The restless engram: Consolidations never end. *Annual Review of Neuroscience, 35,* 227–247.

Dudycha, G. J., & Dudycha, M. M. (1933). Some factors and characteristics of childhood memories. *Child Development, 4,* 265–278.

Duenwald, M. (2002, September 12). Students find another staple of campus life: Stress. *New York Times.* http://www.nytimes.com/2002/09/17/health/students-find-another-staple-of-campus-life-stress.html?pagewanted=all&src=pm

Duff, M. C., Kurczek, J., Rubin, R., Cohen, N. J., & Tranel, D. (2013). Hippocampal amnesia disrupts creative thinking. *Hippocampus, 23,* 1143–1149.

Duñabeitia, J. A., Hernández, J. A., Antón, E., Macizo, P., Estévez, A., Fuentes, L. J., & Carreiras, M. (2014). The inhibitory advantage in bilingual children revisited: Myth or reality? *Experimental Psychology, 61,* 234–251.

Duncan, G. J., Yeung, W. J., Brooks-Gunn, J., & Smith, J. R. (1998). How much does childhood poverty affect the life chances of children? *American Sociological Review, 63,* 406–423.

Duncker, K. (1945). On problem-solving. (L. S. Lees, Trans.). *Psychological Monographs, 58*(5), i–113.

Dunham, Y., Chen, E. E., & Banaji, M. R. (2013). Two signatures of implicit intergroup attitudes: Developmental invariance and early enculturation. *Psychological Science, 6,* 860–868. https://doi.org/10.1177/0956797612463081

Dunlap, K. (1919). Are there any instincts? *Journal of Abnormal Psychology, 14,* 307–311.

Dunlop, S. A. (2008). Activity-dependent plasticity: Implications for recovery after spinal cord injury. *Trends in Neurosciences, 31,* 410–418.

Dunlosky, J., & Rawson, K. A. (2012). Overconfidence produces underachievement: Inaccurate self-evaluations undermine students' learning and retention. *Learning and Instruction, 22,* 271–280.

Dunlosky, J., Rawson, K. A., Marsh, E. J., Nathan, M. J., & Willingham, D. T. (2013). Improving students' learning with effective learning techniques: Promising directions from cognitive and educational psychology. *Psychological Science in the Public Interest, 14*(1), 4–58.

Dunn, J. C., & Kirsner, K. (2011). The search for HMAS Sydney: II. Analysis and integration of survivor reports. *Journal of Applied Cognitive Psychology, 25,* 513–527.

Dunphy, D. C. (1963). The social structure of urban adolescent peer groups. *Sociometry, 26,* 230–246.

Dutton, D. G., & Aron, A. P. (1974). Some evidence for heightened sexual attraction under conditions of high anxiety. *Journal of Personality and Social Psychology, 30,* 510–517.

Dutton, E., van der Linden, D., Lynn, R. (2016). The negative Flynn effect: A systematic literature review. *Intelligence, 59,* 163–169.

Duval, S., & Wicklund, R. A. (1972). *A theory of objective self-awareness.* Academic Press.

Dworkin, E. R., Menon, S. V., Bystrynski, J., & Allen, N. E. (2017). Sexual assault victimization and psychopathology: A review and meta-analysis. *Clinical Psychology Review, 56,* 65–81.

Eagly, A. H., & Wood, W. (1999). The origins of sex differences in human behavior: Evolved dispositions versus social roles. *American Psychologist, 54,* 408–423.

Eagly, A. H., Ashmore, R. D., Makhijani, M. G., & Longo, L. C. (1991). What is beautiful is good, but … : A meta-analytic review of research on the physical attractiveness stereotype. *Psychological Bulletin, 110,* 109–128.

Eastwick, P. W. (2009). Beyond the Pleistocene: Using phylogeny and constraint to inform the evolutionary psychology of human mating. *Psychological Bulletin, 135,* 794–821.

Eastwick, P. W., Eagly, A. H., Finkel, E. J., & Johnson, S. E. (2011). Implicit and explicit preferences for physical attractiveness in a romantic partner: A double dissociation in predictive validity. *Journal of Personality and Social Psychology, 101*(5), 993–1011. https://doi.org/10.1037/a0024061

Eastwick, P. W., Finkel, E. J., Mochon, D., & Ariely, D. (2007). Selective versus unselective romantic desire: Not all reciprocity is created equal. *Psychological Science, 18,* 317–319.

Eaton, W. W., Shao, H., Nestadt, G., Lee, B. H., Bienvenu, O. J., & Zandi, P. (2008). Population-based study of first onset and chronicity of major depressive disorder. *Archives of General Psychiatry, 65,* 513–520.

Ebbinghaus, H. (1908). *Psychology: An elementary textbook.* Heath.

Ebbinghaus, H. (1964). *Memory: A contribution to experimental psychology.* Dover. (Original work published 1885)

Ecklund, E. H., Scheitle, C. P., & Pennsylvania, T. (2007). Religion among academic scientists: Distinctions, disciplines, and demographics. *Social Problems, 54*(2), 289–307. https://doi.org/10.1525/sp.2007.54.2.289.290

Eddy, D. M. (1982). Probabilistic reasoning in clinical medicine: Problems and opportunities. In D. Kahneman, P. Slovic, & A. Tversky (Eds.), *Judgments under uncertainty: Heuristics and biases* (pp. 249– 267). Cambridge University Press.

Edgerton, V. R., Tillakaratne, J. K. T., Bigbee, A. J., deLeon, R. D., & Roy, R. R. (2004). Plasticity of the spinal neural circuitry after injury. *Annual Review of Neuroscience, 27,* 145–167.

Edwards, W. (1955). The theory of decision making. *Psychological Bulletin, 51,* 201–214.

Efferson, C., Lalive, R., & Fehr, E. (2008). The coevolution of cultural groups and ingroup favoritism. *Science, 321,* 1844–1849.

Eguchi, A., Isbister, J. B., Ahmad, N., & Stringer, S. (2018). The emergence of polychronization and feature binding in a spiking neural network model of the primate ventral visual system. *Psychological Review, 125,* 545–571.

Eich, J. E. (1995). Searching for mood dependent memory. *Psychological Science, 6,* 67–75.

Eichenbaum, H. (2008). *Learning & memory.* W. W. Norton.

Eichenbaum, H., & Cohen, N. J. (2001). *From conditioning to conscious recollection: Memory systems of the brain.* Oxford University Press.

Eimas, P. D., Siqueland, E. R., Jusczyk, P., & Vigorito, J. (1971). Speech perception in infants. *Science, 171,* 303–306.

Ein-Gar, D., Shiv, B., & Tormala, Z. L. (2012). When blemishing leads to blossoming: The positive effect of negative information. *Journal of Consumer Research, 38,* 846–859. https://doi.org/10.1086/660807

Einstein, G. O., & McDaniel, M. A. (1990). Normal aging and prospective memory. *Journal of Experimental Psychology: Learning, Memory, and Cognition, 16,* 717–726.

Einstein, G. O., & McDaniel, M. A. (2005). Prospective memory: Multiple retrieval processes. *Current Direction in Psychological Science, 14,* 286–290.

Eisenberg, N., Fabes, R. A., Guthrie, I. K., & Reiser, M. (2000). Dispositional emotionality and regulation: Their role in predicting quality of social functioning. *Journal of Personality and Social Psychology, 78,* 136.

Eisenberger, N. I., Lieberman, M. D., & Williams, K. D. (2003). Does rejection hurt? An fMRI study of social exclusion. *Science, 302,* 290–292. https://doi.org/10.1126/science.1089134

Eisenegger, C., Haushofer, J., & Fehr, E. (2011). The role of testosterone in social interaction. *Trends in Cognitive Sciences, 15*(6), 263–271. https://doi.org/10.1016/j.tics.2011.04.008

Eisenegger, C., Naef, M., Snozzi, R., Heinrichs, M., & Fehr, E. (2010). Prejudice and truth about the effect of testosterone on human bargaining behaviour. *Nature, 463,* 356–359.

Ekman, P. (1965). Differential communication of affect by head and body cues. *Journal of Personality and Social Psychology, 2,* 726–735.

Ekman, P. (1972). Universals and cultural differences in facial expressions of emotion. In J. K. Cole (Ed.), *Nebraska Symposium on Motivation, 1971* (pp. 207–283). University of Nebraska Press.

Ekman, P. (2016). What scientists who study emotion agree about. *Perspectives on Psychological Science, 11*(1), 31–34.

Ekman, P., & Friesen, W. V. (1968). Nonverbal behavior in psychotherapy research. In J. M. Shlien (Ed.), *Research in psychotherapy* (Vol. 3, pp. 179–216). American Psychological Association.

Ekman, P., & Friesen, W. V. (1971). Constants across cultures in the face and emotion. *Journal of Personality and Social Psychology, 17,* 124–129.

Ekman, P., & Friesen, W. V. (1982). Felt, false, and miserable smiles. *Journal of Nonverbal Behavior, 6,* 238–252.

Ekman, P., Levenson, R. W., & Friesen, W. V. (1983). Autonomic nervous system activity distinguishes among emotions. *Science, 221,* 1208–1210.

El Haj, M., Gallouj, K., & Antoine, P. (2017). Google Calendar enhances prospective memory in Alzheimer's disease: A case report. *Journal of Alzheimer's disease, 57,* 285–291.

Elbogen, E. B., & Johnson, S. C. (2009). The intricate link between violence and mental disorder. *Archives of General Psychiatry, 66*(2), 152–161.

Eldridge, L. L., Knowlton, B. J., Furmanski, C. S., Bookheimer, S. Y., & Engel, S. A. (2000). Remembering episodes: A selective role for the hippocampus during retrieval. *Nature Neuroscience, 3,* 1149–1152.

Eldridge, M. A., Barnard, P. J., & Bekerian, D. A. (1994). Autobiographical memory and daily schemas at work. *Memory, 2,* 51–74.

Elfenbein, H. A., & Ambady, N. (2002). On the universality and cultural specificity of emotion recognition: A meta-analysis. *Psychological Bulletin, 128,* 203–235.

Elfenbein, H. A., Beaupré, M., Lévesque, M., & Hess, U. (2007). Toward a dialect theory: Cultural differences in the expression and recognition of posed facial expressions. *Emotion, 7*(1), 131–146. https://doi.org/10.1037/1528-3542.7.1.131

Ellemers, N. (2012). The group self. *Science, 336*(6083), 848–852. https://doi.org/10.10.1126/science.1220987

Ellenbogen, J. M., Payne, J. D., & Stickgold, R. (2006). The role of sleep in declarative memory consolidation: Passive, permissive, or none? *Current Opinion in Neurobiology, 16,* 716–722.

Elliott, R., Sahakian, B. J., Matthews, K., Bannerjea, A., Rimmer, J., & Robbins, T. W. (1997). Effects of methylphenidate on spatial working memory and planning in healthy young adults. *Psychopharmacology, 131,* 196–206.

Ellis, A. (1991). *Reason and emotion in psychotherapy.* Carol.

Ellis, B. J., & Garber, J. (2000). Psychosocial antecedents of variation in girls' pubertal timing: Maternal depression, stepfather presence, and marital and family stress. *Child Development, 71,* 485–501.

Ellis, E. M. (1983). A review of empirical rape research: Victim reactions and response to treatment. *Clinical Psychology Review, 3,* 473–490.

Ellis, L., & Ames, M. A. (1987). Neurohormonal functioning in sexual orientation: A theory of homosexuality–heterosexuality. *Psychological Bulletin, 101,* 233–258.

Ellman, S. J., Spielman, A. J., Luck, D., Steiner, S. S., & Halperin, R. (1991). REM deprivation: A review. In S. J. Ellman & J. S. Antrobus (Eds.), *The mind in sleep: Psychology and psychophysiology* (2nd ed., pp. 329–376). Wiley.

Ellsworth, P. C., & Scherer, K. R. (2003). Appraisal processes in emotion. In R. J. Davidson, K. R. Scherer, & H. H. Goldsmith (Eds.), *The handbook of affective science* (pp. 572–595). Oxford University Press.

Elsey, J. W. B., Van Ast, V. A., & Kindt, M. (2018). Human memory reconsolidation: A guiding framework and critical review of the evidence. *Psychological Bulletin, 144,* 797–848.

Emerson, R. C., Bergen, J. R., & Adelson, E. H. (1992). Directionally selective complex cells and the computation of motion energy in cat visual cortex. *Vision Research, 32,* 203–218.

Epel, E. S., Blackburn, E. H., Lin, J., Dhabhar, F. S., Adler, N. E., Morrow, J. D., & Cawthorn, R. M. (2004). Accelerated telomere shortening in response to life stress. *Proceedings of the National Academy of Sciences, USA, 101,* 17312–17315.

Epel, E. S., Daubenmier, J., Moskowitz, J. T., Foldman, S., & Blackburn, E. H. (2009). Can meditation slow rate of cellular aging? Cognitive stress, mindfulness, and telomerase. *Annals of the New York Academy of Sciences, 1172,* 34–53.

Epley, N., & Waytz, A. (2010). Mind perception. In S. T. Fiske, D. T. Gilbert, & G. Lindzey (Eds.), *The handbook of social psychology* (5th ed., Vol. 1, pp. 498–541). Wiley.

Epstein, R. (2007a). *The case against adolescence: Rediscovering the adult in every teen.* Quill Driver.

Epstein, R. (2007b). The myth of the teen brain. *Scientific American Mind, 18,* 27–31.

Erffmeyer, E. S. (1984). Rule-violating behavior on the golf course. *Perceptual and Motor Skills, 59,* 591–596.

Ericsson, K. A., & Charness, N. (1999). Expert performance: Its structure and acquisition. In S. J. Ceci & W. M. Williams (Eds.), *The nature–nurture debate: The essential readings* (pp. 200–256). Blackwell.

Erikson, E. H. (1959). *Identity and the life cycle.* International Universities Press.

Eriksson, K., Vartanova, I., Strimling, P., & Simpson, B. (2020). Generosity pays: Selfish people have fewer children and earn less money. *Journal of Personality and Social Psychology, 118*(3), 532–544. https://doi.org/10.1037/pspp0000213

Espy, K. A., Fang, H., Johnson, C., Stopp, C., Wiebe, S. A., & Respass, J. (2011). Prenatal tobacco exposure: Developmental outcomes in the neonatal period. *Developmental Psychology, 47*(1), 153–169. https://doi.org/10.1037/a0020724

Estes, A., Munson, J., Rogers, S. J., Greenson, J., Winter, J., & Dawson, G. (2015). Long-term outcomes of early intervention in 6-year-old children with autism spectrum disorder. *Journal of the American Academy of Child and Adolescent Psychiatry, 54,* 580–587.

Etcoff, N. (1999). *Survival of the prettiest: The science of beauty.* Doubleday.

Evans, A. D., & Lee, K. (2013). Emergence of lying in very young children. *Developmental Psychology, 49*(10), 1958–1963. https://doi.org/10.1037/a0031409

Evans, G. W. (2006). Child development and the physical environment. *Annual Review of Psychology, 57,* 423–451.

Evans, G. W., & Stecker, R. (2004). Motivational consequences of environmental stress. *Journal of Environmental Psychology, 24,* 143–165.

Evans, J. St. B., Barston, J. L., & Pollard, P. (1983), On the conflict between logic and belief in syllogistic reasoning. *Memory & Cognition, 11*, 295–306.

Evans, S. W., & Kim, P. (2012). Childhood poverty and young adults' allostatic load: The mediating role of childhood cumulative risk exposure. *Psychological Science, 23*(9), 979–983. https://doi.org/10.1177/0956797612441218

Exner, J. E. (1993). *The Rorschach: A comprehensive system.* Vol. 1. *Basic Foundations.* Wiley.

Eysenck, H. J. (1957). The effects of psychotherapy: An evaluation. *Journal of Consulting Psychology, 16*, 319–324.

Eysenck, H. J. (1967). *The biological basis of personality.* Charles C. Thomas.

Eysenck, H. J. (1990). Biological dimensions of personality. In L. A. Pervin (Ed.), *Handbook of personality: Theory and research* (pp. 244–276). Guilford Press.

Falk, R., & McGregor, D. (1983). The surprisingness of coincidences. In P. Humphreys, O. Svenson, & A. Vari (Eds.), *Analysing and aiding decision processes* (pp. 489–502). North Holland.

Fan, R., Varol, O., Varamesh, A., Barron, A., van de Leemput, I. A., Scheffer, M., & Bollen, J. (2019). The minute-scale dynamics of online emotions reveal the effects of affect labeling. *Nature Human Behaviour, 3*(1), 92–100. https://doi.org/10.1038/s41562-018-0490-5

Fancher, R. E. (1979). *Pioneers in psychology.* W. W. Norton.

Fantz, R. L. (1964). Visual experience in infants: Decreased attention to familiar patterns relative to novel ones. *Science, 164*, 668–670.

Farah, M. J., & Rabinowitz, C. (2003). Genetic and environmental influences on the organization of semantic memory in the brain: Is "living things" an innate category? *Cognitive Neuropsychology, 20*, 401–408.

Farah, M. J., Hutchinson, J. B., Phelps, E. A., & Wagner, A. D. (2014). Functional MRI-based lie detection: Scientific and societal challenges. *Nature Reviews Neuroscience, 15*(2), 123–131. http://www.ncbi.nlm.nih.gov/pubmed/24588019

Farah, M. J., Illes, J., Cook-Deegan, R., Gardner, H., Kandel, E., King, P., ... Wolpe, P. R. (2004) Neurocognitive enhancement: What can we do and what should we do? *Nature Reviews Neuroscience, 5*, 421–426.

Faraone, S. V., Perlis, R. H., Doyle, A. E., Smoller, J. W., Goralnick, J. J., Holmgren, M. A., & Sklar, P. (2005). Molecular genetics of attention-deficit/hyperactivity disorder. *Biological Psychiatry, 57*, 1313–1323.

Farooqi, I. S., Bullmore, E., Keogh, J., Gillard, J., O'Rahilly, S., & Fletcher, P. C. (2007). Leptin regulates striatal regions and human eating behavior. *Science, 317*, 1355.

Farooqi, I. S., Matarese, G., Lord, G. M., Keogh, J. M., Lawrence, E., Agwu, C., & O'Rahilly, S. (2002). Beneficial effects of leptin on obesity, T cell hyporesponsiveness, and neuroendocrine/metabolic dysfunction of human congenital leptin deficiency. *Journal of Clinical Investigation, 110*(8), 1093–1103.

Farrar, M. J. (1990). Discourse and the acquisition of grammatical morphemes. *Journal of Child Language, 17*, 607–624.

Farrelly, D., Lazarus, J., & Roberts, G. (2007). Altruists attract. *Evolutionary Psychology, 5*, 313–329.

Favazza, A. (2011). *Bodies under siege: Self-mutilation, nonsuicidal self-injury, and body modification in culture and psychiatry.* Johns Hopkins University Press.

Fazio, L. K., Brashier, N. M., Payne, B. K., & Marsh, E. J. (2015). Knowledge does not protect against illusory truth. *Journal of Experimental Psychology. General, 144*, 993–1002.

Fechner, G. T. (1966). *Elements of psychophysics* (H. E. Alder, Trans.). Holt, Rinehart and Winston. (Original work published 1860)

Feczer, D., & Bjorklund, P. (2009). Forever changed: Posttraumatic stress disorder in female military veterans, a case report. *Perspectives in Psychiatric Care, 45*, 278–291.

Fedorenko, E., Behr, M. K., & Kanwisher, N. (2011). Functional specificity for high level language processing in the human brain. *Proceedings of the National Academy of Sciences, 108*(39), 16428–16433. https://doi.org/10.1073/pnas.1112937108

Fehr, E., & Gaechter, S. (2002). Altruistic punishment in humans. *Nature, 415*, 137–140.

Fein, S., Goethals, G. R., & Kugler, M. B. (2007). Social influence on political judgments: The case of presidential debates. *Political Psychology, 28*, 165–192.

Feinberg, M., Willer, R., & Schultz, M. (2014). Gossip and ostracism promote cooperation in groups. *Psychological Science, 25*(3), 656–664. https://doi.org/10.1177/0956797613510184

Feinberg, T. E. (2001). *Altered egos: How the brain creates the self.* Oxford University Press.

Feingold, A. (1992a). Gender differences in mate selection preferences: A test of the parental investment model. *Psychological Bulletin, 112*, 125–139.

Feingold, A. (1992b). Good-looking people are not what we think. *Psychological Bulletin, 111*, 304–341.

Feinstein, J. S., Buzza, C., Hurlemann, R., Follmer, R. L., Dahdaleh, N. S., Coryell, W. H., ... Wemmie, J. A. (2013). Fear and panic in humans with bilateral amygdala damage. *Nature Neuroscience, 16*(3), 270–272.

Feldman, D. E. (2009). Synaptic mechanisms for plasticity in neocortex. *Annual Review of Neuroscience, 32*, 33–55.

Felleman, D. J., & Van Essen, D. C. (1991). Distributed hierarchical processing in the primate cerebral cortex. *Cerebral Cortex, 1*, 1–47.

Feng, P., Huang, L., & Wang, K. (2014). Taste bud homeostasis in health, disease, and aging. *Chemical Senses, 39*(1), 3–16. https://doi.org/10.1093/chemse/bjt059

Ferguson, C. J. (2010). Blazing angels or resident evil? Can violent video games be a force for good? *Review of General Psychology, 14*(2), 68–81. https://doi.org/10.1037/a0018941

Ferguson, C. J., Copenhaver, A., & Markey, P. (2020). Reexamining the findings of the American Psychological Association's 2015 Task Force on Violent Media: A meta-analysis. *Perspectives on Psychological Science, 15*(6), 1423–1443. https://doi.org/10.1177/1745691620927666

Fernald, A., Marchman, V. A., & Weisleder, A. (2013). SES differences in language processing skill and vocabulary are evident at 18 months. *Developmental Science, 16*, 234–248.

Fernandez Nievas, I. F., & Thaver, D. (2015) Work-life balance: A different scale for doctors. *Frontiers in Pediatrics, 3*, 115.

Fernbach, P. M., Rogers, T., Fox, C. R., & Sloman, S. A. (2013). Political extremism is supported by an illusion of understanding. *Psychological Science, 24*(6), 939–946.

Ferrari, A. J., Santomauro, D. F., Herrera, A. M. M., Shadid, J., Ashbuagh, C., ... Whiteford, H. A. (2022). Global, regional, and national burden of 12 mental disorders in 204 countries and territories, 1990–2019: A systematic analysis for the Global Burden of Disease Study 2019. *Lancet Psychiatry, 9*(2), 137–150. https://doi.org/10.1016/S2215-0366(21)00395-3

Ferretti, M. T., Iulita, M. F., Cavedo, M., Chiesa, P. A., Dimech, A. S., Chadha, A. S., ... Hampel, H. (2018). Sex differences in Alzheimer's disease: The gateway to precision medicine. *Nature Reviews Neuroscience, 14*, 457–469.

Ferster, C. B., & Skinner, B. F. (1957). *Schedules of reinforcement.* Appleton-Century-Crofts.

Festinger, L. (1957). *A theory of cognitive dissonance.* Stanford University Press.

Festinger, L., & Carlsmith, J. M. (1959). Cognitive consequences of forced compliance. *Journal of Abnormal and Social Psychology, 58,* 203–210.

Festinger, L., Schachter, S., & Back, K. (1950). *Social pressures in informal groups: A study of human factors in housing.* Harper & Row.

Field, G. C. (1921). Faculty psychology and instinct psychology. *Mind, 30,* 257–270.

Fields, H. L., & Levine, J. D. (1984). Placebo analgesia: A role for endorphins? *Trends in Neurosciences, 7,* 271–273.

Figlio, D. N., Freese, J., Karbownik, K., & Roth, J. (2017). Socio-economic status and genetic influences on cognitive development. *Proceedings of the National Academy of Sciences, USA, 114*(51), 13441–13446. https://doi.org/10.1073/pnas.1708491114

Finkel, E. J. (2017). *The all-or-nothing marriage: How the best marriages work.* Dutton.

Finkel, E. J., & Eastwick, P. W. (2009). Arbitrary social norms influence sex differences in romantic selectivity. *Psychological Science, 20,* 1290–1295.

Finkel, E. J., Eastwick, P. W., & Reis, H. T. (2017). Replicability and other features of a high-quality science: Toward a balanced and empirical approach. *Journal of Personality and Social Psychology.* https://doi.org/10.1037/pspi0000075

Finkel, E. J., Eastwick, P. W., Karney, B. R., Reis, H. T., & Sprecher, S. (2012). Online dating: A critical analysis from the perspective of psychological science. *Psychological Science in the Public Interest, 13*(1), 3–66. https://doi.org/10.1177/1529100612436522

Finkelstein, K. E. (1999, October 17). In concert, searchers retrieve Yo-Yo Ma's lost Stradivarius. *New York Times.* http://www.nytimes.com/1999/10/17/nyregion/in-concert-searchers-retrieve-yo-yo-ma-s-lost-stradivarius.html

Finn, R. (1991). Different minds. *Discover, 12,* 54–59.

Fiore, A. T., Taylor, L. S., Zhong, X., Mendelsohn, G. A., & Cheshire, C. (2010). Who's right and who writes: People, profiles, contacts, and replies in online dating. *Proceedings of 43rd Hawaii International Conferences on System Sciences* (pp. 1–10). IEEE Computer Society. https://doi.org/10.1109/HICSS.2010.444

Fiorillo, C. D., Newsome, W. T., & Schultz, W. (2008). The temporal precision of reward prediction in dopamine neurons. *Nature Neuroscience, 11,* 966–973.

Fischer, P., Krueger, J. I., Greitemeyer, T., Vogrincic, C., Kastenmüller, A., Frey, D., ... Kainbacher, M. (2011). The bystander-effect: A meta-analytic review on bystander intervention in dangerous and non-dangerous emergencies. *Psychological Bulletin, 137*(4), 517–537. https://doi.org/10.1037/a0023304

Fisher, D. W., Bennett, D. A., & Dong, H. (2018). Sexual dimorphism in predisposition to Alzheimer's disease. *Neurobiology of Aging, 70,* 308–324.

Fisher, R. J., & Ma, Y. (2014). The price of being beautiful: Negative effects of attractiveness on empathy for children in need. *Journal of Consumer Research, 41*(2), 436–450. https://doi.org/10.1086/676967

Fisher, R. P., & Craik, F. I. M. (1977). The interaction between encoding and retrieval operations in cued recall. *Journal of Experimental Psychology: Human Learning and Perception, 3,* 153–171.

Fiske, S. T. (1998). Stereotyping, prejudice, and discrimination. In D. T. Gilbert, S. T. Fiske, & G. Lindzey (Eds.), *The handbook of social psychology* (4th ed., Vol. 2, pp. 357–411). McGraw-Hill.

Fiske, S. T. (2010). *Social beings: A core motives approach to social psychology.* Wiley.

Fiske, S. T. (2018). Stereotype content: Warmth and competence endure. *Current Directions in Psychological Science, 27*(2), 67–73. https://doi.org/10.1177/0963721417738825

Fitch, C. A., & Ruggles, S. (2000). Historical trends in marriage formation: United States, 1850–1990. In L. J. Waite (Ed.), *The ties that bind: Perspectives on marriage and cohabitation* (pp. 59–88). Transaction Publishers.

Flegal, K. M., & Troiano, R. P. (2000). Changes in the distribution of body mass index of adults and children in the U.S. population. *International Journal of Obesity, 24,* 807–818.

Flensborg-Madsen, T., & Mortensen, E. L. (2018). Developmental milestones during the first three years as precursors of adult intelligence. *Developmental Psychology, 54,* 1434–1444.

Fletcher, G. J. O., Simpson, J. A., Thomas, G., & Giles, L. (1999). Ideals in intimate relationships. *Journal of Personality and Social Psychology, 76,* 72–89. https://doi.org/10.1037/0022-3514.76.1.72

Fletcher, P. C., Shallice, T., & Dolan, R. J. (1998). The functional roles of prefrontal cortex in episodic memory: I. Encoding. *Brain, 121,* 1239–1248.

Flores, S., Bailey, H. R., Eisenberg, M. L., & Zacks, J. M. (2017). Event segmentation improves memory up to one month later. *Journal of Experimental Psychology: Learning, Memory, & Cognition, 43,* 1183–1202.

Flynn, E. (2008). Investigating children as cultural magnets: Do young children transmit redundant information along diffusion chains? *Philosophical Transactions of the Royal Society of London Series B, 363,* 3541–3551.

Flynn, E., & Whiten, A. (2008). Cultural transmission of tool-use in young children: A diffusion chain study. *Social Development, 17,* 699–718.

Flynn, J. R. (2012). *Are we getting smarter? Rising IQ in the twenty-first century.* Cambridge University Press.

Foa, E. B., Liebowitz, M. R., Kozak, M. J., Davies, S., Campeas, R., Franklin, M. E., ... Tu, X. (2007). Randomized, placebo-controlled trial of exposure and ritual prevention, clomipramine, and their combination in the treatment of obsessive-compulsive disorder. *Focus, 5,* 368–380.

Foa, E. B., & McLean, C. P. (2016) The efficacy of exposure therapy for anxiety-related disorders and its underlying mechanisms: The case of OCD and PTSD. *Annual Review of Clinical Psychology, 12,* 1–28.

Foa, E. B., & Meadows, E. A. (1997). Psychosocial treatments for posttraumatic stress disorder: A critical review. *Annual Review of Psychology, 48,* 449–480.

Foa, E. B., Liebowitz, M. R., Kozak, M. J., Davies, S., Campeas, R., Franklin, M. E., ... Tu, X. (2007). Randomized, placebo-controlled trial of exposure and ritual prevention, clomipramine, and their combination in the treatment of obsessive-compulsive disorder. *Focus, 5,* 368–380.

Fogassi, L., Ferrari, P. F., Gesierich, B., Rozzi, S., Chersi, F., & Rizzolatti, G. (2005). Parietal lobe: From action organization to intention understanding. *Science, 308,* 662–667.

Ford, B. Q., & Troy, A. S. (2019). Reappraisal reconsidered: A closer look at the costs of an acclaimed emotion-regulation strategy. *Current Directions in Psychological Science, 28*(2), 195–203. https://doi.org/10.1177/0963721419827526

Ford, J. H., DiBiase, H. D., Ryu, E., & Kensinger, E. A. (2018). It gets better with time: Enhancement of age-related positivity effect in the six months following a highly negative public event. *Psychology and Aging, 33*(3), 419–424. https://doi.org/10.1037/pag0000250

Forkstam, C., Hagoort, P., Fernández, G., Ingvar, M., & Petersson, K. M. (2006). Neural correlates of artificial syntactic structure classification. *NeuroImage, 32,* 956–967.

Fornito, A., Zalesky, A., & Breakspear, M. (2015). The connectomics of brain disorders. *Nature Reviews Neuroscience, 16,* 159–172.

Foroni, F., & Semin, G. R. (2009). Language that puts you in touch with your bodily feelings: The multimodal responsiveness of affective expressions. *Psychological Science, 20*(8), 974–980.

Forscher, P. S., Lai, C. K., Axt, J. R., Ebersole, C. R., Herman, M., Devine, P. G., & Nosek, B. A. (2019). A meta-analysis of procedures to change implicit measures. *Journal of Personality and Social Psychology, 117*(3), 522–559. https://doi.org/10.1037/pspa0000160

Fournier, J. C., DeRubeis, R., Hollon, S. D., Dimidjian, S., Amsterdam, J. D., Shelton, R. C., & Fawcett, J. (2010). Antidepressant drug effects and depression severity. *Journal of the American Medical Association, 303,* 47–53.

Fouts, R. S., & Bodamer, M. (1987). Preliminary report to the National Geographic Society on "Chimpanzee intrapersonal signing." *Friends of Washoe, 7,* 4–12.

Fox, M. J. (2009). *Always looking up.* Hyperion.

Fraga, M. F., Ballestar, E., Paz, M. F., Ropero, S., Setien, F., Ballestar, M. L. ... Esteller, M. (2005). Epigenetic differences arise during the lifetime of monozygotic twins. *Proceedings of the National Academy USA, 102,* 10604–10609.

Fragaszy, D. M., Izar, P., Visalberghi, E., Ottoni, E. B., & de Oliveria, M. G. (2004). Wild capuchin monkeys (*Cebus libidinosus*) use anvils and stone pounding tools. *American Journal of Primatology, 64,* 359–366.

Fraley, R. C. (2019). Attachment in adulthood: Recent developments, emerging debates, and future directions. *Annual Review of Psychology, 70*(1), 401–422. https://doi.org/10.1146/annurev-psych-010418-102813

Fraley, R. C., & Roisman, G. I. (2019). The development of adult attachment styles: Four lessons. *Current Opinion in Psychology, 25,* 26–30. https://doi.org/10.1016/j.copsyc.2018.02.008

Franchow, E. I., & Suchy, Y. (2015). Naturally-occurring expressive suppression in daily life depletes executive functioning. *Emotion, 15*(1), 78–89. https://doi.org/10.1037/emo0000013

Francis, D., Diorio, J., Liu, D., & Meaney, M. J. (1999). Nongenomic transmission across generations of maternal behavior and stress responses in the rat. *Science, 286,* 1155–1158.

Frank, M. G., & Stennet, J. (2001). The forced-choice paradigm and the perception of facial expressions of emotion. *Journal of Personality and Social Psychology, 80,* 75–85.

Frankl, V. (2000). *Man's search for meaning.* Beacon Press.

Frati, A., Pesce, A., Palmieri, M., Iasanzaniro, M., Familiari, P., Angelini, A., ... Raco, A. (2019). Hypnosis-aided awake surgery for the management of intrinsic brain tumors versus standard awake-asleep-awake protocol: A preliminary, promising experience. *World Neurosurgery, 121,* e882–891.

Fratkin, J. L., Sinn, D. L., Patall, E. A., & Gosling, S. D. (2013). Personality consistency in dogs: A meta-analysis. *PLoS ONE, 8,* e54907.

Fredman, T., & Whiten, A. (2008). Observational learning from tool using models by human-reared and mother-reared capuchin monkeys (*Cebus apella*). *Animal Cognition, 11,* 295–309.

Fredrickson, B. L. (2000). Cultivating positive emotions to optimize health and well-being. *Prevention and Treatment, 3,* 0001a. https://doi.org/10.1037/1522-3736.3.1.31a

Freedman, J. L., & Fraser, S. C. (1966). Compliance without pressure: The foot-in-the-door technique. *Journal of Personality and Social Psychology, 4,* 195–202.

Freeman, S., Walker, M. R., Borden, R., & Latané, B. (1975). Diffusion of responsibility and restaurant tipping: Cheaper by the bunch. *Personality and Social Psychology Bulletin, 1,* 584–587.

French, H. W. (1997, February 26). In the land of the small it isn't easy being tall. *New York Times.* http://www.nytimes.com/1997/02/26/world/in-the-land-of-the-small-it-isn-t-easy-being-tall.html

Freud, S. (1965). *The interpretation of dreams* (J. Strachey, Trans.). Avon. (Original work published 1900)

Freund, A. M., & Blanchard-Fields, F. (2014). Age-related differences in altruism across adulthood: Making personal financial gain versus contributing to the public good. *Developmental Psychology, 50*(4), 1125–1136. https://doi.org/10.1037/a0034491

Frick, A., Ahs, F., Engman, J., Jonasson, M., Alaie, I., Björkstrand, J., ... Furmark, T. (2015). Serotonin synthesis and reuptake in social anxiety disorder: A positron emission tomography study. *Journal of the American Medical Association Psychiatry, 72,* 794–802.

Frick, R. W. (1985). Communicating emotion: The role of prosodic features. *Psychological Bulletin, 97,* 412–429.

Fridriksson, J., Fillmore, P., Guo, D., & Rorden, C. (2015). Chronic Broca's aphasia is caused by damage to Broca's area and Wernicke's area. *Cerebral Cortex, 25*(12), 4689–4696. https://doi.org/10.1093/cercor/bhu152

Fried, P. A., & Watkinson, B. (2000). Visuoperceptual functioning differs in 9- to 12-year-olds prenatally exposed to cigarettes and marijuana. *Neurotoxicology and Teratology, 22,* 11–20.

Friedman, G. (2020, March 18). Rapper sparks anti-Semitism outcry with Rothschild, "synagogue of Satan" lyrics. *Times of Israel.* https://www.timesofisrael.com/rapper-sparks-anti-semitism-outcry-with-rothschild-synagogue-of-satan-lyrics/

Friedman, J. M. (2003). A war on obesity, not the obese. *Science, 299*(5608), 856–858.

Friedman, J. M., & Halaas, J. L. (1998). Leptin and the regulation of body weight in mammals. *Nature, 395*(6704), 763–770.

Friedman, M., & Rosenman, R. H. (1974). *Type A behavior and your heart.* Knopf.

Friedman, S. L., & Boyle, D. E. (2008). Attachment in U.S. children experiencing nonmaternal care in the early 1990s. *Attachment & Human Development, 10*(3), 225–261.

Friesen, W. V. (1972). *Cultural differences in facial expressions in a social situation: An experimental test of the concept of display rules* (Doctoral dissertation, University of California, San Francisco).

Frijda, N., Kuipers, P., & ter Schure, E. (1989). Relations among emotion, appraisal, and emotional action readiness. *Journal of Personality and Social Psychology, 57*(2), 212–228.

Frith, C. D., & Fletcher, P. (1995). Voices from nowhere. *Critical Quarterly, 37,* 71–83.

Frith, U. (2003). *Autism: Explaining the enigma.* Blackwell.

Fry, D. P. (2012). Life without war. *Science, 336*(6083), 879–884. https://doi.org/10.1126/science.1217987

Fryar, C. D., Gu, Q., Ogden, C. L., & Flegal, K. M. (2016). Anthropometric reference data for children and adults: United States, 2011–2014. *National Center for Health Statistics. Vital Health Stat, 3*(39), 1–46.

Fu, F., Tarnita, C. E., Christakis, N. A., Wang, L., Rand, D. G., & Novak, M. A. (2012). Evolution of in-group favoritism. *Scientific Reports, 2,* Article 460. https://doi.org/10.1038/srep00460

Fu, Q., Dienes, Z., Shang, J., & Fu, X. (2013). Who learns more? Cultural differences in implicit sequence learning. *PLoS ONE, 8*(8), e71625. https://doi.org/10.1371/journal.pone.0071625

Fukui, H., Murai, T., Fukuyama, H., Hayashi, T., & Hanakawa, T. (2005). Functional activity related to risk anticipation during performance of the Iowa gambling task. *NeuroImage, 24,* 253–259.

Funder, D. C. (2001). Personality. *Annual Review of Psychology, 52,* 197–221.

Furmark, T., Tillfors, M., Marteinsdottir, I., Fischer, H., Pissiota, A., Långström, B., & Fredrikson, M. (2002). Common changes in cerebral blood flow in patients with social phobia treated with citalopram or cognitive behavioral therapy. *Archives of General Psychiatry, 59*(5), 425–433.

Fuss, J., Steinle, J., Bindila, L., Auer, M. K., Kirchherr, H., Lutz, B., & Gass, P. (2015). A runner's high depends on cannabinoid receptors in mice. *Proceedings of the National Academy of Sciences, USA, 112*, 13105–13108.

Fuster, J. M. (2003). *Cortex and mind.* Oxford University Press.

Gadermann, A. M., Alonso, J., Vilagut, G., Zaslavsky, A. M., & Kessler, R. C. (2012). Comorbidity and disease burden in the National Comorbidity Survey Replication (NCS-R). *Depression and Anxiety, 29*, 797–806.

Gagnepain, P., Hulbert, J. C., & Anderson, M. C. (2017). Parallel regulation of memory and emotion supports the suppression of intrusive memories. *Journal of Neuroscience, 37*, 6423–6441.

Gais, S., & Born, J. (2004). Low acetylcholine during slow-wave sleep is critical for declarative memory consolidation. *Proceedings of the National Academy of Sciences, USA, 101*, 2140–2144.

Galanter, E. (1962). Contemporary psychophysics. In R. Brown, E. Galanter, E. H. Hess, & G. Mandler (Eds.), *New directions in psychology.* Holt, Rinehart, & Winston, pp 87–156.

Galati, D., Scherer, K. R., & Ricci-Bitt, P. E. (1997). Voluntary facial expression of emotion: Comparing congenitally blind with normally sighted encoders. *Journal of Personality and Social Psychology, 73*, 1363–1379.

Gale, C. R., Batty, G. D., McIntosh, A. M., Porteous, D. J., Deary, I. J., & Rasmussen, F. (2012). Is bipolar disorder more common in highly intelligent people? A cohort study of a million men. *Molecular Psychiatry, 18*(2), 190–194. https://doi.org/10.1038/mp.2012.26

Gale, C. R., Batty, G. D., Tynelius, P., Deary, I. J., & Rasmussen, F. (2010). Intelligence in early adulthood and subsequent hospitalization for mental disorders. *Epidemiology, 21*(1), 70–77. https://doi.org/10.1097/EDE.0b013e3181c17da8

Galef, B. (1998). Edward Thorndike: Revolutionary psychologist, ambiguous biologist. *American Psychologist, 53*, 1128–1134.

Galling, B., Roldan, A., Hagi, K., Rietschel, L., Walyzada, F., & Correll, C. U. (2017). Antipsychotic augmentation vs. monotherapy in schizophrenia: Systematic review, meta-analysis and meta-regression analysis. *World Psychiatry, 16*, 77–89.

Gallistel, C. R. (2000). The replacement of general-purpose learning models with adaptively specialized learning modules. In M. S. Gazzaniga (Ed.), *The new cognitive neurosciences* (pp. 1179–1191). MIT Press.

Gallistel, C. R., & Gelman, R. (1992). Preverbal and verbal counting and computation. *Cognition, 44*(1–2), 43–74. https://doi.org/10.1016/0010-0277(92)90050-r

Gallo, D. A. (2010). False memories and fantastic beliefs: 15 years of the DRM illusion. *Memory & Cognition, 38*, 833–848.

Gallo, D. A. (2006). *Associative illusions of memory.* Psychology Press.

Gallup. (2014a, July 9). Obesity linked to lower social well-being. Retrieved from http://www.gallup.com/poll/172253/obesity-linked-lower-social.aspx

Gallup, G. G. (1977). Self-recognition in primates: A comparative approach to the bidirectional properties of consciousness. *American Psychologist, 32*, 329–338.

Gallup, G. G. (1997). On the rise and fall of self-conception in primates. *Annals of the New York Academy of Sciences, 818*, 73–84.

Gallup, G. G., & Frederick, D. A. (2010). The science of sex appeal: An evolutionary perspective. *Review of General Psychology, 14*(3), 240–250. doi:10.1037/a0020451

Gallup. (2018, October). Two in three Americans now support legalizing marijuana. https://news.gallup.com/poll/243908/two-three-americans-support-legalizing-marijuana.aspx

Galton, F. (1869). *Hereditary genius: An inquiry into its laws and consequences.* Macmillan/Fontana.

Gangestad, S. W., & Haselton, M. G. (2015). Human estrus: Implications for relationship science. *Current Opinion in Psychology, 1*, 45–51.

Ganzel, B. L., Kim, P., Glover, G. H., & Temple, E. (2008). Resilience after 9/11: Multimodal neuroimaging evidence for stress-related change in the healthy adult brain. *NeuroImage, 40*, 788–795.

Garcia, J., & Koelling, R. A. (1966). Relation of cue to consequence in avoidance learning. *Psychonomic Science, 4*, 123–124.

García-García, I., Zeighami, Y., & Dagher, A. (2017). Reward prediction errors in addiction and Parkinson's disease: From neurophysiology to neuroimaging. *Current Neurology and Neuroscience Reports, 17*, 46. https://doi.org/10.1007/s11910-017-0755-9

Garcia-Moreno, C., Jansen, H. A. F. M., Ellsberg, M., Heise, L., & Watts, C. H. (2006). Prevalence of intimate partner violence: Findings from the WHO multi-country study on women's health and domestic violence. *Lancet, 368*(9543), 1260–1269. https://doi.org/10.1016/S0140-6736(06)69523-8

Gardner, M., & Steinberg, L. (2005). Peer influence on risk taking, risk preference, and risky decision making in adolescence and adulthood: An experimental study. *Developmental Psychology, 41*(4), 625–635. https://doi.org/10.1037/0012-1649.41.4.625

Gardner, R. A., & Gardner, B. T. (1969). Teaching sign language to a chimpanzee. *Science, 165*, 664–672.

Gardony, A. L., Brunyé, T. T., & Taylor, H. A. (2015). Navigational aids and spatial memory impairment: The role of divided attention. *Spatial Cognition & Computation, 15*(4), 246–284. https://doi.org/10.1080/13875868.2015.1059432

Garrett, B. L. (2011). *Convicting the innocent: Where criminal prosecutions go wrong.* Harvard University Press.

Gartstein, M. A., Prokasky, A., Bell, M. A., Calkins, S., Bridgett, D. J., Braungart-Rieker, J., ... Seamon, E. (2017). Latent profile and cluster analysis of infant temperament: Comparisons across person-centered approaches. *Developmental Psychology, 53*(10), 1811–1825. https://doi.org/10.1037/dev0000382

Gates, G. J. (2017). In U.S., more adults identifying as LGBT. *Gallup.* https://news.gallup.com/poll/201731/lgbt-identification-rises.aspx

Gathercole, S. E. (2008). Nonword repetition and word learning: The nature of the relationship. *Applied Psycholinguistics, 27*, 513–543.

Gazzaniga, M. S. (2006). Forty-five years of split brain research and still going strong. *Nature Reviews Neuroscience, 6*, 653–659.

Ge, D., Fellay, J., Thompson, A. J., Simon, J. S., Shianna, K. V., Urban, T. J., ... Goldstein, D. B. (2009). Genetic variation in il28b predicts hepatitis C treatment-induced viral clearance. *Nature, 461*, 399–401.

Ge, X. J., & Natsuaki, M. N. (2009). In search of explanations for early pubertal timing effects on developmental psychopathology. *Current Directions in Psychological Science, 18*, 327–331.

Ge, X. J., Conger, R. D., & Elder, G. H. (1996). Coming of age too early: Pubertal influences on girls' vulnerability to psychological distress. *Child Development, 67*, 3386–3400.

Ge, X. J., Conger, R. D., & Elder, G. H., Jr. (2001). Pubertal transition, stressful life events, and the emergence of gender differences in adolescent depressive symptoms. *Developmental Psychology, 37*(3), 404–417. https://doi.org/10.1037/0012-1649.37.3.404

Gendron, M., Crivelli, C., & Barrett, L. F. (2018). Universality reconsidered: Diversity in making meaning of facial expressions.

Current Directions in Psychological Science, 27(4), 211–219. https://doi.org/10.1177/0963721417746794

Gendron, M., Roberson, D., van der Vyver, J. M., & Barrett, L. F. (2014). Perceptions of emotion from facial expressions are not culturally universal: Evidence from a remote culture. *Emotion, 14,* 251–262. https://doi.org/10.1037/a0036052

Genschow, O., Westfal, M., Crusius, J., Bartosch, L., Feikes, K. I., Pallasch, N., & Wozniak, M. (2021). Does social psychology persist over half a century? A direct replication of Cialdini et al.'s (1975) classic door-in-the-face technique. *Journal of Personality and Social Psychology, 120*(2), e1–e7. https://doi.org/10.1037/pspa0000261

George, O., & Koob, G. F. (2017). Individual differences in the neuropsychopathology of addiction. *Dialogues in Clinical Neuroscience, 19*(3), 217–229.

Geraci, A., & Surian, L. (2011). The developmental roots of fairness: Infants' reactions to equal and unequal distributions of resources. *Developmental Science, 14,* 1012–1020. https://doi.org/10.1111/j.1467-7687.2011.01048.x

Gerbasi, M. E., & Prentice, D. A. (2013). The self- and other-interest inventory. *Journal of Personality and Social Psychology, 105*(3), 495–514. https://doi.org/10.1037/a0033483

Gershoff, E. T. (2002). Corporal punishment by parents and associated child behaviors and experiences: A meta-analytic and theoretical review. *Psychological Bulletin, 128,* 539–579.

Geschwind, D. H. (2009). Advances in autism. *Annual Review of Medicine, 60,* 67–80.

Gesiarz, F., Cahill, D., & Sharot, T. (2019). Evidence accumulation is biased by motivation: A computational account. *PLOS Computational Biology 15*(6), e1007089. https://doi.org/10.1371/journal.pcbi.1007089

Gibb, B. E., Alloy, L. B., & Tierney, S. (2001). History of childhood maltreatment, negative cognitive styles, and episodes of depression in adulthood. *Cognitive Therapy and Research, 25,* 425–446.

Gibson, C. E., Losee, J., & Vitiello, C. (2014). A replication attempt of stereotype susceptibility (Shih, Pittinsky, & Ambady, 1999): Identity salience and shifts in quantitative performance. *Social Psychology, 45*(3), 194–198. https://doi.org/10.1027/1864-9335/a000184

Gick, M. L., & Holyoak, K. J. (1980). Analogical problem solving. *Cognitive Psychology, 12,* 306–355.

Giedd, J. N., Blumenthal, J., Jeffries, N. O., Castellanos, F. X., Liu, H., Zijdenbos, A., ... Rapoport, J. L. (1999). Brain development during childhood and adolescence: A longitudinal MRI study. *Nature Neuroscience, 2,* 861–863.

Gierlach, E., Blesher, B. E., & Beutler, L. E. (2010). Cross-cultural differences in risk perceptions of disasters. *Risk Analysis, 30,* 1539–1549.

Gigerenzer, G., & Hoffrage, U. (1995). How to improve Bayesian reasoning without instruction: Frequency formats. *Psychological Review, 102*(4), 684–704. https://doi.org/10.1037/0033-295X.102.4.684

Gignac, G. E., & Bates, T. C. (2017). Brain volume and intelligence: The moderating role of intelligence measurement quality. *Intelligence, 64,* 18–29.

Gigone, D., & Hastie, R. (1993). The common knowledge effect: Information sharing and group judgment. *Journal of Personality and Social Psychology, 54,* 959–974.

Gilbert, D. T. (1991). How mental systems believe. *American Psychologist, 46,* 107–119.

Gilbert, D. T. (1998). Ordinary personology. In D. T. Gilbert, S. T. Fiske, & G. Lindzey (Eds.), *The handbook of social psychology* (4th ed., Vol. 2, pp. 89–150). McGraw-Hill.

Gilbert, D. T. (2006). *Stumbling on happiness.* Knopf.

Gilbert, D. T., Brown, R. P., Pinel, E. C., & Wilson, T. D. (2000). The illusion of external agency. *Journal of Personality and Social Psychology, 79,* 690–700.

Gilbert, D. T., King, G., Pettigrew, S., & Wilson, T. D. (2016). Comment on "Estimating the reproducibility of psychological science." *Science, 351*(6277). https://doi.org/10.1126/science.aad7243

Gilbert, D. T., & Malone, P. S. (1995). The correspondence bias. *Psychological Bulletin, 117,* 21–38.

Gilbert, D. T., Pelham, B. W., & Krull, D. S. (1988). On cognitive busyness: When persons perceivers meet persons perceived. *Journal of Personality and Social Psychology, 54,* 733–740.

Gilbert, S. J. (2015). Strategic offloading of delayed intentions into the environment. *The Quarterly Journal of Experimental Psychology, 68,* 971–992.

Gilbertson, M. W., Shenton, M. E., Ciszewski, A., Kasai, K., Lasko, N. B., Orr, S. P., & Pitman, R. K. (2002). Smaller hippocampal volume predicts pathological vulnerability to psychological trauma. *Nature Neuroscience, 5,* 1242–1247.

Gilkerson, J., Richards, J. A., Warren, S. F., Montgomery, J. K., Greenwood, C. R., Oller, D. K. ... Paul, T. D. (2017). Mapping the early language environment using all-day recordings and automated analysis. *American Journal of Speech-Language Pathology, 26*(2), 248–265. https://doi.org/10.1044/2016_AJSLP-15-0169

Gillespie, C. F., & Nemeroff, C. B. (2007). Corticotropin-releasing factor and the psychobiology of early-life stress. *Current Directions in Psychological Science, 16,* 85–89.

Gillette, J., Gleitman, H., Gleitman, L., & Lederer, A. (1999). Human simulation of vocabulary learning. *Cognition, 73,* 135–176.

Gilmore, A. W., Quach, A., Kalinowski, S. E., Gonzalez-Araya, E., Gotts, S. J., Schacter, D. L., & Martin, A. (2021). Evidence supporting a time-limited hippocampal role in retrieving autobiographical memories. *Proceedings of the National Academy of Sciences USA, 118*(12), e2023069118. https://doi.org/10.1073/pnas.2023069118

Gilovich, T. (1991). *How we know what isn't so: The fallibility of human reason in everyday life.* Free Press.

Gino, F., & Pierce, L. (2009). The abundance effect: Unethical behavior in the presence of wealth. *Organizational Behavior and Human Decision Processes, 109*(2), 142–155. https://doi.org/10.1016/j.obhdp.2009.03.003

Ginzburg, K., Solomon, Z., & Bleich, A. (2002). Repressive coping style, acute stress disorder, and posttraumatic stress disorder after myocardial infarction. *Psychosomatic Medicine, 64,* 748–757.

Giovanello, K. S., Schnyer, D. M., & Verfaellie, M. (2004). A critical role for the anterior hippocampus in relational memory: Evidence from an fMRI study comparing associative and item recognition. *Hippocampus, 14,* 5–8.

Gladue, B. A. (1994). The biopsychology of sexual orientation. *Current Directions in Psychological Science, 3,* 150–154.

Glanzer, M. & Cunitz, A. R. (1966). Two storage mechanisms in free recall. *Journal of Verbal Learning and Verbal Behavior, 5,* 351–360.

Glass, D. C., & Singer, J. E. (1972). *Urban stress.* Academic Press.

Glenwick, D. S., Jason, L. A., & Elman, D. (1978). Physical attractiveness and social contact in the singles bar. *Journal of Social Psychology, 105,* 311–312.

Glick, D. M., & Orsillo, S. M. (2015). An investigation of the efficacy of acceptance-based behavioral therapy for academic procrastination. *Journal of Experimental Psychology: General, 144,* 400–409.

Glynn, L. M., & Sandman, C. A. (2011). Prenatal origins of neurological development: A critical period for fetus and mother. *Current Directions in Psychological Science, 20*(6), 384–389. https://doi.org/10.1177/0963721411422056

Gneezy, U., & Rustichini, A. (2000). A fine is a price. *Journal of Legal Studies, 29,* 1–17.

Godden, D. R., & Baddeley, A. D. (1975). Context-dependent memory in two natural environments: On land and underwater. *British Journal of Psychology, 66,* 325–331.

Goehler, L. E., Gaykema, R. P. A., Hansen, M. K., Anderson, K., Maier, S. F., & Watkins, L. R. (2000). Vagal immune-to-brain communication: A visceral chemosensory pathway. *Autonomic Neuroscience: Basic and Clinical, 85,* 49–59.

Goel, V. (2007). Anatomy of deductive reasoning. *Trends in Cognitive Sciences, 11,* 435–441.

Goel, V., & Dolan, R. J. (2003). Explaining modulation of reasoning by belief. *Cognition, 87,* 11–22.

Goff, L. M., & Roediger, H. L., III. (1998). Imagination inflation for action events: Repeated imaginings lead to illusory recollections. *Memory & Cognition, 26,* 20–33.

Golden, R. L., Furman, W., & Collibee, C. (2016). The risks and rewards of sexual debut. *Developmental Psychology, 52*(11), 1913–1925. http://doi.org/10.1037/dev0000206

Goldenberg, A., Weisz, E., Sweeny, T. D., Cikara, M., & Gross, J. J. (2021). The crowd-emotion amplification effect. *Psychological Science, 32*(3), 437–450. https://doi.org/10.1177/0956797620970561

Göldi, M., & Rasch, B. (2019). Effects of targeted memory reactivation during sleep at home depend on sleep disturbances and habituation. *NPJ Science of Learning, 4,* 5. http://doi.org/10.1038/s41539-019-0044-2

Goldin, C., & Rouse, C. (2000). Orchestrating impartiality: The impact of "blind" auditions on female musicians. *American Economic Review, 90*(4), 715–741.

Goldman, M. S., Brown, S. A., & Christiansen, B. A. (1987). Expectancy theory: Thinking about drinking. In H. T. Blane & K. E. Leonard (Eds.), *Psychological theories of drinking and alcoholism* (pp. 181–266). Guilford Press.

Goldstein, M. (2017, November 9). TSA misses 70% of fake weapons but that's an improvement. *Forbes.* https://www.forbes.com/sites/michaelgoldstein/2017/11/09/tsa-misses-70-of-fake-weapons-but-thats-an-improvement/?sh=4c356bad2a38

Golinkoff, R. M., Hoff, E., Rowe, M. L., Tamis-LeMonda, C.S., & Hirsh-Pasek, C. (2019). Language matters: Denying the existence of the 30-million-word gap has serious consequences. *Child Development, 90*(3), 985–992. https://doi.org/10.1111/cdev.13128

Gontier, N. (2008). Genes, brains, and language: An epistemological examination of how genes can underlie human cognitive behavior. *Review of General Psychology, 12,* 170–180.

Gonzaga, G. C., Keltner, D., Londahl, E. A., & Smith, M. D. (2001). Love and the commitment problem in romantic relations and friendship. *Journal of Personality and Social Psychology, 81,* 247–262.

Gonzalez-Mule, E., Carter, K. M., & Mount, M. K. (2017). Are smarter people happier? Meta-analyses of the relationships between general mental ability and job and life satisfaction. *Journal of Vocational Behavior, 99,* 146–164. https://doi.org/10.1016/j.jvb.2017.01.003

Good, C., Aronson, J., & Inzlicht, M. (2003). Improving adolescents' standardized test performance: An intervention to reduce the effects of stereotype threat. *Journal of Applied Developmental Psychology, 24*(6), 645–662. https://doi.org/10.1016/j.appdev.2003.09.002

Goodale, M. A., & Milner, A. D. (1992). Separate visual pathways for perception and action. *Trends in Neurosciences, 15,* 20–25.

Goodale, M. A., Milner, A. D., Jakobson, L. S., & Carey, D. P. (1991). A neurological dissociation between perceiving objects and grasping them. *Nature, 349,* 154–156.

Goodfellow, I., Bengio, Y., & Courville, A. (2016). Introduction. In *Deep learning* (Chap. 1, pp. 1–26). MIT Press.

Gootman, E. (2003, March 3). Separated at birth in Mexico, united at campuses on Long Island. *New York Times.* http://www.nytimes.com/2003/03/03/nyregion/separated-at-birth-in-mexico-reunited-at-campuses-on-li.html?_r=0

Gopnik, A. (2012). Scientific thinking in young children: Theoretical advances, empirical research, and policy implications. *Science, 337*(6102), 1623–1627. https://doi.org/10.1126/science.1223416

Gopnik, M. (1990a). Feature-blind grammar and dysphasia. *Nature, 344,* 715.

Gopnik, M. (1990b). Feature blindness: A case study. *Language Acquisition: A Journal of Developmental Linguistics, 1,* 139–164.

Gorczynski, P., & Faulkner, G. (2011). Exercise therapy for schizophrenia. *Cochrane Database of Systematic Reviews, 5,* CD004412.

Gordon, P. (2004). Numerical cognition without words: Evidence from Amazonia. *Science, 306,* 496–499.

Gordon, R. A. (1997). Everyday life as an intelligence test: Effects of intelligence and intelligence context. *Intelligence, 24*(1), 203–320. https://doi.org/10.1016/S0160-2896(97)90017-9

Gorno-Tempini, M. L., Price, C. J., Josephs, O., Vandenberghe, R., Cappa, S. F., Kapur, N., & Frackowiak, R. S. (1998). The neural systems sustaining face and proper-name processing. *Brain, 121,* 2103–2118.

Goshe, K. M., Mortimer, J. A., Smith, C. D., Markesbery, W. R., & Snowdon, D. A. (2002). Hippocampal volume as an index of Alzheimer neuropathology. *Neurology, 58*(10), 1476–1482. https://doi.org/10.1212/wnl.58.10.1476

Gosling, S. D. (1998). Personality dimensions in spotted hyenas (*Crocuta crocuta*). *Journal of Comparative Psychology, 112,* 107–118.

Gosling, S. D. (2008). Personality in non-human animals. *Social and Personality Psychology Compass, 2,* 985–1001.

Gosling, S. D., Rentfrow, P. J., & Swann, W. B., Jr. (2003). A very brief measure of the Big-Five personality domains. *Journal of Research in Personality, 37,* 504–528.

Gotlib, I. H., & Joormann, J. (2010). Cognition and depression: Current status and future directions. *Annual Review of Clinical Psychology, 6,* 285–312.

Gottesman, I. I. (1991). *Schizophrenia genesis: The origins of madness.* Freeman.

Gottesman, I. I., & Hanson, D. R. (2005). Human development: Biological and genetic processes. *Annual Review of Psychology, 56,* 263–286.

Gottfredson, L. S. (1997). Mainstream science on intelligence: An editorial with 52 signatories, history, and bibliography. *Intelligence, 24,* 13–23.

Gottfredson, L. S. (2003). Dissecting practical intelligence theory: Its claims and evidence. *Intelligence, 31*(4), 343–397.

Gottfried, J. A. (2008). Perceptual and neural plasticity of odor quality coding in the human brain. *Chemosensory Perception, 1,* 127–135.

Gouldner, A. W. (1960). The norm of reciprocity. *American Sociological Review, 25,* 161–178.

Grady, C. L., Haxby, J. V., Horwitz, B., Schapiro, M. B., Rapoport, S. I., Ungerleider, L. G., ... Herscovitch, P. (1992). Dissociation of object and spatial vision in human extrastriate cortex: Age-related changes in activation of regional cerebral blood flow measured with [15O] water and positron emission tomography. *Journal of Cognitive Neuroscience, 4*(1), 23–34. https://doi.org/10.1162/jocn.1992.4.1.23

Graf, P., & Schacter, D. L. (1985). Implicit and explicit memory for new associations in normal subjects and amnesic patients. *Journal of Experimental Psychology: Learning, Memory, and Cognition, 11,* 501–518.

Grant, B. F., Hasin, D. S., Stinson, F. S., Dawson, D. A., Chou, S. P., & Ruan, W. J. (2004). Prevalence, correlates, and disability of personality disorders in the U.S.: Results from the National Epidemiologic Survey on Alcohol and Related Conditions. *Journal of Clinical Psychiatry, 65,* 948–958.

Grasby, K. L., Coventry, W. L., Byrne, B., & Olson, R. K. (2019). Little evidence that socioeconomic status modifies heritability of literacy and numeracy in Australia. *Child Development, 90*(2), 623–637. https://doi-org.ezp-prod1.hul.harvard.edu/10.1111/cdev.12920

Grassian, S. (2006). Psychiatric effects of solitary confinement. *Washington University Journal of Law and Policy, 22,* 1–24.

Gray, H. M., Gray, K., & Wegner, D. M. (2007). Dimensions of mind perception. *Science, 315,* 619.

Gray, J. A. (1970). The psychophysiological basis of introversion–extraversion. *Behavior Research and Therapy, 8,* 249–266.

Gray, J. A. (1990). Brain systems that mediate both emotion and cognition. *Cognition and Emotion, 4,* 269–288.

Green, D. A., & Swets, J. A. (1966). *Signal detection theory and psychophysics.* Wiley.

Green, M. F., Kern, R. S., Braff, D. L., & Mintz, J. (2000). Neurocognitive deficits and functional outcome in schizophrenia: Are we measuring the "right stuff"? *Schizophrenia Bulletin, 26,* 119–136.

Green, S. K., Buchanan, D. R., & Heuer, S. K. (1984). Winners, losers, and choosers: A field investigation of dating initiation. *Personality and Social Psychology Bulletin, 10,* 502–511.

Greenberg, J., Pyszczynski, T., Solomon, S., Rosenblatt, A., Veeder, M., Kirkland, S., & Lyon, D. (1990). Evidence for terror management theory II: The effects of mortality salience on reactions to those who threaten or bolster the cultural worldview. *Journal of Personality and Social Psychology, 58,* 308–318.

Greenberg, J., Solomon, S., & Arndt, J. (2008). A basic but uniquely human motivation: Terror management. In J. Y. Shah & W. L. Gardner (Eds.), *Handbook of motivation science* (pp. 114–134). Guilford Press.

Greenspan, L., & Deardorff, J. (2014). *The new puberty: How to navigate early development in today's girls.* Rodale Books.

Greenwald, A. G. (1992). New look 3: Unconscious cognition reclaimed. *American Psychologist, 47,* 766–779.

Greenwald, A. G., & Nosek, B. A. (2001). Health of the Implicit Association Test at age 3. *Zeitschrift für Experimentelle Psychologie, 48,* 85–93.

Greenwald, A. G., McGhee, D. E., & Schwartz, J. L. K. (1998). Measuring individual differences in implicit cognition: The implicit association test. *Journal of Personality and Social Psychology, 74,* 1464–1480.

Gropp, E., Shanabrough, M., Borok, E., Xu, A. W., Janoschek, R., Buch, T., … Brüning, J. C. (2005). Agouti-related peptide-expressing neurons are mandatory for feeding. *Nature Neuroscience, 8,* 1289–1291.

Gross, J. J. (1998). Antecedent- and response-focused emotion regulation: Divergent consequences for experience, expression, and physiology. *Journal of Personality and Social Psychology, 74*(1), 224–237.

Gross, J. J. (2002). Emotion regulation: Affective, cognitive, and social consequences. *Psychophysiology, 39,* 281–291.

Gross, J. J., & Muñoz, R. F. (1995). Emotion regulation and mental health. *Clinical Psychology: Science and Practice, 2,* 151–164.

Gross, J., Leib, M., Offerman, T., & Shalvi, S. (2018). Ethical free riding: When honest people find dishonest partners. *Psychological Science, 29*(12), 1956–1968. https://doi.org/10.1177/0956797618796480

Grover, S., & Helliwell, J. F. (2019). How's life at home? New evidence on marriage and the set point for happiness. *Journal of Happiness Studies, 20,* 373. https://doi.org/10.1007/s10902-017-9941-3

Groves, B. (2004, August 2). Unwelcome awareness. *San Diego Union-Tribune,* p. 24.

Grün, F., & Blumberg, B. (2006). Environmental obesogens: Organotins and endocrine disruption via nuclear receptor signaling. *Endocrinology, 147,* s50–s55.

Grzyb, T., Trojanowski, J., Grzybała, P., Doliński, D., Folwarczny, M., Krzyszycha, K., & Martynowska, K. (2017). Would you deliver an electric shock in 2015? Obedience in the experimental paradigm developed by Stanley Milgram in the 50 years following the original studies. *Social Psychological and Personality Science, 8*(8), 927–933. https://doi.org/10.1177/1948550617693060

Guerzoni, L., Mancini, P., Nicastri, M., Fabrizi, E., Giallini, I., & Cuda, D. (2020). Does early cochlear implantation promote better reading comprehension skills? *International Journal of Pediatric Otorhinolaryngology, 133,* 109976. https://doi.org/10.1016/j.ijporl.2020.109976

Guilford, J. P. (1967). *The nature of human intelligence.* McGraw-Hill.

Guillery, R. W., & Sherman, S. M. (2002). Thalamic relay functions and their role in corticocortical communication: Generalizations from the visual system. *Neuron, 33,* 163–175.

Gunnery, S. D., Hall, J. A., & Ruben, M. A. (2013). The deliberate Duchenne smile: Individual differences in expressive control. *Journal of Nonverbal Behavior, 37,* 29–41.

Gunns, R. E., Johnston, L, & Hudson, S. (2002). Victim selection and kinematics: A point-light investigation of vulnerability to attack. *Journal of Nonverbal Behavior, 26*(3), 129–158. https://doi.org/10.1023/A:1020744915533

Gurwitz, J. H., McLaughlin, T. J., Willison, D. J., Guadagnoli, E., Hauptman, P. J., Gao, X., & Soumerai, S. B. (1997). Delayed hospital presentation in patients who have had acute myocardial infarction. *Annals of Internal Medicine, 126,* 593–599.

Gusnard, D. A., & Raichle, M. E. (2001). Searching for a baseline: Functional imaging and the resting human brain. *Nature Reviews Neuroscience, 2,* 685–694.

Gustafsson, J.-E. (1984). A unifying model for the structure of intellectual abilities. *Intelligence, 8,* 179–203.

Gutchess, A., & Sekuler, R. (2019). Perceptual and mnemonic differences across cultures. *Psychology of Learning and Motivation, 71,* 131–174. https://doi.org/10.1016/bs.pl,.2019.06.001

Gutchess, A. H., Welsh, R. C., Boduroglu, A., & Park, D. C. (2006). Cultural differences in neural function associated with object processing. *Cognitive, Affective, & Behavioral Neuroscience, 6*(2), 102–109. https://doi.org/10.3758/cabn.6.2.102

Guthrie, R. V. (2000). Kenneth Bancroft Clark (1914–2005). In A. E. Kazdin (Ed.), *Encyclopedia of Psychology* (Vol. 2, p. 91). American Psychological Association.

Guzmán-Vélez, E., & Tranel, D. (2015). Does bilingualism contribute to cognitive reserve? Cognitive and neural perspectives. *Neuropsychology, 29,* 129–150.

Haase, C. M., Heckhausen, J., & Wrosch, C. (2013). Developmental regulation across the life span: Toward a new synthesis. *Developmental Psychology, 49*(5), 964–972. https://doi.org/10.1037/a0029231

Hackman, D. A., & Farah, M. J. (2008). Socioeconomic status and the developing brain. *Trends in Cognitive Sciences, 13,* 65–73.

Hackman, J. R., & Katz, N. (2010). Group behavior and performance. In S. T. Fiske, D. T. Gilbert, & G. Lindzey (Eds.), *The handbook of social psychology* (5th ed., Vol. 2, pp. 1208–1251). Wiley.

Haedt-Matt, A. A., & Keel, P. K. (2011). Revisiting the affect regulation model of binge eating: A meta-analysis of studies using ecological momentary assessment. *Psychological Bulletin, 137*(4), 660–681.

Hagen, L., Krishna, A., & McFerran, B. (2016). Rejecting responsibility: Low physical involvement in obtaining food promotes unhealthy eating. *Journal of Marketing Research, 54*(4), 589–604.

Haggard, P., & Tsakiris, M. (2009). The experience of agency: Feelings, judgments, and responsibility. *Current Directions in Psychological Science, 18,* 242–246.

Haidt, J., & Keltner, D. (1999). Culture and facial expression: Open-ended methods find more expressions and a gradient of recognition. *Cognition and Emotion, 13*(3), 225–266.

Haines, M. M., Stansfeld, S. A., Job, R. F., Berglund, B., & Head, J. (2001). Chronic aircraft noise exposure, stress responses, mental health and cognitive performance in school children. *Psychological Medicine, 31,* 265–277.

Hales, C. M., Carroll, M. D., Fryar, C. D., & Ogden, C. L. (2020). Prevalence of obesity and severe obesity among Adults: United States, 2017–2018. *National Center for Health Statistics Data Brief, No 360.* National Center for Health Statistics.

Halim, M. L., Ruble, D. N., Tamis-LeMonda, C. S., Zosuls, K. M., Lurye, L. E., & Greulich, F. K. (2014). Pink frilly dresses and the avoidance of all things "girly": Children's appearance rigidity and cognitive theories of gender development. *Developmental Psychology, 50*(4), 1091–1101. https://doi.org/10.1037/a0034906

Hallett, M. (2000). Transcranial magnetic stimulation and the human brain. *Nature, 406,* 147–150.

Halliday, R., Naylor, H., Brandeis, D., Callaway, E., Yano, L., & Herzig, K. (1994). The effect of D-amphetamine, clonidine, and yohimbine on human information processing. *Psychophysiology, 31,* 331–337.

Halpern, B. (2002). Taste. In H. Pashler & S. Yantis (Eds.), *Stevens' handbook of experimental psychology: Vol. 1. Sensation and perception* (3rd ed., pp. 653–690). Wiley.

Halpern, D. F., Benbow, C. P., Geary, D. C., Gur, R. C., Hyde, J. S., & Gernsbacher, M. A. (2007). The science of sex differences in science and mathematics. *Psychological Science in the Public Interest, 8*(1), 1–51.

Hambrick, D. Z., Oswald, F. L., Altmann, E. M., Meinz, E. J., Gobet, F., & Campitelli, G. (2013). Deliberate practice: Is that all it takes to become an expert? *Intelligence, 45,* 34–45. https://doi.org/10.1016/j.intell.2013.04.001

Hamilton, A. F. C. (2013). Reflecting on the mirror neuron system in autism: A systematic review of current theories. *Developmental Cognitive Neuroscience, 3,* 91–105.

Hamilton, A. F., & Grafton, S. T. (2006). Goal representation in human anterior intraparietal sulcus. *Journal of Neuroscience, 26,* 1133–1137.

Hamilton, A. F., & Grafton, S. T. (2008). Action outcomes are represented in human inferior frontoparietal cortex. *Cerebral Cortex, 18,* 1160–1168.

Hamilton, D. L., & Gifford, R. K. (1976). Illusory correlation in interpersonal perception: A cognitive basis of stereotypic judgements. *Journal of Experimental Social Psychology, 12,* 392–407.

Hamilton, J. P., Etkin, A., Furman, D. J., Lemus, M. G., Johnson, R. F., & Gotlib, I. H. (2012). Functional neuroimaging of major depressive disorder: A meta-analysis and new integration of baseline activation and neural response data. *American Journal of Psychiatry, 169,* 693–703.

Hamilton, J. P., Glover, G. H., Hsu, J. J., Johnson, R. F., & Gotlib, I. H. (2010). Modulation of subgenual anterior cingulated cortex activity with real-time neurofeedback. *Human Brain Mapping, 32,* 22–31.

Hamilton, W. D. (1964). The genetical evolution of social behaviour. *Journal of Theoretical Biology, 7,* 1–16.

Hamlin, J. K. (2014). The case for social evaluation in preverbal infants: Gazing toward one's goal drives infants' preferences for Helpers over Hinderers in the hill paradigm. *Frontiers in Psychology, 5*(Oct.), 1–9. https://doi.org/10.3389/fpsyg.2014.01563

Hamlin, J. K., Wynn, K., & Bloom, P. (2007). Social evaluation by preverbal infants. *Nature, 450*(7169), 557–559.

Hamlin, J. K., Wynn, K., & Bloom, P. (2011). 3-month-olds show a negativity bias in their social evaluation. *Developmental Science, 13*(6), 923–929. https://doi.org/10.1111/j.1467-7687.2010.00951.x.3-month-olds

Happé, F. G. E. (1995). The role of age and verbal ability in the theory of mind performance of subjects with autism. *Child Development, 66,* 843–855.

Happé, F. G. E., & Vital, P. (2009). What aspects of autism predispose to talent? *Philosophical Transactions of the Royal Society B: Biological Science, 364,* 1369–1375.

Harand, C., Bertran, F., La Joie, R., Landeau, B., Mézenge, F., Desgranges, B., ... Rauchs, G. (2012). The hippocampus remains activated over the long term for the retrieval of truly episodic memories. *PLoS ONE, 7,* e43495. https://doi.org/10.1371/journal.pone.0043495

Harding, C. M., Brooks, G. W., Ashikaga, T., Strauss, J. S., & Brier, A. (1987). The Vermont longitudinal study of persons with severe mental illness: II. Long-term outcome of subjects who retrospectively met DSM-III criteria for schizophrenia. *American Journal of Psychiatry, 144,* 727–735.

Hare, B. (2017). Survival of the friendliest: *Homo sapiens* evolved via selection for prosociality. *Annual Review of Psychology, 68*(1), 155–186.

Hare, R. D. (1998). *Without conscience: The disturbing world of the psychopaths among us.* Guilford Press.

Harlow, H. F. (1958). The nature of love. *American Psychologist, 13,* 573–685.

Harlow, J. M. (1868). Recovery from the passage of an iron bar through the head. *Publications of the Massachusetts Medical Society, 2,* 327–347.

Harmon-Jones, E., Harmon-Jones, C., & Levy, N. (2015). An action-based model of cognitive-dissonance processes. *Current Directions in Psychological Science, 24*(3), 184–189. https://doi.org/10.1177/0963721414566449

Harris, B. (1979). Whatever happened to Little Albert? *American Psychologist, 34,* 151–160.

Harris, D. J., Vine, S. J., Wilson, M. R., McGrath, J. S., LeBel, M.-E., & Buckingham, G. (2018). Action observation for sensorimotor learning in surgery. *British Journal of Surgery, 105,* 1713–1720.

Harris, P. L., de Rosnay, M., & Pons, F. (2005). Language and children's understanding of mental states. *Current Directions in Psychological Science, 14,* 69–73.

Harris, P. L., Johnson, C. N., Hutton, D., Andrews, G., & Cooke, T. (1989). Young children's theory of mind and emotion. *Cognition and Emotion, 3,* 379–400.

Harro, J. (2015). Neuropsychiatric adverse effects of amphetamine and methamphetamine. *International Review of Neurobiology, 120,* 179–204.

Hart, B. L. (1988). Biological basis of the behavior of sick animals. *Neuroscience and Biobehavioral Reviews, 12,* 123–137.

Hart, B., & Risley, T. R. (1995). *Meaningful differences in the everyday experience of young American children.* Brookes.

Hart, C. L. (2013). *High price: A neuroscientist's journey of self-discovery that challenges everything you know about drugs and society.* Harper Collins.

Hart, W., Albarracin, D., Eagly, A. H., Lindberg, M. J., Merrill, L., & Brechan, I. (2009). Feeling validated versus being correct:

A meta-analysis of selective exposure to information. *Psychological Bulletin, 135*, 555–588.

Hartshorne, H., & May, M. (1928). *Studies in deceit.* Macmillan.

Hartshorne, J. K., & Germine, L. T. (2015). When does cognitive functioning peak? The asynchronous rise and fall of different cognitive abilities across the life span. *Psychological Science, 26*(4), 433–443. http://doi.org/10.1177/0956797614567339

Hashash, M., Zeid, M. A., & Moacdieh, N. M. (2019). Social media browsing while driving: Effects on driver performance and attention allocation. *Transportation Research Part F: Traffic Psychology and Behaviour, 63*(2), 67–82. https://doi.org/10.1016/j.trf.2019.03.021

Hasher, L., Goldstein, D., & Toppino, T. (1977). Frequency and the conference of referential validity. *Journal of Verbal Learning and Verbal Behavior, 16*, 107–112.

Hasher, L., & Zacks, R. T. (1984). Automatic processing of fundamental information: The case of frequency of occurrence. *American Psychologist, 39*(12), 1372–1388. https://doi.org/10.1037//0003-066x.39.12.1372

Haslam, C., Wills, A. J., Haslam, S. A., Kay, J., Baron, R., & McNab, F. (2007). Does maintenance of colour categories rely on language? Evidence to the contrary from a case of semantic dementia. *Brain and Language, 103*, 251–263.

Hassabis, D., Kumaran, D., Summerfield, C., & Botvinick, M. (2017). Neuroscience-inspired artificial intelligence. *Neuron, 95*, 245–258.

Hassabis, D., Kumaran, D., Vann, S. D., & Maguire, E. A. (2007). Patients with hippocampal amnesia cannot imagine new experiences. *Proceedings of the National Academy of Sciences, USA, 104*, 1726–1731.

Hasselmo, M. E. (2006). The role of acetylcholine in learning and memory. *Current Opinion in Neurobiology, 16*, 710–715.

Hassin, R. R., Bargh, J. A., & Zimerman, S. (2009). Automatic and flexible: The case of non-conscious goal pursuit. *Social Cognition, 27*, 20–36.

Hassmen, P., Koivula, N., & Uutela, A. (2000). Physical exercise and psychological well-being: A population study in Finland. *Preventive Medicine, 30*, 17–25.

Hasson, U., Hendler, T., Bashat, D. B., & Malach, R. (2001). Vase or face? A neural correlate of shape-selective grouping processes in the human brain. *Journal of Cognitive Neuroscience, 13*, 744–753.

Hatemi, P. K., Gillespie, N. A., Eaves, L. J., Maher, B. S., Webb, B. T., Heath, A. C., ... Martin, N. G. (2011). A genome-wide analysis of liberal and conservative political attitudes. *Journal of Politics, 73*, 271–285.

Hatfield, E. (1988). Passionate and companionate love. In R. J. Sternberg & M. L. Barnes (Eds.), *The psychology of love* (pp. 191–217). Yale University Press.

Häusser, M. (2000). The Hodgkin-Huxley theory of the action potential. *Nature Neuroscience, 3*, 1165. https://doi.org/10.1038/81426

Hawkins, R. X. D., Goodman, N. D., & Goldstone, R. L. (2019). The emergence of social norms and conventions. *Trends in Cognitive Sciences, 23*(2), 158–169.

Haworth, C. M. A., Wright, M. J., Luciano, M., Martin, N. G., de Geus, E. J. C., van Beijsterveldt, C. E. M., ... Plomin, R. (2010). The heritability of general cognitive ability increases linearly from childhood to young adulthood. *Molecular Psychiatry, 15*(11), 1112–1120. https://doi.org/10.1038/mp.2009.55

Havlik, J. L., Vieira Sugano, Y. Y., Clement Jacobi, M., Kukreja, R. R., Clement Jacobi, J. H., & Mason, P. (2022). The bystander effect in rats. *Science Advances, 6*(28), eabb4205. https://doi.org/10.1126/sciadv.abb4205

Hayes, J. E., Bartoshuk, L. M., Kidd, J. R., & Duffy, V. B. (2008). Supertasting and PROP bitterness depends on more than the TAS2R38 gene. *Chemical Senses, 23*, 255–265.

Hayes, K., & Hayes, C. (1951). The intellectual development of a home-raised chimpanzee. *Proceedings of the American Philosophical Society, 95*, 105–109.

Hayes, S. C., Strosahl, K., & Wilson, K. G. (1999). *Acceptance and commitment therapy: An experiential approach to behavior change.* Guilford Press.

Haxby, J. V., Gobbini, M. I., Furey, M. L., Ishai, A., Schouten, J. L., & Pietrini, P. (2001). Distributed and overlapping representations of faces and objects in ventral temporal cortex. *Science, 293*, 2425–2430.

Heavey, C. L., Hurlburt, R. T., & Lefforge, N. L. (2012). Toward a phenomenology of feelings. *Emotion, 12*(4), 763–777.

Hebb, D. O. (1949). *The organization of behavior.* Wiley.

Heberlein, A. S., Adolphs, R., Tranel, D., & Damasio, H. (2004). Cortical regions for judgments of emotions and personality traits from point-light walkers. *Journal of Cognitive Neuroscience, 16*(7), 1143–1158. https://doi.org/10.1162/0898929041920423

Hebl, M. R., & Heatherton, T. F. (1997). The stigma of obesity in women: The difference is Black and White. *Personality and Social Psychology Bulletin, 24*, 417–426.

Hebl, M. R., & Mannix, L. M. (2003). The weight of obesity in evaluating others: A mere proximity effect. *Personality and Social Psychology Bulletin, 29*, 28–38.

Hedges, L. V., & Nowell, A. (1995). Sex differences in mental test scores, variability, and numbers of high-scoring individuals. *Science, 269*(5220), 41–45.

Heerey, E. A., Keltner, D., & Capps, L. M. (2003). Making sense of self-conscious emotion: Linking theory of mind and emotion in children with autism. *Emotion, 3*, 394–400.

Heilmann, K., Kahn, M. E., & Tang, C. K. (2021). The urban crime and heat gradient in high and low poverty areas. *Journal of Public Economics, 197*, 104408. https://doi.org/10.1016/j.jpubeco.2021.104408

Heine, S. J., & Lehman, D. R. (1995). Cultural variation in unrealistic optimism: Does the West feel more invulnerable than the East? *Journal of Personality and Social Psychology, 68*, 595–607.

Heiy, J. E., & Cheavens, J. S. (2014). Back to basics: A naturalistic assessment of the experience and regulation of emotion. *Emotion, 14*(5), 878–891. https://doi.org/10.1037/a0037231

Helliwell, J., & Grover, S. (2014, December). How's life at home? New evidence on marriage and the set point for happiness. NBER Working Paper No. 20794.

Henderlong, J., & Lepper, M. R. (2002). The effects of praise on children's intrinsic motivation: A review and synthesis. *Psychological Bulletin, 128*, 774–795.

Henrich, J. (2018). Human cooperation: The hunter-gatherer puzzle. *Current Biology, 28*(19), R1143–R1145. https://doi.org/10.1016/j.cub.2018.08.005

Henrich, J., Boyd, R., Bowles, S., Camerer, C., Fehr, E., & Gintis, H. (2004). *Foundations of human sociality: Economic experiments and ethnographic evidence from fifteen small-scale societies.* Oxford University Press.

Henrich, J., Heine, S. J., & Norenzayan, A. (2010). Most people are not WEIRD. *Nature, 466*, 29.

Herman, C. P., Roth, D. A., & Polivy, J. (2003). Effects of the presence of others on food intake: A normative interpretation. *Psychological Bulletin, 129*, 873–886.

Herman-Giddens, M. E., Steffes, J., Harris, D., Slora, E., Hussey, M., Dowshen, S. A., & Reiter, E. O. (2012). Secondary sexual characteristics in boys: Data from the pediatric research in office settings network. *Pediatrics, 130*(5), e1058–e1068. https://doi.org/10.1542/peds.2011-3291

Hershfield, H. E., Shu, S., & Benartzi, S. (2020). Temporal reframing and savings: A field experiment. *Marketing Science, 39,* 1039–1051. https://doi.org/10.1287/mksc.2019.1177

Hertenstein, M. J., Holmes, R., McCullough, M., & Keltner, D. (2009). The communication of emotion via touch. *Emotion, 9,* 566–573.

Hertig, M. M., & Nagel, B. J. (2012). Aerobic fitness relates to learning on a virtual Morris water maze task and hippocampal volume in adolescents. *Behavioral Brain Research, 233,* 517–525.

Herz, R. S., & von Clef, J. (2001). The influence of verbal labeling on the perception of odors. *Perception, 30,* 381–391.

Hettema, J. M., Neale, M. C., & Kendler, K. S. (2001). A review and meta-analysis of the genetic epidemiology of anxiety disorders. *American Journal of Psychiatry, 158,* 1568–1578.

Heyes, C. (2016). Born pupils? Natural pedagogy and cultural pedagogy. *Perspectives on Psychological Science, 11*(2), 280–295. https://doi.org/10.1177/1745691615621276

Heyes, C. M., & Foster, C. L. (2002). Motor learning by observation: Evidence from a serial reaction time task. *Quarterly Journal of Experimental Psychology* (A), 55, 593–607.

Heyman, G. M. (2009). *Addiction: A disorder of choice.* Harvard University Press.

Heymsfield, S. B., Greenberg, A. S., Fujioka, K., Dixon, R. M., Kushner, R., Hunt, T., ... McCarnish, M. (1999). Recombinant leptin for weight loss in obese and lean adults: A randomized, controlled, dose-escalation trial. *Journal of the American Medical Association, 282*(16), 1568–1575.

Hibbeln, J. R. (1998). Fish consumption and major depression. *Lancet, 351,* 1213.

Hickok, G. (2009). Eight problems for the mirror neuron theory of action understanding in monkeys and humans. *Journal of Cognitive Neuroscience, 21,* 1229–1243.

Hickok, G. (2014). *The myth of mirror neurons: The real neuroscience of communication and cognition.* W. W. Norton

Higgins, E. T. (1987). Self-discrepancy theory: A theory relating self and affect. *Psychological Review, 94,* 319–340.

Higgins, E. T. (1997). Beyond pleasure and pain. *American Psychologist, 52,* 1280–1300.

Hildt, E. (2019). Artificial intelligence: Does consciousness matter? *Frontiers in Psychology, 10*(1535), 1–3. https://doi.org/10.3389/fpsyg.2019.01535

Hilgard, E. R. (1965). *Hypnotic susceptibility.* Harcourt, Brace and World.

Hilker, R., Helenius, D., Fagerlund, B., Skythe, A., Christensen, K., Werge, T. M., ... Glenthøj, B. (2018). Heritability of schizophrenia and schizophrenia spectrum based on the nationwide Danish twin register. *Biological Psychiatry, 83,* 492–498.

Hill, S. E., Prokosch, M. L., DelPriore, D. J., Griskevicius, V., & Kramer, A. (2016). Low childhood socioeconomic status promotes eating in the absence of energy need. *Psychological Science, 27,* 354–364. https://doi.org/10.1177/0956797615621901

Hillman, C. H., Erickson, K. I., & Kramer, A. F. (2008). Be smart, exercise your heart: Exercise effects on brain and cognition. *Nature Reviews Neuroscience, 9,* 58–65.

Hilts, P. (1995). *Memory's ghost: The strange tale of Mr. M and the nature of memory.* Simon & Schuster.

Hintzman, D. L., Asher, S. J., & Stern, L. D. (1978). Incidental retrieval and memory for coincidences. In M. M. Gruneberg, P. E. Morris, & R. N. Sykes (Eds.), *Practical aspects of memory* (pp. 61–68). Academic Press.

Hirschberger, G., Florian, V., & Mikulincer, M. (2002). The anxiety buffering function of close relationships: Mortality salience effects on the readiness to compromise mate selection standards. *European Journal of Social Psychology, 32,* 609–625.

Hirsh-Pasek, K., Adamson, L. B., Bakeman, R., Owen, M. T., Golinkoff., R. M., Pace, A., ... & Suma, K. (2015). The contribution of early communication quality to low-income children's language success. *Psychological Science, 26,* 1071–1083.

Hirst, W., & Echterhoff, G. (2012). Remembering in conversations: The social sharing and reshaping of memory. *Annual Review of Psychology, 63,* 55–79.

Hirst, W., Phelps, E. A., Buckner, R. L., Budson, A. E., Cuc, A., Gabrieli, J. D. E., ... Vaidya, C. J. (2009). Long-term memory for the terrorist attack of September 11: Flashbulb memories, event memories, and the factors that influence their retention. *Journal of Experimental Psychology: General, 138,* 161–176.

Hirst, W., Phelps, E. A., Meksin, R., Vaidya, C. J., Johnson, M. K., Mitchell, K. J., ... Olsson, A. (2015). A ten-year follow-up of a study of memory for the attack of September 11, 2001: Flashbulb memories and memories for flashbulb events. *Journal of Experimental Psychology: General, 144,* 604–623.

Hitchcock, C., Werner-Seidler, A., Blackwell, S. E., & Dalgleish, T. (2017). Autobiographical episodic memory-based training for the treatment of mood, anxiety and stress-related disorders: A systematic review and meta-analysis. *Clinical Psychology Review, 52,* 92–107. https://doi.org/10.1016/j.cpr.2016.12.003

Hobson, J. A. (1988). *The dreaming brain.* Basic Books.

Hobson, J. A., & McCarley, R. W. (1977). The brain as a dream-state generator: An activation–synthesis hypothesis of the dream process. *American Journal of Psychiatry, 134,* 1335–1368.

Hochberg, L. R., Bacher, D., Jarosiewicz, B., Masse, N. Y., Simeral, J. D., Vogel, J., ... Donoghue, J. P. (2012). Reach and grasp by people with tetraplegia using a neurally controlled robotic arm. *Nature, 485,* 372–377.

Hockley, W. E. (2008). The effects of environmental context on recognition memory and claims of remembering. *Journal of Experimental Psychology: Learning, Memory, and Cognition, 34,* 1412–1429.

Hodgkin, A. L., & Huxley, A. F. (1939). Action potential recorded from inside a nerve fibre. *Nature, 144,* 710–712.

Hodson, G., & Sorrentino, R. M. (2001). Just who favors the ingroup? Personality differences in reactions to uncertainty in the minimal group paradigm. *Group Dynamics, 5,* 92–101.

Hoek, H. W., & van Hoeken, D. (2003). Review of the prevalence and incidence of eating disorders. *International Journal of Eating Disorders, 34,* 383–396.

Hoffrage, U., & Gigerenzer, G. (1996). The impact of information representation on Bayesian reasoning. In G. Cottrell (Ed.), *Proceedings of the Eighteenth Annual Conference of the Cognitive Science Society* (pp. 126–130). Erlbaum.

Hoffrage, U., & Gigerenzer, G. (1998). Using natural frequencies to improve diagnostic inferences. *Academic Medicine, 73,* 538–540.

Hofmann, S. G., & Asmundson, G. J. G. (2008). Acceptance and mindfulness-based therapy: New wave or old hat? *Clinical Psychology Review, 28,* 1–16.

Hofmann, S. G., Asnaani, A., Vonk, I. J. J., Sawyer, A. T., & Fang, A. (2012). The efficacy of cognitive behavioral therapy: A review of meta-analyses. *Cognitive Therapy and Research, 36*(5), 427–440. https://doi.org/10.1007/s10608-012-9476-1

Hofmann, W., Vohs, K. D., & Baumeister, R. F. (2012). What people desire, feel conflicted about, and try to resist in everyday life. *Psychological Science, 23,* 582–588.

Hogan, M. J., & Strasburger, V. C. (2008). Body image, eating disorders, and the media. *Adolescent Medicine: State of the Art Reviews, 19*(3), 521–546, x–xi. http://www.ncbi.nlm.nih.gov/pubmed /19227390

Hoge, M. (2018). *Brainwashed: The bad science behind CTE and the plot to destroy football.* Mascot Books.

Hohler, B. (2017, November 9). Aaron Hernandez's brain was several afflicted by CTE. *Boston Globe.* https://www.bostonglobe.com/sports /patriots/2017/11/09/doctor-details-her-findings-after-examination -aaron-hernandez-brain/USjpN1t5Ic02JPG20heeVN/story.html

Hollins, M. (2010). Somesthetic senses. *Annual Review of Psychology, 61,* 243–271.

Hollon, S. D., DeRubeis, R. J., Andrews, P. W., & Thomson, J. A. (2021). Cognitive therapy in the treatment and prevention of depression: A fifty-year retrospective with an evolutionary coda. *Cognitive Therapy and Research, 45,* 402–417. https://doi.org/10.1007 /s10608-020-10132-1

Holman, E. A., Silver, R. C., Poulin, M., Andersen, J., Gil-Rivas, V., & McIntosh, D. N. (2008). Terrorism, acute stress, and cardio-vascular health. *Archives of General Psychiatry, 65,* 73–80.

Holmbeck, G. N., & O'Donnell, K. (1991). Discrepancies between perceptions of decision making and behavioral autonomy. In R. L. Paikoff (Ed.), *New directions for child development: Shared views in the family during adolescence* (no. 51, pp. 51–69). Jossey-Bass.

Holmes, J., Gathercole, S. E., & Dunning, D. L. (2009). Adaptive training leads to sustained enhancement of poor working memory in children. *Developmental Science, 12,* F9–F15.

Holmes, T. H., & Rahe, R. H. (1967). The social readjustment rat-ing scale. *Journal of Psychosomatic Research, 11,* 213–318.

Holt-Lunstad, J. (2018). Why social relationships are important for physical health: A systems approach to understanding and modifying risk and protection. *Annual Review of Psychology, 69*(1), 437–458.

Holt-Lunstad, J. (2021). The major health implications of social connection. *Current Directions in Psychological Science, 30*(3), 251–259. https://doi.org/10.1177/0963721421999630

Hölzel, B. K., Carmody, J., Vangel, M., Congleton, C., Yerramsetti, S. M., Gard, T., & Lazar, S. W. (2011). Mindfulness practice leads to increases in regained gray matter density. *Psychiatry Research: Neuroimaging, 191*(1), 36–43.

Homonoff, T. (2013, March 27). Can small incentives have large effects? The impact of taxes versus bonuses on disposable bag use. Working Papers (Princeton University. Industrial Relations Section). http://arks.princeton.edu/ark:/88435/dsp014q77fr47j

Hooley, J. M. (2007). Expressed emotion and relapse of psychopathology. *Annual Review of Clinical Psychology, 3,* 329–352.

Hooven, C. (2021). *T: The story of testosterone, the hormone that dominates and divides us.* Henry Holt and Co.

Hoppenbrouwers, S. S., Bulten, B. H., & Brazil, I. A. (2016). Parsing fear: A reassessment of the evidence for fear deficits in psychopathy. *Psychological Bulletin, 142,* 573–600.

Hopper, L. M., Flynn, E. G., Wood, L. A. N., & Whiten, A. (2010). Observational learning of tool use in children: Investigating cultural spread through diffusion chains and learning mechanisms through ghost displays. *Journal of Experimental Child Psychology, 106,* 82–97.

Horn, J. L., & Cattell, R. B. (1966). Refinement and test of the theory of fluid and crystallized general intelligences. *Journal of Educational Psychology, 5,* 253–270.

Horner, A. J., Bisby, J. A., Bush, D., Lin, W.-J., & Burgess, N. (2015). Evidence for holistic episodic recollection via hippocampal pattern completion. *Nature Communications, 6,* 7462. https://doi .org/10.1038/ncomms8462

Horner, V., Whiten, A., Flynn, E., & de Waal, F. B. M. (2006). Faithful replication of foraging techniques along cultural transmission chains by chimpanzees and children. *Proceedings of the National Academy of Sciences USA, 103,* 13878–13883.

Hornsey, M. J. (2020). Why facts are not enough: Understanding and managing the motivated rejection of science. *Current Directions in Psychological Science, 29*(6), 583–591. https://doi.org/10.1177 /0963721420969364

Horrey, W. J., & Wickens, C. D. (2006). Examining the impact of cell phone conversation on driving using meta-analytic techniques. *Human Factors, 48,* 196–205.

Horstmann, K. T., Rauthmann, J. F., Sherman, R. A., & Ziegler, M. (in press). Unveiling an exclusive link: Predicting behavior with personality, situation perception, and affect in a pre-registered experience sampling study. *Journal of Personality and Social Psychology.* https://doi.org/10.31234/osf.io/ztw2n

Hortensius, R., & de Gelder, B. (2018). From empathy to apathy: The bystander effect revisited. *Current Directions in Psychological Science, 27*(4), 249–256. https://doi.org/10.1177/0963721417749653

Hosking, S. G., Young, K. L., & Regan, M. A. (2009). The effects of text messaging on young drivers. *Human Factors, 51,* 582–592.

Howard, J. D., & Kahnt, T. (2018). Identity prediction errors in the human midbrain update reward–identity expectations in the orbitof-rontal cortex. *Nature Communication, 9,* 1611.

Howard, J. H., Jr., & Howard, D. V. (1997). Age differences in implicit learning of higher order dependencies in serial patterns. *Psychology and Aging, 12,* 634–656.

Howard, M. O., Brown, S. E., Garland, E. L., Perron, B. E., & Vaughn, M. G. (2011). Inhalant use and inhalant use disorders in the United States. *Addiction Science & Clinical Practice, 6,* 18–31.

Howes, M., Siegel, M., & Brown, F. (1993). Early childhood memories: Accuracy and affect. *Cognition, 47,* 95–119.

Howlin, P. (2021). Adults with autism: Changes in understanding since DSM-III. *Journal of Autism and Developmental Disorders, 51*(12), 4291–4308. https://doi.org/10.1007/s10803-020-04847-z

Hu, X., Cheng, L. Y., Chiu, M. H., & Paller, K. A. (2020). Promoting memory consolidation during sleep: A meta-analysis of targeted memory reactivation. *Psychological Bulletin, 146,* 218–244. https://doi.org/10.1037/bul0000223

Hua, X., Hibar, D. P., Lee, S., Toga, A. W., Jack, C. R., Jr., Weiner, M. W., ... Alzheimer's Disease Neuroimaging Initiative. (2010). Sex and age differences in atrophic rates: An ADNI study with n = 1368 MRI scans. *Neurobiology of Aging, 31,* 1463–1480.

Huang, J., Perlis, R. H., Lee, P. H., Rush, A. J., Fava, M., Sachs, G. S., ... Smoller, J. W. (2010). Cross-disorder genome-wide analysis of schizophrenia, bipolar disorder, and depression. *American Journal of Psychiatry, 167,* 1254–1263.

Hubel, D. H. (1988). *Eye, brain, and vision.* W. H. Freeman.

Hubel, D. H., & Wiesel, T. N. (1962). Receptive fields, binocular interaction and functional architecture in the cat's visual cortex. *Journal of Physiology, 160,* 106–154.

Hubel, D. H., & Wiesel, T. N. (1998). Early exploration of the visual cortex. *Neuron, 20,* 401–412.

Hudson, J. I., Hiripi, E., Pope, H. G., & Kessler, R. C. (2006). The prevalence and correlates of eating disorders in the National Comorbidity Survey Replication. *Biological Psychiatry, 61*(3), 348–358.

Huesmann, L. R. (2017). An integrative theoretical understanding of aggression: A brief exposition. *Current Opinion in Psychology, 19,* 119–124.

Huesmann, L. R., Moise-Titus, J., Podolski, C.-L., & Eron, L. D. (2003). Longitudinal relations between children's exposure to TV violence and their aggressive and violent behavior in young adulthood: 1977–1992. *Developmental Psychology, 39,* 201–221.

Hughes, A., & Kumari, M. (2019). Testosterone, risk, and socioeconomic position in British men: Exploring causal directionality. *Social Science and Medicine, 220,* 129–140. https://doi.org/10.1016/j.socscimed.2018.11.004 (ePub 2018, November 5).

Hughes, J. R. (2007). A review of sleepwalking (somnambulism): The enigma of neurophysiology and polysomnography with differential diagnosis of complex partial seizures. *Epilepsy & Behavior, 11,* 483–491.

Hughes, S., Power, T., & Francis, D. (1992). Defining patterns of drinking in adolescence: A cluster analytic approach. *Journal of Studies on Alcohol, 53,* 40–47.

Huibers, M. J., Cohen, Z. D., Lemmens, L. H., Arntz, A., Peeters, F. P., Cuijpers, P., & DeRubeis, R. J. (2015). Predicting optimal outcomes in cognitive therapy or interpersonal psychotherapy for depressed individuals using the personalized advantage index approach. *PLoS ONE, 10,* e0140771.

Hull, C. L. (1943). *Principles of behavior.* Appleton-Century-Crofts.

Hunsley, J., Elliott, K., & Therrien, Z. (2014). The efficacy and effectiveness of psychological treatments for mood, anxiety, and related disorders. *Canadian Psychology, 55*(3), 161–176. https://doi.org/10.1037/a0036933

Hunt, E. (2012). What makes nations intelligent? *Perspectives on Psychological Science, 7*(3), 284–306. https://doi.org/10.1177/1745691612442905

Hunt, E. B. (2011). *Human intelligence.* Cambridge University Press.

Hunt, L. L., Eastwick, P. W., & Finkel, E. J. (2015). Leveling the playing field: Longer acquaintance predicts reduced assortative mating on attractiveness. *Psychological Science, 26*(7), 1046–1053. https://doi.org/10.1177/0956797615579273

Hunt, M. (2007). *The story of psychology* (Exp. & Rev. Ed.). Anchor Books.

Hupé, J.-M. (2020). An introduction to synesthesia via Vladimir Nabokov. In M. Bouchet, J. Loison-Charles, & I. Poulin (Eds.) *The Five Senses in Nabokov's Works.* Palgrave Macmillan. https://doi.org/10.1007/978-3-030-45406-7_15

Hupé, J.-M., & Dojat, M. (2015). A critical review of the neuroimaging literature on synesthesia. *Frontiers in Human Neuroscience, 9,* Article 103. https://doi.org/10.3389/fnhum.2015.00103

Hurst, N. (2017). How does human echolocation work? *Smithsonian.com.* https://www.smithsonianmag.com/innovation/how-does-human-echolocation-work-180965063/

Hurvich, L. M., & Jameson, D. (1957). An opponent process theory of color vision. *Psychological Review, 64,* 384–404.

Hussey, E., & Safford, A. (2009). Perception of facial expression in somatosensory cortex supports simulationist models. *Journal of Neuroscience, 29*(2), 301–302.

Hutchison, R. M., Culham, J. C., Everling, S., Flanagan, J. R., & Gallivan, J. P. (2014). Distinct and distributed functional connectivity patterns across cortex reflect the domain-specific constraints of object, face, scene, body, and tool category-selective modules in the ventral visual pathway. *Neuroimage, 96,* 216–236. https://doi.org/10.1016/j.neuroimage.2014.03.068

Huttenlocher, P. R. (1979). Synaptic density in human frontal cortex: Developmental changes and effects of aging. *Brain Research, 163,* 195–205.

Huxley, A. (1932). *Brave new world.* Chatto and Windus.

Huxley, A. (1954). *The doors of perception.* Harper & Row.

Hyde, J. S. (2005) The gender similarities hypothesis. *American Psychologist, 60,* 581–592.

Hyman, I. E., Jr., Boss, S. M., Wise, B. M., McKenzie, K. E., & Caggiano, J. M. (2010). Did you see the unicycling clown? Inattentional blindness while walking and talking on a cell phone. *Applied Cognitive Psychology, 24*(5), 597–607.

Hyman, I. E., Jr., & Pentland, J. (1996). The role of mental imagery in the creation of false childhood memories. *Journal of Memory and Language, 35,* 101–117.

Hyman, I. E., Sarb, B. A., & Wise-Swanson, B. M. (2014). Failure to see money on a tree: Inattentional blindness for objects that guided behavior. *Frontiers in Psychology, 5,* 336. https://doi.org/10.3389/fpsyg.2014.00356

Iacoboni, M. (2009). Imitation, empathy, and mirror neurons. *Annual Review of Psychology, 60,* 653–670.

Iacoboni, M., Molnar-Szakacs, I., Gallese, V., Buccino, G., Mazziotta, J. C., & Rizzolatti, G. (2005). Grasping the intentions of others with one's own mirror neuron system. *PLoS Biology, 3,* 529–535.

Ichheiser, G. (1949). Misunderstandings in human relations: A study in false social perceptions. *American Journal of Sociology, 55*(Pt. 2), 1–70.

Ilska, J., Haskell, M. J., Blott, S. C., Sanchez-Molano, E., Polgar, Z., Lofgren, S. E., ... Weiner, P. (2017). Genetic characterization of dog personality traits. *Genetics, 206*(2), 1101–1111. https://doi.org/10.1534/genetics.116.192674

Imbo, I., & LeFevre, J.-A. (2009). Cultural differences in complex addition: Efficient Chinese versus adaptive Belgians and Canadians. *Journal of Experimental Psychology: Learning, Memory, and Cognition, 35,* 1465–1476.

Inciardi, J. A. (2001). *The war on drugs III.* Allyn & Bacon.

Ingvar, M., Ambros-Ingerson, J., Davis, M., Granger, R., Kessler, M., Rogers, G. A., ... Lynch, G. (1997). Enhancement by an ampakine of memory encoding in humans. *Experimental Neurology, 146,* 553–559.

Inniss, D., Steiger, H., & Bruce, K. (2011). Threshold and subthreshold post-traumatic stress disorder in bulimic patients: Prevalences and clinical correlates. *Eating and Weight Disorders, 16*(1), e30–e36. https://doi.org/10.1007/BF03327518

Inui, A. (2001). Ghrelin: An orexigenic and somatotrophic signal from the stomach. *Nature Reviews Neuroscience, 2,* 551–560.

Inzlicht, M., & Ben-Zeev, T. (2000). A threatening intellectual environment: Why females are susceptible to experiencing problem-solving deficits in the presence of males. *Psychological Science, 11*(5), 365–371. https://doi.org/10.1111/1467-9280.00272

Irvine, J. T. (1978). Wolof magical thinking: Culture and conservation revisited. *Journal of Cross-Cultural Psychology, 9,* 300–310.

Isaacowitz, D. M. (2012). Mood regulation in real time: Age differences in the role of looking. *Current Directions in Psychological Science, 21*(4), 237–242. https://doi.org/10.1177/0963721412448651

Isaacowitz, D. M., & Blanchard-Fields, F. (2012). Linking process and outcome in the study of emotion and aging. *Perspectives on Psychological Science, 7*(1), 3–17. https://doi.org/10.1177/1745691611424750

Isenberg, D. J. (1986). Group polarization: A critical review and meta-analysis. *Journal of Personality and Social Psychology, 50*(6), 1141–1151. https://doi.org/10.1037/0022-3514.50.6.1141

Ittelson, W. H. (1952). *The Ames demonstrations in perception.* Princeton University Press.

Iturrate, I., Chavarriaga, R., Montesano, L., Minguez, J., & del R. Millán, J. (2015). Teaching brain-machine interfaces as an alternative paradigm to neuroprosthetics control. *Scientific Reports, 5,* 13893. https://doi.org/10.1038/srep13893

Iverson, G. L. (2015). Suicide and chronic traumatic encephalopathy. *Journal of Neuropsychiatry & Clinical Neurosciences, 28*(1), 9–16. https://doi.org/10.1176/appi.neuropsych.15070172

Iyadurai, L., Blackwell, S. E., Meiser-Stedman, R., Watson, P. C., Bonsall, M. B., Geddes, J. R., Nobre, A. C., & Holmes, E. A. (2018). Preventing intrusive memories after trauma via a brief intervention training involving Tetris computer game play in the emergency department: A proof-of-concept randomized controlled trial. *Molecular Psychiatry, 23*(3), 674–682. https://doi.org/10.1038/mp.2017.23

Iyengar, S., Konitzer, T., & Tedin, K. (2018). The home as a political fortress: Family agreement in an era of polarization. *The Journal of Politics, 80*(4), 1326–1338. https://doi.org/10.1086/698929

Izard, C. E. (1971). *The face of emotion.* Appleton-Century-Crofts.

Jachimowicz, J. M., Hauser, O. P., O'Brien, J. D., Sherman, E., & Galinsky, A. D. (2018). The critical role of second-order normative beliefs in predicting energy conservation. *Nature Human Behaviour, 2*(10), 757–764. https://doi.org/10.1038/s41562-018-0434-0

Jack, R. E., & Schyns, P. G. (2017). Toward a social psychophysics of face communication. *Annual Review of Psychology, 68,* 269–297. https://doi.org/10.1146/annurev-psych-010416-044242

Jackson, J. S., Knight, K. M., & Rafferty, J. A. (2010). Race and unhealthy behaviors: Chronic stress, the HPA axis, and physical and mental health disparities over the life course. *American Journal of Public Health, 100*(5), 933–939. https://doi.org/10.2105/AJPH.2008.143446

Jacobson, E. (1932). The electrophysiology of mental activities. *American Journal of Psychology, 44,* 677–694.

Jacobson, N. C., & Newman, M. G. (2017). Anxiety and depression as bidirectional risk factors for one another: A meta-analysis of longitudinal studies. *Psychological Bulletin, 143,* 1155–1200.

Jacobson, T., & Hoffman, V. (1997). Children's attachment representations: Longitudinal relations to school behavior and academic competency in middle childhood and adolescence. *Developmental Psychology, 33,* 703–710.

Jaeger, A., Eisenkraemer, R. E., & Stein, L. M. (2015). Test-enhanced learning in third-grade children. *Educational Psychology, 35,* 513–521.

Jairam, V., Yang, D. X., Yu, J. B, & Park, H. S. (2020). Emergency department visits for opioid overdoses among patients with cancer. *Journal of the National Cancer Institute, 112*(9), 938–943. https://doi.org/10.1093/jnci/djz233

James, T. W., Culham, J., Humphrey, G. K., Milner, A. D., & Goodale, M. A. (2003). Ventral occipital lesions impair object recognition but not object-directed grasping: An fMRI study. *Brain, 126,* 2463–2475.

James, W. (1890). *The principles of psychology.* Harvard University Press.

James, W. (1911). *Memories and studies.* Longman.

Jamieson, J. P., Koslov, K., Nock, M. K., & Mendes, W. B. (2013). Experiencing discrimination increases risk-taking. *Psychological Science, 24,* 131–139.

Jamieson, J. P., Mendes, W. B., Blackstock, E., & Schmader, T. (2010). Turning the knots in your stomach into bows: Reappraising arousal improves performance on the GRE. *Journal of Experimental Social Psychology, 46,* 208–212.

Jamison, K. R. (1993). *Touched with fire: Manic-depressive illness and the artistic temperament.* Free Press.

Janicak, P. G., Dowd, S. M., Martis, B., Alam, D., Beedle, D., Krasuski, J., ... Viana, M. (2002). Repetitive transcranial magnetic stimulation versus electroconvulsive therapy for major depression: Preliminary results of a randomized trial. *Biological Psychiatry, 51,* 659–667.

Janis, I. L. (1982). *Groupthink: Scientific studies of policy decisions and fiascoes.* Houghton-Mifflin.

Jasieńska, G., Ziomkiewicz, A., Ellison, P. T., Lipson, S. F., & Thune, I. (2004). Large breasts and narrow waists indicate high reproductive potential in women. *Proceedings of the Royal Society: Biological Sciences, 271,* 1213–1217. https://doi.org/10.1098/rspb.2004.2712

Jausovec, N., & Jausovec, K. (2005). Differences in induced gamma and upper alpha oscillations in the human brain related to verbal performance and emotional intelligence. *International Journal of Psychophysiology, 56,* 223.

Jausovec, N., Jausovec, K., & Gerlic, I. (2001). Differences in event-related and induced electroencephalography patterns in the theta and alpha frequency bands related to human emotional intelligence. *Neuroscience Letters, 311,* 93.

Javadi, A.-H., Emo, B., Howard, L. R., Zisch, F. E., Yu, Y., Knight, R., ... Spiers, H. J. (2017). Hippocampal and prefrontal processing of network topology to simulate the future. *Nature Communications, 8,* 14652. https://doi.org/10.1038/ncomms14652

Jayaraman, S., Fausey, C. M., & Smith, L. B. (2015). The faces in infant-perspective scenes change over the first year of life. *PLoS ONE, 10*(5), e0123780. https://doi.org/10.1371/journal.pone.0123780

Jaynes, J. (1976). *The origin of consciousness in the breakdown of the bicameral mind.* Allen Lane.

Jenkins, H. M., Barrera, F. J., Ireland, C., & Woodside, B. (1978). Signal-centered action patterns of dogs in appetitive classical conditioning. *Learning and Motivation, 9,* 272–296.

Jenkins, J. G., & Dallenbach, K. M. (1924). Oblivescence during sleep and waking. *American Journal of Psychology, 35,* 605–612.

Jessen, N. A., Munk, A. S. F., Lundgaar, I., & Nedergaar, M. (2015). The glymphatic system: A beginner's guide. *Neurochemical Research, 40*(12), 2583–2599. https://doi.org/10.1007/s11064-015-1581-6

Jing, H. G., Madore, K. P., & Schacter, D. L. (2017). Preparing for what might happen: An episodic specificity induction impacts the generation of alternative future events. *Cognition, 169,* 118–128.

Jing, H. G., Szpunar, K. K., & Schacter, D. L. (2016). Interpolated testing influences focused attention and improves integration of information during a video-recorded lecture. *Journal of Experimental Psychology: Applied, 22,* 305–318.

Joel, S., Eastwick, P. W., Allison, C. J., Arriaga, X. B., Baker, Z. G., Bar-Kalifa, E., ... Wolf, S. (2020). Machine learning uncovers the most robust self-report predictors of relationship quality across 43 longitudinal couples studies. *Proceedings of the National Academy of Sciences, 117*(32), 19061–19071. https://doi.org/10.1073/pnas.1917036117

Johansson, G. (1973). Visual perception of biological motion and a model for its analysis. *Perception & Psychophysics 14*(2), 201–211. https://doi.org/10.3758/BF03212378

John, O. P., & Srivastava, S. (1999). The Big Five trait taxonomy: History, measurement, and theoretical perspectives. In L. A. Pervin & O. P. John (Eds.), *Handbook of personality: Theory and research* (2nd ed., pp. 102–138). Guilford Press.

John, O. P., Naumann, L. P., & Soto, C. J. (2008). Paradigm shift to the integrative Big-Five trait taxonomy: History, measurement, and conceptual issues. In O. P. John, R. W. Robins, & L. A. Pervin (Eds.), *Handbook of personality: Theory and research* (3rd ed., pp. 114–158). Guilford Press.

Johns, B., & Uriburu, D. (2021, January 9). Drastic learning loss endangers an entire generation of students. *Bethesda Magazine.* https://bethesdamagazine.com/bethesda-beat/opinion/opinion-drastic-learning-loss-endangers-an-entire-generation-of-students/

Johnson, D. J., Cesario, J., & Pleskac, T. J. (2018). How prior information and police experience impact decisions to shoot. *Journal of Personality and Social Psychology, 115*(4), 601–623.

Johnson, D. R., & Wu, J. (2002). An empirical test of crisis, social selection, and role explanations of the relationship between marital disruption and psychological distress: A pooled time-series analysis of four-wave panel data. *Journal of Marriage and the Family, 64,* 211–224.

Johnson, J. S., & Newport, E. L. (1989). Critical period effects in second language learning: The influence of maturational state on the acquisition of English as a second language. *Cognitive Psychology, 21,* 60–99.

Johnson, K. (2002). Neural basis of haptic perception. In H. Pashler & S. Yantis (Eds.), *Stevens' handbook of experimental psychology: Vol. 1. Sensation and perception* (3rd ed., pp. 537–583). Wiley.

Johnson, M. H., Dziurawiec, S., Ellis, H. D., & Morton, J. (1991). Newborns' preferential tracking of face-like stimuli and its subsequent decline. *Cognition, 40,* 1–19.

Johnson, M. K., Hashtroudi, S., & Lindsay, D. S. (1993). Source monitoring. *Psychological Bulletin, 114,* 3–28.

Johnson, N. J., Backlund, E., Sorlie, P. D., & Loveless, C. A. (2000). Marital status and mortality: The National Longitudinal Mortality Study. *Annual Review of Epidemiology, 10,* 224–238.

Johnson, S. C., Dweck, C. S., & Chen, F. S. (2007). Evidence for infants' internal working models of attachment. *Psychological Science, 18,* 501–2. https://doi.org/10.1111/j.1467-9280.2007.01929.x

Johnson, S. L., Cuellar, A. K., & Miller, C. (2009). Unipolar and bipolar depression: A comparison of clinical phenomenology, biological vulnerability, and psychosocial predictors. In I. H. Gottlib & C. L. Hammen (Eds.), *Handbook of depression* (2nd ed., pp. 142–162). Guilford Press.

Johnson, S. L., Cuellar, A. K., Ruggiero, C., Winnett-Perman, C., Goodnick, P., White, R., & Miller, I. (2008). Life events as predictors of mania and depression in bipolar 1 disorder. *Journal of Abnormal Psychology, 117,* 268–277.

Johnston, L., Bachman, J., & O'Malley, P. (1997). *Monitoring the future.* Institute for Social Research.

Johnstone, E. C., Crow, T. J., Frith, C., Husband, J., & Kreel, L. (1976). Cerebral ventricular size and cognitive impairment in chronic schizophrenia. *Lancet, 2,* 924–926.

Jokela, M., Elovainio, M., Singh-Manoux, A., & Kivimaki, M. (2009). IQ, socioeconomic status, and early death: The US National Longitudinal Survey of Youth. *Psychosomatic Medicine, 71*(3), 322–328. https://doi.org/10.1097/PSY.0b013e31819b69f6

Jones, B. C., Little, A. C., Penton-Voak, I. S., Tiddeman, B. P., Burt, D. M., & Perrett, D. I. (2001). Facial symmetry and judgements of apparent health: Support for a "good genes" explanation of the attractiveness–symmetry relationship. *Evolution and Human Behavior, 22,* 417–429.

Jones, E. E., & Harris, V. A. (1967). The attribution of attitudes. *Journal of Experimental Social Psychology, 3,* 1–24.

Jones, E. E., & Nisbett, R. E. (1972). The actor and the observer: Divergent perceptions of the causes of behavior. In E. E. Jones, D. E. Kanouse, H. H. Kelley, R. E. Nisbett, S. Valins, & B. Weiner (Eds.), *Attribution: Perceiving the causes of behavior* (pp. 79–94). General Learning Press.

Jones, J. (1993). *Bad blood.* The Free Press.

Jones, L. M., & Foshay, N. N. (1984). Diffusion of responsibility in a nonemergency situation: Response to a greeting from a stranger. *Journal of Social Psychology, 123,* 155–158.

Jones, M. J., Moore, S. R., & Kobor, M. S. (2018). Principles and challenges of applying epigenetic epidemiology to psychology. *Annual Review of Psychology, 69,* 459–485.

Jones, S. S. (2007). Imitation in infancy. *Psychological Science, 18*(7), 593–599.

Jonsson, H., & Hougaard, E. (2008). Group cognitive behavioural therapy for obsessive-compulsive disorder: A systematic review and meta-analysis. *Acta Psychiatrica Scandinavica, 117,* 1–9.

Jordan, S. A., Cunningham, D. G., & Marles, R. J. (2010). Assessment of herbal medicinal products: Challenges and opportunities to increase the knowledge base for safety assessment. *Toxicology and Applied Pharmacology, 243,* 198–216.

Jørgensen, K. N., Nesvåg, R., Gunleiksrud, S., Raballo, A., Jönsson, E. G., & Agartz, I. (2016). First- and second-generation antipsychotic drug treatment and subcortical brain morphology in schizophrenia. *European Archives of Psychiatry and Clinical Neuroscience, 266,* 451–460.

Judd, L. L. (1997). The clinical course of unipolar major depressive disorders. *Archives of General Psychiatry, 54,* 989–991.

Judd, T. (2014). Making sense of multitasking: The role of Facebook. *Computers & Education, 70,* 194–202.

Jung-Beeman, M. (2005). Bilateral brain processes for comprehending natural language. *Trends in Cognitive Sciences, 9,* 512–518.

Jung-Beeman, M., Bowden, E. M., Haberman, J., Frymiare, J. L., Arambel-Liu, S., Greenblatt, R., ... Kounios, J. (2004). Neural activity when people solve verbal problems with insight. *PLoS Biology, 2,* 500–510.

Jurewicz, I., Owen, R. J., & O'Donovan, M. C. (2001). Searching for susceptibility genes in schizophrenia. *European Neuropsychopharmacology, 11,* 395–398.

Kaas, J. H. (1991). Plasticity of sensory and motor maps in adult mammals. *Annual Review of Neuroscience, 14,* 137–167.

Kagan, J. (1997). Temperament and the reactions to unfamiliarity. *Child Development, 68,* 139–143.

Kahneman, D. (2011). *Thinking fast and slow.* Farrar, Straus and Giroux.

Kahneman, D., & Deaton, A. (2010). High income improves evaluation of life but not emotional well-being. *Proceedings of the National Academy of Sciences, USA, 107,* 16489–16493.

Kahneman, D., & Tversky, A. (1973). On the psychology of prediction. *Psychological Review, 80,* 237–251.

Kahneman, D., & Tversky, A. (1979). Prospect theory: An analysis of decision under risk. *Econometrica, 47,* 263–291.

Kahneman, D., & Tversky, A. (1984). Choices, values, and frames. *American Psychologist, 39,* 341–350.

Kahneman, D., Krueger, A. B., Schkade, D. A., Schwarz, N., & Stone, A. A. (2004). A survey method for characterizing daily life experience: The day reconstruction method. *Science, 306,* 1776–1780.

Kajonius, P., & Giolla, E. M. (2017). Personality traits across countries: Support for similarities rather than differences. *PLoS ONE, 12*(6), e0179646. https://doi.org/10.1371/journal.pone.0179646

Kalb. J. (2015, January 12). Give me a smile. *New Yorker.*

Kalick, S. M., & Hamilton, T. E. (1986). The matching hypothesis reexamined. *Journal of Personality and Social Psychology, 51,* 673–682.

Kalokerinos, E. K., Greenaway, K. H., & Denson, T. F. (2015). Reappraisal but not suppression downregulates the experience of positive and negative emotion. *Emotion, 15*(3), 271–275. https://doi.org/10.1037/emo0000025

Kamin, L. J. (1959). The delay-of-punishment gradient. *Journal of Comparative and Physiological Psychology, 52,* 434–437.

Kamiya, J. (1969). Operant control of the EEG alpha rhythm and some of its reported effects on consciousness. In C. S. Tart (Ed.), *Altered states of consciousness* (pp. 519–529). Anchor Books.

Kan, P. F., & Kohnert, K. (2008). Fast mapping by bilingual preschool children. *Journal of Child Language, 35,* 495–514.

Kandel, E. R. (2006). *In search of memory: The emergence of a new science of mind.* Norton.

Kang, S. H. K., McDermott, K. B., & Roediger, H. L., III. (2007). Test format and corrective feedback modify the effect of testing on long-term retention. *European Journal of Cognitive Psychology, 19,* 528–558.

Kann, L., McManus, T., Harris, W. A., Shanklin, S. L., Flint, K. H., Queen, B., … Ethier, K. A. (2018). Youth Risk Behavior Surveillance: United States, 2017. *MMWR Surveillance Summaries.* https://www.cdc.gov/healthyyouth/data/yrbs/pdf/2017/ss6708.pdf

Kano, M., Shimizu, Y., Okayama, K., & Kikuchi, M. (2007). Quantitative study of ageing epiglottal taste buds in humans. *Gerodontology, 24*(3), 169–172. https://doi.org/10.1111/j.1741-2358.2007.00165.x

Kanwisher, N. (2000). Domain specificity in face perception. *Nature Neuroscience, 3,* 759–763.

Kanwisher, N. (2010). Functional specificity in the human brain: A window into the functional architecture of the mind. *Proceedings of the National Academy of Sciences, USA, 107,* 11163–11170.

Kanwisher, N., McDermott, J., & Chun, M. M. (1997). The fusiform face area: A module in human extrastriate cortex specialized for face perception. *Journal of Neuroscience, 17,* 4302–4311.

Kaplan, D. M., Rentscher, K. E., Lim, M., Reyes, R., Keating, D., Romero, J., … Mehl, M. R. (2020). Best practices for Electronically Activated Recorder (EAR) research: A practical guide to coding and processing EAR data. *Behavior Research Methods, 52*(4), 1538–1551. https://doi.org/10.3758/s13428-019-01333-y

Kapur, S., Craik, F. I. M., Tulving, E., Wilson, A. A., Houle, S., & Brown, G. M. (1994). Neuroanatomical correlates of encoding in episodic memory: Levels of processing effects. *Proceedings of the National Academy of Sciences, USA, 91,* 2008–2011.

Karau, S. J., & Williams, K. D. (1993). Social loafing: A meta-analytic review and theoretical integration. *Journal of Personality and Social Psychology, 65*(4), 681–706.

Karazsia, B. T., Murnen, S. K., & Tylka, T. L. (2017). Is body dissatisfaction changing across time? A cross-temporal meta-analysis. *Psychological Bulletin, 143*(3), 293–320. https://doi.org/10.1037/bul0000081

Kardes, F. R., & Sanbonmatsu, D. M. (2003). Omission neglect: The importance of missing information. *Skeptical Inquirer, 27,* 42–16.

Karlson, K. (2016). We tested over 100 different Facebook ads in one month: Here's what we learned. https://adespresso.com/blog/test-100-facebook-ads-one-month-what-we-learned/

Karow, A., Pajonk, F. G., Reimer, J., Hirdes, F., Osterwald, C., Naber, D., & Moritz, S. (2007). The dilemma of insight into illness in schizophrenia: Self- and expert-rated insight and quality of life. *European Archives of Psychiatry and Clinical Neuroscience, 258,* 152–159.

Karpicke, J. D. & Aue, W. R. (2015). The testing effect is alive and well with complex materials. *Educational Psychology Review, 27,* 317–326.

Karpicke, J. D. (2012). Retrieval-based learning: Active retrieval promotes meaningful learning. *Current Directions in Psychological Science, 21,* 157–163.

Karpicke, J. D., & Blunt, J. R. (2011). Retrieval practice produces more learning than elaborative studying with concept mapping. *Science, 331,* 772–775.

Karpicke, J. D., & Roediger, H. L., III. (2008). The critical importance of retrieval for learning. *Science, 319,* 966–968.

Kashdan, T. B., Goodman, F. R., Stiksma, M., Milius, C. R., & McKnight, P. E. (2018). Sexuality leads to boosts in mood and meaning in life with no evidence for the reverse direction: A daily diary investigation. *Emotion, 18*(4), 563–576. https://doi.org/10.1037/emo0000324

Kasser, T., & Sharma, Y. S. (1999). Reproductive freedom, educational equality, and females' preference for resource-acquisition characteristics in mates. *Psychological Science, 10,* 374–377.

Kassin, S. M. (2007). Internalized false confessions. In M. Toglia, J. Read, D. Ross, & R. Lindsay (Eds.), *Handbook of eyewitness psychology: Vol. 1, Memory for events* (pp. 175–192). Erlbaum.

Kassin, S. M. (2015). The social psychology of false confessions. *Social Issues and Policy Review, 9,* 25–51.

Kaufman, A. S. (2001). WAIS-III IQs, Horn's theory, and generational changes from young adulthood to old age. *Intelligence, 29,* 131–167.

Kaufman, L. (2009, January 30). Utilities turn their customers green, with envy. *New York Times.* http://www.nytimes.com/2009/01/31/science/earth/31compete.html

Kawabata, M., Pavey, T. G., & Coulter, T. J. (2021). Evolving the validity of a mental toughness measure: Refined versions of the Mental Toughness Questionnaire–48. *Stress & Health, 37*(2), 378–391. https://doi.org/10.1002/smi.3004

Kawakami, K., Dovidio, J. F., Moll, J., Hermsen, S., & Russin, A. (2000). Just say no (to stereotyping): Effects of training in the negation of stereotypic associations on stereotype activation. *Journal of Personality and Social Psychology, 78,* 871–888.

Kayyal, M., Widen, S., & Russell, J. A. (2015). Context is more powerful than we think: Contextual cues override facial cues even for valence. *Emotion, 15*(3), 287–291. https://doi.org/10.1037/emo0000032

Kazdin, A. E. (2018). *Innovations in psychological interventions and their delivery: Leveraging cutting-edge science to improve the world's mental health.* Oxford University Press.

Kazdin, A. E., & Blaise, S. L. (2011). Rebooting psychotherapy research and practice to reduce the burden of mental illness. *Perspectives on Psychological Science, 6,* 21–37.

Keane, T. M., Marshall, A. D., & Taft, C. T. (2006). Posttraumatic stress disorder: Etiology, epidemiology, and treatment outcome. *Annual Review of Clinical Psychology, 2,* 161–197.

Keefe, F. J., Abernathy, A. P., & Campbell, L. C. (2005). Psychological approaches to understanding and treating disease-related pain. *Annual Review of Psychology, 56,* 601–630.

Keefe, F. J., Lumley, M., Anderson, T., Lynch, T., & Carson, K. L. (2001). Pain and emotion: New research directions. *Journal of Clinical Psychology, 57,* 587–607.

Keller, H. (1908). Smell, the fallen angel. In *The world I live in* (Chap. 6, p. 75). Hodder & Stoughton.

Kelley, H. H. (1967). Attribution theory in social psychology. In D. Levine (Ed.), *Nebraska Symposium on Motivation* (Vol. 15, pp. 192–238). University of Nebraska Press.

Kelley, H. H., & Thibaut, J. W. (1978). *Interpersonal relations: A theory of interdependence.* Wiley.

Kelley, M. R., Neath, I., & Surprenant, A. M. (2013). Three more semantic serial position functions and a SIMPLE explanation. *Memory & Cognition, 41,* 600–610.

Kelley, W. M., Macrae, C. N., Wyland, C. L., Caglar, S., Inati, S., & Heatherton, T. F. (2002). Finding the self? An event-related fMRI study. *Journal of Cognitive Neuroscience, 14,* 785–794.

Kelly, G. (1955). *The psychology of personal constructs*. Norton.

Kelly, J. F., Karminer, Y., Kahler, C. W., Hoeppner, B., Yeterian, J., Cristello, J. V., & Timko, C. (2017). A pilot randomized clinical trial testing integrated 12-step facilitation (iTSF) treatment for adolescent substance use disorder. *Addiction, 112*, 2155–2166.

Kelm, Z., Womer, J., Walter, J. K., & Feudtner, C. (2014) Interventions to cultivate physician empathy: A systematic review. *BMC Medical Education, 14*, 219.

Keltner, D. (1995). Signs of appeasement: Evidence for the distinct displays of embarrassment, amusement, and shame. *Journal of Personality and Social Psychology, 68*, 441–454.

Keltner, D., & Buswell, B. N. (1996). Evidence for the distinctness of embarrassment, shame, and guilt: A study of recalled antecedents and facial expressions of emotion. *Cognition and Emotion, 10*, 155–171.

Keltner, D., & Haidt, J. (1999). Social functions of emotions at four levels of analysis. *Cognition and Emotion, 13*, 505–521.

Keltner, D., & Harker, L. A. (1998). The forms and functions of the nonverbal signal of shame. In P. Gilbert & B. Andrews (Eds.), *Shame: Interpersonal behavior, psychopathology, and culture* (pp. 78–98). Oxford University Press.

Kendler, K. S., Hettema, J. M., Butera, F., Gardner, C. O., & Prescott, C. A. (2003). Life event dimensions of loss, humiliation, entrapment, and danger in the prediction of onsets of major depression and generalized anxiety. *Archives of General Psychiatry, 60*, 789–796.

Kendler, K. S., Myers, J., & Prescott, C. A. (2002). The etiology of phobias: An evaluation of the stress–diathesis model. *Archives of General Psychiatry, 59*, 242–248.

Kenrick, D. T., Griskevicius, V., Neuberg, S. L., & Schaller, M. (2010). Renovating the pyramid of needs: Contemporary extensions built upon ancient foundations. *Perspectives on Psychological Science, 5*(3), 292–314. https://doi.org/10.1177/1745691610369469

Kenrick, D. T., Sadalla, E. K., Groth, G., & Trost, M. R. (1990). Evolution, traits, and the stages of human courtship: Qualifying the parental investment model. *Journal of Personality, 58*, 97–116.

Kensinger, E. A., & Schacter, D. L. (2005). Emotional content and reality monitoring ability: fMRI evidence for the influence of encoding processes. *Neuropsychologia, 43*, 1429–1443.

Kensinger, E. A., & Schacter, D. L. (2006). Amygdala activity is associated with the successful encoding of item, but not source, information for positive and negative stimuli. *The Journal of Neuroscience, 26*, 2564–2570.

Kensinger, E. A., Clarke, R. J., & Corkin, S. (2003). What neural correlates underlie successful encoding and retrieval? A functional magnetic resonance imaging study using a divided attention paradigm. *Journal of Neuroscience, 23*, 2407–2415.

Keogh, R., & Pearson, J. (2018). The blind mind: No sensory visual imagery in aphantasia. *Cortex, 105*, 53–60. https://doi.org/10.1016/j.cortex.2017.10.012

Keo-Meier, C. L., Herman, L. I., Reisner, S. L., Pardo, S. T., Sharp, C., & Babcock, J. C. (2015). Testosterone treatment and MMPI–2 improvement in transgender men: A prospective controlled study. *Journal of Consulting and Clinical Psychology, 83*, 143–156.

Kerr, N. L., & Tindale, R. S. (2004). Group performance and decision making. *Annual Review of Psychology, 55*, 623–655. https://doi.org/10.1146/annurev.psych.55.090902.142009

Kershaw, T. C., & Ohlsson, S. (2004). Multiple causes of difficulty in insight: The case of the nine-dot problem. *Journal of Experimental Psychology: Learning, Memory, and Cognition, 30*, 3–13.

Kertai, M. D., Pal, N., Palanca, B. J., Lin, N., Searleman, S. A., Zhang, L., ... B-Unaware Study Group. (2010). Association of perioperative risk factors and cumulative duration of low bispectral index with intermediate-term mortality after cardiac surgery in the B-Unaware trial. *Anesthesiology, 112*(5), 1116–1127.

Kessing, L. V., Bauer, M., Nolen, W. A., Severus, E., Goodwin, G. M., & Geddes, J. (2018). Effectiveness of maintenance therapy of lithium vs other mood stabilizers in monotherapy and in combinations: A systematic review of evidence from observational studies. *Bipolar Disorders, 20*, 419–431.

Kessler, R. C. (2012). The costs of depression. *Psychiatric Clinics of North America, 35*, 1–14.

Kessler, R. C., & Luedtke, A. (2021). Pragmatic precision psychiatry: A new direction for optimizing treatment selection. *JAMA Psychiatry, 78*(12), 1384–1390. https://doi.org/10.1001/jamapsychiatry.2021.2500

Kessler, R. C., & Üstün, T. B. (Eds.). (2008). *The WHO Mental Health surveys: Global perspectives on the epidemiology of mental health*. Cambridge University Press.

Kessler, R. C., Adler, L., Barkley, R., Biederman, J., Connors, C. K., Demler, O., ... Zaslavsky, A. M. (2006). The prevalence and correlates of adult ADHD in the United States: Results from the National Comorbidity Study Replication. *American Journal of Psychiatry, 163*, 716–723.

Kessler, R. C., Angermeyer, M., Anthony, J. C., deGraaf, R., Demyittenaere, K., Gasquet, I., ... Üstün, T. B. (2007). Lifetime prevalence and age-of-onset distributions of mental disorders in the World Health Organization World Mental Health Survey Initiative. *World Psychiatry, 6*, 168–176.

Kessler, R. C., Berglund, P., Demler, M. A., Jin, R., Merikangas, K. R., & Walters, E. E. (2005a). Lifetime prevalence and age-of-onset distributions of DSM–IV disorders in the National Comorbidity Survey replication. *Archives of General Psychiatry, 62*, 593–602.

Kessler, R. C., Demler, O., Frank, R. G., Olfson, M., Pincus, H. A., Walters, E. E., ... Zaslavsky, A. M. (2005b). Prevalence and treatment of mental disorders, 1990 to 2003. *New England Journal of Medicine, 352*(24), 2515–2523.

Kessler, R. C., Pecora, P. J., Williams, J., Hiripi, E., O'Brien, K., English, D., ... Sampson, N. A. (2008). Effects of enhanced foster care on the long-term physical and mental health of foster care alumni. *Archives of General Psychiatry, 65*, 625–633.

Kessler, R. C., Petukhova, M., Sampson, N. A., Zaslavsky, A. M., & Wittchen, H. U. (2012). Twelve-month and lifetime prevalence and lifetime morbid risk of anxiety and mood disorders in the United States. *International Journal of Methods in Psychiatric Research, 21*(3), 169–184.

Kessler, R. C., & Wang, P. S. (2008). The descriptive epidemiology of commonly occurring mental disorders in the United States. *Annual Reviews of Public Health, 29*, 115–129.

Keuler, D. J., & Safer, M. A. (1998). Memory bias in the assessment and recall of pre-exam anxiety: How anxious was I? *Applied Cognitive Psychology, 12*, S127–S137.

Keys, E., & Bhogal, M. S. (2018). Mean girls: Provocative clothing leads to intra-sexual competition between females. *Current Psychology, 37*(3), 543–551. https://doi.org/10.1007/s12144-016-9536-x

Kiefer, M., Schuch, S., Schenk, W., & Fiedler, K. (2007). Mood states modulate activity in semantic brain areas during emotional word encoding. *Cerebral Cortex, 17*, 1516–1530.

Kiehl, K. A., Smith, A. M., Hare, R. D., Mendrek, A., Forster, B. B., Brink, J., & Liddle, P. F. (2001). Limbic abnormalities in affective processing by criminal psychopaths as revealed by functional magnetic resonance imaging. *Biological Psychiatry, 50*, 677–684.

Kihlstrom, J. F., Beer, J. S., & Klein, S. B. (2002). Self and identity as memory. In M. R. Leary & J. P. Tangney (Eds.), *Handbook of self and identity* (pp. 68–90). Guilford Press.

Kim, G., Walden, T. A., & Knieps, L. J. (2010). Impact and characteristics of positive and fearful emotional messages during infant social referencing. *Infant Behavior and Development, 33*, 189–195.

Kim, H. S., & Sasaki, J. K. (2014). Cultural neuroscience: Biology of the mind in cultural contexts. *Annual Review of Psychology, 65,* 487–514. https://doi.org/10.1146/annurev-psych-010213-115040

Kim, U. K., Jorgenson, E., Coon, H., Leppert, M., Risch, N., & Drayna, D. (2003). Positional cloning of the human quantitative trait locus underlying taste sensitivity to phenylthiocarbamide. *Science, 299,* 1221–1225.

Kinney, D. A. (1993). From nerds to normal: The recovery of identity among adolescents from middle school to high school. *Sociology of Education, 66,* 21–40.

Kirchner, W. H., & Towne, W. F. (1994). The sensory basis of the honeybee's dance language. *Scientific American, 270*(6), 74–80.

Kirk, N. W., Fiala, L., Scott-Brown, K. C., & Kempe, V. (2014). No evidence for reduced Simon cost in elderly bilingual and bidialecticals. *Journal of Cognitive Psychology* (Hove), *26*(6), 640–648.

Kirsch, I., Cardena, E., Derbyshire, S., Dienes, Z., Heap, M., Kallio, S., ... Whalley, M. (2011). Definitions of hypnosis and hypnotizability and their relation to suggestion and suggestibility: A consensus statement. *Contemporary Hypnosis and Integrative Therapy, 28,* 107–115.

Kirsch, I., Deacon, B. J., Huedo-Medine, T. B., Scoboria, A., Moore, T. J., & Johnson, B. T. (2008). Initial severity and antidepressant benefits: A meta-analysis of data submitted to the Food and Drug Administration. *PLoS Medicine, 5,* e45.

Kirwan, C. B., Bayley, P. J., Galvan, V. V., & Squire, L. R. (2008). Detailed recollection of remote autobiographical memory after damage to the medial temporal lobe. *Proceedings of the National Academy of Sciences, USA, 105,* 2676–2680.

Kish, S. J., Lerch, J., Furukawa, Y., Tong, J., McCluskey, T., Wilkins, D., ... Bioleau, I. (2010). Decreased cerebral cortical serotonin transporter binding in ecstasy users: A positron emission tomography [^{11}c] DASB and structural brain imaging study. *Brain, 133,* 1779–1797.

Kisilevsky, B. S., Hains, S. M., Lee, K., Xie, X., Huang, H., Ye, H. H., ... Wang, Z. (2003). Effects of experience on fetal voice recognition. *Psychological Science, 14*(3), 220–224. https://doi.org/10.1111/1467-9280.02435

Kiyokawa, S., Dienes, Z., Tanaka, D., Yamada, A., & Crowe, L. (2012). Cross cultural differences in unconscious knowledge. *Cognition, 124*(1), 16–24. https://doi.org/10.1016/j.cognition.2012.03.009

Klarer, M., Arnold, M., Günther, L., Winter, C., Langhans, W., & Meyer, U. (2014). Gut vagal afferents differentially modulate innate anxiety and learned fear. *Journal of Neuroscience, 34,* 7067–7076.

Klein, C. T. F., & Helweg-Larsen, M. (2002). Perceived control and the optimistic bias: A meta-analytic review. *Psychology and Health, 17,* 437–446.

Klein, O., & Snyder, M. (2003). Stereotypes and behavioral confirmation: From interpersonal to intergroup perspectives. In M. P. Zanna (Ed.), *Advances in experimental social psychology* (Vol. 35, pp. 153–234). Elsevier Academic Press. https://doi.org/10.1016/S0065-2601(03)01003-7

Klein, R. A., Ratliff, K. A., Vianello, M., Adams, R. B., Jr., Bahník, Š., Bernstein, M. J., ... Nosek, B. A. (2014). Investigating variation in replicability: A "many labs" replication project. *Social Psychology, 45*(3), 142–152. http://doi.org/10.1027/1864-9335/a000178

Klein, R. M., Christie, J., & Parkvail, M. (2016). Does multilingualism affect the incidence of Alzheimer's disease? A worldwise analysis by country. *SSM – Population Health, 2,* 463–467.

Klein, S. B. (2004). The cognitive neuroscience of knowing one's self. In M. Gazzaniga (Ed.), *The cognitive neurosciences* (3rd ed., pp. 1077–1089). MIT Press.

Klein, S. B., Robertson, T. E., & Delton, A. W. (2011). The future-orientation of memory: Planning as a key component mediating the high levels of recall found with survival processing. *Memory, 19,* 121–139.

Klingberg, T. (2010). Training and plasticity of working memory. *Trends in Cognitive Sciences, 14,* 317–324.

Klump, K. L., Strober, M., Bulik, C. M., Thornton, L., Johnson, C., Devlin, B., ... Kaye, W. H. (2004). Personality characteristics of women before and after recovery from an eating disorder. *Psychological Medicine, 34*(8), 1407–1418. https://doi.org/10.1017/S0033291704002442

Klüver, H., & Bucy, P. C. (1937). "Psychic blindness" and other symptoms following bilateral temporary lobectomy in rhesus monkeys. *American Journal of Physiology, 119,* 352–353.

Klüver, H., & Bucy, P. C. (1939). Preliminary analysis of the temporal lobes in monkeys. *Archives of Neurology and Psychiatry, 42,* 979–1000.

Knowlton, B. J., Ramus, S. J., & Squire, L. R. (1992). Intact artificial grammar learning in amnesia: Dissociation of classification learning and explicit memory for specific instances. *Psychological Science, 3,* 173–179.

Knutson, B., Adams, C. M., Fong, G. W., & Hommer, D. (2001). Anticipation of increasing monetary reward selectively recruits nucleus accumbens. *Journal of Neuroscience, 21,* 159.

Kobasa, S. (1979). Stressful life events, personality, and health: An inquiry into hardiness. *Journal of Personality and Social Psychology, 37,* 1–11.

Koehler, J. J. (1993). The influence of prior beliefs on scientific judgments of evidence quality. *Organizational Behavior and Human Decision Processes, 56,* 28–55.

Koen, J. D., & Rugg, M. D. (2019). Neural dedifferentiation in the aging brain. *Trends in Cognitive Sciences, 23*(7), 547–559. https://doi.org/10.1016/j.tics.2019.04.012

Koffka, K. (1935). *Principles of Gestalt psychology.* Harcourt, Brace and World.

Kohlberg, L. (1958). *The development of modes of thinking and choices in years 10 to 16* (Unpublished doctoral dissertation, University of Chicago).

Kohlberg, L. (1963). Development of children's orientation towards a moral order: I. Sequencing in the development of moral thought. *Vita Humana, 6,* 11–36.

Kohlberg, L. (1986). A current statement on some theoretical issues. In S. Modgil & C. Modgil (Eds.), *Lawrence Kohlberg: Consensus and controversy* (pp. 485–546). Falmer.

Kohler, P. K., Manhart, L. E., & Lafferty, E. (2008). Abstinence-only and comprehensive sex education and the initiation of sexual activity and teen pregnancy. *Journal of Adolescent Health, 42,* 344–351.

Kohls, G., Perino, M. T., Taylor, J. M., Madva, E. N., Cayless, S. J., Troiani, V., ... & Schultz, R. T. (2013). The nucleus accumbens is involved in both the pursuit of social reward and the avoidance of social punishment. *Neuropsychologia, 51*(11), 2062–2069. https://doi.org/10.1016/j.neuropsychologia.2013.07.020

Kolb, B., & Whishaw, I. Q. (2015). *Fundamentals of human neuropsychology* (7th ed.). Worth Publishers.

Kolotkin, R. L., Meter, K., & Williams, G. R. (2001). Quality of life and obesity. *Obesity Reviews, 2,* 219–229.

Komter, A. (2010). The evolutionary origins of human generosity. *International Sociology, 25*(3), 443–464.

Könen, T., Dirk, J., & Schmiedek, F. (2015, February). Cognitive benefits of last night's sleep: daily variations in children's sleep behavior are related to working memory fluctuations. *Journal of Child Psychology and Psychiatry, 56*(2), 171–182. https://doi.org.10.1111/jcpp.12296

Koob, G. F., & Volkow, N. D. (2016). Neurobiology of addiction: A neurocircuitry analysis. *The Lancet Psychiatry, 3,* 760–773.

Kosslyn, S. M., Alpert, N. M., Thompson, W. L., Chabris, C. F., Rauch, S. L., & Anderson, A. K. (1993). Visual mental imagery activates topographically organized visual cortex: PET investigations. *Journal of Cognitive Neuroscience, 5*, 263–287.

Kounios, J., & Beeman, M. (2009). The Aha! moment. *Current Directions in Psychological Science, 18*, 210–216.

Kounios, J., & Beeman, M. (2015). *The eureka factor: Aha moments, creative insight, and the brain.* Random House.

Kounios, J., Frymiare, J. L., Bowden, E. M., Fleck, J. I., Subramaniam, K., Parrish, T. B., & Jung-Beeman, M. (2006). The prepared mind: Neural activity prior to problem presentation predicts subsequent solution by sudden insight. *Psychological Science, 17*, 882–890.

Koutsimani, P., Montgomery, A., & Georganta, K. (2019). The relationship between burnout, depression, and anxiety: A systematic review and meta-analysis. *Frontiers in Psychology, 10*, 284. https://doi.org/10.3389/fpsyg.2019.00284

Kovacs, K., & Conway, A. R. A. (2019). What is IQ? Life beyond "general intelligence." *Current Directions in Psychological Science, 28*(2), 189–194. https://doi.org/10.1177/0963721419827275

Kraemer, H. C., Shrout, P. E., & Rubio-Stipec, M. (2007). Developing the *Diagnostic and Statistical Manual–V*: What will "statistical" mean in *DSM–V? Social Psychiatry and Psychiatric Epidemiology, 42*, 259–267.

Krahé, B. (2020). Risk factors for the development of aggressive behavior from middle childhood to adolescence: The interaction of person and environment. *Current Directions in Psychological Science, 29*(4), 333–339. https://doi.org/10.1177/0963721420917721

Krahé, B., & Busching, R. (2015). Breaking the vicious cycle of media violence and aggression: A test of intervention effects over 30 months. *Psychology of Violence, 5*(2), 217–226. https://doi.org/10.1037/a0036627

Kraus, M. W., Piff, P. K., & Keltner, D. (2011). Social class as culture: The convergence of resources and rank in the social realm. *Current Directions in Psychological Science, 20*(4), 246–250. https://doi.org/10.1177/0963721411414654

Kravitz, D. J., Saleem, K. S., Baker, C. I., & Mishkin, M. (2011). A new neural framework for visuospatial processing. *Nature Reviews Neuroscience, 12*, 217–230.

Kravitz, D. J., Saleem, K. S., Baker, C. I., Ungerleider, L. G., & Mishkin, M. (2013). The ventral visual pathway: An expanded neural framework for the processing of object quality. *Trends in Cognitive Sciences, 17*, 26–49.

Kredlow, M. A., & Otto, M. W. (2015). Interference with the reconsolidation of trauma-related memories in adults. *Depression and Anxiety, 32*, 32–37.

Kreibig, S. D. (2010). Autonomic nervous system activity in emotion: A review. *Biological Psychology, 84*(3), 394–421. https://doi.org/10.1016/j.biopsycho.2010.03.010

Kreider, R. M., & Ellis, R. (2011). *Number, timing, and duration of marriages and divorces: 2009.* U.S. Census Bureau.

Kreider, T. (2013) *We learn nothing: Essays.* Simon & Schuster.

Kreider, T. (2018). *I wrote this book because I love you.* Simon & Schuster.

Kreisel, K. M., Spicknall, I., Gargano, J. W., Lewis, F. M. T., Lewis, R. M. … Weinstock, H. S. (2021). Sexually transmitted infections among US women and men: Prevalence and incidence estimates, 2018. *Sexually Transmitted Diseases, 48*, 208–214. https://doi.org/10.1097/OLQ.0000000000001355

Krems, J. A., Ko, A., Moon, J. W., &Varnum, M. E. W. (2021, May). Lay beliefs about gender and sexual behavior: First evidence for a pervasive, robust (but seemingly unfounded) stereotype.

Psychological Science, 32(6), 871–889. https://doi.org/10.1177/0956797620983829

Kristensen, P., & Bjerkedal, T. (2007). Explaining the relation between birth order and intelligence. *Science, 316*, 1717.

Kroeze, W. K., & Roth, B. L. (1998). The molecular biology of serotonin receptors: Therapeutic implications for the interface of mood and psychosis. *Biological Psychiatry, 44*, 1128–1142.

Kroger, J. (2017, February). Identity development in adolescence and adulthood. *Oxford Research Encyclopedia of Psychology.* http://psychology.oxfordre.com/view/10.1093/acrefore/9780190236557.001.0001/acrefore-9780190236557-e-54

Kruglanski, A. W., Jasko, K., Milyavsky, M., Chernikova, M., Webber, D., Pierro, A., & Di Santo, D. (2018). Cognitive consistency theory in social psychology: A paradigm reconsidered. *Psychological Inquiry, 29*(2), 45–59. https://doi.org/10.1080/1047840X.2018.1480656

Kruk, M. R., Halasz, J., Meelis, W., & Haller, J. (2004). Fast positive feedback between the adrenocortical stress response and a brain mechanism involved in aggressive behavior. *Behavioral Neuroscience, 118*, 1062–1070.

Krupenye, C., Kano, F., Hirata, S., Call, J., & Tomasello, M. (2016). Great apes anticipate that other individuals will act according to false beliefs. *Science, 354*(6308), 110–114.

Ksander, J. C., Paige, L. E., Johndro, H. A., & Gutchess, A. H. (2018). Cultural specialization of visual cortex. *Social Cognitive and Affective Neuroscience, 13*(3), 709–718. https://doi.org/10.1093/scan/nsy039

Kucyi, A., & Davis, K. D. (2015). The dynamic pain connectome. *Trends in Neurosciences, 38*, 86–95.

Kuffler, D. P. (2018). Origins of phantom limb pain. *Molecular Neurobiology, 55*, 60–69.

Kuhl, B. A., Dudukovic, N. M., Kahn, I., & Wagner, A. D. (2007). Decreased demands on cognitive control reveal the neural processing benefits of forgetting. *Nature Neuroscience, 10*, 908–917.

Kuhl, P. K. (2010). Brain mechanisms in early language acquisition. *Neuron, 67*, 713–727.

Kuhl, P., & Rivera-Gaxiola, M. (2008). Neural substrates of language acquisition. *Annual Review of Neuroscience, 31*, 511–534.

Kuhl, P. K., Stevens, E., Hayashi, A., Deguchi, T., Kirtani, S., & Iverson, P. (2006). Infants show a facilitation effect for native language phonetic perception between 6 and 12 months. *Developmental Science, 9*(2), F13–F21. https://doi.org/10.1111/j.1467-7687.2006.00468.x

Kulke, L., von Duhn, B., Schneider, D., & Rakoczy, H. (2018). Is implicit theory of mind a real and robust phenomenon? Results from a systematic replication study. *Psychological Science, 29*, 888–900.

Kunda, Z. (1990). The case for motivated reasoning. *Psychological Bulletin, 108*, 480–498.

Kunda, Z., & Oleson, K. C. (1997). When exceptions prove the rule: How extremity of deviance determines the impact of deviant examples on stereotypes. *Journal of Personality and Social Psychology, 72*, 965–979.

Kundakovic, M., Gudsnuk, K, Herbstman, J. B., Tang, D. L., Perera, F. P., & Champagne, F. A. (2015). DNA methylation of BDNF as a biomarker of early-life adversity. *Proceedings of the National Academy of Sciences, USA, 112*, 6807–6813.

Kunugi, H., Urushibara, T., Murray, R. M., Nanko, S., & Hirose, T. (2003). Prenatal underdevelopment and schizophrenia: A case report of monozygotic twins. *Psychiatry and Clinical Neurosciences, 57*, 271–274.

Kunz, P. R., & Woolcott, M. (1976). Season's greetings: From my status to yours. *Social Science Research, 5*, 269–278.

Kupka, R., Duffy, A., Scott, J., Almeida, J., Balanzá-Martínez. V., Birmaher, B., ... Kapczinski, F. (2021). Consensus on nomenclature for clinical staging models in bipolar disorder: A narrative review from the International Society for Bipolar Disorders (ISBD) Staging Task Force. *Bipolar Disorder, 23*(7), 659–678. https://doi.org/10.1111/bdi.13105

Kuppens, P., Tuerlinckx, F., Russell, J. A., & Barrett, L. F. (2013). The relation between valence and arousal in subjective experience. *Psychological Bulletin, 139*(4), 917–940.

Kurby, C. A., & Zacks, J. M. (2008). Segmentation in the perception and memory of events. *Trends in Cognitive Sciences, 12,* 72–79.

Kvavilashvili, L., Mirani, J., Schlagman, S., Foley, K., & Kornbrot, D. E. (2009). Consistency of flashbulb memories of September 11 over long delays: Implications for consolidation and wrong time slice hypotheses. *Journal of Memory and Language, 61,* 556–572.

Kwon, M.-K., Setoodehnia, M., Baek, J., Luck, S. J., & Oakes, L. M. (2016). The development of visual search in infancy: Attention to faces versus salience. *Developmental Psychology, 52*(4), 537–555. https://doi.org/10.1037/dev0000080

LaBar, K. S., & Phelps, E. A. (1998). Arousal-mediated memory consolidation: Role of the medial temporal lobe in humans. *Psychological Science, 9,* 490–493.

Labella, M. H., & Masten, A. S. (2017). Family influences on the development of aggression and violence. *Current Opinion in Psychology, 19,* 11–13.

Labrie, V., Pai, S., & Petronis, A. (2012). Epigenetics of major psychosis: Progress, problems, and perspectives. *Trends in Genetics, 28,* 427–435.

Lacey, H. P., Smith, D. M., & Ubel, P. A. (2006). Hope I die before I get old: Mispredicting happiness across the adult lifespan. *Journal of Happiness Studies, 7*(2), 167–182. https://doi.org/10.1007/s10902-005-2748-7

Lackner, J. R., & DiZio, P. (2005). Vestibular, proprioceptive, and haptic contributions to spatial orientation. *Annual Review of Psychology, 56,* 115–147.

LaFraniere, S. (2007, July 4). In Mauritania, seeking to end an overfed ideal. *New York Times.* http://www.nytimes.com/2007/07/04/world/africa/04mauritania.html?pagewanted=all

Lai, C. K., Lehr, S. A., Cerruti, C., Joy-Gaba, J. A., Teachman, B. A., Koleva, S. P., ... Hawkins, C. B. (2014). Reducing implicit racial preferences: I. A comparative investigation of 17 interventions. *Journal of Experimental Psychology, General, 143*(4), 1765–1785. https://doi.org/10.1037/a0036260

Lai, Y., & Siegal, J. (1999). Muscle atonia in REM sleep. In B. Mallick & S. Inoue (Eds.), *Rapid eye movement sleep* (pp. 69–90). Narosa Publishing House.

Lake, J. (2009). Natural products used to treat depressed mood as monotherapies and adjuvants to antidepressants: A review of the evidence. *Psychiatric Times, 26,* 1–6.

Lakhan, S. E., & Kirchgessner, A. (2012, March 12). Chronic traumatic encephalopathy: The dangers of getting "dinged." *Springer Plus, 1*(2). https://doi.org/10.1186/2193-1801-1-2

Lakin, J. M. (2013). Sex differences in reasoning abilities: Surprising evidence that male–female ratios in the tails of the quantitative reasoning distribution have increased. *Intelligence, 41*(4), 263–274. https://doi.org/10.1016/j.intell.2013.04.004

Lakshminarayanan, V. R., Chen, M. K., & Santos, L. R. (2011). The evolution of decision-making under risk: Framing effects in monkey risk preferences. *Journal of Experimental Social Psychology, 47*(3), 689–693. https://doi.org/10.1016/j.jesp.2010.12.011

Lam, L. L., Emberly, E., Fraser, H. B., Neumann, S. M., Chen, E., Miller, G. E., ... Kobor, M. S. (2012). Factors underlying variable DNA methylation in a human community cohort. *Proceedings of the National Academy of Sciences, USA, 109*(Suppl. 2), 17253–17260.

Lamm, C., Decety, J., & Singer, T. (2011). Meta-analytic evidence for common and distinct neural networks associated with directly experienced pain and empathy for pain. *Neuroimage, 54*(3), 2492–2502.

Landry, M., Lifshitz, M., & Raz, A. (2017). Brain correlates of hypnosis: A systematic review and meta-analytic exploration. *Neuroscience & Biobehavioral Reviews, 81,* 75–98.

Lane, C., Kanjlia, S., Omaki, A. & Bedny, M. (2015). "Visual" cortex of congenitally blind adults responds to syntactic movement. *Journal of Neuroscience, 35*(37), 12859–12868. https://doi.org/10.1523/JNEUROSCI.1256-15.2015

Lane, J. D., Harris, P. L., Gelman, S. A., & Wellman, H. M. (2014). More than meets the eye: Young children's trust in claims that defy their perceptions. *Developmental Psychology, 50*(3), 865–871. https://doi.org/10.1037/a0034291

Lang, F. R., & Carstensen, L. L. (1994). Close emotional relationships in late life: Further support for proactive aging in the social domain. *Psychology and Aging, 9,* 315–324.

Langlois, J. H., Kalakanis, L., Rubenstein, A. J., Larson, A., Hallam, M., & Smoot, M. (2000). Maxims or myths of beauty? A meta-analytic and theoretical review. *Psychological Bulletin, 126,* 390–423.

Langlois, J. H., Ritter, J. M., Casey, R. J., & Sawin, D. B. (1995). Infant attractiveness predicts maternal behaviors and attitudes. *Developmental Psychology, 31,* 464–472.

Lanphear, B. P. (2015). The impact of toxins on the developing brain. *Annual Review of Public Health, 36*(1), 211–230. https://doi.org/10.1146/annurev-publhealth-031912-114413

LaPierre, S., Boyer, R., Desjardins, S., Dubé, M., Lorrain, D., Préville, M., & Brassard, J. (2012). Daily hassles, physical illness, and sleep problems in older adults with wishes to die. *International Psychogeriatrics, 24,* 243–252.

Larsen, S. F. (1992). Potential flashbulbs: Memories of ordinary news as baseline. In E. Winograd & U. Neisser (Eds.), *Affect and accuracy in recall: Studies of "flashbulb memories"* (pp. 32–64). Cambridge University Press.

Larson, R., & Richards, M. H. (1991). Daily companionship in late childhood and early adolescence: Changing developmental contexts. *Child Development, 62,* 284–300.

Latané, B., Williams, K., & Harkins, S. (1979). Many hands make light the work: The causes and consequences of social loafing. *Journal of Personality and Social Psychology, 37,* 822–832.

Lattal, K. A. (2010). Delayed reinforcement of operant behavior. *Journal of the Experimental Analysis of Behavior, 93,* 129–139.

Lavie, P. (2001). Sleep–wake as a biological rhythm. *Annual Review of Psychology, 52,* 277–303.

Lawrence, N. S., Jollant, F., O'Daly, O., Zelaya, F., & Phillips, M. L. (2009). Distinct roles of prefrontal cortical subregions in the Iowa Gambling Task. *Cerebral Cortex, 19,* 1134–1143.

Lazarus, R. S. (1984). On the primacy of cognition. *American Psychologist, 39,* 124–129.

Lazarus, R. S., & Alfert, E. (1964). Short-circuiting of threat by experimentally altering cognitive appraisal. *Journal of Abnormal and Social Psychology, 69,* 195–205.

Lazarus, R. S., & Folkman, S. (1984). *Stress, appraisal, and coping.* Springer.

Le, B., & Agnew, C. R. (2003). Commitment and its theorized determinants: A meta-analysis of the Investment Model. *Personal Relationships, 10*(1), 37–57. https://doi.org/10.1111/1475-6811.00035

Leader, T., Mullen, B., & Abrams, D. (2007). Without mercy: The immediate impact of group size on lynch mob atrocity. *Personality and Social Psychology Bulletin, 33*(10), 1340–1352.

Leary, M. R. (1990). Responses to social exclusion: Social anxiety, jealousy, loneliness, depression, and low self-esteem. *Journal of Social and Clinical Psychology, 9,* 221–229.

Leary, M. R. (2010). Affiliation, acceptance, and belonging: The pursuit of interpersonal connection. In S. T. Fiske, D. T. Gilbert, & G. Lindzey (Eds.), *The handbook of social psychology* (5th ed., Vol. 2, pp. 864–897). Wiley.

Leary, M. R., & Baumeister, R. F. (2000). The nature and function of self-esteem: Sociometer theory. In M. P. Zanna (Ed.), *Advances in experimental social psychology* (Vol. 32, pp. 1–62). Academic Press.

Lecky, P. (1945). *Self-consistency: A theory of personality.* Island Press.

Lederbogen, F., Kirsch, P., Haddad, L., Streit, F., Tost, H., ... Meyer-Lindenberg, A. (2011). City living and urban upbringing affect neural social stress processing in humans. *Nature, 474,* 498–501.

Lederman, S. J., & Klatzky, R. L. (2009). Haptic perception: A tutorial. *Attention, Perception, & Psychophysics, 71,* 1439–1459.

LeDoux, J. E. (1992). Brain mechanisms of emotion and emotional learning. *Current Opinion in Neurobiology, 2,* 191–197.

LeDoux, J. E., Iwata, J., Cicchetti, P., & Reis, D. J. (1988). Different projections of the central amygdaloid nucleus mediate autonomic and behavioral correlates of conditioned fear. *Journal of Neuroscience, 8,* 2517–2529.

Lee, D. N., & Aronson, E. (1974). Visual proprioceptive control of standing in human infants. *Perception & Psychophysics, 15,* 529–532.

Lee, H. Y., Jamieson, J. P., Reis, H. T., Beevers, C. G., Josephs, R. A., Mullarkey, M. C., ... Yeager, D. S. (2020). Getting fewer "likes" than others on social media elicits emotional distress among victimized adolescents. *Child Development, 91*(6), 2141–2159. https://doi.org/10.1111/cdev.13422

Lee, J. J., Wedow, R., Okbay, A., Kong, E., Maghzian, O., Zacher, M., Nguyen-Viet, T. A., ... Cesarini, D. (2018). Gene discovery and polygenic prediction from a genome-wide association study of educational attainment in 1.1 million individuals. *Nature Genetics, 50*(8), 1112–1121. https://doi.org/10.1038/s41588-018-0147-3

Lee, L., Loewenstein, G., Ariely, D., Hong, J., & Young, J. (2008). If I'm not hot, are you hot or not? Physical-attractiveness evaluations and dating preferences as a function of one's own attractiveness. *Psychological Science, 19,* 669–677.

Lee, M. H., Smyser, C. D., & Shimony, J. S. (2013). Resting-state fMRI: A review of methods and clinical applications. *American Journal of Neuroradiology, 34,* 1866–1872. https://doi.org/10.3174/ajnr.A3263

Lefcourt, H. M. (1982). *Locus of control: Current trends in theory and research* (2nd ed.). Erlbaum.

Legare, C. H., & Nielsen, M. (2015). Imitation and innovation: The dual engines of cultural learning. *Trends in Cognitive Sciences, 19,* 688–699.

Legenbauer, T., Vocks, S., Schäfer, C., Schütt-Strömel, S., Hiller, W., Wagner, C., & Vögele, C. (2009). Preference for attractiveness and thinness in a partner: Influence of internalization of the thin ideal and shape/weight dissatisfaction in heterosexual women, heterosexual men, lesbians, and gay men. *Body Image, 6*(3), 228–234. https://doi.org/10.1016/j.bodyim.2009.04.002

Lehtonen, M., Soveri, A., Laine, A., Järvenpää, J., de Bruin, A., & Antfolk, J. (2018). Is bilingualism associated with enhanced executive functioning in adults? A meta-analytic review. *Psychological Bulletin, 144,* 394–425.

Lemann, N. (1999, March 29). The IQ meritocracy: Our test-obsessed society has Binet and Terman to thank—or to blame. *Time,* 115–116.

Lemay, E. P. (2016). The forecast model of relationship commitment. *Journal of Personality and Social Psychology, 111*(1), 34–52. https://doi.org/10.1037/pspi0000052

Lempert, D. (2007). *Women's increasing wage penalties from being overweight and obese.* U.S. Bureau of Labor Statistics.

Lenton, A. P., & Francesconi, M. (2010). How humans cognitively manage an abundance of mate options. *Psychological Science, 21*(4), 528–533. https://doi.org/10.1177/0956797610364958

Lentz, M. J., Landis, C. A., Rothermel, J., & Shaver, J. L. (1999). Effects of selective slow wave sleep disruption on musculoskeletal pain and fatigue in middle-aged women. *Journal of Rheumatology, 26,* 1586–1592.

Lepage, M., Ghaffar, O., Nyberg, L., & Tulving, E. (2000). Prefrontal cortex and episodic memory retrieval mode. *Proceedings of the National Academy of Sciences, USA, 97,* 506–511.

LePort, A. K. R., Mattfield, A. T., Dickinson-Anson, H., Fallon, J. H., Stark, C. E. L., Kruggel, F., ... McGaugh, J. L. (2012). Behavioral and neuroanatomical investigation of highly superior autobiographical memory (HSAM). *Neurobiology of Learning and Memory, 98,* 78–92.

Lepper, M. R., Greene, D., & Nisbett, R. E. (1973). Undermining children's intrinsic interest with extrinsic rewards: A test of the "overjustification" hypothesis. *Journal of Personality and Social Psychology, 28,* 129–137.

Lerman, D. C., & Vorndran, C. M. (2002). On the status of knowledge for using punishment: Implications for treating behavior disorders. *Journal of Applied Behavior Analysis, 35,* 4312–4464.

Lerman, D. (2006). Consumer politeness and complaining behavior. *Journal of Services Marketing, 20,* 92–100.

Lerner, M. J. (1980). *The belief in a just world: A fundamental delusion.* Plenum.

Leung, A. K. C., Leung, A. A. M., Wong, A. H. C., & Hon, K. L. (2020). Sleep terrors: An updated review. *Current Pediatric Reviews, 16*(3), 176–182. https://doi.org/10.2174/1573396315666191014152136

Leung, A. K.-Y., & Cohen, D. (2011). Within- and between-culture variation: Individual differences and the cultural logics of honor, face, and dignity cultures. *Journal of Personality and Social Psychology, 100*(3), 507–526. https://doi.org/10.1037/a0022151

Levelt Committee, Noort Committee, Drenth Committee. (2012, November 28). *Flawed science: The fraudulent research practices of social psychologist Diederik Stapel.* http://www.tilburguniversity.edu/nl/nieuws-en-agenda/finalreportLevelt.pdf

Levenson, J. M., & Sweatt, J. D. (2005). Epigenetic mechanisms in memory formation. *Nature Reviews Neuroscience, 6,* 108–118.

Levenson, R. W., Cartensen, L. L., Friesen, W. V., & Ekman, P. (1991). Emotion, physiology, and expression in old age. *Psychology and Aging, 6,* 28–35.

Levenson, R. W., Ekman, P., & Friesen, W. V. (1990). Voluntary facial action generates emotion-specific autonomic nervous system activity. *Psychophysiology, 27,* 363–384.

Levin, R., & Nielsen, T. (2009). Nightmares, bad dreams, and emotion dysregulation: A review and new neurocognitive model of dreaming. *Current Directions in Psychological Science, 18,* 84–88.

Levine, L. J., Lench, H. C., Karnaze, M. M., & Carlson, S. J. (2018). Bias in predicted and remembered emotion. *Current Opinion in Behavioral Sciences, 19,* 73–77.

Levine, R. V., & Norenzayan, A. (1999). The pace of life in 31 countries. *Journal of Cross-Cultural Psychology, 30*(2), 178–205.

Levine, T. A., Grunau, R. E., McAuliffe, F. M., Pinnamaneni, R., Foran, A., & Alderdice, F. A. (2015). Early childhood neurodevelopment after intrauterine growth restriction: A systematic review. *Pediatrics, 135*(1), 126–141. https://doi.org/10.1542/peds.2014-1143

Levy, J., Trevarthen, C., & Sperry, R. W. (1972). Perception of bilateral chimeric figures following hemispheric disconnection. *Brain, 95*, 61–78.

Lewandowsky, S., Oberauer, K., & Gignac, G. E. (2013). NASA faked the moon landing: Therefore, (climate) science is a hoax. An anatomy of the motivated rejection of science. *Psychological Science, 24*, 622–633.

Lewin, A., & Roy, K. (2020, October). Securing educational equity: Learning from the lived experiences of Black, Latino, and low-income families during the COVID-19 pandemic and beyond. *University of Maryland School of Public Health.* https://static1.squarespace.com/static/5e83a7b8388c7627b9ee5305/t/5f882437a612636f97a366aa/1602757688203/FINAL--Securing+Educational+Equity+Report+-+Black+and+Brown+Coalition+10-6-20+.pdf

Lewin, K. (1948). Resolving social conflicts: Selected papers on group dynamics. (G. W. Lewin, Ed.). Harper & Row.

Lewin, K. (1951). Behavior and development as a function of the total situation. In K. Lewin (Ed.), *Field theory in social science: Selected theoretical papers* (pp. 791–843). Harper & Row.

Lewis, M. B. (2012). Exploring the positive and negative implications of facial feedback. *Emotion, 12*(4), 852–859.

Lewis, M. D., Hibbeln, J. R., Johnson, J. E., Lin, Y. H., Hyun, D. Y., & Loewke, J. D. (2011). Suicide deaths of active-duty U. S. military and omega-3 fatty acid status: A case control comparison. *Journal of Clinical Psychiatry, 72*, 1585–1590.

Lex, C., Bazner, E., & Meyer, T.D. (2017). Does stress play a significant role in bipolar disorder? A meta-analysis. *Journal of Affective Disorders, 208*, 298–308. https://doi.org/10.1016/j.jad.2016.08.057

Li, C., Cheng, Z., Wu, T., Liang, X., Gaoshan, J., Li, L., ... Tang, K. (2017). The relationships of school-based sexuality education, sexual knowledge, and sexual behaviors: A study of 18,000 Chinese college students. *Reproductive Health, 14*, 103.

Li, G., Kung, K. F., & Hines, M. (2017). Childhood gender-typed behavior and adolescent sexual orientation: A longitudinal population-based study. *Developmental Psychology, 53*(4), 764–777. https://doi.org/10.1037/dev0000281

Li, N. P., van Vugt, M., & Colarelli, S. M. (2018). The evolutionary mismatch hypothesis: Implications for psychological science. *Current Directions in Psychological Science, 27*(1). https://doi.org/10.1177/0963721417731378

Li, N. P., Yong, J. C., Tov, W., Sng, O., Fletcher, G. J. O., Valentine, K. A., ... Balliet, D. (2013). Mate preferences do predict attraction and choices in the early stages of mate selection. *Journal of Personality and Social Psychology, 105*(5), 757–776. https://doi.org/10.1037/a0033777

Li, Y. J., Johnson, K. A., Cohen, A. B., Williams, M. J., Knowles, E. D., & Chen, Z. (2012). Fundamental(ist) attribution error: Protestants are dispositionally focused. *Journal of Personality and Social Psychology, 102*(2), 281–290. https://doi.org/10.1037/a0026294

Liberman, Z., Woodward, A. L., & Kinzler, K. D. (2017). The origins of social categorization. *Trends in Cognitive Sciences, 21*(7), 556–568. https://doi.org/10.1016/j.tics.2017.04.004

Libet, B. (1985). Unconscious cerebral initiative and the role of conscious will in voluntary action. *Behavioral and Brain Sciences, 8*, 529–566.

Lieberman, M. D., Inagaki, T. K., Tabibnia, G., & Crockett, M. J. (2011). Subjective responses to emotional stimuli during labeling, reappraisal, and distraction. *Emotion, 11*, 468–480.

Lieberman, M. D., & Rosenthal, R. (2001). Why introverts can't always tell who likes them: Multitasking and nonverbal decoding. *Journal of Personality and Social Psychology, 80*, 294–310.

Liebowitz, M. R., Gorman, J. M., Fyer, A. J., Levitt, M., Dillon, D., Levy, G., ... Davies, S. O. (1985). Lactate provocation of panic attacks: II. Biochemical and physiological findings. *Archives of General Psychiatry, 42*, 709–719.

Lilienfeld, S. O. (2007). Psychological treatments that cause harm. *Perspectives on Psychological Science, 2*, 53–70.

Lilienfeld, S. O., Lynn, S. J., & Lohr, J. M. (Eds.). (2003). *Science and pseudoscience in clinical psychology.* Guilford Press.

Lindenberger, U., & Baltes, P. B. (1994). Sensory functioning and intelligence in old age: A strong connection. *Psychology and Aging, 9*(3), 339–355. https://doi.org/10.1037/0882-7974.9.3.339

Lindenberger, U., & Baltes, P. B. (1997). Intellectual functioning in old and very old age: Cross-sectional results from the Berlin aging study. *Psychology and Aging, 12*, 410–432.

Lindquist, K., & Barrett, L. F. (2008). Constructing emotion: The experience of fear as a conceptual act. *Psychological Science, 19*, 898–903.

Lindquist, K., Wager, T., Kober, H., Bliss-Moreau, E., & Barrett, L. (2012). The brain basis of emotion: A meta-analytic review. *Behavioral and Brain Sciences, 35*(3), 121–143. https://doi.org/10.1017/S0140525X11000446

Lindquist, S. I., & McLean, J. P. (2011). Daydreaming and its correlates in an educational environment. *Learning and Individual Differences, 21*, 158–167.

Ling, X., Zheng, L., Guo, X., Li, S., Song, S., Sun, L., & Dienes, Z. (2018). Cross-cultural differences in implicit learning of chunks versus symmetries. *Royal Society Open Science, 5*, 180469. https://doi.org/10.1098/rsos.180469

Liou, A. P., Paziuk, M., Luevano, J.-M., Machineni, S., Turnbaugh, P. J., & Kaplan, L. M. (2013). Conserved shifts in the gut microbiota due to gastric bypass reduce host weight and adiposity. *Science Translational Medicine, 5*(178), 178ra41.

Liszkowski, U., Carpenter, M., Striano, T., & Tomasello, M. (2006). 12- and 18-month-olds point to provide information for others. *Journal of Cognition and Development, 7*(2), 173–187. https://doi.org/10.1207/s15327647jcd0702_2

Littlejohns, T. J., Holliday, J., Gibson, L. M., Garrat, S., Oesingmann, N., Alfaro-Almagro, F., ... & Allen, N. E. (2020). The UK Biobank imaging enhancement of 100,000 participants: Rationale, data collection, management and future directions. *Nature Communications, 11*(1), 2624. https://doi.org/10.1038/s41467-020-15948-9

Liu, D., Diorio, J., Tannenbaum, B., Caldji, C., Francis, D., Freedman, A., ... Meaney, M. J. (1997). Maternal care, hippocampal glucocorticoid receptors, and hypothalamic–pituitary–adrenal responses to stress. *Science, 277*, 1659–1662.

Liu, D., Wellman, H. M., Tardif, T., & Sabbagh, M. A. (2008). Theory of mind development in Chinese children: A meta-analysis of false belief understanding across cultures and languages. *Developmental Psychology, 44*, 523–531.

Liu, R. T., Sheehan, A. E., Walsh, R. F. L., Sanzari, S., Cheek, S. M., & Hernandez, E. M. (2019). Prevalence and correlates of non-suicidal self-injury among lesbian, gay, bisexual, and transgender individuals: A systematic review and meta-analysis. *Clinical Psychology Review, 74*, 101783. https://doi.org/10.1016/j.cpr.2019.101783

Liu, S., Ullman, T. D., Tenenbaum, J. B., & Spelke, E. S. (2017). Ten-month-old infants infer the value of goals from the costs of actions. *Science, 358*(6366), 1038–1041. https://doi.org/10.1126/science.aag2132

Livingstone, M., & Hubel, D. (1988). Segregation of form, color, movement, and depth: Anatomy, physiology, and perception. *Science, 240,* 740–749.

LoBue, C., Schaffert, J., & Cullum, C.M. (2020). Chronic traumatic encephalopathy: Understanding the facts and debate. *Current Opinion in Psychiatry, 33*(2), 130–135. https://doi.org/10.1097/YCO.0000000000000580

Locksley, A., Ortiz, V., & Hepburn, C. (1980). Social categorization and discriminatory behavior: Extinguishing the minimal intergroup discrimination effect. *Journal of Personality and Social Psychology, 39,* 773–783.

Loehlin, J. C. (1973). Blood group genes and Negro–White ability differences. *Behavior Genetics, 3*(3), 263–270.

Loftus, E. F. (1993). The reality of repressed memories. *American Psychologist, 48,* 518–537.

Loftus, E. F. (2003). Make-believe memories. *American Psychologist, 58,* 867–873.

Loftus, E. F., & Ketchum, K. (1994). *The myth of repressed memory.* St. Martin's Press.

Loftus, E. F., & Klinger, M. R. (1992). Is the unconscious smart or dumb? *American Psychologist, 47,* 761–765.

Loftus, E. F., & Pickrell, J. E. (1995). The formation of false memories. *Psychiatric Annals, 25,* 720–725.

Lonegran, M. H., Olivera-Figueroa, L. A., Pitman, R. K., & Brunet, A. (2013). Propranolol's effects on the consolidation and reconsolidation of long-term emotional memory in healthy participants: A meta-analysis. *Journal of Psychiatry & Neuroscience, 38,* 222–231.

Lopes, P. N., Grewal, D., Kadis, J., Gall, M., & Salovey, P. (2006). Emotional intelligence and positive work outcomes. *Psichothema, 18,* 132.

Lord, C. G., Ross, L., & Lepper, M. R. (1979). Biased assimilation and attitude polarization: The effects of prior theories on subsequently considered evidence. *Journal of Personality and Social Psychology, 37,* 2098–2109.

Lorenz, K. (1952). *King Solomon's ring.* Crowell.

Lovaas, O. I. (1987). Behavioral treatment and normal educational and intellectual functioning in young autistic children. *Journal of Consulting and Clinical Psychology, 55*(1), 3–9. https://doi-org.proxy1.lib.uwo.ca/10.1037/0022-006X.55.1.3

Low, J., & Watts, J. (2013). Attributing false beliefs about object identity reveals a signature blind spot in humans' efficient mind-reading system. *Psychological Science, 24*(3), 305–311. https://doi.org/10.1177/0956797612451469

Lubinski, D. (2004). Introduction to the special section on cognitive abilities: 100 years after Spearman's (1904) " 'General intelligence,' objectively determined and measured." *Journal of Personality and Social Psychology, 86*(1), 96–111. https://doi-org.ezp-prod1.hul.harvard.edu/10.1037/0022-3514.86.1.96

Lubinski, D. (2009). Cognitive epidemiology: With emphasis on untangling cognitive ability and socioeconomic status. *Intelligence, 37*(6), 625–633. https://doi.org/10.1016/j.intell.2009.09.001

Lubinski, D. (2016). From Terman to today: A century of findings on intellectual precocity. *Review of Educational Research, 86*(4), 900–944. https://doi.org/10.3102/0034654316675476

Lubinski, D., & Benbow, C. P. (2021). Intellectual precocity: What have we learned since Terman? *Gifted Child Quarterly, 65*(1), 3–28. https://doi.org/10.1177/0016986220925447

Luborsky, L., Rosenthal, R., Diguer, L., Andrusyna, T. P., Berman, J. S., Levitt, J. T., ... Krause, E. D. (2002). The dodo bird verdict is alive and well—mostly. *Clinical Psychology: Science and Practice, 9,* 2–12.

Lucas, M., Koff, E., Grossmith, S., & Migliorini, R. (2011). Sexual orientation and shifts in preferences for a partner's body attributes in short-term versus long-term mating contexts. *Psychological Reports, 108*(3), 699–710. https://doi.org/10.2466/07.PR0.108.3.699-710

Lucas, R. E., & Dyrenforth, P. S. (2005). The myth of marital bliss? *Psychological Inquiry, 16*(2/3), 111–115.

Lucas, R. E., Clark, A. E., Georgellis, Y., & Diener, E. (2003). Reexamining adaptation and the set point model of happiness: Reactions to changes in marital status. *Journal of Personality and Social Psychology, 84,* 527–539.

Ludwig, A. M. (1966). Altered states of consciousness. *Archives of General Psychiatry, 15,* 225–234.

Lunke, K., & Meier, B. (2019). Creativity and involvement in art in different types of synesthesia. *British Journal of Psychology, 110*(4), 727–744. https://doi.org/10.1111/bjop.12363

Lunke, K., & Meier, B. (2020). A persistent memory advantage is specific to grapheme-colour synesthesia. *Scientific Reports, 10*(1), 3484. https://doi.org/10.1038/s41598-020-60388-6

Lunn, P. D., Belton, C. A., Lavin, C., McGowan, F. P., Timmons, S., & Robertson, D. A. (2020). Using behavioral science to help fight the coronavirus. *Journal of Behavioral Public Administration, 3*(1), 1–15. https://doi.org/10.30636/jbpa.31.147

Luthar, S. S., & Ciciolla, L. (2016). What it feels like to be a mother: Variations by children's developmental stages. *Developmental Psychology, 52*(1), 143–154. http://doi.org/10.1037/dev0000062

Lyden, J., & Binswanger, I. A. (2019). The United States opioid epidemic. *Seminars in Perinatology.* https://doi.10.1053/j.semperi.2019.01.001

Lyle, K. B., Bego, C. R., Hopkins, R. F., Hieb, J. L., & Ralston, P. A. S. (2020). How the amount and spacing of retrieval practice affect the short- and long-term retention of mathematics knowledge. *Educational Psychology Review, 32,* 277–295. https://doi.org/10.1007/s10648-019-09489-x

Lynn, M., & Shurgot, B. A. (1984). Responses to lonely hearts advertisements: Effects of reported physical attractiveness, physique, and coloration. *Personality and Social Psychology Bulletin, 10,* 349–357.

Lynn, R. (2009). What has caused the Flynn effect? Secular increases in the development quotients of infants. *Intelligence, 37*(1), 16–24.

Lynn, R. (2013). *Who discovered the Flynn effect? A review of early studies of the secular increase of intelligence.* https://doi.org/10.1016/j.intell.2013.03.008

Lyons, D. E., Young, A. G., & Keil, F. C. (2007). The hidden structure of overimitation. *Proceedings of the National Academy of Sciences, 104*(50), 19751–19756. https://doi.org/10.1073/pnas.0704452104

Lyubomirsky, S. (2008). *The how of happiness: A scientific approach to getting the life you want.* Penguin.

Mac Giollabhui, N., Hamilton, J. L., Nielsen, J., Connolly, S. L., Stange, J. P., Varga, S., ... Alloy, L. B. (2018). Negative cognitive style interacts with negative life events to predict first onset of a major depressive episode in adolescence via hopelessness. *Journal of Abnormal Psychology, 127*(1), 1–11. https://doi.org/10.1037/abn0000301

MacCann, C., Joseph, D. L., Newman, D. A., & Roberts, R. D. (2014). Emotional intelligence is a second-stratum factor of intelligence: Evidence from hierarchical and bifactor models. *Emotion, 14*(2), 358–374. https://doi.org/10.1037/a0034755

MacDonald, S., Uesiliana, K., & Hayne, H. (2000). Cross-cultural and gender differences in childhood amnesia. *Memory, 8,* 365–376.

MacGregor, J. N., Ormerod, T. C., & Chronicle, E. P. (2001). Information processing and insight: A process model of performance on the nine-dot and related problems. *Journal of Experimental Psychology: Learning, Memory, and Cognition, 27,* 176–201.

Maclean, P. D. (1970). The triune brain, emotion, and scientific bias. In F. O. Schmitt (Ed.), *The neurosciences: A second study program* (pp. 336–349). Rockefeller University Press.

MacLeod, M. D. (2002). Retrieval-induced forgetting in eyewitness memory: Forgetting as a consequence of remembering. *Applied Cognitive Psychology, 16,* 135–149.

MacLeod, M. D., & Saunders, J. (2008). Retrieval inhibition and memory distortion: Negative consequences of an adaptive process. *Current Directions in Psychological Science, 17,* 26–30.

Macmillan, M. (2000). *An odd kind of fame: Stories of Phineas Gage.* MIT Press.

Macmillan, N. A., & Creelman, C. D. (2005). *Detection theory.* Erlbaum.

Macrae, C. N., Bodenhausen, G. V., Milne, A. B., & Jetten, J. (1994). Out of mind but back in sight: Stereotypes on the rebound. *Journal of Personality and Social Psychology, 67,* 808–817.

Madden, D. J., Turkington, T. G., Provenzale, J. M., Denny, L. L., Hawk, T. C., Gottlob, L. R., & Coleman, R. E. (1999). Adult age differences in the functional neuroanatomy of verbal recognition memory. *Human Brain Mapping, 7*(2), 115–135. https://doi.org/10.1002/(sici)1097-0193(1999)7:2<115::aid-hbm5>3.0.co;2-n

Maddi, S. R., Harvey, R. H., Khoshaba, D. M., Fazel, M., & Resurreccion, N. (2009). Hardiness training facilitates performance in college. *Journal of Positive Psychology, 4,* 566–577.

Maddi, S. R., Kahn, S., & Maddi, K. L. (1998). The effectiveness of hardiness training. *Consulting Psychology Journal: Practice and Research, 50,* 78–86.

Maddux, W. W., Mullen, E., & Galinsky, A. D. (2008). Chameleons bake bigger pies and take bigger pieces: Strategic behavioral mimicry facilitates negotiation outcomes. *Journal of Experimental Social Psychology, 44,* 461–468.

Madigan, S., Atkinson, L., Laurin, K., & Benoit, D. (2013). Attachment and internalizing behavior in early childhood: A meta-analysis. *Developmental Psychology, 49*(4), 672–689. https://doi.org/10.1037/a0028793

Madore K. P., Khazenzon, A. M., Backes, C. W., Jiang, J., Uncapher, M. R., Norcia, A. M., & Wagner A. D. (2020). Memory failure predicted by attention lapsing and media multitasking. *Nature, 587*(7832), 87–91. https://doi.org/10.1038/s41586-020-2870-z

Madore, K. P., Addis, D., & Schacter, D. L. (2015). Creativity and memory: Effects of an episodic specificity induction on divergent thinking. *Psychological Science, 26,* 1461–1468.

Madore, K. P., Thakral, P. P., Beaty, R. E., Addis, D. R., & Schacter, D. L. (2019). Neural mechanisms of episodic retrieval support divergent creative thinking. *Cerebral Cortex, 29,* 150–166.

Maenner, M. J., Shaw, K. A., Bakian, A. V., Bilder, D. A., Durkin, M. S., Esler, A., … Cogswell, M. E. (2021). Prevalence and characteristics of autism spectrum disorder among children aged 8 years: Autism and Developmental Disabilities Monitoring Network, 11 sites. United States, 2018. *MMWR Surveillance Summary, 70*(SS-11), 1–16. https://doi.org/10.15585/mmwr.ss7011a1

Maes, M. (1995). Evidence for an immune response in major depression: A review and hypothesis. *Progress in Neuro-Psychopharmacology and Biological Psychiatry, 19,* 11–38.

Maguire, E. A., Gadian, D. G., Johnsrude, I. S., Good, C. D., Ashburner, J., Frackowiak, R. S. J. & Frith, C. D. (2000). Navigation-related structural change in the hippocampi of taxi drivers. *Proceedings of the National Academy of Sciences, 97*(8), 4398–4403. https://doi.org/10.1073/pnas.070039597

Maguire, E. A., Woollett, K., & Spiers, H. J. (2006). London taxi drivers and bus drivers: A structural MRI and neuropsychological analysis. *Hippocampus, 16,* 1091–1101.

Mahajan, N., Martinez, M. A., Gutierrez, N. L., Diesendruck, G., Banaji, M. R., & Santos, L. R. (2011). The evolution of intergroup bias: Perceptions and attitudes in rhesus macaques. *Journal of Personality and Social Psychology, 100*(3), 387–405. https://doi.org/10.1037/a0022459

Mahon, B. Z., Anzellotti, S., Schwarzbach, J., Zampini, M., & Caramazza, A. (2009). Category-specific organization in the human brain does not require visual experience. *Neuron, 63,* 397–405.

Mahowald, M., & Schenck, C. (2000). REM sleep parasomnias. In M. Kryger, T. Roth, & W. Dement (Eds.), *Principles and practices of sleep medicine* (3rd ed., pp. 724–741). Saunders.

Maier, S. F., & Watkins, L. R. (1998). Cytokines for psychologists: Implications of bidirectional immune-to-brain communication for understanding behavior, mood, and cognition. *Psychological Review, 105,* 83–107.

Maier, S. F., & Watkins, L. R. (2000). The immune system as a sensory system: Implications for psychology. *Current Directions in Psychological Science, 9,* 98–102.

Maillet, D., Beaty, R. E., Jordano, M. L., Touron, D. R., Adnan, A., Silvia, P. J., … Kane, M. J. (2018). Age-related differences in mind-wandering in daily life. *Psychology and Aging, 33*(4), 643–653. https://doi.org/10.1037/pag0000260

Major, B., Mendes, W. B., & Dovidio, J. F. (2013). Intergroup relations and health disparities: A social psychological perspective. *Health Psychology, 32,* 514–524.

Major, B., Spencer, S., Schmader, T., Wolfe, C., & Crocker, J. (1998). Coping with negative stereotypes about intellectual performance: The role of psychological disengagement. *Personality and Social Psychology Bulletin, 24*(1), 34–50. https://doi.org/10.1177/0146167298241003

Makel, M. C., Kell, H. J., Lubinski, D., Putallaz, M., & Benbow, C. P. (2016). When lightning strikes twice: Profoundly gifted, profoundly accomplished. *Psychological Science, 27*(7), 1004–1018. https://doi.org/10.1177/0956797616644735

Makin, J. E., Fried, P. A., & Watkinson, B. (1991). A comparison of active and passive smoking during pregnancy: Long-term effects. *Neurotoxicology and Teratology, 16,* 5–12.

Makris, N., Biederman, J., Monuteaux, M. C., & Seidman, L. J. (2009). Towards conceptualizing a neural systems-based anatomy of attention-deficit/hyperactivity disorder. *Developmental Neuroscience, 31,* 36–49.

Malanchini, M., Rimfeld, K., Allegrini, A. G., Ritchie, S. J., & Plomin, R. (2020, April). Cognitive ability and education: How behavioural genetic research has advanced our knowledge and understanding of their association. *Neuroscience & Biobehavioral Reviews, 111,* 229–245. https://doi.org/10.1016/j.neubiorev.2020.01.016

Malina, R. M., Bouchard, C., & Beunen, G. (1988). Human growth: Selected aspects of current research on well-nourished children. *Annual Review of Anthropology, 17,* 187–219.

Malooly, A. M., Genet, J. J., & Siemer, M. (2013). Individual differences in reappraisal effectiveness: The role of affective flexibility. *Emotion, 13*(2), 302–313. https://doi.org/10.1037/a0029980

Mampe, B., Friederici, A. D., Christophe, A., & Wermke, K. (2009). Newborns' cry melody is shaped by their native language. *Current Biology, 19,* 1–4.

Mandler, G. (1967). Organization and memory. In K. W. Spence & J. T. Spence (Eds.), *The psychology of learning and motivation* (Vol. 1, pp. 327–372). Academic Press.

Mandy, W., & Lai, M. C. (2016). The role of the environment in the developmental psychopathology of autism spectrum condition. *Journal of Child Psychology and Psychiatry, 57,* 271–292.

Mann, J. J. (2005). The medical management of depression. *New England Journal of Medicine, 353,* 1819–1834.

Mann, J. J., Apter, A., Bertolote, J., Beautrais, A., Currier, D., Haas, A., ... Hendin, H. (2005). Suicide prevention strategies: A systematic review. *Journal of the American Medical Association, 294*(16), 2064–2074. doi:10.1001/jama.294.16.2064

Marangell, L. B., Silver, J. M., Goff, D. M., & Yudofsky, S. C. (2003). Psychopharmacology and electroconvulsive therapy. In R. E. Hales & S. C. Yudofsky (Eds.), *The American Psychiatric Publishing textbook of clinical psychiatry* (4th ed., pp. 1047–1149). American Psychiatric Publishing.

Marci, C. D., Ham, J., Moran, E., & Orr, S. P. (2007). Physiologic correlates of perceived therapist empathy and social-emotional process during psychotherapy. *Journal of Nervous and Mental Disease, 195,* 103–111.

Marcia, J. E. (1966). Development and validation of ego-identity status. *Journal of Personality and Social Psychology, 3,* 551–558. https://doi.org/10.1037/h0023281

Marcia, J. E. (1993). The ego identity status approach to ego identity. In J. E. Marcia, A. S. Waterman, D. R. Matteson, S. L. Archer, & J. L. Orlofsky (Eds.), *Ego identity: A handbook for psychosocial research* (pp. 3–21). Springer.

Marcus, G. B. (1986). Stability and change in political attitudes: Observe, recall, and "explain." *Political Behavior, 8,* 21–44.

Marcus, G. (2012, December 3). Neuroscience fiction. *New Yorker.* http://www.newyorker.com/news/news-desk/neuroscience-fiction

Marcussen, K., Gallagher, M., & Ritter, C. (2019). Mental illness as a stigmatized identity. *Society and Mental Health, 9*(3), 211–227. https://doi.org/10.1177/2156869318810326

Margoni, F., & Surian, L. (2018). Infants' evaluation of prosocial and antisocial agents: A meta-analysis. *Developmental Psychology, 54,* 1445–1455.

Markel, H. (2011). *An anatomy of addiction: Sigmund Freud, William Halsted, and the miracle drug cocaine.* Pantheon.

Markus, H. (1977). Self-schemata and processing information about the self. *Journal of Personality and Social Psychology, 35,* 63–78.

Marlatt, G. A., & Rohsenow, D. (1980). Cognitive processes in alcohol use: Expectancy and the balanced placebo design. In N. K. Mello (Ed.), *Advances in substance abuse: Behavioral and biological research* (pp. 159–199). JAI Press.

Marsh, A. (2017). *The fear factor: How one emotion connects altruists, psychopaths and everyone in-between.* Robinson

Marsh, A. A., Rhoads, S. A., & Ryan, R. M. (2018). A multi-semester classroom demonstration yields evidence in support of the facial feedback effect. *Emotion.* https://doi.org/10.1037/emo0000532

Marshall, M. (2021). COVID's toll on smell and taste: What scientists know. *Nature, 589,* 342–343.

Marsolek, C. J. (1995). Abstract visual-form representations in the left cerebral hemispheres. *Journal of Experimental Psychology: Human Perception and Performance, 21,* 375–386.

Martin, A. (2007). The representation of object concepts in the brain. *Annual Review of Psychology, 58,* 25–45.

Martin, A., & Caramazza, A. (2003). Neuropsychological and neuroimaging perspectives on conceptual knowledge: An introduction. *Cognitive Neuropsychology, 20,* 195–212.

Martin, A., & Chao, L. L. (2001). Semantic memory and the brain: Structure and processes. *Current Opinion in Neurobiology, 11,* 194–201.

Martin, J., Rychlowska, M., Wood, A., & Niedenthal, P. (2017). Smiles as multipurpose social signals. *Trends in Cognitive Sciences, 21*(11), 864–877. https://doi.org/10.1016/j.tics.2017.08.007

Martin, M. J., Blozis, S. A., Boeninger, D. K., Masarik, A. S., & Conger, R. D. (2014). The timing of entry into adult roles and changes in trajectories of problem behaviors during the transition to adulthood. *Developmental Psychology, 50*(11), 2473–2484. https://doi.org/10.1037/a0037950

Martins, S. S., Sampson, L., Cerda, M., & Galea, S. (2015). Worldwide prevalence and trends in unintentional drug overdose: A systematic review of the literature. *American Journal of Public Health, 105,* E29–E49.

Martland, H. S. (1928). Punch drunk. *Journal of the American Medical Association, 91*(15), 1103–1107. https://doi.org/10.1001/jama.1928.02700150029009

Marucha, P. T., Kiecolt-Glaser, J. K., & Favagehi, M. (1998). Mucosal wound healing is impaired by examination stress. *Psychosomatic Medicine, 60,* 362–365.

Marufu, T. C., Ahankari, A., Coleman, T., & Lewis, S. (2015). Maternal smoking and the risk of stillbirth: Systematic review and meta-analysis. *BMC Public Health, 15*(1), 239. https://doi.org/10.1186/s12889-015-1552-5

Marzuk, P. M., Tardiff, K., Leon, A. C., Hirsch, C., Portera, L., Iqbal, M. I., ... Hartwell, N. (1998). Ambient temperature and mortality from unintentional cocaine overdose. *Journal of the American Medical Association, 279,* 1795–1800.

Masek, L. R., Paterson, S. J., Golinkoff, R. M., Bakeman, R., Adamson, L. B., Owen, M. T., ... Hirsh-Pasek, K. (2021). Beyond talk: Contributions of quantity and quality of communication to language success across socioeconomic strata. *Infancy, 236*(1), 123–147. https://10.1111/infa.12378

Maslach, C. (2003). Job burnout: New directions in research and intervention. *Current Directions in Psychological Science, 12,* 189–192.

Maslow, A. H. (1937). Dominance-feeling, behavior, and status. In R. J. Lowry (Ed.), *Dominance, self-esteem, self-actualization: Germinal papers by A. H. Maslow* (pp. 49–70). Brooks-Cole.

Maslow, A. H. (1954). *Motivation and personality.* Harper & Row.

Maslow, A. (1943). A theory of human motivation. *Psychological Review, 50,* 370–396.

Mason, M. F., Norton, M. I., Van Horn, J. D., Wegner, D. M., Grafton, S. T., & Macrae, C. N. (2007). Wandering minds: The default network and stimulus-independent thought. *Science, 3154,* 393–395.

Masten, A. S. (2004). Family therapy as a treatment for children: A critical review of outcome research. *Family Process, 18,* 323–335.

Masters, W. H., & Johnson, V. E. (1966). *Human sexual response.* Little, Brown.

Masuda, T., & Nisbett, R. E. (2001). Attending holistically versus analytically: Comparing the context sensitivity of Japanese and Americans. *Journal of Personality and Social Psychology, 81*(5), 922–934. https://doi.org/10.1037//0022-3514.81.5.922

Mather, M., Canli, T., English, T., Whitfield, S., Wais, P., Ochsner, K., ... Cartensen, L. L. (2004). Amygdala responses to emotionally valenced stimuli in older and younger adults. *Psychological Science, 15,* 259–263.

Mather, M., & Carstensen, L. L. (2005). Aging and motivated cognition: The positivity effect in attention and memory. *Trends in Cognitive Sciences, 9*(10), 496–502.

Mathur, M. B., & VanderWeele, T. J. (2019). Finding common ground in meta-analysis "wars" on violent video games. *Perspectives on Psychological Science, 14*(4), 705–708. https://doi.org/10.1177/1745691619850104

Matsumoto, D., & Willingham, B. (2009). Spontaneous facial expressions of emotion of congenitally and noncongenitally blind individuals. *Journal of Personality and Social Psychology, 96*, 1–10.

Mattar, A. A. G., & Gribble, P. L. (2005). Motor learning by observing. *Neuron, 46*, 153–160.

Matthews, G., & Gilliland, K. (1999). The personality theories of H. J. Eysenck and J. A. Gray: A comparative review. *Personality and Individual Differences, 26*, 583–626.

Mattson, C. L., Tanz, L. J., Quinn, K., Kariisa, M., Patel, P., & Davis, N. L. (2021). Trends and geographic patterns in drug and synthetic opioid overdose deaths: United States, 2013–2019. *MMWR. Morbidity and Mortality Weekly Report, 70*(6), 202–207. https://http://dx.doi.org/10.15585/mmwr.mm7006a4

Matzel, L. D., Han, Y. R., Grossman, H., Karnik, M. S., Patel, D., Scott, N., ... Gandhi, C. C. (2003). Individual differences in the expression of a general learning ability in mice. *Journal of Neuroscience, 23*(16), 6423–6433.

Maudsley, H. (1886). *Natural causes and supernatural seemings.* Kegan Paul, Trench.

Mauss, I. B., & Robinson, M. D. (2009). Measures of emotion: A review. *Cognition and Emotion, 23*, 209–237.

Mauss, I. B., Levenson, R. W., McCarter, L., Wilhelm, F. H., & Gross, J. J. (2005). The tie that binds? Coherence among emotion experience, behavior, and physiology. *Emotion, 5*(2), 175–190. https://doi.org/10.1037/1528-3542.5.2.175

Max, A. (2006, September 16). Dutch reach new heights. *USA Today.* http://usatoday30.usatoday.com/news/offbeat/2006-09-16-dutch-tall_x.htm

May, R. (1983). *The discovery of being: Writings in existential psychology.* Norton.

May, T., Brignell, A., & Williams, K. (2021). Parent-reported autism diagnostic stability and trajectories in the Longitudinal Study of Australian Children. *Autism Research, 14*(4), 773–786. https://doi.org/10.1002/aur.2470

Mayberg, H., Lozano, A., Voon, V., McNeely, H., Seminowicz, D., Hamani, C., ... Kennedy, S. H. (2005). Deep brain stimulation for treatment-resistant depression. *Neuron, 45*, 651–660.

Mayer, J. D., Caruso, D. R., & Salovey, P. (1999). Emotional intelligence meets traditional standards for an intelligence. *Intelligence, 27*, 267.

Mayer, J. D., Caruso, D. R., Zigler, E., & Dreyden, J. I. (1989). Intelligence and intelligence-related personality traits. *Intelligence, 13*(2), 119–133. https://doi.org/10.1016/0160-2896(89)90011-1

Mayer, J. D., Roberts, R. D., & Barsade, S. G. (2008). Human abilities: Emotional intelligence. *Annual Review of Psychology, 59*, 507–536.

Maynard-Smith, J. (1965). The evolution of alarm calls. *American Naturalist, 100*, 637–650.

Mayr, E. (1942). *Systematics and the origin of species, from the viewpoint of a zoologist.* Columbia University Press.

McClelland, D. C., Atkinson, J. W., Clark, R. A., & Lowell, E. L. (1953). *The achievement motive.* Appleton-Century-Crofts.

McDaniel, M. A., Thomas, R. C., Agarwal, P. K., McDermott, K. B., & Roediger, H. L. (2013). Quizzing in middle-school science: Successful transfer performance on classroom exams. *Applied Cognitive Psychology, 27*, 360–372.

McDermott, K. B. (2021). Practicing retrieval facilitates learning. *Annual Review of Psychology, 72*, 609–633. https://doi.org/10.1146/annurev-psych-010419-051019

McDermott, K. B., Agarwal, P. K., D'Antonio, L., Roediger, H. L., & McDaniel, M. A. (2014). Both multiple-choice and short-answer quizzes enhance later exam performance in middle and high school classes. *Journal of Experimental Psychology: Applied, 20*, 3–21.

McDonald, A., Haslam, C., Yates, P., Gurr, B., Leeder, G., & Sayers, A. (2011). Google Calendar: A new memory aid to compensate for prospective memory deficits following acquired brain injury. *Neuropsychological Rehabilitation, 21*, 784–807.

McElwain, N. L., Booth-LaForce, C., & Wu, X. (2011). Infant–mother attachment and children's friendship quality: Maternal mental state talk as an intervening mechanism. *Developmental Psychology, 47*(5), 1295–1311. https://doi.org/10.1037/a0024094

McEvoy, S. P., Stevenson, M. R., McCartt, A. T., Woodward, M., Haworth, C., Palamara, P., & Circarelli, R. (2005). Role of mobile phones in motor vehicle crashes resulting in hospital attendance: A case-crossover study. *British Medical Journal, 331*, 428–430.

McFarlane, A. H., Norman, G. R., Streiner, D. L., Roy, R., & Scott, D. J. (1980). A longitudinal study of the influence of the psychosocial environment on health status: A preliminary report. *Journal of Health and Social Behavior, 21*, 124–133.

McGarty, C., & Turner, J. C. (1992). The effects of categorization on social judgement. *British Journal of Social Psychology, 31*, 253–268.

McGaugh, J. L. (2000). Memory: A century of consolidation. *Science, 287*, 248–251.

McGaugh, J. L. (2006). Make mild moments memorable: Add a little arousal. *Trends in Cognitive Sciences, 10*, 345–347.

McGaugh, J. L. (2015). Consolidating memories. *Annual Review of Psychology, 66*, 1–24.

McGovern, P. E., Zhang, J., Tang, J., Zhang, Z., Hall, G. R., Moreau, R. A., ... Wang, C. (2004). Fermented beverages of pre- and proto-historic China. *Proceedings of the National Academy of Sciences, USA, 101*, 17593–17598.

McGowan, P. O., Sasaki, A., D'Alessio, A. D., Dymov, S., Labonté, B., Szyf, M., ... Meaney, M. J. (2009). Epigenetic regulation of the glucocorticoid receptor in human brain associates with childhood abuse. *Nature Neuroscience, 12*, 342–348.

McGowan, P. O., Suderman, M., Sasaki, A., Huang, T. C. T., Hallett, M., Meaney, J. J., & Szyf, M. (2011). Broad epigenetic signature of maternal care in the brain of adult rats. *PLoS ONE, 6*(2), e14739. https://doi.org/10.1371/journal.pone.0014739

McGrath, J., Saha, S., Chant, D., & Welham, J. (2008). Schizophrenia: A concise overview of incidence, prevalence, and mortality. *Epidemiologic Reviews, 30*, 67–76.

McGue, M., & Bouchard, T. J. (1998). Genetic and environmental influences on human behavioral differences. *Annual Review of Neuroscience, 21*, 1–24.

McGuire, P. K., Shah, G. M., & Murray, R. M. (1993). Increased blood flow in Broca's area during auditory hallucinations in schizophrenia. *Lancet, 342*, 703–706.

McIntyre, S. H., & Munson, J. M. (2008). Exploring cramming: Student behaviors, beliefs, and learning retention in the Principles of Marketing course. *Journal of Marketing Education, 30*, 226–243.

McKee, A. C. (2020). The neuropathology of chronic traumatic encephalopathy: The status of the literature. *Seminars in Neurology, 40*(4), 359–369. https://doi.org/10.1055/s-0040-1713632

McKee, A. C., Cantu, R. C., Nowinski, C. J., Hedley-Whyte, E. T., Gavett, B. E., Budson, A. E., ... Stern, R. A. (2009). Chronic traumatic encephalopathy in athletes: Progressive tauopathy after repetitive head injury. *Journal of Neuropathology and Experimental Neurology, 68*, 709–735.

McKetin, R., Ward, P. B., Catts, S. V., Mattick, R. P., & Bell, J. R. (1999). Changes in auditory selective attention and event-related potentials following oral administration of D-amphetamine in humans. *Neuropsychopharmacology, 21,* 380–390.

McLaughlin, K. A., Nandi, A., Keyes, K. M., Uddin, M., Aiello, A. E., Galea, S., & Koenen, K. C. (2012). Home foreclosure and risk of psychiatric morbidity during the recent financial crisis. *Psychological Medicine, 42,* 1441–1448.

McLean, K. C. (2008). The emergence of narrative identity. *Social and Personality Psychology Compass, 2*(4), 1685–1702.

McMahon, C. A., & Bernier, A. (2017). Twenty years of research on parental mind-mindedness: Empirical findings, theoretical and methodological challenges, and new directions. *Developmental Review, 46,* 54–80. https://doi.org/10.1016/J.DR.2017.07.001

McNally, R. J. (2021). Are memories of sexual trauma fragmented? *Memory.* https://doi.org/10.1080/09658211.2020.1871023

McNally, R. J. (2003). *Remembering trauma.* Belknap Press of Harvard University Press.

McNally, R. J., & Clancy, S. A. (2005). Sleep paralysis, sexual abuse, and space alien abduction. *Transcultural Psychiatry, 42,* 113–122.

McNally, R. J., & Geraerts, E. (2009). A new solution to the recovered memory debate. *Perspective on Psychological Science, 4,* 126–134.

McNamara, R. A., Willard, A. K., Norenzayan, A., & Henrich, J. (2019). Weighing outcome vs. intent across societies: How cultural models of mind shape moral reasoning. *Cognition, 182,* 95–108. https://doi.org/10.1016/j.cognition.2018.09.008

McPhetres, J., & Zuckerman, M. (2017). Religious people endorse different standards of evidence when evaluating religious versus scientific claims. *Social Psychology and Personality Science, 8,* 836–842.

Mead, G. H. (1934). *Mind, self, and society.* University of Chicago Press.

Meade, M. L., Harris, C. B., Van Bergen, P., Sutton, J., & Barnier, A. J. (Eds.). (2018). *Collaborative remembering: Theories, research and applications.* Oxford University Press.

Meaidi, A., Jennum, P., Ptito, M., & Kupers, R. (2014). The sensory construction of dreams and nightmare frequency in congenitally blind and late blind individuals. *Sleep Medicine, 15,* 586–595.

Mechelli, A., Crinion, J. T., Noppeney, U., O'Doherty, J., Ashburner, J., Frackowiak, R. S., & Price, C. J. (2004). Neurolinguistics: Structural plasticity in the bilingual brain. *Nature, 431,* 757.

Meder, D., Herz, D. M., Rowe, J. B., Lehericy, S., & Hartwig, R. S. (2019). The role of dopamine in the brain: Lessons learned from Parkinson's disease. *NeuroImage, 190,* 79–93. https://doi.org/10.1016/j.neuroimage.2018.11.021

Medin, D. L., & Schaffer, M. M. (1978). Context theory of classification learning. *Psychological Review, 85,* 207–238.

Medvec, V. H., Madey, S. F., & Gilovich, T. (1995). When less is more: Counterfactual thinking and satisfaction among Olympic medalists. *Journal of Personality and Social Psychology, 69*(4), 603–610.

Mehl, M. R., Vazire, S., Ramirez-Esparza, N., Slatcher, R. B., & Pennebaker, J. W. (2007). Are women really more talkative than men? *Science, 317,* 82.

Mehu, M., & Scherer, K. R. (2015). Emotion categories and dimensions in the facial communication of affect: An integrated approach. *Emotion, 15*(6), 798–811. https://doi.org/10.1037/a0039416

Meindl, J. N., & Casey, L. B. (2012). Increasing the suppressive effect of delayed punishers: A review of basic and applied literature. *Behavioral Interventions, 27,* 129–150.

Meins, E. (2003). Emotional development and attachment relationships. In A. Slater & G. Bremner (Eds.), *An introduction to developmental psychology* (pp. 141–164). Blackwell.

Meins, E., Fernyhough, C., Fradley, E., & Tuckey, M. (2001). Rethinking maternal sensitivity: Mothers' comments on infants' mental processes predict security of attachment at 12 months. *Journal of Child Psychology & Psychiatry & Allied Disciplines, 42,* 637–648.

Mellon, R. C. (2009). Superstitious perception: Response-independent reinforcement and punishment as determinants of recurring eccentric interpretations. *Behaviour Research and Therapy, 47,* 868–875.

Meltzer, A. L., McNulty, J. K., Jackson, G. L., & Karney, B. R. (2014). Sex differences in the implications of partner physical attractiveness for the trajectory of marital satisfaction. *Journal of Personality and Social Psychology, 106*(3), 418–428. https://doi.org/10.1037/a0034424

Meltzer, H. Y. (2013). Update on typical and atypical antipsychotic drugs. *Annual Review of Medicine, 64,* 393–406.

Meltzoff, A. N. (1995). Understanding the intentions of others: Reenactment of intended acts by 18-month-old children. *Developmental Psychology, 31,* 838–850.

Meltzoff, A. N. (2007). "Like me": A foundation for social cognition. *Developmental Science, 10*(1), 126–134. https://doi.org/10.1111/j.1467-7687.2007.00574x

Meltzoff, A. N., & Moore, M. K. (1977). Imitation of facial and manual gestures by human neonates. *Science, 198,* 75–78.

Meltzoff, A. N., Kuhl, P. K., Movellan, J., & Sejnowski, T. J. (2009). Foundations for a new science of learning. *Science, 325,* 284–288.

Meltzoff, A. N., Murray, L., Simpson, E., Heimann, M., Nagy, E., Nadel, J., … Ferrari, P. F. (2018). Re-examination of Oostenbroek et al. (2016): Evidence for neonatal imitation of tongue protrusion. *Developmental Science, 21,* 1–8.

Melzack, R., & Wall, P. D. (1965). Pain mechanisms: A new theory. *Science, 150,* 971–979.

Mendes, W. B., Blascovich, J., Hunter, S. B., Lickel, B., & Jost, J. T. (2007). Threatened by the unexpected: Physiological responses during social interactions with expectancy-violating partners. *Journal of Personality and Social Psychology, 92,* 698–716.

Mendes, W. B., Blascovich, J., Lickel, B., & Hunter, S. (2002). Challenge and threat during social interaction with White and Black men. *Personality & Social Psychology Bulletin, 28,* 939–952.

Mendle, J. (2014). Beyond pubertal timing: New directions for studying individual differences in development. *Current Directions in Psychological Science, 23*(3), 215–219. https://doi.org/10.1177/0963721414530144

Mendle, J., Harden, K. P., Brooks-Gunn, J., & Graber, J. A. (2010). Development's tortoise and hare: Pubertal timing, pubertal tempo, and depressive symptoms in boys and girls. *Developmental Psychology, 46*(5), 1341–1353. https://doi.org/10.1037/a0020205

Mendle, J., Ryan, R. M., & McKone, K. M. P. (2018). Age at menarche, depression, and antisocial behavior in adulthood. *Pediatrics, 141*(1), e20171703.

Mendle, J., Turkheimer, E., & Emery, R. E. (2007). Detrimental psychological outcomes associated with early pubertal timing in adolescent girls. *Developmental Review, 27,* 151–171.

Mendoza-Denton, R. (2014). A social psychological perspective on the achievement gap in standardized test performance between White and minority students: Implications for assessment. *Journal of Negro Education, 83*(4), 465–484. https://doi.org/10.7709/jnegroeducation.83.4.0465

Merikangas, K. R., Wicki, W., & Angst, J. (1994). Heterogeneity of depression: Classification of depressive subtype by longitudinal course. *British Journal of Psychiatry, 164,* 342–348.

Mervis, C. B., & Bertrand, J. (1994). Acquisition of the Novel Name–Nameless Category (N3C) principle. *Child Development, 65,* 1646–1662. doi:10.2307/1131285

Merzenich, M. M., Recanzone, G. H., Jenkins, W. M., & Grajski, K. A. (1990). Adaptive mechanisms in cortical networks underlying cortical contributions to learning and nondeclarative memory. *Cold Spring Harbor Symposia on Quantitative Biology, 55,* 873–887.

Mesoudi, A., Chang, L., Dall, S. R. X., & Thornton, A. (2015). The evolution of individual and cultural variation in social learning. *Trends in Ecology & Evolution, 31,* 215–225.

Messick, D. M., & Cook, K. S. (1983). *Equity theory: Psychological and sociological perspectives.* Praeger.

Meston, C. M., & Buss, D. M. (2007). Why humans have sex. *Archives of Sexual Behavior, 36,* 477–507.

Mestre, J. M., Guil, R., Lopes, P. N., Salovey, P., & Gil-Olarte, P. (2006). Emotional intelligence and social and academic adaptation to school. *Psicothema, 18,* 112.

Metcalfe, J. (2009). Metacognitive judgments and control of study. *Current Directions in Psychological Science, 18,* 159–163.

Metcalfe, J., & Finn, B. (2008). Evidence that judgments of learning are causally related to study choice. *Psychonomic Bulletin & Review, 15,* 174–179.

Metcalfe, J., & Wiebe, D. (1987). Intuition in insight and noninsight problem solving. *Memory & Cognition, 15,* 238–246.

Methven, L., Allen, V. J., Withers, G. A., & Gosney, M. A. (2012). Ageing and taste. *Proceedings of the Nutrition Society, 71,* 556–565.

Meuret, A. E., Kroll, J., & Ritz, T. (2017). Panic disorder comorbidity with medical conditions and treatment implications. *Annual Review of Clinical Psychology, 13,* 209–240.

Meyer, M. L. (2019). Social by default: Characterizing the social function of the resting brain. *Current Directions in Psychological Science, 28*(4), 380–386. https://doi.org/10.1177/0963721419857759

Meyer-Bahlberg, H. F. L., Ehrhardt, A. A., Rosen, L. R., & Gruen, R. S. (1995). Prenatal estrogens and the development of homosexual orientation. *Developmental Psychology, 31,* 12–21.

Mez, J., Daneshvar, D. H., Kiernan, P. T., Abdolmohammadi, B., Alvarez, V. E., Huber, B. R., ... McKee, A. C. (2017). Clinicopathological evaluation of chronic traumatic encephalopathy in players of American football. *Journal of the American Medical Association, 318,* 360–370.

Michaela, R., Florian, S., Gert, G. W., & Ulman, L. (2009). Seeking pleasure and seeking pain: Differences in prohedonic and contrahedonic motivation from adolescence to old age. *Psychological Science, 20*(12), 1529–1535.

Miech, R. A., Johnston, L. D., O'Malley, P. M., Bachman, J. G., Schulenberg, J. E., & Patrick, M. E. (2018). Monitoring the Future national survey results on drug use, 1975–2017: Volume I. Secondary school students. Institute for Social Research, University of Michigan. http://monitoringthefuture.org/pubs.html

Miettunen, J., Immonen, J., McGrath, J. J., Isohanni, M., & Jääskeläinen, E. (2018). The age of onset of schizophrenia spectrum disorders. In G. de Girolamo, P. McGorry, & N. Sartorius (Eds.), *Age of onset of mental disorders* (pp. 55–73). Springer.

Miguel, A. Q. C., McPherson, S. M., Simões, V., Yamauchi, R., Madruga, C. S., Smith, C. L., ... Mari, J. J. (2022). Effectiveness of incorporating contingency management into a public treatment program for people who use crack cocaine in Brazil. A single-blind

randomized controlled trial. *International Journal of Drug Policy, 99,* 103464. https://doi.org/10.1016/j.drugpo.2021.103464

Mikels, J. A., & Shuster, M. M. (2016). The interpretative lenses of older adults are not rose-colored—just less dark: Aging and the interpretation of ambiguous scenarios. *Emotion, 16*(1), 94–100.

Mikkola, S., Salonen, M., Hakanen, E., Sulkama, S., & Lohi, H. (2021). Reliability and validity of seven feline behavior and personality traits. *Animals, 11*(7), 1991. https://doi.org/10.3390/ani11071991

Miklowitz, D. J., & Johnson, S. L. (2006). The psychopathology and treatment of bipolar disorder. *Annual Review of Clinical Psychology, 2,* 199–235.

Mikolajczak, M., Avalosse, H., Vancorenland, S., Verniest, R., Callens, M., van Broeck, N., ... Mierop, A. (2015). A nationally representative study of emotional competence and health. *Emotion, 15*(5), 653–667. https://doi.org/10.1037/emo0000034

Milad, M. R., & Rauch, S. L. (2012). Obsessive-compulsive disorder: Beyond segregated cortico-striatal pathways. *Trends in Cognitive Sciences, 16,* 43–51.

Milev, R. V., Giacobbe, P., Kennedy, S. H., Blumberger, D. M., Daskalakis, Z. J., Downar, J., ... CANMAT Depression Work Group. (2016). Canadian Network for Mood and Anxiety Treatments (CANMAT) 2016 clinical guidelines for the management of adults with major depressive disorder: Section 4. Neurostimulation treatments. *Canadian Journal of Psychiatry, 61*(9), 561–575. https://doi.org/10.1177/0706743716660033

Milgram, S. (1963). Behavioral study of obedience. *Journal of Abnormal and Social Psychology, 67,* 371–378.

Milgram, S. (1974). *Obedience to authority.* Harper & Row.

Milgram, S., Bickman, L., & Berkowitz, O. (1969). Note on the drawing power of crowds of different size. *Journal of Personality and Social Psychology, 13,* 79–82.

Millar, P. R., Serbun, S. J., Vadalia, A., & Gutchess, A. H. (2013). Cross-cultural differences in memory specificity. *Culture and Brain, 1,* 138–157. https://doi.org/10.1007/s40167-013-0011-3

Miller, A. J. (1986). *The obedience experiments: A case study of controversy in social science.* Praeger.

Miller, D. T., & Prentice, D. A. (1996). The construction of social norms and standards. In E. T. Higgins & A. W. Kruglanski (Ed.), *Social psychology: Handbook of basic principles* (pp. 799–829). Guilford Press.

Miller, D. T., & Prentice, D. A. (2016). Changing norms to change behavior. *Annual Review of Psychology, 67*(1), 339–361.

Miller, D. T., & Ratner, R. K. (1998). The disparity between the actual and assumed power of self-interest. *Journal of Personality and Social Psychology, 74,* 53–62.

Miller, D. T., & Ross, M. (1975). Self-serving biases in the attribution of causality: Fact or fiction? *Psychological Bulletin, 82,* 213–225.

Miller, G. A. (1956). The magical number seven, plus or minus two: Some limits on our capacity for processing information. *Psychological Review, 63,* 81–96.

Miller, G. A. (2003). The cognitive revolution: A historical perspective. *Trends in Cognitive Sciences, 7*(3), 141–144.

Miller, K. L., Alfaro-Almagro, F., Bangerter, N. K., Thomas, D. L., Yacoub, E., Xu, J., ... Smith, S. M. (2016). Multimodal population brain imaging in the UK Biobank prospective epidemiological study. *Nature Neuroscience, 19,* 1523–1536.

Miller, N. E. (1960). Motivational effects of brain stimulation and drugs. *Federation Proceedings, 19,* 846–854.

Miller, T. W. (Ed.). (1996). *Theory and assessment of stressful life events.* International Universities Press.

Miller, W. R., & Rollnick, S. (2012). *Motivational interviewing: Helping people change* (3rd ed.). Guilford Press.

Millner, A. J., den Ouden, H. E. M., Gershman, S. J., Glenn, C. R., Kearns, J. C., Bornstein, A. M., ... Nock, M. K. (2019). Suicidal thoughts and behaviors are associated with an increased decision-making bias for active responses to escape aversive states. *Journal of Abnormal Psychology, 128*(2), 106–118. https://doi.org/10.1037/abn0000395

Mills, P. J., & Dimsdale, J. E. (1991). Cardiovascular reactivity to psychosocial stressors. A review of the effects of beta-blockade. *Psychosomatics, 32*, 209–220.

Milne, E., & Grafman, J. (2001). Ventromedial prefrontal cortex lesions in humans eliminate implicit gender stereotyping. *Journal of Neuroscience, 21*, 1–6.

Milner, A. D., & Goodale, M. A. (1995). *The visual brain in action.* Oxford University Press.

Milner, B. (1962). Laterality effects in audition. In V. B. Mountcastle (Ed.), *Interhemispheric relations and cerebral dominance* (pp. 177–195). Johns Hopkins University Press.

Milyavsky, M., Webber, D., Fernandez, J. R., Kruglanski, A. W., Goldenberg, A., Suri, G., & Gross, J. J. (2018). To reappraise or not to reappraise? Emotion regulation choice and cognitive energetics. *Emotion.* https://doi.org/10.1037/emo0000498

Mineka, S., & Cook, M. (1988). Social learning and the acquisition of snake fear in monkeys. In T. Zentall & B. G. Galef, Jr. (Eds.), *Social learning* (pp. 51–73). Erlbaum.

Mineka, S., & Ohman, A. (2002). Born to fear: Non-associative vs. associative factors in the etiology of phobia. *Behaviour Research and Therapy, 40*, 173–184.

Mingroni, M. A. (2007). Resolving the IQ paradox: Heterosis as a cause of the Flynn effect and other trends. *Psychological Review, 114*, 806–829.

Minsky, M. (1986). *The society of mind.* Simon & Schuster.

Minson, J. A., & Mueller, J. S. (2012). The cost of collaboration: Why joint decision making exacerbates rejection of outside information. *Psychological Science, 23*(3), 219–224. https://doi.org/10.1177/0956797611429132

Miranda, J., Bernal, G., Lau, A., Kihn, L., Hwang, W. C., & LaFramboise, T. (2005). State of the science on psychological interventions for ethnic minorities. *Annual Review of Clinical Psychology, 1*, 113–142.

Mirnig, N., Stollnberger, G., Miksch, M., Stadler, S., Giuliani, M., & Tscheligi, M. (2017). To err is robot: How humans assess and act toward an erroneous social robot. *Frontiers in Robotics and AI.* http://www.frontiersin.org/article/10.3389/frobt.2017.00021

Mischel, W. (1968). *Personality and assessment.* Wiley.

Mischel, W. (2004). Toward an integrative science of the person. *Annual Review of Psychology, 55*, 1–22.

Mischel, W., & Shoda, Y. (1999). Integrating dispositions and processing dynamics within a unified theory of personality: The cognitive-affective personality system. In L. A. Pervin & O. P. John (Eds.), *Handbook of personality: Theory and research* (pp. 197–218). Guilford Press.

Mischel, W., Shoda, Y., & Rodriguez, M. L. (1989). Delay of gratification in children. *Science, 244*, 933–938.

Mishra, A., & Mishra, H. (2010). Border bias: The belief that state borders can protect against disasters. *Psychological Science, 21*(11), 1582–1586. https://doi.org/10.1177/0956797610385950

Mishra, A., Mishra, H., & Masters, T. M. (2012). The influence of bite size on quantity of food consumed: A field study. *Journal of Consumer Research, 38*(5), 791–795. https://doi.org/10.1086/660838

Mita, T. H., Dermer, M., & Knight, J. (1977). Reversed facial images and the mere-exposure hypothesis. *Journal of Personality and Social Psychology, 35*, 597–601.

Mitchell, D. B., Kelly, C. L., & Brown, A. S. (2018). Replication and extension of long-term implicit memory: Perceptual priming but conceptual cessation. *Consciousness and Cognition, 58*, 1–9. https://doi.org/10.1016/j.concog.2017.12.002

Mitchell, J. M., Bogenschutz, M., Lilienstein, A., Harrison, C., Kleiman, S., Parker-Guilbert, K., ... Doblin, R. (2021). MDMA-assisted therapy for severe PTSD: A randomized, double-blind, placebo-controlled phase 3 study. *Nature Medicine, 27*(6), 1025–1033. https://doi.org/10.1038/s41591-021-01336-3

Mitchell, J. P. (2006). Mentalizing and Marr: An information processing approach to the study of social cognition. *Brain Research, 1079*, 66–75.

Mitchell, J. P., Heatherton, T. F., & Macrae, C. N. (2002). Distinct neural systems subserve person and object knowledge. *Proceedings of the National Academy of Sciences, USA, 99*, 15238–15243.

Mitchell, K. J., & Johnson, M. K. (2009). Source monitoring 15 years later: What have we learned from fMRI about the neural mechanisms of source memory? *Psychological Bulletin, 135*, 638–677.

Mitchell, R. M., Christianson, E., Ramirez, R., Onchiri, F. M., Horn, D. L., Pontis, L., ... Sie, K. C. Y. (2020). Auditory comprehension outcomes in children who receive a cochlear implant before 12 months of age. *Laryngoscope, 130*(3), 776–781. https://doi.org/10.1002/lary.28061

Miura, I. T., Okamoto, Y., Kim, C. C., & Chang, C. M. (1994). Comparisons of children's cognitive representation of number: China, France, Japan, Korea, Sweden and the United States. *International Journal of Behavioral Development, 17*, 401–411.

Miyamoto, Y., Ma, X., & Petermann, A. G. (2014). Cultural differences in hedonic emotion regulation after a negative event. *Emotion, 14*(4), 804–815. https://doi.org/10.1037/a0036257

Moffitt, T. E. (1993). Adolescence-limited and life-course-persistent antisocial behavior: A developmental taxonomy. *Psychological Review, 100*, 674–701.

Moffitt, T. E. (2005). Genetic and environmental influences on antisocial behaviors: Evidence from behavioral-genetic research. *Advances in Genetics, 55*, 41–104.

Moghaddam, B., & Bunney, B. S. (1989). Differential effect of cocaine on extracellular dopamine levels in rat medial prefrontal cortex and nucleus accumbens: Comparison to amphetamine. *Synapse, 4*, 156–161.

Mojtabai, R., Olfson, M., Sampson, N. A., Jin, R., Druss, B., Wang, P. S., ... Kessler, R. C. (2011). Barriers to mental health treatment: Results from the National Comorbidity Survey replication. *Psychological Medicine, 41*(8), 1751–1761.

Mokdad, A. H., Ford, E. S., Bowman, B. A., Dietz, W. H., Vinicor, F., Bales, V. S., & Marks, J. S. (2003). Prevalence of obesity, diabetes, and obesity-related health risk factors, 2001. *Journal of the American Medical Association, 289*(1), 76–79. https://doi.org/10.1001/jama.289.1.76

Molden, D., Lee, A. Y., & Higgins, E. T. (2009). Motivations for promotion and prevention. In J. Shah & W. Gardner (Eds.), *Handbook of motivation science* (pp. 169–187). Guilford Press.

Möller, I., Krahé, B., Busching, R., & Krause, C. (2012). Efficacy of an intervention to reduce the use of media violence and aggression: An experimental evaluation with adolescents in Germany. *Journal of Youth and Adolescence, 41*(2), 105–120. https://doi.org/10.1007/s10964-011-9654-6

Molloy, L. E., Gest, S. D., Feinberg, M. E., & Osgood, D. W. (2014). Emergence of mixed-sex friendship groups during adolescence: Developmental associations with substance use and delinquency. *Developmental Psychology, 50*(11), 2449–2461. http://doi.org/10.1037/a0037856

Monahan, J. L., Murphy, S. T., & Zajonc, R. B. (2000). Subliminal mere exposure: Specific, general, and diffuse effects. *Psychological Science, 11*, 462–466.

Moncrieff, J. (2009). A critique of the dopamine hypothesis of schizophrenia and psychosis. *Harvard Review of Psychiatry, 17*, 214–225.

Moncrieff, J. (2018). Research on a "drug-centred" approach to psychiatric drug treatment: assessing the impact of mental and behavioural alterations produced by psychiatric drugs. *Epidemiology and Psychiatric Sciences, 27*(2), 133–140. https://doi.org/10.1017/S2045796017000555

Monk, E. P., Jr., Esposito, M. H., & Lee, H. (2021). Beholding inequality: Race, gender, and returns to physical attractiveness in the United States. *American Journal of Sociology, 127*(1), 194–241. https://doi.org/10.1086/715141

Montague, C. T., Farooqi, I. S., Whitehead, J. P., Soos, M. A., Rau, H., Wareham, N. J., ... O'Rahilly, S. (1997). Congenital leptin deficiency is associated with severe early-onset obesity in humans. *Nature, 387*(6636), 903–908.

Montenigro, P. H., Corp, D. T., Stein, T. D., Cantu, R. C., & Stern, R. A. (2015). Chronic traumatic encephalopathy: Historical origins and current perspective. *Annual Review of Clinical Psychology, 11*, 309–330.

Montoya, R. M., & Horton, R. S. (2013). A meta-analytic investigation of the processes underlying the similarity-attraction effect. *Journal of Social and Personal Relationships, 30*(1), 64–94. https://doi.org/10.1177/0265407512452989

Montoya, R. M., Kershaw, C., & Prosser, J. L. (2018). A meta-analytic investigation of the relation between interpersonal attraction and enacted behavior. *Psychological Bulletin, 144*(7), 673–709. https://doi.org/10.1037/bul0000148

Mook, D. G. (1983). In defense of external invalidity. *American Psychologist, 38*, 379–387.

Moon, S. M., & Illingworth, A. J. (2005). Exploring the dynamic nature of procrastination: A latent growth curve analysis of academic procrastination. *Personality and Individual Differences, 38*, 297–309.

Moore, E. G. J. (1986). Family socialization and the IQ test performance of traditionally and transracially adopted Black children. *Developmental Psychology, 22*, 317–326.

Moore, L. D., & Elkavich, A. (2008). Who's using and who's doing time: Incarceration, the War on Drugs, and public health. *American Journal of Public Health, 98*(Suppl. 1), S176–S180. https://doi.org/10.2105/AJPH.98.Supplement_1.S176

Gallup. (2020, November). *Support for legal marijuana inches up to new high of 68%.* https://news.gallup.com/poll/323582/support-legal-marijuana-inches-new-high.aspx

National Center for Health Statistics. (2021). *Health, United States 2019: Table 20.* https://www.cdc.gov/nchs/hus/contents2019.htm

Moran, P., Klinteberg, B. A., Batty, G. D., & Vågerö, D. (2009). Brief report: Childhood intelligence predicts hospitalization with personality disorder in adulthood: Evidence from a population-based study in Sweden. *Journal of Personality Disorders, 23*(5), 535–540. https://doi.org/10.1521/pedi.2009.23.5.535

Moray, N. (1959). Attention in dichotic listening: Affective cues and the influence of instructions. *Quarterly Journal of Experimental Psychology, 11*, 56–60.

Morin, A. (2006). Levels of consciousness and self-awareness: A comparison of various neurocognitive views. *Consciousness & Cognition, 15*, 358–371.

Morin, C. M., Bélanger, L., LeBlanc, M., Ivers, H., Savard, J., Espie, C. A., ... Grégoire, J. P. (2009). The natural history of insomnia: A population-based 3-year longitudinal study. *Archives of Internal Medicine, 169*, 447–453.

Morris, C. D., Bransford, J. D., & Franks, J. J. (1977). Levels of processing versus transfer-appropriate processing. *Journal of Verbal Learning and Verbal Behavior, 16*, 519–533.

Morris, R. G., Anderson, E., Lynch, G. S., & Baudry, M. (1986). Selective impairment of learning and blockade of long-term potentiation by an N-methyl-D-aspartate receptor antagonist, AP5. *Nature, 319*, 774–776.

Morris, T. L. (2001). Social phobia. In M. W. Vasey & M. R. Dadds (Eds.), *The developmental psychopathology of anxiety* (pp. 435–458). Oxford University Press.

Morrow, D., Leirer, V., Altiteri, P., & Fitzsimmons, C. (1994). When expertise reduces age differences in performance. *Psychology and Aging, 9*, 134–148.

Moruzzi, G., & Magoun, H. W. (1949). Brain stem reticular formation and activation of the EEG. *Electroencephalography and Clinical Neurophysiology, 1*, 455–473.

Moscovitch, M. (1994). Memory and working-with-memory: Evaluation of a component process model and comparisons with other models. In D. L. Schacter & E. Tulving (Eds.), *Memory systems, 1994* (pp. 269–310). MIT Press.

Moscovitch, M., Cabeza, R., Winocur, G., & Nadel, L. (2016). Episodic memory and beyond: The hippocampus and cortex in transformation. *Annual Review of Psychology, 67*, 105–134.

Moscovitch, M., Nadel, L., Winocur, G., Gilboa, A., & Rosenbaum, R. S. (2006). The cognitive neuroscience of remote episodic, semantic and spatial memory. *Current Opinion in Neurobiology, 16*, 179–190.

Moulton, E., Barton, M., Robins, D. L., Abrams, D. N., & Fein, D. (2016) Early characteristics of children with ASD who demonstrate optimal progress between age two and four. *Journal of Autism and Developmental Disorders, 46*, 2160–2173.

Moura, A. C. A. de, & Lee, P. C. (2004). Capuchin stone tool use in Caatinga dry forest. *Science, 306*, 1909.

Mroczek, D. K., & Spiro, A. (2005). Change in life satisfaction during adulthood: Findings from the Veterans Affairs Normative Aging Study. *Journal of Personality and Social Psychology, 88*, 189.

Muehlenkamp, J. J., Claes, L., Havertape, L., & Plener, P. L. (2012). International prevalence of adolescent non-suicidal self-injury and deliberate self-harm. *Child and Adolescent Psychiatry and Mental Health, 6*(10). https://doi.org/10.1156/1753-2000-6-10

Mueller, T. E., Gavin, L. E., & Kulkarni, A. (2008). The association between sex education and youth's engagement in sexual intercourse, age at first intercourse, and birth control use at first sex. *Journal of Adolescent Health, 42*(1), 89–96.

Mueller, T. I., Leon, A. C., Keller, M. B., Solomon, D. A., Endicott, J., Coryell, W., ... Maser, J. D. (1999). Recurrence after recovery from major depressive disorder during 15 years of observational follow-up. *American Journal of Psychiatry, 156*, 1000–1006.

Muenter, M. D., & Tyce, G. M. (1971). L-dopa therapy of Parkinson's disease: Plasma L-dopa concentration, therapeutic response, and side effects. *Mayo Clinic Proceedings, 46*, 231–239.

Muggleton, N. K., Tarran, S. R., & Fincher, C. L. (2019). Who punishes promiscuous women? Both women and men are prejudiced towards sexually-accessible women, but only women inflict costly punishment. *Evolution and Human Behavior, 40*(3), 259–268.

Mullen, M. K. (1994). Earliest recollections of childhood: A demographic analysis. *Cognition, 52*, 55–79.

Müller, K., & Schwarz, C. (2018). Fanning the flames of hate: Social media and hate crimes. http://doi.org/10.2139/ssrn.3082972

Murayama, K., Miyatsu, T., Buchli, D., & Storm, B. C. (2014). Forgetting as a consequence of retrieval: A meta-analytic review of retrieval-induced forgetting. *Psychological Bulletin, 140,* 1383–1409.

Murphy, G., Loftus, E. F., Grady, R. H., Levine, L. J., & Greene, C. M. (2019). False memories for fake news during Ireland's abortion referendum. *Psychological Science, 30*(10), 1449–1459. https://doi .org/10.1177/0956797619864887

Murray, C. (2002). *IQ and income inequality in a sample of sibling pairs from advantaged family backgrounds.* Paper presented at the 114th Annual Meeting of the American Economic Association.

Murray, H. A. (1943). *Thematic Apperception Test manual.* Harvard University Press.

Murray, H. A., & Kluckhohn, C. (1953). Outline of a conception of personality. In C. Kluckhohn, H. A. Murray, & D. M. Schneider (Eds.), *Personality in nature, society, and culture* (2nd ed., pp. 3–52). Knopf.

Murty, N. A. R., Teng, S., Beeler, D., Mynick, A., Oliva, A., & Kanwisher, N. (2020). Visual experience is not necessary for the development of face-selectivity in the lateral fusiform gyrus. *Proceedings of the National Academy of Sciences, 117*(37), 23011–23020. https://doi.org/10.1073/pnas.2004607117

Myers, D. G., & Lamm, H. (1975). The polarizing effect of group discussion. *American Scientist, 63*(3), 297–303.

Myles, P. S., Leslie, K., McNell, J., Forbes, A., & Chan, M. T. V. (2004). Bispectral index monitoring to prevent awareness during anaesthesia: The B-Aware randomized controlled trial. *Lancet, 363,* 1757–1763.

Nadasdy, A. (1995). Phonetics, phonology, and applied linguistics. *Annual Review of Applied Linguistics, 15,* 68–77.

Nader, K., & Hardt, O. (2009). A single standard for memory: The case of reconsolidation. *Nature Reviews Neuroscience, 10,* 224–234.

Nader, K., Shafe, G., & LeDoux, J. E. (2000). Fear memories require protein synthesis in the amygdala for reconsolidation after retrieval. *Nature, 406,* 722–726.

Nagasako, E. M., Oaklander, A. L., & Dworkin, R. H. (2003). Congenital insensitivity to pain: An update. *Pain, 101,* 213–219.

Nagell, K., Olguin, R. S., & Tomasello, M. (1993). Processes of social learning in the tool use of chimpanzees (*Pan troglodytes*) and human children (*Homo sapiens*). *Journal of Comparative Psychology, 107,* 174–186.

Nairne, J. S., Pandeirada, J. N. S., & Thompson, S. R. (2008). Adaptive memory: The comparative value of survival processing. *Psychological Science, 19,* 176–180.

Nairne, J. S., Thompson, S. R., & Pandeirada, J. N. S. (2007). Adaptive memory: Survival processing enhances retention. *Journal of Experimental Psychology: Learning, Memory, and Cognition, 33,* 263–273.

Nakazato, M., Murakami, N., Date, Y., Kojima, M., Matsuo, H., Kangawa, K., & Matsukura, S. (2001). A role for ghrelin in the central regulation of feeding. *Nature, 409,* 194–198.

Napier, T. C., Kirby, A., & Persons, A. L. (2020). The role of dopamine pharmacotherapy and addiction-like behaviors in Parkinson's disease. *Progress in Neuro-Psychopharmacology and Biological Psychiatry, 102,* 109942. https://doi.org/10.1016/j.pnpbp.2020.109942

Naqvi, N., Shiv, B., & Bechara, A. (2006). The role of emotion in decision making: A cognitive neuroscience perspective. *Current Directions in Psychological Science, 15,* 260–264.

Nash, G. (2001). The subversive male: Homosexual and bestial images on European Mesolithic rock art. In L. Bevan (Ed.), *Indecent exposure: Sexuality, society and the archaeological record* (pp. 43–55). Cruithne Press.

Nassi, J. J., & Callaway, E. M. (2009). Parallel processing strategies of the primate visual system. *Nature Reviews Neuroscience, 10,* 360–372.

National Academies of Science, Engineering, and Medicine. (2019). *Reproducibility and replicability in science.* The National Academies Press. https://doi.org/10.17226/25303

National Center for Health Statistics. (2014). *Health: United States, 2013. In Brief.* National Center for Health Statistics.

National Center for Health Statistics. (2016a). *Health of Black or African American non-Hispanic population.* Centers for Disease Control and Prevention. http://www.cdc.gov/nchs/fastats/black -health.htm

National Center for Health Statistics. (2016b). *Child health.* Centers for Disease Control and Prevention. http://www.cdc.gov /nchs/fastats/child-health.htm

National Center for Statistics and Analysis. (2020, December). *Overview of motor vehicle crashes in 2019. Traffic Safety Facts Research Note. Report No. DOT HS 813 060.* National Highway Traffic Safety Administration.

National Research Council. (2003). *The polygraph and lie detection.* National Academies Press.

National Science Foundation, National Center for Science and Engineering Statistics. (2018). Doctorate recipients from U.S. universities, 2017. *Special Report NSF 19-301.* https://ncses.nsf.gov /pubs/nsf19301/.

Nattress, K. (2019, May 29). Billie Eilish explains how synesthesia affects her music. *iHeart.* https://www.iheart.com/content/2019-05 -29-billie-eilish-explains-how-synesthesia-affects-her-music/

Nave, G., Jung, W. H., Linnér, R. K., Kable, J. W., & Koellinger, P. D. (2019). Are bigger brains smarter? Evidence from a large-scale pre-registered study. *Psychological Science, 30,* 43–54.

Neimark, J. (2004, July/August). The power of coincidence. *Psychology Today,* pp. 47–52.

Neisser, U. (Ed.). (1998). *The rising curve: Long-term gains in IQ and related measures.* American Psychological Association.

Neisser, U., & Harsch, N. (1992). Phantom flashbulbs: False recollections of hearing the news about Challenger. In E. Winograd & U. Neisser (Eds.), *Affect and accuracy in recall: Studies of "flashbulb memories"* (pp. 9–31). Cambridge University Press.

Neisser, U., Boodoo, G., Bouchard, T. J., Jr., Boykin, A. W., Brody, N., Ceci, S. J., ... Loehlin, J. C. (1996). Intelligence: Knowns and unknowns. *American Psychologist, 51,* 77–101.

Nelson, A. B., & Kreitzer, A. C. (2015). Reassessing models of basal ganglia function and dysfunction. *Annual Review of Neuroscience, 37,* 117–135.

Nemeth, C., & Chiles, C. (1988). Modelling courage: The role of dissent in fostering independence. *European Journal of Social Psychology, 18,* 275–280.

Nes, L. S., & Sergerstrom, S. C. (2006). Dispositional optimism and coping: A meta-analytic review. *Personality and Social Psychology Review, 10,* 235–251.

Neuberg, S. L., Kenrick, D. T., & Schaller, M. (2010). Evolutionary social psychology. In S. T. Fiske, D. T. Gilbert, & G. Lindzey (Eds.), *The handbook of social psychology* (5th ed., Vol. 2, pp. 761–796). Wiley.

Newbold, R. R., Padilla-Banks, E., Snyder, R. J., & Jefferson, W. N. (2005). Developmental exposure to estrogenic compounds and obesity. *Birth Defects Research Part A: Clinical and Molecular Teratology, 73,* 478–480.

Newman, A. J., Bavelier, D., Corina, D., Jezzard, P., & Neville, H. J. (2002). A critical period for right hemisphere recruitment in American Sign Language processing. *Nature Neuroscience, 5,* 76–80.

Newman, J. P., Wolff, W. T., & Hearst, E. (1980). The feature-positive effect in adult human subjects. *Journal of Experimental Psychology: Human Learning and Memory, 6,* 630–650.

Newman, M. G., & Stone, A. A. (1996). Does humor moderate the effects of experimentally induced stress? *Annals of Behavioral Medicine, 18,* 101–109.

Newsome, W. T., & Paré, E. B. (1988). A selective impairment of motion perception following lesions of the middle temporal visual area (MT). *Journal of Neuroscience, 8,* 2201–2211.

Neylan, T. C., Metzler, T. J., Best, S. R., Weiss, D. S., Fagan, J. A., Libermans, A., … Marmar, C. R. (2002). Critical incident exposure and sleep quality in police officers. *Psychosomatic Medicine, 64,* 345–352.

Ng, M., Fleming, T., Robinson, M., Thomson, B., Graetz, N., Margono, C., … Gakidou, E. (2016). Global, regional, and national prevalence of overweight and obesity in children and adults during 1980–2013: A systematic analysis for the Global Burden of Disease Study 2013. *Lancet, 384,* 766–781. https://doi.org/10.1016/S0140-6736(14)60460-8

Ng, Q. X., Venkatanarayanan, N., & Ho, C. Y. X. (2017). Clinical use of *Hypericum perforatum* (St John's wort) in depression: A meta-analysis. *Journal of Affective Disorders, 210,* 211–221. https://doi.org/10.1016/j.jad.2016.12.048

Niaura, R., Todaro, J. F., Stroud, L., Spiro, A., III, Ward, K. D., & Weiss, S. (2002). Hostility, the metabolic syndrome, and incident coronary heart disease. *Health Psychology, 21,* 588–593.

Nicoladis, E., & Genesee, F. (1997). Language development in preschool bilingual children. *Journal of Speech-Language Pathology & Audiology, 21,* 258–270.

Nicolas, S., Andrieu, B., Croizet, J.-C., Sanitioso, R. B., & Burman, J. T. (2013). Sick? Or slow? On the origins of intelligence as a psychological object. *Intelligence, 41*(5), 699–711. https://doi.org/10.1016/j.intell.2013.08.006

Niedenthal, P. M., Barsalou, L. W., Winkielman, P., Krauth-Gruber, S., & Ric, F. (2005). Embodiment in attitudes, social perception, and emotion. *Personality and Social Psychology Review, 9*(3), 184–211.

Niedenthal, P. M., Rychlowska, M., Zhao, F., & Wood, A. (2019). Historical migration patterns shape contemporary cultures of emotion. *Perspectives on Psychological Science, 14*(4), 560–573. https://doi.org/10.1177/1745691619849591

Niederkrotenthaler, T., Tran, U. S., Gould, M., Sinyor, M., Sumner, S., Strauss, M. J., Voracek, M., Till, B., Murphy, S., Gonzalez, F., Spittal, M. J., & Draper, J. (2021). Association of Logic's hip hop song "1-800-273-8255" with Lifeline calls and suicides in the United States: Interrupted time series analysis. *British Medical Journal, 375,* e067726. https://doi.org/10.1136/bmj-2021-067726

Nikolaev, B., & McGee, J. J. (2016). Relative verbal intelligence and happiness. *Intelligence, 59,* 1–7. https://doi.org/10.1016/j.intell.2016.09.002

Nikolaev, B., & Salahodjaev, R. (2016). The role of intelligence in the distribution of national happiness. *Intelligence, 56,* 38–45. https://doi.org/10.1016/j.intell.2016.02.006

Nir, Y., & Tononi, G. (2010). Dreaming and the brain: From phenomenology to neurophysiology. *Trends in Cognitive Sciences, 14*(2), 88–100.

Nisbett, R. E. (2009). *Intelligence and how to get it.* Norton.

Nisbett, R. E., & Cohen, D. (1996). *Culture of honor: The psychology of violence in the South.* Westview Press.

Nisbett, R. E., & Miyamoto, Y. (2005). The influence of culture: Holistic versus analytic perception. *Trends in Cognitive Sciences, 9*(10), 467–473. https://doi.org/10.1016/j.tics.2005.08.004

Nisbett, R. E., Aronson, J., Blair, C., Dickens, W., Flynn, J., Halpern, D. F., & Turkheimer, E. (2012). Intelligence: New findings and theoretical developments. *American Psychologist, 67*(2), 130–159. https://doi.org/10.1037/a0026699

Nisbett, R. E., Caputo, C., Legant, P., & Maracek, J. (1973). Behavior as seen by the actor and as seen by the observer. *Journal of Personality and Social Psychology, 27,* 154–164.

Nissen, M. J., & Bullemer, P. (1987). Attentional requirements of learning: Evidence from performance measures. *Cognitive Psychology, 19,* 1–32.

Noah, T., Schul, Y., & Mayo, R. (2018). When both the original study and its failed replication are correct: Feeling observed eliminates the facial-feedback effect. *Journal of Personality and Social Psychology, 114*(5), 657–664. https://doi.org/10.1037/pspa0000121

Nobes, G., Panagiotaki, G., & Engelhardt, P. E. (2017). The development of intention-based morality: The influence of intention salience and recency, negligence, and outcome on children's and adults' judgments. *Developmental Psychology, 53*(10), 1895–1911. https://doi.org/10.1037/dev0000380

Nock, M. K. (2009). Why do people hurt themselves? New insights into the nature and functions of self-injury. *Current Directions in Psychological Science, 18,* 78–83. https://doi.org/10.1111/j.1467-8721.2009.01613.x

Nock, M. K. (2010). Self-injury. *Annual Review of Clinical Psychology, 6,* 339–363. https://doi.org/10.1146/annurev.clinpsy.121208.131258

Nock, M. K., Borges, G., Bromet, E. J., Alonso, J., Angermeyer, M., Beautrais, A., … Williams, D. (2008). Cross-national prevalence and risk factors for suicidal ideation, plans, and attempts. *British Journal of Psychiatry, 192,* 98–105.

Nock, M. K., Borges, G., & Ono, Y. (Eds.). (2012). *Suicide: Global perspectives from the WHO World Mental Health Surveys.* Cambridge University Press.

Nock, M. K., Green, J. G., Hwang, I., McLaughlin, K. A., Sampson, N. A., Zaslavsky, A. M., & Kessler, R. C. (2013). Prevalence, correlates and treatment of lifetime suicidal behavior among adolescents: Results from the National Comorbidity Survey Replication–Adolescent Supplement (NCSA–A). *Journal of the American Medical Association Psychiatry, 70*(3), 300–310. https://doi.org/10.1001/2013.jamapsychiatry.55

Nock, M. K., Holmberg, E. G., Photos, V. I., & Michel, B. D. (2007). Structured and semi-structured interviews. In M. Hersen & J. C. Thomas (Eds.), *Handbook of clinical interviewing with children* (pp. 30–49). Sage.

Nock, M. K., Kazdin, A. E., Hiripi, E., & Kessler, R. C. (2006). Prevalence, subtypes, and correlates of *DSM–IV* conduct disorder in the National Comorbidity Survey Replication. *Psychological Medicine, 36,* 699–710.

Nolen-Hoeksema, S. (2012). Emotion regulation and psychopathology: The role of gender. *Annual Review of Clinical Psychology,* 161–187.

Norby, S. (2015). Why forget? On the adaptive value of memory loss. *Perspectives on Psychological Science, 10,* 551–578.

Norcross, J. C., & Rogan, J. D. (2013). Psychologists conducting psychotherapy in 2012: Current practices and historical trends among Division 29 members. *Psychotherapy, 50,* 490–495.

Norman, L. J., & Thaler, L. (2019). Retinotopic maps of spatial sound in primary "visual" cortex of blind human echolocators.

Proceedings of the Royal Society B, 286(1912), 20191910. https://doi.org/10.1098/rspb.2019/1910

Norrholm, S. D., & Ressler, K. J. (2009). Genetics of anxiety and trauma-related disorders. *Neuroscience, 164,* 272–287.

Norton, M. I., Frost, J. H., & Ariely, D. (2007). Less is more: The lure of ambiguity, or why familiarity breeds contempt. *Journal of Personality and Social Psychology, 92*(1), 97–105. https://doi.org/10.1037/0022-3514.92.1.97

Nosanchuk, T. A., & Lightstone, J. (1974). Canned laughter and public and private conformity. *Journal of Personality and Social Psychology, 29,* 153–156.

Nosofsky, R. M., Sanders, C., & McDaniel, M. (2018). A formal psychological model of classification applied to natural-science category learning. *Current Directions in Psychological Science, 27,* 129–135.

Nowak, M. A. (2006). Five rules for the evolution of cooperation. *Science, 314,* 1560–1563.

Nuttin, J. M. (1985). Narcissism beyond Gestalt and awareness: The name letter effect. *European Journal of Social Psychology, 15,* 353–361.

Nyborg, H., & Jensen, A. R. (2001). Occupation and income related to psychometric *g*. *Intelligence, 29,* 45–55.

O'Connor, M. R. (2019, June 5). Ditch GPS. It's ruining your brain. *Washington Post.* https://www.washingtonpost.com/opinions/ditch-the-gps-its-ruining-your-brain/2019/06/05/29a3170e-87af-11e9-98c1-e945ae5db8fb_story.html

O'Connor, T. G., & Rutter, M. (2000). Attachment disorder following early severe deprivation: Extension and longitudinal follow-up. *Journal of the American Academy of Child and Adolescent Psychiatry, 39,* 703–712.

O'Laughlin, M. J., & Malle, B. F. (2002). How people explain actions performed by groups and individuals. *Journal of Personality and Social Psychology, 82,* 33–48.

O'Neill, J., Daniel, T. O., & Epstein, L. H. (2016). Episodic future thinking reduces eating in a food court. *Eating Behaviors, 20,* 9–13. https://doi.org/10.1016/j.eatbeh.2015.10.002

Ochsner, K. N. (2000). Are affective events richly recollected or simply familiar? The experience and process of recognizing feelings past. *Journal of Experimental Psychology: General, 129,* 242–261.

Ochsner, K. N., Bunge, S. A., Gross, J. J., & Gabrieli, J. D. E. (2002). Rethinking feelings: An fMRI study of the cognitive regulation of emotion. *Journal of Cognitive Neuroscience, 14,* 1215–1229.

Ofshe, R. J. (1992). Inadvertent hypnosis during interrogation: False confession due to dissociative state, misidentified multiple personality, and the satanic cult hypothesis. *International Journal of Clinical and Experimental Hypnosis, 40,* 125–126.

Okdie, B. M., Ewoldsen, D. R., Muscanell, N. L., Guadagno, R. E., Eno, C. A., Velez, J. A., ... Smith, L. R. (2014). Missed programs (you can't TiVo this one): Why psychologists should study media. *Perspectives on Psychological Science, 9*(2), 180–195. https://doi.org/10.1177/1745691614521243

Okereke, O. I., Vyas, C. M., Mischoulon, D., Change, G., Cook, N. R., Weinberg, A., ... Manson, J. E. (2021). Effect of long-term supplementation with marine omega-3 fatty acids vs placebo on risk of depression or clinically relevant depressive symptoms and on change in mood scores: A randomized clinical trial. *JAMA, 326*(23), 2385–2394. https://doi.org/10.1001/jama.2021.21187

Okuda, J., Fujii, T., Ohtake, H., Tsukiura, T., Tanji, K., Suzuki, K., ... Yamadori, A. (2003). Thinking of the future and the past: The roles of the frontal pole and the medial temporal lobes. *NeuroImage, 19,* 1369–1380.

Olatunji, B. O., & Wolitzky-Taylor, K. B. (2009). Anxiety sensitivity and the anxiety disorders: A meta-analytic review and synthesis. *Psychological Bulletin, 135,* 974–999.

Olausson, P. O., Haglund, B., Weitoft, G. R., & Cnattingius, S. (2001). Teenage child-bearing and long-term socioeconomic consequences: A case study in Sweden. *Family Planning Perspectives, 33,* 70–74.

Olds, J. (1956, October). Pleasure center in the brain. *Scientific American, 195,* 105–116.

Olds, J., & Fobes, J. I. (1981). The central basis of motivation: Intracranial self-stimulation studies. *Annual Review of Psychology, 32,* 523–574.

Olds, J., & Milner, P. (1954). Positive reinforcement produced by electrical stimulation of septal areas and other regions of rat brains. *Journal of Comparative and Physiological Psychology, 47,* 419–427.

Ollers, D. K., & Eilers, R. E. (1988). The role of audition in infant babbling. *Child Development, 59,* 441–449.

Olsson, A., & Phelps, E. A. (2007). Social learning of fear. *Nature Neuroscience, 10,* 1095–1102.

Olsson, A., Kopsida, E., Sorjonen, K., & Savic, I. (2016). Testosterone and estrogen impact social evaluations and vicarious emotions: A double-blind placebo-controlled study. *Emotion, 16,* 515–523.

Oltmanns, T. F., Neale, J. M., & Davison, G. C. (1991). *Case studies in abnormal psychology* (3rd ed.). Wiley.

Olton, D. S., & Samuelson, R. J. (1976). Remembrance of places passed: Spatial memory in rats. *Journal of Experimental Psychology: Animal Behavior Processes, 2,* 97–116.

Onishi, K. H., & Baillargeon, R. (2005). Do 15-month-old infants understand false beliefs? *Science, 308,* 255–258.

Ono, K. (1987). Superstitious behavior in humans. *Journal of the Experimental Analysis of Behavior, 47,* 261–271.

Oostenbroek, J., Suddendorf, T., Nielsen, M., Redshaw, J., Kennedy-Constantini, S., Davis, J., ... Slaughter, V. (2016). Comprehensive longitudinal study challenges the existence of neonatal imitation in humans. *Current Biology, 26,* 1334–1338.

Open Science Collaboration, Nosek, B. A., Aarts, A. A., Anderson, C. J., Anderson, J. E., Kappes, H. B., ... Penuliar, M. (2015). Estimating the reproducibility of psychological science. *Science, 349* (6251), aac4716–aac4716. https://doi.org/10.1126/science.aac4716

Ophir, E., Nass, C., & Wagner, A. D. (2009). Cognitive control in media multitaskers. *Proceedings of the National Academy of Sciences, USA, 106,* 15583–15587.

Orban, P., Lungu, O., & Doyon, J. (2008). Motor sequence learning and developmental dyslexia. *Annals of the New York Academy of Sciences, 1145,* 151–172.

Ormel, J., Petukhova, M., Chatterji, S., Aguilar-Gaxiola, S., Alonso, J., Angermeyer, M. C., ... Kessler, R. C. (2008). Disability and treatment of specific mental and physical disorders across the world: Results from the WHO World Mental Health Surveys. *British Journal of Psychiatry, 192,* 368–375.

Orvell, A., Ayduk, Ö., Moser, J. S., Gelman, S. A., & Kross, E. (2019). Linguistic shifts: A relatively effortless route to emotion regulation? *Current Directions in Psychological Science, 28*(6), 567–573. https://doi.org/10.1177/0963721419861411

Osgood, C. E., Suci, G. J., & Tannenbaum, P. (1967). *The measurement of meaning.* University of Illinois Press.

Oswald, L., Taylor, A. M., & Triesman, M. (1960). Discriminative responses to stimulation during human sleep. *Brain, 83,* 440–453.

Otto, M. W., Henin, A., Hirshfeld-Becker, D. R., Pollack, M. H., Biederman, J., & Rosenbaum, J. F. (2007). Posttraumatic stress disorder symptoms following media exposure to tragic events: Impact of 9/11 on children at risk for anxiety disorders. *Journal of Anxiety Disorders, 21,* 888–902.

Oudiette, D., & Paller, K. A. (2013). Upgrading the sleeping brain with targeted memory reactivation. *Trends in Cognitive Sciences, 17,* 142–149.

Ovalle-Fresa, R., Ankner, S., & Rothen, N. (2021). Enhanced perception and memory: Insights from synesthesia and expertise. *Cortex, 140,* 14–35. https://doi.org/10.1016/j.cortex.2021.01.024

Owens, W. A. (1966). Age and mental abilities: A second adult follow-up. *Journal of Educational Psychology, 57,* 311–325.

Oztekin, I., Curtis, C. E., & McElree, B. (2009). The medial temporal lobe and left inferior prefrontal cortex jointly support interference resolution in verbal working memory. *Journal of Cognitive Neuroscience, 21,* 1967–1979.

Paap, K. R., Johnson, H. A., & Sawi, O. (2015). Bilingual advantages in executive functioning either do not exist or are restricted to very specific and undetermined circumstances. *Cortex, 69,* 265–278.

Paap, K. R., & Sawi, O. (2014). Bilingual advantages in executive functioning: Problems in convergent validity, discriminant validity, and the identification of the theoretical constructs. *Frontiers in Psychology, 5,* 962. https://doi.org/10.3389/fpsyg.2014.00962

Pagnin, D., de Queiroz, V., Pini, S., & Cassano, G. B. (2008). Efficacy of ECT in depression: A meta-analytic review. *Focus, 6,* 155–162.

Paivio, A. (1971). *Imagery and verbal processes.* Holt, Rinehart and Winston.

Paivio, A. (1986). *Mental representations: A dual coding approach.* Oxford University Press.

Palermo, T. M., Eccleston, C., Lewandowski, A. S., Williams, A. C., & Morley, S. (2011). Randomized controlled trials of psychological therapies for management of chronic pain in children and adolescents: An updated meta-analytic review. *Pain, 148,* 387–397.

Palmieri, T. J., Blake, R., Flanery, M. A., & Whetsell, W. (2002). The perceptual reality of synesthetic colors. *Proceedings of the National Academy of Sciences USA, 99*(6), 4127–4131. https://doi.org/10.1073/pnas.022049399

Palombo, D. J., Alain, C., Soderlund, H., Khuu, W., & Levine, B. (2015). Severely deficient autobiographical memory (SDAM) in healthy adults: A new mnemonic syndrome. *Neuropsychologia, 72,* 105–118.

Palombo, D. J., Bacopulos, A., Amaral, R. S. C., Olsen, R. K., Todd, R. M., Anderson, A. K., & Levine, B. (2018). Episodic autobiographical memory is associated with variation in the size of hippocampal subregions. *Hippocampus, 28,* 69–75.

Paluck, B. L., & Green, D. P. (2009). Prejudice reduction: What works? A review and assessment of research and practice. *Annual Review of Psychology, 60,* 339–367.

Pan, S. C., & Rickard, T. C. (2018). Transfer of test-enhanced learning: Meta-analytic review and synthesis. *Psychological Bulletin, 144,* 710–756.

Pandit, J. J., Andrade, J., Bogod, D. G., Hitchman, J. M., Jonker, W. R., Lucas, N., ... Cook, T. M. (2014). The 5th National Audit Project (NAP5) on accidental awareness during general anaesthesia: Summary of main findings and risk factors. *Anaesthesia, 69,* 1089–1101.

Pang, W., Esping, A., & Plucker, J. A. (2017). Confucian conceptions of human intelligence. *Review of General Psychology, 21*(2), 161–169. https://doi-org.ezp-prod1.hul.harvard.edu/10.1037/gpr0000103

Pant, R., Kanjlia, S., & Bedny, M. (2020). A sensitive period in the neural phenotype of language in blind individuals. *Developmental Cognitive Neuroscience, 41,* 100744. https://doi.org/10.1016/j.dcn.2019.100744

Papez, J. W. (1937). A proposed mechanism of emotion. *Archives of Neurology and Pathology, 38,* 725–743.

Papies, E. K., Barsalou, L. W., & Rusz, D. (2020). Understanding desire for food and drink: A grounded-cognition approach. *Current Directions in Psychological Science, 29*(2), 193–198. https://doi.org/10.1177/0963721420904958

Pappa, K., Biswas, V., Flegal, K. E., Evans, J. J., & Baylan, S. (2020). Working memory updating training promotes plasticity & behavioural gains: A systematic review & meta-analysis. *Neuroscience and Biobehavioral Reviews, 118,* 209–235. https://doi.org/10.1016/j.neubiorev.2020.07.027

Pardavila-Belio, M. I., Ruiz-Canela, M., & Canga-Armayor, N. (2019). Predictors of smoking cessation among college students in a pragmatic randomized controlled trial. *Prevention Science, 20*(5), 765–775. https://doi.org/10.1007/s11121-019-01004-6

Park, B., & Hastie, R. (1987). Perception of variability in category development: Instance- versus abstraction-based stereotypes. *Journal of Personality and Social Psychology, 53*(4), 621–635. https://doi.org/10.1037/0022-3514.53.4.621

Park, D. C., & Huang, C.-M. (2010). Culture wires the brain: A cognitive neuroscience perspective. *Perspectives on Psychological Science, 5*(4), 391–400. https://doi.org/10.1177/1745691610374591

Park, D. C., & McDonough, I. M. (2013). The dynamic aging mind: Revelations from functional neuroimaging research. *Perspectives on Psychological Science, 8*(1), 62–67. https://doi.org/10.1177/1745691612469034

Park, D. C., Polk, T. A., Park, R., Minear, M., Savage, A., & Smith, M. R. (2004). Aging reduces neural specialization in ventral visual cortex. *Proceedings of the National Academy of Sciences, USA, 101*(35), 13091–13095. https://doi.org/10.1073/pnas.0405148101

Parker, E. S., Cahill, L. S., & McGaugh, J. L. (2006a). A case of unusual autobiographical remembering. *Neurocase, 12,* 35–49.

Parker, G., Gibson, N. A., Brotchie, H., Heruc, G., Rees, A. M., & Hadzi-Pavlovic, D. (2006b). Omega-3 fatty acids and mood disorders. *American Journal of Psychiatry, 163,* 969–978.

Parker, H. A., & McNally, R. J. (2008). Repressive coping, emotional adjustment, and cognition in people who have lost loved ones to suicide. *Suicide and Life-Threatening Behavior, 38,* 676–687.

Parkin, B. L., Ekhtiari, H., & Walsh, V. F. (2015). Non-invasive brain stimulation in cognitive neuroscience: A primer. *Neuron, 87,* 932–945.

Parkinson, B., & Totterdell, P. (1999). Classifying affect-regulation strategies. *Cognition and Emotion, 13,* 277–303.

Parkinson, C., Walker, T. T., Memmi, S., & Wheatley, T. (2017). Emotions are understood from biological motion across remote cultures. *Emotion, 17*(3), 459–477. https://doi.org/10.1037/emo0000194

Parrott, A. C., Morinan, A., Moss, M., & Scholey, A. (2005). *Understanding drugs and behavior.* Wiley.

Parsons, T. (1975). The sick role and the role of the physician reconsidered. *Milbank Memorial Fund Quarterly, Health and Society, 53*(3), 257–278.

Pascual-Ferrá, P., Liu, Y., & Beatty, M. J. (2012). A meta-analytic comparison of the effects of text messaging to substance-induced impairment on driving performance. *Communication Research Reports, 29,* 229–238.

Pascual-Leone, A., Amedi, A., Fregni, F., & Merabet, L. B. (2005). The plastic human brain cortex. *Annual Review of Neuroscience, 28,* 377–401.

Pascual-Leone, A., Houser, C. M., Reese, K., Shotland, L. I., Grafman, J., Sato, S., ... Cohen, L. G. (1993). Safety of rapid-rate transcranial magnetic stimulation in normal volunteers. *Electroencephalography and Clinical Neurophysiology, 89,* 120–130.

Pasupathi, M., McLean, K. C., & Weeks, T. (2009). To tell or not to tell: Disclosure and the narrative self. *Journal of Personality, 77,* 1–35.

Patall, E. A., Cooper, H., & Robinson, J. C. (2008). The effects of choice on intrinsic motivation and related outcomes: A meta-analysis of research findings. *Psychological Bulletin, 134*(2), 270–300.

Patel, G. H., Sestieri, C., & Corbetta, M. (2019). The evolution of the temporoparietal junction and posterior superior temporal sulcus. *Cortex, 118,* 38–50. https://doi.org/10.1016/j.cortex.2019.01.026

Patihis, L., Frenda, S. J., LePort, A. K. R., Petersen, N., Nichols, R. M., Stark, C. E. L., ... Loftus, E. F. (2013). False memories in highly superior autobiographical memory individuals. *Proceedings of the National Academy of Sciences, USA, 110,* 20947–20952.

Patterson, C. J. (2013). Sexual orientation and family lives. In G. W. Peterson & K. R. Bush (Eds.), *The handbook of marriage and the family.* Springer.

Patton, G. C., & Viner, R. (2007). Pubertal transitions in health. *Lancet, 369,* 1130–1139.

Paulozzi, L. J., Mack, K. A., & Hockenberry, J. M. (2014). Vital signs: Variation among states in prescribing of opioid pain relievers and benzodiazepines. United States, 2012. *Morbidity and Mortality Weekly Report, 63,* 563–568.

Paulus, M. (2016). It's payback time: Preschoolers selectively request resources from someone they had benefitted. *Developmental Psychology, 52*(8), 1299–1306. https://doi.org/10.1037/dev0000150

Pavlidou, E. V., Williams, J. M., & Kelly, L. M. (2009). Artificial grammar learning in primary school children with and without developmental dyslexia. *Annals of Dyslexia, 59,* 55–77.

Pavlov, I. P. (1923a). New researches on conditioned reflexes. *Science, 58,* 359–361.

Pavlov, I. P. (1923b, July 23). Pavloff. *Time, 1*(21), 20–21.

Pavlov, I. P. (1927). *Conditioned reflexes.* Oxford University Press.

Pearce, J. M. (1987). A model of stimulus generalization for Pavlovian conditioning. *Psychological Review, 84,* 61–73.

Pearson, J., & Kosslyn, S. M. (2015). The heterogeneity of mental representation: Ending the imagery debate. *Proceedings of the National Academy of Sciences, USA, 112,* 10089–10092.

Peelen, M. V., & Kastner, S. (2009). A nonvisual look at the functional organization of visual cortex. *Neuron, 63,* 284–286.

Pelham, B. W. (2021). The husband-older age gap in marriage is associated with selective fitness. *Journal of Personality and Social Psychology, 121*(3), 601–632. https://doi-org.ezp-prod1.hul.harvard.edu/10.1037/pspi0000319

Pelham, B. W., Carvallo, M., & Jones, J. T. (2005). Implicit egotism. *Current Directions in Psychological Science, 14,* 106–110.

Pelham, B. W., Harding, M., & Hardin, C. (2020). Psychological challenges to common sense philosophy: Illusions of introspection and free will. In R. Peels, J. de Ridder, & R. van Woudenberg (Eds.), *Psychological challenges to common sense philosophy.* Taylor & Francis.

Pelham, B. W., Mirenberg, M. C., & Jones, J. T. (2002). Why Susie sells seashells by the seashore: Implicit egotism and major life decisions. *Journal of Personality and Social Psychology, 82,* 469–487.

Pelphrey, K. A., Morris, J. P., Michelich, C. R., Allison, T., & McCarthy, G. (2005). Functional anatomy of biological motion perception in posterior temporal cortex: An fMRI study of eye, mouth, and hand movements. *Cerebral Cortex, 15*(12), 1866–1876. https://doi.org/10.1093/cercor/bhi064

Penfield, W., & Rasmussen, T. (1950). *The cerebral cortex of man: A clinical study of localization of function.* Macmillan.

Pennebaker, J. W. (1989). Confession, inhibition, and disease. *Advances in Experimental Social Psychology, 22,* 211–244.

Pennebaker, J. W., & Chung, C. K. (2007). Expressive writing, emotional upheavals, and health. In H. Friedman & R. Silver (Eds.), *Handbook of health psychology* (pp. 263–284). Oxford University Press.

Pennebaker, J. W., Kiecolt-Glaser, J. K., & Glaser, R. (1988). Disclosure of traumas and immune function: Health implications for psychotherapy. *Journal of Consulting and Clinical Psychology, 56,* 239–245.

Pennebaker, J. W., & Sanders, D. Y. (1976). American graffiti: Effects of authority and reactance arousal. *Personality and Social Psychology Bulletin, 2,* 264–267.

Penner, L. A., Albrecht, T. L., Orom, H., Coleman, D. K., & Underwood, W. (2010). Health and health care disparities. In J. F. Dovidio, M. Hewstone, P. Glick, & V. M. Esses (Eds.), *The Sage handbook of prejudice, stereotyping and discrimination* (pp. 472–489). Sage.

Pennycook, G., Cannon, T. D., & Rand, D. G. (2018). Prior exposure increases perceived accuracy of fake news. *Journal of Experimental Psychology: General, 147,* 1865–1880. http://doi.org/10.1037/xge0000465

Pennycook, G., Epstein, Z., Mosleh, M., Arechar, A. A., Eckles, D., & Rand, D. G. (2021). Shifting attention to accuracy can reduce misinformation online. *Nature, 592,* 590–595. https://doi.org/10.1038/s41586-021-03344-2

Pennycook, G., McPhetres, J., Zhang, Y., Lu, J. G., & Rand, D. G. (2020). Fighting COVID-19 misinformation on social media: Experimental evidence for a scalable accuracy-nudge intervention. *Psychological Science, 31*(7), 770–780. https://doi.org/10.1177/0956797620939054

Pepping, C. A., MacDonald, G., & Davis, P. J. (2018). Toward a psychology of singlehood: An attachment-theory perspective on long-term singlehood. *Current Directions in Psychological Science.* https://doi.org/10.1177/0963721417752106

Perenin, M.-T., & Vighetto, A. (1988). Optic ataxia: A specific disruption in visuomotor mechanisms. I. Different aspects of the deficit in reaching for objects. *Brain, 111,* 643–674.

Perera, S., Eisen, R., Bhatt, M., Bhatnagar, N., de Souza, R., & Thabane, L. (2018). Light therapy for non-seasonal depression: Systematic review and meta-analysis. *British Journal of Psychiatry, 2,* 116–126.

Perera, T., George, M. S., Grammer, G., Janicak, P. G., Pascual-Leone, A., & Wirecki, T. S. (2016). The Clinical TMS Society consensus review and treatment recommendations for TMS therapy for major depressive disorder. *Brain Stimulation, 9,* 336–346.

Perilloux, H. K., Webster, G. D., & Gaulin, S. J. C. (2010). Signals of genetic quality and maternal investment capacity: The dynamic effects of fluctuating asymmetry and waist-to-hip ratio on men's ratings of women's attractiveness. *Social Psychological and Personality Science, 1*(1), 34–42. https://doi.org/10.1177/1948550609349514

Perlmutter, J. S., & Mink, J. W. (2006). Deep brain stimulation. *Annual Review of Neuroscience, 29,* 229–257.

Perloff, L. S., & Fetzer, B. K. (1986). Self-other judgments and perceived vulnerability to victimization. *Journal of Personality and Social Psychology, 50,* 502–510.

Perls, F. S., Hefferkine, R., & Goodman, P. (1951). *Gestalt therapy: Excitement and growth in the human personality.* Julian Press.

Perrett, D. I., Burt, D. M., Penton-Voak, I. S., Lee, K. J., Rowland, D. A., & Edwards, R. (1999). Symmetry and human facial attractiveness. *Evolution and Human Behavior, 20,* 295–307.

Perrett, D. I., Rolls, E. T., & Caan, W. (1982). Visual neurones responsive to faces in the monkey temporal cortex. *Experimental Brain Research, 47,* 329–342.

Pessiglione, M., Seymour, B., Flandin, G., Dolan, R. J., & Frith, C. D. (2006). Dopamine-dependent prediction errors underpin reward-seeking behavior in humans. *Nature, 442,* 1042–1045.

Petersen, A. C., & Grockett, L. (1985). Pubertal timing and grade effects on adjustment. *Journal of Youth and Adolescence, 14,* 191–206.

Petersen, J. L., & Hyde, J. S. (2010). A meta-analytic review of research on gender differences in sexuality, 1993–2007. *Psychological Bulletin, 136*(1), 21–38. https://doi.org/10.1037/a0017504

Peterson, C., & Siegal, M. (1999). Representing inner worlds: Theory of mind in autistic, deaf and normal hearing children. *Psychological Science, 10,* 126–129.

Peterson, C., Slaughter, V., Moore, C., & Wellman, H. M. (2016). Peer social skills and theory of mind in children with autism, deafness, or typical development. *Developmental Psychology, 52*(1), 46–57. https://doi.org/10.1037/a0039833

Peterson, C., Wang, Q., & Hou, Y. (2009). "When I was little": Childhood recollections in Chinese and European Canadian grade school children. *Child Development, 80,* 506–518.

Peterson, G. B. (2004). A day of great illumination: B. F. Skinner's discovery of shaping. *Journal of the Experimental Analysis of Behavior, 82,* 317–328.

Peterson, L. R., & Peterson, M. J. (1959). Short-term retention of individual verbal items. *Journal of Experimental Psychology, 58,* 193–198.

Petersson, K. M., Forkstam, C., & Ingvar, M. (2004). Artificial syntactic violations activate Broca's region. *Cognitive Science, 28,* 383–407.

Petitto, L. A., & Marentette, P. F. (1991). Babbling in the manual mode: Evidence for the ontogeny of language. *Science, 251,* 1493–1496.

Petrie, K. P., Booth, R. J., & Pennebaker, J. W. (1998). The immunological effects of thought suppression. *Journal of Personality and Social Psychology, 75,* 1264–1272.

Petrow, S. (2018, May 22). I was a GPS zombie. Here's what happened when I went back to paper maps and serendipity. *USA Today.* https://www.usatoday.com/story/tech/columnist/stevenpetrow/2018/05/22/gps-addict-so-tried-driving-without-apple-google-maps/629814002/

Petty, R. E., & Cacioppo, J. T. (1986). The elaboration likelihood model of persuasion. In L. Berkowitz (Ed.), *Advances in experimental social psychology* (Vol. 19, pp. 123–205). Academic Press.

Petty, R. E., & Wegener, D. T. (1998). Attitude change: Multiple roles for persuasion variables. In D. T. Gilbert, S. T. Fiske, & G. Lindzey (Eds.), *The handbook of social psychology* (4th ed., Vol. 1, pp. 323–390). McGraw-Hill.

Petty, R. E., Cacioppo, J. T., & Goldman, R. (1981). Personal involvement as a determinant of argument-based persuasion. *Journal of Personality and Social Psychology, 41,* 847–855.

Pew Charitable Trust. (2015, February). *Federal prison system shows dramatic long-term growth: Policy decisions contribute to steep risk in inmate population and costs.* https://www.pewtrusts.org/~/media/assets/2015/02/pew_federal_prison_growth.pdf

Pew Research Center for People & the Press. (2009). *Growing old in America: Expectations vs. reality.* http://pewsocialtrends.org/pubs/736/getting-old-in-america

Pew Research Center. (2013, June 13). *A survey of LGBT American attitudes, experiences and values in changing times.* http://www.pewsocialtrends.org/wp-content/uploads/sites/3/2013/06/SDT_LGBT-Americans_06-2013.pdf

Phelps, E. A. (2006). Emotion and cognition: Insights from studies of the human amygdala. *Annual Review of Psychology, 57*(1), 27–53. https://doi.org/10.1146/annurev.psych.56.091103.070234

Phelps, E. A., & LeDoux, J. E. (2005). Contributions of the amygdala to emotion processing: From animal models to human behavior. *Neuron, 48*(2), 175–187. https://doi.org/10.1016/j.neuron.2005.09.025

Phills, C. E., Kawakami, K., Tabi, E., Nadolny, D., & Inzlicht, M. (2011). Mind the gap: Increasing associations between the self and Blacks with approach behaviors. *Journal of Personality and Social Psychology, 100*(2), 197–210. https://doi.org/10.1037/a0022159

Philpot, R., Liebst, L. S., Levine, M., Bernasco, W., & Lindegaard, M. R. (2020). Would I be helped? Cross-national CCTV footage shows that intervention is the norm in public conflicts. *American Psychologist, 75*(1), 66–75. https://doi.org/10.1037/amp0000469

Piaget, J. (1954). *The child's conception of number.* Norton.

Piaget, J. (1965). *The moral judgment of the child.* Free Press. (Original work published 1932)

Piaget, J. (1977). The first year of life of the child. In H. E. Gruber & J. J. Voneche (Eds.), *The essential Piaget: An interpretative reference and guide* (pp. 198–214). Basic Books. (Original work published 1927)

Piantadosi, S. T., & Kidd, C. (2016). Extraordinary intelligence and the care of infants. *Proceedings of the National Academy of Sciences, USA, 113* (2016), 1–6. https://doi.org/10.1073/pnas.1506752113

Piazza, J. R., Charles, S. T., Sliwinski, M. J., Mogle, J., & Almeida, D. M. (2013). Affective reactivity to daily stressors and long-term risk of reporting a chronic physical health condition. *Annals of Behavioral Medicine, 45,* 110–120.

Pietschnig, J., Penke, L., Wicherts, J. M., Zeiler, M., & Voracek, M. (2015). Meta-analysis of associations between human brain volume and intelligence differences: How strong are they and what do they mean? *Neuroscience & Behavioral Reviews, 57,* 411–432.

Piff, P. K., Kraus, M. W., Côté, S., Cheng, B. H., & Keltner, D. (2010). Having less, giving more: The influence of social class on prosocial behavior. *Journal of Personality and Social Psychology, 99*(5), 771–784. https://doi.org/10.1037/a0020092

Piff, P. K., Stancato, D. M., Côté, S., Mendoza-Denton, R., & Keltner, D. (2012). Higher social class predicts increased unethical behavior. *Proceedings of the National Academy of Sciences of the United States of America, USA, 109*(11), 4086–4091. https://doi.org/10.1073/pnas.1118373109

Pina, A. A., Polo, A. J., & Huey, S. J. (2019). Evidence-based psychosocial interventions for ethnic minority youth: The 10-year update. *Journal of Clinical Child & Adolescent Psychology, 48*(2), 179–202. https://doi.org/10.1080/15374416.2019.1567350

Pinel, J. P. J., Assanand, S., & Lehman, D. R. (2000). Hunger, eating, and ill health. *American Psychologist, 55,* 1105–1116.

Pines, A. M. (1993). Burnout: An existential perspective. In W. B. Schaufeli, C. Maslach, & T. Marek (Eds.), *Professional burnout: Recent developments in theory and research* (pp. 33–51). Taylor & Francis.

Pinker, S. (1994). *The language instinct.* Morrow.

Pinker, S. (2003). *The blank slate: The modern denial of human nature.* Viking.

Pinker, S. (2007, March 19). A history of violence: We're getting nicer every day. *The New Republic Online.* https://newrepublic.com/article/64340/history-violence-were getting-nicer-every-day

Pinker, S., & Bloom, P. (1990). Natural language and natural selection. *Behavioral and Brain Sciences, 13,* 707–727.

Pitcher, D., Garrido, L., Walsh, V., & Duchaine, B. C. (2008). Transcranial magnetic stimulation disrupts the perception and embodiment of facial expressions. *Journal of Neuroscience, 28*(36), 8929–8933.

Pjrek, E., Friedrich, M.-E., Cambioli, L., Dold, M., Jäger, F., Komorowski, A., … Winkler, D. (2020). The efficacy of light therapy in the treatment of seasonal affective disorder: A meta-analysis of randomized controlled trials. *Psychotherapy and Psychosomatics, 89*(1), 17–24. https:/doi.org/10.1159/000502891

Plack, C. J. (2018a). Pitch and periodicity coding. In *The sense of hearing* (3rd ed., Ch. 7, pp. 128–148). Routledge.

Plack, C. J. (2018b). Spatial hearing. In *The sense of hearing* (3rd ed., Ch. 9, pp. 171–191). Routledge.

Platek, S. M., Critton, S. R., Myers, T. E., & Gallup, G. G. Jr. (2003). Contagious yawning: The role of self-awareness and mental state attribution. *Cognitive Brain Research, 17,* 223–227.

Plavén-Sigray, P., Hedman, E., Victorsson, P., Matheson, G. J., Forsberg, A., Djurfeldt, D. R., … Cervenka, S. (2017). Extrastriatal dopamine D2-receptor availability in social anxiety disorder. *European Neuropsychopharmacology, 27,* 462–469.

Plomin, R., & Caspi, A. (1999). Behavioral genetics and personality. In L. A. Pervin & O. P. John (Eds.), *Handbook of personality: Theory and research* (Vol. 2, pp. 251–276). Guilford Press.

Plomin, R., & Spinath, F. M. (2004). Intelligence: Genetics, genes, and genomics. *Journal of Personality and Social Psychology, 86,* 112–129.

Plomin, R., DeFries, J. C., McClearn, G. E., & McGuffin, P. (2001). *Behavioral genetics* (4th ed.). W. H. Freeman.

Plomin, R., Haworth, C. M. A., Meaburn, E. L., Price, T. S., Wellcome Trust Case Control Consortium 2, & Davis, O. S. P. (2013). Common DNA markers can account for more than half of the genetic influence on cognitive abilities. *Psychological Science, 24*(4), 562–568. https://doi.org/10.1177/0956797612457952

Plomin, R., Scheier, M. F., Bergeman, C. S., Pedersen, N. L., Nesselroade, J. R., & McClearn, G. E. (1992). Optimism, pessimism, and mental health: A twin/adoption analysis. *Personality and Individual Differences, 13,* 921–930.

Plotnik, J. M., de Waal, F. B. M., & Reiss, D. (2006). Self-recognition in an Asian elephant. *Proceedings of the National Academy of Sciences, USA, 103,* 17053–17057.

Pnevmatikos, D., & Trikkaliotis, I. (2013). Intraindividual differences in executive functions during childhood: The role of emotions. *Journal of Experimental Child Psychology, 115*(2), 245–261. https://10.1016/j.jecp.2013.01.010

Polanczyk, G., de Lima, M. S., Horta, B. L., Biederman, J., & Rohde, L. A. (2007). The worldwide prevalence of ADHD: A systemic review and metaregression analysis. *American Journal of Psychiatry, 164,* 942–948.

Polderman, T. J. C., Benyamin, B., de Leeuw, C. A., Sullivan, P. F., van Bochoven, A., Visscher, P. M., & Posthuma, D. (2015). Meta-analysis of the heritability of human traits based on fifty years of twin studies. *Nature Genetics, 47*(7), 702–709. https://doi.org/10.1038/ng.3285

Poldrack, R. A. (2018). *The new mind readers: What neuroimaging can and cannot reveal about our thoughts.* Princeton University Press.

Poliak, S., & Peles, E. (2003). The local differentiation of myelinated axons at nodes of Ranvier. *Nature Reviews Neuroscience, 4,* 968–980.

Poole, D. A., Lindsay, S. D., Memon, A., & Bull, R. (1995). Psychotherapy and the recovery of memories of childhood sexual abuse: U.S. and British practitioners' opinions, practices, and experiences. *Journal of Consulting and Clinical Psychology, 63,* 426–487.

Pope, A. W., & Bierman, K. L. (1999). Predicting adolescent peer problems and antisocial activities: The relative roles of aggression and dysregulation. *Developmental Psychology, 35,* 335–346.

Posner, M. I., & Raichle, M. E. (1994). *Images of mind.* W. H. Freeman and Company.

Post, R. M., Frye, M. A., Denicoff, G. S., Leverich, G. S., Dunn, R. T., Osuch, E. A., … Jajodia, K. (2008). Emerging trends in the treatment of rapid cycling bipolar disorder: A selected review. *Bipolar Disorders, 2,* 305–315.

Postman, L., & Underwood, B. J. (1973). Critical issues in interference theory. *Memory & Cognition, 1,* 19–40.

Postmes, T., & Spears, R. (1998). Deindividuation and anti-normative behavior: A meta-analysis. *Psychological Bulletin, 123,* 238–259.

Powell, R. A., Symbaluk, D. G., MacDonald, S. E., & Honey, P. L. (2009). *Introduction to learning and behavior* (3rd ed.). Wadsworth Cengage Learning.

Power, M. L., & Schulkin, J. (2009). *The evolution of obesity.* Johns Hopkins University Press.

Prakash, R. S., Voss, M. W., Erickson, K. I., & Kramer, A. F. (2015). Moving towards a healthier brain and mind. *Annual Review of Psychology, 66,* 769–797.

Prasada, S., & Pinker, S. (1993). Generalizations of regular and irregular morphology. *Language and Cognitive Processes, 8,* 1–56.

Pratt, L. A., Brody, D. J., & Gu, Q. (2017). Antidepressant use among persons aged 12 and over: United States, 2011–2014. *NCHS Data Brief, no. 283.* National Center for Health Statistics.

Pressman, S. D., Cohen, S., Miller, G. E., Barkin, A., Rabin, B. S., & Treanor, J. J. (2005). Loneliness, social network size, and immune response to influenza vaccination in college freshmen. *Health Psychology, 24,* 297–306.

Price, C. (2012). A review and synthesis of the first 20 years of PET and fMRI studies of heard speech, spoken language, and reading. *Neuroimage, 62*(2), 816–847. https://doi.org/10.1016/j.neuroimage.2012.04.062

Price, J. L., & Davis, B. (2008). *The woman who can't forget: The extraordinary story of living with the most remarkable memory known to science.* Free Press.

Prince, M., Wimo, A., Guerchet, M., Ali, G.-C., Wu, Y-T, Prina, A. M., & Alzheimer's Disease International. (2015). *World Alzheimer Report 2015: The global impact of dementia. An analysis of prevalence, incidence, cost and trends.* Alzheimer's Disease International.

Prior, H., Schwartz, A., & Güntürkün, O. (2008). Mirror-induced behavior in the magpie (*Pica pica*): Evidence of self-recognition. *PLoS Biology, 6,* e202.

Prochaska, J. J., & Sallis, J. F. (2004). A randomized controlled trial of single versus multiple health behavior change: Promoting physical activity and nutrition among adolescents. *Health Psychology, 23,* 314–318.

Procopio, M., & Marriott, P. (2007). Intrauterine hormonal environment and risk of developing anorexia nervosa. *Archives of General Psychiatry, 64*(12), 1402–1407.

Protzko, J. (2015). The environment in raising early intelligence: A meta-analysis of the fadeout effect. *Intelligence, 53,* 202–210. https://doi.org/10.1016/j.intell.2015.10.006

Protzko, J. (2016). Does the raising IQ/raising g distinction explain the fadeout effect? *Intelligence, 56,* 65–71. https://doi.org/10.1016/j.intell.2016.02.008

Protzko, J., Aronson, J., & Blair, C. (2013). How to make a young child smarter: Evidence from the database of raising intelligence.

Perspectives on Psychological Science, 8(1), 25–40. https://doi.org/10.1177/1745691612462585

Provencal, N., & Binder, E. B. (2015). The neurobiological effects of stress as contributors to psychiatric disorders: Focus on epigenetics. *Current Opinion in Neurobiology, 30,* 31–37.

Provine, R. R. (2000). *Laughter: A scientific investigation.* Viking.

Punjabi, N. M. (2008). The epidemiology of adult obstructive sleep apnea. *Proceedings of the American Thoracic Society, 5,* 136–143.

Puterman, E., Lin, J., Blackburn, E. H., O'Donovan, A., Adler, N., & Epel, E. (2010). The power of exercise: Buffering the effect of chronic stress on telomere length. *PLoS ONE, 5,* e10837.

Pyc, M. A., & Rawson, K. A. (2009). Testing the retrieval effort hypothesis: Does greater difficulty correctly recalling information lead to higher levels of memory? *Journal of Memory and Language, 60,* 437–447.

Pyers, J. E., & Senghas, A. (2009). Language promotes false-belief understanding: Evidence from learners of a new sign language. *Psychological Science, 20*(7), 805–812.

Pyers, J. E., Shusterman, A., Senghas, A., Spelke, E. S., & Emmorey, K. (2010). Evidence from an emerging sign language reveals that language supports spatial cognition. *Proceedings of the National Academy of Sciences, USA, 107,* 12116–12120.

Quiroga, R. (2016). Neuronal codes for visual perception and memory. *Neuropsychologia, 83,* 227–241.

Quiroga, R. Q., Reddy, L., Kreiman, G., Koch, C., & Fried, I. (2005). Invariant visual representation by single neurons in the human brain. *Nature, 435,* 1102–1107.

Qureshi, A., & Lee-Chiong, T. (2004). Medications and their effects on sleep. *Medical Clinics of North America, 88,* 751–766.

Rabbitt, P., Diggle, P., Holland, F., & McInnes, L. (2004). Practice and drop-out effects during a 17-year longitudinal study of cognitive aging. *Journal of Gerontology: Psychological Sciences and Social Sciences, 59*(2), 84–97.

Rabin, L. A., Fogel, J., & Nutter-Upham, K. E. (2011). Academic procrastination in college students: The role of self-reported executive function. *Journal of Clinical and Experimental Neuropsychology, 33,* 344–357.

Race, E., Keane, M. M., & Verfaellie, M. (2011). Medial temporal lobe damage causes deficits in episodic memory and episodic future thinking not attributable to deficits in narrative construction. *Journal of Neuroscience, 31,* 10262–10269.

Radford, E., & Radford, M. A. (1949). *Encyclopedia of superstitions.* Philosophical Library.

Rahe, R. H., Meyer, M., Smith, M., Klaer, G., & Holmes, T. H. (1964). Social stress and illness onset. *Journal of Psychosomatic Research, 8,* 35–44.

Raichle, M. E. (2015). The brain's default mode network. *Annual Review of Neuroscience, 38,* 433–447.

Raichle, M. E., & Mintun, M. A. (2006). Brain work and brain imaging. *Annual Review of Neuroscience, 29,* 449–476.

Raines, J., Holmes, L., Watts-Overall, T. M., Slettevold, E., Gruia, D. C., Orbell, S., & Reiger, G. (2021). Patterns of genital sexual arousal in transgender men. *Psychological Science, 32*(4), 485–495. https://doi.org/10.1177/0956797620971654

Rajaram, S. (2011). Collaboration both hurts and helps memory: A cognitive perspective. *Current Directions in Psychological Science, 20,* 76–81.

Rajaram, S., & Pereira-Pasarin, L. P. (2010). Collaborative memory: Cognitive research and theory. *Perspectives on Psychological Science, 6,* 649–663.

Ramachandran, V. S., & Blakeslee, S. (1998). *Phantoms in the brain: Probing the mysteries of the human mind.* Morrow.

Ramachandran, V. S., & Brang, D. (2015). Phantom touch. In T. J. Prescott, E. Ahissar, & E. Izhikevich (Eds.), *Scholarpedia of Touch* (pp. 377–386). Atlantis Press.

Ramachandran, V. S., Brang, D., & McGeoch, P. D. (2010). Dynamic reorganization of referred sensations by movements of phantom limbs. *NeuroReport, 21,* 727–730.

Ramachandran, V. S., Rodgers-Ramachandran, D., & Stewart, M. (1992). Perceptual correlates of massive cortical reorganization. *Science, 258,* 1159–1160.

Ramirez-Esparza, N., Gosling, S. D., Benet-Martinez, V., & Potter, J. P. (2004). Do bilinguals have two personalities? A special case of cultural frame-switching. *Journal of Research in Personality, 40,* 99–120.

Ramirez-Zamora, A., Giordano, J., Gunduz, A., Alcantara, J., Cagle, J. N. ... Okun, M. S. (2020). Proceedings of the Seventh Annual Deep Brain Stimulation Think Tank: Advances in neurophysiology, adaptive DBS, virtual reality, neuroethics and technology. *Frontiers in Human Neuroscience, 14,* 54. https://doi.org/10.3389/fnhum.2020.00054

Rand, D. G. (2016). Cooperation, fast and slow: Meta-analytic evidence for a theory of social heuristics and self-interested deliberation. *Psychological Science, 27*(9), 1192–1206. https://doi.org/10.1177/0956797616654455

Rand, D. G., & Nowak, M. A. (2016). Human cooperation. *Trends in Cognitive Sciences, 17*(8), 413–425. https://doi.org/10.1016/j.tics.2013.06.003

Randles, D., Inzlicht, M., Proulx, T., Tullett, A. M., & Heine, S. J. (2015). Is dissonance reduction a special case of fluid compensation? Evidence that dissonant cognitions cause compensatory affirmation and abstraction. *Journal of Personality and Social Psychology, 108*(5), 697–710. https://doi.org/10.1037/a0038933

Rapaport, D. (1946). *Diagnostic psychological testing: The theory, statistical evaluation, and diagnostic application of a battery of tests.* Year Book Publishers.

Rasmussen, A. S., & Berntsen, D. (2011). The unpredictable past: Spontaneous autobiographical memories outnumber autobiographical memories retrieved strategically. *Consciousness and Cognition, 20,* 1843–1846.

Ratliff, K. A., & Oishi, S. (2013). Gender differences in implicit self-esteem following a romantic partner's success or failure. *Journal of Personality and Social Psychology, 105*(4), 688–702. https://doi.org/10.1037/a0033769

Raven, J., Raven, J. C., & Court, J. H. (2004). *Manual for Raven's Progressive Matrices and Vocabulary Scales.* Harcourt Assessment.

Raz, N. (2000). Aging of the brain and its impact on cognitive performance: Integration of structural and functional findings. In F. I. M. Craik & T. A. Salthouse (Eds.), *The handbook of aging and cognition* (pp. 1–90). Erlbaum.

Reber, A. S. (1996). *Implicit learning and tacit knowledge: An essay on the cognitive unconscious.* Oxford University Press.

Reber, A. S., & Allen, R. (2000). Individual differences in implicit learning. In R. G. Kunzendorf & B. Wallace (Eds.), *Individual differences in conscious experience* (pp. 227–247). John Benjamins.

Reber, A. S., Walkenfeld, F. F., & Hernstadt, R. (1991). Implicit learning: Individual differences and IQ. *Journal of Experimental Psychology: Learning, Memory, and Cognition, 17,* 888–896.

Reber, P. J. (2013). The neural basis of implicit learning and memory: A review of neuropsychological and neuroimaging research. *Neuropsychologia, 51,* 2026–2042.

Reber, P. J., Gitelman, D. R., Parrish, T. B., & Mesulam, M. M. (2003). Dissociating explicit and implicit category knowledge with fMRI. *Journal of Cognitive Neuroscience, 15*, 574–583.

Recanzone, G. H., & Sutter, M. L. (2008). The biological basis of audition. *Annual Review of Psychology, 59*, 119–142.

Rechtschaffen, A., Gilliland, M. A., Bergmann, B. M., & Winter, J. B. (1983). Physiological correlates of prolonged sleep deprivation in rats. *Science, 221*, 182–184.

Redick, T. S. (2015). Working memory training and interpreting interactions in intelligence interventions. *Intelligence, 50*, 14–20.

Redick, T. S., Shipstead, Z., Harrison, T. L., Hicks, K. L., Fried, D. E., Hambrick, D. Z., ... Engle, R. W. (2013). No evidence of intelligence improvement after working memory training: A randomized, placebo-controlled study. *Journal of Experimental Psychology: General, 142*(2), 359–379. https://doi.org/10.1037/a002908

Reed, D. R. (2008). Birth of a new breed of supertaster. *Chemical Senses, 33*, 489–491.

Reeve, C. L., Heggestad, E. D., & Lievens, F. (2009). Modeling the impact of test anxiety and test familiarity on the criterion-related validity of cognitive ability tests. *Intelligence, 37*(1), 34–41. https://doi.org/10.1016/j.intell.2008.05.003

Regan, P. C. (1998). What if you can't get what you want? Willingness to compromise ideal mate selection standards as a function of sex, mate value, and relationship context. *Personality and Social Psychology Bulletin, 24*, 1294–1303.

Regier, T., & Kay, P. (2009). Language, thought, and color: Whorf was half right. *Trends in Cognitive Sciences, 13*, 439–446.

Reichbach, G. L. (2012, May 16). A judge's plea for pot [op-ed article]. *New York Times.* http://www.nytimes.com/2012/05/17/opinion/a-judges-plea-for-medical-marijuana.html

Reid, V. M., & Dunn, K. (2021). The fetal origins of human psychological development. *Current Directions in Psychological Science, 30*(2), 144–150. https://doi.org/10.1177/0963721420984419

Reid, V. M., Dunn, K., Young, R. J., Amu, J., Donovan, T., & Reissland, N. (2017). The human fetus preferentially engages with face-like visual stimuli. *Current Biology, 27*, 1825–1828.e3.

Reis, H. T., Maniaci, M. R., Caprariello, P. S., Eastwick, P. W., & Finkel, E. J. (2011). Familiarity does indeed promote attraction in live interaction. *Journal of Personality and Social Psychology, 101*(3), 557–570. https://doi.org/10.1037/a0022885

Reiss, D., & Marino, L. (2001). Mirror self-recognition in the bottlenose dolphin: A case of cognitive convergence. *Proceedings of the National Academy of Sciences, USA, 98*, 5937–5942.

Reissland, N. (1988). Neonatal imitation in the first hour of life: Observations in rural Nepal. *Developmental Psychology, 24*, 464–469.

Reiter, E. R., Coelho, D. H., Kons, Z. A., & Costanzo, R. M. (2020). Subjective smell and taste changes during the COVID-19 pandemic: Short term recovery. *American Journal of Otolaryngology, 41*(6), 102639. https://doi.org/10.1016/j.amjoto.2020.102639

Renner, K. E. (1964). Delay of reinforcement: A historical review. *Psychological Review, 61*, 341–361.

Renner, M. J., & Mackin, R. (1998). A life stress instrument for classroom use. *Teaching of Psychology, 25*, 46–48.

Rensink, R. A. (2002). Change detection. *Annual Review of Psychology, 53*, 245–277.

Rensink, R. A., O'Regan, J. K., & Clark, J. J. (1997). To see or not to see: The need for attention to perceive changes in scenes. *Psychological Science, 8*, 368–373.

Repacholi, B. M., & Gopnik, A. (1997). Early reasoning about desires: Evidence from 14- and 18-month-olds. *Developmental Psychology, 33*, 12–21.

Reschke, P. J., Walle, E. A., Knothe, J. M., & Lopez, L. D. (2019). The influence of context on distinct facial expressions of disgust. *Emotion. 19*(2), 365–370. https://doi.org/10.1037/emo0000445

Rescorla, R. A. (2006). Stimulus generalization of excitation and inhibition. *Quarterly Journal of Experimental Psychology, 59*, 53–67.

Rescorla, R. A., & Wagner, A. R. (1972). A theory of Pavlovian conditioning: Variations in the effectiveness of reinforcement and nonreinforcement. In A. H. Black & W. F. Prokasy (Eds.), *Classical conditioning II: Current research and theory* (pp. 64–99). Appleton-Century-Crofts.

Ressler, K. J., & Nemeroff, C. B. (1999). Role of norepinephrine in the pathophysiology and treatment of mood disorders. *Biological Psychiatry, 46*, 1219–1233.

Reuben, A., Sugden, K., Arseneault, L., Corcoran, D. L., Danese, A., Fisher, H. L., ... & Caspi, A. (2020). Association of neighborhood disadvantage in childhood with DNA methylation in young adulthood. *JAMA Network Open, 3*(6), e2060945. https://doi.org/10.1001/jamanetworkopen.2020.609

Revonsuo, A. (2000). The reinterpretation of dreams: An evolutionary hypothesis of the function of dreaming. *Behavioral and Brain Sciences, 23*(6), 877–901. https://doi.org/10.1017/S0140525X00004015

Reynolds, T., Baumeister, R. F., & Maner, J. K. (2018). Competitive reputation manipulation: Women strategically transmit social information about romantic rivals. *Journal of Experimental Social Psychology, 78*, 195–209. https://doi.org/10.1016/j.jesp.2018.03.011

Rice, K. G., Richardson, C. M. E., & Clark, D. (2012). Perfectionism, procrastination, and psychological distress. *Journal of Counseling Psychology, 39*, 288–302.

Richards, B. A., & Frankland, P. W. (2017). The persistence and transience of memory. *Neuron, 94*, 1071–1084.

Richards, M. H., Crowe, P. A., Larson, R., & Swarr, A. (1998). Developmental patterns and gender differences in the experience of peer companionship during adolescence. *Child Development, 69*, 154–163.

Richardson, D. S. (2014). Everyday aggression takes many forms. *Current Directions in Psychological Science, 23*(3), 220–224. https://doi.org/10.1177/0963721414530143

Richters, J., de Visser, R., Rissel, C., & Smith, A. (2006). Sexual practices at last heterosexual encounter and occurrence of orgasm in a national survey. *Journal of Sex Research, 43*, 217–226.

Ridenour, T. A., & Howard, M. O. (2012). Inhalants abuse: Status of etiology and intervention. In J. C. Verster, K. Brady, M. Galanter, & P. Conrod (Eds.), *Drug abuse and addiction in medical illness: Causes, consequences, and treatment* (pp. 189–199). Springer.

Rieger, G., Linsenmeier, J. A., Gygax, L., Garcia, S., & Bailey, J. M. (2010). Dissecting "gaydar": Accuracy and the role of masculinity–femininity. *Archives of Sexual Behavior, 39*, 124–140.

Riggs, J. E. (1993). Stone-age genes and modern lifestyle: Evolutionary mismatch or differential survival bias. *Journal of Clinical Epidemiology, 46*(11), 1289–1291. https://doi.org/10.1016/0895-4356(93)90093-g

Rigoli, F., Rutledge, R. B., Chew, B., Ousdal, O. T., Dayan, P., & Dolan, R. J. (2016). Dopamine increases a value-independent gambling propensity. *Neuropsychopharmacology, 41*, 2658–2667.

Rimer, J., Dwan, K., Lawlor, D. A., Greig, C. A., McMurdo, M., Morley, W., & Mead, G. E. (2012). Exercise for depression. *Cochrane Database of Systematic Reviews, 7*, CD004366.

Rinderu, M. I., Bushman, B. J., & Van Lange, P. A. M. (2018). Climate, aggression, and violence (CLASH): A cultural-evolutionary approach. *Current Opinion in Psychology, 19*, 113–118.

Ringach, D. L., & Jentsch, J. D. (2009). We must face the threats. *Journal of Neuroscience, 29*, 11417–11418.

Rippon, G. (2019). *The gendered brain: The new neuroscience that shatters the myth of the female brain.* Penguin Books.

Risko, E. F., Anderson, N., Sarwal, A., Engelhardt, M., & Kingstone, A. (2012). Every attention: Variation in mind wandering and memory in a lecture. *Applied Cognitive Psychology, 26,* 234–242.

Risko, E. F., & Gilbert, S. J. (2016). Cognitive offloading. *Trends in Cognitive Sciences, 20,* 676–688.

Risman, J. E., Coyle, J. T., Green, R. W., Javitt, D. C., Benes, F. M., Heckers, S., & Grace, A. A. (2008). Circuit-based framework for understanding neurotransmitter and risk gene interactions in schizophrenia. *Trends in Neurosciences, 31,* 234–242.

Ritchey, A. J., & Ruback, R. B. (2018). Predicting lynching atrocity: The situational norms of lynchings in Georgia. *Personality and Social Psychology Bulletin, 44*(5), 619–637.

Ritchie, S. J., & Tucker-Drob, E. M. (2018). How much does education improve intelligence? A meta-analysis. *Psychological Science, 29*(8), 1358–1369. https://doi.org/10.1177/0956797618774253

Rivera, L. A. (2012) Hiring as cultural matching: The case of elite professional service firms. *American Sociological Review, 77,* 999–1022.

Rivers, M. L. (2020). Metacognition about practice testing: A review of learners' beliefs, monitoring, and control of test-enhanced learning. *Educational Psychology Review, 33,* 823–862. https://doi.org/10.1007/s10648-020-09578-2

Rizvi, S. L., Finkelstein, J., Wacha-Montes, A., Yeager, A. L., Ruork, A. K. ... Kleiman, E. M. (2022). Randomized clinical trial of a brief, scalable intervention for mental health sequelae in college students during the COVID-19 pandemic. *Behaviour Research and Therapy, 149,* 104015. https://doi.org/10.1016/j.brat.2021.104015

Rizzolatti, G. (2004). The mirror-neuron system and imitation. In S. Hurley & N. Chater (Eds.), *Perspectives on imitation: From mirror neurons to memes* (pp. 55–76). MIT Press.

Rizzolatti, G., & Craighero, L. (2004). The mirror-neuron system. *Annual Review of Neuroscience, 27,* 169–192.

Rizzolatti, G., & Rozzi, S. (2018). The mirror mechanism in the parietal lobe. *Handbook of Clinical Neurology, 151,* 555–573.

Rizzolatti, G., & Sinigaglia, C. (2010). The functional role of the parieto-frontal mirror circuit. *Nature Reviews Neuroscience, 11,* 264–274.

Roberson, D., Davidoff, J., Davies, I. R. L., & Shapiro, L. R. (2004). The development of color categories in two languages: A longitudinal study. *Journal of Experimental Psychology: General, 133,* 554–571.

Roberts, G. A. (1991). Delusional belief and meaning in life: A preferred reality? *British Journal of Psychiatry, 159,* 20–29.

Roberts, G. A., & McGrady, A. (1996). Racial and gender effects on the relaxation response: Implications for the development of hypertension. *Biofeedback and Self-Regulation, 21,* 51–62.

Robertson, L. C. (2003). Binding, spatial attention and perceptual awareness. *Nature Reviews Neuroscience, 4,* 93–102.

Robins, L. N., Helzer, J. E., Hesselbrock, M., & Wish, E. (1980). Vietnam veterans three years after Vietnam. In L. Brill & C. Winick (Eds.), *The yearbook of substance use and abuse* (Vol. 11). Human Sciences Press.

Robins, R. W., Fraley, R. C., & Krueger, R. F. (Eds.). (2007). *Handbook of research methods in personality psychology.* Guilford Press.

Rodieck, R. W. (1998). *The first steps in seeing.* Sinauer.

Rodman, A. M., Powers, K. E., & Somerville, L. H. (2017). Development of self-protective biases in response to social evaluative feedback. *Proceedings of the National Academy of Sciences, USA, 114*(50), 13158–13163.

Roediger, H. L., III, & Karpicke, J. D. (2006). Test-enhanced learning: Taking memory tests improves long-term retention. *Psychological Science, 17,* 249–255.

Roediger, H. L., III, & Karpicke, J. D. (2018). Reflections on the resurgence of interest in the testing effect. *Perspectives on Psychological Science, 13,* 236–241.

Roediger, H. L., III, & McDermott, K. B. (1995). Creating false memories: Remembering words not presented in lists. *Journal of Experimental Psychology: Learning, Memory, and Cognition, 21,* 803–814.

Roediger, H. L., III, & McDermott, K. B. (2000). Tricks of memory. *Current Directions in Psychological Science, 9,* 123–127.

Roediger, H. L., III, Weldon, M. S., & Challis, B. H. (1989). Explaining dissociations between implicit and explicit measures of retention: A processing account. In H. L. Roediger & F. I. M. Craik (Eds.), *Varieties of memory and consciousness: Essays in honour of Endel Tulving* (pp. 3–39). Erlbaum.

Roelofs, K. (2017). Freeze for action: Neurobiological mechanisms in animal and human freezing. *Philosophical Transactions of the Royal Society of London. Series B, Biological Sciences, 372*(1718), 20160206.

Rogers, C. R. (1951). *Client-centered therapy: Its current practice, implications, and theory.* Houghton Mifflin.

Rogers, S. J., Estes, A., Lord, C., Munson, J., Rocha, M., Winter, J., ... Talbott, M. (2019). A multisite randomized controlled two-phase trial of the Early Start Denver Model compared to treatment as usual. *Journal of the American Academy of Child and Adolescent Psychiatry.* https://doi.org/10.1016/j.jaac.2019.01.004

Rogers, T. B., Kuiper, N. A., & Kirker, W. S. (1977). Self-reference and the encoding of personal information. *Journal of Personality and Social Psychology, 35,* 677–688.

Rohrer, D. (2015). Student instruction should be distributed over long time periods. *Educational Psychology Review, 27,* 635–643.

Roig, M., Skriver, K., Lundbye-Jensen, J., Kiens, B., & Nielsen, J. B. (2012). A single bout of exercise improves motor memory. *PLoS ONE, 7,* e44594. https://doi.org/10.1371/journal.pone.0044594

Roisman, G. I., Masten, A. S., Coatsworth, J. D., & Tellegen, A. (2004). Salient and emerging developmental tasks in the transition to adulthood. *Child Development, 75,* 123–133. http://doi.org/10.1111/j.1467-8624.2004.00658.x

Rolls, E. T. (2015). Taste, olfactory, and food reward value processing in the human brain. *Progress in Neurobiology, 127–128,* 64–90.

Romero-Corral, A., Montori, V. M., Somers, V. K., Korinek, J., Thomas, R. J., Allison, T. G., ... Lopez-Jiminez, F. (2006). Association of body weight with total mortality and with cardiovascular events in coronary artery disease: A systematic review of cohort studies. *Lancet, 368*(9536), 666–678.

Ronay, R., & Galinsky, A. D. (2011). Lex talionis: Testosterone and the law of retaliation. *Journal of Experimental Social Psychology, 47*(3), 702–705. https://doi.org/10.1016/j.jesp.2010.11.009

Roney, J. R., & Simmons, Z. L. (2013). Hormonal predictors of women's sexual desire in normal menstrual cycles. *Hormones and Behavior, 63,* 636–645.

Rosch, E. H. (1973). Natural categories. *Cognitive Psychology, 4,* 328–350.

Rosch, E. H. (1975). Cognitive representations of semantic categories. *Journal of Experimental Psychology: General, 104,* 192–233.

Rosch, E. H., & Mervis, C. B. (1975). Family resemblances: Studies in the internal structure of categories. *Cognitive Psychology, 7,* 573–605.

Rose, S. P. R. (2002). Smart drugs: Do they work? Are they ethical? Will they be legal? *Nature Reviews Neuroscience, 3,* 975–979.

Roseman, I. J. (1984). Cognitive determinants of emotion: A structural theory. *Review of Personality and Social Psychology, 5*, 11–36.

Roseman, I. J., & Smith, C. A. (2001). Appraisal theory: Overview, assumptions, varieties and controversies. In K. R. Scherer, A. Schorr, & T. Johnstone (Eds.), *Appraisal processes in emotion: Theory, methods, research* (pp. 3–19). Oxford University Press.

Rosenbaum, J. E. (2009). Patient teenagers? A comparison of the sexual behavior of virginity pledgers and matched nonpledgers. *Pediatrics, 123*(1), e110–e120.

Rosenbaum, S. (2016, June 9). Models keep getting skinnier and skinnier. *New York Post.* https://nypost.com/2016/06/09/models-keep-getting-skinnier-and-skinnier/

Rosenberg, B. D., & Siegel, J. T. (2018). A 50-year review of psychological reactance theory: Do not read this article. *Motivation Science, 4*(4), 281–300. https://doi.org/10.1037/mot0000091

Rosenberg, M. (1965). *Society and the adolescent self-image.* Princeton University Press.

Rosenfeld, M. J., Thomas, R. J., & Hausen, S. (2019). Disintermediating your friends: How online dating in the United States displaces other ways of meeting. *Proceedings of the National Academy of Sciences, 116*(36), 17753–17758. https://doi.org/10.1073/pnas.1908630116

Rosenheck, R. (2008). Fast food consumption and increased caloric intake: A systematic review of a trajectory towards weight gain and obesity risk. *Obesity Reviews, 9*(6), 535–547.

Rosenkranz, K., Williamon, A., & Rothwell, J. C. (2007). Motorcortical excitability and synaptic plasticity is enhanced in professional musicians. *Journal of Neuroscience, 27*, 5200–5206.

Rosenthal, R., & Fode, K. L. (1963). The effect of experimenter bias on the performance of the albino rat. *Behavioral Science, 8*, 183–189.

Ross, L. (1977). The intuitive psychologist and his shortcomings: Distortions in the attribution process. *Advances in Experimental Social Psychology, 10*, 173–220.

Ross, L., Amabile, T. M., & Steinmetz, J. L. (1977). Social roles, social control, and biases in social-perception processes. *Journal of Personality and Social Psychology, 35*, 485–494.

Ross, M., Blatz, C. W., & Schryer, E. (2008). Social memory processes. In H. L. Roediger III (Ed.), *Learning and memory: A comprehensive reference* (Vol. 2, pp. 911–926). Elsevier.

Rossano, F., Carpenter, M., & Tomasello, M. (2012). One-year-old infants follow others' voice direction. *Psychological Science, 23*(11), 1298–1302. https://doi.org/10.1177/0956797612450032

Roth, B., Becker, N., Romeyke, S., Schäfer, S., Domnick, F., & Spinath, F. M. (2015). Intelligence and school grades: A meta-analysis. *Intelligence, 53*, 118–137. https://doi.org/10.1016/j.intell.2015.09.002

Roth, H. P., & Caron, H. S. (1978). Accuracy of doctors' estimates and patients' statements on adherence to a drug regimen. *Clinical Pharmacology and Therapeutics, 23*, 361–370.

Rothbart, M. K., & Bates, J. E. (2006). Temperament. In W. Damon, R. Lerner, & N. Eisenberg (Eds.), *Handbook of child psychology: Vol. 3. Social, emotional, and personality development* (6th ed., pp. 99–166). Wiley.

Rothbaum, B. O., & Schwartz, A. C. (2002). Exposure therapy for posttraumatic stress disorder. *American Journal of Psychotherapy, 56*, 59–75.

Rotter, J. B. (1966). Generalized expectancies for internal versus external locus of control of reinforcement. *Psychological Monographs: General and Applied, 80*, 1–28.

Rotton, L. (1992). Trait humor and longevity: Do comics have the last laugh? *Health Psychology, 11*, 262–266.

Roy-Byrne, P. P., Joesch, J. M., Wang, P. S., & Kessler, R. C. (2009). Low socioeconomic status and mental health care use among respondents with anxiety and depression in the NCS-R. *Psychiatric Services, 60*(9), 1190–1197. https://doi.org/10.1176/ps.2009.60.9.1190

Rozin, P. (1968). Are carbohydrate and protein intakes separately regulated? *Journal of Comparative and Physiological Psychology, 65*, 23–29.

Rozin, P., & Kalat, J. W. (1971). Specific hungers and poison avoidance as adaptive specializations of learning. *Psychological Review, 78*, 459–486.

Rozin, P., Bauer, R., & Catanese, D. (2003). Food and life, pleasure and worry, among American college students: Gender differences and regional similarities. *Journal of Personality and Social Psychology, 85*, 132–141.

Rozin, P., Dow, S., Moscovitch, M., & Rajaram, S. (1998). What causes humans to begin and end a meal? A role for memory for what has been eaten, as evidenced by a study of multiple meal eating in amnesic patients. *Psychological Science, 9*, 392–396.

Rozin, P., Scott, S., Dingley, M., Urbanek, J. K., Jiang, H., & Kaltenbach, M. (2011). Nudge to nobesity: I. Minor changes in accessibility decrease food intake. *Judgment and Decision Making, 6*, 323–332.

Rozin, P., Trachtenberg, S., & Cohen, A. B. (2001). Stability of body image and body image dissatisfaction in American college students over about the last 15 years. *Appetite, 37*, 245–248.

Rozenblit, L., & Keil, F. C. (2002). The misunderstood limits of folk science: An illusion of explanatory depth. *Cognitive Science, 26*, 521–562.

Rubin, D. C., Deffler, S. A., Ogle, C. M., Dowell, N. M., Graesser, A. C., & Beckham, J. C. (2016). Participant, rater, and computer measures of coherence in posttraumatic stress disorder. *Journal of Abnormal Psychology, 125*(1), 11–25. https://doi.org/10.1037/abn0000126

Rubin, M., & Badea, C. (2012). They're all the same! … but for several different reasons: A review of the multicausal nature of perceived group variability. *Current Directions in Psychological Science, 21*(6), 367–372. https://doi.org/10.1177/0963721412457363

Rubin, Z. (1973). *Liking and loving.* Holt, Rinehart & Winston.

Rubin-Fernandez, P., & Geurts, B. (2012). How to pass the false-belief task before your fourth birthday. *Psychological Science, 24*(1), 27–33. https://doi.org/10.1177/0956797612447819

Rudman, L. A., Ashmore, R. D., & Gary, M. L. (2001). "Unlearning" automatic biases: The malleability of implicit prejudice and stereotypes. *Journal of Personality and Social Psychology, 81*, 856–868.

Ruffman, T., Puri, A., Galloway, O., Su, J., & Taumoepeau, M. (2018). Variety in parental use of "want" relates to subsequent growth in children's theory of mind. *Developmental Psychology, 54*, 677–688.

Ruiz, M., Dojat, M., & Hupé, J.-M. (2020). Multivariate pattern analysis of fMRI data for imaginary and real colours in grapheme-colour synaesthesia. *European Journal of Neuroscience, 52*(5), 3434–3456. doi: 10.1111/ejn.14774.hal-03020119

Running, C. A., Craig, B. A., & Mattes, R. D. (2015). Oleogustus: The unique taste of fat. *Chemical Senses, 40*, 507–516.

Rusbult, C. E., & Van Lange, P. A. M. (2003). Interdependence, interaction and relationships. *Annual Review of Psychology, 54*, 351–375.

Ruscio, A. M., Stein, D. J., Chiu, W. T., & Kessler, R. C. (2010). The epidemiology of obsessive-compulsive disorder in the National Comorbidity Survey Replication. *Molecular Psychiatry, 15*, 53–63.

Russell, B. (1945). *A history of Western philosophy.* Simon & Schuster.

Russell, J., Gee, B., & Bullard, C. (2012). Why do young children hide by closing their eyes? Self-visibility and the developing concept of self. *Journal of Cognition and Development, 13*(4), 550–576. https://doi.org/10.1080/15248372.2011.594826

Russell, J. A. (1980). A circumplex model of affect. *Journal of Personality and Social Psychology, 39*, 1161–1178.

Rutledge, R. B., Lazzaro, S. C., Lau, B., Myers, C. E., Gluck, M. A., & Glimcher, P. W. (2009). Dopaminergic drugs modulate learning rates and perseveration in Parkinson's patients in a dynamic foraging task. *Journal of Neuroscience, 29*, 15104–15114.

Rutter, M., & Silberg, J. (2002). Gene–environment interplay in relation to emotional and behavioral disturbance. *Annual Review of Psychology, 53*, 463–490.

Rutter, M., O'Connor, T. G., & the English and Romanian Adoptees Study Team. (2004). Are there biological programming effects for psychological development? Findings from a study of Romanian adoptees. *Developmental Psychology, 40*, 81–94.

Ryan, R. M., & Deci, E. L. (2000). Self-determination theory and the facilitation of intrinsic motivation, social development, and well-being. *American Psychologist, 55*, 68–78.

Ryle, G. (1949). *The concept of mind.* Barnes & Noble.

Sackett, P. R., Borneman, M. J., & Connelly, B. S. (2008, May–June). *High stakes testing in higher education and employment: Appraising the evidence for validity and fairness. American Psychology, 63*(4), 215–227. https://doi.org/10.1037/0003-066X.63.4.215

Sacks, O. (1995). *An anthropologist on Mars.* Knopf.

Sacks, O. (1996). *An anthropologist on Mars.* Vintage.

Saffran, J. R., Aslin, R. N., & Newport, E. I. (1996). Statistical learning by 8-month-old infants. *Science, 274*, 1926–1928.

Sager, M. (2007). Ray Charles: What I've learned [Interview]. *Esquire.* https://www.esquire.com/entertainment/interviews/a763/esq0803-aug-wil/

Sahakian, B., & Morein-Zamir, S. (2007). Professor's little helper. *Nature, 450*(7173), 1157–1159.

Salmon, D. P., & Bondi, M. W. (2009). Neuropsychological assessment of dementia. *Annual Review of Psychology, 60*, 257–282.

Salovey, P., & Grewal, D. (2005). The science of emotional intelligence. *Current Directions in Psychological Science, 14*(6), 281–285.

Salthouse, T. A. (1984). Effects of age and skill in typing. *Journal of Experimental Psychology: General, 113*, 345–371.

Salthouse, T. A. (1987). Age, experience, and compensation. In C. Schooler & K. W. Schaie (Eds.), *Cognitive functioning and social structure over the life course* (pp. 142–150). Ablex.

Salthouse, T. A. (1996a). General and specific mediation of adult age differences in memory. *Journal of Gerontology: Series B. Psychological Sciences and Social Sciences, 51B*, P30–P42.

Salthouse, T. A. (1996b). The processing-speed theory of adult age differences in cognition. *Psychological Review, 103*, 403–428.

Salthouse, T. A. (2000). Pressing issues in cognitive aging. In D. Park & N. Schwartz (Eds.), *Cognitive aging: A primer* (pp. 43–54). Psychology Press.

Salthouse, T. A. (2001). Structural models of the relations between age and measures of cognitive functioning. *Intelligence, 29*, 93–115.

Salthouse, T. A. (2006). Mental exercise and mental aging. *Perspectives on Psychological Science, 1*(1), 68–87.

Salvatore, J. E., Kuo, S. I.-C., Steele, R. D., Simpson, J. A., & Collins, W. A. (2011). Recovering from conflict in romantic relationships: A developmental perspective. *Psychological Science, 22*(3), 376–383. https://doi.org/10.1177/0956797610397055

Sampson, R. J., & Laub, J. H. (1995). Understanding variability in lives through time: Contributions of life-course criminology. *Studies of Crime Prevention, 4*, 143–158.

Sandberg, P., Boraxbekk, C-J., Zogaj, I., & Nyberg, L. (2021). Ancient mnemonic in a new format: Episodic memory training with method of loci in a smartphone application. *The Journals of Gerontology: Series B, 76*(4), 681–691. https://doi.org/10.1093/geronb/gbaa216

Sander, J., Schupp, J., & Richter, D. (2017). Getting together: Social contact frequency across the life span. *Developmental Psychology, 53*(8), 1571–1588. https://doi.org/10.1037/dev0000349

Santangelo, V., Cavallina, C., Colucci, P., Santori, A., Macri, S., McGaugh, J. L., & Campolongo, P. (2018). Enhanced brain activity associated with memory access in highly superior autobiographical memory. *Proceedings of the National Academy of Sciences, USA, 115*(30), 7795–7800.

Santelli, J. S., Kantor, L. M., Grilo, S. A., Speizer, I. S., Lindberg, L. D., Heitel, J., ... Ott, M. A. (2017). Abstinence-only-until-marriage: An updated review of U.S. policies and programs and their impact. *Journal of Adolescent Health, 61*, 273–280.

Santos, R. E. A., da Silva, M. G., do Monte Silva, M. C. B., Barbosa, D. A. M., Gomes, A. L. D. V., Galindo, L. C. M., ... Ferraz-Pereira, K. N. (2021). Onset and duration of symptoms of loss of smell/taste in patients with COVID-19: A systematic review. *American Journal of Otolaryngology, 42*(2), 102889. https://doi.org/10.1016/j.amjoto.2020.102889

Sara, S. J. (2000). Retrieval and reconsolidation: Toward a neurobiology of remembering. *Learning & Memory, 7*, 73–84.

Sarris, V. (1989). Max Wertheimer on seen motion: Theory and evidence. *Psychological Research, 51*, 58–68.

Sarter, M. (2006). Preclinical research into cognition enhancers. *Trends in Pharmacological Sciences, 27*, 602–608.

Satcher, D. (2001). *The Surgeon General's call to action to promote sexual health and responsible sexual behavior.* U.S. Government Printing Office.

Sauter, D. A., Eisner, F., Calder, A. J., & Scott, S. K. (2010). Perceptual cues in nonverbal vocal expressions of emotion. *Quarterly Journal of Experimental Psychology, 63*(11), 2251–2272. https://doi.org/10.1080/17470211003721642

Savage, C. R., Deckersbach, T., Heckers, S., Wagner, A. D., Schacter, D. L., Alpert, N. M., ... Rauch, S. L. (2001). Prefrontal regions supporting spontaneous and directed application of verbal learning strategies: Evidence from PET. *Brain, 124*, 219–231.

Savage-Rumbaugh, S., & Lewin, R. (1996). *Kanzi: The ape on the brink of the human mind.* Wiley.

Savage-Rumbaugh, S., Shanker, G., & Taylor, T. J. (1998). *Apes, language, and the human mind.* Oxford University Press.

Savic, I., & Lindstrom, P. (2008). PET and MRI show differences in cerebral asymmetry and functional connectivity between homo- and heterosexual subjects. *Proceedings of the National Academy of Sciences, USA, 105*(27), 9403–9408.

Savin-Williams, R. C., & Vrangalova, Z. (2013). Mostly heterosexual as a distinct sexual orientation group: A systematic review of the empirical evidence. *Developmental Review, 33*, 58–88.

Sawa, A., & Snyder, S. H. (2002). Schizophrenia: Diverse approaches to a complex disease. *Science, 295*, 692–695.

Sawyer, S. M., Azzopardi, P. S., Wickremarathne, D., & Patton, G. C. (2018). The age of adolescence. *The Lancet: Child and Adolescent Health, 2*, 223–228.

Scarf, D., Imuta, K., Colombo, M., & Hayne, H. (2012). Golden rule or valence matching? Methodological problems in Hamlin et al. *Proceedings of the National Academy of Sciences, USA, 109*(22), E1426.

Scarpelli, S., Alfonsi, V., Gorgoni, M., Giannini, A. M., & De Gennaro, L. (2021). Investigation on neurobiological mechanisms of dreaming in the new decade. *Brain Sciences, 11*(2), 220. https://doi.org/10.3390/brainsci11020220

Scarr, S., Pakstis, A. J., Katz, S. H., & Barker, W. B. (1977). Absence of a relationship between degree of White ancestry and intellectual skills within a Black population. *Human Genetics, 39*(1), 69–86.

Schaal, B., & Al Aïn, S. (2014). Chemical signals "selected for" newborns in mammals. *Animal Behaviour, 97,* 289–299. https://doi.org/10.1016/j.anbehav.2014.08.022

Schachter, S., & Singer, J. E. (1962). Cognitive, social, and psychological determinants of emotional state. *Physiological Review, 69,* 379–399.

Schacter, D. L., & Szpunar, K. K. (2015). Enhancing attention and memory during video-recorded lectures. *Scholarship of Teaching and Learning in Psychology, 1,* 60–71.

Schacter, D. L. (1996). *Searching for memory: The brain, the mind, and the past.* Basic Books.

Schacter, D. L. (2021). *The seven sins of memory: How the mind forgets and remembers* (Rev. 2nd ed.). Houghton Mifflin Harcourt.

Schacter, D. L. (1987). Implicit memory: History and current status. *Journal of Experimental Psychology: Learning, Memory, and Cognition, 13,* 501–518.

Schacter, D. L. (1999). The seven sins of memory: Insights from psychology and cognitive neuroscience. *American Psychologist, 54*(3), 182–203.

Schacter, D. L. (2001a). *Forgotten ideas, neglected pioneers: Richard Semon and the story of memory.* Psychology Press.

Schacter, D. L. (2001b). *The seven sins of memory: How the mind forgets and remembers.* Houghton Mifflin.

Schacter, D. L. (2012). Adaptive constructive processes and the future of memory. *American Psychologist, 67,* 603–613.

Schacter, D. L., & Addis, D. R. (2007). The cognitive neuroscience of constructive memory: Remembering the past and imagining the future. *Philosophical Transactions of the Royal Society of London, B, 362,* 773–786.

Schacter, D. L., & Curran, T. (2000). Memory without remembering and remembering without memory: Implicit and false memories. In M. S. Gazzaniga (Ed.), *The new cognitive neurosciences* (2nd ed., pp. 829–840). MIT Press.

Schacter, D. L., & Madore, K. P. (2016). Remembering the past and imagining the future: Identifying and enhancing the contribution of episodic memory. *Memory Studies, 9,* 245–255.

Schacter, D. L., & Tulving, E. (1994). *Memory systems, 1994.* MIT Press.

Schacter, D. L., Addis, D. R., & Buckner, R. L. (2008). Episodic simulation of future events: Concepts, data, and applications. *Annals of the New York Academy of Sciences, 1124,* 39–60.

Schacter, D. L., Alpert, N. M., Savage, C. R., Rauch, S. L., & Albert, M. S. (1996). Conscious recollection and the human hippocampal formation: Evidence from positron emission tomography. *Proceedings of the National Academy of Sciences, USA, 93,* 321–325.

Schacter, D. L., Dobbins, I. G., & Schnyer, D. M. (2004). Specificity of priming: A cognitive neuroscience perspective. *Nature Reviews Neuroscience, 5,* 853–862.

Schacter, D. L., Gaesser, B., & Addis, D. R. (2013). Remembering the past and imagining the future in the elderly. *Gerontologist, 59*(2), 143–151. https://doi.org/10.1159/000342198

Schacter, D. L., Guerin, S. A., & St. Jacques, P. L. (2011). Memory distortion: An adaptive perspective. *Trends in Cognitive Sciences, 15,* 467–474.

Schacter, D. L., Harbluk, J. L., & McLachlan, D. R. (1984). Retrieval without recollection: An experimental analysis of source amnesia. *Journal of Verbal Learning and Verbal Behavior, 23,* 593–611.

Schacter, D. L., Wagner, A. D., & Buckner, R. L. (2000). Memory systems of 1999. In E. Tulving & F. I. M. Craik (Eds.), *The Oxford handbook of memory* (pp. 627–643). Oxford University Press.

Schacter, D. L., Wig, G. S., & Stevens, W. D. (2007). Reductions in cortical activity during priming. *Current Opinion in Neurobiology, 17,* 171–176.

Schafer, R. B., & Keith, P. M. (1980). Equity and depression among married couples. *Social Psychology Quarterly, 43,* 430–435.

Schaie, K. W. (1996). *Intellectual development in adulthood: The Seattle Longitudinal Study.* Cambridge University Press.

Schaie, K. W. (2005). *Developmental influences on adult intelligence: The Seattle Longitudinal Study.* Oxford University Press.

Schaller, M. (2018). The parental care motivational system and why it matters (for everyone). *Current Directions in Psychological Science, 27*(5), 295–301. https://doi.org/10.1177/0963721418767873

Schapira, A. H. V., Emre, M., Jenner, P., & Poewe, W. (2009). Levodopa in the treatment of Parkinson's disease. *European Journal of Neurology, 16,* 982–989.

Scheibe, S., Sheppes, G., & Staudinger, U. M. (2015). Distract or reappraise? Age-related differences in emotion-regulation choice. *Emotion, 15,* 677–681. https://doi.org/10.1037/a0039246

Scherer, K. R. (1999). Appraisal theory. In T. Dalgleish & M. Power (Eds.), *Handbook of cognition and emotion* (pp. 637–663). Wiley.

Scherer, K. R. (2001). The nature and study of appraisal: A review of the issues. In K. R. Scherer, A. Schorr, & T. Johnstone (Eds.), *Appraisal processes in emotion: Theory, methods, research* (pp. 369–391). Oxford University Press.

Schiele, M. A., Gottschalk, M. G., & Domschke, K. (2020). The applied implications of epigenetics in anxiety, affective and stress-related disorders: A review and synthesis on psychosocial stress, psychotherapy and prevention. *Clinical Psychology Review, 77,* 101830. https://doi.org/10.1016/j.cpr.2020.101830

Schiff, M., Duyme, M., Stewart, J., Tomkiewicz, S., & Feingold, J. (1978). Intellectual status of working-class children adopted early in upper-middle-class families. *Science, 200,* 1503–1504.

Schiff, R., Sasson, A., Green, H., & Kahta, S. (2021). Artificial grammar learning is facilitated by distributed practice: Evidence from a letter reordering task. *Cognitive Processing.* https://doi.org/10.1007/s10339-021-01048-z

Schildkraut, J. J. (1965). The catecholamine hypothesis of affective disorders: A review of supporting evidence. *American Journal of Psychiatry, 122,* 509–522.

Schiller, D., Monfils, M. H., Raio, C. M., Johnson, D. C., LeDoux, J. E., & Phelps, E. A. (2010). Preventing the return of fear in humans using reconsolidation update mechanisms. *Nature, 463,* 49–54.

Schilling, O. K., Wahl, H.-W., & Wiegering, S. (2013). Affective development in advanced old age: Analyses of terminal change in positive and negative affect. *Developmental Psychology, 49*(5), 1011–1020. https://doi.org/10.1037/a0028775

Schlesinger, J. (2012). *The insanity hoax: Exposing the myth of the mad genius.* Shrinktunes Media.

Schmader, T., Johns, M., & Forbes, C. (2008). An integrated process model of stereotype threat effects on performance. *Psychological Review, 115,* 336–356.

Schmidt, F. L., & Hunter, J. E. (1998). The validity and utility of selection methods in personnel psychology: Practical and theoretical implications of 85 years of research findings. *Psychological Bulletin, 124,* 262–274.

Schmitt, D. P., Allik, J., McCrae, R. R., & Benet-Martínez, V. (2007). The geographic distribution of Big Five personality traits: Patterns and profiles of human self-description across 56 nations. *Journal of Cross-Cultural Psychology, 38*(2), 173–212.

Schmitt, D. P., Jonason, P. K., Byerley, G. J., Flores, S. D., Illbeck, B. E., O'Leary, K. N., & Qudrat, A. (2012). A reexamination of sex differences in sexuality: New studies reveal old truths. *Current Directions in Psychological Science, 21*(2), 135–139. https://doi.org/10.1177/0963721412436808

Schmitt, D. P., Realo, A., Voracek, M., & Allik, J. (2008). Why can't a man be more like a woman? Sex differences in personality traits across 55 cultures. *Journal of Personality and Social Psychology, 94*, 168–182.

Schnorr, J. A., & Atkinson, R. C. (1969). Repetition versus imagery instructions in the short- and long-term retention of paired associates. *Psychonomic Science, 15*, 183–184.

Schoenemann, P. T., Sheenan, M. J., & Glotzer, L. D. (2005). Prefrontal white matter volume is disproportionately larger in humans than in other primates. *Nature Neuroscience, 8*, 242–252.

Schonberg, T., O'Doherty, J. P., Joel, D., Inzelberg, R., Segev, Y., & Daw, N. D. (2009). Selective impairment of prediction error signaling in human dorsolateral but not ventral striatum in Parkinson's disease patients: Evidence from a model-based fMRI study. *NeuroImage, 49*, 772–781.

Schott, B. J., Henson, R. N., Richardson-Klavehn, A., Becker, C., Thoma, V., Heinze, H. J., & Duzel, E. (2005). Redefining implicit and explicit memory: The functional neuroanatomy of priming, remembering, and control of retrieval. *Proceedings of the National Academy of Sciences, USA, 102*, 1257–1262.

Schreiner, T., & Rasch, B. (2015). Boosting vocabulary learning by verbal cueing during sleep. *Cerebral Cortex, 25*, 4169–4179.

Schubert, T. W., & Koole, S. L. (2009). The embodied self: Making a fist enhances men's power-related self-conceptions. *Journal of Experimental Social Psychology, 45*, 828–834.

Schulenberg, J. E., Johnston, L. D., O'Malley, P. M., Bachman, J. G., Miech, R. A., & Patrick, M. E. (2016). *Monitoring the future: National survey results on drug use, 1975–2016: Vol. II. College students & adults ages 19–55.* Institute for Social Research, The University of Michigan. https://doi.org/10.1017/CBO9781107415324.004

Schulreich, S., Gerhardt, H., & Heekeren, H. R. (2016). Incidental fear cues increase monetary loss aversion. *Emotion, 16*(3), 402–412. https://doi.org/10.1037/emo0000124

Schultz, D., Izard, C. E., & Bear, G. (2004). Children's emotion processing: Relations to emotionality and aggression. *Development and Psychopathology, 16*(2), 371–387.

Schultz, W. (2016a). Dopamine reward prediction error coding. *Dialogues in Clinical Neuroscience, 18*, 23–32.

Schultz, W. (2016b). Reward functions of the basal ganglia. *Journal of Neural Transmission, 123*(7), 679–693. https://doi.org/10.1007/s00702-016-1510-0

Schultz, W., Dayan, P., & Montague, P. R. (1997). A neural substrate of prediction and reward. *Science, 275*, 1593–1599.

Schulze, K., Vargha-Khadem, F., & Mishkin, M. (2018). Phonological working memory and FOXP2. *Neuropsychologia, 108*, 147–152. https://doi.org/10.1016/j.neuropsychologia.2017.11.027

Schwartz, B. L. (2002). *Tip-of-the-tongue states: Phenomenology, mechanisms, and lexical retrieval.* Erlbaum.

Schwartz, C. E., Wright, C. I., Shin, L. M., Kagan, J., & Rauch, S. L. (2003). Inhibited and uninhibited infants "grown up": Adult amygdalar response to novelty. *Science, 300*, 1952–1953.

Schwartz, H. A., Eichstaedt, J. C., Kern, M. L., Dziurzynski, L., Ramones, S. M., Agrawal, M., ... Ungar, L. H. (2013). Personality, gender, and age in the language of social media: The open-vocabulary approach. *PLoS ONE, 8*, e73791.

Schwartz, J. H., & Westbrook, G. L. (2000). The cytology of neurons. In E. R. Kandel, G. H. Schwartz, & T. M. Jessell (Eds.), *Principles of neural science* (pp. 67–104). McGraw-Hill.

Schwartz, L., & Yovel, G. (2016). The roles of perceptual and conceptual information in face recognition. *Journal of Experimental Psychology: General, 145*(11), 1493–1511. http://doi.org/10.1037/xge0000220

Schwartz, S., & Maquet, P. (2002). Sleep imaging and the neuropsychological assessment of dreams. *Trends in Cognitive Sciences, 6*, 23–30.

Schwartzman, A. E., Gold, D., & Andres, D. (1987). Stability of intelligence: A 40-year follow-up. *Canadian Journal of Psychology, 41*, 244–256.

Schweizer, T. A., Ware, J., Fischer, C. E., Craik, F. I. M., & Bialystok, E. (2012). Bilingualism as a contributor to cognitive reserve: Evidence from brain atrophy in Alzheimer's disease. *Cortex, 48*, 991–996.

Scott, R. M., & Baillargeon, R. (2017). Early false-belief understanding. *Trends in Cognitive Sciences, 21*, 237–249.

Scoville, W. B., & Milner, B. (1957). Loss of recent memory after bilateral hippocampal lesions. *Journal of Neurology, Neurosurgery, and Psychiatry, 20*, 11–21.

Scribner, S. (1984). Studying working intelligence. In B. Rogoff & J. Lave (Eds.), *Everyday cognition: Its development in social context* (pp. 9–40). Harvard University Press.

Sedlmeier, P., Eberth, J., Schwarz, M., Zimmermann, D., Haarig, F., Jaeger, S., & Kunze, S. (2012). The psychological effects of meditation: A meta-analysis. *Psychological Bulletin, 138*, 1139–1171.

Seeman, T. E., Dubin, L. F., & Seeman, M. (2003). Religiosity/spirituality and health: A critical review of the evidence for biological pathways. *American Psychologist, 58*, 53–63.

Segal, Z. V., & Walsh, K. M. (2016). Mindfulness-based cognitive therapy for residual depressive symptoms and relapse prophylaxis. *Current Opinion in Psychiatry, 29*, 7–12. https://doi.org/10.1097/YCO.0000000000000216

Seligman, M. E. P. (1971). Phobias and preparedness. *Behavior Therapy, 2*, 307–320.

Seligman, M. E. P. (1995). The effectiveness of psychotherapy: The *Consumer Reports* study. *American Psychologist, 48*, 966–971.

Selikoff, I. J., Robitzek, E. H., & Ornstein, G. G. (1952). Toxicity of hydrazine derivatives of isonicotinic acid in the chemotherapy of human tuberculosis. *Quarterly Bulletin of SeaView Hospital, 13*, 17–26.

Selye, H., & Fortier, C. (1950). Adaptive reaction to stress. *Psychosomatic Medicine, 12*, 149–157.

Semenza, C. (2009). The neuropsychology of proper names. *Mind & Language, 24*, 347–369.

Semenza, C., & Zettin, M. (1989). Evidence from aphasia for the role of proper names as pure referring expressions. *Nature, 342*, 678–679.

Senghas, A., Kita, S., & Ozyurek, A. (2004). Children create core properties of language: Evidence from an emerging sign language in Nicaragua. *Science, 305*, 1782.

Senju, A., Maeda, M., Kikuchi, Y., Hasegawa, T., Tojo, Y., & Osanai, H. (2007). Absence of contagious yawning in children with autism spectrum disorder. *Biology Letters, 3*(6), 706–708.

Senju, A., Southgate, V., Snape, C., Leonard, M., & Csibra, G. (2011). Do 18-month-olds really attribute mental states to others? A critical test. *Psychological Science, 22*(7), 878–880. https://doi.org/10.1177/0956797611411584

Senju, A., Southgate, V., White, S., & Frith, U. (2009). Mindblind eyes: An absence of spontaneous theory of mind in Asperger syndrome. *Science, 325,* 883–885.

Serpell, R. (1974). Aspects of intelligence in a developing country. *African Social Research, 17,* 578–596.

Seybold, K. S., & Hill, P. C. (2001). The role of religion and spirituality in mental and physical health. *Current Directions in Psychological Science, 10,* 21–23.

Shah, A., Hayes, C. J., Martin, B. C. (2017). Characteristics of initial prescription episodes and likelihood of long-term opioid use: United States, 2006–2015. *Morbidity and Mortality Weekly Report, 66,* 265–269.

Shah, J. Y., Higgins, E. T., & Friedman, R. S. (1998). Performance incentives and means: How regulatory focus influences goal attainment. *Journal of Personality and Social Psychology, 74,* 285–293.

Shahaeian, A., Peterson, C. C., Slaughter, V., & Wellman, H. M. (2011). Culture and the sequence of steps in theory of mind development. *Developmental Psychology, 47*(5), 1239–1247. https://doi.org/10.1037/a0023899

Shallcross, A. J., Ford, B. Q., Floerke, V. A., & Mauss, I. B. (2013). Getting better with age: The relationship between age, acceptance, and negative affect. *Journal of Personality and Social Psychology, 104*(4), 734–749. https://doi.org/10.1037/a0031180

Shallice, T., Fletcher, P., Frith, C. D., Grasby, P., Frackowiak, R. S. J., & Dolan, R. J. (1994). Brain regions associated with acquisition and retrieval of verbal episodic memory. *Nature, 368,* 633–635.

Shariff, A. F., & Tracy, J. L. (2011). What are emotion expressions for? *Current Directions in Psychological Science, 20*(6), 395–399.

Sharot, T. (2011). *The optimism bias: A tour of the irrationally positive brain.* Pantheon Books.

Shaw, J., & Porter, S. (2015). Constructing rich false memories of committing crime. *Psychological Science, 26,* 291–301.

Shaw, J. S., Bjork, R. A., & Handal, A. (1995). Retrieval-induced forgetting in an eyewitness paradigm. *Psychonomic Bulletin & Review, 13,* 1023–1027.

Shedler, J. (2010). The efficacy of psychodynamic psychotherapy. *American Psychologist, 65,* 98–109.

Sheese, B. E., & Graziano, W. G. (2005). Deciding to defect: The effects of video-game violence on cooperative behavior. *Psychological Science, 16,* 354–357.

Shen, H., Wan, F., & Wyer, R. S. (2011). Cross-cultural differences in the refusal to accept a small gift: The differential influence of reciprocity norms on Asians and North Americans. *Journal of Personality and Social Psychology, 100*(2), 271–281. https://doi.org/10.1037/a0021201

Shepperd, J., Malone, W., & Sweeny, K. (2008). Exploring the causes of the self-serving bias. *Social and Personality Psychology Compass, 2*(2), 895–908.

Sherman, L. E., Hernandez, L. M., Greenfield, P. M., & Dapretto, M. (2018). What the brain "likes": Neural correlates of providing feedback on social media. *Social Neuroscience, 13*(7), 699–707. https://doi.org/10.1093/scan/nsy051

Sherman, L. E., Payton, A. A., Hernandez, L. M., Greenfield, P. M., & Dapretto, M. (2016). The power of the like in adolescence: Effects of peer influence on neural and behavioral responses to social media. *Psychological Science, 27*(7), 1027–1035. https://doi.org/10.1177/0956797616645673

Sherman, S. (2021, July 28). US residents search "loss of taste" online as Delta spreads. *Boston Globe.* https://www.bostonglobe.com/2021/07/28/business/us-residents-search-loss-taste-online-delta-spreads/

Sherry, S. B., & Hall, P. A. (2009). The perfectionism model of binge eating: Tests of an integrative model. *Journal of Personality and Social Psychology, 96*(3), 690–709.

Shiffman, S., Gnys, M., Richards, T. J., Paty, J. A., & Hickcox, M. (1996). Temptations to smoke after quitting: A comparison of lapsers and maintainers. *Health Psychology, 15,* 455–461.

Shih, M., Pittinsky, T. L., & Ambady, N. (1999). Stereotype susceptibility: Identity salience and shifts in quantitative performance. *Psychological Science, 10,* 80–83.

Shimamura, A. P., & Squire, L. R. (1987). A neuropsychological study of fact memory and source amnesia. *Journal of Experimental Psychology: Learning, Memory, and Cognition, 13,* 464–473.

Shin, H., & Ryan, A. M. (2014). Early adolescent friendships and academic adjustment: Examining selection and influence processes with longitudinal social network analysis. *Developmental Psychology, 50*(11), 2462–2472. https://doi.org/10.1037/a0037922

Shin, L. M., Rauch, S. L., & Pitman, R. K. (2006). Amygdala, medial prefrontal cortex, and hippocampal function in PTSD. *Annals of the New York Academy of Science, 1071,* 67–79.

Shinskey, J. L., & Munakata, Y. (2005). Familiarity breeds searching. *Psychological Science, 16*(8), 596–600.

Shiota, M. N., Neufeld, S. L., Yeung, W. H., Moser, S. E., & Perea, E. F. (2011). Feeling good: Autonomic nervous system responding in five positive emotions. *Emotion, 11*(6), 1368–1378. https://doi.org/10.1037/a0024278

Shipstead, Z., Redick, T. S., & Engle, R. W. (2012). Is working memory training effective? *Psychological Bulletin, 138,* 628–654.

Shobe, E. (2021). Achieving testing effects in an authentic college classroom. *Teaching of Psychology.* https://doi.org/10.1177/00986283211015669

Shomstein, S., & Yantis, S. (2004). Control of attention shifts between vision and audition in human cortex. *Journal of Neuroscience, 24,* 10702–10706.

Shore, C. (1986). Combinatorial play: Conceptual development and early multiword speech. *Developmental Psychology, 22,* 184–190.

Siebenbruner, J., Zimmer-Gembeck, M. J., & Egeland, B. (2007). Sexual partners and contraceptive use: A 16-year prospective study predicting abstinence and risk behavior. *Journal of Research on Adolescence, 17,* 179–206. http://doi.org/10.1111/j.1532-7795.2007.00518.x

Siegel, A., Roeling, T. A. P., Gregg, T. R., & Kruk, M. R. (1999). Neuropharmacology of brain-stimulation-evoked aggression. *Neuroscience and Biobehavioral Reviews, 23,* 359–389.

Siegel, E. H., Sands, M. K., Van den Noortgate, W., Condon, P., Chang, Y., Dy, J., … Barrett, L. F. (2018). Emotion fingerprints or emotion populations? A meta-analytic investigation of autonomic features of emotion categories. *Psychological Bulletin, 144*(4), 343–393.

Siegel, S. (1976). Morphine analgesia tolerance: Its situational specificity supports a Pavlovian conditioning model. *Science, 193,* 323–325.

Siegel, S. (1984). Pavlovian conditioning and heroin overdose: Reports by overdose victims. *Bulletin of the Psychonomic Society, 22,* 428–430.

Siegel, S. (2005). Drug tolerance, drug addiction, and drug anticipation. *Current Directions in Psychological Science, 14,* 296–300.

Siegel, S. (2016). The heroin overdose mystery. *Current Directions in Psychological Science, 25,* 375–379.

Siegel, S. (2017, June 28). Solving the heroin overdose mystery: How small doses can kill. *Aeon.* https://aeon.co/ideas/solving-the-heroin-overdose-mystery-how-small-doses-can-kill

Siegel, S., Baptista, M. A. S., Kim, J. A., McDonald, R. V., & Weise-Kelly, L. (2000). Pavlovian psychopharmacology: The associative basis of tolerance. *Experimental and Clinical Psychopharmacology, 8,* 276–293.

Siegrist, M., & Cousin, M. E. (2009). Expectations influence sensory experience in a wine tasting. *Appetite, 52*(3), 762–765. https://doi.org/10.1016/j.appet.2009.02.002

Siemer, M., Mauss, I., & Gross, J. J. (2007). Same situation—different emotions: How appraisals shape our emotions. *Emotion, 7*(3), 592–600. https://doi.org/10.1037/1528-3542.7.3.592

Sievertsen, H. H., Gino, F., & Piovesan, M. (2016). Cognitive fatigue influences students' performance on standardized tests. *Proceedings of the National Academy of Sciences, 113*(10), 2621–2624. https://doi.org/10.1073/pnas.1516947113

Sigman, M., Spence, S. J., & Wang, T. (2006). Autism from developmental and neuropsychological perspectives. *Annual Review of Clinical Psychology, 2,* 327–355.

Sigurdsson, T., Doyere, V., Cain, C. K., & LeDoux, J. E. (2007). Long-term potentiation in the amygdala: A cellular mechanism of fear learning and memory. *Neuropharmacology, 52,* 215–227.

Silvani, A., Calandra-Buonaura, G., Dampney, R. A., & Cortelli, P. (2016). Brain-heart interactions: Physiology and clinical implications. *Philosophical Transactions of the Royal Society, A, 347.* https://doi.org/10.1098/rsta.2015.0181

Silver, I., Mellers, B. A., & Tetlock, P. E. (2021). Wise teamwork: Collective confidence calibration predicts the effectiveness of group discussion. *Journal of Experimental Social Psychology, 96,* 104157. https://doi.org/10.1016/j.jesp.2021.104157

Silverman, A. M., Gwinn, J. D., & Van Boven, L. (2014). Stumbling in their shoes: Disability simulations reduce judged capabilities of disabled people. *Social Psychological and Personality Science, 6*(4), 464–471. https://doi.org/10.1177/1948550614559650

Silverman, C., Strapagiel, L., Shaban, H., Hall, E., & Singer-Vine, J. (2016). Hyperpartisan Facebook pages are publishing false and misleading information at an alarming rate. *Buzzfeed News.* https://www.buzzfeed.com/craigsilverman/partisan-fb-pages-analysis

Simeone, J. C., Ward, A. J., Rotella, P., Collins, J., & Windisch, R. (2015). An evaluation of variation in published estimates of schizophrenia prevalence from 1990–2013: A systematic literature review. *BMC Psychiatry, 15,* 193.

Simons, D. J., & Chabris, C. F. (1999). Gorillas in our midst: Sustained inattentional blindness for dynamic events. *Perception, 28,* 1059–1074.

Simons, D. J., & Levin, D. T. (1998). Failure to detect changes to people during a real-world interaction. *Psychonomic Bulletin & Review, 5,* 644–649.

Simons, D. J., & Rensink, R. A. (2005). Change blindness: Past, present, and future. *Trends in Cognitive Sciences, 9,* 16–20.

Simons, D., Lleras, A., Martinez-Conde, S., Slichter, D., Caddigan, E., & Nevarez, G. (2006). Induced visual fading of complex images. *Journal of Vision, 6,* 1093–1101. https://doi.org/10.1167/6.10.9

Simons, G. (2021, February 22). *Welcome to the 24th edition.* https://www.ethnologue.com/ethnoblog/gary-simons/welcome-24th-edition

Simonton, D. K. (2006). Presidential IQ, openness, intellectual brilliance, and leadership: Estimates and correlations for 42 U.S. chief executives. *Political Psychology, 27*(4), 511–526. https://doi.org/10.1111/j.1467-9221.2006.00524.x

Simonton, D. K. (2014). The mad-genius paradox: Can creative people be more mentally healthy but highly creative people more mentally ill? *Perspectives on Psychological Science, 9*(5), 470–480. https://doi.org/10.1177/1745691614543973

Simpson, J. A. (1987). The dissolution of romantic relationships: Factors involved in relationship stability and emotional distress. *Journal of Personality and Social Psychology, 53*(4), 683–692. http://doi.org/10.1037/0022-3514.53.4.683

Simpson, J. A., Collins, W. A., & Salvatore, J. E. (2011). The impact of early interpersonal experience on adult romantic relationship functioning: Recent findings from the Minnesota Longitudinal Study of Risk and Adaptation. *Current Directions in Psychological Science, 20*(6), 355–359. https://doi.org/10.1177/0963721411418468

Simpson, J. A., Collins, W. A., Tran, S., & Haydon, K. C. (2007). Attachment and the experience and expression of emotions in romantic relationships: A developmental perspective. *Journal of Personality and Social Psychology, 92*(2), 355–367. https://doi.org/10.1037/0022-3514.92.2.355

Simpson, J. A., & Rholes, W. S. (2019). Adult attachment orientations and well-being during the transition to parenthood. *Current Opinion in Psychology, 25,* 47–52. https://doi.org/10.1016/j.copsyc.2018.02.019

Simpson, S. J., & Raubenheimer, D. (2014). Perspective: Tricks of the trade. *Nature, 508,* S66. https://doi.org/10.1038/508S66a

Sinclair, A. H., Hakimi, S., Stanley, M. L., Adock, R. A., & Samanez-Larkin, G. R. (2021). Pairing facts with imagined consequences improves pandemic-related risk perception. *Proceedings of the National Academy of Sciences, 118*(32), e2100970118. https://doi.org/10.1073/pnas.2100970118

Sinclair, R. C., Hoffman, C., Mark, M. M., Martin, L. L., & Pickering, T. L. (1994). Construct accessibility and the misattribution of arousal: Schachter and Singer revisited. *Psychological Science, 5*(1), 15–19. https://doi.org/10.1111/j.1467-9280.1994.tb00607.x

Singer, P. (1975). *Animal liberation: A new ethics for our treatment of animals.* Random House.

Singh, D. (1993). Adaptive significance of female physical attractiveness: Role of waist-to-hip ratio. *Journal of Personality and Social Psychology, 65,* 293–307.

Sirois, F. M. (2015). Is procrastination a vulnerability factor for hypertension and cardiovascular disease? Testing an extension of the procrastination–health model. *Journal of Behavioral Medicine, 38,* 578–589.

Siu, A. L., & U.S. Preventive Services Task Force. (2016). Screening for autism spectrum disorder in young children: U.S. Preventive Services Task Force recommendation statement. *Journal of the American Medical Association, 315,* 691–696.

Skiena, S., & Ward, C. B. (2013). *Who's bigger? Where historical figures really rank.* Cambridge University Press.

Skinner, A. L., Olson, K. R., & Meltzoff, A. N. (2020). Acquiring group bias: Observing other people's nonverbal signals can create social group biases. *Journal of Personality and Social Psychology, 119*(4), 824–838. https://doi.org/10.1037/pspi0000218

Skinner, B. F. (1938). *The behavior of organisms: An experimental analysis.* Appleton-Century-Crofts.

Skinner, B. F. (1948). "Superstition" in the pigeon. *Journal of Experimental Psychology, 38,* 168–172.

Skinner, B. F. (1950). Are theories of learning necessary? *Psychological Review, 57,* 193–216.

Skinner, B. F. (1953). *Science and human behavior.* Macmillan.

Skinner, B. F. (1957). Verbal behavior. Appleton-Century-Crofts.

Skinner, B. F. (1958). Teaching machines. *Science, 129,* 969–977.

Skinner, B. F. (1971). *Beyond freedom and dignity.* Bantam Books.

Skinner, B. F. (1972). The operational analysis of psychological terms. In B. F. Skinner, *Cumulative record* (3rd ed., pp. 370–384). Appleton-Century-Crofts. (Original work published 1945)

Skinner, B. F. (1974). *About behaviorism.* Alfred A. Knopf.

Skinner, B. F. (1979). *The shaping of a behaviorist: Part two of an autobiography.* Knopf.

Skotko, B. G., Levine, S. P., & Goldstein, R. (2011a). Having a brother or sister with Down syndrome: Perspectives from siblings. *American Journal of Medical Genetics Part A, 155*(10), 2348–2359. https://doi.org/10.1002/ajmg.a.34228

Skotko, B. G., Levine, S. P., & Goldstein, R. (2011b). Self-perceptions from people with Down syndrome. *American Journal of Medical Genetics Part A, 155*(10), 2360–2369. https://doi.org/10.1002/ajmg.a.34235

Skvortsova, V., Degos, B., Welter, M.-L., Vidailhet, M., & Pessiglione, M. (2017). A selective role for dopamine in learning to maximize reward but not to minimize effort: Evidence from patients with Parkinson's disease. *Journal of Neuroscience, 37,* 6087–6097.

Slagter, H. A. (2012). Conventional working memory training may not improve intelligence. *Trends in Cognitive Sciences, 16,* 582–583.

Slater, A., Morison, V., & Somers, M. (1988). Orientation discrimination and cortical function in the human newborn. *Perception, 17,* 597–602.

Slaughter, V. (2021). Do newborns have the ability to imitate? *Trends in Cognitive Sciences, 25*(5), 377–387. https://doi.org/10.1016/j.tics.2021.02.006

Sloane, S., Baillargeon, R., & Premack, D. (2012). Do infants have a sense of fairness? *Psychological Science, 23*(2), 196–204.

Sloman, S. A., & Fernbach, P. (2017). *The knowledge illusion: Why we never think alone.* Riverhead Books.

Slotnick, S. D., & Schacter, D. L. (2004). A sensory signature that distinguished true from false memories. *Nature Neuroscience, 7,* 664–672.

Small, D. M., Gerber, J. C., Mak, Y. E., & Hummel, T. (2005). Differential neural responses evoked by orthonasal versus retronasal odorant perception in humans. *Neuron, 47*(4), 593–605.

Smart, E., Smart, L., & Morton, L. (2003). *Bringing Elizabeth home: A journey of faith and hope.* Doubleday.

Smetacek, V. (2002). Balance: Mind-grasping gravity. *Nature, 415,* 481.

Smith, A. R., Chein, J., & Steinberg, L. (2014). Peers increase adolescent risk taking even when the probabilities of negative outcomes are known. *Developmental Psychology, 50*(5), 1564–1568. http://doi.org/10.1037/a0035696

Smith, C. N., Frascino, J. C., Hopkins, R. O., & Squire, L. R. (2013). The nature of anterograde and retrograde impairment after damage to the medial temporal lobe. *Neuropsychologia, 51,* 2709–2714.

Smith, E. E., & Jonides, J. (1997). Working memory: A view from neuroimaging. *Cognitive Psychology, 33,* 5–42.

Smith, E. N., Romero, C., Donovan, B., Herter, R., Paunesku, D., Cohen, G. L., ... Gross, J. J. (2018). Emotion theories and adolescent well-being: Results of an online intervention. *Emotion, 18*(6), 781–788. https://doi.org/10.1037/emo0000379

Smith, M. L., Glass, G. V., & Miller, T. I. (1980). *The benefits of psychotherapy.* Johns Hopkins University Press.

Smith, N., & Tsimpli, I.-M. (1995). *The mind of a savant.* Oxford University Press.

Snedeker, J., Geren, J., & Shafto, C. (2007). Starting over: International adoption as a natural experiment in language development. *Psychological Science, 18,* 79–87.

Snedeker, J., Geren, J., & Shafto, C. (2012). Disentangling the effects of cognitive development and linguistic expertise: A longitudinal study of the acquisition of English in internationally adopted children. *Cognitive Psychology, 65,* 39–76.

Sneed, J. R. (2005). Models of the aging self. *Journal of Social Issues, 61*(2), 375–388.

Sniekers, S., Stringer, S., Watanabe, K., Jansen, P. R., Coleman, J. R. I., Krapohl, E., ... Posthuma, D. (2017). Genome-wide association meta-analysis of 78,308 individuals identifies new loci and genes influencing human intelligence. *Nature Genetics, 49,* 1107. http://dx.doi.org/10.1038/ng.3869

Snowdon, D. A. (2003). Healthy aging and dementia: Findings from the Nun Study. *Annals of Internal Medicine, 139*(5 Pt. 2), 450–454. https://doi.org/10.7326/0003-4819-139-5_part_2-200309021-00014

Snowdon, D. A., Kemper, S. J., Mortimer, J. A., Greiner, L. H., Wekstein, D. R., & Markesbery, W. R. (1996). Linguistic ability in early life and cognitive function and Alzheimer's disease in late life: Findings from the Nun Study. *JAMA, 275*(7), 528–532. https://doi.org/10.1001/jama.1996.03530310034029

Snowdon, R., Thompson, P., & Troscianko, T. (2012). *Basic vision: An introduction to visual perception* (2nd ed.). Oxford University Press.

Snyder-Mackler, N., Sanz, J., Kohn, J. N., Brinkworth, J. F., Morrow, S., Shaver, A. O., ... Tung, J. (2016). Social status alters immune regulation and response to infection in macaques. *Science, 354*(6315), 1041–1045. https://doi.org/10.1126/science.aah3580

Soderstrom, N. C., & Bjork, R. A. (2014). Testing facilitates the regulation of subsequent study time. *Journal of Memory and Language, 73,* 99–115.

Sodian, B., & Kristen-Antonow, S. (2015). Declarative joint attention as a foundation of theory of mind. *Developmental Psychology, 51*(9), 1190–1200. https://doi.org/10.1037/dev0000039

Sokol-Hessner, P., Lackovic, S. F., Tobe, R. H., Camerer, C. F., Leventhal, B. L., & Phelps, E. A. (2015). Determinants of propanolol's selective effect on loss aversion. *Psychological Science, 26,* 1123–1130.

Solomon, D., & Adams, J. (2015). The use of complementary and alternative medicine in adults with depressive disorders: A critical integrative review. *Journal of Affective Disorders, 179,* 101–113. https://doi.org/10.1016/j.jad.2015.03.031

Solomon, S., Greenberg, J., & Pyszczynski, T. (1991). A terror management theory of social behavior: The psychological functions of self-esteem and cultural worldviews. In M. P. Zanna (Ed.), *Advances in experimental social psychology* (Vol. 24, pp. 93–159). Academic Press.

Somerville, L. H., Jones, R. M., Ruberry, E. J., Dyke, J. P., Glover, G., & Casey, B. J. (2013). The medial prefrontal cortex and the emergence of self-conscious emotion in adolescence. *Psychological Science, 24*(8), 1554–1562. https://doi.org/10.1177/0956797613475633

Sommerville, J. A., Schmidt, M. F. H., Yun, J., & Burns, M. (2013). The development of fairness expectations and prosocial development in the second year of life. *Infancy, 18*(1), 40–66.

Son, L. K., & Metcalfe, J. (2000). Metacognitive and control strategies in study-time allocation. *Journal of Experimental Psychology: Learning, Memory, and Cognition, 26,* 204–221.

Song, H., Fang, F., Arnberg, F. K., Mataix-Cols, D., de la Cruz, L. F., Almqvist, C., ... Valdimarsdóttir, U. A. (2019). Stress-related disorders and risk of cardiovascular disease: Population based, sibling controlled cohort study. *British Medical Journal, 365,* 1255.

Song, Y., Ma, J., Wang, H. J., Wang, Z., Hu, P., Zhang, B., & Agardh, A. (2014). Trends of age at menarche and association with body mass index in Chinese school-aged girls, 1985–2010. *Journal of Pediatrics, 165,* 1172–1177.

Sonnby-Borgstrom, M., Jonsson, P., & Svensson, O. (2003). Emotional empathy as related to mimicry reactions at different levels of information processing. *Journal of Nonverbal Behavior, 27,* 3–23.

Soule, E. K., Rossheim, M. E., Cavazos, T. C., Bode, K., & Desrosiers, A. C. (2019). Cigarette, waterpipe, and electronic cigarette use among college fraternity and sorority members and athletes in the United States. *Journal of American College Health, 69*(5), 463–469. https://doi.org/10.1080/07448481.2019.1680555

Southgate, V., Senju, A., & Csibra, G. (2007). Action anticipation through attribution of false belief by two-year-olds. *Psychological Science, 18,* 587–592.

Soveri, A., Antfolk, J., Karlsson, L., Salo, B., & Laine, M. (2017). Working memory training revisited: A multi-level meta-analysis of n-back training studies. *Psychonomic Bulletin & Review, 24,* 1077–1096.

Spearman, C. (1904). "General intelligence," objectively determined and measured. *American Journal of Psychology, 15,* 201–293.

Speisman, J. C., Lazarus, R. S., Moddkoff, A., & Davison, L. (1964). Experimental reduction of stress based on ego-defense theory. *Journal of Abnormal and Social Psychology, 68,* 367–380.

Spelke, E. S. (2005). Sex differences in intrinsic aptitude for mathematics and science: A critical review. *The American Psychologist, 60*(9), 950–958. https://doi.org/10.1037/0003-066X.60.9.950

Spence, C. (2015). On the psychological impact of food colour. *Flavour, 4,* 21. https://doi.org/10.1186/s13411-015-0031-3

Spence, C. (2018). Background colour & its impact on food perception & behaviour. *Food Quality and Preference, 68,* 156–166. https://doi.org10.1016/j.foodqual.2018.02.012

Spencer, L. G. (1929). *Illustrated phrenology: The science and art teaching how to read character; A manual of mental science.* L. N. Fowler & Company.

Spencer, S. J., Logel, C., & Davies, P. G. (2016). Stereotype threat. *Annual Review of Psychology, 67*(1), 415–437.

Sperling, G. (1960). The information available in brief visual presentations. *Psychological Monographs, 74*(11), 1–29.

Sperry, D. E., Sperry, L. L., & Miller, P. J. (2019). Reexamining the verbal environments of children from different socioeconomic backgrounds. *Child Development, 90*(4), 1303–1318.

Sperry, R. W. (1964). The great cerebral commissure. *Scientific American, 210,* 42–52.

Spiegel, A. (2011). How psychology solved a WWII shipwreck mystery. *NPR.* https://www.npr.org/templates/transcript/transcript.php?storyId=140816037

Sporns, O., & Betzel, R. F. (2016). Modular brain networks. *Annual Review of Psychology, 67,* 613–640.

Sprecher, S., & Regan, P. C. (1998). Passionate and companionate love in courting and young married couples. *Sociological Inquiry, 68,* 163–185. https://doi.org/10.1111/j.1475-682X.1998.tb00459.x

Spunt, R. P., Meyer, M. L., & Lieberman, M. D. (2015). The default mode of human brain function primes the intentional stance. *Journal of Cognitive Neuroscience, 27*(6), 1116–1124. https://doi.org/10.1162/jocn_a_00785

Squire, L. R. (1992). Memory and the hippocampus: A synthesis from findings with rats, monkeys, and humans. *Psychological Review, 99,* 195–231.

Squire, L. R. (2009). The legacy of patient HM for neuroscience. *Neuron, 61,* 6–9.

Squire, L. R., & Kandel, E. R. (1999). *Memory: From mind to molecules.* Scientific American Library.

Squire, L. R., & Wixted, J. T. (2011). The cognitive neuroscience of memory since HM. *Annual Review of Neuroscience, 34,* 259–288.

Squire, L. R., Frascino, J. C., Rivera, C. S., Heyworth, N. C., & He, B. J. (2021). One-trial perceptual learning in the absence of conscious remembering and independent of the medial temporal lobe. *Proceedings of the National Academy of Sciences USA, 118*(19), e2104072118. https://doi.org/10.1073/pnas.2104072118

Squire, L. R., Knowlton, B., & Musen, G. (1993). The structure and organization of memory. *Annual Review of Psychology, 44,* 453–495.

Srivistava, S., John, O. P., Gosling, S. D., & Potter, J. (2003). Development of personality in early and middle adulthood: Set like plaster or persistent change? *Journal of Personality and Social Psychology, 84,* 1041–1053.

Sroufe, L. A., Egeland, B., & Kruetzer, T. (1990). The fate of early experience following developmental change: Longitudinal approaches to individual adaptation in childhood. *Child Development, 61,* 1363–1373.

St. Jacques, P. L., & Schacter, D. L. (2013). Modifying memory: Selectively enhancing and updating personal memories for a museum tour by reactivating them. *Psychological Science, 24,* 537–543.

Stachl, C., Au, Q., Schoedel, R., Gosling, S. D., . . . Buhner, M. (2020). Predicting personality from patterns of behavior collected with smartphones. *Proceedings of the National Academy of Science, 117*(30), 17680–17687. https://doi.org/10.1073/pnas.1920484117

Staddon, J. E. R., & Simmelhag, V. L. (1971). The "superstition" experiment: A reexamination of its implications for the principles of adaptive behavior. *Psychological Review, 78,* 3–43.

Stahl, A. E., & Feigenson, L. (2015). Observing the unexpected enhances infants' learning and exploration. *Science, 348*(6230), 91–94. https://doi.org/10.1126/science.aaa3799

Stallman, H. M., & Kohler, M. (2016). Prevalence of sleepwalking: A systematic review and meta-analysis. *PLoS ONE, 11*(11), e0164769. https://doi.org/10.1371/journal.pone.0164769

Stanca, L. (2016). The geography of parenthood and well-being: Do children make us happy, where and why? In J. Helliwell, R. Layard, & J. Sachs (Eds.), *World Happiness Report 2016, Special Rome Edition* (Vol. II, pp. 89–103). Sustainable Development Solutions Network. http://worldhappiness.report/#happiness2016

Stanovich, K. E. (2009). *What intelligence tests miss: The psychology of rational thought.* Yale University Press.

Stanovich, K. E., & West, R. F. (2000). Individual differences in reasoning: Implications for the rationality debate? *Behavioral and Brain Sciences, 23,* 645–726.

Statton, M. A., Encarnacion, M., Celnik, P., & Bastian, A. J. (2015). A single bout of moderate aerobic exercise improves motor skill acquisition. *PLoS ONE.* https://doi.org/10.1371/journal.pone.0141393

Staw, B. M., & Hoang, H. (1995). Sunk costs in the NBA: Why draft order affects playing time and survival in professional basketball. *Administrative Science Quarterly, 40,* 474–494.

Steele, C. M. (1997). A threat in the air: How stereotypes shape intellectual identity and performance. *American Psychologist, 52*(6), 613–629. https://doi.org/10.1037/0003-066X.52.6.613

Steele, C. M., & Aronson, J. (1995). Stereotype threat and the intellectual test performance of African Americans. *Journal of Personality and Social Psychology, 69,* 797–811.

Steele, C. M., & Josephs, R. A. (1990). Alcohol myopia: Its prized and dangerous effects. *American Psychologist, 45,* 921–933.

Steele, H., Steele, M., Croft, C., & Fonagy, P. (1999). Infant-mother attachment at one year predicts children's understanding of mixed emotions at six years. *Social Development, 8,* 161–178.

Stein, D. J., Lim, C. C. W., Roest, A., de Jonge, P., Aguilar-Gaxiola, S., Al-Hamzawi, A., ... Scott, K. M. (2017). The cross-national epidemiology of social anxiety disorder: Data from the World Mental Health Survey Initiative. *BMC Medicine, 15*(1), 143. https://doi.org/10.1186/s12916-017-0889-2

Stein, D. J., Phillips, K. A., Bolton, D., Fulford, K. W. M., Sadler, J. Z., & Kendler, K. S. (2010). What is a mental/psychiatric disorder? From *DSM–IV* to *DSM–V. Psychological Medicine, 40*(11), 1759–1765. https://doi.org/10.1017/S0033291709992261

Stein, M. B., Chavira, D. A., & Jang, K. L. (2001). Bringing up bashful baby: Developmental pathways to social phobia. *Psychiatric Clinics of North America, 24*, 661–675.

Stein, M., Federspiel, A., Koenig, T., Wirth, M., Lehmann, C., Wiest, R., ... Dierks, T. (2009). Reduced frontal activation with increasing second language proficiency. *Neuropsychologia, 47*, 2712–2720.

Steinbaum, E. A., & Miller, N. E. (1965). Obesity from eating elicited by daily stimulation of hypothalamus. *American Journal of Physiology, 208*, 1–5.

Steinberg, L. (2007). Risk taking in adolescence: New perspectives from brain and behavioral science. *Current Directions in Psychological Science, 16*(2), 55–59. https://doi.org/10.1111/j.1467-8721.2007.00475x

Steinberg, L., & Monahan, K. C. (2007). Age differences in resistance to peer influence. *Developmental Psychology, 43*, 1531–1543.

Steinberg, L., & Morris, A. S. (2001). Adolescent development. *Annual Review of Psychology, 52*, 83–110.

Steiner, J. E. (1973). The gustofacial response: Observation on normal and anencephalic newborn infants. In J. F. Bosma (Ed.), *Fourth symposium on oral sensation and perception: Development in the fetus and infant* (DHEW 73–546; pp. 254–278). U.S. Department of Health, Education, and Welfare.

Steiner, J. E. (1979). Human facial expressions in response to taste and smell stimulation. *Advances in Child Development and Behavior, 13*, 257–295.

Stellar, J. R., Kelley, A. E., & Corbett, D. (1983). Effects of peripheral and central dopamine blockade on lateral hypothalamic self-stimulation: Evidence for both reward and motor deficits. *Pharmacology, Biochemistry, and Behavior, 18*, 433–442.

Stellar, J. R., & Stellar, E. (1985). *The neurobiology of motivation and reward.* Springer-Verlag.

Stelmack, R. M. (1990). Biological bases of extraversion: Psychophysiological evidence. *Journal of Personality, 58*, 293–311.

Stemmler, G., Aue, T., & Wacker, J. (2007). Anger and fear: Separable effects of emotion and motivational direction on somatovisceral responses. *International Journal of Psychophysiology, 66*(2), 141–153. https://doi.org/10.1016/j.ijpsycho.2007.03.019

Stephens, R. S. (1999). Cannabis and hallucinogens. In B. S. McCrady & E. E. Epstein (Eds.), *Addictions: A comprehensive guidebook* (pp. 121–140). Oxford University Press.

Steptoe, A., & Zaninotto, P. (2020). Lower socioeconomic status and the acceleration of aging: An outcome-wide analysis. *Proceedings of the National Academy of Sciences, 117*(26), 14911–14917. https://doi.org/10.1073/pnas.1915741117

Stern, J. A., Brown, M., Ulett, A., & Sletten, I. (1977). A comparison of hypnosis, acupuncture, morphine, Valium, aspirin, and placebo in the management of experimentally induced pain. In W. E. Edmonston (Ed.), *Conceptual and investigative approaches to hypnosis and hypnotic phenomena* (Vol. 296, pp. 175–193). New York Academy of Sciences.

Stern, W. (1914). *The psychological methods of testing intelligence* (G. M. Whipple, Trans.). Warwick & York.

Sternberg, R. J. (1986). A triangular theory of love. *Psychological Review, 93*, 119–135.

Sternberg, R. J. (1999). The theory of successful intelligence. *Review of General Psychology, 3*(4), 292–316. https://doi.org/10.1037/1089-2680.3.4.292

Sternberg, R. J. (2006). The Rainbow Project: Enhancing the SAT through assessments of analytical, practical, and creative skills. *Intelligence, 34*(4), 321–350. https://doi.org/10.1016/j.intell.2006.01.002

Sternberg, R. J., & Grigorenko, E. L. (2004). Intelligence and culture: How culture shapes what intelligence means, and the implications for a science of well-being. *Philosophical Transaction of the Royal Society B*, 1427–1434. https://doi.org/10.1093/acprof:oso/9780198567523.003.0014

Stevens, J. (1988). An activity approach to practical memory. In M. M. Gruneberg, P. E. Morris, & R. N. Sykes (Eds.), *Practical aspects of memory: Current research and issues* (Vol. 1, pp. 335–341). Wiley.

Stevens, L. A. (1971). *Explorers of the brain.* Knopf.

Stevenson, R. J. (2017). Psychological correlates of habitual diet in healthy adults. *Psychological Bulletin, 143*(1), 53–90. https://doi.org/10.1037/bul0000065

Stevenson, R. J., & Francis, H. M. (2017). The hippocampus and the regulation of human food intake. *Psychological Bulletin, 143*(10), 1011–1032. https://doi.org/10.1037/bul0000109

Stevenson, R. J., & Wilson, D. A. (2007). Odour perception: An object-recognition approach. *Perception, 36*, 1821–1833.

Stice, E., & Yokum, S. (2016). Neural vulnerability factors that increase risk for future weight gain. *Psychological Bulletin, 142*(5), 447–471. https://doi.org/10.1037/bul0000044

Stickgold, R., Hobson, J. A., Fosse, R., & Fosse, M. (2001). Sleep, learning, and dreams: Off-line memory reprocessing. *Science, 294*, 1052–1057.

Stickgold, R., Malia, A., Maguire, D., Roddenberry, D., & O'Connor, M. (2000). Replaying the game: Hypnagogic images in normals and amnesics. *Science, 290*, 350–353.

Stillman, C. M., Howard, J. H., Jr., & Howard, D. V. (2016). The effects of structural complexity on age-related deficits in implicit probabilistic sequence learning. *Journals of Gerontology Series B, Psychological Sciences and Social Sciences, 71*, 212–219.

Stockman, A., & Sharpe, L. T. (2000). Spectral sensitivities of the middle- and long-wavelength sensitive cones derived from measurements in observers of known genotype. *Vision Research, 40*, 1711–1737. See "cone fundamentals" at http://www.cvrl.org/

Stoet, G., & Geary, D. C. (2018). The gender equality paradox in STEM education. *Psychological Science.* http://journals.sagepub.com/doi/full/10.1177/0956797617741719

Stone, A. A. (2018). Ecological momentary assessment in survey research. In D. L. Vannette & J. A. Krosnick (Eds.), *The Palgrave handbook of survey research* (pp. 221–226). Palgrave Macmillan.

Stone, A. A., Schwartz, J. E., Broderick, J. E., & Deaton, A. (2010). A snapshot of the age distribution of psychological well-being in the United States. *Proceedings of the National Academy of Sciences, USA, 107*(22), 9985–9990. https://doi.org/10.1073/pnas.1003744107

Stone, J., Perry, Z. W., & Darley, J. M. (1997). "White men can't jump": Evidence for the perceptual confirmation of racial stereotypes following a basketball game. *Basic and Applied Social Psychology, 19*(3), 291–306. https://doi.org/10.1207/s15324834basp1903_2

Stone, M. H. (1997). Introduction: The history of obsessive-compulsive disorder from the early period to the turn of the twentieth century. In D. J. Stein & M. H. Stone (Eds.), *Essential Papers on Obsessive-Compulsive Disorder* (pp. 19–33). New York: New York University Press.

Stoodley, C. J., Ray, N. J., Jack, A., & Stein, J. F. (2008). Implicit learning in control, dyslexic, and garden-variety poor readers. *Annals of the New York Academy of Sciences, 1145*, 173–183.

Storm, B. C., Bjork, E. L., Bjork, R. A., & Nestojko, J. F. (2006). Is retrieval success a necessary condition for retrieval-induced forgetting? *Psychonomic Bulletin & Review, 2*, 249–253.

Storms, M. D. (1973). Videotape and the attribution process: Reversing actors' and observers' points of view. *Journal of Personality and Social Psychology, 27*, 165–175.

Stott, D. H. (1983). Brain size and "intelligence." *British Journal of Developmental Psychology, 1*, 279–287.

Strack, F. (2016). Reflections on the smiling registered replication report. *Perspectives on Psychological Science, 11,* 929–930. https://doi.org/10.1177/1745691616674460

Strack, F., Martin, L. L., & Stepper, S. (1988). Inhibiting and facilitating conditions of the human smile: A nonobtrusive test of the facial feedback hypothesis. *Journal of Personality and Social Psychology, 54,* 768–777.

Strawn, J. R., Geracioti, L., Rajdev, N., Clemenza, K., & Levine, A., (2018). Pharmacotherapy for generalized anxiety disorder in adult and pediatric patients: An evidence-based treatment review. *Expert Opinion on Pharmacotherapy, 19,* 1057–1070.

Strayer, D. L., Drews, F. A., & Johnston, W. A. (2003). Cell phone–induced failures of visual attention during simulated driving. *Journal of Experimental Psychology: Applied, 9,* 23–32.

Streissguth, A. (2007). Offspring effects of prenatal alcohol exposure from birth to 25 years: The Seattle Prospective Longitudinal Study. *Journal of Clinical Psychology in Medical Settings, 14*(2), 81–101. https://doi.org/10.1007/s10880-007-9067-6

Streissguth, A. P., Barr, H. M., Bookstein, F. L., Sampson, P. D., & Carmichael Olson, H. (1999). The long-term neurocognitive consequences of prenatal alcohol exposure: A 14-year study. *Psychological Science, 10,* 186–190.

Striano, T., & Reid, V. M. (2006). Social cognition in the first year. *Trends in Cognitive Sciences, 10*(10), 471–476.

Striegel-Moore, R. H., & Bulik, C. M. (2007). Risk factors for eating disorders. *American Psychologist, 62,* 181–198.

Strohmetz, D. B., Rind, B., Fisher, R., & Lynn, M. (2002). Sweetening the till: The use of candy to increase restaurant tipping. *Journal of Applied Social Psychology, 32,* 300–309.

Strosberg, B. B. (2021). Adorno's negative psychology. *Social and Personality Psychology Compass, 15*(2), e12578. https://doi.org/10.1111/spc3.12578

Strueber, D., Lueck, M., & Roth, G. (2006). The violent brain. *Scientific American Mind, 17,* 20–27.

Stuss, D. T., & Benson, D. F. (1986). *The frontal lobes.* Raven Press.

Suchman, A. L., Markakis, K., Beckman, H. B., & Frankel, R. (1997). A model of empathic communication in the medical interview. *Journal of the American Medical Association, 277,* 678–682.

Suddendorf, T., & Corballis, M. C. (2007). The evolution of foresight: What is mental time travel and is it unique to humans? *Behavioral and Brain Sciences, 30,* 299–313.

Suderman, M., McGowan, P. O., Sasaki, A., Huang, T. C. T., Hallett, M. T., Meaney, M. J., ... Szyf, M. (2012). Conserved epigenetic sensitivity to early life experiences in the rat and human hippocampus. *Proceedings of the National Academy of Sciences, USA, 109*(Suppl. 2), 17266–17272.

Sullivan-Singh, S. J., Stanton, A. L., & Low, C. A. (2015). Living with limited time: Socioemotional selectivity theory in the context of health adversity. *Journal of Personality and Social Psychology, 108,* 900–916.

Sundet, J. M., Eriksen, W., & Tambs, K. (2008). Intelligence correlations between brothers decrease with increasing age difference: Evidence for shared environmental effects in young adults. *Psychological Science, 19,* 843–847.

Suradom, C., Suttajit, S., Oon-Arom, A., Maneeton, B., & Srisurapanont, M. (2021). Omega-3 polyunsaturated fatty acid (n-3 PUFA) supplementation for prevention and treatment of perinatal depression: A systematic review and meta-analysis of randomized-controlled trials. *Nordic Journal of Psychiatry, 75,* 239–246.

Susman, S., Dent, C., McAdams, L., Stacy, A., Burton, D., & Flay, B. (1994). Group self-identification and adolescent cigarette smoking: A 1-year prospective study. *Journal of Abnormal Psychology, 103,* 576–580.

Suthana, N., & Fried, I. (2012). Percepts to recollections: Insights from single neuron recordings in the human brain. *Trends in Cognitive Sciences, 16,* 427–436.

Sutin, A. R., Stephan, Y., & Terracciano, A. (2015). Weight discrimination and risk of mortality. *Psychological Science, 26*(11), 1803–1811. https://doi.org/10.1177/0956797615601103

Suzuki, L. A., & Valencia, R. R. (1997). Race–ethnicity and measured intelligence: Educational implications. *American Psychologist, 52,* 1103–1114.

Swami, V., & Tovée, M. J. (2006). The influence of body mass index on the physical attractiveness preferences of feminist and nonfeminist heterosexual women and lesbians. *Psychology of Women Quarterly, 30*(3), 252–257. https://doi.org/10.1111/j.1471-6402.2006.00293.x

Swami, V., & Tovée, M. J. (2008). The muscular male: A comparison of the physical attractiveness preferences of gay and heterosexual men. *International Journal of Men's Health, 7*(1), 59–71. https://doi.org/10.3149/jmh.0701.59

Swann, W. B., Jr. (1983). Self-verification: Bringing social reality into harmony with the self. In J. M. Suls & A. G. Greenwald (Eds.), *Psychological perspectives on the self* (Vol. 2, pp. 33–66). Erlbaum.

Swann, W. B., Jr. (2012). Self-verification theory. In P. Van Lang, A. Kruglanski, & E. T. Higgins (Eds.), *Handbook of theories of social psychology* (Vol. 2, pp. 23–42). Sage.

Swann, W. B., Jr., & Rentfrow, P. J. (2001). Blirtatiousness: Cognitive, behavioral, and physiological consequences of rapid responding. *Journal of Personality and Social Psychology, 81*(6), 1160–1175.

Swayze, V. W., II. (1995). Frontal leukotomy and related psychosurgical procedures before antipsychotics (1935–1954): A historical overview. *American Journal of Psychiatry, 152,* 505–515.

Sweatt, J. D. (2019). The epigenetic basis of individuality. *Current Opinion in Behavioral Sciences, 25,* 51–56.

Sweeny, K., Carroll, P. J., & Shepperd, J. A. (2006). Is optimism always best? Future outlooks and preparedness. *Current Directions in Psychological Science, 15,* 302–306.

Swencionis, J. K., & Fiske, S. T. (2016) Promote up, ingratiate down: Status comparisons drive warmth-competence tradeoffs in impression management. *Journal of Experimental Social Psychology, 64,* 27–34.

Swinkels, A. (2003). An effective exercise for teaching cognitive heuristics. *Teaching of Psychology, 30,* 120–122.

Szechtman, H., & Woody, E. Z. (2006). Obsessive-compulsive disorder as a disturbance of security motivation: Constraints on comorbidity. *Neurotoxicity Research, 10,* 103–112.

Szpunar, K. K. (2010). Episodic future thought: An emerging concept. *Perspectives on Psychological Science, 5,* 142–162.

Szpunar, K. K., Khan, N. Y., & Schacter, D. L. (2013). Interpolated memory tests reduce mind wandering and improve learning of online lectures. *Proceedings of the National Academy of Sciences, USA, 110,* 6313–6317.

Szpunar, K. K., Watson, J. M., & McDermott, K. B. (2007). Neural substrates of envisioning the future. *Proceedings of the National Academy of Sciences, USA, 104,* 642–647.

Tajfel, H., Billig, M. G., Bundy, R. P., & Flament, C. (1971). Social categorization and intergroup behaviour. *European Journal of Social Psychology, 1,* 149–178.

Tajfel, H., & Turner, J. C. (1986). The social identity theory of intergroup behavior. In S. Worchel & W. G. Austin (Eds.), *Psychology of intergroup relations* (pp. 7–24). Nelson.

Tajfel, H., & Wilkes, A. L. (1963). Classification and quantitative judgement. *British Journal of Psychology, 54,* 101–114.

Talhelm, T., Oishi, S., & Zhang, X. (2018). Who smiles while alone? Rates of smiling lower in China than U.S. *Emotion.* https://doi .org/10.1037/emo0000459

Tamir, M., Bigman, Y. E., Rhodes, E., Salerno, J., & Schreier, J. (2015). An expectancy-value model of emotion regulation: Implications for motivation, emotional experience, and decision making. *Emotion, 15*(1), 90–103. http://doi.org/10.1037/emo0000021

Tamir, M., & Ford, B. Q. (2012). Should people pursue feelings that feel good or feelings that do good? Emotional preferences and well-being. *Emotion, 12,* 1061–1070.

Tamminga, C. A., Nemeroff, C. B., Blakely, R. D., Brady, L., Carter, C. S., Davis, K. L., … Suppes, T. (2002). Developing novel treatments for mood disorders: Accelerating discovery. *Biological Psychiatry, 52,* 589–609.

Tanaka, F., Cicourel, A., & Movellan, J. R. (2007). Socialization between toddlers and robots at an early childhood education center. *Proceedings of the National Academy of Sciences, USA, 104*(46), 17954–17958.

Tanaka, K. Z., He, H., Tomar, A., Niisato, K., Huang, A. J. Y., & McHugh, T. J. (2018). The hippocampal engram maps experience but not place. *Science, 361,* 392–397.

Tang, A., Crawford, H., Morales, S., Degnan, K. A., Pine, D. S., & Fox, N. A. (2020). Infant behavioral inhibition predicts personality and social outcomes three decades later. *Proceedings of the National Academy of Sciences, 117*(18), 9800–9807. https://doi.org/10.1073 /pnas.1917376117

Tang, Y.-P., Shimizu, E., Dube, G. R., Rampon, C., Kerchner, G. A., Zhuo, M., … Tsien, J. Z. (1999). Genetic enhancement of learning and memory in mice. *Nature, 401,* 63–69.

Tang, Y. Y., Lu, Q., Fan, M., Yang, Y., & Posner, M. I. (2012). Mechanisms of white matter changes induced by meditation. *Proceedings of the National Academy of Sciences, USA, 109,* 10570–10574.

Tao, L., Jiang, R., Zhang, K., Qian, Z., Chen, P., Lv, Y., & Yao, Y. (2020). Light therapy in non-seasonal depression: An update meta-analysis. *Psychiatry Research, 291,* 113247. https://10.1016/j .psychres.2020.113247

Tao, L., Wang, G., Zhu, M., & Cai, Q. (2021). Bilingualism and domain-general cognitive functions from a neural perspective: A systematic review. *Neuroscience & Biobehavioral Reviews, 125,* 264–295. https://10.1016/j.neubiorev.2021.02.029

Tarantino, N., Tully, E. C., Garcia, S. E., South, S., Iacono, W. G., & McGue, M. (2014). Genetic and environmental influences on affiliation with deviant peers during adolescence and early adulthood. *Developmental Psychology, 50*(3), 663–673. http://doi.org/10.1037 /a0034345

Task Force on Promotion and Dissemination of Psychological Procedures. (1995). Training in and dissemination of empirically validated psychological treatments: Report and recommendations. *Clinical Psychologist, 48,* 3–23.

Taylor, S. E. (1989). *Positive illusions.* Basic Books.

Taylor, S. E. (2002). *The tending instinct: How nurturing is essential to who we are and how we live.* Times Books.

Taylor, S. E., & Brown, J. D. (1988). Illusion and well-being: A social psychological perspective on mental health. *Psychological Bulletin, 103,* 193–210.

Taylor, S. E., & Fiske, S. T. (1975). Point-of-view and perceptions of causality. *Journal of Personality and Social Psychology, 32,* 439–445.

Tellegen, A., Lykken, D. T., Bouchard, T. J., Wilcox, K., Segal, N., & Rich, A. (1988). Personality similarity in twins reared together and apart. *Journal of Personality and Social Psychology, 54,* 1031–1039.

ten Brinke, L., Vohs, K. D., & Carney, D. R. (2016). Can ordinary people detect deception after all? *Trends in Cognitive Sciences, 20*(8), 579–588. https://doi.org/10.1016/j.tics.2016.05.012

Terman, L. M. (1916). *The measurement of intelligence.* Houghton Mifflin.

Tesser, A. (1991). Emotion in social comparison and reflection processes. In J. Suls & T. A. Wills (Eds.), *Social comparison: Contemporary theory and research* (pp. 117–148). Erlbaum.

Tessum, C. W., Paolella, D. A., Chambliss, S. E., Apte, J. S., Hill, J. D., & Marshall, J. D. (2021). $PM_{2.5}$ polluters disproportionately and systematically affect people of color in the United States. *Science Advances, 7*(18), eabf4491. https://doi.org/10.1126/sciadv.abf4491

Teuscher, U., & Teuscher, C. (2007). Reconsidering the double standard of aging: Effects of gender and sexual orientation on facial attractiveness ratings. *Personality and Individual Differences, 42*(4), 631–639. https://doi.org/10.1016/j.paid.2006.08.020

Tews, M. J., Stafford, K., & Tracey, J. B. (2011) What matters most? The perceived importance of ability and personality for hiring decisions. *Cornell Hospitality Quarterly, 52,* 94–101.

Teyler, T. J., & DiScenna, P. (1986). The hippocampal memory indexing theory. *Behavioral Neuroscience, 100,* 147–154.

Thaker, G. K. (2002). Current progress in schizophrenia research: Search for genes of schizophrenia. Back to defining valid phenes. *Journal of Nervous and Mental Disease, 190,* 411–412.

Thakral, P. P., Madore, K. P., Kalinowski, S. E., & Schacter, D. L. (2020). Modulation of hippocampal brain networks produces changes in episodic simulation and divergent thinking. *Proceedings of the National Academy of Sciences USA, 117*(23), 12729–12740. https://doi.org/10.1073/pnas.2003535117

Thakral, P., Madore, K. P., & Schacter, D. L. (2017). A role for the left angular gyrus in episodic simulation and memory. *Journal of Neuroscience, 37,* 8142–8149.

Thaler, K., Delivuk, M., Chapman, A., Gaynes, B. N., Kaminski, A., & Gartlehner, G. (2011). Second-generation antidepressants for seasonal affective disorder. *Cochrane Database of Systematic Reviews,* CD008591.

Thaler, R. H. (1988). The ultimatum game. *Journal of Economic Perspectives, 2,* 195–206.

Thaler, R. H., & Sunstein, C. R. (2008). *Nudge: Improving decisions about health, wealth, and happiness.* Penguin Books.

Thase, M. E., & Howland, R. H. (1995). Biological processes in depression: An updated review and integration. In E. E. Beckham & W. R. Leber (Eds.), *Handbook of depression* (2nd ed., pp. 213–279). Guilford Press.

Thibaut, J. W., & Kelley, H. H. (1959). *The social psychology of groups.* Wiley.

Thoma, B. C., Eckstrand, K. L., Montano, G. T., Rezeppa, T. L., & Marshal, M. P. (2021, March). Gender nonconformity and minority stress among lesbian, gay, and bisexual individuals: A meta-analytic review. *Perspectives on Psychological Science, 16*(6), 1165–1183. https://doi.org/10.1177/1745691620968766

Thomaes, S., Bushman, B. J., Stegge, H., & Olthof, T. (2008). Trumping shame by blasts of noise: Narcissism, self-esteem, shame, and aggression in young adolescents. *Child Development, 79*(6), 1792–1801.

Thomas, A. G., Jonason, P. K., Blackburn, J.D., Kennair, L. E. O., Lowe, R., Malouff, J., Stewart-Williams, S., Sulikowski, D., & Li, N. P. (2020). Mate preference priorities in the East and West:

A cross-cultural test of the mate preference priority model. *Journal of Personality, 88*(3), 606–620. https://doi.org/10.1111/jopy.12514

Thomas, A., & Chess, S. (1977). *Temperament and development.* Brunner/Mazel.

Thompson, C. P., Skowronski, J., Larsen, S. F., & Betz, A. (1996). *Autobiographical memory: Remembering what and remembering when.* Erlbaum.

Thompson, P. M., Giedd, J. N., Woods, R. P., MacDonald, D., Evans, A. C., & Toga, A. W. (2000). Growth patterns in the developing brain detected by using continuum mechanical tensor maps. *Nature, 404,* 190–193.

Thompson, P. M., Vidal, C., Giedd, J. N., Gochman, P., Blumenthal, J., Nicolson, R., … Rapoport, J. L. (2001). Accelerated gray matter loss in very early-onset schizophrenia. *Proceedings of the National Academy of Sciences, USA, 98,* 11650–11655.

Thompson, R. F. (2005). In search of memory traces. *Annual Review of Psychology, 56,* 1–23.

Thorndike, E. L. (1898). Animal intelligence: An experimental study of associative processes in animals. *Psychological Review Monograph Supplements, 2,* i–109.

Thornhill, R., & Gangestad, S. W. (1993). Human facial beauty: Averageness, symmetry, and parasite resistance. *Human Nature, 4,* 237–269.

Thornhill, R., & Gangestad, S. W. (1999). The scent of symmetry: A human sex pheromone that signals fitness? *Evolution and Human Behavior, 20,* 175–201.

Thurber, J. (1956). *Further fables of our time.* Simon & Schuster.

Thurstone, L. L. (1938). *Primary mental abilities.* University of Chicago Press.

Tienari, P., Wynne, L. C., Sorri, A., Lahti, I., Läksy, K., Moring, J., … Wahlberg, K. E. (2004). Genotype–environment interaction in schizophrenia-spectrum disorder: Long-term follow-up study of Finnish adoptees. *British Journal of Psychiatry, 184,* 216–222.

Tilot, A. K., Kucera, K. S., Vino, A., Asher, J. E., Baron-Cohen, S., & Fisher, S. E. (2018). Rare variants in axonogenesis genes connect three families with sound-color synesthesia. *Proceedings of the National Academy of Sciences USA, 115*(12), 3168–3173. https://doi.org/10.1073/pnas.1715492115

Timmerman, T. A. (2007). "It was a thought pitch": Personal, situational, and target influences on hit-by-pitch events across time. *Journal of Applied Psychology, 92,* 876–884.

Tobey, E. A., Thal, D., Niparko, J. K., Eisenberg, L. S., Quittner, A. L., Wang, N. Y., & CDaCI Investigative Team. (2013). Influence of implantation age on school-age language performance in pediatric cochlear implant users. *International Journal of Audiology, 52*(4), 219–229. https://doi.org/10.3109/14992027.2012.759666

Todd, A. R., Bodenhausen, G. V., Richeson, J. A., & Galinsky, A. D. (2011). Perspective taking combats automatic expressions of racial bias. *Journal of Personality and Social Psychology, 100*(6), 1027–1042. https://doi.org/10.1037/a0022308

Todd, P. M., & Gigerenzer, G. (Eds.). (2012). *Ecological rationality: Intelligence in the world.* Oxford University Press.

Todes, D. P. (2014). *Ivan Pavlov: A Russian life in science.* Oxford University Press.

Toga, A. W., Clark, K. A., Thompson, P. M., Shattuck, D. W., & Van Horn, J. D. (2012). Mapping the human connectome. *Neurosurgery, 71,* 1–5.

Tolin, D. F. (2010). Is cognitive-behavioral therapy more effective than other therapies? A meta-analytic review. *Clinical Psychology Review, 30,* 710–720.

Tolman, E. C., & Honzik, C. H. (1930a). "Insight" in rats. *University of California Publications in Psychology, 4,* 215–232.

Tolman, E. C., & Honzik, C. H. (1930b). Introduction and removal of reward and maze performance in rats. *University of California Publications in Psychology, 4,* 257–275.

Tolman, E. C., Ritchie, B. F., & Kalish, D. (1946). Studies in spatial learning: I. Orientation and short cut. *Journal of Experimental Psychology, 36,* 13–24.

Tomasello, M., & Call, J. (2004). The role of humans in the cognitive development of apes revisited. *Animal Cognition, 7,* 213–215.

Tomasello, M., Savage-Rumbaugh, S., & Kruger, A. C. (1993). Imitative learning of actions on objects by children, chimpanzees, and enculturated chimpanzees. *Child Development, 64,* 1688–1705.

Tomkins, S. S. (1981). The role of facial response in the experience of emotion. *Journal of Personality and Social Psychology, 40,* 351–357.

Tondo, L., Vázquez, G. H., & Baldessarini, R. J. (2017). Depression and mania in bipolar disorder. *Current Neuropharmacology, 15*(3), 353–358. https://doi.org/10.2174/1570159X14666160606210811

Tootell, R. B. H., Reppas, J. B., Dale, A. M., Look, R. B., Sereno, M. I., Malach, R., … Rosen, B. R. (1995). Visual-motion aftereffect in human cortical area MT revealed by functional magnetic resonance imaging. *Nature, 375,* 139–141.

Torre, J. B., & Lieberman, M. D. (2018). Putting feelings into words: Affect labeling as implicit emotion regulation. *Emotion Review, 10,* 116–124.

Tracy, J. L., & Beall, A. T. (2011). Happy guys finish last: The impact of emotion expressions on sexual attraction. *Emotion, 11*(6), 1379–1387. https://doi.org/10.1037/a0022902

Tracy, J. L., Randles, D., & Steckler, C. M. (2015). The nonverbal communication of emotions. *Current Opinion in Behavioral Sciences, 3,* 25–30.

Tracy, J. L., Shariff, A. F., Zhao, W., & Henrich, J. (2013). Cross-cultural evidence that the nonverbal expression of pride is an automatic status signal. *Journal of Experimental Psychology: General, 142*(1), 163–180.

Treede, R. D., Kenshalo, D. R., Gracely, R. H., & Jones, A. K. (1999). The cortical representation of pain. *Pain, 79,* 105–111.

Treisman, A. (1998). Feature binding, attention and object perception. *Philosophical Transactions of the Royal Society B, 353,* 1295–1306.

Treisman, A. (2006). How the deployment of attention determines what we see. *Visual Cognition, 14,* 411–443.

Treisman, A., & Gelade, G. (1980). A feature integration theory of attention. *Cognitive Psychology, 12,* 97–136.

Treisman, A., & Schmidt, H. (1982). Illusory conjunctions in the perception of objects. *Cognitive Psychology, 14,* 107–141.

Trivers, R. L. (1972). Parental investment and sexual selection. In B. Campbell (Ed.), *Sexual selection and the descent of man, 1871–1971* (pp. 139–179). Aldine.

Troy, A. S., Saquib, S., Thal, J., & Ciuk, D. J. (2018). The regulation of negative and positive affect in response to daily stressors. *Emotion.* https://doi.org/10.1037/emo0000486

Trull, T. J., & Durrett, C. A. (2005). Categorical and dimensional models of personality disorder. *Annual Review of Clinical Psychology, 1,* 355–380.

Tucker, E. (2003, June 25). Move over, Fido! Chickens are becoming hip suburban pets. *USA Today.* http://usatoday30.usatoday.com/money/2003-06-25-pet-chickens_x.htm

Tucker-Drob, E. M., & Bates, T. C. (2016). Large cross-national differences in gene × socioeconomic status interaction on intelligence.

Psychological Science, 27(2), 138–149. https://doi.org/10.1177
/0956797615612727

Tucker-Drob, E. M., Briley, D. A., & Harden, K. P. (2013).
Genetic and environmental influences on cognition across development and context. *Current Directions in Psychological Science, 22*(5),
349–355. https://doi.org/10.1177/0963721413485087

**Tucker-Drob, E. M., Rhemtulla, M., Harden, K. P., Turkheimer, E.,
& Fask, D.** (2010). Emergence of a gene × socioeconomic status
interaction on infant mental ability between 10 months and 2 years.
Psychological Science, 22(1), 125–133. https://doi.org/10.1177
/0956797610392926

Tulving, E. (1972). Episodic and semantic memory. In E. Tulving
& W. Donaldson (Eds.), *Organization of memory* (pp. 381–403).
Academic Press.

Tulving, E. (1983). *Elements of episodic memory.* Clarendon Press.

Tulving, E. (1985). Memory and consciousness. *Canadian Psychologist,
25,* 1–12.

Tulving, E. (1998). Neurocognitive processes of human memory. In
C. von Euler, I. Lundberg, & R. Llins (Eds.), *Basic mechanisms in
cognition and language* (pp. 261–281). Elsevier.

**Tulving, E., Kapur, S., Craik, F. I. M., Moscovitch, M., & Houle,
S.** (1994). Hemispheric encoding/retrieval asymmetry in episodic
memory: Positron emission tomography findings. *Proceedings of the
National Academy of Sciences, USA, 91,* 2016–2020.

Tulving, E., & Pearlstone, Z. (1966). Availability versus accessibility
of information in memory for words. *Journal of Verbal Learning and
Verbal Behavior, 5,* 381–391.

Tulving, E., & Schacter, D. L. (1990). Priming and human memory
systems. *Science, 247,* 301–306.

Tulving, E., Schacter, D. L., & Stark, H. (1982). Priming effects in
word-fragment completion are independent of recognition memory.
*Journal of Experimental Psychology: Learning, Memory, and Cognition,
8,* 336–342.

Tulving, E., & Thomson, D. M. (1973). Encoding specificity and
retrieval processes in episodic memory. *Psychological Review, 80,*
352–373.

**Turkheimer, E., Haley, A., Waldron, M., D'Onofrio, B., &
Gottesman, I. I.** (2003). Socioeconomic status modifies heritability
of IQ in young children. *Psychological Science, 14,* 623–628.

Turner, D. C., & Sahakian, B. J. (2006). Neuroethics of cognitive
enhancement. *BioSocieties, 1,* 113–123.

**Turner, D. C., Robbins, T. W., Clark, L., Aron, A. R., Dowson, J.,
& Sahakian, B. J.** (2003). Cognitive enhancing effects of modafinil
in healthy volunteers. *Psychopharmacology, 165,* 260–269.

**Turner, E. H., Cipriani, A., Furukawa, T. A., Salanti, G., &
de Vries, Y. A.** (2022). Selective publication of antidepressant trials and its influence on apparent efficacy: Updated comparisons
and meta-analyses of newer versus older trials. *PLoS Med 19*(1),
e1003886. https://doi.org/10.1371/journal.pmed.1003886

Turner, M. E., & Pratkanis, A. R. (1998). Twenty-five years of groupthink theory and research: Lessons from the evaluation of a theory.
Organizational Behavior and Human Decision Processes, 73(2–3),
105–115. https://doi.org/10.1006/obhd.1998.2756

Tversky, A., & Kahneman, D. (1973). Availability: A heuristic for
judging frequency and probability. *Cognitive Psychology, 5,* 207–232.

Tversky, A., & Kahneman, D. (1974). Judgment under uncertainty:
Heuristics and biases. *Science, 185,* 1124–1131.

Tversky, A., & Kahneman, D. (1981). The framing of decisions and
the psychology of choice. *Science, 211,* 453–458.

Tversky, A., & Kahneman, D. (1983). Extensional versus intuitive
reasoning: The conjunction fallacy in probability judgment. *Psychological Review, 90,* 293–315.

Tversky, A., & Kahneman, D. (1992). Advances in prospect theory:
Cumulative representation of uncertainty. *Journal of Risk and Uncertainty, 5,* 297–323.

Twenge, J. M., Campbell, W. K., & Foster, C. A. (2003). Parenthood and marital satisfaction: A meta-analytic review. *Journal of
Marriage and Family, 65,* 574–583.

Twenge, J. M., Sherman, R. A., & Lyubomirsky, S. (2016). More
happiness for young people and less for mature adults: Time period
differences in subjective well-being in the United States, 1972–2014.
Social Psychological and Personality Science, 7, 131–141.

Tyler, T. R. (1990). *Why people obey the law.* Yale University Press.

U.S. Census Bureau. (2021, March 4). *Characteristics of adults in
same-sex and opposite-sex couples by state, 2019.* https://www.census
.gov/library/visualizations/interactive/characteristics-of-adults-in-
same-sex-and-opposite-sex-couples-2019.html

U.S. Census Bureau. (2018). *Historical marital status tables.* https://
www.census.gov/data/tables/time-series/demo/families/marital.html

Umberson, D., Williams, K., Powers, D. A., Liu, H., & Needham, B.
(2006). You make me sick: Marital quality and health over the life
course. *Journal of Health and Social Behavior, 47,* 1–16.

Uncapher, M. R., & Rugg, M. D. (2008). Fractionation of the
component processes underlying successful episodic encoding: A
combined fMRI and divided-attention study. *Journal of Cognitive
Neuroscience, 20,* 240–254.

Ungerleider, L. G., & Mishkin, M. (1982). Two cortical visual
systems. In D. J. Ingle, M. A. Goodale, & R. J. W. Mansfield (Eds.),
Analysis of visual behavior (pp. 549–586). MIT Press.

United Nations Office on Drugs and Crime (2015). *The United
Nations Standard Minimum Rules for the Treatment of Prisoners (the
Nelson Mandela Rules).* Adopted by the General Assembly as General
Assembly resolution 70/175, annex, adopted on 17 December 2015.
Available at: https://www.unodc.org/documents/justice-and-prison
-reform/Nelson_Mandela_Rules-E-ebook.pdf

Unkelbach, C., & Högden, F. (2019). Why does George Clooney
make coffee sexy? The case for attribute conditioning. *Current
Directions in Psychological Science, 28*(6), 540–546. https://doi.
org/10.1177/0963721419859354

Uno, K., & Yokosawa, K. (2020). Apparent physical brightness of
graphemes is altered by their synaesthetic colour in grapheme-colour
synaesthetes. *Scientific Reports, 10*(1), 20134. https://doi.org/10.1038
/s41598-020-77298-2

**Urban, N. B. L., Girgis, R. R., Talbot, P. S., Kegeles, L. S., Xu,
X., Frankie, W. G., ... Laruelle, M.** (2012). Sustained recreational
use of ecstasy is associated with altered pre- and postsynaptic markers of serotonin transmission in neocortical areas: A PET study with
[11c] DASB and [11c] MDL 100907. *Neuropsychopharmacology, 37,*
1465–1473.

Ursano, R. J., & Silberman, E. K. (2003). Psychoanalysis, psychoanalytic psychotherapy, and supportive psychotherapy. In R. E. Hales
& S. C. Yudofsky (Eds.), *The American Psychiatric Publishing textbook
of clinical psychiatry* (4th ed., pp. 1177–1203). American Psychiatric
Publishing.

Uskul, A. K., & Over, H. (2014). Responses to social exclusion in
cultural context: Evidence from farming and herding communities.
Journal of Personality and Social Psychology, 106(5), 752–771. https://
doi.org/10.1037/a0035810

Vacha, E., & McBride, M. (1993). Cramming: A barrier to student
success, a way to beat the system, or an effective strategy? *College
Student Journal, 27,* 2–11.

**Vafaei, A., Ahmed, T., Falcão Freire, A., Zunzunegui, M. V., &
Guerra, R. O.** (2016). Depression, sex and gender roles in older adult
populations: The international mobility in aging studies (IMIAS).
PLoS ONE, 11, e0146867.

Valentine, T., Brennen, T., & Brédart, S. (1996). *The cognitive psychology of proper names: On the importance of being Ernest.* Routledge.

Valentová, J., Roberts, S. C., & Havlíček, J. (2013). Preferences for facial and vocal masculinity in homosexual men: The role of relationship status, sexual restrictiveness, and self-perceived masculinity. *Perception, 42*(2), 187–197. https://doi.org/10.1068/p6909

Valian, V. (2015). Bilingualism and cognition. *Bilingualism: Language and Cognition, 18,* 3–24.

Vallacher, R. R., & Wegner, D. M. (1985). *A theory of action identification.* Erlbaum.

Vallacher, R. R., & Wegner, D. M. (1987). What do people think they're doing? Action identification and human behavior. *Psychological Review, 94,* 3–15.

van Amsterdam, J., Pennings, E., & van den Brink, W. (2020). Fatal and non-fatal health incidents related to recreational ecstasy use. *Journal of Psychopharmacology, 34*(6), 591–599. https://doi.org/10.1177/0269881119897559

van Anders, S. M. (2012). Testosterone and sexual desire in healthy women and men. *Archives of Sexual Behavior, 41,* 1471–1484.

von Békésy, G. (1960). *Experiments in hearing.* McGraw-Hill.

van den Boom, D. C. (1994). The influence of temperament and mothering on attachment and exploration: An experimental manipulation of sensitive responsiveness among lower-class mothers with irritable infants. *Child Development, 65,* 1457–1477.

van den Boom, D. C. (1995). Do first year intervention effects endure? Follow-up during toddlerhood of a sample of Dutch irritable infants. *Child Development, 66,* 1798–1816.

Van Dessel, P., Mertens, G., Smith, C. T., & De Houwer, J. (2019). Mere exposure effects on implicit stimulus evaluation: The moderating role of evaluation task, number of stimulus presentations, and memory for presentation frequency. *Personality and Social Psychology Bulletin, 45*(3), 447–460. https://doi.org/10.1177/0146167218789065

van Dis, I., Kromhout, D., Geleijnse, J. M., Boer, J. M. A., & Verschuren, W. M. M. (2009). Body mass index and waist circumference predict both 10-year nonfatal and fatal cardiovascular disease risk: Study conducted in 20,000 Dutch men and women aged 20–65 years. *European Journal of Cardiovascular Prevention & Rehabilitation, 16*(6), 729–734.

Van Gog, T., Kester, L., Dirkx, K., Hoogerheide, V., Boerboom, J., & Verkoeijen, P. P. J. L. (2015). Testing after worked example study does not enhance delayed problem-solving performance compared to restudy. *Educational Psychology Review, 27,* 265–289.

van Honk, J., & Schutter, D. J. L. G. (2007). Testosterone reduces conscious detection of signals serving social correction: Implications for antisocial behavior. *Psychological Science, 18,* 663–667.

van IJzendoorn, M. H., Juffer, F., & Klein Poelhuis, C. W. (2005). Adoption and cognitive development: A meta-analytic comparison of adopted and nonadopted children's IQ and school performance. *Psychological Bulletin, 131,* 301–316.

van IJzendoorn, M. H., & Sagi, A. (1999). Cross-cultural patterns of attachment: Universal and contextual dimensions. In J. Cassidy & P. R. Shaver (Eds.), *Handbook of attachment: Theory, research and clinical applications* (pp. 713–734). Guilford Press.

Van Lange, P. A. M., & Columbus, S. (2021, May). Vitamin S: Why is social contact, even with strangers, so important to well-being? *Current Directions in Psychological Science.* https://doi.org/10.1177/09637214211002538

Van Laningham, J., Johnson, D. R., & Amato, P. (2001). Marital happiness, marital duration, and the U-shaped curve: Evidence from a five-wave panel study. *Social Forces, 79,* 1313–1341.

Van Overwalle, F. (2009). Social cognition and the brain: A meta-analysis. *Human Brain Mapping, 30*(3), 829–858. https://doi.org/10.1002/hbm.20547

van Praag, H. (2009). Exercise and the brain: Something to chew on. Trends in *Neuroscience, 32,* 283–290.

van Stegeren, A. H., Everaerd, W., Cahill, L., McGaugh, J. L., & Gooren, L. J. G. (1998). Memory for emotional events: Differential effects of centrally versus peripherally acting blocking agents. *Psychopharmacology, 138,* 305–310.

van Vliet, I. M., van Well, E. P., Bruggeman, R., Campo, J. A., Hijman, R., Van Megen, H. J., … Van Rijen, P. C. (2013). An evaluation of irreversible psychosurgical treatment of patients with obsessive-compulsive disorder in the Netherlands, 2001–2008. *Journal of Nervous and Mental Disease, 201,* 226–228.

Vargha-Khadem, F., Carr, L. J., Isaacs, E., Brett, E., Adams, C., & Mishkin, M. (1997). Onset of speech after left hemispherectomy in a nine-year-old boy. *Brain, 120*(Pt. 1), 159–182. https://doi.org/10.1093/brain/120.1.159

Vargha-Khadem, F., Gadian, D. G., Copp, A., & Mishkin, M. (2005). FOXP2 and the neuroanatomy of speech and language. *Nature Reviews Neuroscience, 6,* 131–138.

Vargha-Khadem, F., Gadian, D. G., Watkins, K. E., Connelly, A., Van Paesschen, W., & Mishkin, M. (1997). Differential effects of early hippocampal pathology on episodic and semantic memory. *Science, 277,* 376–380.

Vasilenko, S. A., Maas, M. K., & Lefkowitz, E. S. (2015). "It felt good but weird at the same time": Emerging adults' first experiences of six different sexual behaviors. *Journal of Adolescent Research, 30,* 586–606. http://doi.org/10.1177/0743558414561298

Vazire, S., & Mehl, M. R. (2008). Knowing me, knowing you: The relative accuracy and unique predictive validity of self-ratings and other ratings of daily behavior. *Journal of Personality and Social Psychology, 95,* 1202–1216.

Verstaen, A., Haase, C. M., Lwi, S. J., & Levenson, R. W. (2020). Age-related changes in emotional behavior: Evidence from a 13-year longitudinal study of long-term married couples. *Emotion, 20*(2), 149–163. https://doi.org/10.1037/emo0000551

Vinter, A., & Perruchet, P. (2002). Implicit motor learning through observational training in adults and children. *Memory & Cognition, 30,* 256–261.

Visser, M., Jeffries, E., Embleton, K. V., & Lambon Ralph, M. A. (2012). Both the middle temporal gyrus and the ventral anterior temporal area are crucial for multimodal Semantic processing: Distortion-corrected fMRI evidence for a double gradient of information convergence in the temporal lobes. *Journal of Cognitive Neuroscience, 24,* 1766–1778.

Vitkus, J. (1999). *Casebook in abnormal psychology* (4th ed.). McGraw-Hill.

Volkow, N. D. (2021). To end the opioid crisis, we must address painful social disparities. *Drug and Alcohol Dependence, 222*(S3), 108678. https://doi.org/10.1016/j.drugalcdep.2021.108678

Volkow, N., & Blanco, C. (2021). The changing opioid crisis: Development, challenges, and opportunities. *Molecular Psychiatry, 26*(1), 218–233. https://doi.org/10.1038/s41380-020-0661-4

Volkow, N. D., & Boyle, M. (2018). Neuroscience of addiction: Relevance to prevention and treatment. *American Journal of Psychiatry, 175,* 729–740.

Volkow, N. D., Koob, G. F., & McLellan, A. T. (2016). Neurobiologic advances from the brain disease model of addiction. *New England Journal of Medicine, 374,* 363–371.

Volkow, N. D., McLellan, T., & Blanco, C. (2021, August 3). How academic medicine can help confront the opioid crisis. *Academic Medicine,* epub ahead of print. https://doi.org/10.1097/ACM.0000000000004289

von Bartheld, C. S., Bahney, J., & Herculano-Houzel, S. (2016) The search for true numbers of neurons and glial cells in the human brain: A review of 150 years of cell counting. *Journal of Comparative Neurology, 524*, 3865–3895.

von Bastian, C. C., Souza, A. S., & Gasde, M. (2016). No evidence for bilingual cognitive advantages: A test of four hypotheses. *Journal of Experimental Psychology: General, 145*, 246–258.

Von Frisch, K. (1974). Decoding the language of the bee. *Science, 185*, 663–668.

von Stumm, S., & Plomin, R. (2021). Using DNA to predict intelligence. *Intelligence, 86*, 101530. https://doi.org/10.1016/j.intell.2021.101530

Vondra, J. I., Shaw, D. S., Swearingen, L., Cohen, M., & Owens, E. B. (2001). Attachment stability and emotional and behavioral regulation from infancy to preschool age. *Development and Psychopathology, 13*, 13–33.

Vorster, A. P. & Born, J. (2015). Sleep and memory in mammals, birds and invertebrates. *Neuroscience and Biobehavioral Reviews, 50*, 103–119.

Vrij, A., Granhag, P. A., Mann, S., & Leal, S. (2011). Outsmarting the liars: Toward a cognitive lie detection approach. *Current Directions in Psychological Science, 20*(1), 28–32.

Vukasović, T., & Bratko, D. (2015) Heritability of personality: A meta-analysis of behavior genetic studies. *Psychological Bulletin, 141*, 769–785.

Vygotsky, L. S. (1978). *Mind in society: The development of higher psychological processes.* Harvard University Press.

Wade, K. A., Garry, M., & Pezdek, K. (2018). Deconstructing rich false memories of committing crime: Commentary on Shaw and Porter (2015). *Psychological Science, 29*, 471–476.

Wade, S. E., Trathen, W., & Schraw, G. (1990). An analysis of spontaneous study strategies. *Reading Research Quarterly, 25*, 147–166.

Wadhwa, P. D., Sandman, C. A., & Garite, T. J. (2001). The neurobiology of stress in human pregnancy: Implications for prematurity and development of the fetal central nervous system. *Progress in Brain Research, 133*, 131–142.

Wager, T. D., Rilling, J. K., Smith, E. E., Sokolik, A., Casey, K. L., Davidson, R. J., ... Cohen, J. D. (2004). Placebo-induced changes in fMRI in the anticipation and experience of pain. *Science, 303*, 1162–1167.

Wager, T., & Atlas, L. Y. (2013). How is pain influenced by cognition? Neuroimaging weighs in. *Perspectives on Psychological Science, 8*, 91–97.

Wagner, A. D., Schacter, D. L., Rotte, M., Koutstaal, W., Maril, A., Dale, A. M., ... Buckner, R. L. (1998). Remembering and forgetting of verbal experiences as predicted by brain activity. *Science, 281*, 1188–1190.

Wagner, G., & Morris, E. (1987). Superstitious behavior in children. *Psychological Record, 37*, 471–488.

Wai, J., Putallaz, M., & Makel, M. C. (2012). Studying intellectual outliers: Are there sex differences, and are the smart getting smarter? *Current Directions in Psychological Science, 21*(6), 382–390. https://doi.org/10.1177/0963721412455052

Wainer, H., & Zwerling, H. L. (2006). Evidence that smaller schools do not improve student achievement. *Phi Delta Kappan, 88*(4), 300–303. https://doi.org/10.1177/003172170608800411

Wakefield, J. C. (2007). The concept of mental disorder: Diagnostic implications of the harmful dysfunction analysis. *World Psychiatry, 6*, 149–156.

Walden, T. A., & Ogan, T. A. (1988). The development of social referencing. *Child Development, 59*, 1230–1240.

Waldfogel, S. (1948). The frequency and affective character of childhood memories. *Psychological Monographs, 62*(4), i–39. https://doi.org/10.1037/h0093581

Walenski, M., Europa, E., Caplan, D., & Thompson, C. K. (2019). Neural networks for sentence comprehension and production: An ALE-based meta-analysis of neuroimaging studies. *Human Brain Mapping, 40*(8), 2275–2304. https://doi.org/10.1002/hbm.24523

Walker, N. P., McConville, P. M., Hunter, D., Deary, I. J., & Whalley, L. J. (2002). Childhood mental ability and lifetime psychiatric contact. *Intelligence, 30*(3), 233–245. https://doi.org/10.1016/S0160-2896(01)00098-8

Wallbott, H. G. (1998). Bodily expression of emotion. *European Journal of Social Psychology, 28*, 879–896.

Walsh, K., McCormack, C. A., Webster, R., Pinto, A., Lee, S., Feng, T., ... Monk, C. (2019). Maternal prenatal stress phenotypes associate with fetal neurodevelopment and birth outcomes. *Proceedings of the National Academy of Sciences, 116*(48), 23996–24005. https://doi.org/10.1073/pnas.1905890116

Walster, E., Aronson, V., Abrahams, D., & Rottmann, L. (1966). Importance of physical attractiveness in dating behavior. *Journal of Personality and Social Psychology, 4*, 508–516.

Walster, E., Walster, G. W., & Berscheid, E. (1978). *Equity: Theory and research.* Allyn & Bacon.

Walter, K. V., Conroy-Beam, D., Buss, D. M., Asao, K., Sorokowska, A., Sorokowski, P., . . . Zupančič, M. (2020). Sex differences in mate preferences across 45 countries: A large-scale replication. *Psychological Science, 31*(4), 408–423. https://doi.org/10.1177/0956797620904154

Walton, G. M., & Spencer, S. J. (2009). Latent ability: Grades and test scores systematically underestimate the intellectual ability of negatively stereotyped students. *Psychological Science, 20*, 1132–1139.

Waltzman, S. B. (2006). Cochlear implants: Current status. *Expert Review of Medical Devices, 3*, 647–655.

Wammes, J. D., Ralph, B. C. W., Mills, C., Bosch, N., Duncan, T. L., & Smilek, D. (2019). Disengagement during lectures: Media multitasking and mind wandering in university classrooms. *Computers & Education, 132*, 76–89. https://doi.org/10.1016/j.compedu.2018.12.007

Wammes, J. D., Seli, P., Cheyne, J. A., Boucher, P. O., & Smilek, D. (2016). Mind wandering during lectures: II. Relation to academic performance. *Scholarship of Teaching and Learning in Psychology, 2*, 33–48.

Wamsley, E. J., & Stickgold, R. (2011). Memory, sleep, and dreaming: Experiencing consolidation. *Sleep Medicine Clinics, 6*, 97–108.

Wang, J., Otgaar, H., Santtila, P., Shen, X., & Zhou, C. (2021). How culture shapes constructive false memory. *Journal of Applied Research in Memory and Cognition, 10*(1), 24–32. https://doi.org/10.1016/j.jarmac.2020.12.002

Wang, P. S., Aguilar-Gaxiola, S., Alonso, J., Angermeyer, M. C., Borges, G., Bromet, E. J., ... Wells, J. E. (2007). Use of mental health services for anxiety, mood, and substance disorders in 17 countries in the WHO World Mental Health Surveys. *Lancet, 370*, 841–850.

Wang, P. S., Berglund, P. A., Olfson, M., & Kessler, R. C. (2004). Delays in initial treatment contact after first onset of a mental disorder. *Health Services Research, 39*, 393–415.

Wang, P. S., Berglund, P., Olfson, M., Pincus, H. A., Wells, K. B., & Kessler, R. C. (2005). Failure and delay in initial treatment contact after first onset of mental disorders in the National Comorbidity Survey Replication. *Archives of General Psychiatry, 62*(6), 629–640.

Wang, P. S., Demler, O., & Kessler, R. C. (2002). Adequacy of treatment for serious mental illness in the United States. *American Journal of Public Health, 92*, 92–98.

Wang, Q. (2021). The cultural foundation of human memory. *Annual Review of Psychology, 72*, 151–179. https://doi.org/10.1146/annurev-psych-070920-023638

Wang, S., & Allen, R. J. (2018). Cross-modal working memory binding and word recognition skills: How specific is the link? *Memory, 26*, 514–523.

Wang, S. M., Allen, R. J., Lee, J. R., & Hsieh, C. E. (2015). Evaluating the developmental trajectory of the episodic buffer component of working memory and its relation to word recognition in children. *Journal of Experimental Child Psychology, 133*, 16–28.

Wang, S.-H., & Baillargeon, R. (2008). Detecting impossible changes in infancy: A three-system account. *Trends in Cognitive Sciences, 12*(1), 17–23.

Wang, W., & Parker, K. (2014). Record share of Americans have never married as values, economics and gender patterns change. *Pew Research Center's Social & Demographic Trends Project.* http://www.pewsocialtrends.org/2014/09/24/record-share-of-americans-have-never-married/

Wansink, B., & Wansink, C. S. (2010). The largest last supper: Depictions of food portions and plate size increased over the millennium. *International Journal of Obesity, 34*, 943–944.

Ward, B. W., Dahlhamer, J. M., Galinsky, A. M., & Joestl, S. S. (2014). Sexual orientation and health among US adults: National Health Interview Survey, 2013. *National Health Statistics Reports, 15*, 1–10.

Ward, J. (2013). Synesthesia. *Annual Review of Psychology, 64*, 49–75. https://doi.org/10.1146/annurev-psych-113011-143840

Ward, J., Parkin, A. J., Powell, G., Squires, E. J., Townshend, J., & Bradley, V. (1999). False recognition of unfamiliar people: "Seeing film stars everywhere." *Cognitive Neuropsychology, 16*, 293–315.

Ward, Z. J., Long, M. W., Resch, S. C., Giles, C. M., Cradock, A. L., & Gortmaker, S. L. (2017). Simulation of growth trajectories of childhood obesity into adulthood. *New England Journal of Medicine, 377*(22), 2145–2153. https://doi.org/10.1056/NEJMoa1703860

Warne, R. T., & Burningham, C. (2019). Spearman's g found in 31 non-Western nations: Strong evidence that g is a universal phenomenon. *Psychological Bulletin, 145*(3), 237–272. http://dx.doi.org/10.1037/bul0000184

Warneken, F. (2018). How children solve the two challenges of cooperation. *Annual Review of Psychology, 69*(1), 205–229. https://doi.org/10.1146/annurev-psych-122216-011813

Warneken, F., & Tomasello, M. (2009). Varieties of altruism in children and chimpanzees. *Trends in Cognitive Sciences, 13*, 397–402.

Warren, K. R., & Hewitt, B. G. (2009). Fetal alcohol spectrum disorders: When science, medicine, public policy, and laws collide. *Developmental Disabilities Research Reviews, 15*, 170–175.

Warren, M. T., Wray-Lake, L., Rote, W. M., & Shubert, J. (2016). Thriving while engaging in risk? Examining trajectories of adaptive functioning, delinquency, and substance use in a nationally representative sample of adolescents. *Developmental Psychology, 52*(2), 296–310. https://doi.org/10.1037/a0039922

Warrington, E. K., & McCarthy, R. A. (1983). Category specific access dysphasia. *Brain, 106*, 859–878.

Warrington, E. K., & Shallice, T. (1984). Category specific semantic impairments. *Brain, 107*, 829–854.

Watanabe, S., Sakamoto, J., & Wakita, M. (1995). Pigeons' discrimination of painting by Monet and Picasso. *Journal of the Experimental Analysis of Behavior, 63*, 165–174.

Waters, T. E. A., Fraley, R. C., Groh, A. M., Steele, R. D., Vaughn, B. E., Bost, K. K., ... Roisman, G. I. (2015). The latent structure of secure base script knowledge. *Developmental Psychology, 51*(6), 823–830. https://doi.org/10.1037/dev0000012

Waters, T. E. A., Magro, S. W., Alhajeri, J., Yang, R., Groh, A., Haltigan, J. D., ... Roisman, G. I. (2021). Early child care experiences and attachment representations at age 18 years: Evidence from the NICHD study of Early Child Care and Youth Development. *Developmental Psychology, 57*(4), 548–556. https://doi.org/10.1037/dev0001165

Watkins, L. R., & Maier, S. F. (2005). Immune regulation of central nervous system functions: From sickness responses to pathological pain. *Journal of Internal Medicine, 257*, 139–155.

Watkins, N. W. (2019). (A)phantasia and severely deficient autobiographical memory: Scientific and personal perspectives. *Cortex, 105*, 41–52. https://doi.org/10.1016/j.cortex.2017.10.010

Watson, D., & Pennebaker, J. W. (1989). Health complaints, stress, and distress: Exploring the central role of negative affectivity. *Psychological Review, 96*, 234–254.

Watson, D., & Tellegen, A. (1985). Toward a consensual structure of mood. *Psychological Bulletin, 98*, 219–235.

Watson, J. B. (1913). Psychology as the behaviorist views it. *Psychological Review, 20*, 158–177.

Watson, J. B. (1924). *Behaviorism.* The People's Institute Publishing Co.

Watson, J. B. (1930). *Behaviorism* (Rev. Ed.). University of Chicago Press.

Watson, J. B., & Rayner, R. (1920). Conditioned emotional reactions. *Journal of Experimental Psychology, 3*, 1–14.

Watson, M. R., Chromý, J., Crawford, L., Eagleman, D. M., Enns, J. T., & Akins, K. A. (2017). The prevalence of synaesthesia depends on early language learning. *Consciousness and Cognition, 48*, 212–231. https://doi.org/10.1016/j.concog.2016.12.004

Watson, R. I. (1978). *The great psychologists.* Lippincott.

Watt, H. J. (1905). Experimentelle Beitraege zu einer Theorie des Denkens [Experimental contributions to a theory of thinking]. *Archiv fuer die gesamte Psychologie, 4*, 289–436.

Watts, T. M., Holmes, L., Raines, J., Orbell, S., & Rieger, G. (2018). Gender nonconformity of identical twins with discordant sexual orientations: Evidence from childhood photographs. *Developmental Psychology, 54*, 788–801.

Watzke, B., Rüddel, H., Jürgensen, R., Koch, U., Kristen, L., Grothgar, B., & Schulz, H. (2012). Longer term outcome of cognitive-behavioural and psychodynamic psychotherapy in routine mental health care: Randomised controlled trial. *Behaviour Research and Therapy, 50*, 580–387.

Weaver, I. C. G., Cervoni, N., Champagne, F. A., D'Alessio, A. C., Sharma, S., Seckl, J. R., ... Meaney, M. J. (2004). Epigenetic programming by maternal behavior. *Nature Neuroscience, 7*, 847–854.

Webb, T. L., Miles, E., & Sheeran, P. (2012). Dealing with feeling: A meta-analysis of the effectiveness of strategies derived from the process model of emotion regulation. *Psychological Bulletin, 138*(4), 775–808.

Webber, H. E., Lopez-Gamundi, P., Stamatovich, S. M., De Wit, H., & Wardle, M. C. (2021). Using pharmacological manipulations to study the role of dopamine in human reward functioning: A review of studies in healthy adults. *Neuroscience & Biobehavioral Reviews, 120*, 123–158. https://doi.org/10.1016/j.neubiorev.2020.11.004

Weber, R., & Crocker, J. (1983). Cognitive processes in the revision of stereotypic beliefs. *Journal of Personality and Social Psychology, 45*, 961–977.

Webster Marketon, J. I., & Glaser, R. (2008). Stress hormones and immune function. *Cellular Immunology, 252*, 16–26.

Wegner, D. M. (1989). *White bears and other unwanted thoughts.* Viking.

Wegner, D. M. (1994a). Ironic processes of mental control. *Psychological Review, 101*, 34–52.

Wegner, D. M. (1994b). *White bears and other unwanted thoughts: Suppression, obsession, and the psychology of mental control.* Guilford Press.

Wegner, D. M. (1997). Why the mind wanders. In J. D. Cohen & J. W. Schooler (Eds.), *Scientific approaches to consciousness* (pp. 295–315). Erlbaum.

Wegner, D. M. (2002). *The illusion of conscious will.* MIT Press.

Wegner, D. M. (2009). How to think, say, or do precisely the worst thing for any occasion. *Science, 325*, 48–51.

Wegner, D. M., & Gilbert, D. T. (2000). Social psychology: The science of human experience. In H. Bless & J. Forgas (Eds.), *The message within: Subjective experience in social cognition and behavior* (pp. 1–9). Psychology Press.

Wegner, D. M., & Wenzlaff, R. M. (1996). Mental control. In E. T. Higgins & A. Kruglanski (Eds.), *Social psychology: Handbook of basic mechanisms and processes* (pp. 466–492). Guilford Press.

Wegner, D. M., & Zanakos, S. (1994). Chronic thought suppression. *Journal of Personality, 62*, 615–640.

Wegner, D. M., Ansfield, M., & Pilloff, D. (1998). The putt and the pendulum: Ironic effects of the mental control of action. *Psychological Science, 9*, 196–199.

Wegner, D. M., Broome, A., & Blumberg, S. J. (1997). Ironic effects of trying to relax under stress. *Behavior Research and Therapy, 35*, 11–21.

Wegner, D. M., Erber, R., & Raymond, P. (1991). Transactive memory in close relationships. *Journal of Personality and Social Psychology, 61*, 923–929.

Wegner, D. M., Erber, R. E., & Zanakos, S. (1993). Ironic processes in the mental control of mood and mood-related thought. *Journal of Personality and Social Psychology, 65*, 1093–1104.

Wegner, D. M., Schneider, D. J., Carter, S. R., & White, T. L. (1987). Paradoxical effects of thought suppression. *Journal of Personality and Social Psychology, 53*, 5–13.

Wegner, D. M., Vallacher, R. R., Macomber, G., Wood, R., & Arps, K. (1984). The emergence of action. *Journal of Personality and Social Psychology, 46*, 269–279.

Wegner, D. M., Wenzlaff, R. M., & Kozak, M. (2004). Dream rebound: The return of suppressed thoughts in dreams. *Psychological Science, 15*, 232–236.

Weiner, J. (2017, April 12). The return of Lorde. *New York Times.* https://www.nytimes.com/2017/04/12/magazine/the-return-of-lorde.html

Weiner, W. J., Shulman, L. M., & Lang, A. E. (2013). *Parkinson's disease* (3rd ed.). Johns Hopkins University Press.

Weinstein, N. D. (1980). Unrealistic optimism about future life events. *Journal of Personality and Social Psychology, 39*, 806–820.

Weir, C., Toland, C., King, R. A., & Martin, L. M. (2005). Infant contingency/extinction performance after observing partial reinforcement. *Infancy, 8*, 63–80.

Weiser, M., Zarka, S., Werbeloff, N., Kravitz, E., & Lubin, G. (2010). Cognitive test scores in male adolescent cigarette smokers compared to non-smokers: A population-based study. *Addiction, 105*(2), 358–363. https://doi.org/10.1111/j.1360-0443.2009.02740.x

Weisfeld, G. (1999). *Evolutionary principles of human adolescence.* Basic Books.

Weiss, K. J., & Curcio Alexander, J. (2013). Sex, lies, and statistics: Inferences from the child sexual abuse accommodation syndrome. *Journal of the American Academy of Psychiatry and the Law, 41*, 412–420.

Weissman, D. G., Hatzenbuehler, M., Cikara, M., Barch, D., & McLaughlin, K. A. (2021, November 30). *Antipoverty programs mitigate socioeconomic disparities in brain structure and psychopathology among U.S. youths.* https://doi.org/10.31234/osf.io/8nhej

Weissman, M. M., Markowitz, J. C., & Klerman, G. L. (2000). *Comprehensive guide to interpersonal psychotherapy.* Basic Books.

Weldon, M. S. (2001). Remembering as a social process. In D. L. Medin (Ed.), *The psychology of learning and motivation: Advances in research and theory* (Vol. 40, pp. 67–120). Academic Press.

Wellman, H. M., Fang, F., Liu, D., Zhu, L., & Liu, L. (2006). Scaling theory-of-mind understandings in Chinese children. *Psychological Science, 17*, 1075–1081. https://doi.org/10.1111/j.1467-9280.2006.01830.x

Wenzlaff, R. M., & Wegner, D. M. (2000). Thought suppression. In S. T. Fiske (Ed.), *Annual review of psychology* (Vol. 51, pp. 51–91). Annual Reviews.

Wernicke, K. (1874). *Der Aphasische Symptomenkomplex* [The aphasic symptom complex]. Cohn and Weigart.

Wertheimer, M. (1982). *Productive thinking.* University of Chicago Press. (Original work published 1945)

Wesch, N. N., Law, B., & Hall, C. R. (2007). The use of observational learning by athletes. *Journal of Sport Behavior, 30*, 219–231.

Westbrook, A., & Frank, M. (2018). Dopamine and proximity in motivation and cognitive control. *Current Opinion in Behavioral Science, 22*, 28–34.

Westrin, A., & Lam, R. W. (2007). Seasonal affective disorder: A clinical update. *Journal of Clinical Psychiatry, 19*, 239–246.

Wexler, K. (1999). Maturation and growth of grammar. In W. C. Ritchie & T. K. Bhatia (Eds.), *Handbook of child language acquisition* (pp. 55–110). Academic Press.

Wheeler, M. A., Petersen, S. E., & Buckner, R. L. (2000). Memory's echo: Vivid recollection activates modality-specific cortex. *Proceedings of the National Academy of Sciences, USA, 97*, 11125–11129.

White, D. M., Aufderheide-Palk, C., & Gengoux, G. W. (2021). Clinician delivery of virtual pivotal response treatment with children with autism during the COVID-19 pandemic. *Social Sciences, 10*(11), 414. https://doi.org/10.3390/socsci10110414

White, F. J. (1996). Synaptic regulation of mesocorticolimbic dopamine neurons. *Annual Review of Neuroscience, 19*, 405–436.

White, G. L., Fishbein, S., & Rutsein, J. (1981). Passionate love and the misattribution of arousal. *Journal of Personality and Social Psychology, 41*(1), 56–62. https://doi.org/10.1037/0022-3514.41.1.56

White, G. L., & Kight, T. D. (1984). Misattribution of arousal and attraction: Effects of salience of explanations for arousal. *Journal of Experimental Social Psychology, 20*(1), 55–64. https://doi.org/10.1016/0022-1031(84)90012-X

White, G. M., & Kirkpatrick, J. (Eds.). (1985). *Person, self, and experience: Exploring pacific ethnopsychologies.* University of California Press.

White, L. K., & Booth, A. (1991). Divorce over the life course: The role of marital happiness. *Journal of Family Issues, 12*, 5–21.

White, N. M., & Milner, P. M. (1992). The psychobiology of reinforcers. *Annual Review of Psychology, 41*, 443–471.

Whiten, A. (2021). The burgeoning reach of animal culture. *Science, 372*(6537), eabe6514. https://doi.org/10.1126/science.abe6514

Whiten, A. (2017). Social learning and culture in child and chimpanzee. *Annual Review of Psychology, 68*, 129–154.

Whiten, A., & van de Waal, E. (2018). The pervasive role of social learning in primate lifetime development. *Behavioral Ecology and Sociobiology, 72*, 80. doi.10.1007/s00265-018-2489-3

Whitewell, R. L., Milner, A. D., & Goodale, M. A. (2014). The two visual systems hypothesis: New challenges and insights from visual form agnosic patient DF. *Frontiers in Neurology, 8*(5), 255. https://doi.org/10.3389/fneur.2014.00255

Whorf, B. (1956). *Language, thought, and reality.* MIT Press.

Wibowo, E., & Wassersug, R. (2014). Estrogen in men. *American Scientist, 102,* 452–459.

Wicherts, J. M., Dolan, C. V., Hessen, D. J., Oosterveld, P., van Baal, G. C. M., Boomsma, D. I., & Span, M. M. (2004). Are intelligence tests measurement invariant over time? Investigating the nature of the Flynn effect. *Intelligence, 32*(5), 509–537. https://doi.org/https://doi.org/10.1016/j.intell.2004.07.002

Wicklund, R. (1975). Objective self-awareness. In L. Berkowitz (Ed.), *Advances in experimental social psychology* (Vol. 8, pp. 233–275). Academic Press.

Wiebe, S. A., Fang, H., Johnson, C., James, K. E., & Espy, K. A. (2014). Determining the impact of prenatal tobacco exposure on self-regulation at 6 months. *Developmental Psychology, 50*(6), 1746–1756. https://doi.org/10.1037/a0035904

Wiederman, M. W. (1997). Pretending orgasm during sexual intercourse: Correlates in a sample of young adult women. *Journal of Sex & Marital Therapy, 23,* 131–139.

Wiegner, L., Hange, D., Björkelund, C., & Ahlbirg, G., Jr. (2015). Prevalence of perceived stress and associations to symptoms of exhaustion, depression, and anxiety in a working age population seeking primary care: An observational study. *BMC Family Practice, 16,* 38.

Wiesenthal, D. L., Austrom, D., & Silverman, I. (1983). Diffusion of responsibility in charitable donations. *Basic and Applied Social Psychology, 4,* 17–27.

Wig, G. S., Buckner, R. L., & Schacter, D. L. (2009). Repetition priming influences distinct brain systems: Evidence from task-evoked data and resting-state correlations. *Journal of Neurophysiology, 101,* 2632–2648.

Wiggs, C. L., & Martin, A. (1998). Properties and mechanisms of perceptual priming. *Current Opinion in Neurobiology, 8,* 227–233.

Wilcoxon, H. C., Dragoin, W. B., & Kral, P. A. (1971). Illness-induced aversions in rats and quail: Relative salience of visual and gustatory cues. *Science, 171,* 826–828.

Wiley, J. L. (1999). Cannabis: Discrimination of "internal bliss"? *Pharmacology, Biochemistry, & Behavior, 64,* 257–260.

Wilkinson, L., Teo, J. T., Obeso, I., Rothwell, J. C., & Jahanshahi, M. (2010). The contribution of primary motor cortex is essential for probabilistic implicit sequence learning: Evidence from theta burst magnetic stimulation. *Journal of Cognitive Neuroscience, 22,* 427–436.

Wilks, C. R., Chu, C., Sim, D., Lovell, J., Gutierrez, P., Joiner, T., Kessler, R. C., & Nock, M. K. (2021). User engagement and usability of suicide prevention apps: Systematic search in app stores and content analysis. *JMIR Formative Research, 5*(7), e27018. https://doi.org/10.2196/27018

Willett, F. R., Avansino, D. T., Hochberg, L. R., Henderson, J. M., & Shenoy, K. V. (2021). High-performance brain-to-text communication via handwriting. *Nature, 593,* 249–254. https://doi.org/10.1038/s41586-021-03506-2

Williams, A. C. (2002). Facial expression of pain: An evolutionary account. *Behavioral and Brain Sciences, 25,* 439–488.

Williams, C. M., & Kirkham, T. C. (1999). Anandamide induces overeating: Mediation by central cannabinoid (CB1) receptors. *Psychopharmacology, 143,* 315–317.

Williams, E. H., Bilbao-Broch, L., Dowing, P. E., & Cross, E. S. (2020). Examining the value of body gestures in social reward contexts. *NeuroImage, 222,* 117276. https://doi.org/10.1016/j.neuroimage.2020.117276

Williams, K. D. (2007). Ostracism. *Annual Review of Psychology, 58,* 425–452. https://doi.org/10.1146/annurev.psych.58.110405.085641

Williams, K. D., Nida, S. A., Baca, L. D., & Latané, B. (1989). Social loafing and swimming: Effects of identifiability on individual and relay performance of intercollegiate swimmers. *Basic and Applied Social Psychology, 10,* 73–81.

Willingham, D. T. (2007). Critical thinking: Why is it so hard to teach? *American Educator, 31*(2), 8–19.

Wilson, K., & Korn, J. H. (2007). Attention during lectures: Beyond ten minutes. *Teaching of Psychology, 34,* 85–89.

Wilson, T. D. (2009). Know thyself. *Perspectives on Psychological Science, 4,* 384–389.

Wimber, M., Alink, A., Charest, I., Kriegeskorte, N., & Anderson, M.C. (2015). Retrieval induces adaptive forgetting of competing memories via cortical pattern suppression. *Nature Neuroscience, 18,* 582–589.

Wimber, M., Rutschmann, R. N., Greenlee, M. W., & Bauml, K.-H. (2009). Retrieval from episodic memory: Neural mechanisms of interference resolution. *Journal of Cognitive Neuroscience, 21,* 538–549.

Wimmer, H., & Perner, J. (1983). Beliefs about beliefs: Representations and constraining function of wrong beliefs in young children's understanding of deception. *Cognition, 13,* 103–128.

Winawer, J., Witthoft, N., Frank, M. C., Wu, L., Wade, A. R., & Boroditsky, L. (2007). Russian blues reveal effects of language on color discrimination. *Proceedings of the National Academy of Sciences, USA, 104,* 7780–7785.

Windeler, J., & Kobberling, J. (1986). Empirische Untersuchung zur Einschatzung diagnostischer Verfahren am Beispiel des Haemoccult-Tests [An empirical study of the value of diagnostic procedures using the example of the hemocult test]. *Klinische Wochenscrhrift, 64,* 1106–1112.

Windham, G. C., Eaton, A., & Hopkins, B. (1999). Evidence for an association between environmental tobacco smoke exposure and birthweight: A meta-analysis and new data. *Pediatrics and Perinatal Epidemiology, 13,* 35–57.

Winner, E. (2000). The origins and ends of giftedness. *American Psychologist, 55,* 159–169.

Winocur, G., Moscovitch, M., & Bontempi, B. (2010). Memory formation and long-term retention in humans and animals: Convergence towards a transformation account of hippocampal–neocortical interactions. *Neuropsychologia, 48,* 2339–2356.

Winterer, G., & Weinberger, D. R. (2004). Genes, dopamine and cortical signal-to-noise ratio in schizophrenia. *Trends in Neuroscience, 27,* 683–690.

Wise, R. A. (1989). Brain dopamine and reward. *Annual Review of Psychology, 40,* 191–225.

Wise, R. A. (2005). Forebrain substrates of reward and motivation. *Journal of Comparative Neurology, 493,* 115–121.

Wixted, J. T., & Ebbensen, E. (1991). On the form of forgetting. *Psychological Science, 2,* 409–415.

Wolff, P., & Holmes, K. J. (2011). Linguistic relativity. *WIRES Cognitive Science, 2,* 253–265.

Womick, J., Ward, S. J., Heintzelman, S. J., Woody, B., & King, L. A. (2019). The existential function of right-wing authoritarianism. *Journal of Personality.* https://doi.org/10.1111/jopy.12457

Wong, B. A. (2019, May 10). An Instagram with no "likes" could have a big impact on mental health. *HuffPost.* https://www.huffpost.com/entry/instagram-hiding-likes-mental-health_l_5cd092d3e4b0548b735e50bc

Wong, D. T., Bymaster, F. P., & Engleman, E. A. (1995). Prozac (fluoxetine, Lilly 110140), the first selective serotonin uptake inhibitor and an antidepressant drug: Twenty years since its first publication. *Life Sciences, 57,* 411–441.

Wood, A., Rychlowska, M., & Niedenthal, P. M. (2016). Heterogeneity of long-history migration predicts emotion recognition accuracy. *Emotion, 16*(4), 413–420. https://doi.org/1037/emo0000137

Wood, J. M., Bootzin, R. R., Rosenhan, D., Nolen-Hoeksema, S., & Jourden, F. (1992). Effects of the 1989 San Francisco earthquake on frequency and content of nightmares. *Journal of Abnormal Psychology, 101,* 219–224.

Woods, S. C., Seeley, R. J., Porte, D., Jr., & Schwartz, M. W. (1998). Signals that regulate food intake and energy homeostasis. *Science, 280,* 1378–1383.

Woody, S. R., & Sanderson, W. C. (1998). Manuals for empirically supported treatments: 1998 update. *Clinical Psychologist, 51,* 17–21.

Woolf, V. (1925). *Mrs. Dalloway.* Hogarth Press.

Woumans, E., Santens, P., Sieben, A., Versijpt, J., Stevens, M., & Duyck, W. (2015). Bilingualism delays clinical manifestation of Alzheimer's disease. *Bilingualism: Language and Cognition, 18,* 568–574.

Wrangham, R. W. (2017). Two types of aggression in human evolution. *Proceedings of the National Academy of Sciences, USA, 115*(2), 245–253.

Wraw, C., Deary, I. J., Gale, C. R., & Der, G. (2015). Intelligence in youth and health at age 50. *Intelligence, 53,* 23–32.

Wren, A. M., Seal, L. J., Cohen, M. A., Brynes, A. E., Frost, G. S., Murphy, K. G., ... Bloom, S. R. (2001). Ghrelin enhances appetite and increases food intake in humans. *Journal of Clinical Endocrinology and Metabolism, 86,* 5992–5995.

Wrenn, C. C., Turchi, J. N., Schlosser, S., Dreiling, J. L., Stephenson, D. A., & Crawley, J. N. (2006). Performance of galanin transgenic mice in the 5-choice serial reaction time attentional task. *Pharmacology Biochemistry and Behavior, 83,* 428–440.

Wundt, W. (1912/1973). *An introduction to psychology.* Arno Press.

Wyatt, T. D. (2015). The search for human pheromones: The lost decades and the necessity of returning to first principles. *Proceedings of the Royal Society B: Biological Sciences, 282*(1804), 20142994. https://doi.org/10.1098/rspb.2014.2994

Wyckoff, J. P., Asao, K., & Buss, D. M. (2019). Gossip as an intrasexual competition strategy: Predicting information sharing from potential mate versus competitor mating strategies. *Evolution and Human Behavior, 40*(1), 96–104. https:/doi.org/ezp-prod1.hul.harvard.edu/10.1016/j.evolhumbehav.2018.08.006

Wynn, K., Bloom, P., Jordan, A., Marshall, J., & Sheskin, M. (2018). Not noble savages after all: Limits to early altruism. *Current Directions in Psychological Science, 27,* 3–8.

Xie, W., Campbell, S., & Zhang, W. (2020). Working memory capacity predicts individual differences in social-distancing compliances during the COVID-19 pandemic in the United States. *Proceedings of the National Academy of Sciences USA, 117*(3), 17667–17674. https://doi.org/10.1073/pnas.2008868117

Xu, J. Q., Murphy, S. L., Kochanek, K. D., & Arias, E. (2021). Deaths: Final data for 2019. *National Vital Statistics Reports, 70*(8). https://doi.org/10.15620/cdc:106058

Yamaguchi, S. (1998). Basic properties of umami and its effects in humans. *Physiology and Behavior, 49,* 833–841.

Yamane, G. K. (2007, November 1). Obesity in civilian adults: Potential impact on eligibility for U.S. military enlistment, *Military Medicine, 172*(11), 1160–1165. https://doi.org/10.7205/MILMED.172.11.1160

Yan, K. S., & Dando, R. (2015). A cross-modal role for audition in taste perception. *Journal of Experimental Psychology: Human Perception and Performance, 41*(3), 590–596. https://doi.org/10.1037/xhp0000044

Yang, S., & Sternberg, R. J. (1997). Conceptions of intelligence in ancient Chinese philosophy. *Journal of Theoretical and Philosophical Psychology, 17,* 101–119.

Yang, C., Luo, L., Vadillo, M.A., Yu, R., & Shanks, D. R. (2021). Testing (quizzing) boosts classroom learning: A systematic and meta-analytic review. *Psychological Bulletin, 147,* 399–435.

Yehuda, R., Dasakalakis, N. P., Bierer, L. M., Bader, H. N., Klengel, T., Holsboer, F., & Binder, E. B. (2016). Holocaust exposure induce intergenerational effects on FKBP5. *Biological Psychiatry, 80*(5), 372–380. https://doi.org/10.1016/j.biopsych.2015.08.005

Yeo, B. T. T., Krienen, F. M., Sepulcre, J., Sabuncu, M. R., Lashkari, D., Hollinshead, M., ... Buckner, R. L. (2011). The organization of the human cerebral cortex estimated by intrinsic functional connectivity. *Journal of Neurophysiology, 106,* 1125–1165.

Yik, M., Russell, J. A., & Steiger, J. H. (2011). A 12-point circumplex structure of core affect. *Emotion, 11*(4), 705–731.

Yoeli, E., Hoffman, M., Rand, D. G., & Nowak, M. A. (2013, June). Powering up with indirect reciprocity. *Proceedings of the National Academy of Sciences USA, 110*(Suppl. 2), 10424–10429. https://doi.org/10.1073/pnas.1301210110

Young, J. J., Silber, T., Bruno, D., Galatzer-Levy, I. R., Pomara, N., & Marmar, C. R. (2016). Is there progress? An overview of selecting biomarker candidates for major depressive disorder. *Frontiers in Psychiatry, 7,* 72.

Young, R. M. (1990). *Mind, brain, and adaptation in the nineteenth century: Cerebral localization and its biological context from Gall to Ferrier.* Oxford University Press.

Yu, Y., & Kushnir, T. (2014). Social context effects in 2- and 4-year-olds' selective versus faithful imitation. *Developmental Psychology, 50*(3), 922–933. https://doi.org/10.1037/a0034242

Yucha, C., & Gilbert, C. D. (2004). *Evidence-based practice in biofeedback and neurofeedback.* Association for Applied Psychophysiology and Biofeedback.

Yzerbyt, V., & Demoulin, S. (2010). Intergroup relations. In S. T. Fiske, D. T. Gilbert, & G. Lindzey (Eds.), *The handbook of social psychology* (5th ed., Vol. 2, pp. 1024–1083). Wiley.

Zabelina, D. L. (in press). Imagination. In A. B. Bakker, F. Gander, W. Ruch, & L. Tay (Eds.), *Handbook in positive psychology assessment.* European Association of Psychological Assessment (EAPA).

Zajonc, R. B. (1968). Attitudinal effects of mere exposure. *Journal of Personality and Social Psychology, 9,* 1–27.

Zaki, J., Wager, T. D., Singer, T., Keysers, C., & Gazzola, V. (2016). The anatomy of suffering: Understanding the relationship between nociceptive and empathic pain. *Trends in Cognitive Sciences, 20*(4), 249–259.

Zalsman, G., Hawton, K., Wasserman, D., van Heeringen, K., Arensman, E., Sarchiapone, M., ... Zohar, J. (2016). Suicide prevention strategies revisited: 10-year systematic review. *Lancet Psychiatry, 3*(7), 646–659. https://doi.org/10.1016/S2215-0366(16)30030-X

Zannas, A. S., Wiechmann, T., Gassen, N. C., & Binder, E. B. (2016). Gene-stress-epigenetic regulation of *FKBP5*: Clinical and translational implications. *Neuropsychopharmacology, 41*(1), 261–274. https://doi.org/10.1038/npp.2015.235

Zebrowitz, L. A., & Montepare, J. M. (1992). Impressions of baby-faced individuals across the life span. *Developmental Psychology, 28,* 1143–1152.

Zeithamova D., Schlichting M., & Preston A. (2012). The hippocampus and inferential reasoning: building memories to navigate future decisions. *Frontiers in Human Neuroscience, 6*(70). https://doi.org/10.3389/fnhum.2012.00070

Zeki, S. (1993). *A vision of the brain.* Blackwell Scientific.

Zeki, S. (2001). Localization and globalization in conscious vision. *Annual Review of Neuroscience, 24,* 57–86.

Zeman, A., Dewar, M., & Della Salla, S. (2015). Lives without imagery: Congenital aphantasia. *Cortex, 73,* 278–280. https://doi .org/10.1016/j.cortex.2015.05.019

Zentall, T. R., Sutton, J. E., & Sherburne, L. M. (1996). True imitative learning in pigeons. *Psychological Science, 7,* 343–346.

Zentner, M., & Mitura, K. (2012). Stepping out of the caveman's shadow: Nations' gender gap predicts degree of sex differentiation in mate preferences. *Psychological Science, 23*(10), 1176–1185. https://doi.org/10.1177/0956797612441004

Zerwas, S., & Bulik, C. M. (2011). Genetics and epigenetics of eating disorders. *Psychiatric Annals, 41*(11), 532–538. https://doi.org /10.3928/00485713-20111017-06

Zhang, T. Y., & Meaney, M. J. (2010). Epigenetics and the environmental regulation of the genome and its function. *Annual Review of Psychology, 61,* 439–466.

Zhaoyang, R., Sliwinski, M. J., Martire, L. M., & Smyth, J. M. (2018). Age differences in adults' daily social interactions: An ecological momentary assessment study. *Psychology and Aging, 33*(4), 607–618. https://doi.org/10.1037/pag0000242

Zhong, C.-B., Bohns, V. K., & Gino, F. (2010). Good lamps are the best police: Darkness increases dishonesty and self-interested behavior. *Psychological Science, 21*(3), 311–314. https://doi.org/10.1177 /0956797609360754

Zhou, X., Hetrick, S. E., Cuijpers, P., Qin, B., Barth, J., Whittington, C. J., ... Xie, P. (2015). Comparative efficacy and acceptability of psychotherapies for depression in children and adolescents: A systematic review and network analysis. *World Psychiatry, 14,* 207–222.

Zickfeld, J. H., Schubert, T. W., Seibt, B., Blomster, J. K., Arriaga, P., Basabe, N., ... Fiske, A. P. (2019). Kama muta: Conceptualizing and measuring the experience often labelled being moved across 19 nations and 15 languages. *Emotion, 19*(3), 402–424. https://doi.org/10.1037/emo0000450

Zihl, J., von Cramon, D., & Mai, N. (1983). Selective disturbance of movement vision after bilateral brain damage. *Brain, 106,* 313–340.

Zillmann, D., & Bryant, J. (1974). Effect of residual excitation on the emotional response to provocation and delayed aggressive behavior. *Journal of Personality and Social Psychology, 30*(6), 782–791. https://doi.org/10.1037/h0037541

Zimbardo, P. (2007). *The Lucifer effect: Understanding how good people turn evil.* Random House.

Zimprich, D., & Martin, M. (2002). Can longitudinal changes in processing speed explain longitudinal age changes in fluid intelligence? *Psychology and Aging, 17,* 690–695.

NAME INDEX

Martin, A., 91, 92, 212, 223, 348, 349
Martin, L. L., 298, 301, 304
Martin, L. M., 265
Martin, M., 384
Martin, M. J., 384, 422
Martin, N. G., 320, 382, 447, 568
Martin, V. C., 224
Martinez, M. A., 477
Martinez-Conde, S., 114
Martins, S. S., 256
Martire, L. M., 433
Martis, B., 614
Martland, H. S., 66
Martynowska, K., 507
Marucha, P. T., 522
Marufu, T. C., 401
Marzuk, P. M., 191
Masarik, A. S., 422
Masek, L. R., 338
Maser, J. D., 567
Mashek, D., 490
Maslach, C., 526
Maslow, A. H., 313, 454, 464
Mason, A., 534
Mason, M. F., 169
Mason, P., 478, 480
Masse, N. Y., 82
Massey, C., 498
Masten, A. S., 427, 474, 604
Masters, T. M., 317
Masters, W. H., 319
Masuda, T., 22, 95
Mata, R., 433
Mataix-Cols, D., 523
Matarese, G., 313
Mather, M., 432
Matheson, G. J., 559
Matheson, K., 555
Mathews, T. J., 401
Mathur, M. B., 474
Matisse, H., 262
Matsukura, S., 313
Matsumoto, D., 302
Matsuo, H., 313
Mattar, A. A. G., 276, 279
Mattes, R. D., 151
Mattfield, A. T., 201
Matthews, G., 450
Matthews, K., 396
Mattick, R. P., 396
Matzel, L. D., 374
Maudsley, H., 573
Mauss, I. B., 293, 295, 432
Max, A., 384
May, M. A., 456, 457
May, R., 455
May, T., 582
Maybarg, H. S., 616
Mayberg, H., 615
Mayer, A., 235
Mayer, J. D., 378, 391
Maynard-Smith, J., 479
Mayo, R., 304
Mayr, E., 317
Mayr, U., 432
Mazure, C. M., 95
Mazziotta, J. C., 92
Mazzoni, G., 201
McAdams, L., 429
McAdams, M., 324
McArdle, N., 393
McArthur, L. Z., 486
McAuley, E., 94

McAuliffe, F. M., 401
McAuliffe, K., 420
McBride, M., 284
McCabe, D. P., 287
McCabe, M. P., 487
McCabe, R. B., 488
McCain, J., 468
McCarley, R. W., 182
McCarnish, M., 316
McCarter, L., 293
McCarthy, G., 134
McCarthy, J., 16
McCarthy, K. S., 597
McCarthy, R. A., 348
McCartt, A. T., 117
McClearn, G. E., 100, 381, 388, 540
McClelland, D. C., 323, 441
McCluskey, T., 191
McConville, P. M., 389
McCormack, C. A., 401
McCrae, R. R., 448
McCue, M., 534
McCullough, M., 301
McDaniel, M. A., 232, 286, 347
McDermott, J., 128
McDermott, K. B., 215, 218, 224, 235, 286
McDonald, A., 232
McDonald, K., 592
McDonald, R. V., 256
McDonough, I. M., 430, 431
McElree, B., 219
McElwain, N. L., 416
McEvoy, S. P., 117
McEwan, K., 592
McFall, R. M., 619
McFarlane, A. H., 515
McFerran, B., 318
McGarrah, A., 369
McGarty, C., 494
McGaugh, J. L., 87, 200, 201, 212, 230, 239, 299
McGee, J. J., 373
McGeoch, P. D., 93
McGhee, D. E., 496
McGill, K. L., 515
McGovern, P. E., 607
McGowan, F. P., 357
McGowan, P. O., 99
McGrady, A., 530
McGrath, J. J., 574
McGrath, J. S., 274
McGregor, D., 48
McGue, M., 380, 428, 447
McGuffin, P., 100, 381, 388
McGuire, P. K., 573
McHaffie, J. G., 536
McHugh, T. J., 212
McInnes, L., 384
McInnis, O. A., 555
McIntosh, A. M., 389
McIntosh, D. N., 519
McIntyre, S. H., 285
McKay, A., 426
McKee, A. C., 66, 67
McKenzie, K., 575
McKenzie, K. E., 137
McKetin, R., 396
McKnight, P. E., 320
McKone, K. M. P., 423
McLachlan, D. R., 233
McLaughlin, K. A., 563, 585, 586
McLaughlin, T. J., 537

McLean, C. P., 528, 591
McLean, J. P., 286
McLean, K. C., 226, 461, 542
McLellan, A. T., 187, 193
McMahon, C. A., 416
McMurdo, M., 531
McNab, F., 345
McNally, R. J., 179, 237, 527, 531, 621
McNamara, R. A., 420
McNay, E. C., 313
McNeely, H., 615
McNeil, G., 303
McNeill, D., 232
McNell, J., 157
McNulty, J. K., 486
McPherson, S. M., 599
McPhetres, J., 57, 365
McQuaid, R. J., 555
Meaburn, E. L., 381
Mead, G. E., 531
Mead, G. H., 462
Meade, M. L., 226
Meadows, E. A., 529
Meaidi, A., 184
Meaney, J. J., 99
Meaney, M. J., 96, 98, 99, 100
Mechelli, A., 341
Meder, D., 273
Medin, D. L., 347
Mednick, S. C., 425
Medvec, V. H., 33, 307, 464
Meelis, W., 471
Meeus, W. J., 427, 428
Megan, Duchess of Sussex, 439
Mehl, M. R., 442, 460
Mehu, M., 301
Meier, B., 136
Meindl, J. N., 261
Meins, E., 416
Meinz, E. J., 391
Meiser-Stedman, R., 213
Meissner, C. A., 217
Meksin, R., 87, 239
Meldrum, R. C., 396
Mellers, B. A., 477
Mellon, R. C., 267
Meltzer, A. L., 486
Meltzer, H. Y., 608
Meltzoff, A. N., 403, 410, 413, 493
Melzack, R., 146
Memmi, S., 301
Memon, A., 217, 237
Mendelsohn, G. A., 482
Mendes, W. B., 294, 312, 518, 525, 560
Mendle, J., 423
Mendoza-Denton, R., 21, 392, 393
Mendrek, A., 584
Menon, S. V., 563
Menzler, S., 304
Meoni, L. A., 524
Merabet, L. B., 93
Mercer, S. L., 426
Merikangas, K. R., 559, 562, 567, 579
Merkle, K., 582
Merrill, L., 57
Mertens, G., 484
Mervis, C. B., 346
Merzenich, M. M., 94
Mesoudi, A., 278
Mesquita, B., 303
Messick, D. M., 491

Meston, C. M., 320, 321
Mestre, J. M., 378
Mesulam, M. M., 282
Metcalfe, J., 287, 360
Meter, K., 316
Methven, L., 151
Metzler, T. J., 181
Meuret, A. E., 561
Meyer, M. L., 134, 461, 492, 515
Meyer, T. D., 572
Meyer, U., 535
Meyer-Lindenberg, A., 517, 557
Mézenge, F., 212
Michaela, R., 311
Michaelis, S. S., 609
Michel, B. D., 558
Michelet, T., 276
Michelich, C. R., 134
Mick, E., 580
Miech, R. A., 187
Mierop, A., 378
Miettunen, J., 574
Miezin, F. M., 223
Migliorini, R., 487
Mignone, J., 555
Migrenne, S., 317
Miguel, A. Q. C., 599
Miguel, E., 471
Mikels, J. A., 432
Mikkola, S., 450
Miklowitz, D. J., 572
Mikolajczak, M., 378
Miksch, M., 489
Mikulincer, M., 489
Milad, M. R., 564
Miles, E., 311
Milev, R. V., 614
Milgram, S., 506, 507, 508
Milius, C. R., 320
Milkman, K. L., 498
Mill, J., 572
Millar, P. R., 235
Miller, A. J., 507
Miller, C., 570
Miller, D. T., 464–465, 480, 504
Miller, G. A., 15, 17, 208
Miller, G. E., 99, 387, 522, 532, 542
Miller, I., 356, 572
Miller, K. L., 106
Miller, N. E., 313, 471
Miller, P. J., 338
Miller, T. I., 619
Miller, T. W., 515
Miller, W. R., 538
Miller-Johnson, S., 387
Millner, A. J., 586
Mills, C., 117
Mills, J., 511
Mills, P. J., 78
Milne, A. B., 497
Milne, E., 497
Milner, A. D., 125
Milner, B., 20, 86, 211, 220
Milun, R., 472
Milyavsky, M., 312, 510
Minear, M., 431
Mineka, S., 276, 277, 559, 574
Mingroni, M. A., 386
Mink, J. W., 615
Minsky, M., 16, 160
Minson, J. A., 477
Mintun, M. A., 105
Mintz, J., 574

SUBJECT INDEX

Note: Page numbers followed by f indicate figures; those followed by t indicate tables.

selectivity of, 162–163
self-consciousness, 164–165, 165f
sleep and. *see* Sleep
thought suppression and, 170, 170f
transience of, 163
unconscious mind and, 171–173
unity of, 162
Consent, informed, 60–61
Consequences, 599
Conservation, in cognitive development, 408
Consistency, 510–512
Consistency bias, 237
Consolidation, of memories, 212, 215
Construct validity, 32
Constructs, 556
Consumer psychologists, 24
Content morphemes, 331–332
Context
emotional expression and, 303
in operant conditioning, 261
reinstatement, 217
Continuity, perceptual organization and, 129f, 130
Continuous reinforcement, 264
Contralateral control, 90
Control
to avoid demand characteristics, 34, 34f
contralateral, 90
hardiness and, 541
of learning, 287–288
locus of, 458t, 459
mental, 170, 170f
perceived, over stressful events, 517–518
stimulus, in operant conditioning, 261–262
Controlled Drugs and Substances Act, 195
Conventional antipsychotics, 608
Conventional stage of moral development, 419, 419f
Cooperation, 474–479
definition of, 474
groups and, 476–479
riskiness of, 474–476, 475f
Coping
rational, 528
repressive, 527
Core network, 224, 225f
Cornea, 119, 120f
Coronary heart disease. *see* Cardiovascular health
Corpus callosum, 90, 90f, 102, 103
Correlation, 39–42, 40t
causation and, 42–49, 43f
direction and strength of, 41–42, 42f
graphing, 41f
natural, 42
patterns of variation and, 39–42
third-variable problem and, 43
Correlation coefficient, 41
Cortisol, stress and, 520
Counselling psychologists, 594
Counsellors, 594
Couples therapy, 604
COVID-19 pandemic
learning loss and, 288–289
misinformation about, 365, 366
perceived vs. actual risk, 357
psychological treatment and, 606
taste and smell senses, 152, 153–154
CR. *see* Conditioned response
Creative intelligence, 377
Creative thinking, divergent, 225
Creativity, 360–362
in bipolar disorders, 571
episodic memory and, 224–225

CRISPR (clustered regularly interspaced short palindromic repeats), 396
Critical thinking
about evidence, 56–59
experiments and, 56–59
Critical-incident stress debriefing (CISD), 621, 622t
The Critique of Pure Reason (Kant), 4f
Crystallized intelligence, 377, 386
CS. *see* Conditioned stimulus
CTE. *see* Chronic traumatic encephalopathy
Cue exposure therapies, 256
Cues
depth, 131–132, 132f
retrieval, 215–217
verbal and nonverbal, 308t
Cultural explanations, 553
Cultural Formation Interview (CFI), 552
Cultural idioms of distress, 553
Cultural neuroscience, 94–95
Cultural psychology, 20–22, 94
Cultural syndromes, 553
Cultural tools, 412
Cultural worldview, 326–327
Culture
adolescence and, 422
aggression and, 473–474
altruism and, 481–482
beauty and, 486
brain plasticity and, 94–95
childhood amnesia and, 231
definition of, 20
drawing from categories. *see* Stereotyping
discovering, 411–413
display rules, 307
diversity and nonverbal expression, 307
doing favors for strangers and, 481–482
emotional expression and, 305
implicit learning and, 283
intelligence and, 378–379, 391–394
mental disorders and, 552–553, 552f
selectivity in mating and, 482–483
"Cumulative recorder," 11
Current concerns, 168–169, 169f
suppression of, 169–170, 170f
Current state, 358, 359
CUSS. *see* College Undergraduate Stress Scale
Cutting, 587
Cytokines, 535

DARE programs, 621, 622t
Darwin's theory of natural selection, 8
Data-based approach to intelligence, 375, 376–377, 376f, 377f
Day residue, 180
Daydreaming, 169, 169f
DBS. *see* Deep brain stimulation
Deafness. *see* Hearing loss
Debriefing, in research, 61
Deception
insincere facial expressions and, 307
lie detection and, 307–309
lying, 307–309, 308t
in research, 61
Decision criterion, 116
Decision making, 350–357
availability heuristic and, 351, 351f
brain and, 355–356, 356f
conjunction fallacy and, 352–353, 352f
conscious vs. unconscious, 173
errors in, 354–355
framing effects and, 353

judging frequencies and probabilities and, 350–351
optimism bias and, 353–354
rational choice theory and, 350
representativeness heuristic and, 351–352
Declaration of Helsinki, 60
De-differentiated, 431
Deep brain stimulation (DBS), 614–615, 615f
Default network, in brain, 108, 169, 169f
Defense mechanisms, 453, 453t
Degree of relatedness, 97
Deindividuation, 478
Deintensification, display rules and, 307
Déjà vu, 233
Delayed reinforcement and punishment, 260–261, 260f
Delta waves, 175, 175f, 176
Delusions
in bipolar disorders, 570
in schizophrenia, 573–574
Demand characteristics, 33–34
Demerol, 191
Demyelinating diseases, 68
Dendrites, 68, 69f, 71f
Deoxyribonucleic acid (DNA), 96–97, 96f
Dependence, physical and psychological, on drugs, 186
Dependent personality disorder, 583t
Dependent variable, 45, 45f
Depressants, 188–190, 189t
Depressive disorders, 566–570
bipolar, 570–572, 610–611
brain in, 568–569, 569f
cognition and, 569
costs of, 592
double depression, 567
major (unipolar depression), 550, 567
negative thoughts and, 569–570
neurotransmitters and, 568, 569f
omega-3 fatty acids and, 612f
persistent, 567
postpartum, 567–568
risk for, 567–568
seasonal affective disorder, 567, 611–612
stigma, 566
stress and, 568
treatment effectiveness, 616
treatment of, 194
Depth
illusions of, 132–133, 133f
visual perception of, 130–133
Depth cues
binocular, 132, 132f
monocular, 131, 132f
Description, 35–39
graphic representations and, 36–37
statistics and, 37–39, 37f
Descriptive statistics, 37–39, 37f
Desires, cognitive development and, 410
Development, 398–436
in adolescence. *see* Adolescence
in adulthood. *see* Adulthood
cephalocaudal rule and, 403–404
in childhood. *see* Childhood
cognitive. *see* Cognitive development
in infancy. *see* Infancy
moral, 418–420, 419f
motor, 403–404, 404f
perceptual, 402–403
prenatal, 399–400, 400f
proximodistal rule and, 404
psychosocial, stages of, 427–429, 427t